EVERYMAN'S LIBRARY

EVERYMAN,
I WILL GO WITH THEE,
AND BE THY GUIDE,
IN THY MOST NEED
TO GO BY THY SIDE

EVELYN WAUGH

Waugh Abroad
Collected Travel Writing

with an Introduction by
Nicholas Shakespeare

EVERYMAN'S LIBRARY

266

First included in Everyman's Library, 2003
© Evelyn Waugh. Published by arrangement with PFD on behalf of
the Evelyn Waugh Trust.
Details of original publication are given in the Select Bibliography
on page xxvii
Introduction, Bibliography and Chronology © Everyman's Library,
2003
Typography by Peter B. Willberg

ISBN 1-85715-266-2

A CIP catalogue record for this book is available from the
British Library

Published by Everyman's Library,
Gloucester Mansions, 140A Shaftesbury Avenue,
London WC2H 8HD

Distributed by Random House (UK) Ltd.,
20 Vauxhall Bridge Road, London SW1V 2SA

Printed and bound in Germany
by GGP Media, Pössneck

E V E L Y N   W A U G H

CONTENTS

MAPS

viii

INTRODUCTION

———

As soon as I set out on my own, things began to go slightly against me.
(Ninety-Two Days)

In January 1932, Evelyn Waugh's American publisher, John Farrar, wrote to a friend: 'One very important literateur said to me the other day, "I think you have the most important of the young English writers in Evelyn Waugh, but my God, will you stop him writing travel books!"' The writer Waugh looked up to as a mentor, P. G. Wodehouse, expressed a similar concern in his review of *A Handful of Dust*. 'What a snare this travelling business is to the young writer. He goes to some blasted jungle or other and imagines that everybody will be interested in it.'

On the face of it, Waugh didn't think much of his travel books either. He found *Remote People* 'very dull' and *Robbery Under Law* like 'an interminable Times leader of 1880' ('People will say Waugh is done for; it is marriage and living in the country has done it.') Of *Waugh in Abyssinia* he wrote: 'If the book is boring its readers nearly as much as it is boring me to write it it will create a record in low sales ...' while *A Tourist in Africa* struck its author as 'very poor stuff ... hard going because I can only be funny when I am complaining about something'.

One reason he judged writing these books a bitter chore is that they were undertaken to earn money, usually after he had completed a novel, and to involve minimum expenditure on his part. If a hotel or a shipping line was willing to give Waugh advantageous terms he did not blush to commend them in print. Likewise could Waugh be hired as a propagandist for the appropriate Catholic or Conservative cause. In 1935 the pro-Mussolini *Daily Mail* employed him as a war correspondent to cover favourably the Italian invasion of Abyssinia. Two years later he entered into a secret deal with Clive Pearson to write a book excoriating the corrupt and anti-clerical government of Mexico. For the price of £989 plus generous expenses, Waugh was happy to present a withering case against General Cárdenas who had confiscated the Pearson family's oilfields.

Writers have to make a living, and it would be unfair to share in Waugh's denigration of his own travel books on account of the circumstances of their commissioning. As he put it in *Ninety-Two Days*: 'Though most of us would not write except for money we would not write any differently for more money.' This is true especially of Waugh, who even as a hired hand rarely penned a dead sentence. His travel books, here collected for the first time, are valuable for a number of reasons. They show the raw matter of the novels which emerged out of them, notably *Black Mischief*, *Scoop* and *A Handful of Dust*. They constitute a thousand pages of that English prose which Graham Greene likened to the Mediterranean before the war: so clear you could see to the bottom. And where the material is thin – and sometimes it is so thin as to be transparent too – it has the effect of galvanizing Waugh to reveal himself in ways that he achieved only indirectly in fiction.

It was Waugh's firm belief that the novelist deals with action and dialogue. The travel writer, on the other hand, has to endure menacing periods of inaction and silence. His greatest problem: how to fill these unforgiving moments and avoid the 'stark horrors of boredom'. Waugh's solution was to digress, and his digressions expose both the finest and the indefensible traits in his character. That is why if one wishes to discover Waugh's creed in Waugh's words, whether it be his opinions on politics, religion, architecture, journalism, novel writing, or simply what constitutes his notion of Englishness, one has to turn to his travel writing.

*

In 1933, a group of naked Amazonian Indians who had never before seen a white man met a young Englishman in a red blanket, lame in both feet, and covered from head to toe in insect bites. Their thoughts are not recorded by the Englishman, who spoke no word of Kopinang, but it is hard to picture a more misleading ambassador of his race than the thirty-year-old Evelyn Waugh.

There was always a discrepancy between how Waugh saw himself and how the world perceived him. In his own eyes he was an innocent abroad. On the banks of the Murabang, he travelled under the preferred of all his guises, as an 'amateur observer' in the mould of one of his fictional characters: a William Boot, say, or a Tony Last, who 'had no very ambitious ideas about travel', but who, cruelly abandoned by his wife, had escaped the savages of Mayfair to mingle with their remoter cousins in the jungles of Brazil, where he hoped to discover a Lost City. 'He had a clear picture of it in his mind. It was Gothic in character, all vanes and pinnacles, gargoyles, battlements, groining and tracery, pavilions and terraces, a transfigured Hetton ...'

Waugh mentions on at least two occasions a film in his youth that may have suggested to him his role model. The film opens 'superbly' with either Harold Lloyd or Buster Keaton (Waugh's memory is untypically fuzzy on this point), as a convalescent millionaire, arriving in a South American revolution and progressing placidly down the main street, bowing left and right, while a battle rages around him. 'As the dead and wounded double up before him, he raises his hat in acknowledgement of what he takes to be their bows of welcome.'

The world did not share this perception of him. In 1930 the explorer Wilfred Thesiger encountered Waugh at an embassy reception in Addis Abbaba, and, like many people, detested him on sight. Thesiger was about to set off on an expedition into the untamed Danikil country. Waugh was quite keen to head out in the same direction, but his personality militated against grasping the opportunity to attach himself to Thesiger's party. Waugh, dressed in grey suede shoes, a floppy bow-tie and wide trousers, appeared to the seasoned traveller as a 'little pip-squeak'. Thesiger thought him 'flaccid and petulant'.

Once in Asmara, a place of only seven unattached white women among 60,000 men, a gallant Italian guide named Franchi was deluded by Waugh's christian name into procuring a bunch of crimson roses and rushing in a state of 'amorous excitement' to meet him at the airport. To find there a trousered and unshaven man of diminutive height must, accepts Waugh, have been 'a hideous blow'. Others who bumped into Waugh on his globe-trotting mistook him variously for his brother Alec, for a German bank clerk who had lately boxed the ears of his orderly, and for a sweetly-toned harmonium.

It is easy to mistake Waugh for who is he not, but who is he? And what drives him to take refuge in what he calls 'the still-remote regions of the earth'?

Waugh, the reader soon enough realizes, is not of that band of travellers popularized by Hilaire Belloc and incarnated today in Patrick Leigh Fermor, lone and self-sufficient walkers who know where they are going as well as something of the culture through which it contents them to pass. He ridicules such an idealistic relationship between man and nature. 'In the haversack on his back he carries a map and garlic sausage, a piece of bread, a sketch book, and a litre of wine. As he goes he sings songs in dog Latin ...' Waugh's own journeys tend to track the course of the racing tortoises he once encountered on Corfu: 'The chief disability suffered by tortoises as racing animals is not their slowness so much as their confused sense of direction.' The first line of *Labels* – 'I did not really know where I was going' – describes the impulse behind most of Waugh's travels. As Selina Hastings, his most recent biographer, remarks: he cared very little where he went so long as it was away.

The nearest he comes to emulating Wilfred Thesiger is in *Ninety-Two Days*. The book describes one of remarkably few journeys he makes on his own, or without an English companion; an expedition by boat and on horseback through the northern Amazon that strips him bare.

'But why British Guiana?' he is asked of his destination.

'I was at difficulties to find an answer, except that I was going *because* I knew so little ...'

*

Evelyn Waugh spent his first twelve years of adult life, as he put it, 'intermittently on the move'. Several reasons explain his restlessness, but one constant remained his preferred method of transport. 'It always seems odd to me that anyone, for any reason, should choose to travel by land when he can go by water.' Waugh made no bones about his susceptibility to comfort. A ship possessed obvious advantages over the aeroplane, which 'belittles everything it discloses'. On the outward journey he could read about his destination; on the return journey, grind out the first chapter or two. In between, with minimum effort, he could investigate a few ports of call and select those he wanted to return to afterwards.

Above all, a ship provided a matchless opportunity to gather material. Waugh's attention was never much drawn to flora, fauna or wildlife; the South American jungle he found 'endlessly monotonous', and natural wonders such as sunset over Mount Etna caused him physically to recoil: 'Nothing I have ever seen in Art or Nature was quite so revolting.' His imagination was sparked chiefly by homo sapiens, with his eye sharpened on the discrepancy between what a man promises and what he delivers. 'I soon found my fellow passengers and their behaviour in the different places we visited a far more absorbing study than the places themselves,' he writes in *Labels*. Thirty years later, stiffly perambulating the decks of the *Rhodesia Castle*, he has found little reason to change his mind. 'As happier men watch birds, I watch men. They are less attractive but more various.' Unchanged, too, are his motives for leaving home. He has come abroad, he declares, 'with the intention of eschewing "problems" and of seeking only the diverting and the picturesque'.

*

Waugh's first travel book, like his last, takes the shape of a cruise undertaken to avoid the ghastliness of England in February. Aged twenty-six, recently married to Evelyn Gardner and not yet sure of his profession – he still had aspirations to be an artist – he contemplated a voyage on a cargo boat around the Black Sea. 'Would anyone like travel articles about that?' he asked his agent, A. D. Peters. 'I shall be quite pleased to adapt my plans to editorial taste.' He informed him: 'I am growing a moustache.'

Instead of the Black Sea, Peters negotiated free passages for Waugh and his wife aboard a Norwegian liner touring the

Mediterranean, the expenses to be paid for by articles collected as a book. Conceived in the spirit of *Decline and Fall*, his recently published first novel, Waugh looked forward to debunking the type of earnest rural travel writer he had grown up reading, such as Hilaire Belloc, H. V. Morton and S. P. B. Mais. He planned to call the result *The Quest of a Moustache*.

The cruise had a romantic element, too. Waugh had not been able to find the time or money for a proper honeymoon. The voyage with his wife was intended to be a delayed celebration of their marriage as well as a chance for her to recuperate, the arctic English winter having given She-Evelyn, as she was known, a bad dose of German measles and flu.

The Waughs' departure on 10 February 1929 was reported in the *Daily Sketch*. Waugh made it clear that he thought of his future as a draughtsman; he hoped to bring back enough sketches for an exhibition, 'and, if it is successful, abandon writing for painting.'

Her voyage on the *Stella Polaris*, so far from improving She-Evelyn's health, made it infinitely worse. Soon she was coughing up blood. Unaccustomed to women, still less to looking after them, Waugh found himself emotionally at sea. He wrote a postcard to Pansy Lamb, his wife's old flat-mate, saying by the time she received it She-Evelyn would be likely dead.

Few reading his playful account of the liner's progress around the Mediterranean will guess the dreadful background. In the United States the book was published with the title *A Bachelor Abroad* and that is how its narrator appears, as a single, amused, generally sceptical observer who falls in with an English couple on their honeymoon. 'The young man was small and pleasantly dressed and wore a slight, curly moustache; he was reading a particularly good detective story with apparent intelligence. His wife was huddled in a fur coat in the corner, clearly far from well.' Waugh names them Geoffrey (possibly after his wife's brother-in-law) and Juliet (after her sister). 'Every quarter of an hour or so they said to each other, "Are you quite sure you're all right, darling?" And replied, "Perfectly, really I am. Are *you*, my precious?" But Juliet was far from being all right.'

At Port Said, She-Evelyn was taken by stretcher to the British Hospital looking 'distressingly like a corpse', and diagnosed with double pneumonia and pleurisy. There she remained a month. In a foreshadowing of his fictional alter ego Tony Last, Waugh visited her bedside and, puffing on his pipe, doggedly read to her P. G. Wodehouse, which, dipping in and out of fever, she had grave difficulty in understanding. Her incomprehension deepened with the arrival on the scene of Alastair Graham, with whom Waugh had had a homosexual liaison at Oxford (and to whom he intended to dedicate his *Labeliad*, as he now described the book). A few weeks later she felt well enough to visit Graham's house in Athens, where it further alarmed her to observe Waugh's delight in his friend's effeminate behaviour, concluding in an outburst of high camp with Mark Ogilvie-Grant. 'Their new habit is to talk Greek in a cockney accent.'

The honeymoon was over even as the *Stella Polaris* set course for London. The foghorn that sounds in the last paragraph, as the ship, nearing home, enters a sea-mist, was 'a very dismal sound, premonitory, perhaps, of coming trouble ...' The words were written just as Waugh learned that his wife had fallen in love with another man. He would never again be so playful.

*

Best of his travel books, *Labels* illustrates the bathyscope of Englishness within which Waugh habitually floats and which allows him, preferably while luncheoning from a Fortnum & Mason's hamper, to ogle at passing oddities; in other words, at anything that nourishes his taste for the comic, the lunatic and the grotesque.

Nothing satisfies him more than to stumble through the dark vault of a Naples church in order to view a mummified corpse with its stomach slit open:

'The little girl thrust her face into the aperture and inhaled deeply and greedily. She called on me to do the same.

"Smell good," she said. "Nice." '

Unlike more curious writers, Waugh travels to have his biases confirmed, choosing destinations where his prejudices are most likely to be annoyed. 'When we go abroad we take our opinions with us; it is useless to pretend, as many writers do, that they arrive with minds wholly innocent of other experience; are born anew into each new world ...' In this sense the world becomes Waugh's oyster. The more he samples it, the more closely it grows to resemble the image that he supposed Africa held for the Romans, a novelty but also a distorting mirror in which familiar objects are reflected 'in perverse and threatening forms'. The tension in his prose suggests a need to keep vigilant at each step.

Wherever he goes, Waugh adopts the air of a detached and confident narrator for whom England is the touchstone and all that departs from it a source of puzzled fascination. ('It takes some time to overcome the English habit of pocketing change unchecked.') This touchstone is his most cumbersome baggage. He is not absolutely joking when he writes: 'It is just worth considering the possibility that there may be something valuable behind the indefensible and inexplicable assumption of superiority by the Anglo-Saxon race.' He is deadly serious in his opinion that England is the appropriate custodian of the Holy Places.

For the most part, though, he is hilarious. Unawed by advance publicity, he runs down sacred cows with the eagerness of his driver to Nazareth: 'He never smiled except at the corners, or when, as we swept through a village, some little child, its mother wailing her alarm, darted in front of us. Then he would stamp on the accelerator and lean forward eagerly in his seat.'

And so he finds Paris: 'very much like High Wycombe indefinitely extended'.

The Casino in Monte Carlo: 'like Paddington Station in the first weeks of August'.

The sphinx: 'an ill-proportioned composition of inconsiderable aesthetic appeal', with an expression reminiscent of Aleister Crowley.

The Acropolis: 'a Stilton cheese into which port has been poured'.

The Serai in Constantinople: 'somewhat resembles Earl's Court Exhibition'.

Cape Town: 'a hideous city that reminded me of Glasgow'.

And so on, the impression being conveyed that the real Africa (or Mexico, or Guiana) is somewhere else and, frankly, the Africans can keep it; not that too many natives cross Waugh's path:

'Of the Abyssinians we saw very little except as grave, rather stolid figures at the official receptions.'

'In Kenya it is easy to forget that one is in Africa.'

'One does not see many Africans in Salisbury; fewer it seemed than in London.'

Waugh registers foreigners only when they trespass into his culture; either by misspelling his language, as in the case of his guide in Cairo, or by pronouncing it incorrectly.

'Chief, do you want to see this boy's arse?' asks a man in the Amazon, offering him a horse.

'I misunderstood him and said no, somewhat sharply.'

It doesn't cross his mind to learn the language of a country. Martha Gellhorn, prior to travelling through Turkey, taught herself the expression: 'Fuck off, I'm old enough to be your grandmother.' This is a step too far for Waugh. 'I had learned an Arabic phrase which sounded like *Ana barradar.* I don't know what it meant, but I had used it once or twice in Cairo with fair success.'

Not that he would have applied, but these days Waugh is unlikely to have flourished in a job interview at a British or American university. The twenty-first century would turn up its nose at his vulgarity, racism and political incorrectness. And yet to dismiss him on this count is splendidly to miss Waugh's point. He spares no one: Jews, blacks, Americans, and least of all his fellow Englishmen.

The foreigners who guarantee Waugh's attention are not the natives, but transposed figures like himself, middle-class expatriates who present him with a chance to display his peerless ear for dialogue. He is on top form in a mock English tavern in Ndola, plunged back among displaced and dilapidated countrymen, in altercation with a misanthropic philosopher and a barman who asks him if he knows Ed Stanley of Alderly. Or among a group of thirty Americans whom he encounters at Sakkara in a subterranean tunnel called the Serapeum, which the guide explained was the burial place of sacred bulls:

'Oh, ladies and gentlemen, I longed to declaim, dear ladies and gentlemen, fancy crossing the Atlantic Ocean, fancy coming all this way in the heat, fancy enduring all these extremities of discomfort and exertion; fancy spending all this money, to see a hole in the sand where, three thousand years ago, a foreign race whose motives must for ever remain inexplicable interred the carcasses of twenty-four bulls. Surely the laugh, dear ladies and gentlemen, is on us.'

*

The defection of She-Evelyn with a 'ramshackle oaf' named John Heygate was a shock from which Waugh never recovered and had two immediate consequences. It determined his profession; and it precipitated his conversion to Catholicism. On 29 September 1930 he was received into the Roman Catholic Church, his only godparent the charwoman on duty.

Waugh's conversion, about which he never entertained the smallest humour or doubt, sprang from his clear conviction of the truth of the Catholic faith. She-Evelyn believed he had the tendency in him always to become a Catholic, whatever her behaviour. This is quite possible. He was descended from a line of clergymen. Already in *Labels* he had revealed a religious temperament, in the rapture he felt before certain tombs and churches. At any rate, after his wife's desertion life became to Waugh 'unintelligible and unendurable without God'; in the words of his fellow convert Graham Greene, 'he needed to cling to something solid and strong and unchanging'.

Unaltered for two thousand years, the Church was a safe, well-constructed raft onto which he could pile his anguish as well as all his frustrated romanticism. He clung to it with total submission; 'this little island of order and sweetness in an ocean of rank barbarity', as he wrote of a convent in Kampala. His religious faith now underpinned his journeys and confirmed the course of his reverence. Never again would he laugh at the troglodytic inclinations of the Holy Family.

Displaced, humiliated, rudderless, Waugh in the aftermath of his conversion scratched about for another foreign adventure. This time he travelled not merely to escape the English winter; like Tony Last in *A Handful of Dust*, he was going away 'because it seemed to be the conduct expected of a husband in his circumstances, because the associations of Hetton were for the time poisoned for him, because he wanted to live for a few months away from people who would know him or Brenda, in places where there was no expectation of meeting her or Beaver ...'

In the autumn of 1930 he set sail for Addis Ababa to report for *The Times* on the coronation of Haile Selassie. The package tourist who ridiculed fellow passengers in *Labels* graduates in *Remote People* to a foreign correspondent pricking the pomposity of baroquely dressed diplomats. In his accuracy of aim he has something in common with his German driver, who keeps a rifle ready across the wheel so that he can inflict 'slight wounds on the passing farmers at point blank range'. Notorious among his targets are the head of the British Legation, Sir Sydney Barton, a blunt Ulster Protestant who had served in China (where he earned the nickname 'Gunboat Barton' after despatching the cable: 'Trouble at Weihaiwei. Send two cruisers'); and Barton's daughter Esmé, parodied in *Black Mischief* as the promiscuous Prudence Courteney, who crashes in the jungle eventually to be served up to her unsuspecting lover in an aromatic stew. (Unreported by Waugh goes Esmé's revenge. Five years later, he returned to Addis Ababa and was sitting in Le Perroquet, one of the city's two cinema nightclubs, when a young woman marched up to his table, paused, and hurled her champagne into his face.)

Remote People shares obvious similarities with its African sequel, *Waugh in Abyssinia* , in which Waugh casts himself as a hopeless war correspondent mocking the antics of other journalists. Both books are shot through with delicious set-pieces, but what is noticeable is the creeping vein of seriousness. Travel has begun to sweat out his politics, a brand of Conservatism that finds repugnant any rocking of his boat and results, with each succeeding journey abroad, in what George Orwell considered Waugh's disadvantage as a writer: his 'holding false (indefensible) opinions'. Nowhere are these more blatant than in his views on Mussolini. Practically unique among English journalists, Waugh champions the Fascist leader for his ambitions to conquer Abyssinia. In Rome he interviews him off the record and is impressed: Mussolini is exactly the kind of Holy Emperor the modern world needs, a benign civilizer who might bring to a race of homicidal naked cannibals the consolations of Mother Rome.

Waugh's inflexible version of Catholicism is every bit as buoyant as the pride he takes in his Englishness. From *Remote People* on, his journeys assume the character of pilgrimages (*The Holy Places*), of penances (*Ninety-Two Days*), and of proselytizing missions (*Robbery Under Law*). In 1938, following the annulment of his first marriage, he visits Mexico for two months with his new wife Laura. 'Let me ... warn the reader that I was a Conservative when I went to Mexico and that everything I saw there strengthened my opinions.' Once again his political attitude is coloured by his religious sensibilities, but this time at a cost to his art.

'I can only be funny when I am complaining about something.'

In *Robbery Under Law*, he disregards his readers' patience and commits the solecism of becoming dull. 'The worst sufferings I can boast were from bed-bugs in luxury hotels and a film producer at luncheon.' Waugh at his most serious is not necessarily Waugh at his best. Denied the comfort of an Anglo-Saxon kicking-horse (he couldn't very well choose his new wife, still less his benefactor Clive Pearson), he picks an unworthy opponent in the form of his guidebook's author. Sparring with the absent T. Philip Terry, of whose religious attitudes he furiously disapproves, Waugh's focus blurs. One moment Mexico is a 'little republic', the next a 'huge country'. From his visit in the same year, Graham Greene produced his best novel. Waugh produces a partisan history lesson. Even to the reader who remains unaware that this is a book commissioned by the Pearson family, Waugh's questions smack of someone in receipt of a brown envelope. In the same way that the living-room in Puebla springs open, at the touch of a button, to the concealed cell of the Mother Superior, everything leads back to his Catholicism.

Waugh's uncritical homage recalls the Mexican peasants at Guadalupe before the image of the Virgin: 'men who remained apparently interminably on their knees with their arms stretched out on either side of them ... rapt, their lips moving, their eyes open fixed on the picture.'

In this posture, more or less, Waugh expresses his regard for the Empress Helena, a kind old lady possibly born in Colchester, who as Empress Dowager made a journey to Jerusalem from which, he tells us earnestly, 'spring all relics of the true cross'.

*

Alone of Waugh's early travel books, *Robbery Under Law* finds no place in his 1946 anthology of travel writing, *When The Going Was Good*. And yet it contains some of the clearest definitions he ever made about his shifting personas.

On Waugh the restless explorer:

'I believe that man is, by nature, an exile and will never be self-sufficient or complete on this earth; that his chances of happiness and virtue, here, remain more or less constant through the centuries and, generally speaking, are not much affected by the political and economic conditions in which he lives ...'

On Waugh the foreign correspondent:

'His trade is to observe, record and interpret ... His hope is to notice things which the better experienced accept as commonplace and to convey to a distant public some idea of the aspect and feel of a place which hitherto has been merely a geographical or political term ...'

On Waugh without God:

'Given propitious circumstances, men and women who seem quite orderly, will commit every conceivable atrocity ... we are all potential recruits for anarchy. Unremitting effort is needed to keep men living together at peace.'

He presents the profoundly unpeaceful Mexican situation as a cautionary tale in which a once great civilization – greater than the Unites States at the turn of the twentieth century – has succumbed, within the space of a single generation, to barbarism. In Mexico's fate, he sees a morality play and a warning. Civilization is under constant assault, he reminds us, and barbarism, in this instance characterized by Communism, never finally defeated. On the eve of the Second World War, he suggests that what is happening in Mexico, now every year becoming hungrier, wickeder, more hopeless, could happen soon to us all.

'The jungle is closing in and the graves of the pioneers are lost in the undergrowth; the people are shrinking back to the river banks and railheads; they are being starved in the mountains and shot in back yards, dying without God.'

*

There is a particular sadness about Waugh's post-war travel writings that is only partly explained by the fulfilment of his prediction. Visiting Israel with Christopher Sykes to research *The Holy Places*, he has no pride in England as he had in 1935. Everything is monotonous. Tourism and politics have laid waste everywhere. And so he turns back, his eyes goggled on the past. Where as a young man he sought remote people, now he seeks remote epochs; Italy at the time of Augustus Hare; Jerusalem at the time of Helena; anywhere, in fact, before the advent of the wireless, 'the canvasses of Mr Francis Bacon', and interior decorators. 'I will tell you what I have learned in the forest, where time is different,' Tony Last raves to the planter Mr Todd in his delirium. 'There is no City. Mrs Beaver has covered it with chromium plating and converted it into flats.'

A Tourist in Africa exposes Waugh as a testy and rheumatic convalescent in the manner of his character Gilbert Pinfold, shunning the modern world for showy ruins, and stumbling around Genoa with an antiquated 1875 guidebook in the company of Lady Diana Cooper, whom he presents to the reader as Mrs Stitch, the suggestion hard to resist that he rather prefers his fictional creation. Aboard the *Rhodesia Castle* he behaves like a pompous dug-out who insists on wearing a dinner-jacket and complains loudly, at every opportunity, about the background music. As on the *Stella Polaris* years before, he is accosted by a woman who mistakes him for his brother. His loyalest reader (whom he pictures as female) could mistake him for a package tourist of exactly the sort he derided for spoiling the civilized world.

More than anything, Waugh's last travel book underlines

the pitfalls of the freebie. When he starts to dispense unlikely expressions of kindness and gratitude, he generates the suspicion that he has gone soft in the bonce. Staying in Salisbury at Government Lodge, he is driven to admiring the garden 'that has been the particular contribution of the Governor's wife'. No longer is his eye alert to discrepancies, least of all his own. 'I am both ignorant and blasé about tropical fauna,' he announces with just a trace of pride. And on the next page: 'The successive belts of vegetation are a joy to the botanist.' Cape Town, which he had once disparaged as reminding him of Glasgow, is now 'the decent old city'.

A Tourist in Africa is so thin that, according to Hastings, Waugh half-heartedly suggested to his publisher he insert adverbs before all adjectives to pad it out. Instead, he stuffs it with feeble digests of guidebooks scanned while on board ship. 'The chief hotel stands near the railway station. Luggage is carried there through a tunnel under the traffic, which during the day is thick and fast.' He gets as near to writing dead prose as at any time in his career. In the past he would have changed by a single word the energy of the following sentence; now he lets it pass, as if he has slumped into the sort of travel writer he scorned as he embarked on his first cruise. 'There is plenty to delight the mere sight-seer.'

Just when one thinks Waugh is done for he comes closest to discovering his Lost City. On 18 March 1959, moments before sunset, he arrives at the remarkable stone ruins of Great Zimbabwe. As is his habit, he tries to appropriate them; he pictures the African landscape round about as having the aspect of 'Devon parkland' while parts of the temple suggest to him 'Cotswold buttresses'. But all of a sudden metaphor and simile fail him. No one, he realizes, has the bluest clue about what went on at this site. A dense jungle has overgrown it; any attempt to explain its purpose, even the original shape, must remain conjectural. For the first time in three decades of travelling, of ogling, of raising his Anglo-Saxon eyebrow, Waugh is forced to admit: '... "the Temple" at Zimbabwe leaves the visitor from Europe without any comparison'. It is the moment when, transcending his rampant subjectivity and ethno-centrism, he becomes a proper traveller.

The experience releases him into a rare flight of ecstasy. Next day he proceeds to the Serima Mission and there visits a little school of art, 'one of the most exhilarating places in Africa'. The sight of two master craftsmen in their mid-twenties, and their series of intricate ochre-carvings, has a tremendous uplifting effect as if, here in the middle of nowhere, he has stumbled on the dream Tony Last had of Hetton. 'Quite soon,' writes Waugh, 'there will be at Serima one of the most beautiful and original churches of the modern world.' The visit stimulates him to analyse the spiritual dimension of his own profession, which he describes elsewhere in terms of a craftsman putting an experience into shape and communicable form exactly as a carpenter does. At the Serima Mission, Waugh is reinforced in his belief that 'Art is the catechism and prayer in visible form.'

In this transcendent mood he makes an eloquent summary of the consolations of the writer. Still in Rhodesia, Waugh climbs a modest hill called 'the View of the World' and there on its summit, faced by an unbroken horizon, he is moved to contrast the achievement of the politician with that of the artist: 'the one talking about generations yet unborn, the other engrossed in the technical problems of the task at hand; the one fading into a mist of disappointment and controversy, the other leaving behind a few objects of permanent value that were not there before him and would not have been there but for him.'

Waugh's remarks are a modest reminder of the experiences he has amassed in thirty years of travel, and put into shape in this volume. Without them we would have no William Boot; no Prudence Courteney; no Mr Todd reading Dickens to Tony Last, as Waugh once read P. G. Wodehouse to his wife.

But implicit in his observations from 'the View of the World' is a caution. He closes his last travel book with a warning no less dismal or premonitory than the foghorn that sounds at the end of *Labels*: 'Cruelty and injustice are endemic everywhere.' Today, as a British national – the badge that once guaranteed him access to the world – Waugh would not be allowed to cross the border into Zimbabwe, the country that was renamed after its ruins.

INTRODUCTION

In 1942, Evelyn Waugh was in a Nissen hut on a Scottish moor. 'All I asked in that horrible camp was freedom to travel. That, I should like to claim, is what I fought for . . .' A century after his birth, it must be fought for again.

Nicholas Shakespeare

SELECT BIBLIOGRAPHY

LETTTERS, DIARIES AND ESSAYS

AMORY, MARK, ed., *The Letters of Evelyn Waugh*, Weidenfeld & Nicolson, 1980.

DAVIE, MICHAEL, ed., *The Diaries of Evelyn Waugh*, Weidenfeld & Nicolson, 1976.

GALLAGHER, DONAT, ed., *The Essays, Articles and Reviews of Evelyn Waugh*, Methuen, 1983.

COOPER, ARTEMIS, ed., *Mr. Wu and Mrs. Stitch: The Letters of Evelyn Waugh and Diana Cooper*, Hodder & Stoughton, 1991.

MOSLEY, CHARLOTTE, ed., *The Letters of Nancy Mitford and Evelyn Waugh*, Hodder & Stoughton, 1996.

Waugh is one of the great letter-writers.

BIOGRAPHY AND PERSONAL REMINISCENCE

DEEDES, WILLIAM, *War with Waugh*, Macmillan, 2003.

DONALDSON, FRANCES, *Evelyn Waugh. Portrait of a Country Neighbour*, Weidenfeld & Nicolson, 1967. A well-written, warm and honest portrait of Waugh from the late forties.

HASTINGS, SELINA, *Evelyn Waugh: A Biography*, Sinclair-Stevenson, 1994. Lively and sympathetic.

PATEY, DOUGLAS LANE, *The Life of Evelyn Waugh: A Critical Biography*, Blackwell, 1998. An intelligent intellectual biography.

PRYCE-JONES, DAVID, ed., *Evelyn Waugh and His World*, Weidenfeld & Nicolson, 1973. Essays and photographs by friends on different aspects of Waugh.

ST JOHN, JOHN, *To the War With Waugh*, Leo Cooper, 1973. Written by a fellow-member of the Royal Marines.

STANNARD, MARTIN, *Evelyn Waugh: The Early Years 1903–1939*, Dent, 1986, and *Evelyn Waugh: No Abiding City 1939–1966* Dent, 1992. Admirably industrious and full documentation, marred by a lack of sympathy.

SYKES, CHRISTOPHER, *Evelyn Waugh: A Biography*, Collins, 1975. Factually inaccurate, but with the vitality and insight of critical friendship.

WAUGH, ALEC, *My Brother Evelyn & Other Profiles*, Cassell, 1967.

TRAVEL

PRIMARY TEXTS

Labels, A Mediterranean Journal, Duckworth, 1930; US edition: *A Bachelor Abroad, A Mediterranean Journal*, Cape, Smith, New York, 1930.

Remote People, Duckworth, 1931; US edition: *They Were Still Dancing*, Farrar & Rinehart, New York, 1932.

Ninety-Two Days, The Account of a Tropical Journey Through British Guiana and Part of Brazil, Duckworth, 1934; Farrar & Rinehart, New York, 1934.

Waugh in Abyssinia, Longman, Green & Co., 1936; Longman, Green & Co., New York, 1936.

Robbery Under Law: The Mexican Object-Lesson, Chapman & Hall, 1939; US edition: *Mexico: An Object Lesson* Little, Brown, Boston, 1939.

The Holy Places, The Queen Anne Press, 1952; Queen Anne Press and British Book Center, New York, 1953.

A Tourist in Africa, Chapman & Hall, 1960; Little, Brown, Boston, 1960.

SECONDARY TEXTS

FLEMING, PETER, *Brazilian Adventure*, Cape, 1933 (Northwestern University Press, 1999).

GREENE, GRAHAM, *Journey without Maps*, Heinemann, 1936; *The Lawless Roads*, Longman, 1939; *The Power and the Glory*, Heinemann, 1940; *The Heart of the Matter*, Heinemann, 1948.

MAIS, S. P. B., *Mediterranean Cruise Holiday*, Alvin Redman, 1953.

STEER, GEORGE, *Caesar in Abyssinia*, Hodder & Stoughton, 1937.

THESIGER, WILFRED, *Desert, Marsh and Mountain*, Collins, 1979.

CHRONOLOGY

DATE	AUTHOR'S LIFE	LITERARY CONTEXT
1898	Birth of Alec Waugh, Evelyn's brother.	
1903	28 October: birth of Evelyn Waugh to Arthur and Catherine Waugh in Hampstead.	James: *The Ambassadors.* Shaw: *Man and Superman.*
1904		Conrad: *Nostromo.*
1905		James: *The Golden Bowl.* Forster: *Where Angels Fear to Tread.*
1908		Forster: *A Room with a View.* Bennett: *The Old Wives' Tale.* Grahame: *The Wind in the Willows.*
1910	Attends Heath Mount Preparatory School.	Forster: *Howards End.*
1911	Begins keeping a diary.	Lawrence: *The White Peacock.* Beerbohm: *Zuleika Dobson.*
1912		Beerbohm: *A Christmas Garland.* Brooke: *Collected Poems.* Shaw: *Pygmalion.*
1913		Lawrence: *Sons and Lovers.* Proust: *A la Recherche du temps perdu* (to 1927). Conrad: *Chance.*
1914		Joyce: *Dubliners.*
1915		Ford: *The Good Soldier.* Conrad: *Victory.* Buchan: *The Thirty-nine Steps.* Woolf: *The Voyage Out.*
1916		Joyce: *A Portrait of the Artist as a Young Man.*
1917	Alec Waugh's *Loom of Youth* published. Evelyn attends Lancing College, Sussex.	Yeats: *The Wild Swans at Coole.* Eliot: *Prufrock and Other Observations.*
1918		Brooke: *Collected Poems.*
1919		Shaw: *Heartbreak House.* Beerbohm: *Seven Men.* Firbank: *Valmouth.*
1920		Pound: *Hugh Selwyn Mauberley.*

Emmeline Pankhurst founds the Women's Social and Political Union.

Russo-Japanese war. Franco-British *entente cordiale*.
Liberal government in Britain: Campbell-Bannerman Prime Minister. First Russian revolution.

Asquith becomes Prime Minister.

Death of Edward VII.

Coronation of George V. Agadir crisis. Industrial unrest in Britain.

Outbreak of World War I.
Asquith forms coalition government with Balfour.

Easter Rising in Dublin. Lloyd George becomes Prime Minister.

Bolshevik revolution in Russia. US joins war.

Armistice. Women over 30 gain vote.
Versailles peace conference.

League of Nations formed. Prohibition in the US.

DATE	AUTHOR'S LIFE	LITERARY CONTEXT
1921		Huxley: *Crome Yellow*. Pirandello: *Six Characters in Search of an Author*.
1922	January: attends Hertford College, Oxford, as a Scholar reading History. Begins contributing graphics, and later pieces to undergraduate magazines.	Joyce: *Ulysses*. Eliot: *The Waste Land*. Housman: *Last Poems*. Fitzgerald: *The Beautiful and the Damned*.
1923		Cummings: *The Enormous Room*. Firbank: *The Flower Beneath the Foot*. Huxley: *Antic Hay*.
1924	Leaves Oxford with a third-class degree. Begins novel, *The Temple at Thatch*. Makes film, *The Scarlet Woman*. Attends Heatherley's Art School, London.	Forster: *A Passage to India*. Shaw: *Saint Joan*. Ford: *Parade's End* (to 1928).
1925	Schoolmaster at Arnold House, Llanddulas, Denbighshire (January–July). Destroys *The Temple at Thatch* on Harold Acton's criticism. Attempts suicide. Writes 'The Balance'. Begins as schoolmaster in Aston Clinton, Berkshire (September).	Fitzgerald: *The Great Gatsby*. Kafka: *The Trial*.
1926	*P.R.B.: An Essay on the Pre-Raphaelite Brotherhood 1847–1854* privately printed. 'The Balance' published.	Faulkner: *Soldier's Pay*. Nabokov: *Mary*. Henry Green: *Blindness*. Firbank: *Concerning the Eccentricities of Cardinal Pirelli*.
1927	Sacked from Aston Clinton (February). Story for *The New Decameron* commissioned; writes 'The Tutor's Tale: A House of Gentlefolks'. Temporary schoolmaster in London, also contributing to *The Daily Express*. Meets Evelyn Gardner (April). Writes *Rossetti, His Life and Works*. Takes carpentry lessons. Proposes to Evelyn Gardner (December).	Woolf: *To the Lighthouse*. Hemingway: *Men Without Women*. Dunne: *An Experiment with Time*.
1928	Begins writing *Decline and Fall*. *Rossetti* published (April). Marries Evelyn Gardner (June). *Decline and Fall* published (September).	Lawrence: *Lady Chatterley's Lover*. Woolf: *Orlando*. Yeats: *The Tower*. Lewis: *The Childermass*. Nabokov: *King, Queen, Knave*.

CHRONOLOGY

Establishment of USSR. Stalin becomes General Secretary of the Communist party Central Committee. Mussolini marches on Rome. Coalition falls and Bonar Law forms Conservative ministry.

Baldwin becomes Prime Minister. Women gain legal equality in divorce suits. Hitler's coup in Munich fails. German hyper-inflation.

First Labour government formed by Ramsay MacDonald. Hitler in prison. Death of Lenin. Baldwin becomes Prime Minister again after a Conservative election victory.

Locarno conference.

British general strike. First television demonstrated.

Lindbergh makes first solo flight over Atlantic.

Hoover becomes US President. Stalin de facto dictator in USSR: first Five Year Plan. Women's suffrage in Britain reduced from age 30 to age 21.

DATE	AUTHOR'S LIFE	LITERARY CONTEXT
1929	Mediterranean cruise with his wife (February–March). *Vile Bodies* begun. Marriage breaks down (July). Divorce (September).	Faulkner: *The Sound and the Fury*. Cocteau: *Les Enfants terribles*. Hemingway: *A Farewell to Arms*. Henry Green: *Living*. Priestley: *The Good Companions*. Remarque: *All Quiet on the Western Front*.
1930	*Vile Bodies* published (January). Received into the Catholic Church; *Labels, A Mediterranean Journal* published (September). Travels to Abyssinia to report coronation of Haile Selassie for *The Times* (October–November); travels in East and Central Africa.	Eliot: *Ash Wednesday*. Faulkner: *As I Lay Dying*. Nabokov: *The Defence*.
1931	Returns to England (March). *Remote People* completed (August) and published (November). *Black Mischief* begun (September).	Faulkner: *Sanctuary*. Woolf: *The Waves*.
1932	Working on film scenario for Ealing Studios (January–February). Writes 'Excursion in Reality' (March). *Black Mischief* completed (June) and published (October). Sails for British Guiana (December).	Huxley: *Brave New World*. Faulkner: *Light in August*. Betjeman: *Mount Zion*. Nabokov: *Glory*.
1933	Travels in British Guiana and Brazil (January–May). Writes 'The Man Who Liked Dickens' (February). Meets 'white mouse named Laura' Herbert at Herbert family home in Italy (September). 'Out of Depth' and *Ninety-Two Days* written (October–November).	Malraux: *La Condition humaine*. Stein: *The Autobiography of Alice B. Toklas*.
1934	In Fez, Morocco, begins *A Handful of Dust* (January–February). *Ninety-Two Days* published (March) and *A Handful of Dust* completed (April). Expedition to Spitzbergen in the Arctic (July–August). *A Handful of Dust* published (September). Begins *Edmund Campion: Jesuit and Martyr* (September); writes 'Mr Crutwell's Little Outing' and 'On Guard'.	

CHRONOLOGY

DATE	AUTHOR'S LIFE	LITERARY CONTEXT
1935	Completes *Campion* (May); writes 'Winner Takes All' (July). Travels to Abyssinia to report on imminent Italian invasion for *The Daily Mail* (August–December).	Isherwood: *Mr. Norris Changes Trains.* Eliot: *Murder in the Cathedral.* Odets: *Waiting for Lefty.* Graham Greene: *England Made Me.*
1936	Writes *Waugh in Abyssinia* (April–October). Annulment to first marriage agreed by Rome (July); engagement to Laura Herbert. Returns to Abyssinia to report on Italian occupation (July–September). *Waugh in Abyssinia* published. *Scoop* begun (October).	Faulkner: *Absalom, Absalom!* Nabokov: *Despair.*
1937	Marriage to Laura Herbert (17 April); honeymoon in Italy. Decides to rewrite *Scoop* (July). Moves into Piers Court, Stinchcombe, Gloucestershire (August).	Hemingway: *To Have and Have Not.* Orwell: *The Road to Wigan Pier.* Sartre: *La Nausée.* Betjeman: *Continual Dew.* Steinbeck: *Of Mice and Men.*
1938	Birth of daughter, Teresa Waugh (March). *Scoop* published (May). Two trips, both with Laura: to Hungary (May) and Mexico (August–October). Writes 'An Englishman's Home' and begins *Robbery Under Law: The Mexican Object-Lesson.*	Graham Greene: *Brighton Rock.* Beckett: *Murphy.* Orwell: *Homage to Catalonia.*
1939	Completes *Robbery Under Law*; writes 'The Sympathetic Passenger' (May). Begins *Work Suspended*. *Robbery Under Law* published (June). Birth of son, Auberon Waugh (November). Joins Royal Marines (December) and abandons *Work Suspended.*	Joyce: *Finnegans Wake.* Eliot: *The Family Reunion.* Steinbeck: *The Grapes of Wrath.* Henry Green: *Party Going.* Auden: *Journey to a War.* Isherwood: *Goodbye to Berlin.*
1940	Expedition to Dakar, West Africa (August–September). Transfers to Commandos in Scotland (November). Birth and death of daughter, Mary Waugh (December).	Hemingway: *For Whom the Bell Tolls.* Graham Greene: *The Power and the Glory.* Dylan Thomas: *Portrait of the Artist as a Young Dog.* Faulkner: *The Hamlet.* Henry Green: *Pack my Bag: A Self-Portrait.* Betjeman: *Old Lights for New Chancels.*

CHRONOLOGY

Italy invades Abyssinia. Anti-Jewish Nuremberg laws passed in Germany.

Spanish civil war begins. Abdication crisis in Britain. Hitler and Mussolini form Rome–Berlin Axis. Moscow 'Show Trials' begin. Blum forms Popular Front ministry in France.

Japanese invade China. Baldwin retires and Neville Chamberlain becomes Prime Minister.

Germany annexes Austria. Munich crisis.

Nazi-Soviet pact. Germany invades Czechoslovakia and Poland; Britain and France declare war (September 3).

Germany invades Norway and Denmark. Churchill becomes Prime Minister. Dunkirk. Italy declares war on Britain and France. Fall of France. Battle of Britain. The Blitz.

DATE	AUTHOR'S LIFE	LITERARY CONTEXT
1941	Sails for service in Egypt (February); raid on Bardia (April). At Battle of Crete (May). Disillusioned with war. July–August, on circuitous route home, writes *Put Out More Flags*. Rejoins Royal Marines (September).	Acton: *Peonies and Ponies*. Fitzgerald: *The Last Tycoon*.
1942	*Put Out More Flags* published. Transfers to Blues, Special Service Brigade; birth of daughter, Margaret Waugh (June). *Work Suspended* published (December).	Anouilh: *Eurydice*. Sartre: *Les Mouches*. Camus: *L'Etranger*, *Le Mythe de Sisyphe*.
1943	Transferred to London (March). Father dies (June).	Davies: *Collected Poems*. Henry Green: *Caught*.
1944	Given leave to write (January); begins *Brideshead Revisited* (January–June). Birth of daughter, Harriet Waugh (May). On British Military Mission to the Partisans in Yugoslavia (from July).	Eliot: *Four Quartets*. Anouilh: *Antigone*. Camus: *Caligula*. Sartre: *Huis Clos*.
1945	Returns to London (March). *Brideshead Revisited* published and *Helena* begun (May). Demobbed; returns to Piers Court.	Broch: *The Death of Virgil*. Betjeman: *New Bats in Old Belfries*. Orwell: *Animal Farm*. Henry Green: *Loving*. Mitford: *The Pursuit of Love*.
1946	*When the Going was Good* published (selection from previous travel books). Travels to Nuremberg (March) and Spain (June). Writes 'Scott-King's Modern Europe' and *Wine in Peace and War*.	Rattigan: *The Winslow Boy*. Cocteau: *L'Aigle à deux têtes*. Henry Green: *Back*. Dylan Thomas: *Deaths and Entrances*.
1947	Visits New York and Los Angeles for projected film of *Brideshead Revisited* (January–March). Writes 'Tactical Exercise'. Writes first draft of *The Loved One* (May–July). Birth of son, James Waugh (June). Visits Scandinavia (August–September).	Mann: *Doctor Faustus*. Camus: *La Peste*. Diary of Anne Frank is published. Henry Green: *Concluding*.

CHRONOLOGY

USSR is invaded. Japanese attack Pearl Harbor. US joins war.

Fall of Singapore. Germans reach Stalingrad. Battle of El Alamein.

Germans retreat in Russia, Africa and Italy.

Allied landings in Normandy. Red Army reaches Belgrade and Budapest. Butler's Education Act.

Hitler commits suicide. Germany surrenders. World War II ends after atom bombs are dropped on Hiroshima and Nagasaki. United Nations founded. Attlee forms Labour government.

Nuremberg trials. 'Iron Curtain' speech by Churchill. Beginning of Cold War.

Independence of India and Pakistan. Warsaw Communist conference.

DATE	AUTHOR'S LIFE	LITERARY CONTEXT
1948	*The Loved One* published (February). Begins lecture tour in USA (October).	Eliot: *Notes Towards the Definition of Culture.* Graham Greene: *The Heart of the Matter.* Faulkner: *Intruder in the Dust.* Henry Green: *Nothing.* Acton: *Memoirs of an Aesthete.*
1949	Returns from America (March). 'Compassion' published.	Orwell: *Nineteen Eighty-Four.* De Beauvoir: *The Second Sex.* Graham Greene: *The Third Man.* Mitford: *Love in a Cold Climate.* Miller: *Death of a Salesman.*
1950	Birth of son, Septimus Waugh (July). *Helena* published. Last visit to America.	Hemingway: *Across the River and into the Trees.* Eliot: *The Cocktail Party.* Henry Green: *Doting.*
1951	Middle East tour for *Life Magazine* (January–March). Writes *Men at Arms* (June–December).	Salinger: *The Catcher in the Rye.* Powell: *A Question of Upbringing* (the first of the 12 novels comprising *A Dance to the Music of Time* (1952–75). Mitford: *The Blessing.*
1952	Writes *The Holy Places* and 'Love Among the Ruins'. *Men at Arms* published (September). Christmas in Goa.	Beckett: *Waiting for Godot.* Miller: *The Crucible.*
1953	Begins *Officers and Gentlemen* (March).	Hartley: *The Go-Between.*
1954	Voyage to Ceylon and mental breakdown (February). Contributes to "U" and "non U" debate. Death of his mother (December).	
1955	*Officers and Gentlemen* published (May). Trip to Jamaica, writing *The Ordeal of Gilbert Pinfold* (from December).	Nabokov: *Lolita.* Miller: *A View from the Bridge.* Graham Greene: *Loser Takes All, The Quiet American.* Murdoch: *Under the Net.*
1956	Moves to Combe Florey, Taunton, Somerset.	Beckett: *Molloy.* Camus: *La Chute.* Faulkner: *Requiem for a Nun.* Mitford, Waugh, Betjeman et al: *Noblesse Oblige.*

CHRONOLOGY

HISTORICAL EVENTS

Marshall Aid: US contributes $5.3 billion for European recovery. Soviet blockade of West Berlin: Allied airlifts begin (to 1949). State of Israel founded. Apartheid introduced in South Africa. Yugoslavia under Tito expelled from Comintern. National Health Service inaugurated in Britain.

Federal and Democratic Republics established in Germany. People's Republic of China proclaimed. Korean war begins (to 1953). NATO founded.

McCarthy witch hunts – persecution of Communists throughout US.

Conservatives return to power in Britain. Burgess and Maclean defect to USSR.

Death of George VI: accession of Elizabeth II.

Stalin dies and is succeeded by Khrushchev.

Vietnam war begins. Nasser gains power in Egypt.

West Germany joins NATO.

Suez crisis. Invasion of Hungary by USSR.

DATE	AUTHOR'S LIFE	LITERARY CONTEXT
1957	*Pinfold* completed (January) and published (July). First plans for *Unconditional Surrender* (July).	Camus: *L'Exil et le Royaume*. Pasternak: *Doctor Zhivago*. Pinter: *The Birthday Party*. Nabokov: *Pnin*. Spark: *The Comforters*.
1958	Travels to Rhodesia (February–March), collecting material for—	Betjeman: *Collected Poems*.
1959	*The Life of the Right Reverend Ronald Knox* published (October).	Spark: *Memento Mori*. Eliot: *The Elder Statesman*. Graham Greene: *The Complaisant Lover*. Beckett: *Endgame*.
1960	*A Tourist in Africa* published.	Spark: *The Ballad of Peckham Rye*. Updike: *Rabbit, Run*. Pinter: *The Caretaker*. Betjeman: *Summoned by Bells*.
1961	*Unconditional Surrender* published (September). Trip to West Indies with his daughter Margaret (November–February).	Graham Greene: *A Burnt-Out Case*. Albee: *The American Dream*. Huxley: *Religion without Revelation*. Mitford: *Don't Tell Alfred*. Spark: *The Prime of Miss Jean Brodie*.
1962	Working on *A Little Learning*. Begins 'Basil Seal Rides Again' (August).	Albee: *Who's Afraid of Virginia Woolf?* Isherwood: *Down There on a Visit*.
1963	Publication of 'Basil Seal Rides Again'.	Stoppard: *A Walk on Water*. Pinter: *The Lover*. Spark: *The Girls of Slender Means*.
1964	Serial publication of *A Little Learning* (June–July).	Sartre: *Les Mots*. Ayme: *The Minotaur*. Isherwood: *A Single Man*.
1965	War trilogy revised and published as *Sword of Honour* (September).	Pinter: *The Homecoming*. Albee: *Tiny Alice*.
1966	Evelyn Waugh dies on Easter Sunday, 10 April, at Combe Florey.	Albee: *A Delicate Balance*.

CHRONOLOGY

LABELS

A MEDITERRANEAN JOURNAL

M/Y Stella Polaris, 1929

*With love to Bryan and Diana Guinness
without whose encouragement and
hospitality this book would not
have been finished*

AUTHOR'S NOTE

So far as this book contains any serious opinions, they are those of the dates with which it deals, eighteen months ago. Since then my views on several subjects, and particularly on Roman Catholicism, have developed and changed in many ways.

E. W.

ILLUSTRATIONS

ROUTE MAP

CHAPTER 1

I DID NOT really know where I was going, so, when anyone asked me, I said to Russia. Thus my trip started, like an autobiography, upon a rather nicely qualified basis of falsehood and self-glorification. The statement cannot be held to be wholly deceptive because it was potentially true, and also it was made without any informative motive at all. I wanted to go to Russia very much, and someone once persuaded me that, if you went on for long enough saying that you would go somewhere, you always got there eventually. For the fortnight before I left England and for as long after that as I was heading east, I kept saying I was going to Russia; I told three gossip writers of my intention and they printed it in their papers; I told a very polite young man at Cook's office that I was going there and wasted a great deal of his time in looking up steamship routes in the Black Sea; I even, provisionally and with many cautious reservations, booked a passage from Constanza to Odessa and obtained letters of introduction to people who were reputed to have influence with the Soviet Embassy at Angora. But the spell did not work; I never got nearer to Russia than the eastern mouth of the Bosphorus.

I do not suppose that the self-glorification did me very much good either; that is a part of the business of writing which I have not fully mastered. I suppose that by the time this book is published it will be quite a common and simple thing to go to Russia for a holiday. At the time of which I am writing – February 1929 – there was a Conservative majority in the House of Commons and it was a very adventurous project indeed. Now, one of the arts of successful authorship is preventing the reading public from forgetting one's name in between the times when they are reading one's

7

books. It is all very puzzling because, as far as I can see, there are only two respectable reasons for reading a book written by someone else; one is that you are being paid to review it, and the other that you are continually meeting the author and it seems rude not to know about him. But clearly there are masses of people to whom neither of these reasons apply. They read books because they have heard the author's name. Now, even if you are very industrious, you cannot rely on writing more than two books a year, which will employ your public, as it is called, for about six hours each. That is to say, that for every hour in which you employ your reader's attention, you are giving her a month to forget you. It would be very difficult to organise even a marriage on that basis, still more one's financial career. So you have to spend half your leisure in writing articles for the papers; the editors buy these because people read your books, and people read your books because they see your articles in the papers. (This is called a vicious circle by those who have not got into the running.) The rest of your leisure you have to spend in doing things which you think other people will think interesting. My hope was that, when someone saw in the gossip page that I was going to Russia, she would say, what a very interesting young man, and, I must get his life of Dante Gabriel Rossetti out of the circulating library. Well, even this did not happen to any appreciable extent, so I must begin this book, which is going to aim at what the reviewers call the uncompromising sincerity and frankness of youth, by admitting that the whole lie was a flop.

However, I did succeed in getting away from England, and that was all I really cared about. In February 1929 almost every cause was present which can contribute to human discomfort. London was lifeless and numb, seeming to take its temper from Westminster, where the Government, conscious of failure, was dragging out the weeks of its last session. Talking films were just being introduced, and had set back by twenty years the one vital art of the century. There was not even a good murder case. And besides this it was intolerably cold. The best seller of the preceding months had been Mrs Woolf's *Orlando*, and it seemed almost as though Nature were setting out to win some celestial Hawthornden Prize by imitation of that celebrated description of the Great Frost. People shrank, in those days, from the icy contact of a cocktail glass, like the Duchess of Malfi from the dead hand, and crept stiff as automata from their draughty taxis into the nearest tube railway station, where they stood, pressed together for warmth, coughing and sneezing among the evening papers. Intense cold seems peculiarly insupportable in a great city, where one's converse with the seasons is wholly capricious and unrelated to the natural processes of germination and decay.

So I packed up all my clothes and two or three very solemn books, such as Spengler's *Decline of the West*, and a great many drawing materials, for two of the many quite unfulfilled resolutions which I made about this trip were that I was going to do some serious reading and drawing. Then I got into an aeroplane and went to Paris.

I had been up before. During what proved to be my last term at Oxford, an ex-officer of the R.A.F. appeared in Port Meadow with a very dissolute-looking Avro biplane, and advertised passenger flights for seven and sixpence or fifteen shillings for 'stunting'. On a very serene summer evening I went for a 'stunt' flight. It was a memorable experience. Some of the movements merely make one feel dizzy, but 'looping the loop' develops in the mind clearly articulated intellectual doubts of all preconceived habits of mind about matter and movement. There used to be a very terrifying thing at Wembley called the Great Racer. 'Looping the loop' is that thing prolonged to its logical extreme. There were moments on the Great Racer, when the car was in full flight, during which one's nerves reached the highest point of excitement, trembling between ordinary healthy terror and mad panic. Just at that zenith of emotion the car always slackened in speed or changed its direction, so that a few seconds of comparative calm were interspersed between the successive crises. In 'looping', the aeroplane shoots steeply upwards until the sensation becomes unendurable and one knows that in another moment it will turn completely over. Then it keeps on shooting up and does turn completely over. One looks down into an unfathomable abyss of sky, while over one's head a great umbrella of fields and houses has suddenly opened. Then one shuts one's eyes. My companion on this occasion was a large-hearted and reckless man; he was President of the Union, logical, matter-of-fact in disposition, inclined towards beer and Ye Olde Merrie Englande, with a marked suspicion and hostility towards modern invention. He had come with me in order to assure himself that it was really all nonsense about things heavier than air being able to fly. He sat behind me throughout, muttering, 'Oh, my God, oh, Christ, oh, my God.' On the way back he scarcely spoke, and two days later, without a word to anyone, he was received into the Roman Church. It is interesting to note that, during this aeroplane's brief visit to Oxford, three cases of conversion occurred in precisely similar circumstances. I will not say that this aeronaut was directly employed by Campion House, but certainly, when a little later, he came down in flames, the Jesuits lost a good ally, and to some people it seemed as if the Protestant God had asserted supremacy in a fine Old Testament manner.

My flight to Paris was not at all like this. It was disagreeable but quite unexciting. I was taken with one other passenger in a chara-banc from the London office to Croydon. The ticket seemed very cheap until they weighed my luggage and got me to understand how much there was to pay. Then I wished I was going by train. The other passenger was a smartly dressed woman of early middle age; she had only a small attaché case with her. We got into conversation in the charabanc. She said she made this journey on business every week. She was in business in Paris. When you were very busy with business it saved time to fly. I suppose business women never get bored with the idea of their being business women. It is an adventure all the time.

The charabanc took us to a large station with a waiting-room and ticket office, a buffet and a passport office and a bookstall. It was rather a surprise to leave this building and find a grass field and a huge aeroplane. The business woman and I climbed up a ladder into the aeroplane. It was not the newest sort because they are more expensive. Low wicker arm-chairs were arranged on each side of a narrow gangway. At the back was a funny little lavatory. The floor sloped steeply uphill when the machine was on the ground. The windows were small and filled with sliding panes of glass. These, I discovered when we started, kept opening of their own accord through the vibration. The body of the aeroplane was built over the planes, so that we could not see out very easily.

The pilot and the mechanic got in, and we started our flight. Although, presumably, we were travelling a great deal faster than the old Avro in Port Meadow, there was practically no sensation of speed. We seemed to float along in the gentlest way possible. The only movement of which I was conscious was the sudden dropping into air pockets, and this was sensible to the stomach rather than the eye. The chief discomforts of air travelling were, I discovered, those which had drawn me from London, only intensified very severely – cold and noise. The roar of the propellers was shattering. I followed the advice of the company and put cotton wool in my ears, but even so had a headache for some hours afterwards. The cold is worst about one's feet, which are provided with fur-lined footbags. The things which amused me most were (1) the spectacle of a completely horizontal rain storm, and (2) of the pilot telephoning our positions (it seemed extraordinary that they could hear him at Le Bourget when we could scarcely hear him within a few feet), and (3) the look of frightful scorn on the face of the business woman when, soon after we left Le Touquet, I was sick into the little brown paper bag provided for me. One does not feel nearly as ill being air-sick as sea-sick; it is very much more sudden and decisive, but I was acutely embarrassed about my bag. If we had been over the channel it would have been different, but I could not bring myself to throw it out of the window over the countryside. In the end I put it down the little lavatory. As this opened directly into the void the effect was precisely the same, but my conscience was easier in the matter.

The view was fascinating for the first few minutes we were in the air and after that very dull indeed. It was fun to see houses and motor cars looking so small and neat; everything had the air of having been made very recently, it was all so clean and bright. But after a very short time one tires of this aspect of scenery. I think it is significant that a tower or a high hill are all the eminence one needs for observing natural beauties. All one gains from this effortless ascent is a large scale map. Nature, on an elusive principle, seems usually to provide its own view-points where they are most desirable. The Citadel at Cairo, or Canoni Point at Corfu, or the top of the mountain road above Catarro, lose nothing at all of their supremacy from the knowledge that we can now always go higher if we want to, but, on the contrary, seem rather to gain by their peculiar fitness and adequacy. There was one sight, however, which was unforgettable – that of Paris lying in a pool of stagnant smoke, looking, except for the Eiffel Tower, very much like High Wycombe indefinitely extended. After the exaggerated cleanliness and sparkle of the preceding country, this exaggerated sombreness and squalor, called up (particularly to me, who had lately been sick) all the hatred and weariness which the modern megalopolitan sometimes feels towards his own civilisation.

Then we saw below us the aerodrome of Le Bourget, marked out as though for some game. The aeroplane went far beyond it, and only the obvious calmness of the business woman, who closed with a snap the little note-book which she had been filling with sums during the journey, reassured me that we were not being misled. Then we turned round, banking over and descending rapidly, till it seemed as though our wing must catch on the top of the hangars; then a slight bumping and a feeling of buoyancy proclaimed that we were on the ground; we ran forward more slowly and came to rest in front of the station. Here our passports and luggage were examined and we were transferred to a charabanc, which presently deposited us and our luggage in the middle of Paris at the very inconvenient hour when everyone has just finished his luncheon.

There were several friends in Paris whom I wanted to see, but at the moment I did not feel up to coping with telephones or *concierges*; nor did I feel inclined to start looking for rooms; so, rather extravagantly, I drove to the Crillon. I asked for the cheapest bedroom and bath-room they had. There was a very nice little one for 180 francs, said the man at the reception counter. I said I wanted a cheaper one. He said I could have the same room for 140, so I took it. It was, as he said, very nice, with plenty of electric lights and cupboards and a comfortable bed. But I did not really feel I was abroad at all. When one has got accustomed to a certain kind of approach – the trains and boats and queues and customs and crowd – a new route seems very unconvincing. So I undressed, had a very hot bath, and went to sleep. It was not until I woke up and found it was quite dark that I really felt that I was in Paris. Then I ordered some tea and began telephoning from my bed.

I need hardly say that directly I felt strong enough, which was before noon next day, I left the Crillon for cheaper accommodation. My next hotel was remarkably less comfortable. It was exactly facing into the Metro, where it runs very noisily above ground, and the bed was, I think, stuffed with skulls. The only furniture was a bidet and a cupboard full of someone else's underclothes. There were some false teeth under the pillows, and the door opened oddly, being permanently locked and detached from both hinges, so that it could only be moved at the wrong side just far enough to admit of one squeezing through. However, it was cheaper than the Crillon, costing in fact only 18 francs a night. I was rescued from here after a night or two and removed to the cheapest way of living of all – as a guest in a seventeenth-century apartment near the Quai d'Orsay. I stayed in Paris altogether about ten days before moving on south.

Now, Paris is a very well-known city – next to Rome, I suppose, the best-known in the world – and it is one which has come to bear all kinds of romantic labels for all kinds of people. I have called this book *Labels* for the reason that all the places I visited on this trip are already fully labelled. I was no adventurer of the sort who can write books with such names as *Off the Beaten Track in Surrey* or *Plunges into Unknown Herts*. I suppose there is no track quite so soundly beaten as the Mediterranean seaboard; no towns so constantly and completely overrun with tourists as those I intend to describe. But the interest I have found in preparing this book, which I hope may be shared by some of its readers, was that of investigating with a mind as open as the English system of pseudo-education allows, the basis for the reputations these famous places have acquired.

The characteristic thing about Paris is not so much the extent – though that is vast – as the overwhelming variety of its reputation. It has become so overlaid with successive plasterings of paste and proclamation that it has come to resemble those rotten old houses one sometimes sees during their demolition, whose crumbling frame of walls is only held together by the solid strata of wall-papers.

What, after all these years, can we say about Paris? There is a word, 'bogus', which I have heard used a great deal with various and often inconsistent implications. It seems to me that this scrap of jargon, in every gradation of meaning, every innuendo, every allusion and perversion and 'bluff' it is capable of bearing, gives a very adequate expression of the essence of modern Paris.

Paris is bogus in its lack of genuine nationality. No one can feel a foreigner on Monte Carlo, but Paris is cosmopolitan in the diametrically opposite sense, that it makes everyone a foreigner. London, deficient as it is in all the attributes which make a town habitable, is, at least, British. It is our own family skeleton in our own cupboard. Bath and Wells and Birmingham are all implicit in London in a way in which Tours or Tarascon or Lyons are not implicit in Paris; the febrile ardours of French political life, the tenacity and avarice and logic and militancy of French character, seem out of place and improbable in the French capital. And sensitive Frenchmen confess to a feeling of awkwardness there. In England and Germany and the United States people flock to the great towns because they do express the life of the country. London is squalid and coarse, but Englishmen can feel at ease there, as, no doubt, they would still feel at ease in revisiting their homes, even though their mother drank and the butler had fits in the dining-room. Parisians, except the wealthy and elegant, have their eyes for the most part turned away from Paris. When they have collected enough tips they will buy some land in the country and play dominoes in the evening at the chief café of a provincial town. It is in Paris that money must be made, but is best spent in the provinces. They are stuck there for the time being, and impatient to get away. Sometimes in the evening, when the shops and offices are just closing and the Americans are beginning to file into the cocktail bars, I have stood in the Place de la Concorde, attempting vainly to attract a taxi, and seen the whole of Paris like one traffic jam, imprisoned by the increasing confluence of vehicles, and every horn trumpeting for release.

The fiction of Paris, conceived by Hollywood and the popular imagination, seems yearly to impose its identity more and more as the real city of Richelieu and Napoleon and Verlaine fades into the distance. This fictitious city expresses itself in dress parades, studios, and night clubs.

The first of these, because it is modern and commercialised, seems to me by far the most interesting. There is an inscrutable world, of which one occasionally catches a tantalising glimpse or reflection, behind the industry of making women's clothes, which seems to promise, to anyone happy enough to penetrate into that close society, a rich and almost virgin literary soil. The high diplomacy of the *couturiers*; the espionage of the *copistes*; the wicked senators' wives who smuggle their maids into the mannequin shows; the secrets and intrigues and betrayals in the *ateliers*; the simple private lives of mannequins and *vendeuses*; the genius who lives in an attic and conceives robes he will never see for beautiful women he will never meet; the great designer who steals his ideas; the life of the frock as its character is shaped and modified and enriched by the impact of each personality through whose mind it passes; its eventual emergence into reality – what a world to sack! One of the acute problems of authorship to-day is to find any aspect of social organisation about which one can get down one's seventy thousand words without obvious plagiarism; novelists are driven to stake out their own countries or counties, preserving a squatter's right upon Sussex farms, or high society, or sailors or tropical ne'er-do-wells or black men or pirates; or they hunt for improbable themes of women turned into foxes, or men who live for centuries and finally turn into women, or about little children who commit murder. Why not a novel in which the heroine is a dress, instead of its wearer?

That Paris shall be the centre of this enticing world is simply one of the accidents of commercial organisation; talent and reputation find it convenient to concentrate there. There is nothing essentially modish in the atmosphere of Paris, any more than there is anything specifically medical in the atmosphere of Harley Street. In almost all matters except the business of dress-making, Parisian taste is notably lower and less progressive than Berlin or Vienna or even London. The French, through the defects rather than the qualities of their taste, are saved from the peculiarly English horrors of folk dancing, arts and crafts, and the collection of cottage antiquities, only to fall victim, one false thing driving out another, to the worst sort of sham modernity. If the choice is inevitable between pewter-*cum*-warming-pan-*cum*-timbered-gables and the glass of M. Lalique, it is surely better to be imposed upon by a past which one has not seen than by a present of which one is oneself a part? The hand of M. Lalique is heavy on Paris, and oh, those iridescent balls at *Le Bœuf sur le Toit*!

During my visit to Paris I drove to see the Rue Mallet Stevens, which was then still under construction. It is a poignant example of the Parisian aptitude for missing the point of an artistic impulse. Confronted by that dismal metamorphosis of the German bourgeois utilitarian ideal into terms of Parisian *chic*, I felt very proud of the Underground stations of the London suburbs.

Then there is the Trilby tradition, still a vital reality in popular imagination. How many hearts still beat faster beneath paint-smudged pinafores at the thought of this life of artistic activity! But Paris never, even in the very glorious eighties, quite succeeded in getting painting under its full control. Sincere attempts are always being made to organise the art market, like dress designing, on strictly commercial lines, but here considerations other than mere mode and scarcity keep obtruding themselves. There is gambling among art dealers, and genuine enthusiasm, and incidentally Paris is one of the most difficult towns of Europe in which to sell a painting. Paris always just fails to standardise the fashion in art. It does, however, succeed in fostering experiment. There are preposterous pictures in Paris as there are not preposterous frocks, but there is also the possibility of discovery. In this hope I spent a chilly morning in the Rue de la Boëthie, going from exhibition to exhibition, but was confronted everywhere by a deadly predominance of those two Laliques of painting, Laurencin and Foujita. There was a more entertaining exhibition across the river, organised by M. Waldemar George in the Rue Bonaparte. He called it, I think quite justly, a 'Panorama of Contemporary Art'. It was very French. Picabia and Ernst hung cheek by jowl; these two abstract painters, the one so defiant and chaotic, probing with such fierce intensity into every crevice and convolution of negation, the other so delicately poised, so impossibly tidy, discarding so austerely every accident, however agreeable, that could tempt disorder, seemed between them to typify the continual conflict of modern society. There were some decorative canvases whose counterparts I was later to see at Cnossos. There was a picture in which the paint was moulded in low relief. In a corner, displayed before black velvet curtains, hung the apotheosis of bogosity – a head made in white wire, so insignificant in form and character, so drab and boring and inadequate that it suggested the skeleton of a phrenologist's bust. The workmanship was fairly neat, and resembled in many ways the kind of barely ingenious handicraft pursued in hospitals by the disabled, who are anxious to employ their fingers without taxing their intellect or senses. It was called *Tête: dessin dans l'espace*, by M. Jean Cocteau; near it stood a magnificent sculpture by Maillol.

In an exhibition of such gross and almost wanton catholicity, claiming to represent *une action impartiale mais point neutre, orientée vers les formes qu'à defaut d'autres termes on qualifie de modernes, de vivantes*, I was proud to observe that my country, too, was not unrepresented, for there on the table among so much that was perplexing and disconcerting, I was delighted to find a prettily decorated edition of the poems of Mr Humbert Wolfe.

But it is not with M. Poiret or M. Cocteau that most people associate the name of Paris. Wherever *La Vie Parisienne* circulates – furtively smuggled from hand to hand in public schools, stickily thumbed in messes and club rooms in remote quarters of the globe – there are good young men saving up their money for a beano in 'Gay Paree'. And certainly some honour is due to the organisers of Paris night life. Montmartre is a kind of Wembley Exhibition of what anyone has at any time ever thought to be at all pleasurable. Even the ordinary pseudo-respectable round of night clubs – Ciro's, Florence's, the Plantation, Shéherazade, the Grand Ecart, and the rest – are not quite wholly dismal. One cannot help noticing that their patrons look scarcely half as bored as they do in London, and on consideration I found three good reasons for this partial absence of gloom. One is that a great many of those one sees round one are destitute Russians and Viennese who are paid to sit there and look gay; another is that there are so many other places to go on to that one escapes that claustrophobia one is liable to in London, when one's host has signed one in and paid vast guest fees and one knows he is there for the next two hours without hope of release; another is that lots of people are tipsy.

It is one of the modern pseudodoxia epidemica that 'you never see a drunk man in France'. As a race, it is true, the French tend to have strong heads, weak stomachs, and a rooted abhorrence of hospitality. But it is a revelation to see the Paris-Americans drink. The difference between them and the English makes an interesting example of the effects of legislation on appetite. Every true-born Briton lives under a fixed persecution mania that someone is always trying to prevent him from getting a drink. Of course, this is true, but the significant thing is how little they have succeeded. They have been at it now for nearly a hundred and fifty years, and it is still the easiest thing in the world to get drunk in England, and, if that is what is desired, to remain drunk for weeks at a time. (A far more just cause of complaint, which I commend to the Ye-Olde-Merrie-Englande School of grumblers, is that someone is always trying to put us to bed.) If one wishes to drink in London it is possible, by acquainting oneself with the vagaries of the licensing laws, to do so without resorting to any more underhand means than passing oneself off as a bona fide market porter, for eighteen hours in the twenty-four. If this dull intervening period is spent on a travelling railway train with restaurant or pullman accommodation, one can fill one's whole life with a happy round of toping. However, the Merrie-Englanders have so eloquently upheld the cause of freedom that a subdued but smouldering resentment is now one of our national characteristics. Once the Englishman abroad has fully assured himself of the fact that he can buy wine or beer or spirits whenever he wants them, it is usual to see him adopting the routine to which he is accustomed. He does not rise up early in the morning to follow after strong drink, or deny himself his usual allowance of sleep for the delight of quaffing some champagne after bedtime. Not so the Americans, to whom each new bottle comes with an aura of fresh romance. They endow the ancient and prosaic business of wine-selling with the glamour the Englishman reserves for the ancient and prosaic business of brothel-keeping. It is these dazzled Americans, and not only the tourists but the residents, who keep the night life of Paris going.

The thing which chiefly distinguishes the night life of Paris from that of London is that it can be indefinitely prolonged and almost indefinitely varied. But even in its wide variety, there breaks in on one's appreciation the still small voice of the débutante, whispering 'bogus'.

I spent a night with some kind, generous, and wholly delightful Americans. They wanted to show me a place called 'Brick-Top's', which was then very popular. We dined at Ciro's, where the food was delicious and the clientele almost unmixed American. It was no good going to Bricky's, they said, until after twelve, so we went to Florence's first. We drank champagne because it is one of the peculiar modifications of French liberty that one can drink nothing else. Florence's was full of what apparently were well-known people, and here I was introduced to a snobbery that was new to me and is, as far as I have seen, quite unknown in London; that is, the hierarchy of the high demi-monde, the kept women of very rich men, who are all famous, and, without having any social position or set of friends, are able to make the reputation for smartness of dress shops and restaurants. I modestly greeted a few simple and shabby acquaintances of my own while these celebrities were being pointed out to me.

Then we went to an underground public house called the New York Bar. When we came in all the people beat on the tables with little wooden hammers, and a young Jew who was singing made a joke about the ermine coat which one of our party was wearing. We drank some more, much nastier, champagne and went to Brick-Top's, but when we got there, we found a notice on the door saying, 'Opening at four. Bricky', so we started again on our rounds.

We went to a café called *Le Fétiche*, where the waitresses wore dinner-jackets and asked the ladies in the party to dance. I was interested to see the fine, manly girl in charge of the cloakroom very deftly stealing a silk scarf from an elderly German.

We went to the Plantation, where the paintings on the walls are first rate, and to the Music Box, where it was so dark we could hardly see our glasses (which contained still nastier champagne), and to Shéherazade, where the waiters are very impressive. They brought us five different organs of lamb spitted together between onions and bay leaves, all on fire at the end and very nice to eat.

We went to Kasbek which was just like Shéherazade.

Finally, at four, we went to Brick-Top's, a really intimate and delightful negro cabaret. Brick-Top came and sat at our table. She seemed the least bogus person in Paris. It was broad daylight when we left; then we drove to the Halles and ate fine, pungent onion soup at Le Père Tranquille, while one of the young ladies in our party bought a bundle of leeks and ate them raw. I asked my host if all his evenings were like this. He said, no, he made a point of staying at home at least one night a week to play poker.

Now all this is recorded, not to show what a devil of a fellow I am when I am on the spree, but to make clear my point about bogosity, because all this feverish gumping from place to place would be justifiable, and indeed admirable, if each excursion, besides providing one with different decorations, did actually give one a different atmosphere. Later, in Athens, I spent a more modest but somewhat similar evening, and there each place we visited had its own clientele and its own definable character. It was during about the third halt in the pilgrimage I have just described that I began to recognise the same faces crossing and re-crossing our path. There seemed to be about a hundred or so people in Montmartre that night, all doing the same round as ourselves. In each cabaret the professional dancers employed by the house varied (in identity, but very little in type), but the clientele was substantially the same. During an evening's amusement in London one suffers almost every kind of boredom, but not that. The system by which London night clubs really are clubs, to which one is introduced and elected, tends to preserve a certain integrity of atmosphere. People do not want to multiply subscriptions indefinitely, and for the most part confine themselves to membership of one cocktail and one dancing club. The system of guest fees encourages them to choose the same clubs as the majority of their friends, so that each set has what practically amounts to an established headquarters and rendezvous. Another advantage which the club system gives to London over Montmartre, is that when one's subscription is paid one has the right of membership to eat and drink what one likes.

Le champagne obligatoire of Montmartre is no doubt an economic necessity to the proprietors, but it is an exasperating imposition to those who honestly prefer beer or other wines; moreover, the champagne is notoriously of the most dubious sort.

Two incidents of this visit to Paris live vividly in my memory, and comfort me during sleepless nights, plays, gossip about people I do not know, good advice from my agent about the 'sort of stuff you can put across editors', and the hundred and one other occurrences of daily life when one has to look to oneself for support and consolation.

One of these was the spectacle of a man in the Place Beauveau, who had met with an accident which must, I think, be unique. He was a man of middle age and, to judge by his bowler hat and frock coat, of the official class, and his umbrella had caught alight. I do not know how this can have happened. I passed him in a taxi-cab, and saw him in the centre of a small crowd, grasping it still by the handle and holding it at arm's length so that the flames should not scorch him. It was a dry day and the umbrella burnt flamboyantly. I followed the scene as long as I could from the little window in the back of the car, and saw him finally drop the handle and push it, with his foot, into the gutter. It lay there smoking, and the crowd peered at it curiously before moving off. A London crowd would have thought that the best possible joke, but none of the witnesses laughed, and no one to whom I have told this story in England has believed a word of it.

The other incident happened at a night club called *Le Grand Ecart*. To those who relish the flavour of 'Period', there is a rich opportunity for reflection on the change that came over this phrase when the Paris of Toulouse-Lautrec gave place to the Paris of M. Cocteau. Originally it means the 'splits' – that very exacting figure in which the dancer slides her feet farther and farther apart until her body rests on the floor with her legs straight out on either side of her. It was thus that La Goulou and La Mélonite – 'the Mænad of the Decadence' – and all the jolly girls of the Moulin Rouge were accustomed to complete their *pas seul*, with a roguish revelation of thigh between black silk stocking and frilled petticoat, while the late impressionists applauded through a haze of absinthe. It is not so to-day. It is the name of a night club with little coloured electric bulbs, decorated with coils of rope and plate glass mirrors; on the tables are little illuminated tanks of water, with floating sheets of limp gelatine in imitation of ice. Shady young men in Charvet shirts sit round the bar repairing with powder-puff and lipstick the ravages of grenadine and *crème de cacao*. I was there one evening in a small party. A beautiful and splendidly dressed Englishwoman – who, as they say, shall be nameless – came to the next table. She was with a very nice-looking, enviable man who turned out later to be a Belgian baron. She knew someone in our party and there was an indistinct series of introductions. She said, 'What did you say that boy's name was?'

They said, 'Evelyn Waugh.'

She said, 'Who is he?'

None of my friends knew. One of them suggested that she thought I was an English writer.

She said, 'I knew it. He is the one person in the world I have been longing to meet.' (You must please bear with this part of the story: it all leads to my humiliation in the end.) 'Please move up so that I can come and sit next to him.'

Then she came and talked to me.

She said, 'I should never have known from your photographs that you were a blond.'

I should not have known how to answer that, but fortunately there was no need as she went straight on. 'Only last week I was reading an article by you in the *Evening Standard*. It was so beautiful that I cut it out and sent it to my mother.'

I said, 'I got ten guineas for it.'

At this moment the Belgian baron asked her to dance. She said, 'No, no. I am drinking in the genius of this wonderful young man.' Then she said to me, 'You know, I am psychic. The moment I came into this room to-night I *knew* that there was a *great personality* here, and I knew that I should find him before the evening was over.'

I suppose that real novelists get used to this kind of thing. It was new to me and very nice. I had only written two very dim books and still regarded myself less as a writer than an out-of-work private schoolmaster.

She said, 'You know, there is only one other great genius in this age. Can you guess his name?'

I suggested Einstein? No.... Charlie Chaplin? No.... James Joyce? No.... Who?

She said, 'Maurice Dekobra. I must give a little party at the Ritz for you to meet him. I should feel I had at least done something to justify my life if I had introduced you two great geniuses of the age. One must do something to justify one's life, don't you think, or don't you?'

Everything went very harmoniously for a time. Then she said something that made me a little suspicious, 'You know, I so love your books that I never travel without taking them all with me. I keep them in a row by my bed.'

'I suppose you aren't by any chance confusing me with my brother Alec? He has written many more books than I.'

'What did you say his name was?'

'Alec.'

'Yes, of course. What's your name, then?'

'Evelyn.'

'But . . . but they said you wrote.'

'Yes, I do a little. You see, I couldn't get any other sort of job.'

Her disappointment was as frank as her friendliness had been. 'Well,' she said, 'how very unfortunate.'

Then she went to dance with her Belgian, and when she sat down she went to her former table. When we parted she said vaguely, 'We're sure to run into one another again.'

I wonder. And I wonder whether she will add this book, and with it this anecdote, to her collection of my brother's works by the side of her bed.

CHAPTER 2

MY NEXT MOVE was to Monte Carlo, where I had arranged to join a ship called the *Stella Polaris*, which was to carry me to Constantinople, for I still adhered to my resolution of reaching Russia through the Black Sea. I had spent a good deal more money in Paris than I had meant to, and had lost a little through minor dishonesties (if one has a careless disposition and mild appearance, one has to add about ten per cent. on to all one's expenses in France and twenty in Italy, because it seldom occurs to the inhabitants of these countries with whom the tourist comes into contact to offer the correct change until the incorrect has been refused. It takes some time to overcome the English habit of pocketing change unchecked), so I did not travel in a luxurious train or a luxurious manner. A railway journey is always disagreeable to me, and I would sooner suffer to the full, and enjoy the contrast when I reach a house or a ship, than spend a great deal of money in rendering it very slightly more supportable. Accordingly I booked a *couchette*, which, I am told, is the way Frenchmen always travel. It is a carriage for four, with two berths which open from the wall above the seats. You can lie full length on these, covered with rugs. It is one better than sitting up all night and not much more expensive.

My companions in this carriage were a French business man – a commercial traveller, I should think – and a rather sweet-looking young English couple – presumably, from the endearments of their conversation and marked solicitude for each other's comfort, on their honeymoon, or at any rate recently married. The young man was small and pleasantly dressed and wore a slight, curly moustache; he was reading a particularly good detective story with apparent intelligence. His wife was huddled in a fur coat in the corner, clearly

24

far from well. I was to meet this couple again on my travels, so I may as well at once give them the names by which I later learned to call them; they were Geoffrey and Juliet.

Every quarter of an hour or so they said to each other, 'Are you quite sure you're all right, darling?' And replied, 'Perfectly, really I am. Are *you*, my precious?' But Juliet was far from being all right. After we had travelled for about an hour, Geoffrey produced a thermometer and took her temperature. They had some difficulty in reading it and translating the Centigrade degrees into Fahrenheit; when they did succeed, they discovered that it registered 104°. Geoffrey was scared, but not nearly as scared as Juliet. The person who was most scared of all was the French commercial traveller. His eyes narrowed at the sight of the thermometer and he shrank back in his corner as though he could ward off infection with his copy of *Le Journal*; an epidemic of 'flu was raging at this time in London and Paris, and I must admit that I, too, felt profound repugnance towards this unfortunate young couple. I began to visualise myself stranded alone in a Riviera nursing-home. Accordingly, when I found myself in conversation with Geoffrey a little later, I gave him what was, apart from my own interest, the perfectly sound advice to move Juliet into a *wagon-lit* for the night. He went down the corridor to look for the *conducteur*. Juliet and the Frenchman and I sat in our corners in an atmosphere of very intense fear and hostility. After a long time Geoffrey came back; he had endured the series of insults to which one is always subjected in a French railway train and secured a transfer. There was only one bed vacant, and it was in a double compartment divided only by a curtain. Geoffrey said that the other occupant was a man, but that he had three books of devotion ranged on the shelf by his pillow, so that he was undoubtedly wholly respectable. So he put Juliet to bed, and spent most of the evening sitting with her in the sleeper.

I met him again in the restaurant car, where we ate the very bad dinner opposite each other at the same table. He had some rather dim job in London; Juliet had been ill and a sister of hers was paying their expenses on a Mediterranean pleasure cruise. They were booked for the *Stella Polaris*; it was the first time he had been farther abroad than Florence; now Juliet had got 'flu; he was very despondent and I attempted to cheer him with cognac; I told him that I, too, was going in the *Stella Polaris* on my way to Russia; he was suitably impressed by my destination.

We returned to our *couchette*, where the Frenchman was putting on four or five brightly coloured woollen jerseys preparatory to turning in for the night.

How that man snored and grunted!

I slept very little, and when I did was bored by the most prosaic kind of dreams; when daylight came through the edges of the blinds I went out into the corridor. We had travelled through a storm during the night and the windows were completely obscured by frozen snow. A very young priest, who cannot long have left his seminary, was standing in the corridor, steadying himself against the window bars. His chin was blue and his face very pale; he dabbed his nose with a handkerchief.

An hour later, while Geoffrey and I were drinking coffee in the restaurant car, I heard a very sad story about this priest. He was the other occupant of Juliet's *wagon-lit*. He had dined with the late service and returned to his carriage to find Juliet just getting into bed. He had stood in the doorway for one half-minute, his eyes wide with shock. Juliet had made things worse by giving him a feverish smile of welcome. Then, without a word, he fled. He had spent the whole night standing in the corridor, and the night air seemed to have been effective in purging him of any worldly thoughts that the encounter provoked.

The train was an hour or so late owing to the snow, but was very fortunate compared with other trains of that week; the Blue Train next day was held up for nearly six hours, and the Simplon-Orient for several days.

I parted from Geoffrey and Juliet at Monaco. They were going on to Monte Carlo, but I had decided to get out at Monaco because, I was told, the hotels were cheaper, and it would be more convenient for boarding the *Stella Polaris*, though I had inadvertently registered my luggage to Monte Carlo, from where I had it rescued later in the day.

The station at Monaco is very small and unpretending. The only porter I could find belonged to an hotel with a fairly reputable sounding name. He took my suitcase and led me through the snow, down the hill to his hotel. It was a miserable-looking *pension* in a side street. There was a small lounge full of basket chairs in which elderly Englishwomen sat sewing. I asked the porter whether there was not a better hotel at Monaco. Why, yes, he said, all the hotels in Monaco were better than this one. So he picked up my suitcase again and we went out into the snow, pursued by a manageress, and soon reached a large hotel facing the harbour. I do not advise anyone to stay at this hotel, which is neither cheap, smart, quiet, nor comfortable, and the only meal I ate there was the sort of food one has on a railway train. However, as I was out all day, I spent four nights there without any acute dissatisfaction. I learned later that I should have gone to the Monégasque.

After luncheon the snow stopped, and the afternoon turned out intensely cold but bright and clear. I took a tram up the hill to Monte Carlo. The sound of firing came from the bastion below the promenade where '*Tir aux Pigeons*' was advertised. Feeling that if I intended to write a book it was my duty to see all the sights conscientiously (this feeling quickly wore off), I paid a few francs and descended in a gilt lift to the terrace. It was terribly cold. Some kind of match was in progress; the competitors were for the most part South Americans with papal titles. They made very interesting gestures with their elbows as they waited for the little cages to collapse and release the game; they also had interesting gestures of vexation and apology when they missed. But this was rare. The standard of marksmanship was high, and while I was there only three birds, fluttering erratically with plucked tail and wings, escaped the guns, to fall to the little boys below, who wait for them on the beach or in rowing-boats and pull them to pieces with their fingers. Often when the cages fell open the birds would sit dazed among the débris, until they were disturbed with a bowl; then they would rise clumsily and be brought down, usually by the first barrel, when they were about ten feet from the ground. On the balcony above the terrace sat one of the Casino pigeons, privileged and robust, watching the destruction without apparent emotion. The sport seemed unattractive, lacking, as it does, even the artificial spontaneity or artificial utility of English and Scottish shooting parties. The only convincing recommendation which I heard of it came from one of the visitors at the Bristol who remarked that it was not cricket; but even that is only very negative praise.

On the way back down the hill I stopped at the Sporting Club and became a temporary member, and it was here that I learned the solution of a minor problem which had often vexed me. I was always reading in my newspapers about 'clubmen', and it made me wonder who this mysterious race were and if I had ever seen one. Clearly they were rapidly becoming extinct, because, though the papers were full of their deaths, I never read of their births or appointments. I felt it was sad to live in this age and not to see them. One day I should read of the death of the last clubman and should know it was too late. I wondered how many clubs one had to belong to before one could be described as a clubman, or whether it was enough merely to sleep and eat one's meals at a club. The problem presented itself in an acute form when I applied to the secretary of the Sporting Club for temporary membership. He was a gracious and elegant young man, and he said it would be a delight and honour for me to join his club. He began to fill in my *dossier*. Name? Address? Nationality? Profession? Then he sat with the point of his fountain pen poised over the space marked 'Club'. I said that I did not belong to a club in London. He looked disappointed and embarrassed. Surely, he said, I must belong to the Authors' Club. I tried to explain the paradox of English social organisation by which it is possible to write books and yet not be a member of the Authors' Club. He clearly did not understand. There were in his mind only two possible explanations; either I was a crook trying to pass myself off as an author, or else I was a renegade and discredited author, an outcast from his fellows, a plagiarist and infringer of copyrights, an illiterate, misleading, and mischievous author, one, no doubt, whose books were bound in plain wrappers and might not be sent through the post. He was very sorry, the secretary said, but only clubmen were eligible for the Sporting Club. The Sporting Club was affiliated to all the leading clubs of Europe and America. The idea of this gay little cocktail-bar-*cum*-gambling-den being in affiliation with, say, the National Liberal Club seemed to me noteworthy. Then, as I turned to go, the vision which this conversation had called up of red leather chairs and old men asleep behind periodicals reminded me of an episode in my past.

'I am a life member of the Oxford Union,' I said. 'No doubt you are affiliated with that society?'

'Why, certainly,' said the secretary. All his good nature returned to him. He made out a little card of membership for me and bowed me to the door.

And the moral of this story is that we are, one and all, clubmen, without our knowledge, and it only comes out when we die.

And the discovery of this fact shows how travel broadens the mind.

That night I dined at the Sporting Club. The dinner was delicious and less expensive than the three or four leading restaurants. I saw, but did not dare to speak to, Joseph, who is one of the famous servants of Europe; he lends money to famous beauties and knows the secrets of the *noblesse industrielle*. After dinner I played roulette and won a hundred francs or so. I went up with them to the Casino, which, by comparison, seemed very shabby. The cinema producer's version of the *salles privées*, with jewelled courtesans and ribboned grand-dukes, is a thing of the past. Nowadays, in the evening, these famous rooms look like Paddington Station in the first weeks of August. There are rows of very dowdy spinsters playing the minimum stake methodically upon the even chance; young men in tweeds who look like, and probably are, accountants on their holiday; a few avaricious retired soliders, and numerous ugly Germans. I admired the dexterity of the croupiers, particularly those who deal out cards with flat wooden batons. I went back into the other rooms called 'The Kitchen', and played for a little. No one tried to filch my winnings. I, on the other hand, absent-mindedly collected a large pile of valuable square counters belonging to a governess opposite; I hastily restored them, but it was clear from the things she said very audibly under her breath that she had little faith in my apologies. I lost my hundred francs and another hundred and then went back to bed.

In spite of the frost, which showed no sign of breaking, I enjoyed the next three days very well. Once I went up to the palace gardens and visited the aquarium, which is less like a cinema than the one in

London, and more like a fish-shop. On another day I took the funicular railway to La Turbie and walked through deep snow to Eze for luncheon. There were two rival restaurants immediately facing each other. I asked advice from an inhabitant as to which was the better, but he said that that was a matter I must decide for myself. This seemed a foolish answer, as there was no way in which I could judge except by having two preliminary luncheons and then a third in the house of my choice, so I did not try to decide but took the one on the left without bothering any more about it, and was rewarded by a perfectly adequate meal and half a bottle of fizzing wine called Royal Provence, which I learned to like some years ago in Tarascon. Most of my meals I had in small restaurants in Monaco and Monte Carlo and Beausoleil. There was a delightful one on the quay, called Stallé's, which was not quite as cheap as it looked, and another on the harbour front, called Marina, where dinner cost only 10 francs and the landlord was anxious to please; another I went to in Monte Carlo was called Giardino's. The food there was good, and it had a small garden with a roof of trellis and vines which I learned to enjoy when I returned later in the summer, but there was a rather self-conscious clientele, many of them from the Russian ballet, and the whole place reminded me too closely of Soho.

Great excitement prevailed during my last day as a result of the visit of three destroyers; two of them were Italian and one British, the *Montrose*. The Italians arrived in the early morning and woke up the principality by firing salutes. The *Montrose* adhered more rigidly to etiquette and caused offence to some of the Monegasques by her unadvertised approach. The three ships lay alongside the quay, and the crowds never tired of comparing them. There was very little doubt about the superior smartness of the *Montrose*, but the salvo of guns had put public opinion warmly on the side of the Italians, and they collected by far the larger audience; incidentally, there always seemed to be more going on in them, and the uniform of their chief officer – I do not know what his rank can have been – outdid in grandeur even the Monegasque sergeants of police. I saw Geoffrey once for a few minutes in the Casino. He was very worried about Juliet, but her sister had cabled more money and she now had an attendant doctor and nurse trying to get her fit to travel in the *Stella*.

A thing which excited my particular admiration was the way in which the Casino authorities dealt with the snow. There was a heavy fall every night I was there, sometimes continuing nearly until midday, but always, within an hour of it stopping, every trace had disappeared. The moment that the last flake had fallen there appeared an army of busy little men in blue overalls armed with brooms and hoses and barrows; they sluiced and scraped the pavements and brushed up the lawns; they climbed up the trees with ladders and shook down the snow from the branches; the flower beds had been overlaid with wire frames, straw, and green baize counterpanes; these were whipped off, revealing brightly flowering plants which were replaced, the moment they withered in the frost, by fresh supplies warm from the hot-houses. Moreover, there was no nonsense about merely tidying the unseemly deposit out of the way; one did not come upon those dirty drifts and banks of snow which survive in odd corners of other places weeks after the thaw. The snow was put into barrows and packed into hampers and taken right away, across the frontier perhaps, or into the sea, but certainly well beyond the imperium of the Casino.

This triumph of industry and order over the elements seems to me typical of Monte Carlo. Nothing could be more supremely artificial, except possibly the india rubber bathing beach which they had just decided to instal, but there is a consistency and temperance and efficacy about the artificiality of Monte Carlo which Paris so painfully lacks. The immense wealth of the Casino, derived wholly and directly from man's refusal to accept the conclusion of mathematical proof; the absurd political position of the state; the newness and neatness of its buildings; the absolute denial of poverty and suffering in this place, where sickness is represented by fashionable invalids and industry by hotel servants, and the peasantry in traditional costume come into town to witness in free seats at the theatre ballets of *Le pas d'acier* and *Mercure*; all these things make up a principality which is just as real as a pavilion at an International Exhibition. It might, indeed, actually be some such pavilion in an exposition arranged in time instead of in space – the Palace of Habitable Europe in the early twentieth century; it seems to me to bear just that relation to our own lives to-day which Mr Belloc's idea of mediæval Christendom, or the sixth form masters' Greek city state, bear to the actual lives of the Greeks at the time of Pericles, or the Christians in the time of St Thomas Aquinas.

CHAPTER 3

THE ARRIVAL OF the *Stella Polaris* caused every bit as much excitement in Monaco as the three destroyers had done. She came in late in the evening, having encountered some very heavy weather on her way from Barcelona. I saw her lights across the harbour and heard her band faintly playing dance music, but it was not until next morning that I went to look closely at her. She was certainly a very pretty ship, standing rather high in the water, with the tall, pointed prow of a sailing yacht, white all over except for her single yellow funnel, and almost ostentatiously clean; a magnificent Scandinavian seaman stood at the foot of the gangway, and I could see above him on the main deck the officer of the watch saying good-bye to two or three of the passengers. So far I was agreeably impressed, but I reserved judgment, for she has the reputation of being what is called 'the last word' in luxury design, and I am constitutionally sceptical of this kind of reputation.

During that day I had some opportunity of observing my future fellow passengers, for they mostly arrived early or spent the night before embarkation at the Bristol. Vast quantities of luggage appeared in the vestibule bearing the blue and white labels of the *Stella*; some of this belonged to those who had been on the preceding cruise and were on their way home; these fraternised in the lounge and the cocktail bar with the prospective passengers, and I heard on all sides comparisons of the rigours of the storm as it had been felt in the Mediterranean and the Blue Train. I saw them in the restaurants and the Casino and driving out on the Corniche in hired motor cars – clearly diverse in origin and experience, but imbued, nevertheless, with a certain recognisable conformity of interests which makes them a necessary part of the study of any conscientious analyst of

33

modern social conditions, for they are a type selected and developed by a series of conditions which are wholly peculiar to the present age, and must form part of our 'period' as surely as gossip-writers or psycho-analysts.

I do not really know how genuine or valuable this sense of period is. It is a product of the English public school and University educa-tion; it is, in fact, almost its only product which cannot be acquired far better and far more cheaply elsewhere. Cultured foreigners are lacking in it, and so are those admirably informed Englishmen whose education has been at secondary schools, technical colleges, and the modern Universities, or at the Royal Naval Colleges of Dartmouth and Greenwich. I am inclined to think that it is practic-ally valueless. It consists of a vague knowledge of History, Literature, and Art, an amateurish interest in architecture and costume, of social, religious, and political institutions, of drama, of the biograph-ies of the chief characters of each century, of a few memorable anecdotes and jokes, scraps of diaries and correspondence and family history. All these snacks and titbits of scholarship become fused together into a more or less homogeneous and consistent whole, so that the cultured Englishman has a sense of the past, in a continuous series of clear and pretty *tableaux vivants*. This Sense of the Past lies at the back of most intelligent conversation and of the more respectable and worse-paid *genre* of weekly journalism. It also colours our outlook on our own age. We wonder what will be the picture of ourselves in the minds of our descendants; we try to catch the flavour of the period; how will this absurd little jumble of antagonising forces, of negro rhythm and psycho-analysis, of mech-anical invention and decaying industry, of infinitely expanding means of communication and an infinitely receding substance of the communicable, of liberty and inertia, how will this ever cool down and crystallise out? How shall we look in the fancy-dress parties and charity pageants of 2030? So we go through our lives generalising and analysing, and that, anyway, gives us an imper-sonal and rather comforting attitude towards them.

Pleasure cruising is a development of the last twenty years. Before that only the very rich, who owned their own yachts, could afford this leisurely pottering from port to port. It is a new sort of travel and it has produced a new sort of traveller, who is without any doubt, a considerable contributor to our period.

Our sense of the past informs us of two kinds of Englishmen abroad in the last century. First there is the survivor of the grand tour; he is invariably male; a young man fresh from the University, well born and wealthy, travelling usually in his own coach, with his own servants; he may have friends with him, or a tutor; he always has a pair of pistols and a great many letters of introduction; a courier has ridden before him to prepare his rooms; he dines at the British embassies and legations and is presented at foreign courts; he admires the Italian marbles, the Opera; the gardens and parks seem to him in no way superior to his own home; he keeps a journal; he has rather adventurous love affairs; perhaps he fights a duel; he goes through France, Italy, Austria, and Germany in this way, dancing, observing, commenting; then he returns after a year or eighteen months with trunks full of presents for his sisters and cousins, and perhaps some pieces of sculpture to dispose about the house, or an antique bronze or some engravings; he is fully equipped for the duties of legislation, and does not, except in his memory, repeat the experience.

But by about 1860 middle-class prosperity and mechanical transport had produced a new type; the Jones, Brown, and Robinson of the picture books, the Paterfamilias of Punch. Paterfamilias, as a rule, travels with his wife and without his children; often there are other adult members of his family with him – a sister or a brother-in-law; he wears a heavy tweed overcoat and a tweed cap with ear flaps in winter; in summer he gets very hot; he has lived all his life in England and has worked very hard and done well; he is over 'on the Continent' for three weeks or a month; he is very jealous of his country's prestige, but he thinks it is better preserved by a slightly blustering manner with hotel proprietors and a refusal to be 'done' than by his predecessor's scrupulous observance of etiquette; he is very suspicious of foreigners, chiefly on the grounds that they do not have baths, disguise their food with odd sauces, are oppressed by their rulers and priests, are dishonest, immoral, and dangerous, and talk a language no one can make head or tail of; he is made to ride upon a donkey far too small for him and suffer other similar indignities; the question of cigar smoke in railway carriages is with him one of particular cogency; with his arrival begins the ignoble trade of manufacturing special trinkets for tourists, horrible paper-weights of local wood or stone, ornaments of odious design, or bits of cheap jewellery for him to take back as souvenirs. The noble prod-ucts of his age are Baedeker's guide books and Cook's travel agency. Hard on his heels comes the travelling spinster; astute in tracking the English Protestant chaplain; expert in the brewing of bedroom tea; she has arrowroot and biscuits in her Gladstone bag and a warm wrap to put on at sundown; inadequate sanitation is wedded in her mind with the superstitions of Popery. A new stage has been marked. English people have discovered that it is quite cheap to live abroad.

At the beginning of this century Mr Belloc invented a new traveller; again a male type, though it is disastrously aped by eman-cipated women. 'All the world is my oyster,' said Mr Belloc, 'since men made railways and gave me leave to keep off them.' The pilgrim on the path to Rome wears very shabby clothes, and he carries a very big walking stick. In the haversack on his back he carries a map and garlic sausage, a piece of bread, a sketch book, and a litre of wine. As he goes, he sings songs in dog Latin; he knows the exaltation of rising before day-break and being overtaken by dawn many miles from where he slept; he talks with poor people in wayside inns and sees in their diverse types the structure and unity of the Roman Empire; he has some knowledge of strategy and military history; he can distin-guish geographical features from scenery; he has an inclination towards physical prowess and sharp endurances; he maintains a firm reticence upon the subject of sex.

That was in the days when it was an unusual experience to have marched with an army; since then there has been the war.

There has also been the motor car. Tourist traffic is no longer confined to the railways. There are very few roads in Europe now where one can walk without a furtive circumspection; one may sing away for a mile or so, then there is a roar at one's heels and one is forced to leap for the gutter in a cloud of dust. The pilgrim has become the pedestrian. But to a certain extent the influence of the *Path to Rome* still determines the travel experiences of a great number of intelligent Englishmen. There is a new type of traveller which is represented by nearly all the young men and women who manage to get paid to write travel books. One comes into frequent and agreeable contact with him in all parts of the world; his book, if finished, is nearly always worth reading. It is his duty, he feels, to the publisher who has advanced him his expenses, to have as many outrageous experiences as he can. He holds the defensible, but not incontrovertible, opinion that poor and rather disreputable people are more amusing and representative of national spirit than rich people. Partly for this reason and partly because publishers are, by nature, unwilling to become purely charitable, he travels and lives cheaply and invariably runs out of money. But he finds a peculiar relish in discomfort. Bed bugs, frightful food, inefficient ships and trains, hostile customs, police and passport officers, consuls who will not cash cheques, excesses of heat and cold, night club champagne, and even imprisonment are his peculiar delights. I have done a certain amount of this kind of travelling, and the memory of it is wholly agreeable. With the real travel snobs I have shuddered at the mention of pleasure cruises or circular tours or personally conducted parties, of professional guides and hotels under English management. Every Englishman abroad, until it is proved to the contrary, likes to consider himself a traveller and not a tourist. As I watched my luggage being lifted on to the *Stella* I knew that it was no use keeping up the pretence any longer. My fellow passengers and I were tourists, without any compromise or extenuation; but we were tourists – and this brings us back to our original argument – of a new kind.

The word 'tourist' seems naturally to suggest haste and compulsion. One thinks of those pitiable droves of Middle West school teachers whom one encounters suddenly at street corners and in public buildings, baffled, breathless, their heads singing with unfamiliar names, their bodies strained and bruised from scrambling in and out of motor charabancs, up and down staircases, and from trailing disconsolately through miles of gallery and museum at the heels of a facetious and contemptuous guide. How their eyes haunt us long after they have passed on to the next phase of their itinerary – haggard and uncomprehending eyes, mildly resentful, like those of animals in pain, eloquent of that world-weariness we all feel at the dead weight of European culture. Must they go on to the very end? Are there still more cathedrals, more beauty spots, more sites of historical events, more works of art? Is there no remission in this pitiless rite? Must reverence still be done to the past? As each peak of their climb is laboriously scaled, each monument on the schedule ticked off as seen, the horizon recedes farther before them and the whole landscape bristles with inescapable beauties. And as one sits at one's café table, playing listlessly with sketch book and apéritif, and sees them stumble by, one sheds not wholly derisive tears for these poor scraps of humanity thus trapped and mangled in the machinery of uplift.

There is nothing of this kind about pleasure cruising; indeed, the qualities which struck me most about this system of travel were its outstanding comfort and leisure. The first day out of Monaco we spent at sea, arriving at Naples early the next morning. As I walked round the decks and lounge with Geoffrey – he had got Juliet on board, but she was confined to her cabin with acute neuralgia – and studied our fellow passengers and the way in which they passed their day, we realised how admirably it all fitted into place and filled a need in modern life. Ships can be very dirty and uncomfortable – I once travelled second class on a Greek steamer from Patras to Brindisi – but even the worst kind of ship has some advantages over the best kind of hotel. The servants are almost always better, probably because they bear a more direct personal responsibility for your comfort; also one escapes that haphazard and disorganised avarice which is a characteristic of hotel life; a ship is not itself a money-making thing. You have bought your ticket at the office on shore and paid them the money. The ship's business is to carry you where you want to go and to make you as comfortable as they can on the journey; they do not count your baths and your cups of tea; there are not regiments of uniformed little boys, spinning swing doors and expecting tips. There is an integrity and decency about a ship which one rarely finds on land except in very old-fashioned and expensive hotels. As far as I can see, a really up-to-date ship has every advantage over an hotel except stability and fresh meat. By any standard the comfort of the *Stella* was quite remarkable. She is a Norwegian owned six-thousand-ton motor yacht, carrying, when full, about two hundred passengers. As one would expect from her origin, she exhibited a Nordic and almost glacial cleanliness. I have never seen anything outside a hospital so much scrubbed and polished. She carried an English doctor and nurse; otherwise the officers and crew, hairdresser, photographer, and other miscellaneous officials were all Norwegian. The stewards came of that cosmopolitan and polyglot race, Norwegian, Swiss, British, Italian, which supply the servants of the world. They maintained a Jeeves-like standard of courtesy and efficiency which was a particular delight to the English passengers, many of whom had been driven abroad by the problem of servants in their own homes. The passengers, too, were of all nationalities, but British strongly predominated, and English was the official language of the ship. The officers seemed to speak all languages with equal ease; several of them had first gone to sea in windjammers; sitting out between dances after dinner, while the ship ran on smoothly at fifteen knots into the warm darkness, they used to tell hair-raising stories of their early days, of typhoons and calms and privations; I think that when they were getting a little bored by their sheltered lives they found these reminiscences consoling.

My cabin was large and furnished like a bedroom; Juliet and Geoffrey were on the deck above me and, thanks to Juliet's sister, occupied a suite of great luxury, with a satinwood panelled sitting-room and their own bath-room. There were four of these in the ship, besides about a dozen state-rooms with private bath-rooms. The smoking-room, lounge, and writing-rooms were much like those to be found in any modern ship. The decks were exceptionally broad and there was a very comfortable deck bar sheltered on three sides from the wind. The dining-room had the advantage over many ships that it could seat all the passengers at once, so that meals did not have to be arranged in two services. These, allowing for the limitations of cold storage, were admirable, and almost continuous in succession. It seems to be one of the tenets of catering on board ship that passengers need nutrition every two and a half hours. On shore the average civilised man, I suppose, confines himself to two or at the most three meals a day. On the *Stella* everybody seemed to eat all the time. They had barely finished breakfast – which included on its menu, besides all the dishes usually associated with that meal, such solid fare as goulash and steak and onions – before tureens of clear soup appeared. Luncheon was at one o'clock and was chiefly remarkable for the cold buffet which was laden with every kind of Scandinavian delicatessen, smoked salmon, smoked eels, venison, liver pies, cold game and meat and fish, sausage, various sorts of salad, eggs in sauces, cold asparagus, in almost disconcerting profusion. At four there was tea, at seven a long dinner, and at ten dishes of sandwiches, not of the English railway-station kind, but little rounds of bread covered with caviare and *foie gras* with eggs and anchovies. Drinks and tobacco were sold, of course, duty free, and were correspondingly cheap. There were some interesting Scandinavian spirits, drunk as apéritifs, which made me feel rather sick.

Besides these purely fleshly comforts, there was the great satisfaction of not having to fuss about anything. For the real travel snob, recurrent clashes with authority at customs houses and police stations are half the fun of travelling. To stand for hours in a draughty shed while a Balkan peasant, dressed as a German staff officer, holds one's passport upside down and catechises one in intolerable French about the Christian names of one's grandparents, to lose one's luggage and one's train, to be blackmailed by adolescent fascists and pummelled under the arms by plague inspectors, are experiences to be welcomed and recorded. But for the simpler sort of traveller there is more comfort in handing his passport to the purser on the first evening of the cruise in the confidence that he will be able to walk down the gangway and saunter off into any town he comes to without molestation or delay. Moreover, nobody, however hard-boiled, can really enjoy the incessant packing and unpacking which is entailed in independent travelling, or the nuisance of carrying about with one from hotel to hotel, steamer and *wagon-lit*, an ever increasing collection of dirty clothes. When, as you will read if you persevere so far with this essay, I rejoined the *Stella* later after six weeks on my own, almost the chief satisfaction was to fill my laundry bag, hang up my suits on proper hangers and arrange my brushes and bottles on the dressing-table, and push my trunk under the bed in the knowledge that it would not be wanted again until I reached England.

The passengers for the most part could be divided into two sorts. There were those who were simply travelling on holiday, and there were those who were out to see the world and improve their minds. The first of these were strongly in the majority, and it is for them that pleasure cruising is most aptly suited. They were the elderly people, either singly or in couples, who always avoid English winters. Twenty years ago they would simply have gone to Egypt or Morocco or Southern Europe and spent two months in an hotel. The system of pleasure cruises provides them with greater comfort and a more frequent change of scene at about the same expense. Besides them there were one or two invalids, like Juliet, convalescent after illness or operations. There was also a newly married couple of rather demonstrative disposition. I cannot think of a more extraordinary milieu in which to spend a honeymoon, but these two seemed quite at ease, however shy they made the rest of us feel.

The sight-seers were another matter. For their benefit there was a lecturer who used to give informative addresses in the dining-room after tea. Most of them were girls whose mothers and fathers came under the first heading; between ports they read guide books, played deck games, danced, and fell in love with the officers; many of them kept diaries. A pleasure ship is not the best way to do sight-seeing, but it is by no means a bad one. It depends entirely on what one wants to see. Clearly in a museum or picture gallery the means of conveyance which brought you there are negligible; so far as they affect you at all, the only quality one asks is that they shall not be too tiring. The same applies in an almost equal degree to obviously show places such as Pompeii, but when the object of one's visit is to see places of natural beauty such as the Greek Islands or the Dalmatian Coast, there is a great deal to be said for a less luxurious approach. One of the chief objections is that your time in each place is strictly limited; it is very nice to spend a single day at Gibraltar, but two days at Venice are valueless from the point of view of getting an adequate impression. One cannot curtail or prolong one's stay in accordance with one's sympathies; one can, however, very conveniently reconnoitre for future journeys and decide what places one wishes to visit again at one's leisure.

Another objection is that one's arrival inevitably coincides with a large influx of other visitors, which causes an unnatural outbreak of rapacity among the inhabitants of smaller towns; one is inclined to accept an impression that the whole Mediterranean sea-board is peopled exclusively by beggars and the vendors of souvenirs. Moreover, every place you visit is comparatively crowded; this applies very little to a small ship like the *Stella*, but in the case of the large cruising liners the effect is disastrous to any real appreciation of the country. Places like Venice and Constantinople swallow up this influx without undue indigestion, but the spectacle, which I once saw on a previous visit, of five hundred tourists arriving by car to observe the solitude of a village in the Greek mountains is painful and ludicrous.

Even when you are travelling in a small ship and berthed at a large town, you see a great deal of your fellow passengers on shore; you find them bowing to you in shops and churches and night clubs; they blush with the utmost embarrassment when discovered in less reputable resorts, and wink knowingly at you next morning; they borrow money in Casinos, explaining that they are 'cleaned out' and know that their number is bound to turn up next time. They consult you about tips and stop you in the street to show you things they have bought, and according to your temperament this can be an amusement or a bore. I soon found my fellow passengers and their behaviour in the different places we visited a far more absorbing study than the places themselves.

One particularly interesting type which abounds on cruising ships is the middle-aged widow of comfortable means; their children are safely stored away at trustworthy boarding-schools; their servants are troublesome; they find themselves in control of more money than they have been used to; their eyes stray to the advertisements of shipping companies. And how artistically these are phrased. One of the compensating discoveries one makes when, for any reason, one finds a period of celibacy imposed on one, is that everyone one meets, and many of the commonplace events and occurrences of daily life, become suffused in a delicious way with an air of romance. (I have no doubt that much of the radiant happiness evident in religious communities comes from this source. What a lot of nonsense people will talk about sex repression. In many cases an enforced and unrationalised celibacy does give rise to those morbid conditions which supply material for the jollier passages in the Sunday newspapers. But in healthier psychological organisms, a sublimated sex motive may account for a vast proportion of the beneficial activities of man; copulation is not the only laudable expression of the procreative urge – certainly not copulation in which the procreative motive has been laboriously frustrated. The Christian virtues of charity and chastity have from old time an indissoluble alliance – but all this is hardly to the point.) These widows, then, celibate and susceptible, read the advertisements of steamship companies and travel bureaux and find there just that assembly of phrases – half poetic, just perceptibly aphrodisiac – which can produce at will in the unsophisticated a state of mild unreality and glamour. 'Mystery, History, Leisure, Pleasure', one of them begins. There is no directly defined sexual appeal. That rosy sequence of association, desert moon, pyramids, palms, sphinx, camels, oasis, priest in high minaret chanting the evening prayer, Allah, Hichens, Mrs Sheridan, all delicately point the way to sheik, rape, and harem – but the happily dilatory mind does not follow them to this forbidding conclusion; it sees the direction and admires the view from afar. The actual idea of abduction is wholly repugnant – what would the bridge club and the needlework guild say when she returned? – but the inclination of other ideas towards it gives them a sweet and wholly legitimate attraction.

I do not think these happier travellers are ever disappointed in anything they see. They come back to the ship from each expedition with their eyes glowing; they have been initiated into strange mysteries, and their speech is rich with the words of the travel bureau's advertising manager; their arms are full of purchases. It is quite extraordinary to see what they will buy. At every port some peculiar trinket is peddled, tortoiseshell at Naples, shawls at Venice, vile jewellery at Tangier, tortoises and sponges and olive-wood animals at Corfu, beads and Turkish delight and unseemly picture postcards at Port Said; there is a mysterious trade done at Constantinople in English small change; at Majorca they sell kindergarten basket-work and straw hats, at Algiers binoculars and carpets, at

Athens frightful marble statuettes. It is hard to escape without buying something; the widows buy anything they are offered. I suppose it is the housekeeping habit run riot after twenty years of buying electric-light bulbs and tinned apricots and children's winter underwear. They become adept in bargaining and may be seen in the lounge over their evening coffee, lying prodigiously to each other, like the fishermen of comic magazines, comparing prices and passing their acquisitions from hand to hand amid a buzz of admiration and competitive anecdote. I wonder what happens to all this trash. When it reaches England and is finally unpacked in the grey light of some provincial morning, has it lost some of its glamour? Does it look at all like the other bric-a-brac displayed in the fancy goods emporium down the street? Is it distributed among relatives and friends to show that they are not forgotten during the voyage? – or is it treasured, every bit of it, hung upon walls and displayed on occasional tables, a bane to the house-parlourmaid but a continual reminder of those magical evenings under a wider sky, of dance music and the handsome figures of the officers, of temple bells heard across the water, of the inscrutable half light in the bazaars, of Allah, Hichens, and Mrs Sheridan?

There was a series of land excursions organised on board the *Stella* by a patient and very charming Norwegian ex-sea-captain in a little office on the promenade deck, and one of the questions most exhaustively discussed among the passengers was whether these were worth while. I went on one or two of them, and I think that, for those whose main object is to save themselves as much trouble as possible, they are an excellent thing. If one has little experience of travelling and no knowledge of the language of the country one is inevitably cheated a great deal. All the ruffians of every nation seem to concentrate themselves in the tourist traffic. The organised ex-peditions worked smoothly and punctually; there were always enough cars and enough luncheon; everyone always saw all that had been promised him. I shall describe some of these trips in more detail later. At Naples, where I set out entirely alone with a very little knowledge of Italian, I wished very much that I had joined one of the parties.

We ran into the bay early on Sunday morning, and moored alongside the quay. There was a German-owned tourist ship in the harbour, which we were to see several times during the next few weeks, as she was following practically the same course as ourselves. She was built on much the same lines as the *Stella*, but the officers spoke contemptuously of her seaworthiness. She had capsized, they said, on the day she was launched, and was now ballasted with concrete. She carried a small black aeroplane on her deck, and the passengers paid about five guineas a time to fly over the harbour. At night her name appeared on the boat deck in illuminated letters. She had two bands which played almost incessantly. Her passengers were all middle-aged Germans, unbelievably ugly but dressed with courage and enterprise. One man wore a morning coat, white trousers, and a beret. Everyone in the *Stella* felt great contempt for this vulgar ship.

By the time that we had finished breakfast, all the formalities of passport and quarantine offices were over, and we were free to go on shore when we liked. A number of English ladies went off in a body, carrying prayer-books, in search of the Protestant church. They were outrageously cheated by their cab driver, they complained later, who drove them circuitously and charged them 85 lire. He had also suggested that instead of going to matins they should visit some Pompeian dances. I, too, was persecuted in a precisely similar way. As soon as I landed a small man in a straw hat ran to greet me, with evident cordiality. He had a brown, very cheerful face, and an engaging smile.

'Hullo, yes, you sir. Good morning,' he cried. 'You wanta one nice woman.'

I said, no, not quite as early in the day as that.

'Well then, you wanta see Pompeian dances. Glass house. All-a-girls naked. Vair artistic, vair smutty, vair French.'

I still said no, and he went on to suggest other diversions rarely associated with Sunday morning. In this way we walked the length of the quay as far as the cab rank at the harbour entrance. Here I took a small carriage. The pimp attempted to climb on to the box, but was roughly repulsed by the driver. I told him to drive me to the cathedral, but he took me instead to a house of evil character.

'In there,' said the driver, 'Pompeian dances.'

'No,' I said, 'the cathedral.'

The driver shrugged his shoulders. When we reached the cathedral the fare was 8 lire but the supplement showed 35. I was out of practice in travelling, and after an altercation in which I tried to make all the wrong points, I paid him and went into the cathedral. It was full of worshippers. One of them detached himself from his prayers and came over to where I was standing.

'After the mass. You wanta come see Pompeian dances?'

I shook my head in Protestant aloofness.

'Fine girls?'

I looked away. He shrugged his shoulders, crossed himself, and relapsed into devotion. . . .

At dinner that evening at the Captain's table the lady next to me said, 'Oh, Mr Waugh, the custodian at the museum was telling me about some very interesting old Pompeian dances which are still performed, apparently. I couldn't quite follow all he said, but they sounded well worth seeing. I was wondering whether you would care to——'

'I'm terribly sorry,' I said, 'I promised to play bridge with the doctor.'

I did not really enjoy those two days in Naples very much. I was ill at ease all the time, and impelled by a restless sense of obligation to see a great deal more than I intelligently could. As a result I wasted money and saw practically nothing. I should have done far better to have joined one of the conducted tours, but I felt snobbish about this, and also I had an idea that I could do things cheaper by myself. A few hours on shore convinced me of the futility of this view. Baedeker's admirable phrase, 'always extortionate and often abusive', applies perhaps more fitly to the Neapolitans than any other race. When I returned in six weeks' time I had become accustomed to depredation and discourtesy and was able to visit the places I wanted to see in a fairly calm state of mind. During these first wet days at Naples I came very near to that obsession by panic and persecution mania which threatens all inexperienced travellers. I refused the services of official guides with undue curtness, only to fall victim to illiterate touts who trotted at my side in a fog of garlic fumes, explaining the architecture to me in a flood of unintelligible English or attempting to sell me trays full of souvenirs. After the first morning I knew that I was beginning to develop that haunted look I had seen so often in the tourist's eye. I saw very little. I went to the museum and derived some amusement from the spectacle of my fellow passengers furtively applying for tickets to the Gabinetta Pornographica. I stood for some time before what must be one of the most lovely gateways in the world – the triumphal arch of Alphonso of Aragon in the Castel Nuovo, and neither of the two postcard sellers who chattered at my side could quite dispel the delight and exaltation it aroused. I walked for some time about the streets of the old town, where Baedeker commends the 'diverse scenes of popular life'. Small boys with long brown legs were bowling oranges about on the wet lava. The girls, at the orders of the priests, wore thick, dirty stockings. Bedding and washing hung from the windows as soon as the rain stopped; the uneven alleys rose in steps between high tenement houses; the smells were varied and intense but not wholly disagreeable. There were shrines at most of the street corners, honoured with artificial bouquets. Rudimentary trades were being pursued in dark workshops. The women gossiped and scolded at their doors and windows and innumerable balconies. I am not ashamed of enjoying this walk. The detestation of 'quaintness' and 'picturesque bits' which is felt by every decently constituted Englishman, is, after all, a very insular prejudice. It has developed naturally in self-defence against arts and crafts, and the preservation of rural England, and the preservation of ancient monuments, and the transplantation of Tudor cottages, and the collection of pewter and old oak, and the reformed public house, and the Ye Olde Inne and the Kynde Dragone and Ye Cheshire Cheese, Broadway, Stratford-on-Avon, folk-dancing, Nativity plays, reformed dress, free love in a cottage, glee singing, the Lyric, Hammersmith, Belloc, Ditchling, Wessex-worship, village signs, local customs, heraldry, madrigals, wassail, regional cookery, Devonshire teas, letters to *The Times* about saving timbered alms-houses from destruction, the preservation of the Welsh language, etc. It is inevitable that English taste, confronted with all these frightful menaces to its integrity, should have adopted an uncompromising attitude to anything the least tainted with ye oldeness.

But in a Latin country no such danger exists in any considerable degree. In England, the craze for cottages and all that goes with them only began as soon as they had ceased to represent a significant part of English life. In Naples no such craze exists because the streets are still in perfect harmony with their inhabitants. With his unfailing discernment Baedeker points firmly and unobtrusively to the essential – 'the diverse scenes of popular life'.

I spent the rest of the day visiting churches, most of which were shut. This was a surprise to me, as I had come to accept the statement so frequently advanced by Roman Catholics in England that their churches are always open for devotion in contrast to the Protestant parish church. I had a list, compiled from Baedeker and Mr Sitwell's *Southern Baroque Art*, of those I wished to see. It was one of the exasperating traits of the Neapolitan cab drivers to nod happily at their directions, drive on an elaborate and I have no doubt circuitous route until they arrived before the façade of the building whose frescoes I wished to see, and then, turning round on the box, smile genially, make the motion of locking a door, and say, '*Chiusa, signore.*' The Church of Sansevero was the only one I succeeded in entering that afternoon, and it amply repaid the trouble we took to find it. The name was new to my driver, but after many enquiries we found a small door in a back street. He left the carriage and went off to fetch the custodian, returning after a great delay with a lovely little bare-footed girl who carried a bunch of large keys. We left the slum and stepped into a blaze of extravagant baroque. The little girl pattered round, enumerating the chapels and tombs in a voice of peculiar resonance. The sculpture there is astonishing, particularly Antonio Corradini's 'La Pudicizia' – a gross female figure draped from head to foot in a veil of transparent muslin. I do not see how imitative ingenuity can go further; every line of face and body is clearly visible under the clinging marble drapery; the hands and feet alone are bare, and the change of texture between the marble which represents flesh and the marble which represents flesh closely covered with muslin is observed with a subtlety which defies analysis.

While I was going round, my driver took the opportunity of saying a few prayers. The action seemed slightly out of place in this church, so cold and ill-kept and crowded with all but living marble.

When I had made a fairly thorough tour, the little girl lit a candle and beckoned me to a side door, her face, for the first time, alight with genuine enthusiasm. We went down a few steps and turned a corner. It was completely dark except for her candle, and there was a strong smell of putrefaction. Then she stepped aside and held up the light for me to see the object of our descent. Two figures of death stood upright against the wall in rococo coffins, their arms folded across their chests. They were quite naked and dark brown in colour. They had some teeth and some hair. At first I thought they were statues of more than usual virtuosity. Then I realised that they were exhumed corpses, partially mummified by the aridity of the air, like the corpses at St Michan's in Dublin. There were man and woman. The man's body was slit open, revealing a tangle of dry lungs and digestive organs. The little girl thrust her face into the aperture and inhaled deeply and greedily. She called on me to do the same.

'Smell good,' she said. 'Nice.'

We went up into the church.

I asked her about the corpses. 'They are the work of the priest,' she said.

Next day I wasted a great deal of time at the aeroplane station trying unsuccessfully to induce a very amiable Italian, to whom I had an introduction, to give me a free flight to Constantinople. After luncheon I drove to Pozzuoli to see a very boring volcanic eruption. The guide who took me round pretended that he could set the gas alight with a piece of smouldering tow. He was about six feet six in height, and wore an astrakhan collar on his overcoat. He seemed so crestfallen at the obvious failure of his demonstration that I felt impelled to cheer him up with a few words of admiration. But this is the wrong line to take with Italians. You should always belittle their goods and they will respect you. The slightest courtesy renders you contemptible. From the moment my guide thought he had taken me in with his pathetic scientific experiment he became domineering and querulous (I remember an almost precisely similar incident in the chemistry laboratory at my school).

On the way back I visited the aquarium. I do not know its value among ichthyologists, but as an 'artistic entertainment' it seemed to me very much inferior to the one in London; it smelt. I had tea at Bertolini's, still alone and still very much depressed. The whole bay of Naples and Vesuvius were blotted out by mist.

We sailed that evening during dinner. I came upon poor Geoffrey disconsolately reading *l' Illustration* in the smoking-room. Juliet's neuralgia was better, but her temperature was still high. She had not eaten any dinner. He seemed to have spent most of the day cabling to her sisters.

We reached Messina early next morning, and almost all the passengers went off in motor cars to Taormina, rejoining the ship late in the afternoon at Catania. Geoffrey and I went on shore, and drove round the town in a little horse carriage, visiting the meagre concrete buildings that are slowly rising to replace the desolation of the great 1908 earthquake. It is astonishing how little has been done and in what a niggardly manner. It is a magnificent site for a town, with its long open bay and background of hills and vineyards. The new commercial and residential streets are devoid of any beauty or dignity. The churches make some half-hearted attempts to attract – particularly San Juliano, where the baptistry in concrete Gothic is clean and tall and well conceived. In the square opposite the cathedral, against the background of corrugated iron and builders' litter, stands, apparently uninjured, the very lovely Renaissance fountain by Montorsoli. Its grace and richness of design and the patina of the marble were all the more moving for the ramshackle squalor of their surroundings. This contrast was still more noticeable in the cathedral. We entered through a builders' yard, heaped with fragments of sculpture. The interior was full of scaffolding, and workmen were trotting about busily on all sides pushing barrows, carrying sacks of cement and steel girders. The huge baroque altar and reredos, covered in some places with sacking, in others by dust and fragments of stone, glowed between the scaffolding, while exquisite shrines of inlaid marbles were being gradually pieced together against the raw concrete walls. We walked about for some time in the twilight of the cathedral, unmolested by guides or custodians, and only a little scared by the occasional cataracts of tools and masonry which fell from the ceiling round our feet. We rejoined the ship and lunched almost alone with the officers, while we cruised down to Catania in calm water. The weather was now very fine. We sat on the boat deck and studied the shore through binoculars. Taormina was clearly visible, and the flow of lava from a recent volcanic eruption. The little train that ran down to Catania seemed to make a great deal more smoke than Etna.

Catania looked dirty and uninviting from the sea. A motor boat came out to meet us full of harbour officials, quarantine officers, passport inspectors, and so on, most of them in very fine uniforms with cloaks and swords and cocked hats. The companion ladder was let down for them, but there was some swell on in the harbour and they found difficulty in boarding. As the boat rose towards the ladder the officials stretched out their hands to the rail and towards the massive Norwegian seaman who was there to assist them. Some succeeded in catching hold, but each time their courage failed them just when the boat was at its highest; instead of stepping firmly from the motor boat, they gave a little hop and then let go. It was not a very exacting feat; all the passengers returning from Taormina accomplished it without mishap, including some very elderly ladies. The Sicilians, however, soon abandoned the attempt, and contented themselves with driving twice round the ship as though to show that they had never really intended coming on board, and then returned to their offices.

Geoffrey and I went ashore for an hour or two. The people seemed urban and miserable, particularly the children, who hung about in little joyless groups at the street corners as only grown men do in happier places. We looked at some interesting baroque churches, one with a concave façade which, I think, is unusual, and saw some fine, murky Caravaggios in the San Nicolo Museum. We were unable to obtain access to the church, however, to see the frescoed roof which Mr Sitwell describes in *Southern Baroque Art*. Geoffrey insisted on investigating a partially excavated Greek theatre of no particular interest.

That evening we headed east with two clear days at sea before reaching Haifa. During these days Juliet developed pneumonia, so I saw little of Geoffrey. Deck games broke out all over the ship. The most exacting of these was called 'deck tennis'; the players stood in pairs on opposite sides of a high net and tossed a rope ring backwards and forwards. Many of the passengers attained an astonishing degree of agility in this occupation. Less fortunate ones rendered themselves ludicrous and unpopular by throwing the rings overboard. Some played with such vigour and persistence that they strained their backs and arms, slipped on the deck and bruised their knees, chafed raw places in the skin of their hands, struck each other in the face, twisted their ankles, and sweated profusely.

There was a milder game which consisted in throwing rope rings over a stump, and a still milder one of propelling wooden quoits along the deck with specially constructed bats, like brooms without bristles. Another was called 'Bull Board'; in this the competitors threw rubber discs on to a black board divided into numbered squares. The gentlest and easiest of all was played by dropping rope rings into a bucket. This was strong favourite among the older passengers, who might be seen furtively practising it whenever they thought the decks were deserted.

A committee was formed, of which I found myself a very helpless member, to organise these sports into a tournament. Each of us was put in charge of one of the games and was responsible for hunting out the competitors and introducing them to their partners and opponents in the heats. In this way everyone on board soon knew everyone else, and was able to verify all his previous speculations about his fellow travellers' origins and inclinations. It was interesting to notice that while the English, on the whole, threw themselves zealously into all the business of organising, scoring, and refereeing, they were disposed to treat the games themselves with discernible casualness and frivolity. The other nationalities, however, and particularly the Scandinavians, devoted every energy wholeheartedly to the cause of victory.

I should really like, in the manner of *Goodbye to All That*, to fill in some pages at this point with descriptions of my own athletic prowess, but must instead confess that I was defeated in the first round of every one of these games, and was severely rebuked by my partners on two occasions for more than ordinary clumsiness.

We reached Haifa during the night after the second day of sports. It is a small port of undistinguished appearance, built during the end of the last century, on the south shore of the bay of Acre, at the foot of Mount Carmel. I had never heard of it before I went there, though as a matter of fact it is a town of some commercial importance. Lately its name has appeared in the newspapers as the scene of anti-Jewish rioting. It seemed very peaceful on the morning of our arrival; there was no other big shipping in the harbour and a light fall of rain kept most of the inhabitants indoors. They are a mixed and somewhat soft-tempered race, composed of Jews, Armenians, Arabs, Turks, and a great many Germans. A large cement works in the outskirts of the town provides the livelihood of most of them. The houses are square and white without any pretensions to ornament; most of them give the impression of being unfinished. To the south, Mount Carmel appeared through the mist, a bulky headland less than two thousand feet in height, crowned with a monastery. Behind the town the highlands of Galilee were just visible, crest upon crest fading away into the grey sky in successive gradations of obscurity.

Warned by my experience in Naples, I had arranged to go with the organised expedition to Nazareth, Tiberias, and Mount Carmel. Accordingly, I landed immediately after breakfast with the rest of the *Stella* party. The cars were waiting for us on the quay-side. I was put into the front seat of a Buick next to the driver, who had a sallow, intellectual face and European clothes. Most of the other drivers wore the *taboosh*; the dragoman in charge of the expedition had huge moustaches that stood out from his face, so that the ends were clearly visible from behind him like the horns of a bison. The few loafers who appeared to stare at us wore the voluminous Turkish trousers which are designed by the faithful to provide accommodation in case of the sudden rebirth of the Prophet. Later we passed several families in Arab costume and a convoy of camels. I had always associated them before with sand and sun and date palms. They seemed out of place in this landscape, for, except for an occasional clump of cactus by the side of the road, these misty purple hills, this gentle downpour of rain, this plethora of Jews, these drab conifers, might surely have been from some grouse-laden corner of the Scottish highlands. It raised a curious confusion in the mind by this association of Bonny Prince Charlie with the 'glamour of the inscrutable East'.

The driver of our motor car was a restless and unhappy man. He smoked 'Lucky Strike' cigarettes continuously, one after the other. When he lit a new one he took both hands off the wheel; often he did this at corners; he drove very fast and soon outdistanced all the other cars. When we most nearly had accidents he gave a savage laugh. He spoke almost perfect English with an American accent. He said he could never eat or drink when he was out with the car; he smoked instead; last month he had driven a German gentleman to Baghdad and back; he had felt ill after that. He never smiled except at the corners, or when, as we swept through a village, some little child, its mother wailing her alarm, darted in front of us. Then he would stamp on the accelerator and lean forward eagerly in his seat. As the child skipped clear of our wheels, he would give a little whistle of disappointment through his teeth and resume his despondent but polite flow of anecdote. This man had no religious beliefs, he told me, no home, and no nationality. He was an orphan brought up in New York by the Near East Relief Fund; he did not know for certain, but he supposed his parents had been massacred by the Turks. He liked America; there were a lot of rich people there, he said. After the war he had tried to get American citizenship, but they had turned him out. He had some very bitter trouble about some 'papers'; I could not quite understand what. They had sent him to colonise Palestine. He did not like Palestine because there were so few rich people there. He hated the Jews because they were the poorest of all, so he had become a Mohammedan. He was allowed a dozen wives but remained unmarried. Women took up time and money. He wanted to get rich and then spend all his time going from one place to another until he died. Perhaps if he became very rich they would let him become an American citizen. He would not settle in America, but he would like, when he travelled about, to say he was American; then everyone would respect him. He had been to London once; that was a good town, full of rich people. And Paris; that was nice, too, plenty of rich people there. Did he like his present job? What else was there to do in a stinking place like the Holy Land? His immediate ambition was to get a job as steward in a ship; not a stinking little ship, but one full of rich people like the *Stella Polaris*. I liked this man.

We went to Cana of Galilee, where a little girl was offering wine jars for sale. They were the authentic ones used in the miracle. If they were too big she had a smaller size indoors; yes, the small ones were authentic, too. Then we drove on to Tiberias, a small fishing village of cubic houses on the Sea of Galilee. There were the ruins of some kind of fort and a white domed public bath of steaming mineral water. We were led into this bath. In the courtyard a kind of picnic was going on; an Arab family sitting on the ground and eating bread and raisins. It was almost dark in the bath; the naked bathers lay about in the steam undisturbed by our intrusion. We lunched at Nazareth in an hotel managed by Germans, and ate omelettes, rissoles, and pork, and drank an uncommendable wine called Jaffa Gold. During luncheon the rain stopped. We went to visit the holy places. Mary's Well, in the central square of the town, is the most likely of these to be genuine. It is a communal fountain of obvious antiquity and traditional design; the present fabric may not date from the beginning of the Christian era, but there is a strong probability that a well of similar design has always occupied the same spot. The villagers coming to draw water must bear a strong resemblance to those of two thousand years ago, except that, instead of the earthenware ewers depicted by Mr Harold Copping, they now carry petrol tins on their heads. The Church of Annunciation is of modern construction and meagre design, but it is approached through a pretty courtyard containing fragments of early erections. We were shown the site of the Annunciation and Joseph's Workshop; both these were caves. A cheerful Irish monk with a red beard opened the gates for us. He was as sceptical as ourselves about the troglodytic inclinations of the Holy Family. The attitude of my fellow travellers was interesting. This sensible ecclesiastic vexed them. They had expected someone very superstitious and credulous and mediæval, whom they would be able to regard with discreet ridicule. As it was, the laugh was all on the side of the Church. It was we who had driven twenty-four miles, and had popped our tribute into the offertory box, and were being gently humoured for our superstition.

Outside the church a brisk trade was done in olive-wood paper-weights. Small boys flung themselves at our feet and began cleaning our shoes. A nun sold lace doyleys. An old woman wanted to tell our fortunes. We struggled through these Nazarenes and got back to the cars. Our driver was smoking by himself. The other drivers were ignorant fools, he said. He wasn't going to waste his time talking to them. He looked with derision at the souvenirs we had bought.

'They are of no interest,' he said, 'none whatever. But if you really wished to buy them you should have told me. I could have got them for you at a tenth of the price.' He lunged out with a spanner and rapped an old man over the knuckles who was trying to sell us a fly-whisk. Then we drove on. The hills were covered with asphodel and anemones and cyclamen. We stopped him, and I got out to pick a bunch for Juliet.

'They will all die before you get back to the ship,' said the driver.

We went back to Haifa, and through the town to the Monastery on Mount Carmel. This has little to show of any architectural interest, as it has been subject to successive demolitions and spoli-ations since its foundation. The British Governor of Acre in the Napoleonic wars carried off all its treasure, and the Turks used it as a hospital in 1915. There are some shocking frescoes representing the history of the order, by one of the present brothers. The cave, however, over which it is built, known as Elijah's Cave, is a spot of peculiar sanctity, being revered alike by Jews, Mohammedans, and Christians. The Carmelites are one of the few important Latin orders in the East, and they observe that peculiar liaison between Christianity and paganism that is such a feature in the Eastern Churches. During one week in the year, the Arabs bring their children to Carmel, and the monks bless them and perform the ceremony of shaving their heads. During this week the whole hillside is turned into an encampment; the Arabs bring presents of oil, incense, and candles. No attempt is made to convert them to Christianity; they go away, as they came, with camels and horses and numerous wives, thoroughly conscientious Mohammedans. (An interesting book might be written on this subject. At Sinai I am told there is a mosque inside the monastery cloister, and the bell for mass is rung daily by the Mohammedan priest.) An English monk, with the diction and tone of voice of an archdeacon, showed us over. There was a picture postcard stall in the cloister kept by a monk who attempted to give me the wrong change.

We left Haifa for Port Said at dinner-time, and ran almost immediately into heavy weather. The battens, called 'fiddles' by the good sailors, were put out on the tables, and the stewards went round the cabins disposing all breakable objects on the floor. There was no dancing that evening. Poor Geoffrey had spent the day with the ship's doctor securing the services of a nurse. They secured a squat young woman of indeterminable nationality, who spoke English of a sort and had had hospital training. She spent the first half-hour scrubbing Juliet and tumbling her from one side of the bed to the other till her temperature rose to formidable heights. Then she scraped her tongue with a nail file. Then she was very sick and retired to her cabin, and poor Geoffrey, who had been up all the night before, shared another night's vigil with the stewardess (whom the nurse addressed as 'sister'). They sent this nurse back by train from Port Said. It was the first time she had been at sea. Despite the fact that she had spent the whole of her voyage prostrate in her cabin, she expressed the utmost delight in her experience and applied to the doctor for a permanent position on board. After she had gone Geoffrey found an odd document in the cabin. It was a sheet of the ship's notepaper. At the very top, above the crest, was a line of very unsteady pencil handwriting. 'Pneuminia (*La Grippe*) is a very prevalent epidemic Disease in the spring it is.'

Many of the passengers left the *Stella* at Haifa and went on to Egypt by way of Damascus and Jerusalem, rejoining her eight days later at Port Said. The others stayed on board for the night and left next morning by train for Cairo and Luxor. Geoffrey, Juliet, and I, and the two other invalids, were left on board after the first day at Port Said. Everyone on board values this week of inaction in the middle of the cruise. The officers change into mufti and go shopping at Simon Arzt; the sailors and stewards go ashore in jolly batches of six and seven. It is about the only opportunity they have for prolonged land excursions; several of them went up to Cairo for the day.

Those who are on duty are employed in renewed prodigies of cleaning, polishing, and painting. We were filled up with fuel and water. The band played on shore in one of the cafés. The Captain gave luncheon-parties to officials and friends. The sun was brilliant and warm without being too hot, and for the first time we were able to sit comfortably on deck without scarves or greatcoats, and watch the continual coming and going of the big ships in the canal basin.

This was a spectacle of inexhaustible variety. Often there would be as many as four or five first-class liners in the harbour at one time, English, French, German, Italian, Dutch; cargo ships of all sizes from all parts of the world; emigrant ships, troop ships, tourist ships. The ferry boat paddled backwards and forwards, taking gangs of black and incredibly ragged workmen to the coal yards on the east side. There were always innumerable little rowing-boats circling round the ship in the hope of picking up a fare, their boatmen keeping up a soft halloing of self advertisement; there were the coolies trotting up and down the ladders with sacks of coal, chanting in time and apparently quite unhurried by the whacks and smacks of their overseer; there were the dredgers ceaselessly at work, day and night, with a sound like sea lions at feeding-time; there were fast motor launches filled with harbour officials, always dashing from ship to shore, and almost upsetting with their wash the unstable rowing-boats. Beyond all this bustle we could see the low buildings of the town, a few trees, and, standing out from the shore on its own promontory, the domed and arcaded offices of the canal company; next to it, and modestly emulous in design, stands Navy House, from whose balconies the wives of British officers watch with wistful eyes the P. & O. ships bearing their sisters home on leave, while on the terrace below them Tommies in shirt-sleeves dangle baited hooks into the water and wait with indomitable tenacity the rare advent of some wholly uneatable little fish.

The only disturbing element in this happy week was Juliet, who was by this time very seriously ill. The doctor pronounced her unfit for travel, and she was accordingly lowered in a stretcher and taken ashore to the British hospital. I accompanied the procession, which consisted of the ship's doctor, carrying warm brandy and a teaspoon, an officer, Geoffrey, half distracted with anxiety, a dense mob of interested Egyptians, Copts, Arabs, Lascars, and Sudanese, and a squad of ambulance men, two of whom fought the onlookers while the others bundled Juliet – looking distressingly like a corpse – into a motor van. These last men were Greeks, and refused all payment for their services. It was sufficient reward that they were allowed to wear uniform. They must be the only people in the whole of Egypt who have ever done anything for nothing. I met one of them some weeks later marching with a troop of Boy Scouts, and he fell out of the ranks and darted across the road to shake my hand and ask me news of Juliet in French far worse than my own.

It was a melancholy journey to the hospital, and a still more melancholy walk back with Geoffrey. The British hospital lies at the far end of the sea front. We passed a game of football, played enthusiastically upon an uneven waste of sand, by Egyptian youths very completely dressed in green and white jerseys, white shorts, striped stockings, and shiny black football boots. They cried "ip-'ip-'ooray' each time they kicked the ball, and some of them blew whistles; a goat or two wandered amongst them, nosing up morsels of lightly buried refuse.

We stopped on the terrace of the Casino Hotel for a drink, and a conjuror came and did tricks for us with live chickens. These are called 'gully-gully men' because of their chatter. They are the worst possible conjurors but excellent comedians. They squat on the ground, making odd clucking noises in their throats and smiling happily, and proceed with the minimum of deception to pop things in and out of their voluminous sleeves; their final trick is to take a five-piastre piece and drop that up their sleeve, but it is a good entertainment the first two or three times. There was a little Arab girl in the town who had taught herself to imitate them perfectly, only, with a rare instinct for the elimination of inessentials, she used not to bother about the conjuring at all, but would scramble from table to table in the cafés, saying, 'Gully-gully,' and taking a chicken in and out of a little cloth bag. She was every bit as amusing as the grown-ups and made just as much money. On this particular after-noon, however, Geoffrey was not to be consoled so easily, and the performance seemed rather to increase his gloom. We went back to the ship, and I helped him pack up his luggage and move it to his hotel.

Two days later I decided to join him. The news from the Black Sea was discouraging; heavy storms were raging, some of the ports were still icebound, and very few ships were running regularly; everyone I met told me that it would take at least six weeks to get a Soviet visa. What with this and a feeling of genuine compassion towards Geoffrey and Juliet, I gave up all idea of Russia and determined rather on the less ambitious enterprise of compiling the first travel book to deal extensively and seriously with Port Said; accordingly, I settled there for the next month, and this chapter contains a summary of my investigations.

The town is built on a dead flat patch of sand bounded on the north by the Mediterranean Sea, on the east by the Suez Canal, on the south by Lake Menzaleh, and trailing off westward in a series of indeterminate sand dunes to the Nile Delta. It is thus an island joined to the mainland by a strip of sand between Lake Menzaleh, and the Canal, just broad enough for railway-lines and a high road. On its Mediterranean front it is 'making land' yearly at an astonishing speed, and it is on this recently formed northern territory that the European quarter has been built. The principal arterial thoroughfare in the centre of the town, joining the Arab quarter to the harbour, still bears the name Quai du Nord from the time when it formed the extremity of the town. The principal buildings, the Governor's House, the Casino Hotel, the British and Egyptian hospitals, the schools, and the houses of the richest inhabitants were all built before the war upon the new sea front, and already a vast, firm *plage* has crept up between the road and the sea, ripe for further development; this causes some anxiety, particularly to the hotel proprietors, who depend upon ready access to the sea as an important palliation of their other many inadequacies.

The hotel where Geoffrey and I stayed was on the front – a brand new concrete building kept by a retired English officer and his wife. We chose it because it was near the hospital and comparatively cheap; it was recommended by all the British colony in Port Said on the grounds that it was the only place where you could be certain of not meeting any 'gyppies'. The people we did meet were certainly

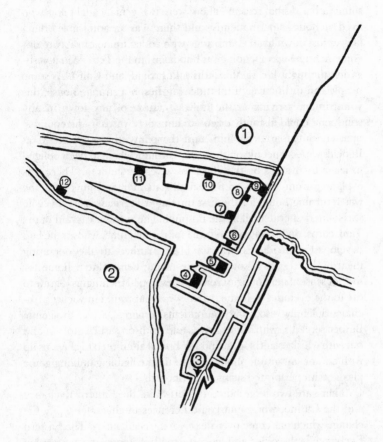

SKETCH MAP OF PORT SAID SHOWING

very British but far from gay. Few people stay in Port Said except for
some rather dismal reason. There were two genial canal pilots who
lived at Bodell's permanently, and there was an admirable young
lawyer just down from Cambridge who added immeasurably to our
enjoyment; he was spending his holiday from the Temple in investigating the night life of Alexandria, Port Said, and Cairo. As some
people can instinctively find the lavatories in a strange house, this
young man, arriving at the railway station of any town in any
continent, could instantly orientate himself towards its disreputable
quarter. But apart from him and the pilots, the other guests at
Bodell's were all people on their way through who had been obliged
to leave their ships by the illness of wives or children. There was
a planter from Kenya with a small daughter and governess; he
was returning home for the first time after fourteen years; his wife
was lying desperately ill in the hospital. There was a captain in the
Tank corps, on his way out to India for the first time, whose wife had
developed appendicitis and had been rushed to the operating
theatre. There was a soldier's wife taking her children home for
the hot season; her youngest son had developed meningitis. I grew to
dread the evenings at home, when we all sat round in wicker arm-
chairs dolefully discussing the patients' progress, while the gentle
Berber servants, with white gowns and crimson sashes, stole in and
out with whiskies and sodas, and Mr Bodell attempted to cheer us up
with an ancient gramophone and an unintelligible gambling game
played with perforated strips of cardboard.

There are two large hotels in Port Said, the Eastern Exchange
and the Casino, whose marked differences in character typify the
change which has come over the town in recent years. The Eastern
Exchange is the older and less esteemed; it stands at a busy street
corner among the shops and cafés and rises above them in tier upon
tier of glass-fronted, steel-framed balconies. The bar is very large,
and full of rather decayed leather arm-chairs and steel pillars.
A great deal of heavy drinking goes on there, and the whole place
has a distinctly dissolute air. The servants are all Sudanese or
Berbers in native costume; shop girls from Simon Arzt's store
dance there in the evenings; it is unusual to see anyone in evening
dress; Egyptian officials give parties there; English commercial

agents stay there and jolly groups of officers from the liners; the food is by far the best in the town and the drinks expensive but pure. The bedrooms are for the most part arranged in large, under-furnished suites. There was always a bustle of coming and going, people recognising old acquaintances, quarrelling with the servants, consulting the blackboard on which were chalked up the times of the departure of ships.

The Casino stands at the corner of the sea front and the harbour, well away from the shops and cafés, among shipping offices, apartment houses, and government buildings, looking out along the breakwater to the Lesseps statue. It is solidly and pompously built of concrete, and advertises a minute but carefully tended garden at the back. It would like, if it could, to achieve an air of the French Riviera. The servants are mostly Europeans and Greeks in shabby evening suits; the food is poor. On gala nights there is a *boule* table, the proceeds of which go to local charities.

Every Saturday evening there is a dance to which printed invitations are issued, and the European society of Port Said turns up in force, very self-conscious in dinner jackets and tulle. Balloons, cardboard trumpets, dolls, and artificial noses are distributed. Every consulate has its table and maintains a certain diplomatic reserve. Next to them in social importance come the three British doctors, the two lawyers, the chaplain, the A.S.C. officers and their wives from Navy House, the British head of police, the shipping office and bank managers. Anyone in British service counts higher than anyone in Egyptian service. The nurses from the hospital are eagerly pursued as partners. But the standards of Port Said society, though wide, are rigid. At the Casino one sees the young men at Cook's office who sell railway tickets, but not the young men at Simon Arzt's who sell sun helmets. Egyptians are not excluded but very few of them attend. Sometimes passengers off the liners appear, inclined to gaiety after the dull canal passage. These are welcomed but freely criticised. While I was there a young woman from an outward-bound P.&O. danced without stockings. I daresay she is still being discussed. There was also a young man who put on a *taboosh* and was officially rebuked by a glance from the British consul. Nearly all the gentlemen of Port Said drink a little too much on these Saturday evenings, and may be seen at half-past eleven next morning sitting round in the club with cups of Bovril and Worcester sauce – declaiming ungratefully against the Casino's whisky.

This club is a very important part of Port Said life. All tolerably respectable British male residents are members, and strangers are hospitably enrolled for the period of their visit. Everyone we encountered, Mr Bodell, the doctors at the hospital, the chaplain, the manager of the bank where we cashed our letters of credit, kindly volunteered to introduce us to the club. It occupies the floor above the Anglo-Egyptian Bank, and consists of a billiard-room, writing-room, smoking-room, balcony, and bar. It is furnished with large arm-chairs and photographs of the Royal Family and of generals and admirals in the last war. The smell of deodorisers predominates until evening, when tobacco smoke takes its place. Bridge, snooker, and poker dice (for drinks) are the chief occupations; *Punch*, the *Illustrated Sporting and Dramatic News*, and the weekly edition of the *Daily Mirror* the chief intellectual interests. Conversation is vigorous and emphatic, though limited in scope. There seemed an abundance of genuine, if undiscriminating, good-fellowship. 'All the trouble in this town is made by the women,' one of the members told me, and, except for some mild intrigues at the time of the committee election, I saw nothing but harmony and concord on all sides.

It seemed to me that the life led by these oversea business men and officials was in every way agreeable and enviable when compared with its counterpart in modern England. There was, of course, no nonsense of tropical romance; no indomitable jungle, no contact with raw nature, no malaria, delirium tremens, or 'mammy-palaver'; no one showed the smallest inclination to 'go native'; no one was eating out his heart for the lights of Piccadilly or yew walks of a manorial garden; they did not play their bridge with greasy cards or read and re-read a year-old newspaper; no one was 'trying to forget'. One must go to other parts of Africa for that. Port Said is highly respectable and almost up to date. They certainly did not read new books, but then they did not read old books either; they had gramophone records of musical plays still running in London; their newspapers were ten days old, but they had their own *Tatler*, an illustrated gazette of English and American society called the *Sphinx*. (Incidentally, it was in this paper that I noticed a device which I recommend to the English illustrated Press. There was a photograph of four pleasant, plain people blinking into the sunlight, reproduced twice in the same issue with different names beneath each.) The routine of the day was leisured, broken by a very long luncheon interval during which the younger people played tennis and their elders dozed; everyone assembled at the club at six o'clock to read the papers and chat. In the evening there were rehearsals for amateur theatricals and a great many dinner-parties. At one of these my hostess, on leaving the dining-room, paused at the door to say, 'Good-bye, darling men, and keep your naughty stories for us.'

The women seemed peculiarly care-free; they live in manageable modern flats and are served by quiet native men-servants, whose response to all orders, however ill-comprehended, is a deferential inclination of the head and a softly spoken 'All right.' No one is troubled by social aspirations because there is no direction in which to aspire; everyone knows everyone else, and there are no marked disparities of income. No one wants particularly to keep a car, as there is nowhere to drive except the French club at Ismailia.

The men live within five minutes' walk of their work, they have none of that feverish bustling in and out of railway trains and omnibuses which embitters middle-class life in London. More than this, they are, almost without exception, the employees of important firms; they act merely as local agents, with strictly limited responsibilities and nicely defined powers, enjoying absolute security of income, and looking forward to regular degrees of promotion and ultimate superannuation and pension. They are thus serenely ignorant of the anxieties that beset the small company director; the yearly struggle to present a plausible balance sheet to the shareholders' meeting; the harassed perusal of the national budget which may, by some new incidence of taxation, close carefully prepared markets and turn a marginal profit into a dead loss. They live in a Utopian socialist state untroubled by the ardours and asperities of private enterprise. I think many of them were conscious of the peculiar felicity of their lives. Certainly, those who had lately been home on leave had returned with a slightly dissatisfied air. England was changing, they said; damned Bolshies everywhere. 'You have to come outside England,' one of them told me, 'to meet the best type of Englishman.'

I saw practically nothing of the French colony, but I imagine that their life is very similar. They have their own club, but I think that most of their social interests centre in Ismailia, a newly built residential town up the canal. The French consul was the only man I ever saw win consistently at *boule* at the Casino. There were a great number of Greeks, but all of a poorer class, artisans, hairdressers, and the keepers of small shops. They have the largest church in a town bristling with ecclesiastical architecture. Except for Simon Arzt and one admirable French confectioner, the shops are uninteresting and mainly in Coptic or Egyptian hands. Simon Arzt's is a magnificent emporium selling almost everything you could hope to find in Harrods at a considerably higher price. It opens for all big ships, no matter at what hour of the night they come in.

One of the curses of Port Said, and, indeed, of the whole of Egypt, is the street hawking. One cannot sit down for a moment at any café without being beset by tiny Arab urchins, mostly with moist ophthalmic eyes and nasty skin diseases, who attempt to clean your shoes. Mere verbal refusal has no force to discourage. They squat at your feet crying, 'Clin-büts, clin-büts,' and tapping the backs of their brushes together. The experienced resident then kicks them as hard as he can, and they put out their tongues and go on to the next table; the visitor pretends not to notice, and, taking this as a commission, they then proceed to befoul his socks and trouser-ends with black paste. Nor is it sufficient protection to allow the first comer to do this and be done with him; not only will a queue of little boys wait until he has finished and then begin their importunacy, but the same boy will be back in twenty minutes and attempt to clean them all over again. The nuisance gradually abates as one's reputation as a kicker spreads; after a fortnight Geoffrey and I were known as self-reliant and violent customers and lived unmolested, but when, after three weeks, Juliet was well enough to come out with us, the boot-boys, with laudable discernment, decided that we would not want to show temper before the white lady, and renewed their persecution until the end of our visit. Juliet thought them rather angels.

I suppose that this cleaning of boots is the early training for the more ambitious salesmanship which menaces one's peace of mind in the open air. These elder pests usually stay at home when there is no ship in, but that is a rare remission. They peddle European newspapers, chocolates, cigarettes, bead necklaces, amber and ivory cigarette-holders, cigarette cases of inlaid brass and gun metal, *appliqué* embroidery from debased hieroglyphic designs, and picture postcards of unexampled lewdness which they flourish very embarrassingly under one's eyes. Geoffrey bought a packet and sent them in heavily sealed envelopes to various acquaintances in England, thereby, I believe, rendering both himself and them liable to criminal prosecution. The original plates of the photographs are, I learned later, of some antiquity, having been made for sale at the first International Exhibition at Paris and being brought to Port Said for the celebrations at the opening of the Suez Canal. There have been innumerable imitations since, of course, but it seemed to me that these earlier examples left little room for improvement; and it was interesting to observe that, for all their nudity, they are unmistakably 'dated' by that indefinable air of period which we have already discussed.

Besides these there were the 'gully-gully' men and numberless fortune-tellers; the latter carried with them printed extracts from testimonials purporting to be written by Lord Allenby, Lord Plumer, Lord Lloyd, and other distinguished Englishmen, but their predictions were invariably monotonous and non-committal. Europeans have a superstitious respect for Oriental soothsayers which the town Arabs have been quick to commercialise; all camel-boys regularly offer to tell their customers' fortunes before proceeding to offer other, and often less acceptable, services.

The dragomans who infest the tourist quarter of Cairo are of a very much higher class; they all speak at least one European language tolerably well, have a superficial but fairly extensive knowledge of antiquities, and exhibit great courtesy and social charm. They are richly clothed and live in some degree of comfort, usually with four or five wives. Most of them have small farms in the country where they retire at the close of the tourist season. As there is nothing at all in Port Said which any intelligent tourist

could wish to see, there are very few dragomans. I only met one –
a fine ingratiating rascal with a great black moustache and gold
teeth. He took me to the mosque – a tawdry, modern building,
overlaid like a teashop with cheap Oriental decorations – and
offered to procure me some hashish. I gave him thirty piastres; he
returned with admirably simulated circumspection and slipped
a packet into my hand, telling me on no account to open it in the
street. I bore this furtively back to Bodell's and opened it in my
bedroom with Geoffrey and the Cambridge solicitor. Inside we
found a ten-piastre tin of amber cigarettes. The laugh was on me.
We made several other attempts to obtain hashish, which is
a common commodity in an Arab town, but were always met by
expressions of blank incomprehension. Every European is assumed
to be a spy until it is proved to the contrary, and we were no doubt
known to be on amicable terms with the commissioner of police.
The drug trade, however, is one of wide ramifications in Egypt.
The hashish crop is grown in French Syria and brought either by
rail to Cantara or by sea to Port Said. Every imaginable device is
employed to smuggle it through the customs, and apparently pregnant Arab wives are subjected to a rigorous pummelling which often
results in the discovery of bales of contraband under their black
gowns; once in the country the distribution is apparently undetect-
able, and all important seizures of stock take place at the frontier.
It seems to me that it would be well worth the while of some
enterprising European to organise this side of the business. Tourist
baggage is submitted to a very cursory scrutiny. All that is necessary
would be to assemble a dozen or so Europeans at Damascus with
large trunks heavily encrusted with hotel and steamship labels.
These could be half filled with hashish and cocaine, concealed in
sponge bags, boots and shoes, soap boxes, hollow books, and the
many other undutiable articles of luggage that are never examined.
The gang would then book a round tour to Cairo with a perfectly
genuine and unsuspicious guide from one of the reputable travel
agencies. One such convoy would be enough to provide a handsome profit for all concerned. As far as I can see, it could be repeated
with judicious changes of personnel for as long as the organisers
required.

Another and very much safer way of making a fortune, which I have been commending to all my avaricious friends, is to start a night club in Port Said. At present there is nothing of the kind. Large ships are continually arriving for a stay of two or three hours and disgorging a horde of fairly wealthy passengers. Port Said still retains a reputation for low life, and half of them at least are avid to see it. They come prancing on shore. Gambling? Why, certainly, there is the *boule* table in aid of Christian charities at the Casino. Dancing? This way to the Eastern Exchange Hotel. Drinking? Here is a clean, airy café – Bass, Guinness, Johnny Walker, English spoken. Theatre? Why, yes. The Port Said Amateur Operatic Society are performing *The Mikado*, or else there are three excellent American dramas of mother love at the three cinemas. It is not at all what they have been led to expect. So they go off to the Casino and dance for an hour, buy a few frightful trinkets of embroidery or brass work, and go back disconsolately to their ships. I firmly believe that anyone enterprising enough to give them what they want could become a rich man in one season. There are no licensing laws, and he could follow the economical example, set by the proprietors of the fashionable resorts of London and Paris, of making his own champagne downstairs in the basement. Rents are low, particularly in the old part of the town round the docks, where the houses are wooden, two-storied buildings with slightly romantic associations. The 'Eldorado' Cinema with its double tier of matchboard boxes would serve excellently. I should imagine that it had been built for this purpose in Port Said's disreputable days. It is, in construction, almost exactly like those breath-taking dancing saloons in films about the Klondyke gold rush. It would be easy to collect a sufficiently amusing cabaret of Arab *can-can* dancers, snake charmers, and so on. A few outcasts might be imported from the 'Blue Lantern' and ranged round the walls to give the place a nasty look. 'Jungle-wallahs', returning from lonely outposts of commerce, would find it delightfully civilised and up-to-date, while at the next table parties of tourists and officials going out for the first time would sit no less entranced at this introduction to the glamour of the East.

It is only since the war, and largely, I understand, owing to the efforts of the present head of police, that Port Said has become so respectable. From the years when it first grew up round the mouth of the canal it became a harbour for all the most thorough-going type of international riff-raff, and its reputation as a sink of iniquity grew with the town's importance. And, as is always the case, the literary myth survives long after the event. While I was at Bodell's he showed me a recently published magazine story about Port Said, describing the 'evil-smelling, green canal winding its way between the narrow alley ways where sin and crime walk unashamed'. Well, the canal could never have wound its way among the alleys, nor, I think, was it ever evil-smelling or green, but from all the older residents told me, it was certainly quite true about sin and crime walking unashamed until the militant cleaning up by Teale Bey. Robbery with violence and murder were common occurrences in the streets, and people were unwilling to venture out after dark even into the European quarter, except in twos and threes. Now it is nearly as safe as Plymouth, and very much safer than Marseilles or Naples. Prostitution, which was one of the most prominent features of the town, has sunk to negligible dimensions. Up to and during the war there were brothels in the chief streets round the harbour and over the leading cafés and shops. To-day they are all localised, as in most Oriental towns.

Geoffrey, the Cambridge solicitor, and I spent two or three evenings investigating this night-town, called by the residents 'red lamp district'. It lies at the farthest extremity of the town on the shore of Lake Menzaleh, round the little wharf and goods yard of the Menzaleh canal, separated from the shops and offices and hotels by a mile or so of densely populated Arab streets. It is very difficult to find by day, but at night, even without our solicitor's peculiar gifts, we should have been led there by the taxis full of tipsy sailors and stewards, or grave, purposeful Egyptians, that swept by us in the narrow thoroughfare.

We set out after dinner one evening, rather apprehensively, with a carefully calculated minimum of money, and life-preservers of lead, leather, and whale-bone, with which our solicitor, surprisingly, was able to furnish us, we left watches, rings, and tie-pins on our dressing-tables, and carefully refrained from alarming Juliet with the knowledge of our destination. It was an interesting walk. An absurd tram runs up the Quai du Nord, drawn by a mare and a donkey. We followed this for some way and then struck off to the left through Arab Town. These streets presented a scene of astonishing vivacity and animation. Little traffic goes down them and there is no differentiation of pavement and road in the narrow earthen track; instead, it is overrun with hand-barrows selling, mostly, fruit and confectionery, men and women bargaining and gossiping, innumerable bare-footed children, goats, sheep, ducks, hens, and geese. The houses on either side are wooden, with overhanging balconies and flat roofs. On the roofs are ramshackle temporary erections for store-rooms and hen-houses. No one molested us in any way, or, indeed, paid us the smallest attention. It was Ramadan, the prolonged Mohammedan fast during which believers spend the entire day from sunrise to sunset without food or drink of any kind. As a result the night is spent in feverish feasting; nearly everyone carried a little enamelled bowl of a food resembling some kind of milk pudding, into which he dipped between bites of delicious-looking ring-shaped bread. There were men with highly decorated brass urns selling some kind of lemonade; there were women carrying piles of cakes on their heads. As we progressed the houses became more and more tumble-down and the street more narrow. We were on the outskirts of the small Sudanese quarter where a really primitive life is led. Then suddenly we came into a rough, highly lighted square with two or three solid stucco-fronted houses and some waiting taxis. One side was open to the black, shallow waters of the lake, and was fringed with the masts of the little fishing-boats, called, I believe, *makaris*. Two or three girls in bedraggled European evening dress seized hold of us and dragged us to the most highly lighted of the buildings; this had 'Maison Dorée' painted across its front, and the girls cried, 'Gol'-'ouse, gol'-'ouse,' 'Vair good, vair clean.' It did not seem either very good or very clean to me. We sat in a little room full of Oriental decorations and drank some beer with the young ladies. Madame joined us, a handsome Marseillaise in a green silk embroidered frock; she cannot have been more than forty, and was most friendly and amusing. Four or five other young ladies came in, all more or less white; they sat very close together on the divan and drank beer, making laudably little effort to engage our attention. None of them could talk any English, except, 'Cheerioh, Mr American.' I do not know what their nationality was. Jewesses, Armenians, or Greeks, I suppose. They cost 50 piastres each, Madame said. These were all European ladies. The other, neighbouring houses, were full of Arabs – horrible, dirty places, she said. Some of the ladies took off their frocks and did a little dance, singing a song which sounded like ta-ra-ra-boom-ty-ay. There was a jolly-sounding party going on upstairs, with a concertina and glass-breaking, but Madame would not let us go up. Then we paid for our drinks and went out.

Then we went next door to a vastly more plebeian house called Les Folies Bergères, kept by a gross old Arab woman who talked very little French and no English. She had a licence for eight girls, but I do not think hers was a regular establishment. On our arrival a boy was sent out into the streets, and he brought back half a dozen or so Arab girls, all very stout and ugly and carelessly daubed with powder and paint. They sat on our knees and embarrassed us rather, so we made our escape, promising to fetch some friends and return. There was another large house, called Pension Constantinople, which we surveyed from outside but did not enter. All round were the little alleys where the free-lance prostitutes lived. These were one-roomed huts like bathing cabins. The women who were not engaged sat at their open doors sewing industriously, and between stitches looking up and calling for custom; many had their prices chalked on the door-posts – 25 piastres in some cases, but usually less. Inside iron bedsteads were visible, and hanging banners worked with the crests of British regiments. Their trade is only among the poorest class of Arab, but sitting, as they were, silhouetted against the light, many of them suggested an attraction which their more sumptuously housed competitors lacked, something of that now banal mystery which captivated the imaginations of so many writers of the last century to the furtive drabs of the northern city streets.

On our way back we came upon another gaily illuminated building called Maison Chabanais. We went in, and were surprised to encounter Madame and all her young ladies from the Maison Dorée. It was, in fact, her back door. Sometimes, she explained, gentlemen went away unsatisfied, determined to find another house, then as often as not they found the way round to the other side, and the less observant ones never discovered their mistake. She was an enterprising, humorous woman, and several times after this we visited her in the evening for a glass of beer and a chat; as long as we paid for the beer she never bothered us to extend our patronage further.

Arab Town, at any hour of the day or night, was a fascinating place to us, and it was astonishing to discover how ignorant the English colony were about it, and how uninterested. Many of them had never been there at all. Although it was only a few streets away, they were as vague about it as Londoners are about Limehouse. They had an idea that it smelled and crawled with bugs, and that was enough for them, though they showed a tolerance of my interest, remarking that every chap has his own game; I was one of those writing johnnies, so of course I had to nose round a bit collecting local colour; jolly interesting too for a chap who was interested in that sort of thing; they would read about it all in my book when that came out; meanwhile, snooker and whisky-soda for them. But it was not local colour or picturesque bits, or even interest in the habits of life of another race, which drew me there day after day, but the intoxicating sense of vitality and actuality. I do not suppose that this part of Port Said is more interesting than any other Oriental town; indeed, probably much less so, but it was the first I visited and the only one where I stayed for any length of time. Their intensely human joviality and inquisitiveness, their animal-like capacity for curling up and sleeping in the dust, their unembarrassed religious observances, their courtesy to strangers, their uncontrolled fecundity, the dignity of their old men, make an interesting contrast with all the wrangling and resentment of northern slums, lightened by fitful outbursts of hysteria. You cannot walk down a poor street in England without hearing some woman in a rage or some child in tears. I do not remember once hearing either of these things in Port Said.

While we were there, Ramadan came to an end with the feast of Bajiram. All the children were given new clothes – those that could not afford a frock wearing a strip of tinsel or bright ribbon, and paraded the streets on foot or in horse-cabs. The streets of Arab Town were illuminated and hung with flags, and everyone devoted himself to making as much noise as he could. The soldiers fired cannonade after cannonade of artillery; civilians beat drums, blew whistles and trumpets, or merely rattled tin pans together and shouted. This went on for three days.

There was a fair and two circuses. Geoffrey and I and the head of the hospital went to the circus one evening, much to the bewilderment of the club. The hospital nurses were very shocked at our going. 'Think of the poor animals,' they said. '*We* know the way the gyppies treat their animals.' But, unlike European circuses, there were no performing animals.

We were the only Europeans in the tent. The chairs were ranged on rather unstable wooden steps ascending from the ring to a considerable height at the back. Behind the back row were a few heavily curtained boxes for the women; there were very few there; most of the large audience consisted of young men, a few of them in ready-made suits of European pattern, but all wearing the red *taboosh*. A number of small boys were huddled between the front row and the ringside, and a policeman was employing his time in whisking these off the parapet with a cane. The seats seemed all to be the same price; we paid 5 piastres each and chose places near the back. Attendants were going about between the rows selling nuts, mineral waters, coffee, and hubble-bubbles. These were of the simplest pattern, consisting simply of a cocoanut half full of water, a little tin brazier of tobacco, and a long bamboo mouthpiece. The doctor warned me that if I smoked one of these I was bound to catch some frightful disease; I did so, however, without ill effect. The vendor keeps several alight at a time by sucking at each in turn. We all drank coffee, which was very thick and sweet and gritty.

The show had begun before we arrived, and we found ourselves in the middle of a hugely popular comic turn; two Egyptians in European costume were doing crosstalk. It was, of course, wholly unintelligible to us; now and then they smacked or kicked each other, so I have no doubt it was much the same as an English music-hall turn. After what seemed an unconscionable time the comedians went away amid thunderous applause, and their place was taken by a very pretty little white girl in a ballet dress; she cannot have been more than ten or twelve years old; she danced a Charleston. Later she came round and sold picture postcards of herself. She turned out to be French. To those that enjoy moralising about such things there is food for reflection in the idea of this African dance, travelling across two continents from slave to gigolo, and gradually moving south again towards the land of its origin.

Then there were some Japanese jugglers, and then an interminable comic turn performance by the whole company. They sang a kind of doleful folk song and then, one at a time, with enormous elaboration of 'business', came in and lay down on the ground; after all the grown-ups were settled the little girl came in and lay down too; finally a tiny child of two or three tottered in and lay down. All this took at least a quarter of an hour. Then they all got up again, still singing, one at a time in the same order, and went out. After that there was an interval, during which everyone left his place and strolled about in the ring as people do at Lord's between the innings. After this a negro of magnificent physique appeared. First he thrust a dozen or so knitting-needles through his cheeks, so that they protruded on either side of his head; he walked about among the audience bristling in this way and thrusting his face into ours with a fixed and rather frightful grin. Then he took some nails and hammered them into his thighs. Then he stripped off everything except a pair of diamanté drawers, and rolled about without apparent discomfort on a board stuck with sharp carving-knives.

It was while he was doing this that a fight began. It raged chiefly round the exit, which was immediately below our seats. The heads of the combatants were on a level with our feet, so that we were in a wholly advantageous position to see everything without serious danger. It was difficult to realise quite what was happening; more and more of the audience joined in. The negro got up from his board of knives, feeling thoroughly neglected and slighted, and began addressing the crowd, slapping his bare chest and calling their attention to the tortures he was suffering for them. The man on my right, a grave Egyptian with a knowledge of English, with whom I had had some conversation, suddenly stood up, and leaning across all three of us struck down with his umbrella a resounding blow on the top of one of the fighting heads; then he sat down again with unruffled gravity and devoted himself to his hubble-bubble.

'What is the fight about?' I asked him.

'Fight?' he said. 'Who has been fighting? I saw no fight.'

'There.' I pointed to the seething riot in the doorway which seemed to threaten the collapse of the entire tent.

'Oh, that!' he said. 'Forgive me, I thought you said "fight". That is only the police.'

And sure enough, when the crowd eventually parted some minutes later, there emerged from its depths two uncontrollably angry police constables whom the onlookers had been attempting to separate. They were ejected at last to settle their quarrel outside; the crowd began sorting out and dusting their fallen fezes; everything became quiet again, and the big negro resumed his self-lacerations in an appreciative calm.

Various forms of acrobatics followed in which the little French girl displayed great intrepidity and style. It was in full swing when we left, and apparently continued for hours nightly until the last comer felt he had had his money's worth. One day after this we saw the French child in the town, seated at a table in the confectioner's with her manager, eating a great many chocolate éclairs with a wan and emotionless face.

During Bajiram,[1] the railways sold return tickets to Cairo at half price, so the solicitor and I went up for a night in a very comfortable pullman carriage. The line runs for some time between the lake and the canal, then, with desert on one side, to Cantara, the junction for Jerusalem and the site of one of the largest base camps of the last war, and then through the Nile valley to Cairo. This last part of the journey was particularly beautiful after the weeks we had spent in the colourless surroundings of Port Said; acres and acres of brilliant green crops stretched out on either side of us, divided by little dykes of running water which blinded oxen filled, pacing round and round the wells in their narrow circle; camels were swaying along the roads, laden with great bundles of vegetation. Everything gave an impression of effortless opulence and biblical fertility. Agriculture on

---

1 I am not sure if this is the most correct spelling of the word. It is pronounced Biram. There seem to be two or three Europeanised spellings for almost every Arabic word.

this superb soil is a very different art from that harsh struggle for subsistence among the rocky small holdings of Southern Europe.

We arrived at Cairo in the late afternoon and went to look for an hotel. All the hotels in Egypt are bad, but they excuse themselves upon two contrary principles. Some maintain, legitimately, that it does not really matter how bad they are if they are cheap enough; the others, that it does not really matter how bad they are if they are expensive enough. Both classes do pretty well. We sought out one of the former, a large, old-fashioned establishment under Greek man- agement in the Midan el-Khaznedar, called the Hotel Bristol et du Nil, where rooms even in the high season are only 80 piastres a night. My room had three double beds in it under high canopies of dusty mosquito netting, and two derelict rocking chairs. The windows opened onto a tram terminus. None of the servants spoke a word of any European language, but this was a negligible defect since they never answered the bell.

Dennis – as it would be more convenient to name my companion – had been to Cairo before and was anxious to show me the sights, particularly, of course, those of the 'red light district'. We walked along the Sharia el-Genaineh to Shepheard's for cocktails. This street, which runs along one side of the Ezbekiyeh Gardens, is notable for its beggars, who line the railings exhibiting their sores and deformities, and clutching at the clothes of the passers-by. Shepheard's was full of exhausted tourists, just back from their round of sight-seeing. We went on to dinner at the St James's restaurant, which Dennis knowingly called 'Jimmy's'. This is a tolerable imitation of a small English grill-room, with bottles of Worcester sauce, ketchups, and relishes on the tables. After dinner, inevitably, we sought out the houses of ill fame. These all lie in the triangle of slum behind the Sharia el-Genaineh. At their doors and above the entrances to the alleys were pasted notices saying, 'Out of Bounds to all Ranks of H.M. Forces'. The reason for this interdic- tion, we learned, was not so much to protect the morals or health of the troops as the peace of the inhabitants. Just after the war the Australians, in their fun, threw a young woman to her death out of a top-story window, and then refused even to pay the normal charges of the establishment. Decent Egyptians refused to frequent places where that kind of thing was likely to occur, so that the brothel-keepers were obliged to seek protection from the military authorities. That, at any rate, was the story we were told.

The whole quarter was brilliantly illuminated in honour of the holiday. Awnings of brightly coloured cotton, printed to imitate carpets, were hung from window to window across the streets. Rows of men and women sat on chairs outside the houses watching the dense crowds who sauntered up and down. Many small cafés were occupied by men drinking coffee, smoking, and playing chess. This district, in addition to its disreputable trade, is the centre of a vivid social life; men were dancing deliberate and rather ungainly folk dances in some of the cafés. There was plenty of music on all sides. Except for a picket of military police, we saw no Europeans; nobody stared at us or embarrassed us in any way, but we felt ourselves out of place in this intimate and jolly atmosphere, like gate-crashers intruding on a schoolroom birthday party. We were just about to go when Dennis met an acquaintance – an Egyptian electrical engineer who had been in the ship with him coming out. He shook us both warmly by the hand and introduced the friend who was with him; they linked their arms with ours and all four of us paraded the narrow street in this way, chatting amicably. The engineer, who had been trained in London for some important post connected with telephones, was very anxious that we should form a good impression of his town, and was alternately boastful and apologetic. Did we find it very dirty? We must not think of them as ignorant people; it was a pity it was a holiday; if we had come at any other time he could have shown us things people never dreamed about in London; did we love a lot of girls in London? He did. He showed us a pocket-book stuffed with photographs of them; weren't they peaches? But we must not think Egyptian girls were ugly. Many had skins as fair as our own; if it had not been a holiday, he could have shown us some beauties.

He seemed a popular young man. Friends greeted him on all sides and he introduced us to them. They all shook hands and offered us cigarettes. As none of them spoke any English these encounters were brief. Finally he asked us if we would like some coffee, and took us into one of the houses.

'This is not so dear as the others,' he explained, 'some of them are terrible what they charge. Just like your London.'

It was called the High Life House, the name being painted up in English and Arabic characters on the door. We climbed a great many stairs and came into a small room where three very old men were playing on oddly shaped stringed instruments. A number of handsomely dressed Arabs sat round the walls munching nuts. They were mostly small landed proprietors, our host explained, up from the country for the festival. He ordered us coffee, nuts, and cigarettes and gave half a piastre to the band. There were two women in the room, a vastly fat white creature of indistinguishable race, and a gorgeous young Sudanese. Would we like to see one of the ladies dance, he asked. We said we would, and suggested the negress. He was puzzled and shocked at our choice. 'She has such a dark skin,' he said.

'We think she is the prettier,' we said.

Courtesy overcame his scruples. After all, we were guests. He ordered the negress to dance. She got up and looked for some castanets without glancing in our direction, moving very slowly. She cannot have been more than seventeen. She wore a very short, backless, red dance dress with bare legs and feet. When she moved it was clear that she had nothing on under her frock. She wore several gold bracelets round her ankles and wrists. These were quite genuine, our host assured us. They always put all their savings into gold ornaments. She found her castanets and began dancing in an infinitely bored way but with superb grace. The more inflammatory her movements became, the more dreamy and detached her expression. There was no suggestion of jazz about her art – merely a rhythmic, sinuous lapsing from pose to pose, a leisurely twisting and vibrating of limbs and body. She danced for a quarter of an hour or twenty minutes, while our host spat nut-shells contemptuously round her feet; then she took up a tambourine and collected money, giving a faintly discernible nod at each donation.

'On no account give her more than half a piastre,' said our host.

I had nothing smaller than a 5-piastre piece, so I put that into her collection, but she received it with unmoved indifference. She went out to conceal her winnings and then sat down again, and, taking a handful of nuts, began munching and spitting, her eyes half closed and her head supported on her fist.

Our host was clearly finding us something of an encumbrance by now, so after prolonged exchanges of courtesy and good fellowship we left him for the European quarter. Here we picked up a taxi and told him to drive us to a night club. He took us to one called Peroquet, which was full of young men in white ties throwing paper streamers about. This was not quite what we were looking for, so we drove on right out of the town and across the river to Ghizeh. The place of entertainment here was called Fantasio, and there was a finely liveried commissionaire outside. A number of slot machines in the vestibule, however, removed any apprehensions about its smartness. It was a dreary place. The tables were divided into pens by low wooden partitions; about three quarters of them were empty. On a stage at the end of the hall a young Egyptian was singing what sounded like a liturgical chant in a doleful tenor. With brief pauses, this performance continued as long as we were there. There was a magnificent-looking old sheik in one of the boxes, incapably drunk. (It is all nonsense about Mohammedans not drinking.)

After half an hour of the Fantasio even Dennis's enthusiasm for night life became milder, so we engaged an open horse-carriage and drove back under the stars to the Bristol and Nile. Next day we went out to the scent-makers' bazaar in the Mouski and bought some scent for Juliet, and caught the midday train back to Port Said. We lunched in the pullman and ate, among many other delicacies, some excellent little bitter cucumbers, served hot.

There were many other stimulating and delightful experiences in Port Said – tea at the vicarage, dinner at the consulate, cocktails at Navy House – which approximate too nearly to English life to warrant discussion in a book of travel. There was an evening when the club entertained the ward-room of a visiting battleship; and on that occasion I was slapped on the back, as I entered the bar, by a red-headed youth who said, 'Will you take a drink with the senior service, sir?' What does he know of England who only England knows? When I come to write my novel of Port Said life there will be many such incidents to recount, but for the purpose of this present book only one other episode in my visit deserves mention. That is the trip which Dennis and I took on the Menzaleh canal to a fishing village called Matarieh.

The Menzaleh canal is a term used to dignify the navigable track across the lake from Port Said to Damietta where the bottom has been artificially deepened in places to a few feet, and the shallows marked off with piles. There is daily service down this shallow trough worked by a paddle steamer and a motor launch. Matarieh is a convenient half-way point. One starts at eight in the morning on the steamer and arrives at noon. In an hour the motor launch on its way from Damietta picks one up and takes one back to Port Said by five o'clock. Except for the manager of the canal company, only one other English resident had ever been on this journey; he was the retiring doctor, who, in his first weeks, had set out that way in the hopes of shooting snipe, and had 'collared a jolly good bag, too'.

Mr Bodell gave us sandwiches, and the manager came to see us off from the quay opposite the Maison Dorée. It was a fine, sunny day. The only other first-class passengers were two American missionary women who sat in their cabin sewing. Dennis and I had brought beer, tobacco, and books; the manager lent us two easy chairs from the office.

'Paddle steamer' gives a wrong idea of this boat. It had nothing in common with the floating club-houses of the Nile or the Mississippi except its means of propulsion. This was a single paddle set in the stern, which acted also as a dredger, churning up sand and gravel from the bottom as we went along. Our boat had no name. It was built in two stories, with a flat roof and flat bottom; it drew about nine inches of water. The lower floor was engine-room, hold, and second-class saloon rolled into one. Twenty or thirty Arabs and Egyptians, men, women, and children, sprawled among heaps of fuel and a cargo of sacks. The top floor was approached by an iron ladder. Here there were two cabins and some breadth of grubby deck. This ship had once been to sea; the manager had brought it himself from Alexandria to Port Said in the first months of the war, with six terrified and sea-sick Egyptians on board.

The canal led past many flat islands, some mere sand-dunes, others covered with grass. On one there was a large ruined mosque.

There were hundreds of little fishing-boats all over the lake, most of them apparently navigated by small boys; they are of identically the same construction as those depicted in hieroglyphic drawings – fish-shaped, with a single sail on a long flexible cross beam and short mast. There were also fishermen wading about with hand nets like those used for shrimping. The catch from this lake are the very tasteless little fish that are inevitable at any Port Said dinner-table. Once or twice we narrowly escaped collision with some of the fishing-boats, and once we ran aground and had to be pushed off by hand. It was a delightful, lazy morning in the sun.

Matarieh seemed very remote indeed from Cairo or Port Said; a little collection of one-storied cabins built on a promontory and joined by a strip of railway-line to the mainland. I suppose our arrival there was nearly as surprising as would be the arrival in a Dorset village of an Arab sheik in native costume. At any rate, it created enormous excitement. The clerk of the canal company received us with great courtesy and a few words of English; he bowed us into the hut which served as his office; and gave us each a bag of pea-nuts and some ginger beer. There was a framed photograph of the Great Pyramid on his desk. We attempted to walk round the village, but soon collected the entire population at our heels. They followed at a few paces' distance, giggling and nudging one another; when we stopped, they stopped; when we turned round and glared at them, they backed away and attempted to take cover. Dennis took a snapshot of them which, unfortunately, failed to develop. Their attitude was certainly not hostile, nor, I think, really derisive; it was merely uncontrolled curiosity of the kind which impels English women to jostle round one as one goes into a wedding, but it was acutely embarrassing, so we returned to the Menzaleh Canal Navigation Company's office, when the agent was most apologetic.

'This is a dirty hole,' he said. 'All full of savage sailors – like in resemblance to your own Malta.' (Those were his exact words. We could all make up remarks of that kind; the only reason why this one is worth recording is that it happens to be genuine.)

Presently the motor launch came to take us back. There was one other passenger with us, a finely dressed Arab with a big gold-topped walking-stick. He was sitting back in the stern seat, eating bread and olives; his four wives and nine or ten children were travelling second class, separated from us by a wicker screen. When he had finished his luncheon he offered some to us, and, when we refused, passed the remains through to them. The women poked henna-stained fingers through the lattice, asking for cigarettes. Dennis was carrying a shooting-stick which attracted his curiosity. He could speak no English, but we demonstrated its use in dumb show. He was delighted and made a little joke, pretending to sit on the nob of his own cane; the chief point of that joke was that he was vastly fat. Two of his wives were squinnying through the grill, and burst out laughing too, but were quickly silenced by some words of reprimand, uttered very sternly in Arabic. When we arrived at Port Said we saw him get into a carriage and drive away, leaving his women to follow on foot with the luggage. A right-minded, high-principled man.

CHAPTER 4

SHORTLY BEFORE EASTER the doctors pronounced Juliet fit to move, so we packed up and left Port Said for Cairo. Before going we made our adieux to the various people who had befriended us. This was no modern, informal leave-taking, but a very solemn progression from house to house with little packs of calling cards marked 'p.p.c.' in the corner. I had heard scathing comments from time to time at Port Said dinner-parties on people who neglected these polite observances.

The journey was unremarkable except to Juliet, who was not used to the ways of Egyptian porters. These throw themselves upon one's baggage like Westminster schoolboys on their Shrove Tuesday pancake, with this difference, that their aim is to carry away as small a piece as possible; the best fighter struggles out happily with a bundle of newspapers, a rug, an air-cushion, or a small attaché case; the less fortunate share the trunks and suitcases. In this way one's luggage is shared between six or seven men, all of whom clamorously demand tips when they have finally got it into the train or taxi. Juliet was shocked to see her husband and myself defending our possessions from attack with umbrella and walking-stick; when the first onslaught was thus checked and our assailants realised that we had not newly disembarked, we were able to apportion it between two of them and proceed on our way with dignity.

We had booked rooms at Mena House on the grounds that desert air and a certain degree of luxury were essential to Juliet's recovery. It is the one of the grand hotels of Egypt that comes nearest to justifying their terrific charges. Shepheard's, Mena, the Semiramis, the Continental, the Grand Hotel at Heliopolis, the Palace at Luxor,

and one or two others are all owned by the same company. Most of
them shut for the summer, and the company make it their aim to
amass in the four months of the Egyptian high season the profit
which places of more equable climate distribute over the entire year.
Mena seems to me by far the best value. It stands outside the town
beyond Ghizeh, immediately below the Great Pyramid. The road
out to it is a great place for motor-speeding, and there is usually
a racing car or so piled up at the side of the road any time one goes
along, for Egyptians, particularly the wealthier ones, are reckless
with machinery. We passed two on our way out with Juliet, one
about two hundred yards from the road in a field of cucumbers, with
two *fellahin* eyeing it distrustfully. Trams run all the way out to the
pyramids, but they are crowded and slow and are very little used by
Europeans or Americans. At the tram terminus there are a mob
of dragomans, a great number of camels and mules for hire, a
Greek-owned café, a picture-postcard shop, a photographic shop,
a curiosity shop specialising in scarabs, and Mena House. This is
a large building in pseudo-Oriental style, standing in a vast and very
lovely garden. When one is paying more than one can really afford,
one is inclined to become over-critical. Mena seemed to me lacking
in most of the things which distinguish a first-rate from a second-rate
hotel; the meals were pretentious and mediocre; there were never
enough pens in the writing-rooms; I wanted another table in my
bedroom and had to make three applications before it appeared;
Juliet had dinner in bed, and instead of bringing up each course
separately, they left them all together on a tray outside her door to
get cold; my bill was made out wrong and the office staff received the
correction ungratefully; there were far too many servants in the hall
and not enough in the bedrooms – I could continue this series of
quite justifiable complaints for some time, but I think it would make
dull reading. We grumbled a good deal while we were there, but the
fact remains that we enjoyed ourselves, and against all the disadvantages which I have retailed we must set the very great beauty of the
surroundings. On three sides the desert began immediately below
the garden wall and stretched out to the horizon in wave upon wave
of sand, broken during the day by miasmas and little patches of
iridescence. The pyramids were a quarter of a mile away, impressive

by sheer bulk and reputation; it felt odd to be living at such close quarters with anything quite so famous – it was like having the Prince of Wales at the next table in a restaurant; one kept pretending not to notice, while all the time glancing furtively to see if they were still there. The gardens were grossly luxuriant, a mass of harsh greens and violets. Round the house they were studded with beds, packed tight with brilliantly coloured flowers, like Victorian paper-weights, while behind and beyond were long walks bordered by gutters of running water, among orchards and flowering trees heavy with almost overpowering scent; there were high cactus hedges and a little octagonal aviary, and innumerable white-robed gardeners, who stood up from their work and bowed and presented buttonholes when a visitor passed them. There was a stable of good horses for hire, besides camels and donkey-carts; there were tennis courts, billiard tables, swimming pool, golf links (among other amenities an English Protestant chapel and chaplain), and, above all, perfectly soundless nights, which one cannot find anywhere in Cairo.

There was also plenty of life, particularly at the weekends. The residents were mostly elderly and tranquil, but for luncheon and tea all kinds of amusing people appeared. Huge personally con-ducted luxury tours of Americans and northern Englishmen, Aus-tralians in *jodhpurs* with topees and fly-whisks, very smart Egyptian officers with vividly painted motor cars and astonishing courtesans – one in a bright green picture frock led a pet monkey on a gold chain; it wore a jewelled bracelet round its neck and fleaed its rump on the terrace while she had her tea. On Easter Monday they had what they called a gymkhana, which meant that all the prices were raised for that afternoon. Apart from this it was not really a success. There was a gentlemen's camel race which was very easily won by an English sergeant who knew how to ride, and a ladies' camel race for which there were no competitors, and a ladies' donkey race won by a noisy English girl of seventeen, and a gentlemen's donkey race for which there were no competitors, and an Arabs' camel race the result of which had clearly been arranged beforehand, and an Arabs' donkey race which ended in a sharp altercation and the exchange of blows. There was an English tourist who tried to make a book; he stood on a chair and was very facetious, but gave such short odds that there were no takers. There was a lady of rank staying in the hotel who gave away the prizes – money to the camel- and donkey-boys and hideous works of Egyptian art to the Euro- peans. On another evening there was a ball, but that too was ill attended, as it happened to coincide with a reception at the Resi- dency, and no one was anxious to advertise the fact that he had not been invited there.

Geoffrey's and my chief recreations were swimming and camel- riding. We used to ride most days for two hours, making a wide circle through the Arab village and up the ancient track past the Sphinx and the smaller pyramids. It is a delightful way of getting about, combining, as it does, complete security with an exhilarating feeling of eminence. A camel bite leads in most cases to the worst kind of blood-poisoning, and it was a little alarming at first when our mounts turned round and snapped their long green-coated teeth at our knees, but after the first morning we learned to sit cross-legged in the correct Arab fashion, and to guide them with their single hemp reins, while the camel-boys trotted behind and whacked them with a cane. To please their customers, the boys called their beasts by American names – 'Yankydoodle', 'Hitchycoo', 'Red-Hot Momma', etc. They were most anxious to please in every way, even to seizing our hands and foretelling by the lines in our palms illimitable wealth, longevity, and fecundity for both of us.

It was an interesting point of Egyptian commercial organisation that a guide hired outside the gates of the hotel cost 8 piastres an hour, while one engaged through the hall porter asked 25 piastres. Geoffrey, Juliet, and I went round the local antiquities with a kindly old bedouin called Solomon, but there is little of interest that has not been taken to the museum at Cairo, as these places were all excav- ated before the modern policy was initiated of leaving relics *in situ*. The pyramids are less impressive when seen close. They are a fine sight from the parapet of the citadel at Cairo, where all five groups of them can be seen standing up in the distinct border of the Nile valley, but, as one approaches, one sees that the original facing has only adhered in a few patches, and the whole now give the impression of immense cairns of stone rather than of buildings. The Sphinx is an ill-proportioned composition of inconsiderable æsthetic appeal; and its dramatic value has been considerably diminished since its base was disinterred. The mutilations of its face give it a certain interest. If one had come upon it unexpectedly in some unexplored region, one could be justified in showing mild enthusiasm, but as a piece of sculpture it is hopelessly inadequate to its fame. People from the hotel went out to see it by moonlight and returned very grave and awestruck; which only shows the mesmeric effect of publicity. It is just about as inscrutable and enigmatic as Mr Aleister Crowley.

One Friday, Solomon came to tell us about some religious dances that were to be performed in the neighbourhood; did we want to see them? Juliet did not feel up to it, so Geoffrey stayed at home with her and I went off alone with Solomon. We rode to the farther end of the plateau on which the pyramids stand, and then down into a sandy hollow where there were the entrances to several tombs. Here we left our camels in charge of a boy and climbed into one of the holes in the hillside. The tomb was already half full of Arabs; it was an oblong chamber cut in the rock and decorated in places with incised hieroglyphics. The audience were standing round the walls and packed in the recesses cut for the coffins. The only light came through the door – one beam of white daylight. The moment we arrived the dance began. It was performed by young men, under the direction of a sheik; the audience clapped their hands in time and joined in the chant. It *was* a dull dance, like kindergarten Euryth-mics. The youths stamped their feet on the sandy floor and clapped their hands and swayed slowly about. After a short time I signed to Solomon my readiness to leave, and attempted to make as unobtru-sive a departure as possible so as not to disturb these ungainly devotions. No sooner, however, had I reached the door than the dance stopped and the whole company came trooping out crying for 'bakshish'. I asked Solomon whether it was not rather shocking that they should expect to be paid by an infidel for keeping their religious observances. He said, rather sheepishly, that some tip was usual to the sheik. I asked where the sheik was. 'Sheik. Me sheik,' they cried, all running forward and beating their chests. Then the old man appeared. I gave him the piastres and they promptly transferred their attention to him, seizing his robes and clamouring for a share. We mounted our camels and rode away. Even then two or three urchins pursued us on foot crying, 'Bakshish! Bakshish! Me sheik!'

As we went back I asked Solomon, 'Was that a genuine religious dance?'

He pretended not to understand.

'You did not like the dance?'

'Would they have done that dance if you had not brought me?'

Solomon was again evasive. 'English and American lords like to see dance. English lords all satisfied.'

'I wasn't satisfied,' I said.

Solomon sighed. 'All right,' he said, which is the Arab's reply to all difficulties with English and American lords. 'Better dance another day.'

'There won't be another day.'

'All right,' said Solomon.

But I did not tell Geoffrey and Juliet it had been a bogus dance. They wished they had come when I told them how interesting it had been.

Another expedition which I made alone was to Sakkara, the enormous necropolis some way down the Nile from Mena. There are two pyramids there, one, rising in steps, which is considerably older than the pyramid at Ghizeh, and a number of tombs; one of them, named unpronounceably the Mastaba of Ptahhotep, is exquisitely decorated in low relief. It is ill-lighted, and a slightly impatient custodian waits on one with candles and magnesium wire; the low ceiling is entirely covered with the initials of tourists written with candle smoke. Another still more beautifully sculptured chamber is called more simply the Mastaba of Ti. As I emerged from this vault I came upon a large party of twenty or thirty indomitable Americans dragging their feet, under the leadership of a dragoman, across the sand from a charabanc. I fell in behind this party and followed them underground again, this time into a vast subterranean tunnel called the Serapeum, which, the guide explained, was the burial-place of the sacred bulls. It was like a completely unilluminated tube railway station. We were each given a candle, and our guide marched on in front with a magnesium flare. Even so, the remote corners were left in impenetrable darkness. On either side of our path were ranged the vast granite sarcophagi; we marched very solemnly the full length of the tunnel, our guide counting the coffins aloud for us; there were twenty-four of them, each so massive that the excavating engineers could devise no means of removing them. Most of the Americans counted aloud with him.

One is supposed, I know, to think of the past on these occasions; to conjure up the ruined streets of Memphis and to see in one's mind's eye the sacred procession as it wound up the avenue of sphinxes, mourning the dead bull; perhaps even to give licence to one's fancy and invent some personal romance about the lives of these garlanded hymn-singers, and to generalise sagely about the mutability of human achievement. But I think we can leave all that to Hollywood. For my own part I found the present spectacle infinitely stimulating. What a funny lot we looked, trooping along that obscure gallery! First the Arab with his blazing white ribbon of magnesium, and behind him, clutching their candles, like penitents in procession, this whole rag-tag and bobtail of self-improvement and uplift. Some had been bitten by mosquitoes and bore swollen, asymmetrical faces; many were footsore, and limped and stumbled as they went; one felt faint and was sniffing 'salts'; one coughed with dust; another had her eyes inflamed by the sun; another wore his arm in a sling, injured in heaven knows what endeavour; every one of the party in some way or another was bruised and upbraided by the thundering surf of education. And still they plunged on. One, two, three, four . . . twenty-four dead bulls; not twenty-three or twenty-five. How could they remember twenty-four? Why, to be sure, it was the number of Aunt Mabel's bedroom at Luxor. 'How did the bulls die?' one of them asks.

'What did he ask?' chatter the others.

'What did the guide answer?' they want to know.

'How *did* the bulls die?'

'How much did it cost?' asks another. 'You can't build a place like this for nothing.'

'We don't spend money that way nowadays.'

'Fancy spending all that burying bulls. . . .'

Oh, ladies and gentlemen, I longed to declaim, dear ladies and gentlemen, fancy crossing the Atlantic Ocean, fancy coming all this way in the heat, fancy enduring all these extremities of discomfort and exertion; fancy spending all this money, to see a hole in the sand where, three thousand years ago, a foreign race whose motives must for ever remain inexplicable interred the carcasses of twenty-four bulls. Surely the laugh, dear ladies and gentlemen, is on us.

But I remembered I was a gate-crasher in this party and remained silent.

We often drove into Cairo by the hotel bus and did sight-seeing. We went to the museum. It is some indication of the official Egyptian attitude towards tourists that the price for admission to this collection drops from 10 piastres to one piastre at the end of the Cairo season. The Egyptians have never taken the smallest interest in their antiquities; they have remained an invading race throughout the centuries of their occupation, and have consistently been either neglectful or actively destructive of the civilisation of their predecessors. When in the last century European antiquarians, at their own expense and often at considerable personal risk, began excavating and preserving the works of art that had survived the generations of depredation and decay, the Egyptians suddenly woke to the fact that their waste lands contained treasures of the highest commercial value. Even then everything was left to the private enterprise of French and English scholars; Egypt has not produced a single first-rate Egyptologist, contenting herself with the more modest office of fattening on the visitors who came to examine the achievements of their fellow countrymen. So churlish is their attitude, moreover, towards the founders of their prosperity that nowhere in the official catalogue of the Tutankhamen discoveries, nor, so far as I could see, in the galleries themselves, was there any mention of the names of Lord Carnarvon or Mr Howard Carter. In distributing blame, however, it is only fair to credit British commercial enterprise with the gradual erosion by yearly inundation of the lovely little temple of Philæ.

The important point about Egyptian works of art, which seems rarely to be appreciated by tourists or archæologists, is that they really *are* works of art.

There seem to me few things more boring than the cult of mere antiquity. I would view with the utmost equanimity the obliteration

of all those cromlechs and barrows and fosses of our remote ancestors which litter the English countryside; whenever I see Gothic
lettering on the ordnance survey map I set my steps in a contrary
direction. I wish all the rectors who spend their days in scratching up
flint arrow-heads and bits of pottery and horrible scraps of tessellated pavement would bury them again and go back to their prayers.
But Egyptian antiquities are quite another matter. There is nothing
here to evoke that patronising interest with which we arm ourselves
in our surveys of ancient British remains.... How clever of Dr So-
and-So to guess that that little splinter of bone in the glass case was
not really a little splinter of bone but a Pictish needle – and how
clever of the Picts all those years ago to think of making a needle out
of a little splinter of bone.... There is nothing of that in our appreciation of Egyptian remains, particularly the incomparable collection recently unearthed in the tomb of Tutankhamen. Here we are
in touch with a civilisation of splendour and refinement; of very
good sculpture, superb architecture, opulent and discreet ornament,
and, so far as one can judge, of cultured and temperate social life,
comparable upon equal terms with that of China or Byzantium or
eighteenth-century Europe, and superior in every artistic form to
Imperial Rome or the fashionable cultures of the Minoans or the
Aztecs.

The neglect of Egyptian art by the English artistic public seems to
me to be due to two causes. One, the very simple one, that the
unremitting avarice of the Egyptian race makes it impossible for
many people of culture to afford to visit them, and secondly, that the
romantic circumstances of the Tutankhamen discovery were so
vulgarised in the popular Press that one unconsciously came to
regard it less as an artistic event than as some deed of national
prowess – a speed record broken, or a birth in the Royal Family;
after the discovery came the death of Lord Carnarvon, and the
public imagination wallowed in superstitious depths. By the time
that adequate photographs began to appear it was impossible to
dissociate them from all the irrelevant bubble of emotion and
excitement. In the mind of the public the tomb of Tutankhamen
became a second Queen's Doll's House full of 'quaint' and
'amusing' toys. The fact that a rich and beautiful woman, even

though living very long ago, should still require the toilet requisites of a normal modern dressing-table was greeted with reverberations of surprise and delight and keenly debated controversies in the Press about the variable standards of female beauty. The fact that idle men, very long ago, passed their time in gambling and games of skill was a revelation. Everything of 'human' interest was extensively advertised, while the central fact, that the sum of the world's beautiful things had suddenly been enormously enriched, passed unemphasised and practically unnoticed.

Mr Howard Carter's books and the official catalogue give a complete inventory of the treasures, and there is nothing to be gained by my including here a paraphrase of these accurate and restrained accounts; but I must mention as works of outstanding beauty and nobility the two life-size figures of the king which were found in the ante-chamber, on either side of the entrance to the sepulchre (cases 5 and 6, Nos. 181 and 96); they are carved in wood and covered partly with gold leaf and partly with black varnish; except for a difference in head-dress they are nearly identical. The king is represented in the act of walking, a tall stick in one hand, a mace in the other; his eyes, gold-lined, stare straight before him; he is travelling with the wind, which blows his skirt tight about his legs at the back and throws it stiffly forward in front. These two figures seem to me unique in sculpture as a perfectly satisfactory statement of the motion of walking. It is interesting to compare them with Mr Tait McKenzie's solution of the same problem in the war memorial at Cambridge.

Next, and second only to these in value, I should put the wooden chest (case 20, No. 324), painted on the top with hunting scenes and on the side panels with battle pictures of the king's victory over his northern and southern enemies, the Asiatics and Nubians. In the brilliant draughtsmanship of these miniatures one sees the sudden flowering into genius of the stiff, scriptural decoration, hitherto regarded as the Egyptians' whole contribution to graphic art. Nothing that I have seen in Persian painting is more vigorously conceived or tactfully disposed than the design of these panels. There is also a carved wooden chair (case 22, No. 3), which seems to me more satisfactory in design and more sensitive in execution than any article of furniture produced in Europe in any age. The jewellery, though made with obvious taste and discretion, seemed to demand less attention than it received; the beds are supremely elegant; the coffins very fine and rich in general effect, but monotonous and uninspired in detail; all the sculpture is admirable, particularly a big dog and some little gilt goddesses; the alabaster vases are not every-one's cup of tea; I thought them a bore, but better judges than me find them delightful. But without illustrations this commentary must become tedious, and has already extended beyond the limits I intended for it. It would be interesting if some publisher or public body would send out Mr Roger Fry or some other cultured and articulate critic to write a review of these works from a purely æsthetic attitude. It seemed to me a collection which ought to form a necessary part of every artistic education.

There is another museum in Cairo devoted to Arab art. It was practically empty on the morning when I visited it, and I was thus enabled to go round at my leisure, undisturbed. It is a much less popular collection among European tourists, and I confess I sympa-thise with its neglect. To a Western mind there is something particu-larly stultifying about the succession of intricate geometrical devices that characterise Arab art. The attendants were most amiable. One of them was in charge of a room reconstructed from a mediæval Arab dwelling-house. It was his office, whenever a visitor arrived, to switch on the electric lights in the pierced brass lantern and behind the coloured glass windows, and to set the little fountain playing in the middle of the marble floor. This was obviously a source of great pride to him, and he stood bowing and grinning in sympathy with our expressions of delight. The greater part of the collection consists of woodwork – lattices of *mashrabieh* and door panels of inlaid arabesques. There is also a room full of brass lamps, all designed and decorated with the same patience and lack of enterprise; some incised plaster work; some leather book-bindings, and a little pottery.

I was moved by something of the Crusader's zeal for cross against crescent, as I reflected that these skilful, spiritless bits of merchandise were contemporary with the Christian masterpieces of the Musée Cluny. The period of Arab supremacy in Egypt coincides almost exactly with the dominion of Latin Christianity in England; during those centuries when the Christian artists were carving the stalls of our cathedrals and parish churches, these little jigsaw puzzles were being fitted together beyond the frontiers, by artificers whose artistic development seemed to have been arrested in the kindergarten stage, when design meant metrical symmetry and imagination the endless alternation, repetition, and regrouping of the same invariable elements. Living as we are under the impact of the collective inferiority complex of the whole West, and humbled as we are by the many excellencies of Chinese, Indians, and even savages, we can still hold up our heads in the Mohammedan world with the certainty of superiority. It seems to me that there is no single aspect of Mohammedan art, history, scholarship, or social, religious, or political organisation, to which we, as Christians, cannot look with unshaken pride of race.

The Arabs come nearest, perhaps, to exciting our admiration, in their architecture. Driving about the streets of the old town we continually came upon buildings of great sweetness and attraction – squat onion-shaped domes; high pointed domes like Saracen helmets; white minarets like wedding-cake decorations or ornamental bone penholders; little white-washed courtyards with trees growing in them and fountains; great stone doorways canopied with stalactite vaulting; fretted plaster façades; cloisters with gilded and painted beams; balconies screened from the street with black *mashrabieh*; ruined tombs silted up with sand; vast, densely populated courts with mosaic walls and pavement – all these make a direct but somewhat superficial appeal to our affections. I tried to go round the principal mosques in an intelligent and critical manner, but found that there was too much to assimilate that was odd and unfamiliar. I began to sympathise with American visitors to Europe. We, who have grown up in life-long familiarity with a mature culture, have, to some extent, an instinctive discrimination of the genuine from the spurious in our own civilisation. We can perceive uncertainty in an artistic motive; we know when an idea is new and vital and when the artist has become bored, imitative, and repetitive. We do not confuse nineteenth- with thirteenth-century Gothic; we can relate the art of our own continent to its history; heraldry and ecclesiastical symbolism throw out allusions which we can recognise. To those who are born in a new country and brought up among half-finished institutions, three hundred years ago is much the same as five hundred; one cathedral much the same as another, be it Norman, Gothic, or Baroque; one Virgin and Child much the same as another, be it by Cimabue, Filippo Lippi, or Mantegna. The date in the guide book, four numerals in a row, is unrelated to the fact, and therefore hard to remember, easy to confuse ludicrously. 'Did you say B.C. or A.D.?' is quite a common question from tourist to guide.

In just this way I found myself floundering hopelessly in my attempts to grasp the essentials of Arab architecture. I would memorise a list of dynasties and dates in the morning and forget them before luncheon; I confused the features of one building with those of another, and, looking at photographs later, was often unable to remember which buildings I had seen and which I had not. It would clearly take more than the three weeks at my disposal to get any kind of coherent impression, so in the end I was content to give up the attempt, treating the places we visited as so many spots of natural beauty. In this way I passed the time pleasantly if unprofitably.

One of the religious buildings which interested me most was the University of El Azhar, the centre of Moslem scholarship. Moslem scholarship consists in learning by heart long passages of theology. El Azhar is a large establishment, dating from the early fourteenth century, with more than ten thousand students of all ages and nationalities, and three or four hundred dons. We watched some of them at work, squatting, packed together, in a vast, pillared hall, rocking on their heels and repeating with half-closed eyes verse after verse of the Koran. Even Oxford seemed comparatively vital by contrast.

The citadel, too, repaid the precipitous ascent. The alabaster mosque of Mohammed Ali is enormous and vulgar, like a music-hall, but there is an arresting cast-iron fountain in the outer court, presented by Louis Philippe; there is also a charming deserted palace, the site of the murder of the Mamluks, with nineteenth-century mural decorations in grisaille. The view across Cairo to Ghizeh and the Nile valley, with the groups of pyramids clearly standing out against the desert, and the hundreds of domes and minarets bristling out of the city at one's feet, is a memorable experience.

As I wished to see a little more of Egypt before leaving, I drove down to Helwan for a couple of nights. It is an inconsiderable cluster of villas and hotels existing simply for the spa. I stayed in an excellent English *pension*, called the English Winter Hotel; the beds in the garden were edged with bottles; there were two lemurs in cages; the other guests were a colonel, two bishops, and an archdeacon, all very British. Before I had been there two hours I knew everything there was to know about their rheumatism.

The road from Helwan to Cairo runs along the Nile bank past a large convict settlement, a very palatial royal villa, and an ancient Coptic church, and enters Cairo through a very interesting quarter which many tourists omit to visit. That is Masr el Atika, Old Cairo or Babylon, the Coptic settlement built in the days of persecution within the walls of the old Roman garrison station. In this constricted slum there are five mediæval Coptic churches, a synagogue, and a Greek Orthodox convent. The Christians seem to differ in decency very little from their pagan neighbours; the only marked sign of their emancipation from heathen superstition was that the swarm of male and juvenile beggars were here reinforced by their womenfolk, who in the Mohammedan quarters maintain a modest seclusion. The churches, however, were most interesting, particularly Abu Sergh, which has Corinthian columns taken from a Roman temple, Byzantine eikons, and an Arabic screen. It is built over the cave where the Holy Family – always troglodytic – are said to have spent their retirement during Herod's massacre of the innocents. The deacon, Bestavros, showed us over. When he had finished his halting exposition and received his tip, he said, 'Wait one minute. Get priest.'

He hurried into the vestry and brought out a patriarchal old man with a long grey beard and large greasy bun of grey hair, obviously newly awakened from his afternoon nap. This priest blinked, blessed us, and held out his hand for a tip; then, lifting up his skirts, he tucked the two piastres away in a pocket and made off. At the vestry door he stopped. 'Go getting bishop,' he said.

Half a minute later he returned with a still more venerable figure, chewing sunflower seeds. The pontiff blessed us and held out his hand for a tip. I gave him two piastres. He shook his head.

'He is a bishop,' explained Bestavros, 'three piastres for a Bishop.'

I added a piastre and he went away beaming. Bestavros then sold me a copy of a history of the church written by himself. It is such a very short work that I think it worth reproducing here with spelling and punctuation exactly as it was printed.

A BRIEF HISTORY
of
ABU SARGA CHURCH

By
MESSIHA BESTAVROS
ABU SARGA CHURCH

This Church was built in the year A.D. 1171 by a man whose name was Hanna El Abbah the secretary of Sultan Salah-El-Din El-Ayoubi.

The Church contains 11 marble pillars each containing a panting of one of the apostles and one granite pillar without capital, panting or cross alladvig Judes who betrayed our Lord.

The alter for the holy comminion contains 7 Maszaic steps (the 7 degrees of bishops). The screen of the alter is made of carved ivory.

On the North of wich were are tow nice penals of carved wood: one shows the last supper and the other Bethlehm. On there Southern sides St. Demetrius, St. Georges and St. Theodore.

The cript was cut out of a solid rock 30 years B.C. Mearly which was used as a shelter for strangers. When the Holy Family moved from Jernsalim to Egypt to hide themselves from King Herod they found this cript where they remained until the death of King Herod.

When St. Mark started preaching in Alexandria at 42 A.D. and we the Pharos who embraced the religion of Christ used this criot as a church for a period of 900 years till this church built on its top. On the other side of the cript you can see the fount where Christian

children are baptised by emersion in water for 3 times. This church
contains manu Byzantian painitings of the 9th & 10th centuries.

MESIHA BESTAVROS,
Deacon.

Opposite old Babylon is Roda Island, with a pretty, derelict
garden and an old Nilometer.

CHAPTER 5

I PARTED FROM Geoffrey and Juliet at Port Said. They had cabled to Juliet's sister for more money and, as soon as it arrived, set off for Cyprus in a Khedivial Line ship. She left late at night, and I saw them off and drank some vermouth with them in a gaily upholstered saloon; the ship was coaling at the time and everything was slightly grimy; the other passengers were Greeks. I had to climb across two coal barges to get back to my boat. As we rowed back across the harbour, whose black waters reflected row upon row of bright portholes where the big ships lay at anchor, and whose air echoed with the singing of the coolies and the shouts of the porters and boatmen and the howling of the dredgers, my meditations were disturbed by a vigorous attempt on the part of the two oarsmen to blackmail me into increasing the price we had already agreed upon for the journey. They stopped rowing and we drifted about in the dark, arguing. I had learned an Arabic phrase which sounded like '*Ana barradar.*' I do not know what it meant, but I had used it once or twice in Cairo with fair success. I kept repeating it at intervals during the conversation. In the end they started rowing again and, when we reached the shore, I gave them their original price. It was interesting to notice that they bore no malice about it, but sent me away with smiles and bows and the entreaty that I would use their boat again (which was painted on the back seat with a U.S. flag and the title 'Gene Tunney'). This very sensible attitude seemed to show the advantages of not having an inherited Protestant conscience. When an Englishman attempts to be extortionate and fails, he keeps up his grumble until one is out of earshot, and, I believe, does bear a genuine personal grudge against one for the rest of that day. He does not admit, even to himself, that he was 'trying it on' or accept defeat with good grace. Arabs and, I imagine, most Oriental races, have no conception of the 'fair price' or of absolute values of exchange. Hence, no doubt, the Jews' superiority over Europeans in finance. The English boatman prefers to kick his heels day after day on the quay-side, rather than take less for his labour than he has convinced himself is right. He very rarely attempts to get more, even if his passengers look rich and their need for his service acute. When he does, it is only after convincing himself that the increased demand is actually the normal one. When he is caught out his conclusion is that his customer was no gentleman to make such a fuss about a shilling. It is the same with writers, who will all gladly starve their wives and tailors rather than accept less than their fifteen guineas a thousand words, while at the same time maintaining an undertone of complaint against the ignorance and meanness of editors and publishers.

Next day I, too, left Port Said in the P. & O. ship *Ranchi* for Malta. On leaving Egypt, as a final nip of avarice, one is obliged to pay a few shillings 'quarantine tax'. I should have paid a similar levy on landing, but, as I came off the *Stella*, no one asked me for it. Accordingly I had to pay double on leaving. No one seems to know anything about this imposition, what statute authorised it and how much of what is collected ever finds its way into the treasury, or what bearing it has upon 'quarantine'. Many residents maintain that it is purely a bit of fun on the part of the harbour officials, who have no legal right to it whatever. Anyway, it seems to me a model of revenue collection, as the sum is not large enough to raise protests from any but the most truculent and is demanded when delay is least desirable, just when one is most harassed with getting one's luggage through the customs, catching trains or boats, and landing in a new country.

Thanks to the kind offices of the local manager, I was able to obtain a second-class berth. The residents in Port Said said: 'You meet a first-rate lot of people travelling second class since the war. A jolly sight better than in the first class, particularly on the ships from India – the first class is all *nouveaux riches*. You meet some pretty rough diamonds in the Australian ships. But you'll find second class on the *Ranchi* as good as first class on a foreign line. My wife travels second class when she goes home.'

But my motive really was less the ambition to meet nice people than to save money. As it was, the second-class fare – twelve pounds for the two days' voyage to Malta – seemed extremely expensive. After my extravagances at Mena House I was beginning to get worried again about money, so I thought of what still seems to me an ingenious device. Before leaving Cairo I wrote – on the note-paper of the Union Club, Port Said – to the managers of the two leading hotels in Valletta, the Great Britain and the Osborne, between whom, I was told, there existed a relationship of acute rivalry, and enclosed a publisher's slip of Press cuttings about my last book; I said to each that I proposed to publish a travel diary on my return to England; I had heard that his was the best hotel in the island. Would he be willing to give me free accommodation during my visit to Malta in return for a kind reference to his establishment in my book? They had not had time to answer by the time I embarked at Port Said, but I went on board hoping that at Valletta I should experience some remission of the continual draining of money that I had suffered for the last two months.

It is one of the unsatisfactory things about ships that you never know when they are going to arrive. The *Ranchi* was advertised to sail some time on Sunday and was expected early in the afternoon. On Sunday morning she was announced for nine o'clock that evening. Finally she came in well after midnight and stayed only two hours. During those two hours the town, which, as usual, was feeling the ill-effects of its Saturday night at the Casino, suddenly woke again into life. Simon Arzt's store opened; the cafés turned on their lights and dusted the tables; out came the boot-cleaners and postcard sellers; the passengers who had stayed on board through the canal came ashore and drove round in two-horse carriages; those who had left the ship at Aden for a few hours at Cairo, and had spent all that afternoon on the quay in a fever of apprehension that they might miss her, scuttled on board to their cabins; half the residents of Port Said had business of some kind to transact on board. I went down to the harbour in a bustle that was like noon in the City of London. I am quite sure that I have never spent a more boring four hours in my life than those between dinner and the arrival of the *Ranchi*, sitting with my luggage in the deserted hall of

Bodell's *pension*. The sudden brightness of the streets and the animation on all sides seemed quite unreal. I went on board, found my
steward and my cabin, disposed of my luggage, and went on deck for
a little. The passengers who had done the Aden–Cairo–Port Said
dash were drinking coffee, eating sandwiches, and describing the
pyramids and Shepheard's Hotel. 'Two pounds ten, simply for
a single bed and no bathroom. Think of that!' they said with obvious
pride. 'And we rode on camels – you should just have seen me. How
Katie would have laughed, I said. And the camel-boy told my
fortune, and we had a coffee made actually in the temple of the
Sphinx. You *ought* to have come. Well, yes, perhaps it was a little
exhausting, but then we've plenty of time at sea to make up for it.
And there was the sweetest little boy who cleaned our shoes. And we
went into a mosque where the Mohammedans were all saying their
prayers – so quaint. And would you believe it – at Shepheard's they
charged 15 piastres – that's over three shillings – for a cup of early
morning tea, and not very good tea at that. You *ought* to have come,
Katie!'

Before we sailed, I went down to my cabin and went to bed. The
man who was sharing it with me, a kindly, middle-aged, civil engineer, was already undressing; he wore combinations. I woke once
when the engines started, dozed and woke again as we ran clear of
the breakwater and began to roll, and then fell soundly asleep, to
wake next morning on the high seas with a hundred Englishmen all
round me, whistling as they shaved.

We had cold, sunless weather and fairly heavy seas during the
next two days. I rather wished that I had gone first class. It was not
that my fellow passengers were not every bit as nice as the Port Said
residents had told me they would be, but that there were so many of
them. There was simply nowhere to sit down. The lounge and
smoking-room were comfortable and clean and well ventilated
and prettily decorated and all that, but they were always completely
full. On the decks there were no deck-chairs except those the
passengers provided for themselves; the three or four public
seats were invariably occupied by mothers doing frightful things to
their babies with jars of vaseline. It was not even possible to walk
round with any comfort, so confined and crowded was the single

promenade deck. It is impossible to walk happily on a rolling ship unless one has ready access to one or other rail for support, and these were always lined with military men in overcoats. Children were everywhere. It was the beginning of the hot season in India, and the officers' wives were taking them back to England in shoals; the better sort lay and cried in perambulators; the worse ones fell all over the deck and were sick; these ones, too, appeared in the dining-room for breakfast and luncheon and were encouraged by their mothers to eat. There was an awful hour every evening at about six o'clock, when the band came down from the first-class deck to play Gilbert and Sullivan to us in the saloon; this visitation coincided exactly with the bathing of the elder children below; the combination of soap and salt water is one of the more repugnant features of sea travel, and the lusty offspring of sahib and memsahib shrieked their protest till the steel rafters and match-board partitions echoed and rang. There was no place above or below for a man who values silence.

Apart from the overcrowding, the second-class accommodation on the *Ranchi* was, as they had said, a great deal better than the first-class of many ships. The cabins were comfortable, the food unpretentious and wholesome, and one only had to have the band for one hour in the day. The other passengers were mostly soldiers on leave or soldiers' wives, leavened with a few servants of first-class passengers, some clergymen, and three or four nuns. The valets wore neat blue suits throughout the voyage, but the soldiers had an interesting snobbism. During the day, though cleanly shaved and with carefully brushed hair, they cultivated an extreme freedom of dress, wearing khaki shorts and open tennis shirts and faded cricket blazers. At dinner, however, they all appeared in dinner jackets and stiff shirts. One of them told me that the reason he travelled second class was that he need not trouble about clothes, but that he had to draw the line somewhere. On the other side of the barrier we could see the first-class passengers dressed very smartly in white flannels and parti-coloured brown and white shoes. Among them there was a youth who knew me hurrying back to contest a seat in the Conservative interest at the General Election. He kept popping over the rail to have cocktails with me and tell me about the lovely first-class girls he danced and played quoits with. He cost me quite a lot in cocktails. He often urged me to come over and see all the lovely girls and have cocktails with him. 'My dear chap,' he used to say, 'no one will dare to say anything to you while you're with *me*. I'd soon fix it up with the Captain if they did.' But I kept to my own bar. Later this young man, in his zeal to acquit himself splendidly before the first-class girls, clambered up one of the davits on the boat deck. He was reported to the Captain and seriously reprimanded. P. & O. ships are full of public school spirit. He did very badly indeed in the election, I believe, reducing an already meagre Conservative poll almost to extinction.

Just before luncheon on the third morning, we came in sight of Malta. There was some delay about landing because one of the passengers had developed chicken-pox. There was only one other passenger disembarking. We had to go and see the medical officer in the first-class saloon. He had infinite difficulties about the pro-nunciation of my name. He wanted to know the address I was going to in Malta. I would only tell him that I had not yet decided between the two hotels. He said, 'Please decide now. I have to fill in this form.'

I said I could not until I had seen the managers.

He said, 'They are both good hotels, what does it matter?'

I said, 'I want to get in free.'

He thought I was clearly a very suspicious character, and told me that on pain of imprisonment, I must report daily at the Ministry of Health during my stay at Valletta. If I did not come the police would find me and bring me. I said I would come, and he gave me a quarantine form to keep. I lost the form that evening and never went near the Ministry of Health and heard no more about it.

We went ashore in a lighter and landed at the Custom House. Here I was met by two young men, both short, swarthy, and vivacious, and each wearing a peaked cap above a shiny English suit. One had 'The Osborne Hotel' in gold on his cap, the other 'The Great Britain Hotel'. Each held in his hand a duplicate letter from me, asking for accommodation. Each took possession of a bit of my luggage and handed me a printed card. One card said:

THE OSBORNE HOTEL
STRADA MEZZODI
Every modern improvement.   Hot water.   Electric light.

Excellent Cuisine.

PATRONISED BY H.S.H PRINCE LOUIS OF BATTENBERG
AND THE DUKE OF BRONTE

The other said:

THE GREAT BRITAIN HOTEL
STRADA MEZZODI
Every modern improvement.   Hot and cold water.   Electric light.

Unrivalled cuisine.   Sanitation.

THE ONLY HOTEL UNDER ENGLISH MANAGEMENT

(a fact, one would have thought, more fit to be concealed than advertised).

I had been advised in Cairo that the Great Britain was really the better of the two, so I directed its representative to take charge of my luggage. The porter of the Osborne fluttered my letter petulantly before my eyes.

'A forgery,' I explained, shocked at my own duplicity. 'I am afraid that you have been deluded by a palpable forgery.'

The porter of the Great Britain chartered two little horse-carriages, conducted me to one, and sat with the luggage in the other. There were low, fringed canopies over our heads so that it was impossible to see out very much. I was aware of a long and precipitous ascent, with many corners to turn. At some of these I got a glimpse of a baroque shrine, at others a sudden bird's-eye view of the Grand Harbour, full of shipping, with fortifications beyond. We went up and round, along a broad street of shops and more important doorways. We passed groups of supremely ugly Maltese women wearing an astonishing black head-dress, half veil and half umbrella, which is the last legacy to the island of the conventual inclinations of the Knights of St John. Then we turned off down a narrow side street and stopped at the little iron and glass porch of the Great Britain Hotel. A little dark passage led into a little dark lounge, furnished like an English saloon bar, with imitation leather arm-chairs, bowls of aspidistra on fumed oak stands, metal-topped tables, and tables with plush coverings, Benares brass work, framed photographs, and ash-trays stamped with the trade-marks of various brands of whisky and gin. It was an old house, how old I cannot say, but certainly not later than the middle of the eighteenth century, and its construction seemed in conflict with this scheme of decoration. Do not mistake me; it was not remotely like an old-fashioned hotel in an English market town; it was a realisation of the picture I have always in my mind of the interiors of those hotels facing on to Paddington station, which advertise '5s. Bed and Breakfast' over such imposing names as Bristol, Clarendon, Empire, etc. My heart fell rather as I greeted my host in this dingy hall, and continued to fall as I ascended, story by story, to my bedroom. The worst of it, however, was in this first impression, and I think I am really doing my duty honourably to the proprietor in warning people of it and exhorting them not to be deterred. For I can quite conscientiously say that the Great Britain *is* the best hotel in the island. There are no luxurious hotels. I went later to look at the Osborne and felt that I had done one better than H.S.H. Prince Louis of Battenberg and the Duke of Bronte. The food at the Great Britain was good; there was a large variety of wine and spirits; the lavatories and bathrooms quite adequate; the servants particularly willing and engaging. As an example of good service I may quote that one evening, being tired and busy, I decided to dine in my room. At Mena House, where there were hosts of servants and a lift, as I have noted, the dinner was brought up in one load and left outside the door; at the Great Britain every course was carried separately up three flights of stairs by the panting but smiling *valet de chambre*.

Before I left, the proprietor of the hotel asked me, rather suspiciously, what I intended to say about him. I replied that I would recommend him to the readers of my book.

They had had another writer, he told me, who had come to stay as his guest; he wrote for a paper called *Town and Country Life*; he had written a very nice piece indeed about the Great Britain. They had had the article reprinted for distribution.

The proprietor gave me a copy.

That, he said, was the kind of article that did a house good. He hoped mine would be as much like that as I could make it.

It was a funny article. It began: 'The beautiful and prolific foliage, exotic skies, and glorious blue waters, a wealth of sunshine that spells health and happiness, and the facilities for enjoying outdoor sports, all the year round, are a few of the reasons that has made Malta so popular. Picturesque scenery, and people, complete as fascinating an array of attractions as the heart of the most blasé, could wish for.' It continued in this way for a column, with the same excess of punctuation; then it gave a brief survey of Maltese history and a description of the principal sights, for another column. Then it started on the Great Britain Hotel. 'No expense,' it said, 'has been spared to make the Public Rooms as comfortable as possible ... the Management boasts that its meals equal in the excellence of its food, cooking and serving, those served at London's hostelries and restaurants ... special pains are taken to see that all beds are most comfortable and only best material used ...' and so on for a column and a half. It finished with this sentence: 'The luxuries of modern civilisation have all been embodied in the building and organisation of the Great Britain Hotel, Valletta, Malta, where the visitor is able to revel in the joys of a healthy happy stay amidst the fascinations of a modern palace set in Nature's own setting of sea and foliage, and here are to be obtained sunshine and warmth the whole year round.'

I will not be outdone in gratitude. If my appreciation is more temperately expressed it is none the less genuine. Let me state again, the Great Britain may be less suitably placed for golfers than Gleneagles; the bathing may be better from the Normandie; one can shop more conveniently from the Crillon, the Russie is set in a prettier square, one meets more amusing company at the Cavendish, one can dance better at the Berkeley and sleep better at Mena and eat better at the Ritz, but *the Great Britain Hotel, Valletta, Malta, is the best on the island*; further comparisons seem rather to confuse the issue.

Malta was quite different from what I had imagined. I expected it to be much more British and much more breezy. I expected a great many white flag-staffs and band-stands and very clean streets, and officers' wives with Sealyham terriers, and white-washed buildings with verandahs and little brass cannon and lookout towers with spiral iron staircases. I did not associate in my mind a naval base with baroque architecture, and, without giving much thought to it, I supposed the sailors were illimitably supplied with English nursery maids to walk with along the front and take to the cinema; it was odd to see them swaggering down precipitous alleys with prostitutes who talked a mixture of Arabic and Italian. I expected to find a Sabbath-keeping, undemonstrative Protestantism, one English church full of fairly recent memorial tablets, and a chaplain or two carrying tennis rackets. I found the most ardently Catholic people in Europe; a place where the Church owns a third of the soil, and monks, nuns, priests, novices, prelates, and religious processions emerge in serried masses at every corner. I daresay things seem different when the fleet is in; while I was there the harbour was empty except for a submarine, a target carrier, and the usual mercantile shipping. In these circum-stances I got the impression of a place far less British than Port Said. It is true that I saw a cricket match being played, and that Gieves have a shop in Strada Mezzodi, and that notices are displayed at the Custom House and the railway station advertising the addresses of the local secretaries of the Society for the Prevention of Cruelty to Animals and the Girls' Friendly Society, and that English money is used, and that the *cafés chantants* call themselves music-halls, and that instead of cafés there are public houses with a row of handles behind the bar and barmaids who draw up pint glasses of metallic-tasting draught bitter, but in spite of all this there seemed something superficial about the British occupation. After all, we have only been there for a little over a hundred years, and we came, not as colonists among savages, but as the mandatories of an outpost of high European culture. But trivial as has been the English influence to alter the essentially Mediterranean character of the island, this tenancy by a first-class naval power has been the means of preserv-ing almost the whole of its charm. Malta in the nineteenth century might so easily have become neutralised and internationalised, or, worse still, the Order of St John might have been reconstituted on an archaic-heraldic-churchy basis and the island have lapsed into bogus autonomy as a carefully nurtured 'quaint survival'.

Nothing, of course, could destroy its importance as a sea port and coaling station, but the three lovely towns of the Grand Harbour, Valletta, Senglea, and Vittoriosa, might very easily indeed have fallen to the water-colour artists. They have all the ingredients of the picturesque – ancient buildings, fortifications, narrow and precipitous streets, national costume, local religious festivals, and an unconscionably romantic history; the climate would have proved very much more favourable to retired æsthetes than the Riviera; only the acquisitive instincts of British nineteenth-century diplomacy saved Malta from developing into such a thing as does not bear thinking of – a nightmare island combining and epitomising all the unendurable characteristics of Capri, Rye, and Carcassonne. The occupation by the British Navy has prevented all that; the fortifications have not been allowed to crumble and grow mossy; they are kept in good order, garrisoned and, whenever it was expedient, ruthlessly modified; roads have been cut through them and ditches filled up. Nothing, except the one museum in the Auberge d'Italie, has been allowed to become a show place; everything is put to a soundly practical purpose. There is a governor in the Grand Master's Palace, monks in the monasteries, marines and naval officials in the principal houses, a police station in the Knights' Hospital, a modern signalling station perched on the roof of the Auberge de Castille.

I spent too little time in Malta, and look forward eagerly for an opportunity to revisit it. Most of my days were spent in exploring Valletta, with the aid of a small book called *Walks in Malta*, by F. Weston, which I bought for two shillings at Critien's, the big stationer's shop. I found it a slightly confusing book at first until I got used to the author's method; after that I became attached to it, not only for the variety of information it supplied, but for the amusing Boy-Scout game it made of sight-seeing. 'Turning sharply to your left you will notice . . . ' Mr Weston prefaces his comments, and there follows a minute record of detailed observation. On one occasion, when carrying his book, I landed at the Senglea quay, taking it for Vittoriosa, and walked on for some time in the wrong town, hotly following false clues and identifying 'windows with fine old mouldings', 'partially defaced escutcheons', 'interesting iron-work balustrades', etc. for nearly quarter of a mile, until a clearly non-existent cathedral brought me up sharp to the realisation of my mistake.

Valletta is built on a high peninsula between two deep creeks which form the natural harbours of Marsamuscetto and the Grand Harbour; the south-east bank of the latter is broken by three smaller and narrower creeks which throw out, at right angles to Valletta, the two peninsulas on which are built the towns of Vittoriosa and Senglea. The north-west bank of the Marsamuscetto Harbour is again broken by creeks into two peninsulas; Forts Tigné and Manoel stand on these points; Fort St Elmo at the head of Valletta and Fort St Angelo at Vittoriosa. Thus, wherever one walks upon the high ground and cavaliers of Valletta, one is confronted with a magnificent prospect of water, shipping, a high and broken coast-line, fortifications, and behind these again the rising hills of the interior.

A ferry plies regularly between the three towns. There is very little to see at Senglea except the view it affords of the other two and a delightful sixteenth-century observation tower carved with a huge eye and ear. Vittoriosa has a fine main street with a good deal of Norman work here and there among the houses, a large convent with one of the links which bound St Lawrence to his gridiron, a bishop's palace and an inquisitor's palace, a good Renaissance church, but the most interesting thing is the disposal of the streets in relation to the fortifications. Vittoriosa is much older than Valletta and was planned in the days of bow and arrow; for this reason the streets that lead inwards from the walls to the centre of the town afford the assaulting party no opportunity for a single victorious charge, but turn backwards and forwards at right angles, each turn a bow-shot from the last, so that the retreating defenders could loose a flight of arrows and instantly take cover, reload, wait the appearance of their enemies, fire again, and again take cover. (All this was explained to me by Mr Weston.)

Valletta was built to withstand bombardment with firearms, and is a model of seventeenth-century military science. I should imagine that even to-day it would be impregnable to infantry until it had first been pounded to pieces from the air or sea. When Napoleon took it, by treachery, his chief of staff is said to have remarked to him, 'It is well, general, that there was someone within to open the gates to us. We should have had trouble in working our way through had the place been empty.'

With Mr Weston's help it is amusing to trace out the particular purpose of each rampart and ditch and cavalier, but the chief interests in Valletta are artistic. Until the beginning of the eighteenth century the Knights of St John were enormously wealthy; at the time of their dissolution they were practically bankrupt and had already been obliged to dispose of some of their treasures; Napoleon's troops carried away most of what was left and lost it in Aboukir Bay, but, in spite of this wholesale depredation, the residue is dazzling in its splendour.

It is hard to form any temperate idea of the magnificence of the Knights' lives in the seventeenth and eighteenth centuries, when even the common sailors in hospital ate off silver plate. It must be remembered that in Malta alone of the cultured states of Europe slave labour was extensively employed for all public works. Mohammedan prisoners, with shaved heads and pig-tails, worked in the quarries and on the fortifications and were herded at night into a common prison. The Knights were an international aristocracy curiously combining the careers of monk and soldier of fortune. One wonders what odd rites of initiation were practised in the Auberges; what friendships and jealousies sprang up among these celibate warriors.

If only there had been some Maltese Guardi or Longhi or Canaletto to record the life of the island for us. It is in the Cathedral of St John, the conventual church of the order, that one gets most idea of its original splendour. This is not a wholly attractive building. Outside it is austere and almost shabby; inside there is no single spot where the eye can rest for one moment that is not ablaze with decoration. The barrel vaulting of the roof is frescoed by Mattia Preti with a series of rich and vigorous baroque compositions. His work was new to me at this time, though since then I have encountered his name repeatedly. He has fearlessly attacked the problem set by the curvature of the surface and has worked prodigies of perspective, enhancing his effects by painting false shadows across the mouldings between the bays. Malta is full of his work, but the ceiling of St John's is by far the grandest and best preserved.

Gafa, the sculptor, is another artist whom I had not heard of before. Indeed, to the best of my knowledge there is no work of his outside the island. I saw a lovely, effeminate head of St John by him and a terrific marble group of the Baptism of our Lord. He died before this was finished and the final touches were left to Bernini, who was engaged on the high altar. There is also a fine Caravaggio in the church, which the verger points out as being by Michelangelo.

The floor is completely carpeted with the inlaid marble tomb-stones of the more august knights; there are more than four hundred of them, all heraldic and rococo, many with figures of death as supporters. All round the church are the chapels of the different Languages, most of them with elaborate marble altars and canopies. There is not one piece of plain stone left in the building. The parts of the wall that are not overlaid with marble are carved in high relief with rather boring decorative panels which give an effect of sculp-tured lodging-house wall-paper. The Chapel of the Language of Auvergne has massive silver gates and screen which escaped pillage by Napoleon through their being painted black and taken for iron. Among its other treasures the cathedral owns a piece of the true cross, a thorn from the crown of thorns, and some of the finest tapestry in Europe, which is only brought out on a few days of the year – alas, on none of the days of my visit.

Another sight to which I was denied access was the Dominican Chapel of Bones at the end of the town. Apparently some midship-men had played bowls with the skulls, so the building was locked up even from more responsible visitors. It was possible to obtain an order to view it, I was told, but I felt ashamed to apply, having no possible business there beyond casual curiosity.

I discovered two interesting quarters of Malta for myself. One was the district at the end of the Strada Reale below the Castle of St Elmo, where the seamen go for their recreation. It was full of brilliantly painted public houses and *cafés chantants*. In the absence of the fleet everything was very quiet, but I should think it would repay a visit at a more popular time.

The other must, I should think, be the most concentrated and intense slum in the world. It is called the Manderaggio and consists of a huge pit quarried out on the north-west edge of the town. It was intended originally for an artificial land-locked creek for the protection and repair of small boats, but the work was abandoned before it reached sea level. In this crater the poorest of the population have made their home for the last three hundred years. It is approached from the west end of the Strada San Giovanni, down stone steps under a low arch that reminds one of the Adelphi Arches in London. Until quite recent years it was a place where the police could offer no protection; since then it has been scoured clean of its more militant criminality and it is about as safe as the *vieux port* at Marseilles. It is wise to go with some kind of escort, however, as none of the inhabitants speak a word of any European language, and the labyrinth of streets is so intricate that only those whose families have inhabited it for generations have any sense of its geography. Not a single street in the Manderaggio is accessible to wheeled traffic; most of them are narrow passages in which two can barely pass without brushing against each other; many of them are mere tunnels and flights of steps, roofed over with dwelling-houses; half of them are blind alleys leading through infinite deviations, round hair-pin bends, and up and down precipitous inclines to a dead stop; the houses are jumbled, literally, on top of each other and densely populated; some of them are caves cut in the face of the cliff, some are poised on buttresses over a drop of a hundred feet, some are in cellars approached by steps from the level of the gutter; needless to say, the dirt and smell are overpowering. As is the case with most slums the population seems to consist solely of the extremely young and the extremely old. I suppose that all the active men are down in the harbour. I did not attempt a visit after dark, when, I suppose, the real life of the Manderaggio begins. I am keeping that and the sailor quarter for another and less solitary excursion.

I went inland one day on an absurd railway to Notabile or Citta Vecchia, the old capital of the island. There I saw numerous ancient buildings, many of them of Norman construction, three churches, a cathedral containing a portrait of the Madonna painted by St Luke and a good della Robbia plaque, an infinitely boring

Roman villa with a well-preserved tessellated pavement, a consump-
tives' hospital, the cave where St Paul stayed on his visit to Publius
(though this would seem anything but a courteous lodging), and
a catacomb full of very dilapidated Byzantine frescoes which the
custodian described as Phœnician – a term used among Maltese
archæologists to describe any work earlier than the Norman occupation.

About this time I began making enquiries at the shipping offices
for a berth from Malta in any direction, and was told that these
could very rarely be guaranteed, particularly at the present season.
Preference was always given to passengers booking a long passage.
One just had to take one's chance. I was getting a little impatient
with the proprietor of the Great Britain, who had, in the last two
days, developed a habit of popping suddenly out of his office whenever I sat down to have a drink, and saying, "Ullo, 'ullo. And 'ow's
that book getting along? You don't seem to be seeing much of the
island,' adding encouragingly: 'You couldn't see a 'alf of it, not if
you was to spend a life-time 'ere, you couldn't.' I became aware
of a slight claustrophobic itch at the back of my mind, to which I am
always liable on small islands, and in this mood one day, less than
a week after my arrival, I leant over the Cavalier of St James, looking
down into the Grand Harbour. Then I saw below, among the
fishing-boats and cargo ships and nondescript official launches
and lighters, a very radiant new arrival; a large white motor vessel,
built like a yacht with broad, clean decks and a single yellow funnel.
I took the funicular down to the Custom House and looked at
her from the quay. She was the *Stella Polaris*, on her second cruise
from the one I had abandoned at Port Said. As I stood there
the motor launch left her side and ran up to the quay, the Norwegian
cross fluttering at its stern. Three or four passengers landed, carrying
cameras and sunshades. With them was the purser. I greeted
him and asked where they were bound. He said for Constantinople,
Athens, Venice, and the Dalmatian coast. Was there a spare berth?
He said there was. The *Stella* was not due to sail until next afternoon,
but within an hour I had made my adieux at the Great Britain, paid
my drink account, tipped the kind and tireless servants, assured the
proprietor that he should have my warmest commendations to

the British public, and moved my luggage down to the harbour. That afternoon I unpacked, sent a vast pile of clothes to the laundry, folded and hung up my suits, set in order the mass of papers I had accumulated, notes, photographs, letters, guide books, circulars, sketches, caught and killed two fleas I had picked up in the Manderaggio, and went above, very contentedly, to renew my acquaintance with the deck bar steward.

CHAPTER 6

ON OUR WAY east we stopped for the day at Crete. The little harbour of Candia was too small for the *Stella*, so we anchored outside in the bay, well sheltered by the headland of Cape Paragia and the island of Dia. Inside the fortified breakwater, with its finely carved Venetian lion, lay a jumble of ramshackle shipping – a small fishing fleet, two or three coastal sailing-boats, and some incredibly dissolute tramp steamers which ply between Piræus and the islands. A cargo of wine was being loaded into one of these, bottled in goat-skins. These were quite black and stretched taut and hard. A strong stench, part vinous, part goaty, rose from them. A slightly superior vintage was being rolled on in casks. The wine of Crete is lowly esteemed by connoisseurs.

The inhabitants, who had assembled to stare at us, were a good-looking race, particularly the old men, who had noble aquiline noses and great grey beards. They wore waistcoats covered with braid and rather greasy tassels, and coloured handkerchiefs round their heads; some of them had very tight corduroy trousers and others very loose blue ones of Turkish pattern. The young men seemed different in type, being stockier and swarthier, but as most of them were sailors, or seamen of some kind, I suppose it is probable that they were not Cretans at all. The women assumed that decent unobtrusiveness that usually survives for a generation or two after Moslem domination.

There is one main street in the town and a labyrinth of divergent alleys. There is the façade of a ruined Venetian palace, and a battered Venetian fountain carved with lions and dolphins. There is also a mosque, built up in places with capitals and fragments of carved stone work from other Venetian buildings. The top has been knocked off the minaret and the building has been turned into a cinematograph, where, by an odd coincidence, a film was being exhibited named *L'Ombre de Harem*. The shops sold, mostly, hunks of very yellow and grey meat, old Turkish watches, comic German picture-postcards, and brightly patterned lengths of printed cotton.

I accompanied a party of fellow passengers to the museum to admire the barbarities of Minoan culture. Except for one or two examples of animal sculpture, particularly a stone frieze of cattle and a substantially restored bull's head with fine sweeping horns, I saw nothing to suggest any genuine æsthetic feeling at all. It is interesting to notice how often a simplification and stylisation of animal form is the intermediate stage between Art and Arts and Crafts. Young women in England who delight to make the nastiest kind of pot, will sometimes model very pretty lambs and calves.

It is less easy to come to a firm decision about the merits of Minoan painting, since only a few square inches of the vast area exposed to our consideration are earlier than the last twenty years, and it is impossible to disregard the suspicion that their painters have tempered their zeal for accurate reconstruction with a somewhat inappropriate predilection for covers of *Vogue*. Without some determined sacrifice of diffidence, some frank assertion of personal taste, it would have been impossible to cope at all with the problem of making a large, decorative composition out of the few discoloured fragments at the archæologists' disposal. It is ungrateful to complain, but I do think that it is now harder, rather than less hard, to form any clear impression of Minoan painting.

We chartered a Ford car and drove with a guide to Cnossos, where Sir Arthur Evans (our guide referred to him always as 'Your English Lord Evans') is rebuilding the palace. At present only a few rooms and galleries are complete, the rest being an open hillside scarred with excavations, but we were able to form some idea of the magnitude and intricacy of the operation from the plans which were posted up for our benefit on the chief platform. I think that if our English Lord Evans ever finishes even a part of his vast undertaking, it will be a place of oppressive wickedness. I do not think that it can be only imagination and the recollection of a bloodthirsty mythology which makes something fearful and malignant of the cramped galleries and stunted alleys, these colonnades of inverted, conical pillars, these rooms that are mere blind passages at the end of sunless staircases; this squat little throne, set on a landing where the paths of the palace intersect; it is not the seat of a law-giver nor a divan for the recreation of a soldier; here an ageing despot might crouch and have borne to him, along the walls of a whispering gallery, barely audible intimations of his own murder.

That afternoon I went for a walk alone, by the coast for a mile or so along a strip of railway-track to a quarry or cement works of some kind, then inland by the banks of a stream on a very English footpath lined with rankly growing wild flowers and thistles and bearded barley, and so back to the town, where I got lost in the environs and mocked by a troop of small children. There was one pretty incident of my visit which I only discovered later. I took a camera with me to Cnossos and left it in the car when we went over the excavations. I remember being mildly surprised later in the day, when I came to photograph the harbour, to see by the number that I had exposed more of the film than I thought. When it came back from the ship's photographic shop after being developed I was surprised to find a picture I had never taken; it was incorrectly focused and the perspective was crazily distorted by the angle at which the camera had been held. Nevertheless, it was recognisable as the Ford car in which we had driven to Cnossos, with the driver sitting very upright at the wheel. He must have induced one of his friends to take it while we were at the palace, and I thought it argued a nice nature in the man. He could not have hoped either to receive a print or even to see our surprise when the result of his little joke became visible. If he had merely wished to meddle with an unaccustomed piece of mechanism he would have left the film exposed at the same place, and so ruined both his own and my next photograph. I like to think that he wished to add a more durable bond to our relationship than the fleeting obligation of two hours' hire; he wanted to emphasise his individual existence as a separate thing from the innumerable, impersonal associations of the tourist. I am sure he was amused at the thought of the little surprise he had stored up for us, when we cursorily paid him his fare and went back to our ship. I expect he experienced something of the satisfaction which those eccentric (and regrettably rare) benefactors derive from sending bank-notes anonymously to total strangers. If only his technical ability had come up to his good nature, I would have reproduced his portrait in this book, but I am afraid that, in the only form I possess, it would do him no further credit.

We spent the night at anchor and sailed early next morning so as to pass the Cyclades in daylight. The islands were beautiful, and all the passengers assembled on deck with telescopes and binoculars to watch their passage. One of them told me that on Santorini there still survives a Venetian colony, speaking a slightly debased six-teenth-century Italian. They are mostly the descendants of noble families; although sunk economically to the status of peasants they still live in the ruins of their palaces, with mouldering escutcheons over their doors – a whole town of Tesses of the D'Urbervilles – and have never intermarried with the Greeks, towards whom they exhibit an inherited superiority, little justified by their present condition.

We passed a new island, recently erupted from the sea – a heap of smoking volcanic matter, as yet quite devoid of life. Then past Naxos, Paros, and Mykonos into the Aegean, and so north to the Dardanelles, making fifteen knots through a calm sea. 'Can't you just see the quin-quē-remes?' said an American lady to me, as we leant on the rail, near each other. 'From distant Ophir,' she added, 'with a cargo of ivory, sandalwood, cedarwood, and sweet white wine.' I could not, but with a little more imagination I think I might easily have seen troopships, full of young Australians, going to their death with bare knees.

We were in the Hellespont when I awoke next morning, and passed Suvla Bay and Gallipoli before noon. The sea was pale green and opaque with the ice water that was coming down from the Black Sea. The Sea of Marmora was choppy; we ran under cold winds and a grey sky, broken by fitful bursts of sunlight. In the early afternoon we came in sight of Constantinople.

Owing to some confusion by the harbour authorities, we were unable immediately to obtain a berth on the Galata quay, so we employed the two hours' delay in cruising up the Bosphorus to the mouth of the Black Sea. It was too early in the year to see this at its best, but even on this cloudy and bleak afternoon the shore was attractive enought to keep us on deck in our overcoats. It seemed to me rather like the river banks of Devon, the Dart, for instance, or the estuary at Bideford, with their low green hils, covered with parkland and woods and dotted with villas and country houses.

We passed flight after flight of small birds, moving very fast and low just over the surface of the water, and uttering sad little cries. I was told that they are peculiar to these waters. Little is known about their habits, where they build or where they come from; they are never seen to rest inland. It is reported, quite credibly it seemed to me, by the local fishermen that these are the souls of the Christian soldiers and sailors, Russian, Venetian, English, Australian, Greek, who in the centuries have fallen on Turkish soil, attempting to reconquer the great Christian capital from the Mohammedans. They fly backwards and forwards looking for Christian ground to rest on, always hoping that the vows they took may have been fulfilled by their successors.

It was getting dark by the time that we came back to the mouth of the Golden Horn. A low sea mist was hanging about the town, drifting and mingling with the smoke from the chimneys. The domes and towers stood out indistinctly, but even in their obscurity formed a tremendous prospect; just as the sun was on the horizon it broke through the clouds, and, in the most dramatic way possible, threw out a great splash of golden light over the minarets of St Sophia. At least, I think it was St Sophia. It is one of the delights of one's first arrival by sea at Constantinople to attempt to identify this great church from the photographs among which we have all been nurtured. As one approaches, dome after dome comes into view, and receives, each in its turn, little gasps of homage. Finally, when the whole immense perspective has been laid before us, two buildings contend for recognition. The more imposing one is the Mosque of Ahmed I. One can identify it by its distinction, unique except for the Kaaba at Mekka, of having six minarets. A more convincing way, however, of carrying one's point, is to say, 'That' – pointing wherever you choose – 'is Agia Sophia.'

'Agia' will always win the day for one. A more recondite snobbism is to say 'Aya Sophia', but except in a very sophisticated circle,
who will probably not need guidance in the matter at all, this is liable
to suspicion as a mere mispronunciation.

I spent the next day with a party of fellow passengers visiting the
more obvious sights of the town – all of them far too famous to
require description. It was an interesting example of the new regime
in Turkey, that the dragoman assigned to us by the Natta tourist
agency was a woman, a very plain, plump, self-possessed little
person, who instructed us in a manner of maddening gentleness
and forbearance, as though she were conducting a school treat of
young children who had to be amused but kept well in hand. She
had none of the flattery or invention of the male guide, and seemed
to lack any genuine curiosity about the subjects she spoke of. Some
sort of guide is necessary in Constantinople if one does not speak
Turkish. She certainly piloted us quite successfully to a great number
of interesting places in a short space of time. We saw Agia Sophia,
a majestic shell full of vile Turkish fripperies, whose whole architectural rectitude has been fatally disturbed by the reorientation of the
mihrab. We saw the famous blue mosque, where the effect of the fine
blue-green tiles of the walls, mostly, I think, of Persian workmanship,
is hurt by the crude Reckitt's blue of the painting and the characterless vulgarity of the patterns inside the dome. In Cairo I have noted
the pride and superiority which a Western mind must feel when
confronted with Arabic art; this feeling is intensified and broadened
a hundred times in relation to everything Turkish. They seem to
have been unable to touch any existing work or to imitate any
existing movement without degrading it. It will be interesting to
see, now that they have stumbled upon woman's suffrage and
secularism, what their natural genius for vilification will make of
those two essentially Western anomalies. We visited the great underground cistern, which is still the principal reservoir of the town, with
its forest of marble columns. It is now lighted by electricity, and fails
to give the same impression of illimitable extent which is recorded by
those earlier travellers who rowed round it by torchlight. It is a fine,
big cistern, however, and well worth seeing. We went to see a fort
called Seven Towers. This, our guide informed us, was used for

imprisoning 'criminals, foreign ambassadors, and so forth'. We visited a military museum in a descrated Christian basilica. It was like the hall of the worst kind of English country house, full of suits of armour, embroidered velvet banners and saddle-cloths, drums and trumpets, extravagantly ornamented firearms, and bayonets and daggers tastefully and ingeniously arranged in stars and rosettes and suns. We lunched at the Tokatlian, where the *hors d'œuvres* were described on the menu as 'various tidbits'. Here the hall porter approached me in a fatherly manner, and, as we might offer a cigarette card or a postage stamp to a little boy, asked if I would like to have the label of an hotel at Therapia to stick on my trunk. I was pleased to notice at the end of the cruise, when the luggage was stacked on the quay at Harwich, that many of my fellow passengers had been sympathetic to this suggestion. After luncheon we went to the Great Bazaar, which, owing largely to the edict forbidding Oriental clothes, is far less superficially exciting than the Mouski at Cairo. It is very much better, however, for actual shopping. I could not afford to buy anything myself, but I saw many delightful objects, eikons from Asia Minor, pretty eighteenth-century clocks and snuff boxes, Oriental embroideries, nineteenth-century colour prints, ingenious mechanical toys from the disbanded harems, etc., which others had bought at fairly reasonable prices.

After this, with only about two hours to spare, we went to the Serai, the palace of the Sultans, now converted into a public museum; the attendants are mostly the survivors of the royal eunuchs. One was a dwarf; he had a funny little shrivelled up, sexless face and a big black overcoat which brushed the ground and came very near to tripping him up once or twice. None of them were as big and fat as I had imagined. In the bad times before the secure establishment of the Kemalist regime, I am told that there was a big demonstration meeting held by the agitated eunuchs to protest against the abolition of polygamy; there was also about that time a procession of pimps demanding a higher percentage to cover the increased cost of living. Apparently the emancipation of women, there as elsewhere, had put a good deal of unfair amateur competition against the regular trade. This may or may not be true. It did not seem to me my business to investigate statements of this kind, but simply to scribble them down in my note-book if they seemed to me amusing. But then, I have had three weeks in Fleet Street at one stage in my career. That is what people mean, I expect, when they say that newspaper training is valuable to an author.

The most striking thing about the Serai (regarded as a building and apart from the collections now exhibited there) is its astonishing discomfort. It somewhat resembles Earl's Court Exhibition, consisting, not of a single building, but of a large enclosed area, laid out roughly with lawns and trees, and strewn fortuitously with kiosks and pavilions of varying date and design. It is simply a glorified nomad encampment. Constantinople is by no means warm. The site was chosen for its political and geographical importance rather than for the serenity of its climate. Although on practically the same latitude as Naples, it is exposed to cold winds from the Steppes, and snow is not uncommon. Yet, in the five centuries of Turkish occupation, it seems never to have occurred to the sultans, with vast wealth and unlimited labour at their disposal, to provide any kind of covered corridor between the various rooms of their chief residence. Their highest aspirations towards physical luxury were confined to sprawling among gaudy silk cushions and munching sweetmeats while the icy wind whistled through the lattice-work over their heads. No wonder they took to drink. The treasures of the royal household, however, are staggering. Some idea of the economy of the Serai can be gained from the fact that the officials of the Kemalist party, when making a tour of the buildings in the first months of their occupation, came upon a room stacked from floor to ceiling with priceless sixteenth-century porcelain, still in the original contemporary wrappings in which it had arrived by caravan from China. It had been no one's business to unpack it, and there it had lain through the centuries. Theft and embezzlement must have been continuous and unchecked in the household. The astonishing thing is the amount of treasure that has survived the years of imperial bankruptcy. There are huge uncut emeralds and diamonds, great shapeless drops full of flaws, like half-sucked sweets; there is a gold throne set with cabuchons of precious stone; a throne of inlaid mother-o'-pearl and tortoiseshell; there are cases of jewelled pipe mouthpieces, and of dagger-hilts, watches, cigar-holders, snuff boxes, hand-mirrors, brushes, combs – twenty or thirty of each, all supremely magnificent; there is a dressing-table presented by Catherine the Great, encrusted all over, every inch of it, with rose-coloured paste jewels; there is a dressing-table presented by Frederick the Great, covered with alabaster and amber; there is an exquisite Japanese garden and temple made of filigree gold and enamel; there is a model paddle steamer, made of red and white gold with diamond port-holes and ruby and emerald pennons; there is the right hand and the skull of St John the Baptist; there are jewels to be worn in turbans and jewels to be worn round the neck on chains and jewels to be worn by women and jewels to be played with and tumbled listlessly between the fingers from hand to hand. They are not, of course, of equal quality; even to my most inexpert eye it was clear that many of the stones, most impressive by their bulk, would emerge quite inconsiderable from the hands of a modern stone-cutter. Even so, their value, if they are genuine, should be enough to rescue any budget. The guide made a round estimate of each object in turn as being worth 'more than a million dollars'. One cannot help doubting, however, whether, in the prolonged period of Turkish insolvency, some depredations were not made upon this hoard. It would have been so easy to prise out a cabuchon emerald or so with the finger-nail and replace it with a jujube, that I feel it must have been done from time to time – who knows how often?

Immediately in front of me in our tour of inspection there travelled a very stout, rich lady from America, some of whose conversation I was privileged to overhear. Whatever the guide showed her, china, gold, ivory, diamond or amber, silk or carpet, this fortunate lady was able casually to remark that she had one like that at home. '*Why*,' she would say, 'whoever would have thought that *that* was of any value. I've got three like that, that Cousin Sophy left me, bigger, of course, but just the same pattern, put away in one of the store-rooms. I must have them out when I get back. I never looked on *them* as being anything much.'

But she had to admit herself beaten by the right hand and skull of St John the Baptist.

During this visit I did not bother at all about the classical antiquities, but returned to the Serai again next day for a prolonged inspection. I also had my hair cut in a very up-to-date shop in Pera, opposite the Tokatlian. It had a front in the latest Parisian taste that might have been designed by M. Lalique himself, and a window full of the bottles of Guerlain and Chanel, and complete outfits of Elizabeth Arden. Inside there were rows of marble basins with numerous silver taps; there were silver ovens for heating towels; electric cables and switches for every kind of friction and ultra-violet ray; there were chairs like operating tables which could be tilted to any angle by pressure of the foot; the brushes, the moment they were used, were dropped into a shoot like cards at a Casino, from which they emerged later sterilised and sealed up in air-proof paper wrappings. There were hairdressers in white overalls, and manicurists trotting about with little stools and boxes of instruments. Yet I am sorry to say that with all these attractions the place smelled very strongly of drains, the water from the hot spray was tepid and discoloured, and the electrical machines emitted long blue sparks, crackled, and did no more.

I lunched at the Embassy, a fine, stately building constructed in the last century on the model, so I was told, of the Reform Club in London, and soon to be reluctantly abandoned for the desolation of Angora. Osbert and Sacheverel Sitwell were there, combining a gay enthusiasm for the subtleties of Turkish rococo with unfathomable erudition about Byzantine archæology and the scandals of Ottoman diplomacy. Back to the Serai after luncheon, and then to the *Stella*. We sailed that afternoon just before sunset.

The chief subject of conversation on board that evening was an accident which had occurred in the harbour. The ferry steamer which travels between Galata and Scutari, on the other side of the Bosphorus, had run on to the rocks in the morning mist; the passengers had been removed without loss of life but only just in time. There was a newcomer in the *Stella* – a very elegant Greek who wore an Old Etonian tie and exhibited an extensive acquaintance with the more accessible members of the English peerage. He had been on board the ferry boat at the time of the disaster, and he gave a very interesting account of his experience. The ship had been crowded with labourers going across to their work. At the first impact the Captain and his chief officer leaped into the only boat and made off. Later in the day the Captain resigned his command, on the grounds that this was the third time it had happened in eighteen months and his nerves were not what they had been. Left to themselves the passengers, who were a motley race of Turks, Jews, and Armenians, fell into a state of mad panic. The only helpful course would have been to sit absolutely firm and hope for rescue. Instead they trotted moaning from side to side, swaying the ship to and fro and shaking it off the rocks on which it was impaled. My informant sat, frozen with terror, on one of the seats, in expectation of almost immediate capsize. He was here met by a stout little man, strutting calmly along the deck with a pipe in his mouth and his hands plunged into the pockets of his ulster. They observed each other with mutual esteem as the frenzied workmen jostled and shouted round them.

'I perceive, sir,' said the man with the pipe, 'that you, too, are an Englishman.'

'No,' answered the Greek, 'only a damned foreigner.'

'I beg your pardon, sir,' said the Englishman, and walked to the side of the ship, to drown alone.

Fortunately, however, there was no drowning. Boats came out from the shore and removed all the passengers before the ship foundered.

The Greek was travelling only as far as Athens. I spent most of next day in his company. He asked me searching questions about 'æstheticism' at Oxford. He had been at the House, but remarked with a shade of regret that he had not found any 'æstheticism' in his day. Was it because of 'æstheticism' that Oxford did so badly at athletics. I said, no, the evil was deeper than that. I didn't mind telling another Oxford man, but the truth was, that there was a terrible outbreak of drug-taking at the University.

'Cocaine?'

'Cocaine,' I said, 'and worse.'

'But do the dons do nothing to stop it?'

'My dear man, the dons are the origin of the whole trouble.'

He said that there had been practically no drug-taking at the House in his time.

He renewed the attack later in the day. Would I come down to his cabin to have a drink?

I said I would have a drink with him by all means, but in the deck bar.

He said, 'I can see you are Scottish because of your blue eyes. I had a very dear friend who was a Scotchman. You remind me a little of him.'

Later, he said, would I come to his cabin to look at a silver Turkish inkpot. I said no, but I would love to see it on deck. It was very ugly.

When he disembarked he invited me to luncheon at the Grande Bretagne. I said yes, but next day he did not turn up.

We arrived just before dinner and moored in Phaleron Bay. That evening there was a fancy-dress ball on board. Some of the passengers had brought very elaborate costumes with them, others hired simple ones from the ship's barber; others contented themselves with a false nose or a mask, but everyone did something, even the oldest. Prizes were awarded for the best dresses. After the band had gone to bed various groups split up and disappeared with bottles of champagne to continue the party in their cabins. The purser was in very good form that evening – a man of rare social gifts and unflagging spirit.

I had been to Athens once before, at a time when I had never been farther from England than Paris. I shall not easily forget the romance of my first arrival. I came from Marseilles in the *Patris II*, a Hellenic national ship of fairly recent construction. It was in winter and we had rough weather most of the way. I shared a cabin with a Greek currant merchant who did not move from his bed during the five days' voyage. The only other English-speaking first-class passenger was a blustering American engineer. I sat on deck most of the time, feeling rather ill and reading James's *Varieties of Religious Experience*. At intervals the American and I drank *mastika*. He said if one ever drank *mastika* one returned to Greece; sometimes I went and looked over at the 'deck passengers', huddled under improvised tents, scratching their feet, and always eating. Piræus was our first stop. Sun had set and the harbour was all alight when we came in. There was a long delay before we could land. The rowing boats came out all round us packed so tight that one could have walked ashore, all the boatmen shouting for custom. The friends I was visiting had come out to meet me, and sat bobbing below and shouting up, 'Evelyn'. They had brought their valet with them to deal with the luggage – a man of singular ferocity who had been a hired assassin at Constantinople under the old regime. He and the boatmen took up the cry 'EE-lin! EE-lin!'

Then my luggage got into the hands of the wrong boatman, and he and that valet had a fight which the valet won very easily by means of an outrageous but wholly conclusive foul blow. Then we went ashore and drove very quickly from Piræus to Athens, along a road cleft and scarred as if by bombardment, in a very ramshackle Morris car which had no lamps or brakes or hooter, but was freed from police molestation by a diplomatic number and a little Union Jack between the places where the headlights ought to have been.

It was the Orthodox Christmas Day, and the streets were full of people shaking hands and kissing and letting off fireworks in each other's eyes. We went straight to a night club kept by a one-legged Maltese, who gave us cocktails made out of odd drugs and a spirit of his own distilling.

Later the *première danseuse* of the cabaret came out and sat at our table and warned us on no account to touch the cocktails. It was too late.

Later still I drove round the city in a taxi-cab on I forget what errand, and then back to the night club. The taxi-driver followed me to our table. I had given him as a tip over ten pounds in drachmas, my watch, my gloves, and my spectacle-case. It was too much, he protested.

The rest of my visit was rather overshadowed by this introduction to Athenian life. In fact, it was not until I had been very sea-sick on the way home that I fully recovered from the effects of that evening. That was in my undergraduate days, and it makes me feel unnaturally old to recall them.

But even now, in comparative maturity, my second visit to Athens coincided with my introduction to a new sort of drink. As soon as I landed I took a taxi into the town, to visit a friend called

Alastair who lived at this time in a little house in the eastern quarter, under the slopes of Lycabettus, in a side street off the Kolonaki Square. This house was full of mechanical singing birds and eikons, one of which, oddly enough the most modern, had miraculous powers. One of Alastair's servants gave notice, on the grounds that it used to stretch an arm out of the picture and bang him over the head when he neglected his work. Alastair was not yet dressed. I told him that I had had a late night, drinking after the ball with some charming Norwegians, and felt a little shaken. He then made me this drink, which I commend to anyone in need of a wholesome and easily accessible pick-me-up. He took a large tablet of beet sugar (an equivalent quantity of ordinary lump sugar does equally well) and soaked it in Angostura Bitters and then rolled it in Cayenne pepper. This he put into a large glass which he filled up with champagne. The excellences of this drink defy description. The sugar and Angostura enrich the wine and take away that slight acidity which renders even the best champagne slightly repugnant in the early morning. Each bubble as it rises to the surface carries with it a red grain of pepper, so that as one drinks one's appetite is at once stimulated and gratified, heat and cold, fire and liquid, contending on one's palate and alternating in the mastery of one's sensations. I sipped this almost unendurably desirable drink and played with the artificial birds and musical boxes until Alastair was ready to come out. I had another friend in Athens called Mark, and with these two I spent two very delightful days, sleeping in Alastair's house and rejoining the *Stella* just before she sailed. I did not revisit the Tower of Winds or the Temple of Theseus or the Acropolis, and will say nothing about them here, except to remark about the last that it is not 'snow-white', as I have seen it described by quite responsible observers, but a singularly beautiful tone of very pale pinkish brown; the nearest parallel to it in Nature that I can think of is that of the milder parts of a Stilton cheese into which port has been poured. We did, however, after lunching at the Grande Bretagne, drive out to the church at Daphne. I think I should be trespassing too dangerously upon Mr Robert Byron's ground if I were to venture upon any eulogy of these superb mosaics. They have had a disturbed history, what with the arrows of the Crusaders – who were moved by the theological differences of the Western and Eastern patriarchates to shoot away the eyes from the vast head of Christ in the dome – the Turks, who lit log fires in the nave, and, in quite recent times, the missiles of lunatics, who used to resort there from a neighbouring institution, and employed the time between their devotions in throwing stones and old bottles at the glittering ceiling; large parts of them, however, have survived intact and constitute one of the finest existing monuments of Byzantine art.

From Daphne we drove along the Eleusis road, pursued at times by savage sheep-dogs, and then turned off by the cart road below Mount Ægaleos to an isolated café overlooking the bay of Salamis. It was Sunday afternoon, and there were several other parties sitting under the Hawaiian thatched arbour. There was a photographer making little tin-type photographs which, when developed, usually revealed his own thumb print and little else. There were two students, male and female, in football shorts and open shirts, with rugged staffs and haversacks. There was a very happy family of Athenian bourgeoises. They had a baby with them. This they first sat on the table, then on the top of their car; then they put it upside down on a chair; then it was lifted on to the roof of the café, then it was put astride a clothes line and rocked gently backwards and forwards, then it was put into the bucket of the well and let down out of sight, then it was given a bottle of gaseous lemonade, a more perilous drink in Athens than in any town in the world. To all these efforts towards its entertainment it responded with chirrups of happy laughter and big, frothy bubbles dribbling down its chin. There was also a limousine containing two very *mondaine* young ladies, who would not come into the open, but sat back hardly visible among cut velvet upholsteries and were waited upon by two adolescent military officers; now and then the window would be let down and jewelled fingers would appear, haughtily discarding a sheet of silver paper or a banana skin.

Mark and Alastair and I sat in the shade and drank a carafe of resinated white wine and ate Turkish delight, while the photographer capered before us with his camera and caused us to purchase enough copies of his thumb print to convict him of any crime in the Greek statute book.

We went back to the *Stella* for dinner and then returned to see the night life. First we went to an underground café decorated with pseudo-Russian frescoes. Here we saw most of the English colony, engaged in those fervent intrigues, part social, part political, part personal, which embellish and enrich Athenian life more than that of any capital in Europe. But the entertainment was confined to one pianist in Georgian peasant dress. We asked if there was to be no cabaret. 'Alas,' said the manageress. 'Not to-night. Last night there was a German gentleman here, and he bit the girls so terribly in the legs that to-night they say they will not dance!'

From there we went to the Folies Bergères, which was very chic and Parisian; the waiter tried to induce us to order champagne, and a Hungarian Jewess performed Oriental dances in a Chu-Chin-Chow slave market costume, modestly supplemented with pink cotton tights. Mark's boredom soon became uncontrollable, so we called for our bill, paid them half what they demanded (which they accepted with every manifestation of gratitude), and left.

We walked across the gardens to the poorer part of the town. Of the many smells of Athens two seem to me the most characteristic – that of garlic, bold and deadly like acetylene gas, and that of dust, soft and warm and caressing like tweed. It was in this dusty smell that we walked in the garden, but garlic met us at the bottom of the steps which led from the street to the door of the ΜΠΑΡ[1] ΘΕΛΛΑΤΟΕ; it was garlic sweetened, however, by the savour of roast lamb. There were two lambs impaled horizontally on spits, sizzling over an open charcoal fire. The atmosphere was one of Dickensian conviviality. Only men were present, most of them peasants come up from the country for the night. They all smiled greetings to us, and one of them sent three mugs of beer across to our table. This began a tremendous round of ceremonious health-drinking which was still going on by the time we left. It is the commendable practice of the Greeks never to serve drink without food, usually a little bit of garlic sausage, or bad ham on the end of a match; these appear in little saucers, and our table was soon strewn with them.

---

1 There is no B sound in the modern Greek, B being pronounced like V. One of the simpler delights of Greek is one's continual discovery of English words in Greek characters. Cinema has come back to them after a long journey spelled with a Σ.

Two men in the corner were playing guitars of a kind, and others were dancing, with very severe expressions on their faces but a complete lack of self-consciousness. They were Pyrrhic dances of indefinable antiquity. Four of them danced together, going through the various figures with great solemnity. If one of them made a false move it was as though he had dropped a catch in an English cricket match; they accepted his apologies in as sporting a spirit as they could assume, but it clearly was a grave wrong, not lightly to be dismissed or expiated except by prodigies of accuracy in the future. Moreover, as in cricket, the amateur status was jealously preserved. So far from taking a hat round after the performance, the dancers themselves paid a few halfpence to the band. There was keen competition to dance, the fours being already made up and eagerly waiting for their turn to take the floor. The only fight which occurred that evening was occasioned by one rather tipsy young man attempting to perform out of his turn. They all set on him and pummelled him for his bad manners, but later it was made up and they drank his health. I had not since I left England, and seldom before that, found myself in a company so lacking in avarice. No one made the smallest attempt to get anything out of us, but, on the contrary, repeatedly offered us beer and cigarettes and would take nothing except as an exchange of courtesy. Alastair reminded me of how we had once gone into a small pub in a fishing village in North Devon. Five or six fishermen were sitting round the parlour sipping half-pints of cider. We ordered ourselves a half-pint each and asked the landlord to provide a round of drinks. When we asked for the reckoning he told us twelve shillings. They had each asked for a treble whisky. We did not think any the worse of them. Except during the salmon season they could never afford spirits. We were clearly rich to them. Still, the atmosphere at the Thellatos was different.

As the evening went on the conversation became more animated. I was, of course, quite unable to follow it, but Alastair said it was mostly about politics; an uninstructed discussion but full of high feeling. There was an elderly man with a curly grey beard who was much moved. He roared and pounded on the table with his fist; he pounded on his glass, broke it, and cut himself. He stopped

arguing and began to cry. Immediately everyone else stopped arguing too and came over to comfort him. They wrapped a grubby
handkerchief round his hand, which was not, I think, at all seriously
injured. They gave him beer and bits of bad ham on matches; they
patted him on the back and put their arms round his neck and kissed
him. Soon he was smiling again and the discussion was resumed, but
as soon as he showed signs of excitement, they warned him with
smiles, by moving his mug farther across the table.

At last, after a great many adieux, we climbed up the steps again
into the fresh air, and so home under the orange-trees through the
warm darkness that smelled like tweed.

Next morning Alastair had to go to the Chancery to decode
telegrams, so Mark and I went shopping in Shoe Lane – the street
in the old Turkish quarter where all the second-hand dealers have
their stalls. Mark continued some negotiations which, he told me,
had already been protracted for three weeks, concerning the purchase of a grotto constructed by Anatolian refugees out of cork and
looking-glass and pieces of sponge; only the price prevented me
from buying a marble statuette of an association footballer.

The *Stella* was sailing at noon for Venice, and I narrowly escaped
missing the last launch from the shore, Mark delaying me by the gift
of three religious postcards, a balloon, and a basket of black olives.

Immediately after luncheon we passed through the Corinth
canal, which, for some reason I could not understand, attracted
many of the passengers more than anything they had yet seen on
their travels. It took some time to go through, but they remained on
deck, photographing it and talking about it and making water-
colour sketches of its featureless stone sides, while I went to my
cabin and dozed; I had a good deal of sleep to make up and this
seemed an opportunity.

We reached Corfu early next morning and spent the day there. It
is a long, thin, hilly island separated from the mainland by a narrow
channel, just opposite the Greek-Albanian border. It has one fair-
sized, comparatively wealthy town, a mountain of 3,000 feet, and
two lakes. In classical times it was called Kerkyra; Odysseus was
shipwrecked here and met Nausicaa by a little brook on the south-
west side of the island. Later it belonged to the Venetians, who built

the now dilapidated fortifications of the harbour; in the nineteenth century the English held it and built the admirable roads which distinguish it from the other Greek islands; thanks to the scarcity of wheeled traffic these are still in excellent repair. It now belongs to the Greeks, who have attempted to revert to its earlier name, so that 'Kerkyra' is now carved by the convicts on the olive-wood animals which are hawked everywhere in the streets. I do not know whether this paragraph of rather rudimentary information may seem an impertinence. I can only assume in my reader the same ignorance that I had myself when I first went there.

Frankly I had never heard of the place when, after my first visit to Greece, I stopped there for a few hours in a vile ship called the *Yperoke*, where I was travelling second class in barely conceivable discomfort. It seemed to me then one of the most beautiful places I had ever seen. So much was I impressed, that when, later, I found myself writing a novel about someone very rich, I gave her a villa in Corfu, as I thought that, when I was rich, that was one of the first things I would buy. I still think so, and if enough people buy this book I shall fulfil my intention. It is full of lovely villas, many of them for sale. Before the war the harbour was much frequented by private yachts, and during the season the shores were peopled by a very gay cosmopolitan society. It has become less fashionable since the collapse of the Central Powers, but all the more habitable. Do let me urge you, gentle reader, if you have only borrowed this book from a library, to buy two or three copies instantly so that I can leave London and go and live peacefully on this island.

The chief merchandise of the island seemed to be live tortoises and the olive-wood animals I have mentioned, as made by the convicts in the prison. Several passengers in the *Stella* bought tortoises, few of which survived the voyage; tortoise races became an added attraction to the deck games. The chief disability suffered by tortoises as racing animals is not their slowness so much as their confused sense of direction. I had exactly the same difficulty when I used to take part in sports at my school, and was repeatedly disqualified for fouling the other competitors.

There are, as far as I know – and Baedeker by his silence seems to confirm this – no antiquities or sites of historic interest in Corfu.

There are walks and drives among the natural beauties of the hills and streams and sea-coast and lake, and the artificial beauties of rich little farms, slightly disorderly in their exuberant fertility. There is a town sparkling with unembarrassed, provincial sociability, cafés, concert halls, a theatre, a good hotel, arcaded streets of shops, the seat of two archbishops, Latin and Orthodox, a casino, a garrison of soldiers, innumerable sailors of all nationalities, a harbour full of shipping. There is a temperate and endearing climate. I cannot conceive why rich people go and live on the French Riviera when there are places like Corfu left in the world.

I did not do very much during our day there, as, indeed, there is very little to do. I pottered round the town and harbour renewing my feelings of envy and aspiration. After luncheon I drove in a horse-carriage along the Vide Imperatore Guglielmo, which is bordered by groves of olive, rose, and orange-trees, to the little balustraded platform called, in the old style, Canone Point, or, in its Hellenised version, ΣΤΟΠ ΚΑΝΟΝΙ. This is the extreme point of the peninsula that runs out from the town, enclosing the fiord called Lake Kaliki-copulo. There used to be a battery here of one gun. Now there is a café-restaurant. The bank falls steeply down to the water, where there are two tiny islands, the one wooded, containing a villa that was once, I think, a monastery; the other is very small and is completely occupied by a minute chapel, two cypress-trees, and a parsonage. It is accessible from the beach by stepping-stones. I went down to it. There were two little bells in the tower, and, inside, some quite black eikons and a hen laying an egg. The priest appeared magically, rowing a boat full of vegetables from the opposite bank. His son sat in the stern with bare legs crossed under him, nursing a tin of Californian peaches. I gave some money to the church expenses and climbed up the hill path to the café. One or two other passengers had arrived from the *Stella*. I joined them, and ate sponge fingers and drank some delicious Corfiote wine, that looks like the juice of blood oranges and tastes like cider and costs, or should cost when one is not obviously a tourist, about twopence. A band appeared, of two guitars and a fiddle. The fiddler was quite young but blind. They played, 'Yes,

Sir, That's My Baby', in the oddest way conceivable, and laughed aloud with pleasure at the money they collected.

In my very brief visit I became more attached to Corfu than any place I can think of. I was sorry to leave, but I think that there, more than anywhere, I felt the disadvantage of arriving on a pleasure ship. At Venice I was quite unconscious of any such feeling. The moment she was anchored in the mouth of the Grand Canal, the *Stella* simply became an unusually comfortable hotel. We spent two days there and then sailed for Ragusa.

What can I possibly write, now, at this stage of the world's culture, about two days in Venice, that would not be an imperti-nence to every educated reader of this book? Am I to say that it consists of an archipelago of one hundred and thirty-five islands transected by a hundred and forty-five canals; that on one of these islands stands a church, dedicated to St Mark, filled with mosaics of peculiar splendour; that on another of these islands there is a disused sailors' hostel, called the Scuola San Rocco, with frescoes on its walls and ceiling by Jacopo Tintoretto (1512–1594); that the Venetians were once a virtuous and a very wealthy race who had 'learned Christianity from the Greeks, chivalry from the Normans, and the laws of human life and toil from the ocean itself'; that nowadays they are less virtuous and less wealthy, and subsist, in fact, entirely upon the foreigners who come to admire the works of their fore-fathers? Or shall I say that I ate *scampi* at Cavaletto and felt no ill effects; that I went to a prettily decorated rococo night club, called Luna, which had been a gambling-room in the time of Goldoni; that a lady I was with had a gold cigarette case stolen from her by a gondolier; that I met Berta Ruck in the Piazzetta and later Adrian Stokes, and walked with him in the rain over innumerable little bridges to visit places of interest that happened always to be shut; how when the rain became intolerable we took refuge in a black-smith's shop next door to a Palladian church, and when Adrian asked the youth in charge of the shop what time the church opened, he replied scornfully, how was he to know, he was in the next parish; how the same youth asked whether the canals in London had been frozen over that winter; how I went back with Adrian to tea in a very grand apartment on the Giudecca full of Titians and

Tiepolos, and Adrian told me that Ruskin was all wrong about the dates of some of the buildings he most admired; how for a long time I could not think what it was that made the life of Venice seem so different from any other town, until I realised that there was no traffic, and that half the children of the town had never seen any horses except the bronze ones outside St Mark's, and Adrian told me that when, some months ago, a motor car had been landed on its way to the Lido, the crowd was so great to see it that two people were pushed over into the water and nearly drowned; how I discovered that an acquaintance of mine was a legendary figure in Venice, well thought of among the poor as the eccentric English milord who had bought up all the cauliflowers in the vegetable market and floated them down the Grand Canal; how I purchased a Tauchnitz edition of *St Mark's Rest* at Alinari's, and reflected that unlike most men of letters, Ruskin would have led a much more valuable life if he had been a Roman Catholic?

No, it seems to me a moment for humility. Perhaps if I made my home in Venice for twenty years and attained a perfect command of mediæval Italian; if I spent months in public and private libraries translating and collating original sources; if I learned almost everything about the chemistry of painting, scraped bits off frescoes and had them analysed, made X-ray studies of them, and trotted all over Europe comparing them with other versions; if I steeped myself in the latest æsthetic theories; if I became adept at particularising among all manner of conflicting and incongruous influences, tracing in one and the same object, here the Byzantine, there the Moorish, there the Catholic, Frankish, or Norman motive; if I became a master of the subtle art of attribution, able delicately to shift reputation from shoulder to shoulder and identify the technique of one anonymous mason from the baser imitations of another – then perhaps I might decently contribute a chapter here to what has already been written by those who have mastered all these accomplishments. Meanwhile, since there seems no probability of my ever becoming anything more considerable than one of a hundred globe-trotting novelists, I will pass on to Ragusa.

I think I may, without offence, assume in many of my readers an incomplete acquaintance with this town. It is now called Dubrovnik,

a somewhat unhelpful change, after the manner of new nationalities, which coincided with the rechristening of Cattaro, Kotor and
Spalato, Split. It has until quite lately had an interesting and honourable history, being one of the free city states of the west which,
generation after generation, by courage and guile and good fortune,
was enabled to maintain its integrity against barbarian influence. It
was founded originally by the fugitives driven by heathen invasion
from Salona and Epidamus; these established an aristocratic administration of forty-five senatorial families and an elected rector, more
or less parallel to the Council and Doge at Venice. They owed
nominal allegiance to the Emperor at Byzantium until the Fourth
Crusade, and after that to Venice, but they were in all practical
matters self-governing and independent. They became wealthy
through general trade and the salt mines at Stagno, and at the
middle of the seventeenth century had a population of 33,000, with
360 vessels and a standing army of 4,000. They were obliged to live
throughout the whole of this period in a state of perpetual defence,
first against the Slavs, Bosnians, and Serbs, and later against the
Turks, who became masters of the entire mainland, hemming them
in precariously between the mountains and the sea. In 1667 Ragusa
suffered a plague and earthquake which reduced it, in one catastrophe, from a thriving city to a small coast town. It recovered slowly
and incompletely, and at the end of the eighteenth century passed
into the hands of the Austrians, but, although no longer politically
considerable, it remained Catholic, aristocratic, and cultured, immeasurably aloof from its savage neighbours. It was the simple task
of the allied statesmen of the Peace Conference to undo the work of
a thousand years and hand it over to its traditional enemies, the
mongrel kingdom of the Jugo-Slavs.

There is a little harbour under the walls of Ragusa, but larger
ships anchor off Gravosa, the commercial landing-stage a short
tram-ride from the town. The day of our visit was a religious festival
of the Eastern calendar, and the shops were therefore compulsorily
closed. This was a real hardship on the inhabitants, to whom the
arrival of a big ship is a rare and exceedingly lucrative occurrence;
the overwhelming majority of them, all, in fact, except the Serbian
officials and garrison, are Roman Catholics, for whom the day had

no significance. The Slav officials, however, who, I think, are made to feel very conscious of their social inferiority in these imperial towns, were closely on the lookout for any infringement of the law, and it was only with difficulty that we could obtain access to the public buildings.

The chief of these are the Rector's Palace and the Sponza, or Custom House. These are naturally quite small and, after Venice, comparatively simple, but they are well preserved, dignified and peculiarly charming in design, and full of fine workmanship. The Rector's Palace is attributed to Michelozzo Michelozzi, the architect of the Palazzo Riccardi at Florence. The Custom House has a window and balcony of graceful fourteenth-century Venetian Gothic. There are also small Dominican and Franciscan monasteries, the latter containing an exquisite little romanesque cloister, planted in the centre with a garden of orange-trees, cactuses, and evergreens from which rise a little fountain and the statue of a saint. The churches, except for the crude and modern Orthodox cathedral, are all interesting; Santa Maria Maggiore contains two very dubious paintings attributed to Titian and Andrea del Sarto; San Salvatore has a lovely sixteenth-century façade; the cathedral is good early eighteenth-century baroque. There are remains of several of the noble houses, with armorial carvings over the doors, but most of these have sunk into poor hands and are split up into tenement dwellings; that the aristocratic tradition survived, however, was clear from the bearing of several very dowdy and very august grandes dames whom I observed at their prayers, and from the general courtesy and dignity of the townspeople. Most of these were smartly dressed and vivacious in manner, exchanging greetings and jokes at the cafés and promenading the broad main street of the town – called, inevitably, the Stradone – with a delightfully modified swagger. There were a few country people in from the hills, looking very clean and starched in their peasant costumes, the men with highly decorative daggers sticking from their sashes. There was a band playing in the evening in the main square outside the walls, and down in Gravosa they let off some fireworks, but whether in honour of the *Stella*'s arrival or of the Orthodox festival I was unable to discover. That evening we sailed down the coast to Catarro.

Catarro has been exposed to much the same historical influences as Ragusa, though her history is less eminent. She was never a free town except for thirty years at the beginning of the fifteenth century. Before that time she was held from 1185 successively by the Nemanja dynasty of Serbs, Lewis the Great of the Hungarian-Croat Empire, and the Bosnian King Tvrtko I. In 1420 she came again under Western influence, and was held by Venice until 1797, when the Austrians took possession of her, and, except for a brief interlude during the Napoleonic period when Russia and France had her in turn, remained in possession until the Peace Conference. The original Roman population became extensively diluted by Slav blood during the Middle Ages, but it is interesting to note, in view of modern Slavonic pretensions, that when the Venetians took over the town, Western culture had so far survived that all documents were still in Latin, and Italian was the language of the courts of law. From 1420 until 1918 the town was wholly under Western influence, until, with Ragusa and the rest of the Dalmatian coast, it was bundled into Jugo-Slavia.

Like Ragusa, it suffered from earthquakes and plagues, and has never recovered its mediæval population. It is a smaller town than Ragusa, much less attractive architecturally, built on a triangle of alluvial soil at the end of a deep fiord. Owing to the strict limit imposed on expansion by the nature of the site, the streets are extremely narrow and the houses jumbled on top of each other; there is none of the spaciousness of Ragusa, and no equivalent to the Stradone; the people seemed poorer, less leisurely, less sociable with each other, less courteous to strangers; they stared and begged when we came ashore as they had not done at Ragusa. Nevertheless, it looked very attractive from the water, huddled at the foot of a great rock cleft away from the wooded hillside. A fortified stone wall climbed up this crag, protecting the town from the rear and making a triangle, with the sea front for base and the Citadel of St John as the apex, 260 metres up. Half-way up to the summit is a little chapel clearly visible from below.

Catarro is full of churches – there are said to have been thirty at one time – all of them Roman Catholic except two; one of these is the repulsive modern Serbian-Orthodox cathedral of St Nicholas, and the other the fine twelfth-century church of St Lucas, which the Catholics handed over to Orthodox refugees from Turkish persecution in the middle of the seventeenth century. The largest and oldest Catholic church is St Tryphon's, but it has little to commend it except antiquity. St Tryphon is little known outside the town of his burial; his most renowned exploit was the cure of a widow's son who had been bitten by a basilisk, an incident which is attractively recorded in the fourteenth-century ciborium of the high altar. St Joseph's has a picture they claim is by Veronese, and St Mary's a crucifix of wood, plaster, and canvas attributed to Michelangelo; the Franciscan Church of St Clara has a very gorgeous baroque altar of coloured marble. The secular buildings are picturesque but boring. I do not think it is a town where anyone except the most hardened water-colourist would want to stay for very long.

There is a very good road built by the Austrians that leads up from Catarro to Cetinje, the capital of Montenegro. On the atlas the distance looks very small, but the ascent is so steep that there are between twenty and thirty hairpin bends before it reaches the pass in the mountains and leads down to the plateau on which Cetinje stands. From the *Stella*'s deck one could trace the path up the mountain-side, twisting backwards and forwards among the rocks and scrub until it was lost to sight three thousand feet up. I joined the *Stella* expedition, and it took us two and a half hours' hard driving to cover the distance, which, as the crow flies, measured on the map, is rather under eight miles.

We started soon after breakfast in five or six cars, and arrived just at luncheon time. To avoid running in each other's dust, the drivers, as soon as we started, spaced themselves out at long intervals along the road. The ascent in places was so steep, and the road so carefully graded that we could shout to the parties above and below, although there was, perhaps, a half-mile of road between us, as though to someone in the upper windows of a house. By the time we reached the summit the *Stella* and the fiord in which she lay had grown minute and unreal, and a great stretch of the Adriatic coast lay exposed behind us, and in front and on either side ridge upon ridge of mountain.

The road ran straight for some distance; the air was cold and clear; there were patches and drifts of snow in sheltered places and no sign of human habitation. No sign of human habitation, but many signs of human activity. I have but a very slight acquaintance with mountainous country, so I cannot tell whether I am recording a commonplace of all such districts or whether what surprised me so much was indeed peculiar to Montenegro. That was that the boulders and cliffs that comprised the landscape all round us were varied at quite frequent intervals by deep, usually circular craters and basins, with rocky sides and a flat surface of soil at the bottom, no bigger in many cases than the floor of a large room, at the most not thirty yards in diameter. Yet in the majority of cases these little pot-holes of earth, so inaccessible from farm or market, bore every indication of being rudely but carefully cultivated. The crop, whatever it was, was still quite immature, just regular lines of green shoots protruding a few inches above the soil, but it was quite clearly no accidental growth. It puzzled me very much to think who could be the farmer of these ungrateful acres.

Presently the road began to descend slightly, and then ran quite straight across a plain of arable land into Cetinje. Since it is the capital of a large province, and was until quite recently the capital of an independent kingdom, it is seemly to speak of Cetinje as a town, though actually it is no more than a large village, spaciously laid out and ornamented by one or two public buildings, no larger certainly than might be found in most English villages, but in this part of the world uncommonly large for anything except a town of some importance. The palace is about the size of the average English rectory; its largest room is occupied by a billiard table, which so far eclipsed the other concomitants of royalty in the eyes of the neighbouring highlanders that the palace became known, not as the house of the king, but as Billjarda, the house of the billiard table. This billiard table added very considerably to the prestige of the royal family, but it had the disadvantage of entirely filling the only room suitable for official receptions. These, indeed, occurred so rarely that the inconvenience was trifling; when, however, someone did come to visit the King of Montenegro, or some event of national importance such as the christening or marriage of a child had to be celebrated, the

German legation, which was in every way more commodious, used to be borrowed for the party.

Another building of prominence was, or rather had been, the hotel, for this had caught fire some time before our visit and been totally demolished. Fortunately no one was staying there at the time; but, indeed, it would have been a peculiarly unfortunate coincidence if there had been, since fires and visitors are equally unusual events at Cetinje. Our arrival, therefore, in six dusty motor cars, had been carefully prepared for, and Montenegrins from all over the province had put on their best clothes and come into town to see the tourists and, if they could, make a little money. On the occasion of the first conducted tour arriving in Cetinje, some thirty or so years ago, the king himself had ridden out to greet them at the head of his household cavalry, and had so frightened the tourists by his salvoes of blank cartridges, a little wildly fired from the hip, that it was all the guides could do to persuade them to drive on into the town and attend the banquet prepared for them. There was no such demonstration for us, but the urchins of the country gave us a gentler welcome by throwing bunches of wild flowers into our laps as we drove past their houses.

As I have remarked, the hotel had lately been destroyed; luncheon was therefore served on trestle tables in the House of Parliament. It is only fair to say that this was no very serious degradation to the building, since even in the days of the kingdom it had combined a double office, being the legislature by day and the theatre by night. There was a stage at the end, surmounted by a crowned cypher, and on one of the walls hung a large, symbolic oil-painting, representing a man in Montenegrin national costume who held in one hand the fasces and in the other the mane of a live lion. This emblem of nationality reminded me strongly of the cartoons which appeared during the war. At one time, I remember, there was a strongly supported movement to make much of Montenegro. There was, if I remember rightly, a Montenegrin flag day, and 'Brave little Montenegro' for a very short time was a phrase of almost equal potency to 'Brave little Belgium' or 'Russian Steamroller'.

Luncheon was very bad indeed, even though it was cooked in the office of the commissar of police; the wine was a dark-coloured local vintage, not red but not exactly black, the colour one's fountain-pen makes when one dips it accidentally into the red inkpot; it was very sour and left a temporarily indelible stain on the tongue and teeth. After luncheon we walked round the broad lanes of the town, and visited the shops, where the stock of peasant textiles (indistinguishable from the products of Hampstead arts and crafts) was supplemented for the occasion by all kinds of curios, some of them crosses and bits of jewellery but mostly daggers and pistols with elaborately decorated hilts and butts. I presume that these were brought in by the owners and sold for them on heaven knows what exorbitant commission. It seemed to me rather pathetic to see them there, because among Balkan peoples these are often the only possessions of value, and are a real source of pride, being handed down from father to son, as symbols of family importance as well as of personal valour and independence. Most of them, I think, would have been of doubtful efficiency in prosecuting the blood feuds which enliven Montenegrin life. Indeed, I expect that it is futile to sentimentalise about them. Most likely the owners were saving up to buy cartridges for a stolen army rifle, and so snipe the neighbours in a more deadly manner from behind their pig-styes.

The drive back was quicker and far more hazardous than the ascent. There was just time for a swim in the fiord before the *Stella* sailed again.

CHAPTER 7

DURING THE NEXT few days on our way back to Monte Carlo we were rarely out of sight of land for long. We stopped once more at Catania, Messina, and Naples. As before, a large party went up by train to Taormina. I remained on the *Stella* as I had done two months before. I cannot account for this disinclination to see Taormina. I think it was chiefly meanness and the fear of embarrassing some friends of mine whom I believed to be spending their honeymoon there. Also, the Straits of Messina are very beautiful, and it always seems odd to me that anyone, for any reason, should choose to travel by land when he can go by water.

I do not think I shall ever forget the sight of Etna at sunset; the mountain almost invisible in a blur of pastel grey, glowing on the top and then repeating its shape, as though reflected, in a wisp of grey smoke, with the whole horizon behind radiant with pink light, fading gently into a grey pastel sky. Nothing I have ever seen in Art or Nature was quite so revolting.

We passed Stromboli late in the evening. Everyone came out on deck in the hope of seeing an eruption, but was unrewarded.

We reached Naples on Ascension Day. This was always a great festival at my school. It was the only whole holiday in the year. We used to go in large bodies to a village called Bramber where there is a museum of stuffed monstrosities – two-headed hens, five-legged sheep, and so forth. It usually rained. It was also a great festival at Naples. The churches were all draped in white silk and blazing with electric-light bulbs. I was able to see much that had been locked away from me on my first visit.

I went to Pompeii, which everyone knows all about. I thought that the most interesting thing I saw was the plaster cast of the suffocated dog. I had heard a great deal about the pornographic frescoes which characterise many of the houses, and was surprised to find them, in most cases, mere scribbles, no better than D. H. Lawrence's, clearly not the work of the professional decorators who had made such an elegant job of the other rooms. Only one, in the house of Vetii, was at all amusing, and that only by the standard of American 'strip' draughtsmanship. In the most recently excavated streets, the discoveries have been left in their places, instead of being removed to the museum at Naples; this is naturally by far the most interesting quarter of the town. The guide who conducted us had a great clean-shaven jowl and pop-eyes; he might have been assassinated anywhere in mistake for Mussolini. It is very curious how the lower orders often grow to resemble the public figures of their generation. Gladstones are only just beginning to die out in England; there was a don at my college exactly like a prominent murderer.

The next day I drove out to luncheon at the Capucini Hotel at Amalfi, and home by Sorrento – a road of wonderful charm and variety.

On the night we left Naples there was a *diner d'adieu*. The most respected passenger made a speech proposing the health of the Captain and officers and thanking them for the safety and comfort of the voyage; the Captain responded and we all sang 'Auld Lang Syne'. Next morning we arrived at Monaco.

This was the end of the cruise. Luggage appeared on deck, supplemented by oddly shaped bundles of souvenirs piled up during the voyage. The passengers busied themselves in retrieving their passports, changing cheques, tipping the stewards, saying good-bye to the Captain and officers, saying good-bye to each other, and promising to meet again. My packing was only half done. I looked hopelessly at the heaps of clothes, books, and photographs on my bed. I thought despondently of the odious P.L.M. journey before me, of eating my meals in the restaurant car with my wine and my soup being rocked and splashed on the tablecloth, and the knives and forks jingling, and the servants jostling past in the corridors; of the sleepless night in a grossly expensive sleeper or propped upright in the corner of a carriage; of the fœtid early morning air of the train, the unshaven grimy feeling; of creeping round Paris in the Ceinture; of the bleak quay at Calais and the bleaker quay at Dover, of all the dirt and indignity of travelling by rail. Then I pushed my trunk back under my bed.

The *Stella* had finished her Mediterranean season and was due to start back in two days to Norway to revictual for her summer cruises in the fiords. Her route now lay round the Spanish coast, touching at Algiers and Mallorca, to Harwich, a cruise of fourteen days. I decided to remain on board.

In the interval between the two cruises the ship was devoted to another terrific spring cleaning. I slept in my cabin and took my meals on shore. Monte Carlo was practically deserted; the Sporting Club was closed; the Russian ballet had packed up and left for their last season in London; the dress shops had either already closed or were advertising their end of the season sales; there were shutters up in most of the villas and hotels; a few invalids encumbered the promenades in their bath-chairs; Mr Rex Evans had ceased to sing. And I wondered, as I pottered about those serene and sunny streets or sat drowsily in the shade of the Casino Gardens, at that provision of destiny which has made rich people so rigidly liturgical in their movements that they will come to Monte Carlo in the snow because that is the time ordained for their arrival in rubric and calendar, and will leave as soon as it becomes habitable for their grubby great shambling cities in the north; and how unlike rich people are to the lilies of the field, who do not divide time by any metrical system, but will joyfully put out buds at the first intimation of spring, and lose them, almost immediately, in the intervening frost.

Two days later the new passengers came on board; there were three or four of us left from the preceding cruise, and we watched the new arrivals critically and decided that we did not think very much of them. They certainly did not look prepossessing next day, after a night of heavy seas in the Gulf of Lyons, but bore slightly discontented faces, as though attributing the bad weather to negligence on the part of someone in authority. We sailed along the coast all the morning – while a charming Catalan whose acquaintance I had made, pointed out, very eagerly, the summer villas of his friends and relations – and reached Barcelona at two o'clock in the afternoon. At the mouth of the harbour and all along the breakwater lay a fleet of rafts, from which depended strings of mussels, fattening in sewage. We berthed alongside the quay in the inner basin.

It was a week too early for the Barcelona Exhibition, but there was plenty to see. There is a street called the Ramblas, with old houses and churches on each side and a broad promenade in the middle dividing the two narrow lanes of traffic. This promenade is full of seats and trees and kiosks for selling newspapers and cigarettes and picture-postcards; at all hours of the day it is full of soldiers and townspeople, saluting and gossiping, but its chief beauty is the flower stalls, which colour and perfume the whole length of the street. These are best about midday, before the stock has been depleted by purchasers, or grown dusty and limp. There is a cathedral of Spanish Gothic, the windows of which have been reduced to little slits and peep-holes of stained glass; the darkness of the interior is almost impenetrable, and the little light there is, is so unnatural that it seemed not to be a real building at all but a stage setting – perhaps for the temptation of Marguerite in *Faust*, or for *The Hunchback of Notre Dame*, or the final act of some historical drama in which the heroine, penitent, renounces the world and becomes a nun – the sentimentalised caricature of the Gothic of Chartres or Beauvais. There is a frightful hill called Tibidabo, laid out as a pleasure garden with a restaurant and café, a hall of slot machines, an unfinished oratory of fantastic design, and a Great Wheel. There is an excellent taxi company called 'David', whose drivers speak French and refuse tips; there are also various free-lance taxi-drivers of menacing aspect, who speak no foreign language, manipulate the taxi-meter to their own advantage, and demand large tips. There are numerous fine houses in the old part of the town, with wrought-iron gates and pretty courtyards. There is, I believe, though I was too tired after our rough passage to investigate it, a riotous night life in the streets round the docks. I had two meals on shore at quiet restaurants and found the prices high and the cooking execrable. The wine, however, was quite good. At one of the restaurants, a very humble place, little more than a cabman's eating-house, I saw a young private soldier drink from a flask that had a spout, finely pointed at the end, protruding from its side. He held it at arm's length, tilting it so that a very delicate stream of wine shot from it with some force. This he caught in his mouth by negligently protruding his lower lip. The wine splashed against his teeth and gurgled down his throat without a drop being spilled. Then, with a deft twist of the wrist, he stopped the flow, catching the last drips, and passed the flask across the table to his companion, who drank in the same manner, but more clumsily, directing the stream first into his eye and then down his chin, to the delight of everyone in the restaurant. It looks very difficult to drink like that, and is, I believe, more difficult than it looks, but it must be very delicious when one has learned.

But the glory and delight of Barcelona, which no other town in the world can offer, is the architecture of Gaudi. In England we scarcely know the meaning of Art Nouveau. Mr John Betjeman, the chief living authority on the subject, traces it chiefly in the decorative motive of the roots of the water-lily, which became prominent in this country at about the time of William Morris's death; I have seen pewter work, too, of about 1900, in which tulips and dock leaves have been very happily rendered; there are stencil designs in some early numbers of the *Studio* in which one can discern the repressed but resilient aspirations of the movement, but with us, as with the Parisians, decadence proved the more vital force. The peacock's feather and the green carnation outshine the tulip and the water-lily root. Then, after a warm but inconclusive flirtation with Holland – when painters made heavily patterned pictures of windmills and umber sails, and put tiles round their hearths and pot-bellied jugs of burnished copper in their windows – English decorative fancy went whirling off among timber and thatch and black old oak. But this was not the case with the Catalans who responded to the movement with all the zeal of their exuberant but wholly undiscriminating nature. They never concerned themselves with the Decadence or with archaism. Art Nouveau came to them at a time of commercial expansion and political unrest, and they took it to themselves and made it their own, even christening it and importing it into Florida under their own name, as the Neo-Catalan style. In its new guise it has even, in recent years, come back to England. Near to where I am writing this, on the south coast of England, there is a small colony of villas and bungalows extending from Bognor Regis for about a mile along the edge of the beach. They are mostly empty during the winter months, so that I can lean on their gates and study them without causing annoyance or suspicion, and in their very new and, I trust, impermanent structure I have been able to discern many features that are fundamentally Neo-Catalan. There is the same eagerness to attract attention, though this, I think, may be more a commercial than an artistic impulse. They are built not as homes, but as holiday pavilions to be let on short leases at extravagant rents during the bathing season; their aim is to catch the eye with a prominent exterior and leave the interior to chance, in the confidence that the tenants will spend most of the day sprawling on the sand. They exhibit the same irresponsible confusion of architectural styles, here Gothic, here Tudor, here Classical. They exhibit the same abhorrence of an unvariegated line, whenever it is structurally possible substituting machicolation or sweeping curvature. They exhibit the same predilection for very bright colours and iridescent surfaces, more particularly those achieved by glazed tiles or a mosaic of broken china and pebbles embedded in cement. This last is one of the chief decorative devices of Neo-Catalan architecture; there are examples of it sparkling and blazing all over Barcelona, but Gaudi alone was able to use it with precision and enterprise and make of it the craft which, in New York, is reverently known as 'Tiffany bath-room'.

Gaudi bears to these anonymous contractors and job-builders something of the same relation as do the masters of Italian baroque to the rococo decorators of the Pompadour's boudoir, or Ronald Firbank to the author of *Frolic Wind*. What in them is frivolous, superficial, and *chic* is in him structural and essential; in his work is apotheosised all the writhing, bubbling, convoluting, convulsing soul of the Art Nouveau.

I could discover very little about his life save that it began in Barcelona, was for the most part spent there, and ended there less than five years ago, when the aged and partially infirm master was run down and killed by an electric tram-car in the main boulevard of the town. In his later years he did very little creative work, devoting his failing energies to supervising the construction of the great

Church of the Holy Family, which I shall shortly describe. The period of his grossest and wildest output is the last two decades of the last century; it was then that his art, cautiously maturing, broke through all preconceived bounds of order and propriety, and coursed wantonly over the town, spattering its riches on all sides like mud.

But, indeed, in one's first brush with Gaudi's genius, it is not so much propriety that is outraged as one's sense of probability. My interest in him began on the morning of my second and, unfortunately, my last day in Barcelona. I was walking alone and without any clear intention in my mind, down one of the boulevards when I saw what, at first, I took to be part of the advertising campaign of the Exhibition. On closer inspection I realised that it was a permanent building, which to my surprise turned out to be the offices of the Turkish Consulate. Trees were planted in front of it along the pavement, hiding the lower stories. It was the roof which chiefly attracted my attention, since it was coloured peacock-blue and built in undulations, like a rough sea petrified; the chimneys, too, were of highly coloured glazed earthenware, and they were twisted and bent in all directions like very gnarled fruit-trees. The front of the building, down to the level of the second row of windows, was made of the mosaic of broken china I have described above, but thoughtfully planned so that the colours merged in delicate gradations from violet and blue to peacock-green and gold. The eaves overhung in irregular, amorphous waves, in places attenuated into stalactites of coloured porcelain; the effect was that of a clumsily iced cake. I cannot describe it more accurately than that because, dazzled and blinded by what I subsequently saw, my impression of this first experience, though deep, is somewhat indistinct. I went all round it with a camera trying to find an aspect I could photograph, but the trees and the sun combined to frustrate me.

I knew now what I wanted to see in Barcelona; hiring one of the David taxis, I made the driver understand that I wanted to go to any other building like this one. He took me to a large apartment house not far away, called, I think, the Casa Miláy Camps. I verified the fact later at a photograph shop that this was by the same architect as the Turkish Consulate, and that his name was Gaudi. I was able to take snapshots of this building which I have before me as I write, but the impression they give is far less eccentric than the reality. It has the same undulating roof of coloured tiles, but Gaudi has here intro-duced the innovation that the curves of the sky-line do not corres-pond in any way at all to the curves of the top of the walls. The chimney-stacks are all different in design, some being decorated in spirals, others in diamonds, others in vertical ribs, but of somewhat the same shape, like great bee-hives, from the top of which protrude little asymmetrical chimney-pots. The walls of the building, which stands at a corner, are faced with rough sandstone, pierced by six courses of windows. These are made to look like caves, having no sharply defined outlines or any straight line anywhere about them, sides, top, and bottom being all wildly and irrelevantly curved, as if drawn by a faltering hand. The ground plan, too, is designed with the same undulating boundaries. Perhaps the most unexpected thing about this building is the ironwork; the front door is composed of glass panes set in an iron frame of uncompromising irregularity, like the cuts in a jigsaw puzzle or the divisions in that thing known to gardeners as a 'crazy pavement', while outside many of the windows have wrought-iron balustrades that are fearless tangles of twisted metal, like the wreckage of an aeroplane that has fallen burning from a great height and has suddenly been cooled with hosings of cold water.

There are undoubtedly other houses by Gaudi in Barcelona, and somewhere in the district, I was told, one could see a bishop's palace of his design, but in the short time at my disposal I was obliged to concentrate myself upon his two major works, the Parc Güell and the Templo de la Sagrada Familia. Both of these lie some little way out of the town. Parc Güell is a public garden and recreation ground; it is also the name of the surrounding suburb, so that it was a little time before I could make my taxi-driver understand which I wanted; this difficulty was increased by my own ignorance. I had simply been told that there was Gaudi work at the Parc Güell; no more. We drove up several streets of villas, all extravagantly Neo-Catalan but lacking in just that quality which I had already learned to recognise as the master's. The moment we came into sight of the entrance gates of the gardens there was no more doubt; this was the real thing. I paid off the taxi and entered up a double flight of china-mosaic steps, between curving machicolated walls, decorated in a gay check pattern of coloured tiles, at the base of which was a little fountain and a kind of totem pole of mosaic.

I think that the whole gardens were laid out by Gaudi; certainly all the architectural features are unmistakably his. There is a great terrace on which the children play games, with a fine crinkled edge of the typical broken china mosaic; there is a battlemented wall built of rough stones and clinkers, and embellished with plaques of the word 'Güell' in contorted, interlacing letters; there is a kind of pergola supported on a colonnade of clinker pillars set askew and at all angles to each other; there is a turret, surmounted by a wrought-iron stand supporting a cross; there is a little lodge that is a gem of Gaudism, looking like a fairy cabin from the worst kind of Rackhamesque picture book. I was able to obtain a very happy snapshot of the last two features, which I reproduce here (Plate I, fig. 1). It gives the impression that the turret and lodge form parts of the same building; actually they are some fifty or so yards apart. Almost everything in the photograph is noteworthy, but I would draw the attention of all serious students to (1) the curvature of the ground plan of the lodge, (2) the surface of the walls composed of rough stones, (3) the rough stone shaft at the corner, (4) the mosaic shaft in the centre of the window and the curved shape of the window, (5) the 'sugar-icing' eaves and patterned mosaic roof, (6) the high, arching machicolation of the roof, (7) the horned gables, (8) the chimney-pot, (9) the sugar-icing eaves and machicolation on turret, (10) the 'fairy pavilion' outside staircase, (11) the proportions of the base of the cross of the spire. The whole of Gaudi's secular architecture seems to me summarised in these two buildings, and as I looked at them I could not help being struck by the kinship they bore to the settings of many of the later U.F.A. films. The dream scene in *Secrets of the Soul*, the Oriental passages in *Waxworks* particularly, seem to me to show just the same inarticulate fantasy.

Only a small part has as yet been built of the great Church of the Holy Family, which was to have been Gaudi's supreme achievement, and unless some eccentric millionaire is moved to interpose in the near future, in spite of the great sums that have already been

PLATE I

FIG. 2 South door, exterior

FIG. 1 Lodge at Parc Güell

PLATE II

Interior of the Church of the Holy Family

squandered upon it, the project will have to be abandoned. The vast undertaking was begun with very small funds and relied entirely upon voluntary contributions for its progress. The fact that it has got as advanced as it has, is a testimony to the great enthusiasm it has aroused among the people of the country, but enthusiasm and contributions have dwindled during the last twenty years, until only ten men are regularly employed, most of their time being taken up in repairing the damage caused to the fabric by its exposure; there are already menacing cracks in the towers; immense sums would be required to finish the building on the scale in which it was planned, and the portions already constructed fatally compromise any attempt at modification. It seems to me certain that it will always remain a ruin – and a highly dangerous one unless the towers are removed before they fall down.

All that is finished at present is the crypt, a part of the cloisters, the south door, two of the towers, and part of the east wall. There is a model in the crypt of the finished building, which was shown in Paris at one of the International Exhibitions but did not attract any great international support. The church is to be circular with a straight, gabled south front, forming a tangent touching the circumference, not, as might be supposed, at its centre, but at a point some way to the east of the central main door; beyond the high altar is to be a baptistry with a very high, pointed dome, fretted and presumably glazed.

Plate II gives a fair idea of the interior – if that is not a slightly ridiculous phrase to apply to a single arc of wall – of the structure as it stands to-day; the dais and steps enclosed by the east wall is the site of the high altar; the scaffolding between the two middle towers is, of course, temporary; in the finished model a fifth, very much smaller pinnacle rises between them from over the porch and reaches to about half the height of the present scaffolding; the two inner towers are intended to be considerably taller than the outer ones; all four are surmounted by mosaic pinnacles of typical Gaudi design, one of which I reproduce here (Plate III, fig. 1). Note the 'Hosanna Excelsis'. Like many architects, Gaudi used bands of lettering as a decorative motive, and devised a type suitable to the style of the buildings.

Note also in Plate II the cottages in the right foreground with undulating roofs, and the perverse lamp standard to the left of them.

Fig. 2, Plate I, shows the south door below the towers from the other side. It is the most elaborate piece of sculpture in the church. It will be seen that Gaudi has again introduced his 'sugar-icing' motive, translating it from tile and mosaic into carved stone, giving an effect as though the whole work had been arrested in an early stage of liquefaction. As they ascend, in fact, the forms all become less carefully defined; the birds and animals, figures and foliage of the lower stages being cut with the utmost elaboration of detail, while the birds towards the summit emerge vaguely as though their finer edges had already begun to melt; above these again come the heavens, indicated by stars strewn among the signs of the zodiac; fig. 2, Plate III, shows Gemini and Taurus so lightly adumbrated as to be barely distinguishable. Fig. 3, Plate III, gives the detail of the windows above the door; note the delicately rendered rosaries and medallions.

It will be seen from this that Gaudi has employed two very distinct decorative methods in his sculpture, the one so evanescent and amorphous, the other so minute and intricate, that in each case one finds a difficulty in realising that one is confronted by cut stone, supposing instinctively that the first is some imperfectly moulded clay and the second ivory or mahogany. The descent into the crypt renders one most conscious of this conflict. Here the architecture is, structurally, an austere and rather unlovely Gothic, and the decoration strictly formal in design, though indefatigably naturalistic in execution. The door of the cloisters, called the Puerta de Rosario (Plate III, fig. 4), is another and more exaggerated example of this manner. As can be seen from this photograph, it is like an old-fashioned paper-lace Easter card, translated with infinite labour and virtuosity into a third dimension.

There is a sacristan employed to show visitors over the building, and it is only by their contributions that the work continues at all. He told me that it makes a very strong appeal to the peasants of the neighbourhood, who come in large numbers to wonder at the cleverness of the carving. Tourists for the most part are unsympathetic, he said, expressing their impatience with the eccentricities of

PLATE III

FIG. 1 Detail of pinnacle

FIG. 2 Detail of south door

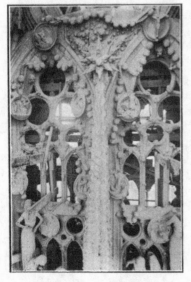

FIG. 3 Detail of window

FIG. 4 Detail of Puerta de Rosario

'modern art'. I do not say that if I were rich I could not find a better way of devoting my fortune, but I do think that it would be a pity to allow this astonishing curiosity to decay. I feel it would be a graceful action on the part of someone who was a little wrong in the head to pay for its completion.

I could easily have employed a happy fortnight at Barcelona tracking down further examples of Gaudism. He designed many things besides houses, I believe, making it his special province to conceive designs for tables and chairs and other objects of common utility which would render them unfit for their ostensible purposes. He is a great example, it seems to me, of what art-for-art's-sake can become when it is wholly untempered by considerations of tradition or good taste. Picabia in Paris is another example; but I think it would be more exciting to collect Gaudis.

There is a large book on Gaudi published in Barcelona which I could not at the time afford to buy; nor, if I had bought it, should I have been able to read it, since it is written in Spanish. But I should dearly like to have gone round with this book, identifying the illustrations and making photographs and sketches of my own; perhaps even to have read a paper or produced a monograph upon the subject.

But the *Stella* was due to sail that evening, and my passage was booked to England.

CHAPTER 8

WE HAD RATHER a nasty crossing to Mallorca, where we spent the next day. I have heard people being very eloquent about the charm of this island, but I must confess that I found it disappointing. It may be that, after moving as rapidly from place to place as we had been doing lately, one's palate becomes vitiated with an excess of variety, so that one misses the subtler and more fugitive qualities which reveal themselves shyly to more leisured travellers, and one requires the pungent flavour of Gaudi to arouse one's appetite for further sight-seeing. Or it may be that those who have come to love the Balearic Isles so deeply are inexperienced, and judge them by contrast with the Isles of Wight or of Man, or perhaps they have been fortunate there in love and see them suffused by their own memories. Whatever the reason, I was a little bored. Mallorca seemed a pretty, sleepy little island and Palma a pretty, sleepy little town; for the same kind of attraction I rather prefer Tarascon or Wells. I walked about the town in the morning and saw the cathedral, where there was nothing to see, and the market where there was nothing to buy. I had an *apéritif* in a shady café in the main square; it was rather expensive; nothing in Palma was as cheap as I had been led to suppose; the taxis were almost as exorbitant as those of Oxford. In the afternoon I went for a drive into the interior of the island, along lanes bordered with thorn hedges and banks of rich red loam, like the west of England. The taxi-driver's brother was gardener at the country villa of one of the important citizens of the town; he took me to see the garden, which was built on the side of a little valley, with two or three springs bubbling up in it and falling down in ornamental cascades to the stream at the bottom of the hill; the woods on the opposing slope were full of nightingales. The villa itself was a lovely old house, built round a *patio* in the Spanish manner; behind it the hill ascended steeply, with rocky paths, rose-trees, grottoes, and more waterfalls and rivulets. One grotto had a marble Venus inside it, and all round the walls, and in the ceiling and floor, were little concealed jets, which could be turned on all together, suddenly, from outside, drenching Venus and the visitor in a dozen delicate spouts of water. I have seen bath-rooms equipped like this in the houses of rich people in England. This form of practical joke was not uncommon in Europe in the eighteenth century, but I believe that it was originally learned from the Moors. In the Alcazar Palace at Seville there is a maze set in one of the tessellated pavements, the centre and goal of which is a little fountain. As the unwary guest leaned over it to trace his way through the intricate corners and blind alleys of the puzzle, his host would turn on the tap and souse him. It is now out of order, and perhaps is deliberately left in this condition so that the custodian shall not be tempted to bring ridicule on the tourists. I think that, if one had nothing else to do, it would be fun to collect practical jokes of this kind. I know a house in Ireland which has in its hall a carved oak chair of nineteenth-century construction; as one sits down in it, iron clamps fly out from the arms and imprison one's thighs inextricably until one is released by a trigger from behind; this toy can be very painful indeed to stout people; nowadays ingenuity seems to take milder forms, mostly in association with music boxes which play inside decanters or cigarette boxes or rolls of toilet paper.

It was the Norwegian Independence Day, and the *Stella* was dressed with hundreds of little flags. That evening there were speeches at dinner, and after the dancing a very heavenly party, to which I was invited, given by the officers and the Scandinavian passengers. The first officer made a patriotic speech in Norwegian and then in English, and then he made a speech in English in praise of England and then translated his speech into Norwegian. Then I made a speech in English in praise of Norway, and one of the passengers translated my speech into Norwegian; then she made a speech in English and Norwegian in praise of England and Norway and quoted Kipling. It was all delightful. Then we went down to the lower deck, where the crew were having a tremendous supper of Norwegian *delicatessen* and sugar cakes and champagne; one of them was in a rostrum made of flags; he was delivering a patriotic speech. Then we all drank each other's health and danced; it was by no means a calm sea. Then we went up to the Captain's cabin and ate a dish called *eggdosis*, but I do not know how it was spelt. It was made of eggs and sugar and brandy whipped up into a firm cream. Then we went to the cabin of the lady who had translated my speech – she had one of the suites-de-luxe, of the kind which Geoffrey and Juliet had occupied – and there we made more speeches, oddly enough most of them in French.

I woke up feeling a little ill after Independence Day, and found that we had arrived in Algiers and were berthed alongside the Quai de Marine in the Port de Commerce, and that the deck was already covered with stalls as though for a charity bazaar. They were selling filigree gold jewellery, binoculars, and carpets. The jewellery was vile; the binoculars were mostly of well-known makes and, being duty free, were astonishingly cheap; several passengers bought pairs, but I do not know whether or not they succeeded in getting them past the Customs at Harwich. The carpets, too, were very cheap; some were shiny, of European manufacture; others were native workmanship of rough striped wool like horse blankets. The water in the harbour was dense with floating refuse; young men swam about, butting and churning back with their arms the scum of empty bottles, sodden paper, grape-fruit skins, and kitchen waste, and calling for coins to be thrown to them.

The town is built along the slopes of the west side of the Bay of Algiers. Except for the little triangle of mean streets around and below the Kasbar quarter, it has grown up in the second half of the last century on a typically French provincial model. There is a Place de la République, planted with magnolia-trees and bamboos, surrounded by cafés and restaurants; broad, arcaded boulevards lead out of this, with offices, shops, and apartment houses. French posters are on all the hoardings, advertising Geugeot, Dubonnet, Savon Palmolive, Citroën, Galeries Lafayette; an expanse of garden suburb stretches out to the south; there is a fine park laid out with tropical plants; a Bois de Boulogne; a Shakespeare Chemin; a nine-hole golf course and a Chemin du Golfe; the wooded hills above the town are dotted with larger villas, barracks, and forts.

A fortnight before our arrival the Foreign Legion had been in quarters here, but had now been moved up-country. I should have liked to see this company of exiled chivalry – all, I like to think, suffering for the good name of others, all of exalted and romantic origin. The taxi-driver to whom I spoke of them gave an unenthusiastic account. They got so little pay, he said, that there was nothing they could ever afford to do, except to stand about at the street corners and spit; they were for the most part tough, undersized young criminals of very limited intellect; he was glad to see the backs of them. But taxi-drivers, as a race, are always constitutionally misanthropic.

An expedition drove off from the *Stella* to visit a valley of monkeys, but I remained behind in the town, where there seemed quite enough to employ one's attention for a couple of days. It was particularly interesting after Port Said, which, except for the determining fact of French administration, should have had much in common. The great difference was the apparent absence of racial and colour distinctions in Algiers. It is by no means a predominantly Moorish population. Baedeker gives the figures in 1911 as 33,200 Mohammedans, 12,500 Jews, and 35,200 Europeans, mostly Italians and Spaniards. In the last twenty years the balance has been shifted still further against the Mohammedans by the steady influx of French traders and officials and the development of the higher slopes as a winter resort for the rich of all nations. Even the Kasbar, the ancient Oriental quarter, is invaded by Maltese and low-class Mediterraneans of various races. The Moors, however, have made no attempt at imitation, either of the clothes or manners of the Europeans. There is no Kemalist nonsense about votes for women and bowler hats. The men remain polygamous, and walk about the streets gravely conversing with each other, very dignified figures indeed, in large, padded turbans and long cloaks, carrying tall walking-sticks; while their wives trot behind, veiled in white, their eyes circled with smears of paint and their fingers steeped in henna. The men mix absolutely freely with Europeans of their own class; the white porters and street scavengers exchange cigarette ends with their coloured colleagues, while, in the chief cafés, handsomely robed Moorish landowners sit unembarrassed at the next tables to naval and military officers and frock-coated *légionnaires*, listening to the band, drinking their vermouth and Cassis, reading the French journals, and exchanging greetings on all sides. What is it, I wonder, which gives the Anglo-Saxons, alone among the colonists of the world, this ungenerous feeling of superiority over their neighbours? Why did the British residents at Port Said warn me against the hotels which might harbour 'gyppies'? At the restaurant where I lunched on the second morning, there was a delightful party at the next table – a dapper little Frenchman and his wife and three Moors with long beards, great aquiline noses, and very humorous, wrinkled eyes. One of these was host. They were all clearly enjoying their luncheon immensely, and drinking a lot of local *vin rosé*. The Frenchwoman was flirting mildly with her host, and her husband was making very successful jokes which I could not quite overhear, although I strained all my attention to do so.

This was a very charming restaurant. I omitted to record the name in my note-book, but it is easy enough to find, a little way down the Boulevard de la République. There are tables inside and on the pavement, among shrubs in pots, overlooking the harbour. It was very Marseillais in character; an elderly woman stood behind a table opening crumpled little bright green oysters; there were heaps of rather dangerous-looking lobsters and *écrevisses*. I ate *bouillabaisse* and *œufs la Turque*, and drank some Algerian white wine. I do not believe that Algerian wine is really very nice. It was evidently a very popular restaurant; every table was occupied; but perhaps that was because it happened to be Whit Sunday.

After luncheon I climbed rather heavily up to the Kasbar. There is a fine view from there over the town and harbour and the whole Bay of Algiers; the houses are very old and the alleys narrow and precipitous; it has that vivid street life that one sees in every old town which has a slum quarter inaccessible to traffic; there was one street and a little terrace given up to houses of ill-fame – all very gay with bright paint and tiles, and crowded thick at every door and window with plain, obese young women in gaudy clothes. If I had come there fresh from England I should have found it amusing enough, but as a spectacle of Oriental life it was less exciting than Cairo on Bajiram night, and as an example of mediæval town-planning less formidable than the Manderaggio at Valletta.

There was very little begging or street hawking except the inevitable swarm of boot-cleaners, and no native dragomans. Except on the harbour front one could walk about unmolested; there, however, one had to run the gauntlet of a great number of guides – nasty, jaunty young men for the most part, dressed in European suits and straw hats, bow ties, and Charlie Chaplin moustaches; they spoke French and some English, and were, I imagine, of vaguely European extraction. Their particular trade was organising parties to see native dances – *fêtes Mauresques* – and an intolerable nuisance they were over it. Many of the passengers from the *Stella* went off with them and came back with very different reports of the entertainment. Some appeared to have seen decorous and perfectly genuine performances in the courtyards of one or other of the mediæval Moorish houses; they described a native band with drums and wind instruments and a troupe of veiled dancing girls who went through the figures of various traditional tribal dances; they said it was a little monotonous, but they seemed quite satisfied with their evening. Another party, including two Englishwomen, were led to the top floor of a house of ill-fame, where they were sat round the walls of a tiny room. Here they waited for some time in the light of a small oil lamp, becoming more and more uneasy, until the curtains of the door were suddenly thrust aside and a very large, elderly Jewess pranced in among them, quite naked except for a little cheap jewellery, and proceeded to perform a *danse de ventre* on the few yards of floor that separated them. The verdict of one of the Englishwomen on this experience was: 'Well, I am quite glad in a way to have seen it, but I should certainly never wish to go again.' Her companion refused to discuss the subject at all, from any angle, with anyone, and for the rest of the voyage entirely avoided the company of the gentlemen who had escorted her that evening.

But there was one party who had a still sadder time of it. They were five Scots people in early middle age, three women and two men, inter-related in some way that I never had occasion to define. These were caught by a very shady guide who took them up to the

Kasbar in a taxi-cab. He charged them 200 francs for this drive, which they politely paid without question. He then took them to a house in a blind alley, knocked on the door three times, and excited their uneasiness by saying, 'This is very dangerous. You are safe as long as you are with me, but on no account get separated or I cannot answer for the consequences.' They were admitted one at a time and charged 100 francs each. The door was shut behind them and they were led down to a cellar. The guide explained to them that they must order coffee, which they did at the cost of 20 francs a head. Before they had tasted it a revolver shot sounded just outside the door.

'Run for your lives,' said the guide.

They scampered out and found their taxi, which, by apparent good fortune, was waiting for them.

'No doubt the ladies are feeling unsettled by their experience. Would they like a little cognac?'

He then directed the car, which cost another 200 francs, to one of the ordinary cafés of the town and gave them each a tot of *eau-de-vie*. He settled the bill for them and explained that it had come to 25 francs a head and 10 francs for the tip.

'That is the advantage of coming with me,' he explained. 'I do the tips for you and you are not put upon. There are many cheats in this town who would take advantage of your inexperience if you were alone.'

He then saw them back to the ship, reminding them discreetly that the fees for his evening's services were 100 francs or whatever they liked to make it. They were still so bewildered and agitated that they gave him a hundred and fifty, thanking him very much and congratulating themselves on the narrow escape they had had. Only later, talking it over among themselves, did the suspicion arise that perhaps the charges had been unduly heavy, and that the house from which they had made their escape might, in fact, be the guide's own home, and that his wife or small son or a kindly neighbour had fired the pistol for them.

I think it did them great credit that they did not conceal this dismal story, but told it to everyone on board, half resentfully but half humorously.

'I'd like to go back and have a few words with that merchant,' remarked the men of the party, but, alas, by that time we had left Algiers.

We sailed that night and were at sea until late the next evening, when we came in to Malaga. It was cold and grey and windy all that day. It is depressing to wake up to rough weather with the plates creaking and doors banging and things rolling about overhead. Many people stayed in their cabins. Those that came up sat about moodily, wrapped in rugs, with novels which they left open across their knees for long periods at a time. A few of the sturdier ones attempted deck games, but the movement of the ship took all pleasure from them as competitions, leaving only the satisfaction of bravado. I am a fairly good sailor and did not actually feel ill. I must admit, however, that I had very little appetite that day for food, wine, or tobacco. At the best, rough weather is profoundly irritating to the nerves, as it renders almost all activity laborious and ineffectual. I was very glad to see harbour lights and people walking about under the trees, watching us as we came in.

We spent two days here, to enable those who wished to go up to Granada. I stayed on board, mainly because I was short of money; there is very little to see or do in Malaga, though it is an agreeable, compact little town, smelling strongly of burnt olive oil and excrement. It looks very pretty from the sea, with an avenue of trees along the front, and behind them the white limestone cathedral and steep little hills, one of them crowned by some dissolute fortifications. But one has seen the best of it before one lands. The cathedral is a nice clean piece of sixteenth-century architecture, still unfinished, though work went on at it intermittently until the middle of the eighteenth century. It reminded me strongly of the chapel at Hertford College, evoking long suppressed memories to me of all those gentle and wise men who directed my youth with who can tell what insight and sympathy, and of all the smug, sheep-faced undergraduates praying for success in their pass schools, and above them, crouching in his stall, the venerable figure of my history tutor, ill at ease in his starched white surplice, biting his nails, and brooding, I have no doubt, on all the good he intended for each one of us. But these were the most flimsy of ghosts; there was no one like that in the cathedral at Malaga; only a riotous troop of begging choir boys, and paralysed old women, and a dull verger.

Two streets to the east of the cathedral is a little hill called Alcazabar, covered with tumble-down cottages and some indistinguishable Moorish remains. This is peopled with gypsies and goats, and it is from here, when the wind is in that quarter, that the town gets its smell.

There is a wine called Malaga, a species of dark, sweet sherry, which I have drunk and disliked in England. I drank some here, hoping it would be better, but found it very nasty. It is drunk locally in big bumpers as an *apéritif*, in accordance with that paradoxical Latin taste which prescribes something sweet and thick and pungent at this time of the evening; though whether it is preferable to cloy the palate in this way, or to paralyse it with iced spirits in the fashion of my own country, I leave for the gourmets to decide. There were two or three clubs in the town, along the main thoroughfare, but these were built like cafés, open to the street, with only a low rail between the passers-by and the members; stout, easy-looking men who sat all day in arm-chairs, smoking cheroots and staring at the traffic. No doubt this is a regular institution in Andalusia; it was new to me and seemed noteworthy and laudable.

In spite of the bad weather we had encountered on the way there, our two days at Malaga turned out bright and warm. There was an excellent bathing-place a mile or so down the coast, to which I went with the second officer and a few of the passengers; there were bright little cabins and a steep beach and a café-restaurant, but the water was still deadly cold. On my second afternoon I drove out in a one-horse carriage to a pretty park and garden of the Hacienda de San José and the villa of La Concepcion, and walked about on grey shingle paths under semi-tropical trees between brilliant green banks, scattered in places with Roman antiquities of broken marble.

Late the second evening the expedition returned from Granada, dusty and tired and rather cross. As soon as they were safely embarked we sailed again, this time through calm waters, and arrived during the early hours of the morning at Gibraltar.

All over the world there are rock formations in which people profess to see the likeness of natural objects – heads of crusaders, dogs, cattle, petrified beldams, etc. There is an idea, started, I believe, by Thackeray, that the Rock of Gibraltar looks like a lion. 'It is the very image,' he said, 'of an enormous lion, crouched between the Atlantic and the Mediterranean, and set there to guard the passage for its British mistress.' Everyone else on board was instantly struck by the felicity of this image, so I suppose that it must be due to some deficiency in my powers of observation that to me it appeared like a great slab of cheese and like nothing else.

An English policeman with helmet, whistle, truncheon, and rolled mackintosh cape was on duty at the landing-stage. I think this man pleased the English passengers more than anything they had seen in their travels. 'It makes one feel so safe inside,' said one of the ladies; but I cannot for the life of me think what she meant by that.

I will not say that I did not know any town could be so ugly as the town of Gibraltar; to say that would be to deny many bitter visits in the past to Colwyn Bay, Manchester, and Stratford-on-Avon; but I will say that I had forgotten much, and that Gibraltar was a shock, and sudden sharp reminder of what I was returning to. In the past three months I had seen so many towns of widely different origin and circumstance, but all distinguished in some way by fine architecture or a gracious setting or a seemly and individual habit of life. Baedeker, always slow to condemn, remarks of Gibraltar that 'the streets are narrow and dark and are relieved by few squares . . . the cleanness of the town and the absence of beggars produce a pleasant impression' and of the Anglican cathedral he reticently confines himself to the statement that it is 'built in the Moorish style'; he reminds those in search of entertainment that a military band plays near the Assembly Rooms on Sundays and Wednesdays between the hours of three and five in the afternoon. His bald, unemphasised account of the little peninsula is one of the most able passages in the whole of his works, and suggests more censure than all the adjectives I can assemble.

The only place that I can think of at all like the town of Gibraltar, is Shoreham-by-Sea in Sussex, but this comparison will mean little, I suppose, to most English people. For those, however, who have at any time had occasion to pass through it, or, worse, to stop there,

I will add this modification – that they must think of Gibraltar as a Shoreham deprived of its two churches, and scoured of all the ramshackle, haphazard characteristics which make it relatively tolerable. It is Shoreham, with a touch of Aldershot, transplanted to the east coast of Scotland or the north coast of Wales; Shoreham emptied of those mild, nondescript old men with beards, who potter about the side of the estuary, spitting into the mud flats; Shoreham never brightened by those passing charabancs and carloads of south coast trippers.

I walked for some time about those very clean streets, feeling that there could be no town in the world without something of interest somewhere. The shop windows displayed little except seedy shaving brushes and tarnished cutlery and indefinable objects stitched on to cards; there were chemists' shops selling English aperients and patent pills; a paper-shop selling threepenny novelettes and twopenny weeklies; a few curiosity shops with a stock oddly composed of little Victorian and Edwardian knick-knacks – descended presumably from officers' villas – and flaring modern embroideries and beaten metal from Tangier. There was a tobacconist selling Dunhill pipes and tobacco-jars ornamented with regimental and naval devices. I passed some sailors' wives standing near a milliner's window; they shrank as I passed as though I had brought with me some of the polluted air of Malaga. Most of them, I learned later, keep strictly to their houses when there are 'trippers about', like Hampstead residents on bank-holidays.

As I was walking along very disconsolately I found a notice which said, 'To Brighter 'Bralter ☞'. I followed it for some way until I came to another, similar announcement, and so, in pursuit of pleasure, I began a kind of lugubrious treasure hunt, following these clues through the length of that town. At last I came to the South Port Gate and a neat little cemetery, where are buried a number of men who fell at Trafalgar. Many of the graves were of pretty, Wedgwood pattern, with urns and delicate carved plaques. Somewhat farther ahead, in a kind of recreation ground, preparations were being made with tents and awnings for some kind of gymkhana. I felt, however, that the posters had at least led me to the one tolerable spot on the Rock. In the afternoon I went for a little drive in a horse-carriage, to a dismal neck of sand, quarter of a mile broad, called Neutral Ground, which divides the English and Spanish territory. I wonder what would be the legal consequences of putting up some bungalows there and starting a little lawless colony.

Gibraltar claims this other distinction, that it is the only place in Europe inhabited by wild monkeys. I saw none, but they are said to frequent the higher slopes in large numbers; indeed, at one time they became a great cause of offence, pinching and biting the garrison, snatching at hats, firing off cannon at unsuitable moments, chattering impudently in the faces of high officials, and openly demonstrating the facts of life before the officers' children; the governor accordingly had them exterminated, upon which such an outcry went up on all sides, demanding where were the traditions of English seamanship, and what would become of our domination in the Atlantic, and how could Gib. be looked on as the key to the Mediterranean, now that it was robbed of its monkeys, that he was obliged to import a fresh stock from Africa, who rapidly repopulated the Rock and restored popular confidence.

Nothing could have been less like Gibraltar than our next stop, Seville. We arrived at the mouth of the Guadalquivir at about noon, but had to wait for some time, as ships of the *Stella*'s capacity are only able to cross the bar at high-water. The river is navigable as far as Seville by vessels of twenty-three-foot draught. I should think that we came very near to the maximum. The only other ship we met of the same size was the *Meteor*, a cruising steam-ship belonging to the same company as ourselves; she was berthed next to us by the river bank, and some of us went over to visit her; many of the *Stella*'s officers had been transferred from her, and I had heard a great deal about her from them, who often spoke of their experiences on 'the good old *Meteor*', and also from my elder brother, who had once travelled in her to Norway; she is a pretty ship, built on much the same lines as the *Stella*, though less up-to-date in her equipment.

It is over fifty miles to Seville from the open sea, and we had necessarily to make slow progress in the narrow, meandering river. The banks on either side were low; at first we travelled between sandy flats covered with rough pasture and herds of black cattle;

later these gave place to trees and occasional farms and villages, the inhabitants of which turned out to wave; the water was brown and quite opaque, like breakfast coffee, as I have sometimes found the bath-water in remote country houses. After the blustering of the Atlantic this gentle progression was at first soothing, then irritating, and then towards evening very soothing again. It was quite dark by the time we reached our destination and moored against the grassy right bank of the river; this, too, seemed odd after so many diverse harbours, to be lying alongside a towing path, like a college barge on the Isis.

As I remarked when I first set out in the *Stella*, one of the chief advantages of this sort of travelling is that it enables one to sample a great many places quite effortlessly, and choose those one wants to return to afterwards. Seville is certainly a town for a prolonged visit. In the two days that we were there, I was only able to get a glimpse at a few of the obvious show places and a few hints at the life of the people. This year, or next year, or later, I shall go back there. At present it seems to me impertinent to write very much about it. It is certainly one of the most lovely cities I have ever seen; only a general diffidence about the superlative prevents me from saying the most lovely. I can think of many with more lovely things in them, but none that has the same sweetness and refinement combined with activity and good sense; it seems to avoid every sort of vulgarity, even that of the professional beauty. I did not begin to master the geography of the town, and remember it now in a series of isolated magic lantern slides. The cathedral is magnificent; one of the finest in Europe; a great, spacious, Gothic church full of superb sculpture hidden in dark corners and behind metal gates. The dome was never a great success technically, as it has twice fallen in since it was originally built; the last restoration was by Casanova, in the late eighties, and it is hoped that he has succeeded in making it relatively permanent; just outside the cathedral is a large *patio*, once the courtyard of a mosque, in which hangs a stuffed crocodile sent by the Sultan of Egypt to Alfonso the Learned, with a suit for the hand of his daughter.

The Alcazar palace is very pretty, with delicately carved wood, open plaster work like lace, and beautiful Oriental tiles; it must be a great joy to those who can feel any genuine enthusiasm for Moorish work, and it is worth noticing that this, like most of the best Moorish houses in Seville, was constructed after the Christian occupation. The gardens of the Alcazar, with pavilion, grotto, and fountains, cannot help delighting the most hard-boiled Westerner.

The other most famous building is the Giralda, a square tower built of Roman brick; this was originally the minaret of the mosque, but the Christians added a belfry, a small dome, and a bronze figure of Faith. At the time of our visit, it was illuminated in the evenings by flood-lights, in honour of the Spanish-American Exposition.

This exhibition had only just opened, and many of the buildings were still unfinished. It must not be supposed, however, that the project had been hurriedly or frivolously undertaken. The 1913 edition of Baedeker's *Spain and Portugal* mentions that large portions of the park were at that time closed for the preparations. The war delayed matters, but after the war work was begun again, deliberately and thoroughly. Everything was done on a solid and permanent basis. The pavilions are not mere lath and plaster erections, designed to last a dry summer; they are massive palaces of brick and stone, which are to be used later, I believe, for an Andalusian University. We were presented on landing with a prettily decorated prospectus written in English, which remarked: 'Five hundred years from now the descendants of those who visit this Exposition will see with their own eyes these very same buildings, mellowed by the passing ages, but equal to their present grandeur in lines and in massive construction.' Some of the buildings certainly will profit by mellowing, being at present very gay indeed in bright patterned brick work and coloured tiles; a little too gay, perhaps, for their 'massive construction' and the academic future ordained for them. Their contents, however, were magnificent. The Colonial and South American pavilions were not yet open, but I spent a delightful afternoon quite alone in the two great art galleries. One of these contained a remarkable collection of paintings by the Spanish masters – Velásquez, Zubarán, El Greco, Goya, and a great number whose names are rarely heard outside their native country. Most of these are normally either inaccessible in private houses or to all intents and purposes equally hidden in the obscure chapels of Spanish cathedrals. A series of four fantastic paintings by an anonymous artist of the eighteenth century particularly attracted me; they were named after the seasons, and represented, from a distance, female heads which, on closer examination, turned out to be composed entirely of ingeniously painted arrangements of the fruits and flowers of each quarter of the year; this, I suppose, is the ancestry from which are descended the picture-postcards one sees sometimes on stalls, of race-horses whose anatomy is curiously determined by the interlaced limbs of four or five nude female figures. The other gallery, which also was empty except for one very young and one very old priest, making a brisk tour side by side, was full of Spanish applied arts; beautiful carved Calvaries, reredoses, choir stalls; gold and silver pyxes, monstrances and tabernacles and communion plate; candlesticks and crucifixes – most of these lent from cathedral treasuries. There was also a gorgeous series of tapestries lent by the king from the Escurial. And, so far from suffering the bargain-sale scramble of a loan collection in London, one was able to walk round these superb galleries absolutely alone.

But the whole exhibition was like that. Tourists had so far not arrived in any appreciable quantities, and the Sevillians after sixteen years' preparation were bored with the whole business. There were elements of ill-feeling in their neglect. They considered that the price of admission was too high and that they had been unrighteously defrauded of the use of their favourite park. There was no organised boycott, but it just so happened that no Sevillians went to their exhibition. There was a model railway, with a miniature steam-engine, which took an empty train round and round the ground; there was an *Attracion* Park in which a great wheel revolved, empty; there were switch-backs and scenic railways on which empty cars swooped and swerved through breath-taking descents; there were silent rifle ranges with heaps of ammunition lying undischarged and mountains of bottles unbroken; in the evening the gardens were brilliantly illuminated; the trees were filled with electric-light bulbs in the shape of apples, oranges, and clusters of bananas; ingeniously concealed flood-lamps made the lawns luminous and many coloured; electric lights were hidden under the water-lilies on the lake; illuminated fountains sparkled high in the air, like soundless and inexhaustible fireworks. It would have been a fascinating scene even in a Wembley crowd; on the night of my visit there was not another figure stirring anywhere; I felt as if I had achieved the Nonconformist ideal of being the only righteous soul saved in the universe; quite, quite alone in the whole of paradise. I suppose it really is not wholly gracious to emphasise this particular feature of the exhibition, as it can clearly not have come about by any deliberate intention of the organisers. To compliment them on it is somewhat like the polite painter who I once overheard, while being shown round the infinitely nurtured and tended garden of an acquaintance, congratulate his host on the excellence of his 'soft, mossy lawns'. Rather a touching paragraph in the prospectus said: 'In view of the large number of visitors expected at Seville throughout the Exposition, several new hotels and two garden-cities have been constructed ... suited equally, in their variety, to the millionaire and to the most moderate purses. ... Seville will accommodate some 25,00 visitors simultaneously throughout the Exposition.' It certainly merited the concurrence of 250,000, but I was very thankful that I saw it as I did, before anyone else arrived.

I had no meals on shore in Seville but sampled several vintages of Manzanilla in the cafés; it is a very dry species of sherry, served as a rule with a little piece of smoked boar's-head; the inferior brands taste like the smell of evening newspapers, but the best is very fine and delicate. There was a reception on the *Stella* for the Archbishop of Andalusia and various chaplains and officials; they drank glasses of champagne and ate iced cake and smoked cigars; conversation was impeded by our ignorance of Spanish and their ignorance of all other languages, but everyone smiled continuously and it had every evidence of being a success as a party; this, it may be remarked, happened just before luncheon.

Exigencies of the tide made it necessary for us to leave in the early afternoon of our second day. We turned, after prolonged and skilful manœuvring, and sailed back down the river to the coast, crossing the bar into the Gulf of Cadiz at high tide that night. Early next morning we rounded Cape St Vincent. From then onwards, with a brief call at Lisbon, we headed straight up the Atlantic coast for England.

'I do not find Lisbon so pretty town as I have been tinking about,'
remarked one of my Swedish friends as we leant over the rail,
watching the lights of the harbour disappear behind us. He had
lost heavily at the Casino, and I think that had embittered him. For
me Lisbon was a very agreeable surprise. There is no European
capital of any antiquity about which one hears so little; I know
practically nobody else who has ever been there even for a day.
And yet it is readily accessible; it has a romantic and honourable
history intimately allied, if that is any commendation nowadays,
with our own; a unique style of architecture, and inhabitants of
marked racial peculiarities.

It lies in a beautiful natural harbour, where the river Tagus
suddenly swells out into a great lake before narrowing again into
the little bottle-necked mouth. The town is built on the side of
a range of low hills, with domes and towers on most of the highest
points; the water front is equalled only by that of Dublin in the
purity of its architecture. It was built in the middle of the eighteenth
century, after the demolition of the earlier buildings in the great
earthquake. The central feature is the lovely Praça do Commercio,
a square open on its fourth side to the water's edge, with a fine
equestrian statue in the middle; behind this extends the Cidade
Baixa, excellent eighteenth-century streets, rectangularly planned;
behind them again lies the Rocio, a square known to generations of
English sailors as 'Roly-Poly Square'; the great new boulevard,
Avenida da Liberdade, runs from the Rocio to the northern extremity of the town, and on either side the eastern and western quarters
rise on two densely populated hills.

Before luncheon I drove out with two fellow passengers to the
Convent dos Jeronymos de Belem, a fine sixteenth-century building
just outside the town on the coast road. This was my introduction to
the Arte Manuelina – the style of architecture evolved in Portugal at
the time of her commercial greatness. It is well described in the
words of Baedeker as 'the fantastic style of the time of Emmanuel
I the Great, a picturesque blend of late-Gothic, Moorish, and
Renaissance features with *motifs* from the gorgeous edifices of the
East Indies'. Belem is the only perfect example of this style in Lisbon,
as buildings of this kind are naturally unsuited to withstand even the

strains of their own weight, and all the others came hopelessly to grief in the great earthquake of 1755. It is a comic but not disagreeable manner of building, and antiquity has mellowed and refined the undue opulence of its decoration. The few attempts I saw to revive it in modern times seemed peculiarly infelicitous. It is the sort of architecture, one feels, that was never really intended to be built at all; it is a painter's and draughtsman's architecture, of the kind one sees in the background of northern sixteenth-century paintings and wood engravings, in which slender pillars, all fretted and twisted, support vast stretches of flamboyant fan-tracery; it is the sort of decoration one can imagine more easily in cast steel than in stone. Since 1834 this building has been converted into an orphanage, and the fabric seemed to have suffered somewhat in consequence; the elaborately carved stalls in the church were crumbling with dry rot. We went out into the cloisters; it was play-time, and hundreds of male orphans were tearing up and down, rolling each other in the gravel, kicking and hitting each other, and throwing small stones in each other's faces; the noise, reverberating through the vaulted roof, was deafening; our ears sang with it for half an hour afterwards; I trembled for the security of these fragile pinnacles, that intricate fretwork of carved stone. One of the orphans very politely conducted us round; he spoke English accurately, and was, it so happened, coal black. It is one of the interesting things about the Portuguese that the lower orders all show more or less marked negro characteristics. This is attributed to the extensive inbreeding in the Portuguese African colonies, and also to the policy, said to have been prosecuted by the great Pombal, of introducing a stud of negroes to repopulate the country after the ravages of the great earthquake.

I spent the afternoon driving about the town. It has not yet recovered from its earthquake, and most of the chief churches are left as ruins. In one of them, now used as a museum, I saw some interesting Peruvian mummies. At the top of a very high hill is the chapel of Nossa Senhora do Monte, much frequented by those who admire fine views, and also by women who wish to bear children, for in one of the side chapels is preserved an ancient stone seat which will cure the most stubborn case of barrenness, it is said, if the patient only sits on it for half a minute. There is also a very rich Jesuit church, called Sao Roque, well worth a visit on account of its frescoed ceiling, in which an almost unique trick of perspective has been employed; the plain vaulted roof is painted to represent elaborate architectural groining, with, between the false stone work, a series of frescoes conceived on quite different planes from their actual surface; a painting, as it were, of a painting. From all points of observation except one, the effect is barely intelligible; when, however, one stands in the centre of the floor, all the lines recede into their right places and an almost completely successful illusion is achieved. There is a false dome by Mantegna designed on a similar principle, and, of course, many compositions into which this kind of trick has been unobtrusively inserted, but I do not know of any example so complete and ingenious. It is only since the discovery of photography that perspective has ceased to be an art.

We sailed late that evening. Next day we were in a choppy sea, with a cold wind blowing from the shore, and that night we came into the Bay of Biscay; the ship developed a slow roll which caused serious discomfort to many. A great number of the passengers remained on deck during luncheon, nourishing themselves with dry biscuits and quarter-bottles of champagne. The roll went on undiminished until we rounded Cape Finisterre late in the afternoon.

In the channel news reached us by wireless of the results of the first day's count of the General Election; everyone prophesied a sweeping Labour victory, and the deepest gloom and apprehension settled upon the English passengers; many of the elder ones began wondering whether it would be wise to land.

The sea was quite calm now that we were out of the Bay of Biscay, but we ran into recurrent banks of fog which held up our progress; there was talk of our not getting in until late the next afternoon.

That evening there was a small party in the Captain's cabin, consisting of the officers off duty and two or three of the Scandinavian passengers and myself; we drank each other's health and exchanged invitations to visit each other in our countries. After a time I went out from the brightly lighted cabin on to the dark boat deck. For the moment the night was clear and starry. I was carrying my champagne glass in my hand, and, for no good reason that I can now think of, I threw it out over the side, watched it hover for a moment in the air as it lost momentum and was caught by the wind, then saw it flutter and tumble into the swirl of water. This gesture, partly, I suppose, because it was of its own moment, spontaneous and made quite alone, in the dark, has become oddly important to me, and bound up with the turgid, indefinite feelings of home-coming.

For to return to one's own country, even after the shortest absence, is, in its way, an emotional business. I had left in the depth of winter and was coming back to late spring; then, if ever, England is still a lovely country. To-morrow I should have a number of telephone calls to make; I should have to see my publishers about this book; I should have to order some new clothes; I should have to attend to a great heap of correspondence – bills and Press cuttings mostly, perhaps a few invitations.

I do not know on quite what terms we now deal with the emotions that were once called patriotism. Clearly we can feel very little martial ardour, or acquisitive ambition, or a pride of possession in other people's territory. And yet, although everything one most loves in one's own country seems only to be the survival of an age one has not oneself seen, and though all that one finds sympathetic and praiseworthy in one's own age seems barely represented at all in one's own country, there still remains a certain uncontaminated glory in the fact of race, in the very limits and circumscription of language and territorial boundary; so that one does not feel lost and isolated and self-sufficient. It seems to me that there is this fatal deficiency about all those exiles, of infinitely admirable capabilities, who, through preference or by force of untoward circumstances, have made their home outside the country of their birth; it is the same deficiency one finds in those who indulge their consciences with sectarian religious beliefs, or adopt eccentrically hygienic habits of life, or practise curious, newly classified vices; a deficiency in that whole cycle of rich experience which lies outside personal peculiarities and individual emotion.

So, suitably moralising, I came near the end of my journey.

While I still stood on the boat deck we ran into another belt of mist. The engines changed to slow and then to dead slow, and the fog-horn began dolefully sounding the half-minutes.

In twenty minutes we were clear again, and running under the stars at full speed.

I woke up several times in the night to hear the horn again sounding through the wet night air. It was a very dismal sound, premonitory, perhaps, of coming trouble, for Fortune is the least capricious of deities, and arranges things on the just and rigid system that no one shall be very happy for very long.

We came into harbour at Harwich early next morning; a special train was waiting for us; I lunched in London.

REMOTE PEOPLE

CONTENTS

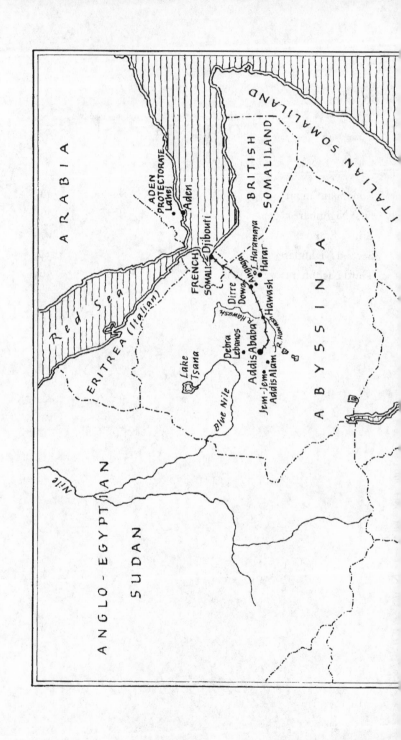

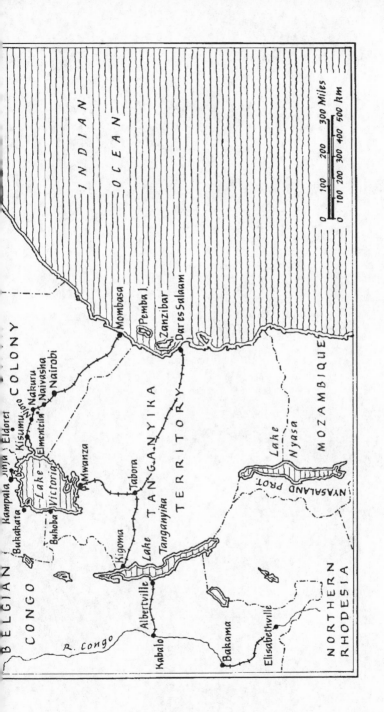

ETHIOPIAN EMPIRE

CHAPTER 1

THEY WERE STILL dancing when, just before dawn on October 19th, 1930, the *Azay le Rideau* came into harbour at Djibouti. The band – a pitiably hot quartet in alpaca dinner-jackets – had long ago packed up their instruments and retired to their remote and stifling cabin. An Anamite boy was swabbing the deck and pushing into the scuppers sodden masses of paper streamers. Two or three stewards were at work pulling down the flags and festoons of coloured lights with which the ship had been decorated. One couple remained.

The girl was a second-class passenger to Mauritius; she was clearly of mixed blood, and she had chosen to wear the costume of a Tyrolean peasant, hired for the night from the ship's barber. Her partner was an officer in the French Foreign Legion; he wore an ill-fitting white uniform, open at the throat; he was quite young, blue-chinned, slightly pot-bellied, shorter than she by several inches. Their feet moved slowly over the wet boards to the music of a portable gramophone; at intervals they stopped, and unclasped each other, to rewind the instrument and reverse the single record.

For two days of gross heat the ship had been *en fête*. There had been deck-games, races for the children, a tombola with two-franc tickets and such prizes as could be procured on board – bottles of vermouth and eau-de-Cologne, tins of tobacco, sweets, lumps of coral, and ornamental cigarette-holders from Port Said. An autographed photograph of Marshal d'Esperez had been put up to auction and sold, amid wild applause, to a Press photographer for 900 francs; a cinema film had been exhibited by one of the passengers, with a faltering light on a screen that flapped restlessly in the hot breeze; there had been a horse-race decided by throw of dice, with a pari-mutuel and many hotly disputed results; at the deck bar there had been frequent orders for champagne, shared among families of French officials, six or eight of them to a bottle. Finally, on the last evening of the voyage, the fête had culminated in a fancy-dress dinner, a concert, and a ball.

It was a widely diverse company who had been thus indulged. There sat at my table a red-headed American on his way to Saigon, where he hoped to sell agricultural machinery; his watch-chain was loaded with Masonic insignia, he wore a ring of the interlaced initials of some other commercial secret society, he had Froth Blowers' cuff-links, and a Rotarian wheel in his buttonhole. No doubt he needed some such evidence of good-fellowship to aid his salesmanship, for he was unable to speak a word of French and was obliged to have the menu translated to him by his neighbour, the Italian proprietor of the third-best hotel in Madras. There was also an English girl who wore green sandals, and her mother who carried everywhere a small but assertive lapdog, which formed the basis of many complaints from those who were scandalised by her daughter's carmine toenails. There was a large number of French colonial officials, their wives and disorderly children, who make up the bulk of a normal Messageries Maritimes passenger list, on this occasion reinforced by a draft of the Foreign Legion on their way to preserve discipline in Indo-China. The men travelled fourth class, sprawling about the lower deck by day, battened down in the hold at night. They were mostly Germans and Russians; in the evening they formed into little groups and sang songs. They had a band of drums and mouth-organs which came up to play in the first-class saloon on the evening of the concert. The drum was painted with the device 'Mon Jazz'. Two of them climbed through a port-hole one night in the Suez Canal and escaped. Next day a third tried to follow their example. We were all on deck drinking our morning apéritifs when we heard a splash and saw a shaven-headed figure in shirt-sleeves scrambling up the bank behind us. He had no hat and the sun was at its strongest. He ran through the sand, away from the ship, with gradually slackening speed. When he realised that no one was pursuing him he stopped and turned round. The ship went on. The last we saw of him was a figure stumbling after us and waving his arms. No one seemed the least put out by the occurrence.

My cabin steward usually had some story to tell me of daily life on the lower deck. One day two of the legionaries began fighting and were put in the cells; another day a Chinaman went mad in the night and tried to commit suicide; another day there had been a theft on board, and so on. I think he used to invent a great deal to amuse me.

Besides this normal traffic of the line, there were about twenty of us bound for Djibouti on our way to Abyssinia for the emperor's coronation. My own presence there requires some explanation. Six weeks before, I had barely heard Ras Tafari's name. I was in Ireland, staying in a house where chinoiserie and Victorian Gothic contend for mastery over a Georgian structure. We were in the library, discussing over the atlas a journey I proposed to make to China and Japan. We began talking of other journeys, and so of Abyssinia. One of the party was on leave from Cairo; he knew something of Abyssinian politics and the coming coronation. Further information was contributed from less reliable sources; that the Abyssinian Church had canonised Pontius Pilate, and consecrated their bishops by spitting on their heads; that the real heir to the throne was hidden in the mountains, fettered with chains of solid gold; that the people lived on raw meat and mead; we looked up the royal ramily in the *Almanack de Gotha* and traced their descent from Solomon and the Queen of Sheba; we found a history which began: 'The first certain knowledge which we have of Ethiopian history is when Cush the son of —— ascended the throne immediately after the Deluge'; an obsolete encyclopaedia informed us that, 'though nominally Christian, the Abyssinians are deplorably lax in their morals, polygamy and drunkenness being common even among the highest classes and in the monasteries'. Everything I heard added to the glamour of this astonishing country. A fortnight later I was back in London and had booked my passage to Djibouti. Two days later I was in a railway train going to Gloucestershire, where I met a friend who works on the staff of a London daily newspaper. I began boasting to him of my trip. My only anxiety was whether, as a tripper, I should be able to obtain access to the more interesting ceremonies. He said he thought that it might be arranged for me to go in some subordinate position to assist the paper. Accordingly, on my return from the weekend I saw his foreign editor and emerged from the interview for the first time in my life a fully accredited journalist, with a miniature passport authorising me to act as special correspondent during the ten days' coronation celebrations at Addis Ababa. Five days later I was on board the *Azay le Rideau* at Marseille, and ten days after that I was standing on deck in my pyjamas watching the dawn break over the low coastline of French Somaliland and over the haggard couple dancing to the gramophone.

Sleep had been impossible for some time, as the servants of the Egyptian delegation had been at work assembling their masters' luggage immediately opposite the door of my cabin. Tin trunk after tin trunk was dragged out with loud military commands from the servant in charge and loud unmilitary remonstrances from his subordinates. It seemed hardly conceivable that five men could have so many clothes. And after the tin trunks came the great crates which contained the King of Egypt's present to the emperor. These had appeared on board at Port Said under escort of an armed patrol, and throughout the voyage had been guarded with some ostentation; their contents had been the object of wild speculation among the passengers, our imaginations wallowing in a profusion of biblical opulence – frankincense, sardonyx, madrepore, and porphyry. In point of fact, as appeared later, they contained a handsome but unexceptional suite of bedroom furniture.

There were three other delegations on board, from France, Holland, and Poland; a fourth, the Japanese, was awaiting our arrival at Djibouti. When not exchanging ceremonious introductions,[1] or pacing the decks at great speed, these envoys occupied themselves with finely emblazoned dispatch-cases, writing, typing and annotating their complimentary addresses.

At first sight there is something a little surprising in this sudden convergence on Abyssinia of the envoys of the civilised world, and I think that the Abyssinians were as surprised as anyone. After the sudden death of the Empress Zauditu in the spring of the

---

1 One of the first discoveries I made in my new profession was that nearly everyone in public life is obsessed by the fear that his name will be spelled wrong. As soon as it became known that I was a journalist – on board, and later at Addis Ababa – I was again and again approached by diffident officials tendering cards engraved with their names and correct titles.

year, immediately subsequent to the defeat of her husband Ras Gougsa, Ras Tafari notified the Powers that he proposed, as soon as he decently could, to assume the title of Emperor of Ethiopia, and included in this announcement, in the case of those few nations who maintained diplomatic representatives at his Court, an invitation to attend the ceremonies. A few years before, he had been crowned Negus; on that occasion his immediate neighbours had taken a few days' holiday to visit him, and there had been a mild exchange of courtesies by telegram. Something a little more conspicuous was expected of the imperial coronation, but the response of the world Powers exceeded Ethiopian expectation in a manner that was both gratifying and embarrassing. The states less directly interested in African affairs construed the notification as an invitation, and those with important local interests seized the opportunity for a display of cordiality and esteem out of all proportion to anything their previous relations with the country had given reason to expect. Two govern-ments sent members of their royal families; the United States of America sent a gentleman of experience in the electric installation trade; the Governors of British Somaliland, the Soudan, Eritrea, the Resident at Aden, a marshal of France, an admiral, three airmen, and a marine band all appeared in various uniforms and orders. Substantial sums of public money were diverted to the purchase of suitable gifts; the Germans brought a signed photograph of General von Hindenburg and eight hundred bottles of Hock; the Greeks a modern bronze statuette; the Italians an aeroplane, the British a pair of elegant sceptres with an inscription composed, almost correctly, in Amharic.

Why all this fuss? Many people, even those intimately involved, were asking themselves this question. The simpler Abyssinians in-terpreted it as a suitable tribute to Abyssinian greatness; the kings of the world were doing homage. Others, a little more versed in world affairs, saw in it some plot against Abyssinian integrity – the *ferangi* had come to spy out the land. Honest colonists all over Africa grumbled at this absurd display of courtesy towards a mere native. At the legations themselves there was some restlessness; all this would still further complicate the task of impressing on the Abyssi-nians their real unimportance in the greater world; but what could they do? If some Powers chose to send dukes and princes, sceptres and aeroplanes, what could the others do but follow as best they could? Who started the stampede? And the Abyssinian Government may have wondered a little apprehensively how all these august gate-crashers were to be accommodated, and how the expenses of hospitality were to be met out of an irregular revenue and a depreciated currency. Why all this fuss?

One need not explore any deep political cause for a plausible explanation. Addis Ababa is not a place where great diplomatic reputations are easily won, the potentates of the Foreign Office do not keep any very keen scrutiny to see how their cadets are shaping in that rare altitude. Diplomatic appointments there may be a suitable reward for an industrious consul-general, but it is scarcely the foundation of a career. Who could blame these officials if occasionally there crept into their dispatches phrases tending to estimate with some generosity the importance of the land of their exile? Is Abyssinia not the source of the Blue Nile? May there not be vast mineral wealth in those unprospected hills? And if, in the trivial course of compound life, that unvarying round of modest entertainment, there suddenly came to the women of the diplomatic corps – poor half-sisters of the great ladies of Washington or Rome – the possibility of sudden splendour, of royalty and gold braid, curtseys and champagne and handsome ADCs, who can blame them if they strengthened their menfolk in urging the importance of really imposing special representation at the festivities?

And need one wonder if states very remote from Africa – sledded Polaks and blond Swedes – decided to join in the party? If the glamour of Abyssinia had drawn me there from a life of comparative variety and freedom, why not them from their grey chanceries? Gun-cases among their trunks of uniform showed that they intended to make the most of their jaunt, and several of them, I know, had paid their own fares. 'Nous avons quatre citoyens ici, mais deux sont juifs,' one attaché explained to me, and proceeded to demonstrate the apparatus with which, during his sojourn in Africa, he hoped to add to his already extensive collection of butterflies.

*

Day broadened rapidly and the dancers finally separated and went off to bed. Lighters came out from shore and coaling began. Planks stretched between the ship and the barges. One of them broke, throwing the Somali coolies heavily on to the coal – a drop of ten feet or more. One lay on his back groaning after the others had got up. The foreman threw a lump of coal at him. He groaned and turned on to his face; another lump, and he staggered to his feet and resumed work. Somali boys came swimming round the ship calling for money to be thrown them. Passengers appeared on deck.

We lay well out in the bay. Between us and the landing-stage lay the wreck of a large cargo boat, heeled over on her side, swept clear, and corroded by the tide. She is mentioned in Armandy's *La Désagréable Partie de Campagne*.

Soon it began to rain.

Great uncertainty prevailed as to how or when we should get to Addis Ababa. The purser had been most reassuring. He had wired to the station informing them of the number of passengers, he said. A special train would be ready for us that day. There were conflicting rumours about, however. Those who had some previous acquaintance with Abyssinia remarked that things could not conceivably be as smooth as that. Report circulated that there was to be a special train, but that it was only for the delegations; a further report that there were to be two trains, one that morning for delegations, one in the evening for unofficial passengers; that a shipload of passengers were arriving that day from Aden from a P. & O. liner, and that there was very little hope of accommodation; that all unofficial traffic had been stopped until after the coronation. The delegations themselves knew nothing of their arrangements except that they were expected to luncheon at the governor's house.

We waited our turn to go ashore with some anxiety. The coolies droned dismally up and down the unstable planks; the little boys in the water cried for francs, or appeared shivering on deck, offering to amuse us by jumping back again; guns on shore boomed the salutes as the Government launch fetched each delegation in turn. The warm rain poured down steadily.

Eventually we were free to land. There was another Englishman
travelling to Addis Ababa, an elderly gentleman on his way to the
legation as a private visitor. Throughout the voyage he had studied
a formidable little book about tropical hygiene, and passed on to me
much disquieting information about malaria and black-water, cholera and elephantiasis; he used, over his cigar in the evenings, to
explain how hook-worms ate their way from the soles of the feet to
the internal organs, how jiggers laid their eggs under the toenails,
and retailed the symptoms of slow paralysis with which the spirillum
tick might infect us.

Together we put our luggage in charge of the French-speaking
native porter of the Hôtel des Arcades and went to the English vice-
consul – an amiable young shipping-clerk – who told us that there
were in fact two trains that evening, but both of them were reserved
for delegations; the next train was three days later; that was
reserved for the Duke of Gloucester; there was another one three
days after that – reserved for Prince Udine. He could hold out very
little hope of our getting up to Addis, but he would see what could be
done. In a state of mind born of this information we drove to the
Hôtel des Arcades. Our topis were soft on our heads, our white suits
clinging about our shoulders. The porter said I must go with him to
the customs. We arrived there to find a damp native soldier on guard
with water running down his rifle. The customs officer was at the
reception at Government House, he said. He could not tell what
time he would return or whether he would return at all that day. By
means of the hotel porter I pointed out that we must have our
luggage to change into dry clothes. Nothing could be moved until
the officer returned, he said. The porter, without more ado, picked
up the nearest pieces and began piling them into the taxi. The guard
remonstrated, but the porter continued undeterred. Then we drove
back to the hotel.

This was a two-storied building with an arcaded front of shabby
stucco; at the back a wooden staircase led to two broad verandahs on
to which the two or three bedrooms opened. There was a lemon-tree
in the yard inhabited by a misanthropic black monkey. The propri-
etress was a handsome Frenchwoman abounding in commercial
good nature. She gave us warm water and a room to change in, and

made light of our troubles. It was her peculiar fortune to subsist upon the inadequacies of the Franco-Ethiopian railway service, for no one voluntarily spends long in Djibouti.

This fact, sufficiently clear from our earliest impression, became clearer when, after luncheon, the rain having stopped, we drove for a tour of the town. We bumped and rocked along in a one-horse cab through pools of steaming mud. The streets, described by the official guide book as 'elegant and smiling', were mere stretches of waste-land between blocks of houses. These, in the European quarter, were mostly built on the same plan as the hotel, arcaded and decaying.

'They look as though they might fall down any minute,' remarked my companion as we drove past one more than usually dissolute block of offices, and while we looked they actually did begin to fall. Great flakes of stucco crumbled from the front; a brick or two, toppling from the coping, splashed into the mud below. Some scared Indian clerks scampered into the open, a Greek in shirt-sleeves appeared from the house opposite, a group of half-naked natives rose from their haunches and, still scouring their teeth with sticks of wood, gazed apprehensively about them. Our driver pointed excitedly with his whip and admonished us in Somali. It had been an earthquake which, in the more sensible motion of the cab, had escaped our notice.

We jolted on past a whitewashed mosque to the camel-market and native quarter. The Somalis are a race of exceptional beauty, very slender and erect, with delicate features and fine, wide-set eyes. Most of them wore a strip of rag around their waists, and a few coils of copper wire on wrists and ankles. Their heads were either shaven or dyed with ochre. Eight or nine harlots besieged our carriage until whipped away by the driver; innumerable naked children splashed through the mud after us, screaming for baksheesh. Some splendid fellows with spears, in from the country, spat contemptuously as we passed. We came to the outskirts of the town, where the huts, formerly grass-thatched, mud-built squares, became little domed structures like inverted birds' nests, made out of twigs, grass, rags, and flattened tins, with one hole through which a man might crawl on his belly. We returned by the sea front past a few fairly ordered goods yards and corrugated-iron sheds. I stopped at the post office and conscientiously cabled back to my employers the arrival of the various delegations. When I returned to the hotel I found the vice-consul there with the good news that he had obtained a carriage for us in the first special train that evening. Elated though we felt, the heat was still overpowering; we went to sleep.

At evening, with the knowledge of our imminent departure, Djibouti suddenly became more tolerable. We visited the shops, bought a French novel with an inflammatory wrapper, some Burma cheroots, and changed some money, getting, in return for our tattered and grimy notes of the Banque d'Indo-Chine, massive silver dollars of superb design.[1]

Most recent books about Abyssinia – and I had read many between West Meath and Marseille – contain graphic descriptions of the train journey between Djibouti and Addis Ababa. Normally there is a weekly service which does the journey in three days; the two nights are spent in hotels at Dirre-Dowa and Hawash. There are several good reasons for not travelling at night; one is that the lights in the train are liable to frequent failure; another that during the rainy season it is not unusual for parts of the line to get washed away; another that the Galla and Danakil, through whose country the line passes, are still primarily homicidal in their interests, and in the early days of the railway formed a habit, not yet wholly eradicated, of

1 The Marie Thérèse thaler, ousted elsewhere in Africa by the meagre rupee or the sordid East African shilling, is still the basic coin of Abyssinia. It is not the most commodious form of currency. It varies in value with the price of silver, and gives opportunity for a great deal of rather shady speculation. Notes are issued by the Bank of Abyssinia against a silver deposit. Even at Dirre-Dowa, two stations down the line from Addis, the local branch of the bank charges a three per cent discount in cashing them, and except in the capital or on the railway they are quite valueless. I saw a small caravan setting out for three months in the interior which carried two mule-loads of dollars for current expenses. It is the coin which the people are used to, and they insist on having it. The Menelik dollar went out of circulation because no one wanted it. The half and quarter dollar are accepted after prolonged scrutiny. There are two issues, in one of which the lion's tail is straight, while in the other it curls back at the tip; both are of equally pure silver, but the second is usually refused, even as a tip. A hundred years ago the Marie Thérèse thaler was the coin of the Arab trader from Tangier to Manchuria. Now its general use survives only in Arabia and Ethiopia. It is still minted in Vienna from the 1780 die, a gracious survival which forms, however, a very deceptive introduction to Ethiopian manners.

taking up steel sleepers here and there to forge into spear-heads.[1]
During coronation week, however, it was found necessary, if the
rolling-stock was to be adequate to the additional traffic, to run
through trains. We left Djibouti after dinner on Friday and arrived
at Addis on Sunday morning. There was, of course, no restaurant
car and the few wagon-lits were occupied by the delegations, but my
companion and I had each the side of a first-class carriage to
ourselves; we stopped for meals at wayside buffets; it was a fairly
comfortable journey.

We passed in the darkness the intolerable desolation of French
Somaliland – a country of dust and boulders, utterly devoid of any
sign of life, and arrived at Dirre-Dowa at dawn. This orderly little
township sprang up during the construction of the railway on the
land conceded to the French company, and has lived on the railway
ever since with slightly diminishing prosperity. It contains two
hotels, a café, and a billiard-saloon, a few shops and offices, a bank,
a flour-mill, one or two villas, and the residence of an Abyssinian
governor. Bougainvillaea and acacia-trees border the streets. Twice
a week the arrival of a train stirs up a few hours' activity; travellers
arrive for the hotels; luggage is carried about the street; postal
officials sort out the mail; commercial agents put on their sun-
helmets and saunter down with their invoices to the goods office;
then, like a small island when the mail-boat steams out of harbour,
Dirre-Dowa relapses into its large siesta.

This, however, was no ordinary week. Not since 1916 – the civil
war before the last – when Lej Yasu's Mohammedan followers were
massacred just over the hills at Harar – had Dirre-Dowa known so
many radically disturbing events as this succession of special trains
bringing the emperor's visitors to the coronation. Flagstaffs painted
with the Abyssinian colours had been planted down the main streets,
and lines of yellow, red, and green flags strung between them; motor

1 There are also frequent raids on the telegraph wires, pieces of which are much
valued as bangles and bracelets. Shortly before the coronation, for the convenience of
the Press, the Government seized a number of men who may have been implicated in
the business, cut off a hand and a foot apiece, and exhibited them, one at each halt
down the line. No doubt the example was salutary, but the telegraph service remained
very irregular.

cars had been brought by train from the capital – for there are no roads outside the town – to convey the delegates to breakfast; the irregular troops of the whole province had been mobilised to line the way.

It was a grand and startling spectacle. My companion and I waited behind for some minutes in our carriage until the formal greetings were at an end and the delegates were clear of the station. Then we crossed the platform into the square. It was quite empty and quite silent. On three sides stood the Abyssinian soldiers; in front, where the main avenue led up to the governor's house, the last of the cars was just disappearing; as far as one could see stood the ranks of motionless, white-clothed tribesmen, bareheaded, bare-footed, with guns on their shoulders; some had olive skins and keen aquiline features; others were darker, with thick lips and flat noses showing the infection of slave blood; most of them were of good height and strong physique; all wore curly black beards. Their dress was the invariable costume of the country – a long white shirt, white linen breeches loose above the knee and tight at the calves like jodhpurs, and the *chamma*, a white shawl worn like the toga over one shoulder, and a bandoleer of cartridges prominently displayed. In front of each section stood their chief in the gala dress so frequently photographed for the European Press. This, varying in grandeur with the wearer's wealth, consisted of a head-dress of lion's mane and gold ornament, a lion's skin, a brilliantly striped shirt, and a long sword curving out behind for some three feet or more; in some cases the lion's skin was represented by a garment of embroidered satin, like a chasuble, slit in front and behind in conventionalised tail and legs. It was a memorable experience to emerge, after the Latin holiday-making on the *Azay le Rideau*, the scramble at Djibouti, and the unquiet night in the train, into the sweet early morning air and the peace cast by these motionless warriors; they seemed at once so savage and so docile; great shaggy dogs of uncertain temper held for the moment firmly at leash.

We breakfasted at the hotel, and smoked a pipe on the terrace, awaiting the return of the delegates. Presently the soldiers who had been squatting on their haunches were called to attention; the cars came down the hill bearing diplomats handsomely refreshed by

a banquet of porridge, kippers, eggs, and champagne. We returned
to the train and resumed our journey.

From now until Hawash, where we arrived at sundown, the line
ran through mile upon mile of featureless bush country – thorn,
scrub, and flat, brownish mimosa-trees, and dust, ant-hills, a few
vultures, now and then a dry watercourse or outcrop of stone,
nothing else, hour upon hour. At intervals we stopped for water at
stations consisting of a single shed and barbed-wire compound; here
there was always a guard drawn up to meet us, two or three
uniformed railway police and the local chief with his levy of sometimes a dozen, sometimes fifty, men. At noon we lunched in a tent at
a halt named Afdem; luncheon consisted of four courses of meat
variously prepared. We waited four hours at Hawash, from six until
ten, while mechanics experimented with the lighting of the train; an
armed guard squatted at the door of each coach. There are several
sheds at Hawash, two or three bungalows of railway officials,
a concrete platform, and an inn. After dinner we sat in the yard of
the inn on hard little chairs, or paced about the platform or stumbled
between the steel sleepers of the permanent way; there was no
village or street; it was better to keep in the open as there were
fewer mosquitoes; the lights in the carriage windows flashed feverishly on and off. Presently a group of ragged Gallas appeared and
began to dance; two performed in the centre of the circle; the others
stood round singing, stamping their feet and clapping their hands;
they acted a lion hunt in dumb show. The guards wanted to drive
them away, but the Egyptian Minister restrained them and gave
a handful of dollars to the dancers; this set them going more eagerly
and they spun about in the dust like tops; they were extremely fierce
men, their long hair matted with butter and mud, and their thin,
black bodies hung with scraps of skin and sacking.

At last the lighting was put right and we started again. Hawash
lies at the foot of the highlands; throughout the night we climbed
steadily. Each time we were jolted into consciousness between
intermittent periods of sleep, we found the air fresher and the
temperature lower, and by early morning we had wrapped ourselves
in rugs and overcoats. We breakfasted before dawn at a place called
Mojo and resumed our journey just as the first light began to break.

It revealed a profound change in the landscape; the bush and plain had disappeared, and in its place there extended crests of undulating downland with a horizon of blue mountains. Wherever one looked were rich little farms, groups of circular thatched huts inside high stockades, herds of fine humped cattle browsing in deep pastures, fields of corn and maize being worked by families; camel caravans swayed along the track by the railway, carrying fodder and fuel. The line still mounted, and presently, between nine and ten, we came in sight, far ahead of us, of the eucalyptus-woods that surround Addis Ababa. Here, at a station named Akaki, where an Indian merchant maintains a great warehouse and a ras had constructed a great part of what was to be an hotel, we stopped again to allow the delegates time to shave and put on their uniforms. Tin trunks and dressing-cases appeared again, valets ran between the luggage-van and the sleeping-cars. The Dutch Minister soon appeared at the side of the line in cocked hat and gold braid, the Egyptian in *tarboosh* and epaulettes, the Japanese in evening coats and white waistcoats and top hats; the chiefs inspected their subordinates; then all got into the train again and proceeded. We puffed up the winding track for another half-hour and at last arrived at Addis Ababa.

The station is a large, two-storied, concrete building with a single covered platform. Red carpet had been put out, and before the carpet were drawn up a very different body of troops from those we had passed on the way. These were squat, coal-black boys from the Soudanese border. They wore brand-new, well-cut, khaki uniforms; the lion of Judah shone in polished brass on cap badges and buttons; with bayonets fixed and rifles of recent pattern. Beside them a band of bugle and drums, with a little black drummer poising crossed sticks above the big drum. But for the bare feet below their puttees, they might have been the prize platoon of some Public School OTC. In front of them with drawn sword stood a European officer. This was a squad of Tafari's own guard. Hardly had the blood congealed on Gougsa's mangled corpse, or the bereaved empress succumbed to her sudden chill, before orders had been issued for the formation of this corps. Officers had come from Belgium to undertake the training. The men had been recruited from Tafari's own scattered provinces, bound to the throne by direct feudal allegiance. In six months he had trained a regiment of them – the nucleus of an organised national army.

As the train stopped, the guard presented arms; the head chamberlain advanced in a blue satin cloak to greet the delegations, and the band struck up. This, too, was an innovation. It is my misfortune to be quite insensible to music, but I was told by all who heard them that the tunes played as each delegation was received were, in practically all cases, easily recognisable. One thing I did realise, and that was their unusual length; there was no skimping of difficulties, every anthem was played through thoroughly verse by verse. The Poles came out easy winners in prolixity. Finally the Ethiopian anthem was played; we heard this so often during the next ten days that it became vaguely familiar, even to me. (It began like the Hymn 'Lights above celestial Salem', but ended quite differently.)

Eventually the last delegation disappears. The Minister's daughters have come from the British Legation to meet the train. They ask me what arrangements have been made for my accommodation, and I reply, to the best of my knowledge, none. Consternation. They say that the town is completely full. It will be impossible to get a room now. It is possible there may be a tent somewhere at the legation; it is conceivable that one of the hotels will let me pitch it in the yard. We get into the car and mount the hill into the town. Half-way up we pass the Hôtel de France. At the entrance stands the supremely Western figure of Irene Ravensdale in riding habit. We stop to greet her. I run indoors and ask the manager whether there is, by any chance, a vacant room. Why, yes, certainly. It is not a very good room, it is in an outhouse behind the hotel; but, if I care to take it, it is mine for two pounds a day. I accept eagerly, sign the register, and rejoin Irene. The legation car and the luggage has disappeared. Instead, the street is full of Abyssinians arriving from the country on mules, slaves trotting all round them, clearing and obstructing the way. We return to the hotel, lunch, and go to sleep. Later the luggage turns up in the charge of a good-hearted young Englishman, who, having failed as a coffee farmer, has been engaged temporarily at the legation as general help. The preposterous *Alice in Wonderland* fortnight has begun.

CHAPTER 2

IN FACT, IT is to *Alice in Wonderland* that my thoughts recur in seeking some historical parallel for life in Addis Ababa. There are others: Israel in the time of Saul, the Scotland of Shakespeare's *Macbeth*, the Sublime Porte as one sees it revealed in the dispatches of the late eighteenth century, but it is in *Alice* only that one finds the peculiar flavour of galvanised and translated reality, where animals carry watches in their waistcoat pockets, royalty paces the croquet lawn beside the chief executioner, and litigation ends in a flutter of playing-cards. How to recapture, how retail, the crazy enchantment of these Ethiopian days?

First let me attempt to convey some idea of the setting. Addis Ababa is a new town; so new, indeed, that not a single piece of it appears to be really finished. Menelik the Great chose the site forty years ago and named it, when it was still a hillside encampment, 'The New Flower'. Till then the Government had shifted between the ancient, priest-ridden cities of the north, mobile according to the exigencies of fuel, but morally centred on Axum, the ecclesiastical capital, as the French monarchy centred on Rheims. Menelik was the first king to break the tradition of coronation at Axum, and at the time even his vast military prestige suffered from the breach. It is mentioned by contemporary writers as a source of weakness; actually it was a necessary part of his policy. He was no longer merely king of the Christian, Amharic highlanders, he was emperor of a great territory embracing in the west the black pagan Shankallas, in the east the nomad anthropophagous Danakils, in the south-east the Ogaden Desert inhabited by Somalis, and in the south the great belt of cultivable land held by the Mohammedan Gallas. At Addis

Ababa he found the new centre for his possessions, still in the highlands among his own people, but on their extreme edge; immediately at its foot lies the territory of the wretched Guratchi, the despised, ill-conditioned people who provide the labour for building and sweeping; Hawash is the land of the Gallas. Addis Ababa is the strategic point for the control of these discordant dominions. Lej Yasu contemplated a further, more radical change. It appears to have been his purpose, or the purpose of his counsellors, to reorientate the empire from Harar and build up a great Mohammedan Power which should in the event of the victory of the Central Powers in Europe, enclose the whole Somali coastline. It was an intemperate ambition which needed no European intervention to encompass its downfall. The exact circumstances of his failure may, perhaps, never be known, nor the extent to which these plans were even clearly formulated. It is certain that he was in correspondence with the Mad Mullah in British Somaliland. It is widely believed that he had in his last years frankly apostatised from the Church; his father's Mohammedan origin added colour to this report, and proof was supplied in the form of his portrait wearing a turban which purported to have been taken at Harar. Many, however, declare that this conclusive piece of evidence was fabricated in Addis Ababa by an Armenian photographer. Whatever the truth of these details, the fact is clear that the unfortunate young man fell, not, as is usually said, through his grosser habits of life, which, indeed, tended rather to endear him to his humbler subjects, but through his neglect of what must remain for many years to come the strength of the Ethiopian Empire – its faith and the warlike qualities of the Amharic hillsmen. Lej Yasu has not been seen since 1916. He is said to be living, listless and morbidly obese, under Ras Kassa's guardianship at Fiche, but a traveller who lately passed the reputed house of his capitivity remarked that the roof was out of repair and the entrance overgrown with weeds. People do not readily speak of him, for the whole country is policed with spies, but more than one European who enjoyed the confidence of his servants told me that the name is still greatly respected among the lower orders.

He has, through his mother, the true blood of Menelik. They describe him as a burly young man with compelling eyes, recklessly generous and superbly dissipated. Tafari's astute diplomacy strikes some of them as far less kingly.

There was no constitution in Ethiopia. The succession was determined in theory by royal proclamation, in practice by bloodshed. Menelik had left no male and no legitimate children. Lej Yasu's mother was his daughter and he had nominated Lej Yasu. In the circumstances, Lej Yasu had named no successor and there was thus no indisputable heir. By right of Menelik's blood, his second daughter reigned as the Empress Zauditu, but her religious duties occupied more of her attention than the routine of government. A regent was necessary; three or four noblemen had, by descent, equal claims to the office. The most important of these was Ras Kassa, but deeply concerned with religion and the management of his estates, he was unambitious of wider obligations. The danger which confronted the country was that Menelik's conquests would again disintegrate into a handful of small kingdoms, and that the imperial throne would become a vague overlordship. In such a condition, Abyssinian independence could scarcely hope to survive the penetration of European commercial interests. The rases appreciated the position and realised that there was only one man whose rank, education, intellect, and ambition qualified him for the throne. This was Ras Tafari. Accordingly, by their consent and choice, he became Negus. With the general public, outside his own provinces, his prestige was slight; he was distinguished neither by the blood of Menelik nor any ostentatious feat of arms. Among the rases he was *primus inter pares*; one of themselves chosen to do a job, and answerable to them for its satisfactory execution. From this precarious position in the years that followed, Tafari gradually built up and consolidated his supremacy. He travelled in Europe; he was at pains to impress visiting Europeans with his enlightenment. He played on the rivalries of the French and Italian representatives, and secured his own position at home by advancing his country's position in the world. He obtained admission to the League of Nations; everywhere he identified himself with his country, until Europe came to look to him as its natural ruler.

Even so, he had to fight for his throne. In the spring of 1930 a powerful noble named Ras Gougsa[1] rebelled. He was the husband of the empress; they had been divorced, but maintained cordial and intimate relations. Tafari's army was victorious, and, in the blood-thirsty rout, Gougsa was himself slain. The empress died suddenly next day, and Tafari, with the assent of the rases, proclaimed himself emperor, fixing for his coronation the earliest date by which preparations could adequately be made. The coronation festivities were thus the final move in a long and well-planned strategy. Still maintaining his double ruff of trumping at home with prestige abroad, abroad with his prestige at home, Tafari had two main motives behind the display. He wished to impress on his European visitors that Ethiopia was no mere agglomeration of barbarous tribes open to foreign exploitation, but a powerful, organised, modern state. He wanted to impress on his own countrymen that he was no paramount chief of a dozen independent communities, but an absolute monarch recognised on equal terms by the monarchies and governments of the great world. And if, in the minds of any of his simpler subjects, courtesy and homage became at all confused, if the impression given was that these braided delegates (out for a holiday from their serious duties, an unusual pageant, and perhaps a few days' shooting) had come in their ruler's name to pay tribute to Ethiopian supremacy – so much the better. The dismembered prisoners of Adowa were still unavenged. The disconcertingly eager response of the civilised Powers gave good colour to this pretension. 'We did not think so much of Tafari,' remarked the servant of one Englishman, 'until we learned that your king was sending his own son to the coronation'; and there can be no doubt that the other rases, confronted at close quarters with the full flood of European diplomacy, realised more clearly that other qualities were needed for the government of a modern state than large personal property and descent from Solomon. This very exuberance, however, of European interest tended to hinder the accomplishment of the emperor's first ambition. The gun-cases were his undoing, for in the days that

1 There is a Ras Gougsa, quite unconnected with the rebel, who is still living. He acted as host to the American delegation during the coronation.

followed the celebrations, when the delegations were scattered on safari about the interior of the country, they had the opportunity of observing more than had been officially prepared for them. They saw just how far the emperor's word ran in the more distant parts of his dominions; they saw the frail lines of communication which bound the Government to its outposts; they saw something of the real character of the people, and realised how inadequate an introduction to the national life were the caviare and sweet champagne of Addis Ababa.

I have said above that the coronation was fixed for the earliest date by which preparations could be made. This statement needs some qualification and brings me back from this political digression to the description of Addis Ababa with which I began the chapter, for the first, obvious, inescapable impression was that nothing was ready or could possibly be made ready in time for the official opening of the celebrations six days hence. It was not that one here and there observed traces of imperfect completion, occasional scaffolding or patches of unset concrete; the whole town seemed still in a rudimentary stage of construction. At every corner were half-finished buildings; some had been already abandoned; on others, gangs of ragged Guraghi were at work. It is difficult to convey in words any real idea of the inefficiency to which low diet and ill-will had reduced these labourers. One afternoon I watched a number of them, twenty or thirty in all, under the surveillance of an Armenian contractor, at work clearing away the heaps of rubble and stone which encumbered the courtyard before the main door of the palace. The stuff had to be packed into wooden boxes swung between two poles, and emptied on a pile fifty yards away. Two men carried each load, which must have weighed very little more than an ordinary hod of bricks. A foreman circulated among them, carrying a long cane. When he was engaged elsewhere the work stopped altogether. The men did not sit down, chat, or relax in any way; they simply stood stock-still where they were, motionless as cows in a field, sometimes arrested with one small stone in their hands. When the foreman turned his attention towards them they began to move again, very deliberately, like figures in a slow-motion film; when he beat them they did not look round or remonstrate, but quickened their movements just perceptibly; when the blows ceased they lapsed into their original pace until the foreman's back being turned, they again stopped completely. (I wondered whether the Pyramids were built in this way.) Work of this nature was in progress in every street and square of the town.

Addis Ababa extends five or six miles in diameter. It lies at a height of eight thousand feet, with a circle of larger hills to the north of it, culminating at Entoto in a mountain of about ten thousand. The station is at the southern extremity of the town, and from it a broad road leads up to the post office and principal commercial buildings. Two deep watercourses traverse the town, and round their slopes, and in small groves of eucalyptus scattered between the more permanent buildings, lie little clusters of *tukals*, round native huts, thatched and windowless. Down the centre of the main thoroughfares run metalled tracks for motor-traffic, bordered on either side by dust and loose stones for mules and pedestrians; at frequent intervals are sentry-boxes of corrugated iron, inhabited by drowsy, armed policemen; there are also police at point duty, better trained than most of the motor-drivers in European signals of control. Attempts are even made, with canes and vigorous exchanges of abuse, to regulate the foot-traffic, a fad which proves wholly unintelligible to the inhabitants. The usual way for an Abyssinian gentleman to travel is straight down the middle of the road on mule-back with ten or twenty armed retainers trotting all round him; there are continual conflicts between the town police and the followers of the country gentleman, from which the police often come out the worse.

Every man in Abyssinia carries arms; that is to say, he wears a dagger and bandoleer of cartridges round his waist and has a slave-boy walking behind with a rifle. There is some question about the efficacy of these weapons, which are mostly of some antiquity. Some are of the Martini type, probably salvaged from the field of Adowa, others are comparatively modern, bolt-action weapons and old, English service-rifles. They have percolated through singly from Somaliland and been brought in, disguised as other merchandise, by such romantic gun-runners as Arthur Rimbaud and M. de Montfried. Cartridges are a symbol of wealth and, in the interior, a recognised medium of exchange; their propriety for any particular brand of firearm is a matter of secondary importance; often the brass ammunition displayed in the bandoleers will not fit the rifle carried behind, and there is usually a large percentage of expended cartridges among it.

The streets are always a lively scene; the universal white costume being here and there relieved by the brilliant blues and violets of mourning or the cloaks of the upper classes. The men walk about hand in hand in pairs and little groups; quite often they are supporting some insensible drunkard. Women appear in the markets, but take no part in the general street-lounging of their men. Occasionally a woman of high degree passes on a mule; under a vast felt hat her face is completely bandaged over with white silk, so that only the two eyes appear, like those of a hooded rider of the Ku Klux Klan. There are numerous priests, distinguished by long gowns and high turbans. Sometimes the emperor passes in a great red car surrounded by cantering lancers. A page sits behind holding over his head an umbrella of crimson silk embroidered with sequins and gold tassels. A guard sits in front nursing a machine-gun under a plush shawl; the chauffeur is a European wearing powder-blue livery and the star of Ethiopia.

There are open fields immediately round the station, broken on one side by the thin roof of the public baths, where a spring wells up scalding hot. It is from here that the water is conveyed in petrol-cans for our baths at the hotel. On the other side of the road stands the execution shed. Public hanging has recently been abolished in Tafari's own provinces, and the gibbet-tree before the cathedral cut down to make room for a little (unfinished) garden and a statue of Menelik. Homicides are now shot behind closed doors, though the bereaved relatives still retain the right of carrying out the sentence. No distinction is made in Abyssinian law between manslaughter and murder; both are treated as offences against the family of the dead man. It is for them to choose whether they will take blood-money or blood; the price varies with the social status of the deceased, but is usually about a thousand dollars (£70 or £80). Occasionally the murderer prefers to die rather than pay. There was a case in Addis Ababa shortly before our arrival in which the bargaining was continued in the execution shed right up to the firing of the shot; the relatives abating their price dollar by dollar, the murderer steadfastly refusing to deprive his children of their full inheritance.

As part of the general policy for tidying up the town for the arrival of the visitors, high stockades have been erected, or are being erected, down all the streets, screening from possibly critical eyes the homes of the poorer inhabitants. Half-way up the hill stands the Hôtel de France, a place of primitive but cordial hospitality, kept by a young Frenchman and his wife who have seen better days as traders in hides and coffee at Djibouti. At the top of the hill, in front of the post office, two main roads branch out to right and left, the one leading to the Gebbi (Tafari's palace), the other to the native bazaar and Indian quarter. Work is in progress at the crossroads making a paved and balustraded island round a concrete cenotaph which is destined to commemorate the late empress. A fourth road leads obliquely to Gorgis, the cathedral of St George.

The buildings are mostly of concrete and corrugated iron. There is another large hotel kept by a Greek, the Imperial, most of which has been requisitioned for the Egyptian delegation. There are two or three small hotels, cafés, and bars, kept either by Greeks or Armenians. There is another large hotel under construction. It was being made specially for the coronation, but is still hopelessly unready. It is here that the Marine band of HMS *Effingham* are put up. A night-club advertises that it will open shortly with a cabaret straight from the Winter Garden Theatre in Munich; it is called Haile Selassie (Power of the Trinity). This is the new name which the emperor has assumed among his other titles; a heavy fine is threatened to anyone overheard referring to him as Tafari. The words have become variously corrupted by the European visitors to 'Highly Salacious' and 'I love a lassie' – this last the inspiration of an RAC mechanic.

The bank and the manager's house are the two most solid buildings in the town; they stand behind a high wall in a side street between the two hotels. Round them are the two or three villas of the European traders, the bank officials, and the English chaplain. The shops are negligible; wretched tin stores, kept by Indians and Armenians, peddling tinned foods, lumps of coarse soap, and tarnished hardware. There is one shop of interest near the bank, kept by a French-speaking Abyssinian. It is called 'Curiosities' and exhibits anything from monkey-skins and cheap native jewellery to Amharic illuminated manuscripts of antiquity. Here I bought a number of modern Abyssinian paintings, mostly either hunting-scenes or intensely savage battle-pictures. Painting is more or less a hereditary craft in Abyssinia. It is in regular demand for ecclesiastical decoration. The churches of Abyssinia are all built on the same plan of a square inner sanctuary enclosed in two concentric ambulatories; sometimes the outside plan is octagonal, sometimes circular. It is very rarely that anyone except the priests is allowed to see into the sanctuary. Attention is concentrated on its walls, which are covered with frescos. The designs are traditional and are copied and recopied, generation after generation, with slight variation. When they begin to grow shabby and the church can afford it, a painter is called in to repaint them, as in Europe one calls in the paperhanger. In the intervals of executing these commissions the more skilful painters keep their hands in by doing secular work on sheets of linen or skins; these too are traditional in composition, but the artist is allowed more freedom in detail. His chief concern is to bring the old patterns up to date, and this he does, irrespective of historical propriety, by the introduction of topis, aeroplanes, and bombs. The secretary of the American Legation gave me a particularly delightful representation of the death of the Harar giant; this story is a very early mediæval legend, probably connected with the wars against the Arabs, but the artist has drawn the giant-slayers with the khaki uniforms and fixed bayonets of Tafari's latest guard – a happy change after the stale, half-facetious, pre-Raphaelite archaism that seems ineradicable in English taste.

The Gebbi is a great jumble of buildings on a hill to the east of the town. At night, during coronation week, it was lit up with rows of electric bulbs, but by day it presented a slightly dingy appearance. The nucleus consists of a stone building containing a throne-room and banqueting-hall; a glazed corridor runs down one side, many of the panes were broken and all were dirty; the front is furnished with a double staircase and portico, clearly of classic sympathies. It was made for Menelik by a French architect. (It might well have been the hôtel de ville of some French provincial town.) In front of this is an untidy courtyard, irregular in shape, littered with loose stones and blown paper, and, all round it, sheds and outbuildings of all kinds and sizes; tin guard-houses, a pretty thatched chapel, barnlike apartments of various Court officials, servants' quarters, laundry and kitchens, a domed mausoleum in debased Byzantine style, a look-out tower and a barrack square. High walls encircle the whole, and the only approach, through which came alike butchers and ambassadors, is through two heavily guarded doors. In spite of this, the precincts seemed to be always full of loafers, squatting and squabbling, or gaping at the visitors.

The American Legation is not far from the centre of the town, but the British, French, and Italians all live beyond the racecourse, five or six miles out. Menelik chose the site of the concession, and the reason usually given for their remoteness is to ensure their safety in case of trouble. In point of fact, they are wholly indefensible, and, if an attack were ever made on them, would be unable to withstand half a day's siege. The social result, for better or worse, has been to divorce the diplomatic corps from the general life of the town. It may be this that Menelik desired.

It is now possible to reach the British Legation by car; until quite lately guests rode out to dinner on mules, a boy running in front with a lantern. Indeed, as further preparation for the visitors, the road from the town had been strewn with stones, and a motor-roller of the latest pattern brought from Europe; this machine was sometimes seen heading for the legations, but some untoward event always interposed, and the greater part of the way was left to be rolled by the tyres of private cars. It was an expensive and bumpy journey.

The legation stands in a small park with the consulate next to it, and on either side of the drive a little garden city has sprung up of pretty thatched bungalows which accommodate the other officials. During the coronation a camp was pitched in the paddock for the staffs of the various visitors, and periodic bugling, reminiscent of an ocean liner, added a fresh incongruity to the bizarre life of the little community. At normal times this consisted of the Minister, lately arrived from Shanghai, a Chinese scholar whose life's work had been in the Far East; the secretary, lately arrived from Constantinople; the consul, lately arrived from Fez, an authority and enthusiast in Mohammedan law (none of these had yet had time to learn any Amharic); the archivist, who had spent five or six years at Addis and knew how to mark out tennis-courts; the vice-consul, who performed prodigies of skill in sorting out luggage and looking up trains, despite the fact that he was all the time seriously ill from the after-effects of blackwater fever, and the oriental secretary, whom a perfect command of Amharic and fair smattering of English made invaluable as official interpreter.

Besides the officials and officers of all grades who now swelled the household, a substantial family party of uncles, aunts, and cousins had come out from England to see the fun. Housekeeping assumed a scale unprecedented in Addis Ababa, but all moved smoothly; a cook was specially imported from London who, happily enough, turned out to be named Mr Cook; the invitation cards from the British Legation greatly surpassed those of all other nations in thickness, area, and propriety of composition, and when it was discovered that by an engraver's error the name *Haile* had become *Hailu* (the name of the most formidable of the rival rases) no pains were spared to correct each card in pen and ink; the Duke's luggage was no sooner lost by one official than it was recovered by another. Everything bore witness to the triumph of Anglo-Saxon organisation.

Outside the legations was a personnel of supreme diversity. There was the Caucasian manager of the Haile Selassie Casino; the French editor of the *Courier d'Éthiope*, an infinitely helpful man, genial, punctilious, sceptical; an Englishman in the employ of the Abyssinian Government, debonair of appearance, but morbidly ill at ease in the presence of journalists before whom he might betray himself into some indiscretion; a French architect married to an Abyssinian; a bankrupt German planter obsessed by grievances; a tipsy old Australian prospector, winking over his whisky and hinting at the mountains full of platinum he could tell you about if he cared to. There was Mr Hall, in whose office I spent many frantic hours; he was a trader, of mixed German and Abyssinian descent, extremely handsome, well dressed, and monocled, a man of imperturbable courtesy, an exceptional linguist. During the coronation he had been put in a little tin house next to the Casino and constituted chief, and, as far as one could see, sole member, of a *bureau d'étrangers*. It was his week's task to listen to all the troubles of all the foreigners, official or unofficial, to distribute news to the Press, issue tickets and make out lists for the Abyssinian functions; if the Italian telegraph company took an hour's rest, it was Mr Hall who heard the complaints; if an officious police officer refused someone admittance to some grand stand, Mr Hall must see to it that the officer was reprimanded; if His Majesty's Stationery Office forgot to issue the text of the coronation service, Mr Hall promised everyone a copy; if a charabanc had not arrived to take the band to the racecourse, if there had not been enough coronation medals to go round the church, if, for any reason or no reason, anyone in Addis Ababa was in a bad temper – and at that altitude the most equable natures become unaccountably upset – off he went to Mr Hall. And whatever language he cared to speak, Mr Hall would understand and sympathise; with almost feminine delicacy he would calm him and compliment him; with masculine decision he would make a bold note of the affair on his pad; he would rise, bow, and smile his pacified visitor out with every graceful assurance of goodwill – and do absolutely nothing about it.

Of the Abyssinians we saw very little except as grave, rather stolid figures at the official receptions. There was Ras Hailu, owner of the rich province of Gojam, reputed wealthier than the emperor himself; a commanding figure, dark complexioned, and his little pointed beard dyed black, and slightly insolent eyes. Among his many great possessions was a night club two miles out on the Addis Alem road. He had planned this himself and, wishing to be up-to-date, had given it an English name. It was called 'Robinson'. There was the venerable Ras Kassa and Moulungetta, the commander-in-chief of the army, a mountain of a man with grey beard and bloodshot eyes; in full-dress uniform with scarlet-and-gold cloak and lion's mane busby, he looked hardly human; there was George Herui, son of the Minister of Foreign Affairs, the product of an English university – a slight young man dressed with great elegance either in European clothes or in the uniform of a Court page; his father stood high in the emperor's confidence; George's interest, however, seemed mainly Parisian.

Apart from the officials and journalists who pullulated at every corner, there were surprisingly few visitors. At one time Messrs Thomas Cook & Company were advertising a personally conducted tour, an announcement which took a great deal of the romance out of our expedition. The response was considerable, but when their agent arrived it soon became apparent that the enterprise was inpracticable; there was no certainty of transport or accommodation, and, with soaring prices and fluctuating currency, it was impossible to give an estimate of the expenses involved. So the tour was cancelled, but the agent remained, a cocksure, dapper little Italian, an unfailing source of inaccurate information on all local topics.

There was a slightly class-conscious lady with a French title and an American accent, who left the town suddenly after a luncheon-party at which she was not accorded her proper precedence. There was the American professor, who will appear later in this narrative, and two formidable ladies in knitted suits and topis; though unrelated by blood, long companionship had made them almost indistinguishable, square-jawed, tight-lipped, with hard, discontented eyes. For them the whole coronation was a profound disappointment. What did it matter that they were witnesses of a unique stage of the interpenetration of two cultures? They were out for Vice. They were collecting material, in fact, for a little book on the subject, an African *Mother India*, and every minute devoted to Coptic ritual or displays of horsemanship was a minute wasted. Prostitution and drug traffic comprised their modest interests, and they were too dense to find evidence of either.

But perhaps the most remarkable visitors were the Marine band. At first the emperor had intended to import a European dance-band from Cairo, but the estimate for fees and expenses was so discouraging that he decided instead to issue an invitation to the band of HMS *Effingham* to attend the coronation as his guests and to play at the various functions. They arrived on the same day as the Duke of Gloucester, under the command of Major Sinclair, strengthened by a diet of champagne at breakfast, luncheon, tea, and dinner throughout their journey, and much sage advice about the propriety of their behaviour in a foreign capital. At Addis they were quartered in a large, unfinished hotel; each man had his own bedroom, furnished by his thoughtful hosts with hairbrushes, clothes-hangers, and brand-new enamelled spittoons.

Perhaps no one did more to deserve his star of Ethiopia than Major Sinclair. Eschewing the glitter and dignity of the legation camp, he loyally remained with his men in the town, and spent anxious days arranging appointments that were never kept; his diary, which some of us were privileged to see, was a stark chronicle of successive disappointments patiently endured. '*Appointment 9.30 emperor's private secretary to arrange for this evening's banquet; he did not come. 11. Went as arranged to see master of the king's music; he was not there. 12. Went to see Mr Hall to obtain score of Ethiopian national anthem – not procurable. 2.30. Car should have come to take men to aerodrome – did not arrive . . .*' and so on. But, in spite of every discouragement, the band was always present on time, irreproachably dressed, and provided with the correct music.

One morning in particular, on which the band played a conspicuous part, remains vividly in my memory as typical of the whole week. It was the first day of the official celebrations, to be inaugurated by the unveiling of the new Menelik memorial. The ceremony was announced for ten o'clock. Half an hour before the time, Irene Ravensdale and I drove to the spot. Here, on the site of the old execution-tree, stood the monument, shrouded in brilliant green silk. Round it was a little ornamental garden with paving, a balustrade, and regular plots, from which, here and there, emerged delicate shoots of newly sown grass. While some workmen were laying carpets on the terrace and spreading yellow sunshades of the kind which cover the tables at open-air restaurants, others were still chipping at the surrounding masonry and planting drooping palm-trees in the arid beds. A heap of gilt arm-chairs lay on one side; on the other a mob of photographers and movietone men were fighting for places. Opposite the carpeted terrace rose a stand of several unstable tiers. A detachment of policemen were engaged furiously laying about them with canes in the attempt to keep these seats clear of natives. Four or five Europeans were already established there. Irene and I joined them. Every ten minutes or so a police officer would appear and order us all off; we produced our *laissez-passers*; he saluted and went away, to be succeeded at a short interval by a colleague, when the performance was repeated.

The square and half a mile of the avenue approaching it were lined with royal guards; there was a band formed up in front of them; the Belgian colonel curvetted about on an uneasy chestnut horse. Presently, punctual to the minute, appeared Major Sinclair and his band. They had had to march from their hotel, as the charabanc ordered for them had failed to appear. They halted, and Major Sinclair approached the Belgian colonel for instructions. The colonel knew no English, and the major no French; an embarrassing interview followed, complicated by the caprices of the horse, which plunged backwards and sideways over the square. In this way the two officers covered a large area of ground, conversing inconclusively the while with extravagant gestures. Eventually Irene heroically stepped out to interpret for them. It appeared that the Belgian colonel had had no orders about the English band. He had his own band there and did not want another. The major explained he had direct instructions to appear in the square at ten. The colonel said the major could not possibly stay in the square; there was no room for him, and anyway he would have no opportunity of playing, since the native band had a programme of music fully adequate for the whole proceedings. (Knowing that band's tendency to repetition, we could well believe it.) At last the colonel conceded that the English band might take up a position at the extreme end of his troops at the bottom of the hill. The officers parted, and the band marched away out of sight. A long wait followed, while the battle between police and populace raged round the stand. At last the delegations began to arrive; the soldiers presented arms; the native band played the appropriate music; the Belgian colonel was borne momentarily backwards through the ranks, capered heroically among the crowd, and reappeared at another corner of the square. The delegations took up their places on the gilt chairs under the umbrellas. A long pause preceded the emperor's arrival; the soldiers still stood stiff. Suddenly up that imposing avenue there appeared a slave, trotting unconcernedly with a gilt chair on his head. He put it among the others, looked round with interest at the glittering uniforms, and then retired. At last the emperor came; first a troop of lancers, then the crimson car and silk umbrella. He took up his place in the centre of the Court under a blue canopy; the band played the Ethiopian national anthem. A secretary presented him with the text of his speech; the cameramen began snapping and turning. But there was a fresh delay. Something had gone wrong. Messages passed from mouth to mouth; a runner disappeared down the hill.

One photographer, bolder than the rest, advanced out of the crowd and planted his camera within a few yards of the royal party; he wore a violet suit of plus-fours, a green shirt open at the neck, tartan stockings, and parti-coloured shoes. After a few happy shots of the emperor he walked slowly along the line, looking the party critically up and down. When he found anyone who attracted his attention, he took a photograph of him. Then, expressing his satisfaction with a slight inclination of the head, he rejoined his colleagues.

Still a delay. Then up the avenue came Major Sinclair and the Marine band. They halted in the middle of the square, arranged their music, and played the national anthem. Things were then allowed to proceed according to plan. The emperor advanced, read his speech, and pulled the cord. There was a rending of silk and a vast equestrian figure in gilt bronze was partially revealed. Men appeared with poles and poked away the clinging folds. One piece, out of reach of their efforts, obstinately fluttered over the horse's ears and eyes. The Greek contractor mounted a ladder and dislodged the rag.

The Marine band continued to play; the delegations and court-iers made for their cars; the emperor paused, and listened attentively to the music, then smiled his approval to the major before driving away. As the last of the visitors disappeared, the people broke through the soldiers, and the square became a dazzle of white tunics and black heads. For many days to come, numbers of them might be seen clustering round the memorial and gazing with puzzled awe at this new ornament to their city.

CHAPTER 3

UNTIL LATE ON the preceding afternoon, wild uncertainty prevailed about the allocation of tickets for the coronation. The legations knew nothing. Mr Hall knew nothing, and his office was continuously besieged by anxious journalists whose only hope of getting their reports back in time for Monday's papers was to write and dispatch them well before the event. What could they say when they did not even know where the ceremony would take place?

With little disguised irritation they set to work making the best of their meagre material. Gorgis and its precincts were impenetrably closed; a huge tent could be discerned through the railings, built against one wall of the church. Some described the actual coronation as taking place there; others used it as the scene of a state reception and drew fanciful pictures of the ceremony in the interior of the cathedral, '*murky, almost suffocating with incense and the thick, stifling smoke of tallow candles*' (Associated Press); authorities on Coptic ritual remarked that as the coronation proper must take place in the inner sanctuary, which no layman might glimpse, much less enter, there was small hope of anyone seeing anything at all, unless, conceivably, exceptions were made of the Duke of Gloucester and Prince Udine. The cinema-men, whose companies had spent very large sums in importing them and their talking apparatus, began to show signs of restlessness, and some correspondents became almost menacing in their representations of the fury of a slighted Press. Mr Hall, however, remained his own serene self. Everything, he assured us, was being arranged for our particular convenience; only, he admitted, the exact details were still unsettled.

Eventually, about fourteen hours before the ceremony was due to start, numbered tickets were issued through the legations; there was

216

plenty of room for all, except, as it happened, for the Abyssinians themselves. The rases and Court officials were provided with gilt chairs, but the local chiefs seemed to be wholly neglected; most of them remained outside, gazing wistfully at the ex-Kaiser's coach and the tall hats of the European and American visitors; those that succeeded in pushing their way inside were kept far at the back, where they squatted together on their haunches, or, in all the magnificent trappings of their gala dress, dozed simply in distant corners of the great tent.

For it was there, in the end, that the service took place. 'Tent', however, gives an incomplete impression of this fine pavilion. It was light and lofty, supported by two colonnades of draped scaffold-poles; the east end was hung with silk curtains, behind which a sanctuary had been improvised to hold the tabor from the cathedral. A carpeted dais ran half the length of the floor. On it stood the silk-covered table that bore the regalia and the crown neatly concealed in a cardboard hat-box; on either side were double rows of gilt chairs for the Court and the diplomatic corps, and at the end, with their backs to the body of the hall, two canopied thrones, one scarlet for the emperor and one blue for the empress.

Their Majesties had spent the night in vigil, surrounded inside the cathedral by clergy, and outside by troops; when they entered the tent it was from behind the curtains by means of a side door leading directly from the cathedral. One enterprising journalist headed his report '*Meditation Behind Machine-Guns*', and had the gratifying experience when he was at last admitted into the precincts, of finding his guess fully justified; a machine section was posted on the steps covering each approach. Other predictions were less happy. Many correspondents, for instance, wrote accounts of the emperor's solemn progress from the palace at sundown; actually it was late at night before he arrived, and then with the minimum of display. The Associated Press postponed the event until dawn, and described it in these terms: '*As their Majesties rode to church through the dusty streets of the mountain capital, which were packed with tens of thousands of their braves and chieftains, the masses uttered savage cries of acclaim. Scores of natives were trampled in the dust as the crowd surged to catch sight of the coronation party.*'

It was highly interesting to me, when the papers began to arrive from Europe and America, to compare my own experiences with those of the different correspondents. I had the fortune to be working for a paper which values the accuracy of its news before everything else; even so I was betrayed into a few mistakes. Telegraphic economy accounts for some of these, as when 'Abuna', the title of the Abyssinian primate, became expanded by a zealous subeditor into 'the Archbishop of Abuna'. Proper names often came through somewhat mangled, and curious transpositions of whole phrases occasionally took place, so that somewhere between Addis Ababa and London I was saddled with the amazing assertion that George Herui had served on Sir John Maffey's staff in the Soudan. Some mistakes of this kind seem inevitable. My surprise in reading the Press reports of the coronation was not that my more impetuous colleagues had allowed themselves to be slapdash about their details or that they had fallen into some occasional exaggeration of the more romantic and incongruous aspects of the affair. It seemed to me that we had been witnesses of a quite different series of events. 'Getting in first with the news' and 'giving the public what it wants', the two dominating principles of Fleet Street, are not always reconcilable.

I do not intend by this any conventional condemnation of the 'Yellow Press'. It seems to me that a prig is someone who judges people by his own, rather than by their, standards; criticism only becomes useful when it can show people where their own principles are in conflict. It is perfectly natural that the cheaper newspapers should aim at entertainment rather than instruction, and give prominence to what is startling and frivolous over what is important but unamusing or unintelligible. 'If a dog bites a man, that's nothing; if a man bites a dog, that's news.' My complaint is that in its scramble for precedence the cheap Press is falling short of the very standards of public service it has set itself. Almost any London newspaper, today, would prefer an incomplete, inaccurate, and insignificant report of an event provided it came in time for an earlier edition than its rivals. Now the public is not concerned with this competition. The reader, opening his paper on the breakfast-table, has no vital interest in, for instance, Abyssinian affairs. An aeroplane accident or boxing-match are a different matter. In these cases he simply wants to know the result as soon as possible. But the coronation of an African emperor means little or nothing to him. He may read about it on Monday or Tuesday, he will not be impatient. All he wants from Africa is something to amuse him in the railway train to his office. He will be just as much amused on Tuesday as on Monday. The extra day's delay makes the difference, to the correspondent on the spot, of whether he has time to compose a fully informed account (and, in almost all cases, the better informed the account the more entertaining it will be to the reader). Or at least it makes this difference. Events in a newspaper become amusing and thrilling just in so far as they are given credence as historical facts. Anyone, sitting down for a few hours with a typewriter, could compose a paper that would be the ideal of every news-editor. He would deal out dramatic deaths in the royal family, derail trains, embroil the country in civil war, and devise savage and insoluble murders. All these things would be profoundly exciting to the reader so long as he thought they were true. If they were offered to him as fiction they would be utterly insignificant. (And this shows the great gulf which divides the novelist from the journalist. The value of a novel depends on the standards each book evolves for itself; incidents which have no value as news are given any degree of importance according to their place in the book's structure and their relation to other incidents in the composition, just as subdued colours attain great intensity in certain pictures.) The delight of reading the popular newspapers does not come, except quite indirectly, from their political programmes or 'feature articles', but from the fitful illumination which glows in odd places – phrases reported from the police courts, statements made in public orations in provincial towns – which suddenly reveal unexpected byways of life. If these were pure invention they would lose all interest. As soon as one knows that they are written with conscious satire by some bright young reporter in the office, there is no further amusement in the astounding opinions so dogmatically expressed in the correspondence column.

In Addis Ababa, for the first time, I was able to watch the machinery of journalism working in a simplified form. A London office is too full and complicated to enable one to form opinions on any brief acquaintance. Here I knew most of the facts and people involved, and in the light of this knowledge I found the Press reports shocking and depressing. After all, there really was something there to report that was quite new to the European public; a succession of events of startling spectacular character, and a system of life, in a tangle of modernism and barbarity, European, African, and American, of definite, individual character. It seemed to me that here, at least, the truth was stranger than the newspaper reports. For instance, one newspaper stated that the emperor's banqueting-hall was decorated with inlaid marble, ivory, and malachite. That is not very strange to anyone who has been into any of the cheaper London hotels. In actual fact there were photographs of Mr Ramsay MacDonald and M. Poincaré, and a large, very lifelike oil-painting of a lion, by an Australian artist. It all depends on what one finds amusing. In the same way the royal coach was reported to have been drawn from the church by six milk-white horses – a wholly banal conception of splendour. If the reporters had wanted to say something thrilling, why did they not say gilded eunuchs, or ostriches with dyed plumes, or a team of captive kings, blinded and wearing yokes of elephant tusk? But since custom or poverty of imagination confined them to the stables, why should they not content themselves with what actually happened, that the ex-Kaiser's coach appeared at the church equipped with six horses (they were not white, but that is immaterial) and a Hungarian coachman in fantastic circus livery, but that, as they had never been properly trained, they proved difficult to manage and at the first salute of guns fell into utter confusion, threatening destruction to the coach and causing grave alarm to the surrounding crowds; that finally two had to be unharnessed, and that this was not accomplished until one groom had been seriously injured; that next day in the procession the coachman did not appear, and the emperor resumed his crimson motor car – a triumph of modernism typical of the whole situation?

This is what I saw at the coronation:

The emperor and empress were due to appear from their vigil at seven in the morning. We were warned to arrive at the tent about an hour before that time. Accordingly, having dressed by candlelight, Irene and I proceeded there at about six. For many hours before dawn the roads into the town had been filled with tribesmen coming in from the surrounding camps. We could see them passing the hotel (the street lamps were working that night) in dense white crowds, some riding mules, some walking, some moving at a slow trot beside their masters. All, as always, were armed. Our car moved slowly to Gorgis, hooting continuously. There were many other cars; some carrying Europeans; others, Abyssinian officials. Eventually we reached the church and were admitted after a narrow scrutiny of our tickets and ourselves. The square inside the gates was comparatively clear; from the top of the steps the machine-guns compromised with ecclesiastical calm. From inside the cathedral came the voices of the priests singing the last phase of the service that had lasted all night. Eluding the numerous soldiers, policemen, and officials who directed us towards the tent, we slipped into the outer ambulatory of the church, where the choir of bearded and vested deacons were dancing to the music of hand drums and little silver rattles. The drummers squatted round them; but they carried the rattles themselves and in their other hand waved praying-sticks.[1] Some carried nothing, but merely clapped their empty palms. They shuffled in and out, singing and swaying; the dance was performed with body and arms rather than with the feet. Their faces expressed the keenest enjoyment – almost, in some cases, ecstasy. The brilliant morning sun streamed in on them from the windows, on their silver crosses, silver-headed rods, and on the large, illuminated manuscript from which one of them, undeterred by the music, was reciting the Gospels; the clouds of incense mounted and bellied in the shafts of light.

Presently we went on to the tent. This was already well filled. The clothes of the congregation varied considerably. Most of the men were wearing morning coats, but some had appeared in evening dress and one or two in dinner-jackets. One lady had stuck an American flag in the top of her sun-helmet. The junior members of the legations were there already, in uniform, fussing among the

---

[1] These are long rods with crooked handles; the Abyssinians prostrate themselves frequently, but do not kneel in prayer; instead, they stand resting their hands on the stick and their forehead on their hands.

seats to see that everything was in order. By seven o'clock the
delegations arrived. The English party, led by the Duke of Gloucester and Lord Airlie in hussar and lancer uniforms, were undoubtedly
the most august, though there was a very smart Swede carrying
a silver helmet. It happened that our delegation was largely composed of men of unusually imposing physique; it was gratifying both
to our own national loyalty (an emotion which becomes surprisingly
sensible in remote places) and also to that of the simpler Abyssinians,
who supposed, rightly enough, that this magnificent array was there
with the unequivocal purpose of courtesy towards the emperor; I am
rather more doubtful, however, about the impression made on the
less uneducated classes. They have deep suspicions of the intentions
of their European neighbours, and the parade of our own war lords
(as Sir John Maffey, Sir Harold Kittermaster, Sir Stewart Symes,
Admiral Fullerton, and Mr Noble, in full uniform, may well have
appeared in their eyes) was little calculated to allay them. It is
perhaps significant to note that important commercial contracts
and advisory positions at Court have recently been accorded to
the least demonstrative of the visiting nations – the United States
of America. However, it is churlish to complain that our public
servants are too handsome, and, as far as the coronation ceremonies
went, they certainly added glamour to the pageant.

It was long after the last delegate had taken his place that the
emperor and empress appeared from the church. We could hear the
singing going on behind the curtains. Photographers, amateur and
professional, employed the time in taking furtive snapshots. Reporters dispatched their boys to the telegraph office with supplementary
accounts of the preliminaries. By some misunderstanding of the
instructions of the responsible official, the office was closed for the
day. After the manner of native servants, the messengers, instead of
reporting the matter to their masters, sat, grateful for the rest, on the
steps gossiping until it should open. It was late in the day that
the truth became known, and then there was more trouble for
Mr Hall.

The ceremony was immensely long, even according to the original schedule, and the clergy succeeded in prolonging it by at least
an hour and a half beyond the allotted time. The six succeeding days

of celebration were to be predominantly military, but the coronation day itself was in the hands of the Church, and they were going to make the most of it. Psalms, canticles, and prayers succeeded each other, long passages of Scripture were read, all in the extinct ecclesiastical tongue, Ghiz. Candles were lit one by one; the coronation oaths were proposed and sworn; the diplomats shifted uncomfortably in their gilt chairs, noisy squabbles broke out round the entrance between the imperial guard and the retainers of the local chiefs. Professor W., who was an expert of high transatlantic reputation on Coptic ritual, occasionally remarked: 'They are beginning the Mass now,' 'That was the offertory,' 'No, I was wrong; it was the consecration,' 'No, I was wrong; I think it is the secret Gospel,' 'No, I think it must be the Epistle,' 'How very curious; I don't believe it was a Mass at all,' '*Now* they *are* beginning the Mass . . .' and so on. Presently the bishops began to fumble among the bandboxes, and investiture began. At long intervals the emperor was presented with robe, orb, spurs, spear, and finally with the crown. A salute of guns was fired, and the crowds outside, scattered all over the surrounding waste spaces, began to cheer; the imperial horses reared up, plunged on top of each other, kicked the gilding off the front of the coach, and broke their traces. The coachman sprang from the box and whipped them from a safe distance. Inside the pavilion there was a general sense of relief; it had all been very fine and impressive, now for a cigarette, a drink, and a change into less formal costume. Not a bit of it. The next thing was to crown the empress and the heir apparent; another salvo of guns followed, during which an Abyssinian groom had two ribs broken in an attempt to unharness a pair of the imperial horses. Again we felt for our hats and gloves. But the Coptic choir still sang; the bishops then proceeded to take back the regalia with proper prayers, lections, and canticles.

'I have noticed some very curious variations in the canon of the Mass,' remarked the professor, 'particularly with regard to the kiss of peace.'

Then the Mass began.

For the first time throughout the morning the emperor and empress left their thrones; they disappeared behind the curtains into the improvised sanctuary; most of the clergy went too. The stage was empty save for the diplomats; their faces were set and strained, their attitudes inelegant. I have seen just that look in crowded second-class railway carriages, at dawn, between Avignon and Marseille. Their clothes made them funnier still. Marshal d'Esperez alone preserved his dignity, his chest thrown out, his baton poised on his knee, rigid as a war memorial, and, as far as one could judge, wide awake.

It was now about eleven o'clock, the time at which the emperor was due to leave the pavilion. Punctually to plan, three Abyssinian aeroplanes rose to greet him. They circled round and round over the tent, eagerly demonstrating their newly acquired art of swooping and curvetting within a few feet of the canvas roof. The noise was appalling; the local chiefs stirred in their sleep and rolled on to their faces; only by the opening and closing of their lips and the turning of their music could we discern that the Coptic deacons were still singing.

'A most unfortunate interruption. I missed many of the verses,' said the professor.

Eventually, at about half-past twelve, the Mass came to an end and the emperor and empress, crowned, shuffling along under a red and gold canopy, and looking as Irene remarked, exactly like the processional statues of Seville, crossed to a grand stand, from which the emperor delivered a royal proclamation; an aeroplane scattered copies of the text and, through loud speakers, the Court heralds reread it to the populace.

There was a slightly ill-tempered scramble among the photographers and cinema-men – I received a heavy blow in the middle of the back from a large camera, and a hoarse rebuke, 'Come along there now – let the eyes of the world see.'

Dancing broke out once more among the clergy, and there is no knowing how long things might not have gone on, had not the photographers so embarrassed and jostled them, and outraged their sense of reverence, that they withdrew to finish their devotions alone in the cathedral.

Then at last the emperor and empress were conducted to their coach and borne off to luncheon by its depleted but still demonstratively neurasthenic team of horses.

Having finished the report for my paper, which I had been composing during the service, I delivered it to the wireless operator at the Italian Legation; as I began to search for my car the Belgian major rose up and began insulting me; I could not quite understand why until I learned that he mistook me for a German bank-clerk who apparently had lately boxed the ears of his orderly. My Indian chauffeur had got bored and gone home. Luncheon at the hotel was odious. All food supplies had been commandeered by the Government, M. Hallot told us; it was rather doubtful whether the market would open again until the end of the week. Meanwhile there were tinned chunks of pineapple and three courses of salt beef, one cut in small cubes with chopped onion, one left in a slab with tomato ketchup, one in slices with hot water and Worcestershire sauce; the waiters had gone out the night before to get drunk and had not yet woken up.

We were all in a bad temper that night.

Six days followed of intensive celebration. On Monday morning the delegations were required to leave wreaths at the mausoleum of Menelik and Zauditu. This is a circular, domed building of vaguely Byzantine affinities, standing in the Gebbi grounds. Its interior is furnished with oil-paintings and enlarged photographs of the royal family, a fumed oak grandfather clock, and a few occasional tables of the kind exhibited in shop windows in Tottenham Court Road; their splay legs protruded from under embroidered linen tablecloths, laid diagonally; on them stood little conical silver vases of catkins boldly counterfeited in wire and magenta wool. Steps led down to the vault where lay the white marble sarcophagi of the two potentates. It is uncertain whether either contains the body attributed to it, or indeed any body at all. The date and place of Menelik's death are a palace secret, but it is generally supposed to have taken place about two years before its formal announcement to people; the empress probably lies out under the hill at Debra Lebanos. At various hours that morning, however, the delegations of the Great Powers dutifully appeared with fine bundles of flowers, and, not to be outdone in reverence, Professor W. came tripping gravely in with a little bunch of white carnations.

There was a cheerful, friendly tea-party that afternoon at the American Legation and a ball and firework display at the Italian, but the party which excited the keenest interest was the *gebbur* given by the emperor to his tribesmen. These banquets are a regular feature of Ethiopian life, constituting, in fact, a vital bond between the people and their over-lords, whose prestige in time of peace varied directly with their frequency and abundance. Until a few years ago attendance at a *gebbur* was part of the entertainment offered to every visitor in Abyssinia. Copious first-hand accounts can be found in almost every book about the country, describing the packed, squatting ranks of the diners; the slaves carrying the warm quarters of newly slaughtered, uncooked beef; the dispatch with which each guest carves for himself; the upward slice of his dagger with which he severs each mouthful from the dripping lump; the flat, damp platters of local bread; the great draughts of *tedj* and *talla* from the horn drinking-pots; the butchers outside felling and dividing the oxen; the emperor and nobles at the high table, exchanging highly seasoned morsels of more elaborate fare. These are the traditional features of the *gebbur* and, no doubt, of this occasion also. It was thus that the journalists described their impressions in glowing paraphrases of Rhey and Kingsford. When the time came, however, we found that particular precautions had been taken to exclude all Europeans from the spectacle. Perhaps it was felt that the feast might give a false impression of the civilising pretensions of the Government. Mr Hall loyally undertook to exercise his influence for each of us personally, but in the end no one gained admission except two resolute ladies and, by what was felt to be a very base exploitation of racial advantage, the coloured correspondent of a syndicate of negro newspapers.

All that I saw was the last relay of guests shambling out of the Gebbi gates late that afternoon. They were a very enviable company, quite stupefied with food and drink. Policemen attempted to herd them on, kicking their insensible backs and whacking them with canes, but nothing disturbed their serene good temper. The chiefs were hoisted on to mules by their retainers and remained there blinking and smiling; one very old man, mounted back to front, felt feebly about the crupper for his reins; some stood clasped together in silent, swaying groups; others, lacking support, rolled contentedly in the dust. I remembered them that evening as I sat in the supper-room at the Italian Legation gravely discussing the slight disturbance of diplomatic propriety caused by the emperor's capricious distribution of honours.

There were several parties that week, of more or less identical composition. At three there were fireworks, resulting in at least one nasty accident; at one, a cinema which failed to work; at one, Gilla dancers who seemed to dislocate their shoulders, and sweated so heartily that our host was able to plaster their foreheads with bank-notes; at another, Somali dancers shivered with cold on a lawn illuminated with coloured flares. There was a race meeting, where the local ponies plunged over low jumps and native jockeys cut off corners; the emperor sat all alone under a great canopy; the royal enclosure was packed and the rest of the course empty of spectators; a totalisator paid out four dollars on every winning three-dollar ticket; both bands played; Prince Udine presented an enormous cup and the emperor a magnificent kind of urn whose purpose no one could discover; it had several silver taps and little silver stands, and a great tray covered with silver cups of the kind from which grape-fruit is eaten in cinema-films. This fine trophy was won by a gentleman, in gilt riding-boots, attached to the French Legation, and was used later at their party for champagne. There was a certain amount of whispering against French sportsmanship, however, as they had sent back their books of sweepstake tickets with scarcely one sold. This showed a very bad club spirit, the other legations maintained.

There was a procession of all the troops, uniformed and irregular, in the middle of which Irene appeared in a taxi-cab surprisingly surrounded by a band of mounted musicians playing six-foot pipes and banging on saddle drums of oxhide and wood. The people all shrilled their applause, as the emperor passed, in a high, wailing whistle.

There was the opening of a museum of souvenirs, containing examples of native craftsmanship, the crown captured by General Napier at Magdala and returned by the Victoria and Albert

Museum, and a huge, hollow stone which an Abyssinian saint had worn as a hat.

There was a review of the troops on the plain outside the railway station. Although we had been privileged to see almost every member of His Majesty's forces almost every day, this was a startling display for those, like myself, who had never seen a muster of tribesmen in Arabia or Morocco. The men converged on the royal stand from all over the plain, saluting him with cries and flourishes of arms, the little horses and mules galloping right up to the foot of the throne and being reined back savagely on to their haunches, with mouths dripping foam and blood.

But no catalogue of events can convey any real idea of these astounding days, of an atmosphere utterly unique, elusive, unforgettable. If in the foregoing pages I have seemed to give undue emphasis to the irregularity of the proceedings, to their unpunctuality, and their occasional failure, it is because this was an essential part of their character and charm. In Addis Ababa everything was haphazard and incongruous; one learned always to expect the unusual and yet was always surprised.

Every morning we awoke to a day of brilliant summer sunshine; every evening fell cool, limpid, charged with hidden vitality, fragrant with the thin smoke of the *tukal* fires, pulsing, like a live body, with the beat of the tom-toms that drummed incessantly somewhere out of sight among the eucalyptus-trees. In this rich African setting were jumbled together, for a few days, people of every race and temper, all involved in one way or another in that complex of hysteria and apathy, majesty and farce; a company shot through with every degree of animosity and suspicion. There were continual rumours born of the general uncertainty; rumours about the date and place of every ceremony; rumours of dissension in high places; rumours that, in the absence at Addis Ababa of all the responsible officials, the interior was seething with brigandage; rumours that Sir Percival Phillips had used the legation wireless; that the Ethiopian Minister to Paris had been refused admittance to Addis Ababa; that the royal coachman had not had his wages for two months and had given in his notice; that the airmen from Aden were secretly prospecting for a service between the capital and the coast; that one of the legations had refused to receive the empress's first lady-in-waiting; above all, there was the great Flea Scandal and the Indiscretion about the Duke of Gloucester's Cook.

I had an intimation of that affair some days before it was generally known. Two journalists were drinking cocktails with me on the hotel terrace on the evening before the coronation. One of them said, 'We got a jolly good story this morning out of ——,' naming an amiable nitwit on the Duke of Gloucester's staff. 'It isn't in your paper's line, so I don't mind telling you.'

The story was plain and credible; first, that the old Gebbi in which His Royal Highness was quartered was, like most houses in Ethiopia, infested with fleas; secondly that the German cook was unable to obtain due attention from the native servants and came to complain of the fact. She paced up and down the room passionately, explaining her difficulties; when she turned her back it was apparent that in her agitation she had failed to fasten her skirt, which fell open and revealed underclothes of red flannel; the English party were unable to hide their amusement, and the cook, thinking that the ridicule was part of a scheme of persecution, stormed out of the house, leaving the party without their breakfast.

'You sent that back?' I asked.

'You bet your life I did.'

I felt there might be trouble.

Two days later the local correspondent of one of the news agencies received the following message from London: '*Investigate report fleas Gloucester's bed also cook red drawers left Duke breakfastless.*' He hurried with this cable to the legation and, on the Minister's advice cabled back, '*Insignificant incident greatly exaggerated advisable suppress.*'

But it was too late. The papers of the civilised world had published the story. The emperor's European agents had cabled back news of the betrayal; the emperor had complained to the legations. Stirring reports were in circulation that the emperor required every journalist to leave the country, bag and baggage, within twenty-four hours; that Lady Barton was revising her dance list; that the kantaba had cancelled his banquet; that no more stars of Ethiopia were to be dealt out until the culprit was discovered. Phrases such as 'breach of hospitality', 'gross ill-breeding', 'unpardonable irregularity', 'damned bad form' volleyed and echoed on every side. At a party that evening the ADC who had caused the trouble was conspicuously vigorous in his aspirations to 'kick the bounder's backside, whoever he is'. We all felt uneasy for nearly a day, until the topic was succeeded by the French Legation's shabby behaviour over the sweepstake tickets, and the grave question of whether the emperor would attend Marshal d'Esperez's private tea-party.

One morning, a few days later, Irene and I were sitting outside the hotel drinking apéritifs and waiting for luncheon; we were entertained by the way in which the various visitors treated a pedlar who diffidently approached them with a bundle of bootlaces in one hand and an enamelled *pot de chambre* in the other. Suddenly a taxi drove up, and a servant wearing the palace livery jumped out and emptied a large pile of envelopes into Irene's lap. Two were addressed to us. We took them and handed back the rest, which the man presented, to be sorted in the same way, at the next table. It was not perhaps the most expeditious method of delivery, but, as he was unable to read, it is difficult to think of what else he could have done.

The envelopes contained an invitation to lunch with the emperor that day at one o'clock; as it was then after half-past twelve we disregarded the request for an answer and hurried off to change.

Professor W. had spoken to me of this party some days before, saying with restrained relish, 'On Saturday I am lunching with the emperor. There are several things I shall be interested to discuss with him.' But, as it turned out, he had little opportunity for conversation. There were about eighty guests and many empty places, showing that the messenger had not been able to finish his round in time (indeed, it is no unusual thing in Addis Ababa to receive cards of invitation many hours after the event). They were the European officials in the Abyssinian Government, European residents, journalists, and private visitors whose names had been sent in by the legations; the European officers of the army, a few Abyssinian notables, the wives of visiting consuls, and so on. At first we stood in the glazed corridor which ran down one side of the main building. Then we were ushered into the throne-room, bowed and curtseyed, and ranged ourselves round the walls while *byrrh* and vermouth and cigars were carried round. There was something slightly ecclesiastical in the atmosphere.

The emperor then led the way into the dining-room. We tramped in behind him in no particular order. He seated himself at the centre of the top table; three tables ran at right angles to him, resplendent with gold plate and white-and-gold china. Typewritten name-cards lay on each plate. Ten minutes or so followed of some confusion as we jostled round and round looking for our places; there was no plan of the table, and as most of us were complete strangers we were unable to help each other. The emperor sat watching us with a placid little smile. We must have looked very amusing. Naturally no one cared to look at the places next to the emperor, so that when at last we were all seated the two most honoured guests were left to sidle forlornly into the nearest empty places. Eventually they were fetched. Irene sat on one side and the French wife of the Egyptian consul on his other. I sat between an English airman and a Belgian photographer. A long meal followed, of many courses of fair French cooking and good European wines. There was also *tedj* and the national beverage made from fermented honey. We had sent out for some, one evening at the hotel, and found it an opaque yellowish liquid, mild and rather characterless. The emperor's *tedj* was a very different drink, quite clear, slightly brown, heavy, rich, and dry. After luncheon, at Irene's request, we were given some of the liqueur distilled from it – a colourless spirit of fine flavour and disconcerting potency.

Only one odd thing happened at luncheon. Just as we were finishing, a stout young woman rose from a seat near the back and made her way resolutely between the tables until she planted herself within a few yards of the emperor. I understand that she was a Syrian Jewess employed in some educational capacity in the town. She carried a sheaf of papers which she held close to her pince-nez with one plump hand while she raised the other above her head in a Fascist salute. Conversation faltered and ceased. The emperor looked at her with kindly inquiry. Then, in a voice of peculiar strength and stridency, she began to recite an ode. It was a very long complimentary ode, composed by herself in Arabic, a language wholly unintelligible to His Majesty. Between verses she made a long pause during which she fluttered her manuscript; then she began again. We had just begun to feel that the performance would really prove interminable, when, just as suddenly as she had begun, she stopped, bobbed, turned about, and, with glistening forehead and slightly labouring breath, strode back to her place to receive the congratulations of her immediate neighbours. The emperor rose and led the way back to the throne-room. Here we stood round the walls for a quarter of an hour while liqueurs were served. Then we bowed in turn and filed out into the sunshine.

That evening at the hotel two soldiers appeared with a huge basket of coloured Harari work for Irene from the emperor. In it was a fine outfit of native woman's clothing, consisting of a pair of black satin trousers of great girth, an embroidered cloak, a hand-woven *chamma*, and a set of gold ornaments.

One moment of that week is particularly vivid in my memory. It was late at night and we had just returned from a party. My room, as I have said, was in an outhouse at a little distance from the hotel; a grey horse, some goats, and the hotel guard, his head wrapped in a blanket, were sleeping in the yard as I went across. Behind my room, separated from the hotel grounds by wooden palings, lay a cluster of native *tukals*. That evening there was a party in one of them – probably celebrating a wedding or funeral. The door faced my way and I could see a glimmer of lamplight in the interior. They were singing a monotonous song, clapping in time and drumming with their hands on petrol-tins. I suppose there were about ten or fifteen of them there. I stood for some time listening. I was wearing a tall hat, evening clothes and white gloves. Presently the guard woke up and blew a little trumpet; the sound was taken up by other guards at neighbouring houses (it is in this way that they assure their employers of their vigilance); then he wrapped himself once more in his blanket and relapsed into sleep.

The song continued unvarying in the still night. The absurdity of the whole week became suddenly typified for me in that situation – my preposterous clothes, the sleeping animals, and the wakeful party on the other side of the stockade.

CHAPTER 4

IT WAS DURING our third week in Addis Ababa, when the official celebrations were over and the delegations were being packed off to the coast as fast as the Franco-Ethiopian Railway's supply of sleeping-cars would allow, that Professor W. suggested to me that we should make an expedition together to Debra Lebanos.

This monastery has for four centuries been the centre of Abyssinian spiritual life. It is built round a spring where the waters of Jordan, conveyed subterraneously down the Red Sea, are believed to well up endowed with curative properties; pilgrims go there from all parts of the country, and it is a popular burial-ground for those who can afford it, since all found there at the Last Trump are assured of unimpeded entry into Paradise.

It was the dry season, so that the road could be attempted by car. Professor Mercer had recently made the journey and had come back with photographs of a hitherto unknown version of Ecclesiastes. Ras Kassa had driven from Fiche only two weeks before and renewed the bridges for the occasion, so that we had little difficulty in finding a driver willing to take us. Permission had first to be obtained from Kassa to use the road. Professor W. obtained this and also a letter of commendation from the Abuna. An escort of soldiers was offered us, but refused. The expedition consisted simply of ourselves, a bullet-headed Armenian chauffeur, and a small native boy, who attached himself to us without invitation. At first we were a little resentful of this, but he firmly refused to understand our attempts at dismissal, and later we were devoutly grateful for his presence. The car, which did things I should have thought no car could possibly do, was an American make which is rarely seen in Europe. When we had packed it with our overcoats, rugs, tins of petrol, and provisions, there was just room for ourselves. The hotel supplied beer and sandwiches and olives and oranges, and Irene gave us a hamper of tinned and truffled foods from Fortnum & Mason. We were just starting, rather later than we had hoped, when Professor W. remembered something. 'Do you mind if we go back to my hotel for a minute? There's just one thing I've forgotten.' We drove round to the Imperial.

The thing he had forgotten was a dozen empty Vichy-bottles. 'I thought it would be courteous,' he explained, 'to take some holy water back to Ras Kassa and the Abuna. I'm sure they would appreciate it.'

'Yes, but need we take quite so much?'

'Well, there's the patriarchal legate, I should like to give him some, and Belatingeta Herui, and the Coptic patriarch at Cairo ... I thought it was a nice opportunity to repay some of the kindness I have received.'

I suggested that this purpose could be more conveniently achieved by giving them *tedj*, and that from what I had seen of Abyssinians they would much prefer it. Professor W. gave a little nervous laugh and looked anxiously out of the window.

'Well, why not fill my empty beer-bottles?'

'No, no, I don't think that would be quite suitable. I don't really like using Vichy-bottles. I wish I had had time to scrape off the labels,' he mused. 'I don't *quite* like the idea of holy water in Vichy-bottles. Perhaps the boy could do it tomorrow – before they are filled, of course.'

A new aspect of the professor's character was thus revealed. My acquaintance with him until that day was limited to half a dozen more or less casual encounters at the various parties and shows. I had found him full of agreeably ironical criticism of our companions, very punctilious, and very enthusiastic about things which seemed to me unexceptionable. 'Look,' he would say with purest Boston intonation, 'look at the exquisite grace of the basket that woman is carrying. There is the whole character of the people in that plaited straw. Ah, why do we waste our time looking at crowns and canons? I could study that basket all day.' And a wistful, faraway look would come into his eyes as he spoke.

Remarks of that kind went down very well with some people, and I regarded them as being, perhaps, one of the normal manifestations of American scholarship. They were compensated for by such sound maxims as 'Never carry binoculars; you only have to hand them over to some wretched woman as soon as there is anything worth seeing.' But this worldly good sense was a mere mask over the essential mystical nature of the professor's mind; one touch of church furniture, and he became suddenly transfused with reverence and an almost neurotic eagerness to do all that could be expected of him, with an impulsive and demonstrative devotion that added a great deal to the glamour of our expedition together.

Those bottles, however, were an infernal nuisance. They clinked about the floor, making all the difference between tolerable ease and acute discomfort. There was nowhere to rest our feet except on their unstable, rolling surface. We drew up our knees and resigned ourselves to cramp and pins and needles.

Debra Lebanos is practically due north of Addis Ababa. For the first mile or two there was a clearly marked track which led out of the town, right over the summit of Entoto. It was extremely steep and narrow, composed of loose stones and boulders; on the top of the hill was a little church and parsonage, the ground all round them broken by deep ravines and outcrops of stone. 'Whatever happens,' we decided, 'we must make quite certain of coming over here by daylight.'

From Entoto the way led down to a wide plain, watered by six or seven shallow streams which flowed between deep banks at right angles to our road. Caravans of mules were coming into the town laden with skins. Professor W. saluted them with bows and blessings; the hillmen answered him with blank stares or broad incredulous grins. A few, more sophisticated than their companions, bellowed, 'Baksheesh!' Professor W. shook his head sadly and remarked that the people were already getting spoiled by foreign intrusion.

It took two or three hours to cross the plain; we drove, for the most part, parallel to the track, rather than on it, finding the rough ground more comfortable than the prepared surface. We crossed numerous dry watercourses and several streams. At some of these there had been rough attempts at bridge-building, usually a heap of

rocks and a few pieces of timber; in rare cases a culvert ran under-
neath. It was in negotiating these that we first realised the astonishing powers of our car. It would plunge nose first into a precipitous
gully, shiver and stagger a little, churn up dust and stones, roar, and
skid, bump and sway until we began to climb out, and then it would
suddenly start forward and mount very deliberately up the other
side as though endowed with some peculiar prehensile quality in its
tyres. Occasionally, in conditions of scarcely conceivable asperity,
the engine would stop. Professor W. would sigh and open the door,
allowing two or three of his empty bottles to roll out on to the
running-board.

'Ah, ça n'a pas d'importance,' said the driver, prodding the boy,
who jumped out, restored the bottles, and then leant his shoulder
against the back of the car. This infinitesimal contribution of weight
seemed to be all the car needed; up it would go out of the river-bed,
and over the crest of the bank, gaining speed as it reached level
ground; the child would race after us and clamber in as we bumped
along, a triumphant smile on his little black face.

At about eleven we stopped for luncheon by the side of the last
stream. The boy busied himself by filling up the radiator by the use
of a small cup. I ate sandwiches and drank beer rendered volatile by
the motion of the car. The professor turned out to be a vegetarian;
he unwrapped a little segment of cheese from its silver paper and
nibbled it delicately and made a very neat job of an orange. The sun
was very powerful, and the professor advanced what seemed, and
still seems, to me the radically unsound theory that you must wear
thick woollen underclothes if you wish to keep cool in the tropics.

After leaving the plain we drove for three hours or so across
grassy downland. There was now no track of any kind, but occasional boundary-stones hinted at the way we should follow. There
were herds grazing, usually in the charge of small naked children. At
first the professor politely raised his hat and bowed to them, but the
effect was so disturbing that after he had sent three or four out of
sight, wailing in terror, he remarked that it was agreeable to find
people who had a proper sense of the menace of motor transport,
and relapsed into meditation, pondering, perhaps, the advisability
of presenting a little holy water to the emperor. The route was

uneventful, broken only by occasional clusters of *tukals*, surrounded by high hedges of euphorbia. It was very hot, and after a time, in spite of the jangle of the bottles and the constriction of space, I fell into a light doze.

I awoke as we stopped on the top of a hill; all round us were empty undulations of grass. 'Nous sommes perdus?' asked the professor. 'Ça n'a pas d'importance,' replied the driver, lighting a cigarette. The boy was dispatched, like the dove from Noah's ark, to find direction in the void. We waited for half an hour before he returned. Meanwhile three native women appeared from no-where, peering at us from under straw sunshades. The professor took off his hat and bowed. The women huddled together and giggled. Presently fascination overcame their shyness and they approached closer; one touched the radiator and burned her fingers. They asked for cigarettes and were repelled, with some very forceful language, by the driver.

At last the child returned and made some explanations. We turned off at right angles and drove on, and the professor and I fell asleep once more.

When I next woke, the landscape had changed dramatically. About half a mile from us, and obliquely to the line of our path, the ground fell away suddenly into a great canyon. I do not know how deep it was, but I should think at least two thousand feet, descending abruptly in tiers of sheer cliff, broken by strips and patches of timber. At the bottom a river ran between green banks, to swell the Blue Nile far in the south; it was practically dry at this season except for a few shining channels of water which split and reunited on the sandy bed in delicate threads of light. Poised among trees, two-thirds of the way down on a semi-circular shelf of land, we could discern the roofs of Debra Lebanos. A cleft path led down the face of the cliff and it was for this that we were clearly making. It looked hopelessly unsafe, but our Armenian plunged down with fine intrepidity.

Sometimes we lurched along a narrow track with cliffs rising on one side and a precipice falling away on the other; sometimes we picked our way on broad ledges among great volcanic boulders; sometimes we grated between narrow rock walls. At last we reached a defile which even our driver admitted to be impassable. We climbed out along the running-boards and finished the descent on foot. Professor W. was clearly already enchanted by the sanctity of the place.

'Look,' he said, pointing to some columns of smoke that rose from the cliffs above us, 'the cells of the solitary anchorites.'

'Are you sure there are solitary anchorites here? I never heard of any.'

'It would be a good place for them,' he said wistfully.

The Armenian strode on in front of us, a gallant little figure with his cropped head and rotund, gaitered legs; the boy staggered behind, carrying overcoats, blankets, provisions, and a good half-dozen of the empty bottles. Suddenly the Armenian stopped and, with his finger on his lips, drew our attention to the rocks just below us. Twenty or thirty baboons of both sexes and all ages were huddled up in the shade.

'Ah,' said Professor W., 'sacred monkeys. How very interesting!'

'Why do you think they are sacred? They seem perfectly wild.'

'It is a common thing to find sacred monkeys in monasteries,' he explained gently. 'I have seen them in Ceylon and in many parts of India . . . Oh, why did he have to do that? How very thoughtless!' For our driver had throne a stone into their midst and scattered them barking in all directions, to the great delight of the small boy behind us.

It was hot walking. We passed one or two *tukals* with women and children staring curiously at us, and eventually emerged on to an open green ledge littered with enormous rocks and a variety of unimposing buildings. A mob of ragged boys, mostly infected with disagreeable skin diseases, surrounded us and were repelled by the Armenian. (These, we learned later, were the deacons.) We sent the boy forward to find someone more responsible, and soon a fine-looking, bearded monk, carrying a yellow sunshade, came out of the shadow of a tree and advanced to greet us. We gave him our letter of introduction from the Abuna, and after he had scrutinised both sides of the envelope with some closeness, he agreed, through our Armenian, who from now on acted as interpreter, to fetch the head of the monastery. He was away some time and eventually returned with an old priest, who wore a brown cloak, a very large white turban, steel-rimmed spectacles, and carried in one hand an old black umbrella and in the other a horsehair fly-whisk. Professor W. darted forward and kissed the cross which swung from the old man's neck. This was received rather well, but I felt too shy to follow his lead and contented myself with shaking hands. The monk then handed his superior our letter, which was tucked away in his pocket unopened. They then explained that they would be ready to receive us shortly, and went off to wake up the other priests and prepare the chapter house.

We waited about half an hour, sitting in the shade near the church, and gradually forming round us a circle of inquisitive ecclesiastics of all ages. The Armenian went off to see about his car. Professor W. replied to the questions that were put to us, with bows, shakes of the head, and little sympathetic moans. Presently one monk came up and, squatting beside us, began to write on the back of his hand with a white pencil in a regular, finely formed Amharic script. One of the letters was in the form of a cross. Professor W., anxious to inform them all that we were good Christians, pointed to this mark, then to me and to himself, bowed in the direction of the church, and crossed himself. This time he made a less happy impression. Everyone looked bewildered and rather scared; the scribe spat on his hand, and hastily erasing the text, fell back some paces. There was an air of tension and embarrassment, which was fortunately disturbed by our Armenian with the announcement that the council of the monastery were now ready to receive us.

Apart from the two churches, the most prominent building was a tall, square house of stone, with a thatched roof and a single row of windows set high up under the eaves; it was here that we were led. A small crowd had collected round the door, which was covered with a double curtain of heavy sackcloth. The windows also were heavily screened, so that we stepped from the brilliant sunshine into a gloom which was at first completely baffling. One of the priests raised the door-curtain a little to show us our way. A single lofty room constituted the entire house; the walls were of undisguised stone and rubble, no ceiling covered the rafters and thatch.

Preparations had clearly been made for us; carpets had been spread
on the earthen floor, and in the centre stood two low stools covered
with rugs; twelve priests stood ranged against the wall, the head of
the monastery in their centre; between them and our seats stood
a table covered with a shawl; the only other furniture was a cupboard
in the far corner, roughly built of irregularly stained white wood, the
doors secured with a staple and padlock. We sat down and our
chauffeur-interpreter stood beside us jauntily twirling his cap.
When we were settled, the head of the monastery, who apparently
also bore the title of abuna, brought our letter of introduction out of
his pocket and, for the first time, opened it. He read it first to himself
and then aloud to the company, who scratched their beards,
nodded, and grunted. Then he addressed us, asking us what we
wanted. Professor W. explained that we had heard from afar of the
sanctity of the place and the wisdom and piety of the monks, and
that we had come to do reverence at their shrine, pay our duty and
respect to them, and take away some account of the glories of the
monastery of which all the world stood in awe. This pretty speech
was condensed by our chauffeur into three or four harsh vocables,
and greeted with further nods and grunts from the assembly.

One of them asked whether we were Mohammedans. It seemed
sad that this question was necessary after all Professor W.'s protestations. We assured him that we were not. Another asked where we
had come from. Addis Ababa? They asked about the coronation,
and Professor W. began a graphic outline of the liturgical significance of the ceremony. I do not think, however, that our chauffeur
was at very great pains to translate this faithfully. The response,
anyway, was a general outburst of chuckling, and from then onwards, for about ten minutes, he took the burden of conversation
from our shoulders and speedily established relations of the utmost
geniality. Presently he began shaking hands with them all and
explained that they would like us to do the same, a social duty
which Professor W. decorated with many graceful genuflections
and reverences.

The professor then asked whether we might visit the library of
which the world stood in awe. Why, certainly; there it was in the
corner. The abuna produced a small key from his pocket and

directed one of the priests to open the cupboard. They brought out five or six bundles wrapped in silk shawls, and, placing them with great care on the table, drew back the door-curtain to admit a shaft of white light. The abuna lifted the corners of the shawls one after another and revealed two pieces of board clumsily hinged together in the form of a diptych. Professor W. kissed them eagerly; they were then opened, revealing two coloured lithographs, apparently cut from a religious almanac printed in Germany some time towards the end of the last century, representing the Crucifixion and the Assumption, pasted on to the inner surfaces of the wood. The professor was clearly a little taken aback. 'Dear, dear, how remarkably ugly they are,' he remarked as he bent down to kiss them.

The other bundles contained manuscripts of the Gospels, lives of the saints, and missals, written in Ghiz[1] and brightly illuminated. The painting was of the same kind as the frescos, reduced to miniature. Sometimes faces and figures had been cut out of prints and stuck into the pages with a discomposing effect on their highly stylised surroundings. They told us with great pride that the artist had been employed at Addis Ababa on some work for the late empress. Professor W. asked whether there were not some older manuscripts we might see, but they affected not to understand. I remembered hearing from George Herui that it was only after very considerable difficulties that Professor Mercer had unearthed his Ecclesiastes. No doubt there were still reserves hidden from us.

It was then suggested that we should visit the sacred spring. Our Armenian here sidled unobtrusively out of the way; he had had enough exercise for one day. Professor W. and I set out with a guide up the hillside. It was a stiff climb; the sun was still strong and the stones all radiated a fierce heat. 'I think, perhaps, we ought to take off our hats,' said the professor; 'we are on very holy ground.'

I removed my topi and exposed myself to sunstroke, trusting in divine protection; but, just as he spoke, it so happened that our guide stopped on the path and accommodated himself in a way which made me think that his reverence for the spot was far from fanatical.

---

1 The ecclesiastical language, unintelligible to all the laity and most of the priest-hood. It is written in Amharic characters.

On our way we passed a place where overhanging cliffs formed a shallow cave. Water oozed and dripped all round, and the path was soft and slippery. It is here that the bodies of the faithful are brought; they lay all about, some in packing-cases, others in hollow tree trunks, battened down with planks, piled and tumbled on top of each other without order; many were partially submerged in falls of damp earth, a few of these rough coffins had broken apart, revealing their contents. There were similar heaps, we were told, on the other parts of the hillside.

We had a fine view of the valley; our guide pointed out a group of buildings on the far side. 'That is the convent for the women,' he explained. 'You see it is quite untrue that we live together. The houses are entirely separate. We do not cross the valley to see them, and they do not cross to us. Never. It is all a lie.' He wanted to make this point quite clear.

At last we reached the spring, which fell in a pretty cascade to join the river far below at the bottom of the valley. Most of the water, however, had been tapped, and was conveyed in two iron pipes to bathing-places near the monastery. We climbed down again to see them. One, built especially for Menelik, was a little brick house with a corrugated-iron roof. The old empress had frequently come here, and since her death it had not been used. We peered through the window and saw a plain kitchen-chair. There was a rusty spout in the ceiling from which a trickle of water fell on to the brick floor and drained away through the waste-pipe in one corner. The other bath was for public use. The pipe was fitted with a double spout, directing two streams of water on to either side of a brick wall. One side was for men and the other for women, and a three-sided screen was built round each. The floor was made of cement. A boy was in there at the time of our visit, swilling himself down with as much puffing and spluttering as if he were under any purely secular shower-bath.

As we turned back, our Armenian and a monk met us with a message from the abuna – should they kill a goat, a sheep, or a calf for our dinner? We explained that we had full provision for our food. All we required was shelter for the night and water to wash in. The Armenian explained that it was usual to accept something. We suggested some eggs, but were told that they had none. They urged a goat very strongly. Meat is a rare luxury in the monastery, and they were, no doubt, eager to take the opportunity of our visit for a feast. The professor's vegetarian scruples, however, were unconquerable. At last they suggested honey, which he accepted readily. The question of our accommodation was then discussed. There was a hut or a tent. The Armenian warned us that if we slept in the hut we should certainly contract some repulsive disease, and if in the tent, we might be killed by hyenas. He had already made up his own mind, he said, to sleep in the car. We returned to the monastery, and the abuna led us in person to see the hut. It was some time before the key could be found; when the door was at last wrenched open, an emaciated she-goat ran out. The interior was windowless and fetid. It appeared to have been used as a kind of lumber-room; heaps of old rags and broken furniture encumbered the floor. A swarm of bees buzzed in the roof. It was not quite ready, the abuna explained; he had not expected guests. It could, of course, be prepared, or would we think it inhospitable if he offered us the tent? We declared that the tent would be wholly satisfactory, and so, with evident relief, the abuna gave instructions for its erection. It was now nearly sunset. A spot of ground was chosen near the house where we had been received, and a very decent bell-tent pitched. (It was the property of the old empress, we learned. She had often slept there on her visits to the spring.) The floor was covered with hay and the hay with rugs. A little boat-shaped oil-lamp was hung from the tent-pole; our rugs, provisions, and bottles were brought in and laid on one side. We were then invited to enter. We sat down cross-legged and the abuna sat beside us. He looked enormous in the tiny light; the shadow from his great turban seemed to fill the whole tent. The chauffeur squatted opposite us. The abuna smiled with the greatest geniality and expressed his best wishes for our comfort; we thanked him heartily. Conversation lapsed and we all three sat smiling rather vacantly. Presently the flap was lifted and a monk came in wearing a heavy brown burnous and carrying an antiquated rifle. He bowed to us and retired. He was a guard, the abuna explained, who would sleep outside across the door. Another smiling pause. At last supper arrived; first a basket containing half a dozen great rounds of native bread, a tough, clammy substance closely resembling crêpe rubber in appearance; then two earthenware jugs, one of water, the other of *talla* – a kind of thin, bitter beer; then two horns of honey, but not of honey as it is understood at Thame; this was the product of wild bees, scraped straight from the trees; it was a greyish colour, full of bits of stick and mud, bird dung, dead bees, and grubs. Everything was first carried to the abuna for his approval, then to us. We expressed our delight with nods and more extravagant smiles. The food was laid out before us and the bearers retired. At this moment the Armenian shamelessly deserted us, saying that he must go and see after his boy.

The three of us were left alone, smiling over our food in the half darkness.

In the corner lay our hamper packed with Irene's European delicacies. We clearly could not approach them until our host left us. Gradually the frightful truth became evident that he was proposing to dine with us. I tore off a little rag of bread and attempted to eat it. 'This is a very difficult situation,' said the professor; 'I think, perhaps, it would be well to simulate ill-health,' and holding his hands to his forehead, he began to rock gently from side to side, emitting painfully subdued moans. It was admirably done; the abuna watched him with the greatest concern; presently the professor held his stomach and retched a little; then he lay on his back, breathing heavily with closed eyes; then he sat up on his elbow and explained in eloquent dumb show that he wished to rest. The abuna understood perfectly, and, with every gesture of sympathy, rose to his feet and left us.

In five minutes, when I had opened a tinned grouse and a bottle of lager and the professor was happily munching a handful of ripe olives, the Armenian returned. With a comprehensive wink, he picked up the jug of native beer, threw back his head, and, without pausing to breathe, drank a quart or two. He then spread out two rounds of bread, emptied a large quantity of honey into each of them, wrapped them together, and put them in his pocket. 'Moi, je puis manger comme abyssin,' he remarked cheerfully, winked at the grouse, wished us good night, and left us.

'Now at last,' said the professor, producing a tin of Keating's powder, 'I feel in the heart of Ethiopia.' He sprinkled the rugs and blankets, wrapped his head in a pale grey scarf, and prepared to settle down for the night. We had had a tiring day, and after smoking a pipe I decided to follow his example. The lamp was flickering and smoking badly and threatened at any moment to burn through its own string and set us on fire. I blew it out, and was just becoming drowsy when the abuna returned, carrying a lantern, to see whether the professor felt any better. We all smiled inarticulately for some time, and the professor pointed to the half-empty beer-jug and the horns of honey as proof of his recovery. The abuna noted them with evident satisfaction, and then his eye, travelling round the tent, was attracted by the Keating's powder which lay like thick dust over the floor and bedding. He called in the guard and rather crossly pointed out this evidence of neglect. The man hastily produced a broom and brushed out the tent. Then, when everything was in order, and after many bows, smiles, and blessings, he left us to sleep.

But I, at any rate, slept very little. It was a deadly cold night and a bitter wind sprang up, sweeping the valley and driving under the tent and through our thin blankets, while outside the door the guard coughed and grunted. I was out before dawn and watched the monastery waking into life. There seemed very little order. The monks emerged from the huts in ones and twos and pottered off to work in the fields and woods. A certain number of them went down to the church, where the professor and I followed them. They sat about outside until a priest appeared with the keys; then a service began, apparently quite at haphazard. Two or three would start intoning some kind of psalm or litany, and others seemed to join in as they thought fit; two or three were reading aloud from large manuscripts supported on folding rests; others leant on their praying-sticks or squatted in corners muttering. Now and then one would stop on his way to work, kiss the door on the inner wall, and pass on. The frescos of the inner sanctuary were hung with green curtains; one of the priests pointed to them and explained in dumb show that they would be drawn for our inspection later in the day.

We returned to our tent for breakfast. Beer and anchovies seemed rather discouraging after our chilly night, but there was no alternative except tinned loganberries and *foie gras*. The guard came in, finished the beer, and ate some bread and honey. He showed great interest in our belongings, fingering everything in turn – the tin-opener, electric torch, a pocket-knife, a pair of hairbrushes. I let him play with the sword-stick I happened to have brought with me; he in exchange showed me his rifle and bandoleer. About half the cartridges were empty shells; the weapon was in very poor condition. It could not possibly have been used with any accuracy, and probably not with safety. I asked whether he had ever killed anything with it; he shook his head, and produced a large, rather blunt dagger, which he stabbed into the earth.

Presently the chauffeur came to assure us that he had spent a very comfortable night and felt fairly confident that he would be able to extricate the car from its position on the path, where it blocked all approach to the monastery and was causing a good deal of trouble to the herdsmen in charge of the community's cattle. We told him to remain at hand to act as interpreter, and soon a priest came to conduct us to the churches. There were two of these; the main building, where we had already been, and a small shrine, containing a cross which had fallen from heaven. The professor thought this might be a piece of the true cross brought there from Alexandria after the Arab invasion, and showed great interest and veneration; we were not allowed to see it, but as a special concession we were shown the shawl in which it was wrapped.

In the main church we paid a fee of seven dollars to have the frescos unveiled. They had lately been repainted in brilliant colours and the priest was justly proud of the renovation. On one wall were portraits of Ras Kassa, Menelik, and the late empress. It was clear that these heads had been copied from photographs, with the curious result that they stood out solidly, in carefully articulated light and shade and great fidelity of detail, against a composition of purely conventional pre-Renaissance design. Another wall was filled with rider saints. The professor made a plan of it and took down their names. We were then shown some brass processional crosses and some illuminated missals, none of any great antiquity. It was, in fact, a curious feature of Debra Lebanos that, although the community had been the centre of Abyssinian spiritual life since very early days in the conversion of the country, and had been settled on this spot for several centuries, they seem to have preserved no single object from the past. It may be that their treasures have all been pillaged in the continual invasions and disorders of Abyssinian history, or that they have been sold from time to time in moments of financial need, or perhaps simply that they did not choose to show them to strangers.

One thing, however, we did see of the greatest interest. That was the sanctuary. We might not, of course, enter it, but the priest drew back the curtain for us and allowed a short glimpse of the dark interior. In the centre stood the tabor, which is both altar-stone and tabernacle, a wooden cupboard built like a miniature church in three tiers, square at the base, from which rose an octagonal story surmounted by a circular dome. Round the tabor, in deep dust, for the sanctuary is rarely, if ever, swept out, lay an astonishing confusion of litter. There was no time to take in everything, but, in the brief inspection, I noticed a wicker chair, some heaps of clothes, two or three umbrellas, a suitcase of imitation leather, some newspapers, and a teapot and slop-pail of enamelled tin.

It was about ten o'clock when we left the church; there was a Mass at one o'clock, which we were both anxious to attend, which would not be over until half-past two or three. We were thus undecided about our movements. We might spend another night there and start back early next day for Addis Ababa; we might go and see Fiche, Kassa's capital fifteen miles away, and spend a night in the car there, or we might start immediately after Mass and try to get to Addis that night. The chauffeur favoured the last plan and was hopeful of his ability, now that he knew the way, of doing the journey in five or six hours. We had not provisions to last us in any comfort for two days, and I was reluctant to fall back on Abyssinian food. Together we persuaded the professor to attempt the journey; if the worst came to the worst we could spend the night on the plain; a prospect to which the chauffeur added romance with gloomy stories of wild beasts and brigands. As the sun mounted, it became intensely hot. We lay in the tent smoking and dozing until the abuna came to conduct us to Mass.

I will not attempt any description of the ritual; the liturgy was quite unintelligible to me, and, oddly enough, to the professor also. No doubt the canon of the Mass would have been in part familiar,

but this was said in the sanctuary behind closed doors. We stood in
the outer ambulatory. A carpet was placed for us to stand on and we
were given praying-sticks, with the aid of which we stood throughout the two hours of service. There were twenty or thirty monks
round us and some women and babies from the *tukals*. Communion
was administered to the babies, but to no one else. Many of the
monks were crippled or deformed in some way; presumably they
were pilgrims who had originally come to the spring in the hope of
a cure, and had become absorbed into the life of the place. There
seemed to be very little system of testing vocations in the community.
The priests and deacons wore long, white-and-gold cloaks and
turbans, and had bare feet. Now and then they emerged from the
sanctuary, and once they walked round in procession. The singing
was monotonous and more or less continuous, accompanied by
a drum and sistrums.[1] For anyone accustomed to the Western rite
it was difficult to think of this as a Christian service, for it bore that
secret and confused character which I had hitherto associated with
the non-Christian sects of the East.

I had sometimes thought it an odd thing that Western Christianity, alone of all the religions of the world, exposes its mysteries to
every observer, but I was so accustomed to this openness that I had
never before questioned whether it was an essential and natural
feature of the Christian system. Indeed, so saturated are we in this
spirit that many people regard the growth of the Church as a process
of elaboration – even of obfuscation; they visualise the Church of the
first century as a little cluster of pious people reading the Gospels
together, praying and admonishing each other with a simplicity to
which the high ceremonies and subtle theology of later years would
have been bewildering and unrecognisable. At Debra Lebanos
I suddenly saw the classic basilica and open altar as a great positive
achievement, a triumph of light over darkness consciously accomplished, and I saw theology as the science of simplification by which
nebulous and elusive ideas are formalised and made intelligible and
exact. I saw the Church of the first century as a dark and hidden
thing, as dark and hidden as the seed germinating in the womb;

1 Silver rattles.

legionaries off duty slipping furtively out of barracks, greeting each other by signs and passwords in a locked upper room in the side street of some Mediterranean sea port; slaves at dawn creeping from the grey twilight into the candle-lit, smoky chapels of the catacombs. The priests hid their office, practising trades; their identity was known only to initiates; they were criminals against the law of their country. And the pure nucleus of the truth lay in the minds of the people, encumbered with superstitions, gross survivals of the paganism in which they had been brought up; hazy and obscene nonsense seeping through from the other esoteric cults of the Near East, magical infections from the conquered barbarian. And I began to see how these obscure sanctuaries had grown, with the clarity of the Western reason, into the great open altars of Catholic Europe, where Mass is said in a flood of light, high in the sight of all, while tourists can clatter around with their Baedekers, incurious of the mystery.

By the time Mass was over, our chauffeur had succeeded in the remarkable and hazardous feat of backing the car up the path. We said goodbye to the abuna and climbed the ravine, attended by a troop of small deacons. When we at last reached the top the professor took from his pocket a handful of half-piastre pieces with which he had secretly provided himself. He ordered the children to line up, and our boy cuffed and jostled them into some kind of order. Then he presented them with a coin apiece. They had clearly not expected any such donation, but they quickly got the hang of the business, and, as soon as they were paid, queued up again at the back. Our boy detected this simple deception and drove away the second-comers. When each had received his half-piastre, and some had grabbed two, there were still a number of coins left over. 'Do you think,' asked the professor rather timidly, 'that it would be very vulgar and tripperish to make them scramble for them?'

'Yes,' I said.

'Of course it would,' said the professor decidedly. 'Quite out of the question.'

The deacons, however, continued to caper round us, crying for more and clinging to the car, so that it became impossible to start without endangering several lives. 'Ça n'a pas d'importance,' said the chauffeur inevitably, cranking up the engine. The professor, however, preferred a more humane release. 'Perhaps, after all...' he said, and threw his handful of money among the children. The last we saw of Debra Lebanos was a scrambling of naked black limbs and a cloud of dust. It was interesting to be in at the birth of a tradition. Whoever in future goes to Debra Lebanos will, without doubt, find himself beset by these rapacious children; Professor W. had taught them the first easy lesson of civilisation. It is curious how Americans, however cultured, seem incapable of neglecting this form of instruction.

Our journey back for the first three hours was uneventful. We made good time on the downs, and darkness found us at the beginning of the plain. From then onwards progress was slow and uncertain. Four or five times we lost the track and continued out of our way until a patch of bush or marsh brought us up short. Twice we got stuck and had to push our way out; two or three times we were nearly overturned by sudden subsidences into the watercourses. It was these channels that enabled us to find our way, for they all ran at right angles to our route. When we reached one the Armenian and the boy would take opposite sides and follow the bank down until one of them reached the crossing; there would then be whistles and signals and we resumed the right road.

At each check, the professor made up his mind to stop. 'It is quite impossible. We shall never find the road until daylight. We may be going miles out of our way. It is dangerous and futile. We had far better spend the night here and go back at dawn.'

Then the driver would return with news of success. 'J'ai décidé; nous arrêtons ici,' the professor would say.

'Ah,' came the invariable response, 'vous savez, monsieur, ça n'a pas d'importance.'

Throughout the journey the boy sat on the mudguard in front, picking out the rare stones and hoof-marks which directed us. Once, however, the Armenian despaired. We had all walked round and round for half an hour in widening circles, searching the completely blank earth with electric torches. We came back defeated. It was now about ten o'clock and bitterly cold. We were just discussing how we could possibly keep ourselves warm during the coming eight hours, when the boy saw lights ahead. We drove on and ran straight into a caravan bivouacked round a campfire. Our arrival caused great consternation in the camp. Men and women ran out of the tents or sprang out of the ground from huddled heaps of blankets; the animals sprang up and strained at their tethers or tumbled about with hobbled legs. Rifles were levelled at us. The Armenian strode into their midst, however, and, after distributing minute sums of money as a sign of goodwill, elicited directions.

Our worst check was within sight of Addis, on the top of Entoto. This part of the journey had seemed perilous enough by daylight, but by now we were so stiff and cold as to be indifferent to any other consideration. Twice we pulled up within a few feet of the precipice, the boy having fallen asleep on the mudguard where he sat. We got stuck again with two wheels in the air and two in a deep gully, but eventually we found the road and at that moment ran out of petrol. Two minutes earlier this disaster would have been insuperable. From now on, however, it was all downhill, and we ran into the town without the engine. When at last we reached the professor's hotel we were too tired to say good night. He silently picked up his bottles of holy water and, with a little nod, went up to his room, and I had fallen asleep before he was out of sight. A sulky night-porter found us a can of petrol and we drove on to the Hôtel de France. The manager was sitting up for me with a boiling kettle and a bottle of rum. I slept well that night.

CHAPTER 5

IN LONDON, FULL of ingenuous eagerness to get aboard, I had booked my ticket through to Zanzibar, between which island and Djibouti the Messageries Maritimes maintain a fortnightly service. Now, with everyone else going home, I began to rather regret the arrangement and think wistfully of an Irish Christmas. The next ship, the *Général Voyson*, was not due for ten days, and the prospect of spending the time either at Addis Ababa or Djibouti was unattractive. The difficulty (and of course the charm) of Abyssinia is the inaccessibility of the interior. I should dearly have liked to make a journey north to Axum or Lallibella, but this would require camping-equipment and the organisation of a caravan; it would take many weeks and more money than I could conveniently afford; even so, I would have attempted it if I had been able to find a companion, but no one seemed ready to come, and it seemed futile to set out alone in complete ignorance of the geography and language of the country. I was on the point of forfeiting my ticket and joining the Italian ship by which Irene was sailing north, when Mr Plowman, the British consul at Harar, who with his family was visiting the capital for the coronation, very kindly suggested that I should return with him and break my journey at his home for a few days. No suggestion could have been more delightful. There was glamour in all the associations of Harar, the Arab city-state which stood first among the fruits of Ethiopian imperialism, the scene of Sir Richard Burton's *First Steps in Africa*, the market where the caravans met between coast and highlands; where Galla, Somali, and Arab interbred to produce women whose beauty was renowned throughout East Africa. There is talk of a motor-road that is to connect it with the railway, but at present it must still be approached by the tortuous hill-pass and small track along which Arthur Rimbaud had sent rifles to Menelik.

Except for one overpowering afternoon spent scrambling with Irene through the forest of Jemjem in hopeless pursuit of black-and-white monkeys, the last days before we left Addis were agreeably quiet and enabled us to readjust our rather feverish impressions of the town and its inhabitants. On the morning of November 15th we left by the last of the special trains. The departure took place with far less formality than the arrivals. There was no band, but the platform was crowded with the whole European population. Even our Armenian chauffeur came to see us off; the carriage in which I travelled was filled with little bunches of flowers hung there by the servants of one of the British officials who was going home on leave. Mr Hall was there with eye-glass and top hat. He trusted that anything I wrote about Abyssinia would be friendly and sympathetic. I assured him that it would be so.

Next day at dawn we arrived at Dirre-Dowa, and the Plowmans and I took leave of our fellow passengers. We had all spent a practically sleepless night, and for the greater part of that hot Sunday we remained in our rooms at Bollolakos' hotel. I went to Mass at a church full of odious French children, washed in a sandy bath, slept, and wrote an article on Abyssinian politics to post to my paper. As I sealed up the envelope I had the agreeable feeling of being once more a free man. I could now come and go as I liked. I could meet people without seeing in their eye the embarrassed consciousness that they were talking to 'the Press'; it affected people in various ways, some were reticent to the verge of rudeness, others so expansive as to be almost tedious, but no one, I found, treated a journalist quite as a fellow human being.

We dined that evening in a pleasant little party consisting of the Plowmans and their governess, the Cypriot manager of the local bank, Mr Hall's brother, who was in business at Dirre-Dowa, and his wife, an English lady who wore a large enamelled brooch made in commemoration of the opening of Epping Forest to the public and presented to her father who was, at the time, an alderman of the City of London. We sat in the open under an orange-tree and drank chianti and gossiped about the coronation, while many hundreds of small red ants overran the table and fell on to our heads from above.

The Plowmans' horses had not arrived that day, so that their start would have to be delayed until Tuesday morning and their arrival at Harar until Thursday. The director of the railway had wired to the station-master at Dirre-Dowa to reserve mules and servants for me, and I decided to avail myself of them next day and reach Harar a day ahead of my hosts. I felt that it was, in a way, more suitable to enter the town alone and unofficially.

Accordingly, I set out early next morning, riding a lethargic grey mule, accompanied by a mounted Abyssinian guide who spoke French, an aged groom who attached himself to me against my express orders, and a Galla porter, of singularly villainous expression, to carry my luggage. We had not been going long before this man, easily out-distancing our beasts, disappeared into the hills with great lurching strides, the bag containing my passport, letter of credit, and all of my essential clothes balanced negligently on his head. I became apprehensive, and the guide was anything but reassuring. All Gallas were dishonest, he explained, and this one was a particularly dirty type. He disclaimed all responsibility for engaging him; that had been done by the station-master; he himself would never have chosen a man of such obvious criminal characteristics. It was not unusual for porters to desert with the luggage; there was no catching them once they got over the hills among their own people; they had murdered an Indian not long ago in circumstances of peculiar atrocity. But it was possible, he added, that the man had merely hurried on to take his *khat*.[1]

This was, in fact, what had happened. We came upon him again some hours later, squatting by the roadside with his lap full of the leaves and his teeth and mouth green with chewing; his expression had softened considerably under the influence of the drug, and for

---

1 This is a herb of mildly intoxicating properties eaten extensively by Arabs and the Mohammedan peoples of East Africa. Its effect is temporarily stimulating, but enervating in the long run. Habitual *khat* chewers are said to be more satisfactory as workmen, but less satisfactory as husbands. It is bitter in taste, rather like sorrel. I ate a leaf or two without noticing any effect; the real addict browses every morning on a great bundle.

the rest of the journey he was docile enough, trailing along behind us in a slightly bemused condition.

For the first few miles we followed the river-bed, a broad stretch of sand which for a few hours in the year is flooded from bank to bank with a turgid mountain torrent, which sweeps down timber and boulders and carries away the accumulated refuse of the town. It was now nearing the end of the dry season and the way was soft and powdery; it was heavy going until we reached the foot of the caravan route. There is a short cut over the hills which is used by foot passengers and riders who are much pressed for time; on the guide's advice we chose the longer and more leisurely road which winds in a long detour round the spur and joins the rock path at the summit. It is about four hours from the hotel to the uplands by this road. The mules took things easily; it was necessary to beat them more or less continually to keep them moving at all. At the top we paused for a rest.

Behind us, as far as we could see, the country was utterly desolate; the hillside up which we had climbed was covered with colourless sand and rock, and beyond, on the other side of the valley, rose other hills equally bare of dwelling or cultivation. The only sign of life was a caravan of camels, roped nose to tail, following us a mile or so below. In front of us everything was changed. This was Galla country, full of little villages and roughly demarcated arable plots. The road in places was bordered with cactus and flowering euphorbia-trees; the air was fresh and vital.

Another three hours brought us to a native inn, where the boys hoped to get some food. The landlord, however, told us that the local governor had recently cancelled his licence, an injustice which he attributed to the rivalry of the Greek who kept the rest house at Haramaya. He provided them with a tin can full of *talla*, which the two Christians drank; the Mohammedan religiously contenting himself with another handful of *khat*. Then we went on. In another four hours we were in sight of the lake of Haramaya, a welcoming sheet of light between two green hills. It was here that we proposed to break the journey for a night. It is not difficult to ride through in one day on a pony; it is quite possible on a mule, but most people prefer to wait until the next morning. It is another four hours on, and four hours at that stage seem barely supportable. Moreover, the gates of the city are shut at sundown and it is sometimes difficult to obtain admission after that time. I was tired out, and at the sight of water the mules for the first time showed some sign of interest. Indeed, it became impossible to keep them to the path, so I left the boys to water them and walked the last mile round the lake to the rest house.

This was a single-storied, white building comprising a dining-room, kitchen, verandah, and four minute bedrooms. The accommodation was very simple; there was, of course, no bath or sanitation and no glass in the windows. There was, however, a most delightfully amiable young Greek in charge of it, who got me a meal and talked incessantly in very obscure English. It was now about three o'clock. Seeing that I was tired, he said he would make me a cocktail. He took a large glass and poured into it, whisky, crème de menthe, and Fernet Branca, and filled up with soda-water. He made himself a glass of the same mixture, clinked glasses, and said, 'Cheerioh, damned sorry no ice.' As a matter of fact, it was surprisingly refreshing. After luncheon I went to my room and slept until late in the evening.

We dined together on tinned spaghetti and exceedingly tough fried chicken. He prattled on about his home in Alexandria and his sister who was taking a secretarial course and his rich uncle who lived at Dirre-Dowa and had set him up in the inn. I asked what the uncle did, and he said he had a 'monopole'; this seemed to be a perfectly adequate description of almost all commerical ventures in Abyssinia. I could not gather what he monopolised; whatever it was seemed extremely profitable and involved frequent excursions to Aden. The nephew hoped to succeed to the business on his uncle's retirement.

While we were dining, two heavily armed soldiers appeared with a message for my host. He seemed mildly put out by their arrival, explaining with great simplicity that he was involved in an affair with an elderly Abyssinian lady of high birth; she was not very attractive, but what choice had he in a remote place like this? She was generous, but very exacting. Only that afternoon he had been with her and here were her retainers come to fetch him again. He gave them each a cigarette and told them to wait. When they had finished smoking, they returned; he offered them more cigarettes, but they refused; apparently their mistress was impatient; the young man shrugged and, excusing himself with the phrase (typical of his diction) 'You won't allow me, won't you?' went away with them into the darkness. I returned to my bed and slept.

Next morning we rode into Harar. The way was full of traffic, caravans of camels, mules and asses, horsemen, and teams of women bent double under prodigious loads of wood. There were no carts of any kind; indeed, I think that they are quite unknown in Abyssinia, and that the railway engine was the first wheeled vehicle to appear there. After three hours' gentle ride we came in sight of the town. Approached from Haramaya it presents a quite different aspect from the drawing in Burton's *First Steps in Africa*; there it appears as he saw it coming fom the Somali coast, perched on a commanding hill; we found it lying below us, an irregular brown patch at the foot of the hills. In the distance rose the flat-topped mountain which the Abyssinians have chosen for their refuge in the event of the country rising against them; there is a lake of fresh water at the summit, and a naturally fortified camp which they hope to hold against the Galla until relief arrives from their own highlands. No one may visit the place without a permit from the local dedej-match.

A few buildings – the British consulate, Lej Yasu's deserted palace, a Capuchin leper settlement, a church, and the villas of one or two Indian merchants – have spread beyond the walls; outside the main gate a few women squatting beside little heaps of grain and peppers constituted a market; there was a temporary and rather unstable arch of triumph presented to the town by the firm of Mohammedali in honour of the coronation. A guard was posted at the gate; there was also an octroi, where we had to leave the luggage until the officer should return from his luncheon some hours later.

As in most mediæval towns, there was no direct street in Harar leading from the gates to the central square. A very narrow lane ran, under the walls, round numerous corners before it turned inwards and broadened into the main street. On either side of this passage stood ruined houses, desolate heaps of stone and rubble, some of them empty, others patched up with tin to accommodate goats or poultry. The town, like the numerous lepers who inhabit it, seemed to be dying at its extremities; the interior, however, was full of vitality and animation.

There are two inns in Harar, boasting the names of Leon d'Or and Bellevue; both universally condemned as unsuitable for European habitation. Any doubt I might have had about which to patronise was dissolved, as soon as we turned into the main street, by a stout little man in a black skull-cap, who threw himself at my bridle and led me to the Leon d'Or. During my brief visit I became genuinely attached to this man. He was an Armenian of rare character, named Bergebedgian; he spoke a queer kind of French with remarkable volubility, and I found great delight in all his opinions; I do not think I have ever met a more tolerant man; he had no prejudice or scruples of race, creed, or morals of any kind whatever; there were in his mind none of those opaque patches of inconsidered principles, it was a single translucent pool of placid doubt; whatever splashes of precept had disturbed its surface from time to time had left no ripple; reflections flitted to and fro and left it unchanged.

Unfortunately his hotel was less admirable. Most of his business was done in the bar, where he sold great quantities of colourless and highly inflammatory spirit distilled by a fellow countryman of his and labelled, capriciously, 'Very Olde Scotts Whisky', 'Fine Champayne', or 'Hollands Gin' as the taste of his clients dictated. Next to the bar was a little dining-room where two or three regular customers (also fellow countrymen) took their greasy and pungent meals. The bedrooms were built round a little courtyard, where some pathetic survivals of a garden were discernible amid the heaps of kitchen refuse with which it was littered. This building had formerly been the town house of an Abyssinian official. It was rarely that anyone came to stay; usually not more than one in any three weeks, he said; but, as it happened, there was a second guest at that moment, a French clerk on business from the Banque d'Indo-Chine at Djibouti. I lunched with this young man, who was a punctilious, mannerly person; the hot wind had chapped his lips so that he was unable to smile – an affliction which made him seem a little menacing in light conversation. It was he who first put into my head the deplorable notion of returning to Europe across the Congo by the west coast. The proprietor waited on us in person, and made it hard to escape the forbidding dishes: we both felt moderately ill after every meal.

That afternoon I went for a walk round the town and saw that a large part of it was in decay. The most prominent buildings were the modern Government House, the French hospital, Mohamme-dali's offices, a Capuchin mission cathedral, and an ancient mosque with two whitewashed minarets; the rest of the place was made up of a bunch of small shops, a few Armenian, Greek, and Indian stores, single-roomed dwelling-houses, mostly standing back behind grubby little yards, and numerous *tedj* houses, combined brothels and public houses which advertise themselves with a red cross over the door – a traditional sign which caused some misunderstanding when the Swedish medical mission first established itself in the country.

The appearance of the buildings and the people was wholly foreign to Abyssinia; a difference which was emphasised on this particular afternoon by the fact that all the Abyssinians were indoors at a party at Government House, so that the streets were peopled almost exclusively by turbaned Harari. The beauty of the women was dazzling – far exceeding anything I had expected. The native women I had seen at Addis Ababa had been far from attractive; their faces had been plump and smug, their hair unbecomingly heaped up in a black, fuzzy mass, glittering with melted butter, their figures swollen grotesquely with a surfeit of petticoats. The women of Harar are slender and very upright; they carry themselves with all the grace of the Somalis, but, instead of their monkey-like faces and sooty complexions, they had golden brown skins and features of the utmost fineness. Moreover, there was a delicacy about their clothes and ornaments which the Somalis entirely lacked; their hair was plaited into innumerable tight little ropes and covered with bright silk shawls; they wore long trousers and silk shawls wound under their arms, leaving their shoulders bare. Most of them had bright gold ornaments. Burton admits their beauty, but condemns their voices as harsh and outstandingly displeasing. I cannot conceive what prompted this statement; indeed, compared with those of Arab women, they seemed soft and sweet. (No sound made by mankind is quite so painful as the voices of two Arab women at variance.) An alliance might be formed with any of these exquisite people, the Armenian informed me later, for four thalers a month and board. That it was possible that the parents might expect more in the case of a foreigner. This sum, however, covered the girl's services in the house, so that it was a perfectly sound investment if I intended making a stay of any length in the town. I explained that I was only there for three days. In that case, he said, it was obviously more convenient to confine myself to married women. There were certain preliminary formalities to be gone through with an unmarried girl which cost time and money.[1]

I visited the leper settlement; a little collection of *tukals* outside the walls, in the charge of a French priest. Four or five sleep in each hut, an arrangement which the old priest explained in what seems to me a very terrible phrase, 'You understand, monsieur, that it takes several lepers to make one man.'

I went to the cathedral and there met the Bishop of Harar, the famous Monsignor Jerome, of whom I had heard many reports in Addis Ababa. He has been in the country for forty-eight years, suffering, at first, every kind of discouragement and persecution, and attaining, towards the middle of his career, a position of great influence at Court. He acted as Tafari's tutor, and many people attributed to him, often in harsh terms, the emperor's outstanding skill as a political tactician. Lately, as his pupil's ambitions have become realised, the bishop's advice has been less devotedly canvassed. Indeed, it is doubtful whether it would still be of great value, for he is a very old man now and his mind is losing something of its former grasp of public affairs.

It is his practice to greet all visitors to his church, but I did not know this at the time and was greatly startled when he suddenly swooped in upon me. He was tall and emaciated, like an El Greco saint, with very long white hair and beard, great roving eyes, and

[1] The Harari, in common with the Somalis and most of the Gallas, practise infibulation.

a nervous, almost ecstatic smile; he advanced at a kind of shuffling jogtrot, fluttering his hands and uttering little moans. After we had been round the church, which was shabby and unremarkable enough, he invited me into his divan to talk. I steered the conversation as delicately as I could from church expenses to Arthur Rimbaud. At first we were at cross purposes, because the bishop, being a little deaf, mistook my '*poète*' for '*prêtre*', and inflexibly maintained that no Father Rimbaud had ever, to his knowledge, ministered in Abyssinia. Later this difficulty was cleared up, and the bishop, turning the name over in his mind, remembered that he had, in fact, known Rimbaud quite well; a young man with a beard, who was in some trouble with his leg; a very serious man who did not go out much; he was always worried about business; not a good Catholic, though he had died at peace with the Church, the bishop understood, at Marseille. He used to live with a native woman in a little house, now demolished, in the square; he had no children; probably the woman was still alive; she was not a native of Harar, and after Rimbaud's death she had gone back to her own people in Tigre ... a very, very serious young man, the bishop repeated. He seemed to find this epithet the most satisfactory – very serious and sad.

It was rather a disappointing interview. All the way to Harar I had nurtured the hope of finding something new about Rimbaud, perhaps even to encounter a half-caste son keeping a shop in some back street. The only significant thing I learned from the bishop was that, living in Harar, surrounded by so many radiant women, he should have chosen a mate from the stolid people of Tigre – a gross and perverse preference.

That evening, at about six o'clock, Mr Bergebedgian suggested that we might go to the Abyssinian party which had now finished luncheon and was settling down to an evening's music at Government House. He himself was an indispensable guest, as he had promised the loan of an Aladdin lamp, without which they would be left in complete darkness. Accordingly, we set out and were received with great warmth by the acting governor. A considerable sum had apparently been granted to the municipality to be spent on rejoicings for the coronation, an object which was rightly interpreted as meaning a series of parties. They had been going on for a fortnight and would continue until the dedejmatch returned from the capital. As a symbol of the origin of the feast, a kind of altar had been built, at one end of the room, on which stood a large photograph of Tafari surrounded by flowers. About fifty Abyssinians in white *chammas* sat round on the floor, already fairly drunk. Green chairs of the kind one finds in public parks were set for us at a velvet-covered round table. The acting governor sat with us and poured out extravagant glasses of whisky. Slaves trotted about among the other guests, distributing bottles of German beer. With the appearance of our lamp the entertainment began. An orchestra emerged, furnished with three single-stringed fiddles. The singer was an Abyssinian woman of startling girth. She sang in a harsh voice, panting for breath between each line. It was an immensely long ballad of patriotic sentiment. The name Haile Selassie recurred with great regularity. No one paid any more attention than they would have at a musical party in Europe, but she sang on cheerfully, through the buzz of conversation, with an expression of settled amiability. When a gate-crasher was detected and expelled with some disorder, she merely turned round and watched the proceedings, still singing lustily. At the end of her song she was given some beer and many friendly smacks on the behind. The whisky was reserved for us and for a few favoured guests; the host singled these out, called for their glasses, and poured it into their beer from the bottle on the table.

The second song was a great deal longer than the first; it was of the kind, popular in European cabarets, which introduces references to members of the audience. Each name was greeted with cheers and a good deal of boisterous back-smacking. The host asked our names and repeated them in her ear, but they came out so distorted, if they came out at all, as to be wholly unrecognisable. After about two hours, Mr Bergebedgian said he must return to the inn and see to the dinner. This was the signal for a general movement; three or four notables were invited to the table, wine-glasses produced, a dish of sponge fingers, and finally a bottle of champagne. We drank each other's health, making graceful unintelligible little speeches in our own languages. Then, after much handshaking, we returned to the inn, leaving our Aladdin lamp at the party.

After a profoundly indigestible dinner, Mr Bergebedgian joined us – the unsmiling clerk and myself – in a glass of a disturbing liqueur labelled 'Koniak'. Presently he said, would we like to go to another party? There was a wedding in the town. We said we should like to go very much. This time our expedition was attended with grave precautions. First, Mr Bergebedgian buckled on bandoleer and revolver-holster; then he went to the cash-desk and produced a heavy automatic pistol, charged the magazine, and tucked it into place; then he reached under the bar and drew out four or five wooden clubs, which he dealt out to his servants; the bank-clerk showed a revolver, I my sword-stick; he nodded approval. It was all very much like Rat's preparation for the attack on Toad Hall. Then he barred up the house, a process involving innumerable bolts and padlocks. At last, attended by three servants with staves and a storm lantern, we set out. Things were safer at Harar than they used to be, he explained, but it was wiser to take no risks. As we emerged into the street, a hyena flashed red eyes at us and scuttled off. I do not know how hyenas have got their reputation for laughing. Abyssinia is full of them; they come into the towns at night scavenging and performing the less valuable service of nosing up corpses in the cemeteries; they used to bay all round the hotel at Addis Ababa, and the next night, which I spent in a tent in the Plowmans' garden, was disturbed by a small pack of them crunching bones within a few yards of my bed, but not once did I hear anything approaching a laugh.

The streets were pitch black – not a lighted window showed anywhere – and except for hyenas, dogs, and cats fighting over the refuse, totally deserted. Our way led down a narrow passage, between high, crumbling walls, which was sometimes graded in steps and sometimes sloped steeply inwards to a dry gutter. Our first stop was at the house of a Greek grocer. We beat on the shutters, behind which a crack of light was immediately extinguished. Mr Bergebedgian called his name, and presently a little peep opened and a pair of eyes appeared. Some civilities were exchanged, and then, after much drawing of bolts, we were admitted. The grocer offered us 'koniak' and cigarettes. Mr Bergebedgian explained that we wanted him to accompany us to the party. He refused, explaining that he had to make up his books. Mr Bergebedgian, accordingly, borrowed some small silver (a loan which, I observed, was duly noted in the accounts) and we took our leave. More black, empty alleys. Suddenly a policeman rocketed up from the gutter where he had been taking a rest, and challenged us with some ferocity. Mr Bergebedgian replied with a mock flourish of his revolver; some light exchange of chaff and back-chat followed, in the course of which the policeman decided to join the party. After a few minutes we found another policeman, huddled in his blanket on the counter of a deserted greengrocer's stall; they shook him awake and brought him along with us. At last, we reached a small courtyard, beyond which, from a lighted door, came the sound of singing.

No doubt we looked rather a formidable gang as we stalked in bristling with weapons, but it was probably the sight of the two policemen which caused most alarm. Anyway, whatever the reason, wild panic followed our entry. There was only one door, through which we had come, and a stream of Harari girls dashed past us, jostling, stumbling, and squealing; others cowered away under their shawls or attempted to climb the steps which led to a little loft. Mr Bergebedgian repeatedly explained our pacific intentions, but it was some time before confidence was restored. Then a young man appeared with chairs for us and the dance was resumed.

The house consisted of a single room with a gallery full of coffee sacks at one end approached by a ladder. This corner was the kitchen. A large stove, built of clay and rubble, stood under the ladder, and two or three earthenware jars and pots lay on and around it. Opposite the door the floor was raised in a carpeted dais which extended in a narrow ledge down the adjoining wall. It was here that our chairs were set. The few men of the party lounged round the door; the girls squatted together on the dais; the dance took place in the well of the floor to the music of the girls, singing, and the beating of hand drums. It was a pretty scene, lit by a single oil-lamp; the walls were decorated with coloured wickerwork plates; a brazier of charcoal and incense stood in one corner; a wicker dish of sweets was passed from one delicate henna-stained hand to another among the girls on the dais.

The dance was of the simplest kind. One girl and two men stood opposite each other; the girl wore a shawl on her head and the men held their *chammas* over the lower part of their faces. They shuffled up to each other and shuffled back; after several repetitions of this movement they crossed over, revolving as they passed each other, and repeated the figure from opposite sides. As the girl came to our end, Mr Bergebedgian pulled her shawl off. 'Look,' he said, 'hasn't she got nice hair?' She recovered it crossly and Mr Bergebedgian began teasing her, twitching it back every time she passed. But he was a soft-hearted fellow and he desisted as soon as he realised that he was causing genuine distress.

This was the bride's house that we were in; a second party was in progress in another part of the town at the home of the bridegroom. We went to visit it and found it precisely similar in character, but very much larger and more splendid. Clearly the girl had made a good match. These parties are kept up every night for a week before the wedding; the bride's friends and relations in her home, the bridegroom's in his. They do not mix until the actual wedding-day. For some reason which I could not fathom they had lately come under ban of the law; hence the consternation at our arrival. We stayed for about an hour and then returned to our hotel. The policemen came in with us and hung about until they were given a tumblerful each of neat spirit. Sleep was difficult that night, for the pillows were hard as boards, and through the windows, devoid of glass and shutters, came the incessant barking of dogs and hyenas and the occasional wailing horns of the town guard.

Next morning the bank-clerk rode away and Mr Bergebedgian took me for a walk in the town. He was a remarkable guide. We went into the shops of all his friends and drank delicious coffee and smoked cigarettes; he seemed to have small financial transactions with all of them, paying out a thaler here, receiving another there. We went into the law-courts, where we saw a magistrate trying a case about real property; for some reason both litigants and all the witnesses were in chains; the plaintiff was a Galla who pleaded his

own cause through an interpreter. He became so eager about his
wrongs that the interpreter was unable to keep up with him, and
after repeated admonishments left him to finish his own case in his
own tongue. Behind the court was a lion in a wooden case so small
that he could barely move in it, so foul that the air of the whole yard
was insupportable. We saw the great hall used for the raw-beef
banquets. A group of slave-boys were being instructed in squad
drill by an older boy with a stick. The commands were recognisably
of English origin – presumably imported by some old soldier from
the KAR. We went into the prison, a place of frightful filth, only
comparable to the lion's cage. Mr Bergebedgian, in whose character
there was a marked strain of timidity, was very reluctant to enter,
saying that three or four deaths occurred there every week from
typhus; a flea from one of the prisoners would kill us both. That
evening in my bath I found myself covered with fleabites, and
remembered this information with some apprehension. I was not
really at ease in my mind until the time was over for the disease to
show itself. The cells stood round a small yard; three or four men
were tethered to the wall of each cell, with chains just long enough to
allow of their crawling into the open. Those who were fed by their
families never left the buildings; the others were allowed to earn
their keep by working in gangs on the roads. The lot of the more
neglected seemed by far preferable. Most of the prisoners were there
for debt, often for quite trifling sums; they remained there until they
paid or, more probably, died. There were no less than three prisons
in Harar. My servant got locked up one day for a breach of the
sanitary regulations and I had to pay five dollars to get him out. He
remarked, with some justice, how could one tell that there were any
sanitary regulations in Harar? In his opinion, it was a put-up job
because he was a stranger.

We went into the two or three *tedj* houses. At this stage of the
morning they were fairly empty, some had no customers at all, in
others a few dissipated men, who had slept the night there, squatted
holding their heads, quarrelling with the women about the
reckoning; at only one did we find any gaiety, where a party just
arrived from the country were starting to get drunk; each sat beside
a decanter of cloudy *tedj*, one of them was playing a kind of banjo.

The women were, without exception, grossly ugly. Mr Bergebedgian drew back a sleeve and exhibited a sore on the shoulder of one
of them. 'A dirty lot,' he said, giving her an affectionate pat and
a half-piastre bit.

We went through the bazaar, Mr Bergebedgian disparaging
all the goods in the friendliest way possible, and I bought some
silver bangles which he obtained for me at a negligible fraction
of their original price. We went into several private houses, where
Mr Bergebedgian examined and exhibited everything, pulling
clothes out of the chests, bringing down bags of spice from the
shelves, opening the oven and tasting the food, pinching the girls,
and giving half-piastre pieces to the children. We went into
a workshop where three or four girls of dazzling beauty were at
work making tables and trays of fine, brilliantly patterned basket-
work. Everywhere he went he seemed to be welcome; everywhere he
not only adapted, but completely transformed, his manners to the
environment. When I came to consider the question I was surprised
to realise that the two most accomplished men I met during the six
months I was abroad, the chauffeur who took us to Debra Lebanos
and Mr Bergebedgian, should both have been Armenians. A race of
rare competence and the most delicate sensitivity. They seem to me
the only genuine 'men of the world'. I suppose everyone at times
likes to picture himself as such a person. Sometimes, when I find that
elusive ideal looming too attractively, when I envy among my friends
this one's adaptability to diverse company, this one's cosmopolitan
experience, this one's impenetrable armour against sentimentality
and humbug, that one's freedom from conventional prejudices, this
one's astute ordering of his finances and nicely calculated hospitality, and realise that, whatever happens to me and however I deplore
it, I shall never in actual fact become a 'hardboiled man of the world'
of the kind I read about in the novels I sometimes obtain at book-
stalls for short railway journeys; that I shall always be ill at ease with
nine out of every ten people I meet; that I shall always find something startling and rather abhorrent in the things most other people
think worth doing, and something puzzling in their standards of
importance; that I shall probably be increasingly, rather than de-
creasingly, vulnerable to the inevitable minor disasters and injustices

of life – then I comfort myself a little by thinking that, perhaps, if I were an Armenian I should find things easier.

After luncheon, a very discomforting meal, I assembled my staff and rode out to the consulate on the hillside opposite, where the Plowmans had returned that morning. It was a house of some age, standing in a large garden, and here I spent three restful days.

The consul and I went to another celebration at Government House, an afternoon party for the six or seven European residents – the French doctor, two priests, two Swedish school teachers and the Italian consul. We sat round a table in the same room and drank champagne and ate sponge fingers. I visited Mr Bergebedgian once or twice and saw the religious dances at the church for the feast of St Michael. Then I resumed my travels. I had intended to stay there for only two nights, having an idea that my train to Djibouti left Dirre-Dowa on Saturday evening. I was assured, however, that it was not until Sunday, so I stayed on until Saturday afternoon, resting that night at Haramaya and reaching the station after a tiring but uneventful ride at midday on Sunday.

There I learned that my train had left on the previous evening. The next started on Tuesday morning and arrived at Djibouti about two hours after the advertised time of the *Général Voyron*'s sailing. I telegraphed to the Messageries' agent, begging him to delay the ship, and resigned myself to a tedious weekend.

FIRST NIGHTMARE

WHEN WE HAVE been home from abroad for a week or two, and time after time, in answer to our friends' polite inquiries, we have retold our experiences, letting phrase engender phrase, until we have made quite a good story of it all; when the unusual people we encountered have, in retrospect, become fabulous and fantastic, and all the checks and uncertainties of travel have become very serious dangers; when the minor annoyances assume heroic proportions and have become, at the luncheon-table, barely endurable privations; even before that, when in the later stages of our journey we reread in our diaries the somewhat bald chronicle of the preceding months – how very little attention do we pay, among all these false frights and bogies, to the stark horrors of boredom.

It seems to me that not nearly enough has been said about this aspect of travel. No one can have any conception of what boredom really means until he has been to the tropics. The boredom of civilised life is trivial and terminable, a puny thing to be strangled between finger and thumb. The blackest things in European social life – rich women talking about their poverty, poor women talking about their wealth, week-end parties of Cambridge æsthetes or lecturers from the London School of Economics, rival Byzantinists at variance, actresses off the stage, psychologists explaining one's own books to one, Americans explaining how much they have drunk lately, houseflies at early morning in the South of France, amateur novelists talking about royalties and reviews, amateur journalists, quarrelling lovers, mystical atheists, raconteurs, dogs, Jews conversant with the group movements of Montparnasse, people who try to look inscrutable, the very terrors, indeed, which drive one to refuge in the still-remote regions of the earth, are mere pansies and pimpernels to the rank flowers which flame grossly in those dark and steaming sanctuaries.

I am constitutionally a martyr to boredom, but never in Europe have I been so desperately and degradingly bored as I was during the next four days; they were as black and timeless as Damnation; a handful of fine ashes thrown into the eyes, a blanket over the face, a mass of soft clay knee deep. My diary reminds me of my suffering in those very words, but the emotion which prompted them seems remote. I know a woman who is always having babies; every time she resolves that that one shall be the last. But, every time, she forgets her resolution, and it is only when her labour begins that she cries to midwife and husband, 'Stop, stop; I've just remembered what it is like. I refuse to have another.' But it is then too late. So the human race goes on. Just in this way, it seems to me, the activity of our ant-hill is preserved by a merciful process of oblivion. 'Never again,' I say on the steps of the house, 'never again will I lunch with that woman.' 'Never again,' I say in the railway carriage, 'will I go and stay with those people.' And yet a week or two later the next invitation finds me eagerly accepting. 'Stop,' I cry inwardly, as I take my hostess's claw-like hand. 'Stop, stop,' I cry in my tepid bath; 'I have just remembered what it is like. I refuse to have another.' But it is too late.

From time to time I meet people who say they are never bored; they are of two kinds; both, for the most part, liars. Some are equally entranced by almost all observable objects, a straggle of blossom on a whitewashed wall, chimneys against the sky, two dogs on a muck heap, an old man with a barrow... Precepts of my house master, a very indolent clergyman, rise before me ... 'only a dull boy is ever dull' ... 'the world is so full of a number of things' ...

Others find consolation in their own minds. Whenever they are confronted with a dreary prospect, they tell me, they just slip away from the barren, objective world into the green pastures and ivory palaces of imagination. Perhaps, by a kind of arrested development, some of them really have retained this happy faculty of childhood, but as a rule I find that both these boasts boil down to a simple form of pessimism – the refusal to recognise that any particular human activity can be of greater value than any other one.

Has anyone ever compiled an anthology of bored verse? It would make a pretty Christmas book with Richard Sickert's 'Ennui' as Frontispiece. Shakespeare and the Bible are full of passages that might be quoted; then there is Mr Herbert's housemaid's song from *Riverside Nights*, and the wartime 'Nobody knows how bored we are, and nobody seems to care'. There might be an appendix of suicides' letters which appear constantly in the daily Press and are too soon forgotten, confessions of faith by men in early middle age who say: '*I am fed up and have resolved to end it all. It just goes on and on. Yesterday the clock broke and there is four shillings owing for the milk. Tell Ruby the key of the coal-cellar is under the hat upstairs. There is not any coal. I have not been a bad man, but I couldn't stand it. Give Aunt Loo my love; she was always one of the best. If the milkman says it's more, it is only four shillings.*'

I wish I could write an account worthy of inclusion in that anthology of the four days between Harar and Aden, but the truth is that they have become vague and insignificant. The suffering was genuine enough, but like a mother emerging from twilight sleep, I am left with only the vague impression that nothing much happened.

Nothing much happened. After luncheon I paid off my mules, the guide, the porter, and the old man who had, by sheer persistence at some indefined moment during the journey, become recognised as a legitimate member of my suite.

Then I sat in Mr Bollolakos' hotel.

Outside in the empty streets the white dust lay radiant and miasmic. Inside there was shade. The bar was locked; the servants were all asleep. The courtyard was unendurable. There was only one place to sit – a small square parlour with cement floor and whitewashed walls; in the centre a table with a plush cloth over it, against the walls a rickety wicker couch and two iron rocking-chairs. I had nothing to read except the first volume of a pocket edition of Pope. There are moments when one does not want to read Pope; when one requires something bulky and informative. There was no bookshop or newsagent in the town. Most hotels, however simple, harbour some reading-matter of some sort or other: brochures of advertisement, magazines or novels left by previous visitors, a few postcards on a rack ... At Mr Bollolakos' there was nothing.

For an hour or two I sat in the rocking-chair reading Pope's juvenile poems.

Most of the time I thought about how awful the next day would be.

In my bedroom were three more volumes of Pope and some writing-paper.

But I should have to cross the courtyard to get to my bedroom.

Presently I got more uninterested in Pope's juvenile poems and decided to cross the courtyard. The three volumes of Pope were somewhere at the bottom of my bag; but I found the writing-paper quite easily; also a minute French dictionary I had forgotten about.

I sat for an hour or so and read the French dictionary, rocking the iron chair in the parlour. '*Bourrasque*, f., squall; fit. *Bourre*, f., wadding; trash. *Bourreau*, m., executioner.'. . .

Presently I drew the table up to the wicker couch, rolled back the plush covering, and wrote a great many letters of Christmas greetings to everyone in England whose address I could remember. I said that it was lovely in Abyssinia; that I pitied them in the fogs and monotony of London; that I longed to see them again and hear all their scandal; that I should be home early in the New Year; that I had bought them presents of shocking Abyssinian painting, which I would deliver on my return to England – every word was a lie.

At sunset the servants woke up; the bar was opened; tables were brought out into the courtyard and laid for dinner; Mr and Mrs Hall and the Cypriot bank-manager arrived. I told them that I had no books, and they compassionately lent me some copies of *John o' London's Weekly*. Mr Hall was most amiable. He led me back to his house after dinner and showed me some pastel drawings he had made of Ethiopian sunsets, and a coloured photograph of the Prince of Wales which stood on a draped easel in a corner of the drawing-room. His invitation for the coronation had arrived by yesterday's mail; intrigue in high places had delayed it, he said; there were many members of the commercial community who were jealous of his wife's jewellery; and he nodded significantly to the fine brooch commemorating the opening of Epping Forest to the public.

That night, under my mosquito curtain, I read three issues of *John o' London's Weekly* straight through, word for word, from cover to cover.

Next morning after breakfast I read the fourth. Then I went up to the bank and dragged out the cashing of a small cheque to the utmost limits of politeness; I sent a letter of introduction to the famous M. de Montfried, but learned that he was in Europe. It was still early in the day. I took a dose of sleeping-draught and went to bed again.

That evening the train from Hawash arrived, bringing the old gentleman with whom I had travelled to Addis Ababa and one of the ladies who had been staying at the legation. He was on his way to visit the Plowmans at Harar; she was going to the coast and then to Europe. The latest news from Addis was that everyone felt very tired.

Early next morning the train left for Djibouti. There was none of the formality or facility that had characterised our arrival. Half an hour after the train was due to start, the lady from the legation and I were turned out of the carriages which she had occupied on the previous two days, to make room for the servants of an Abyssinian princess who was running down to the coast for a little shopping. These men were very drunk and employed their time in throwing beer-bottles into the desert from the observation platform. With every mile of the journey the heat and humidity became worse; the country on either side of the line was unrelieved emptiness; we rattled and jolted very slowly along the narrow track, increasing by another hour and a half the delay which the royal party had caused, while the young lady from the legation entertained me with censorious comments on the two or three English and Irish acquaintances whom we found in common.

There was one moment of excitement when, towards sundown, we came in sight of the sea and saw that the *Général Voyron* was still there. She lay far out in the harbour, with steam up, presumably waiting for the train. The line into Djibouti turns and twists among great boulders and dry watercourses, so that sometimes we lost sight of her for ten minutes at a time; with every reappearance she seemed further away. Presently it became clear that she had, in fact, already sailed.

I discussed the question with the Messageries agent, but he was unpenitent. I had said in my telegram that I was coming at five-thirty; he had kept the ship back until six; I had arrived at seven; it was not his affair that the train was late; sometimes on that line trains were several days late. This attitude is described, by those who like it, as Latin logic. It is true that Armenians do not see things in the same terms.

We went to the Hôtel des Arcades. Madame's geniality seemed less comforting that it had done on my first arrival. We visited the British vice-consul to ask about ships and learned that there was one to Europe on Thursday and a small boat to Aden on Saturday; the next Messageries ship to Zanzibar left in a fortnight; he said that there had been several little earthquakes during the last month and showed us a large fissure in the wall of his office.

I returned to the hotel in low spirits. From any point of view the prospect seemed unsatisfactory. The primary need seemed to be immediate escape from Djibouti. I had practically made up my mind to return to Europe when Madame at the hotel came to my rescue. There was an Italian boat leaving for Aden next day; the Messageries ship from Zanzibar would pick me up there. We dined on the pavement and I went to bed more hopefully.

Next day was the most deadly of all. I was awakened at dawn with information that the Italian boat was in, and was leaving in an hour. I dressed in haste, fastened my luggage, and hurried down-stairs. Madame greeted me in a pink *peignoir*. The boy had made a mistake. There was no boat in.

As soon as it was open I went to the Italian shipping office and bought my ticket. Their ship was due at any time, and would leave within an hour or two of her arrival. She was called the *Somalia*. They would ring me up at the hotel as soon as she was sighted. I sat about the hotel all day waiting for their message; it was impossible to go far away. We visited the chief store of the town and bought some books; the Abyssinian princess was there in a heavy green veil, bargaining over a pseudo-Chinese dinner-gong of atrocious construction. At dinner-time the shipping company rang up to say that the *Somalia* was not expected until next morning. Later that evening I discovered that there were three American cinema-men staying at the other hotel; their company was very pleased with them for the pictures they had made of the coronation, and they were pleased with themselves. We went for an exquisitely dismal jaunt together in the native town.

Next day was pretty bad. I was again called at dawn with the news that the *Somalia* was in and would sail directly. This time the information was partially correct. I paid, in my haste without questioning it, an hotel bill of staggering size, and hurried down to the sea. The *Somalia* was there all right, a clean little coastal steamer with accommodation for half a dozen passengers. When I had embarked I learned that she was not sailing until six that evening. I had not the spirit to return to the shore; I watched the liner for Europe arrive, take up the lady from the legation, and steam away. All that day I sat on a swivel chair in the saloon, reading one of the books I had purchased at the store – a singularly ill-informed account of Abyssinia, translated from the English.

Eventually, rather after six o'clock, we sailed, and crossed in fine weather to Aden. There were five of us at dinner that night – the captain, a French clerk, and an Italian official and his wife on their way to Mogadishu. We had nothing much to say to each other. The Italian official made some jokes about sea-sickness; the French clerk gave me some figures, whose significance I have now forgotten, about the coffee trade at Hodeida; the captain was gallant in Italian to the official's wife.

Next morning we arrived at Aden. That was the end of four exceedingly painful days.

BRITISH EMPIRE

CHAPTER 1

PURE MISCHANCE HAD brought me to Aden, and I expected to dislike it. I had, in fact, a fairly clear picture in my mind of what it would be like; a climate notoriously corrosive of all intellect and initiative; a landscape barren of any growing or living thing; a community, full of placid self-esteem, typical in part of Welwyn Garden City, in part of the Trocadero bar; conversation full of dreary technical shop among the men, and harsh little snobberies among the women. I contrasted it angrily with the glamour and rich beauty I expected to find at Zanzibar. How wrong I was.

How wrong I was, as things turned out, in all my preconceived notions about this journey. Zanzibar and the Congo, names pregnant with romantic suggestion, gave me nothing, while the places I found most full of interest were those I expected to detest – Kenya and Aden.

On first acquaintance, however, there was much about the settlement to justify my forebodings. It is, as every passenger down the Red Sea knows, an extinct volcano joined to the mainland by a flat and almost invisible neck of sand; not a tree or flower or blade of grass grows on it, the only vegetation is a meagre crop of colourless scrub which has broken out in patches among the cinders; there is no earth and no water, except what is dragged there in a ceaseless succession of camel-carts through the tunnelled road; the sanitation everywhere – in the hotels, the club, the mess, the private bungalows – is still that of a temporary camp. Architecture, except for a series of water-tanks of unknown age, does not exist. A haphazard jumble of bungalows has been spilt over the hillside, like the litter of picnic-parties after Bank Holiday. Opposite the quay a waste space has been faintly formalised and called a garden, and behind it stands a mean crescent, comprising shipping offices, two hotels, and a few shops peddling oriental trash in silk, brass, and ivory. The chief hotel is as expensive as Torr's at Nairobi; the food has only two flavours – tomato ketchup and Worcestershire sauce; the bathroom consists of a cubicle in which a tin can is suspended on a rope; there is a nozzle at the bottom of the can encrusted with stalactites of green slime; the bather stands on the slippery cement floor and pulls a string releasing a jet of water over his head and back; for a heavy extra charge it is possible, with due notice, to have the water warmed; the hall-porter has marked criminal tendencies; the terrace is infested by money-changers. The only compensating luxury, a seedy, stuffed sea-animal, unmistakably male, which is kept in a chest and solemnly exhibited – on payment – as a mermaid. You would have to search a long time before finding many such hotels in the whole of England.

There are other superficial disadvantages about Aden, notably the division of the settlement into two towns. So far I have been speaking of the district known as Steamer Point; about three miles – an expensive taxi-drive – away lies Crater Town, the centre of such commerce as has survived. This was the original nucleus of the settlement. It is surrounded on three sides by cliffs, and on the fourth by what was once a harbour, now silted up and for a long time closed to all traffic. The original residency stands there, now a guest-house for visiting Arab chiefs; there is also a large derelict barracks, partially demolished, and an Anglican church, built in Victorian Gothic, which was once the garrison chapel, and is still provided with its own chaplain, who reads services there Sunday after Sunday in absolute void. This man, earnest and infinitely kind, had lately arrived from Bombay; he rescued me from the hotel, and took me to stay with him for a few days in his large, ramshackle house on the Crater beach, known to taxi-drivers as 'Padre sahib's bungalow'. A few of the political officers still have quarters round the Crater, and there are a half-dozen or so British commercial agents and clerks: the rest of the population are mixed Asiatics, for the most part Indian, Arab, or Jew, with numerous Somalis and one or two Persians and Parsees, inhabiting a compact series of streets between the water and the hills.

Trade has been declining during recent years. Mokka coffee, which until lately was shipped through Aden, is now taken through Hodeida, while in her former important position as clearing house for skins she has been largely superseded by the small, French and Italian, Red Sea ports who now export directly to Europe. The inanition which descends on everyone in Aden is completing the dissolution; the business men still talk gloomily about the 'world slump', but it is clear to most honest observers that the chances of recovery are extremely small. In these circumstances there would probably be a general movement of Indian traders to East Africa; about sixty per cent of the population, however, consists of Arabic-speaking Mohammedans, who may be expected to survive the exodus. The problem of British policy will then arise: whether Crater Town will decay into an Arab village, crowded in the ruins of the infantry lines and the garrison chapel, like the Arab villages of North Africa among Roman fortifications, a 'picturesque bit' between an administrative post at Steamer Point and an air-base at Khormaksar, where liner passengers may take their Kodaks during an hour on shore, or whether it will be possible to make of it an Arab capital town, forming a centre for education, medical service, and arbitration for the tribes between the Hadramaut and the Yemen. Meanwhile, the town affords a remarkable variety of race and costume. Arabs are represented in every grade of civilisation, from courteous old gentlemen in Government service who wear gold-rimmed spectacles, silk turbans, and light frock coats and carry shabby umbrellas with highly decorated handles, to clusters of somewhat bemused Bedouin straight from the desert; these are, in appearance, very different from the noble savages of romance; their clothes consist of a strip of blanket round the waist, held up by a sash from which protrudes the hilt of a large dagger; their hair is straight, black, and greasy, lying on the back of the head in a loose bun and bound round the forehead with a piece of rag; they are of small stature and meagre muscular development; their faces are hairless or covered with a slight down, their expressions degenerate and slightly dotty, an impression which is accentuated by their loping, irregular gait.

The British political officer introduced me to a delightful Arab who acted as my interpreter and conducted me round Crater Town. He took me to his club, a large upper story, where at the busy time of the commercial day we found the principal Arab citizens reclining on divans and chewing *khat*; later he took me to an Arab café where the lower class congregate; here, too, was the same decent respect for leisure; the patrons reclined round the walls in a gentle stupor, chewing *khat*. 'These simple people, too, have their little pleasures,' my companion remarked.

Later I received an invitation to tea from the president and committee of the club. This time the bundles of *khat* had been removed, and plates of sweet biscuits and dates and tins of cigarettes had taken their place. My friend and interpreter was there, but the president – whose father was chief secretary to the Sultan of Lahej – spoke enough English to make conversation very difficult.

I was introduced to about a dozen Arabs. We sat down in two rows opposite each other. A servant brought in a tray of tea and bottled lemonade. We talked about the distressing conditions of local trade.

Everything would be all right and everyone would be happy, said the Arabs, if only the bank would give longer and larger overdrafts. I remarked that in England we are embarrassed in exactly that way too. They laughed politely. Europeans, they said, could always get all the money they wanted. Even Indians, a race renowned for dishonour and instability, could get larger advances than the Arabs; how was one to live unless one borrowed the money? They had heard it said I was writing a book. Would I, in my book, persuade the bank to lend them more money? I promised that I would try. (Will any official of the Bank of India who reads this book please let the Aden Arabs have more money?)

We talked about London. They told me that the Sultan of Lahej had been there and had met the King-Emperor. We talked about the King-Emperor and pretty Princess Elizabeth. I confess I am pretty bad at carrying on this kind of conversation. There were several long pauses. One of them was broken by the president suddenly saying, 'We all take great sorrow at the loss of your R 101.'

I agreed that it had been a terrible disaster, and remarked that I knew one of the victims fairly well.

'We think it very sad,' said the president, 'that so many of your well-educated men should have been killed.'

That seemed to me a new aspect of the tragedy.

Conversation again languished, until one of the company, who had hitherto taken no part in the conversation, rose to his feet and, tucking up his shirt, exhibited the scars in his side caused by a recent operation for gall stone. This man was local correspondent to a London newspaper. He had lately, he told me, sent the foreign-news editor a complete genealogy of the Imam of Sana, compiled by himself with great labour. Did I know whether it had yet been printed, and, if not, could I put in a word for him in Fleet Street when I returned?

When the time came to leave, the president gave me an inscribed photograph of himself in Court uniform.

One evening there was a fair in Crater. There were stalls selling sweets and sherbet under naphtha flares, and tables with simple gambling-games. One of these was the simplest gambling-game I ever saw. The banker dealt five cards face downwards and the players placed a stake of an anna on one or other of them. When each card had found a backer – two players were not allowed to bet on the same card – they were turned up. The winning card was then paid even money and the banker pocketed three annas a time. There was also a game played for tins of pineapple. Groups of men danced in circles between the stalls. The officer formerly in command of the Aden Levy told me the interesting fact that, when Arab troops are halted for refreshment during a route march, instead of lying down like Europeans, they make up little parties and dance. But I could not see anything specifically invigorating about the mild shuffling and clapping which they performed at this fair.

One unifying influence among the diverse cultures of the Crater was the Aden troop of Boy Scouts. It is true that Arabs cannot be induced to serve in the same patrol with Jews, but it is a remarkable enough spectacle to see the two races sitting amicably on opposite sides of a campfire, singing their songs in turn and occasionally joining each other in chorus. The scoutmaster, an English commercial agent, invited me to attend one of these meetings.

The quarters were a disused sergeants' mess and the former barrack square. My friend was chiefly responsible for the Arab patrol, the Jews having an independent organisation. As I approached, rather late, I saw the latter drilling in their own quarter of the parade ground – a squad of lengthy, sallow boys in very smart uniforms furnished with every possible accessory by the benefaction of a still-wealthy local merchant. The Arabs – with the exception of one resplendent little Persian, for 'Arab' in this connection was held to include all Gentiles, Somali, Arab, and Mohammedan Indians – were less luxuriously equipped. There were also far fewer of them. This was explained by the fact that two of the second-class scouts were just at that time celebrating their marriages.

Tests were in progress for the tenderfoot and other badges. The acquiring of various badges is a matter of primary concern in the Aden troop. Some of the children had their arms well covered with decorations. 'We generally let them pass after the third or fourth attempt,' the scoutmaster explained. 'It discourages them to fail too often.'

Two or three figures crouching against corners of masonry were engaged on lighting fires. This had to be done with two matches; they had been provided by their mothers with horrible messes of food in tin cans, which they intended to warm up and consume. I believe this qualified them for a cookery medal. 'Of course, it isn't like dealing with English boys,' said the scoutmaster; 'if one isn't pretty sharp they put paraffin on the sticks.'

The scoutmaster kept the matchbox, which was very quickly depleted. Breathless little creatures kept running up. 'Please, sahib, no burn. Please more matches.' Then we would walk across, scatter the assembled sticks and tinder, and watch them built up again. It was not a long process. A match was then struck, plunged into the centre of the little pile, and instantly extinguished. The second match followed. 'Please, sahib, no burn.' Then the business began again. Occasionally crows of delight would arise and we were hastily summoned to see a real conflagration. Now and then a sheet of flame would go up very suddenly, accompanied by a column of black smoke. 'Oil,' said the scoutmaster, and that fire would be disqualified.

Later a Somali boy presented himself for examination in scout law. He knew it all by heart perfectly. 'First scoot law a scoot's honour iss to be trust second scoot law...' et cetera, in one breath.

'Very good, Abdul. Now tell me what does "thrifty" mean?'

'Trifty min?'

'Yes, what do you mean, when you say a scout is thrifty?'

'I min a scoot hass no money.'

'Well, that's more or less right. What does "clean" mean?'

'Clin min?'

'You said just now a scout is clean in thought, word, and deed.'

'Yis, scoot iss clin.'

'Well, what do you mean by that?'

'I min tought, worden deed.'

'Yes, well, what do you *mean* by clean?'

Both parties in this dialogue seemed to be losing confidence in the other's intelligence.

'I min the tenth scoot law.'

A pause during which the boy stood first on one black leg, then on the other, gazing patiently into the sun.

'All right, Abdul. That'll do.'

'Pass, sahib?'

'Yes, yes.'

An enormous smile broke across his small face, and away he went capering across the parade ground, kicking up dust over the fire-makers and laughing with pleasure.

'Of course, it isn't quite like dealing with English boys,' said the scoutmaster again.

Presently the two bridegrooms arrived, identically dressed in gala clothes, brilliantly striped silk skirts, sashes, and turbans, little coats and ornamental daggers. They were cousins, about fourteen years of age. They had been married a week ago. Tonight they were going to see their brides for the first time. They were highly excited by their clothes, and anxious to show them to their fellow scouts and scoutmaster.

Meanwhile the Jews had made a huge bonfire on the beach. Both patrols assembled round it and a short concert was held. They sang local songs in their own languages. I asked what they meant, but the scoutmaster was not sure. From what I know of most Arabic songs, I expect that they were wholly incompatible with the tenth scout law.

When, on leaving, I thanked the scoutmaster for his entertainment he said, 'Did you really find it interesting?'

'Yes, indeed I did.'

'Well, then, perhaps you won't think it such cheek what I am going to ask. We thought of starting a patrol magazine. I wondered if you would write us a short story for it. Just some little thing, you know, to do with scouting in different parts of the world.'

I thought it simplest to agree, but I do not feel very guilty at not having kept that promise. After all, I was on a holiday.

I think that perhaps it was the predominance of bachelors at Steamer Point that made the English community there so unusually agreeable. On paper its composition was exactly what one would have assumed – Resident and ADC, some soldiers, a sailor, numerous airmen, India Office and colonial officials; just such a list as has made English colonial stations odious throughout the novel-reading world. It just happened that at Aden they were all peculiarly pleasant individuals. In fact, I think there is never anything essentially ludicrous about English officials abroad; it is the wives they marry that are so difficult; at Aden the centres of social intercourse were in the club and the messes, not at bungalow 'sundowner'-parties. At Zanzibar the club was practically empty from eight o'clock onwards – everyone was at home with his wife; at Aden the bar and the cardroom were full till midnight; there seemed to be no children in the town – at any rate, none were ever mentioned.

There was plenty of entertainment going on. During my brief visit – ten days only in Aden itself – there was a dance at the club, a ball at the residency, and a very convivial party given by the Sappers. There was also a cinematograph performance.

This is a singular feature of Aden life which occurs every Thursday on the roof of the Seamen's Institute. I went with the flight-commander, who had been in charge of the Air Mission at Addis. We dined first at the club with two of his officers. There were parties at the other tables, also bound for the cinema; there were also dinner-parties at many of the bungalows. People entertain for the cinema on Thursday nights as they do for dances in London. It is not a hundred yards from the club to the Seamen's Institute, but we drove there in two cars. Other parties were arriving; a few Somalis loitered round the entrance, watching the procession; the residency car, flag flying on the bonnet, was already there. Upstairs the roof was covered with deep wicker chairs. The front row was reserved for the Resident's party. The other seats were already two-thirds full. Everyone, of course, was in evening dress. It was a warm night, brilliant with stars (though here I may interpolate that there is a lot of nonsense talked about tropical constellations. South of Cairo I never saw a sky that nearly equalled the splendour of a northern clear night. As for the Southern Cross, which one so often sees described as 'a blazing jewel', it is as dim and formless as a handful of glow-worms.)

The first film was a Pathé Gazette, showing the King leaving London for Bognor Regis twenty months previously, and an undated Grand National, presumably of about the same antiquity. A fine old slapstick comedy followed. I turned to remark to my host how much superior the early comedies were to those of the present day, but discovered, to my surprise, that he was fast asleep. I turned to my neighbour on the other side; his head had fallen back, his eyes were shut, his mouth wide open. His cigarette was gradually burning towards his fingers. I took it from him and put it out. The movement disturbed him. He shut his mouth and, without opening his eyes, said, 'Jolly good, isn't it?' Then his mouth fell open again. I looked about me and saw in the half-light reflected from the screen that with very few exceptions the entire audience were asleep. An abysmal British drama followed, called *The Woman Who Did*. It was about a feminist and an illegitimate child and a rich grandfather. The roof remained wrapped in sleep. It is one of the odd characteristics of the Aden climate that it is practically impossible to remain both immobile and conscious.

Later, 'God Save the King' was played on the piano. Everyone sprang alertly to attention and, completely vivacious once more, adjourned to the club for beer, oysters, and bridge.

Everyone was delightfully hospitable, and between meals I made a serious attempt to grasp some of the intricacies of Arabian politics; an attempt which more often than not took the form of my spreading a table with maps, reports, and note-books, and then falling into a gentle and prolonged stupor. I spent only one really strenuous afternoon. That was in taking 'a little walk over the rocks', with Mr Leblanc and his 'young men'.

Nothing in my earlier acquaintance with Mr Leblanc had given me any reason to suspect what I was letting myself in for when I accepted his invitation to join him in his little walk over the rocks. He was a general merchant, commercial agent, and shipowner of importance, the only European magnate in the settlement; they said of him that he thrived on risk and had made and lost more than one considerable fortune in his time. I met him dining at the residency, on my first evening in Aden. He talked of Abyssinia, where he had heavy business undertakings, with keen sarcasm; he expressed his contempt for the poetry of Rimbaud; he told me a great deal of very recent gossip about people in Europe; he produced, from the pocket of his white waistcoat, a Press-cutting about Miss Rebecca West's marriage; after dinner he played some very new gramophone records he had brought with him. To me, rubbed raw by those deadly four days at Dirre-Dowa and Djibouti, it was all particularly emollient and healing.

A day or two afterwards he invited me to dinner at his house in Crater. A smart car with a liveried Indian chauffeur came to fetch me. We dined on the roof; a delicious dinner; iced *vin rosé* – 'It is not a luxurious wine, but I am fond of it; it grows on a little estate of my own in the South of France' – and the finest Yemen coffee. With his very thin gold watch in his hand, Mr Leblanc predicted the rising of a star – I forget which. Punctual to the second, it appeared, green and malevolent, on the rim of the hills; cigars glowing under the night sky; from below the faint murmur of the native streets; all infinitely smooth and civilised.

At this party a new facet was revealed to me in the character of my host. Mr Leblanc the man of fashion I had seen. Here was Mr Leblanc the patriarch. The house where we sat was the top story of his place of business; at the table sat his daughter, his secretary, and three of his 'young men'. The young men were his clerks, learning the business. One was French, the other two English lately down from Cambridge. They worked immensely hard – often, he told me, ten hours a day; often half-way through the night, when a ship was in. They were not encouraged to go to the club or to mix in the society of Steamer Point. They lived together in a house near Mr Leblanc's; they lived very well and were on terms of patriarchal intimacy with Mr Leblanc's family. 'If they go up to Steamer Point, they start drinking, playing cards, and spending money. Here, they work so hard that they cannot help saving. When they want a holiday they go round the coast visiting my agencies. They learn to know the country and the people; they travel in my ships; at the end of a year or two they have saved nearly all their money and they have learned business. For exercise we take little walks over the rocks together. Tennis and polo would cost them money. To walk in the hills is free. They get up out of the town into the cool air, the views are magnificent, the gentle exercise keeps them in condition for their work. It takes their minds, for a little, off business. You must come with us one day on one of our walks.'

I agreed readily. After the torpid atmosphere of Aden it would be delightful to take some gentle exercise in the cool air. And so it was arranged for the following Saturday afternoon. When I left, Mr Leblanc lent me a copy of Gide's *Voyage au Congo*.

Mr Leblanc the man of fashion I knew, and Mr Leblanc the patriarch. On Saturday I met Mr Leblanc the man of action, Mr Leblanc the gambler.

I was to lunch first with the young men at their 'mess' – as all communal *ménages* appear to be called in the East. I presented myself dressed as I had seen photographs of 'hikers', with shorts, open shirt, stout shoes, woollen stockings, a large walking-stick. We had an excellent luncheon, during which they told me how, one evening, they had climbed into the Parsees' death-house, and what a row there had been about it. Presently one of them said, 'Well, it's about time to change. We promised to be round at the old man's at half-past.'

'Change?'

'Well, it's just as you like, but I think you'll find those things rather hot. We usually wear nothing except shoes and shorts. We leave our shirts in the cars. They meet us on the bathing-beach. And if you've got any rubber-soled shoes I should wear them. Some of the rocks are pretty slippery.' Luckily I happened to have some rubber shoes. I went back to the chaplain's house, where I was then living, and changed. I was beginning to be slightly apprehensive.

Mr Leblanc looked magnificent. He wore newly creased white shorts, a silk openwork vest, and white *espadrilles* laced like a ballet dancer's round his ankles. He held a tuberose, sniffing it delicately. 'They call it an Aden lily sometimes,' he said. 'I can't think why.'

There was with him another stranger, a guest of Mr Leblanc's on a commercial embassy from an oil firm. 'I say, you know,' he confided in me, 'I think this is going to be a bit stiff. I'm scarcely in training for anything very energetic.'

We set out in the cars and drove to a dead end at the face of the cliffs near the ancient reservoirs. I thought we must have taken the wrong road, but everyone got out and began stripping off his shirt. The Leblanc party went hatless; the stranger and I retained our topis.

'I should leave those sticks in the car,' said Mr Leblanc.

'But shan't we find them useful?' (I still nursed memories of happy scrambles in the Wicklow hills.)

'You will find them a great nuisance,' said Mr Leblanc.

We did as we were advised.

Then the little walk started. Mr Leblanc led the way with light, springing steps. He went right up to the face of the cliff, gaily but purposefully as Moses may have approached the rocks from which he was about to strike water. There was a little crack running like fork-lightning down the blank wall of stone. Mr Leblanc stood below it, gave one little skip, and suddenly, with great rapidity and no apparent effort, proceeded to ascend the precipice. He did not climb; he rose. It was as if someone were hoisting him up from above and he had merely to prevent himself from swinging out of the perpendicular, by keeping contact with rocks in a few light touches of foot and hand.

In just the same way, one after another, the Leblanc party were whisked away out of sight. The stranger and I looked at each other. 'Are you all right?' came reverberating down from very far ahead. We began to climb. We climbed for about half an hour up the cleft in the rock. Not once during that time did we find a place where it was possible to rest or even to stand still in any normal attitude. We just went on from foothold to foothold; our topis made it impossible to see more than a foot or two above our heads. Suddenly we came on the Leblanc party sitting on a ledge.

'You look hot,' said Mr Leblanc. 'I see you are not in training. You will find this most beneficial.'

As soon as we stopped climbing, our knees began to tremble. We sat down. When the time came to start again, it was quite difficult to stand up. Our knees seemed to be behaving as they sometimes do in dreams, when they suddenly refuse support in moments of pursuit by bearded women broadcasters.

'We thought it best to wait for you,' continued Mr Leblanc, 'because there is rather a tricky bit here. It is easy enough when you know the way, but you need someone to show you. I discovered it myself. I often go out alone in the evenings finding tricky bits. Once I was out all night, quite stuck. I thought I should be able to find a way when the moon rose. Then I remembered there was no moon that night. It was a very cramped position.'

The tricky bit was a huge overhanging rock with a crumbling flaky surface.

'It is really quite simple. Watch me and then follow. You put your right foot here . . . ' – a perfectly blank, highly polished surface of stone – ' . . . then rather slowly you reach up with your left hand until you find a hold. You have to stretch rather far . . . so. Then you cross your right leg under your left – this is the difficult part – and feel for a footing on the other side . . . With your right hand you just steady yourself . . . so.' Mr Leblanc hung over the abyss partly out of sight. His whole body seemed prehensile and tenacious. He *stood* there like a fly on the ceiling. 'That is the position. It is best to trust more to the feet than the hands – push up rather than pull down . . . you see the stone here is not always secure.' By way of demonstration he splintered off a handful of apparently solid rock from above his head and sent it tinkling down to the road below. 'Now all you do is to shift the weight from your left foot to your right, and swing yourself round . . . so.' And Mr Leblanc disappeared from view.

Every detail of that expedition is kept fresh in my mind by recurrent nightmares. Eventually after about an hour's fearful climb we reached the rim of the crater. The next stage was a tramp across the great pit of loose cinders. Then the ascent of the other rim, to the highest point of the peninsula. Here we paused to admire the view, which was indeed most remarkable; then we climbed down to the sea. Variety was added to this last phase by the fact that we were now in the full glare of the sun, which had been beating on the cliffs from noon until they were blistering hot.

'It will hurt the hands if you hang on too long,' said Mr Leblanc. 'One must jump on the foot from rock to rock like the little goats.'

At last, after about three hours of it, we reached the beach. Cars and servants were waiting. Tea was already spread; bathing-dresses and towels laid out.

'We always bathe here, not at the club,' said Mr Leblanc. 'They have a screen there to keep out the sharks – while in this bay, only last month, two boys were devoured.'

We swam out into the warm sea. An Arab fisherman, hopeful of a tip, ran to the edge of the sea and began shouting to us that it was dangerous. Mr Leblanc laughed happily and, with easy powerful strokes, made for the deep waters. We returned to shore and dressed. My shoes were completely worn through, and there was a large tear in my shorts where I had slipped among the cinders and slid some yards. Mr Leblanc had laid out for him in the car a clean white suit, a shirt of green crêpe-de-Chine, a bow tie, silk socks, buckskin shoes, ivory hairbrushes, scent spray, and hair lotion. We ate banana sandwiches and drank very rich China tea.

For a little additional thrill on the way back, Mr Leblanc took the wheel of his car. I am not sure that that was not the most hair-raising experience of all.

Next day – Sunday, December 14th – intolerably stiff in every muscle, bruised, scratched, blistered by the sun, I set out for Lahej, where the Resident had arranged for me to spend two nights as the Sultan's guest to see the assembly of the tributary chiefs on Tuesday. This was to be the second of these assemblies. The first, held in the spring of the preceding year, had been an experiment in what is likely to prove an extremely important development in the Protectorate policy.

Until I came to Aden I did not realise that there was any particular policy there or any problems requiring solution. I saw a small red semi-circle on the map and supposed vaguely that it was a railed off, benevolently administered territory, sequestered from the troubles of the rest of Arabia, and overrun by mission schools, district officers, clinics, prevention-of-cruelty-to-animals inspectors, German and Japanese commercial travellers, Fabian women collecting statistics and all the other concomitants of British imperialism. None of these things can be found anywhere in South Arabia. 'Protectorate' is one of the vaguest terms in the whole political jargon. In Zanzibar it means nothing less than a complete system of direct government; in Aden, until the last two or three years, it has merely meant the doling out or withholding of small stipends to the virtually independent tribal chiefs, who are bound to the Aden Government by thirty separate treaties. There has been no 'protection' in the ordinary sense of the word. At the beginning of the last war the entire territory, up to Khormaksar, was overrun by the Turks and remained in their hands until the Armistice. Even now there are seventy 'protected' subjects living as hostages in the hands of the Imam of Sana and large tracts of 'protected' territory paying him tribute. The boundaries shown in the atlas are practically meaningless; they are nowhere demarcated, but depend on traditional tribal holdings. The surrounding country is on all sides little known and inhospitable. The western border was defined by the 1903–4 boundary commission at the time when the Yemen was in Turkish hands. The Imam has never recognised that agreement and, in fact, openly and constantly violates it; to the north is the Rhub-al-Khali, where boundaries do not count. (It is interesting, at any rate for me, to think that, while Flight-Commander Vachell and I were looking at his large-scale service maps and at that great blank space in them, and he was describing some flights he had made skirting the edge and saying that of all uncharted parts of the world that was likely to keep its integrity the longest, during those very days Mr Bertram Thomas was setting out on his crossing.) On the north-east lies the Hadramaut, still, except for Mukulla, practically *terra incognita*. A recent explorer – Boscawen – reports a series of castles supporting a life of high luxury, inhabited by Arabs who have made fortunes in Java and the Malay States.

The Protectorate is the name for the thirty or so tribes living between these areas. They are entirely separate from Aden Settlement; their affairs are dealt with by the Colonial Office, while Aden itself is under the Bombay Presidency. The Resident at Aden is in charge of both. In the early days of the settlement the policy was initiated of paying money bribes to the immediate neighbours in return for a certain standard of good behaviour. This meant in all cases that they were to refrain from attacking the European and Indian settlers, and in five cases that they were to afford safe communication for the caravans coming down to the coast. It was a makeshift system from the start, but the endemic lethargy of the place prolonged it for nearly a century. Occasionally a more than usually vigorous administrator would attempt to put down internal hostilities by making the stipends conditional upon pacific behaviour, but, for the most part, the Residents seemed to have regarded residence as their primary duty. Until the war, the pressure of Turkish expansion had been the chief consideration. When this was removed there seemed only two logical policies, either to abandon the Protectorate altogether, allow the Imam to overrun it, and make a single agreement with him for the safety of the settlement, or to institute direct administration. There were serious objections to both these courses; the first would be a breach of our treaty obligations – the Shafei sect of the protected tribes are irreconcilably hostile to the Zeidi highlanders – and the second certainly expensive and possibly unsuccessful.

A third course was proposed by Sir Stewart Symes,[1] and adopted as the policy of the British Government. This is to develop the

1 A few weeks after my visit Sir Stewart Symes left Aden to take up the Governorship of Tanganyika.

protectorate upon native and federal lines, resisting the consistent disintegrating tendency of Arab society by giving support always to paramount chiefs, and to unite the tribes into a single responsible body able to cooperate in frontier defence, and bound to the Aden Government by a single collective guarantee instead of the present hotch-potch of treaties. Under this régime Aden Settlement would become the cultural capital of the new State, and educational and medical service would eventually take the place of the old system of cash payments.

An essential part of this scheme is the institution of a *jurga*, or tribal council, on the lines at present in operation in Baluchistan, which will act as a court of arbitration in internal disputes and as a single articulate body with whom the Aden Government can treat. The Sultan of Lahej is, by wealth and position, the natural president, *primus inter pares*, of this council. He is the only chief with prestige enough to assemble the others and with a palace to accommodate them.

The first council was held in the spring of 1929; most of the chiefs attended, bewildered and somewhat suspicious of the whole business. It was the first time in their lives, possibly the first time in the history of the tribes, that so many of them had sat down peaceably together. The new policy was explained to them in simple terms, and a treaty was drawn up and accepted, binding the signatories in general terms to cooperation and amicable relations. Conversations were held between the Resident, the Sultan of Lahej, and the various chiefs. They showed excusable anxiety about their pensions, but on the whole seemed interested. The success or failure of the assembly on Tuesday was regarded as an important indication of the practicability of making it a yearly function. The former signatory chiefs, and some others, had been invited to attend. The meeting was to be at the palace. A temporary British camp was being pitched two miles out of the town, where the Resident would be able to hold informal discussions with individual chiefs during the week.

This, very briefly, is the political situation in the protectorate and the meaning of the assembly of chiefs, and that was why, stiff and sore, I was being bumped along the track from the peninsula to Lahej.

There was once a railway from Aden to Lahej, but it fell out of use and had lately been demolished; a quay at the docks was still littered with rusty rolling-stock and lengths of rail. A young Scotsman was, in fact, at that moment staying at the hotel whose business was to see to their disposal. I had some talk with him. His firm had bought the whole concern, without seeing it, at a bargain price and then sent him out to do the best he could with it. He was doing quite well, he said, patiently selling it bit by bit in improbable quarters of the world. No move had as yet been made to replace it; we – Colonel Lake, the chief political officer, the driver, and I – bounced along in the sand, in a six-wheel army lorry, beside the remains of the track, which still clearly showed the corrugations where the sleepers had lain. It took us about two hours to reach the camp. The Aden Levy had arrived the day before. Some neat little kitchens of grass and wattles had been erected behind a sand dune, out of sight. Great trouble had been taken with the alignment of the camp; an avenue of signalling-flags led up to its centre; the sites for the tents were symmetrically disposed round it. The tents themselves were causing some trouble, particularly a great cubic pavilion that was to be used for the Resident's durbar; there was a high, hot wind blowing; grass and reeds had been scattered about to lay the driving sand, but with little success. Clouds of grit eddied everywhere.

Just as we arrived they got the big tent fixed at last; they stood back to admire it. The subaltern in charge came to greet us. 'Thank heavens we've got that done. We've been at it since five this morning. Now we can have a drink.'

While he was still speaking, the tent bellied, sagged, and fell; the patient little Arabs began their work again, laying foundations of stones, three feet deep, to hold the pegs in the loose sand.

We lunched in the mess-tent, dozed, and then, mounted on camels, Colonel Lake and I rode the remaining two miles into the town. I had already seen it from the air during a flight, frustrated by low clouds, which Vachell and I had attempted to make to Dhala. It was a typical Arab town of dun-coloured, flat-roofed houses and intricate alleyways. The palace was wholly European in conception, smaller than the Gebbi at Addis, but much better planned and better kept; there were pretty formal gardens in front of it, and all round the town lay bright green meadows and groves of coconut and date-palm. There was one large, lately redecorated mosque and the usual small shrines and tombs.

A power station has lately been built and most of the principal houses installed with electricity. This is naturally a matter for great pride and, to draw his visitors' attention more closely to the innovation, the sultan has conceived the rather unhappy plan of building the new guest-house immediately over the electric plant. Fortunately this was not yet finished, so that we were directed to the old guest-house, a pleasant, rather dilapidated villa of pseudo-European style, standing at the extremity of the town on the edge of the fields. Here Colonel Lake left me in the charge of the Arab butler, having elicited the fact that there were two other occupants of the house – German engineers in the sultan's employ. Except for these there were no Europeans of any kind in the town.

The furniture was very simple; in my room, a wash-hand stand with odd china, an iron bedstead with a mosquito-curtain and one collapsible, Hyde Park chair; round the walls were traces of a painted dado, representing looped and fringed curtains and gilt tassels; in the living-rooms, two tables, more Hyde Park chairs, and some iron rocking-chairs, which seem to play an essential part of hospitality in the East, as gilt chairs once did in London. There were also some personal possessions of the German engineers – two or three comic magazines of a year or two back, a fiddle, some tins of fruit and biscuits, Alpine photographs, a gramophone, an album containing photographs of male cinema-stars.

After about an hour they themselves arrived. They were very young men – both twenty-two, I learned later – and they had come in overalls straight from work; they spoke English, one rather better than the other, but both very fluently, loudly, and unintelligibly. Their first concern was to apologise for their appearance. They would be ashamed to speak to me, they said, until they had washed and changed. They had fitted up a kind of shower-bath behind a curtain of sacking at the top of the stairs. Here they hid themselves and spluttered happily for some minutes, emerging later, naked, dripping, and better composed. They dried themselves, combed their hair, put on smart tropical suits, and called for dinner. They produced some bottled amstel from beneath their beds and put it under the shower-bath to cool, and opened a tin of greengages in my honour. They were a most friendly, generous pair.

Dinner consisted of a highly pungent meat stew and salad. The cooking was not good, they explained, and they suspected the butler of cheating the sultan and themselves by confiscating their rations and substituting inferior purchases of his own; however, it did not do to complain; they were well paid and could afford to supplement their meals with biscuits and beer and tinned fruit; they would probably be the ultimate losers in any conflict with the butler. I should find, they said, that their food would make me rather ill. At first they suffered continuously from dysentery and nettle-rash; also the mosquito-curtains were too short and were full of holes. I should probably get a touch of malaria. The salad, they said, helping themselves profusely, was full of typhus.

I retail this information simply and concisely as though it had come to me in so many words. As a matter of fact, it took the whole of dinner in telling, and half an hour or so afterwards. Both spoke simultaneously all the time, and, when the issues became confused, louder and louder. 'We know English so well because we always speak it with our Dutch friends at Aden,' they explained (but again at far greater length and with many misunderstandings and cross purposes). 'It was largely from them that we learned it.'

There were interruptions. Fairly frequently the light turned orange, flickered, and went out, on one occasion, for so long that we all set out to the power station to see what had happened. Just as we left the house, however, we saw the lights go up again, and returned to our conversation. 'Engineer', I realised, was a title covering a variety of functions. Three times messages came from the palace; once, to say that the water-closet had broken and that they were to come and mend it first thing in the morning; again, to say that one of Sultan Achmed's (the Sultan of Lahej's brother) new tractors was stuck in a watercourse; a third, to remark that the lights kept going out. All these things were duly noted down for their attention.

Next morning I had an audience with the sultan. His Highness was an impassive, middle-aged man, wearing semi-European clothes – turban, black frock coat, white linen trousers. As head of the Fadl family, the hereditary rulers of the Abdali tribe and, for a brief period, the former possessors of Aden, he holds by far the most influential position in the protectorate. He is in close personal relationship with the Settlement Government and substantially supported by them.

At the time of our first occupation of Aden, the Fadl family had for about eighty years been independent of the Imam; their position, however, was precarious, and it was directly from them[1] that the Settlement Government inherited the futile system of purchasing the goodwill of the neighbouring tribes with regular monetary bribes. Their connection with the British Government has tended greatly to increase the family's wealth and stability and consequent prestige. They are, in fact, the only really secure house in Southern Arabia, and would have most to lose, of any of the Protectorate tribes, from Zeidi overlordship. There is no resident adviser at Lahej and no attempt at domestic control. Within his own territory the sultan's power is only limited by the traditional law of his own people.

We drank delicious coffee on the balcony overlooking the palace gardens and, with the aid of an interpreter, asked politely after each other's health and the health of our relatives. I commented on the striking modernity of his city – the electric light, the water-supply, the motor-buses; he remarked how much more modern these things were in London. He said that the Resident told him I wrote books; that he had not himself written a book, but that his brother had written a very good one, which I must see before I left Lahej. Conversations through an interpreter always seem to me so artificial that it is hardly worth while thinking for anything to say. He asked after my comfort at the guest-house; I replied that it was luxury itself; he said not so luxurious as London. I was at the moment, just as the Germans had predicted, tortured with nettle-rash. I said that the tranquillity was greater than in London. He said that soon he would have more motor-buses. Then we took leave of each other and I was conducted to Sultan Achmed Fadl.

[1] Treaty between the Company and the Sultan of Lahej 1839 by which the Company made themselves responsible for stipends formerly paid by the sultan to the Fadhli, Yafai, Haushabi and Amiri.

His Highness's brother lived in a small, balconied house on the further side of the main square. He was already receiving company. A British political officer was there, the subaltern who had supervised the collapse of the Resident's durbar tent, and the Haushabi sultan; a secretary was in attendance and numerous servants and guards sat about on the narrow staircase.

The Haushabi sultan was an important young man finely dressed and very far from sane. He sat in a corner giggling with embarrassment, and furtively popping little twigs of *khat* into his mouth. It was not often that his womenfolk allowed him to leave his own district. Sultan Achmed was a good-looking man of about forty, with high, intellectual forehead and exquisite manners; he spoke English well. His habit of life was pious and scholarly. He had private estates, almost as large as his brother's, whose cultivation he supervised himself, experimenting eagerly with new methods of irrigation, new tractors and fertilisers, new kinds of crops – a complete parallel to the enlightened landed gentleman of eighteenth-century England.

He showed me his book: a history of the Fadl family from the remotest times until the death of his father (unfortunately shot by a British sentry during the evacuation of Lahej before the Turkish advance in 1915). It was written in exquisite script, illuminated with numerous genealogies in red and black. He hoped to have a few copies printed for distribution among his friends and relatives, but he did not think it was likely to command a wide sale.

He suggested a drive, and went to change. His motoring-costume consisted of a grey overcoat, white shorts, khaki stockings, particoloured black-and-white shoes, and a grey silk veil. When he gave orders, his servants kissed his knees, and, whenever we stopped during the drive, passers-by hurried to salute him in the same way. His car was not new – I think it must have been one of those devised by the German mechanics from the débris of former accidents – but it carried a crest of ostrich plumes on the bonnet and an armed guard beside the chauffeur. We drove to his country house a mile or two away and walked for some time in his gardens – shrubs flowering in the shade of coconut-palms by the bank of a stream. He ordered a bunch of flowers to be prepared for me, and the gardeners brought a vast bundle of small, sweet-smelling roses and some great spear-shaped white flowers, sheathed in barbed leaves, which gave out a scent of almost stifling richness, reputed throughout Arabia, so the Germans told me later, to act upon women as an aphrodisiac. He also gave me twelve gourds of Dhala honey, eight of which were subsequently stolen by the butler at the guest-house, who thus, with unconscious kindness, relieved me of a particularly unmanageable addition to my luggage, without my incurring any possible self-reproach on grounds of ingratitude.

That afternoon I visited the camp where all the tents were at last firmly in position, and in the evening I sat with the Germans, gradually disentangling from their flow of sound an outline of their really remarkable careers. They had left school at Munich when they were eighteen and, together with a large number of boys of their year, had determined to seek their fortunes. Accordingly they had split up into pairs, made a solemn leavetaking, and scattered all over the globe. They had no money, their only assets being a sketchy knowledge of practical mechanics and, they said, a natural gift for languages. They had worked their way doing odd jobs at garages, through Spain and North Africa to Abyssinia, with the vague intention of sometime reaching India. Two years before at Berbera they had heard that the Sultan of Lahej had just expelled his French engineer for dishonest practices; they had crossed the gulf on the chance of getting the job, had got it, and remained there ever since. They undertook every kind of work, from the mending of punctures in his Highness's tyres to the construction of a ferro-concrete dam on the wadi and the irrigation of his entire estates. They had charge of the electric plant and the water-supply of the town; they mended the firearms of the palace guard; they drew up the plans and supervised the construction of all new buildings; they advised on the choice of agricultural machinery; with their own hands they installed the palace water-closet – the only thing of its kind in the whole of Southern Arabia. When not otherwise engaged, they put in their time patching up abandoned army lorries and converting them into motor-buses. Their only fear was that the sultan might take it into his head to procure an aeroplane; that, they felt, would almost certainly lead to trouble. Meanwhile, they were as happy as the day was long;

they would have to move on soon, however; it would not do to risk Stagnation of the Spirit.

Sultan Achmed combined his gentler pursuits with the office of commander-in-chief of the army, and early next morning he was busy inspecting the guard of honour and inducing a high degree of uniformity in their equipment. Long before the Resident was due to arrive they were drawn up in the palace courtyard, arranged like strawberries on a coster's barrow, with the most presentable to the fore. The chiefs had been arriving on horses and camels throughout the preceding afternoon, and had been quartered according to their rank in various houses about the town. They formed a very remarkable spectacle as they assembled among the fumed-oak furniture and plush upholstery of the sultan's state drawing-room. No one except the Fadl family and their Ministers had attempted European dress. They wore their best and most brilliant robes, and in most cases finely jewelled swords of considerable antiquity. They talked very little to each other, but stood about awkwardly, waiting for the Resident's entry, mutually suspicious, like small boys during the first half-hour of a children's party. Most of them, in spite of interminable genealogies, lived, in their own homes, a life of almost squalid simplicity, and they were clearly overawed by the magnificence of Lahej; some from the remoter districts were bare-footed and they trod the Brussels carpets with very uncertain steps; embarrassment gave them a pop-eyed look, quite unlike the keen, hawk faces of cinema sheiks. While we were waiting, I was introduced to each in turn, and through my interpreter, had a few words with them, asking whether they had had a long journey and what the prospects were for the crops and grazing-land. I was much struck by the extreme youth of the assembly; except for the old Amir of Dhala, few of the chiefs seemed to be much older than myself, while there were one or two small children among them. This I learned was a matter of policy. The tendency of Arab communities is always towards the multiplication of political units, so that the death of a chief is invariably the occasion for discord and disintegration, with consequent neglect and damage of communal property. To mitigate this evil a practice of post-remogeniture has arisen among those tribes in which, as is usually the case, the chieftainship is elective within the ruling family, by choosing the youngest eligible male and thus postponing as far as possible the recurrence of the emergency.

As soon as the Aden party arrived we took our places in the council-room, and the chiefs were formally announced one after another in order of precedence; each in turn shook hands with the Resident and then sat down in the chair assigned to him. Some were at first too shy to go the whole length of the room, and tried to get away with little bows from the door; their companions, however, prodded them on, and they came lolloping up with down-cast eyes to give very hurried greeting and then shoot for a chair. It was all very much like the prize-giving after village sports, with Sir Stewart as the squire's wife and the Sultan of Lahej as the vicar, benevolently but firmly putting the tenants' children through their paces. It was hard to believe that each of them could lead a troop of fighting men into the field and administer an ancient and intri-cate law to a people of perhaps fifteen hundred, perhaps twenty thousand souls.

The Sultan of Lahej made a little speech, in Arabic, opening the conference; then Sir Stewart Symes, first in English and then in Arabic, reminded his audience of the purpose of the meeting and outlined the chief local events of the past eighteen months, explain-ing the motives and activities of the Aden Government. Little was said of a question that was clearly in everyone's thoughts – the Imam of Sana.

Round this somewhat mysterious figure centres one of the chief problems of immediate practical importance in Arabia. Civil and religious prestige, mingling indistinguishably as they do in Moham-medan communities, have combined to give him a unique position in local politics. He traces his descent directly from the Zeidi Imam who, in A.D. 900, migrated south from Iraq and established himself in the Yemen highlands. From time to time, ancestors of his have held practically all the territory from the Hejaz to the Hadramaut. In 1630 they defeated the Turks and became paramount over most of the tribes now included in the protectorate; towards the middle of the eighteenth century there were a series of successful Shafei risings in the lowlands, and, throughout the second half of the nineteenth century, Turkish expansion again confined them to the hills. The present Imam led a revolt in 1904 which was easily subdued by the Turks, and from then until 1918 he accepted a mediatised status, confining himself to the Yemen proper, and resigning claims to authority over the Shafei tribes. Immediately after the war, however, he began a policy of penetration, occupying Shafei towns beyond the frontier agreed on by the 1903-4 Anglo-Turkish boundary commission. In 1928 the British Government were induced to move, and the local Air Force units, cooperating with the local tribesmen, easily forced the Zeidi to evacuate Dhala and other 'protected' areas. Before the process was complete, however, instructions were issued from London to cease action, leaving large Shafei districts and many hostages in the Imam's hands. Since then there have been no official negotiations between the two parties. The Imam's political policy is compromised by his religious position; like the Pope, he shares the embarrassments with the advantages of supernatural sanction. Once having laid claim to the protectorate, he cannot recede except under superior force, and that the London Government are unwilling to employ. The Imam remains at Sana in rather anxious seclusion; two unofficial British travellers were lately received by him, and entrusted with an embassy offering the very comic terms that the British should renounce all treaty obligations with the Shafei tribes, in return for which the Imam was willing to allow them possession of Aden and Perim, provided that it was officially and openly admitted that they were there on his sufferance. The British Government have adopted the superficially dignified attitude of complete aloofness, while the Imam's private troubles pile up. He has a serious Shafei problem within his own dominions round Hodeida, and hostilities are threatening with his Wahabte neighbour, Ibn Saud of the Hejaz. Sooner or later he is bound to sue for British friendship. All this is perfectly satisfactory to the Colonial Office at Whitehall, but it is less easy to induce the actual sufferers in Arabia to take a long-sighted view of the situation. The old Amir of Dhala's brother is a hostage at Sana. The Audli country is in two parts; the northern is a fertile plateau, the southern is desert; the Zeidi are in possession of the entire northern plateau, taxing the people and consuming the crops; the Audli sultan is ten years old – a child, incidentally, of some beauty and exquisite gravity, who sat beside his uncle throughout the conference, superbly dressed, his eyes lined with indigo. There was one old sheik who did not attend the conference this year; he had just heard that his only son, a hostage in the Imam's hands, had been killed in the collapse of the prison roof. 'Trusteeship of weaker races' is a phrase popularly current in Whitehall, where its application involves the bankruptcy of pioneer, white settlers in Africa; when the same idea implies the risk of parliamentary criticism, 'Jingoism' takes its place.

It is very surprising to discover the importance which politics assume the moment one begins to travel. In England they have become a hobby for specialists – at best a technical question in economics, at worst a mere accumulation of gossip about thoroughly boring individuals. One can trip about France or Italy with the utmost delight and profit without holding any views on *L'Action française* or Fascism. Outside Europe one cannot help being a politician if one is at all interested in what one sees; political issues are implicit in everything, and I make no apology for their occasional appearance in these pages. I went abroad with no particular views about empire and no intention of forming any. The problems were so insistent that there was no choice but to become concerned with them.

When the speeches were over, we adjourned to the drawing-room and talked until luncheon. Only the English party and the prime minister lunched with the sultan. It was a very fine banquet, including fresh asparagus served with onion sauce; we drank lemon squash as befitted a Mohammedan function. After luncheon I took leave of the sultan and returned with the Aden party to the settlement. I wish I could have stayed longer. On the next two days the Resident was to hold his durbar in the camp, interviewing those of the chiefs who had matters to discuss with him in private. After that there was to be a day when no British would visit Lahej, in the hope that the chiefs might begin to form understandings with one another and share each other's problems. On the last day there was to be a garden-party at the palace. I wish I could have stayed, but my fortnight at Aden was up. The *Explorateur Grandidier* was due next day, sailing for Zanzibar; if I missed her there was another fortnight to wait. It was six weeks since I had had any mail; I had arranged for everything to be sent to Zanzibar. My plans for the future were still vague, but that tight-lipped young man at Harar had set me considering the idea of crossing Africa to the west coast. And so, what with one thing and another, I decided to move on.

CHAPTER 2

EVERYONE ADMITTED THAT it was an unfortunate time to visit
Zanzibar. Usually in the tropics, if one remarks on the temperature,
the inhabitants assume an air of amused tolerance and say, 'You find
this hot? You ought to see what it's like in such a month.' But
December in Zanzibar is recognised as a bad season.

Throughout my stay I am obsessed by heat; I see everything
through a mist, vilely distorted like those gross figures that loom at
one through the steam of a Turkish bath.

I live at the English Club. Every day, soon after dawn, I am
awakened by the heat; I lie there under my mosquito-net streaming
with sweat, utterly exhausted; I take time summoning enough resolution to turn the pillow dry side up; a boy comes in with tea and
a mango; I lie there uncovered for a little while, dreading the day.
Everything has to be done very slowly. Presently I sit limply in a hip-
bath of cold water; I know that before I am dry of the water I shall
again be damp with sweat. I dress gradually. One wears long
trousers, coat, shirt, socks, suspenders, bow tie, buckskin shoes,
everything in this town. Half-way through dressing I cover my
head with eau-de-quinine and sit under the electric fan. I do this
several times during the day. They are the only tolerable moments.
I go up to breakfast. A Goan steward offers me bacon and eggs, fish,
marmalade. I eat *papai* – an odious vegetable, tasteless and greasy; it
is good for one. I go up to the library and read local history. I try to
smoke. The fan blows fragments of burning tobacco over my
clothes; the bowl of the pipe is too hot to hold. Through the window
a very slight breeze carries up from the streets a reek of cloves, copra,
and rotten fruit. A ship has been in the night before. I send a boy to
the bank to inquire after my mail; there is still nothing. I make notes

about the history of Zanzibar; the ink runs in little puddles of sweat that fall on to the page; I leave hot thumb-prints on the history-book. The plates have all come loose and the fan scatters them about the library. Luncheon is early. I usually sit with a young official who is living at the club during his wife's absence at home. I tease him by putting on an earnest manner and asking him for information which I know he will be unable to give me – 'Are there any reciprocal rights at law between French subjects in Zanzibar and British subjects in Madagascar? Where, in the protectorate Budget, do the rents appear, paid for the sultan's possessions on the mainland? What arrangement was made between the Italian Government and the sultan about the cession of the Somaliland littoral below the River Juba?' – or questions which I know will embarrass him – 'Were the commercial members of Council in favour of the loan from the Zanzibar Treasury to the Government of Kenya? Is it a fact that the sultan pays for his own postage account and the Resident does not; is it a fact that the sultan has money invested abroad which the administration want to trace?' He is very patient and promises to ring up the solicitor-general that afternoon and get the facts I want. After luncheon I go to bed. At two-forty exactly, every afternoon, the warm little wind that has been blowing from the sea, drops. The sudden augmentation of heat wakes me up. I have another bath. I cover my head with eau-de-quinine and sit under the fan. Tea. Sometimes I go to Benediction in the cathedral, where it is cool. Sometimes my official takes me for a drive into the country, through acres of copra-palm and clove-trees and tidy little villages, each with police station and clinic. Sometimes I receive a call from a Turk whom I met on the ship coming here; he talks of the pleasures of Nice and the glories of Constantinople before the war; he wears close-cropped hair and a fez; he cannot wear his fez in Nice, he tells me, because they take him for an Egyptian and charge him excessively for everything. We drink lemon squash together and plan a journey in the Hejaz. 'We will ride and ride,' he says, 'until our knees are cut and bleeding.' He is very interesting about Mohammedanism, which he seems to regard as a family affair of his own, rather as Old Catholics in England regard the Universal Church. It is interesting, too, to discuss

European history with an intelligent man who has learned it entirely from a Mohammedan point of view. The warmth of my admiration for Armenians clearly shocks him, but he is too polite to say so. Instead, he tells me of splendid tortures inflicted on them by his relatives.

Dinner on the club terrace; it is a little cooler now; one can eat almost with pleasure. Often, in the evening, we go out for a drive or visit a *ngoma*. Once I went to the cinema, where, quite unlike Aden, the audience was wide awake – mainly composed of natives, shrieking hysterically at the eccentricities of two drunken Americans. The *ngomas* are interesting. They are Swahili dances, originally, no doubt, of ritual significance, but nowadays performed purely for recreation. Like most activities, native or immigrant, in Zanzibar, they are legalised, controlled, and licensed. A list is kept in the police station of their place and date; anyone may attend. Once or twice, teams of fine negroes from the mainland made their appearance, and gave a performance more varied and theatrical than the local one. Missionaries look askance at the entertainments, saying that they induce a state of excitement subversive of the moral law. One dance we attended took place in absolute darkness; we were even asked to put out our cigars. It was, as far as we could see, a kind of blind-man's-buff; a man stood in the centre enveloped in an enormous conical extinguisher made of thatched grass, while the rest of the company capered round him, making derisive cries, beating tins and challenging him to catch them. The tufted top of his hood could just be seen pitching and swaying across the sky. On another occasion a particularly good mainland party – from somewhere below Tanga I was told – brought a band of four or five tom-tom players. It was odd to see these men throwing back their heads and rolling their eyes and shoulders like trick drummers in a Paris orchestra.

We made an excursion into the brothel quarter, which in Burton's time, and for a generation after, was one of the most famous in the East. Now, however, there is nothing to see or to tempt the young official from domesticity. It is squalid and characterless. Moreover, at the sight of us the women ran into their houses or hid in their yards. It was assumed at once that we were spies, not customers. This is creditable or not to the character of British officialdom, according as you like to look on it.

The only thing which does not appear to be under the benevolent eye of the administrator in Zanzibar is witchcraft, which is still practised surreptitiously on a very large scale. At one time, Zanzibar and Pemba – particularly the latter island – were the chief centres of black art in the whole coast, and novices would come from as far as the great lakes to graduate there. Even from Haiti, it is said, witch doctors will occasionally come to probe the deepest mysteries of voodoo. Nowadays everything is kept hidden from the Europeans, and even those who have spent most of their lives in the country have only now and then discovered hints of the wide, infinitely ramified cult which still flourishes below the surface. No one doubts, however, that it does flourish, and it seems appropriate that it should have its base here in this smug community.

One day my Turkish friend and I drove out to tea at Bububu. This name had lived in my mind ever since a question was asked in the House of Commons about the future of the Bububu railway. I had hoped that perhaps one day Mr Sutro might choose the Zanzibar–Bububu line for a Railway Club dinner. But alas, like the Lahej railway, it has now been abolished and the scraps sold for what they will fetch. One can still discern traces of the impermanent way among the copra-palms on the outskirts of the town.

The village and surrounding estate belong to a stout, bald, very cheerful Arab, a cousin of the sultan's. He drove us out from Zanzibar, pointing on the way to the derelict villas of various of his relatives. His own was far from neat, but large, and set in a beautiful walled garden full of fountains, many of which had been made to work in our honour. The furniture was a curious medley of pseudo-Oriental – which Orientals seem greatly to prefer to the products of their own craftsmen – and pseudo-European. We sat outside on the terrace in the shade of a dense mango-tree, perched on the inevitable Hyde Park chairs, and ate biscuits and preserved ginger. Whisky and soda had been produced for me, the Turk conscientiously confining himself to tea. My host seemed fairly certain that I was in some way connected with the Government – the fact that I bore no official rank making my mission the more important – and he was at some pains to express his dearest loyalty to the British administration. According to the gracious Arab custom, we were loaded with flowers on our return.

I think that, more than the climate, it is the absence of any kind of political issue which makes Zanzibar so depressing. There are no primary problems at all; such difficulties as there are, are mere matters of the suitable adjustment of routine. There are no perceptible tendencies among the people towards nationalisation or democracy. The sultan is the model of all that a figurehead should be; a man of dignified bearing and reputable private life. He has no exclusively valid claim to his office; the British Government put him there, and they pay him a sufficient proportion of his revenue to enable him to live in a modest degree of personal comfort and at the same time support a system of espionage wide enough to keep him in touch with the doings of his protectors. The two main industries of the islands, cloves and copra, are thoroughly prosperous compared with any other form of agriculture on the East African coast. Law and order are better preserved than in many towns in the British Isles. The medical and hygienic services are admirable; miles of excellent roads have been made. The administration is self-supporting. The British Government takes nothing out of the island. Instead, we import large numbers of well-informed, wholly honest members of our unemployment middle class to work fairly hard in the islanders' interest for quite small wages. Gay, easily intelligible charts teach the Swahili peasants how best to avoid hook-worm and elephantiasis. Instead of the cultured, rather decadent aristocracy of the Oman Arabs, we have given them a caste of just, soap-loving young men with Public School blazers. And these young men have made the place safe for the Indians.

British imperialism takes on an odd complexion in some parts of the world. In East Africa its impetus was neither military nor commercial, but evangelical. We set out to stop the slave-trade. For this reason, and practically no other, public opinion forced on the Government the occupation of Zanzibar and the construction of the Uganda railway. In the last two decades of the nineteenth century, zealous congregations all over the British Isles were organising bazaars and sewing-parties with the single object of stamping out Arabic culture in East Africa. There was an alliance between Church and State as cordial as it always should have been, but rarely was, between Papacy and Empire. The Mohammedans were to be driven out with the Martini rifle and Gatling gun; the pagans were to be gently elevated with the hymn-book.

The firearms did their work, and a constant supply of curates flowed to the mission-field. But for every curate there were a dozen grubby amateur law-givers. Throughout Zanzibar and Pemba, Indians have obtained control of the entire retail trade; almost without exception every shop – from the tailor who makes mess-jackets for the Resident's ADC to the petty grocer in a tin shed up country who cheats the peasant out of a few pice in the sale of cigarettes – is in Indian hands. The British bankruptcy law seems to have been devised expressly for Hindu manipulation. From Zanzibar as far as the lakes, every magistrate tells the same story, of Indian traders who set up shop without capital, obtain goods on credit, transmit money to India, go bankrupt for the value of their original stock, and then start again. No Arab or European can compete with them, because they can subsist on a standard of living as low as the natives. But with this difference. What among the natives is a state of decent, primitive simplicity is squalor among the Indian immigrants, because where the natives are bound by tribal loyalties and wedded to their surroundings by a profound system of natural sanctity, the East African Indians are without roots or piety. More than this, in the islands (but not to any import-ant extent on the mainland) the Indians are gradually obtaining possession of the soil. The Arabs are by nature a hospitable and generous race and are 'gentlemen' in what seems to me the only definable sense, that they set a high value on leisure; deprived by the Pax Britannica of their traditional recreations, these qualities tend to degenerate into extravagance and laziness, as they do in any irre-sponsible aristocracy. Following the normal European rake's pro-gress, they run into debt, mortgage their estates. This, under the protection of British law, has been the Indians' opportunity. The courts are continually busy with applications by Indians for posses-sion of Arab property. The former landed gentry either take up positions as managers on their old estates or else drift to the town, where they hang about the cafés in tattered finery, offering their services as guides to tourists. An English legal officer told me he was convinced that, in the great majority of the cases he tried, the money advanced was a very small fraction of the value of the property. What could one do? – the Arabs signed anything without reading it.

No doubt the process was inevitable; it is the Arabs' fault; they have failed to adapt themselves to the economic revolution caused by the suppression of the slave-trade, and they must consequently be submerged. There was nothing the British could have done about it. All this is true, but the fact remains that if the British had not come to East Africa the change would not have taken place. We came to establish a Christian civilisation and we have come very near to establishing a Hindu one. We found an existing culture which, in spite of its narrowness and inflexibility, was essentially decent and valuable; we have destroyed that – or, at least, attended at its destruction – and in its place fostered the growth of a mean and dirty culture. Perhaps it is not a matter for censure; but it is a matter for regret.

So far I have said nothing about the town.

Seen from the sea, as one approaches it, it is pretty, but quite unremarkable. Palm-groves stretch out on either side; the town looks very small and flat. There are no domes or minarets, as the puritanical tenets of the particular sect that is locally espoused forbid display of this kind. The chief houses on the front are the sultan's palace and the 'House of Wonders' – the translation of the Arabic name for the municipal offices; there is a good staircase in this building, but neither it nor the palace show anything of interest from outside. The plan of the town is infinitely involved, a tangle of alleys, winding in and out, turning in their course and coming surprisingly to dead ends or leading back to their points of departure. The houses are solid Arab-work of the seventeenth and eighteenth centuries, mostly with fine doorways of carved wood and massive doors studded with brass bosses. Almost all the interiors have admirable staircases. One excellent quality commends this system of town planning – everything is extremely compact. In towns such as Nairobi, Mombasa, or Kampala, which have grown up since the introduction of hygiene, one is continually involved in expensive taxi rides. At Zanzibar the residency, cathedral, club, bank, post office, hotel, offices, and shops are all within five minutes' walk of one another. The town is, I suppose, as good an example of Arabic eighteenth-century architecture as survives intact anywhere. Liner passengers, trotting round in rickshaws, are apt to attribute greater antiquity to it. I met at least one lady who associated it with biblical time.

Zanzibar in the time of Burton must have been a city of great beauty and completeness. Now there is not a single Arab in any of the great Arab houses; there are, instead, counting-houses full of Indian clerks or flats inhabited by cosy British families and scattered with Egyptian hieroglyphics in appliqué embroidery, Benares brass, cane chairs, school groups, 'finds' from the bazaars, and European children's toys. The alleys, at least in the European quarter, are absurdly clean, and memsahibs go hooting down them in Morris two-seaters.

The modern architecture has mostly been rather happy. The residency and the museum – an interesting collection created and preserved by the delightful Dr Spurier – are the work of an amateur, rather over-impressed by the glamour of his surroundings. My Turkish friend, indeed, could not for some time be persuaded that the museum was not the tomb of some notable, and was accustomed to make appropriate devotions as he passed, until I drew him inside and pointed out the bottled snakes, the decorations of the late sultan, the autographed letters of felicitation from Queen Victoria, Livingstone's medicine chest (which, by the way, contained practically no quinine, but an enormous variety of pharmaceutically valueless poisons), propagandist photographs of unvaccinated children suffering from smallpox, and other objects of interest. The latest buildings, however, designed by the present official architect, seemed to me very good indeed, combining great economy and restraint with a delicate receptiveness to local influences. He has not yet had scope, however, for any work requiring high imagination. It will be a great pity if, while he holds his office, some fanatic does not succeed in destroying the sultan's boring nineteenth-century palace, so that he may have the rebuilding of it. Neither cathedral is of much artistic interest.

I went to Pemba for two nights. It is all cloves, coconuts, and tarmac, very much like the interior of Zanzibar. A small steamboat, the *Halifa*, makes a weekly journey to the north end of the island and back; the crossing takes a night. I disembarked at Mkoani, a green hillside scattered with bungalows; the water below the little landing-stage was clearer than I ever saw sea-water – every pebble, fathoms down, perfectly visible. I drove with the provincial commissioner to Weti, stopping to pay various calls on the way at Chake-Chake and a model estate managed by a community of Quakers. A delightful dinner that night with the doctor and his wife; no nonsense about stiff shirts and mess-jackets; we dined in pyjamas in a garden where preparations were being made for a Christmas-party. This was the only household in the island which possessed an electric-light plant, and the best was being made of it with globes swung from the trees. Next day – Christmas Eve – I sailed back to Chake-Chake, bathed in a party, went to cocktails at two bungalows, and dinner at a third, where a highly acrimonious dispute broke out late in the evening about the allotment of Christmas presents. My hosts were two elderly bachelors. They were giving a joint Christmas-party to the European children of the island, and a fine heap of toys had arrived for them in the *Halifa* for distribution to their guests. They rehearsed the business with chairs for children. 'This will do for So-and-So's little boy,' and 'This for So-and-So's girl,' and 'Have the So-and-So's got two children or three?' At first it was all very harmonious and Dickensian. Then suspicion of favouritism arose over the allocation of a particularly large, brightly painted india-rubber ball. 'Mary ought to have it; she's a sweet little thing.' 'Peter's brother has just gone to school in England. He's terribly lonely, poor kiddy.' The ball was put first on one dump, then on the other; sometimes it rolled off and bounced between them. 'Sweet little thing' and 'Lonely kiddy' became battle-cries as the big ball was snatched backwards and forwards. It was an odd sight to see these two hot men struggling over the toy. Presently came the inevitable 'All right. Do as you like. I wash my hands of the whole thing. I won't come to the party.' Renunciation was immediately mutual. There was a sudden reversal of the situation; each party tried to force the ball upon the other one's candidate. I cautiously eschewed any attempts at arbitration. Finally peace was made. I forget on what terms, but, as far as I remember, the ball was given to a third child and all the other heaps were despoiled to compensate Mary and Peter. They certainly came very well out of the business. Later that evening I went back to the *Halifa*. Some of my new friends came to see me off. We woke up the Goan steward and persuaded him to make lemon squash for us. Then we wished one another a happy Christmas, for it was past midnight, and parted. Early next morning we sailed for Zanzibar, arriving at tea-time. My mail had not yet come.

Christmas seemed very unreal divorced from its usual Teutonic associations of yule logs, reindeer, and rum punch. A few of the Indian storekeepers in the main street had decked their windows with tinsel, crackers, and iridescent artificial snow; there was a homely crèche in the cathedral; beggars appeared with the commendation 'Me velly Clistian boy'; there was a complete cessation of the little club life that had flourished before. I thought that I should have to spend Christmas Night alone, but Dr Spurier introduced me to a delightful party in a flat near the wharf.

Eventually the mail arrived, and I was able to leave for Kenya. I took an almost empty Italian liner named the *Mazzini*. Her main business is done between Genoa and Mombasa. She then makes a week's round trip to Zanzibar, Dar-es-Salaam, and back to Mombasa, and so to Europe. Her few passengers were nearly all restful people taking a few days' holiday on the water. The best thing about this ship was a nice old cinematograph; the worst was a plague of small blackbeetles which overran the cabins and died in vast numbers in the baths. An English lady declared that she had been severely stung by one in the back of the neck – but I find this difficult to believe. She and her husband were from Nairobi. It was the first time they had seen the sea since their arrival in the country eleven years before. The husband was a manufacturer of bricks. The trouble about his bricks, he said, was that they did not last very long; sometimes they crumbled away before they had been laid; but he was hopeful of introducing a new method before long.

We stopped at Dar-es-Salaam. It was hideously hot and there seemed little of interest in the town – some relics of Arab and German occupation, a rash of bungalows, a corrugated-iron bazaar full of Indians. I visited the agent of the Belgian Congo and explained that I had an idea of returning to Europe by way of the west coast. He was sympathetic to the idea and told me of an air service running weekly between Albertville and Boma; the fare was negligible, the convenience extreme. He showed me a timetable of the flight. It was two years old. He had not yet received the new one, but, he assured me, I could be confident that any changes that might have been made would be changes for the better. I believed him.

On the last day of the year we arrived at Mombasa. I had spent a pleasant evening there on my way down. It is a green island, linked to the mainland by a bridge. The English have converted it into a passable reproduction of a garden-city. Kilindini docks lie at some distance outside the town. They are very grand – far finer than anything I had seen since Port Said: there is a Portuguese fort, bits of an Arab quarter, a club, golf links, bathing-beach, some hotels. On this particular morning, however, my whole time was occupied with the immigration officers.

We were called up to interview them in the saloon. They were a pair of chubby nonentities who at home might have secured posts at an inferior private school or in the counting-house of some wholesale drapery business in the Midlands. In Mombasa they were people of authority and very ready to show it. I presented a passport in which a former foreign secretary requested and required in the name of His Majesty that all whom it might concern should allow me to pass freely without let or hindrance and should afford me any assistance and protection of which I might stand in need. I did not need very much. All I wanted was to catch the 4.30 train to Nairobi. On the face of it, it seemed a simple business. Not at all. The foreign secretary's commendation did not seem to be wholly intelligible. I was given a form to fill in. Why was I coming to Kenya? For how long? Whom did I know there? Where was I going to stay? How much money had I got? Under what other aliases was I accustomed to travel? Of what crimes had I been convicted in what countries? I completed the form and handed it over. They read my replies, shaking their heads significantly at one another, and asked me to wait behind while they dealt with the less suspicious passengers. Presently they tackled me again. What proofs had I of the truth of my statements? I went below, unpacked my luggage and brought up letters of credit for a little under two hundred pounds, and introductions to the colonial secretary and the apostolic delegate. My inquisitors held a whispered conference. Then they said that they required a deposit of fifty pounds. Was this obligatory on all visitors? No, but my replies had been unsatisfactory. In what way unsatisfactory? At about this stage an element of mutual dislike became apparent in the tone of our conversation.

'You say that you intend to remain here *about* three weeks. Why do you not say exactly?'

'Because I have not yet decided. It may be five weeks. It may be two. It depends how I like the country.'

'You say your address at Nairobi is "uncertain". What do you mean by that?'

'I mean that I do not know. I have wired to a friend' – naming the chief ADC at Government House – 'asking him to engage a room for me. He has promised to get me one at Muthaiga Club if it is possible. As it is race week there will probably be some difficulty. I shall either be there or at Torr's Hotel. I shall not know which until I reach Nairobi.'

More mutterings. Then:

'Have you got fifty pounds on you in East African currency?'

'No, I can give you a cheque.'

'That will not do. We shall hold your luggage and passport until you pay us fifty pounds in notes.'

'When shall I get it back?'

'When you leave the country.'

'But I shall be leaving through Uganda.'

'You must report to the emigration officer. He will write for it.'

'That will take some time?'

'Probably about a week.'[1]

---

1 As it turned out, the money was eventually refunded to me in London towards the middle of April.

'You mean that I shall have to wait a week at the frontier station.'

'Yes, that is what we mean.'

I drove into the town, cashed a cheque and returned to Kilindini. The immigration officers had now left the ship. I drove back to their office in the town, then back to Kilindini with their permission to land, then back to the town with my luggage.

That is how I spent my morning.

And so I entered Kenya fully resolved to add all I could to the already extensive body of abusive literature that has grown up round that much misunderstood dependency.

CHAPTER 3

BUT MY ILL temper gradually cooled as the train, with periodic derailments (three to be exact, between Mombasa and Nairobi) climbed up from the coast into the highlands. In the restaurant car that evening I sat opposite a young lady who was on her way to be married. She told me that she had worked for two years in Scotland Yard and that that had coarsened her mind; but since then she had refined it again in a bank at Dar-es-Salaam. She was glad to be getting married as it was impossible to obtain fresh butter in Dar-es-Salaam.

I awoke during the night to draw up my blanket. It was a novel sensation, after so many weeks, not to be sweating. Next morning I changed from white drill to grey flannel. We arrived in Nairobi a little before lunch time. I took a taxi out to Muthaiga Club. There was no room for me there, but the secretary had been told of my coming and I found I was already a temporary member. In the bar were several people I had met in the *Explorateur Grandidier*, and some I knew in London. They were drinking pink gin in impressive quantities. Someone said, 'You mustn't think Kenya is always like this.' I found myself involved in a luncheon-party. We went on together to the Races. Someone gave me a cardboard disc to wear in my buttonhole; someone else, called Raymond, introduced me to a bookie and told me what horses to back. None of them won. When I offered the bookie some money he said in rather a sinister way, 'Any friend of Mr de Trafford's is a friend of mine. We'll settle up at the end of the meeting.'

Someone took me to a marquee where we drank champagne. When I wanted to pay for my round the barman gave me a little piece of paper to sign and a cigar.

317

We went back to Muthaiga and drank champagne out of a silver cup which someone had just won.

Someone said, 'You mustn't think Kenya is always like this.'

There was a young man in a sombrero hat, trimmed with snake skin. He stopped playing dice, at which he had just dropped twenty-five pounds, and asked me to come to a dinner-party at Torr's. Raymond and I went back there to change.

On the way up we stopped in the bar to have a cocktail. A man in an orange shirt asked if either of us wanted a fight. We both said we did. He said, 'Have a drink instead.'

That evening it was a very large dinner-party, taking up all one side of the ballroom at Torr's. The young lady next to me said, 'You mustn't think that Kenya is always like this.'

After some time we went on to Muthaiga.

There was a lovely American called Kiki, whom I had met before. She had just got up. She said, 'You'll like Kenya. It's always like this.'

Next morning I woke up in a very comfortable bedroom; the native boy who brought my orange juice said I was at Torr's.

I had forgotten all about Mombasa and the immigration officers.

Another side of Nairobi life: I sit at a table in the offices of the Indian Association, talking to the Indian leaders. They are named Mr Isher Dass, Mr Varma, and Mr Shams-ud-Deen. Mr Isher Dass is very conciliatory; he thanks me often for my open-minded attitude; he says that he hopes my book will be unlike *Mother India*. 'Quite unlike,' I assure him. Mr Varma is very pugnacious; he smokes cigars all the time; bangs the table and snarls. He says that colour prejudice in Kenya has come to such a pass that Indians are made to share the same waiting-rooms with natives. I detect an inconsistency in that argument, but think it best to say nothing for fear of a scene. Mr Varma looks as if he were up to anything. Mr Shams-ud-Deen has a gentler and more incisive mind. He is the only one worth talking to, but Mr Varma makes such a noise that it is impossible to say anything. On the whole it is an unsatisfactory interview, but when I leave they present me with several controversial pamphlets of their own composition. These tell me all they were trying to say. In fact,

I find phrase after phrase occurring which I remembered in their conversation. Clearly they know their case by heart. Raymond finds me reading the pamphlets and remarks that he is all for the blacks, but Indians are more than he can stand; besides they spread jiggers and bubonic plague. Then he drives me out to Muthaiga. The windscreen of his car has been broken overnight, and the body heavily battered. He remarks that someone must have borrowed it.

Another Nairobi scene; an evening picnic in the game reserve from Government House. We consist of the Acting-Governor and his wife; the ADCs, an agricultural expert from England, and the Race Week house-party; the latter includes a whiskered cattle rancher, very tall and swarthy, in the clothes of a Mexican bandit; oddly enough he is called 'Boy'; his wife is slight and smart, with enormous eyes and an adventurous past; she once rode alone from Addis Ababa to Berbera; she too has a queer name – Genessie.

We drive to a place called Lone Tree, disturbing herds of zebra and wildebeeste; their eyes flash bright green, dazzled by our spot-light. We make a detour and see some hyenas – but not as close as the one at Harar – and little jumping creatures called dik-diks. Meanwhile, the servants have lit a great bonfire and put motor cushions round it. We sit down and eat supper, the ADCs doing all the polite drudgery that makes most picnics hideous; presently most of the party fall asleep, except poor Genessie, whom I keep awake with descriptions of Abyssinia (it is only some days later that I realise she knows far more about it than I do).

Already, in the few days I had spent at Nairobi, I found myself falling in love with Kenya. There is a quality about it which I have found nowhere else but in Ireland, of warm loveliness and breadth and generosity. It was not a matter of mere liking, as one likes any place where people are amusing and friendly and the climate is agreeable, but a feeling of personal tenderness. I think almost everyone in the highlands of Kenya has very much this feeling, more or less articulately. One hears them grumbling about trade conditions, about the local government and the home government, but one very rarely hears them abuse the country itself as one hears Englishmen abroad in any other part of the world. It is little to be wondered at if, when they feel their positions threatened, this feeling takes form in expressions of local patriotism which seem fantastic in Whitehall.

I am concerned in this book with first-hand impressions, and wish to avoid, as far as possible, raising issues which it is not in my scope to discuss at length, but personal experiences are dependent on general conditions and I cannot hope to make my emotions about Kenya intelligible unless I devote a few sentences to dissipating some of the humbug which has grown up about it.

One very common idea of Kenya is spread by such books as Frederic de Janzé's *Vertical Land*. I began this chapter with the description of a day spent in the de Janzé circle between Muthaiga and Torr's. My reason for doing so was first that it made a contrast with the churlish officialdom of the coast and secondly that, in point of fact, this happened to be the succession of events as I remember them, on my first day in Nairobi. People were insistent that I should not regard Race Week as typical of the life of the country, because 'the Happy Valley' has come in for too much notoriety in the past. No one reading a book about smart people in London or Paris takes them as representing the general life of the country; but it is exactly this inference which is drawn when a book is written about smart people in Kenya. Even in the set I met at Muthaiga, only a small number are quite so jolly all the year round. 'Boy', for instance, owns the largest cattle farm in the country and, incredible as it sounds, knows almost every beast individually by sight. Of the settler community in general, the great majority are far too busy on their farms to come to Nairobi, exept on an occasional predatory expedition to the bank or the Board of Agriculture.

Another quite inconsistent line of criticism represents the settlers as a gang of rapacious adventurers. Mr Macgregor Ross's *Kenya from Within* did a great deal to popularise this view and, when the more sober London weeklies mention the affairs of East Africa, their comments are more often than not inspired by the same kind of mistaken highmindedness. It is, on the face of it, rather surprising to find a community of English squires established on the equator. By the doctrine, just old-fashioned enough to be prevalent in refined English circles, they have no business there at all; the soil is the inalienable property of the African coloured races, and the sooner it is made untenable for the white settlers, the better. This dogma, it may be noted, is not held to apply everywhere; its strongest advocates are quite ready to hasten the eviction of traditional landowners in their own country, while in the settlement of the Near East, two exercises in arbitrary statesmanship have been attempted which are in principle contradictory both to this attitude and to each other – the transshipment of Jews to Palestine and of Anatolian Christians to Greece.

But, of course, it is futile to attempt to impose any kind of theological consistency in politics, which are not an exact science but, by their nature, a series of makeshift, rule-of-thumb, practical devices for getting out of scrapes. There is in existence a body of serious opinion in England which holds that, in the past, the Africans have been unjustly exploited by European commercial interests, and is anxious to prevent this in future. It is unprofitable to discuss the question of abstract 'rights' to the land; if one does, one is led into all kinds of ethnological byways – have the Nilotic immigrant tribes any more 'right' in East Africa than the British? One must confine oneself to recent history and rough justice. There is one general principle which one may accept; that the whole of history, from the earliest times until today, has been determined by the movements of peoples about the earth's surface; migratory tribes settled and adapted their cultures to new conditions; conquest, colonisation, commercial penetration, religious proselytising, topographical changes, land becoming worked out, pastures disappearing, harbour silting up – have preserved a constant fluidity of population. It is useless to pretend that, suddenly, at the beginning of the Boer War, the foundation of the Third International, or at this or that time in recent history, the piano stopped and the musical chairs were over, the lava stream cooled and congealed, and the whole process was at an end, for no other reason than that the enlightened people of Northern Europe – having lost their belief in revealed religion and falling back helplessly for moral guidance on their own tenderer feelings – have decided that it is Wrong. The process will go on, because it is an organic process in human life. One nation may artificially restrain its people from going to a certain place; it may bring about the ruin of those who do. But in the end the future of European settlement in Central Africa will depend on the suitability of the country for the foreign system of cultivation by large, individual landowners, on the ability of the immigrant races to maintain efficiency in an alien climate, to propagate there, and on the re-establishment of the world's markets on a basis which will enable them to sell their produce at a price high enough to maintain their standard of living. On first acquaintance, and for a few months' visit, the climate of the Kenya highlands is slightly intoxicating but wholly agreeable. It is still uncertain, however, whether Nordic people will be able to live permanently at that altitude and on that latitude. Until the second generation have grown up, it is impossible to say. Many of the children I met seemed perfectly normal in health, and peculiarly self-reliant; in others there seemed to be a somewhat morbid alternation of listlessness and high excitement. There is as yet no adequate secondary education. Those who can afford it, send their children to school in England.

It must be remembered that only a part – about two thousand families in all – of the small European population can be regarded as citizens of the colony. The officials and commercial agents serve their term and then retire to England; the settlers look upon the country as their permanent home; the two groups can scarcely be expected to regard local policy from the same point of view or with the same concern. The officials are sure of their pay and their pensions; the settlers mostly depend on local prosperity for their entire livelihood. They are people who bought their farms and sunk the whole of their capital in them; during the good years they re-invested the greater part of their profits in building, buying more land, machinery and stock. From many European accounts you might suppose that all they had done was to drive out a few scared natives and take possession of fully equipped properties, as though they were an invading army occupying an agricultural English county. Very large grants of land were made to early settlers, such as Lord Delamere, who had the means to develop them. Except in the case of pasturage the land was, as it stood, valueless for cultivation on a large scale; it consisted for the most part of tracts of bush country which had to be cleared either by hand or by machinery imported at great expense from abroad; there were no roads by which the products could be brought to market. It is, in fact, one of the many grounds for Indian complaint that the farmers have been obliged to undertake the task bit by bit, and that even now the greater part of the land distributed to Europeans is still waiting for full development. While the present uncertainty persists there is little inducement to the settlers to add to their commitments. Large fortunes have been made in the past by speculating in real estate at Mombasa and Nairobi. Throughout the country as a whole, how-ever, investment in land – whether it has taken the form of clearing and planting free grants of virgin soil or of the actual purchase of already developed farmland – has, in the past ten years, proved barely profitable and during the last eighteen months, uniformly disastrous. It is not big business enterprise which induces the Kenya settlers to hang on to their houses and lands, but the more gentle motive of love for a very beautiful country that they have come to regard as their home, and the wish to transplant and perpetuate a habit of life traditional to them, which England has ceased to accommodate – the traditional life of the English squirearchy, which, while it was still dominant, formed the natural target for satirists of every shade of opinion, but to which now that it has become a rare and exotic survival, deprived of the normality which was one of its determining characteristics, we can as a race look back with unaffected esteem and regret. I am sure that, if any of them read this book, they will deny with some embarrassment this senti-mental interpretation of their motives. It is part of the very vitality of their character that they should do so. They themselves will say simply that farming was impossible in England, so they came to Kenya, where they understood that things were better; they will then grouse a little about the government, and remark that after all, bad as things are, it is still possible to keep a horse or two and get excellent shooting – things only possible at home for those who spend the week in an office. That would be their way of saying what I have just said above. The Kenya settlers are not cranks of the kind who colonised New England, nor criminals and ne'er-do-wells of the kind who went to Australia, but perfectly normal, respectable Englishmen, out of sympathy with their own age, and for this reason linked to the artist in an unusual but very real way. One may regard them as Quixotic in their attempt to re-create Barsetshire on the equator, but one cannot represent them as pirates and land-grabbers.

That particular charge, so often put forward by African National-ists, would in any case apply directly only to a tiny section of the existing white population, the vast majority of whom came into the country after the question of inalienable native reserves had been, one hopes, finally settled. Even if grossest injustice had been done by the original settlers, it could hardly be expiated by a corresponding injustice to their successors. The question is not one of importance in the present situation. It may, however, be remarked that as a matter of fact there has never been an example of colonisation carried out with so little ill-will between the immigrant and the indigenous races, or with such scrupulous solicitude for the weaker party. At the time of the construction of the Uganda railway, vast tracts of the present colony of Kenya were completely uncultivated and unin-habited. Walls of desert were the only protection which the agricul-tural tribes could put up against the warrior tribes. It was from these neutral areas that a large proportion of the European farms were developed. In cases where natives were found in possession, they were asked to mark out the territory which they habitually used, allowance was made for their expansion and their whole area was made over to them before any claims by colonists were considered in the neighbourhood. That, at any rate, was the principle. It is impossible to say how far in practice there may have been corrup-tion or mild coercion; whether the natives invariably understood that, in making their claims, they were limiting themselves perma-nently within the boundaries they drew out. It is, on the face of it, probable that in the general large process there were occasional failures to apply the principle in absolute purity; but there is no evidence that failure was at all extensive, except in the case of the Masai. No one can reasonably pretend that their treatment was just or expedient. It may be said, with perfect truth, that the Masai are a race of bullies; that the only international law they ever recognised was that of superior strength, and that they were treated according to their own morality. The fact remains that their wholesale eviction from Laikipia in 1904, where they had been induced to migrate with explicit guarantees of permanent possession, was gravely dishonourable according to European morality, and a blunder in statesmanship which was aggravated by the uncertainty with which it was carried out. The superb physique of the race fits them for the part of noble savage which nationalists have been eager enough to assign to them, and they remain the least responsive people in East Africa to the benevolent attentions of the Colonial Office. They have been prevented in their traditional pastime of murdering their pacific neighbours by the ingenious device of confiscating their shields (which thus renders them and their herds defenceless against lion). When, as compensation, they were offered the privilege of participation in the late war, they refused, providing the only example of wholly successful conscientious objection. Lately, however, a new opening has been found for them as cinema actors. Shields are dealt out – a restoration which on one occasion at least, resulted in a fine resumption of bloodshed – and they are sent out before a barrage of well-protected cameramen to spear lion in the bush for the amusement of European and American audiences, sheltering their courtships from the rain.

Everyone I met was anxious to impress on me that there was no 'native problem'; that the whole thing was invented in London and Bombay. It would be absurdly pretentious after a few weeks in the country to make any general statement on a question as broad as that. What I can say with conviction, however, is that all the European settlers I met, while eschewing Colonial Office uplift, had a sense of responsibility towards their native employees, and a half humorous sympathy with them, which compared strikingly with the attitude of most European capitalists towards factory hands. People abused their native servants in round terms and occasionally cuffed their heads, as they did their English servants up to the end of the eighteenth century. The idea of courtesy to servants, in fact, only came into being when the relationship ceased to be a human one and became purely financial. The cases of cruelty of white to black, quoted by Mr Macgregor Ross, are mere examples of pathological criminality which can be found anywhere without distinction of race; white people are cruel to white, black to black, white to black, and when prestige is inoperative, black to white. The cases in *Kenya from Within* have some significance in their bearing on the way in which justice is administered in African courts, but none on the relationship of white masters to black servants. When the settlers say that there is no native problem, they mean that they can see nothing essentially incompatible between the welfare of the two races. I am sure that they are perfectly sincere in saying this. On the other hand they are alarmed by the Duke of Devonshire's term 'paramountcy'.[1]

I went to a pantomime in Nairobi, performed (incidentally extremely well) by amateurs. The comic man, dressed as the Widow Twankey or an ugly sister of Cinderella's, I forget which, had as one of his chief recurrent gags the line 'I will have paramountcy'. The word rankles and it is clearly embarrassing to the settlers that it should have been used by a Conservative Minister. If it had been coined by that most ridiculed nobleman, Lord Passfield of Passfield Corner, it could have been pigeon-holed as 'Labour' and forgotten; coming from the Duke of Devonshire it seems a betrayal of their cause in the quarter where they most expected support. There is a slight infection of persecution mania about all political thought in the colonies, just as there is megalomania in Europe. Words like 'paramountcy' are inflammatory. In its context the term is a typical assertion of public highmindedness with no particular application. '*Primarily Kenya is an African territory and His Majesty's Government think it necessary definitely to record their considered opinion that the interests of the African natives must be paramount and that if, and when, those interests and the interests of the immigrant races should conflict, the former should prevail.*' There is very little menace in 'paramountcy', stated in this vaguely pious way. So far as the East African European interests are threatened by the policy declared in the White Paper of 1923, it seems to me to be in quite a sufficient direction; the insistence of the integrity of the territory as a whole introduces an essentially foreign bureaucratic attitude opposed to what is the present disposition of those on the spot to regard the white settled highlands and the native

1 Kenya White Paper 1923.

reserves as different states in a federation. There is no question of the white settlers being handed over to the rule of natives; there was a question of natives being ruled by settlers. There were serious objections to this and the object of the White Paper was to assert that the home government would not contemplate such a devolution of authority. A slightly sinister note, if one wishes to find one, lies in the ascription of the settled highlands to the 'primarily African' territory.

The relationship of settler to native is primarily that of an employer of labour, and there is no reason why this should not become easier rather than less easy as the second generation of natives grow up who are accustomed to the idea of white neighbours and curious to see more of the world than life in the reserves can offer. The fear apparent in the White Paper that officials are being used for semi-compulsory recruitment of labour, or that local taxation was assessed with the motive of driving natives outside the reserves to work, seems to have little foundation enough, and should, in the normal course of progress, rapidly disappear.

The Indian question, however, is a different matter. There was very nearly armed rebellion on the issue in 1923, and the ill feeling then aroused is still present, sometimes subterraneously complicating and embittering simple questions, often frankly apparent on both sides. The trouble is both social and political. The more educated, professional Indians resent their exclusion from the social life of the Europeans; they are not admitted to the hotels, bars or clubs of the colony and, in practice though not by law, they are segregated in railway trains and the residential quarters of towns. They are not allowed to occupy or speculate in land in the highlands. They outnumber the Europeans by rather more than two to one. In the allotment of non-official seats in the legislative council, provision is made for eleven elected Europeans and five elected Indians.[1] Education is kept separate between the races, each community being taxed at a different rate for the support of its own schools.[2] There is very little hope of high promotion for Indians

[1] Also for one Arab and one missionary nominated to represent native interests.

[2] There is also a liquor tax devoted to education, divided proportionately between the two communities.

in government service. There is a long list of 'grievances', which Mr Varma spat out at me as though I were individually responsible for them all; until in fact I began to wish that I were. He resented the fact that separate lavatories were provided for Indians in trains; he said that, as a member of the British Empire he insisted on owning land in the highlands. I asked whether he set great store by his membership of the Empire and he said he did not. I asked him whether the cultivation of a highland farm would not interfere with his practice in Nairobi. For reply he quoted figures that seemed to show that an Indian who owned a farm near the Nandi escarpment had done better with his coffee than his European neighbours. When, later, I asked his European neighbours they said that the farm was notorious for miles round as the breeding-place of every pest which afflicted their crops. It is impossible to find out the truth when you really get down to the brass tacks of racial antagonism. Most of the 'grievances' involved no particular hardship, except deprivation of European intercourse, for which it is hard to believe Mr Varma had any sincere aspiration.

The situation is that the settlers want Kenya to consist of white people, owning the soil and governing themselves, and Indians to be foreigners, allowed full freedom of trade but divorced from the life of the country; the Indians want it to be an Indian colony governed on the wretched old principle of head-counting, which they have pulled out of the pie of European education. Both sides are capable of hypocrisy in their bandying about of the phrase 'native welfare' to support their claims. I do not think that the most whole-hearted supporter of Indian Nationalism would claim that the East African Indians were suitable 'trustees' for a 'people not yet able to stand by themselves under the strenuous conditions of the modern world',[1] nor, I think, would Major Grogan maintain that the majority of settlers came to Kenya primarily to protect the pagans from Hindu influence.

At the time of writing, the situation, complicated by the commission on closer Union, is in an impasse. The Indians refuse to take up the seats allotted them in the council; the business of government is

---

1 Kenya White Paper.

managed by the official Europeans and criticised by the elected ones. The Indians hold out for a common electoral roll; the Hilton Young Commission – whose whole report was an example of the futility of the attempt to scrutinise evidence by a body who were not previously agreed upon their political principles – advised a common franchise, if adopted with the consent of the European community. It is probable that Mr Varma would refuse his common franchise if it came to him with European consent, and it is quite certain that European consent will not be forthcoming. Meanwhile, no one finds the lack of Indian cooperation a serious embarrassment, except the Government of India, who have been at greater difficulty in persuading Indians in India of the essentially harmonious natures of the two races, and of the advantages accruing to membership of the British Empire, while events are following this course in East Africa.

It is barely possible to explain to North Europeans the reality of race antagonism. For so many generations the Mediterranean peoples have been at war with the infidel that they have learned to accept it calmly as a normal thing, and therefore seem often to be immune from it, as Turks are said at advanced age to become immune from syphilis. But the Northern races, confronted with the danger of domination or infection by a coloured race, tend to go a little mad on the subject. The fear of Indians, Negroes, Japanese or Chinese obsesses one or other of all the branches of the Nordic race who, by leaving their own sea mists and twilight, have exposed themselves to these strangers. Anglo-Saxons are perhaps worse than any. It is easy enough for Anglo-Saxons in London, whose only contact with coloured peoples is to hear gramophone records of spirituals, or occasionally share a 'bus with a polite, brown student, to be reasonable about the matter and laugh at the snobbery of their cousins in India or shudder at the atrocities of their more distant cousins in Virginia, but the moment they put on a topi, their sanity gently oozes away. 'You can see *he* hasn't been out before,' someone remarked to me in an outward-bound liner as we observed an Englishman offering some mild, normal courtesy to a negro first-class passenger. Alas, it was true. In East Africa as yet there are no negroes in positions where they could possibly contemplate equality with the whites; Anglo-Saxon sanity remains undisturbed in that direction. But when some newly arrived Anglo-Saxon advises equal franchise with Indians (on a basis of qualification by education which will still enable the Anglo-Saxon to keep dominance in practice though resigning it in theory), then there is a talk about kidnapping the Governor and the 'Boston tea-party'. It is not a matter one can be censorious about. Gentle reader, you would behave in just the same way yourself after a year in the tropics. It is just a lack of reasoning – I will not call it a failing – to which our race is prone as the Malays are prone to periodical fits of homicidal mania. The reciprocal feeling which people like Mr Varma have about Anglo-Saxons is every bit as unbalanced. It really is not a thing to censure, but it is something to be remembered when considering the temperament of this equatorial Barsetshire. And one other point – it is just conceivable that they might be right. When over a long period a great number of otherwise respectable people consistently deny the conclusions of their own reason on some particular point, it may be a disease like roulette, or it may be a revelation like the miracles of Lourdes. It is just worth considering the possibility that there may be something valuable behind the indefensible and inexplicable assumption of superiority by the Anglo-Saxon race.

As I have said above, it is uncertain whether the kind of life which the Kenya settlers are attempting to re-establish is capable of survival; whether there may not be in the next twenty-five years a general Withdrawal of the Legions to defend Western civilisation at its sources. But, whatever its future, it is an experiment in transplanted social institutions as interesting in its way as the Spanish settlement of America or the Norman baronies of the Levant.

At the end of Race Week, Raymond and I left Nairobi and drove through the Rift Valley to Lake Naivasha. A bad road; red earth cut into deep ruts; one of the best roads in the country. On the way we pass other settlers returning to their farms; they wear bright shirts and wide felt hats; they drive box-body cars, in most cases heaped with miscellaneous hardware they have been buying at the capital; groups of Kikuyu, the women with heavy luggage on their backs supported by a strap round their foreheads; their ears are slit and ornamented; their clothes of copper-coloured skins; the men have mostly made some effort at European dress in the form of discarded khaki shorts or an old hat. They attempt a clumsy kind of salute as we pass, smiling and saying 'Jambo bwana', rather as children in England still wave their pocket handkerchiefs to trains. I have heard it said that you can tell the moment you cross into Kenya from Uganda or Tanganyika territory by the sulky, oppressed demeanour of the natives. That seemed to me true, later, of the South African Union but without foundation in Kenya. Perhaps the observation was first made by someone crossing from the south directly into the Masai reserve; anyway, journalists in London have found it a convenient remark to repeat.

The scenery is tremendous, finer than anything I saw in Abyssinia; all round for immense distances successive crests of highland. In England we call it a good view if we can see a church spire across six fields; the phrase, made comic by the Frankaus of magazine fiction, 'Wide Open Spaces', really does mean something here. Brilliant sunshine quite unobscured, uninterrupted in its incidence; sunlight clearer than daylight; there is something of the moon about it, the coolness seems so unsuitable. Amber sunlight in Europe; diamond sunlight in Africa. The air fresh as an advertisement for toothpaste.

We are going to stay with Kiki. She lives in a single-storied, very luxurious house on the edge of the lake. She came to Kenya for a short Christmas visit. Someone asked her why she did not stay longer. She explained that she had nowhere particular to go. So he gave her two or three miles of lake front for a Christmas present. She has lived there off and on ever since. She has a husband who shoots most sorts of animals, and a billiard-room to accommodate their heads. She also has two children and a monkey, which sleeps on her pillow. There was an English general staying in the house. He had come all the way from England to shoot a rare animal called a bongo; he had meant to spend all the winter that way. He got his bongo the first week on safari. He felt rather at a loose end. The General was delightful. One day after dinner we talked about marriage and found ourselves in agreement on the subject. (A little while ago I was lunching at a restaurant in London when I was suddenly hit hard between the shoulders and someone said 'Jambo bwana'. It was the General. I asked him to luncheon next week, and secured numerous beautiful girls to talk to him. He never came.)

It was lovely at Naivasha; the grass ran down from the house to the water, where there was a bathing-place with a little jetty to take one clear of the rushes. We used to swim in the morning, eat huge luncheons and sleep in the afternoon. Kiki appeared soon after tea. There were small, hot sausages at cocktail time. Often, very late after dinner, we went into the kitchen and cooked eggs. (There is an important division between the sort of house where you are allowed to cook after midnight, and the house where, if you are hungry, dry sandwiches are shown you, between decanters.) Once Kiki and I went for a walk as far as some ants, fifty yards up the garden. She said, 'You must just feel how they can sting,' and lifted a very large one on to the back of my hand with a leaf. It stung frightfully. More than that, several others ran up the leg of my trouser and began stinging there.

In Kenya it is easy to forget that one is in Africa; then one is reminded of it suddenly, and the awakening is agreeable. One day before luncheon we were sitting on the terrace with cocktails. Kiki's husband and the General were discussing someone they had black-balled for White's; Raymond was teaching chemin-de-fer to Kiki's little boy; there was a striped awning over our heads and a gramo-phone – all very much like the South of France. Suddenly a Kikuyu woman came lolloping over the lawn, leading a little boy by the hands. She said she wanted a pill for her son. She explained the sort of pain he had. Kiki's husband called his valet and translated the explanation of the pain. The valet advised soda mint. When he brought it, the woman held out her hand but they – to the woman's obvious displeasure – insisted on giving it directly to the child. 'Otherwise she would eat it herself the moment she was round the corner.' Apparently the Kikuyu have a passion for pills only equalled in English Bohemia; they come at all hours to beg for them, usually on the grounds that their children are ill, just as Europeans beg for sixpences.

After a time Kiki made a sudden appearance before breakfast, wearing jodhpurs and carrying two heavy bore guns. She had decided to go and kill some lions.

So Raymond and I went to his house at Njoro.

One does not – or at any rate I did not – look upon farming as the occupation of a bachelor, perhaps only because I had so often seen the words 'Farmer's Wife' staring at me from hoardings or perhaps through some atavistic feeling of sympathetic magic that fertility in promoting crops and family were much the same thing. Whatever the reason, the large number of bachelor farmers was, to me, one of the surprising things about Kenya. Raymond is one, though perhaps he is more typically bachelor than farmer. I spent about a fortnight with him off and on at Njoro; sometimes he was away for a day or two, sometimes I was. A delightful if rather irregular visit. His cook was away all the time. There was a head boy called Dunston who spent most of the day squatting outside cooking bath water on a wood fire. I learned very few words of Swahili. When I woke up I said, 'Woppe chickule, Dunston?' which meant, 'Where is food, Dunston?' Dunston usually replied, 'Hapana chickule bwana,' which meant, 'No food, my lord.' Sometimes I had no breakfast; sometimes I found Raymond, if he was at home, sitting up in bed with a tin of grouse paste and a bottle of soda-water, and forced him to share these things with me; sometimes if the telephone was working I rang up Mrs Grant, the nearest neighbour, and had breakfast with her. We used to lunch and dine at the Njoro golf club or with the neighbours: very friendly dinner-parties, Irish in character, to which we bounced over miles of cart-track in a motor van which Raymond had just acquired in exchange for his car; it was full of gadgets designed to help him capture gorillas in the Eturi forest – a new idea of Raymond's, prompted by the information that they fetched two thousand pounds a head at the Berlin Zoo – but was less comfortable than the car for ordinary social use.

The houses of Kenya are mainly in that style of architecture which derives from intermittent prosperity. In many of them the living-rooms are in separate buildings from the bedrooms; their plan is usually complicated by a system of additions and annexes which have sprung up in past years as the result of a good crop, a sudden burst of optimism, the influx of guests from England, the birth of children, the arrival of pupil farmers, or any of the many chances of domestic life. In many houses there is sadder evidence of building begun and abandoned when the bad times came on. Inside they are, as a rule, surprisingly comfortable. Up an unfenced cart-track, one approaches a shed made of concrete, match-boarding, and corrugated iron, and, on entering, finds oneself among old furniture, books, and framed miniatures.

There are very few gardens; we went to one a few miles outside Njoro where an exquisite hostess in golden slippers led us down grass paths bordered with clipped box, over Japanese bridges, pools of water-lilies, and towering tropical plants. But few settlers have time for these luxuries.

Boy and Genessie, with whom I spent a week-end, have one of the 'stately homes' of Kenya; three massive stone buildings on the crest of a hill at Elmenteita overlooking Lake Nakuru, in the centre of an estate which includes almost every topographical feature – grass, bush forest, rock, river, waterfall, and a volcanic cleft down which we scrambled on the end of a rope.

On the borders a bush fire is raging, a low-lying cloud by day, at night a red glow along the horizon. The fire dominates the week-end. We watch anxiously for any change in the wind; cars are continually going out to report progress; extra labour is mustered and dispatched to 'burn a brake'; will the flames 'jump' the railroad? The pasture of hundreds of head of cattle is threatened.

In the evening we go down to the lakeside to shoot duck; thousands of flamingo lie on the water; at the first shot they rise in a cloud, like dust from a beaten carpet; they are the colour of pink alabaster; they wheel round and settle further out. The head of a hippopotamus emerges a hundred yards from shore and yawns at us. When it is dark the hippo comes out for his evening walk. We sit very still, huddled along the running-boards of the cars. We can hear heavy footsteps and the water dripping off him; then he scratches himself noisily. We turn the spotlight of the car on him and reveal a great mud-caked body and a pair of resentful little pink eyes; then he trots back into the water.

Again the enchanting contradictions of Kenya life; a baronial hall straight from Queen Victoria's Scottish Highlands – an open fire of logs and peat with carved-stoned chimney-piece, heads of game, the portraits of prize cattle, guns, golf-clubs, fishing-tackle, and folded newspapers – sherry is brought in, but, instead of a waist-coated British footman, a bare-footed Kikuyu boy in white gown and red jacket. A typical English meadow of deep grass; model cow-sheds in the background; a pedigree Ayrshire bull scratching his back on the gatepost; but, instead of rabbits, a company of monkeys scutter away at our approach; and, instead of a smocked yokel, a Masai herdsman draped in a blanket, his hair plaited into a dozen dyed pig-tails.

I returned to Njoro to find Raymond deeply involved in preparations for his gorilla hunt; guns, cameras, telescopes, revolvers, tinned food, and medicine chests littered tables and floors. There was also a case of champagne. 'You have to have that to give to Belgian officials – and, anyway, it's always useful.'

That evening I dined with the Grants. They had an English-woman staying with them whose daughter had been in the party at Genessie's. She was a prominent feminist, devoted to the fomentation of birth-control and regional cookery in rural England, but the atmosphere of Kenya had softened these severe foibles a little; she was anxious not to be eaten by a lion. It had been arranged that we should all climb Mount Kilimanjaro together; this plan, however, was modified, and, instead, we decided to go to Uganda. I wanted to visit Kisumu before leaving Kenya, so it was decided that they should pick me up there on the following Sunday. Next day I watched Raymond loading his van, and that evening we had a heavy evening at the Njoro club. Early the day after, I took the train for Kisumu.

It was here that I had one of the encounters that compensate one for the blank, nightmare patches of travelling. I was going second class. My companion in the carriage was a ginger-haired young man a few years older than myself; he had an acquaintance with whom he discussed technicalities of local legislation; later this man got out and we were left alone. For some time we did not speak to each other. It was a tedious journey. I tried to read a copy of Burton's *Anatomy of Melancholy* which I had stolen from Raymond's shelves. Presently he said, 'Going far?'

'Kisumu.'

'What on earth for?'

'No particular reason. I thought I might like it.'

Pause. 'You're new in the country, aren't you?'

'Yes.'

'I thought you must be. Kisumu's bloody.'

Presently he said again: 'What have you seen so far?'

I told him briefly.

'Yes, that's all most visitors see. They're delightful people, mind you, but they aren't typical of Kenya.'

Two or three stations went by without any further conversation. Then he began getting together his luggage – a kit bag, some baskets, a small packing-case, and an iron stove-pipe. 'Look here. You won't like Kisumu. You'd far better stay with me the night.'

'All right.'

'Good.'

We got out at a station near the Nandi escarpment and transferred his luggage to a Ford van that was waiting some distance away in charge of an Indian shopkeeper.

'I hope you don't mind; I've got to see my brother-in-law first. It isn't more than thirty miles out of the way.'

We drove a great distance along a rough track through country of supreme beauty. At crossroads the signposts simply bore the names of the settlers. Eventually we arrived at the house. There were several people there, among them a man I had been at school with. Until then my host and I did not know each other's names. There was an Italian garden, with trimmed yew hedges and grass, balustraded terrace, and a vista of cypresses; in the distance the noble horizon of the Nandi hills; after sundown these came alight with little points of fire from the native villages; the household was playing poker under a thatched shelter. My host transacted his business; we drank a glass of Bristol Cream and continued the journey. It was now quite dark. Another very long drive. At last we reached our destination. A boy came out to greet us with a lantern, followed by an elderly lady – my host's mother-in-law. 'I thought you were dead,' she said. 'And who is this?'

'He's come to stay. I've forgotten his name.'

'You'll be very comfortable; there's nothing in the home to eat and there are three swarms of bees in the dining-room.'

Then, turning to her son-in-law: 'Belinda's hind-quarters are totally paralysed.'

This referred, not, as I assumed, to her daughter, but, I learned later, to a wolfhound bitch.

We went up to the house – a spacious, single-storied building typical of the colony. I made some polite comment on it.

'Glad you like it. I built most of it myself.'

'It is the third we have had in this spot,' remarked the old lady. 'The other two were destroyed. The first caught fire; the second was struck by lightning. All the furniture I brought out from England was demolished. I have had dinner prepared three nights running. Now there is nothing.'

There was, however, an excellent dinner waiting for us after we had had baths and changed into pyjamas. We spent the evening dealing with the bees, who, at nightfall, had disposed themselves for sleep in various drawers and cupboards about the living-room. They lay in glutinous, fermenting masses, crawling over each other, like rotten cheese under the microscope; a fair number flew about the room stinging us as we dined; while a few abandoned outposts lurked among the embroidered linen sheets in the bedrooms. A subdued humming filled the entire house. Baths of boiling water were brought in, and the torpid insects were shovelled into them by a terrified native boy. Some of the furniture was carried out on to the lawn to await our attention in the morning.

Next day we walked round the farm – a coffee plantation. Later, a surveyor of roads arrived and we drove all over the countryside pointing out defective culverts. During the rains, the old lady told me, the farm was sometimes isolated from its neighbours for weeks at a time. We saw a bridge being built under the supervision, apparently, of a single small boy in gum-boots. Poor Belinda lay in a basket on the verandah, while over her head a grey and crimson parrot heartlessly imitated her groans.

The surveyor took me to the station for the afternoon train to Kisumu – a town which proved as dreary as my host had predicted – numerous brand-new, nondescript houses, a small landing-stage and railway junction, a population entirely Indian or official. The hotel was full; I shared a bedroom with an Irish airman who was prospecting for the Imperial Airways route to the Cape. Next day, Sunday, I went to church and heard a rousing denunciation of birth-control by a young Mill Hill Father. The manager of the hotel took me for a drive in his car to a Kavirondo village where the people still wore no clothes exept discarded Homburg hats. Then Mrs Grant arrived with the feminist and her daughter.

We drove to Eldoret and stayed at one more house, the most English I had yet seen – old silver, family portraits, chintz-frilled dressing-tables – and next day crossed the frontier into Uganda.

CHAPTER 4

IN ITS WHOLE character, Uganda is quite distinct from Kenya. It is a protectorate not a colony. Instead of the estates of white settlers, one finds evidence of European interest, in seminaries, secondary schools, 'homes', welfare centres, Christian missions of all denominations, theological colleges, and innumerable frantic cyclists.

Long before the coming of Arabs or English, the Baganda people had attained a fair degree of organisation. They had, and still have, a centralised monarchy, an hereditary aristocracy, a complex and consistent system of law. They are quick-witted – so much so that Sir Harry Johnston had described them as 'the Japanese of Africa' – and ambitious of education. They have accepted Christianity, some as a mere constituent part of the glamorous Western civilisation they covet, others with genuine spiritual fervour. They have thrown themselves eagerly into theological controversy, hurtling texts backwards and forwards like shuttlecocks; there are several magazines in Kampala, edited and written by natives, devoted almost exclusively to this form of journalism. They take a lively interest in the technicalities and theories of local government, land tenure, and trade organisation. The national costume is a model of decency – a single white gown which covers them completely to neck, wrist, and ankle. They have a written language which can boast a literature of sorts; in addition to which many of them speak both English and Swahili.

Of course, this culture is remarkable only in comparison with their savage neighbours in Kenya, Tanganyika, and the Congo, and it is confined to a minority among the Baganda. The population of the Protectorate is still for the most part made up of completely unsophisticated peasant cultivators. The inhabitants of an ordinary Baganda village do not show evidence of any special superiority;

339

they do differ radically, however, from their neighbours in having a conscious national unity and a progressive intelligentsia. They are being educated towards the old-fashioned ideal of representative institutions, and official British policy abhors the idea of a permanent white population which might embarrass this development, as it will do in Kenya.

There was nothing, however, to mark the frontiers of the two territories. We crossed some time during the morning and arrived at Jinja in the late afternoon. It would be tedious to describe each of the lakeside settlements; they vary in size, but are all identical in character, neat, sanitary, straggling; a landing stage and an office; sometimes a railway station and an hotel; sometimes a golf links; genial, official nonentities, punctilious and slightly patronising. Entebbe is drearier than most; Jinja slightly gayer; Kisumu is the norm.

At Jinja there is both hotel and golf links. The latter is, I believe, the only course in the world which posts a special rule that the player may remove his ball by hand from hippopotamus footprints. For there is a very old hippopotamus who inhabits this corner of the lake. Long before the dedication of the Ripon Falls it was his practice to take an evening stroll over that part of the bank which now constitutes the town of Jinja. He has remained set in his habit, despite railway-lines and bungalows. At first, attempts were made to shoot him, but lately he has come to be regarded as a local mascot, and people returning late from bridge parties not infrequently see him lurching home down the main street. Now and then he varies his walk by a detour across the golf links and it is then that the local rule is brought into force.

There were several big-game hunters staying in the hotel, so that there was not room for all of us. Accordingly I went off to the Government rest-house. These exist all over Africa, primarily for the convenience of travelling officials, but private individuals may make use of them, if they are empty. They vary in range from small hotels to unfurnished shelters. At Jinja there was a bedstead and mattress, but no sheets or blankets. I had just made a collection of the overcoats of the party when we saw a black face grinning at us from below the hotel steps. It was Dunston, hat in hand, come to report the loss of Raymond. He and the neighbour who was joining his gorilla hunt had gone on in a car, leaving Dunston and the native driver to follow in the van. Somewhere they had missed the road. Anyway, here was the van with the rifles and provisions and 'Hapana bwana de Trafford'. Dunston wanted instructions. We told him to take bwana de Trafford's blankets to the rest-house, make up the bed, and then wait for further instructions. Meanwhile we wired to Eldoret, Njoro, and Nairobi, reporting the position of Raymond's lorry. I do not know whether he ever found it, for we left next morning for Kampala.

Here I said good-bye to my companions and established myself at the hotel. I was becoming conscious of an inclination to return to Europe and wanted to get down to Albertville and the Belgian air service as soon as I could. A kind-hearted young travel agent tried to persuade me to pay him £60 to arrange my route through Lake Kivu, but I found in the end that it would be quicker and a great deal cheaper to stick to the regular service round Lake Victoria to Mwanza; from there to Tabora and Kigoma, and so across Lake Tanganyika to my goal. From now on, this record becomes literally a 'travel book'; that is to say that it deals less with the observation of places than with the difficulties of getting from one place to another.

There were still five days, however, to put in before the lake steamer called for Mwanza, and these days I spent in a *milieu* that was mainly ecclesiastical, for the missions hold most of the strings of Uganda policy.

In reaction from the proselytising fervour of fifty years ago, there is at the moment a good deal of distrust of foreign missions. Many officials, in unofficial moments, will confess that if they had their way they would like to clear all the missionaries out of the country; many private persons told me that they would never engage a 'mission boy' as a servant – they were always dishonest and often insolent. By an anti-imperialist interpretation of history, missionaries are regarded as the vanguard of commercial penetration. Romantics with a taste for local colour denounce them as the spoil sports who have clothed the naked and displaced fine native carving with plaster statuettes of the Sacred Heart. More serious sociologists maintain that tribal integrity, and with it the whole traditional structure of justice and morality, is being undermined by the suppression of tribal initiation ceremonies. Many good churchmen in Europe are not, I think, free from a slight resentment at the large sums yearly subscribed and dispatched for the doubtful benefit of remote corners of the globe, which might be employed at home on work of immediate and obvious importance. From all sides, criticism is being directed against these heroic outposts. One cannot remain a night in Kampala without finding one's sympathies involved on one side or the other.

Of course, from the theological aspect, there is no room for doubt; every soul baptised, educated in the Faith and upheld by the sacraments in Christian life, whether it inhabits a black or white body, is so much positive good. Moreover, since growth is a measure of life, it is impossible that the Faith should not spread – expansion is organically inseparable from its existence. But theological arguments have little efficacy in modern controversy. It seems to me that this can be conceded to the general scepticism about Westernisation: that had it been possible to prevent alien influence – European, Arab, or Indian – from ever penetrating into Africa; could the people have lived in invincible ignorance, developing their own faith and institutions from their own roots; then, knowing what a mess we have made of civilisation in Europe and the immense compensating ills that attend every good we have accomplished, we may say that it would have been a mischievous thing, as long as there were any pagans left in Europe, to try and convert Africa. But it is quite certain that, in the expansive optimism of the last century, Africa would not have been left alone. Whether it wanted or not, it was going to be heaped with all the rubbish of our own continent; mechanised transport, representative government, organised labour, artificially stimulated appetites for variety in clothes, food, and amusement were waiting for the African round the corner. All the negative things were coming to him inevitably. Europe has only one positive thing which it can offer to anyone, and that is what the missionaries brought. In Uganda the missionaries got there before the trader or the official, and it is to this priority that they owe their unique position as managers of the entire elementary and secondary education of a country in which education is regarded as the highest function of government.

Kampala is built on seven hills, three of which are occupied by ecclesiastical buildings. There is the great cathedral at Ruaga, the Mill Hill mission at Nsambia, and, opposite them, the Church Missionary Society's cathedral – a really beautiful domed building, made entirely by native workmen. On a fourth is Makerere College, a secular institution, where the prize students of the mission schools receive a fairly advanced education. It is hoped that eventually this will form the nucleus of an East African university. Meanwhile the entrance examinations are hotly contested. Rivalry is intense between the Catholic missions and the CMS. It is not forty years since the last religious war was fought there. The occasional lapses into polygamy of the native Protestant clergy are greeted by the Catholic laity with unchristian delight, and the Makerere class lists are watched as a fair indication of the relative merits of the two faiths.

At the time of the religious war the issues had become fatally confused with the question of nationality. Today the Catholic missions have become thoroughly cosmopolitan; at Ruaga they are mainly French, but Bishop Camplin at Nsambia is a Scotsman, Mother Kevin at Kokonjiro is Irish, the Teaching Brothers are, many of them, Canadian, and Father Janssen, the parish priest of Kampala, is Dutch. It was Father Janssen who acted as my guide during the five days at Kampala; an unforgettable figure, with vast beard, gaitered legs, and pipe of foul Boer tobacco, who drove about the town on a motor-bicycle defending the purity of his converts, when necessary, by force. He had built most of his church with his own hands, making clever counterfeits of wood-carving with the aid of a cement-mould and a paint-pot. With him I went round fever wards, maternity homes, schools, and seminaries; a gallant, indefatigable, inflexible man. His only personal ambition was to get away from the smug amenities of Kampala into the wilds, preferably to the head-hunters of Borneo, where he had begun his service.

We went out together to luncheon at Kokonjiro, a convent of native girls presided over by two European nuns and a woman doctor. They wear habit and live by strict rule; here they are trained as nurses and school teachers. At the convent they manage a small farm and hospital, and in recreation time do skilled needlework. It does not sound very remarkable to a reader in Europe; it is

astounding in Central Africa – this little island of order and sweetness in an ocean of rank barbarity; all round it for hundreds of miles
lies gross jungle, bush, and forest, haunted by devils and the fear of
darkness, where human life merges into the cruel, automatic life of
the animals; here they were singing the offices just as they had been
sung in Europe when the missions were little radiant points of
learning and decency in a pagan wilderness. The only thing which
upset the calm of Kokonjiro was the ravages of white ants in the
sanctuary steps.

On the way back we stopped at a boys' school kept by Teaching
Brothers; a loutish class were at work on the history syllabus of
Makerere. The subject that afternoon was 'The Rivalry between
Venice and Genoa in the Sixteenth Century'. Professor Huxley, in
African View, derided the teaching of Latin at the Tabora seminary. It
seems to me that the Makerere history syllabus is a far more notable
example of unimaginative education. Swahili, his local dialect, and
the kind of colloquial English he is likely to learn in the secular
schools do not give the African a vehicle he can use with precision
when his mind comes to interest itself in the more complex aspects of
his own existence; Latin, intrinsically, is of value to him. But what
sort of significance can the details of European history have to a man
who will most probably never leave his own territory, and has never
seen more than a handful of Europeans in his life?

I left Kampala on the following Sunday afternoon. The *Rusinga*,
in which I travelled down the lake, was a comfortable little boat
staffed with four smart officers who wore white and gold uniforms in
the mornings and blue and gold at night. The voyage was uneventful; at Entebbe we ran into a plague of small fly; an Indian clerk in
new boots paced the deck all night and kept me awake. On Tuesday
we reached Bukoba and took on several more passengers; for the
first time we came under grey skies, a pleasant experience after the
invariable white glare of the preceding months. From now on we
were in the rains. Bukoba was German built, before the war. It has
rather more character than the other lake stations, with acacia
avenues and substantial little houses with sturdy porticoes. On
Wednesday I disembarked at Mwanza, where I spent a day and
a half in a grubby hotel kept by a Greek. It is a deadly little town

populated chiefly by Indians. I had to share a room with a CMS chaplain. At meals I sat with him and an elderly 'tough-egg' from Manchester, engaged in the cotton trade. At least he was so engaged until Thursday morning. He had come down from the south to meet his local manager. When he returned from the interview I asked, with what I hoped would be acceptable jocularity, 'Well, did you get the sack?'

'Yes,' he answered, 'as a matter of fact, I did. How the devil did you know?'

An unfortunate episode.

Later at luncheon he got rather drunk and told some very unsuitable anecdotes about a baboon. The missionary went off immediately to write letters in the bedroom. That evening we took the train to Tabora and arrived at noon next day. I travelled with the missionary, a cultured and courteous man. We talked about the language problem. A conference was sitting at that time, and had just decided to make Kiswahili compulsory throughout the three territories of Kenya, Uganda, and Tanganyika. On the whole, local opinion seems to favour this policy, though at first sight there seems little to commend it except the consideration that all the officials have learned the language at some pains and do not want to see their industry wasted. It is clearly desirable that there should be a *lingua franca*. Most of the local dialects are quite inadequate for educated employment. There is, for example, no word in Kikuyu for 'virgin' and no stage of Kikuyu womanhood with which any parallel to it can be drawn. This, as may be imagined, has caused considerable difficulty to missionaries. My travelling companion's point was that it was essential that Africans should speak a language of African origin; this seemed unduly doctrinaire. The same policy was defended to me on other grounds by the editor of a local newspaper, who maintained that it tended to preserve race superiority if English remained occult.

We also discussed the rite of female circumcision, which is one of the battlegrounds between missionaries and anthropologists. The missionary told me of an interesting experiment that was being made in his district. 'We found it impossible to eradicate the practice,' he said, 'but we have cleansed it of most of its objectionable features. The operation is now performed by my wife, in the whole-some atmosphere of the church hut.'

Perhaps it is by arrangement with the hotel proprietors that every change of train involves the delay of a night or two. It was not until late on Sunday evening that I could get my connection to Kigoma. Even in Africa the hotel at Tabora is outstandingly desolate. It is very large and old. In the optimistic days of German imperialism it was built to provide the amusement of an important garrison. It is now rapidly falling to pieces under the management of a dispirited Greek. One enters from the terrace into a large, double ballroom from which open a dining-room and a bar; music-stands and a broken drum lie on a dais at one end. In the centre is a threadbare billiard table. The bedrooms are in a wing; they open into a cool arcaded corridor; each is provided with a balcony and a bath-room. The paint had long ago worn off the bath; the tap would neither turn on or off, but dripped noisily day and night; the balcony had been used as a repository for derelict chairs; two panes of glass in the windows had been broken and stuffed with rag. My only companion here was a commercial traveller in cigarettes. We spent a long afternoon together playing poker-dice for shilling points. At the end of the day we were all square.

The town is not without interest. It reflects the various stages of its history. Fine groves of mango remain to record the days of Arab occupation, when it was the principal clearing station for slaves and ivory on the caravan route to the coast. Acacia-trees, a fort, and that sad hotel remain from the days of German East Africa. It was for some time the base of von Letow's gallant campaign; it was here that he coined his own gold – the Tabora sovereign much coveted by collectors. England's chief contribution is a large public school for the education of the sons of chiefs. This institution, erected at vast expense as a sop to the League of Nations, from which we hold the mandate, is one of the standing jokes of East Africa. Bishop Michaud, who very kindly called on me and drove me about in his car, took me to inspect it. It is a huge concrete building of two stories, planted prominently on one of the most unsuitable sites in the territory for the agricultural demonstrations that are the princi-pal feature of its training. At first it was intended exclusively for future chiefs, but now it has been opened to other promising natives. They wear crested blazers and little rugger caps; they have prefects and 'colours'; they have a brass band; they learn farming, typewriting, English, physical drill, and public-school *esprit de corps*. They have honour boards, on which the name of one boy is inscribed every year. Since there were no particular honours for which they could compete – Makerere was far above their wildest ambitions – it was originally the practice of the boys to elect their champion. Elections, however, proved so unaccountably capricious that nomination soon took their place. I was invited to attend a *shari* (the local word for any kind of discussion). This was a meeting of the whole school, at which the prefects dealt with any misdemeanours. They sat in chairs on a dais; the school squatted on the floor of the great hall. Three boys were called up: two had smoked; one had refused to plough. They were sentenced to be caned. Resisting strongly, they were pinioned to the ground by their friends while the drill-sergeant, an old soldier from the KAR, delivered two or three strokes with a cane. It was a far lighter punishment than any at an English public school, but it had the effect of inducing yells of agony and the most extravagant writhings. Apparently this part of the public-school system had not been fully assimilated.

We drove out to the ruins of the Arab house where Stanley and Livingstone had spent three weeks together. On the way we passed the residence of a local chief whose history illustrates the difference between English and African ideas of justice. A few months before my arrival he had been arrested for very considerable defalcations of public accounts. There was not the smallest doubt of his guilt in anyone's mind. He was sent down to the coast for trial, and there acquitted upon some purely technical legal quibble. To the European this seemed an excellent example of British impartiality; anyone, black or white, guilty or not guilty, got a fair trial according to law on the evidence submitted. To the native there was only one explanation; he had bribed or intimidated his judges. Under German administration, justice was often ruthless, but it was delivered arbitrarily by the officer on the spot, and the sentence executed immediately in a way that the natives understood; English justice, more tender and sophisticated, with its rights of appeal and delays of action, is more often than not confusing and unsatisfactory to the African mind.

That evening an opinionated little Austrian sizal-farmer arrived at the hotel, full of ridicule of British administration. He had just returned to the farm he had worked before the war, as Germans and Austrians are now doing in large numbers. He was confident that after a few more years of British mismanagement the territory would have to be handed back to Germany. 'Before the war,' he said, 'every native had to salute every European or he knew the reason why. Now, with all this education . . .' He was as boring as any retired colonel in an English farce.

On Saturday evening the cigarette traveller and I went to an Indian cinema. We saw a very old Charlie Chaplin film, made long before his rise to eminence, but full of all the tricks that have now become world famous; there was even an unhappy ending – his renunciation of love in favour of the handsome bounder. There was also a scene which was clearly the first version of the exquisite passage in *Gold Rush* where he eats the old boot; he is sitting under a tree, about to begin his luncheon, when a tramp steals it; Charlie shrugs his shoulders, picks a handful of grass, peppers and salts it, and eats it with delicacy; then he pours water into a can, rinses the tips of his fingers as though in a finger bowl, and dries them on a rag – all performed with a restrained swagger.

This was followed by an Indian film – a costume piece derived from a traditional fairy-story. A kindly Indian next to us helped us with the plot, explaining, 'That is a bad man,' 'That is a elephant,' etc. When he wished to tell us that the hero had fallen in love with the heroine – a situation sufficiently apparent from their extravagant gestures of passion – he said, 'He wants to take her into the bushes.'

The church at Tabora was very beautiful; a great thatched barn, with low, whitewashed walls and rough wooden pillars daubed with the earth colour of the country. It was packed next day with a native congregation who sang at Mass with tremendous devotion. That afternoon I went for another drive with the bishop, and late in the evening caught the train for Kigoma.

SECOND NIGHTMARE

I ARRIVED AT Kigoma in the morning of February 2nd, a haphazard spatter of bungalows differing very little from the other lakeside stations I had passed through, except in the size and apparent disorder of its wharfs and goods yard. The lake steamers belong to the Belgian Chemin de Fer des Grands Lacs; notices everywhere are in French and Flemish; there are the offices of Belgian immigration authorities, vice-consulate, and customs; a huge unfinished building of the Congo trading company. But the impression that I had already left British soil was dissipated almost at once by the spectacle of a pair of Tanganyika policemen, who stood with the ticket collector at the station door and forcibly vaccinated the native passengers as they passed through.

It was now about noon and the heat was overpowering. I was anxious to get my luggage on board, but it had to be left at the customs sheds for examination when the official had finished his luncheon. A group of natives were squatting in the road, savages with filed teeth and long hair, very black, with broad shoulders and spindly legs, dressed in bits of skin and rag. A White Father of immense stature drove up in a box-body lorry containing crates, sacks, and nuns for transshipment; a red and wiry beard spread itself over his massive chest; clouds of dense, acrid smoke rose from his cheroot.

There was a little Greek restaurant in the main street, where I lunched and, after luncheon, sat on the verandah waiting for the customs office to open. A continual traffic of natives passed to and fro – most of them, in from the country, far less civilised than any I had seen since the Somalis; a few, in shirts, trousers, and hats, were obviously in European employment; one of them rode a bicycle and fell off it just in front of the restaurant; he looked very rueful when he got up, but when the passers-by laughed at him he began to laugh too and went off thoroughly pleased with himself as though he had made a good joke.

By about three I got my luggage clear, then after another long wait bought my ticket, and finally had my passport examined by British and Belgian officials. I was then able to go on board the *Duc de Brabant*. She was a shabby, wood-burning steamer, with passenger accommodation in the poop consisting of a stuffy little deck-saloon, with two or three cabins below and a padlocked lavatory. The short deck was largely taken up by the captain's quarters – an erection like a two-roomed bungalow, containing a brass double bedstead with mosquito-curtains, numerous tables and chairs, cushions, photograph frames, mirrors, clocks, china and metal ornaments, greasy cretonnes and torn muslin, seedy little satin bows and ribbons, pots of dried grasses, pin-cushions, every conceivable sort of cheap and unseamanlike knick-knack. Clearly there was a woman on board. I found her knitting on the shady side of the deck-house. I asked her about cabins. She said her husband was asleep and was not to be disturbed until five. Gross snorting and grunting from the mosquito-curtains gave substance to her statement. There were three people asleep in the saloon. I went on shore again and visited the Congo agency, where I inquired about my aeroplane to Leopoldville. They were polite, but quite unhelpful. I must ask at Albertville.

Soon after five the captain appeared. No one, looking at him, would have connected him in any way with a ship; a very fat, very dirty man, a stained tunic open at his throat, unshaven, with a straggling moustache, crimson-faced, gummy-eyed, flat-footed. He would have seemed more at home as proprietor of an *estaminet*. A dozen or so passengers had now assembled – we were due to sail at six – and the captain lumbered round examining our tickets and passports. Everyone began claiming cabins. He would see to all that when we sailed, he said. When he came to me he said, 'Where is your medical certificate?'

I said I had not got one.

'It is forbidden to sail without a medical certificate.'

I explained that I had been given a visa, had bought a ticket, had had my passport examined twice by British and Belgian officials, but that no one had said anything to me about a medical certificate.

'I regret it is forbidden to travel. You must get one.'

'But a certificate of what? What do you want certified?'

'It is no matter to me what is certified. You must find a doctor and get him to sign. Otherwise you cannot sail.'

This was three-quarters of an hour before the advertised time of departure. I hurried on shore and inquired where I could find a doctor. I was directed to a hospital some distance from the town, at the top of the hill. There were, of course, no taxis of any kind. I set out walking feverishly. Every now and then the steamer gave a whistle which set me going at a jog-trot for a few paces. At last, streaming with sweat, I reached the hospital. It turned out to be a club house; the hospital was about two miles away on the other side of the town. Another whistle from the *Duc de Brabant*. I pictured her sailing away across the lake with all my baggage, money, and credentials. I explained my difficulty to a native servant; he clearly did not at all understand what I wanted, but he caught the word doctor. I suppose he thought I was ill. Anyway, he lent me a boy to take me to a doctor's house. I set off again at high speed, to the disgust of my guide, and finally reached a bungalow where an Englishwoman was sitting in the garden with needlework and a book. No, her husband was not at home. Was it anything urgent?

I explained my predicament. She thought I might be able to find him on the shore; he might be there at work on his speed-boat, or else he might be playing tennis, or perhaps he had taken the car out to Ujiji. I had better try the shore first.

Down the hill again, this time across country over a golf course and expanses of scrub. Sure enough, at one of the landing stages about a quarter of a mile from the *Duc de Brabant*, I found two Englishmen fiddling with a motorboat. One of them was the doctor. I shouted down to him what I wanted. It took him some time to find any paper. In the end his friend gave him an old envelope. He sat down in the stern and wrote: '*I have examined Mr*' – 'What's your name?' – '*Waugh, and find him free from infectious disease, including omnis t.b. and trypansiniasis. He has been vaccinated.*' – 'Five shillings, please.'

I handed down the money; he handed up the certificate. That was that.

It was ten past six when I reached the *Duc de Brabant*, but she was still there. With a grateful heart I panted up the gangway and presented my certificate. When I had got my breath a little I explained to a sympathetic Greek the narrow escape I had had of being left behind. But I need not have hurried. It was a little after midnight before we sailed.

The boat was now very full. On our deck there were four or five Belgian officials and their wives, two mining engineers, and several Greek traders. There was also a plump young man with a pallid face and soft American voice. Unlike anyone I had seen for the past month, he wore a neat, dark suit, white collar and bow tie. He had a great deal of very neat luggage, including a typewriter and a bicycle. I offered him a drink and he said, 'Oh no, thank you,' in a tone which in four monosyllables contrived to express first surprise, then pain, then reproof, and finally forgiveness. Later I found that he was a member of the Seventh Day Adventist mission, on his way to audit accounts at Bulawayo.

The waist and forecastle were heaped with mail-bags and freight over which sprawled and scurried a medley of animals and native passengers. There were goats and calves and chickens, naked negro children, native soldiers, women suckling babies or carrying them slung between their shoulders, young girls with their hair plaited into pig-tails, which divided their scalps into symmetrical patches, girls with shaven pates and with hair caked in red mud, old negresses with bundles of bananas, over-dressed women with yellow and red cotton shawls and brass bangles, negro workmen in shorts, vests, and crumpled topis. There were several little stoves and innumerable pots of boiling banana. Bursts of singing and laughing.

They laid the tables in our saloon for dinner. We sat tightly packed at benches. There were three or four small children who were fed at the table. Two ragged servants cooked and served a very bad dinner. The captain collected the money. Presently he passed round a list of those to whom he had given cabins. I was not among them, nor was the American missionary nor any of the Greeks. We should have slipped him a tip with our tickets, I learned later. About a dozen of us were left without accommodation. Six wise men laid themselves out full length on the saloon benches immediately after dinner and established their claim for the night. The rest of us sat on our luggage on the deck. There were no seats or deck-chairs. Luckily it was a fine night, warm, unclouded, and windless. I spread an overcoat on the deck, placed a canvas grip under my head as a pillow and composed myself for sleep. The missionary found two little wooden chairs and sat stiff backed, wrapped in a rug, with his feet up supporting a book of Bible-stories on his knees. As we got up steam, brilliant showers of wood sparks rose from the funnel; soon after midnight we sailed into the lake; a gentle murmur of singing came from the bows. In a few minutes I was asleep.

I woke up suddenly an hour later and found myself shivering with cold. I stood up to put on my overcoat and immediately found myself thrown against the rail. At the same moment I saw the missionary's two chairs tip over sideways and him sprawl on the deck. A large pile of hand luggage upset and slid towards the side. There was a tinkle of broken china from the captain's quarters. All this coincided with torrential downpour of rain and a tearing wind. It was followed in a second or two by a blaze of lightning and shattering detonation. A chatter of alarm went up from the lower deck, and various protests of disturbed livestock. In the half-minute which it took us to collect our luggage and get into the saloon we were saturated with rain. And here we were in scarcely better conditions, for the windows, when raised, proved not to be of glass, but of wire gauze. The wind tore through them, water poured in and slopped from side to side. Women passengers came up squealing from their cabins below, with colourless, queasy faces. The saloon became intolerably over-crowded. We sat as we had at dinner, packed in rows round the two tables. The wind was so strong that it was impossible, single-handed, to open the door. Those who were ill – the American missionary was the first to go under – were obliged to remain in their places. The shriek of the wind was so loud that conversation was impossible; we just clung there, pitched and thrown, now out of our seats, now on top of one another; occasionally someone would fall asleep and wake up instantly with his head thumped hard against table or wall. It needed constant muscular effort to avoid injury. Vile retchings occurred on every side. Women whimpered at their husbands for support. The children yelled. We were all of us dripping and shivering. At last everyone grew quieter as alarm subsided and desperation took its place. They sat there, rigid and glum, gazing straight before them or supporting their heads in their hands until, a little before dawn, the wind dropped and rain ceased beating in; then some of them fell asleep, and others slunk back to their cabins. I went out on deck. It was still extremely cold, and the little boat bobbed and wallowed hopelessly in a heavy sea, but the storm was clearly over. Soon a green and silver dawn broke over the lake; it was misty all round us, and the orange sparks from the funnel were just visible against the whiter sky. The two stewards emerged with chattering teeth and attempted to set things to order in the saloon, dragging out rolls of sodden matting and swabbing up the water-logged floor. Huddled groups on the lower deck began to disintegrate and a few cocks crowed; there was a clatter of breakfast cups and a welcome smell of coffee.

It was raining again before we reached harbour and moored against an unfinished concrete pier, where dripping convicts were working, chained together in gangs. Albertville was almost hidden in mist; a blur of white buildings against the obscurer background. Two rival hotel proprietors stood under umbrellas shouting for custom; one was Belgian, the other Greek. Officials came on board. We queued up and presented our papers one at a time. The inevitable questions: Why was I coming into the Congo? How much money had I? How long did I propose to stay there? Where was my medical certificate? The inevitable form to fill in – this time in duplicate: Date and place of father's birth? Mother's maiden name? Maiden name of divorced wife? Habitual domicile? By this time I had learned not to reveal the uncertainty of my plans. I told them I was going direct to Matadi and was given a certificate of entry which I was to present to the immigration officer at the frontier. It took two hours before we were allowed to land.

Quite suddenly the rain stopped and the sun came out. Everything began to steam.

*

I spent two nights at Albertville. It consists of a single street of offices, shops, and bungalows. There are two hotels catering for visitors in transit to and from Tanganyika; no cinemas or places of amusement. There are white people serving in the shops, and white clerks at the railway station; no natives live in the town except a handful of dockers and domestic servants. The food at the hotel is fairly good; better than I have had for several weeks. The Belgian manager is amiable and honest. I spend my time making inquiries about the air service. No one knows anything about it. One thing is certain, that there has never been an air service at Albertville. They think there was one once at Kabalo; that there still may be. Anyway, there is a train to Kabalo the day after tomorrow. There is no alternative; one can either take the train to Kabalo or the boat back to Kigoma; there are no other means of communication in any direction. With some apprehension of coming discomfort, I purchase a ticket to Kabalo.

The train left at seven in the morning and made the journey in a little under eleven hours, counting a halt for luncheon at the wayside. It is an uneven line; so uneven that at times I was hardly able to read. I travelled first class to avoid the American missionary, and had the carriage to myself. For half the day it rained. The scenery was attractive at first; we pitched and rocked through a wooded valley with a background of distant hills, and later along the edge of a river broken by islands of vivid swamp. Towards midday, however, we came into bush country, featureless and dismal; there was no game to be seen, only occasional clouds of white butterflies; in the afternoon we jolted over mile upon mile of track cut through high grass, which grew right up on either side of the single line to the height of the carriages, completely shutting out all view, but mercifully shading us from the afternoon sun. There was a shower-bath attached to the first-class coach, an invaluable contribution to the comfort of a hot day's journey which might well be commended to the PLM. It was fantastic to discover, on a jolting single line in Central Africa, decencies which one cannot get on the Blue Train. It is perhaps fair to remark that the shower-bath was not, nor apparently had been for some time, in working order; but I have long ceased to hope for any railway carriage that will offer

a tolerable water system. It seems to be well understood by coach
designers in all parts of the world that the true measure of luxury
consists in the number of unnecessary electric light switches and
different coloured bulbs.

It was just before sundown when we reached Kabalo, a place of
forbidding aspect. There was no platform; a heap of wood fuel and
the abrupt termination of the line marked the station; there were
other bits of line sprawling out to right and left; a few shabby trucks
had been shunted on to one of these, and apparently abandoned;
there were two or three goods sheds of corrugated iron and a dirty
little canteen; apart from these, no evidence of habitation. In front of
us lay the Upper Congo – at this stage of its course undistinguished
among the great rivers of the world for any beauty or interest; a broad
flow of water, bounded by swamps; since we were in the rainy season,
it was swollen and brown. A barge or two lay in to the bank, and
a paddle steamer, rusted all over, which was like a flooded Thames
bungalow more than a ship. A bit of the bank opposite the railway-
line had been buttressed up with concrete; on all sides lay rank
swamp. Mercifully, night soon came on and hid this beastly place.

I hired a boy to sit on my luggage, and went into the canteen.
There, through a haze of mosquitoes, I discerned a prominent
advertisement of the Kabalo–Matadi air service; two or three railway officials were squatting about on stiff little chairs swilling tepid
beer. There was a surly and dishevelled woman slopping round in
bedroom slippers, with a tray of dirty glasses. In answer to my
inquiry, she pointed out the patron, a torpid lump fanning himself
in the only easy chair. I asked him when the next aeroplane left the
coast; everyone stopped talking and stared at me when I put this
question. The patron giggled. He did not know when the *next* would
leave; the *last* went about ten months ago. There were only three
ways of leaving Kabalo; either by train back to Albertville or by river
up or down stream. The *Prince Leopold* was due that evening for
Bukama; in a day or so there would be a boat down the river; if I took
that, I could, with judicious alternations of boat and rail, reach
Matadi in under a month.

At this stage one of the railway officials interposed helpfully.
There were trains from Bukama to a place called Port Francqui.

If I wired, and if the wire ever reached its destination, I could arrange for the Elisabethville–Matadi air service to pick me up there. Failing that, I could get from Bukama on to the newly opened Benguela railway and come out on the coast at Lobita Bay in Portuguese West Africa. In any case, I had better go to Bukama. Kabalo, he remarked, was a dull place to stay in.

Two hours passed and there was no sign of the *Prince Leopold*. We ate a frightful (and very expensive) meal in the canteen. The Seventh Day Adventist came in from the railway-line, where he had been sitting in the dark to avoid the sight and smell of beer-drinking. He was travelling by the *Prince Leopold*, too. Another two hours and she arrived. We went on board that night and sailed at dawn.

The journey took four days. It was not uncomfortable. There was heavy rain half the time and the temperature was never insupportable. I had a cabin to myself, and I fought boredom, and to some extent overcame it, by the desperate expedient of writing – it was there, in fact, that I ground out the first two chapters of this book.

The *Prince Leopold* was a large paddle-steamer, twice the size of the *Rusinga*, with half the staff. The captain and a Greek steward seemed to do all the work; the former young and neurotic, the latter middle-aged and imperturbable, both very grubby. It was a great contrast to all those dapper bachelors on Lake Victoria, with their white collars and changes of uniform. The captain had married quarters in the top story (one could only regard it as a floating house, not as a ship); his strip of deck was fringed with pots of ferns and palm; below him was the European passengers' deck, two rows of tiny cabins, an observation platform, and a bath-room; the ground floor was occupied by cargo and native passengers. We stopped two or three times a day at desolate little stations, where a crowd of natives and two sickly Belgian agents would come down to greet us. Sometimes there was a native village; usually nothing except a single shed and a pile of timber. We delivered mail, took up cargo, and occasionally effected some change of passengers. These were all Greek or Belgian; either traders or officials; except for the inevitable round of handshaking each morning there was very little intercourse. The Seventh Day Adventist became slightly ill; he attributed his discomfort to the weakness of the tea. The scenery was utterly dreary. Flat papyrus-swamps on either side broken by rare belts of palm. The captain employed his time in inflicting slight wounds on passing antelope with a miniature rifle. Occasionally he would be convinced that he had killed something; the boat would stop and all the native passengers disembark and scramble up the side with loud whoops and yodels. There was difficulty in getting them back. The captain would watch them, through binoculars, plunging and gambolling about in the high grass; at first he would take an interest in the quest, shouting directions to them; then he would grow impatient and summon them back; they would disappear further and further, thoroughly enjoying their romp. He would have the siren sounded for them – blast after blast. Eventually they would come back, jolly, chattering, and invariably empty-handed.

We were due to arrive at Bukama on Sunday (February 8th). The train for Port Francqui did not leave until the following Tuesday night. It was customary for passengers to wait on board, an arrangement that was profitable to the company and comparatively comfortable for them. I was prevented from doing this by a violent and inglorious altercation with the captain, which occurred quite unexpectedly on the last afternoon of the journey.

I was sitting in my cabin, engrossed in the affairs of Abyssinia, when the captain popped in and, with wild eye and confused speech, demanded to be shown the ticket for my motor-bicycle. I am convinced that he was sober, but I am less sure of his sanity. I replied that I had no motor-bicycle. 'What, *no* motor-bicycle?' 'No, *no* motor-bicycle.' He shook his head, clicked his tongue and popped out again. I went on writing.

In half an hour he was back again; this time with a fellow passenger who spoke English.

'The captain wishes me to tell you that he must see the ticket for your motor-bicycle.'

'But I have already told the captain that I have no motor-bicycle.'

'You do not understand. It is necessary to have a ticket for a motor-bicycle.'

'I have no motor-bicycle.'

They left me again.

Ten minutes later the captain was back. 'Will you kindly show me your motor-bicycle.'

'I have no motor-bicycle.'

'It is on my list that you have a motor-bicycle. Will you kindly show it to me.'

'I have no motor-bicycle.'

'But it is on my list.'

'I am sorry. I have no motor-bicycle.'

Again he went away; again he returned; now, beyond question, stark crazy. 'The motor-bicycle – the motor-bicycle! I must see the motor-bicycle.'

'I have no motor-bicycle.'

It is idle to pretend that I maintained a dignified calm. I was in a tearing rage, too. After all we were in the heart of the tropics where tempers are notoriously volatile.

'Very well, I will search your luggage. Show it to me.'

'It is in this cabin. Two suitcases under the bunk; one bag on the rack.'

'Show it to me.'

'Look for it yourself.' As I say, an inglorious schoolboy brawl.

'I am the captain of this ship. Do you expect me to move luggage?'

'I am a passenger. Do you expect me to?'

He went to the door and roared for a boy. No one came. With a trembling hand I attempted to write. He roared again. Again. At last a sleepy boy ambled up. 'Take those suitcases from under the bunk.'

I pretended to be writing. I could hear the captain puffing just behind me (it was a very small cabin).

'Well,' I said, 'have you found a motor-bicycle?'

'Sir, that is my affair,' said the captain.

He went away. I thought I had heard the last of the incident. In half an hour he was back. 'Pack your bag. Pack your bag instantly.'

'But I am staying on board until Tuesday.'

'You are leaving at once. I am the captain. I will not allow people of your kind to stay here another hour.'

In this way I found myself stranded on the wharf at Bukama with two days to wait for my train. A humiliating situation, embittered by the Seventh Day Adventist, who came to offer his sympathy.

'It doesn't do to argue,' he said, 'unless you understand the language.' Damn him.

I thought I had touched bottom at Kabalo, but Bukama has it heavily beaten. If ever a place merited the epithet 'God-forsaken' in its literal sense, it is that station. An iron bridge spans the river leading from the European quarter to the desolated huts of the native navvies who built it. Two ruined bungalows stand by the waterside and the overgrown Government rest-house, whose use has been superseded by the *Prince Leopold*; it is still nominally open, and it was here that I should have to stay if I decided to wait for the Port Francqui train. It is unfurnished and, presumably, infested with spirillum tick. Some distance from the landing-point lies the jumble of huts that serve as ticket and goods office of the Katanga railway. A road leads up the hill, where there are two abandoned offices and a Greek bar and general store. At the top of the hill is the administrative port – a flag-staff, the bungalow of the resident official, and a small hospital round which squatted a group of dejected patients enveloped in bandages. A platoon of native soldiers shuffled past. The heat and damp were appalling, far worse than anything I had met in Zanzibar. At sundown, swarms of soundless, malarial mosquitoes appeared. I sat in the Greek bar, with sweat splashing down like rain-water from my face to the floor; the proprietor knew only a few words of French. In these few words he advised me to leave Bukama as soon as I could, before I went down with fever. He himself was ashen and shivering from a recent bout. There was a train some time that evening for Elisabethville. I decided to take it. The Seventh Day Adventist, I found, was travelling with me.

We had a long wait, for no one knew the time when the train was expected. The station was completely dark except for one window at which a vastly bearded old man sold the tickets. Little groups of natives sat about on the ground. Some of them carried lanterns, some had lighted little wood fires and were cooking food. There was a ceaseless drumming in the crowd – as difficult to locate as the song of a grasshopper – and now and again a burst of low singing. At ten o'clock the train came in. The carriage was full of mosquitoes; there was no netting; the windows were jammed; the seats hard and extremely narrow. Two Greeks ate oranges all through the night. In this way I went to Elisabethville.

Elisabethville has really no part in this Nightmare. The two days I spent there were placid and wholly agreeable. I arrived early in the afternoon on the day after my departure from Bukama and stayed there until late on the Wednesday evening. I lived in an hotel kept by an ex-officer with a fine cavalry moustache. There was decent wine, good cigars, and very good food. There was a large, cool room in which to work, and a clean bath-room; in the town I found a bookshop and an excellent cinema. The only nightmarish thing was the disorganisation of my plans – but these had been so frequently changed during the past month that I had ceased to put any trust in their permanence.

The air service proved definitely and finally to be useless to me. There was, it is true, some prospect of an aeroplane leaving for the coast during the next week or two, provided that enough passengers demanded it. Since the fare was slightly in excess of that charged by Imperial Airways for the whole journey from London to Cape Town, it seemed to me unlikely that there would be much custom. The 'newly opened' railway to Lobita Bay was closed again. It had only been possible in the dry season when motor-transport could bridge the unfinished gap at the Belgian end of the line. I could return to Bukama and go to the coast via Port Francqui and Leopoldville, catching a Belgian steamer at Boma; but, paradoxically enough, the quickest way to Europe – and by this time I was hard in the grip of travelphobia – was hundreds of miles out of the way through the Rhodesias and the Union of South Africa. There I could get a fast mail-boat from Cape Town to Southampton. The journey had already vastly exceeded my original estimate and I was uncomfortably short of money;[1] accordingly I decided to follow this route.

1 Since expenses are always an important part of travel, it may be of interest to remark that, from the date I left England in October 1930, until my return in March 1931, the total cost of my journey, including a good many purchases of tropical clothes, local painting, carving, etc., and consistent losses at all games of skill and chance, came to a little short of £500.

I had some difficulty in explaining, to the satisfaction of the immigration officer whose permission was necessary before I could leave the Congo, why I diverged so much from the itinerary outlined in my certificate of entry. In the end, however, he understood my difficulties and gave me leave to depart. In the meantime I worked, rested, and enjoyed the comfort and tranquillity of Elisabethville. How reassuring are these occasional reconciliations with luxury. How often in Europe, after too much good living, I have begun to doubt whether the whole business of civilised taste is not a fraud put upon us by shops and restaurants. Then, after a few weeks of gross, colonial wines, hard beds, gritty bath-water, awkward and surly subordinates, cigars from savage Borneo or the pious Philippines, cramped and unclean quarters, and tinned foodstuffs, one realises that the soft things of Europe are not merely rarities which one has been taught to prefer because they are expensive, but thoroughly satisfactory compensations for the rough and tumble of earning one's living – and a far from negligible consolation for some of the assaults and deceptions by which civilisation seeks to rectify the balance of good fortune.

Six days in the train with little to relieve the monotony. At Bulawayo I bought a novel called *A Muster of Vultures*, in which the villain burned away his victims' faces with 'the juice of a tropical cactus'; at Mafeking I bought peaches; once our windows were bedewed with spray from the Victoria Falls; once everything was powdered deep in dust from the great Karoo Desert; once we took in a crowd of desperate men dismissed from the Rhodesian copper-mines; two were known to be without tickets or passports and there was a frantic search for them by bare-kneed police officers, up and down the corridors and under the seats; one of them stole nine shillings from the half-caste boy who made up the beds. When we changed on to a new train at Bulawayo there were white stewards in the dining-car; after so many months it seemed odd and slightly indecent to see white men waiting on each other. Currency consisted chiefly of threepenny bits (called 'tickies') and gold sovereigns; also of a variety of notes issued by different banking corporations.

At last we arrived in Cape Town; a hideous city that reminded me of Glasgow; trams running between great stone offices built in Victorian Gothic; one or two gracious relics of the eighteenth century; down-at-heel negroes and half-castes working in the streets; dapper Jews in the shops.

I had about forty pounds left in my pocket. A boat was sailing that afternoon. I could either wire to London for more money and await its arrival or I could take a third-class ticket home. I left that day. For £20 I bought a berth in a large and clean cabin. There were two other occupants; one a delightful man from North Devon who had been working on the railway; the other a Jew boy from a shop. The stewards treated us with superiority, but good nature; the food was like that of an exceptionally good private school – large luncheons, substantial meat teas, biscuit suppers. There was a very fat Welsh clergyman travelling in the third class with us. His congregation came to see him off. They sang hymns on the quayside, which he conducted with extravagant waving of his arms until we were out of earshot. Chiefly they sang one whose refrain was 'I'm sailing home', but they had been a little deluded by the felicity of these words, for the general theme of the composition was less appropriate. It referred, in fact, not to the journey from Cape Town to England, but to death and the return of the soul to its Creator. However, no one seemed depressed by this prediction, and the clergyman's wife sang it with great feeling long after her husband had stopped beating the time.

It was a pleasant voyage. In the evenings we played 'pontoon', a simplified form of *vingt-et-un*, a game which in itself is far from complex. In the mornings we boxed or played 'pontoon'. There were frequent sing-songs, led by a troop of disgruntled dirt-track racers whose season in South Africa had been a failure.

We stopped at St Helena, where I should not the least object to being exiled, and at Tenerife, where everyone bought very foul cigars. A day later, however, we ran into rough and very cold weather and the cigar-smoking fell off noticeably. There were heavy seas for the rest of the voyage, and most of the women remained below. A sports committee was organised, and proved the occasion for much bad blood; the Welsh clergyman in particular came in for criticism, on the ground that a man with a child of his own had no business to organise the children's fancy-dress party. 'He'll give his own little boy the best prize,' they said. 'Who wouldn't?' He replied by saying that he would have them know that, when he came out, a special presentation had been made to him by his fellow passengers in thanks for his public-spirited management of the deck-games. They said, 'That's as may be.' He said he would sooner give up the whole thing than have his honour questioned. It was all most enjoyable.

Eventually, on March 10th, we berthed at Southampton.

THIRD NIGHTMARE

ON THE NIGHT of my return I dined in London. After dinner we were in some doubt where to go. The names I suggested had long ceased to be popular. Eventually we decided, and drove to a recently opened supper-restaurant which, they said, was rather amusing at the moment.

It was underground. We stepped down into the blare of noise as into a hot swimming-pool, and immersed ourselves; the atmosphere caught our breath like the emanation in a brewery over the tanks where fermentation begins. Cigarette-smoke stung the eyes.

A waiter beckoned us to a small table, tight-packed among other tables, so that our chairs rubbed backs with their neighbours. Waiters elbowed their way in and out, muttering abuse in each other's ears. Some familiar faces leered through the haze; familiar voices shrilled above the din.

We chose some wine.

'You'll have to take something to eat with it.'

We ordered seven-and-sixpenny sandwiches.

Nothing came.

A negro in fine evening clothes was at the piano, singing. After-wards, when he went away, people fluttered their hands at him and tried to catch his eye. He bestowed a few patronising nods. Someone yelled, 'He's losing his figure.'

A waiter came and said, 'Any more orders for drinks before closing time?' We said we had had nothing yet. He made a face and pinched another waiter viciously in the arm, pointing at our table and whispering in Italian. That waiter pinched another. Eventually the last-pinched waiter brought a bottle and slopped out some wine into glasses. It frothed up and spilt on the tablecloth.

We looked at the label and found that it was not the wine we had ordered.

Someone shrilled in my ear: 'Why, Evelyn, where *have* you been? I haven't seen you about anywhere for days.'

My friends talked about the rupture of an engagement which I did not know was contracted.

The wine tasted like salt and soda water. Mercifully a waiter whisked it away before we had time to drink it. 'Time, if you please.'

I was back in the centre of the Empire, and in the spot where, at the moment, 'everyone' was going. Next day the gossip-writers would chronicle the young MPs, peers, and financial magnates who were assembled in that rowdy cellar, hotter than Zanzibar, noiser than the market at Harar, more reckless of the decencies of hospitality than the taverns of Kabalo or Tabora. And a month later the wives of English officials would read about it, and stare out across the bush or jungle or desert or forest or golf links, and envy their sisters at home, and wish they had the money to marry rich men.

Why go abroad?

See England first.

Just watch London knock spots off the Dark Continent.

I paid the bill in yellow African gold. It seemed just tribute from the weaker races to their mentors.

NINETY-TWO DAYS

The writer, at Takutu River

With love to Diana

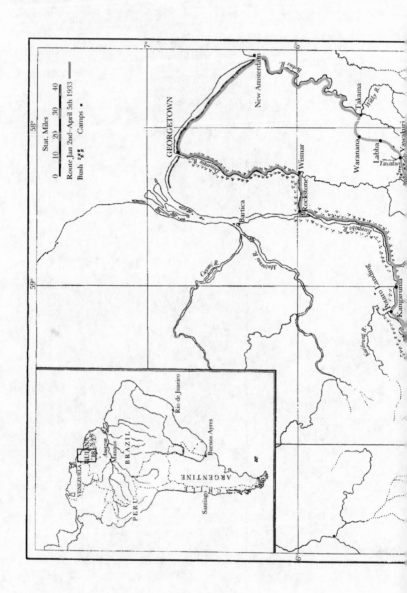

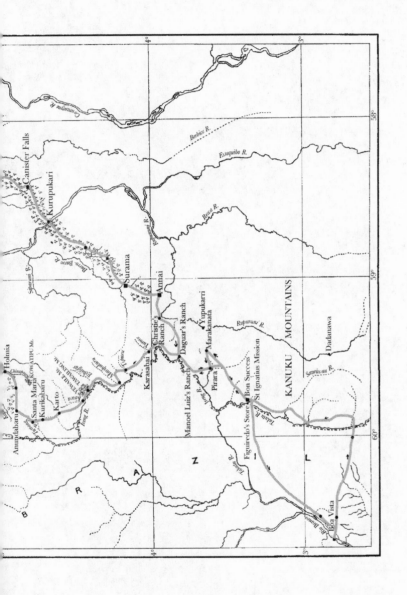

A map of British Guiana and part of Brazilian savannah, showing the author's route

CONTENTS

ILLUSTRATIONS

From photographs taken by the Author

376

CHAPTER 1

Reasons for visiting Guiana – and for writing about it – family connexion with Trinidad – Georgetown – History of Rupununi – Mr Bain – departure.

October 12th, 1933.
At last, relentlessly, inevitably, the lugubrious morning has dawned; day of wrath which I have been postponing week by week for five months.

Late last evening I arrived at the house I have borrowed and established myself in absolute solitude in the deserted nurseries; this morning immediately after breakfast I arranged the writing-table with a pile of foolscap, clean blotting paper, a full inkpot, folded maps, a battered journal and a heap of photographs; then in very low spirits I smoked a pipe and read two newspapers, walked to the village post office in search of Relief nibs, returned and brooded with disgust over the writing-table, smoked another pipe, and wrote two letters, walked into the paddock and looked at a fat pony; then back to the writing-table. It was the end of the tether. There was nothing for it but to start writing this book.

I read the other day that when his biographer revealed that Trollope did his work by the clock, starting regularly as though at an office and stopping, even in the middle of a sentence, when his time was up, there was an immediate drop in his reputation and sales. People in his time believed the romantic legend of inspired genius; they enjoyed the idea of the wicked artist – Rossetti unhinged by chloral, closeted with women of low repute, or Swinburne sprawling under the table; they respected the majestic and august, Tennyson, Carlyle and Ruskin in white whiskers and black cloaks; what they could not believe was that anyone who lived like themselves, got up and went to bed methodically and turned out a regular quantity of work a day, could possibly write anything worth reading. Nowadays, of course, opinion is all the other way. The highest tribute one can pay to success is to assume that an author employs someone else to write for him. Most Englishmen dislike work and grumble about their jobs and writers now make it so clear they hate writing, that their public may become excusably sympathetic and urge them to try something else. I have seldom met a male novelist who enjoyed doing his work, and never heard of one who gave it up and took to anything more congenial. I believe it would have been better for trade if writers had kept up the bluff about inspiration. As it is, the tendency is to the opposite exaggeration of regarding us all as mercenary drudges. The truth I think is this – that though most of us would not write except for money, we would not write any differently for more money.

All this is, in a sense, an apology for the book I am going to write during the coming, miserable weeks. It is to be a description of the way I spent last winter and, on the face of it, since there were no hairbreadth escapes, no romances, no discoveries, it seems presumptuous to suppose that I shall interest anyone. Who in his senses will read, still less buy, a travel book of no scientific value about a place he has no intention of visiting? (I make a present of that sentence to any ill-intentioned reviewer.) Well, the answer as I see it, is that man is a communicative animal; that probably there are a certain number of people who enjoy the same kind of things as I do, and that an experience which for me was worth six months of my time, a fair amount of money and a great deal of exertion, may be worth a few hours' reading to others. Just as a carpenter, I suppose, seeing a piece of rough timber feels an inclination to plane it and square it and put it into shape, so a writer is not really content to leave any experience in the amorphous, haphazard condition in which life presents it; and putting an experience into shape means, for a writer, putting it into communicable form.

When anyone hears that a writer is going to do something that seems to them unusual, such as going to British Guiana, the invariable comment is, 'I suppose you are going to collect material for a book,' and since no one but a prig can take the trouble to be always explaining his motives, it is convenient to answer, 'Yes,' and leave it at that. But the truth is that self-respecting writers do not 'collect material' for their books, or rather that they do it all the time in living their lives. One does not travel, any more than one falls in love, to collect material. It is simply part of one's life. Some writers have a devotion for rural England; they settle in Sussex, identify themselves with the village, the farm, and the hedgerow and, inevitably, they write about it; others move into high society; for myself and many better than me, there is a fascination in distant and barbarous places, and particularly in the borderlands of conflicting cultures and states of development, where ideas, uprooted from their traditions, become oddly changed in transplantation. It is there that I find the experiences vivid enough to demand translation into literary form.

So for the next month or two I shall be reliving my journey in Guiana and Brazil. Not that it has ever been out of my memory. It has been there, ill digested, throughout a crowded and fretful summer, obtruding itself in a fragmentary way at incongruous moments. Now, in this seaside nursery, it will be all laid out, like the maps and photographs and drawings on the writing-table, while falling leaves in the autumnal sunshine remind me that it will soon be time to start out again somewhere else.

December, 1932.

Warm sun, calm water, a slight following wind; after a week of heavy seas it was at last possible to write. Passengers, hitherto invisible, appeared from below and started playing deck games. There was no band. The ship was small, old and slow, a cargo boat carrying a few passengers and not caring much about them. It was not until the sea became smooth that one saw how slow she was. A more comfortable ship would have necessitated transhipping at Trinidad.

The company was, presumably, typical of the route; three or four planters returning to the islands, men of old-fashioned appearance, thin brown faces and bulky watch-chains; two parsons, one white, one black, both affable; two English soaks doing the 'round trip' for the good of their health, both surly when sober; some nondescript women of various colours rejoining husbands or visiting brothers; an agreeable English family on holiday, every day of their winter carefully planned in advance; a genteel young negress with purple lips; a somewhat cranky young man from the Philippines who had an attachment for islands. Very few were going as far as Georgetown.

The first night of the voyage was as depressing a time as I have known in adult life. We sailed from London Docks. It was intensely cold; the heating apparatus was out of order and the bar was closed until we were at sea. Most people have some reason to be sad when it actually comes to leaving. At dusk there was a boat drill; depressed, mutually suspicious passengers paraded in rows opposite ragged and shivering lascars; all round us colourless water and colourless Thames-side factories. That was the low spot of the journey; everything after it was a holiday.

For those of us who were good sailors, that is to say. From the time we got into the Channel until a day past the Azores, the boat rolled and wallowed extravagantly. There are many other disadvantages in rough weather besides sea-sickness; the noise is incessant; every movement becomes an exertion; it is difficult to sleep; the stewards become facetious. Rough weather performs the highly desirable function, however, of keeping the children quiet; for it is notorious that children, at sea in fine weather, are one of the traveller's most severe trials.

During the first ten days I began to read up a little more about the place I was going to. I could scarcely have known less to start with, and when people immediately before my departure asked, 'But why British Guiana?' I was at difficulties to find an answer, except that I was going *because* I knew so little; and also because it has always attracted me on the map.

When I was at school there was no question of Geography being taught badly or not enough; it simply was not taught at all and arriving as a History scholar at Oxford I earned the immediate and implacable disapproval of my tutor through revealing that I did not know which way the Rhine flowed. Since then I have picked up a little, but far less, I imagine, than a bright elementary schoolboy knows. I looked at the *Times* shipping news to-day and read that the *Bideford* had left Henjam and arrived at Basidu, the *Cumberland* was at Beppu, the *Dauntless* at Ushuwaia, the *Fitzroy* at Lerwick, the *Ladybird* at Kiukiang, and the *Scarborough* at New Bedford, and reflected despondently that none of these places meant a thing to me. I am shaky about solstices and equinoxes. If required to explain how tides worked I should find myself in hopeless confusion. On the other hand I do greatly enjoy browsing over atlases, and for years the Guianas have fascinated me.

It always seemed odd that those three little gobs of empire should survive in the general explosion of South American self-government. Cayenne was always in the news through its association with Devil's Island; Dutch Guiana conveyed nothing, but that is scarcely surprising since no normally educated Englishman knows anything about Dutch colonies; British Guiana seemed absurdly remote. One is always meeting Canadians and Australians; everyone has cousins in Kenya and Nigeria and Rhodesia, South Africans seem to have controlled English life twenty-five years ago; people are constantly going and coming to and from the Malay States and India; one way or another most of the Empire (and particularly Tristan da Cunha) comes to one's notice at some time; but I never remember hearing anything at all about Guiana.

Then I met a sailor who told some astonishing stories about the natives of New Guinea, and, as I had listened inattentively to the first part of the conversation, that set me thinking about Guiana. By the time I discovered my mistake I had got interested in the place for other reasons. I bought a large map of it and found it all blanks and guesses; I found that a friend of mine had had an uncle there as a missionary; another had himself made a journey up one of the rivers to Kaieteur Falls, one of the finest, most inaccessible, and least advertised natural wonders of the world. I met someone else who had business interests all along the coast and spoke of a journey anywhere in the interior as a very reckless undertaking. I collected the few books that dealt with the country. And so gradually a vague, general idea began to take shape in my mind of a large empty territory stretching up three great rivers and their tributaries to shadowy, undefined boundaries; most of it was undeveloped and unsurveyed, large areas quite unexplored; except for a tract of grass land on the Brazilian frontier, and an inhabited fringe along the coast, it was all forest or swamp; there was no railway or road into the interior, the only means of communication being by boat up rivers broken every few miles by rapids and falls; the coast population contained every conceivable race, chiefly Portuguese, negro and East Indian; the greater part of the colony had no permanent inhabitants, except shy little communities of aboriginal Indians; except on the coast there had been practically no European settlement and little enough there; and a few place-names, later to become real, stuck in my mind as words – Bartika, Wismar, Rupununi, Takutu.

There had been a constitution but finding it unworkable, they reverted to Crown Colony Government. The coastal strip was much like any West Indian island slightly down at heel; the interior, virgin forest of the sort that stretches over half the continent. So much I had gathered from conversation and cursory reading. It was new country to me and after alternating panics that it would prove impossibly arduous or impossibly dull, I abandoned the other winter projects that had been floating vaguely in my mind – the Solomon Islands, fox-hunting, carpentry classes, Iraq and Mexico – and took my ticket to Georgetown, with two small suitcases, a camera, a letter of credit and no clear plan of what my procedure would be when I arrived.

My fellow passengers from Georgetown were not encouraging. They were mildly excited at first when they learned that anyone who wrote books was coming to their country, and with that pathetic belief in the might of the pen which one continually meets in out of the way places, hoped that I should persuade the Imperial Government to 'do something' about local trade conditions. The country was stiff with gold and diamonds, they said, which only needed 'development'. When I told them that I wanted to go up country, they lost interest. Of course there was always Kaieteur, they said, quite a lot of tourists went there; three or four a year; they believed it was very pretty when you got there but it cost a great deal and you might be drowned or get fever; or there was the Rupununi savannah; several white people lived there and even a white woman, but it cost a great deal to get there and you might be drowned on the way or get fever; besides it was only at certain seasons you could get there at all. I had far better winter in Trinidad, they said, where there was an excellent new country club, horse-races and a lot of money about, or at Barbados, where the bathing was unrivalled.

And to be honest I did gaze rather wistfully as each of the islands in turn disappeared behind us. The first was Antigua and, coming on it as we did after twelve days of unbroken horizons, it remains the most vivid and most glamorous. Not that there was anything particularly remarkable about it – steep little hills covered in bush, a fringe of palm along the beach, brilliant blue water revealing, fathoms down, the silver sand of its bed; an old fort covering the bay; a shabby little town of wooden, balconied houses, its only prominent building a large plain Cathedral rebuilt after an earthquake, with shining towers and a good pitch-pine interior; inquisitive black urchins in the street; women in absurd sun hats, the brims drooping and flapping over their black faces, waddling along on flat feet; ragged negroes lounging aimlessly at corners; baskets of highly coloured fish for sale – purple and scarlet like markings of a mandril; ramshackle motor cars; and in the churchyard the memorials of a lost culture – the rococo marble tombs of forgotten sugar planters, carved in England and imported by sailing ship in the golden days of West Indian prosperity.

It is significant that marble, that most grand and delicate of all building material, the substance of almost all sculpture, has to-day become the symbol of the vulgar and garish – the profiteers of *Punch circa* 1920, Lyons Corner House and the Victor Emanuel Memorial; it is part of the flight from magnificence to which both the 'ye-olde'-pewter-and-sampler æsthetic and its more recent counterpart, the 'modern'-concrete-and-steel-tube, have given impetus. A broken column in the Syrian desert, an incised slab overwhelmed in the gross vegetation of the South American bush remain as spoors of something gracious that passed that way centuries before. I thought how delightful it would be to make a study of the trade in marble and rare stones, tracing the course round the Mediterranean cities of the porphyry galleys from the hottest quarries in the world on the Red Sea coast; a trade so active that practically no porphyry has been quarried since and all the pedestals and urns of Napoleonic bric-a-brac were made, so I am told, of stone cut in the time of Caligula. But this is the kind of thing one thinks about only when one is travelling; all the time that I am abroad I make resolutions to study one thing or another when I get back – Portuguese, map-making, photography; nothing ever comes of it. Perhaps it is a good thing to preserve one's ignorance for old age.

We stopped only a day at Antigua to put down passengers and cargo; one of the things we brought to the islands was holly for their Christmas decorations. It looked odd being tossed down into the lighters under a blazing sky, so completely dissociated from its traditional concomitants of Yule logs and whisky punch and Santa Claus stamping off the snow. But it was not my first Christmas in the tropics; I knew it all – the cablegram forms specially decorated with berries and robins, the puzzled native children before the crib in the Church, 'auld lang syne' on the gramophone, the beggars trotting hopefully behind one in the street saying 'Happy Clistmas – me velly Clistian boy'; the prospect of hot plum pudding on a windless, steaming evening. But everyone all the world over has something to be melancholy about at Christmas, not on account of there being anything intrinsically depressing about the feast but because it is an anniversary too easily memorable; one can cast back one's mind and remember where one was, and in what company, every year from the present to one's childhood.

For the last week of the voyage the life of the ship disintegrated. Most of the day we were on land; the decks were crowded with agents; passengers disappeared and new ones arrived on short journeys between the islands; even the soaks in the bar once got as far as the nearest hotel ashore. I should like to write about the islands, particularly Barbados with its castellated churches, 'poor white' descendants of Monmouth's army, its excellent ghost story and over-rated cooking – but there is a reason why I should not. My brother Alec is also fond of travelling and like me, poor fish, he lives by writing books, so on one of our rare but agreeable meetings we made a compact each to keep off the other's territory; with a papal gesture he made me a present of the whole of Africa and a good slice of Asia in exchange for the Polynesian Islands, North America and the West Indies. When he saw in a newspaper that I was going to Guiana he sent me a sharp note claiming that the West Indies included any places on the mainland of West Indian character – i.e., sugar estates, slaves, rum and pirates – and recommending British Honduras. We compromised on my promising to get up country as soon as I could and to pay as little attention as possible to what I passed on the way. It is an odd thing about my brother and me that though we scarcely ever meet each other in England and seem to share none of the same friends, I often come upon his tracks abroad. This occurred in Trinidad in quite a startling way.

I was sitting, an hour or so after our arrival, on the verandah of the principal hotel, talking to some acquaintances I had picked up.

It seemed to me a good hotel; there was plenty of coming and going and a constant fanfare of motor horns, two men competed to take your hat and did not give you a number, a blackboard announced the local sailings, there was a stall selling American illustrated magazines at a greatly enhanced price, drinks were extremely expensive, there were numerous servants doing nothing and half the tables were occupied by lonely and fretful men waiting for people who had not turned up; it had in fact all the characteristics – whether you like them or not is a different matter – that the rough and tumble of life has taught one to associate with a good hotel.

We had a round or two of swizzles and then one of my new friends said, 'I say, your name is mud in this joint.'

'It stinks,' said the other.

Now one may or may not be used to this sort of thing by the end of one's stay in a place, but this seemed too early days for anyone to have taken against me; it sounded like mere prejudice; so I asked the reason.

'Well, that book you wrote,' he said, 'laying into this hotel. I don't say you were wrong, but you can hardly expect them to like it here.'

Then I remembered that in one of his books my brother had dealt at some length with the discomforts he had suffered in an hotel in Trinidad. Apparently this busy place where we were sitting was the original of his 'Baracuta'. There had been a legal action about it, not against him but against a member of the local parliament who had quoted him. And while this was being explained to me, a message arrived that the manager had heard I was in the hotel and was coming to talk to me. A difficult moment.

'He's quite a decent chap,' my companions explained, 'except when he gets roused.'

'Here he comes.'

A stocky, neat man, not, as it happened, unlike my brother, was approaching in a purposeful way. 'Good evening, Mr Waugh,' he said. 'I heard you were here. Boy, take an order for drinks,' and then turning with what I took to be an ugly glint in his eye he said, 'I hope you like my hotel better than your brother did.'

We had a drink and talked uncomfortably about my destination in Guiana. There was clearly going to be no chucking out, but there was still the glint in the manager's eye.

Presently I said, 'I hope Alec's book didn't cause you much trouble.'

'Trouble. I got two hundred and fifty quid damages for it. I could do with some more trouble like that. Boy, take an order for drinks.' Then I realised that the glint was far from menacing. We had some more drinks and he made me a member of his country club. Finally he said, 'Look here, I feel I owe your family something for the good turn your brother did me. Why go back to the ship? They'll be taking on cargo all night and it'll be as noisy as hell. Stay here as my guest.'

I murmured that I had brought no luggage ashore. 'That's all right. I'll fix you up.'

So that night after a heavy evening at the country club – which was all stiff shirts and white waistcoats and saxophones and as urban as the Embassy – I went back to a large suite at the 'Baracuta' and found put out for me silk pyjamas, a dressing-gown gayer than I should have dared choose for myself, a new toothbrush, and a note begging me to call for anything else I needed. An exemplary manner in which to accept criticism.

Blue water ends at Trinidad; there and from there onwards the sea is murky; opaque, dingy stuff the colour of shabby stucco, thick with mud sweeping down from the great continental rivers – the Orinoco, the Essequibo, the Demerara, the Berbice, the Courantyne; all along the coast their huge mouths gape amidst dune and mangrove, pouring out into the blue Caribbean the waters of the remote highlands. Later I was to tramp across part of the great continental divide, where the tributaries of the Amazon and Essequibo dovetail into one another, tiny cascading brooks, confusing in an unmapped country because they seemed always to be flowing in the direction one did not expect; I was to wade through them or scramble over them on slippery tree trunks in the forest where they were ruby clear, wine-coloured from the crimson timber; I was to paddle tedious days down them when they had become deep and black; leaving them months later, as I saw the water become blue and clear again I was to feel touched with regret, for they had become for a time part of my life. But now as we approached the mainland I only felt mildly depressed that bathing had ceased to be attractive.

Depression deepened as rain set in; a monotonous tropical downpour, always dreary, most monotonous and most depressing when one is on the water. We were already a day late and now we missed the tide by an hour and had to lie at anchor in the rain and a slight fog, waiting to cross the bar into Demerara. There was a lightship faintly visible a mile or so away. They told me without pride that it was a new one. There were now only a handful of passengers left, all pretty impatient at the delay.

Next day, before noon, we arrived. There was nothing to see. The town lies at the mouth of the Demerara on the right bank; opposite are low, green mangrove swamps. Half a dozen small ships lay alongside the quay. We steamed up and then drifted down to our berth with the current. Low wooden sheds and low roofs beyond them; everything quite flat; rain streamed down ceaselessly. I have never seen a less attractive harbour; hope dried up in one at the sight of it; only the heavy reek of sugar occupied the senses.

Landing was simple. There was none of the jaunty cross-examination which usually greets a British subject when he arrives on British territory; an elderly negro in a straw hat glanced at our passports; the Customs officers opened nothing; we passed through the sheds, which were full of bees attracted to the sugar bags, and out into the water-logged street; a taxi splashed and skidded to the hotel; the windows were obscured by rain.

A bare bedroom with white wooden walls, a large bed with mosquito netting, a rocking chair, a faint smell of 'Flit'. There I was.

People sometimes ask me, no doubt by way of politeness and to make conversation, 'But when you arrive alone at these

out-of-the-way places, what do you *do*? I mean how do you *start?*'
Well, apart from its conversational value in keeping one going
another ten minutes, that is a good question and I have often
wondered if there is a satisfactory answer. On this particular occasion the first thing I did was to change my hotel. Not that there was
anything wrong with the one that had been chosen for me, in the
sense that Alec found things wrong with his 'Baracuta'. Residents
considered it the best in the town. The man with business interests
mentioned before had booked me a room there; it was clean and
quiet and select and full in the sea breeze, but it simply would not do.
I have picked up enough about travelling to know that when one
arrives in a strange town the thing one needs is a very noisy and busy
hotel, with people from out of town popping into the bar for drinks
and elderly men telling stories until late into the night. There was
one like that in Georgetown and I got into it that afternoon. It was
kept by a dashing, handsome fellow with a military title, half Irish
and half Portuguese, with a fine swagger and plenty of talk. There
I removed my luggage to a bare bedroom with white wooden walls,
a large bed with mosquito netting, a rocking chair and a faint smell
of 'Flit', and felt comforted by the change.

Two coloured reporters arrived from local newspapers to interview me. They had followed me on bicycles from the other hotel.
(This, let me hasten to say, is no indication of fame. All first-class
passengers are given column interviews on arrival at Georgetown.)
They looked rather damp and had none of the breezy technique of
their trade. They took down all I said laboriously as though I were
a witness at an Archbishop's Court.

Was it true that I was a writer? Yes.

A writer who had published books or just a writer? I told them
that I did write books but that I had also been a reporter for three
weeks on the *Daily Express*. The London *Express*? That clearly impressed them, confirming what I have always maintained, that most
fools can get a book published but it takes a particular kind of fool to
hold down a job on a daily paper.

Was I going to write about Guiana? One of them had a cutting
from a London paper in which I had facetiously said that
I understood the beetles in Guiana were as big as pigeons and that

one killed them with shot-guns. Had I really come to shoot beetles, they asked. They were afraid I should be disappointed. The beetles were certainly remarkably large, but not as large as that.

Had I any views about the mineral resources of the country? When I confessed that I had not, they were clearly nonplussed; this was their stock, foolproof question, because most visitors to Georgetown came there with some idea of prospecting for diamonds or gold. They gazed at me with reproach. I volunteered the information that I was going up country.

'Ah, to Kaieteur?'

I then inwardly took the vow which I very nearly kept, that I would in no circumstances visit that very famous waterfall. I told them that my route was so far uncertain but that I hoped to travel up into Brazil and out by the Amazon. They took it all down but they looked incredulous. Then they shut up their note-books and wished me a happy journey. They knew better than me. I was going to Kaieteur all right.

So I was left to tackle the old problem of getting through the afternoon, which, next to the problem of getting through the morning, is one of the hardest a lonely man can set himself.

There was nothing particular to do; there never is on occasions of this kind, so I did what one always does. I wrote my name in the book at Government House, presented my only letter of introduction (the recipient was away; they always are), sent off some affectionate cablegrams (decorated with holly and robins this time and at a reduced rate, in honour of Christmas) and, since the rain had stopped, set out on foot to see the town.

Perhaps it was the name Georgetown, so like that of an Irish country house, that made me expect something different. Anyway for no better reason that I can think of, I had pictured the place small and solid like the town at St Helena. Instead it was all made of wood and very large; large in the tiresome sense that everything was a long way from everything else. The main streets were very broad, with grass and trees down the centre, and the houses all 'stood in their own grounds'. The shops were large departmental stores and seemed all to be called either Booker's or Foggarty's; the club, for which I had found a temporary membership card awaiting me, was a vast barn entirely empty. The Museum took some finding; it was an upper floor smelling of must and containing a few cases of Indian work, some faded photographs and the worst stuffed animals I have seen anywhere. There was a large Catholic Cathedral, concrete and unfinished, and numerous timber churches in the box-of-bricks style of architecture. The people seemed all black or brown; the black noisy and shabby, the brown subdued and natty. There had once been trams but they had ceased working. That at first sight was Georgetown.[1]

Subsequent closer acquaintance could not improve the architecture but it revealed a number of very likeable qualities in the life of the place. Acknowledgements of kindness received tend to make rather tedious reading but it would be churlish to omit any reference to the cordiality and help which I encountered from every kind of person in British Guiana; much of this will, I hope, be apparent in the ensuing narrative; one thing I would like to remark on particularly. It is delightful but not uncommon to receive some hospitality from British officials abroad; it is because His Excellency the Governor and Lady Denham extended to me so much more than the formal courtesies of their position, that I should like to offer them here my explicit and especial thanks.

It was December 22nd when I landed, and January 3rd when I left for the interior. Most of this time, with the exception of three delightful days spent in the Governor's launch on an expedition up the Essequibo mouth to Mazaruni station, was spent in trying to make some sort of plans for the future. Christmas was both a good and a bad time for this purpose; good because most of the people from up country had come down to town for the celebrations; bad because they took the holidays seriously in Georgetown and most of the shops and offices were shut most of the time. Most of my

---

1 Doubtless some local patriot will complain that I give a wrong impression; that there is a cricket club, a golf club, a promenade along the sea front and a spacious botanical gardens. That is all true. I have nothing against the amenities of the place. Just the reverse, that it is disappointing to travel a long way and find at the end of one's journey, a well-laid-out garden city.

information came casually from conversation in the hotel bar; indeed so much of one's help comes in that way that I wonder how teetotallers ever get about at all.

Gradually I picked up some of the vocabulary of the place and since I shall be using it in future, it will be as well to give some explanation. First as to the races. In East Africa people are divided into Europeans, Indians and natives. In Guiana the word 'native' is never used. The aboriginal Indians are called Indians or 'bucks'. The Indians, that is to say the descendants of the indentured immigrants from India, are called East Indians; there are great numbers of these, mostly in agricultural village communities along the coast; then there are the negro and mulatto descendants of emancipated slaves who are usually spoken of as blacks and coloured people. I never heard 'nigger' used except familiarly by one black to another. Creole is used of anybody, black, coloured or white, born in the West Indies, and also of animals bred there. Then there are the whites, who in Guiana are practically all temporary inhabitants, officials and business men on a job; there is no white Creole aristocracy such as one finds in the islands. The English are, I should say, a minority even among the whites, who come from every country in Europe but chiefly from Portugal via Madeira. In the census returns a column is headed 'European or Portuguese,' a distinction not particularly relished by the Portuguese; they have most of the money in the country, but there are extremely few people in Guiana who are at all rich by European standards.

There are other words peculiar to the colony, many of Dutch or Indian origin; a landing-stage is a 'stelling', a fallen tree, a 'tacuba'; a stream, a 'creek'; a bush path, a 'line'; 'bush' is used for forest as in other parts of the world (I never heard 'jungle' used); open country is 'savannah'; the broad chopping knives used for clearing the lines are called cutlasses; puma and jaguar are called 'tigers'; a halfpenny is a 'cent' and fourpence a 'bit' (this is due to the tiresome currency calculated in dollars and usually worked in pounds and shillings); most curious word of all was that for the blacks who go in little unorganised parties up the rivers to prospect for alluvial gold or diamonds; they are called 'pork knockers' because, it is said, when they are in funds they come into the stores and knock on the counter

demanding pork (but this seems as unsatisfactory as most etymo-
logical derivations).

Few of the people I talked to had even the most cursory acquaintance with the bush, though most of them could name someone who
at one time or another had been up to Kaieteur; they were mostly
discouraging and, like the books I had read coming out, for quite
contradictory reasons; half regarding the expedition as a mild and
rather tedious picnic and half as a precipitate and painful suicide.
There is always the conviction at the back of people's minds in this
part of the world that no stranger can be up to much good, so in
order to dispel the suspicion that I was after diamonds, I gave it out,
as was indeed the truth, that I wanted to take photographs of the
primitive Indians. Here again they were discouraging. 'You'll find
them all playing gramophones and working sewing-machines.
They're all civilised now. We know what you want,' they said with
winks, 'you want to take the girls naked. Well, your best plan is to go
up to Bartika and get a few of the tarts there to pose for you. You can
get the proper feather ornaments from the Self Help shop. That's
what most of the American scientific expeditions do.' Across the
Brazilian border I might find something to interest me, but not in
Guiana, they said.

I later enquired in more responsible quarters and learned that
this was far from being the truth; one whole tribe the Wei-Weis
still live in absolute seclusion, though the difficulties of reaching
these alone were insuperable, but I was to find later among the
Wapishianas, Patamonas and Machusis, people with only the most
superficial contact with civilisation. But it was all a little discouraging
and I realised that though people were anxious enough to help, they
could do nothing until I told them what I wanted. I could not just say
I wanted to see interesing things because they had no idea what
would interest me. It was up to me to fix on a destination and
they would tell me how to get there. I had a note of introduction
to a Jesuit missionary on the Takutu River and from what I had
heard in London about the circumstances of his life, it sounded good
enough. There were three Takutu Rivers marked on my map, but
two were merely guesses, sketched in tentatively with dotted lines,
while one was marked firmly as a place of known importance, so

I assumed, correctly as it turned out, that this was the one I wanted. It ran through the furthest extremity of the Rupununi savannah forming the boundary between British Guiana and Brazil. Accordingly I made this my objective.

Something should here be said about the history of the Rupununi. It is the only considerable piece of open country in the colony, cut off from the coast by forest and forming, geographically, a part of the big plain which stretches into Brazil beyond the Rio Branco. It was first visited by the explorer Schomburgh in the middle of the last century, claimed vaguely for the British Government with other tracts later ceded to our neighbours, and then left to oblivion until it was rediscovered by a highly romantic character named Mr Melville. This gentleman, who died a few years back, was a parson's son from Jamaica. His story, as told me by one of his daughters, was that after various unsuccessful attempts at gold washing he was found by some Wapishiana Indians dying of fever in the upper Essequibo. He expressed a desire to die in open country and they accordingly carried him to the Rupununi savannah where he made an immediate recovery. The Indians at that time had no trade connection at all with the coast. Melville began bartering in a small way, taking down a yearly boat to Georgetown loaded with hammocks and other examples of Indian workmanship and bringing back fish hooks, axe heads, patent medicines and other desirable commodities. He won the Indians' confidence, married among them, and presently began keeping cattle on a gradually increasing scale until by 1914 he was living in patriarchal authority at a large ranch named Dadanawa.

There was at this time no connection with the coast except by boat down the Essequibo, a journey always arduous, often dangerous and sometimes impossible. His cattle were all sold over the border into Brazil and the country was to all appearance Brazilian; the few other ranchers were Brazilian, Portuguese was the language, there was no representative of government except Melville himself who had been presented with the title of magistrate; there was no attempt to collect customs duties on the trade across the Takutu.

Then with the outbreak of war came a sudden demand for beef. It became necessary to find a way for the Rupununi cattle to reach the Georgetown market. It is impossible to navigate the Essequibo with large boats; the long-debated railway to the interior was no nearer being begun; accordingly it was decided to cut a trail down the already existing Indian line from the beginning of the bush at Anai, to the highest navigable point, Takama, on the Berbice River. The route ran over countless deep creeks; there was no question of making a road for wheeled vehicles but simply a track down which the beasts could be got alive and fattened up again at pasture on the coast. There were numerous, serious objections to the plan, notably the immense leakage through animals accustomed to the savannah, stampeding into the bush from which they could never be re- covered, and also through their dying of exhaustion and lack of food on the ten days' drive. However Melville sold out his whole interests while the scheme was still popular and handed over his huge territory to a newly formed Rupununi Development Company which has carried on a precarious existence ever since. Meanwhile Melville's family still hold complete predominance in the district, all the key positions being held by his sons and sons-in-law.

The cattle trail is one of the chief grumbles of the colony; that and the new road which the present Government is constructing from Bartika to Kaieteur, presumably because these are its chief recent activities and bar politics all over the world consist of grumbling at the Government. In most dependencies I have found that the Public Works Department was the chief butt of conversation; in Guiana it was always the Lands and Mines.

As soon as I decided to make for Takutu I was advised to go and see Bain, the Commissioner for the district, who by good chance was in Georgetown for Christmas. So with the Governor's introduction I sought him out in the boarding-house where he was staying. He was a middle-aged, emaciated man, creole with some Indian blood. Like everyone else in the colony he had at one time worked gold and diamonds; like most other people he had also been a surveyor, a solider, a policeman and a magistrate; he had lately returned to the last avocation which included most of the other functions. He received me with great kindness and vivacity, telling me that the Rupununi was the most beautiful place in the world and that anyone with a gift for expression should be able to make a book about it.

He was himself returning in a day or two by the cattle trail as far as Kurupukari which was well on my way. He had a boat of stores leaving almost at once from Bartika which he expected to find awaiting him. He offered me a place in that.

'It ought to get there before me,' he said. 'I do not know about the rains. Perhaps it will take four days, perhaps eight. But it must get there because it is full of barbed wire I need. Unless of course it's wrecked,' he added. 'Mr Winter's boat was totally destroyed in the rapids the day before yesterday.'

I had no idea where Kurupukari was, but it sounded as good as anywhere else. When I got back I looked for it on the map. Mr Bain had spoken very quickly so that when I found Yupukarri right up on the savannah I was highly delighted. It was not for two days that I found Kurupukari about a hundred miles away from it. Then I realised that I was in for a longer journey than I had anticipated, and trebled my order for stores.

These were a difficulty, partly because, under the present arrangement, I was to leave before the end of the New Year holidays which meant that I had only one day in which to get everything, but chiefly because I had no idea what I should need. Again opinion was contradictory, some people saying, 'Just take a gun and live by that,' and others, 'Don't count on getting *anything* up country. The ranchers live on farine.'

I had no idea what farine was but I felt I should need something else. Mr Bain simply said, 'You should be like me. I can go for days without eating – like a camel. That is the way to live in the bush.'

I had already begun to guess that travelling in an empty country was going to be very different from Africa where labour is almost unlimited. It was not a case for luxurious 'chop boxes' of varied delicacies. I realised that moving stores from place to place was going to be a problem – how great a problem I did not know until later. So I concentrated on necessaries – flour, sugar, corn beef, potatoes, rum and so on – bought hammock, gun, mosquito net and blanket, delivered them to the firm who were organising Mr Bain's boat and settled down to enjoy the last two days in Georgetown.

From that moment onwards I did not have an hour's certainty of plan. It was arranged that I should take Tuesday's steamer to Bartika and start in the boat on Wednesday; then I discovered by chance that there was no steamer on Tuesday; wires were sent and the boat delayed until Thursday.

Then Mr Bain rang up to say he was sending a black policeman with me who was to act as my servant; that sounded all right until the agents rang up to say that now the policeman was coming there would only be room for 100 lbs of my stores. There was nothing to do except countermand three-quarters of them.

Then the agents rang up to say, did I realise that it was an open boat and that since the rains were on it was imperative to take a tarpaulin. Desperate and unsuccessful attempts to secure a tarpaulin with every shop in Georgetown closed.

Then Mr Bain rang up to say that the agents said it was an open boat and that the rains were on. I should be soaked to the skin every day and undoubtedly get fever and he could not take the responsibility of sending me in it.

Then I went to see Mr Bain and he said I had better come to Takama with him and perhaps there would be a horse to get me to Kurupukari.

Then I rang up the agents and said that since the boat was relieved of my weight they were to put all my stores on board.

Then Mr Bain rang up to say that he had come to the conclusion that I could have the horse which he had meant to pack with his personal stores; instead he would send them by boat.

Then I rang up the agents and said they were to take from my stores the weight equivalent to the personal stores Mr Bain was sending by boat.

All these, and other less remarkable alarms, occurred at intervals of two or three hours. I may also note that for each telephone call successfully put through there were five or six failures; that I never left the hotel for an hour without finding messages on my return to ring up Mr Bain and the agent urgently; that whenever I rang them up they had just gone out; and that on the last day I was lying in severe pain, poisoned with a local delicacy called 'crab-back' and imagining that I had cholera. Taken all in all it was a disturbed departure.

There was plenty going on in Georgetown that week.

An unknown Dutchman shot himself on Christmas morning in his room at the rival hotel, on account of feeling lonely.

A gentleman known to his friends as 'the Blood of Corruption' was arrested on numerous charges. He was the leader of a criminal organisation called 'the Beasts of Berlin'. They had taken the name from a cinema film; none of them had the remotest idea what Berlin was; they just liked the name. But they were perfectly serious criminals for all that.

There was a race-meeting in heavy rain and, on New Year's Eve, a large number of dances. At my hotel there was a Caledonian Ball, characterised by a marked male predominance, pipers, and quite elderly men sitting giggling on the ballroom floor; there was also a more decorous function at the club where I ate the poisoned 'crab-back'. There were several 'swizzle parties', an institution which dates from long before the North American cocktail party, starts at six and goes on till midnight. There was a negro masquerade – an unorganised and more or less spontaneous exhibition of joviality; the gayer spirits dressed up in comic fancy dress and clowned about in Camp Street, each followed by a small court of admirers. There was said to be a 'Komfa' dance (I do not know if that is the right spelling). These dances, the direct descendants of the African 'Ngoma', still take place from time to time along the coast in out-of-the-way bits of waste ground, usually at the full moon; they are illegal for they usually conclude with an orgy and are apparently associated with voodooism. A young engineer whom I had met on the boat, had news of one from one of his workmen. We drove about in search of it for the greater part of one evening but failed to locate it.

Through all this the preparations for the journey up country, the buying of chlorodyne and bandages, gun caps and cartridge cases, flour and kerosene, seemed fantastic and unsubstantial, and the empty forest, a few miles away, infinitely remote, as unrelated to the crowded life of the coast as it was to London. Most journeys, I think, begin and all end with a sense of unreality. Even when eventually I found myself in the train for New Amsterdam, sitting opposite Mr Bain, with our improbable baggage piled up round us, it still required an effort to convince me that we were on our way.

CHAPTER 2

Mr Bain's conversation – New Amsterdam – the Berbice – Mr Bain's solicitude – Yetto at a party – the savannah – Mr Bain's missing links – the bush – a snake – Kurupukari – farine and tasso – arrival of stores.

IT IS SAID that the railway along the Guiana coast is the oldest in the Empire. It runs in pretty, flat country over creeks and canals and through gay, ramshackle villages. The stations still bear the names of the old sugar estates but these are mostly split up now into small holdings growing coco-nut and rice. The further one goes from Georgetown towards New Amsterdam, the blacker become the inhabitants, of purer negro type and more cheerful manners. Berbice men look on Demerarans as wasters; the Demerarans look on them as bumpkins.

It was just dark by the time Mr Bain and I reached New Amsterdam. We had the carriage to ourselves and our baggage. Most of the way Mr Bain talked.

I do not know how the legend originated that the men who administer distant territories are 'strong and silent'. It is all against the testimony of observed fact. Some may start strong and even retain a certain wiriness into middle life, but most of them, by the time they have attained any eminence in the King Emperor's service, are subject to one or more severe complaints. As for their silence, it seems to vary in exact inverse ratio to their distance from civilisation. For silence one must go to the pie-faced young diners-out of London; men in the wide open spaces are, in my experience, wildly garrulous; many of them, I have noticed, contract the habit of talking to themselves or to dogs and natives, equally ignorant of their language. What is more, they will talk on all subjects – highly personal reminiscences, their dreams, diet and digestion, science, history, morals and theology. But pre-eminently of theology. It seems to be the obsession waiting round the corner for all lonely men. You start talking bawdy with some breezy, rum-drinking tramp skipper and in ten minutes he is proving or disproving the doctrine of original sin.

Mr Bain, though indefatigable in his duty, was not strong; frequent attacks of fever had left him bloodless and fleshless, and besides this he suffered from constant, appalling bouts of asthma which kept him awake for all but an hour or two every night. Nor was he silent. During the stimulating fortnight I was to spend in his company he talked at large on every conceivable topic, eagerly, confidently, enthusiastically, not always accurately, sometimes scarcely coherently, inexhaustibly; with inspired imagination, with dizzy changes of thought and rather alarming theatrical effects, in a vocabulary oddly compounded of the jargon he was accustomed to use among his subordinates and the longer, less habitual words he had noticed in print. As I have said, he talked of everything at one time or another, but mostly either in metaphysical speculation or in anecdote. He himself always figured prominently in the latter and it was in these that his gestures became most dramatic. The dialogue was all in *oratio recta*; never 'I ordered him to go at once,' but 'I say to him, "Go! plenty quick, quick. Go!" ' and at the words Mr Bain's finger would shoot out accusingly, his body would stiffen and quiver, his eyes would blaze until I began to fear he would induce some kind of seizure.

One engaging and lamentably uncommon trait in Mr Bain's reminiscences was this, that besides, like half the world, remembering and retailing all the injustices he had encountered, he also remembered and retained every word of approbation; the affection he had received from his parents as a boy; the prize given him at school for his geometry; the high commendation he had had at the technical college for his draughtsmanship; numberless spontaneous expressions of esteem from various acquaintances throughout his life; the devotion of subordinates and the confidence of superiors; the pleasure the Governor took in his official reports; testimonies from delinquents to the impartiality, mercy, and wisdom of his judicial sentences – all these were fresh and glowing in his memory and all or nearly all, I was privileged to hear.

Many of his stories I found to strain the normal limits of credulity – such as that he had a horse which swam under water and a guide who employed a parrot to bring him information; the bird would fly on ahead, said Mr Bain, and coming back to its perch on the Indian's shoulder whisper in his ear what he had seen, who was on the road and where they could find water. I do not think that there was any conscious effort to deceive. I think that like many raconteurs he drew no clear distinction between what had actually occurred and what he had told a fair number of times as a good story. But most people dislike the idea that they are having their legs pulled and I soon fell into what now seems to me an ungenerous and exasperating habit of cross-examination, which usually disinterred some closely concealed nucleus of verbal truth.

At sundown it became cold and clammy in the carriage; clouds of mosquitoes came in from windows and corridor, biting us to frenzy. Mr Bain remarked gloomily that they were probably all infected with malaria. Everyone has different theories about quinine; Mr Bain recommended constant, large doses, observing parenthetically that they caused deafness, insomnia and impotence.

We transferred from the train to a ferry steamer and drifted rather disconsolately across to the town. There was a boarding-house kept by a white gentleman in reduced circumstances; here we dined in a swarm of mosquitoes; the house had run out of drink during the New Year celebrations. After dinner to avoid the mosquitoes we walked about the streets for an hour. They were empty and ill-lit. New Amsterdam, eighty years ago, was a prosperous, if sleepy, town with a club and its own society; now there is barely a handful of whites quartered there, the rest having been driven out by mosquitoes and the decay of the sugar trade. At a street corner we met a Jordanite haranguing a few apathetic loafers and a single suspicious policeman. He wore a long white robe and a white turban and he waved a wand of metal tubing; a drowsy little boy sat beside him holding a large Bible. The Jordanites are one of the many queer sects that flourish among negroes. They derive their name not as might be supposed from the river, but from a recently deceased Mr Jordan from Jamaica; their object seemed partially pious, partially political; they are said to favour polygamy. The present speaker ran round in little circles as he spoke, 'What for you black men afraid ob de white man? Why you ascared ob his pale face and blue eye? Why do you fear his yellow hair? Because you are all fornicators – dat is de reason. If you were pure of heart you need not fear de white man.'

Then he saw us and seemed rather embarrassed. ''Nother text boy.' But the boy was asleep over the Bible. He cracked him sharply on the head with his wand and the child hastily read a verse of Ezekiel and the preacher took up on another subject.

'The black man got a very inferior complex,' remarked Mr Bain as we resumed our walk.

Next day we started at dawn. There was a great rainbow over the town. On the way to the quay I noticed a charming old Lutheran Church, relic of the Dutch occupation, that had been invisible the night before.

A lazy, uneventful day in the paddle steamer up the Berbice River. Monotonous vegetable walls on either bank, occasionally broken by bovianders' cabins.[1] Now and then an unstable, dug-out canoe would shoot out from the green shadows and an unkempt, bearded figure would deliver or receive a parcel of mail. We slung our hammocks on deck. There was a steward who made gin-swizzles of a kind and served revolting meals at intervals of two hours. On the whole a tolerable day's journey.

Our only companions on the top deck were a Belgian rancher, his Indian wife, some of their children, and his wife's sister. They were the first Indians I had seen. Since they had taken up with a European they wore hats and stockings and high-heeled shoes, but they were very shy, guarding their eyes like nuns, and giggling foolishly when spoken to; they had squat little figures and blank, mongol faces. They had bought a gramophone and a few records in town which kept them happy for the twelve hours we were together. Conversation was all between Mr Bain and the rancher, and mostly about horses. I never approach any new horse (and few familiar ones for that matter) without some sinking in self-esteem, so I listened with more than polite interest. Quite different standards of quality

---

1 Boviander is the name given to the people of unpredictable descent – mostly Dutch, Indian and negro mixtures – who live in isolated huts all along the lower waters of the big rivers; they generally have a minute clearing where they grow manioc or maize; they fish, and spend most of their time, like the water rat in *Wind in the Willows*, 'messing about in boats'.

seemed to be observed here from those I used to learn from Captain Hance.

'I tell you, Mr Bain, that buckskin of mine was the finest mare bred in this district. You didn't have to use no spur or whip to her. Why before you was on her back, almost, she was off like the wind and *nothing* would stop her. And if she didn't want to go any particular way *nothing* would make her. Why I've been carried six miles out of my course many a time, pulling at her with all my strength. *And* how she could rear.'

'Yes, she *could rear*,' said Mr Bain in wistful admiration, 'it was lovely to see her.'

'And if she got you down she'd roll on you. She wouldn't get up till she'd broken every bone in your body. She killed one of my boys that way.'

'But what about my Tiger.'

'Ah, he was a good horse. You could see by the way he rolled his eyes.'

'Did you ever see him *buck*? Why he'd buck all over the corral. And he was wicked too. He struck out at you if he got a chance.'

'That was a *good* horse, Tiger. What became of him?'

'Broke his back. He bolted over some rocks into a creek with one of the boys riding him.'

'Still you know I think that for *bucking* my Shark . . .'

And so it went on. Presently I asked in some apprehension, 'And the horse I am to ride to-morrow. Is he a *good* horse too?'

'One of the strongest in the country,' said Mr Bain. 'It will be just like the English Grand National for you.'

So the day wore on. The steward trotted about with frightful helpings of curried fish; later with greyish tea and seed cake; later with more fish and lumps of hard, dark beef. The Indian ladies played their gramophone. The rancher had a nap. Mr Bain told me more. At last, about seven, we arrived at our destination, and descended in the dark into a dug-out canoe.

'Be careful, be careful, if you're not used to them you will certainly be drowned,' Mr Bain admonished me, thus giving the first evidence of what, for the next few days, was going to prove a somewhat tiresome solicitude for my safety. The trouble was this. The Governor had requested Mr Bain to look after me and, in his kindness, had stressed the fact that the conditions of the country were new to me and that he took a personal interest in my welfare. Mr Bain, in his kindness, interpreted this to mean that something very precious and very fragile had been put into his charge; if any accident were to befall me the Governor would never forgive it; danger, for one of delicate constitution, lurked in every activity of the day. If I helped to saddle the placid pack ox he would cry out, 'Stand back, be careful, or he will kick out your brains.' If I picked up my own gun he would say, 'Be careful, it will go off and shoot you.'

Fortunately this scrupulous concern began to wear thin after three days' travel, but during those three days it came as near as anything could to straining my affection and gratitude towards him.

The dug-out, paddled by an indiscernible figure in the stern, swept away from the ship across the dark water; the opposite bank was lightless. We scrambled up the slippery bank (Mr Bain urging me anxiously not to fall down) and could just make out a rise in the ground surmounted by some kind of building; the boatman brought up a lantern and we climbed further. Mr Bain in the meantime asking fretfully, 'Yetto? Where's Yetto? I told him to be here with my hammock.'

'Yetto come with de horses this morning. Now him go bottom-side to a party. Him no say nothing about de hammock.'

'Yetto proper bad man,' said Mr Bain lapsing into vernacular. 'Him proper Congo.'

Thus in circumstances of discredit and terms of opprobrium I first heard the name of someone to whom I was later to become warmly attached.

We climbed the little hill and reached a thatched shelter, open at the sides, where two figures lay asleep in hammocks. They woke up, sat up and stared at us. A black man and his wife. Mr Bain asked them if they knew what Yetto had done with his hammock.

'Him gone to de party.'

'Where dis party?'

'Down to de river. Indian house. All de boys at de party.'

So we went down to look for Yetto. We paddled almost noise-lessly down stream, keeping into the bank. It was an effort to balance in the narrow, shallow craft. Eventually we heard music and hauled in under the bushes.

The party was in a large Indian hut. It was cosmopolitan in character, being made up of Brazilian *vaqueiros* (cowboys), bovianders, blacks and a number of clothed and semi-civilised Indians. Two Brazilians were playing guitars. The hostess came out to greet us.

'Good night,' she said, shaking hands and leading us in. It was not etiquette to ask for Yetto at once so we sat on a bench and waited. A girl was walking from guest to guest with a bowl of dark home-brewed liquor; she handed a mug to each in turn, waiting while they drank and then refilling it for the next. Two or three negroes were dancing. The Indians sat in stolid rows, silently, soft hats pulled down over their eyes, staring gloomily at the floor. Now and then one would get up, stroll apathetically across to a girl and invite her to dance. The couple would then shuffle round in a somewhat European manner, separate without a word or a glance and resume their seats. The Indians, I learned later, are a solitary people and it takes many hours' heavy drinking to arouse any social interests in them. In fact the more I saw of Indians the greater I was struck by their similarity to the English. They like living with their own families at great distances from their neighbours; they regard strangers with suspicion and despair; they are unprogressive and unambitious, fond of pets, hunting and fishing; they are undemonstrative in love, unwarlike, morbidly modest; their chief aim seems to be on all occasions to render themselves inconspicuous; in all points, except their love of strong drink and perhaps their improvidence, the direct opposite of the negro. On this particular evening however their only outstanding characteristic was inability to make a party go.

After a time Yetto was detected drinking guiltily in a corner. He was a large middle-aged black of unusual ugliness. He was not ugly in the way a handsome negro is ugly. He was comic; huge feet and hands, huge mouth, and an absurd little Hitler moustache. He talked with a breadth of creoled intonation that for the first few days was quite unintelligible to me. Mr Bain and he talked at some length about the hammock; a conversation in which 'you proper Congo' occurred frequently. Then he left the party and came away with us to find it. At last at about ten o'clock Mr Bain and I were established in the rest house.

Sleep was not easy. A hammock is one of the most agreeable things for an hour's rest, but it needs practice to adapt it for a night, particularly when it is tied to the same framework as three others, whose occupants with every movement set it vibrating. The hammocks used in Guiana are all of Indian manufacture, woven in thick cotton threads; they are light enough to roll up and tie behind one's saddle and have the particular property that they wrap round the body and 'give' at any change of position. They are so much the cleanest and most portable sort of bed that I wonder they are not more used in other parts of the world. But they take some getting used to. It is not difficult to fall out of them, they are extremely draughty and if you do go to sleep in the wrong position you are liable to wake up stiff in the back. Later I learned the correct way to lie, diagonally instead of vertically; later too I had harder days behind me. On this particular night I slept little. Nor did poor Mr Bain who sat hour after hour with his head between his knees, gasping for breath in the throes of asthma. The black couple, however, made up for us both with enormous, rhythmic snores.

Next morning Yetto and some other boys appeared with the horses and the misgivings which I had been suffering ever since the conversation of the previous day, rapidly subsided. They were some very small ponies and they stood placidly in the corner of the corral cropping the tops off the arid tufts of grass; they were too lethargic even to switch away the horse flies that clustered on their quarters; mine had been attacked by a vampire bat during the night and bore a slaver of blood on his withers. I never rode a good horse all the time I was on the savannahs; partly, of course, because in no quarter of the globe do people readily lend or hire good horses to a stranger, but chiefly because there are very few of them. Most of the ranches own large herds which are loosed at grass for three-quarters of the year. When some are needed the *vaqueiros* are sent out to lasso them and bring them in; they are ridden for a week or two until they begin to show signs of collapse (through the heat of the climate and the cut of the Brazilian saddles they are very easily galled) and then turned out again. They are nearly all promiscuously bred, unshod and grass fed. Generally, when first in from the savannah, they bucked a little, shied, and were a nuisance for half an hour; after that they settled down to the regular four-mile-an-hour jog-trot; after the fourth hour they had to be spurred and whipped to keep them in motion at all.

Mr Bain had various duties to occupy him; the packing of the ox took some care, and it was noon before we were ready. The black man, who had shared the rest house the night before, was coming with us. He was manager of the ranch ten or twelve miles away, which was to be our first stop. We mounted and made to start off. My pony would not move.

'Loosen de reins,' they said.

I loosened the reins and kicked him and hit. He took a few steps backwards.

'Loosen de reins,' they said.

Then I saw how they were riding, with the reins hanging quite loose, their hands folded on the front of the saddle. That is the style all over this part of the world; the reins are never tightened except in an occasional savage jerk; the aids are given on the neck instead of on the bit. Drama in movement is the object aimed at; the *vaqueiros* like a horse that as soon as they mount him will give two or three leaps in the air and then start off at a gallop; it does not matter how short a time the gallop lasts provided he takes them out of sight of the spectator; then after many hours' monotonous jogging they will spur him into life when they approach either ranch or village, arrive at the gallop, the horse's mouth lathered with foam, rein him back on to his hocks and dismount in a small dust storm. I had seen this often enough in the old days of the cinema, but had not realised that it occurred in real life.

We set off across the plain cantering a little but mostly jogging at what for many weeks was to be my normal travelling gait. The country was dead flat and featureless except for ant-hills and occasional clumps of palm; the ground was hard earth and sand tufted

Bridling of Rupununi horse

with dun-coloured grass; thousands of lizards scattered and darted under the horses' feet; otherwise there was no sign of life except the black crows who rose at our approach from the carcasses strewn along the track, and resettled to their feast behind us. Here and in the forest we passed a carcass every half-mile. Many were recently dead, for the last drive had lost forty per cent., and these we cantered past holding our breath; others were mere heaps of bone picked white by the ants, the mound of half-digested feed always prominent among the ribs.

During the ride Mr Bain discoursed to the black rancher about history; I listened fitfully for my horse was continually dropping behind, but I was never out of earshot of the voice, voluble, rhapsodic, now rising to some sharp catastrophe, now running on evenly, urgently, irresistibly in the shimmering noon heat.

I caught bits ' . . . once you see there was nothing but water. It says so in the Bible. Water covered the face of the earth. Then He divided the land from the waters. How did He do that, Mr Yerwood? Why, by killing de crabs, and all de shells of de crabs became ground down by the tides and became sand. . . . '

' . . . then there was Napoleon. He was only a little corporal but he divorced his wife and married the daughter of an Emperor. Mark my words, Mr Yerwood, all dose Bolshevists will be doing that soon. . . . '

' . . . and why did the English take so long to subdue de little Boers. Because dey were so sporting. When dey take prisoners dey let dem go again for to give dem another chance. . . . '

We reached our destination in about two hours and found three sheds and a wired corral. It was less than I had expected. Through the influence of the cinema, 'ranch' had taken on a rather glorious connotation in my mind; of solid, whitewashed buildings; a courtyard with a great tree casting its shadow in the centre and a balustraded wall, wrought-iron gates, a shady interior with old Spanish furniture and a lamp burning before a baroque Madonna, and lovely girls with stock-whips and guitars. I do not say that I had expected to find this at Waranana; in fact it would have greatly surprised me; but I did feel that the word 'ranch' had taken a fall.

Various dependants of Mr Bain's were awaiting him here – policemen returning to duty, woodmen in charge of keeping the trail open; he also had stores and saddlery and some horses, left behind on his previous journey. All these he attended to so that by next morning everything was ready for us to start out. A moody young policeman named Price was handed over to me (or me to him), to act as my personal servant. Yetto was never far away, grinning sheepishly and constantly reprimanded. He held an uncertain position, partly government runner, partly groom, partly cook, partly porter.

Mr Yerwood killed a chicken for us and, after we had dined, joined us and drank some of our rum. He and Mr Bain talked about animals, their stories growing less probable as the evening progressed. Finally Mr Yerwood described a 'water-monkey' he had once seen; it was enormous and jet black; it had a grinning mouth full of sharp teeth; it swam at a great speed; its habit was to submerge itself and wait for bathers whom it would draw down and pound to pieces on the rocks at the bottom. Just such an occurrence had happened to a friend of Mr Yerwood's; every bone in his body was broken when it floated to the surface, Mr Yerwood said.

Not to be outdone, Mr Bain related how once, when walking in the late afternoon in the neighbourhood of Mount Roraima, he had encountered two Missing Links, a man and his wife slightly over normal size but bowed and simian in their movements; they were naked except for a light covering of soft reddish down; they had stared at Mr Bain a full half-minute, then said something he did not understand, and strolled off into the bush. After that there was little to be said on the subject of animals. It was ten o'clock – late for the district – so we took to our hammocks, leaving the lamp burning as a protection against vampire bats.

It would be tedious to record the daily details of the journey to Kurupukari. Mr Bain managed everything; I merely trotted beside him; we took six days from the ranch, averaging about fifteen miles a day. Mr Bain often explained how, in normal conditions, he did the whole journey in two stages at full gallop all the way. On this occasion we had to keep pace with the pack oxen and the walking men, and anyway I do not think our ponies were up to much more. All the time we only passed one human being – a Portuguese – speaking Indian, padding along on foot, going down to the river on some inscrutable errand. For two days we travelled over grass land and then entered the bush on crossing the Yawakuri River. Immediately our entire conditions changed; it was cool and quite sunless. The green, submarine darkness of the jungle has been described frequently enough but it can never, I think, be realised until one has been there. The trail was as broad as an English lane with vast, impenetrable walls of forest rising to a hundred and fifty feet on either side; the first twenty feet from the ground were dense under-growth, then the trunks of the trees emerged, quite bare, like archi-tectural columns rising vertical and featureless until they broke into the solid roof of leaves, through which appeared only rare star points of direct sunlight. There were always men working to keep the trail clear of fallen timber and there were always trees lying across it at frequent intervals. Usually some kind of line had been chopped round these through the bush and we would dismount and lead our horses. There were also creeks every few miles, low at this time of year, so that we could ride through them. In the wet season, Mr Bain said, you had to crawl across a tacuba leading a swimming horse, carry your baggage across and load and reload your pack animals four or five times a day. Sometimes the trail had been completely cleared with a 'corduroy' of logs through the marshy places; elsewhere only the undergrowth had been chopped away and the trees stood up in the middle of the path; once we came to a place where the virgin forest had been burned and a second growth of low bush had taken its place; there was loose white sand here, blinding to the eyes after the gloom of the forest and heavy going for the horses.

Everyone who has ever been there, has remarked on the appar-ent emptiness of the bush. The real life, so naturalists write, takes place a hundred feet up in the tree-tops; it is there that you would find all the flowers and parrots and monkeys, high overhead in the sunlight, never coming down except when there is a storm. Occa-sionally we would find the floor of the trail strewn with petals from flowers out of sight above us. I have not a naturalist's trained observation and no doubt missed many things that he would have seen; certainly I saw little enough; one jaguar slinking away ahead of us, two or three acouris, a large rodent that makes possible but dull eating, some tortoises that the boys eagerly collected for meat, an incredible number of ants; ants of all sizes and shades, alone and in endless caravans; they were everywhere; it was impossible to find a square three inches of ground anywhere without an ant in it; you could not throw away the dregs of your mug without drowning one.

We met the first snake on our first day in the bush. Mr Bain and I were riding abreast a mile or so ahead of the baggage. He was telling me his views on marriage ('... whom God has joined together let no man put asunder. Yes. But tell me this. Who is God? God is love. So when a couple have ceased to love one another...') when he suddenly reined up and said in a melodramatic whisper: 'Stop. Look ahead. Dere is a terrible great snake.' It was in the days when he still regarded my safety as peculiarly precarious. 'Don't come near – it may attack you.'

Sure enough about twenty yards ahead was a very large snake, curled up in the middle of the trail.

'What kind is it?'

'I never saw anything like him before. Look at his terrible great head,' hissed Mr Bain.

It certainly was a very odd-looking head from where we sat, swollen and brown and quite different in appearance from the mottled coils. Mr Bain dismounted and I followed. Very stealthily, step by step he approached the creature. It did not move and so, emboldened, he began to throw pieces of dead wood at it. None of them fell within six feet of their mark. He approached closer, motioning me back apprehensively. Then the snake suddenly raised his neck, retched and for a moment it appeared as though his head had fallen off. Then it became clear what had happened. We had surprised a python in the act of slowly swallowing a large toad. It had got down the back legs and was slowly sucking in the body when it had been disturbed; the 'terrible great head' was the toad's body half in and half out of the jaws. The python averted its own delicately pointed face and slipped away into the bush;

the toad showed little gratitude or surprise at his escape, but dragged himself rather laboriously under a log and sat down to consider his experience.

But if there was little to see there was a great deal to hear; always, but particularly from sunset until dawn, the bush was alive with sounds. We used to turn in early, usually between seven and eight, because there was nothing to do after dark; there were no chairs to sit in or table to sit at; the lantern light was too dim for reading. As soon as we finished supper we rolled up in our hammocks and there was nothing to do but lie and listen for ten or eleven hours. There were the immediate sounds of poor Mr Bain's asthma; of the boys squatting round their fire, sometimes singing, more often arguing, always quite unintelligible when they were among themselves; there were our own beasts grazing in the corral and limping about at hobble; often we would hear the crash of dead timber falling in the forest near us, but around and above and through all these were the sounds of the bush. As I have said, I am no naturalist; Mr Bain's experienced ear was able to pick out innumerable voices that to me were merged in the general chatter, but even to me there were some sounds that were unmistakable; there were the 'howler' monkeys; I never saw one except stuffed in a museum – he was a small ginger creature – but we heard them roaring like lions most days; in the far distance it was like the noise of the dredgers that once used to attend me lying sleepless night after night at Port Said. There were the frogs, some shrill like those in the South of France, others deep and hoarse. There was a bird which mooed like a cow, named, appositely enough, the 'cow-bird', and another which struck two sharp metallic notes as though with a hammer on a copper cistern; this was called the 'bell-bird'; there was a bird that made a noise like a motor bicycle starting up; a kind of woodpecker drilling very rapidly with his beak; there were others of various kinds who whistled like errand boys. There was one which repeated 'Qu'est ce qu'il dit?' endlessly in a challenging tone. There was one insect which buzzed in a particular manner. 'Listen,' said Mr Bain one day, 'that is most interesting. It is what we call the "six o'clock beetle", because he always makes that noise at exactly six o'clock.'

'But it is now quarter past four.'

'Yes, that is what is so interesting.'

At one time and another in the country I heard the 'six o'clock beetle' at every hour of the day and night.

But experienced 'bush men' say that they can tell the time as accurately by the sounds of the bush, as a mariner can by the sun.

On the whole this part of the journey was comfortable enough. We had ample stores, every evening there was a creek to wash in; nothing went seriously wrong with the animals or the boys; there was no rain. At night we lay in the rest houses that have been put up every fifteen miles or so for the *vaqueiros* driving down the cattle. These are simply thatched shelters, sometimes with floors and breast-high walls; there was no furniture and sometimes we found the fabric of the place half demolished by bucks who, with their peculiar improvidence, had chopped it up for firewood rather than step five yards to the bush outside; often too we found the houses foul with the remains of bad fish and meat left by the previous occupants; once a cow had died to windward of us whom it had been no one's business to remove. Yetto's cooking was unbelievable and consisted mainly of boiling up corned beef with vast quantities of red peppers and rock salt. But, as I have said, it was on the whole a comfortable week and a delightful one. There was enough exertion to make one glad when one had reached the day's destination; the new scenery, utterly unlike anything I had seen before, was a continual pleasure. Mr Bain's company was a full enough experience in itself. When on the seventh day we reached Kurupukari I was sorry that this stage of the journey was over.

Kurupukari was marked large on the map and had figured constantly in our conversation for the past week. I had little idea, however, of what to expect and vaguely imagined something like the lake stations at Victoria Nyanza or Lake Tanganyika – a pier, a government office, the commissioner's residence, half a dozen corrugated-iron store-houses, a shop or two, a post office, a handful of native huts and a flag-staff. What I found was a surprise. There was a flag-staff, certainly, lying flat in the grass, still under construction; it was completed and erected during my stay; later Mr Bain hopes to obtain a flag for it. But there was no landing, no habitations, only a single wooden house standing in a clearing on a slight hill.

Rest house on cattle trail

Essequibo from Kurupukari House

The Essequibo bends there, so that the place had the look of a peninsula; the river even at this season was immense, and the wooded islands round which it divided and converged made it seem larger still; a broad creek flowed into it immediately opposite the station; there were sand dunes and rocks, submerged at full flood, but now high and dry, confusing one's sense of direction; there were cascades and patches of still lake so that one seemed to be surrounded by a system of ornamental waters, and across its vast and varied expanse one could see the green precipices of forest and appreciate, as one could not when directly beneath them, the freakish height of the trees and the gay dapple of blossom at their summit.

The house, like most in the country, was of one story, raised on piles ten or twelve feet from the ground. There were steps leading to a verandah; in the interior was a single, large room, with partitioned cubicles at the sides. This room was the law court, dignified with a dais, a witness stand and a dock; in one of the cubicles was an iron bedstead which I occupied, the others had struts for the hammocks; the verandah was the living-room with a table and two arm-chairs, it was also the government office; some tattered, printed regulations, a calendar and an obsolete map hung on the walls; there was a desk with pigeon-holes for licences, forms, stamps; here were transacted the multifarious functions of local government; a tax was levied on passing cattle, grants of land were registered, pilots' certificates were endorsed, letters were accepted for the irregular river service to the coast. A resident black sergeant of police took charge of them. Under us, between the supporting piles, there lived, under the minimum of restraint, a dozen or so convicts. These were mostly Indians serving sentence for cattle stealing; they were sent out daily to work on the trail armed with cutlasses, under the supervision of a single policeman or under no supervision at all; they were sometimes sent as messengers on two- or three-day journeys alone into the bush; they slept under a more solid shelter than in their homes and ate more regularly and more copiously and all returned the fatter and prouder for their contact with civilisation.

Mr Bain's cubicle had a cupboard, without lock, in which he kept or attempted to keep, a few personal possessions; on the walls were pasted some pictures of film stars cut out of magazines and a few picture-postcards. Any passing rancher would and constantly did, occupy the room, for the house was a regular rest house on the trail and it was usually a matter of a day or so to get a drive across the river (once there had been a flat-bottomed ferry boat to facilitate the operation but that had lately been sunk and the last few drives had had to swim across with deplorable losses). Everyone in fact who passed on any occasion used the house as a matter of right; the captains and bosuns of the river boats squatted about chatting in the courtroom; bucks in for a gun licence spent a day or two getting the latest river gossip; ballata[1] collectors waited here for transport. This busy place was the nearest thing Mr Bain had to a home, a curious contrast to the trim little official residences of British Africa. In all his huge district there was not one place which Mr Bain could lock up; his life was spent eternally jogging up and down the cattle trail and across the plain to the ultimate frontier station at Bon Success, hanging his hammock in the *vaqueiros'* shelters or putting up the night at the scattered little ranch houses of the savannah, living from year's end to year's end in camp conditions except for rare official visits to a Georgetown boarding-house. It was not everybody's job.

Unsatisfactory news awaited us at Kurupukari; our boat from Bartika had not arrived and Mr Bain, who had hitherto been unreasonably confident about it, suddenly became correspondingly depressing. That was the way in the bush, he said, one had to be used to things like that; there was not much water in the river, no doubt they were having a difficult time at the rapids; it might be weeks before they arrived; they might never arrive at all; that was probably it – the boat had been wrecked and the men all drowned; the barbed wire and the stores anyway would be lost beyond hope. How right he had been to bring me up the trail . . . and so on.

Meanwhile we were reduced to the milder discomforts of a state of siege; of a siege in the early days, that is to say, before the garrison get properly down to eating their own wounded. We had a box and

1 A substitute for rubber used principally for submarine cables; periodically a thriving trade product in the forest. The Indians bleed it from trees, and exchange it with representatives of a local company for cloth, hardware, etc.

a half of biscuits and a tin of milk; otherwise we had exhausted all our tinned stores. We were entirely out of butter, potatoes, flour, sugar, rum and tobacco. It was uncomfortable, particularly as there seemed no certainty of relief, but there was no danger of starvation. There were several bullocks grazing outside the house, one of which Mr Bain had killed and dried; a boviander across the water grew a little maize; and there were great sacks of *farine* for the convicts' rations. Both this and the dried beef need a word or two of explanation since they are the staple diet of the cattle country and less palatable or satisfying food I never struck in any part of the world.

Farine is a vegetable product made from cassava root. It is tantalising to speculate how it ever came to be discovered, for cassava in its natural state is poisonous and a fairly elaborate process of pulping and squeezing and drying is necessary to convert it to an edible condition. When and how, in the unchronicled days before the first European explorers of the sixteenth century, did the Indians conceive the idea? After what failures and experiments? How did the taste and knowledge spread among the countless antagonistic nationalities? For over a great part of the continent, among tribes utterly dissimilar in race and habit are found the same cultivated cassava crops, the same ingenious wicker tubes, that contract and expand in its manufacture. There seems no answer to this or to the other more immediate question; why, now that most parts are comparatively accessible and other cereals can be introduced, do not only the Indians but the foreign settlers persist in planting this one vegetable that takes most trouble to prepare and is most repulsive when prepared? I asked several people and they said vaguely that it was the food of the country; that the boys expected it; that one got used to it in time. For I used 'edible' in the same sense as it is used in the bush as qualifying any substance not actively lethal; turtles' eggs are considered 'edible', so are lizards and the fat white grubs which inhabit the heart of some palm trees; on the way up Mr Bain would frequently offer me bitter little berries or tasteless, mushy fruits as 'bush food'. *Farine* was very difficult to manage. It is like coarse sawdust in appearance; a granulated, tapioca-coloured substance of intense hardness and a faint taste of brown paper. It is eaten quite alone, or with hot water to soften it or more luxuriously with milk or the water in which the *tasso* has been boiled.

Tasso is the dry beef mentioned above. It is the incarnation of every joke ever made about meat at schools or messes or charitable institutions. It would certainly cause a mutiny in any English prison. It is prepared in this way. The killing of a beast is an event of some importance in the immediate neighbourhood. Indians get news of it and appear mysteriously like gulls round a trawler when the catch is cleaned. A few choice morsels are cut away and cooked and eaten fresh. The Indians carry off the head and the entrails. The rest is sliced into thin slabs, rolled in salt and hung up to dry. A few days of sun and hot savannah wind reduce it to a black, leathery condition in which it will remain uncorrupt indefinitely. Even the normally omnivorous ants will not touch it. It is rolled up and tied to the back of one's saddle; it is even, so I was told, put under the saddle above the blanket to keep it tender and protect the horse from galling. When the time comes to eat it, it is scrubbed fairly clean of dust and salt and boiled in water. It emerges softened but fibrous and tasteless. I can conceive it might be possible for a new-comer to stomach a little *farine* with a rich and aromatic stew; or a little *tasso* with plenty of fresh vegetables and bread. The food of the savannah is *farine* and *tasso* and nothing else.

For four days there was no sign of the boat. I went out with a gun but did not see any game. It had all migrated, Mr Bain said, on account of the dry weather and the boviander's hunting. Lack of tobacco was making us short of temper. There seemed no point in hanging on indefinitely; if the boat had been sunk we should not hear news of it for weeks. I decided to take some *tasso* and biscuits and set off for Anai at the end of the cattle trail, where the resident policeman was said to keep hens. From him I could get enough provisions to take me to the first ranch and so move on by stages to Bon Success where there was a Portuguese store. From there it was only a few miles to the mission house. Mr Bain could lend me a riding horse and a pack horse as far as Anai, and Yetto all the way. A policeman was also going up to duty at Bon Success who would carry a certain amount of baggage. It would be a far less comfortable journey than the first week had been, but it was possible. Anything was better than staying on without books or provisions at Kurupukari. Then when all this was decided, late on the last afternoon, one of the convicts reported the sound of a motor. Mr Bain and I hurried down to the river bank. He too could hear it plainly, though it was half an hour before a sound reached my duller ears. Pessimistic to the last, Mr Bain said it was probably some other boat, but in the end, just at sundown it came into sight, a grey blob very slowly approaching. Their sharper eyes – Mr Bain's and the little cluster of convicts and police – instantly recognised it as ours. In another half-hour it was there. An open boat low in the water, with an outboard engine. Nothing could be unloaded that night. There was a crew of four or five, each with a story to tell. They camped near the boat and long into the night we could hear them arguing and boasting over their fire. We went to bed suffused as though by wine with renewed geniality.

The unloading took all the morning and as I saw my stores packed bit by bit against the wall of my cubicle I began to despair of ever moving them. But Yetto was confident that he and the horse and the policeman could manage them with ease. We swam the horses across the river that afternoon and hobbled them in the corral on the opposite bank so that they would be ready to start the next day. The pack horse took unkindly to the water and swallowed a good deal on the way across.

Everything seemed set for my departure. I had even some kind of plan evolved for my ultimate route. It was possible, said Mr Bain, to take a canoe from Bon Success down the Takutu to Boa Vista. That meant nothing to me but Mr Bain explained that it was an important Brazilian town – next to Manaos the most important town in Amazonas. He had never been there himself but he knew those who had and in his description he made it a place of peculiar glamour – dissipated and violent; a place where revolutions were plotted and political assassinations committed; from there regular paddle steamers plied to Manaos – a city of inexpressible grandeur, of palaces and opera houses, boulevards and fountains, swaggering military in spurs and white gloves, cardinals and millionaires; and from there great liners went direct to Lisbon. Mr Bain made a very splendid picture of it all – so graphic and full of passages so personal and penetrating that it was difficult to accept his assurance that he knew it only by repute. His eyes flashed as he told me of it and his arms swept in circles. I felt that it was a singularly fortunate man who went to Boa Vista and Manaos.

On the eve of my departure Mr Bain and I had an intimate and convivial dinner. Next morning I sent the stores across with Yetto and the policeman; they were to arrange the pack horse's load and their own and start ahead of me. Soon after midday I went across myself. Mr Bain came to see me off. We found and saddled the horse; I mounted and after many expressions of mutual good will, I rode off alone up the trail.

CHAPTER 3

Difficulties of transport – second start – Yetto, Price and Sinclair – Jagger –
Yetto's better days – Surana – Anai – an ill-natured horse – a mystic.

AS SOON AS I set out on my own, things began to go slightly against
me; I was pursued by no cataclysmic doom but by a series of mild
mishaps which began within half an hour of my saying good-bye to
Mr Bain.

I was jogging happily up the trail, feeling for the first time a little
like an explorer when I met the neighbouring boviander squatting
moodily on a tree stump beside a pile of tins that were obviously
a part of my stores. The man grinned amiably and took off his hat.
'Yetto and Price say to take dese back,' he explained. 'Horse no can
carry. Him lie down all de time.'

'Lies down?'

'All de time. Dey beat him with a stick and him goes little little
way and den him lie down again. Him no get top side. De boys make
pack lighter.'

I looked at the pile and saw that with a minimum of discrimination, they had abandoned my entire meat ration. There seemed
nothing to be done. I picked out half a dozen tins, rolled them up in
the hammock at the back of my saddle and told the man to present
the rest to Mr Bain with my compliments. Then I rode on less
contentedly.

About six miles farther on I came upon the pack horse unsaddled
and hobbled, his pack lying on the ground near him. I shouted for
Yetto who eventually appeared from the bush where he and Price
had been having a nap.

'Him weary,' said Yetto. 'Him no carry pack topside.' We undid
the loads and rearranged them, sifting out everything unessential
from the heap. An Indian boy had appeared mysteriously and
I entrusted to him the stores we could not take, to carry back to

419

Kurupukari. Then I rode on ahead to the shelter where we should spend the night. I waited two hours and there was no trace of the baggage. Then I resaddled my horse and rode back. About a mile from where I had left them, Yetto and Price were sitting on a fallen tree eating *farine*. The horse was grazing near them, the packs were on the ground.

'Dat horse am sick. Him no go at all.'

It was now late afternoon. There was nothing for it but to return to Kurupukari, so I left Price to guard the stores, told Yetto to follow with the pack horse and rode back again to the river.

That ride remains one of the most vivid memories of the cattle trail. Checked and annoyed as I was, the splendour of the evening compensated for everything. Out on the savannah there is no twilight; the sun goes down blazing on the horizon, affording five or ten minutes of gold and crimson glory; then darkness. In the forest night opens slowly like a yawn. The colours gradually deepened, the greens pure and intense to the point of saturation, the tree trunks and the bare earth glowing brown; the half shades, the broken and refracted fragments of light all disappeared and left only fathomless depths of pure colour. Then dusk spread; distances became incalculable and obstacles detached themselves unexpectedly and came suddenly near; and while it was almost night in the trail the tops of the trees were still ablaze with sunlight, till eventually they too darkened and their flowers were lost. And all the pattering and whistling and chattering of the bush at night broke out loudly on all sides, and the tired little horse – who was doing a double journey and, being always on the move, had no instinct for home – suddenly pricked his ears and raised his head and stepped out fresh as though his day were only just beginning.

It was black night when I reached the corral. I hobbled him, took off his bridle and saddle and carried them down to the water's edge. The other bank showed no light. After prolonged shouting I heard an answering call and twenty minutes later a canoe appeared suddenly at my feet. We paddled to the house and I sent the man reluctantly back for Yetto. Mr Bain received me without surprise. He never thought I would get far alone.

Next day there was more reorganisation. The pack horse was clearly unfit for the journey so the sergeant hired me a donkey named Maria and a vain young negro named Sinclair, who had been hanging about without apparent purpose in and out of the house for some days. I was still obliged to abandon a great part of my stores. One of the heaviest items was the ammunition and gun; it was a cheap Belgian weapon I had bought at the ironmongers in Georgetown but it had exercised a fascination over the sergeant ever since I arrived; I had seen him playing with it, holding it to his shoulder and squinting down the barrel. Now he offered to buy it and the ammunition for twenty-five dollars, which was about what I had paid. I let him have it, and from then onwards never passed a day without seeing quantities of game.

Next day we set out again and reassembled at the place where I had left the stores, Yetto, Price, Sinclair, the horse, Maria, and myself, and began dividing up the loads and the duties. For his half-dollar a day a boy is assumed to be able to carry about fifty pounds for about twenty miles. It was Yetto's boast, of which the others were quick to take advantage, that he could carry a hundred pounds for fifty miles. I used to see them piling things on to Yetto's back and him taking them with pride and good humour. Relations were somewhat complicated by the fact that Price was not really under my orders at all. He was going to duty at Bon Success. He was new to the bush and did not like it. I made him groom and gave him the lamp and cooking utensils to carry. Sinclair was an odious youth anyway, but he knew a little about cooking. The other two hated him and on the last days went without food altogether rather than take it from him. He asked if he might drive the ass and I said yes. He then made the point that it was impossible both to carry a pack and drive the ass who strayed all over the path and needed constant goading along. In point of fact Maria did nothing of the sort. She quickly got wise to the fact that if she stayed behind with the boys, they unslung their loads as soon as I was out of sight, and put them on her back. Accordingly she used to break away and trot along happily beside the horse. This was maddening for me, because every few miles her pack would work loose and she would start scattering bits of luggage along the trail and I would have to stop and rearrange things.

Every evening Yetto had complaints against Sinclair. 'Chief, dat boy no good at all. Him too young; him not know discipline.' Every day I used to decide to pay him off and send him back; then I used to think of Yetto's detestable cooking and hesitate. And on these occasions Sinclair always succeeded in putting me in a good temper. He would appear with my towel just when I wanted it; he would find a lime-tree and unasked prepare me rum and lime when I returned from my bath in the creek; he knew exactly the things I should want, map, journal, fountain-pen, glasses, and laid them out just where I needed them beside the hammock. So in spite of the fact that I knew him to be lazy, untruthful, disloyal, sulky and conceited, he remained in my service to the end as far as the frontier.

To this rather absurd little band there attached himself a spectral figure named Jagger. I had seen him, too, moping on the steps at Kurupukari and heard Mr Bain upbraiding him on more than one occasion on some obscure subject connected with the post office. He was a coloured youth in the technical Georgetown sense of the word and in that sense only; for I never saw a face so devoid of a nameable hue. It was a ghastly *grisaille* except for his eyes which were of a yellowish tinge, the colour of trodden snow, and circled with pink. He loped along with us carrying his own food and belongings; never asking for anything except company, always eager to help with advice. He spoke accurate and elaborate English, in a toneless, lisping voice that would have sounded supercilious had it not been accompanied by his expression of inflexible misery and self-disgust. He was ragged, destitute and extremely ill and was making for the Rupununi district as his last resource; going, he said, to visit friends, which was probably another way of saying that he was about to join that curious race of tramps who wander about the cattle country, there and in Brazil, living indefinitely on the open hospitality of the ranches.

His father had been a man of some substance. Jagger had been educated at a school and university in Scotland; he had married a Portuguese girl and cut rather a dash for some time in Georgetown. I never fully mastered the history of his downfall which was

Sinclair, Price and Yetto

Rupununi Vaqueiro with ox-head

connected in some way with litigation, wills and moneylenders. Yetto explained it quite simply, 'Him was robbed by his brudders.'

He had fever badly, and on the second day arrived at the midday halt well behind the others, and dragging himself along unsteadily. He hung up his hammock, rolled into it and lay with averted face, unwilling to eat or talk. As I rode on that afternoon I began to worry about Jagger. It really looked as though he might be going to die on our hands; in his present state he would never reach the savannah on foot. Here I felt was the time for a Christian gentleman to show his principles; to emulate Sir Philip Sidney.

'Yetto,' I said that evening, 'I think that to-morrow Jagger had better ride my horse. I can easily walk the next few stages.'

'Dat's all right, chief,' said Yetto. 'Him not come on.'

'Not come on?'

'Him plenty sick. Him stay in his hammock, back where us had breakfast.'

'But will he be all right?'

'Oh yes, chief, him'll be all right. Him sick, dat's all.'

Later that evening half a dozen *vaqueiros* arrived with a drove of fifty cattle. I gave them quinine for Jagger and instructions to look after him, but I never heard whether or no he reached the savannah.

Various unsensational incidents stand out in my memory of this phase of the journey. A torrential rain-storm in which I arrived soaked through and through at the shelter two hours ahead of the outfit. I had been warned of the dangers in that climate of sitting about wet, so I stripped and made a fire. I must have looked an unseemly figure, stark except for hat and riding boots, scrabbling in the bush for dead wood. I had not made a fire since I was a boy scout fifteen years before. Contrary to all expectation it burned magnificently; I hung up my clothes round it on wooden props and they were soon steaming. Then I realised a thing that ought to have been obvious – that a fire needs constant refuelling. I went out again into the rain looking for wood, but without a cutlass could get very little. Then with very little compunction I tore up a large patch of the bark floor and substantial bits of the structure of the house and burned those. A week before I had been bitterly commenting on the Indians who had done the same, pointing out that it showed a peculiar trait in their racial character – a listlessness, improvidence, a wantonness, irresponsible egotism, arrested development – I had found numerous epithets to describe my contempt for their destructive habits.

A meeting on the trail with three Englishmen; one a rancher with a reputation for eccentricity; the other two naturalists who for some years had been tramping about tropical America in the pay of that last and now defunct survivor of the 'Fairy Godmother Departments', the Empire Marketing Board. The three were coming down together on foot. One had dysentery and looked deathly; the other two by contrast abnormally robust. They had just shot a 'bush turkey'. We stewed it and ate it together and then parted company, though not before one of the naturalists had caught a peculiar fly in the nostril of my horse.

A scare about a 'bad cow' which is what in England would be called a wild steer. This we learned about from the *vaqueiros* mentioned above to whose good attention I committed the wretched Jagger. The 'bad cow' had broken away from the drive and was last seen champing defiantly in the middle of the trail six or seven miles in front of us. There were deep creeks on either side of him which he was unlikely to cross alone, so that he would probably be in about the same place on the next day. He would charge at sight, the *vaqueiros* said. Accordingly I rode warily and with some misgiving when I got to the danger area. But it was all right. A tiger had got him the night before and the crows were already clustered round his carcass just where the *vaqueiros* said I would find him.

During the first week's ride, when I had been with Mr Bain, continually entertained by the fresh spate of his reminiscences, I had had practically no conversation with the boys. Now in the evenings, and particularly after wet days when I issued a ration of rum, I found them very sound company, particularly Yetto. I wish I could reproduce his manner of speech, but to attempt it would mean torturing the reader with phoneticisms. It was difficult to follow, being full of vowel sounds of immense breadth; the diction was creolese with a curious admixture of rather unusual words such as 'weary' and 'matrimony'.

Like most people in the colony Yetto had done a variety of jobs in his time. He had formed one of the police guard of honour when the Prince of Wales visited Georgetown and the Prince had shaken hands with him. He had once set out on an ill-fated expedition to Cuba – a story which was introduced by: 'Chief, did you ever know a black man from Grenada named Adams?'

'No, I'm afraid not.'

'Him stole twenty dollars off of me.'

Adams had taken charge of the joint funds and absconded in Trinidad. Yetto had been married but had not liked it. He had seen the Georgetown riots. But the high summit of his experience had been a lucky strike as a 'pork knocker'. He had come back to Georgetown with $800 and had spent it in six weeks.

'Why, chief, me took an automobile and drove round and round de town with three girls and me give them gold bangles and went to all de best rum shops and hotels. But me didn't drink no rum, no chief, nor beer either. It was gin and whisky all de time. Me didn't get no sleep for days, driving round all night with the girls.'

'But tell me, Yetto, did you get any better girls for all this money you were spending?'

'No, chief, just de same girls but me like to see dem happy. Dey was fine girls but you could get dem for a dollar a night. But me give dem gold bangles and gin and whisky and a drive round and round in an automobile. All de girls plenty fond of Yetto when he had de money. . . . But me was young den. Now me learned wisdom.'

'What would you do if you had the money now?'

There was a pause and I expected Yetto to tell me that he would buy a farm or a shop and settle down from the arduous and unsettled life he was now living. 'Well, chief, me tell you dis. Me would spend all de money on myself. Me would buy fine clothes and rings. Den de girls would go wid me for de hope of what me was going to give dem. And in de end me would give dem nothing.' And he opened his vast mouth and roared with laughter, his gold teeth flashing in the firelight.

But his pleasures had not been wholly philistine. During that rapturous six weeks an Italian opera singer had given a concert in Georgetown (. . . shadow and spangle of cheap tragedy . . . the ageing

prima donna, Grand Dukes and English Milords behind her, pitifully touring like faint and ever widening ripples in a lake, in the
company of her seedy and devoted manager, yearly to more
remote and less lucrative audiences to the final, tartarean abyss of
a Georgetown concert hall....)

'De cheapest ticket was two dollars but me went with my girl.
Dere was all white people dere and de way her sung was wonderful,
wid a different coloured dress for each song and dey was in all de
languages, French and English and Italian and German and Spanish. Dat lady knew everything. Her made us cry.'

The last time that Yetto had come up the trail, had been in the
company of a government vet. and his wife and the presence of the
lady gave the occasion a peculiar lustre in Yetto's eyes. It had been
altogether a very magnificent expedition with collapsible camp
tables, picnic baskets and a cocktail shaker. They had travelled ten
miles a day on foot with a troop of porters. Every place where they
had halted was sanctified in Yetto's eyes. 'Dis is where Mrs McDougal
shot an accouri.' ... 'Dis is where Mrs McDougal was so weary
dat Mr McDougal had to take off her boots.' ... 'Dis is where
Mrs McDougal had a bath.' ... Yetto had not missed a detail of
her habits or idiosyncrasies. 'Mrs McDougal had a great fancy for
me. Her took my snapshot. Her said, "Now I must take Yetto," and
her did. Doctor McDougal promised to send me a print. To-morrow
me show you de very tree where Mrs McDougal took my snapshot.
When we get to Takama her say, "I don't know what we should
have done without Yetto." Dere's nothing me wouldn't do for
Mrs McDougal.'

On the third day from Kurupukari we crossed a dry creek and
came into a little savannah named after the creek, Surana, where
there was a large Indian village. These were sophisticated Macushis
who were in constant contact with the ranches and the traffic of the
trail. The men all wore shorts, grubby singlets and felt hats, the
women cotton dresses. Some of them spoke a little English, some
Portuguese; most of them had worked for Europeans at one time or
another; there was a black man living among them, married to one
of their girls. Altogether a highly cosmopolitan and contaminated
lot, but even so, they had retained some of the characteristics of their

race, particularly in the plan, or rather absence of plan, of the village.

'Large' must be interpreted in the local sense, in which a dozen huts make an important place, twenty something quite exceptional. Indeed I never saw a village as large as that though later in the Wapishiana country I slept at one where, I was told later, no less than twenty-two huts could be counted from one spot. But I arrived there after dark and set off at the first glimmer of dawn so that I never knew until later the size of the place.

About a dozen or fifteen huts could be seen at Surana. I believe there were others out of sight. The trail ran straight down the middle of the savannah, a bare streak. Half a dozen houses were built near it, but at considerable distances from one another. Tiny, meandering footpaths ran between them. Other huts lay half a mile or so away and, as always in Indian villages, there was a ruin or two and a house under construction. It was all very different from the compact, stockaded townships of Africa. A polite English-speaking young man came out to meet me and showed me an empty mud and thatched hut where I could spend the night, and the water hole, half a mile distant where I could wash. Later some of the women brought me a present of bananas. It was a hospitable place. Many of them assembled to stare and talk to the boys.

'Dey all love Yetto,' said Yetto.

That evening after supper Sinclair came to me leading an Indian and said, 'Chief, do you want to see this boy's arse?'

I misunderstood him and said no, somewhat sharply.

'Fine, young "arse",' said Sinclair. 'Your "arse" plenty weary. You want new "arse" to go Bon Success.' He further explained that Surana was so much beset by bats and tigers that the Indians left all their horses and cattle on the other side of the bush at Anai. The boy would come with us next day, and if I liked the look of his horse I could have it at a dollar a day for the rest of the journey. I should be needing two horses, because Maria had to go back to Kurupukari, so I closed with the offer.

Next day we reached Anai on the edge of the savannah. It was exhilarating to see open country again after the cramped weeks in the forest and the view from Anai at late evening was peculiarly fine;

to the west lay the Pakaraima Mountains; far away to the south the wooden tops of the Kanuku hills were just visible on the horizon; at our feet and before us lay the level savannah dotted with 'sand-paper' trees and broken in places by islands of bush; a high wind was blowing from the south.

Anai itself was simply a house, like the one at Kurupukari only slightly more dilapidated for no one lived there, the policeman in residence preferring a cosy outbuilding. There was glass in some of the windows for it had once been intended for a commissioner's residence but the boarding of the walls had warped and shrunk so that the wind whistled through the rooms, and I was obliged to put my pipe inside a boot before I could get it alight.

'Dat house is so healthy,' said Yetto, 'dat yo shiver all night.'

There were other occupants on the evening of my arrival; a surly Syrian, with a flabby white face, grotesque in riding clothes. He was a Georgetown business man who had lately acquired a share in the ranch of an aged Brazilian negro and had been up to see to his interests; with him was a villainous-looking, wizened little Brazilian *vaqueiro*.

'Dat a very cruel man. Him tie up de Indians all night and beat dem until Mr Bain stop him.'

The Syrian asked me of the news in Georgetown and then said 'What about the war?'

I supposed he meant the threatened breach between Colombia and Venezuela and I gave a vague description of the situation. 'No, no, I mean the war in Europe.'

'Unless it has broken out in the last fortnight there isn't one. Who did you think were fighting?'

'All of them. You know, Germany and Italy and Russia and France and so on. That was what I heard. One of the boys got it from a *vaqueiro* who had heard it on the wireless at Boa Vista.' He sighed listlessly. 'Well, I'm glad there's nothing in it. Not that it affects me much.'

There was also a pleasant Spaniard named Orella and his wife coming down with a small drive of cattle. The wife was one of the daughters of Melville. They sent their love to the various relatives of theirs I should meet in the savannah, for, as I said earlier, almost

First view of savannah from Anai

Anai House. Sinclair with Chestnut stallion

everyone of importance in the Rapununi has some tie with the Melville family. The Spaniard and I dined together, leaving the Syrian and his *vaqueiro* to another table.

Yetto's predictions about the healthiness of the place proved quite accurate. It was deadly cold after the soft, close nights of the forest.

Next day was full of incident. I had arranged for horses the night before; a pack horse from the policeman and a riding horse from the Indian who had followed us from Surana. At dawn they went out to catch them but it was two hours before they brought them in. The policeman's horse was a stocky little grey, the Indian's a fiery chestnut stallion, larger than most of the local animals and six times more lifelike. He came in stepping high and tossing his head and was a difficulty from the first. He shied away from any attempt to saddle him until we made the discovery that he was blind on the off side, having lately had his eye kicked in by a mare to whom his advances had been unwelcome. The bridle was altogether more difficult; he was not used to a bit and resisted by the simple expedient of rearing, striking out with his forefeet and throwing himself over on to his back. When he had done this twice, nearly braining the Indian and slewing his saddle rakishly under his belly, we gave up the idea of the bit and borrowed a Brazilian bridle with a barbed metal nose-piece. He took to that more kindly and at length, the saddle readjusted, fretted restlessly from foot to foot, his single eye rolling in a challenging fashion, ready to be mounted. Mr Orella who had been watching proceedings meditatively from the verandah gave it as his opinion that this was a fresh horse. However he allowed me to mount and as soon as I was in the saddle set off at a canter in the desired direction. After a mile he settled down to a brisk trot and I was able to enjoy the scenery and congratulate myself on at last having got a good ride.

The trail led along the foot of the hills, passed through them down a little valley and emerged again into the open grass land; there is usually a strong, blustering wind on the savannah. It was like being by the sea, to emerge into bright light and wide horizons after the twilit green tunnel through which we had come. I jogged along in the happiest frame of mind; if I had known how to, I should have sung. Suddenly after about ten miles the stallion stopped dead. I had no whip or spurs; I undid the leather hobble from his cheek strap and beat him; I kicked him as hard as I could. He stood four square and immovable. I thought something must be wrong with his harness, so dismounted and examined it; everything was in order. I tried to look at his feet but nothing would induce him to lift a hoof from the ground. I looked round for a stick but there was nothing in sight except sand and grass. I remounted and began the battle with heels and hobble. When I was practically exhausted he suddenly started off again and trotted another two miles. He was an odd horse. After two miles we reached a belt of bush; it was here, by a creek, that I had arranged to wait for the boys to catch up and cook breakfast. At the opening of the bush a thin log lay across the path. The stallion stopped again. The battle was resumed, but here I had the advantage for I was able to break off a stick. The stallion's answer was the one unfailing expedient. Quite slowly he stood up on his hind legs and performed the back somersault that he had been practising at Anai that morning. With an agility which I did not think it likely I could ever repeat, I managed to fall clear of him. He rolled for a little, shedding a stirrup leather; struck out with all four feet hopefully but inaccurately; then quietly got up, stepped over the log and began cropping the bush on the other side.

What with the fight and the fall I was fairly exhausted and felt thankful that this was our stopping place. I tethered him, unsaddled him, found the missing leather and decided that in the afternoon I would ride the grey and see how the boys could manage with a pack saddle on the stallion.

I was deadly thirsty and went down to the creek for water. It was perfectly dry except for one fetid puddle. I got a certain ignoble consolation from thinking that probably the horse was thirsty too. Then I lit a pipe and waited.

Yetto was the first to turn up and he immediately began on a story of Sinclair's misdoings that in my present rather dizzy state was quite unintelligible. Its conclusion, anyway, was that Yetto and Price had left Sinclair with the pack horse and that Sinclair did not know the way. Presently Price came loping in. He told me the story about

Sinclair but it still made no sense. I sent him and Yetto up and down stream to see if there was a pool anywhere fit to drink. They came back after an hour without having found anything. At last Sinclair and the pack horse arrived. He began on his story but I had not the patience for it. I said I would hear it that night; meanwhile I was far too thirsty to eat anything; he was to saddle the pack horse and put the pack on the chestnut. I was going straight on.

It was a painful ride, the first of many that were to follow. The heat was intense, glaring up off the earth so that my face was skinned under the shade of a broad-brimmed hat. Exhaustion was infectious; I felt it seeping up from the stumbling horse, seeping down into him from me. Constant urging was necessary to keep him at a trot. When he fell into a walk the dead hardness of the saddle was intolerable. Above all there was thirst. Later I had many longer and hotter days without water, but this was the first of them and I was fresh from the deep shade and purling creeks of the forest. The trail, clear enough in places, would sometimes dwindle and peter out among patches of dried sedge; then it was necessary to cast round in widening circles until I picked it up again after a loss of time and strength. Often it would split and divide into two equally prominent branches. Then it was a matter of guessing to decide on the route; sometimes I went wrong and found the track I had been following led only to a dried water hole; then again it was necessary to cast for the real trail. In this way I must have covered nearly double the real distance, when at about five in the afternoon, I arrived at my destination.

This was the ranch of a man named Christie. I knew nothing about him except what I had been told the previous evening; that he was very old and 'very religious'. His religion, I was warned, took the form that he did not participate in the open hospitality of the savannah. He allowed – he could scarcely have prevented it – passers-by to hobble their horses in his corral and sleep under his shelter, but that was the full extent of his goodwill. Most people, riding through, if they could rely on their horses, made a double stage of it and got through to Anai in one day; others hung their hammocks in the open by the creek where I had left Yetto and the boys. However there was no question of that for me; even if I had not had followers on foot, the horse could not have made any further effort; he was barely able to get so far. I had to risk the religious atmosphere and put up at Christie's.

Visibility is poor on the savannah by reason of the 'sand-paper' trees. These low shrubs, six or ten feet in height, are scattered loosely all over the country at intervals of twenty yards or so; sometimes they are thicker and from a distance give the impression of a copse, but when approached always resolve into isolated units; they throw almost no shade; their leaves are very rough on one side and it is from this peculiarity that they get their name; their wood is brittle and useless for any practical purpose. Their only good quality, that I was able to discover, was the element of surprise that they gave to travelling. In some countries one sees the day's objective from the start; it is there in front of one, hour after hour, mile after mile, just as remote, apparently, at noon as it had been at dawn; one's eyes dazzle with constant staring. The 'sand-paper' trees often hid a house from view – particularly the low, dun houses of the district – until one was practically inside it. Then there would be a sudden, exultant, a scarcely credulous, inward leap of delight as one realised at the worst and almost desperate hour of the day, that one's distress was over. Horse and I were both unsteady with fatigue when an Indian home came into view quite near us. Then another, with some women squatting in front. They ran in and hid at my approach but I rode up to the door and shouted into the darkness, making the motions of drinking. After some giggling and nudging one of them brought me out a calabash of cold water. Then I said 'Christie' and they repeated 'Christie' and giggled some more. Finally one of them came out and pointed in the direction I should take. Another twenty minutes brought me to the ranch. It was a handful of huts, thrown out haphazard on the ground like the waste stuff of a picnic party. There was no one about. I dismounted and walked round. The central and largest house was only half built but there was another near it with dilapidated thatch, open at all sides, which was distinguishable from the others by a plank floor, raised a couple of feet from the earth. Here, reclining in a hammock and sipping cold water from the spout of a white enamelled teapot, was Mr Christie.

He had a long white moustache and a white woolly head; his face was of the same sun-baked, fever-blanched colour as were most faces in the colony but of unmistakable negro structure. It is illegal for blacks – or for that matter, whites, unless they get permission – to settle in Indian country and I learned that for the first ten years or so of his residence there had been repeated attempts by the government to evict him; after that they had let him be. I greeted him and asked where I could water my horse. He smiled in a dreamy, absent-minded manner and said, 'I was expecting you. I was warned in a vision of your approach.'

He climbed out of the hammock, looked about for shoes, found only one, and hobbled across to shake hands with me.

'I always know the character of any visitors by the visions I have of them. Sometimes I see a pig or a jackal; often a ravaging tiger.'

I could not resist asking, 'And how did you see me?'

'As a sweetly toned harmonium,' said Mr Christie politely.

He pointed out the tenuous straggle of footpath that led to the water hole. I took off saddle and bridle and led the horse down by his rope halter. He whinnied at the smell of water and we both drank immoderately; he was trembling in the legs and lathered in sweat but, I was glad to find, not galled. I sluiced him down, turned him into the corral, and left him happily rolling in the dust. Then I slung my hammock under a shelter near Mr Christie's house and fell asleep until, two hours later, the rest of my party arrived. They had my change of clothes with them. As soon as they arrived I got out of boots and breeches, had a bath and a mug of rum. I drank a lot of rum that evening; how much I did not realise until next morning when I discovered the empty bottle. Sinclair, knowing that there was a row in the air, had picked a handful of limes on his way. He filled up the mug assiduously with rum and limes and brown sugar and cold, rather muddy water. I did not investigate the boys' quarrel and Sinclair did not get the sack. The sweet and splendid spirit, the exhaustion of the day, its heat, thirst, hunger and the effects of the fall, the fantastic conversations of Mr Christie, translated that evening and raised it a finger's breadth above reality.

The lamp stood on the floor in the middle of the shelter so that all the faces were illumined as faces are not meant to be seen; from below with cheek bones casting shadows across their eyes and strong light under the brows and chin and nostrils. Everyone in the vicinity came round to watch me eat supper. Mr Christie stalked round and round the lamp telling me about God.

He asked me whether I were a 'believer' and I said yes, a Catholic.

'There are *some* good Catholics,' conceded Mr Christie, 'they are far from the truth but they are in the right direction. Only the other evening I was looking at the choir of the blessed singing before the throne of God and to my great surprise, I recognised the late Bishop of Guiana . . . but they take too much on themselves. Their ministers like to be called "father". There is only one "Father" – the one above.'

'Have you the same objection to children addressing their male parent in that way?'

'It is a terrible thing to be a male parent' – Mr Christie had a large family by an Indian mistress – 'Verily it is written' – and he quoted some text I cannot remember to the effect that children are a curse. 'Why only the other day my eldest son begat a child by a woman of no cultivation. He even speaks of marrying her.'

'But living as you do out here in the savannah, is lack of cultivation a very serious matter?'

'It is very serious when she will not sing,' said Mr Christie severely.

We spoke of the uncle of some friends of mine who had worked in this district as a missionary and retired to England as the result of a complete breakdown.

'That man had the devil in him,' said Mr Christie. 'Do you know what he did? He boiled a chicken in the place where I used to say my prayers. I have never been there since. It was defiled.'

I told him that the priest had since recovered his health and was working on the South Coast.

'No, no, I assure you that the contrary is the case. He appeared to me the other night and all the time he spoke to me his head rolled about the floor in a most horrible manner. So I knew he was still mad.'

Every Sunday he preached for four or five hours to the neighbouring Indians. I asked him whether his work among them was successful. 'No, not successful, you could not call it successful. I have been here for thirty years and so far have made no converts at all. Even my own family have the devil in them.'

He told me that he was at work on a translation of the scriptures into Macushi, 'but I have to change and omit a great deal. There is so much I do not agree with . . . but I am not worried. I expect the end of the world shortly.' Some years back he had seen a number flashed in the sky and that was the number of days remaining. I asked him how he knew that that was the meaning of the number.

'What else could it be?' he asked.

As I sat soaking rum he told of numerous visions. How when his mistress died he had heard a voice from heaven say, 'The old horse is dead.'

'It did not mean that she was like a horse. In some ways she was very pretty. It meant no more riding for me.'

Lately he had been privileged to see the total assembly of the elect in heaven.

'Were there many of them?'

'It was hard to count because you see they had no bodies but my impression is that there were very few.'

I asked if he believed in the Trinity. 'Believe in it? I could not live without it. But the mistake the Catholics make is to call it a mystery. It is all quite simple to me.' He told me how the Pope had had a French admiral murdered and his heart sent to Rome in a gold box; also that Freemasons stole bodies out of the cemetery and kept them in a cellar below every Lodge. You could always tell a Freemason, he said, because they had VOL branded on their buttocks. 'It means volunteer, I suppose,' he said. 'I can't think why.'

Presently some of the onlookers in the outer circle came into the hut and squatted down round the lamp. I had some cocoa made and handed round. One of Mr Christie's daughters had married an East Indian. The man put a naked child on my knee and attempted to interest me in a row he was having with the policeman at Anai about illicit tobacco selling. It was all a trumped-up charge, he said, the result of spite. But I was not in the mood to follow his difficulties.

After a little I fell asleep and woke up to find the party still going on and Mr Christie still talking of visions and mystic numbers. When I next awoke they had all gone away, but I could hear Mr Christie prowling round in the darkness outside and muttering to himself.

CHAPTER 4

Daguar's ranch – Hart's ranch – St Ignatius Mission – Figuiredo – the Boundary Commission.

NEXT DAY WAS easy going. I started early and did the twenty-odd miles to the next ranch before midday. The first half of the ride was pleasantly cool, none of it was particularly disagreeable, for it is not until afternoon, when the ground has got hot, that the savannah becomes unendurable. When it is possible the *vaqueiros* stay under cover and sleep from one until three. The horse was tired after the bad time he had had the day before but he made the journey successfully, with a little pushing in the last five miles, at the regular four mile an hour savannah trot.

The ranch I was making for, was the property of a Georgetown Chinaman named Mr Wong, who was one of Yetto's heroes on account of his reputation for high play at cards. The manager, to whom I had a note of introduction from Mr Bain, was a Portuguese called d'Aguar or Da Guar or Daguar – opinion on the savannah differed about the spelling. Anyway he was a swarthy, genial man, with a well-trained Indian mistress and a totally untrained little boy of repulsive habits. The ranch was of very simple nature, three wattle and mud huts in a wire enclosure, earth-floored, thatch-roofed; one of them with a small verandah just long enough to sling a hammock, but the enclosure was swept clean daily and there was a garden beyond growing several sorts of vegetable. He was clever with his fingers and the eaves of the huts were hung with bridles and whips of plaited hide and ornamented saddles of his own making; most of the ranchers are leather-workers during the wet season when the plains are water-logged, and the damp in the air makes the raw hide malleable. There was a certain swagger in Daguar's clothes, too; he had a big-brimmed, leather-bound Brazilian hat, large silver buckles down the sides of his leggings and

437

a silver-hilted knife stuck into one of them; large spurs were strapped on to his bare, horny heels.

There were several pets, too; a grey monkey tied by his loins in the shade, a macaw and two or three green parrots on the rooftop, a gentle, perfectly tame deer, which he had caught as a baby and gelded. There were some cigarette cards nailed upon the supports of the house. The child, though naked, had an immense length of black hair coiled in a bun like an orthodox priest's, some artificial toys, made in Germany and bought in Georgetown. The Indian girl had a heliotrope dress of a material that glittered like wet seaweed, which she hastened to put on in our honour on my arrival. It was clearly a home on which was expended exceptional pride and care.

I asked the way to wash and was shown a path through the vegetable garden into a belt of bush. I went down and, pushing through, suddenly found a sharp precipice at my feet and a dark, swift river of some breadth. It was unexpected and dramatic after the great stretch of arid savannah all round. On the opposite side there was the same clay cliff and a fringe of bush; that was Brazil. I had not taken in – for the ranch was not marked on the map – that I was already at the frontier and that this was the Ireng. I was to see plenty of this river later on and grow to hate it. At the time I did not like it for the descent was slippery and coming up, clean from one's bath, one was covered with clay on hands and knees; also because I was bitten by countless small flies; also because I found the first tick on my body. Later I grew to think nothing of them, but I found this first one repulsive with his head deep and tenacious in my flesh and his body swollen to the size of a pea. I burned him off and left the Ireng with some revulsion.

The bites itched all the afternoon. Daguar explained that the cabouri fly was troublesome in this district even in dry weather. In the rains it was impossible to go out of doors without gloves and a towel muffled round the head. They are odious little insects, so small that they easily penetrate any ordinary mosquito curtain; they breed in running water and attack in great numbers. Several books about the neighbourhood describe them as completely covering every exposed surface of the writer, so that no skin was visible at all. You cannot feel their bite until they have finished sucking; then they leave a little black spot behind them and a circle of burning flesh. But they are less formidable than the mosquito because, so far as is known, they do not carry fever, they will not bite through even the thinnest clothes, they are instantly dispersed by wind or darkness.

Insects played a fairly prominent part in my experience through-out all this period. For the preceding week I had been discomforted by *bêtes rouges*, a minute red creature which brushes off the leaves of the bush on to one's clothes and finds its way below one's skin where it causes unendurable itching. My arms and legs were covered with these in spite of crab oil and antiseptic soap and I scratched until I was raw. I cured them temporarily at St Ignatius but picked them up again as soon as I was on the move. It is quite accurate to say that in the weeks from leaving Kurupukari until some time after my final return to Georgetown, there was not a two-inch square on my body that was not itching at some time of the day or night.

When the boys arrived I told Yetto to cook breakfast[1] but he said that Mrs Daguar was getting me some. Presently she brought it, a dish of fried eggs, minced tasso fried with herbs, bananas and delicious Brazilian coffee; she had china and cups and glasses and knives and forks and even a tablecloth. I asked her how she became such an excellent cook and she said she had worked for one of the Melvilles before she took up with Daguar. I had with me a number of Woolworth necklaces and bracelets which I had bought in London for barter and was in some doubt whether this woman was too grand to like them. However, I tried one on the child and the mother was so evidently delighted that I gave another to her with complete success. That and a glass of rum to Daguar put us all on a very friendly basis and he volunteered to lend me another horse to take me to Mr Hart's, the ranch where I was bound next day.

A Portuguese family came to call that afternoon with a guitar which they played. They all came in and solemnly shook hands with me – about eight of them – on arrival and on departure. (I suppose English people abroad must be constantly giving offence by not shaking hands often enough. It never occurs to us. I once travelled

---

1 Luncheon was always called breakfast in this country.

in a French ship where every passenger shook every other passenger's hand every morning.)

Two wild-eyed, shaggy Patamona Indians also arrived in a canoe
from upstream, trying to trade a monkey for some gunpowder, for
Wong's ranch is at one extreme angle of the savannah, the nearest
civilised spot to the Pakaraima district.

The boys spent the afternoon washing clothes and drying them
in the sun. Yetto was still as cheerful as ever but Price had got
noticeably thinner since I first met him at Takama. He did not like
his rations and he did not like walking and he did not like Sinclair.
I think it was this last trouble that upset him more than anything.
Half the bad feeling was because Sinclair took for himself and never
shared out whatever was left over from my meals – and I noticed
that he always prepared twice as much as I needed. But there were
only two more days to Bon Success where I should be leaving all
three of them and I did not propose to involve myself in their
squabble.

Next day a fresh horse and an early start brought me to Pirara by
eleven in the morning. On the map a large lake is marked, called
Amuku. I was surprised not to see this but learned that it had never
existed. Schomburgh, the explorer, had camped there in the last
century and found a patch of land temporarily inundated; the
cartographers have recopied it from one another ever since.

The village of Pirara, on the other hand – another prominent
feature of the map – did once exist, not indeed in recent memory but
in reliable records. Now both Amuku and Pirara are bare savannah
and the name Pirara is used of the ranch about five miles to the east
of the place marked on the map, owned by Mr Hart, an American
married to another of the Melville daughters. It is one of the most
imposing and important houses in the district, *the* most important
next to Dadanawa. Its unique and most famous feature is a wind
wheel which draws water and works a variety of machines in the
workshop. This is a landmark all over the plain, though to my
inexperienced eye it was indistinguishable from a palm tree except
at the shortest range. It seriously worried me in fact, because Daguar
had told me that I should see it from, at the very least, ten miles off

Mr Hart's ranch at Pirara

and, not seeing it, I began to think that I was on the wrong trail, and fretted increasingly until at length, of the countless tall trees with circular summits one seemed outstandingly rigid and symmetrical and gradual approach revealed it as Mr Hart's wind wheel.

Mr Hart was still away – it was his disastrous drive whose carcasses we had encountered all the way up the trail – but Mrs Hart received me with the utmost kindness. She had a tumultuous family of sons under the precarious control of an attractive, Creole governess in shorts; lithe and vital as an adolescent Josephine Baker. Their school hours seemed mostly spent in reciting the rosary and getting whipped.

The house, like all tropical houses, was a collection of separate buildings; the main one was shingle built, with floors, doors and even ceilings; I was given the schoolroom for my hammock; there were framed pictures on the walls, looking-glasses and several shelves of books. Across the yard was a shower bath. There were large fruit-trees all round – mangos, soursap, grape-fruit, lemon and orange, breadfruit and custard apple; there was a flower garden with pebble paths; there was fresh pork for breakfast; most sensational of all there was a motor truck standing outside, as unexpected and incongruous an object as it would have been in the Piazza at Venice. It was the only mechanical vehicle between Georgetown and Manoas. It had belonged, I was told, to a German who had once been taken with the idea that crops up fruitlessly from time to time, of improving Boa Vista. After his rout Mr Hart bought it and with infinite difficulty got it to Pirara. He could seldom afford to use it himself on account of the enormous price of benzine in the neighbourhood and indeed there were few directions in which it could have been driven. At the moment, however, it was doing service for the Government in carrying Boundary Commission stores from their dump at Yupukarri to Bon Success.

I heard a good deal about this Boundary Commission and later came into contact with part of it. Like all activities of Government it was, no doubt unjustly, one of the jokes of the colony. It is notorious that South American States are in frequent conflict about inaccessible bits of territory. At the beginning of this century Brazil claimed the whole of the Rupununi savannah, while there was very nearly war between Great Britain and Venezuela over the North-West frontier. Arbitrators were able to avert hostilities in both cases, but the boundaries as defined by them remained vague, as they were plotted on blank or conjectural maps in reference to hills or rivers that had never been surveyed and whose existence in some cases was only assumed from Indian report. A joint commission of the states involved had accordingly gone out to survey and demarcate the frontiers, to find which of the numerous confluent streams of the Takutu and Courantyne were in fact the rivers and which the tributaries, whether the brown patches marked on all the maps as Akarai Mountains corresponded to any real geographical feature, and other disputed points that could only be decided by first-hand investigation. The Brazilians had been led to expect a detachment of Royal Engineers and suffered some disappointment and resentment, it was freely said in the colony, when, the two parties having painfully converged and established contact, they discovered a number of local surveyors racially representative of the mixed population of Georgetown. The Commission had been at work for some time, but had so far only surveyed the single section of the line that was already accurately known; their main achievement to date was the division of Mount Roraima, where the British, Brazilian and Venezuelan boundaries meet, so that the colony was left with only a precipitous face of bare rock, and the brass plate erected by Lady Clementi to commemorate her visit there, became foreign property. Their activities however had necessitated a good deal of moving of stores and consequent recruiting of labour from villages hitherto untouched by civilisation, with the result that wages in the form of celluloid combs, printed cottons, and even gramophones were to be found in unlikely places. There was also the secondary effect, much complained of by the ranchers, that labour was scarce, for the Indians only come out to work when they need some specific object, usually a gun or ammunition, and could subsist happily on the glut of Government stores for months to come.

As I have mentioned there were books at Pirara – a curious library, much ravaged by ants, filled, like the boxes outside second-hand booksellers', with works on every conceivable subject, hygiene, carpentry, religion, philosophy, and among them a number of fairly recent best-sellers left presumably from time to time by passing travellers. As I was looking through them I came upon a local mission magazine in which were extracts from the diaries of Father Carey-Elwes, the priest who had first penetrated into the Indian villages of the border and hill country. Two days dealt with the writer's first acquaintance with Mr Christie many years before, and I was enchanted to discover a description corresponding almost exactly to my own experience; enchanted and somewhat relieved, for in the last two days I had begun to doubt whether the whole of that fantastic evening had not been an illusion born of rum and exhaustion. One anecdote seemed to me so delightful that I cannot forbear to repeat it. At the end of his stay Father Carey-Elwes offered his host one of the medals of Our Lady which he carried for distribution among his converts. The old man studied it for a moment and returned it saying (I quote from memory), 'Why should I require an image of someone I see so frequently? Besides, it is an exceedingly poor likeness.'

Next day's journey lay through Bon Success where Mr Teddy Melville lived; he is one of Mrs Hart's brothers and holds the Government rank of Ranger. She had not seen him for some time and accordingly kindly offered to drive me there in the motor van. Sinclair and Price were by now visibly exhausted by their unwonted exercise and comparatively easy as my own journey had been, I too had grown tired in the successive wearying days on horseback, the continuous saddling and bridling, watering and grooming, the early start to avoid the heat of the day, the stiff and sticky wait until the rest of the party arrived with soap and change of clothes – so I gratefully accepted her offer.

Daguar's horse and the stallion – somewhat sobered by now – were to be called for by Yetto and Sinclair on their return journey. There is a casualness in the rancher's treatment of horses, other than their own favourite mounts, that at first seemed surprising after the exaggerated importance with which they are treated in England. Very few people on the savannah could tell you exactly how many horses they possessed or where they were. At the annual round-ups they are identified by their brands, sorted out and taken home. For the rest of the time they wander at pasture, often straying twenty or thirty miles. Borrowed horses are left about and fetched when needed like books in England. Of course a horse in that country is worth about a tenth of its price in England. One can buy a reasonably strong eight-year-old pony for five pounds or less.

We did the twenty miles or so to Bon Success in a third of the time it would have taken by horse but during that time the going was incomparably rougher. Mrs Hart, a son, the driver and myself sat on the wooden seat in front; the boys lay with the luggage behind and we were all thrown up and down and from side to side as the car jolted over the grass beside the trail. Ground that seemed smooth enough on foot was scarcely passable on wheels. I soon realised why no one else thought it worth while investing in a car. There were two considerable creeks to get through. We had to cut dried wood and lay a way across them, then haul the car up the opposite bank with chain and pulleys. But we got to Bon Success well before noon and breakfasted with Teddy Melville and his enchanting little Brazilian wife. We slept for an hour and then drove on up the course of the Takutu another two miles to St Ignatius, where I was to spend ten days as the guest of Father Mather, the kindest and most generous of all the hosts of the colony.

He was at work in his carpenter's shop when we arrived and came out to greet us, dusting the shavings off his khaki shirt and trousers, and presenting a complete antithesis of the 'wily Jesuit' of popular tradition. Like all his Society, Father Mather is a self-effacing man and I think he would not relish any further personal description. He is a skilled and conscientious craftsman; everything he does, from developing films to making saddles, is done with patient accuracy. Most of the simple furniture of the living-room was his work – firm, finely jointed and fitted, delicately finished, a marked contrast to the botched, makeshift stuff that prevailed even in Georgetown. He loves and studies all natural things, in particular woods and birds about which he has huge stores of first-hand knowledge. It is very rarely that he goes down to the coast; when he does the river-side scenery – to me unendurably monotonous –

Father Mather at St Ignatius Mission

provides a luxurious orgy of observation; occasionally some call will take him into the hills, but for the most part his work keeps him in the desolate surroundings of St Ignatius, and his researches are confined to the insects that collect round his reading-lamp in the evenings.

I paid off Yetto, Sinclair and Price and they went away, Price to the station at Bon Success, Yetto and Sinclair back down the trail, for blacks are not encouraged to stay long among the Indians. Before they left they each asked to be photographed and in turn wore Yetto's old cloth cap and Price's spotted handkerchief for their portraits. Mrs Hart had tea, chatted for an hour and drove off. The first phase of the journey was over.

All the time I was in Guiana I found myself remarking on the contrast it offered to Africa. St Ignatius was very unlike the missions I had seen there – the crowded compounds, big school houses with their rows of woolly black heads patiently absorbing 'education'; the solid presbyteries and packed, devout congregations; the native priests and nuns, methodical in white linen and topees; the troops of black children veiled for their first Communion; the plain chant and the examination papers. It was as lonely an outpost of religion as you could find anywhere. If it had not been for the Calvary on the river bank, it might have been one of the smaller ranches. It was, in fact, a ranch also, for without cattle no one can live on the savannah; and the head *vaqueiro* was later to prove of the greatest service to me. Like all the savannah houses it was invisible from quite a short distance. The main building was made of wattle mud, thatch, timber and corrugated iron; a home far smaller and less imposing than Pirara or Anai, but, unlike them, distinguished by a second story with a gallery of loose planks running the length of it. The walls of the upper rooms came short of the eaves and the high savannah wind swept and eddied through them, while the timbers swayed and creaked and the thatch and iron above seemed to heave and belly, so that at night one felt as though one were at sea in a sailing ship. Downstairs there was a single small living-room, a kitchen, and store-rooms; above there were not only bedrooms but, in one of them, an iron bedstead, mattresses, and pillow, where I was put to sleep. This, a bright reading-lamp, bread and pure English conversation were luxuries I found here which I had greatly missed on the journey up.

Near the house was a small church built of tin and thatch and furnished with a few benches six inches high from the mud floor; it was open at the west end for light and ventilation, and in spite of every discouragement and a barrier of wire netting, a hen used regularly to lay her eggs behind the altar. Some way from the church stood Father Mather's workshop where every kind of odd job in leather, iron and wood was brilliantly performed. Further away still was a little shelter used as a school house for a dozen or so Indian children who appeared irregularly to learn from a kindly Indian teacher. There were several Indian houses scattered within a mile's radius of the mission who kept a close liaison with it. There was a wired corral and a *vaqueiros'* hut. There was a large, slightly dilapidated barn where visiting Indians put up.

Here Father Mather lived quite alone for the greater part of the year. Another priest, Father Keary, used the home as his headquarters but except in the wet weather he was continually on circuit among the villages. Father Mather kept the home going and managed the ranch and stores; he attended to the Indians in the immediate vicinity and dispensed medicines and first aid. Most of the ranchers on the British side, and all the Brazilians were Catholics and he saw to their needs, baptising and marrying and burying them. He repaired the boats and harness and the fabric of the house. He had once been desperately ill from fever and had frequent slighter recurrences; he had constant toothache for he was two hundred miles from the nearest dentist; he was one of the happiest men I met in the country.

I have often observed that the servants of the religious are, as a class, of abnormally low mentality. I do not know why this should be – whether it is that good people in their charity give jobs to those whom no one else will employ, or whether, being poor, they get them cheap, or whether they welcome inefficient service as a mortification, or whether unremitting association with people of superior virtue eventually drives sane servants off their heads. Whatever the explanation, that is usually the state of affairs. Father Mather's establishment, however, was an exception. It is true that there was an idiot Macushi boy who constantly obtruded a moon face round the door at meal times, asking for tobacco, but he was employed only on casual labour outside the house. The two Indian widows who cooked, wove hammocks, drove the guinea fowl out of the bedrooms and generally 'did for us' were exemplary people. So was David Max y Hung, the head *vaqueiro* mentioned above. This pious and efficient young man spoke two Indian languages, English and Portuguese, perfectly. He was half Chinese, half Arawak Indian and his wife was Brazilian. He was away at a round-up at the time of my arrival (every ranch sends a representative to every round-up to identify his own cattle and see that there is no tampering with the brands) and it was his absence that prolonged my stay so pleasantly, for on the first evening Father Mather explained to me that it was quite hopeless to think of reaching Boa Vista by canoe at that season. It was easy, however, to ride there, and on David's return I could have horses and David himself for a guide. So I stayed on, glad of the rest and learning hourly from Father Mather more about the country, for a week until David returned, and a final three days while horses were being got in and baggage repacked.

They were peaceful and delightful days. Mass at seven in the little church where sometimes half a dozen Indians would appear, always the school teacher and the idiot boy; then coffee; then Father Mather would go off to his workshop and I would sit and read in a long chair in the windswept gallery or make tracings from maps at the table downstairs. There were a quantity of maps of varying value, mostly roughly sketched plans of journeys in the hills and round the savannah, and gradually I was able to correct my official map until it had some semblance of accuracy. Breakfast at noon and then Father Mather returned to his business. At sundown we used to go down to the river to wash (one does not do much swimming in these rivers because they are full of dangerous creatures – sting ray, electric eels and carnivorous fish); supper at seven, and after supper we smoked and talked until bedtime about Guiana or England while Father Mather sorted out photographs or insects or feathers. During these evenings I learned to cut up, consume and eventually even to enjoy the pungent black tobacco of the district.

There were pets, of course; a misanthropic and rather menacing 'bush turkey' which strutted about the gallery, shaking his scarlet dewlap; two toucans with vast, disproportionate beaks, shaped and coloured like toys; they used to appear at meal times and catch pieces of bread with astonishing accuracy; if neglected they asserted their presence by pecking one sharply in the leg. There was a mischievous little mocking-bird who upset everything and to whom I became particularly attached; he was killed by a cat during my stay. There was also a huge toad who inhabited the house, though he can scarcely be described as a pet; he had quarters behind a kerosene tin and woke up at sunset with a series of deep barks; he never appeared except by lamplight when he would come out, flopping along heavily; he had an unaccountable taste for burning cigarette ends which he would snap up and swallow with an insatiable appetite.[1]

There were a few callers because the mission lay on the cattle trail to Dadanawa and it is uncivil in that district to pass any house without stopping to greet the inhabitants. The manager of the company's ranch came to coffee one morning. He was riding a fine, corn-fed horse, and habitually did the journey from Bon Success to Dadanawa in one day. On another occasion Mr Gore, the next neighbour up the trail passed us with a drove of cattle and stopped for supper. He had had a wandering life and told stories of the Yukon gold rush, but he had now married an Indian and settled in the Rupununi for good. Teddy Melville came by with an ostentatiously armed policeman, on his way to investigate a story of 'pork knockers' in Indian territory beyond Wichabai. And besides more formal visitors there were usually a dozen or so nondescript strangers hanging about the house. Some were Brazilians, in or out of jobs, or calling on relatives at ranches this side of the border; others were Indians come to trade, bringing in pelts, honey, *farine*, game or fish to exchange for cloth or shot. There was never any bargaining with these traders. They took what they were offered with completely impassive faces. Usually Father Mather led them

---

[1] I mentioned this phenomenon later to Mr Winter, who told me he had once seen a toad eat a burning cigar end outside an hotel in Georgetown but that no one would ever believe him.

into the store and let them see what he had. They could go on choosing until they had made up the value of what they had brought. Occasionally they would have taken all that attracted them before they had exhausted their credit. Then they would make as though to go and he would force some further object on them. They would take it listlessly like everything else, and drift away to their homes. Sometimes there were Indians with injuries or illnesses asking for medical attention. Sometimes they had no apparent motive in their visit but had come for a few days' gossip, or were halting on a journey, moved invisibly like the tides, on some unexplained, pointless errand.

The life of the Brazilian frontier must, I should think, be unique in the British Empire. In its whole length from Mount Roraima to the Courantyne – a distance of about five hundred miles – Bon Success is the only British Government station, and that is under the admirable management of Mr Melville, who is half Indian by birth and married to a Brazilian. On the other side there is no representative of law nearer than Boa Vista. There is no comic *Beachcomber* administrator dressing at night for dinner and whistling his old school song as the colours are lowered at sunset; there are no flags, no military, no customs, no passport examinations, no immigration forms. The Indians have probably very little idea of whether they are on British or Brazilian territory; they wander to and fro across the border exactly as they did before the days of Raleigh.

Throughout the whole district, too, there is only one shop and that is in two parts, half in Brazil and half in British Guiana. The proprietor is a Portuguese named Mr Figuiredo. He lives immediately opposite Mr Melville and he takes good care to keep his dealings strictly legal. On his own side of the river he sells things of Brazilian origin, hardware, ammunition, alcohol in various unpalatable forms, sugar and *farine*, a few decayed-looking tins of fruit and sweets, tobacco, horses, saddlery and second-hand odds and ends extorted from bankrupt ranchers; on the British side he sells things brought up from Georgetown, mostly male and female clothing, soaps and hair oils, for which the more sophisticated Indians have a quite unsophisticated relish, and brands of patent medicines with engraved, pictorial labels and unfamiliar names – 'Radways Rapid Relief', 'Canadian Healing Oil', 'Lydia Pynkham's Vegetable Product'. If a Brazilian wants anything from the British side he and Mr Figuiredo paddle across the river and he buys it there; and vice versa. Any guilt of smuggling attaches to the customer.

Father Mather and I went to breakfast with Mr Figuiredo one day. He gave us course after course of food – stewed *tasso* with rice, minced *tasso* with *farine*, fresh beef with sweet potatoes, fresh pork, fried eggs, bananas, tinned peaches and creme de Cacao of local distillation. His women folk were made to stand outside while we ate, with the exception of one handsome daughter who waited. After breakfast we went into the shop and Mr Figuiredo made an effortless and unembarrassing transition from host to shopkeeper, climbing behind the counter and arguing genially about the price of coffee. He has no competition within two hundred miles and his prices are enormous; many ranchers pay their wage bill in chits on his store; even allowing for the expense and risk of transport his profits must be exceptional, but he lives in a very simple fashion, dressing always in an old suit of pyjamas and employing his family to do the work of the house. His ambition is to save enough to leave Brazil altogether and retire to Portugal.

Once or twice Father Mather and I paid visits to neighbouring Indians, but even these comparatively civilised people were very elusive; at one little group of houses all the men were away on a hunting expedition; at another the whole population had migrated to their cassava fields in the hills. Those we met were intensely shy except for one elderly woman who was reputed to be a 'piai woman'.[1] She had an old felt hat, long straggling hair and a filthy calico dress; her upper lip was tattooed with a blue moustache. She was extremely friendly, kissed our hands and gave us a calabash of home-brewed liquor.

After a week David returned from the round-up – suave, spectacled, faultlessly efficient – and took over the arrangements for my journey to Boa Vista. The ranches on the other side lay along the banks of the Takutu and the Rio Branco; this, though circuitous, was

[1] Witch.

the normal route which could be done in five or six days. It was possible, however, to travel direct across the savannah in three days and, to David's unexpressed regret, I decided to do this. My luggage was now reduced to a rucksack and a canvas grip, so that its transport presented no serious difficulty. I was assured of ample provisions at Boa Vista and for the short crossing would take the luck of the country. Father Mather added bread and chocolate. On the morning of our departure he made me two presents, typical of him and of the country. I had casually mentioned, early in my stay, that I wished I had brought with me some kind of case for my camera. Later I noticed him measuring it but did not know the reason until he appeared with a perfectly fitting case, covered with deer skin and lined with flannel, on a foundation of galvanised iron; there was even a waterproof envelope for it kept in place by a band cut from an old bicycle tyre. He also gave me two pieces of rare local wood shaped up for conversion into walking-sticks, gummed over and wrapped in waterproof paper to protect them from damage.

David's Brazilian brother-in-law Francisco joined us; the luggage was divided – unequally, for I took only hammock, blanket and change of clothes – between our three horses. Then after breakfast on February 1st, we set off for the border. The sun was obscured and a light drizzle of rain was falling.

CHAPTER 5

Brazilian savannah – amenities of Boa Vista – attempts to improve Boa Vista – 'the Company' – Father Alcuin – Mr Steingler – the boundary commissioner – horse-dealing – the new Prior – escape from Boa Vista.

THE FORD WAS about three miles upstream from St Ignatius. As I have said, there were no formalities of any sort in crossing the boundary; our horses waded through the shallow water, stretching forward to drink; half-way over we were in Brazil. A lurch and scramble up the opposite bank; we forced our way through the fringe of bush, leaning low in the saddle to guard our faces from the thorn branches; then we were out into open country again, flat and desolate as the savannah we had left; more desolate, for here there was no vestige of life; no cattle track, no stray animals; simply the empty plain; sparse, colourless grass; ant-hills; sand-paper trees; an occasional clump of ragged palm; grey sky, gusts of wind, and a dull sweep of rain.

We rode on until sunset, Francisco in front showing the way, then myself; at the back David who had chosen the worst horse. I never saw anyone take so much trouble with his horse as Francisco. Every few miles he would dismount, slacken the girths and peer under his saddle for signs of galling. Brazilian saddles are built on a wooden frame, padded with straw like the packing of wine bottles. He had a ragged blanket below the straw which he would repeatedly shake out and refold. I got impatient at these frequent stops but Francisco proved right in the end for he was the only one of us who got his horse to Boa Vista with a whole back.

At sunset the horses raised their heads and quickened their pace. It was intensely dark and we could only follow by the creaking of the harness ahead. At length we came to a stop and a blacker darkness in front proved to be a *vaqueiros'* out-station. Francisco and David called out in Portuguese and were presently answered by a man's voice. Some minutes later a very small light appeared in the hands of

Midday halt at Dry Creek on Brazilian savannah. David and Francisco unsaddling.

Marco receiving coffee from Brazilian ranchers (lame pack-horse in background)

a small boy. It revealed a typical thatched shelter with mud floor and breast-high mud walls, of the sort to which I had by now grown accustomed; also an elderly man who came out to shake our hands. In the shadows were half a dozen hammocks whose occupants peered at us and rolled over again to sleep. A second light glowed dimly beyond, in a room where the women had been roused to make us some supper. Francisco and David led off the horses to water at a near-by creek; the small boy dragged out a box for me to sit on; finding I could not speak Portuguese the elderly man contented himself by sitting astride his hammock and staring at me gloomily. After about ten minutes the boy brought me a minute cup of black coffee, thick and sweet, as coffee is always made in the countries that grow and understand it. There was a table at one side of the room, built on piles driven into the floor; when David and Francisco returned the man motioned us to draw up our boxes and sit there; the lamp stood in the centre. It consisted of a little bowl of beef fat with a couple of inches of wick hanging over the edge and giving a smoky, orange flame. A woman brought in a tin pot of stewed *tasso* and another of *farine*. We had our own plates, knives and forks. David and Francisco helped themselves liberally. I attempted, in politeness, to eat a little but found it impossible to swallow. David, with an explanation to our host of this curious English taste, produced the bread. I soaked a slice in the tasteless, greasy water of the stew and ate it. Later when the others were in their hammocks I supplemented this meagre dinner with some of Father Mather's chocolate.

The thatch above our heads was very old and partially rotten. Even in the flickering light of the dip we could see moving across it the shadows of lizards and huge spiders; presumably it was also full of scorpions. Its reek was overpowering – a mixture of wet spaniel and turnip fields, so pungent that for hours I could not sleep and even contemplated taking my hammock outside and looking for other shelter under the trees. Eventually, however, I lost consciousness and was awakened at grey dawn by David to say that the horses were saddled and that we had a long day in front of us.

It proved to be by far the hardest day I had yet done. The rain had passed over and the sun came up, blinding and burning; there was no wind. With two brief halts we rode steadily until half an hour before sunset. Two hours after our start we stopped at an Indian house to make tea and eat some dry bread. After that, until evening, we got no water. The stream where we stopped at noon was dry except for a few thick puddles, good enough for washing down the horses but not fit for drinking. Without water, I found, one lost all appetite for food, and I left the stale bread and tinned sausage untouched in my pocket.[1] All through the blazing afternoon I found that I thought of nothing except drinking. I told myself very simple stories which consisted of my walking to the bar of my club and ordering one after another frosted glasses of orange juice; I imagined myself at a plage, sipping ice-cold lemon squashes under a striped umbrella, beside translucent blue water. I constructed 'still lives' of bottles and syphons, glass goblets of bitter Hereford cider, jugs of peaches soaking in hock and champagne, even effervescing tumblers of liver salts. It was interesting that the drinks I thought of were nearly all fruity – no foaming tankards of ale or cellar-cool wine.

At last that day, like all others, came to an end. When I was unsteady in the saddle with exhaustion and the sun lay low and straight in our eyes, we came to a flowing creek and a hut beyond it. The horses could not be got past the water, nor had we any inclination to urge them. We drank mug after mug of the cold stream and then, very stiffly, climbed up the bank to greet our host, a curly-headed half-caste. As he was bringing out the inevitable *farine* and *tasso*, I slung my hammock; sat down in it to wait; lay down, and awoke in my clothes eleven hours later to find dawn breaking and the horses already saddled.

The next two days were easy going and uneventful except for our passing a black jaguar and an ant bear. The jaguar was a mere shadow, slipping away from us in the distance; I did not learn until later that it was a beast of some rarity. The ant bear, though common enough, was vastly more impressive, like something from an earlier phase of creation; the size and colour of an Irish wolf-hound with an

1 For some reason no one travels with water in this country; chiefly I suppose because every ounce of weight is considerable, and also because at most times in the year the place is well watered. Anyway the pint or so of tepid liquid which one could have taken in a flask would have been negligible against the thirst of twelve hours in the sun.

absurdly attenuated nose, and a tail as long as itself, curled and feathery; it loped along lethargically within a few yards of us, either oblivious or indifferent to our approach.

We had now reached the inhabited Rio Branco district and we slept at a large ranch house, distinguished by a primitive sugar mill, round which an ox plodded to the constant shouting of an Indian boy. A rich smell of toffee arose from the copper cauldrons. The process resulted in stone-hard cakes of candy, one of which was presented to each of us on leaving and happily gnawed up by David and Francisco. The proprietor dispensed patriarchal hospitality to twenty or more strangers and workmen. We dined in three shifts, the company waiting patiently on benches to take the first vacant place at the table; they were of all races and ranks, including a one-eyed negro, a deaf and dumb Indian, and an elegant young man in imitation silk pyjamas who hiccoughed extravagantly. The fare was the usual *farine* and *tasso*, enriched with milk and treacle. David did all the conversation necessary at these visits, performing greetings and introductions and expressing our thanks with infinite courtesy and giving an impression of such distinction that, here, we were allowed to sling our hammocks in the verandah of the house instead of in the crowded shed outside. On the fourth day we reached the bank of the Rio Branco at an empty hut immediately opposite Boa Vista.

Since the evening at Kurupukari when Mr Bain had first mentioned its name, Boa Vista had come to assume greater and greater importance to me. Father Mather had only been there once, and then in the worst stage of malignant malaria, so that he had been able to tell me little about it except that some German nuns had proved deft and devoted nurses. Everybody else, however, and particularly David, had spoken of it as a town of dazzling attraction. Whatever I had looked for in vain at Figuiredo's store was, he told me, procurable at 'Boa Vist''; Mr Daguar had extolled its modernity and luxury – electric light, cafés, fine buildings, women, politics, murders. Mr Bain had told of the fast motor launches, plying constantly between there and Manaos. I had come to regard it as Middle Western Americans look on Paris, as Chekhov peasants on St Petersburg. In the discomfort of the journey there, I had looked forward to the soft living of Boa Vista, feeling that these asperities were, in fact, a suitable contrast, preparing my senses for a fuller appreciation of the good things in store. So confident was I that when we first came in sight of the ramshackle huddle of buildings on the further bank, I was quite uncritical and conscious of no emotion except delight and expectation.

The river was enormously broad and very low; so low that as we gazed at the town across sand dunes and channels and a fair-sized island it seemed to be perched on a citadel, instead of being, as was actually the case, at the same dead level as the rest of the plain. Two *vaqueiros* were lying in hammocks by the bank, and from these David elicited the information that a boat was expected some time in the next few hours to ferry them across. There was a corral by the hut into which we turned the horses; then we carried the saddles and baggage down the precipitous path to the water's edge and settled ourselves to wait. The *vaqueiros* studied us with an air that I came to recognise as characteristic of Boa Vista; it was utterly unlike the open geniality of the ranches; conveying, as it did, in equal degrees, contempt, suspicion and the suggestion that only listlessness preserved us from active insult.

With David's assistance, I began some inquiries about accommodation. There was none, they said.

'But I understood there were two excellent hotels.'

'Ah, that was in the days of the Company. There was all kinds of foolishness in the days of the Company. There is nowhere now. There has not been an hotel for two years.'

'Then where do strangers stay?'

'Strangers do not come to Boa Vist'. If they come on business, the people they have business with put them up.'

I explained that I was on the way to Manaos and had to wait for a boat. They showed complete indifference, only remarking that they did not know of any boat to Manaos. Then one of them added that possibly the foreign priests would do something for me – unless they had left; last time he was in Boa Vist' the foreign priests were all sick; most people were sick in Boa Vist'. Then the two men started talking to each other, with the obvious desire of terminating our conversation.

My enthusiasm had already cooled considerably by the time we saw a boat put out from the opposite shore and make slowly towards us. The owner of the boat had business at the ranch on our side and made no difficulty about lending it. We all got in, his boy, David, Francisco, I, the two surly *vaqueiros*, the saddles and the baggage, so that the gunwales were only an inch clear of the water. Then partly paddling, partly wading and pushing, we made our way across. There were women squatting on the further shore, pounding dirty linen on the rocks at the water's edge. We hauled our possessions up the steep bank and found ourselves in the main street of the town. It was very broad, composed of hard, uneven mud, cracked into wide fissures in all directions and scored by several dry gulleys. On either side was a row of single-storied, whitewashed mud houses with tiled roofs; at each doorstep sat one or more of the citizens staring at us with eyes that were insolent, hostile and apathetic; a few naked children rolled about at their feet. The remains of an overhead electric cable hung loose from a row of crazy posts, or lay in coils and loops about the gutter.

The street rose to a slight hill and half-way up we came to the Benedictine Mission. This at any rate presented a more imposing aspect than anything I had seen since leaving Georgetown. It was built of concrete with a modestly ornamented façade, a row of unbroken glass windows, a carved front door with an electric bell, a balustraded verandah with concrete urns at either end; in front of it lay a strip of garden marked out into symmetrical beds with brick borders.

We approached rather diffidently for we were shabby and stained with travelling and lately unaccustomed to carved front doors and electric bells. But the bell need have caused us no misgiving for it was out of order. We pressed and waited and pressed again. Then a head appeared from a window and told us, in Portuguese, to knock. We knocked several times until the head reappeared; it was Teutonic in character, blond and slightly bald, wrinkled, with a prominent jaw and innocent eyes.

'The gentleman is a stranger too. He speaks Portuguese in a way I do not understand,' said David. 'He says there is a priest but that he is probably out.'

I was used to waiting by now, so we sat on the doorstep among our luggage until presently an emaciated young monk in white habit appeared up the garden path. He seemed to accept our arrival with resignation, opened the door and led us in to one of those rooms only found in religious houses, shuttered, stuffy and geometrically regular in arrangement; four stiff chairs ranged round four walls; devotional oleographs symmetrically balanced; a table in the exact centre with an embroidered cloth and a pot of artificial flowers; everything showing by its high polish of cleanliness that nuns had been at work there.

The monk was a German-Swiss. We spoke in halting French and I explained my situation. He nodded gloomily and said that it was impossible to predict when another boat would leave for Manaos; on the other hand a new Prior was expected some time soon and that boat must presumably return one day. Meanwhile I was at liberty to stay in the house if I chose.

'Will it be a question of days or weeks?'

'A question of weeks or months.'

David interposed in alternate Portuguese and English that he thought the Boundary Commission had a boat going down in a few days; he would go into the town and enquire. I explained to the monk that if this were the case I would gladly accept his invitation; if there were no Commission boat I would return with David to Guiana. With rather lugubrious courtesy the monk, who was named Father Alcuin, showed me a room and a shower bath; explained that he and the other guest had already breakfasted; sent across to the convent for food for me. I ate the first palatable meal since I had left St Ignatius, changed and slept. Presently David returned with reassuring information. The Commission boat was passing through in four or five days; a week after that there would be a trade launch. He smiled proudly both at bringing good news and because he had bought a startling new belt out of his wages. Then he and Francisco bade me good-bye and went to rest with the horses on the other bank of the river.

Already, in the few hours of my sojourn there, the Boa Vista of my imagination had come to grief. Gone; engulfed in an earthquake, uprooted by a tornado and tossed sky-high like chaff in the wind, scorched up with brimstone like Gomorrah, toppled over with trumpets like Jericho, ploughed like Carthage, bought, demolished and transported brick by brick to another continent as though it had taken the fancy of Mr Hearst; tall Troy was down. When I set out on a stroll of exploration, I no longer expected the city I had had in mind during the thirsty days of approach; the shady boulevards; kiosks for flowers and cigars and illustrated papers; the hotel terrace and the cafés; the baroque church built by seventeenth-century missionaries; the bastions of the old fort; the bandstand in the square, standing amidst fountains and flowering shrubs; the soft, slightly swaggering citizens, some uniformed and spurred, others with Southern elegance twirling little canes, bowing from the waist and raising boater hats, flicking with white gloves indiscernible particles of dust from their white linen spats; dark beauties languorous on balconies, or glancing over fans at the café tables. All that extravagant and highly improbable expectation had been obliterated like a sand castle beneath the encroaching tide.

Closer investigation did nothing to restore it. There was the broad main street up which we had come; two parallel, less important streets, and four or five more laid at right angles to them. At a quarter of a mile in every direction they petered out into straggling footpaths. They were all called Avenidas and labelled with names of politicians of local significance. The town had been planned on an ambitious scale, spacious, rectangular, but most of the building lots were still unoccupied. There was one fair-sized stores, a little larger and a little better stocked than Figuiredo's, half a dozen seedy little shops; an open booth advertising the services of a barber-surgeon who claimed to wave women's hair, extract teeth and cure venereal disease; a tumbledown house inhabited by the nuns, an open school house where a fever-stricken bearded teacher could be observed monotonously haranguing a huge class of listless little boys; a wireless office, and a cottage where they accepted letters for the post; there were two cafés; one on the main street was a little shed, selling *farine*, bananas and fish, there were three tables in front of it, under a tree, where a few people collected in the evening to drink coffee in the light of a single lantern; the second, in a side street, was more attractive. It had a concrete floor and a counter where one could buy cigarettes and nuts, there were dominoes for the use of habitués and besides coffee, one could drink warm and expensive beer.

The only place, besides the Benedictine Priory, which had any pretensions to magnificence was the Church, a modern building painted in yellow and orange horizontal stripes, with ornate concrete mouldings; there were old bells outside, and inside three sumptuous altars, with embroidered frontals and veils, carved reredoses, large, highly coloured statues, artificial flowers and polished candlesticks, decorated wooden pews, a marble font bearing in enormous letters the name of the chief merchant of the town, a harmonium; everything very new, and clean as a hospital – not a hen or a pig in the building. I was curious to know by what benefaction this expensive church had come into being and was told that, like most things, it had started 'in the days of the Company'.

I discovered one English-speaking person in the town; a singularly charmless youth, the illegitimate son of a prominent Georgetown citizen whom I had met there at Christmas time. This served as a fragile link between us, for the young man told me that he hated his father and had thought of shooting him on more than one occasion. 'Now I have been married and have written five times for money and had no answer.'

He was completely fleshless like all the inhabitants of Boa Vista, with dank, black hair hanging over his eyes, which were of slightly lighter yellow than the rest of his face. He spoke in a melancholy drawl. He was almost the only person I saw doing any work in the whole town. He drove a motor launch for the storekeeper and owned a small blacksmith's shop where he made branding irons and mended guns. Most of the other inhabitants seemed to have no occupation of any kind, being caught up in the vicious circle of semi-starvation which makes people too apathetic to exert themselves for more. Perhaps they picked up a few casual wages during the flood season when boats ran from Manaos fairly frequently and the ranchers came in for stores and needed labour for shipping their cattle. All the time that I was there I scarcely saw anyone except the school teacher earn anything – or spend anything. Even in the café the majority of customers came to gossip and play dominoes and went away without ordering a cup of coffee. At some miles distant was a settlement of soldiers who brought a few shillings into the town; they were reservists bedded out with wives on small allotments. An aged town clerk presumably received some sort of wages; so no doubt did the itinerant government vet. who appeared from time to time; so did the wireless operator and an official of villainous aspect called the 'Collector'. But the other thousand-odd inhabitants spent the day lying indoors in their hammocks and the evenings squatting on their doorsteps gossiping. Land was free, and, as the nuns proved, could produce excellent vegetables, but the diet of the town was *farine*, *tasso* and a little fish, all of which were of negligible cost. But it was far from being the care-free, idyllic improvidence one hears described of the South Sea Islands. Everyone looked ill and discontented. There was not a fat man or woman anywhere. The women, in fact, led an even drearier life than the men. They had no household possessions to care for, no cooking to do, they left their children to sprawl about the streets naked or in rags. They were pretty – very small and thin, small-boned and with delicate features; a few of them took trouble with their appearance and put in an appearance at Mass on Sundays in light dresses, stockings and shoes, and cheap, gay combs in their hair.

From fragmentary and not altogether reliable sources I picked up a little of the history of Boa Vista. It was a melancholy record. The most patriotic Brazilian can find little to say in favour of the inhabitants of Amazonas; they are mostly descended from convicts, loosed there after their term of imprisonment as the French loose their criminals in Cayenne, to make whatever sort of living they can in an inhospitable country. Practically all of them are of mixed Indian and Portuguese blood. There is no accurate census but a recent medical survey in the *Geographical Magazine* reports that they are dying out, families usually becoming sterile in three generations; alien immigrants, mostly German and Japanese are gradually pushing what is left of them up country; Boa Vista is their final halting place before extinction. The best of them go out into the ranches; the worst remain in the town.

They are naturally homicidal by inclination, and every man, however poor, carries arms; only the universal apathy keeps them from frequent bloodshed. There were no shootings while I was there; in fact there had not been one for several months, but I lived all the time in an atmosphere that was novel to me, where murder was always in the air. The German at the Priory constantly slept with a loaded gun at his bedside and expressed the same surprise at seeing me going shopping without a revolver, as a Londoner might show if one went out without a hat; the blacksmith, partly no doubt owing to his avocation, spoke of little else; one of his main preoccupations was altering trigger springs so that they could be fired quick on the draw.

There was rarely a conviction for murder. The two most sensational trials of late years had both resulted in acquittals. One was the case of a young Britisher who had come across from Guiana, panning gold. He had no right there and one evening in the café tipsily expressed his willingness to shoot anyone who interfered with him. The boast was recognised as constituting provocation when, a few nights later, he was shot in the back and robbed, while entering his house.

The other case was more remarkable. Two respected citizens, a Dr Zany and a Mr Homero Cruz were sitting on a verandah talking, when a political opponent rode up and shot Dr Zany. His plea of innocence, when brought to trial, was that the whole thing had been a mistake; he had meant to kill Mr Cruz. The judges accepted the defence and brought in a verdict of death from misadventure. It was the first time in my life that I found myself in contact with a society in which murder was regarded as being as common and mildly regrettable as divorce in England; there was no glamour in it; I found it neither heroic nor horrifying; instead it seemed to spring from some species of arrested development.

The officials at Boa Vista live at so safe a distance from supervision and are so badly paid, that inevitably they make what profits they can from bribes. Fortunately my meagre baggage and travel-torn appearance did not excite their cupidity. I heard several stories later of their extortion that were probably true. Twice lately British ranchers had come down by motor launch, in the flood season, to buy provisions. In each case the officer in charge had attempted to seize his boat under pretext that some regulation had been contravened, and the ranchers had had to make their escape by night, in one case under fire.

From time to time attempts have been made to raise the condition of the town. A little before the War a German appeared with ample capital and began buying cattle. He offered and paid a bigger price than the ranchers had ever before received; he fitted out a fleet of large motor launches to take the beasts down to market at Manaos, the scheme being that if he could organise a regular supply and get them down quickly and in good condition their value would compensate for the higher rate; he even sent a man across the border with a bag of sovereigns to buy cattle at Dadanawa. The project was perfectly sound financially and would have brought considerable advantage to the district, but it was destined to failure. Before the first convoy had reached the market, he had been shot and killed by an official whom he had neglected to bribe. The defence was that he had been shot while evading arrest on a charge of collecting turtles' eggs out of season. The murderer was exonerated and the boats never reappeared at Boa Vista.

A more recent enterprise had been that of 'the Company', so frequently referred to. I never learned the full story of this fiasco, for the Benedictines were deeply involved in it and I did not like to press the question at the Priory. The blacksmith gravely assured me that the scandal had been so great that the Archbishop had been taken to Rome and imprisoned by the Pope. There certainly seemed to have been more than ordinary mismanagement of the affair. Father Alcuin never mentioned it except to say that things had not gone as well as they had hoped. So far as I could gather the facts are these:

A year or two ago, inflamed by charitable zeal, the wealthy Benedictines at Rio conceived the old plan of bringing prosperity and self-respect to Boa Vista. Geographically and politically the town held the key position to the whole, immense territory of the Northern Amazon tributaries. The monks saw that instead of its present position as a squalid camp of ramshackle cut-throats, it might be a thriving city, a beacon of culture illuminating the dark lands about it, a centre from which they could educate and evangelise the Indians, a place that might typify the now very dubious superiority of the civilised life. They imagined it, even, as a miniature ecclesiastical state where industry, commerce and government should be in the benevolent hands of the Church; a happy dream, glowing with possibilities of success to those imperfectly acquainted with the real character of Boa Vista.

Accordingly 'the Company' was launched, under the highest ecclesiastical patronage, financed by Benedictine money and managed by the brother of one of the hierarchy. The method by which the town was to be raised to prosperity was, again, sensible enough to anyone who expected normal working conditions. Instead of the cattle being transported to the slaughter-houses at Manaos, they were to be butchered on the spot and tinned. Cheap corned beef, it was assumed, would rapidly take the place of the unnourishing *tasso* and would provide a more valuable and more manageable export than live cattle. The factory would provide regular and remunerative employment to all in the district and, following the best tradition of big business, 'the Company' would also provide the necessaries and amusements on which their wages should be spent; the profits, rapidly circulating, would be used in public services. No one had any ulterior motive; the whole scheme was for the glory of God and the comfort of the people of the place. In Rio, on paper, it all seemed faultless. Operations were begun on a large scale.

The canning factory was built and installed with the best modern machinery, an electric plant was set up, providing the streets and the houses with light; a fine Church, a hospital and a small school were built; there was soon to be a larger school, a Priory and a convent; liberal wages were paid out, two hotels and a cinema opened; a refrigerator provided Boa Vista with the first ice it had ever seen. Everything seemed to be going admirably.

But the monks at Rio had reckoned without the deep-rooted, local antagonism to anything godly or decent; a prejudice which at the moment was particularly inflamed by the unforeseen arrival of an irresponsible American with a rival scheme for improvement.

His more ambitious proposal was to run a motor road and railway through the impassable bush that separated the town from Manaos, a project more or less equivalent in magnitude to the making of the Panama Canal. Finding that concessions had already been granted to the Benedictines which made his already impracticable railway legally impossible, he fell back on explaining to the inhabitants the great advantages of which they had been deprived, the higher wages he would have paid, the greater prosperity which he would have initiated. The citizens, naturally disposed to see a sinister purpose in any activity, however small, had already become suspicious of the great changes that were taking place. The American emphasised the foreign birth of most of the Order and the relationship between the manager of the Company and the high ecclesiastic in Rio with the result that by the time the monks and nuns reached their new home, they found everyone fairly convinced that a swindle was being perpetrated at their expense. It was only with difficulty and some danger that they succeeded in landing, being attacked with hostile demonstrations and showers of stones.

From then onwards everything went against the Benedictines who were insulted and boycotted. The canning factory proved a failure; no one would use the ice – an unnatural, impermanent substance, typical of everything foreign; dishonest stuff that had lost half its weight even before you got it home – they didn't want the hospital, much preferring to sicken and die in their hammocks in the decent manner traditional to the place; no one paid his electric light bill and the plant had to be stopped. The priests went down with fever and, one by one, had to be sent back to Manaos. 'The Company' became bankrupt and all further work was stopped. No Priory was built, no big school, no convent. At the time of my arrival things were at their lowest ebb. Father Alcuin was the last priest left and he was so ill that only supernatural heroism kept him at his work. Often he was only able to totter to the Church to say his Mass and then retire to bed in high fever for the remainder of the day. The palatial house in which he was living, was the building originally intended for the hospital. Its two big wards were now occupied by a carpenter engaged in making benches for the Church, and a government vet. who fitted up a laboratory there, which he used from time to time between his rounds of the ranches; he was investigating a prevalent form of paralysis in horses which he attributed to worms. Whatever minute flicker of good still survived in the town, was preserved by the nuns, silent, devoted, indefatigable, who lived in appalling quarters near the river bank, kept a school for the handful of bourgeois daughters, and nursed a negro and an aged diamond prospector who had arrived separately in a dying condition from up country and were in no mood to respect the prejudices of the town. It was, as I have said, the lowest point; a new Prior was expected daily to reorganise things and set them to rights.

The Priory – as the hospital was now called – was no exception to the rule formulated in the last chapter, that the religious are served by idiots. A single Indian boy of impenetrable stupidity looked after us. He had a round brown face and a constant, mirthless grin which revealed rows of sharply filed teeth. He giggled when observed and would, in occasional bursts of confidence, produce for inspection a grubby sheet of lined paper on which he had tried to copy an alphabet written for him by Father Alcuin. He was absolutely honest, and dazed with delight when, on leaving, I gave him a small tip. His chief duty was to fetch the meals from the convent kitchen, quarter of a mile away. They arrived cold and dusty, but with surprising regularity. He also rang the angelus and could always be found by the bell rope half an hour before the time, waiting for the clock hands to reach the appointed place. The rest of his day was spent in talking to a captive monkey that was tethered to a tree in the garden, or in gaping, hour after hour, at the jars of worms which filled the vet.'s laboratory.

The only other occupant of the house was the German who had first greeted our arrival; a man typical, except in his eccentricities, of the men of his race whom one encounters in remote places all over the globe; part of the great exodus of disillusioned soldiers and students that followed the defeat of 1918, from Germany and the German colonies. I have encountered them, wistful and denationalised as Jews, in Abyssinia, Arabia and East Africa, and they make real to me some of the claptrap of Nazi patriotism.

Mr Steingler was not a particularly attractive man. I never discovered what he was doing in Boa Vista. He had a minute and unprofitable plantation up the River Uraricuera where he lived in complete solitude and, I gathered from his conversation, great privation. He spoke vaguely of business he had to do in the town and would often go shuffling off to gossip at the stores; he spoke of some mail he was expecting but when eventually the boat arrived from Manaos, there was nothing in it for him; he would sometimes announce his imminent departure, but always stayed on. He said he did not like to leave while Father Alcuin was so ill. The truth was I think that he could not bear to leave a place where there were people to talk to him in German; and he liked the food. He was a demonstratively greedy man and used to give great boyish whoops and guffaws of delight as he helped himself to the dishes, for at his farm, as he often explained, he had only *farine* and *tasso*.

It was only by slow degrees that he had come to his present condition. He had had a good job with a commercial firm in Manaos; then he had come to Boa Vista in the days of 'the Company'; then he had wandered off on his own up country. It is possible that he was staying on at the Priory because absolute destitution awaited him at his farm.

He was a firm atheist and did not disguise his contempt for the activities of his hosts. I tried to point out to him once that it was particularly fortunate for him that some people still had such curious notions – the nuns had nursed him through a grave illness the year before – but he said 'No, it is nonsense. It is only for children,' and of the new Prior who was coming, 'No doubt it is a step in his career.'

His appearance was extremely odd, for he carried himself with the stiff back of an infantryman while his loose sandals made him drag his feet in an incongruous manner, when he walked. He wore a shiny and threadbare suit of blue serge, a 'boater' straw hat, a crumpled white collar and a narrow black tie. His ankles were bare and his sandals of his own manufacture. He invariably carried an absurd little ebony cane with a dented silver crook. We went to the café together most nights but he would seldom accept a drink, saying at first that he could not drink beer when it was not iced; later I realised it was because he could not afford it himself and in this one form would not take hospitality he could not return (a peculiarly irritating form of priggishness), so to cover his pride I used to invent reasons – that a boat was expected, that Father Alcuin was better, that it was my birthday – and then he would drink the warm beer with relish and laugh loudly at whatever was said.

We talked in a laborious mixture of French and English, of neither of which languages Mr Steingler had much command; indeed he seemed to be barely intelligible in any language; his fluent Portuguese seemed to cause endless misunderstandings at the café and even his German seemed to puzzle Father Alcuin. The difficulty lay chiefly in discovering which of his many languages Mr Steingler was trying to speak. Conversation at meals was always uneasy, for Father Alcuin knew no English and only the most formal French; most of the time he and Mr Steingler would stumble along in German, occasionally explaining some obscure point in Portuguese; then, feeling that I was being left out of things, they would attempt to draw me in. Mr Steingler would suddenly bow towards me, beam, and make curious animal sounds in the roof of his mouth.

Most of us, when speaking a foreign language, make some attempt to imitate the accents of the country; heaven knows, it is usually a pitiable attempt bearing the most meagre and shadowy likeness to the true sounds, but at least it is an indication that we *are* speaking an alien tongue, a warning light to the listener to pay closer attention; a salute of formal courtesy, like the running up of the country's flag in a foreign port. Not so Mr Steingler who made no difference of any kind in his pronunciation whether he talked German or English, French or Portuguese. Moreover, he had, through prolonged denationalisation, largely forgotten from what languages his vocabulary derived, and would come out with such disconcerting questions as, 'Commons dites-vous "manquer" en French?'

As a rule Father Alcuin was too ill to eat; when he was in fever he kept to his room but in the days of intermission he usually sat at table with us, drinking a little soup. I do not think he ever liked me much or understood what I was doing in his house, but he accepted my presence without complaint as he accepted all the other hardships of Boa Vista. He used to get a little outside news from the wireless operator and retail it to us; also alarming rumours such as that the unemployed were sacking London and that an unprecedented epidemic of influenza was killing off the French like flies. Only on the subject of Freemasons did he show any violent emotion. It is possible that they had taken some sinister hand in the fiasco of 'the Company', for the organisation assumes forces in South America that would appal their respectable brothers in England.

Was it really true that the King of England was a Mason?

I replied that I thought he was.

'Is that how he became King? Did the Masons put him on the throne?'

'No, he is king by legal hereditary right.'

'Then how did the poor man fall into their power?'

It was useless to explain that English Masons were for the most part headmasters and generals with, as far as I knew, no criminal activities.

'That is what they say until they have you in their power. And the Prince of Wales, is he a Mason too? Is that why he does not marry? Do the Masons forbid it?'

I think he began to suspect me of secret Masonry after a time, in spite of my conscientious assistance at Sunday Mass.

The Church was, considering the villainy of the place, surprisingly well attended; largely I suppose because the nasal singing of the girls' school provided the only kind of entertainment of the week. These children, shepherded to their places by the nuns, were dressed up in clean muslin veils and, the wealthier of them, long white cotton gloves; they wore innumerable medals and coloured ribbons and sashes, proclaiming their different degrees of piety. They sang sugary little vernacular hymns in tremulous, whining voices. They occupied the greater part of the Church. Beside them were the elderly women in best dresses and clean stockings. What with this weekly blossoming of femininity, and the concrete architectural ornaments of the building, the candles and the artificial flowers, Sunday Mass was the nearest thing to a pretty spectacle that Boa Vista provided, and the men assembled in fair numbers to enjoy it. They did not come into the Church for that is contrary to Brazilian etiquette, but they clustered in the porch, sauntering out occasionally to smoke a cigarette. The normal male costume of the

town was a suit of artificial silk pyjamas, which many of the more
elegant had washed weekly, so that on Sundays they carried themselves with an air of great refinement and caution. Some minutes
before the Elevation they might be seen unfolding their handkerchiefs and spreading them on the bare boards of the floor; then,
when the bell rang, they would delicately kneel on one knee, rise,
shake out the handkerchief, refold it and tuck it away in the breast
pocket. This, however, was the practice only of the most pious; the
majority remained throughout propped against the walls, staring at
the napes of the girls' necks. A priest told me that when he was new
to the country he had remonstrated with the men, telling them that
this was no fashion in which to hear Mass.

'We haven't come to hear Mass,' they had replied, fingering the
revolver butts in their holsters. 'We're here to see you don't interfere
with our women.'

No other event marked the passing of the days.

In a previous travel book I once remarked that I was bored for
some days on a Congo river steamer. Not only did the reviewers
take hold of this as a suitable text for their criticism, but I received
a handful of cross letters from strangers saying, no doubt with
good sense, that if travelling bored me I had far better stay at
home and, anyway, give up writing about it; some suggested that it
was, to them, the height of adventure to drift through the rain
between featureless mangrove swamps and that it was an intolerable
injustice that I, who could afford to do so, should not provide others
with the romance I could not appreciate. So I will not repeat my
mistake. I will not say I was bored in Boa Vista but merely remark
that I found very little to occupy my time. There was an edition of
Bossuet's sermons and a few lives of the Saints in French, for me to
read; I could walk to the wireless office and learn that no news
had been heard of the Boundary Commissioner's boat; I could
visit the English-speaking blacksmith and watch him tinkering
with antiquated automatic pistols. This young man would not
come with me to the café on account of his having recently beaten
the proprietor – an act of which he was inordinately proud, though it
can have required no great courage since he was a very old man and
slightly crippled. I could give bananas to the captive monkey and

I could study the bottled worms in the laboratory; I could watch the carpenter in his rare moments of industry, sawing up lengths of plank. There was really quite a number of things for me to do, but, in spite of them all, the days seemed to pass slowly.

The blacksmith, who knew all that was going on in the town promised to tell me as soon as the Commissioner's boat was sighted, but it so happened that he forgot to do so, and I only learned from Mr Steingler, one morning after I had been six days in the Priory, that it had arrived the previous evening and was due to leave in an hour; the Commissioner was at that moment at the wireless station. I hurried off to interview him. Things might have been less difficult if Father Alcuin had been able to accompany me but it was one of the days when he was down with fever. Alone I was able to make no impression. The Commissioner was an amicable little man, in high good humour at the prospect of a few days' leave in Manaos, but he flatly refused to have me in his boat. I cannot hold it against him. Everyone in that district is a potential fugitive from justice and he knew nothing of me except my dishevelled appearance and my suspicious anxiety to get away from Boa Vista. I showed my passport and letters of credit, but he was not impressed. I besought him to cable to Georgetown for my credentials, but he pointed out that it might take a week to get an answer. I offered him large wads of greasy notes. But he was not having any. He knew too much about foreigners who appeared alone and unexplained in the middle of Amazonas; the fact of my having money made me the more sinister. He smiled, patted my shoulder, gave me a cigarette, and sharp on time left without me.

I cannot hold it against him. I do not think that the British Commissioners would have done any more for a stray Brazilian. But it was in a despondent and rather desperate mood that I heard his boat chugging away out of sight down the Rio Branco.

From then onwards my only concern was to find some other means of getting away from Boa Vista. The trade boat of which David had spoken became increasingly elusive as I tried to pin its proprietor down to any definite statement of its date of departure. He was the manager of the chief store, a low-spirited young man named Martinez. I went to see him every day to talk about it; he seemed glad of a chat but could hold out only the vaguest hopes for me. The boat had to arrive first. It should be on its way with the new Prior; when it came, there would be time enough to discuss its departure. All sorts of things had to be considered – cargo, mail, other passengers. Day after day went by until all faith I had ever cherished in the trade boat, slowly seeped away. Ordinary vexation at the delay began to give place to anxiety, for everyone in the town seemed to spend at least three days a week in fever, and I had no wish to catch it; the malaria of that district takes a peculiarly disagreeable and persistent form. It seemed to me a poor gamble to risk becoming semi-invalid for life for the dubious interest of a voyage down the Rio Branco. So I abandoned the idea of Manaos and decided to return to Guiana and visit Dadanawa.

This journey, so simple from British territory, where one was supported by the goodwill of the mission and the ranchers, presented endless difficulties from the other side. There was a large ranch, surviving from the days of 'the Company', which still belonged to the Benedictines, but with the arrival of the Prior imminent, Father Alcuin could not take the responsibility of hiring me horses. Mr Martinez said he could arrange it but days passed and no horses appeared. He found me a guide, however, in the person of a good-natured boy named Marco; he was fifteen or sixteen, in from the country, and had been hanging round the store for some weeks in search of employment; this youth, after a house-to-house enquiry lasting several days, eventually secured the hire of a horse for himself, belonging, as it turned out, to Mr Martinez and quartered at the ranch on the other side of the river. I still needed another horse – if possible two – and provisions. Mr Martinez had some tins of sweet biscuits and sardines, another shop had two tins of sausage; the nuns made bread and cheese. These would comfortably take us the three days' ride to Dadanawa. Horses were still an unsolved difficulty when help came from an unexpected quarter.

Mr Steingler had hitherto listened apathetically to my complaints, merely remarking from time to time, 'Les peuples ici sont tous bêtes, tous sauvages; il faut toujours de patience,' until one day the thought came to him that there might be something in it for him. He opened the subject cautiously, saying one evening that even if I secured a horse, it would be impossible to get a saddle; both were equally important. I agreed. He then went on to say that it so happened that he had a very good saddle himself, one that he would not readily part with to anyone, a particularly fine, new saddle of European workmanship, a rare and invaluable possession in a country like this. However, seeing my difficulty, and feeling the kinship that one European feels for another in a savage country, he was willing to part with it to me.

He took me to his room and dragged it out from under his bed. It was made on the English pattern but clearly of the most slipshod local workmanship; moreover it was of great age and in deplorable condition, half unsewn, with padding as hard as metal, every leather frayed and half worn through, several buckles missing. I asked him what he wanted for it.

Between European gentlemen, he said, it was impossible to bargain over money. He would call in a friend to make an assessment. The friend was the carpenter from the next room who was transparently in the racket up to his eyes. He turned over the saddle, praised it (embarrassing himself and Mr Steingler by inadvertently detaching another buckle while he spoke) and said that, all things considered, 20,000 *Reis* (£5) would be a moderate price. A new saddle, made on the ranches, with elaborate ornamental tooling, cost rather less than that in the country, but European gentlemen could not bargain over money. Besides I saw a possibility of advantage to myself. I accepted the assessment and then began in my turn, to point out that necessary as a saddle was, and much as I admired this particular one of Mr Steingler's, it was of very little use to me without a horse. I would buy it at his price, if he would find me a mount to put under it.

From that moment onwards Mr Steingler worked for me indefatigably. He set out there and then in his boater hat, twirling his ridiculous cane, and by evening was able to report that the Collector had the very horse for me; a beast of some age, he admitted, but immensely strong, big-boned, well-conditioned; just what was needed for savannah travelling. We went to see him. He was of much the same quality as the saddle and curiously enough, commanded exactly the same price. Presumably 20,000 *Reis* was a unit in their minds, the highest figure to which avarice could aspire. I bought him on the spot. I do not know what rake-off Mr Steingler got on the transaction, or whether he merely wished to keep in with the Collector. I preferred to be thought a mug and get away, rather than to achieve a reputation for astuteness and risk spending an unnecessary hour in Boa Vista.

That evening Mr Steingler did a further bit of business, by producing the town clerk, a venerable old man with a long white beard, who was willing to hire me a pack horse he owned in the corral on the further bank – 4,000 *Reis* for the journey to Dadanawa. I paid him and went to bed well contented with the prospect of immediate escape.

Next morning I bade farewell to Father Alcuin. The plans for my departure had been freely discussed at table for over a week, but had not penetrated the feverish trance in which the poor monk lived. He was greatly surprised, and when I handed him a donation to the house to cover my board and lodging, he woke suddenly to the fact that he had exerted himself very little on my behalf; it was then that he revealed, what before he had kept carefully hidden, that he had a wooden pack saddle which he could put at my disposal. Thus equipped and blessed I felt that I was at last on my way.

But it was not to be as easy as that; the forces of chaos were still able to harass my retreat and inflict some damaging attacks. The next two days, in fact, were slapstick farce, raised at moments to the heights of fantasy by the long-awaited appearance of the Prior.

News of his approach and imminent arrival came on the morning of the day that I had fixed for my departure. Instantly the Priory was overrun by nuns. They worked in the way nuns have, which is at the same time subhuman and superhuman; poultry and angels curiously compounded in a fluttering, clucking, purposeful scurry of devoted industry; they beat up the Prior's mattresses and dusted every crevice of his quarters, they trotted to and fro with wicker rocking chairs and clean sheets, they lined the corridor to his room with potted shrubs, put palm leaves behind all the pictures, arranged

embroidered tablecloths on every available shelf and ledge, decorated the bookcase with artificial flowers, built a triumphal arch over
the front door and engrossed programmes for a hastily organised
concert. I regretted very much that I should not be there to see his
reception.

My plans were that I should cross the river in the afternoon with
the grey cob I had bought from the Collector; see to the rounding in
of the other two horses, sleep by the corral on the further side and
start for Dadanawa first thing the next morning.

Mr Martinez had organised the crossing, for which he had hired
me a canoe and another boy, whom I was to meet with Marco at
three o'clock. At half past four they arrived; the other boy turned out
to be a child of eight or nine. Mr Martinez explained that he was
taking the place of his elder brother who had fever that day.

We carried the saddles and baggage down the bank, found the
canoe, which when loaded was dangerously low in the water. The
descent at the usual landing-place was too steep for a horse, so it was
arranged that the small boy and I should paddle to a point up stream
where the bank shelved down more gently, where Marco would
meet us with the horse. It was half past five when we reached the
place and found no sign of Marco. The sun sets at six. For half an
hour the small boy and I sat hunched in the canoe – I cramped and
fretful, he idly playful with my belongings – then we paddled back in
the darkness to the landing-place. Sundry whistlings and catcalls
ensued until presently Marco loomed up through the shadows
riding the grey. We neither spoke a word of the other's language
but by repetitions and gestures, and that telepathy which seems to
function between two people who have something of urgency to
communicate, we got to understand that the horse had taken some
catching, that Marco was quite ready to try swimming him across in
the dark, that I thought this lunacy, that the baggage was to be left
where it was, that Marco was to sling his hammock by the bank and
guard it all night, that I would come at dawn and we would cross
over then. I cannot explain how we discussed all this, but in the end
the situation was well understood. Then I hurried back to the Priory
which I had left a few hours before with so many formal thanks and
good wishes.

In my vexation I had entirely forgotten about the Prior. I now came to the refectory, ten minutes late for dinner, out of breath and wet to the knees, to find him sitting at table. He was, as it happens, in the middle of the story of his own sufferings on the way up. It was a problem of good manners of the kind that are solved so astutely on the women's pages of the Sunday papers. What should I do? It was clearly impossible to escape unobserved, for the Prior had already fixed me with a look of marked aversion. I could not slip into a chair with a murmured apology for my lateness, because some explanation of my reappearance was due to Father Alcuin, and of my existence to my new host, the Prior. There was nothing for it but to interrupt the Prior's story with one of my own. He did not take it too kindly. Father Alcuin attempted to help me out, explaining rather lamely that I was an Englishman who had waited here on the way to Manaos.

Then what was I doing attempting to cross the Rio Branco in the dark? the Prior demanded sternly.

I said I was on my way to Dadanawa.

'But Dadanawa is nowhere near Manaos.'

Clearly the whole thing seemed to him highly unsatisfactory and suspicious. However, with the charity of his Order he bade me sit down. The idiot boy removed the soup plates and the Prior resumed his story. In honour of his arrival a fish course had been added to the dinner; nothing could have been less fortunate for he had lived on fish for the last ten days and on that particular sort of coarse and tasteless fish that was now offered him. He glared at it resentfully over his spectacles and ordered it to be removed. Mr Steingler watched it go with evident distress.

The Prior was no doubt a very good man, but he did not add to the ease of the refectory. He was thoroughly exhausted by his journey and in no mood to bustle off to the nuns' concert. He had already formed a low opinion of Mr Steingler and my arrival confirmed him in his general disapproval. He was there on a mission of reorganisation and Mr Steingler and myself were obviously the kind of thing that had to be investigated and cleaned up. He finished his narration of delays and discomforts, took a dislike against the pudding, and before Mr Steingler had nearly finished his first helping, rose to recite an immensely long grace. Then with hostile adieux, stumped away grumbling to the celebrations at the school.

Next day at dawn I saw him on his way to Mass and he was more amicable. I bade him good-bye with renewed thanks and went down to the river. The small boy and Marco were there; the baggage was intact; after an hour's perilous and exhausting work we got the canoe and the horse across to the other side; the child paddled back and I settled down to wait until Marco had collected the other horses. The pack horse was easily identified by some *vaqueiros* who were waiting there. He was a wretched creature, down in the pasterns, but our baggage was very light and it seemed probable that he would get it to Dadanawa. Mr Martinez's horse could not be found. After two hours Marco returned, smiling and shrugging and shaking his head.

Back to Boa Vista once more. We had to wait until noon for a canoe. I arrived at the Priory once more, a good quarter of an hour late for luncheon. The Prior's doubts of my honesty became doubts of my sanity. Once more I made my adieux, repeating the same thanks with increased apologies. Mr Martinez, at last roused to activity, decided to accompany me himself to the other side and find the horse. He issued a number of peremptory orders which were lethargically obeyed. His motor launch was brought up, four or five men recruited, and a formidable expedition set out. After some hours, the horse was discovered straying some miles distant, lassoed and led in. Then a further disaster occurred. A large sow which had been nosing round the baggage for some time discovered a way in to the kit bag and ate the whole of the bread and cheese on which I had been counting as my main sustenance in the next few days.

Back to Boa Vista; back to the Priory, just as they were finishing dinner. The Prior now regarded me with undisguised despair. I was able, however, to buy another loaf and more cheese from the convent. Next morning, without further contact with my hosts, I slipped out of the Priory and left Boa Vista for the last time in Mr Martinez's motor launch.

CHAPTER 6

Leaving Boa Vista – change of route – lost on the savannah – pleasures of travelling – change of route – Karasabai – Tipuru.

THERE WAS A fringe of palm about a mile from the corral, which in floodtime marked the river's edge, but before we had reached it the red roofs of Boa Vista were already out of view. Looking back, and finding the town invisible, I felt myself freed from the dead weight that I had been carrying about with me all the blank, fourteen days of my sojourn, but the gaiety and inward radiance were of short duration, for the mist of frustration which had enveloped all my dealings with the place still hung about us and followed us like the clouds of cabouri fly for the whole of that journey.

The horses had looked discouraging from the start but I had learned, since the first day at Takama, to expect ill-looking animals and even to get fair service from them. These, however, were well below the second-class of savannah horses. The best of them was the grey cob I had bought from the Collector; he was old and lazy and disposed to lie down in protest when the saddle was put on his back, but he was in reasonable working condition. Later he developed a gall high on his back, but we were able to improvise a rope crupper, padded with rag under the tail, which held the saddle back from the place, so that sometimes ridden and sometimes loaded with the pack, he alone finished the journey with us. Marco's horse was young and weak and had not been out at grass long enough since his last bout of work, but the boy was light and rode him easily, so that at a slow pace he was good for some days. The town clerk's pack horse was hopeless. How hopeless we did not realise until at the fifth mile he went dead lame in the off fore. There was now no question of taking him to Dadanawa, the only problem was whether he could make the nearest ranch. We were more than half-way, so that it would have been useless to turn back.

We lightened his pack to a negligible weight, dividing it between our two mounts (mine of course lying down in protest) and at walking pace dragged him painfully on across the savannah. We passed no water that day; every creek was a gulley of cracked mud; although we covered less than ten miles we took over seven hours in doing it.

It would be tedious to describe the next two days in detail. Our first halt was at a ranch where all the men were away on a round-up except an aged, one-eyed *vaqueiro*. Although only a few miles from Boa Vista, the people seemed of a different race. A stout lady received us hospitably and three or four daughters saw to our needs, bringing out coffee and chairs, and giggling discreetly at us from the shadows. Marco had none of the debonair grace of David. He would hang back diffidently, afraid to enter and, since I had no means of communicating with them, my intercourse with our various hosts and hostesses was limited to smiles and bows. He was able to secure the loan of a horse, however, to replace the lame pack horse which we turned into their corral to await his return. It took him and the one-eyed man three hours to find it so that we had already lost the good hours of the morning before we resumed our travels. Altogether we had lost a full day's stage in the first twenty-four hours. This was a serious matter as we were carrying a minimum of supplies and the bread speedily became uneatable, carried, as it was, in a canvas bag under the full blaze of the sun. Another thirsty, monotonous day brought us to a little out-station where a bearded man, bare to the waist but heavily armed, was cooking some fresh pork. We dined with him and slung our hammocks outside his hut. Next day in another six or seven hours we reached a ranch where a man with a face like El Greco's St Ignatius was making a pair of leggings. Martinez's horse was by now good for very little and this was our last chance of getting a remount before Dadanawa. I saw Marco tackling him on the question and after long discussion, it was evident that the request was being refused. However he brought us luncheon – the inevitable *farine* and *tasso* – and seemed to be genial enough. I expressed admiration of his leather work with various grimaces and nods. We had only a handful of biscuits left from our stores and one tin of sausage. I opened the tin, turned it out on a plate and offered it to our host. He refused, but while I ate I noticed that he studied the plate with keen interest. I renewed the offer and this time he leant across, cut off a piece with his clasp knife and tasted it suspiciously. He liked it and finished the plate. Those sausages won us a horse, for after the meal he beckoned to Marco and I saw with delight that he had taken a lasso off its peg in the wall of the house. They went out together and returned in half an hour with a sturdy little skewbald mare. Whenever we made a change of horses I took the best, gave Marco the second and put the pack, which now weighed barely sixty pounds, on to the most tired – this was by now the Collector's grey. With renewed vigour we set out again and late in the afternoon forded the Takutu and rode up on to British soil, at a place where a large creek flowed out.

At sunset we found an Indian hut. If things had gone better we should have been already at Dadanawa, but there was two days' ride still before us. We had a few dusty biscuits and the vague hope of finding provisions among the Indians on the way. The house where we camped was empty of food except for a little sour milk and *farine*. It was no mere fastidious distaste that kept me from eating *farine*; I had found on the journey to Boa Vista that it made me ill; accordingly I ate the last of the biscuits and went to bed hungry and slightly anxious for the future.

Hope and good spirits returned at dawn next day. There had been no light in the hut the evening before so that I had not been able to look at the map or attempt to fix our position. Now I began to take in our surroundings. Neither the ford was marked nor any of the ranches on the Brazilian side; all I had to go by was the position of the creek, and two large groups of bush-clad hills that lay immediately to the east of us. It came to me that these must be the Kanuku Mountains and the Kusads; our position lay midway between them, and the creek beside which we were camped must be the substantial river marked on the map as the Sauriwau. I verified this by asking the Indian, pointing to the creek and saying 'Sauriwau?' He nodded emphatically. In that case the reason was clear why we had taken so long in reaching the Takutu, for instead of striking dead east from Boa Vista in the direct line for Dadanawa, we had turned north and were a good forty miles out of our way. The cattle trail to Dadanawa, as marked on the map, ran by the

Sauriwau and this no doubt explained Marco's divagation. On these calculations we were only twenty miles from St Ignatius. I had no particular reason for going to Dadanawa except the desire to visit the manager whom I had greatly liked in Georgetown and the curiosity of seeing the home in which old Melville had reigned. In our present position of short provisions and two exhausted horses, the obvious course was to make straight for my old host at St Ignatius. I was unable to explain my reasoning to Marco and the map meant nothing to him, but by pointing north and saying 'Ignatio' and 'Bon Success' I got him to understand the change of plan. He was puzzled but acquiescent, so leaving him to manage the pack, I set out ahead on the fresh horse, a clearly marked trail before me, the knowledge that it was impossible to miss the way if I kept between the Takutu and the Kanuku Mountains, and the confident expectation of surprising Father Mather at his twelve o'clock breakfast.

The air was clear and cool and the horse stepped out vigorously. As I gradually rounded the spur of the hills on my right I watched them assume the contour that I seemed to know so well; the high dark line that I had seen day after day from St Ignatius. After an hour or so the path I was following narrowed to a single line and finally disappeared, but this did not greatly worry me. I knew my direction and sooner or later I should come upon the main trail once more, so I rode on from half past six until half past eleven without much concern; then I began to feel it was time I came upon some familiar landmarks. There was a village which Father Mather and I had visited on foot, that could not be far away. Some Indian huts, suddenly emerging from the screen of sand-paper trees, raised my hopes but when I approached them I realised they were not those I expected. I rode up to one of them and a few women scuttled inside at my approach. I tried to question them, pointing in the direction I was going and saying 'Ignatius' and 'Bon Success', but could get no indication of answer. At another hut a man leapt on his horse and cantered away at my approach. I rode on with some misgivings.

A line of hills had appeared on the horizon in front of me, presumably the Pakaraimas, and I reflected that I had never known them appear so close. The sun was now well up and the heat was overpowering; the horse had lost his freshness and could not be got out of a walk; the ground on all sides was the cruellest – dried marshland broken into hard hummocks – with no sign of a path anywhere; I had had no meal for twenty-four hours and felt suddenly dizzy. My fear was that I had ridden past the mission and should turn back south-west to find it. Marco, who had everything with him including my hammock, was some miles behind. It is easy in that district to pass within quarter of a mile of someone and not see him. Since I was off the trail there was no probability of his picking me up if I stopped to wait.

The horse could go no further so I dismounted and led him. The only reasonable plan seemed to be to make for the river which must lie somewhere to my left; there at least we could get water and there, if anywhere, would be the landmarks I needed. So very painfully and unsteadily we began walking across the baked sedge. The horse pulled back from the halter and I was obliged to remount; he stumbled on, utterly beaten. It was one of the low spots of the journey. I had been given a medal of St Christopher before I left London. I felt that now, if ever, was the moment to invoke supernatural assistance. And it came. At that moment we reached water – a broad creek flowing east to west. When we had both drunk we started out again, slightly revivified, down stream; and there the real miracle occurred in the appearance of an Indian hut standing among palm trees a hundred yards in front. Outside was an old Wapishiana saddling an ox. I came up to him and made signs that I wanted to eat. 'Good morning,' he said. 'You hungry? Come inside, please.'

A child unsaddled the horse and took him down to water. I entered and sat on the Indian's hammock. Presently his wife brought me cassava bread, three eggs and half a roast bird about the size of a grouse. At first I was too exhausted to be surprised at my reception. After I had eaten all I was offered my mind felt clearer. The old man came in and said, 'Where you going?'

'St Ignatius.'

'Me going that way too. Going Bon Success to see Mr Teddy. Me work for Mr Teddy's father. Taking bwi (ox) there this afternoon.'

'Is it far?'

'Not far. Get there to-morrow.'

Then it began to break in on me that I was far further astray than I had thought. I still did not understand how. I pointed to the hills I had passed.

'But those are the Kanukus.'

'No, no, those Kanukus,' and he pointed to the blue line of mountains on the horizon ahead of me.

But I was too tired to discuss the question further. I lay back in the old man's hammock and shut my eyes, and it was then, in the hour's rest I took, half awake and wholly exhausted, that I slowly turned over in my mind what had happened and realised that an hour before I had been in serious danger of being lost and that when I could go no further four fortunate events had coincided in a way that seemed unlikely to recur often on the normal theory of probability; one, that I had found a house at all at that particular spot in a sparsely inhabited region, secondly that it belonged to an Indian who understood English, thirdly that he should have food in his house,[1] and fourthly and oddest of all that he should be going on the same road as I, on the same day – a journey which he probably did not make twice in five years.

The Problem may be stated mathematically thus: *Suppose that this particular district is crossed, on an average, by two strangers a year; one in every two hundred Indians knows some English; one in every fifty Indian houses possesses surplus food; most Indians go to Bon Success once in every five years; there is one Indian house every fifteen miles; on February 21st, 1933, a stranger's horse gave out within quarter of a mile of an Indian house, whose owner spoke English, had food, and was that day setting out for Bon Success. When is this likely to recur?* (supposing for the sake of the calculation that all strangers' horses give out at some stage of the journey). As I see it there is a $1:182.5$ chance that there will be a traveller on any given day; $1:5,475$ chance that his horse will stop within quarter of a mile, either side of a house; a $1:1,095,000$ chance that the particular inhabitant will speak English; a $1:54,750,000$ chance that he will

[1] A state surprisingly uncommon. Indians usually eat all they have as soon as they get it.

also have food – and so on. But I am no mathematician, and possibly the question is not as simple as it looks. Anyway, I prefer to regard the incident as a benevolent intervention of St Christopher's.

We set out at three that afternoon, the old Indian leading on his ox. He had with him a small boy who in spite of their disparity of age, was apparently his son. This child rode my horse, who now refreshed, seemed well able to carry him. I was more than once humiliated to observe what far better value the Indians got from their horses than I could; it was not due solely to their slighter weight, but to the way they rode, sitting forward, balanced on the fork of their legs, swaying with each step, bare heels gently drumming the flanks, the leathers – or more often the loops of rope – let down to the full stretch – and only the great toe hooked into the stirrup. Probably my stolid, arm-chair English style of riding took more out of the animals than my weight and my heavy boots. In this case the child sat bare-back and the horse trotted along beside us as gaily as if he had been following free. I rode the little mare that had been intended for the boy.

In this fashion we struck up a fair pace to the north-east across thick grass land and presently came to the trail I had lost earlier in the day. Towards sunset we came to a belt of palm-trees, a creek, and beyond them a deserted house, and there astride the ruinous roof and signalling ecstatically to us, was Marco. Up till then, for no very good reason, I had rather disliked the youth; now his genuine delight at my reappearance and the way in which he manifested it, seizing both my hands and grinning all over his ugly little face, established a cordiality which, though it could not develop greatly, owing to my ignorance of Portuguese, persisted until he bade me farewell some days later, laden with the preposterous purchases for which he had exchanged his wages at Mr Figuiredo's. We made another rearrangement by which the Indian took my grey and put the packs on to his ox, and then rode on together until about two hours after dark when we reached the Sauriwau where I had supposed us to be camping the night before. (Incidentally the name on the map appeared to be wrong for everyone spoke of it as Sawari Wau.[1]) There was a large village here, I learned later; in the darkness we could see only one campfire. The inhabitants came out to greet us but they had no food for us or accommodation so we camped in the open and set out again before dawn, without dinner or breakfast.

That day we followed the trail round the foot of the Kanuku Mountains which I had thought myself to be on the day before. By noon we reached Mr Gore's ranch. He was away but his Indian wife gave us food of which I was by then in some need, and after resting there for the full heat of the afternoon, reached St Ignatius before dark. The Indian and his son took payment for their help in the form of red cotton, fish hooks, a knife, a necklace and a highly coloured celluloid comb, and rode on to Bon Success.

Father Keary was at the mission, revictualling for another tour. He was a tall, ex-army chaplain, with the eyes of a visionary, a large grizzled beard, an Irish brogue, a buoyant and hilarious manner. He set off towards the hills on the day after my arrival.

I stayed on with Father Mather, resting, reading Dickens, writing letters to England, all of which were delivered several weeks after my own return, and making plans for departure. I was reluctant to go back to the coast by my old route, both because it is always tedious to retrace one's steps and because I felt I had seen too much of horses and the cattle trail and not enough of the bush and the rivers, but the objections to every alternative seemed so cogent, that laziness had almost impelled me to do so, when Teddy Melville passed by with the report that owing to disease in the savannah, an embargo had been placed on all animals crossing at Kurupukari. I should have to go by foot from there to the Berbice. That decided me; if I had to walk, I would walk in a more interesting direction. There was a line over the Pakaraima Mountains to a village called Kurikabaru which was the furthest point of the mission itinerary. Father Mather had once made the journey and Father Keary went there annually.

1 The greater number of the Indian names on the map are incorrect, largely owing to the explorers having employed guides from tribes unfamiliar with the districts they were crossing. Also in many cases to misread notes. Even the famous Kaieteur falls owe their name to a clerical error. It should be Kaieteuk, the k and r being similar in the handwriting of Mr Barrington Brown who discovered them. I have adopted the prevalent usages throughout.

From Kurikabaru it was no great distance to the Upper Potaro where Mr Winter whom I had met in Georgetown, was working for diamonds; his claim was the furthest point of penetration from the Essequibo. The intervening district was crossed by the Roraima line, up which the Boundary Commission had had their stores carried the previous year, so that the trail was bound to be still easily traceable. Moreover it was the route followed by the Clementis on their journey some years back which was described and roughly mapped in a copy of the *Geographical Journal*. One could take a horse and pack bullock for the first four days from St Ignatius; after that it would not be difficult to recruit droghers from village to village.

I could have done nothing without Father Mather, but with his help everything became smooth. It took some time, however, to make preparations, a guide had to be procured, animals brought in, stores packed; it was ten days before I was again on the move.

During this placid interlude it was inevitable that I should often reflect on the pains and compensations of the sort of life I was living, and was going to live for some weeks more, and to contrast them with the things that are written and spoken about it. There is room for a good deal of debunking of the subject. I do not mean of the delight of travel. That is a different question altogether for it is a delight just as incommunicable as the love of home. I mean the opinion which one frequently meets that the greatest physical and mental well-being can be attained only in the wild parts of the world. We have all been shaken by it at one time or another. Perhaps we have been discussing architecture when a Voice, as though from another world, has broken in with, 'Well the finest roof I ever want to see is my own tarpaulin, pitched in the bush beside my own camp-fire, and the knowledge that there's not another human habitation within a hundred miles of it'; or discussing food, and the Voice has said, 'I never enjoy anything so much as sitting down after a twenty-mile trek to a billy-can full of cocoa and a freshly killed piece of hartebeest cooked in an old tobacco tin.' In an instant the conversation is destroyed; the little restaurant in the Dordogne, about which you were going to speak so lyrically, is left unsung, and in the awkward silence such interruptions cause, every heart begins to sink slightly and the suspicion grows whether perhaps all our ideas of good living are not a delusion, and that perhaps these decisive people from the desert *do* really know more than we about our own business.

Well I have spent long enough time in the wilds to call that particular bluff. There are a hundred excellent reasons for rough travelling, but good living is not one of them.

Lying at ease in the gallery at St Ignatius I began to tabulate some of the fallacies thus put forward.

For instance, *that one felt free*; on the contrary there seemed no limit to the number of restrictions with which the 'open life' hampered one. Every personal possession became an encumbrance to be weighed and considered, as so many more pounds to transport; like a snowball growing into an avalanche the difficulties accumulated; additional baggage meant additional labour, which in its turn required more rations and more labour to carry the rations. As for freedom of movement, there were before me at the moment two directions only in which it was possible to travel with any hope of arriving at a destination.

That one was untrammelled by convention; I have never understood this, for I seem to know quite a variety of people, of all kinds of interests and degrees of wealth, and none of them seems burdened by these conventions of civilisation one hears so much about. If the cliché refers merely to personal appearance, is it really more onerous to wear a bowler hat than a topee, to shave in the morning than to spend half an hour, every evening, picking ticks off one's body? The toilet of the tropics with all its hygienic precautions is every bit as elaborate as dressing for dinner. Or if it is the strain of social intercourse, surely it is easier to remember the few rules of conduct in which one has been trained from the nursery, than to adapt oneself to the unpredictable politenesses, the often nauseating hospitality of savages?

That one eats with a gay appetite and sleeps with the imperturbable ease of infancy. Nonsense. Of course after my Brazilian crossing I fell with particular relish on the bread and marmalade and eggs and fresh beef of the mission, but these things are always delicious everywhere. However hungry I was I found it difficult to swallow and impossible to digest the *farine* and *tasso* of the ranches. If anything, hunger makes one's sense of taste all the keener, so that one finds things disagreeable which one would at other times accept. It is worth noticing that children, the only people in civilisation who are constantly hungry, are also the most fastidious and can only under the heaviest compulsion be made to eat things they dislike. There was only one commodity which I found enjoyable in camp which I should not normally have liked; strong, very sweet tea, made with condensed milk. As for sleep, I scarcely had a single good night in the open; exhaustion does not necessarily make for sleepiness; with one's whole body on fire with insect bites, one's face above the blanket cold in the wind, incessant animal noises on all sides, it was exceptional if one got two hours' unconsciousness on end.

I noted these down at the time, together with other fallacies, intending to make an article of them, but later I thought that perhaps I was stalking a tree and that fewer people than I supposed were taken in by that kind of boasting; and later I fell to wondering whether there were any pleasures I had found in that country which I had missed in Europe, and decided that there were two. The first was washing; not that I do not wash in Europe or that I find it distasteful, but that the mild pleasure derived from one's warm bath before dinner at home differs in kind rather than degree from the exquisite almost ecstatic experience of washing in the tropics after a long day's journey; it was as keen a physical sensation as I have ever known, excluding nothing, to sit on a tacuba across a fast-flowing mountain creek, dabble one's legs knee deep and pour calabash after calabash of cellar-cool water over one's head and shoulders, to lie full length on the polished rocks and let the stream flow over one, eddying and cascading; even to write about it brings back a faint tremor of that full exultation, the ripple and splash of the water, the sharp tang of the germicidal soap. It was a pleasure that was renewed nearly every day; a thing to remember and aspire towards, in the blind heat and dryness and disappointment of noon.

The other pleasure I discovered, oddly enough, was reading; or rather rediscovered, for I seem to recall having experienced some pleasure in this occupation as a child. But never since; I have read numerous books for various reasons – to acquire information; out of curiosity to see what they were like; out of politeness because

I knew the author; I have dipped into most best-sellers to make up
my mind whether they were justly or unjustly successful, and as soon
as I knew, I have put them aside; I have raced through detective
stories because the problems they set leave an itch for completion,
an instinct of the kind that makes one wish to put things straight on
the chimney-piece of a strange house; I have read books because
I was being paid to review them, but I had not for ten years read
a book for the mere pleasure of the process. At Father Mather's
I began to read with this motive and by good chance the books he
had were just those which were meant to be read in that way and
when I left him I took away a copy of *Nicholas Nickleby* and read it
with avid relish during the ensuing journey, bit by bit while the light
lasted, grudging the night every hour of her splendour and the day
its toil, which kept me from this new and exciting hobby.

Alas, both these pleasures have eluded me since I came back to
Europe. I have read several books, for the old reasons and in the old
way; I have taken numberless baths of all temperatures; but the
rapture is gone, irrecapturable, except by great effort and at a long
distance.

A guide was eventually found for me in one of the near-by
villages; a plump, docile Macushi named Eusebio, who pretended
to a greater knowledge of English than he actually had and
answered 'Yes' to everything whether he had understood or not.
He was remarkable for having no personal possessions of any sort,
and his first act was to borrow a large part of his wages in advance to
fit himself out with clothes, cup, plate, knife, tobacco, and a grey felt
hat for the journey.

He was a soft young man and he did not travel well, but
I promised him that, if he gave satisfaction, I would take him to
Georgetown with me and this hope kept him going through the
rough places.

Tireless to the last in his kindness, Father Mather supplied me
with provisions from his own stores and supervised my packing,
making coverings for the more perishable things, performing prodigies of dexterity with elastic bands and waterproof wrapping;
I obtained *farine* and dried meat for the droghers' rations from

Figuiredo; also gunpowder, caps and shot to supplement my Woolworth trinkets in the more remote villages where money does not
run; also a curious substance in a flat tin, labelled Marmalade, which
when opened proved to be a purplish glucose jelly of most disagreeable nature. David rounded up a pack ox and a strong little horse
for the first days of the journey. Everything was ready by March 4th
and early on the 5th we set out for Pirosha under an agreeably
cloudy sky.

The trail was clear enough and after giving a lead to the ox across
the Mocu-Mocu creek, I rode on ahead, leaving Eusebio to follow at
his own pace, which was leisurely and irregular, a poor two miles an
hour, for the animal lumbered from side to side, browsing as he
went.

The first two stages were along the way I had come, through
Mr Hart's and Daguar's ranches, and should have been without
incident had I not again gone astray and in this way involved myself
in the heaviest day's ride I had yet made. It was the old nursery
trouble of being 'too clever by half'. I had left soon after seven
and by twelve should have been within a short distance of Hart's,
when there was a fork in the trail, on the far side of a creek; two
equally prominent tracks diverging. My natural inclination would
have been to take the one on the left, and I should have been right;
false ingenuity, however, supervened, for in the bed of the creek
there were marks of motor-tyres. I knew that Mr Hart's was the
only car in the district so I cast round and eventually picked up the
tracks again on the right-hand road. I followed the tyres mile
after mile, surprised at the length of the journey but confident
that in the end they would lead me to the ranch; there were
frequent divisions in the way and I began to enjoy the game of
finding the faint impress of the treads in the hard earth, and to
applaud my own perception. At two o'clock thatched roofs came
into sight, but they were not those of the ranch; instead was a little
Macushi village with the trail leading through it and beyond to the
horizon.

The headman came out to meet me. He knew no English and
had no food, but he was able to point out my way to me. I rested for
half an hour, and to entertain me, he produced a basket full of

carefully folded spills of paper. These – unreadable, of course, to him – were all the documents that had come to the village from time to time – marriage licences from passing missionaries, a writ to some-one to appear at court at Anai, several gun licences and an illumi-nated confirmation card – all charms of mysterious potency, paternally stored away in the eaves of his hut.

I rode back, at an acute angle from the way I had come, and finally reached Hart's at half past five; the little horse which had covered a good forty miles, trotted bravely to the last. I had supposed that Eusebio would be there before me and there might be some concern at my disappearance, but the Harts had seen nothing of him. While I was gratefully eating cheese and drinking tea they explained the mistake I had made. I had been within a mile of the house when I had followed the car tracks, made in a recent direct journey with Government stores between Yupukarri and Bon Success.

Eusebio turned up at eight o'clock, having delayed on the road to cook and devour an armadillo which he had caught.

I thought that the horse could do with a day's rest, so sent Eusebio ahead to Daguar's and spent another night at Hart's. Mr Hart was at home this time, a kindly, middle-aged American of wide experience, whose heart was more in woodwork than in cattle. In the evening I participated in a scene of curiously patri-archal piety; Mr Hart assembled the whole household, including sleepy children, the Creole governess like Josephine Baker, and the old Wapishiana grandmother, and together we walked up and down in the moonlight, loudly reciting the rosary; Mr Hart calling on each of us in turn to lead the devotions. It was a performance which in normal surroundings would have paralysed me with shyness, but here it was not embarrassing, for the oddness of the company and the moonlit landscape made the occurrence half real and impersonal.

After Daguar's, which I reached without misadventure at noon the next day, the journey entered on another phase. So far it had been increasingly strange and slightly more adventurous each week. The road I was now starting on promised to be by far the most interesting. It ran, very roughly, parallel with the Ireng, along the west of the Pakaraima Mountains, passing first through fairly well-populated Macushi country, then through an uninhabited hinterland, and then to the villages of the Patamonas; then, turning east there was another empty stretch until I should strike Mr Winter's camp, who was prospecting somewhere in the upper Potaro district. Except Father Keary, on his annual round, no European or coast Creoles ever normally went into this country. A fair number of the men worked or had worked from time to time for Europeans, either collecting ballata or, less commonly, acting as droghers, but the villages themselves were untouched by civilisation except at second or third hand. The line of communication to Roraima temporarily established by the Boundary Commission a year before, had provided more work than usual and in consequence there was a momentary glut of cheap hardware and Japanese cotton which gave some appearance of sophistication, but these perishable luxuries are no doubt already disappearing and the communities reverting to their primitive character which was only very superficially disturbed.

Daguar was able to find me a mounted Indian to act as guide, so I sent Eusebio off that day, to sleep on the road and meet me at Karasabai, the first village.

I had ridden to Daguar's with Teddy Melville who was on his way from Hart's to Anai. We stopped on the way at a ranch I had always thought of as Marie Louise's, but which I found was really Manoel Luiz's; this Brazilian negro had at a great age recently married a Portuguese girl from Georgetown and had, in her honour, repainted the front of his house so that it resembled a circus booth, with Union Jacks, heads of oxen and ill-counterfeited marble. He urged us to stay to breakfast, but I remembered the cooking at Daguar's and insisted on going on, where we were rewarded with fresh pork stewed in milk. We rested, in some discomfort from cabouri flies, until, with nightfall, they disappeared. Next day the guide and I set out for the hills.

From now onwards the Government map, which had at the best of times been barely adequate, became quite without value, nothing on it except the course of the Ireng having any relation to the lie of the country. The trail wound in and out through belts of bush, across dry creeks, round patches of swamp, and up narrow hill passes; its general direction was north-east for the first ten miles or so and then, sharply turning, north-west for another ten. At first I was fired with the ambition of making a compass traverse of the route and stopped to note every change of direction and topographical feature, and to check our ascent with an aneroid, but I found the conditions so diverse and the way so intricate that I abandoned the project after a day or two. While it lasted, however, the practice made me observant of the country as I had not been before and heightened my enjoyment of the change of scenery. That, now I advert to it, should certainly be included with Washing and Reading as one of the delights of this journey. In Europe, with modern communications, you take it as a matter of course as you accept the shifting of canvas trees between the acts of a pantomime; you fall into a doze, while monotonous fields of stubble swim past the carriage window, and wake up amid lakes and mountains, or else you travel by aeroplane when all scenery is meaningless as a page from an atlas, as flat and as conventionally coloured, while between you and it lie fathoms of air and sunlight. But here every change was achieved by effort. I have already remarked on the tartarean plunge on entering the forest and of the bird-like sense of liberation on leaving it. Now I found myself in the greatest transition of all, the emergence from monotony to change. For weeks I had seen nothing but savannah, sometimes a horizon of hills further away or nearer, but day after day the same road across absolutely flat plain, the same dun dapple of earth and grass, the whiter ruts of the cattle trail, the coffering of dried sedge, squat sand-paper trees or tattered spinsterish palms. From now onwards the way was kaleidoscopic. Each of the numberless turns of the path, each emergence from bush, disclosed a new spectacle, sometimes a dozen hilltops like the domes of Istanbul, sometimes a bare precipice of grass, a wooded channel, a rocky ascent, a black wall of forest, a grassy saucer sheltering a cluster of huts, a horseshoe of odd, conical hills, the glitter and black shadow of water as a loop of Ireng appeared suddenly at one's feet, or a mountain stream tumbling to join it in a cataract over the smooth rocks – all negligible enough from a train window, but stimulating at a time when some encouragement was particularly valuable to get one on from one point to the next.

Except for one sharp ascent among rocks and loose pebbles where we dismounted and led our horses, we were able to ride all the way from Daguar's to Karasabai, making good time. In something less than four hours we came to a spur from which we could see a wide panorama of hill country, the Ireng, dark and menacing, far away to the left, and immediately below us to the right the village of Karasabai. We crossed the Yurore creek and arrived just as Eusebio was unsaddling the pack ox. The village stood half-way up a large grass-covered valley lying north and south, encircled on three sides by high hills – a stadium more than an amphitheatre, for it ran back to some depth. To the north the hills were covered in bush, on the other sides bare. There were ten huts together and three roofs visible at a distance; one house stood on piles with a ladder leading to its door, the others were square, single-roomed structures of wattle and thatch of the sort I had seen all over the savannah. Eusebio had already found quarters for us in one of them; there was a little corral with a wooden paling enclosing some cows and half a dozen calves; there was also a long mud house, kept empty and used as a church when Father Keary visited the place. Eusebio told me that he was on the same road as us, had slept there the night before, and that we should meet him at Tipuru the next day.

The chief man of the place offered me formal hospitality in the shape of *cassiri* in a tin bowl of European manufacture. I put it to my lips and passed it on to Eusebio. *Cassiri* is the drink of the country from time immemorial.[1] (It is curious how propagandists always talk as though alcohol had been introduced to the backward races by unprincipled traders and imperialists, referring ironically to the joint import of gin and hymn-books. In point of fact almost every race had discovered it for themselves, centuries before European explorers appeared on the scene at all and used it on a large scale for frequent, prolonged orgies, beside which the most ambitious American parties appear austerely temperate.) It is made from sweet cassava roots, chewed up by the elder members of the community

---

1 There is also another similar drink named Piwari.

and spat into a bowl. The saliva starts fermentation, and the result is a thick, pinkish liquor of mildly intoxicating property. I was a little sceptical about the orgiastic nature of the ceremonial *cassiri* parties, until I saw the vat in which it is kept. There is one or more in every village, according to its size. There were two at Karasabai in the back of the hut where we were quartered and I took them at first to be boats, for they consisted – like most of the craft on those rivers – of entire tree trunks hollowed out. Before a party – and Father Keary told me with regret that the tendency was for the parties to become more frequent – the whole village chews and spits indefatigably, until the vat or vats are completely full. Then after the fermentation has been under way for some time, they all assemble and drink the entire quantity. It usually takes some days, beginning sombrely like all Indian functions, warming up to dancing and courtship, and ending with the whole village insensibly drunk.

The people crowded out to greet us, one by one presenting themselves and shaking hands with shy manners and downcast eyes; then they formed a close circle and stared from noon until sunset without intermission. When one looked directly at them they looked away, but immediately resumed their emotionless scrutiny when one was occupied elsewhere. They were not hostile or amused or, it seemed, particularly observant; they stared as yokels stare over gates. They watched every object unpacked without apparent curiosity; when I left the open hut none of them attempted to touch the baggage or play with it as they would have done in most parts of Africa. The only thing which moved them was my camera from which they fled in alarm. They were all unattractive, squat and dingy, with none of the grace one expects in savages. They seemed to have singularly little interest in personal adornment. Their hair was lank and ragged with none of the ochre powder, bone combs and skewers, the high architectural coiffes, poodle-like shavings beloved by the African. A few had lines and spots of blue tattooing on the face, but none of the intricate incised and embossed ornament, the monstrous structural operations to nose, lips and ears, the backs and breasts scarred and pitted in pattern like Venetian leather work, that makes negro beauty so formidable to a new-comer. Most of them had a hole pierced in the lower lip, stuck with a quill or piece of wood. Each had a necklace on which was strung his *bena* (a charm consisting usually of some part of an animal – tooth or bone), the religious medal he was given at baptism and a miscellaneous collection of things that had taken his or her fancy – nuts, teeth, beads, buttons, coins, gun-caps; the women had the lower part of the leg, below the knee and above the ankle, tightly bandaged with fibre or beads, to swell out the calf, which is regarded as a centre of attraction in this country as are the breasts in Europe, the feet in China, and the buttocks in most parts of Africa. A few of the men, those that had recently been out to work, wore shorts and vests but most of them were naked except for the *lap*, a red cotton loin cloth; the women, without exception, had soiled, colourless dresses.

These I learned were only worn in the presence of strangers. In her own village – which practically means her family, for the community is inextricably inter-related – an Indian woman goes naked except for a little bead apron six or seven inches square. Often when approaching a village I used to see the women scurry into their houses and emerge clothed; only very rarely did they appear in front of me or the droghers – for an Indian from another tribe or even another village is a stranger every bit as alarming as a white man – without their dresses and when they did so it was because they were poor and had no stuff, not because they were less modest. Still less was it because they were less Christianised.

That is another complaint of propagandists, that the Christian missionaries teach the natives to be ashamed of their bodies and by distributing petticoats, deprive them of all the moral and hygienic advantages of nudism. There may be some truth in this legend somewhere. I have read accounts of the activities of American Baptists in the South Seas that seem to support it, but as far as my personal experience goes I have found the reverse to be true. I have talked to Dutch, French, German and English missionaries, Protestant and Catholic, in widely different parts of the world and found them either indifferent or mildly opposed to the clothing of their converts. If they give them clothes it is because they know it is the most welcome present they can offer, for the truth is, not that dresses are forced upon them, but that the moment they have set eyes on a fully dressed woman most savages will as readily give their love to the trader as their souls to the missionary in order to imitate her; if petticoats are going at the mission house, she will be baptised, confirmed, taught the story of Noah's Ark or the ten commandments, to get one, for clothing appeals equally to the two usually contradictory instincts of modesty and ostentation. In the case of the Guiana Indians, with exception of those like the hostess at Daguar's who have become definitely civilised, the motive seems to be entirely modesty. They have a shrinking from anything that makes them obtrusive. They wore their grubby linen without any of the swagger and provocation of a negress, for it was no adornment, merely a shield between them and an alien world.

Eusebio reported that there were no supplies to be got in the village, Father Keary's party having exhausted whatever there had been, so I breakfasted off biscuits, sardines and tea. My audience never left me but I soon grew used to their presence and was able to wash, eat, write or sleep without regard to them. In the late afternoon I strolled round the village, followed at a short distance by most of the inhabitants. There were several women suckling children, two weaving hammocks, another spinning cotton on a little hand bobbin; a man was mending a blow-pipe. I had read about these weapons in detective stories and had imagined them – as obviously had the authors – as short instruments easily concealed about the person. This one was about eight foot long; the dart they use is the size of a pen – I had imagined a barely visible thorn – but it is true that they shoot with amazing accuracy. It is also true that the Indians have the secret of the 'deadly vegetable poison which defies analysis', that appears so often in the more old-fashioned shocker, but the difficulty of obtaining the poison is gradually driving the blow-pipe out of use. Various explorers from time to time have obtained bits of the poison and recipes for its concoction but none, I think, have proved genuine; they usually contain numerous magical ingredients such as ants and scorpions, but the bases are without doubt certain obscure plants which the Indians take pains to hide. If, in some exceptional moment of indiscretion, they give a name, the enquirer is little the wiser, for it is one unknown to botany and the secret of its location is never divulged. There are, of course, numerous common plants that are poisonous and are openly used for polluting streams for fishing but there is more than one that the Indians know about and will not reveal. None of them are common, but it is handed down orally among the piai men, where they can be found. Father Keary once encountered a party of his converts on a journey many days from their village. He asked them what they were doing and they at first demurred; finally they confessed that they were on an expedition to collect a certain bark with which to make away with an unpopular man in their community. He induced them to turn back but he never learned what the tree was or where it grew. Reliable authorities who have seen the arrow poison in use, describe it as a dark paste, a minute portion of which in an open wound, causes immediate paralysis and death. There is said to be another poison which causes insanity but the evidence for this is less conclusive. The general tendency since the introduction of firearms seems to be for poison to go out of favour among hunters and to be confined solely to the use of homicides and fishermen.

At one house a man lay in his hammock, apparently in the best of health but being attended with all the circumstances of illness. A woman with a very small baby at her breast was holding a calabash to his lips for him to drink. I asked Eusebio what was the matter and he explained that the man's wife had lately given birth to a child. I had read about this convention and heard it spoken of by Father Mather and the ranchers. It is prevalent amongst most of the tribes of the country, particularly the Wapishiana, and forms a curious contrast to the views on procreation taken in other equally savage parts of the world.

Here, as among most primitive peoples, parturition is a comparatively easy process; a few hours before it and a few hours after the mother will be sturdily trotting about seeing to the business of the home. The father, on the other hand is laid up for some weeks, keeps to his hammock, is tenderly nursed, and receives the congratulations and sympathy of his relatives and neighbours. The explanation given by those anthropologists who have noticed the practice, is that the soul of the child is linked with the father's so that while it is in the precarious stage of early infancy any risk he takes may endanger it. That is purely a hypothesis, because of course the

Indians have neither the vocabulary or inclination for metaphysical discussion. The fact, however, is indisputable, and it is interesting as forming a contrast to another anthropological hypothesis which became popular on the publication, some years ago, of Professor Malinowski's *Sexual Life of Savages*. That book, well written and superbly illustrated, enjoyed a success far beyond the ordinary public of anthropological students. It dealt with a universally absorbing subject and it printed love songs which general readers found agreeably indelicate. It treated conscientiously and brilliantly, of one group of savages – the Trobriand Islanders and described, among many other significant things, how they had no knowledge at all of the paternal contribution to procreation. The hypothesis based on this, was the familiar one, that man has evolved his social organisation from a matriarchal herd. Now partly because, as I have said, the book found its way to unsophisticated readers and partly because its title was *The Sexual Life of Savages* in general rather than of *Trobriand Islanders* in particular, countless 'Outline' educated people, jumped at the belief that the Trobriand Islanders' ignorance was universal to primitive man and the herd hypothesis established.

Of course anthropologists are no more unprejudiced than any other scientist – or any amateur observer like myself. Most work in that field comes either from inquirers, flushed with the agnosticism of the provincial universities, and firmly convinced beforehand that man's idea of God and right conduct have evolved from the vague speculations of an animistic, matriarchal herd, or from missionaries fresh from their seminaries, equally well convinced that man is descended from a single monogamous, monotheistic pair, and that when erroneous beliefs are prevalent it is because people have deteriorated with the ages and muddled and forgotten what was once a clear, revealed fact. Both parties jump at any peculiarity that seems to support their views. When Christian anthropologists discovered that the temptation of Adam and Eve by the serpent in the Garden of Eden was a myth widely held outside the Jewish nation, they pointed to that fact as proving that, since all were descended from Adam and Eve, all had the tradition of their origin, though only the Jews had been enabled to keep it completely free from contamination; the other party, less logically but no less triumphantly, said that it proved that Genesis was not an inspired book, if people who had not read it believed what it told. I have met ecclesiastics who maintained that the widespread dislike of snakes and the peculiar prominence given them above all other creatures, in many cults, was also a product of the Garden of Eden tradition.

However that may be, it seems worth pointing out for what it is worth that the ideas of parental responsibility of the primitive Guiana Indians[1] are the direct opposite of those of the Trobriand Islanders, and that no theory based on the latter can neglect consideration of the former.

My guide from the savannah would go no further, but Eusebio found me another mounted Indian, so that next morning I was again able to ride on ahead and leave him to follow with the ox. We started half an hour after dawn and rode up the valley to where in its north-east it narrowed into a defile. It was marshy at the top and there was a creek to ford. Some bush closed in round us but the trail was clear and we could keep up a steady trot; there were open patches but for the most part that day's journey was through bush, up a series of little passes, climbing all the time, occasionally so sharply that we had to dismount. We passed an Indian family on the trail, the men in front armed with bows and arrows, the women behind carrying the luggage. Once the way opened into a wide valley, wooded on all sides but grass at the bottom and in the centre of it, two knolls, one crowned by a hamlet of three round houses. At eleven o'clock we left the bush and came into downland, successive crests of low, grass-covered waves with the trail clearly marked across them. Another half-hour's bush ride brought us to Tipuru.

It was a particularly attractive place, built on the summit of one of the little hills, where an outcrop of rock broke through the grass, and extending down one side of it towards the stream after which it was named. The houses were substantially built and so compact together that the trodden earth between them had almost the nature of village streets. At Karasabai the houses had mostly been open on

1 The Guiana Indians as far as is known never participated at all, or had any contact with, the high civilisation of the Indians in mediæval Peru.

Macushi Indian and child at Marakanata village

three sides, but here the mud walls were built up into the eaves to keep out cabouri fly and the interiors were dark and warm. The mission owned a house and a church in the village and some cows in the corral, for this was an important village, both by reason of its size and its position, which made it the terminus beyond which horses and pack animals could not be taken and consequently the recruiting place for droghers on the long march in the mountains. Here too the people from the outlying hamlets could assemble if they had children to baptise – for hazy as most of the Indians may be on the more elaborate truths of Christianity, they are all keen for baptism. The headman – chief is too large a term – was a fine-looking old man, unique among all the Indians I saw in the possession of a stubble of grey beard.

When Father Keary's surprise at my arrival had somewhat abated, we breakfasted together in the hut reserved for him. His presence made everything a great deal easier for me, for now I was able to entrust the horse and pack ox to the men he was sending back to St Ignatius; he would also be able to help me collect droghers, a process over which I had anticipated considerable difficulty. That afternoon, after he had spent an hour in the Church teaching the children the rosary in Macushi, we went round the village but even with Father Keary's help and his head boy Antonio, we found droghers difficult to procure. The Indian men do not like carrying loads, regarding it as woman's work, and the women will not travel without their men, so that one was obliged to engage and feed, and carry the rations for twice the labour one required. I also needed a hunter and no one in the village seemed to possess arms, so that after two hours' laborious negotiations it looked as though the journey would not be possible, at any rate until we had sent into the surrounding country for additional help.

It was then that Father Keary proposed that we should combine our expeditions. He had in any case to go two-thirds of the way in the same direction; his original intention was to spend three or four days in each village but he could easily, he said, travel straight through and make longer visits on his return journey; moreover the country between the last of his villages and Mr Winter's camp was unknown to him and he would like the opportunity to explore it.

I agreed eagerly and so it was arranged. To help with our provisions Father Keary ordered a cow to be slaughtered.

This was all that was needed to overfill the cup of local excitement. The tension, apparent all through the afternoon, at last snapped. Two white men had arrived in two days, each with strange Indians, and now a cow was to be killed. Blank little mongolian faces creased noticeably at the corners of eyes and mouth in expressions of, to them, wild emotion. The meat was chopped up, salted and packed, and the offal distributed. In an hour everyone in the place from the smallest children to the oldest grandparents, had possessed himself of a handful of steaming entrails and was trotting to and fro, in and out of the houses talking in a manner that would have been extremely morose in any other country in the world, but here was an almost hysterical outburst of animation.

While the village were feasting that night, Antonio told us a curious story, that there were skulls and bones hidden among the rocks about quarter of a mile away. He had not seen them himself, nor had anyone whom he knew, but it was certain they were there. He did not know how long they had been there, but threw his head back and made the inevitable whining noise by which an Indian conveys distance, in time or space, greater than he can compute. They were the bones, he said, of Arakuna Indians from whom the Macushis had taken the village generations ago.

It was an odd story, new to Father Keary and contrary to what is generally held about these hill Indians, that they have no military traditions. It was the only time that Antonio ever volunteered information or told us any but the most practical and generally inaccurate details of the distances and directions of streams and camping places. It is possible he was moved to boast by pride in his own village and wished to explain that it was different from the others. Usually if one asked him anything about the beliefs or habits of his people he would look away and, perhaps, snigger.

CHAPTER 7

On foot in the hills – cabouri fly – Kenaima – Karto – djiggas – Kurikabaru – Santa Maria – Anundabaru – Mr Winter – base treatment of Eusebio.

WE SET OUT on foot next morning across the Tipuru, walking one behind the other in a single file which presently spaced out until we straggled a good half-mile from first to last. The organisation was in Father Keary's hands and I had been witness to some of the difficulties that attended it, so I was not critical; there did seem, however, to be more people in our party than our needs warranted. First there was a sturdy gnome-like woman of great age, who, since she was a slow walker, always set off alone an hour before the rest of the party, was passed half-way and finished a constant but undismayed last. She carried nothing except her own belongings, a slab of meat, and a few cooking-pots; her interest in coming seemed to be change of air, healthy exercise and the pleasure of observing two foreigners in discomfort; also the half-dollar a day in trade goods, which she received in common with the more heavily burdened members of the expedition. Then followed Antonio who as guide and interpreter was too proud to carry anything except a gun and a cutlass; behind him plodded his wife bowed double with his luggage, her own, and a fair share of the general rations; she was one of the few attractive Macushi women I saw, stocky and drab but with a very sweet, childlike face and long loose hair which blew round her head on the hilltops. Then came Father Keary and myself, and behind four other droghers and Eusebio. He showed a clear aversion to taking a load and usually escaped without anything heavier than the things I needed on the road – hammock, towel, change of clothes, rations for the next meal, and the rapidly depleted bottle of Lisbon brandy which I had bought from Figuiredo. Even so he started reluctantly, looked pathetic all day, and often ended only a few paces ahead of the old woman. The heavy stuff, Father Keary's altar equipment and the *farine* rations, were borne by two brothers, very large and muscular for their race, shock-headed, with lowering cave-man brows and loud, unexpected laughs; they were more untamed than their companions, whom they seemed to despise, and ate apart from them.

They all went barefoot except over the rocks when they would produce flat sandals of palm bark. Father Keary and I wore rubber-soled canvas boots. There is no satisfactory alternative to my know-ledge, for we were in a country where one is wading streams five or six times a day and then rapidly becoming dry in direct tropical sun, but the softness of the soles, though it prevented blistering to some extent, made the feet easily bruised on loose stones and the trellis of root in the bush.

We walked for about five hours with a ten-minute rest half-way at a village of five houses named Shimai, and finally made camp by the Maripakuru creek, a short distance from its confluence with the Ireng; there we found a solitary skeleton house, half built and then deserted, and slung our hammocks under the thatched section of its roof. Our day's progress seemed discouraging for the trail had wound in and out of the bush, up creeks to find suitable fords, over steep passes and round spurs, climbing all the way, so that though we had covered a lot of ground and were thoroughly tired, our actual distance from Tipuru seemed negligible.

The cabouri fly here were unbearable so that though we wrapped our hands in handkerchiefs – gloves were one of the highly desirable things it had not occurred to me to bring – and swathed our necks and faces in towels, there was no sleep and little real rest until sunset. We had no lamp with us, so it was necessary to eat by daylight, and even the small amount of uncovering necessary to enable us to swallow and to handle spoon and knife, made meals, hungry as we were, wholly unwelcome. The bath was delicious so long as one remained submerged, but any limb that appeared over the surface of the water was instantly covered with voracious flies. Cabouri will not attack one so long as one is in motion, and I found it on the whole more agreeable to walk up and down, in spite of stiffness and soreness of feet, than to lie tormented in the hammock. Antonio went out with his gun but came back empty-handed, but we

Antonio's wife

Macushi chief of Tipuru village (note carsava bread drying on roof)

still had fresh meat from the kill at Tipuru so this did not worry us. The truth became clear later, when we were in some need of food, that he was a thoroughly incompetent hunter; moreover the moment he was out of his own country he became timid, and made excuses to avoid leaving the party.

The life of every Indian in these parts is overshadowed by an ever present, indefinable dread, named *Kenaima*. I met plenty of people, from a self-confident woman graduate in Trinidad, to a less certain mineralogist who had lived half his life among Indians, who were willing to explain *Kenaima* to me and each told me something different. All the books on the country mention *Kenaima*, many at some length. Its existence and importance cannot be doubted; baptism and even continual contact with Europeans do little to dispel its terror; it is as deep-rooted in the belief of the clothed, English-speaking Indians who work timber at Batika and Mazaruni, as of the unsophisticated people in the Pakaraima Mountains, but no one has yet discovered what exactly constitutes it. All unexplained deaths are attributed to *Kenaima*, certain places are to be avoided on account of *Kenaima*, strangers may *be Kenaimas*, people can set a *Kenaima* on you, you are in danger of *Kenaima* if you associate with men of another tribe. Various ceremonial acts are necessary to propitiate *Kenaima*. It is certainly something malevolent and supernatural, that is all that can be said certainly of it.

It is as well to be highly sceptical of all statements made about primitive beliefs, particularly at the present moment when so much information is being confidently doled out to the public at third hand in the innumerable popular 'Outlines' of culture. These are usually *précis*, with the qualifications omitted, of weightier books which for the most part are collections of untravelled scholars; the authority ultimately depends on evidence of explorers and travellers and only those who have some acquaintance with the difficulties of obtaining this evidence, know what sort of value to attribute to it. At least two-thirds of it is derived from interrogations conducted either through interpreters (the most unsatisfactory form of conversation even on the simplest matters) or with an incomplete knowledge of the language. In any case the languages do not as a rule possess a vocabulary or syntax capable of accuracy, being devoid of abstract terms. And even was it possible for the primitive man to express what he believed – it is hard enough for the highly educated – he is invariably reluctant to do so. Even in the practical questions of direction – as appeared when I asked the Indian at Takutu ford whether I had reached the Sauriwau creek – his natural inclination is to tell the inquirer what he thinks he wishes to hear. This is still more the case in dealing with intimate and embarrassing questions about his private beliefs.

I encountered a very clear instance of this fallibility of opinion in the case of *Kenaima*. Two Europeans who had exceptional opportunities of studying Indians, had earned their confidence, and had certainly devoted most of their life to them, gave me completely contradictory explanations of the belief. One said that it was the power of evil, the abstract malevolent and destructive principle in life, working for its own end, sometimes in concrete form either human or animal, in order to injure and kill; the other that it was the art by which a human enemy was able to develop supernatural advantages, become a beast, like the leopard men, werewolves, etc., of universal reputation, travel immense distances instantaneously, go without food, become invisible, and so on, in order to accomplish his revenge. I can imagine either of these statements finding its way into a text-book and becoming part of the material for anthropological hypothesis. Both cannot be wholly true and probably neither is. Possibly *Kenaima* is supernatural evil, always present and active, which can on occasions be canalised by magic and used for a human motive, in which case the revenger is possessed by evil to such an extent that for the time being he *is Kenaima*. That is merely a guess. I quote the two confidently definite explanations as being noticeable contributions to the general scepticism that is one of the more valuable fruits of travel.

Another rather more arduous march left us still depressingly close to the point of our departure; as on the day before we scrambled up and down, through bush where the trail was almost lost and had to be cleared step by step with cutlasses, turning on our tracks, and wading through creeks – one of them the Echilifar, deep and very fast so that it was hard to keep our feet. As before whenever we attempted to rest, we were beset with cabouris. At half past eleven we reached a hut inhabited by a negress who had been brought up by one of the servants of the Boundary Commission and left there. She gave us fresh milk and four addled eggs. We put up our hammocks in her house and the shade and swaddlings of handkerchiefs and towels gave us some respite from fly. After an hour and a half we resumed the march; at half past four Antonio gave a loud holla, which was taken up by the following men, and we came in sight of a village of three huts, apparently nameless; there was a fourth partially ruinous hut which we were offered for our camp and unwisely accepted; unwisely because the place was alive with fleas, djiggas and ticks.

We seemed popular here for the people greeted us with unusual cordiality, and besides the ceremonial bowl of *cassiri* laid out for us on the ground a great dish of cassava bread (not unlike oat cake) and earthenware bowls of peppers and stewed leaf (not unlike spinach). I was intensely thirsty and seeing Father Keary drink some of the *cassiri*, did so too. It was agreeable and enormously refreshing, so that always after this, when it was offered, I drank a pint or more with increasing appreciation.

Attempting to check our position on the map by inquiries from Antonio, I found that we were even nearer Tipuru than I had thought, for the two mountains Yewaile and Tawaling, marked several miles apart, are, according to Antonio, two humps on the same spur of hill, and our whole afternoon's march had been merely to encircle this. Father Keary did not share the geographical interests of the early missionaries of his Society and was wholly oblivious to his position or direction. It was his habit to spend most of the day's march telling his beads, quietly following Antonio from one sphere of his true activity to the next. Before supper that evening he baptised a child and married the parents.

We were able to purchase two cocks here with Woolworth bracelets, one of which we killed for supper and the other carried on alive for the next day. It is a curious fact that though most Indian households keep a few fowls they do not use them or their eggs for food; indeed the birds which live frugally on what they can pick up round the houses, are barely eatable. They are kept because the

Indians find the crowing of the cocks at night a comforting sound, likely to scare away *Kenaimas*, and also as measure of time, for they crow pretty regularly at an hour's interval from midnight until dawn.

The night was one of exceptional discomfort, for the moonlight streamed through the ruined roof of the hut, brightly illuminating the interior, with the result that the cabouris kept awake; there were also mosquitoes in fair numbers (I was not using my net at the time and did not wish to disturb the boys to find it among the baggage) and they, with the fleas already mentioned, made sleep difficult; the djiggas and ticks were also at work but did not cause immediate pain. All that was needed to complete the discomfort of night was rain, and this began in a steady downpour some hours before dawn, just when the setting of the moon offered some relief from the cabouris. The boys crowded into the hut but were little better off, for there was no roof of any consequence; so we lit a small fire and sat scratching and shivering until daylight. Father Keary said Mass in the smoky gloom of one of the houses, and we set out again in the rain, scarcely at all refreshed by our night's rest.

That day's march was three long and steep climbs, with two small descents, one to cross the Yowiparu creek, and the other to a bush valley beside the Kowa River where we made camp. We stopped to eat some bananas at the summit of one of the hills but were too tired to trouble about having a meal prepared before supper; then we killed our own cock and ate it in the inevitable swarm of cabouris. But the bush where we camped was tall and dense so that the moonlight did not penetrate to us; the flies disappeared at sunset and we got ten hours' undisturbed sleep.

Next day, for the first time, we seemed to make real progress; the line lay more or less straight, mounting all the way, mostly through open country. We left camp at 6.45 and, taking an hour and a half's rest between 11 and 12.30, reached Karto, the first of the Patamona villages at 4.45. The last few hours were very painful, first climbing a hillside of sharp pebbles in the full glare of the afternoon sun, and then crossing a dead flat tableland of hot, iron-hard earth.

There were three houses at Karto and an open shelter where we slept. The people were cheerful and hospitable, bringing out, as

Father Keary receiving cassiri from Patamona Indian

before, *cassiri*, peppers, cassava bread and vegetable. Here, for the first time, we met women wearing no clothes except their little bead aprons. There were no cabouris or mosquitoes here, but there was little sleep, for the old bites were continuously at work; we were at a considerable height and it was bitterly cold after sundown; also the djiggas, inflamed by the day's walk, began to make themselves felt.

These are small insects which live in and round houses; they work their way through one's boots to the soles of one's feet where they drill holes and lay their eggs, preferably under the toe-nails or any hard piece of skin; the process is painless or at least unnoticeable among the numerous other bites that torment one. In a day the eggs have begun to grow; they continue to do so at great rapidity, raising a lump which is at first irritating and later painful. If allowed to remain they hatch out into maggots in the foot and serious poisoning sets in. Their removal is a perfectly simple process if performed by someone native to the place; the eggs are in a little, onion-shaped envelope and it is essential that this shell be removed unbroken, otherwise an egg remains and hatches out. People who live in places liable to djiggas usually have their feet examined by their servant every evening after their bath. He opens up the hole with a pin and dexterously picks out the bag of eggs intact. I had seen Antonio and his wife attending each other in this way several times during the journey. I felt two or three djiggas during the night and asked Antonio to get them out next morning. When he came to do so he found a dozen more and got them all out without difficulty; the operation was practically painless.

It had painful consequences, however, for when I came to walk I found that what with the bruising of the day before and the several small punctures, I was exceedingly lame in both feet. Fortunately we had not far to go and with the help of numerous swigs of brandy, and two sticks, I was able to hobble along at about half the usual pace and four times the usual effort, and just made Kurikabaru, the next village, before giving out, feeling that I had in some measure atoned for whatever suffering I had inflicted on the town clerk's horse on the journey from Boa Vista.

We spent two nights at Kurikabaru; a little hut was at our disposal, built of bark and divided into four minute cubicles, dark and draughty. I spent most of the time there, lying in my hammock. It was a bleak village, thirteen huts scattered on a desolate hilltop, and the people were impoverished and dour. There was rain some of the time and a continuous, raw wind; the height by the aneroid was a little under three thousand feet; I slept with shirt, trousers, and stockings over my pyjamas, but even then was cold at night under the blanket. There was dust and refuse blowing about all day when the rain did not keep it down. The people kept to their houses, huddled in the wood-smoke. The Macushi droghers were ill at ease there and my three wished to go home; loads had grown lighter – in fact we were now uncomfortably short of provisions – and they could easily be spared. Eusebio stayed on and I engaged a Patamona man to carry what was left of my things.

Paying the droghers was a complicated process as it had to be done in powder, packed in little red flasks, shot, gun-caps and necklaces; in the end I had not enough to go round for I had been frivolously open-handed at the beginning of the journey, making presents to anyone with an amiable manner. The droghers had to take dollar notes for some of their wages; they accepted them with the apparent lassitude they maintained in all their dealings and tucked them away in their loin cloths, from which *cache*, if they had not disintegrated, as seemed probable, during the journey, they would no doubt pass from hand to hand from the hills to the savannah until eventually they reached Mr Figuiredo.

I also sent a messenger ahead to find Mr Winter with a note warning him of our approach, and throwing myself on his kindness for provisions and transport down the Potaro.

Provisions were running short. When I had given the droghers rations for their return journey, we were left without meat and barely enough *farine* to last the boys four days. Of the personal stores of Father Keary and myself, there was a fair amount of coffee, some rapidly coagulating sugar, two cupfuls of rice, one-eighth of a bottle of brandy, a tin of sardines and a tin of salmon. There was nothing to be got in Kurikabaru except a few bananas. In these circumstances it was impossible to stay on there so we set out again on the second day. On the last evening a hunter came in with a small deer, of which we were able to secure a leg.

Patamona wife removing djiggas from her husband's feet

Patamona child at Kurikabaru

It was hunger rather than restored fitness that decided us on the march. The holes from the djiggas were now mostly healed over, but I was suffering from an inflamed toe where one of them had become slightly poisoned. It was astonishing and slightly ludicrous that so small a disability could affect one so much – a single minute limb, shiny, rosy and increased by half of an inch at the most in girth, made one dead lame; walking was acutely unpleasant; not only was every step very painful but the effort to the rest of the body was absurdly magnified so that an hour's march exhausted one as much as four hours of normal progress. It was annoying too for the rest of the expedition who were obliged to adapt their pace to my limp, for it is every bit as distressing to be held back on a march as to be pushed on.

Fortunately the next stage was a very short one, and by cutting the side out of my boot to ease the swelling, I was able to make it in four hours. We left the open hills now and entered the forest which stretches from there, unbroken, to the coast; there were no more invigorating changes of view, prospects of river and mountain suddenly disclosed and as suddenly shut out as though the curtain had fallen on the act of a play; no shifting of horizon, five miles distant at dawn, fifty miles distant at noon; no confidence, no possibility of surprise, that urged one up the steepest and most fiery hillside with eagerness to see what was beyond; instead there was a twilit green tunnel, leaves on each side and overhead, leaves in front that had to be cut clear as we advanced, and underfoot slippery leaf-mould or a cruel network of bare roots.

We were still crossing Amazon waters; the creeks we crossed and recrossed were tributaries of the Tumong, which in its turn ran into the Ireng, and so by the Rio Branco past Boa Vista into the Rio Negro, the Amazon, and the South Atlantic. During the next two days we passed the continental divide where the waters start flowing towards the Carribean, feeding the Potaro and Essequibo, but there was no clearly defined watershed; the streams dovetailed into one another, the source of the Kowa, which is Amazon water, being north of the source of the Murabang which runs eventually to the Essequibo; the official map of this river system was wildly inaccurate, and what with my complaints about the complexity of the geography, and my lameness, I must, I think, have proved a very tiresome travelling companion to Father Keary.

There was nothing to give beauty or excitement to that morning's journey, except a fine waterfall which we came to un-expectedly; a sunless pool, over-arched with branches into which a stream fell sheer, twenty or thirty feet, but no rainbows shone round it and the spray rose dull as sea mist, to meet the falling water.

Our camp that afternoon was the least attractive we had yet made. We came on an acre of cleared ground surrounded on all sides by bush. There had once been a village there in the days of Father Carey-Elwes, and since it had no name when he discovered it, he christened the place Santa Maria. Now there was only one house and the desolation was accentuated by the tattered ruin of a shelter erected two years back by the Boundary Commissioners, and now reduced to a half-capsized skeleton of beams and rafters, and a few shreds of waterproof cardboard hanging forlornly from what had been the roof. There was no flowing water here; instead a patch of marsh which deepened towards the centre into a shallow and opaque pool. We camped in the bush near it, slinging our hammocks among a variety of biting and stinging flies and a million or so ants, which rapidly invaded our provisions until we hung them too from the trees.

The space round the house was unswept, littered with bones and rags and broken earthenware; the people remarkable in their pov-erty and unkempt condition even among their race. The younger members were little used to visitors and hid indoors, crowding about the sides of the door, sometimes emerging and then darting back with silly giggling. The older ones attempted to show some hospital-ity but the *cassiri* they brought out was warm and only half fer-mented.

I had expected to find my messenger here with a reply from Mr Winter, but there was no sign of him. The people reported that he had passed through two days before but he had his bow and arrows with him and they supposed he had seen game. Nothing will deflect an Indian from following food. I had heard that often a whole boat's crew would desert if they saw a herd of bush pig, and follow it for days, returning after an orgy of meat-eating to their employers and quite uncomprehending the vexation they might have aroused.

The people at Santa Maria did not know exactly where Mr Winter was. He was within two days' journey, they said, but he had left his home at Anundabaru some years ago.

In all these depressing circumstances there was one hopeful feature – a fat little stallion trailing his halter, at grass near the house. The Indians were not only willing to hire him out, but would accept a dollar note in payment. This solved the only pressing problem which was how, in my crippled condition, I was going to get to Mr Winter's before supplies gave out. There was, of course, no saddle or bridle, so I set out next morning soon after sunrise, a relieved, if highly comic figure, riding bare-back with Antonio leading the horse by his rope.

The bush line led up the Tumong, sometimes along the bank, sometimes meandering away from it, three times crossing it and finally, in contravention of everything the map suggested, leaving it on our left. There were also numerous smaller streams to cross, all running through precipitous little glens. It was possible to ride for about half the way, on the alternate half-miles that lay along the tops of the ridges; climbs in and out of the valley had to be done on foot, the stallion being left to find his own perilous way through them, from rock to rock, over fallen or under half-reclining tree trunks, but always emerging steaming and patient on the opposing summit. The riding was far from pleasurable for the line was, in its best places, but head high for foot passengers and the breadth of a single file, and in its worst, totally obscured, so that to the normal discomfort of bare vertebrae was added constant scratching and whipping across the face, and buffeting of the legs against tree trunks which, on the injured side, were agonising. It provided, however, the necessary stimulus of expectancy, for while I was riding – face down blind on the horse's neck and nervously anticipating more jostling than ever came to the swollen foot – I longed avidly to walk, and while I walked – hobbling one pace to every two up and down the sides of the valleys – I longed to ride; and as the intervals between changes were of short duration there were frequently recurring moments of delight when I first found myself astride the sharp ridge and sweaty sides of the horse, and first on my foot again, when it became necessary to dismount. In this way after an hour's rest between eleven and twelve we reached our destination before four o'clock.

On the way we met my returning messenger who had had no sport on his journey but had taken three nights instead of one for the sake of his own ease. He brought a large key and attached to it a note from Mr Winter which read: *Delighted you are coming. You will find me half a day's good walking from Anundabaru. Your boy seems to have taken a long time coming which was unfortunate as I sent my boat down to Kangaruma for mail at six this morning. If he had arrived earlier I would have held it back. However, no doubt it will return and in the fullness of Patamona time can go down again. Of course stay here with me till then. You have come at a bad time as I am extremely short of provisions. Here is the key of Anundabaru House where you can camp on the way, but it is probably in bad repair.*

Earlier in the year I might have regarded this as a major misfortune, but I was by now so well used to the checks and annoyances of travelling that I was unable to blame the messenger very heartily. After all it would have been an unnatural coincidence if I *had* caught the boat and, as it turned out, there was a rough fifteen miles' walk between Mr Winter's camp and the river, which I would have been in no condition to undertake at that moment.

For nearly a mile square round Anundabaru the trees were all down, having been demolished by a Government botanist who wished to test a theory that a tropical rainforest would not burn. By good fortune the house escaped the conflagration. The earth was still black with wood ash but bracken had grown up to a height of six or ten feet. A wood shack stood in the centre near the Anundabura creek. It was a modest building but seemed spacious after the huts where we had slept lately, and, since it was the first building of sawn wood since Hart's, remarkably civilised. It was built on piles, with three rooms and a little verandah. An Indian, settled near it, had utilised the lower story as a store and shelter for livestock.

We climbed the somewhat rickety steps and as we were supervising the arrangement of baggage, Antonio pointed out that our trouser legs were covered with fleas. So were all our clothes, and a closer scrutiny revealed that the earth between the bracken and the house was covered with them, as densely as though by ants;

enormous creatures twice the usual size hopping everywhere in the dust. But their bulk was their undoing for we were able to pick them off before they had done much biting.

That night at supper Father Keary and I finished the last of our provisions, keeping only a few bananas for next morning's breakfast. We went to our hammocks as usual at sunset and were peacefully asleep when, at about nine, rain began. It was then clear what Mr Winter meant when he warned us that the house might be in bad repair. It happened that I had the worse room, and I awoke to find water pouring in on me and to hear it on all sides. It was absolutely dark and the matches on the floor by my side were already sodden and useless. I began a difficult investigation, treading carefully round the floor in the hope of finding a dry patch. Presently I heard Father Keary awake, striking matches in his room. We lit a scrap of ballata that we found lying about, and by its light were able to see the extent of our discomfort. There was a long dry strip in Father Keary's room where he could hang his hammock. We assembled the more perishable luggage – photographic films, note-books, matches, etc., under this. My room was completely swamped except for one corner, about a yard square. Here the ballata gave out, but by striking matches we were able to hang the hammock in a U with the centre, when it was weighted down, just clear of the floor. Here I sat with my head on my knees until dawn, damp, sleepless, and uncharitably intolerant of the stertorous snores which rose above the splash of the water from Father Keary's room next door.

It was still raining pitilessly at dawn next morning. I went down to see how the boys had fared, who had camped in the Indian's hut. They too were wet and depressed, huddled round the fire in an atmosphere thick with smoke and steam, reeking of men, animals and wet thatch.

The little creek by the house had swollen overnight into a broad, swift torrent of brown water, full of mud and leaves and dead wood. There were a number of larger creeks between there and Mr Winter's and a brief consultation with Antonio convinced me that they and the slippery state of the ground made it impossible to take the stallion any further. Accordingly, so as not to hold up the expedition, I set out first with one man as guide, expecting to be caught up by the others before I reached Mr Winter's. As it turned out, however, I got there a few minutes before them, for the cold water through which we were constantly passing, eased my foot and the rough nature of the line made the journey more of an obstacle race than a walk – a matter of scrambling over tree trunks and rocks, using hands as much as feet; this nearly equalised our chances.

I had met Mr Winter on a convivial evening at Christmas-time in the Georgetown hotel, and he now greeted me as an old friend. He was equally genial to Father Keary, offering him every facility if he wished to include the camp, where a considerable village had grown up, in his annual itinerary. But with practical clarity he explained his present position. He was down to the last bin in all provisions and could do nothing towards rationing the boys. He could put me up until I found a means of getting down river; he could give Father Keary a fowl and some eggs for his own use, but he had no *farine*, dried meat or rice to spare. In the circumstances Father Keary had to make an immediate retreat to Kurikabaru which, without the handicap of my lameness, could be done comfortably in two days. There he would probably be able to collect cassava and yams. It was not a very satisfactory prospect and I watched him go with concern – but there was no possible alternative.

About one concomitant arrangement I felt some personal guilt. Eusebio had to go back too. The unfortunate youth had endured all the discomforts of the march – and he made it abundantly plain that he took them as great discomforts – in the hope of visiting George-town, and now that all the stiffest walking was over, and there remained, for the most part, only a leisurely river journey, well suited to his disposition, he found himself headed back, all the way he had come, through the hills again, down to the savannah and his native village. I paid him a large compensation, but both of us knew that the other knew that no compensation could really suffice. I am still ashamed at his betrayal, but, again, there was no alternative. Not only was Mr Winter unable to feed him, but he expressly refused to have a Macushi in his camp, upsetting his Patamona workmen. The labour supply was precarious and at any untoward happening the Indians were liable to melt away silently to their villages.

As he unpacked for me, Eusebio's face betrayed that reproach, wistfulness and melancholy, that only plump and rather ignoble faces can adequately express.

Poor Eusebio! I am sure Georgetown would have the worst possible effect on him, but I hope he gets there some time, in some fashion, and does not for ever nurture resentment for my breach of faith.

CHAPTER 8

Diamond washing and selling – Upper Potaro – a bad family – Kaieteur –
Lower Potaro – Amatuk.

WE HAD DESCENDED constantly from Kurikabaru but Winter's
camp stood at a considerable height; high enough to be cool most of
the day and cold between midnight and dawn. There was usually
a mist for the first three or four hours of day, which gradually lifted
revealing the great bulk of Mount Kowatipu, five or six miles away
across the valley. This was a long, flat-topped spur, with sharply
precipitous, bush-clad cliffs. There was said to be a lake on its
summit, but no white man has ever been there and no Indian has
first-hand knowledge of it.

The camp was built on a cleared hilltop between the valleys of
the Mikraparu creek and the Murabang River, which runs into the
Kopinang, officially regarded as a tributary of the Potaro, but
according to Winter, who is one of the few men who have visited
it, the real river, carrying a far greater volume of water than the
stream marked on the maps as the upper Potaro. It was the Mikraparu creek which Winter was working for alluvial diamonds.

The camp consisted of a bark store-house, a little hut with
thatched roof and stake walls which we used as a dining-room and
a larger house under construction where we slept; this room had
a floor and walls made of bark, and a roof of waterproof paper. It
was entirely constructed by a Patamona Indian named Thomas who
had recently left his wife on account of her having given birth to
twins – certain evidence of infidelity to an Indian mind. Winter had
been there two or three years and already had a lime and a pau-pau
tree bearing well; there were also a large number of hens whose eggs
formed an important part of our diet. As he had warned me,
provisions were low, particularly flour, rice and sugar. We began
in great luxury with bacon, tinned butter, tinned milk, and toast, but

Mr Winter's camp (Mount Kowatipu in background)

Mr Winter's hunter (note baby accouni in child's hands)

after a week were reduced to yams and eggs and whatever the hunters brought in.

Winter kept two hunters in his employment who were paid by results. Sometimes they would bring in two or three bush cows in a week, he said, and then there would be meat rations for the whole camp. While I was there they were unlucky, often bringing nothing at all; occasionally, however, they would kill an excellent bird called mahm, not unlike a pheasant in size and flavour, or a water rodent called labba, that tasted like pork. Bush turkey and bush pig, the other most abundant game, were flesh of no particular flavour or quality.

Winter had never tasted *cassiri* and was sceptical of my praise of it. However he had some made and the two women who looked after the house knew a method of fermenting it which did not involve spitting. He agreed with me that it was excellent. We also unearthed in his store a keg of crude spirit that had been sent originally for making embrocation; with brown sugar and limes it made a fiery aperitif which we used to drink at sundown after our baths.

Scattered at some distance from the house were the huts inhabited by the fluctuating body of Indian workers. It was a year-old experiment to employ Indians, which so far was giving excellent results. Negroes had to be transported to and from the coast and paid comparatively high wages on their journey; while at work they expected rations of meat, dried fish, sugar, rice, and flour. The Indians drifted into camp with wives and children, worked for a month or two until they had acquired the object they coveted, usually a gun, and then drifted back to their homes. While they were there they lived simply, happy enough as long as they had plenty of *farine* and yams and an occasional orgy of meat, and their wives and older children joined in the work. It seemed an idyllic arrangement. They were thriftless with their possessions and easily broke them or exchanged them for something of far lower value which happened to take their fancy, and so would return eventually to do another spell of work. Winter was extraordinarily clever in coaxing labour out of the villagers.

Whenever he went to Georgetown he came back with some new supply of novelties, knowing that once these began circulating in the villages and it became known that they were obtainable at his store, he would begin tapping sources he could never reach himself. He had a great success shortly after Christmas with some mechanical mice, emerald-green drawers, and a gramophone. When I first arrived my hat and red blanket excited great cupidity, everyone asking Winter how long he would have to work to earn one like them and why he had never seen them in the store. There was a kindergarten atmosphere about the camp; the little wives would often stop in their work to play. Any at all painful accident, such as a boy falling from a ladder and breaking his rib, was greeted with an outburst of wild merriment.

These Indians were mostly from the Kopinang banks and had never seen missionaries, policemen or white men of any kind before. They arrived naked and went away heavily swathed in calico; a few even took hats and high-heeled shoes, but I got the impression that they were attracted by them as toys rather than finery and that when they got home they would be put away and played with, not flaunted before their less travelled neighbours. It was astonishing to see how easily these very simple people adapted themselves to the mechanism of the trommel but they worked without system, as though it were all part of a game; when shovelling earth they would throw one spadeful high and the next low, sometimes several in quick succession, sometimes a few very slowly. I never saw less coercion in any country in the world. Had any been attempted there would have been no complaints or protests; the Indians would simply have left the wages due to them, packed up and gone away, as they have often treated impatient travellers in the past. They have by nature and upbringing no sense of authority. In most languages the first word one learns is 'sir'; few of the Indian languages – I think none – have any term of subservience or respect. The chiefs of the villages have no power and no privileges. They are elected for any sort of eminence – in one case because the man was cited as witness in a police case and came back from Anai with such prestige that the former chief was instantly deposed – and exercise no judicial function. Nor are they supported by contributions from the village. You do not in Indian villages find those luxurious old men, common enough in Africa, squatting at ease among a dozen wives and sniffing an ammonia bottle while his hut is piled up with yams and manioc by his subjects. Every now and then a black 'pork knocker' will work his way up into Indian country and attempt to assert himself in a village, taking up with the women and bullying the men. The Indians are afraid of the blacks on account of their size and strength and for a little will do what they are told. Then they lose patience and one of two things happens; either they all decamp silently and leave him to starve or he is stealthily murdered, poisoned or shot full of arrows in the back. Several black adventurers have come to a bad end in this way, but that has been mostly in Macushi country. The Kopinang people have lived unmolested.

While I was at Winter's, however, a report came in of a party of 'pork knockers' who were working down the Yawong on the other side of Mount Kowatipu; they had conscripted the Indians whom Winter had sent for from Baramakatoi to cut lines round his concession and were using them as droghers. They were said to be making for Brazil.

The law against black immigration into the native reserves can, of course, rarely be enforced. No policeman or officer of the government had ever passed through the country where I now was. The nearest policeman was at Bartika, ten days' journey away and the nearest magistrate at Bon Success. It was in fact an extremely lonely camp, with no neighbours at all. The nearest white man was at Mazaruni station, a few miles from the coast. There was no through traffic; I was the first guest Winter had entertained since his settlement there. Moreover it is getting more lonely. Ten years before there had been East Indian and Portuguese stores all down the Potaro between Kaieteur and Kangaruma. Now there are none at all. There had also been a German planter at the mouth of the Chinapowu whose estate was largely marked on the map, but, as I was to find later, there was no trace of it except some bamboos and fruit-trees, smothered and reverting to wilder forms in the bush.

I spent ten days waiting for Winter's boat to return, during which my foot slowly mended. After a week the nail came off and I was perfectly well; until then I kept to my hammock most of the day.

Winter was a delightful host and companion; middle-aged, genial, cynical, personally optimistic. Race, pure white Creole; education, technical, engineering and surveying mostly in the United States and Canada; married, with wife and family in Barbados whom he visited whenever he could; religion, Anglo-Israelite; politics, socialist turned conservative on finding himself a capitalist and employer of labour; general contempt and suspicion of all officials; generous, businesslike, witty; personally optimistic for he always examined his sieve with the expectation of finding the large stone that was going to make his fortune.

As my foot got better I often went down with him to the workings. He was washing for alluvial gold and diamonds in the bed of the Mikraparu, and to do this had dammed and canalised the little creek. The dam was made of timber and mud, held together with ropes of bush vine and attached to the surrounding trees, and the piping that conducted the water to the trommel was of hollowed wood. With the exception of a small hand-pump, worked by a deaf and dumb girl, the entire mechanism had been constructed on the spot. It had the appearance of a drawing by Mr Heath Robinson, but it seemed to work. The trommel was a horizontal, cylindrical sieve made of wire gauze of varying mesh; it was rotated by hand, two girls spinning it with wooden handles. The gravel from the bed of the stream was brought up in barrows and emptied into the trommel where it was washed down by the water from the stream. As it went down all the heavier and smaller stones fell through into a tray. At the end of the sieve only large pebbles emerged and were shovelled into a heap by two more girls. The hard work of digging out the gravel and wheeling it up to the trommel was done by their men.

The gold dust, being the heaviest constituent of the mud in the tray, went to the bottom and passed through a mercury trap where it was collected; any larger nuggets remained with the mud, in which would also be the diamonds, and were washed down into another fine sieve called a jig. This was gently swayed up and down in a tank of water until all the soluble matter had disappeared. The product was a sieve full of very fine gravel containing whatever diamonds and gold nuggets had been in the load. The whole process was

Mr Winter's diamond workings at Mikraparu Creek

Mr Winter's diamond workings at Mikraparu Creek

exceedingly simple. I never knew if the Indians had any clear idea of the purpose of the various tasks set them; they performed them in the half listless, half frivolous manner I have indicated. A black foreman named Gerry worked at the digging with the men and generally kept operations in motion in Winter's absence. His main job was to get the Indians out of their hammocks in the morning and to blow a whistle for them to stop at the end of the day.

The only skilled labour was Winter's, in searching the jig; it was full of beryls, clear white stones which when wet and glistening seemed to me indistinguishable from the diamonds. These on the days I went, were invariably minute and singularly unimpressive. A good day's yield was six or seven carats in twenty-five stones, most of them tarnished and opaque, and two or three fragments of gold the size of rice grains. These were all put carefully into a cartridge case, weighed and sealed up. (The diamonds were cleaned up with hydrofluoric acid and boiled in *aqua regia* before they reached the market.) I never acquired any skill in picking them out though the usual maxim is that though it is possible to mistake another stone for a diamond, it is impossible ever to mistake a diamond for anything else. It is said to have a metallic sheen that belongs to no other stone, but I always needed to have it shown to me before I recognised it.

The diamond trade of Guiana is on a far smaller scale and organised in a more haphazard fashion than in the great diamond fields of South Africa. There are no large corporations controlling the output; no smuggling and illicit diamond buying. The workers are all solitary prospectors or handfuls of friends trying their luck in common. Very few of them have any knowledge of geology; they work up the rivers and creeks until their rations are exhausted or until they have made a strike good enough to warrant their return to the coast. They then celebrate their good fortune in a few months' high living and either look for other work, or drift back again to the bush in the hope of another success. No fortunes have ever been made there. The market is in the hands of Jews and Portuguese in Georgetown, most of whom have agents buying for them up river. If an agent is thought by his employers to have paid too much for a stone, he is liable to have it returned to him and the price stopped out of his wages. Some sellers make a habit of going from one jeweller to another with their diamonds in the hope of finding a higher offer. They are completely in the hands of the buyers because few of them understand the subtleties of colouring that determine the value of a stone. But they gain little by their negotiations, for a buyer does not like to take a stone after he has once made an offer, for it means that his bid has been the highest and that he is paying more than his rivals' valuation.

There are certain stones of known defects that have been changing hands in the colony for years. As soon as any new-comer appears in the market they are all offered to him. One in particular is famous; a twenty-four-carat stone of negligible value on account of flaws and discolouration. The original discoverer boiled it in *aqua regia* and produced on it a series of minute surface cracks which gave it a dull whitish appearance, that on casual inspection might belong to a good stone in rough condition. A buyer paid $100 a carat for it as a gamble (the normal value would be $210) and had it returned to him by the merchants at headquarters. However, he was able to sell it again before the story got round, and since then it has been bought and resold four or five times, the last holder being faced with a dead loss until some stranger appears to take it off him. It is like the knave of clubs in the nursery game of 'Black Sambo'.

Winter had innumerable stories of the country which he used to recount with superb pungency over supper, and as we sat in our hammocks in the evening. There was one of a cook of his who had come to him highly qualified, a fugitive from her home. She had been taken by a missionary at an early age and taught the domestic arts and virtues in a Georgetown college. At adolescence she became haunted by the claustrophobia that affects all Indians when they come to town, and, urged by her instinct, made for her native bush. But she was by now neither civilised nor primitive. She arrived after long absence at her mother's house, armed with her certificate for proficiency on the pianoforte, umbrella in hand, sun bonnet on her head. She found a strange, naked woman who was her mother, eagerly welcoming her to a one-roomed hut, full of wood-smoke and poultry. More than this she found a naked young man who had been selected by her mother as a husband. Numerous suitors appeared, attracted by the glamour of her urban education, but all equally savage, uncouth, and unacceptable. A common enough situation in countries where educational experiments are practised, but in this case distinguished by a less usual conclusion. The original suitor, at last losing patience with her superiority and aloofness, married the mother and the two proceeded to make the hut still less habitable for her. So she packed up her umbrella and bonnet and musical diploma, and enjoyed a brief elopement with a passing catechist. After which she became Mr Winter's cook and so excellently had she been taught at her coast school that he was at the moment making strenuous efforts to retrieve her from the holiday she was taking among the negro boating community down river.

But most of Winter's stories depended for their point on his belief in the incompetence and dishonesty of all Government officials, and so cannot suitably be transcribed here. Moreover they need the surroundings in which they were told, the lamplight in the half-finished shed, the surrounding campfires of the Indian huts, and beyond them, invisible in the dark, but sensible, the forest and the dominant cliffs of Kowatipu.

Much of this chronicle – perhaps, it may seem, too much – has dealt with the difficulties of getting from place to place. But that seems to me unavoidable for it is the preoccupation of two-thirds of the traveller's waking hours, and the matter of all his nightmares. It is by crawling on the face of it that one learns a country; by the problems of transport that its geography becomes a reality and its inhabitants real people. Were one to be levitated on a magic carpet and whisked overnight from place to place, one would see all that was remarkable but it would be a very superficial acquaintance, and, in the same way, if one leaves the reader out of one's confidence, disavowing all the uncertainties of the route, the negotiations, projects and frustrations, making of oneself one of those rare, exemplary dragomans who disguise every trace of effort and present themselves before their employers with a plan completely tabulated, hampers packed, conveyances assembled, servants in attendance, one may show them some pretty spectacles and relate some instructive anecdotes, but one will not have given them what was originally offered when one was engaged – a share in the experience of travel, for these checks and hesitations constitute the genuine flavour.

I feel this strongly about those who travel in aeroplanes. They take with them, wherever they go, from start to finish, a single series of problems involving fuel, mechanism and air conditions. The features of geography and the character of the people are involved incidentally and indirectly. If one travels in the manner of the country, taking horses or cars where possible, walking when necessary, getting rations and labour where one can, using regular services of transport when one comes across them and fitting out expeditions of one's own where no facilities exist, one identifies oneself with the place one is visiting in a way that is impossible to the, perhaps, more courageous fliers. That, anyhow, is how I was travelling. There had hitherto been two main phases of the journey; by horse in the cattle country and by foot in the hills. Now I was to start on another, by boat down the rivers.

The situation was this: all regular service for mail and the delivery of stores, up stream from the coast, stopped at a depot named Kangaruma on the lower Potaro. It was there that Winter's stores were awaiting him. Between Kangaruma and the mouth of the Chinapowu – a day's march from his camp and the highest navigable point of the river – there were three obstacles, Amatuk falls, Waratuk falls, and the Kaieteur. It was possible by unloading it and carefully paying it out on a rope to get a boat over Waratuk. Amatuk and, of course, Kaieteur were impossible. Thus, in getting down, three separate boats were needed, one from Chinapowu to Kaieteur, another from Kaieteur to Amatuk, a third from Amatuk to Kangaruma. In getting stores up stream droghers were needed to carry them from landing to landing; in the case of Kaieteur this was a formidable process as there was a two-mile portage, half of which was a sharp precipice. The river above Amatuk is uninhabited so that the labour had to be sent down and brought back with the stores. It was again needed to carry them from Chinapowu to the camp up a fifteen-mile trail part of which was also precipitous. Thus 'sending down for stores' was not so simple a process as the words suggest. There was a further difficulty – that Winter owned only two of the three boats needed; between Amatuk and Kangaruma the only boat belonged to a Portuguese, ominously named Diabolo; there was no reason to suppose that it would be at Amatuk when we arrived; moreover its owner was in a position of absolute monopoly and able to exact any charge he liked for its use. Winter's negro foreman spoke gloomily of Diabolo's ill-nature.

I mentioned in the last chapter that Winter had sent a man down to Kangaruma for mail. He now eagerly awaited his return so that the boats could be used to send down for stores. On the eighth day the man came, a black named Sobers, and on the tenth we started out. There was difficulty about collecting droghers; some passing Indians were recruited but two of them fell sick before starting so that in the end two men had to be taken away from the digging. Eventually the party consisted of these two, Sobers who was now being sent back to the coast for good, his usefulness being superseded by the Kopinang Indians, the black foreman Gerry, myself, and a Patamona family consisting of father and mother, son aged eight or nine and a dog, which they insisted at the last minute on bringing with them; they were an unattractive trio, even apart from their dog. The woman was slatternly and ill-favoured even for one of her race, with gross bandy legs, filthy and ragged clothes; the males wore only the lap; they had hair like chows and furtive, unfriendly eyes. I engaged Sobers, a muscular ruffian with gold teeth, as my own servant; the Indians were under the orders of Gerry, and I was in the position of passenger in the boat.

The walk from Mikraparu to Chinapowu was through bush line and across creeks, little different from the way from Anundabaru except that there was one steep descent down which we slipped from tree trunk to tree trunk, and that I was no longer lame. I wondered how the droghers managed to get their burdens up that hillside on the return journey.

At Chinapowu there were a few remains of a Boundary Commission store-house and some deserted Indian huts rapidly falling to ruin. Of the plantation house of Holmia no sign remained. The Clementis on their Roraima journey in 1916 recorded that it was then just visible in the encroaching bush. The cleared ground was now ten feet deep in a second growth from which emerged in gross and rudimentary forms a few descendants of cereals and fruit-trees.

There was one building, deserted, but still more or less intact, which had been built as a trading station at the time when all that district was being worked for ballata; it was substantially built of sawn wood; inside there were still the shelves on which the stock had been displayed, a counter and a rusted weighing-machine. The floor was filthy and crawling with djiggas, but I swept the counter clear and lay on that until some time after the blacks and me, the Indians turned up with my hammock. I had divided the copy of *Martin Chuzzlewit*, giving Winter, who was out of all reading matter, the part I had read. I now enjoyed the last chapters until the light failed and it was necessary to try to sleep.

The boat was a small flat-bottomed craft just capable of carrying us all and the luggage. It was beached high above the level of the river; we got it emptied out and afloat soon after daybreak but were obliged to delay until half past seven by the Indian family who insisted on making up the fire which they had kept smouldering under their hammocks all through the night, and cooking themselves some maize cobs they had found in the bush – relics of Holmia. Kaieteur was a full day's journey and it was important to make it before nightfall, so that this delay aggravated the antipathy I had felt for them ever since I discovered their intention of travelling with a dog. (This sentiment may perhaps shock animal lovers, but let them remember that Indian pets are far more odious even than those of Europeans, and are the chief disseminators of fleas, ticks and djiggas.)

Our boat was not built for speed, and weighed deep as we were, made slow progress even with the help of the stream. The two blacks rowed with immense energy, taking a pleasure in their strength. They fitted up rowlocks, tied paddles to wooden poles, and used them as oars. The two Indian boys paddled fairly consistently but the family sat in the stern with their dog, making little attempt to help. The man complained that he was sick, and when we handed paddles to the woman and boy they trailed them listlessly in the water for a little, then shipped them, and opened a clothful of putrid fish which they proceeded to munch for the greater part of the day. They were bush people unused to the river. I would gladly have left them behind, but they were needed as droghers for Winter's stores.

Boat on upper Potaro

Potaro landing

Instead I attempted to set a good example by paddling myself and within half an hour regretted it bitterly. It has always seemed to me an unnatural form of propulsion in which one is pulling against one's own weight and exhausting half one's strength in forming a fulcrum. After an hour, I gave it up and the Patamonas went on placidly eating their revolting food, occasionally offering some particularly uneatable morsel to the dog.

The river banks were absolutely devoid of habitation; familiar walls of forest on either side. Sobers and Gerry exchanged reminiscences of various camping-grounds (for it is a two- or three-day journey up stream from Kaieteur to Chinapowu) and of phenomenal conditions of flood or drought that they had known. The water was deep sepia in colour and absolutely smooth; every feature of the forest wall was duplicated there in minute detail – trunk and bush vine, tangled undergrowth, bare root, and the blossoming cumulus of the summit – except when, occasionally, we reached a place where the surface was dappled with real petals, white, yellow and pink, floating past us, strewn profusely and irregularly from the tree-tops over a large area, single and in clusters, as though they were flowering in a meadow.

It was after five when we reached Kaieteur. The landing was, of course, some way above the falls and leaving the boys to secure the boat and bring up the luggage, I hurried forward on foot to see them before it was dark. I had expected to be led there by the sound, but it was scarcely perceptible until one reached the brink and even there, so great was the depth, that only a low monotone rose to greet one.

The path led across a rock plateau totally unlike the surrounding country, bare except for cactuses and a few flowers, scattered with quartz, pebbles and sponge-like growths of crystal. A faint path led to the edge of the precipice and there a natural platform of rock allowed me to lie and study the extraordinary scene.

It has been described in detail by several travellers. I had arrived at the best time of day, for then, in late afternoon, the whole basin and gorge were clear of mist. The river was half full. Some visitors have toiled up to find only a single spout of water over which they were able to stand astride. A Russian artist went there to paint it and

was obliged to fill in the river from photographs and his imagination. That evening the whole centre of the lip was covered, and
the water gently spilled over it as though from a tilted dish. At the
edge it was brown as the river behind it, rapidly turning to white and
half-way down dissolving in spray so that it hung like a curtain of
white drapery. It fell sheer from its seven hundred-odd feet, for the
cliff had been hollowed back in the centuries and the edge jutted
over an immense black cavern. At the foot dense columns of spray
rose to meet it so that the impression one received was that the water
slowed down, hesitated, and then began to reascend, as though
a cinema film had been reversed. And not only reversed, but taken
in slow motion, for just as aeroplanes hurtling like bullets through
the air seem from the ground to be gently floating across the sky, so
the height here delayed and softened the vast fall, like the mason's at
Buckfast, who, tumbling off the triforium, is said to have been
caught half-way down by angels, lowered gently and set on his feet
in the nave, breathless, bewildered but unhurt.

The basin below was heaped with rocks, reduced by distance to
little boulders, among which the water was breaking in a high sea,
wave after wave set in being by the fall, emanating outwards and
smashing into spray against the banks like an incoming tide; half
a dozen or so minor cataracts were visible down the gorge before the
river regained its tranquillity.

But more remarkable, perhaps, than the fall itself was the scene
in which it stood. The scale was immense, so that the margin of
forest shrank to a line of shrub and it was only by an effort that one
could remind oneself that these were the great ramparts that had
towered over us all day. The cleavage, too, was so abrupt that it
appeared unnatural; as though two sections in a composite panorama had been wrongly fitted; above was the placid level on which
we had travelled, below for miles ahead the river could be followed,
shot black and silver ribbon, gently winding between bush-clad hills,
and here, in the middle a sharp break where the edges, instead of
coming together, lay apart, clumsily disjointed.

I lay on the overhanging ledge watching the light slowly fail, the
colour deepen and disappear. The surrounding green was of density
and intenseness that can neither be described or reproduced;

a quicksand of colour, of shivering surface and unplumbed depth, which absorbed the vision, sucking it down and submerging it. When it was quite dark I found my way back to the others.

There was a rest house in fair condition at the top of Kaieteur; this, and the one at Amatuk had been erected at the time when a Georgetown company projected a regular tourist service, which had come to nothing. (A lady named Mrs McTurk carried on the good will of the concern and made the arrangements for anyone who wished to go up, but no caretaker or store was now kept at the falls.) There were numerous names and initials carved on the walls and Sobers said it was lucky to leave some trace of one's occupation. Gerry, however, was sceptical, saying, 'Most of dey is dead already.'

The most recent inscription was dated in January of that year and said, '*Alfredo Sacramento, Author and Globe Trotter starved here.*'

I had heard this man's story from Winter. He was a Portuguese who appeared in Georgetown about Christmas-time, with no claims to authorship but many to globetrotting. He was supporting himself by selling his own portrait on signed postcards. It is not a unique means of livelihood. I met a bearded Dane in Venice doing the same thing and every now and then I see a brief interview in the English papers with someone who has successfully circumnavigated the earth in this way. Most of these travellers carry a recommendation, genuine or spurious, from some university professor, which, translated into six languages, proclaims their literary promise. Armed with this and a suitcase full of photographs of themselves in exploring costume, they set out to travel round the world. I do not know if any of them ever write books when they get home; their experience is mostly a monotonous round of café touting, incarceration and deportation, rows at consulates and immigration offices. (We gave the bearded Dane a list of addresses at which he should call when he came to England, but I have not yet heard of his arrival.)

Sacramento quickly exhausted the patience and curiosity of Georgetown and, taking up with some blacks in a rum shop, was told golden legends of the hospitality of the Indians and ranchers. Asking how he could get there, he was told that from Kaieteur there was a clear road through to Brazil, with Indian villages at every halt, where, though they were unlikely to buy his portrait, the people would feed him and help him on his way. The poor fellow believed all that he was told and began making enquiries about how he could reach Kaieteur. As it happened there was in Georgetown at the time a Canadian doctor, who, reading about Kaieteur in a magazine devoted to popular education, had impetuously taken a passage to Guiana and asked at the railway station for a ticket to the falls. Disgusted but undeterred by discovering the expedition to be more elaborate than he had expected, he was then arranging for a boat to take him up. The boat captains are always glad of an extra hand upstream, so Sacramento was able to get a free passage on condition of his using a paddle and helping with the droghing. Accordingly he travelled up with the doctor to Kaieteur, who, when he had looked at the falls and taken a spool of photographs, descended (incidentally cracking a rib en route) and left Sacramento alone at the top. On looking about for the road he had been promised he found it to be non-existent; the plateau ended in impenetrable bush; the only craft at the landing was Winter's boat – far too heavy to be launched, still less propelled upstream, single-handed. So Sacramento found himself without provisions or hope of escape until the next tourist should arrive, perhaps in six months' time.

Fortunately for him Winter was on his way back to the diamond working, and ten days later met Sacramento, by then within a fine distance of death from starvation and poisoning from the roots and berries he had been attempting to eat. Winter fed him by increasing degrees, until he was restored to a fair state of health and then sent him back to Amatuk in his boat, but Sacramento took the kindness with little gratitude. With returning strength, his wanderlust came back to him and he could not be persuaded that the road into Brazil was quite impossible to a man without guides and provisions, that the Indians were scattered, elusive and quite unwilling, even when they were able, to give food to strange foreigners. Sacramento went back under compulsion, alive, but full of resentment.

It was interesting to notice the reactions to Kaieteur of the different members of the party. Gerry and the two Indian boys had seen it before and did not bother to look again. Sobers had been there seven times but always went down to see it, with genuine awe and appreciation of its beauty. The Patamona family had never been there before and did not take the smallest interest in it; instead they lit the fire under their hammocks and lay alternately dozing and munching *farine* without putting themselves quarter of a mile out of the way to see it. One book says that the Indians think it haunted by *Kenaima* and when obliged to approach, put pepper in their eyes to blind themselves, but I heard no confirmation of this and I think the Patamonas' reluctance to visit it came from mere stupidity and lack of imagination.

Next morning, as soon as it was light, Sobers and I went down to the fall, this time not to the ledge from which I had seen it the night before, but down another line to the water edge, where we were able to walk on dry rocks to the very brink of the fall. But at that time the whole basin and gorge were full of mist that blotted out everything except the rush of brown water at our feet.

As before the bad family lay long in their hammocks and pottered about with wood embers and fish preparing a lengthy breakfast. There was a long, very steep, rocky descent to Tokeit landing. On the way we passed a snake, coiled up asleep in the trail; bathed at the bottom and launched the boat, while we waited for the Indians to arrive. The boat proved to be of the same build as the one we had used the day before, but about half its size, and quite incapable of carrying the whole of the party. Accordingly I decided to leave the bad family behind. They accepted their desertion with the same brutish apathy they had shown to all our proceedings. They had rations for two days which we were able to supplement very slightly from the remaining stores. It would be at least five days, probably longer, before Gerry returned from Kangaruma to relieve them. Meanwhile they were better off than Alfredo Sacramento because they had a bow and arrows with them; there were fish in the river and no doubt game in the bush, and, anyway, periodic fasts are common enough experiences in their own villages. Nevertheless I felt guilty, though less guilty than I had done in the case of Eusebio. Some of the party *had* to be left behind and they and their dog were the most easily spared. They squatted at the water's edge and watched us till we were out of sight.

Lightened as we were, the boat was dangerously low in the water and our progress correspondingly slow. It was windless in the gorge and now we began to feel the weight of the descent we had made. Days and nights grew hotter, the nearer we approached the coast. After Kangaruma there was no need for a blanket at night, and the briskness we had felt in the hills gave way to lassitude.

The gorge which from Kaieteur had the appearance of a single cleft, was revealed on closer acquaintance as a series of wooded hills. The river wound in and out between them until at noon we reached Waratuk. At high flood these rapids could be shot, but at this season it had the effect of a dam of boulders spanning the river with, between each, a sharp cataract, bubbling over rocks in a series of little falls and whirlpools. The broadest channel was on the left bank. We drew the boat in, unloaded it and carried the stores to a sand beach that lay in still water quarter of a mile down stream. Here the Indians and I waited while Gerry and Sobers handled the boat over the rapids. They tied a rope to the stern, hitched it round a boulder, and Sobers took the end, slowly paying it out under Gerry's orders. Gerry stood at the bows, and, sometimes jumping from stone to stone, sometimes wading thigh-deep in the surf, steered them between the rocks. If he had lost his footing and loosed his hold on the boat for a moment it would have been swept sideways and stove in. The whole operation took about twenty minutes and was done with astonishing dexterity and absence of fuss. In a few days' time Gerry would have the far more difficult task of taking the boat up, without Sobers' help. I wondered how he would manage it; so I think did Gerry, looking contemptuously at the frail little Indians who would be his companions.

We cooked lunch on the sand-bank, rested for an hour and then reloaded the boat and set out again. In about three hours we reached Amatuk, where the boat was no further use to us and had to be beached. It was here that trouble might be expected with Mr Diabolo. He lived on the right bank some way below the falls and we heard ourselves hailed from behind and saw some blacks fishing among the rocks. They appeared to be friends of Sobers'. In a few minutes one of them appeared in a boat and rowed over to us. He was a youth of unmistakably criminal appearance, but he greeted

Sobers and Gerry with great warmth, and bowed politely to me. We got into the boat with our baggage, picked up the fishermen and presently made for a house on the further bank. This I gathered was Mr Diabolo's boat, and that was Mr Diabolo's house. Mr Diabolo was away so both these had been appropriated by our friends who were 'pork knockers' washing the gravel of a worked-out diamond claim that had once belonged to Winter. They were as open-handed to us as they had been to themselves, and readily let us have the use of the boat for our journey to Kangaruma on the next day. The presence of the friendly 'pork knockers' was doubly fortunate for it solved the problem which had worried my conscience far more than the discomfort of the bad Patamona family; that was, how, without them, Winter's stores were to be carried in reasonable time up Amatuk and Waratuk. For a dollar a head the blacks agreed to take on the job.

They also urged us to sleep in Mr Diabolo's house, but there was another slightly lower down, belonging to Mrs McTurk where I thought I should be more comfortable. It was built on a small island in the middle of the river; at flood time this was submerged and the house stood up in midstream on its piles just clear of the water. There was an arm-chair there, the first I had seen for many weeks, and a shelf of tattered novels. An aged negro lived there as caretaker and exacted a toll of one dollar for its use. The vampires in that house were thicker than I had found them anywhere, and kept me awake by fluttering round my mosquito net and hanging to it, trying to nose a way in.

But the arm-chair and the row of old novels, and the caretaker with his white woolly head, his respectful English, and his expectation of a tip, were all symbols of the return to civilisation; another phase of the journey – the last but one – was over.

CHAPTER 9

Lower Potaro – Kangaruma – regular communications – Tumatumari – Rockstone – Wismar – Georgetown – conclusion.

COMPARED WITH THE country above Kaieteur, the lower Potaro was populous and civilised. With every splash of the paddles we drew nearer to Georgetown; not only in mileage, but in the air and temper of our surroundings; we passed other boats manned by negroes in felt hats, vests and short trousers; we were among people who spoke English and knew the value of money; the buildings were graced with corrugated iron, wire fencing, asbestos and sawn planks. But it was a broken and fugitive civilisation. Not here those firm, confident tentacles of modernity that extend to greet the traveller, no tractors making their own roads as they advance; no progressive young managers projecting more advanced stations of commerce, opening up new districts, pushing forward new settlements and new markets; no uniformed law asserting itself in chaos.

Instead we had overtaken civilisation in its retreat; the ground was worked out, the beaches sifted of their treasure, the trees bled to death for ballata, the stores derelict and once busy stations in process of evacuation. It was as though modernity had put out sensitive snail-horns and, being hurt, had withdrawn them. The wounds in the bush – surface scratches negligible to its vast bulk and power – were healing over and the place returning to the solitude and desolation frivolously disturbed.

There had once been a police station below Amatuk and a handful of shops trading rum and rations for gold dust, diamonds and ballata. These and the clusters of shacks round them had all been abandoned in the retrocession; the rain and the ants and the omnivorous bush were pulling them to pieces and overwhelming them. They were very ignoble ruins; not the majestic façades of the burned-out houses of Southern Ireland or the overgrown capitals

536

and pediments that remain when a real civilisation comes to its end; bare frames of rotten timber and misshapen tin or most desolate of all, rusted and half-buried heaps of useless machinery. For it was a destructive and predatory civilisation that we were meeting and it was disappearing like the trenches and shell-craters of a battlefield.

At Kangaruma I came once more into contact with regular communications, though not, let it be said, communications highly organised or very direct. Here the river made a wide detour over impassable waterfalls. A broad trail had been cut through to Potaro landing and the intervening creeks roughly bridged, forming the straight five-mile base of a triangle. A lorry covered this journey when freight warranted and the state of its mechanism permitted it. As often as not the vehicle was out of order and passengers were obliged to walk; this had been the case when Sobers was last there and he expressed little confidence in its restoration. From Potaro landing a launch with an outboard engine plied, when required, to Tumatumari, where there was a village and another waterfall. From Tumatumari there was another motor launch owned by an East Indian which journeyed irregularly to Rockstone on the Essequibo where there had once been a village and a railway service to Wismar. Trains no longer ran, but the line remained and it was possible to cross either by foot or on a truck pushed by hand or, if one was fortunate, drawn by a motor tractor. Wismar was a place of some importance on the Demerara, where an American company were working for bauxite, and from there bi-weekly steamers sailed to Georgetown. It will be clear that the journey involved a number of somewhat uncertain connexions. It was, however, a definite line of communication and in that differed from anything I had encountered since leaving the Berbice.

There was also an alternative route down the Government's new road to Bartika, which met the Potaro at a point between Potaro landing and Tumatumari. Something has been said of this enterprise already and comment is apposite here after what I have written above about the abandonment of the district, for there certainly was a large scheme making for its development. The next ten years or so will show which will be victor, the bush or the road. It is being done at what is, for the Colony, great expense and on a considerable scale, and is, in its way, a courageous attempt. If it is unsuccessful, the defeat will mean the abandonment at any rate for a generation, probably for ever, of the 'opening up' of the interior; the colony will resign itself to the limits of a single strip of seaboard and leave the huge territory at its back in the primeval integrity it has always maintained.

The arguments against its success may be stated as follows: that it was too late in coming; twenty years earlier when the Potaro was busy with 'pork knockers', ballata bleeders and quite a few gold seekers working on a large scale, it might have been of immense value; by now the district was too far decayed and its resources exhausted; that it was unreliable from an engineering point of view, being built on sand over a substructure of roots; it would subside and collapse, the sand would wash away and the Government would be faced with the alternative of abandoning wheeled traffic or spending a great sum annually in its upkeep; that since it was a ridge road – running partly along natural hills and partly on an artificial viaduct – there was little prospect of settlers cultivating its borders for the difficulties of transporting produce to the road level would counter-balance the advantage of rapid transit; that even as it was the journey to Georgetown took as long that way as by Rockstone, for it was a two-day land journey and boats ran from Bartika just as infrequently as from Wismar; moreover the journey was one of excruciating discomfort with every possibility of a breakdown on the way and an indefinite delay in the bush. At the time Sobers, who found a mournful pleasure in multiplying the probable difficulties of our journey, had come up, there had been a two weeks' cessation of the lorry service.

Whatever the ultimate advantages of the new road, I decided in the immediate circumstances to follow the river route. At Kangaruma the prospect was more hopeful than Sobers had led me to expect, for the lorry to Potaro landing was in order and due to start on the next day and there seemed a very fair chance of all the connexions fitting and my getting to Georgetown on the fourth day.

There was a shop at Kangaruma where I was able to purchase tinned butter (at seven and sixpence a pound), corned beef, potatoes, fairly fresh bread, tobacco, beer and other luxuries. There was a clean room kept for visitors, a good bathing creek, and, most remarkable of all, a pile of newspapers, the weekly edition of an illustrated daily dating to within a month of my arrival. I had not seen an English paper later than the one I read on board ship on the morning of my departure from London. Inevitably, I had come to expect every kind of public and private cataclysm, the fall of governments, outbreak of wars and revolutions, the assassination of the royal family, the marriage, parenthood, divorce and death of all my friends. Actually, of course, it was a very short time and nothing of particular note had occurred. But, even so, it was the newspapers more than anything else that brought it home to me that my journey was coming to an end.

It did not end without some remaining asperities. Now that one was back among organised communications, all the civilised man's impatience at delay returned and each stage of the journey was attended by several hours' irritation during which the various negroes responsible came nearly to blows in apparently pointless altercations. The lorry, however, was ready next morning and after immense preliminary agitation of the starting handle, was got to work and arrived at its destination late but intact.

I left Gerry and the Indians sorting out Winter's stores. Sobers, as arranged, came on with me. From Amatuk onwards our relations became remote; he said 'Chief' more often when talking to me and took off his cap whenever he came into a room where I was sitting. There had been an inevitable transition; we were no longer travelling companions but servant and master.

There was a long wait at Potaro landing while the captain of the boat and the driver of the lorry attempted to remove part of the engine which had to be taken down river for repairs. They quarrelled with one another, shouted at the tops of their voices, and knocked the car about in a way which must have shortened its already precariously protracted existence, by a considerable time. Finally when they had battered and hammered and wrenched and roared themselves hoarse they gave up the attempt as hopeless and we chugged down towards Tumatumari. After a mile or two we came to Garroway stream, the present terminus of the Government road. There was a large labour camp there and the beginnings of a bridge which, if the venture continues, will carry the road up to Kaieteur. We took on mail and a couple more passengers, and reached Tumatumari at half past one.

This had once been a considerable town with an hotel, police station and resident commissioner; now it was a ramshackle negro village of wooden huts sprawling along one street that led past the falls between the two landings. The only man of any authority was an aged and amiable black who combined the offices of postmaster, school teacher and preacher. There was a little rest house, maintained for the use of visiting officials, to which he gave me the keys. He also lent me a romance of colonial life written by a black schoolmaster and printed in Trinidad – a curiously ingenuous tale of the finally reconciled conflict of love and duty.

There were a dozen or so stores in the village licensed to buy gold and sell rum, and a chattering black population who lived on supplying recreation to 'pork knockers'. At first there was no news of the Rockstone boat whose timetable, apparently, depended on the caprice of the bosun. 'Him starts when him likes,' they said. 'De captain very old and him can't see much.'

But it arrived that afternoon with a handful of passengers. One of them had brought a live pig. He was a speculator in pork and it was his practice to borrow a pig from the station clerk at Rockstone, bring it to Tumatumari, and lead it about the village, hawking for orders. The price was fixed beforehand. If he got enough orders for meat to cover his fare and show a small profit, he killed the pig, divided it up and returned to pay its owner. If there was no adequate market he led the animal back disconsolately to Rockstone and was the loser by the expense of his journey. On this occasion the demand was brisk and the beast's death squeals disturbed the evening.

I went down to the landing, interviewed the all-powerful bosun and extorted a promise from him to sail at seven the next morning. It was essential to make an early start if we were to catch the Wismar boat which left early the following morning. A few hours' delay might mean the loss of four days in a town where I was reluctant to spend much time.

Next morning at seven, however, there was no sign of activity at the landing and the stores we were taking down still lay in a heap on shore. I recruited Sobers and some other passengers and got the boat loaded, but the bosun still maintained that he was unable to start; the mail-bag had not arrived. I went up to the post office and found it open and the postmaster still accepting letters which arrived in a dilatory fashion every quarter of an hour. Everyone who bought a stamp felt herself – they were mostly women – entitled to a several minutes' gossip. A large printed order announced that on the mornings when the mail left, the office was closed at 6.30 a.m. I pointed this out and demanded that the bag be sent down to the boat. The postmaster explained that he had to sort all the letters out first, complete his own correspondence and seal up the bag. Meanwhile more negresses came slopping up, flat-footed, to buy postal orders and chat about their families. It was eleven before we started.

It took us ten hours to Rockstone without a stop. I sat under an awning amidships. There was one other first-class passenger, a large black lady of some importance, for she wore shoes and gold earrings and travelled with a bag of peppermints and a thermos flask of cold water. The men at the back lit a fire on a piece of iron and cooked luncheon on the way.

After we reached the Essequibo the scenery became painfully monotonous – a vast breadth of water bordered by forest and broken occasionally by islands of bush. After dark my companion slept, sprawling over most of the seat.

Rockstone was another deserted town. The large wooden house built as an hotel was falling to pieces; beside it stood the barrack-like quarters that had been used by the railway employees. The only inhabitant, now, was the East Indian railway clerk who lived in the derelict station. I explained to him the urgency of my catching the Demerara boat. He was full of sympathy, remarking that Rockstone and Wismar were full of mosquitoes and no place in which to spend unnecessary nights. He was himself shaking with fever. It was impossible, however, to get across that night, he said, as the tractor was out of order.

I interviewed the bosun of the boat who seemed the only active man about, and the driver of the tractor; they were both despondent until I offered five dollars between them if I caught the ship next morning. That secured their attention and for some hours grinding noises, sudden reports and showers of sparks came from the stationary tractor. Meanwhile the other passengers, about twelve in all, had retired to sleep, some of them hanging hammocks from convenient posts, some making little nests among the heaps of goods which littered the yard, others sprawling, without compromise, across the platform. I put up my hammock in the booking-office and went to sleep with little expectation of getting to Wismar until next day.

Just before midnight, however, the clerk began running up and down the platform shaking the sleepers and blowing his whistle. The tractor was working.

We all climbed with our luggage into an open trolley and with a grating of gears and overwhelming issue of exhaust gas, the tractor started.

It was a slow journey; the oil-lamp that hung in front of us illumined little except the two rails. The bush had originally been cut back some distance on either side to protect the line from falling timber, but a luxurious second growth now grew round and over us. Two or three times we were obliged to stop and remove fallen branches and shovel away a small landslide. After two hours it came on to rain heavily and the passengers drew a tarpaulin sheet over us, completely excluding air and view. Personally I would have preferred a wetting. I have occasionally heard it debated whether negroes have an unpleasant smell. These certainly had. I have also heard it said that white men are as disagreeable to them as they are to us; I can only say that my fellow passengers on this journey were not fastidious and showed no desire to avoid proximity with me. I could have wished they had.

But it came to an end at last, a little before dawn. The Demerara boat was at the quayside and we went on board at once and dozed in a swarm of mosquitoes.

Next day we sailed down stream with a perceptible sea breeze in our faces, past sugar plantations, bovianders' huts, East India villages – characteristic riverside scenery. Early that afternoon I was back in Georgetown.

The journey was over and here the book might well come to an end. There is no occasion for a purple passage. I have written throughout a direct and, I hope, accurate, day-to-day chronicle of a journey over strange ground and in circumstances that were – to me – unusual. It makes no claim to being a spiritual odyssey. Whatever interior changes there were – and all experience makes some change – are the writer's own property and not a marketable commodity. I had been ninety-two days away from letters and the normal amenities of life; it had been an arduous and at times arid experience. I had taken enough strenuous exercise and suffered enough mild privation to justify myself in spending the rest of the year in indolence and self-indulgence. I had one grave breach of faith – poor Eusebio – on my conscience. I had contributed to the generally distasteful impressions of the new Prior of Boa Vista. I had caused unavoidable pain to several horses. I had added to my treasury of eccentrics the fantastic figure of Mr Christie. I had seen several different sorts of life being led – rancher, missionary, Indian, diamond hunter – which I could never have imagined. I had added another small piece to the pages of the atlas that were real to me. For me it had been abundantly worth while and it seems to me conceivable that an account of it may interest some people. I might make this the end of the book and abandon for good the nursery where I have been working, but I think it would be in keeping with its desultory nature, to complete it, as it has been written, with some final, unambitious paragraphs about the remaining days.

There was some time to wait in Georgetown before there was a ship home. Even then I had to break my voyage at Trinidad. In Georgetown I met an agreeable character called 'Professor' Piles who lived by selling stuffed alligators. He had a peculiar fascination over them and over snakes, and loved both species dearly. He used to go out to the creeks and call them; it went greatly against his sentiments to kill them, but he had to live. Once he had been put in prison at Mazaruni and had secured release by the simple expedient of summoning every snake in the neighbourhood. Every morning when the warders came to his cell they found it full of assembled reptiles. They would accompany him at recreation and at work to the great detriment of good order and discipline, so that eventually the Governor was obliged to order his release. I bought a crate full of baby alligators from him to take back as presents to the children of my friends. They have not been a great success. One child said, foolishly I thought, 'Is it a rabbit?' and another − a girl − called it 'Evelyn' and proceeded to tear it to pieces; a third said, 'Is it real?' and on being told that it was asked, 'Is it dead?' His interest was then exhausted and he returned to his bricks.

I renewed the acquaintances I had made at Christmas and paid formal calls of farewell, feeling a little patronising towards the town dwellers who let themselves be shut in between forest and sea, and never adventured into the country behind them.

'Have you been up to Kaieteur?'

'Not exactly, but I passed it coming down, on my way back.'

There was the inevitable disappointment of getting my films back from the developers. I had taken two dozen rolls and packed them with every precaution Father Mather or I could devise, but many of them had got spoiled during the journey. A large number, too, were failures as pictures. Without exception all the photographs taken in the bush and in the cattle trail were worthless, pitch dark with glaring blots of light. Even those in which the exposure had been successful were disappointing, for compositions which had seemed full of interest when I took them, now appeared drab and insignificant. All the landscapes, except those of river scenery, were despoiled of their beauty, the hills flattened out, the trees barely distinguishable, the valleys without form. The Indians had been, as I have described, elusive subjects, but I had taken numerous snapshots of them unawares, by the device which I may commend to the more careful manipulations of others facing the same problem; you stand or sit facing at right angles to your subject and holding the camera sideways, turned towards them, looking ahead but all the time glancing down and sighting the lens by means of the finder. The Indians rarely suspected that they were being taken, nor alas, would these suspicions have been aroused in most cases if they had seen the results, which, though amusing souvenirs, were few of them recognisable as portraits and fewer still reproducable as the illustrations for which they were primarily intended.

Out of 192 exposures, barely fifty were of any real interest.

From Georgetown to Trinidad in a smart Canadian ship, full of sea-sick boy scouts on their way to a Jamboree, and convivial golfers going to a tournament in Barbados.

It was Holy Week so I went out to stay in a little Benedictine monastery in the hills behind Port of Spain. They maintain a guest house where many people go for the cool air. I sat at table with a lady anthropologist with whom I involved myself in acrimonious arguments about Indian character. She would not have it that they were cowards, and she knew much more of them than I did; but I still think I was right.

I feel that this book has too much ecclesiastical flavour already; otherwise I could well devote a chapter to the Easter festivals at Mount St Benedict. On Good Friday pilgrims of all races and creeds assembled to kiss the Cross from all parts of the island – Hindus, Protestants, Chinese – and for Easter morning the church and courtyard of the monastery were packed with a dense crowd. They began arriving at about ten on Saturday evening and all through the night we could hear the chatter and the padding of bare feet as they climbed past the guest house. The first Mass was said before dawn and after it the great crowd formed a procession, each carrying a candle in a coloured paper shade. As the only white man present I found a torch thrust into my hands to carry in front of the Host. The line of coloured lights wound down the steeply graded hill road and climbed back again to the Church and just as we reached the summit again day began to break over the hills and there was a feeling of New Year.

From Trinidad I took a comfortable Dutch ship to Southampton. There was some slight discussion at the Customs as to whether stuffed alligators were dutiable as furniture, but in the end these were allowed in as scientific specimens. After a change of luggage in London I went straight to Bath and spent a week there alone in an hotel. Spring was breaking in the gardens, tender and pure and very different from the gross vegetation of the tropics. I had seen no building that was stable or ancient for nearly six months. Bath, with its propriety and uncompromised grandeur, seemed to offer everything that was most valuable in English life; and there, pottering composedly among the squares and crescents, I came finally to the end of my journey.

WAUGH IN ABYSSINIA

For
Kitty & Perry
who, I have no doubt, will affect to
recognise thinly disguised and rather
flattering portraits of themselves
in this narrative;
with my love

CONTENTS

NOTE

This morning, after the final proofs of the first chapter had gone to press, there have appeared in the English newspapers some notices of Marshal de Bono's book on the war. I have not seen the book. The notices consist of a few quotations isolated from their context, interspersed in a highly tendentious commentary, and surmounted by sensational headlines. They may well prove misleading. At the moment I see no reason to alter any of the conclusions reached in this chapter.

E. W.

OCTOBER 9TH, 1936.

CHAPTER 1

THE INTELLIGENT WOMAN'S GUIDE TO
THE ETHIOPIAN QUESTION

1

'Although the benefits of a civilised Protectorate are very evident, it is, I confess, with a feeling almost of sadness that I reflect that since I said farewell to Johannis at Afgol, on December 16, 1887, no other European can ever grasp the hand of an Independent Emperor of Ethiopia.'

These words, published in 1892 in Mr Gerald Portal's account[1] of his embassy to Abyssinia – an undertaking, like most others in that country, accomplished only at the expense of acute privation and some danger, embarrassed by the treachery of native guides and the ceremonious discourtesies of native noblemen; like most others, fruitless of result – record what an informed and, on the whole, sympathetic observer in the last century foresaw as the inevitable development of Ethiopian history.

He was writing at the close of a decade which had been marked by sensational changes in the constitution of Africa; changes still active whose only logical outcome was the division and occupation of the entire continent by the people of Europe. In the previous decade Livingstone and Stanley had made their momentous journeys across hitherto totally unknown country. Livingstone had inspired a resurgence of missionary spirit comparable, though in many respects dissimilar, to that of the sixteenth century – Catholics, Lutherans, Anglicans, Baptists had followed the laborious stages of his great journey, eager to reclaim the Africans from slavery and superstition. Stanley appealed more particularly to the commercial ambitions of his age. The industrial revolution, which had begun by giving more wealth to nearly everybody, had reached its second

---

1 *My Mission to Abyssinia*, by Gerald H. Portal, C.B. (1892).

stage in which enormous, yearly increasing accumulations of surplus capital were falling into a small, yearly diminishing number of hands; the need of the time was for new sources of raw material, new markets, but, more than anything, for new fields of profitable investment. It was in his private capacity as a capitalist that Stanley's patron, King Leopold of Belgium, founded the International African Association. But in the 'eighties the exploitation of Africa took on a national and political complexion. France in the arduous years that followed the Prussian war saw a possibility of recovering in Africa the prestige she had lost in Europe. England, concerned primarily with safeguarding the route to India, possessed of ample territories in the temperate zones for the settlement of her surplus population, at first hung back, repeatedly and explicitly discouraging expansion of her coastal trading stations, until forced into competition by Germany.

It was not until 1884 that Bismarck disclosed his ambitions of African Empire; from the moment that he did so he became the dominating engineer of the partition. Africa was enormous; there was room for everyone; its wealth was illimitable; there, looming preternaturally large in the mists of legend and travellers' tales, lay the solution that Europe was seeking; there the ambitions and energies that with disastrous regularity rose to threaten the progress of civilisation, might have full and harmless scope. His concern, while obtaining all for his own people which generations might require, was that the frictions aroused in the scramble should not imperil the settlement of Europe so recently and satisfactorily achieved. The Congress of Berlin met in the winter of 1884 and the Powers discussed their claims and intentions. All were agreed upon the basic assumption: Africa was open to partition; any part of it that was held only by its own natives was a no-man's-land which any European might claim. Boundaries were to be on a strictly national basis;[1] it only remained to define the rules by which they should be drawn.

---

[1] The Congo Free State was brought into being, but from the first was mainly and soon exclusively Belgian.

Ten years earlier, when European interest was limited to a fringe of coastal trading stations, it had been vaguely held that, as mineral rights are prolonged from the earth's surface to its centre, the hinterland of these stations was legitimately theirs for an indefinite depth, if and when expansion should seem desirable. Such a theory was clearly applicable only to a circular and perfectly homogeneous continent; it had, moreover, the grave objection that considerable strips of the African coast were claimed on historic grounds by weak and, it was believed, retrograde states such as Portugal and Zanzibar. At Berlin an attempt was made to define what constituted 'effective occupation' and 'spheres of influence'. In practice, however, boundaries continued to be marked by the process of local adventure by explorers and leisurely adjustment in their respective Chanceries.

The most remarkable feature of the partition was the speed with which it was accomplished. In less than ten years the whole of pagan Africa was in the hands of one or other of the European Powers. Explorers pushed on from village to village armed with satchels of draft treaties upon which hospitable chiefs were induced to set their mark; native interpreters made gibberish of the legal phraseology; inalienable tribal rights were exchanged for opera hats and musical boxes; some potentates, such as the Sultan of Sokoto, thought they were accepting tribute when they were receiving a subsidy in lieu of their sovereign rights,[1] others that it was the white man's polite custom to collect souvenirs of this kind; if, when they found they had been tricked, they resisted the invaders, they were suppressed with the use of the latest lethal machinery: diplomats in Europe drew frontiers across tracts of land of which they were totally ignorant, negligently overruling historic divisions of race and culture and the natural features of physical geography, consigning to the care of one or other white race millions of men who had never seen a white face. A task which was to determine the future history of an entire continent, requiring the highest possible degrees of scholarship and statesmanship, was rushed through in less than ten years.

1 *The Dual Mandate in British Tropical Africa*, by Lord Lugard (1922).

But the avarice, treachery, hypocrisy and brutality of the partition are now a commonplace which needs no particularisation. Indeed the popular view is to exaggerate the criminality; to accept the fact as something inexcusable but irreparable; a great wrong, never to be repeated, committed in another, more barbarous age. It is worth remembering, at the present crisis, how lately these things were done and also how many of the high qualities of European civilisation appeared in the process. In the lowest category, the financiers who stayed in Europe at their offices were men of daring; what they risked was a small thing but it was what they valued most highly; orthodox big-business distrusted the travellers' tales of African wealth; it was a gamble in which fortunes were lost as well as won. The explorers were doing what no men had done before them; they did not travel at the head of an army but in small companies, often alone, in unknown dangers. Many lost their lives, almost all lost their health, and of the mixed motives which impelled them – adventure, patriotism, science – avarice was usually the least important and the least rewarded. There were the administrators, who, for small salaries, brought justice and order into wicked places, and, in the highest category of all, priests and nuns, missionaries of every sect and doctors, whose whole lives were an atonement for the crimes of their countrymen. It is worth remembering that these achievements were not exclusively or even predominantly British.

It is worth remembering indeed, in the present circumstances, the particular nature of the reproach which attaches to England. France, Germany and Belgium were the more ruthless; we the more treacherous. We went into the shady business with pious expressions of principle; we betrayed the Portuguese and the Sultan of Zanzibar,[1] renouncing explicit and freshly made guarantees of their territory; we betrayed Lobenguela and other native rulers in precisely the same method but with louder protestations of benevolent intention than our competitors; no matter into what caprice of policy our electorate chose to lead us, we preached on blandly and continuously; it was a trait which the world found difficult to tolerate; but we are still preaching.

1 *The Partition of Africa*, by J. Scott Keltie (1893).

2

In 1930 many Europeans exercised the privilege of grasping the hand of an Independent Emperor of Abyssinia.

On November 2 of that year Ras Tafari Makonnen was crowned King of Kings, Lion of Judah, Emperor Haile Selassie I at Addis Ababa. Delegations from the entire civilised world were present to wish him, in the name of their countries, a long and prosperous reign and to assure him of their friendly intentions. The Duke of Gloucester, attended by the Governors of the surrounding territories, represented Great Britain; the Prince of Udine, Italy; Marshal d'Esperez, France. Not only these great neighbouring Powers, but states as remote in their interests as Holland and Poland chose to interpret the announcement of the succession as an invitation; everyone was eager to observe this unique monarchy which had defied all predictions and retained its independence. Abyssinian hospitality was strained almost unendurably in their accommodation. It was widely believed among the populace that these braided figures had come to pay homage.

The new Emperor was treated to every mark of independent royalty. Press photographers and cinema men jostled before him, divesting the prolix solemnities of almost all their decency. Presents of biblical diversity were heaped upon him – hock from Germany, statuary from Greece, bedroom furniture from Egypt. Distant editors were demanding stories of 'barbaric splendour' and, while earnest palace officials were trying to interest the visiting correspondents in the new programme of administrative reform and social service, the cable office was glutted with press messages describing the rough and often shoddy pageantry in terms that would have been barely applicable to the court of Suleiman the Magnificent or of the Mogul Emperors of India.

Except at the military reviews the Abyssinians were not conspicuous. At the coronation itself only a few dozen were present – the great Rases, who sat among the delegations on the dais, gorgeous, rather morose personages in comic gilded coronets, and a handful of smaller chiefs who had fought their way past the royal guards and now dozed fitfully on the floor in far corners of the pavilion. Besides these, the European visitors were aware of the existence, at a great distance, of a dense, half-human rabble that was constantly held at bay by the police; a mass of curly black heads that were for ever being whacked with staves; a great tide of grubby white garments which flowed into the city at dawn from the surrounding hillside and ebbed out at nightfall, assisted in all its motions by unremitting direction from canes and rifle butts.

The focal point, the still hub of all the turmoil, was Tafari himself; a small, elegant figure, Oriental rather than African, formal, circumspect, inscrutable; he moved like a vested statue carried in a religious procession; he sat upright and impassive among the sprawling and fidgeting European delegates; it scarcely seemed possible that anyone could take pleasures as sadly as he took those of his European guests; at the racecourse he spoke to no one, but sat under his canopy, motionless except for a slight inclination in acknowledgement of the salutes of the winning riders; in the ballroom he sat by the wall, his tiny, polished shoes just clear of the dancers.

That crowded week was the consummation of months of feverish activity, years of quiet plotting. A few days earlier he had been driving about the city, directing in person the planting of the flag-staffs, the erection of triumphal arches; he had discussed every detail of the extravagant entertainment. He was able, now, to sit and enjoy his triumph. For years he had been playing a delicate game between the Powers and his own people; abroad and to foreign visitors he had shown himself as the descendant of a historic line of Christian kings and queens, representative of an ancient civilisation, a statesman who would distil all that was most valuable in the modern world, the friend of missionaries, doctors and schoolmasters; he had explained his country as a mediæval state, a cohesive whole held together by the intricate bonds of feudalism, its occasional disorders as those which had beset Europe seven centuries ago – the over-mighty subject, a too dominant clergy. At home he had presented himself as the man who understood the ways of the foreigner, to whom his people must surrender their ancient rights of local independence if they were to retain any independence at all. He could make no pre-eminent claim to authority on grounds of heredity; the real Emperor was in chains, few people knew where. Tafari was the man chosen for a job; one of many great noblemen elected by the others, one of themselves, set the task for which they knew he was suited, to continue the tortuous, dangerous policy that had so far succeeded, of playing off the Powers against each other. It was thus that Abyssinia, contrary to all reasonable prediction, had survived so far, not only intact but enormously augmented.

But in Tafari's mind – pathetically compounded of primitive simplicity and primitive suspicion, of the traditional Christian right-eousness, that had found occasional expression even in characters as intemperate as the Emperor Theodore's, and traditional savage hostility to European standards – there was a belief, half formed, never fully operative, that there had lately been a change in the constitution of the world. Abyssinia had survived through the rival-ries of the Powers; now these rivalries were at an end; old wrongs had been forgotten, the map had finally been drawn, rolled up, sealed, at Versailles and Geneva. The Powers still maintained their mission to rule Africa; they had consecrated it in the phrase of the League Covenant: '*The well being and development of peoples not yet able to stand by themselves under the strenuous conditions of the modern world form a sacred trust of civilisation . . . best entrusted to advanced nations.*' Germany, by her defeat in battle, was held to have proved herself unworthy of this trust and her share was redistributed, great parts being given to the Boers – with the single exception of the Abyssinians the most notoriously oppressive administrators of subject peoples in Africa.[1] But Abyssinia remained unappropriated. More than that, through the good offices of her old enemies the Italians, she had inexplicably – miraculously, it might well appear to a people as confident of Divine favour as the Abyssinians – stepped into place beside the conquerors. She was a member of the League of Nations, admitted on equal terms to the councils of the world, her territory guaranteed absolutely and explicitly; that vast and obscure agglomeration of feudal fiefs, occupied military provinces, tributary sultanates, track-less no-man's-lands roamed by homicidal nomads; undefined in

[1] The massacre by air bombing of the Bondelzwarts, a primitive race in ex-German South-West Africa, by the South African mandatory government, on the grounds that 'they could not or would not pay a tax on their dogs', was mentioned at Geneva in 1923, but resulted in no reproof or compensation.

extent, unmapped, unexplored, in part left without law, in part grossly subjugated; the brightly coloured patch in the schoolroom atlas marked, for want of a more exact system of terminology, 'Ethiopian Empire', had been recognised as a single state whose integrity was the concern of the world. Tafari's own new dynasty had been accepted by the busy democracies as the government of this area; his enemies were their enemies; there would be money lent him to arm against rebels, experts to advise him; when trouble was brewing he would swoop down from the sky and take his opponents unawares; the fabulous glories of Prester John were to be reincarnate; roads, telephones, tractors, chemical manures, clinics, colleges and new hygienic gaols.

Forty years of confused history, in Africa and Europe, lay between Tafari and Johannis. It was during this period that the Ethiopian Empire came into existence.

3

At the beginning of the nineteenth century Abyssinia consisted of the four mountain kingdoms of Amhara, Shoa, Tigre and Gojjam, situated in almost complete isolation from outside intercourse; their neighbours were hostile pagans and Mohammedans of negro and Hamitic race; the Abyssinians[1] were Christians of mixed Semitic and Hamitic blood; they believed they had migrated from Arabia at some unrecorded date, probably before the Christian era; they employed a common literary language, Ghiz, which had some affinity with ancient Armenian, and spoke dialects derived from it, Tigrean and Amharic; they shared a common culture and feudal organisation and recognised a paramount King of Kings as their nominal head; from time to time in their history the King of Kings had asserted effective government and extended his rule to the outlying tribes; in the century before Mohammed he had controlled

---

1 The name, a corruption of the Arabic Habasha, is variously derived as meaning 'Mongrels' and as 'members of the Arabian Habashat tribe'. Hamitic and Semitic have now little precise meaning. Professor Kolmodin of Upsala denies that Abyssinians originated from Arabia. Malaya and Oceania have been suggested as their source.

a great part of the Red Sea coast and the Yemen; there are ancient traditions of a golden age in which he had ruled from Khartoum to Nyassa, but by 1818, when, it is thought, Kassa was born, the office had become purely titular, shared often by several claimants at once, and the four kingdoms were practically autonomous; they were at constant war against one another, against their neighbours, and against internal rebels. Kassa was the son of a minor Amhara chief; his mother lived by selling *kosso*, a specific against tapeworm, in the streets of Gondar; like most Abyssinians with any claim to gentle birth he traced his descent from Solomon and the Queen of Sheba. From living by brigandage in the low countries, Kassa succeeded in making himself King of Kings, under the name of Theodore, and for the first time in centuries established a central monarchy over the whole country; in later life he became an alcoholic and in his cups imprisoned at Magdala a handful of European adventurers, including two who had been given British consular privileges. In 1867 an expedition was sent to rescue them under Lord Napier, and next year, at the cost of £9,000,000, was successful. Theodore committed suicide at the moment of defeat and the British troops left the country to another period of chaos. In 1872 the Ras of Tigre became King of Kings under the name of John (the Johannis whose independent hand was grasped by Mr Gerald Portal). He was much pestered during his short reign by European bagmen and died, very gloriously, at the moment of victory over the Dervishes. His reign is notable as marking the beginning of the struggle for empire between the Italians and the Abyssinians which resulted in the wars of 1895 and 1935. The nature of this struggle has never been widely understood in Europe.

The Italians first established themselves in the Red Sea by the purchase – by a private trading company which was later absorbed by the state – of the small port of Assab on the edge of the Danakil country. In 1885, at the invitation of the British, they settled further west at Massawa. The collapse of Turkish-Egyptian power before the Mahdi was promising a redistribution in this part of Africa (it had the double effect of laying open to occupation a number of important towns both on the coast and in the interior and at the same time leaving an extremely dangerous neighbour in the Soudan; the pressure on the flank of both parties by the Mahdists must be taken into account throughout the succeeding years). We had temporarily used Massawa to assist the evacuation of the Soudan garrisons; it was a place of few attractions, troublesome and expensive to maintain, but in the existing condition of competitive expansion it was certain that our evacuation would immediately result in its occupation by another Power; always anxious for the safety of our route to India, we preferred that it should fall to a small and friendly state, rather than to France. Accordingly we persuaded the Italians to take on our responsibility, pointing out that though the town itself was far from desirable it offered a fine starting-point for the exploitation of the interior. From then, for fifty years, our policy was to encourage Italian penetration in Abyssinia.

The hinterland between Massawa and Tigre was at that time one of the most insecure districts in Africa and Italian progress met with some reverses, the worst of which was the massacre at Dogeli of a part-military part-scientific exploring expedition of 500 men by an ambush of 20,000 Tigreans; but at Johannis's death in 1889 Abyssinia again seemed to disintegrate and offer an opportunity for Italian intervention of the kind that was proving successful all over Africa.

The mismanagement of this opportunity has been fully examined from every point of view.[1] The radical causes were indecision and false economy by the parliamentary government in Rome, undue and ignorant interference with the men on the spot, contradictory policy pursued by the men on the spot due largely to the difficulties of communication between the Italians treating with Menelik and those treating with Mangasha, a fatal but very natural underestimation of the abilities of Menelik, and a less excusable failure to realise the basic unity that lay below the superficial antagonisms of the Abyssinian rulers.

Johannis had acknowledged two successors, Menelik, Ras of Shoa, and Mangasha of the Tigre, his illegitimate son, both of

[1] Perhaps the best source for the English reader is *The Campaign of Adowa and the Rise of Menelik*, by G. F.-H. Berkeley (1902).

whom commanded a very powerful following. Menelik was little known in the north, but while Johannis was busy with the Dervishes and the Italians he had been making sensational conquests in the non-Abyssinian countries in the west and south, among the Kaffa and Galla peoples, the most important of which was the Emirate of Harar, an ancient, wealthy and cultured Arab city state, recently evacuated by its Egyptian garrison, over which he put his nephew Ras Makonnen. From then onwards Harar suffered from direct Abyssinian rule more continuously and acutely than any part of the empire. Menelik, in these expeditions, was furnished with arms and advice by a number of more or less shady Europeans, the majority of whom were French; his soldiers were better equipped and better organised than any in Africa. Any enemy of his could count on support from his Mohammedan neighbours, in particular from the powerful Sultan of Aussa and the Somalis of the Ogaden.

Mangasha had the prestige which still surrounded the historic north, the sacred city of Axum, the original home of the Abyssinian people; he had moreover the loyalty – about the only unqualified loyalty discernible in the whole affair – of the great warrior Ras Alula, who, immediately on Johannis's death, drove out Menelik's agent Seyoum. The factions were thus, apparently, equally matched and Italian policy alternated disastrously between the two; their forces meanwhile pushed forward and occupied what, in 1935, constituted the Italian colony of Eritrea, including large sectors of purely Abyssinian highland. When Baldissera, the leader of this advance, resigned, the Italian party in favour of a Shoan alliance was left supreme. Accordingly two treaties were concluded with Menelik, acknowledging his position as Emperor, establishing a protectorate of his dominions, and fixing a frontier between it and the Italian colony. This situation was accepted by the European Powers, and when in December 1889 Menelik announced his accession, he was informed by Great Britain and Germany that he had acted improperly in addressing himself to them directly instead of through the Italian government. In March 1890 Abyssinia was represented by Italy at the second Congress of Brussels. Atlases of the period mark an area broken only by the French 'Protectorate of

Tajurra' (French Somaliland) and an indefinite British strip on the south coast of the Gulf of Aden, as 'Italian Abyssinia'. The matter, however, was far from being settled. There were ambiguities in the Amharic version of the treaty of Ucciali, of which Menelik quickly took advantage. Count Antonelli, who had arranged it, hurried back to Shoa. Negotiations were resumed with all the cumbrous machinery of the Abyssinian court – the prevarications and evasions, the diplomatic illnesses, the endless exchanges of irrelevant compliments, the lethargy and cunning of which Menelik was a master. At length it was agreed that he should accept a protectorate for five years and the Italians should give up some of the ground they had won in Tigre. The matter was settled and signed; Antonelli examined the document with his interpreter and discovered that its provisions were exactly contrary to what had been decided – a complete renunciation by Italy of all rights in Abyssinia. Menelik regretted that there had been a misunderstanding but refused to reopen the matter. It was a trick that would have been childish enough, were it not backed by a daily increasing armed strength. Still the Roman government could not decide on resolute action. Negotiations were begun through other channels. Finally, in February 1893, in a supremely ill-considered attempt at conciliation, the Italians made Menelik a present of a huge consignment of cartridges. He at once formally denounced the treaty of Ucciali. He had got all he wanted. A month later he sent a declaration to the Powers asserting his independence and defining his frontiers so that they included two provinces under Italian administration and vast tracts of neighbouring country where his troops had not hitherto set foot. The Italians had not only armed their enemy but they had antagonised their remaining allies. The caravan of ammunition had proceeded slowly from Harar, attracting a maximum of attention. All over the Aussa and the Ogaden it was known that the Italians were betraying them; from Tigre Mangasha came to make his submission. Four years before the Tigreans had refused Menelik entrance to Axum for his coronation; now they allowed him to introduce men of his own into all their commands. He could contemplate war without misapprehension.

Nothing can be further from historical fact than to picture Menelik as a black Bruce, recklessly defying a powerful invader. He had calculated his chances and his opportunities astutely. He was well informed about the relative strengths of the European Powers. He was no savage chief to whom any white face was a divine or diabolic portent. He knew that the Italians were a poor people, with no recent military tradition; their government was hampered by the ineptitude in handling parliamentary forms consistently shown by the Mediterranean peoples. The British had spent £9,000,000 on their expedition against Theodore; Rome now reluctantly voted £750,000. Menelik knew that if the British met with a reverse, as they had at Khartoum, they would draw on their limitless reserves and, in their own time, return in overwhelming strength; if the Italians failed, they would fail decisively.

The defeat, in the spring of 1896, *was* decisive but far from ignominious; at the opening of the campaign Baratieri fought a masterly action against the Dervishes, while Tosselli subdued the Tigre in three days. In 1895 the Italians held the line Adowa–Makale–Adigrat and in 1896 had an advance post at Amba Alagi. Then Menelik arrived in the north in overpowering strength; his speed of mobilisation had been beyond the calculations of European strategists; until the last disastrous days the Italians were completely unaware of the numbers that were coming against them; each man carrying his own rations and ammunition, trotting indefatigably along the mountain tracks from all corners of the four kingdoms, a force of 100,000 men had silently assembled. Up to the last moment, even after the Italian retreat had begun, Ras Makonnen, the father of Haile Selassie, was flirting with Italian proposals to desert; finally he threw himself, with the Harar garrison, on to Menelik's side. At Adowa, on March 1, Baratieri's army was annihilated by a well-equipped force outnumbering it by eight to one. During the preceding retreat and in the hopeless final engagement acts of courage on the part of the Italian officers and of fidelity on the part of the native troops were performed which would have lent glory to any army. Nearly 1,000 white troops were killed and 4,000 or 3,000 askaris; few wounded survived; the white prisoners who were brought to Menelik himself were well treated and eventually released.[1]

Glutted with victory, Menelik's army began to disperse and he was unable to follow up his advantage; the Italians rallied, defeated the Dervishes, reconquered Kasala and checked the Abyssinian advance at Tukruf, while another force moved to the relief of Adigrat. Till then Menelik had hoped to clear Tigre of the invaders; he now came to terms and a boundary was drawn, which remained in force until October 1935, leaving a substantial corner of Abyssinia within the colony of Eritrea. In return Italy withdrew all claims to a protectorate.

In the twelve years which followed Menelik created the Ethiopian Empire.[2] The process was closely derived from the European model; sometimes the invaded areas were overawed by the show of superior force and accepted treaties of protection; sometimes they resisted and were slaughtered with the use of the modern weapons which were being imported both openly and illicitly in enormous numbers; sometimes they were simply recorded as Ethiopian without their own knowledge. The history of the reign becomes a monotonous succession of the place-names of conquered territories. Already, before the Italian war, Menelik had taken possession of huge Galla and Guraghi territories to the south-west of Shoa. In 1897 he sent an expedition into Kaffa, captured the king, and absorbed the country. In 1898 Makonnen defeated and secured the nominal allegiance of the Somali tribes of the Ogaden. In the same year a Frenchman in Menelik's employ, Léon Danegon, returned to Addis Ababa after a triumphal expedition at the head of 15,000 Abyssinian soldiers, which had penetrated nearly to the shores of Lake Rudolf; he presented Menelik with an itinerary specifying the tribes and villages visited, all of which were promptly

1 In an attempt to minimise the savagery of the victorious army, it is claimed that only thirty white prisoners were castrated. The truth is that only thirty survived and returned to Rome; innumerable others were reckoned among those killed in action; a few are said to have lived but to have preferred, in shame, to remain in Africa.

2 In the following pages 'Abyssinian' will be used to qualify the Amharic-speaking, Semitic, Christian peoples of the four mountain kingdoms; 'Ethiopian' the tribes and naturalised immigrants (of whom there were a considerable number) subject to their rule.

declared Ethiopian territory. A similar expedition, twice as strong, led by a Russian, had been sent out the previous year; it now returned to report the submission of the kings and peoples of Ghimirra. Kadaret, Kallabat, Fazogli were captured by his nephew Tasama, accompanied by French, Swiss, and Russian advisers, and the Ethiopian flag was planted on the banks of the White Nile. In 1899 Borana, a long strip of lowland on the Soudanese border, Beni Shangul, Gunza and Gubba, were conquered, and a second attempt was made on the Ogaden, where 9,000 Somalis were killed in a battle south of Jijiga. In 1900 there were further submissions by the Nilotic peoples north of Lake Rudolf; a campaign was launched against the Aussa, who did not submit until 1909, at the same time as the Sultanates of Teru and Biru. During this period there were three formidable risings in Tigre; Gojjam was put under Shoan rule in 1901 after its king had been poisoned. In 1903 there was another campaign against the Ogaden.[1] In 1913 Menelik died after having spent his later years in a partially comatose condition; he left his country with nominal dominion over an area three or four times its size, inhabited by a complex variety of peoples all totally dissimilar to it in religion, language, race and history.

It is impossible to give any general survey of the government of the subject provinces; material is scanty and conditions varied so radically from place to place that the observations of no particular traveller can be accepted as having any universal application. In general it may be said that, with the exception of the Hararis, the Mohammedan peoples came off the most lightly; the Sultan of Jimma retained virtual independence until 1933; the Danakils, Aussa and Somalis were left in their savage condition, unworried except by the occasional visits of Imperial tax-gatherers – an event which had more the complexion of a raid by brigands than an administrative act. The pagan peoples of the south and west were treated with wanton brutality unequalled even in the Belgian Congo. Some areas were depopulated by slavers; in others Abyssinian garrisons were permanently quartered on the people, whose duty it was to support them and their descendants. Abyssinian officials,

1 *A History of Ethiopia*, by Sir E. A. Wallis Budge (1928).

with retinues which varied in size from a royal guard to a standing army, lived upon the work and taxes of the original inhabitants; their function was not to protect but to hold in subjection; fighting was the only occupation they recognised. It was not a question of a tolerable system being subject to abuse, but of an intolerable system. When, in the days of the mobilisation, reports appeared in Europe of the movements of 'the army of Kambata' or 'the army of Sidamo', an impression was given of national solidarity that was entirely fictitious. If the subject peoples were willing to fight for the Abyssinians, it was argued, their rule could not be as oppressive as the Italians pretended. In fact these provincial armies were the Abyssinian garrisons recalled for service, as British forces might be withdrawn from Egypt or Palestine; their very number, swarming past the Emperor, hour after hour, capering and boasting on their way to the front, testified to the dead weight of the Abyssinian occupation.

Here was imperialism devoid of a single redeeming element. However sordid the motives and however gross the means by which the white races established – and are still establishing – themselves in Africa, the result has been, in the main, beneficial, for there are more good men than bad in Europe and there is a predisposition towards justice and charity in European culture; a bias, so that it cannot for long run free without inclining to good; things which began wickedly have turned out well. The very feature which to-day seems most odious in the original depredations – the unctuous avowals of high principle with which they were made – has itself provided a check. The significance of the Congo atrocities is not so much that they were committed as that they were exposed and suppressed; there is a conscience in Europe which, when informed and aroused, is more powerful than any vested interest. Even in the terms of nineteenth-century liberalism there has been more gain than loss to the African natives. It was to the interest of the exploiters to preserve the exploited from the endemic ravages of plague, famine and massacre to which they were heirs, to educate them for profitable contacts with an advanced machinery of commerce and administration; waste lands have been made fertile, hunted peoples have been made secure, vile little tyrannies have been abolished. The Abyssinians had nothing to give their subject peoples, nothing to teach them. They brought no crafts or knowledge, no new system of agriculture, drainage or roadmaking, no medicine or hygiene, no higher political organisation, no superiority except in their magazine rifles and belts of cartridges. They built nothing; they squatted in the villages in the thatched huts of the conquered people, dirty, idle and domineering, burning the timber, devouring the crops, taxing the meagre stream of commerce that seeped in from outside, enslaving the people. It was not, as in the early days of the Belgian Congo, that bad men with too much power, too far from supervision, were yielding to appetites of which their own people denied them satisfaction. The Abyssinians imposed what was, by its nature, a deadly and hopeless system. In the tin-roofed offices at Addis Ababa the *Jeunesse d'Ethiopie*[1] drew up occasional programmes of reform; there was a model province at Asfa Tafari conveniently near the railway-line to allow visiting Europeans a cursory inspection; palace officials were always ready to explain in glib French how, bit by bit, the whole Empire was to be brought under a new and enlightened system – these things affected the nation as little as might a committee of women welfare workers in Europe passing a resolution deploring the use of tobacco. Even in the *Jeunesse d'Ethiopie* itself there was little real desire for change; a weekly visit to the cinema, a preference for whisky over *tedj*, toothbrush moustaches in place of the traditional and imposing beards, patent leather shoes and a passable dexterity with fork and spoon were the Western innovations that these young men relished; these, and a safe climb to eminence behind the broad, oxlike backs of the hereditary aristocracy. Perhaps the Emperor himself thought of something more ambitious; perhaps a handful of his circle vaguely shared his thoughts; but the governing class as a whole were immovable. Something, it was realised, had to be done to ensure the support of the mysterious, remote, incalculably powerful organisation at Geneva, of which Abyssinia had become a part, something on paper, neatly typewritten in French and English. Tricking the European was a national craft; evading issues,

---

1 The society of 'progressive' Abyssinians.

promising without the intention of fulfilment, tricking the paid foreign advisers, tricking the legations, tricking the visiting international committees – these were the ways by which Abyssinia had survived and prospered.

It was generally supposed among her neighbours that Ethiopia would disintegrate at the death of Menelik, and in provision for this they made an agreement in 1906 renouncing competitive action in the subsequent resettlement. France and England had no desire for extensive additions of territory, contenting themselves with a guarantee of their interests in the railway zone and the Blue Nile respectively. (England, as was shown in the judiciously revealed Maffey report, has not changed her ambitions since.) The principle of 1891 was reaffirmed that the greater part of Ethiopia lay within Italy's legitimate sphere of influence. In an exchange of notes between the British and Italian governments in December 1925 the understanding was made more explicit; Great Britain undertook to support the constantly evaded Italian request to build a railway through Western Ethiopia connecting her two colonies, recognised an exclusive Italian economic influence in West Abyssinia and the whole territory to be crossed by the railway, and promised to support all Italian demands for concessions in that territory. There was complete agreement between all parties. If Ethiopia broke up, Italy was to assume whatever political authority she desired; if it remained intact she was to develop it by means of peaceful economic penetration.

Ethiopia did not break up on Menelik's death. There were grave disorders, but government of a kind was maintained. The crisis did not come until the summer of 1916, when, at the height of the European war, no one could contemplate an expensive campaign in Africa. Lij Yasu, Menelik's successor, was deposed after a series of engagements and risings which continued sporadically until his death in 1935. He fell because he attempted to reorientate his empire. He was predominantly Mohammedan by blood (his father was a superficially Christianised Mohammedan chief; his mother, Menelik's daughter by a Mohammedan wife) and he conceived the idea of a vast East African Mohammedan state, under German-

Turkish auspices, embracing the territories of the allied Powers. He tried to break the domination of the Abyssinians of the four Christian kingdoms and was broken by them. In the succeeding period the power was precariously shared between the Empress, the Shoan military party, represented by the veteran Fitaurari Hapta Giorgis, the Church represented by the Coptic Abuna – all strongly conservative – and Ras Tafari, the son of Ras Makonnen. It ended, not without bloodshed, in Tafari achieving supreme power.

At the peace conference, as is notorious, Italy received an inconsiderable fraction of the colonial advantages which had been promised her as the price of entering the war upon the side of the allied Powers, but she was in no mood for imperialistic adventures. The situation envisaged in the 1906 agreement had not fully come into being. Accordingly, she decided to encourage Abyssinian aspirations towards unity and reform, and with this end overcame British opposition and secured Abyssinia membership of the League of Nations. From then onwards her policy was an economic and cultural imperialism of the kind which the United States of America have imposed upon their unprogressive Latin neighbours and of which the Treaty of Friendship, signed in 1928, was intended to be the charter. It was the frustration of this policy which provoked the war of 1935.

In the spring and summer of 1935, while both sides were preparing for war and negotiations for peace were being made at Rome, Paris and Geneva in an atmosphere of increasing futility, the Italian Bureau of Propaganda issued a series of documents in English and French itemising the acts of offence perpetrated by the Abyssinians, which attracted little sympathy among the public to which they were addressed. The public utterances of Signor Mussolini had been rhetorical and uncompromising,[1] those of the Emperor of Abyssinia studiously temperate. The cinema-going public of Europe was accustomed to the spectacle of Signor Mussolini in exuberant baroque attitudes; of the Emperor hierarchic and remote as a figure from

---

1 'Let no one hold any illusions in or out of Italy. We are tolerably circumspect before we make a decision, but once a decision is taken we march ahead and do not turn back . . . Better live as a lion one day than a hundred years as a sheep. . . . We must go forward until we achieve the Fascist Empire,' etc.

a Byzantine ikon; troops and war materials were daily being shipped from Italy to East Africa with the maximum of ostentation; the Abyssinians moved barefoot through unfrequented passes. For fifteen years the civilised world had been contemplating askance the destructive force of its scientific discoveries. In these circumstances complaints about Abyssinian 'aggression' seemed patently absurd, and neither at Geneva nor in Europe at large were they seriously considered. 'Aggression' was an unfortunate phrase, borrowed from the vocabulary of the League of Nations. There was never any positive intention among responsible Abyssinians to overrun the Italian colonies and add them to the Ethiopian Empire; they talked of these things in their cups, but the Emperor, certainly, indulged in no fancies of that kind. There was, however, a firm determination to restrict to a minimum all intercourse between the two nations and to treat the Italians as the least rather than the most favoured of their three neighbours. They neither wanted Italy's friendship nor feared her enmity. Membership of the League of Nations corresponded exactly to the present of ammunition to Menelik in 1893; the Italians had armed Abyssinia against themselves; they had earned no recompense and no gratitude. Abyssinia had no further use for them. The days were past when a disorderly and undeveloped country needed to put herself under the particular protection of a great Power; what need had Abyssinia for Italian friendship when she had been given the friendship of the entire world? This was the argument of the Court and *Jeunesse d'Ethiopie*, but in the huts of the soldiers and the tin-roofed palaces of the provincial governors it ran differently; it was thumped out on the oxhide war-drums and chanted by the minstrels, chuckled about over the horns of *tedj*; the Italians were the white men of Adowa; at every feast day throughout the country the veterans paraded in gala dress, rolling their eyes, whirling their swords, slavering at the mouth, stamping themselves into delirium as they re-enacted the slaughter of that day, yelling of the white blood they had shed. The Italians were one with Kafa and the Shankalla, Guraghi and Galla, a conquered people, slaves. It was all very remote from the council chambers at Geneva, from the manifest accumulations of girders and wire and explosives on the quays of Massawa and Mogadishu, but it was the essential temper of the people which, refined and formalised, found its way into the official dealings of the Emperor and ministers.

The Italian complaints may be summarised as stating that Ethiopia was barbarous and xenophobic and that she had not fulfilled her engagements to Italy under the 1928 Treaty of Friendship. Of the truth of the first point there was never any serious doubt among informed people. Slavery and slave-raiding were universal; justice, when executed at all, was accompanied by torture and mutilation in a degree known nowhere else in the world; the central government was precarious and only rendered effective by repeated resort to armed force; disease was rampant. All were agreed upon the truth of these statements. The Covenant of the League assumed, and in some particulars specified, a cultural standard for its members to which Abyssinia nowhere approximated. The central government minimised, but admitted the existence of the problem. They contended that the solution lay within the country; in a generation Abyssinia would reform herself. There was no unanimity among foreign observers as to how much reliance could be placed on these assurances. In the absence of evidence most resorted to sentiment in forming their opinions. On the one side were the missionaries of all races and creeds. These were naturally disposed to credulity and charity. They preferred to believe the best of everyone; they were, moreover, bound to the Emperor by particular ties of gratitude: he gave them property and protection; some – one in particular who has been most eloquent in pleading the Ethiopian cause[1] – had taken the foolhardy step of assuming Ethiopian nationality; the work they were doing was, in most cases, so patently altruistic that they encountered little hostility and some cooperation from their native superiors. Incongruously allied with these were the Europeans who deplored all European influence in Africa, and rejoiced to find an 'unspoiled' area; who would have liked to preserve Ethiopia, in the way that national parks are isolated and preserved for animals, as a sanctuary for savages; extreme lovers of the picturesque who

---

1 Immediately after the Italian occupation this man issued a retraction of his accusations. Although his original statements were given immense publicity in the English press, the retraction passed unnoticed.

fostered lepers and eunuchs and brigand chiefs, as their milder
brothers encouraged sulky yokels in England to perform folk dances
on the village green. Added to these were a handful of travellers who
had had the rare good fortune to be politely treated by the Abyssinians and were chivalrously disinclined to abuse the hospitality they
had received. These were the elements which constituted the pro-
Abyssinian party until the great campaign of 1935 started, when the
Socialists of Europe, in their hatred of the internal administration of
Italy, nearly succeeded in precipitating world war in defence of an
archaic African despotism.

The anti-Abyssinian party consisted of those who had done or
attempted to do jobs in the country; it varied in composition from
the consuls who were concerned in securing fulfilment of obligations
towards their nationals and the cosmopolitan adventurers who had
tried to trick the natives and found themselves tricked. These were
convinced that there was no possibility of reform through the ordinary governmental channels and that European help would never
be generally acceptable or effective as long as Abyssinia was an
unconquered country. The xenophobia of the people was an insuperable barrier to all free cooperation. This is the feature of the
country which has most impressed visiting writers – particularly
the French. Djibouti has always been haunted by interested gossips
who warn travellers of the dangers they will encounter up the line.
Most people are disposed to settle high political questions in terms of
the treatment they have received in casual encounters during their
travels; a dishonest taxi-driver or an overbearing policeman embit-
ter international relations more than the perfidy of governments.
The English, on the whole, are intensely xenophobic, and for this
reason their sympathies are most easily aroused on behalf of nations
with whom they have least acquaintance. All of them know something about the French and the Italians. They have been over-
charged for their luncheon in Paris; they have been made to walk
on the other side of the street in Rome. But only an infinitesimal
number have suffered the indignities of travelling in Abyssinia.
Those that have are inclined to be intemperate about it. The essence
of the offence was that the Abyssinians, in spite of being by any
possible standard an inferior race, persisted in behaving as superiors;

it was not that they were hostile, but contemptuous. The white man, accustomed to other parts of Africa, was disgusted to find the first-class carriages on the railway usurped by local dignitaries; he found himself subject to officials and villainous-looking men at arms whose language he did not know, who showed him no sort of preference on account of his colour, and had not the smallest reluctance to using force on him if he became truculent. There were, of course, large tracts of Ethiopia where any stranger, white or Abyssinian, was liable to be murdered on sight. Few travellers penetrated to those regions, and those who did were conscious that they were doing something highly dangerous. It was less glamorous to be in danger, as not infrequently happened, of being knocked down by a policeman in the streets of the capital. The Abyssinians were constantly coming to blows; any direction of traffic was performed with buffeting and whipping; an arrest invariably involved a fight; an evening's entertainment often resulted in the discharge of firearms, broken heads and chains for the whole party. It was the normal tenor of Abyssinian life, and Europeans, if they came to the country, were expected to share in it. Abyssinians rarely travelled, even within their own boundaries; the number who had been to Europe was minute. They judged Europeans as they saw them in Ethiopia, and what they saw did not impress them. The results aggravated the cause, for only Europeans negligent of their own dignity could maintain any relations with them. The Legations, anxious to preserve their own prestige, dissociated themselves as far as they could from their less reputable nationals; jealous of each other's influence they studiously avoided common action to support the rights that had been guaranteed to foreigners by treaties. The Abyssinians formed their opinion of Western civilisation from the deportment of journalists, press photographers and concession-hunters. The formidable dossier prepared by the Italians of outrages upon European dignity – partly acts of mob-hooliganism but chiefly of violence by the police – does not so much prove hostility as a sense of equality. They treated visitors rather better than their own people, but not so much better as to make the country agreeable.

Towards Europeans who wished to settle and make money in the country they adopted a less equitable manner. It was illegal for foreigners to own land in Ethiopia, but it was always possible to acquire by purchase temporary concessions for almost any kind of undertaking. The prospector had only to bribe his way into the presence of the responsible official, put down his deposit and lay his finger on any part of the map to receive permission to mine or farm there. It was when he arrived at the chosen place that his difficulties began; he would find his concession was already held under various titles by a dozen rival claimants, native and foreign; he would find labourers impossible to keep in decent discipline; he would find neighbours who pilfered and raided, against whom he could obtain no redress; he would find local officials who evinced scant regard for the documents he had obtained at Addis, and expected substantial sums to tolerate his existence among them; he would find himself taxed and hampered at every stage of his communications, and involved in litigation which ended only in his despair. Addis was always full of more or less undeserving Europeans who had been reduced to destitution by this process. There were a few mills, a brewery, a few plantations, whose white owners continued to struggle for a living; in the north an eminently workable potash concession was reduced to bankruptcy. In other parts of Africa Europeans had found things too easy; here conditions were deliberately made intolerable. The result was that the national resources of the country were unexplored and unexploited even to the extent that the Abyssinians imported tropical products, such as sugar, rather than adventure themselves into the lowlands where they might be produced or allow more enterprising races to undertake the work for them. Inevitably, the unknown became the focus for legends; frustrated cupidity acted as a spur to imagination, people spoke of vast deposits of gold and platinum, of untapped wells of oil, while the only foreigners, mostly Asiatic and Levantine, to make a living from the country were the traders and small monopolists, and they were in constant embarrassment through the difficulties put in their way by the courts of collecting their debts. Everyone who had any dealings with the Imperial Family – the Indian who took command photographs of the Princesses, the Russian who put the electric lighting into the new palace, the dentist, the chef – were kept waiting hopelessly, indefinitely for their money. The rases and officials copied the Emperor. The law courts were conducted with the same policy. Decisions given in favour of foreigners were only after the maximum of delay, if at all, put into execution. Under the capitulations, generally known as the Klobukowski Treaty, special tribunals had been set up to deal with cases between Ethiopians and foreigners in which the respective consuls sat. It was the custom to balance the accounts periodically and pay to whichever party had the larger credit the balance in his country's favour. Shortly after the coronation, under the present régime, the time came to settle the score between the British consul at Addis Ababa and the Ethiopian officials; a large undisputed sum was outstanding in the British favour. The Ethiopian officials maintained that it was irregular for them merely to pay the difference; each side must appear with his full reckoning. Accordingly the British consul arrived with members of the Legation guard bearing in sacks of silver dollars the total sum due. It was counted out in the presence of the Ethiopians – a lengthy process – who then remarked that they had not their money with them; they would take the British dollars and bring theirs next week. The consul refused and the sacks were carried back to the Legation compound. A week later the Ethiopian judges said that they now had their money ready. The same procedure took place; the Ethiopians again tried to take the money, promising theirs on the next day; again the sacks were carried back under guard. At the third meeting the British consul said that he proposed to pay by cheque; the Ethiopians agreed, snatched the paper from his hands across the table and, with profuse promises that their money was on the way, watched him leave the court, satisfied that they had succeeded in outwritting the foreigner. The consul stopped the cheque by telephone, and from then onwards for two years the special tribunal ceased to sit.

Mildly comic incidents of this kind were of frequent occurrence in the very centre of Haile Selassie's government; prolonged and multiplied all over the country they assumed a more offensive complexion. The Soudanese and Kenya frontiers were kept in a state of expensive vigilance by their turbulent neighbours. But the British were a race whom, on the whole, the Abyssinians liked and respected; the Italians were suspected and despised; they were, moreover, a race whom recent developments of patriotic ardour, combined with the memory of past humiliations, made particularly sensitive to insult. They were a race whose colonial aspirations were concentrated in that part of the globe. Great Britain and France with their diffuse interests were not easily to be provoked to an unremunerative war. The Italians were waiting for an opportunity to demonstrate their new virility. The repeated grave annoyances were doubly offensive to them since, by the Treaty of Friendship of 1928, they had every reason to regard themselves as especially privileged.

It was evident, within six years of its having been made, that the Abyssinians had no intention of maintaining the spirit of that treaty. Italy had expected tangible commercial advantages. Her ambitions were clear and, judged by the international morality of America, Japan or any of the League Powers, legitimate. Abyssinia could not claim recognition on equal terms by the civilised nations and at the same time maintain her barbarous isolation; she must put her natural resources at the disposal of the world; since she was obviously unable to develop them herself, it must be done for her, to their mutual benefit, by a more advanced Power. By the 1928 Treaty, Italy believed that she had been chosen for this office. Abyssinia required technical advisers for her administration, whom Italy expected to supply; Abyssinia needed additional and cheaper means of access to the sea, which Italy offered through her colonies, granting a free zone in the port of Assab. In all these matters Italian expectations were disappointed. Little scope was given for Italian commercial enterprise. Of the many foreigners engaged by Haile Selassie as advisers and experts only one Italian was chosen and that for a minor post. The new arterial road, which was specifically provided in the 1928 agreement, joining Dessye with Assab was abandoned and, instead, Haile Selassie concentrated on opening communications with the British territories in Kenya and Somaliland. The construction of a wireless station at Addis Ababa was undertaken by an Italian company, heavily subsidised by the Italian government, but on completion was handed over to the management of a Swede and a Frenchman. A large hospital – the only building of any architectural merit in Addis Ababa – was erected with Italian money, partly voted by the government, partly subscribed by private Italian philanthropists, but pressure was exerted to prevent Abyssinians availing themselves of it. Italian social service throughout the country was suppressed; Ethiopians were forbidden to attend the consulate doctors; even Ethiopian cattle were kept from the Italian vets who were attempting to treat with prophylaxis the cattle plague that was ravaging the herds of both empires. The Ethiopian government persisted, as it had done for nearly forty years, in evading its promise to demarcate the Italian frontiers. Complaints of illegal imprisonment, injury and murder of Italian subjects accumulated and were left unsatisfied; insults to Italian diplomats and consuls and attacks on their property and servants went unpunished.

Some responsibility for the subsequent disaster must rest with the other European Legations at Addis Ababa, who constantly refused to take common action but pursued the old policy of competing for Ethiopian favour in their own small schemes of advantage. It is doubtful whether any warning was given to the Emperor of the change of temper between democratic and Fascist Italy; of the claustrophobia, aggravated by the universal economic depression, which now inclined her to welcome rather than shun an appeal to force. Whatever was said was qualified by the assurance that the Emperor was covered by the protection of the League and by the ignorant confidence of his army in their ability to defeat the Italians as they had defeated them before. It was in these circumstances, in December 1934, when Italy had finally despaired of achieving her objects by peaceful means and had already begun to sound the Powers tentatively about their attitude to her expansion in Africa; when she was actually in search of a diversion from internal distress, that the Abyssinians chose to attack the military post at Walwal.

It is uncertain how far this piece of folly was directed from Addis Ababa, and how far it was the spontaneous act of the troops on the spot. The committee which examined the evidence at Geneva came to no conclusion. What is certain is that it was not a tribal raid of the kind that was common along that frontier but a serious battle fought by a properly constituted Abyssinian force from the north.

Walwal is a watering-place and pasture without regular inhabitants, frequented at various seasons by the tribes of British and Italian Somaliland and the Ethiopian Ogaden. The treaties defining the frontier were mutually contradictory and the ground had never been surveyed, but the place undoubtedly lay in the Ethiopian sphere. Nothing, however, had been done by the Abyssinian authorities to make their possession in any way effective. By its character it was a natural battleground for tribal warfare, involving peoples under Italian protection, and in the absence of any Abyssinian police post the Italians had established one there, without protest of any kind, five years before. No attempt was made to conceal its existence, and the Anglo-Abyssinian boundary commission[1] who visited it on November 23 must have known what they would find. They arrived at the head of a large force – far in excess of any normal protective escort – which had assembled behind their caravan. Its numbers have been variously estimated; probably there were about six hundred Abyssinian soldiers, drawn from the garrisons of the Galla–Somali borders. Realising that there was going to be trouble, the British commissioners withdrew with their normal escort, leaving this extraordinary force behind to fight it out; there was thus no impartial witness to determine the disputed point of who fired the first shot. Whatever the Italian legal position, they were certainly on the defensive tactically. The battle took place on December 5 and the Abyssinians were defeated. It was then that they decided to resort to arbitration and the Italians decided to resort to war. There were attempts at ambush on Italian patrols in the Ogaden on December 28 and January 8, and on January 29 an attack in force on the Italian garrison at Afdub; both sides began to prepare for war on a larger scale; but while the Abyssinians enlisted European sympathy by a scrupulous regard for the formalities of peaceful negotiation, the Italians boasted from the first that they proposed to fight – in their own time and in the manner which suited them best.

---

1 I have never seen any satisfactory explanation of what this commission was doing there, 80 miles off its course.

No one except Signor Mussolini knows exactly what form he intended the war to take. There are indications that it was originally planned as a punitive demonstration; the transport and disembarkation of immense loads of war material was accomplished with great ostentation, but until the autumn of 1935, when hostilities had actually begun, little was done to improve the roads between Massawa and the front line. My own belief – and this is purely personal and conjectural – is that as late as the beginning of summer, 1935, Signor Mussolini had no intention of making war upon a national scale or of attempting the military conquest of the whole Ethiopian Empire. I believe that Italian agents throughout Ethiopia had been sounding the loyalty of the local chiefs, had paid large subsidies to them and had secured a system of treaties and verbal understandings which led them to expect a practically bloodless settlement. It was Signor Mussolini's hope that before Christmas his envoy at Geneva would be able to present the League with evidence of a series of voluntary submissions, and to claim that there had been no act of aggression or conquest – merely an exchange of allegiance by the people themselves; that all that was necessary to precipitate mass desertions was a demonstration of overwhelming force which would be performed mainly in the air. A few sharp encounters with modern methods of war would bring the Abyssinians to realise their necessarily inferior and dependent station; they were then to be left as a sovereign state, consisting of Shoa, Amhara, Gojjam and the greater part of Tigre. Adowa should remain in Italian hands as a monument that the defeat of 1896 had been avenged; the Abyssinian subject-races would be transferred to Italian protectorate. In Addis Ababa the Italian representative should assume a position similar to that once held by the British High Commissioner in Egypt; the internal order of the country should be taken from the charge of the local magnates and put under a national gendarmerie, officered by Italians; England and France should be allowed to enjoy the same position as they had occupied before except that Signor Mussolini was willing to facilitate the construction of the dam at Lake Tsana which had up till then been delayed by the Abyssinians. The neighbouring territories would have been saved much expense and anxiety through the establishment of an orderly rule on their frontiers; the subject peoples would have gained by changing to progressive and comparatively humane masters; the Abyssinians themselves would have preserved the traditional forms of their independence and participated in the profits resulting from the development of their resources.

This policy certainly underestimated the duplicity of the Abyssinian rulers with whom Italy had been in contact, and the confidence in their superiority of the Abyssinian troops, but I believe that the misfortunes that have fallen upon both peoples – the slaughter and terror on one side, the crippling expenditure on the other – are primarily due to the policy pursued by the British government.

The Emperor believed that if he could win the support of the League, there would be decisive action on his behalf; he transmitted this to his simpler subjects in the assertion that England and France were coming to fight against Italy, so that even those who had least love of Abyssinian rule feared to declare themselves against what seemed to be the stronger side.

The Italians, in the face of sanctions and a campaign of peevish and impotent remonstrance in England, felt their national honour to be challenged and their entire national resources committed to what, in its inception, was a minor colonial operation of the kind constantly performed in the recent past by every great Power in the world.

At the time of writing[1] the papers are filled with reports of the death agonies of the Abyssinian people and scholars are demonstrating in the correspondence column their ingenuity in composing Greek epitaphs for them. No one can doubt that an immense amount of avoidable suffering has been caused, and that the ultimate consequences may be of world-wide effect.

1 April 1936.

CHAPTER 2

ADDIS ABABA DURING THE LAST DAYS OF
THE ETHIOPIAN EMPIRE

1

IN THE SUMMER of 1935 the *Evening Standard* published a cartoon representing the Throne of Justice occupied by three apes who squatted in the traditional attitude, each with his hands covering his eyes, ears or mouth; beneath was the legend, '*See no Abyssinia; hear no Abyssinia; speak no Abyssinia.*'

This may have expressed the atmosphere of Geneva; it was wildly unlike London. There the editorial and managerial chairs of newspaper and publishing offices seemed to be peopled exclusively by a race of anthropoids who saw, heard and spoke no other subject. Few of them, it is true, could find that country on the map or had the faintest conception of its character; those who had read Nesbitt believed that it lay below sea-level, in stupefying heat, a waterless plain of rock and salt, sparsely inhabited by naked, homicidal lunatics; those who had glanced through Budge pictured an African Tibet, a land where ancient, inviolable palaces jutted on to glaciers, an immemorial régime hedged by intricate ceremonial, a mountain solitude broken only by monastic bells calling across the snowfields from shrine to shrine; the editor of one great English paper believed – and for all I know still believes – that the inhabitants spoke classical Greek.

But Abyssinia was News. Everyone with any claims to African experience was cashing in. Travel books whose first editions had long since been remaindered were being reissued in startling wrappers. Literary agents were busy peddling the second serial rights of long-forgotten articles. The journal of a woman traveller in Upper Egypt was advertised as giving information on the Abyssinian problem. Files were being searched for photographs of any inhospitable-looking people – Patagonian Indians, Borneo head-hunters,

583

Australian aborigines – which could be reproduced to illustrate Abyssinian culture. Two English newspapers chose their special correspondents on the grounds that they had been born in South Africa. In the circumstances anyone who had actually spent a few weeks in Abyssinia itself, and had read the dozen or so books which constituted the entire English bibliography of the subject, might claim to be an expert, and in this unfamiliar but not uncongenial disguise I secured employment with the only London newspaper which seemed to be taking a realistic view of the situation, as a 'war correspondent'.

There followed ten inebriating days of preparation, lived in an attitude of subdued heroism before friends, of knowledgeable discrimination at the tropical outfitters. There was a heat wave at the time ('Nothing to what *you're* going to, Sir,' they said). I trod miasmic pavements between cartographers and consulates. In the hall of my club a growing pile of packing-cases, branded for Djibouti, began to constitute a serious inconvenience to the other members. There are few pleasures more complete, or to me more rare, than that of shopping extravagantly at someone else's expense. I thought I had treated myself with reasonable generosity until I saw the luggage of my professional competitors – their rifles and telescopes and ant-proof trunks, medicine chests, gas-masks, pack saddles, and vast wardrobes of costume suitable for every conceivable social or climatic emergency. Then I had an inkling of what later became abundantly clear to all, that I did not know the first thing about being a war correspondent.

2

After the bustle, ten tranquil days on the familiar route. The *Golden Arrow* half seen through the feverish twilight of 6 A.M. Gerard Street gin; acquaintances on the boat ('We are going to Cannes. Where are you?' 'Addis Ababa'); sleep between Calais and Paris; an acquaintance in the during-car ('I am going to Antibes. Where are you?' 'Addis Ababa'); cool early morning at the Marseilles docks, succeeded by a day of burning heat; sailing at sunset. Five days in the Mediterranean, of calm water and cool breezes; the familiar depressing spectacle of French colonial domesticity on the Messageries decks; stud poker at night with two matey Americans, an exquisitely polite Siamese and a bumptious Dutchman. Port Said at midnight; Simon Arzt's coming to life; a fellow journalist slipping away to cross-examine the harbour master. Sultry days in the Canal; the Dutchman's manners at the card table becoming increasingly offensive. Finally, on August 19, Djibouti; the familiar stifling boulevards; spindly, raffish Somalis; the low-spirited young man at the Vice-consulate; the tireless, hopeless street pedlars; the familiar rotund Frenchmen, their great arcs of waistline accentuated with cummerbunds; the seedy café clientèle, swollen at this moment by refugees – Dodecanean mostly – from up the line and by despondent middle-aged adventurers negotiating for Ethiopian visas; the familiar after-dinner drive to the café in the palm grove; the fuss about train and luggage. A torrid, almost sleepless night. On the 20th, shortly before midday, we crossed the Ethiopian frontier.

The occupants of the railway carriage were typical of the rising tide of foreigners which was then flowing from all parts of the world to the threatened capital.

There were six of us, sipping iced Vichy water from our thermos flasks and gazing out bleakly upon a landscape of unrelieved desolation.

One of them had been my companion from London, a reporter from a Radical newspaper. I saw him constantly throughout the succeeding months and found his zeal and industry a standing reproach. I did not know it was possible for a human being to identify himself so precisely with the interests of his employers. He never stopped working; he was continually jotting things down in a little note-book; all events for him had only one significance and standard of measurement – whether or no they constituted a 'story'. He did not make friends; he 'established contacts'. Even his private opinions were those of his paper; the situation, obscure to most of us, was crystal clear to him – the Emperor was an oppressed anti-fascist. His editor had told him that he must wear silk pyjamas under his clothes if he wished to avoid typhus; he never neglected to do so. He carried with him everywhere an iodine pencil with which he painted fleabites and scratches, so that he soon presented a somewhat macabre piebald spectacle. In the final reckoning he probably sent back sounder information than many of us.

My other colleague was a vastly different character. From time to time he gave us visiting-cards, but we never remembered his name, and for the next few weeks he became a prominent and richly comic figure in Addis life, known to everyone as 'the Spaniard'. He was vivacious and swarthy and stout, immensely talkative and far from intelligible in English, French and German. His equipment, as he proudly admitted, was largely acquired at a sixpenny store. He changed his clothes in the train, putting on breeches and a pair of chocolate-coloured riding-boots which laced up the front, and a Boy Scout's belt and revolver holster. He then placed a tin aneroid on the seat beside him and proclaimed the changes of altitude with boyish excitement, peeling and devouring one by one throughout the journey an enormous basket of slightly rotten bananas.

It was clear to us that Spanish journalism was run on quite different lines from English. From the moment we left Marseilles he had been composing articles for his paper – one about Haifa, two about de Lesseps, one about Disraeli. 'I have a very good history of Africa in German,' he explained. 'When I have nothing to report I translate passages from that. Mine is the most important paper in Spain, but it is a great thing for them to send a correspondent as far as this. They must have news all the time.' He had no cabling facilities at the Radio and was obliged to pay for all his dispatches in cash, a transaction which involved him in endless counting and recounting of coins and notes. While the rest of us were leading a life agreeably unembarrassed by the financial cares that occupy so much attention in normal travel, the Spaniard was in a chronic high fever of anxiety about his expenditure; for many days after his arrival at Addis Ababa he was to be found with a stub of pencil and sheet of paper working out how many thalers he should have got for his francs at Djibouti and brooding sceptically over the results; he was apparently an easy prey for the dishonest; his cabin, he complained, was rifled on board ship and a wad of money stolen; at Djibouti he had a still odder misfortune; he gave me his pocket-book to guard while he went for a swim and on his return maintained that a thousand francs had disappeared from it. He bewailed the loss at length and in piteous terms, saying that he was saving it for a present to his little daughter. But I made no offer to reimburse him and he soon recovered his jollity. It was a great surprise to him to discover that three of the English journalists beside myself were new and probably temporary members of our staffs and that all except one were entirely new to the work of foreign correspondent. 'I am the most important and expensive man on my paper,' he said.

'English editors would not send anyone whose life they valued on a job of this kind,' we told him.

'I have my revolver. And the boots are snake-proof. How much do you think they cost?'

Someone suggested ten shillings.

'*Very* much less,' he said proudly.

He was one of the few people who, I really believe, thought that the coloured races were dark skinned because they did not wash. 'Look at his black thumb holding my plate!' he would exclaim with loathing when native servants waited on him. But he was of a volatile nature and his displeasure never lasted. He did not intend to stay long in Ethiopia, because, he explained, he was his paper's Paris correspondent and it was impossible to do both jobs satisfactorily at the same time. 'I shall merely make a rapid tour of the front on a motor bicycle,' he said.

In the absence of any more probable alternative, it was later put about in Addis Ababa, where everyone was credited with some sinister activity, that the Spaniard was a papal spy.

The fourth member of the party was a sturdy American doctor who had come to offer his services to the Ethiopian Red Cross. With him was Mr Prospero, whom he had rescued from an indefinite sojourn in the Djibouti hotel. Mr Prospero was photographer for an American news reel. A few weeks before he had been a contented resident in Japan, where he owned a house, a dog; had lately paid the last instalment on a saloon car, and employed his time making pictures of cherry blossom and court ceremonial. At a few hours' notice he had been whisked away from this life of lotus eating and deposited, penniless – his funds having been cabled in advance to Addis – at Djibouti, than which there can be no town in the world less sympathetic to strangers desirous of borrowing a railway fare. His life thereafter was a protracted martyrdom gallantly but gloomily endured, which seemed to typify the discouragement which in less degrees we all suffered. At Addis he was accommodated at the Imperial Hotel in a ground-floor room immediately next to the only entrance; as more camera men arrived, they joined him there with camp beds and mountains of technical apparatus until the little room, heaped with cameras and crumpled under-clothes, packing-cases of film and half-empty tins of baked beans, presented a scene hideously compounded of workshop, warehouse and slum dormitory. I saw Mr Prospero constantly, and always in distress; now soaked to the skin pathetically grinding the handle of his camera in an impenetrable pall of rain; now prostrate under the bare feet of a stampeding mob, like a football in a rugger scrum, now lamed, now groaning with indigestion, now shuddering in high fever. He became a figure from classic tragedy, inexorably hunted by hostile fates. After we had been in Addis Ababa some time a copy of a poster arrived from America advertising his news reel. It represented a young man of military appearance and more than military intrepidity standing calmly behind his camera while bombs burst overhead and naked warriors rolled interlocked about his knees. In vast letters across this scene of carnage was printed:

'O.K., BOYS, YOU CAN START THE WAR NOW
PROSPERO IS THERE.'

The sixth and by far the gayest of us was an Englishman who was soon, suddenly, to become world famous: Mr F. W. Rickett. He had joined our ship at Port Said and throughout the succeeding week had proved a light-hearted companion. From the first he was invested with a certain mystery. Anyone travelling to Addis Ababa at that moment attracted some speculation. Mr Rickett spoke openly of a 'mission', and when tackled by the Radical on the subject hinted vaguely that he was bringing Coptic funds to the Abuna. He spoke more freely about a pack of hounds which he had in the Midlands, and when, as often happened, he received lengthy cables in code, he would pocket them nonchalantly, remarking, 'From my huntsman. He says the prospects for cubbin' are excellent.' The Radical and I put him down as an arms salesman of whom large numbers were said to be frequenting Addis Ababa. In the gaudy reports of his concession which flooded the papers of the world a fortnight later great emphasis was laid upon Mr Rickett's 'unobtrusive entrance' into the country and his residence at 'an obscure boarding-house'. Nothing could have been further from his intentions or expectations. He had ordered the one luxury carriage of the Ethiopian railway and treasured the most extravagant hopes about its character – even to the belief that it contained a kitchen and cook. He had, in fact, very kindly offered me a place in it. But when we got to the station we found that we had to take our places in the ordinary coach. In the same way he had ordered a suite at the Imperial Hotel. It was only when we found there was no other accommodation, that we went to Mrs Heft's excellent *pension*. Moreover, as will later appear, he had no desire, once it was signed, to keep his *coup* a secret. It was by chance that it became the single sensational scoop of the entire war. Mr Rickett was far too genial to concern himself with matters of that kind.

The day wore on, more oppressive after luncheon at a wayside buffet; the little train jerked and twisted through an unendurable country of stone and ant-hills. There were no signs of rain here, the sand was bare, the few tufts of scrub colourless as the surrounding stone; the watercourses were dry. At sunset we stopped for the night at Diredawa, an orderly little town created by and subsisting on the railway; it was entirely French in character and population, divided by the dry river-bed from a ramshackle native quarter. I remembered how gratefully I had left it five years before. Now in the cool of the evening, with the lights of the hotel terrace revealing sombre masses of flowering bougainvillaea it seemed agreeable enough. The head of the railway police came up from the station with us for a drink. He was one of the new school of Ethiopian official – clean shaven, khaki-clad, French-speaking. He told us the latest news from Europe. Mr Eden had walked out of the Paris discussions. That meant that England was going to fight against Italy, he said. 'That depends on the League of Nations,' we said.

'No, no. It is because you do not want Italy to be strong. It is good. You know that Ethiopia cannot threaten you. We are friends. Together we will defeat the Italians.'

We did not disabuse him; instead we accepted our temporary popularity as easily as we could, clinked glasses and drank to peace.

Next morning at dawn we resumed our places in the train and reached Addis that evening.

I little suspected what a large part in our lives that stretch of line was going to play in the coming months. I covered it six times before Christmas and learned every feature – the transition from desert to downland, the view of the lakes, the cinder fields, the Awash gorge, the candle-lit hotel at Awash where on every journey but this one the train deposited us for the night, the stations where there was an ostrich, a beggar who recited prayers, a little girl who mimed, the painted arch of the lake hotel at Bishoftou which told that the climb was nearly over and that we were in measurable distance of Addis, the silly coon-face of the ticket collector outside the window as he climbed along the running-boards to enquire who wanted to lunch at the buffet. But at this time we all assumed that, when war was declared, we should at once be isolated. On the first day Awash bridge would be bombed and the line cut in a hundred places. The Abyssinians were at work already in the manner, at once both laborious and haphazard, which characterised all their enterprises, getting together materials for alternative bridges and loop lines, but no one had any reliance on them. We had all planned routes of escape to Kenya or the Soudan. At the beginning of October every train that left for Djibouti was reported as the last until even the most persevering among the journalists lost interest. If anything had been needed to rob the situation in which we found ourselves of any remaining vestige of heroic glamour it was this regular, unimpaired service to the coast. No one, except the few informed French officials, expected this. Of the various fates which from time to time we predicted for Haile Selassie – rescue by British aeroplanes, death in battle, murder, suicide – no one, I think, ever seriously suggested what was actually to happen; that in the final catastrophe, desperate and disillusioned, betrayed by the League, deserted by his army, hunted by insurgent tribesmen, with his enemies a day's march from the Palace and their aircraft regularly reconnoitring over his head, he would quietly proceed to the station, board the train and trip down to Djibouti by rail. The least romantic of us never suggested that.

3

Addis Ababa on the eve of war seemed little changed in character and appearance from the city I had known five years before. The triumphal arches that had been erected for the coronation had grown shabbier but they were still standing. The ambitious buildings in the European style with which Haile Selassie had intended to embellish his capital were still in the same rudimentary stage of construction; tufted now with vegetation like ruins in a drawing by Piranesi, they stood at every corner, reminders of an abortive modernism, a happy subject for the press photographers who hoped later to present them as the ravages of Italian bombardment. The usual succession of public holidays paralysed the life of the country; we arrived on the eve of one of them and for two days were unable to cash cheques or collect our luggage from the customs. There was a new Palace and some new shops. The lepers, driven into the villages for the coronation, had returned; that was the most noticeable change.

The newspapermen in their more picturesque moods used often to write about the cavalcades of fighting men who swept through 'the narrow streets of the mountain capital', evoking for their readers the compact cities of North Africa. In fact the streets were very broad and very long. Everything lay at a great distance from everything else. The town was scattered over the hillside like the litter of a bank holiday picnic party.

One chief thoroughfare, curving sharply where it crossed the river, led from the old Gibbi (Menelik's Palace) to the irregular space before the post office which constituted the hub of the town. Here, on a drab little balustraded concrete island, stood one of the four public monuments of the town, a gilt three-pointed star on a concrete pedestal. Two rival cinemas stood on either side soliciting patronage through the voices of two vastly amplified gramophones, which played simultaneously from sunset until long after midnight, when the hyenas and wild dogs usurped the silence, howling over the refuse heaps, disinterring the corpses in the public cemetery. Other streets branched off from here, leading variously to Giorgis (the Cathedral), the commercial quarter, the hotels and the wireless station. A broad road led down to the railway, a strip of tarmac down the centre, at the sides mule tracks deep in mud during the rains, rutted and dusty during the dry season. In front of the station stood another monument, a gilt Lion of Judah. The third was near Giorgis, an equestrian statue of Menelik, which I had seen unveiled at the time of the coronation (it was a morning rendered remarkable by the rivalry of two brass bands; at the moment of unveiling, as happens from time to time in more northerly countries, the flag failed to respond and had to be torn off in sections by a Greek contractor on a step ladder; one fragment proved inaccessible, a square of vivid green artificial silk which continued to flutter gaily about the eyes and ears of the gilt horse). The fourth was a concrete phallus copied from one of the antiquities of Axum and, incongruously, embellished with a clock at the summit. It stood in the cross roads at the furthest end of the main thoroughfare, dominating a taxi rank of decrepit and flea-infested vehicles which had now been relegated to the use of Asiatics. The taxis in the fashionable quarter of the town were also flea-infested, but brand-new and as fast as the roads would allow. There was a great number of them, brought up by train, native driven, their fares so wildly augmented for the new arrivals that the old residents were obliged with the utmost reluctance to pursue their business on foot.

The frontage of the main streets was broken by many empty building-lots and − a more depressing spectacle − by abandoned foundations and the ruins of recent fires. (An insurance company had lately begun operations in Addis Ababa and the result had been a holocaust of important business premises.) Between them stood shops, offices, cafés and private houses, for the most part of one story, all roofed with corrugated iron, built of concrete or timber. A few shops had windows of plate glass. The most prosperous sold tins of food and bottles of deleterious spirits. A stationer's shop displayed European papers and indecent postcards; there were Goanese tailors and Armenian bootmakers; an ironmonger's dealing in frail-looking firearms and very solid knuckle-dusters; a German confectioner's; beyond the bazaar quarter stood the huge emporium of the firm of Mohamedally.

The entire trade of the town was in alien hands, for the most part Levantine and Indian. I do not think there was a single shop or office managed by an Abyssinian. The artisans were Arab and Sikh. Even the porters on the railway were Arabs. There was no Abyssinian middle class. The lowest manual labour and the highest administrative posts were reserved for them; bullying and being bullied. They had no crafts. It was extraordinary to find a people with an ancient and continuous habit of life who had produced so little. They built nothing; they made no gardens; they could not dance. For centuries Africa has offered Europe successive waves of æsthetic stimulus. Of the gracious, intricate art of Morocco or the splendour of Benin, the Abyssinians knew nothing; nor of the dark, instinctive art of the negro – the ju-ju sculpture, the carved masks of the medicine man, the Ngomas, the traditional terrifying ballet which the dancing troops carry from the Great Lakes to the islands of Zanzibar and Pemba. To lounge at the door of his hut counting his cartridges, to indulge in an occasional change of wife, to have a slaveboy in attendance to trot behind his mule carrying his cheap Belgian rifle, to be entertained, now and then, by his chief to a surfeit of raw beef and red pepper and damp grey bread, to boast in his cups of his own bravery and the inferiority of all other races, white, black, yellow and brown – these after centuries of self-development were the characteristic pleasures of the Abyssinian.

In the Church alone his æsthetic feelings found expression. Compared with the manifestations of historic Christianity in any other part of the world, West or East, the decoration was shoddy, the ceremony slipshod, the scholarship meagre, but, at least, it was something unique in the life of the people. By its interminable liturgy, its school of fine penmanship and direct didactic painting, its lore of customary right and wrong, it fostered a tradition independent of, and antagonistic to, the ideals of Addis Ababa – the push and polish of the *Jeunesse d'Ethiopie.*

Those who are inclined to lament the passing of a low but individual culture should remember that it was already marked down for destruction. In Persia and Turkey, to-day, we see the triumph of native progressive parties, accompanied by the swift obliteration of native piety and of almost all that made native life characteristic and beautiful. The Abyssinian progressive party was still uncertain of its strength. It aimed at breaking the influence of the clergy; most of its members were personally irreligious, but they had not yet begun openly to attack the beliefs on which the influence of the clergy was based. Specifically Christian formulæ were still preserved in many of their utterances. But the Church and the particular brand of development at which the *Jeunesse d'Ethiopie* aimed could not have subsisted together. The people had been tenacious of their faith against centuries of invasion; they were bound to it by the routine and special occasions of their life. It is probable that the *Jeunesse d'Ethiopie* would have fallen. If they had failed, Europe would have intervened. If they had succeeded, they would have created a country that was independent, powerful, uniform and utterly drab.

4

There were several hotels in Addis Ababa, all, at the time of our arrival, outrageously prosperous. The 'Splendide', at which we all assumed we should stay – the Radical had had the name painted in large white letters on his medicine chest – was completely full with journalists and photographers living in hideous proximity, two or three to a room even in the outbuildings. It was a massive, shabby building of sepulchral gloom, presided over by a sturdy, middle-aged, misanthropic Greek, who had taken it over as a failing concern just before the troubles. There was something admirable about the undisguised and unaffected distaste with which he regarded his guests and his ruthless disregard of their comfort and dignity. Some attempted to be patronising to him, some dictatorial, some ingratiating; all were treated with uniform contempt. He was well aware that for a very few months nothing that he did or left undone could affect his roaring prosperity; after that anything might happen. The less his guests ate the greater his profits, and from his untidy little desk in the corner he watched with sardonic amusement the crowds of dyspeptic journalists – many of them elderly men, of note in their own country – furtively carrying into his dining-room paper bags of fresh bread, tins of tuck and pocketsful of oranges and bananas, like little boys trooping in to tea at their private schools. Mr Kakophilos never apologised and very rarely complained. Nothing of the smallest value was endangered in the scenes of violence which became increasingly frequent as the journalists made themselves at home. When his guests threw their bedroom furniture out of the window, he noted it in the weekly bill. If they fired their revolvers at the night watchman he merely advised the man to take careful cover. Menageries of unclean pets were introduced into the bed-rooms; Mr Kakophilos waited unconcerned until even their owners could bear their presence no longer. His was the chief hotel of the town and nothing could shake its status. Here, intermittently, the government posted its *communiqués*; here the Foreign Press Association held its acrimonious meetings; here every evening, when the wireless station was shut, we all assembled, in seedy wicker chairs in the large, bare, flea-ridden hall, to drink and grumble.

The Deutsches Haus, where Mr Rickett and I were taken, was humbler and very much more hospitable. It stood near the Splendide in a side street, but its immediate surroundings were not imposing. Opposite was a tannery run by a Russian Prince, from which, when the wind was in the wrong quarter, there came smells so appalling that we were obliged to shut our windows and scatter in different parts of the town; sometimes a lorry of reeking pelts would be left all day at our gates; once, for some purpose connected with his hideous trade, His Highness acquired a load of decomposing cows' feet. He was a debonair figure, given to exotic tastes in dress. When he first arrived at Addis he was asked to luncheon at the British Legation and the guard turned out for him. A few days later he opened a house of ill fame. Now he was mainly, but not exclusively, interested in the fur trade. He often spoke wistfully of a convoy of girls who had been on order from Cairo since the battle of Walwal but were held up somewhere, mysteriously and unjustly, in the customs.

On either side of the Deutsches Haus stood the quarters of native prostitutes, single-roomed, doorless cabins from which issued occasional bursts of raucous squabbling and of more raucous light music. Cotton curtains hung over the entrances which were drawn back when the inhabitants were disengaged, to reveal a windowless interior, a wood fire, a bed and usually a few naked children and goats. In the old days the curtains bore the time-honoured device of the red cross, but lately a government order had caused it to be removed. It was still to be seen in the provinces, but at Addis only the upright remained and a cleaner strip where the bar had been unpicked. The ugliness of these women was a constant source of wonder to us, not, indeed, on account of their natural disadvantages, because that is a matter of common observation in their profession all over the world, but of their neglect of any possible means of embellishment. I asked my interpreter what were the charges at these houses.

'For me,' he said, 'it is a thaler because I am a British subject. If an Abyssinian gives a thaler he goes again and again until there is a quarrel.'

Quarrels seemed fairly frequent, to judge by the sounds which greeted us at all hours of the day on the way to the Deutsches Haus.

But though the surroundings were forbidding, the hospitality inside the gates (which were kept by a grizzled warrior armed with a seven-foot spear) was delightful. Mrs Heft was one of the Germans who had drifted to Abyssinia from Tanganyika when it was confiscated by the British government after the war. There were a large number of her compatriots in the town, mostly in very poor circumstances, employed as mechanics or in petty trade. The Deutsches Haus was their rendezvous where they played cards and occasionally dined. The Hefts could never quite get used to the disregard of small economies or the modest appetites of her new boarders. Many of our demands seemed to her painfully complex. 'The journalists pay well,' she confided. 'But they are very difficult. Some want coffee in the morning and some want tea, and they expect it always to be hot.' But she worked untiringly in our service.

She was a housewife of formidable efficiency. Daily from dawn until noon a miniature market was held on the steps of the dining-room. Half a dozen native hawkers squatted patiently, displaying meat, eggs and vegetables. Every half-hour she or Mr Heft would emerge, disparage the goods, ask the price, and, in simulated rage, tell the salesmen to be off. Eventually, when it was time to start cooking luncheon, she made her purchases.

Mr Heft had a deafening little car, which at any moment of the day or night he would take out for our use. There was also a hotel taxi, which the bearded chauffeur used as a crèche for his baby. When his services were required he would whisk the infant out of the back seat and nurse it as he drove.

There were two geese loose in the yard who attacked all comers. Mr Heft was always promising to kill them, but they were still alive when I left the country. There was also a pig, which he did kill, from which Mrs Heft made a magnificent abundance of sausages and *patés*. The food, for Addis, was excellent. Mr Heft hovered over the tables at meal times watching all we ate. 'No like?' he would say, in genuine distress, if anyone refused a course. 'Make you eggies, yes?'

The Hefts' bedroom opened from the dining-room, and it was there that everything of value in the house was kept. If one wanted change for a hundred-thaler note, an aspirin, a clean towel, a slice of sausage, a bottle of Chianti, the wireless bulletin, a spare part for a car, a pack of cards, one's washing or one's weekly bill, Mrs Heft dived under her bed and produced it.

I always suspected that in his rare moments of leisure Mr Heft was doing a little journalism on his own account. There were few people in Addis who, in course of time, did not find themselves on the pay roll of one or more of the various news agencies.

The Deutsches Haus soon became the headquarters of most of the English journalists and photographers. We employed our own servants, decorated our rooms with monkey-skin rugs from the Russian Prince and native paintings from the itinerant artists, and were, on the whole, tolerably comfortable. *The Times* and the Reuter's correspondents rented houses. The Americans, more Baedekerminded, stayed resolutely with Mr Kakophilos.

There were two places of entertainment in the town, *Le Select* and the *Perroquet*, usually known by the names of their proprietors, Moriatis and Idot. Both had a bar and a talking cinema. Mme Idot had also a kitchen and put it about that her cooking was good. From time to time she would placard the town with news of some special delicacy – *Grand Souper. Tripes à la mode de Caen* – and nostalgic journalists would assemble in large numbers, to be bitterly disillusioned. She came from Marseilles, Mme Moriatis from Bordeaux. They were bitter rivals, but while Mme Moriatis affected ignorance of the other's existence, Mme Idot indulged in free criticism. 'Poor woman!' she would say. 'What does she think she is doing here? She should go back to Bordeaux. She has a face like Lent.' M. Moriatis was a very handsome cad-Greek; M. Idot a hideous cad-Frenchman. Both, by repute, whipped their wives, but Mme Idot professed to enjoy it. Mme Idot shed an atmosphere of false gaiety, Mme Moriatis of very genuine gloom. One talked gravely to Mme Moriatis about the beauties of France and the wickedness of Abyssinian character; she was always apologising for the inadequacy of her entertainment and one tried to encourage her. 'It is not *chic*,' she would say very truly. 'It is not as I should like it. If the Italians were here we should have dancing at the aperitif time and upstairs an hotel with bath-rooms – completely European.' Everyone pinched Mme Idot and slapped her behind, told her that her films were unendurable and her wines poisonous. *Le Select* had pretensions to respectability and occasionally held charity matinées attended by members of the diplomatic corps. There was no nonsense of that kind about the *Perroquet*. Both prospered on the contrast, because, after an hour in either place, one longed for the other.

There were three hospitals in the town – two of them American, one Italian. There was a mosque and countless churches – Abyssinian, Armenian, Greek Orthodox, Catholic, Church of England, Adventist. There were government offices and the ramshackle palaces of wealthy Abyssinian rases. There was an hotel near the railway station, built over a hot spring, where, if one could face the leper who guarded its approach – a woman of nightmare, unique even in a land of appalling spectacles – one could get a bath. And behind and around all these buildings lay the *tukals* of the native inhabitants, clusters of thatched huts packed in the hollows and gulleys which broke the hillside, among the great groves of eucalyptus. They seemed to have little part in the life of the city; one could live there for weeks and scarcely be aware of their existence. From them, in early morning, the crowds emerged which all day long sauntered about the streets, picking their way bare-footed from stone to stone of the rough pavements. There was curfew an hour or so after sunset; then any native was liable to arrest. By dinner time they had entirely disappeared, like office workers from the City of London, and the streets were given up to aliens and hyenas.

5

Most visitors to Addis Ababa arrive feeling ill. The sudden rise from coast level to eight thousand feet, the change of temperature from the heat of the Red Sea to the cold nights and sunless days of the plateau in the rainy season, the food and, if they are imprudent, the water they have consumed at the railway buffets during the ascent, all contribute to disturb the hardiest constitution. On this occasion our distress was aggravated by the feverish and futile bustle in which all our colleagues appeared to be living, and the unplumbed lethargy of the native customs officials which prevented us getting to our luggage and warm clothes until late on the third day after our arrival. I had mild dysentery and a heavy cold, and lay in my room for two days, dizzy, torpid and acutely miserable, until a series of peremptory cables from Fleet Street roused me to a sense of my responsibilities: *Require comprehensive cable good colourful stuff also all news*, shortly followed by *Please indicate when can expect comprehensive cable*, followed by *Presume you are making arrangements getting stuff away* and *What alternative means communication in event breakdown?*

The method by which telegrams were distributed gave limitless opportunity for loss and delay. They were handed out to the messengers in bundles of about a dozen. The men were unable to read and their system of delivery was to walk round the town to the various hotels and places where foreigners might be expected to congregate and present their pile of envelopes to the first white man they saw, who would look through them, open any that might seem of interest, and hand back those that were not for him. Often it took more than a day for a message to reach us and, as the commands of Fleet Street became more and more fantastically inappropriate to the situation and the inquiries more and more frivolous, we most of us became grateful for a respite, which sometimes obviated the need of reply.

However, on the third day one of these messengers found his way to my room with the first, very reasonable request, so I left my bed and set out rather shakily into the pouring rain to look for 'colour'.

First steps as a war correspondent were humdrum – a round of the Legations with calling-cards, a sitting at the photographer's to obtain the pictures needed for a journalist's pass, registration at the Press Bureau.

This last was a little tin shed at the further extremity of the main road. It might well have been classed among the places of entertainment in the town. Here morning and afternoon for the first six weeks, until everyone, even its organisers, despaired of it ever performing any helpful function, might be found a dozen or so exasperated journalists of both sexes and almost all nationalities, waiting for interviews. It was an office especially constituted for the occasion. At the head of it was a suave, beady-eyed little Tigrean named Dr Lorenzo Taesas. He was a man of great tact and many accomplishments, but since he was also Judge of Special Court, head of secret police, and personal adviser to the Emperor, it was very rarely that he attended in person. His place was taken by another Tigrean, named David, equally charming, a better linguist, an ardent patriot, who was unable on his own authority to make the most trivial decision or give the simplest information. 'I must ask Dr Lorenzo,' was his invariable answer to every demand. In this way a perfect system of postponement and prevarication was established. If one approached any government department direct, one was referred to the Press Bureau. At the Press Bureau one was asked to put one's inquiry in writing, when it would be conveyed to the invisible Dr Lorenzo. At this early stage the Abyssinians had no reason to be hostile to the Press. Most of them in fact – and particularly the Emperor – were eager to placate it. But this was the manner in which Europeans had always been treated in the country. Just as many white men see a negro as someone to whom orders must be shouted, so the Abyssinians saw us as a people to be

suspected, delayed, frustrated in our most innocent intentions, lied
to, whenever truth was avoidable, and set against one another by
hints of preferential treatment. There was no ill-will. The attitude
was instinctive to them; they could not alter it, and closer acquaintance with us gave them good reason to stiffen rather than relax.

Almost all those impatient figures on Dr Lorenzo's doorstep were
after one thing. We wanted to get up country. Travelling in Ethiopia,
even in its rare periods of tranquillity, was a matter of the utmost
difficulty. Many writers have left accounts of the intricate system of
tolls and hospitality by which the traveller was passed on from one
chief to another and of the indifference with which the Emperor's
laissez-passer was treated within a few miles of the capital. Now, with
torrential rains all over the highlands flooding the streams and
washing away the mule tracks, with troops secretly assembling and
migrating towards the frontiers, with the subject peoples, relieved of
their garrisons, turning rebel and highwaymen, the possibilities of
movement in any direction were extremely slight. But, at any rate
for the first weeks after our arrival, we most of us cherished a hope,
and the Press Bureau constantly fostered it, that we should get to the
fighting. No one ever got there. My last sight of Lorenzo, more than
three months later at Dessye, was of a little figure, clad in khaki then
in place of his dapper morning coat, surrounded by a group of
importunate journalists in the Adventist Mission compound, promising that very soon, in a few days perhaps, permission would be
granted to go north. Actually it was only when the front came to
them, and the retreat of the government headquarters could not
keep pace with the Italian advance, that any of them saw a shot fired.

But meanwhile there still lingered in our minds the picture we
had presented of ourselves to our womenfolk at home, of stricken
fields and ourselves crouching in shell holes, typing gallantly amid
bursting shrapnel; of runners charging through clouds of gas, bearing our despatches on cleft sticks. We applied, formally, for permission to travel, absolving the government of all responsibility for our
safety, and awaited an immediate reply.

The Radical, who knew his job, had no illusions of the kind. The
court, the government offices and the Legations were the 'news
centres'. His place was near the wireless office. Not so my immediate

neighbour in the Deutsches Haus, an American who proclaimed his imminent departure for the Tigre. A squad of carpenters was noisily at work under our windows boxing his provisions, his caravan of the sturdiest mules was stabled nearby. He had already discarded the dress of a capital city and strode the water-logged streets as though he were, even at that moment, pushing his way through unmapped jungle. Poor chap, he was one of the group surrounding Lorenzo at Dessye.

6

It was the general belief, shared by the Abyssinians, that the main campaign would be fought in the south. There would be a small advance in great strength from Asmara, a ceremonial entry into Adowa, the erection of some kind of monument to the fallen in the war of 1896; then troops would be transferred by sea to Mogadishu and from there would drive up the comparatively easy country of the Fafan valley to Jijiga, Harar and the railway. This was what the military experts predicted. In the circumstances, with the northern roads impassable, the best plan seemed to be to move south and see as much as was possible of the line of this advance. Three journalists had already been some way, one of them a considerable way, in that direction. Facilities were becoming rarer and we were warned by David that we should now get no further than Harar; but I had hopes, based on my acquaintance with the officials of five years back, that the men on the spot might prove more amenable. Even if we were obliged to stay in Harar there seemed a prospect of better news than in Addis, for there were exciting rumours from there of Italian propaganda among the Mohammedans. In Addis everything seemed to be at a standstill.

Mr Rickett, it is true, held out hopes of a story. He was clearly up to something and drove off every now and then to interview such very dissimilar dignitaries as the Abuna[1] and Mr Colson, the American financial adviser of the Emperor. I thought it impertinent to inquire

---

[1] The Egyptian head of the Abyssinian Church. His predecessor had been a man of great personal influence, but the present Abuna was unambitious and far from well.

further. On the second day of our visit he had promised me an important piece of news on Saturday evening. Saturday came and he admitted, rather ruefully, that he had not been able to arrange anything; it would probably be next Wednesday, he said. It seemed clear that he was involved in the endless postponements of Abyssinian official life, from which the American doctor was also suffering with undisguised annoyance, and that in ten days' time I should find him at the Deutsches Haus, still negotiating. Accordingly, with Patrick Balfour, an old friend who had preceded me as correspondent for the *Evening Standard*, I decided to leave by the Monday train.

In the meantime we attempted to collect what little news there was in Addis. Troops were drilling on many of the roads; there was no other place for them, for the fields were water-logged and there was no dry parade ground. A great deal was written about the smartness of the Imperial Guard – the Belgian-trained force of Haile Selassie's own creation, which had been in existence for about six years. They shaved their faces and wore tidy uniforms; the cavalry rode well-matched, well-groomed ponies, the infantry usually marched in step and refrained from chatter when standing at attention. They formed an outstanding contrast to the general shabbiness of the town and to the wild feudal levies. But they would have gained little credit as a contingent at an O.T.C. camp in England, and in comparison with the Somali Camel Corps or the K.A.R. they were rabble.

There were volunteers also from the town and surrounding district about three thousand strong, who were paid a thaler or two a week, when they had not forfeited the sum in fines for lateness or undiscipline. There was something pathetically futile about their training. They lived at home with their wives and, at dawn, began to pour in, many from farms at some distance. When they had been paraded and counted they were marched two miles to the old armoury and issued with rifles. These had to be returned again at evening and carefully counted. There was an inherent disposition for the Abyssinian, as soon as he was given a new rifle, to take to the hills with it. The least that might be expected was that he would shoot up a *tedj* house. So a large part of the day was occupied in distributing and collecting the arms. The remainder was spent in arms drill and march discipline on the European model. As there was practically no road outside the city where four men could march abreast, and as the one quality in which Abyssinian troops were sensationally effective was in their habit of movement – breaking up over miles of country, foraging and resting at will, now strolling pensively, now trotting, covering prodigious distances daily – this forming of fours, dressing by the right, keeping step, wheeling and halting to command seemed quite without purpose.

And yet it is hard to suggest what could have taken its place. There was far too little ammunition for target practice. The country all round was a swamp where it was impossible to exercise in open order. They had only a few weeks to prepare. They were mostly detribalised by their residence in and near the capital; the drill at least taught them to obey their new superiors. It also acted as an intoxicant and spur to patriotism. The children took it up, and could be seen drilling one another in front of their homes. Even some of the women, in the houses round the Deutsches Haus, might be seen saluting and practising right and left turns. But it seemed an incomplete preparation for meeting a modern mechanical army.

There was a meeting of high-born ladies in premises that had formerly been a night club to discuss the formation of a local Red Cross unit. Patriotic speeches were made and a subscription collected. There were rumours brought me by a sibilant Greek most of which were so obviously false as to need no investigation. There was a morning of great excitement when it was believed, wrongly, that a member of the Italian Legation had been ambushed by natives. There were strongly supported and quite untrue reports that a legion of Egyptian volunteers was on its way to fight for the Abyssinians. There were untrue stories of a munition factory that was being opened by an English engineer, and of an army of women that was secretly drilling in the provinces. There was a genuine financial crisis and a run on the bank. There were demands from Fleet Street for daily items of 'spot news'.

It was with great relief that, on Monday morning, August 26 – in the entirely purposeless secrecy with which the journalists in Addis invested all their movements – Patrick and I set out for Harar.

CHAPTER 3

HARAR AND JIJIGA

1

THE TRAIN TO Diredawa was full of refugees. All the trains at this time carried a fair number. There was never, except immediately after the outbreak of the war, any real panic, but the men of the foreign community were being quietly advised by their consuls to get their families out of the country, and those who could were winding-up their affairs and following. Only the Italians had been told to go quickly, and most of them had gone before I came. They left in high spirits, confident of a speedy and glorious return. The Greeks from Rhodes and the Dodecanese formed a more sombre body. Many of these had been born in Abyssinia; almost all had come to the country as Greek or Turkish nationals. It was the only home they had known; they were artisans earning a better living than they could have got among their own people. Then, by changes in the map that were incomprehensible to them, they found that they had suddenly become Italians, and now they were being hustled down to the coast with the prospect of being recruited into labour gangs or soldiers to fight against the country of their adoption. There were several of them in our train, wistfully sucking oranges in the second-class coach.

In the first class were a large party of Levantine women and children, plump and pallid as though modelled in lard. After a noisy and emotional leave-taking they subsided into their places and sobbed quietly for an hour, then began to cheer up and expand, opened their cases and produced thermos flasks and bags of sweet-meats until they gradually spread over the whole coach an atmosphere of sticky domesticity.

The only male was one of the former mystery men of Addis, who was reputed to be an Englishman, an engineer, and the future organiser of the Emperor's munition factory. He told us that he found journalists very inquisitive people, but his story, for what it was worth, had now 'broken', so that we were able to join him at cut-throat bridge without embarrassing him with further questions. After fifteen hours we reached Diredawa and Mr Bololakos' hotel. Early next morning the mystery man and the emigrants proceeded to the coast and Patrick and I were left to make our arrangements for going to Harar.

Until three years before, the journey took two days. One rode out on mule-back, first for a sultry hour along the river-bed, then by a precipitous track up the hillside among thorn and boulders, out into open downland, through corn crops and coffee fields to the rest house on Lake Harramaya, where one spent the night; on the next day, along the broad, frequented caravan route to the walled city. Now there was a motor road.

It was this road which constituted one of the particular griev-ances of the Italians. In the 1928 agreement the Abyssinians had promised to make their second outlet to the sea from Dessye to Assab; instead they had chosen to link the railway with Berbera in British Somaliland. A stream of motor lorries now followed this route, carrying out coffee and skins, bringing in, it was believed, arms and ammunition. It formed, too, the main line of communi-cation with the Ethiopian Ogaden, the channel by which supplies would reach troops at Sasa Baneh and Gerlogubi. Jijiga was the junction where the ways divided, one to Hargeisa and British Somaliland, the other down the Fafan valley; it was therefore expected to be the main objective of the autumn campaign.

For centuries before Menelik Harar was an independent Emir-ate, a city state founded by Arabs from across the Red Sea, who held sway over a large and fertile province inhabited by peaceable Moslem Gallas. They held the caravan route between the coast and the interior and made their city the emporium of a rich trade in coffee and slaves. The Harari people spoke their own language, wore a distinctive costume, and exhibited a very high standard of culture in comparison with their rough neighbours. They were rigid in their faith and hostile to foreign influence. The Emir's family claimed high, Sherifian descent and already showed signs of decadence when Burton – the first white man in their history – visited them in the middle of the last century. He came, as he admits in his account of the expedition,[1] with the intention of preparing the way for English occupation. His description of the city and its people was no doubt somewhat modified by his desire to make out a good case for interference. He represents them as vicious, tyrannical and rather squalid. The Hararis, naturally enough, look back to the days of their independence as a golden age, the Baghdad of Haroun al Raschid. No doubt it differed little from the other Moslem Sultanates which once covered the African coast and trade routes; a despotism that was sometimes benevolent and sometimes oppressive according to the disposition of the reigning monarch, but qualified always by the integrity of Koranic law; Harar had its shrine which formed a centre of pilgrimage; its market where goods of exotic value were displayed; a place of riches and security which easily became a splendid legend among the surrounding barbarians. Even in 1935, after a generation of Abyssinian misrule and Indian and Levantine immigration, it retained something of the gracious fragrance of Fez or Meknes.

Burton's ambition was disappointed. During the brief experiment of Khedival imperialism, Harar fell under Egyptian rule; for a few months it was garrisoned by Indian troops and flew the Union Jack. Then it was abandoned to its fate and captured by the Shoans under Menelik.

In the first stages of the Franco-Ethiopian Railway it was proposed to join Harar with Djibouti, but the work stopped short at Diredawa, the enterprise came in danger of failure, and, when the line was continued, it was run direct to the capital. Harar was then under French influence; a French mission and leper settlement were established there and the town became the headquarters of romantic smugglers of whom Rimbaud is the most illustrious. But its wealth rapidly declined. The railway had usurped the place of the camel-track as the main trade route. The Shoan rulers fastened themselves upon the dying body and drained it of vitality. The Emir's family lived in poverty and obscurity; the position of

[1] *First Steps in East Africa*, by Sir Richard Burton.

the sheiks became purely titular. Abyssinians lounged and swaggered in every office; as the revenue from trade fell, the duties were increased to support them; the Galla peasants, bringing their baskets of produce to market, found their meagre profits absorbed in customs-dues. The Abyssinian garrison lived on the free labour of the conquered people; the Harari women carried their water and wood. Christian manners and morals[1] defiled the holy places.

When I visited the town in 1930 it was clearly declining fast. The fringe of houses immediately inside the walls were empty and ruinous, as though, like the lepers that thronged the streets, Harar were already dead and decaying at its extremities.

The motor road did something to revive its importance, but at the expense of its charm. We left Diredawa shortly before midday, having been delayed by the necessity of obtaining passes to cross the provincial boundary. Patrick and I and his servant had now been joined by another Englishman, an old acquaintance named Charles G., who had come out primarily in search of amusement. He had arrived in the small hours of the morning, the train from Djibouti having been twice delayed – once by a two-mile wash-out of the track, once by the impatience of the engine-driver, who had started off after the midday halt leaving all his passengers still lunching at the buffet. There was also a youthful and very timid Abyssinian nobleman, who wanted a lift and raised entirely vain hopes of his being useful to us.

We left in two cars and, twisting and groaning up the countless hairpin bends and narrow embankments of the new road, were very soon at the top of the pass, which formerly had taken four hours of arduous riding. Here was a military post, a barricade and new corrugated-iron gates, which were later described by many poetic correspondents as 'the ancient "Gates of Paradise"'.

---

1 Koranic law forbids prostitution. The rows of *tedj* houses in Harar were all staffed by Abyssinian women. Under Abyssinian rule the liquor trade became a valuable source of revenue. The older Hararis complained bitterly of the consequent demoralisation of the younger generation. It is worth noticing, however, that Burton, fresh from the austere standard of Arabia, was shocked by the almost universal drunkenness he found in Harar.

They certainly emphasised the contrast between the Harar province and the surrounding wilderness. Behind lay the colourless, empty country which one saw from the train; mile after mile of rock and dust, ant-hill and scrub, and, on the far horizon, the torrid plain of the Danakil desert, where the Awash river petered out in a haze of heat. In front, beyond the surly Abyssinian guard, the uplands were patterned with standing crops, terraces of coffee, neat little farms in flowering stockades of euphorbia, the pinnacles of their thatched roofs decorated with bright glass bottles and enamelled chamber-pots. We passed one considerable village, dominated, as all such places were, by an Abyssinian squatter, and in less than four hours after our departure from Diredawa were in sight of the walls and minarets of Harar.

Perhaps I had been unduly eloquent in describing to my companions the beauties that awaited us. I had come to Harar, as Patrick and I were coming now, fresh from the straggling, nondescript, tin and tarmac squalor of Addis Ababa, and it had seemed like a city from the 'Arabian Nights'. Five years' absence had enhanced the glamour of that revelation. I spoke of it as a place of gardens and good manners and fine craftsmanship and described how, when the five great gates were closed at sunset, I had set out, heavily armed, with an Armenian publican, through a labyrinth of pitch-black streets, to a wedding party, where on a herb-strewn floor, in soft lamplight and clouds of incense, I had seen modest, light-hearted girls dancing formal and intricate figures. I had talked at some length about those girls; they had all the slender grace of the Somalis, their narrow hips, broad, straight shoulders and high, pointed breasts, but instead of their sooty, monkey faces had skins of warm golden-brown and soft, delicately carved features; they wore their hair in a multitude of plaits and covered it with brilliant silk shawls; another shawl was bound under their arms, leaving the shoulders and arms bare, and from knee to ankle were revealed slim calves, in tight trousers of bright spiral stripes, like sugar-sticks in a village post office. Their feet and the palms of their hands were dyed with henna. They were the débutantes of the town, unmarried girls of good family, the bridesmaids at the coming wedding. It was a unique spectacle for a Moslem city.

After all I had remembered, and all I had said, the reality was a little disappointing. There had been changes. The first sight to greet us, as we came into view, was a vast, hideous palace, still under construction; a white, bow-fronted, castellated European thing like a south coast hotel. It stood outside the walls, dominating the low, dun-coloured masonry behind it. The walls had been breached and, instead of the circuitous approach of mediæval defence, the narrow, windowless lane which had led from the main gates, under the walls, bending and doubling until it reached the centre of the town, a new, straight track had been driven through. There was an hotel, too, built in two stories, with a balcony, a shower-bath and a chamber of ineffable horror, marked on the door, *W. C.* It was kept by a vivacious and avaricious Greek named Carassellos, who, every-one said, for no reason at all, was really an Italian. This building, where we took rooms, had been erected immediately in front of the Law Courts, and the space between was a babel of outraged litigants denouncing to passers-by the venality of the judges, the barefaced perjury of the witnesses, and the perversions of the legal system, by which they had failed in their suits. About twice every hour they would come to blows and be dragged inside again by the soldiers to summary punishment.

But the main change seemed to be in the proportions of Abyssinians to Hararis. It was at the moment, by all appearance, an Abyssinian town. Great numbers of troops were being drafted there. A Belgian training school was established. Abyssinian officials had been multiplied for the crisis, and with their women and children filled the town. The Hararis were rapidly melting away; those that could afford it, fled across the frontiers into French and British territory, the majority to the hills. They were a pacific people who did not want to get involved on either side in the coming struggle; particularly, they did not want their women to get into the hands of the Abyssinian soldiers. In place of the lovely girls I had described, we found the bare, buttered, sponge-like heads, the dingy white robes, the stolid, sulky faces and silver crosses of the Abyssinian camp followers.

That afternoon the Abyssinian youth we had conveyed from Diredawa brought three educated friends to tea with us. It was a very dull little party. We learned later that here and in Addis Ababa any native who was seen conversing with a white man was liable to immediate arrest and cross-examination about what had been said. This restricted social intercourse to an exchange of the simplest commonplaces. Our guests wore European clothes, hats and shoes. I was unable to place one of them and asked him, as delicately as I could, whether he were Mohammedan or Christian. 'I do not believe any of that nonsense,' he said. 'I am educated.'

Later the chief of the police dropped in for some whisky. He was an officer of the old school, greatly given to the bottle. He was suffering at the time from a severe cold and had stuffed his nostrils with leaves. It gave him a somewhat menacing aspect, but his intentions were genial. Very few journalists had, as yet, visited Harar, and the little yellow cards of identity from the Press Bureau, which were an object of scorn in Addis, were here accepted as being evidence, possibly, of importance. Patrick's servant, whose French was fluent but rarely intelligible, acted as interpreter. That is to say, he carried on a lively and endless conversation, into which we would occasionally intrude.

'What is he saying, Gabri?'

'He says he has a cold. He hopes you are well.'

Then they would carry on their exchange of confidences. The end of this interview, however, was a promise that we should have a pass to take us as far as Jijiga.

2

Next day Fleet Street asserted itself again. A cable arrived for me saying, *Investigate Italian airplane shot down Harar*. There was absolutely no truth in the report. Had anything of the kind happened, the town would have been buzzing with the news. But the morning had to be spent disproving it. I visited the Italian Consulate – furtively, because an incessant watch was kept at the gates – learned the latest uncompromising utterances from Rome which had just come over the wireless, and left by a side door in the compound.

There were more signs of military activity at Harar than in Addis. In the plain outside the walls two or three hundred camels were waiting to be moved south as transport animals, while in an outdoor circus ring Somalis were training others for riding. About five thousand Shoan troops were being drilled in Belgian methods and, in imitation of them, a company of Harari youths, fired with an uncharacteristic and very brief enthusiasm, had taken to marching about for an hour each morning, before they went to work. The Emperor had visited Harar a few weeks before, as he did yearly, for the province was a personal fief granted by Menelik to his father, and had attempted with some apparent success to conciliate Moslem opinion. There were promises of a new deal in the south and the creation of a Moslem Ras. Prayers were being offered in the mosques for Abyssinian victory and two sheiks sent round the tribes to preach a holy war against the Europeans. It was not until much later, on my return to the district, that I began to suspect how superficial this harmony was. At the moment everyone we met was anxious to impress on us the reality of Ethiopian unity. We were told of great numbers of deserters who were coming over from Italian Somaliland with their rifles and ammunition to offer their services to the Emperor. Actually, I think, in these weeks immediately before the outbreak of war there was a steady trickle across the frontier in both directions. The Somalis are a moody people who had little affection for either conqueror. They were ready to enlist temporarily with anyone who would give them a new rifle. The propaganda department of both sides, throughout the autumn and early winter, until Desta's defeat in January made it apparent which was the winning side, were constantly issuing lists of the Somali chiefs who had made their submission or organised a revolt in the rival territories.

3

During our day of waiting for permission to go to Jijiga, Patrick and I each engaged a spy. They were both British 'protected persons', who had for a long time made themselves a nuisance at the Consulate. That was their only point in common.

Mine, Wazir Ali Beg, was an Afghan, an imposing old rascal with the figure of a metropolitan policeman and the manner of a butler.

He wrote and spoke nearly perfect English. At some stage of his life he had been in British government service, though in what precise capacity was never clear – probably as a consulate dragoman somewhere. Lately he had set up in Harar as a professional petition writer. He put it about among the British Indians, Arabs and Somalis who thronged the bazaar that he was a man of personal influence in the Consular Court, and thus induced them to part with their savings and brief him to conduct their cases for them. To me he represented himself as the head of a vast organisation covering the Ogaden and Aussa countries. He never asked for money for himself but to 'reimburse' his 'agents'. On the occasion of our first meeting he gave me an important piece of news: that a party of Danakil tribesmen had arrived at Diredawa to complain to the Governor of Italian movements in their territory; a force of native and white troops had penetrated the desert south-west of Assab and were making a base near Mount Moussa Ali. It was the verification of this report, a month later, which provoked the order for general mobilisation and precipitated the war. Wazir Ali Beg had a natural *flair* for sensational journalism and was so encouraged by my reception of this report that he continued to recount to me by every mail more and more improbable happenings, until, noticing letters in his scholarly hand addressed to nearly every journalist in Addis Ababa, I took him off my pay roll. He then used my letter of dismissal to put up his prices with his other clients, as evidence of the sacrifices he was making to give them exclusive service.

Patrick's spy was named Halifa, but he was soon known to the European community as Mata Hari. He was an Aden Arab whose dissolute appearance suggested only a small part of the truth. He approached us that evening without introduction on the balcony of the hotel, squatted down on his haunches very close to us, glanced furtively about him, and with extraordinary winks and gestures of his hands expressed the intention of coming with us to Jijiga as interpreter.

His frequent appearances at the Consular Court were invariably in the capacity of prisoner, charged with drunkenness, violence and debts of quite enormous amounts. He made no disguise of the fact that most of his recent life had been spent in gaol. When he found that this amused us, he giggled about it in a most forbidding way. He wore a huge, loose turban which was constantly coming uncoiled like the hair of a drunken old woman, a blue blazer, a white skirt and a number of daggers. Gabri, Patrick's Abyssinian servant, took an instant dislike to him. 'Il est méchant, ce type arabe,' he said, but Gabri, once outside the boundaries of his own country, was proving a peevish traveller. He did not at all like being among Mohammedans and foreigners. Harar he could just bear on account of the abundance of fellow countrymen, but the prospect of going to Jijiga filled him with disgust. The chief of police had already given us two effeminate little soldiers, who trotted at our heels wherever we went, weighted down by antiquated rifles, looking as though they would burst into tears at every moment of crisis. We felt we could do with an addition to our party, so Mata Hari was engaged. Our association with him did us no good in the eyes of the chief of police, and largely contributed, I think, to the subsequent expulsion of Charles G.; but he added vastly to our amusement.

4

After protracted negotiations we had taken seats in a coffee lorry, bound for Hargeisa. There were the usual delays as the Somali driver made a last-minute tour of the town in the endeavour to collect additional passengers, and it was soon clear that we should not reach Jijiga by nightfall. Our two soldiers began nervously to complain of danger from brigands, but the journey was uneventful and we reached Jijiga, hungry and shaken, at ten o'clock that evening. For the first half the road ran through hill country, eminently suitable for a guerilla defence: the surface was abominable and almost every mile we passed through narrow defiles where a charge of dynamite could hold up a mechanised column; the hillside was strewn with boulders and densely overgrown with bush, affording limitless cover. It seemed the sort of country that a handful of men could hold against an army.

Later in the afternoon we emerged into the open plain. It seemed easy to predict the course of the war – the rapid occupation of Jijiga, a pitched battle beyond, ending in an overwhelming victory for the

Italians, wild acclamation at Rome and the expectation of the fall of Harar; then a resolute rearguard action in the hills, indefinite delay, stubborn, expensive fighting while the long line of communication was constantly harassed by Ogaden tribesmen; then the rains again, and withdrawal to winter quarters in Jijiga. How wrong we were!

Rain came on at sunset and for four hours we made slow progress. The headlights pierced only a few feet of darkness; we skidded and splashed through pools of mud. Our driver wanted to stop and wait for dawn, saying that, even if we reached Jijiga, we should find ourselves locked out. We induced him to go on and at last came to the military post at the outskirts of the town. Here we found another lorry, full of refugees, which had passed us on the road earlier in the day. They had been refused admission and were now huddled together in complete darkness under sodden rugs, twenty or thirty of them, comatose and dejected. Our soldiers climbed down and parleyed; the driver exhibited the consular mailbag which he was carrying; Patrick and I produced our cards of identity. To everyone's surprise the barrier was pulled back and we drove on to the town. It was to all appearances dead asleep. We could just discern through the blackness that we were in a large square, converted at the moment to a single lake, ankle-deep. We hooted, and presently some Abyssinian soldiers collected round us, some of them drunk, one carrying a storm lantern. They directed us into a kind of pound; the gates were shut behind us and the soldiers prepared to return to bed.

There was no inn of any kind in Jijiga, but the firm of Mohamedally kept an upper room of their warehouse for the accommodation of the Harar consul on his periodic visits. We had permission to use this and had wired the local manager to expect us. His representative now appeared in pyjamas, carrying an umbrella in one hand and a lantern in the other. 'Good night,' he said, greeting us. 'How are you?'

Fresh trouble started, which Mati Hari tried to inflame into a fight, because the soldiers in command refused to let us remove our bags. They had to be seen by the customs officer, who would not come on duty until next morning. As they contained our food, and we had had nothing to eat since midday, the prospect seemed discouraging. The Indian from Mohamedally's told us it was hopeless and that we had better come to our room. Mata Hari, Charles and I set out with one of our own soldiers to find the customs officer. We knocked up his house, where they refused to open the door but shouted through the keyhole that the customs office was at the French House. A handful of Abyssinians had now collected in the darkness. Mata Hari did all he could to provoke them to violence, but our Harari guard was more conciliatory and eventually we were led, through what appeared to be miles of mud, to another house, which showed a light and a posse of sentries. The nature of the 'French House' was not at the moment clear. Sounds of many loud voices came from the interior. After Mata Hari had nearly got himself shot by one of the sentries, the door opened and a small Abyssinian emerged, clean shaven, dressed in European clothes, horn-spectacled; one of the younger generation. We later learned that he was new to his position, having spent the previous year in prison on a charge of peculation. He came with us to the lorry, apologising in fluent French for the inconvenience we had suffered. Our bags were surrendered and the Indian led us to our room, where, after supper, we slept on the floor until daybreak.

5

One of the wonders of travel is where native servants sleep. They arrive at any hour in a strange place and seem immediately to be surrounded by hospitable cousins-in-law, who embrace them, lead them home and for the rest of the stay batten upon one's stores. Our party broke up and disappeared cheerfully into the night; all except Gabri, who did not like Jijiga. He was intensely xenophobic where Somalis were concerned; he would not eat anything himself, saying that the food was not suitable for an Abyssinian; he nearly starved us by refusing to buy provisions on the grounds that the prices were excessive.

Mati Hari seemed to have slept in the mud, to judge by his appearance next morning, but perhaps he had merely found his fight. He came to our room in a kind of ecstasy, almost speechless with secrecy. He had news of the highest importance. He could not say it aloud, but must whisper it to each of us in turn. Count Drogafoi, the French Consul, had been thrown into prison. We asked him to repeat the name. He shook his head, winked and produced a stub of pencil and a piece of paper. Then, glancing over his shoulder to make sure he was not observed, he wrote the word, laboriously, in block capitals, DROGAFOI. It was to Droga-foi's house, he said, that we had been the night before. They were going to shoot Drogafoi that day. They had also arrested twelve Roman Catholics; these would be sewn up in skins and burned alive. There were four Maltese Popes in the town. They would probably be shot too. He would return shortly, he said, with further infor-mation, and with that and another meaning wink he tip-toed down-stairs.

In a somewhat puzzled state of mind we sat down to a breakfast of tinned partridge and Chianti. While we were still discussing what, if any, possible truth could be concealed in this story, the customs officer, our friend of the night before, came to introduce himself by name – Kebreth Astatkie – and to inquire about our welfare. Dedjasmach Nasebu, the Governor of Harar, was in Jijiga that day, he told us, on his way south, and would be pleased to see us. Accordingly we set out on foot for the Gibbi.

Rain had stopped and the town presented a more cheerful appearance. It consisted of a single main square and two side streets. It had been laid out, not many years back, by the father of the young man we had brought from Diredawa. It served two purposes; a caravanserai on the Berbera–Harar road and military outpost and administrative centre on the fringe of the Ogaden. The Gibbi and Mohamedally's warehouse were the only buildings of more than one story. The single European in the town, besides the mysterious Drogafoi and the Maltese Popes, was a Greek, whom Mata Hari pointed out to us, riding a bicycle.

'That is the Alcohol,' he explained; an imposing title which, we found later, meant that he owned the local liquor monopoly.

We also discovered the identity of the Maltese Popes; they were four Franciscan friars who ran an impoverished little mission – a cluster of native huts, half a mile outside the town.

The Gibbi, like most Abyssinian official buildings, was a nonde-script assembly of tin-roofed sheds, the largest of which had some upper rooms, reached by an outside staircase. Two half-grown lions were tethered outside the main door; the slave in charge wrestled with one of them for our benefit, and was rewarded with a thaler and a deep scratch on the thigh. There was the inevitable small army of ragged retainers, squatting on their heels, nursing their old rifles.

We were first shown into the presence of the governor of Jijiga, Fitaurari Shafarah, an officer of the old school, who sat, surrounded by local notables, in a very small room, hung with carpets; the shutters were closed and the atmosphere stupefying. He was a grizzled, gloomy little man who had been present at the battle of Walwal and had gained some discredit there, through being dis-covered, at the height of the action, squatting in his tent selling cartridges to his own troops. (It was not so much the trade itself that was resented as the fact that he put up the price when the Abyssinians seemed to be in difficulties.) His own interpreter intro-duced us, and after the exchange of a few civilities we sat in un-broken silence for rather more than half an hour. Eventually we were led into the open and upstairs to Nasbu's quarters. The Dedjasmach wore European uniform and spoke French. Like every-one else in Abyssinia who spoke French – with the single exception of the Emperor – he was clean shaven. He was well up in European affairs. We drank coffee together and discussed the constitution of the Committee of Five, the Committee of Thirteen, the Council of the League, and such topics as, in those days, seemed important.

Patrick then asked him what truth there was in the story that a Frenchman had been arrested in Jijiga.

'A Frenchman arrested?' he inquired with innocent incredulity. 'I will ask about it.'

He clapped his hands and sent a servant for Kebreth. They talked together for a few seconds in Amharic, discussing, presum-ably, what it was wise to give away; then he said, 'Yes, it appears that something of the sort has occurred,' and proceeded to tell us the whole story, while Kebreth produced from various pockets about his person a collection of all the relevant documents.

Drogafoi was a Count Maurice de Roquefeuil du Bousquet, who had come to Ethiopia nine years before in search of a livelihood; for the last three years he had been working a mica concession a few miles out of Jijiga; three months ago he had married a French widow from Diredawa. For some time the police had been keeping a watch on his house. He was said to live in guilty splendour, but when Patrick and I visited his home later we found two simple and clearly impoverished little rooms. The main cause for suspicion was the fact that Somalis from the neighbouring tribes resorted there, with whom he could have had no legitimate business. On the day before our arrival, an elderly Somali woman had been arrested leaving his house and, when she was searched, a film tube was found in her armpit, which, she confessed, she was taking to the Italian Consulate at Harar. Kebreth showed us the contents: a snapshot of some motor lorries and five pages of inaccurate information (of the kind which Wazir Ali Beg used regularly to write to me) describing the defences of Jijiga.

The Count and Countess had been arrested and their house searched. Kebreth said it was full of correspondence with Italian officers across the frontier, and of the names of native agents who were now being rounded up. He showed us the Count's passport and finally the Count himself, who, with his wife, was now under guard in an outbuilding of the Gibbi. As a large proportion of the Count's agents were boys who had been educated at the mission school, unfounded suspicion had also fallen upon the Franciscan friars. We took photographs of the Gibbi and the Count's house, of the lion cubs and the place of his imprisonment, of the slave in charge of the lions and the captain of the guard. Kebreth gave us a postcard of the Count posed against a studio background of drapery and foliage which he had confiscated among other more incriminating papers. A dramatic moment came when we expressed a wish to photograph the detective responsible for the arrest.

'You wish to photograph the detective?' said Kebreth. 'He stands before you. It was I.'

So we photographed Kebreth too, beaming through his horn-rimmed spectacles, and returned to Mohamedally's with the feeling that we were on to a good thing. It seemed to have all the ingredients of a newspaper story – even an imprisoned 'bride'. Moreover, there was no possibility of any other journalist having got it. We happily imagined cables arriving for our colleagues in Addis. '*Badly left Roquefeuil story*' and '*Investigate imprisoned countess Jijiga*'. It was now Friday morning. If we were to reach the Saturday papers it must be cabled by seven o'clock. Patrick and I feverishly typed out our reports while Charles engaged a car to take them to the nearest wireless station at Hargeisa, in British Somaliland, and Kebreth obligingly made out a pass for his journey.

6

When our cables were safely on their way, Patrick and I walked out into the town and there had another stroke of good luck. It was midday and the people were trooping into the little mosque to their prayers. A car drove up and there emerged a stocky figure in a black cossack hat. It was Wehib Pasha, a Turkish veteran of the Gallipoli campaign, one of the major mystery men of the country. He had left Addis in the greatest secrecy. There had been rumours that he was bound for the Ogaden. Some said he was on a religious mission, to preach a Moslem crusade against the Italians; others that he was to be the new Moslem Ras, whose appointment was hinted at. Patrick had interviewed him in Addis and found him profoundly uncommunicative.

His disgust at seeing us was highly gratifying. He shot into the mosque and sent his secretary-companion – an elegant Greek youth with a poetic black beard and immense, sorrowful eyes – to inform us that we were not to follow him about, and that if we took any photographs he would have our cameras destroyed. We sent Mata Hari into the mosque after him and told him to make inquiries in the market about what the Pasha was doing. The reply, which we got some hours later, disentangled from Mata Hari's more obvious inventions, was that the Pasha had recruited a large labour gang and was leaving next day for the south in a train of lorries, to dig lion pits for the Italian tanks. This was the first news, I think, which anyone got of the construction of the famous defensive line which was believed to be holding up Graziani's Northern advance for the entire war. Actually these well-planned earthworks were never used, for instead of an orderly retreat, the Abyssinians fell back in hopeless rout and could not be persuaded to man them.

Feeling that our trip to Jijiga had been a triumphant success, Patrick and I made our arrangements with a half-caste lorry driver to return next day to Harar. There remained the delicate question of whether or no we should tip Kebreth. Gabri and Mata Hari, when consulted, said of course all officials must be tipped on all occasions; Gabri alone showed some anxiety that we would give too much. Accordingly when Kebreth came in that evening for a drink with us, Patrick produced a note and with great tact suggested that we should be glad if he would distribute a small sum to the poor of the town in acknowledgement of our enjoyable visit.

Kebreth had no respect for these euphemisms; he thanked us, but said with great composure that times had changed and Ethiopian officials now received their wages regularly.

Five hours' delay next morning in getting on the road. Our half-caste driver made one excuse and then another – he had to take some mail for the government, he was awaiting another passenger, the municipal officer had not yet signed his pass. At last Mata Hari explained the difficulty; there was shooting on the road; a handful of soldiers in the manner of the country had taken to the bush and were at war with the garrison. 'This driver is a very fearful man,' said Mata Hari.

Presently, when the half-caste had at last been taunted into activity by our staff, the danger passed. Less than a mile outside the town we met soldiers coming back, dragging some very battered prisoners. 'Perhaps they will be whipped to death. Perhaps they will only be hanged,' said Mata Hari.

We lunched on the road at de Roquefeuil's mica works – a dingy little jumble of sheds and a derelict car. To our embarrassment the owner himself suddenly appeared under the guard of two lorry loads of soldiers. He had come to remove his personal belongings before being sent north. He sent out a message to us, to remind us that we were on private property. We drove on and arrived at Harar in the late evening.

*

We were still in a mood of self-approval. We wondered whether any of our messages had yet arrived in London and whether Patrick had got in first with the Saturday evening edition, or I on Monday morning. We expected cables of congratulation. There was a cable for me. It said, '*What do you know Anglo American oil concession?*' Evidently our messages had been delayed; but as there was no possible competitor, we were not alarmed. I replied, '*Apply local agent for commercial intelligence Addis,*' and, still in good humour, went up to dine at the Consulate.

Next morning there was another cable, a day old: '*Must have fullest details oil concession.*' I replied: '*Absolutely impossible obtain Addis news Harar.*' Before luncheon there was a third: '*Badly left oil concession suggest your return Addis immediately.*'

It was now clear that something important had happened in our absence, which eclipsed our stories of Roquefeuil and Wehib Pasha. A two-day train left Diredawa for Addis on Tuesday morning. In low spirits Patrick and I arranged for our departure.

Harar had suddenly lost its charm. News of the events at Jijiga had filtered through in wildly exaggerated forms; the town was inflamed with spy-mania. Mata Hari was promptly gaoled on the evening of his return. We bought him out, but he seemed to expect hourly re-arrest and became completely incoherent with secrecy. The chief of police may have had some reprimand for allowing us to go to Jijiga or perhaps it was only that his cold was worse; whatever the reason, his manner had entirely changed towards us and he was now haughty and suspicious. Mr Carassellos was in a condition of infectious agitation. Half his friends had just been arrested and cross-examined under suspicion of complicity with de Roquefeuil. He was expecting the soldiers to come for him any minute.

Roquefeuil and the native prisoners arrived on Sunday night. Throughout the day on Monday, Mata Hari popped in on us with fragments of unlikely news about his trial; that he was in the common prison, that the Emperor was coming in person to supervise his execution; that he had boasted, 'In seven days' time this town will be in the hands of Italy and I shall be avenged.' But the story had lost its interest for us.

7

No one in Harar knew anything about an oil concession. The first information we received was at Diredawa, where a young official explained that the Emperor had leased most of the country to America. At Awash we learned that Mr Rickett was associated with the business. At Addis, on Wednesday night, we found that the story was already stale. Patrick and I, the Reuters and *The Times* correspondents had all been away. The *Morning Post* correspondent had not yet arrived; thus the Radical and the *Daily Telegraph* correspondent were the only English-born journalists in Addis. They and the American agency, Associated Press, had had the scoop to themselves. It was a sensational story which, for a few days, threatened to influence international politics.

Mr Rickett, as the agent of a group of American financiers, had secured from the Emperor a concession for mineral rights of unprecedented dimensions. The territory affected was that bordering on the Italian possessions over which the Italian troops would presumably seek to advance, and which, presumably, they hoped to annex. The concessionaires admitted absolute Abyssinian sovereignty over the area and held it on a direct lease from the Emperor. Much, perhaps most, of the rights involved had already been ceded from time to time to other interests, but it was in keeping with Abyssinian tradition to disregard this. The significant feature, at the time, was the fact that Mr Rickett was an Englishman, and that in the early reports his principals were described as an Anglo-American company. Apprehensions were immediately aroused in Italy, and to a less degree in France, that England, who was at the moment adopting an increasingly censorious attitude towards Italian ambitions, was herself bent on economic annexations in Ethiopia, and was merely using the League of Nations to gain commercial preference. In fact there was absolutely no truth in this, although it was, in the circumstances, a very natural suspicion. Mr Rickett had not called at the Legation and the British Minister in Addis was completely unaware of his existence. During his stay he had, to my knowledge, met only one British official, and him the most junior, at dinner with Patrick and myself, when their conversation had been exclusively frivolous. No English capital, I believe, was involved in the venture. The purity of English motives was completely unaffected by the Rickett concession. There is, however, some room for reflection on the Emperor's behaviour.

It is popular now to regard him as completely ingenuous and completely dignified; a noble savage betrayed by his belief in the reality of the white man's honour. The Rickett concession shows him in a somewhat different form. It was made in direct contradiction to the previous policy of his reign, at the moment when he was declaring in highly felicitous and highly impressive terms an absolute and exclusive reliance on the Covenant of the League. He had already appealed to America as a signatory of the Kellogg Pact and learned that he could expect no support there. He was now attempting to buy that support. It was a shrewd attempt, but it came too late. Had the concession been made in 1934, it is difficult to see how the United States government could have permitted Italian occupation. As it was, in September 1935, with war already inevitable, the State Department at Washington intervened against him and forbade the ratification of the concession. By doing so they virtually recognised Italy's right to conquer, for, while he was still a sovereign ruler, they refused to recognise the Emperor's right to grant concessions within his own dominions. The Emperor had reverted to the traditional policy of balancing the self-aggrandisement of the white peoples one against another, and it failed. After that he was left with no cards to play except international justice, collective security and the overweening confidence of his fighting forces. He played the first two astutely enough; the third turned out to be valueless. No possible reproach can attach to him for his negotiation with Mr Rickett. It might have proved masterly. But it does to some extent dispel the sentimental haze which, to liberal eyes, threatens to obscure his highly complex character.

CHAPTER 4
WAITING FOR THE WAR

ON OUR RETURN to Addis Ababa we found the temporary white population still further increased. Of my original companions Mr Rickett and the American doctor had both left; the one happy in the brief delusion that his mission had been a success, the other fully conscious of failure and indignant at the neglect and suspicion of the Abyssinian officials whom he had hoped to help. Their rooms at the Deutsches Haus were immediately snapped up. All the hotels were already overcrowded, the Splendide was a slum, the tide of journalists was still in flood. A week later (New Year's Day, 1928, in the Abyssinian calendar, which had fallen behind the rest of Christendom during the centuries of isolation) another boat train arrived, packed with pressmen, including two internationally celebrated correspondents of the Hearst organisation. Two more trains before the outbreak of war brought up the number of accredited journalists and photographers to rather more than a hundred. They showed almost every diversity which the human species produces. There was a simian Soudanese, who travelled under a Brazilian passport and worked for an Egyptian paper; there was a monocled Latvian colonel, who was said at an earlier stage of his life to have worked as ringmaster in a German circus; there was a German who travelled under the name of Haroun al Raschid, a title, he said, which had been conferred on him during the Dardanelles campaign by the late Sultan of Turkey; his head was completely hairless; his wife shaved it for him, emphasising the frequent slips of her razor with tufts of cotton-wool. There was a venerable American, clothed always in dingy black, who seemed to have strayed from the pulpit of a religious conventicle; he wrote imaginative despatches of great length and flamboyancy. There was an Austrian, in Alpine costume,

625

with crimped flaxen hair, the group leader, one would have thought, of some Central European Youth Movement; a pair of rubicund young colonials, who came out on chance and were doing brisk business with numberless competing organisations; two indistinguishable Japanese, who beamed at the world through horn-rimmed spectacles and played interminable, highly dexterous games of ping-pong in Mme Idot's bar. These formed an exotic background that was very welcome, for the majority of the regular pressmen were an anxious, restless, mutually suspicious crowd, all weighed down with the consciousness that they were not getting the news. They were expected to cable daily (all, that is to say, except the Spaniard, who, born in a happier and more leisured tradition, was content to post occasional thick packages of closely written manuscript), and the wireless station could only cope with the accumulations of copy by periodic closures.

The Americans were, on the whole, in easier circumstances, for their Press has created so voracious an appetite in its readers for impertinent personal details, that they can even swallow such information about the people who are employed to discover it. They were thus able to glut the service with expansive pages of autobiography about their state of health and habits of life, reactions and recreations, while the more practical Europeans were kept in pursuit of 'spot news'.

It was a disheartening quest. The situation throughout the whole of September was perfectly clear. Everyone was waiting for Italy at her own convenience to begin the war. There were committee meetings and conversations in Europe. News of them was published belatedly in our cyclostyle bulletin at the wireless office. No one, least of all the Abyssinians, believed they would deflect the Italians from their intentions. Until an 'act of aggression' had actually taken place nothing could be done; it would then appear what sort of support, if any, Great Britain and France were prepared to give. It was probable, as in fact occurred, that news of the beginning of hostilities would be published in Europe before we heard of it in Addis Ababa. Meanwhile we were required to provide daily items of interest to keep public attention engaged.

There were reports from all over the country of extensive troop movements. The order for general mobilisation had not been made, but the local chiefs were collecting forces and moving them as unostentatiously as possible towards various points of concentration. A strong party, headed by Ras Moulungeta, were known to be in favour of immediate general mobilisation. The Emperor's policy at the moment was to avoid any movement that the Italians could interpret as being aggressive or menacing; it was believed that the order had been signed, printed, and then suspended. The news of its promulgation was cabled back almost daily by one or other of the special correspondents: '*War drums beating in the North – the Emperor raises the Standard of Solomon.*' Almost daily enquiries came from Fleet Street, '*What truth general mobilisation?*' Like almost every important event in the war it was so often anticipated and so often denied that, when it actually happened, it had lost all its interest.

Occasionally troops came through Addis and entrained for Diredawa, but for the most part they remained out of sight. It was reported that in many places they had come without provisions and were plundering the farms on their route; in the Galla country, in particular, there had been serious disturbances and some loss of life. But there was no possibility of leaving the city to investigate. No answer was given to our applications for leave to travel. We were obliged to rely for information about what was happening in the interior upon the army of Greek and Levantine spies who frequented Mme Moriatis's bar. Most of these men were pluralists, being in the pay not only of several competing journalists at once but also of the Italian Legation, the Abyssinian secret police, or both. They were equally ignorant, but less scrupulous than ourselves. We could retail their lies, even when we found them most palpable, with the qualification, 'It is stated in some quarters' or 'I was unofficially informed'. There is a slight difference, I discovered, in the professional code of European and American journalists. While the latter will not hesitate, in moments of emergency, to resort to pure invention, the former must obtain their lies at second hand. This is not so much due to lack of imagination, I think, as lack of courage. As long as someone, no matter how irresponsible or discredited, has made a statement, it is legitimate news, but there must always be some source, 'which has hitherto proved satisfactory', on which the blame can later be laid.

The rains showed no signs of lifting, but they provided another topic for our cables; grey clouds hung low over the city, shutting out the surrounding hills; at irregular, incalculable intervals they broke in a deluge which rang so loud on the iron roofs as to stop conversation during the day, and at night to give the illusion that one was travelling by train through a tunnel; there was little drainage in the town, and during the storms many of the side streets became cataracts; there was often thunder and sometimes hail; but now and then, once a week perhaps, there would be a few minutes' fitful sunshine and a patch of blue sky. That provided a story. Some correspondents described crowds of natives gathering, gazing up, apprehensive that a fleet of aeroplanes might emerge and begin the bombardment. (It is interesting to remember, in view of the outcry of pained surprise which later greeted the practically bloodless bombardment of Harar, that at this time almost everyone in Addis, Abyssinian and foreign alike, expected that the capital would immediately become a target not only for bombs but gas. Most of the population dug shelters in their gardens; others were made by the municipality; instructions were issued to the population that they were to take cover in the hills; many of the more timid correspondents shifted their quarters on the outbreak of war and slept with gas masks beside their beds.)

The railway station was a centre of minor information. An increased service was running at the time and trains left for the coast two or three times in the week. All had refugees on board – one day the women of the Swedish community, another the German – as the consulates arranged for the evacuation. Half the white population and practically all the Press were on the platform for each departure. There was seldom any very sensational occurrence; sometimes an Indian would be arrested smuggling dollars; there were always tears; once or twice an Abyssinian dignitary left on an official mission, attended by a great entourage, bowing, embracing his knees, and kissing him firmly on his bearded cheeks. At any time there was a fair amount of rough and tumble at the Addis terminus between Arab porters and station police. This served to give colour to the descriptions of panic and extravagant lamentation which were dutifully cabled to Fleet Street.

The arrivals in the evening were more interesting, for anyone visiting Addis at this season was a potential public character, perhaps another Rickett. Two humane English colonels excited feverish speculation for a few days until it was discovered that they were merely emissaries of a World League for the Abolition of Fascism. There was a negro from South Africa who claimed to be a Tigrean, and represented another World League for the abolition, I think, of the white races, and a Greek who claimed to be a Bourbon prince and represented some unspecified and unrealised ambitions of his own. There was an American who claimed to be a French Viscount and represented a league, founded in Monte Carlo, for the provision of an Ethiopian *Disperata* squadron, for the bombardment of Assab. There was a completely unambiguous British adventurer, who claimed to have been one of Al Capone's bodyguard and wanted a job; and ex-officer of the R.A.F. who started to live in some style with a pair of horses, a bull terrier and a cavalry moustache – he wanted a job too. All these unusual characters were good for a paragraph.

The more respectable soldiers of fortune were, as was traditionally right, of Swiss nationality. Several of them secured posts of responsibility. There was also a gang of Belgian ex-officers, who were a great embarrassment to the charming Belgian minister, the *doyen* of the Addis diplomats. For five years there had been an official military mission from Belgium, seconded from their regiments to train the Imperial Guard. These were under orders to leave the country in case of war. The new-comers were there in defiance of their superiors. Some were Congo veterans, some young subalterns in search of adventure. They were engaged for vague general services and given quarters in the Empress's bath-house, from which they emerged now and then in parties of half a dozen, to sit, a gloomy, uniform row in white bum-shavers, along Mme Moriatis's bar. Their presence was not recognised by their fellow officers of the official mission; few of them were even given any serious occuption. In a few weeks their enthusiasm for the Abyssinian cause was noticeably cooler.

The government offices, particularly the Gibbi and the Foreign Office, were places which the Radical described as 'News Centres'. It was frequently necessary to visit them to test the opinion of 'official circles' on the various proposals for a peaceful settlement which periodically cropped up as rumour in Europe and were urgently transmitted to us by wireless. These were disheartening expeditions. The official one sought was seldom available; one waited about in corridors and ante-rooms thronged with squatting, sodden, undisguisedly hostile soldiers, eventually to be received by some irresponsible, infinitely evasive deputy. The inaccessibility of the officials was due partly to their natural bent towards prevarication, but more to the lack of competent personnel, which was fatal to the Addis bureaucratic system. Half the officials were men of hereditary eminence and imperturbable, aristocratic lassitude; they spent the greater part of their day in eating and sleeping and when disturbed gave either of the traditional excuses that they were at prayer or had taken their *kosso*. The two or three comparatively businesslike men – the handful of genuine exponents of the ideals of the *Jeunesse d'Ethiopie* – were given such a multiplicity of posts that they had time for none of them. In this way urgent business was indefinitely held up, while parasites like ourselves were left in complete confusion.

There was also a mysterious and, I am now inclined to believe, non-existent force of Yemen Arabs which made a fitful appearance in our despatches. By some accounts they were still in the Yemen and were waiting orders for the attack from the Imam of Sana. They were to cross the Red Sea in a fleet of dhows, fall upon Assab and massacre the garrison, then join with the Aussa Sultan in a drive up the Italian coastline as far as Massawa. Another version had it that they were already in Addis, organised as a fighting corps. They were constantly reported as parading at the palace and offering their arms and fortune in the Emperor's service. There was in fact a number of venerable old traders from the Yemen, dotted about the bazaar quarter. If two of them sat down together for a cup of coffee it was described as a military consultation.

By every post, until I told him to stop, Wazir Ali Beg sent me a budget of news. Like our own reports, some of it was fantastic rumour, some trivial gossip, with, here and there embedded, a few facts of genuine personal observation.

'*An Arab sweet seller of Diredawa,*' he wrote, '*left here for Djibouti about a month ago. Some Italian engaged him and gave him some packets of mortal poison and a big sum of money. This man was instructed to put each packet of poison in Water Reservoir of Diredawa. A Somali woman gave information about this to the Abyssinians. Many poison packets and a sum of 5,200 francs were found on this Arab. He has been taken in chains to Addis Ababa. He is very short of stature and his hair have turned gray. The Emperor has rewarded this Somali woman and ordered that she be paid a sum of $1,000.*'

When news was scanty he would sometimes fill up his page with such items as '*News has been given me just now that the Somalis number 15 thousand men and there is no account of the number of Abyssinians going from all sides,*' or with darker hints: '*I have news in my possession of the utmost importance. I have not forgotten your instructions, these news will be very dangerous to put on paper. I may only tell you these in person or send a special messenger.*'

On the last occasion he wrote to me – three weeks before the outbreak of hostilities – he reported a battle: '*The Manager of Messrs Mohamedaly and Co. and another trader informed me that there was news of a big clash between Somalis, Dankalis and white Italian soldiers near Assab. 500 white wounded soldiers were brought to Djibouti and 200 Italians are reported dead. If I had money I would at once have gone to Djibouti myself. But I trust these gentlemen as they are men of position.*' I had less trust than Wazir Ali Beg in these gentlemen of position, and as this letter was shortly followed by the suggestion of an enormous increase in his retaining fee and the assertion, which I knew to be false, that he had declined several offers of profitable employment from other journalists, I decided to drop him. He had no difficulty in finding other correspondents and, as the situation became darker and reporting more speculative, Wazir Ali Beg's news service formed an ever-increasing part of the morning reading of the French, English and American newspaper publics.

Whenever Mata Hari was out of prison, he too wrote. Patrick has already published the correspondence elsewhere, but, with his permission, I cannot forbear to quote a few extracts.

'THE ETHUPIAN NEWS OF THE 11TH SEPTEMBER

Troubles at 3 p.m.

Soldiers. *Fieghts near Bazara doors some of the Soldiers entered Bazara house as some brack heads bloods come out* . . .

Dagash Mazh *said the Ethupian troops will assault the Italian troops before the time of the rain* . . .

Dagash Mazh *regarding to the lecture of the 8th advise the soldiers, regret to say, at 3 p.m. the soldiers to their misfortune and endignity on the peoples, robing the vegetables, etc.*

Truck *passed on to leg of one Somalee.*

News *from the Arabic news papers, the warfare will be between six Governments shortly.*

Somali Merchant Mahmood Warofaih *made trench in his garden and put his money, few day repeat to see his money and not found, at once come mad.*'

This last trouble was by no means peculiar to Mahmood Warofaih. During the crisits it seemed to be happening all over the country. The gardener at the Deutsches Haus suffered in exactly that way and showed every sign of losing his reason until, to the disappointment of the other servants, who were enjoying the spectacle immoderately, Haroun al Raschid charitably reimbursed him.

The Foreign Press Association held occasional meetings, which until its final dissolution became increasingly disorderly as the weeks of proximity and competition produced an elaborate web of personal and racial antipathies. The meetings took place at the Splendide Hotel, in the evening when the wireless was shut, or was supposed to be shut, for the day. Discussion was bilingual and required constant interpretation. The intention was to establish a method of negotiation with the Ethiopian government. The result was to destroy whatever slight unity among themselves, or prestige among the officials, the journalists ever possessed. The meetings, however, were highly enjoyable, having a character of combined mock-trial and drinking bout. The Americans and French did most of the talking; the English endeavoured to collect the subscriptions and maintain some semblance of constitutional order. The Spaniard was elected a member of committee, with acclamation. The Radical made a conscientious and rather puzzled treasurer. The Americans were facetious or ponderously solemn, according as their drink affected them. There was one of them who was constantly on his feet crying: 'Mr Chairman, I protest that the whole question is being treated with undesirable levity.' Every now and then the French walked out in a body and formed an independent organisation.

Our chief function was to protest. We 'protested unanimously and in the most emphatic manner' or we 'respectfully represented to the Imperial Government' that the cabling rates were too high, that the Press Bureau was inconveniently situated and inadequately staffed, that a negro aviator had insulted a French reporter, that preferential treatment was given to certain individuals in the despatch of late messages, that the official bulletins were too meagre and too irregular; we petitioned to be allowed to go to the fronts, to be told definitely whether we should ever be allowed to go there. No one paid the smallest attention to us. After a time the protesting habit became automatic. The Association split up into small groups and pairs protesting to one another, cabling their protests to London and Geneva, scampering round to the palace and protesting to the private secretaries of the Emperor at every turn of events. But that was later; in these early days the Foreign Press Association showed some of the light-heartedness of a school debating society.

One of the events which attracted most attention was the arrival, early in September, of the reinforcements to the Sikh guard at the British Legation. As the constituents of this force had been exactly and publicly specified some time before in London, it was odd to see the ingenuity with which journalists sought to conceal themselves about the station and transcribe the names of the officers' uniform cases. One even hired a balcony overlooking the line and sat there all day in the hope of seeing their train come in.

It had been decided, with a minimum of common sense, that the arrival should be kept secret; the train, which was known to have left Diredawa, was left in a siding, some way down the line, until nightfall, when all the approaches to the station and Legation were elaborately cleared. If a simple statement, such as was made in London, had been issued, describing the numbers and equipment of the company, there would have been little excitement aroused. As it was, in a population like that of Addis, credulous, suspicious and given to the most extravagant exaggerations, wild rumours were circulated and believed. The Emperor had given repeated assurances, pledging his personal honour for the safety of all Europeans in his country. When eventually he fled precipitately, throwing open his arsenal to the mob, everyone was profoundly thankful for the presence of the Sikhs (even those who were most eloquently contemptuous of the Italian reliance on native troops), but at the time, when everything was surprisingly well controlled and there was still a disposition among new-comers to believe what the Abyssinians told them, the arrival of a guard of unknown dimensions and the creation, it was believed, of an armed stronghold at the British Legation, seemed to be a slight on the Imperial hospitality which earned the nickname of 'Barton's Folly'. How wrong we were!

The Italian Legation, meanwhile, was in a unique situation, representing a government that, although not at war, had expressed its intention of going to war within a few weeks. The Minister, Count Vinci, had little of the manner of a professional diplomat. He was stocky, cheerful, courageous, friendly and slightly mischievous; he seemed thoroughly to enjoy his precarious position. He rode out daily into the town, alone or in the company of a single groom. His enemies said that he was seeking to provoke an 'incident'. He entertained liberally, and at his table there was an atmosphere of ease and humour lacking elsewhere in Addis. He was surrounded by spies, both his own and those of the government. For months now the secret police had instituted a surveillance, which came very near to persecution, of his native servants. In Addis and at the provincial consulates they were frequently arrested on one charge or another, questioned and often held in chains. Vinci cheerfully entered his claims for explanation at the Foreign Office, in the certainty that they would receive no attention. Every day he or the first secretary went to the little Fascist club they had formed in the bazaar quarter and sat alone, receiving anyone who cared to interview him. He and his suite still appeared conspicuously at the public functions. As far as he was concerned, negotiations with the Emperor were at an end. Any settlement there might be, would be made in Europe. His immediate business was to maintain the dignity of the future conquerors and to get his nationals out of the country before the trouble started. His only anxiety was the safety of the provincial consuls. There were five regular consulates – at Adowa, Gondar, Harar, Dessye and Debra Markos – and a commercial agency at Magalo. At most of these there were two or three Europeans – a dispenser, wireless operator, besides the normal officials – and a small native guard, sometimes of local troops, sometimes of Italian Eritrean subjects. At this season their journey to the frontier might take several weeks. On September 7 Vinci applied to the Ethiopian Foreign Office for their permission to withdraw. The permission was neither refused nor given; to travel without it, even in normal times, would have been highly dangerous. Belatingetta Herui, the Foreign Minister, prevaricated, maintaining that the consuls must come to Addis, not travel directly, and more conveniently, to the frontier. He did not wish them to have the opportunity of seeing the Ethiopian concentrations of troops and frontier defences. On September 18 Vinci declared that if he did not receive the permission at once, he would instruct his consuls to start their journey without it, and that the Abyssinians must take responsibility for any 'incident' that might occur. It was not until September 22 that facilities were at length given. It was for this reason that two of the consuls were still on the road at the time of the bombardment of Adowa.

The news of the British naval concentration in the Mediterranean, which convulsed Europe, made little impression in Addis. The single outside event which caused much discussion was the decision of the Committee of Five. Their recommendations reached the Emperor on September 19. He was entertaining the Press to dinner that evening and we expected that some statement might be made on the subject. It was clear, as soon as the terms became known, that they offered no satisfactory solution but that they strengthened the position which the Emperor had adopted of scrupulous legality and devotion to League principles. They recognised and satisfied Italy's complaint that Ethiopia was a bad neighbour; they provided for extensive reforms under European advice, a regular budget, economic development, a national police system. They represented, in fact, the avowed programme of the *Jeunesse d'Ethiopie*. There were two grave objections to them. They offered Italy nothing. The

Emperor was to be free to choose his own European advisers, and it was perfectly evident that, after the antagonism inflamed by the events of the preceding months, none of these would be Italian. The rectifications of frontier suggested were valueless, particularly if they were made as compensation for a corridor to the coast, which would deflect trade from the routes which the Italians were seeking to establish through their own territory. After the demonstrative preparations which had been made, the acceptance of these recommendations by Italy would have been a humiliating withdrawal in the face of threatened coercion. The second objection was that the solution they offered to Ethiopia's internal disorder would not have worked in practice. The predominant class – and, I believe, a fair number of the *Jeunesse d'Ethiopie* themselves – would have believed that they had achieved a diplomatic triumph; danger was averted; the new Geneva ju-ju had worked; the white man was tricked again. They would have settled back complacently into their traditional manner of life. The new commissioners would have found themselves frustrated at every turn. The only white men with whom the Ethiopians worked harmoniously were Levantine adventurers. The single Englishman – a man of high principles, experience and notable tact – who had held an advisory post among them found his position untenable and had resigned. If the new advisers were conscientious men they would sooner or later have been obliged to invite armed intervention, in which case a mandate would have to be given to one or other of the Powers, or, at the worst, to a condominium of more than one (an experiment by the League which is proving disastrous in the Pacific). An unconquered Abyssinia would never accept effective reform.

Nothing was said about the proposals at the Emperor's banquet, but it was an interesting evening. It was the first time that I had been inside the new Gibbi, which the Emperor had recently built on the outskirts of the city. The old Gibbi of Menelik, still used for many court functions and for the officers of the personal staff, was the centre of the Imperial rule. This was a private residence, designed especially for the entertainment of Europeans. The old Gibbi had character. It was ramshackle and without plan; a central, semi-European, stone hall, surrounded by a great village of sheds and huts, timber and tin and thatch, with a chapel, a mausoleum, a slaughter-house, barracks and prisons, courts of justice, huge, irregular parade grounds, cages of lions, stables jumbled together on the stockaded hillside. The new Gibbi was like the villa of a retired Midland magnate. It had been furnished and arranged throughout by a firm of London decorators. They had laid the linoleum and displayed the silver-framed photographs. Nothing had been done to add the smallest personal touch.

The footmen wore European liveries. Until a few days before there had been a Swiss chef, but the Abyssinians, even those most eloquent in their desire to suppress slavery, could never accustom themselves to the practice of paying their servants. Having received no wages for many months, the chef gave notice and set up for himself in a little pension-restaurant in the town. The Emperor summoned him back for the Press banquet; he refused to come, so they arrested his entire domestic staff. Still he would not come, so the dinner was provided, I believe, by the ruthless Mr Kakophilos.

The electric light failed seven times in the course of the evening. This mischance was attributed to M. Idot, who had been observed mingling furtively among the guests. It was said that the Emperor had intended to give a cinema show after dinner and M. Idot wanted to deflect his guests to the *Perroquet*. In this he was certainly successful. It was a rowdy night both there and at Mme Moriatis's.

The Emperor made other attempts to relieve the tedium of our vigil. The displays of modernity which had formed one of the lighter elements of the coronation were once more revived. We woke up one morning to find the town placarded with trilingual proclamations against cruelty to animals. '*Considering*,' the English version read, '*that cruelty and ill-treatment against tamed and utile animals are incompatible with human dignity, the Municipality informs the public that it is formally forbidden to ill-treat animals.*'

A few days later a model prison was opened. This project had captivated the Imperial imagination some years before; plans had been got out by a Swiss contractor and foundations laid; then, as on most Ethiopian undertakings, work had ceased. Now, with a hundred inquisitive foreigners in the town, it was resumed with feverish activity.

There were several existing less ambitious prisons in Addis from which European visitors are rigorously excluded. Minor malefactors, hopping cheerfully about in chains and collecting the money for their release by begging, were a common sight in the country, but an attempt had been made in Addis to keep them out of sight of the photographers, who had a way of sending home their pictures labelled 'Slaves on the way to market'.

On my previous visit I had got inside the prison at Harar. Later, an Italian agent with a camera had done the same, and the results provided several pages in the Geneva dossier and the various pamphlets issued by the Ministry of Propaganda in Rome. The result was not an improvement in the prison but, in future, its absolute inaccessibility to white investigators. It was an appalling spectacle. I am told that the crates in which they confine Manchurian criminals are more disagreeable still, but the Harar gaol remains in my memory as the lowest pit of human misery to which I have ever penetrated. The prisoners were mostly there in discharge of small debts; three or four deaths occurred weekly, I was informed, from typhus. The cells were little hutches built round an open yard, as foul as human habitation could make it. Three or four men were tethered to the wall of each cell, by chains just long enough to allow of their crawling into the open. (It was also common – though I did not see an example myself – for prisoners to be manacled wrist-to-ankle, and left doubled up for months at a time.) They were provided with no food except what their relatives chose to provide. They had no occupation of any kind, but squatted day after day, sick or well, quite hopeless.

The Emperor's new prison offered a standard of comfort not only immeasurably superior to the homes of his law-abiding subjects, but also to most of the Addis hotels. There were shower-baths and a laundry, a recreation-room provided with educational works, a dining-room with benches and tables set with enamel ware. Each bunk was provided with a pyjama suit, which was, I believe, sent back to the stores from which it had been borrowed immediately after the official opening.

This took place in the last week in September, on the first fine day we had seen. The sun shone brilliantly on the new concrete; the clouds had lifted and a vast panorama of rolling downland, of blue hilltops, each crowned with a farm or conical church, and of deep green valleys, was suddenly revealed. The new prison lay at a little distance from the city; we drove to it through fields of new yellow flowers. The Legations, the Press, the photographers, the whole white population, the general staff and the Court were all present. As Vinci walked round behind the Emperor, someone remarked that he was choosing his cell.

The Governorship of the prison was conferred upon one of the progressive, already fully employed, young clerks of the *Jeunesse d'Ethiopie*. We asked him about its future use. Perhaps wishing to enhance its importance, he said it was for the punishment of murderers and high-born rebels. When the last visitor had driven away the gates were locked, a handful of soldiers left on guard, and for the remainder of Haile Selassie's brief reign the place was deserted and forgotten; reports and photographs of the Emperor's enlightened innovation flooded the European and American press; it had done its work. Malefactors were still expeditiously hustled off to the old, secret prisons.

The more impressive celebrations were those which formed a part of the traditional calendar and had not been specially planned for the edification of the journalists. There was the New Year's day, already mentioned, a domestic feast, for which each household made a little bonfire in the mud outside its doors and danced at nightfall in the rain, clapping, stamping and chanting a monotonous African song. For two days before the whole town became a meat market. They were slaughtering at every corner and the children ran about the streets carrying handfuls of fresh entrails. The rich ate beef and entertained their followers; the poor had mutton. Everyone seemed to be carrying a lamb across his shoulders, or pushing a sheep, wheelbarrow fashion on its fore legs. A series of banquets was given daily at the Palace – the traditional entertainment of the troops and their chiefs, raw beef, red peppers and *tedj* – but no Europeans were allowed to enter, in the ingenuous apprehension that the exhibition of table manners might shock them and undermine the impression

created by the new prison and the humane ordinance of the municipality against ill-treating animals.

September 28 was the feast of Maskal, preceded a week earlier
by the Emperor's Maskal, and on the day before by a great military
review. The origins of this feast are lost in somewhat speculative
folklore. It is the Spring festival which marks, or is designed to
mark, the end of the rains. Its essential feature is the setting up
on the eve, and the burning at dawn next day, of the Maskal
staff, identical, presumably, with the European maypole. Since the
conversion of the country, the day has been Christianised, and
the pole is taken to represent the wood of the cross. It is, of course,
a purely Abyssinian festival, in which the Moderns and Pagans
have no share. It was observed all over the Empire, wherever
there was an Abyssinian garrison, and with particular pomp in
Addis Ababa.

The ceremony a week before was a personal religious function of
the Emperor's, attended by the Court, the Legations and, at this
final celebration, by the Press. It was remarkable as the first time that
Vinci and the Emperor had met since Vinci's refusal, after an anti-
Italian speech of the Emperor's, to attend his birthday reception in
July. In some quarters his presence that morning was taken as an
augury of peaceful settlement.

The occasion gave the special correspondents the chance, for
which their editors had long been waiting, to compose some 'good
colourful stuff' of the kind which had been used so extravagantly
during the coronation. What was more surprising was that many of
them seemed genuinely impressed by what they saw.

The ceremony took place in the old Gibbi in a great shed, not
unlike an aeroplane hangar, where the raw beef banquets were
normally held. The room was lit by windows from which were peeling
patches of gelatine, in coloured patterns counterfeiting stained glass.
Petrol cans, painted pale green, held ragged little palms. At the far
end was a great, gilt, canopied divan-throne, in the style which once
graced the old Alhambra Music Hall. Here the Emperor sat, with
two great bundles of drapery, the Abuna and the Abyssinian prelate,
on either side of him. The three were dignified and impressive;
two pet dogs sniffed and scratched at their feet. Nosegays of wild

flowers were distributed to the waiting assembly. Glittering bunches of priests and deacons began to assemble. The camera was kind to them, for their robes at close quarters were of the shoddiest material – gaudy Japanese vegetable silks, embroidered with sequins and tinsel; there were gilt crowns and bright umbrellas. Presently they formed themselves into a double row and began to dance a kind of clumsy and rather lugubrious Sir Roger de Coverley, swaying from side to side and slowly waving their silver-headed prayer sticks. There was a jingle of silver sistrums and a rhythmic hand drumming, a prolonged, nasal chanting. After a time the Abuna rose from his throne and began an address in Arabic, which his interpreter declaimed in stentorian Amharic. It was a homily upon the significance of the Holy Cross. At length, after about an hour, the Emperor and his suite retired and the ecclesiastics came into the open and posed obligingly to the camera men.

It was customary for apologists to liken the coronation of Ethiopia to that of mediæval Europe; there were close parallels, of a kind, to be drawn between Ethiopia, with its unstable but half-sacred monarchy, the feudal fiefs and the frequent insurrections, the lepers and serfs, the chained and tortured captives, the isolation and ignorance, the slow *tempo*, and our own high and chivalrous origins; parallels so close that many humane people accepted them as identical. On this particular morning of the Emperor's Maskal the comparison seemed to be fruitful. We had seen the highest expression of historic Abyssinian culture; this was the Church's most splendid and solemn occasion, in the heart of the Imperial Court. It was natural to consider, as one drove back to one's typewriter, what a ceremony of the kind was like in mediæval Europe; of the avenues of fluted columns, branching high overhead into groined and painted roof, each boss and capital a triumph of delicate sculpture, the sweet, precise music, the embroidered vestments, the stained and leaded windows to which later artists look, hopeless of emulation, the learning and austerity of the monastic orders, the royal dignity of the great Churchmen, of a culture which had created an object of delicate and individual beauty for every simple use; metal, stone, ivory and wood worked in a tradition of craftsmanship which makes succeeding generations compete for their humblest product. It was significant to turn from that to the artificial silk and painted petrol cans of Addis Ababa.

A week later, on the eve of Maskal proper, was held the last annual review of the Imperial Guard. This, like the guard itself, was the innovation of Haile Selassie's, which happily reconciled the traditional ceremony of setting up the Maskal pole with the new order.

It took place in the circular space where the Menelik memorial stood, in front of Giorgis. A grandstand had been erected in the inevitable decorative scheme of corrugated iron and artificial silk. The Maskal was planted early in the day by the municipal authorities, without any particular ceremony. It was a tall post, crowned at the summit with a bunch of wild flowers. In a burst of belated energy gangs of workmen were employed, almost until the moment of the Emperor's arrival, patching the worst fissures in the rough pavement. The bazaar was closed for the festival. Dense crowds of peasants had been thronging the streets since dawn. The irregular troops of the immediate neighbourhood had assembled under their chiefs to take part in the display. Many of them carried wands, in the traditional fashion, to cast at the foot of the Maskal.

The ceremony was planned to start soon after midday. There was no knowing how long it would last. The morning was clear and sunny and the majority of the journalists preferred to get their day's work done before proceeding to the show. They typed out expansive descriptions, deposited them at the wireless bureau and took their places in a shelter provided for them at the side of the Imperial stand. Mr Prospero and the other cinema men had set up their apparatus under the statue of Menelik. The diplomatic corps began to arrive; Vinci and all his suite once again in attendance.

A tremor of anxiety passed through the journalists' stand when, shortly before the Emperor's arrival, the sky became suddenly overcast and an intensely cold wind stirred the gaudy draperies. At one o'clock it began to rain, then to thunder, then to hail. It was the heaviest and longest storm of the season. The whole square was soon submerged. Twenty yards away poor Mr Prospero was barely visible through the torrent of falling water, pathetically holding a little deer-stalker hat over the lens of his camera.

At half past one the Emperor arrived in field uniform accompanied by an escort of sodden lancers. He took his place on the throne and sat immobile, staring into the rain. It was already evident that the roof over our heads was designed more for ornament than protection; water poured in from numerous multiplying and widening holes. A few journalists had brought their typewriters with them. They attempted to write their copy, but the paper turned to pulp under the keys. Still nothing happened. It was necessary for the Abuna to inaugurate the ceremony by walking three times round the Maskal; nothing would induce him – an elderly, infirm man, born in a happier climate – to leave the dry spot his deacons had found for him in the shelter. (Next day it was officially announced in his name – since he himself was unable to leave his bed – that rain on Maskal day, though unusual, was the happiest possible augury for Abyssinian prosperity.)

The tedium of waiting was relieved by a vigorous but losing battle waged by the police against a soaking and very uncompanionable rabble of poor whites, half-castes and Indians, who began filtering over the railings into the Press stand. Every half-hour or so Mr David, at our earnest request, would push his way in with a posse of police and denounce the gate-crashers. They would be pushed outside into the hail, protesting vehemently in Greek, Armenian, Amharic and French, and, as soon as his back was turned, come clambering back. It was not much drier inside than out, but their racial pride was involved in the struggle.

At last, at quarter past three, the rain slackened perceptibly. The Abuna emerged, and, with a dejected air, walked round the Maskal, casting a wand at its base. The Emperor and his younger son, the Duke of Harar, followed. Then, as the downpour again increased in violence, the parade began.

The troops varied in character from the Imperial Guard, uniformed, shaven, tolerably smart, to the irregular feudal levies. Both these were impressive. Between them in degree of training were the new volunteers whom we had seen drilling in the street. These struck an unhappy compromise; some of them had uniforms, but none had yet acquired the carriage of regular soldiers. There was nothing at all ridiculous about the totally undisciplined little companies, who cheered and stumbled and chattered and jostled round their chiefs; but the volunteers, laboriously attempting to keep the step, with their caps at odd angles, and expressions on their faces of extreme self-consciousness, made a very silly show.

The procession was arranged in alternate bodies of disciplined and undisciplined troops, ending with the very smart cavalry regiment of the Imperial Guard and sixteen motor lorries carrying anti-aircraft machine guns. This arrangement fulfilled a double purpose; it emphasised for the benefit of his own people and the European visitors the difference between the Imperial Guard and the feudal levies, giving a sample of the change which the new régime hoped to effect universally throughout the Empire, and it separated the wilder men from rival companies with whom they might have come into conflict.

The high spirits of the troops seemed unaffected by the weather. In the coming weeks, as the provincial armies passed through the capital on their way to the Northern front, we were to see several such displays. For most of the Press it was then a new experience. The old chiefs, almost without exception, looked superb. Their gala costume varied in magnificence with their wealth. They had head-dresses and capes of lion skin, circular shields and extravagantly long, curved swords, decorated with metal and coloured stuff; their saddles and harness were brilliant and elaborate. Examined in detail, of course, the ornaments were of wretched quality, the work of Levantine craftsmen in the Addis bazaar, new, aiming only at maximum ostentation for a minimum price; there was nothing which bore comparison with the splendour of a North African or Asiatic workmanship. But in their general effect, as they emerged from the watery haze which enclosed us, strutted and boasted before the Emperor, and were hustled away in the middle of their speeches by the Court Chamberlains, those old warriors were magnificent.

Boasting was a particular feature of all these parades. Sometimes it was done by special minstrels, sometimes by the chief himself, who would spur his mule up to the steps of the throne, rein it back on its haunches, brandish his spear and recite the deeds of bloodshed he had achieved in the past and those he proposed to do in the future; sometimes he would dismount and dance before the Emperor with drawn sword, chanting of his prowess. If he were allowed to continue too long in this manner he intoxicated himself and in a kind of ecstasy, sword whirling, eyes turned up, beard and lips spattered with foam, would constitute a serious danger to those near him. (When the Kambata army came through they cut open the head of one of the chamberlains in their enthusiasm.) The greater part of these recitations, my interpreter told me, dealt with the first battle of Adowa; most of the promises of future service were taunts at Italy. Vinci and his staff sat through the wet afternoon listening with polite, if slightly ironical, attention.

An incongruous and more sombre note was struck by the sudden appearance among these flamboyant demonstrators of a bedraggled little procession of shivering school-children, who sang a hymn in quavering, barely audible tones.

The journalists meanwhile were beginning to slip away to the wireless bureau to send, at urgent rates, contradictions of their earlier messages. Still the procession went on. It ended, shortly before sunset, with four Red Cross vans. Perhaps they were appropriate to the last festival of free Abyssinia.

Another week followed, full of whispered rumours; more journalists and cinema men arrived. I bought a petulant and humourless baboon which lived in my room at the Deutsches Haus, and added very little to the interest of these dull days. There were rowdy evenings at *Le Secret* and the *Perroquet*. The Spaniard went back to resume his duties in Paris. Patrick and I gave a dinner-party in his honour, which was overclouded for him by the loss of his sixpenny fountain-pen. 'Who of you has taken my feather?' he kept asking with great earnestness. 'I cannot work without my feather.'

At last, on October 2, came the announcement which had been so often predicted, that general mobilisation would be proclaimed on the morrow. It was preceded by the formal complaint that Ethiopian territory had been violated at Mount Moussa Ali, south-west of Assab on the borders of French Somaliland. An Italian force, as Wazir Ali Beg had reported a month earlier, had established a base on the Ethiopian side of the frontier. Notices were posted inviting the Press to attend 'a ceremony of great importance' which was to be held next day at the old Gibbi. Everybody knew what that meant.

I drove to the Italian Legation, but found them all in a fever of activity. Presumably they had already received news from Eritrea that the war was about to start. It was particularly gay that evening in the bars. Next morning we all assembled at the Palace at half past ten. We were shown straight into an airless gallery and kept there. I remember saying to the Reuter's correspondent, 'Well, now that they *have* at last mobilised, I suppose — and — (naming two abnormally untruthful colleagues who had anticipated the morning's order by ten days) will have to start announcing the bombardment of Adowa.'

No one knew quite what to expect, and even the most daring of the journalists had decided to wait and see what happened before composing their reports. Various almost liturgical ceremonies were expected; we were told in some quarters that the Emperor would set up his standard in person; that his crimson tent would be pitched as a rallying point for the armies; that the great drum of Menelik would be beaten, which had not sounded since 1895.

The drum was there; we could hear it clearly from our place of confinement, beating a series of single thuds, slow as a tolling bell. When eventually the doors were thrown open and we emerged on to the terrace, we saw the drum, a large ox-hide stretched over a wooden bowl. It may or may not have belonged to Menelik; all the whites said that it had and Mr David politely agreed.

A flight of stone steps led from the terrace to the parade ground, where a large, but not very large, crowd had assembled. They were all men. Over his shoulder I watched an American journalist typing out a description of the women under their mushroom-like umbrellas. There were no women and no umbrellas; merely a lot of black fuzzy heads and white cotton clothes. The Palace police were trying to keep the crowd back, but they pushed forward until only a small clearing remained, immediately below the steps. Here Mr Prospero and half a dozen of his colleagues were grinding away behind tripods.

The drum stopped and the people were completely silent as the Grand Chamberlain read the decree. It took some time. He read it very loudly and clearly. At the end there were three concerted bursts of clapping. Then the men made a rush for the Palace; it was unexpected and spontaneous. They wanted to see the Emperor. Most of them had swords or rifles. They flourished these wildly and bore down upon the little group of photographers, who, half fearing a massacre, scuttled for safety, dragging along their cumbrous apparatus as best they could. The crowd caught poor Mr Prospero, knocked him down and kicked him about, not in any vindictive spirit, but simply because he was in the way. One of them eventually put him on his feet, laughing, but not before he had sustained some sharp injuries.

Upstairs the decree, in quite different terms, we found later, was being read to the journalists in French by Dr Lorenzo. He could not make himself heard above the shouting. He stood on a chair, a diminutive, neat, black figure, crying for attention. A great deal of noise came from the journalists themselves. I had seldom seen them to worse advantage. Dr Lorenzo had in his hand a sheaf of copies of the decree. The journalists did not want to hear him read it. They wanted to secure their copies and race with them for the wireless bureau. Lorenzo kept crying in French, 'Gentlemen, gentlemen, I have something of great importance to communicate to you.'

He held the papers above his head and the journalists jumped for them, trying to snatch, like badly brought up children at a Christmas party.

The soldiers had now worked themselves into high excitement and were streaming past, roaring at the top of their voices.

Lorenzo led a dozen of us into the Palace, where in comparatively good order he was able to make his second announcement. He was clearly in a state of deep emotion himself; the little black hands below the starched white cuffs trembled. 'His Majesty has this morning received a telegram from Ras Seyoum in the Tigre,' he said. 'At dawn this morning four Italian war planes flew over Adowa and Adigrat. They dropped seventy-eight bombs, causing great loss of life among the civilian population. The first bomb destroyed the hospital at Adowa, where many women and children had taken refuge. At the same time Italian troops invaded the Province of Agame, where a battle is now raging.'

CHAPTER 5

ANTICLIMAX

1

THE EXCITEMENT BARELY survived the transmission of our cables. By afternoon the cheering crowd had melted away and were dozing silently in their tukals. Shutters were put up on the Greek-Italian grocery store and a guard posted before it, while at the back door journalists competed with the French Legation to buy the last tins of caviare. There were guards at the Italian Legation, the Italian Hospital and mission, the house of the military attaché; these buildings were out of bounds to Ethiopians and, for all practical purposes, to ourselves, for the soldiers in charge were a surly lot; Mr David at the Press Bureau assured us that the guards were there merely for the protection of the Italians, that we had only to show our Press cards to obtain admission; in fact for the first day or two we were turned back in the most uncompromising manner; later their vigilance became milder and Vinci and his staff even accepted invitations to dinner.

His position was to become increasingly anomalous. It had been odd during the preceding month; now that hostilities had actually begun, it was without precedent. The Emperor was reluctant to order his withdrawal, for fear of compromising the posture he had assumed of quaker-like patience. No one knew the exact extent or purpose of the hostilities. Some said the bombardment of Adowa was a local reprisal for the deflection by the Abyssinians of a stream flowing to the Italian lines. No one knew how abruptly or effectively the League of Nations might intervene. In those days of early October, in Addis Ababa at least, it was thought possible that there might be some concerted, exemplary action which would smother the new-born war almost before it had taken independent breath. It was important to keep means of communication open

648

with the enemy. So, for the time being, Vinci stayed on, attended by a somewhat incongruous entourage of nuns and grocers. He had deserved a holiday and he was enjoying it. For four years he had been at an arduous, responsible and unpleasant post, trying to maintain a working method which with each year had been more obviously futile; a routine of constant insult, constant protest, constant evasion; always hampered by the jealousies of his European colleagues. Now the make-believe was over; the uniforms and evening clothes were packed; the journalists who had pestered him were at a distance. With Latin relish he settled down to a few days of leisure.

That afternoon and evening we drove round the town in search of 'incidents', but everything was profoundly quiet. News of the bombardment of Adowa was now all over the bazaars, but it seemed to cause little stir. It would be impertinent to attempt any certain definition of what the people felt. Perhaps the majority of them believed that the war had already been in progress for some time. Adowa was a very long way off. Practically no one in Addis had ever been there. It was known to them by name, as the place where the white men had been so gloriously cut to pieces forty years before. It was inhabited by Tigreans, a people for whom they had little liking. News of its destruction was received in Addis rather as we, in London, read of floods in China or earthquakes in Japan. There seemed a complete absence of indignation, an absence of all emotion except a mild sporting enthusiasm at the prospect of a good season's shooting.

The Europeans, Levantines and Americans, on the other hand, fell into a cold sweat of terror. The Emperor's American adviser had at this time organised a daily tea party of specially sympathetic correspondents, to whom he divulged the government communiqués a day before they were officially issued. This group became a centre from which Ethiopian propaganda radiated. On the afternoon of October 3, 'the Leaker', as he was familiarly known, gave it out that an air raid was expected on Addis that evening. The effect was galvanic. One group of American journalists hastily concluded a deal for the lease of a mansion immediately next door to the Italian Legation. They packed up their stores and luggage and their accumulations of trashy souvenirs and set off in secrecy to their new home. Unfortunately they were contravening a municipal bye-law which forbade a change of address without previous permission. I cannot help suspecting that Mr Kakophilos must have tipped off the police; there was a touch of saturnine triumph in the air with which he welcomed their return, an hour later, under guard, to his hotel. A similar fate befell a neurotic young Canadian who set out to hide on the top of Mount Entoto. Other journalists took refuge in outlying missions and hospitals, or shared their bedrooms with their chauffeurs for fear that, when the alarm came, they might find their cars usurped by black women and children. Others are said to have sat up all night playing stud poker in gas masks. Timidity was infectious. A passing motor bicycle would have us all at the window staring skywards. A few hardened topers remained sober that evening for fear of sleeping too heavily. But the night passed undisturbed by any except the normal sounds − the contending loudspeakers of the two cinemas, the hyenas howling in the cemetery. Few of us slept well. The first two hours after dawn were the most likely time for a raid, but the sun − at last it was full summer − brought reassurance. After a slightly strained week-end we settled down to our former routine. On Monday night there was a bacchanalian scene at Mme Idot's, where, among other songs of international popularity, 'Giovanezza' was sung in a litter of upturned tables and broken crockery.

2

From now until the very end − and, indeed, long after the end − the one department of the Ethiopian government which worked with tolerable efficiency was the propaganda. Its aim, as is usual, was to represent the enemy as both ruthless and ineffective. Mass disloyalty, cowardice, extreme physical weakness and cruelty were the characteristics imputed to the invading armies; restraint, courage, wisdom and uniform success of the defenders; women, children and the medical services the chief victims. These are the normal objectives of a propagandist campaign in time of war; the Ethiopians pursued them tolerably well.

First there were the public utterances of the Emperor. These were drafted for him by his professional white advisers, but it is probable that he took a large share in their composition. They were designed entirely for foreign consumption and were quite admirable. They were repeated throughout the world and more than any single feature of the situation stirred the women, clergy and youths of the civilised races, conservative and socialist alike, to that deep, cordial, altruistic and absolutely ineffective sympathy which has been his reward.

Besides these, the government issued occasional bulletins of news. They were, naturally enough, incomplete and tendentious, but, at first, as far as they went, surprisingly truthful. When they proved false it was generally because the local commanders were lying, not the central government. News of reverses was delayed and suppressed, casualties among the fighting forces minimised and those among non-combatants exaggerated, but I do not know of a case in which the truth was officially denied or a lie categorically affirmed. The bulletins compared very favourably with those issued by any nation in time of war.

It is worth noticing one change of policy among the propagandists. In the early stages of the war, so long, in fact, as the Abyssinian armies appeared to be holding out successfully, attention was constantly called to the desertions of Italian native troops. These were represented as mutinous and eager for revenge against the oppression of their masters. Later, when the break-up of the Abyssinian defence was apparent, a new line was adopted and the myth propagated, and eagerly received in England, that the Italians owed their victory entirely to native soldiers while they themselves remained at a safe distance. Ras Kassa went so far as to give public utterance to the statement that no white troops at all had appeared in the front line. It was a double-edged argument, for, if a measure were needed to judge the relative merits of Abyssinian and Italian imperialism, there could be no more certain one than the subject people's willingness to die for the régime. The Ethiopian subject races revolted at the first opportunity and finally drove the Emperor from the country; the Eritreans followed their white officers with ferocious devotion.

The real work of the propaganda department was done through unofficial channels. To the horde of competing journalists the government communiqués were of negligible importance. They were transmitted instantly in full by Reuter's and the other agencies and gave no material for the special news which the editors were demanding. This had to be procured by other means; it had to be jealously guarded from rivals. It could not be investigated for fear of attracting their attention. An exclusive lie was more valuable than a truth which was shared with others.

A point of this kind was particularly apt for Ethiopian intelligence; it exemplified just what they had always thought about Europeans – an unscrupulous, impatient, avaricious, credulous people – and they exploited it to the full. They worked partly by means of unofficial revelations – usually in hints or guarded agreement with the statements which their interviewer was attempting to impose on them – in official quarters; partly in the employment of foreigners and servants to spread news which they wanted to have believed. The information was given to the journalists singly, so that each imagining himself especially astute or especially privileged, gave it corresponding prominence in his despatch. An example occurred during the first days of the war in the case of the hospital at Adowa.

The first communiqué, read in dramatic circumstances by Dr Lorenzo, asserted that the first bomb of the attack had fallen on 'the hospital', destroying it and killing many women and children. The statement was, presumably, taken from Ras Seyoum's despatch and passed on directly to us and to Geneva without enquiry. When we began to look for details, our doubts were aroused whether there had ever been a hospital there at all. No such thing existed as a native hospital; no Red Cross units had yet appeared in the field; the medical work of the country was entirely in mission hands, either of Catholic orders – Capucins, Lazarists, Consolata – or Swedish and American Protestants. The headquarters of these organisations knew nothing about a hospital at Adowa, nor did the Consulates know of any of their nationals engaged there. The publication of the news was already having the desired effect in Europe; a letter, which caused great amusement when it reached us, appeared in *The Times* expressing the hope that 'the noble nurses had not died in vain', but at Addis Ababa suspicions were aroused that our legs were being pulled. Mr David and Dr Lorenzo, when pressed, had to admit that they knew no more than was disclosed in the first bulletin; there *had been* a hospital – it was now destroyed, they maintained stoutly, and added that it was clearly marked with the red cross; apart from that they had no information.

But suddenly, from other sources, a flood of detail began to reach us. There was an Abyssinian servant who had been treated there two years ago for a pain in his leg by a great number of American doctors and nurses; the hospital was a fine building in the centre of the town.

There was a Greek who knew the place well. It was managed by Swedes and lay at a short distance along the Adigrat road.

There was a Swiss architect and government contractor – a jolly fellow, married to a half-caste; he was responsible for most of the ugliest of the recent public buildings – who was able to give Patrick confidential but absolutely authentic information about the nurse who had been killed; she was of Swedish birth but American nationality; she had been blown to bits. He had heard all about it on the telephone from a friend on the spot.

The most circumstantial story came from an American negro who was employed as aviator by the Ethiopian government. I met him at his tailor's on the Saturday morning, ordering a fine new uniform. He had been at Adowa, he claimed, at the time of the bombardment. More than this, he had been in the hospital. More than this, he had been drinking cocoa with the nurse five minutes before her death. She was a handsome lady, thirty-two years old, five foot five in height. They had been sitting in the hospital – clearly marked by the red cross – when the first bomb had fallen. The airman's first thought, he said, was for the safety of his machine, which was lying a mile outside the town. Except for himself and the doctor there were no other men in the town. It was populated solely by women and children. He had lain near his aeroplane for some hours while the bombs fell. The Italians had flown very badly, he said, and bombed most erratically ('Mr Waugh, do you realise, *I* might have been killed *myself*?'). Eventually he had returned to see the place demolished and the nurse dead. He had then flown back to Addis, where the Emperor had been deeply moved by his story.

When we pointed out to the Press Bureau that neither the Swedish nor American consuls knew of the hospital, Mr David had an ingenious explanation. It was true, he said, that the nurses and doctor had not passed through Addis Ababa and registered there; they had entered the country from Eritrea, whence they had been driven by Italian brutality.

Cables were soon arriving from London and New York: '*Require earliest name life story photograph American nurse upblown Adowa.*' We replied '*Nurse unupblown*,' and after a few days she disappeared from the news. Later, when the Ethiopian government made its comprehensive complaint on the acts against international convention committed by Italian airmen, the Adowa hospital was not mentioned. Its brief vogue, however, was of assistance to one thoroughly deserving Englishman.

Captain P. had arrived some time before and had been having a typically trying time. He was the officer sent in advance by the British Ambulance, voluntarily subscribed and equipped in London for service on the Abyssinian front. His job was to arrange for the arrival of the unit and he came in the expectation of a cordial reception. As the American doctor had found, enthusiasm for the Red Cross was not strong in Abyssinia. News that a subscription had been opened in England was warmly received, but there had been a marked abatement when it was learned that Englishmen intended to come and spend it themselves, to go pushing about behind the lines wasting good money on men who had been fools enough to get incapacitated; worse still, giving equal attention to wounded enemies. More than this, the British, very wisely as events proved, had decided to employ only their own men. They would bring British native orderlies from Kenya and work under advice from Addis Ababa, but as a single, indivisible unit, with their own commissariat and disciplinary system. The scum of the Addis missions, flabby-faced, soft-spoken youths, had already been recruited into an 'Ethiopian Red Cross Corps', and could be seen lounging and giggling in an empty shop on the main street. The authorities wished Captain P. to take these into his unit instead of the men from Kenya.

Negotiations were carried on through the intermediary of the head of one of the missions – a naturalised Ethiopian subject, educated in America, of no defined theological complexion – and were intolerably protracted. Captain P. had come with a pardonable sense of vicarious benefaction. He was greeted with the customary suspicion and delay. On Friday the 4th he was in despair and had delivered his ultimatum that he would leave Addis by the next train unless an agreement was reached. By that evening the Adowa hospital scare was at its height. The Abyssinians suddenly saw the vast possibilities for propaganda in the presence in a dangerous situation of a genuine Red Cross hospital. Their tone changed. Captain P. was informed next day that the British unit would be welcome; indeed, that the Emperor could barely contain his anxiety for its immediate arrival. 'My people are lying wounded in the hills; there is no one to tend them,' he said in a moving speech. So Captain P. set off for Berbera and, rather more than two months later, the gallant ill-starred unit arrived in the country. The 'Ethiopian Red Cross' continued to hang about the city. Some weeks later they were put in charge of an Indian who had a scheme for reconciling Christianity and Mohammedanism, a very pious American youth who left the table if wine was shown him, and two chatty Irishmen, one a doctor, the other a publican, who were embarrassed by no such fad. This corps added one more to the many bright elements of the campaign. It was constantly being ordered to the front, but evening after evening the familiar faces were to be seen in the Addis bars. By the beginning of December they had got to Dessye, where half of the native orderlies were under treatment for venereal disease; others were in chains for breaches of discipline; others were in tears at the prospect of moving nearer the fighting. There were disagreements among the officers, and they occupied separate quarters. After it was all over one of our most august papers conveyed the idea that they had been in the front line from the beginning of the war.

3

News of the capture of Adowa and Adigrat reached us on October 7, long after its publication to the rest of the world. It caused little stir, for the defence of the two towns had never been part of the Abyssinian strategy. The advance appeared to have been held up for three days by scouts and skirmishers. We had all expected a sensationally rapid penetration from north and south. In the Ogaden rain was said to be still falling. There had been bombing there, but, it was reported, barely two out of three bombs exploded; they splashed harmlessly into the mud. Incendiary bombs were extinguished or fizzled like damp fireworks in the marshes. The soldiers, when they spoke of aeroplanes, used feminine suffixes – a grammatical form expressive of supreme contempt. It was pointed out that in those clusters of tents and mud huts a bomb was of greater value than anything it could destroy; a house could be rebuilt in a week-end. As the anxiety for our own safety became calmer, we believed that the great attack had in some way gone off at half-cock.

We still believed that the railway was doomed. On Tuesday the 8th 'positively the last' train left for Djibouti. There was something very like a riot at the station as frantic refugees attempted to board it, and the station police locked out legitimate passengers who had reserved their places. For the first time the scene approximated to the descriptions which, as early as August, had been filling the world's Press. It was now too late to be of interest – another example of the inverted time lag between the event and its publication which marked all our professional efforts in the country. One contrast remains vivid in my memory among the confused impressions of the railway station. A cattle truck packed with soldiers on the way to the southern front; their rifles had been taken away for fear they got into mischief during the journey, but most of them had weapons of a kind; all were in a delirious condition, hoarse, staring, howling for blood. In the next coach sat a dozen Italian nuns on the way to the coast; fresh-faced, composed, eyes downcast, quietly telling their beads.

It was not until October 10 that any action was taken with regard to the Italian Legation. The consul and his staff had arrived from Dessye. There was now only the commercial agent from Magalo on the road. Vinci was unwilling to leave without him; the Emperor made an order for his expulsion. It was one of his few injudicious utterances. Instead of basing the order on the indisputable fact that a state of war existed between the two countries, he coupled it with accusations of personal bad faith against the Minister, espionage and abuse of diplomatic privilege. The sequel was the richly comic incident of October 12.

Vinci's departure was announced for eight in the morning. There was to be nothing unobtrusive about it. The Abyssinians were anxious to demonstrate before the world that they were a highly courteous and civilised nation; all, and more than all, the full formalities were to be observed. A printed order was issued the evening before giving the programme for the day. Train and station were prepared for a ceremony of the most dignified nature. A guard of honour of the household cavalry was waiting at dawn outside the Legation gates. By eight o'clock the diplomatic corps were pacing the carpeted platform. Mr Prospero had erected a platform for his cinema camera. All the photographers were there and all the reporters. Presently the luggage arrived, prominent in its midst a dripping packing-case containing bottled beer on ice, and a caged leopard. The Italian consul and the two secretaries were there, looking as though they had been awakened uncommonly early after an uncommonly late night. But of Vinci, or the military attaché, Calderini, there was no sign.

An hour passed. The British, French and American Ministers conferred anxiously. A rumour began to travel along the platform that there had been a hitch. Some of us struggled through the crowd, found a car and drove to the Italian Legation. The squadron of lancers had dismounted and were squatting by their horses. There was also a picket of infantry and a temporary telephone station. No one was allowed inside the gates. A zealous young colonial reporter climbed the wall; was captured and frog-marched, rather roughly, to imprisonment in the telephone hut. We drove back to the station. The train was still there; the luggage and the leopard were on board; the diplomatic corps had gone home to breakfast. The consul's greenish face appeared apprehensively at a carriage window. At half past ten the train started. At the last moment one of the secretaries jumped out on the off-side and took refuge in an out-building. He was disarmed, arrested and sent on later to join the train further down the line.

Back to the Italian Legation. The Ethiopian Foreign Minister was just leaving, alone; a puzzled black face under a bowler hat. He drove to the Belgian Legation to consult the doyen; what did a highly courteous and civilised nation do, when, in time of war, a Minister refused to accept his passport? The doyen did not know.

All the photographers and the camera men had now assembled outside the gates of the Italian Legation and were picnicking under the hedge. The guards were in a bad temper and there were several scuffles. The colonial had been released and was now alternately protesting and apologising. Inside Vinci and Calderini, having completed a leisurely toilet, took their coffee on the terrace and later settled down to a hand or two of piquet in chancery. All manner of rumours spread through the bazaars: that there was a mine below the Gibbi and Vinci was waiting his moment to press a button and blow it up. David and Lorenzo said, justly, as they had so often said before, that he was 'provoking an incident'.

Vinci and Calderini stayed in Addis for another fortnight. Their attitude was, primarily, that their place was in the country so long as any of their subordinates remained there. Application had been made in good time for the consul's recall. Abyssinian suspicion and obstructiveness had marred the dignified departure that had been planned for them. The order of expulsion had included personal charges; to accept it might be construed as an admission of guilt. But more than these official reasons, there was, I believe, an element of mischief in the matter. As future conquerors, the Italians chose to withdraw their representative, as they had chosen to attack, entirely at their own convenience. They were not going to be hustled out at the command of their future subjects.

They were removed from the Legation and kept in absolute isolation at Ras Desta's house while the Magalo agent made his way slowly – almost imperceptibly – towards the railway-line. Repeated messages were sent from the Emperor to hurry him up. He cut down his day's marches to fifteen, then to twelve, finally to ten miles; it was fatiguing, he said, and he enjoyed collecting butterflies on the way. At last he reached Hadama station, where Vinci joined him and they proceeded together to the coast.

During his captivity the Press Bureau did all they could to render Vinci's position ignominious. Lorenzo and his colleagues said that the reason he could not leave was that he was in an alcoholic stupor; he sat all day drooling over the whisky bottle, talking about his ruined career and the pains of hell. A few correspondents loyally cabled the story back, but few of them believed it and, I think, no English newspaper published it. When, eventually, Vinci emerged, spruce and cheerful, it was to go by the quickest route to Mogadishu, where, for the rest of the war, he commanded a company of native infantry with conspicuous success.

4

Provincial armies now began to appear in the capital, to do homage to the Emperor on the way to the northern front. The first and most formidable were from Kambata; they had been on the march for ten days or more and arrived lean and defiant. Most of them had never been in the city before; they swaggered through the traffic and caused trouble to anyone who obstructed. They threatened the gentle Radical and nearly lynched the two colonials who rode out to their camp to take snapshots; they created some sort of disturbance at the Gibbi, the details of which never came out; a chamberlain was said to have been cut down and several servants injured in the Emperor's presence. They had been told that Ras Seyoum had just retaken Adowa and massacred 30,000 whites, including Mussolini's son. The tale went to their heads. They got very drunk in the *tedj* houses, refused to pay and had several fights with the civic police. Soon they were hustled off to the front without being granted the ceremonial march-past which they expected. Many of them were accompanied by women from their province; squat little negresses padding along beside the column, bowed double under loads of provisions and babies.

The men from Wollaga and Shoa – Ras Moulugetta's own men – were better behaved and were given their parade. It was like the Maskal review. The Emperor and his court sat under a canopy while the men streamed past him, hour after hour. They came in little knots, each man clinging, if he could, to his chief's saddle, rushed to the foot of the throne shouting and dancing and were driven on with canes. I got my interpreter to take down some of the things which they shouted:

'*When he was a calf we drove him away with sticks*' (referring to 1896); '*now he is a fat bull and we will slaughter him and eat him.*'

'*You have kept us too long. All our enemies are already slain by the men of the other provinces.*'

'*Never fear, we will please you. We will soon be at the sea.*'

News of Haile Selassie Gugsa's submission was suppressed at Addis Ababa until several days after it was known in Europe; it reached us first as the rumour that he had tried to desert but had been shot by his own men; in this form it was held by the majority of the natives long after a more truthful version had been issued by the Press Bureau. But it caused no alarm. It was believed that Kassa's Galla cavalry had invaded Eritrea and were harassing the Italian communications. There was an atmosphere of highest optimism everywhere.

It was rumoured that the Emperor would shortly proceed north and make his headquarters at Dessye; that if he did so the Press would be allowed to go too. Meanwhile we were more than ever starved of credible information. A censorship had been imposed which worked irregularly and capriciously. At first it was put in charge of a very young Belgian – one of the ex-officers who had offered their services to the Abyssinians. He knew very little English and on the first morning contented himself with sending back, without any comment except that they could not be sent, all the cables submitted to him and then closing his office for the day. Later he explained that nothing might be sent which mentioned the Emperor, numbers or movements of troops, war news other than the official communiqués, local news which might be of use to the enemy or which reflected upon the standards of Abyssinian civilisation. No particular details would be expunged; the entire message would be stopped which contained any such offensive matter. This ordinance seemed to impose a complete cessation of all our activities and we received it, either gladly or in a frenzy of rage, according as we valued our jobs. Rage predominated. A special meeting was called of the Foreign Press Association, at which, for the first time, almost the entire Press appeared and apparent solidarity was maintained. A protest was drafted in the most uncompromising terms declaring that until we had attention to our grievances we would boycott the wireless and that if we did not receive an answer from the government by the following evening we would ask to be withdrawn. We asked for a new censor who had some acquaintance with the languages he dealt in, who kept regular hours, who would read our cables in our presence and point out what passages he found objectionable, who would impose a more reasonable code. We elected a deputation to wait on Dr Lorenzo with our protest and explain it to him. We would negotiate through this deputation and maintain our strike until they had come to terms. We parted in good humour with the prospect of a holiday. That was at noon. By breakfast time next day a group of correspondents, including one of the elected deputies, had opened private negotiations with the Belgian. From that moment it became clear that the Foreign Press Association was not going to serve any useful purpose. No answer was received to our protest by the time we had specified or for some days afterwards. When it came it was a blunt refusal to consider it. Meanwhile everyone went on working as before. The censor became less draconian and was later superseded by a scholarly-looking Abyssinian. The Foreign Press Association met once more, when two Americans challenged one another to fight and a third was sick. After that it ceased to exist even in name. The Radical gave the money that had been collected to the head of the wireless bureau.

The camera men were even more unhappily placed than the correspondents. Their apparatus rendered them conspicuous and most of the native soldiers had an exaggerated idea of the value which their portraits might be to the enemy. The cinema companies in particular had invested huge sums in their expeditions and were getting very little in return for it.

Two hundred or more of the Addis Ababa prostitutes appeared one day dressed in high-heeled sandals and ultramarine male uniforms. This was a golden opportunity for the photographers, who got them to pose with rifles and swords and sent back the results entitled 'Abyssinian Amazons. Famous Legion of Fighting Women leave for the Front', to the great distress of Dr Lorenzo and Mr David, who hoped, and eventually succeeded in making good copy out of the casualties among the female camp followers.

One group of cinema men purchased the goodwill of a chief who was encamped with his men in the hills behind Addis and were able to stage some fairly effective charades of active service. Later at Dessye the 'Ethiopian Red Cross' lent itself to a vivid imposture, staging a scene of their own heroic services under fire, with iodine to counterfeit blood and fireworks and flares for a bombardment. One prominent photographer had brought out with him a set of small bombs which he was able to discharge from his position at the camera by means of an electric cable. He had some difficulty explaining them at the French customs and I do not know if they were ever used. Those who had worked during the Chinese wars – where, it seemed, whole army corps could be hired cheaply by the day and even, at a special price, decimated with real gunfire – complained bitterly of the standard of Abyssinian venality.

The white population of the town pursued their normal routine of petty and profitless trade. Like all my colleagues I now had two or three of them in my employment bringing me wretched scraps of news, mostly about municipal taxation. Mme Moriatis showed signs of despair, spoke daily of a massacre, and tried to persuade her husband to pack up. One evening when she was showing a French version of 'Peg o' my Heart', her cinema was visited by the pictur-esque retinue of one of the provincial magnates, who came with women, bodyguard and two half-grown lions who were left on the steps in charge of his slaves. The brief run on the bank came to an end. The thaler went up in value; the engine drivers of the railway did a brisk trade in smuggling silver. Various statesmen and warriors returned from exile and were reconciled to the Emperor. The French population organised itself in a defence corps. Issa tribesmen shot down an Italian aeroplane and hid for days, not knowing if they had done well or ill. An Abyssinian airman came very near being shot down by his fellow countrymen at Dessye. An Egyptian Prince arrived to establish a Red Crescent hospital. The Yemen Arabs were reported to be active. We eked out our despatches with such small items of news. Already some correspondents began to talk of leaving, and the most distinguished veteran actually left. The rest of us centred all our hopes on the long-deferred trip to Dessye. Various dates – the anniversary of his accession, St George's Day – were suggested as the time of the Emperor's departure. In the interval of waiting I decided on another visit to Harar.

On our previous journey we found that the further we went from Addis Ababa the milder we found official restrictions; now the case was reversed. Awash, where the train halted for the night, was a military post under the command of a Swiss. A boisterous French adventurer was in charge at Diredawa. We were no longer allowed to sit out after dinner on the hotel verandah; all lights had to be screened. There and at Harar sentries were posted every few yards along the streets and no one was allowed to go out of doors after dark without escort. Charles G. had had the fortune to witness a fight between two of the European police officers. As a result he had lately been expelled on a charge of espionage. His parting act was to buy a slave and give her to Mati Hari as a tip. At Harar the evacuation was almost complete. Few families now slept in the town; most of the stalls in the bazaar were shuttered; those that were open had been deserted by their proprietors and the stock was being sold off by listless underlings. The chief of police, formerly so cordial, now barely troubled himself to acknowledge our greetings. He had taken gravely to the bottle and might be seen daily, from early morning, sunk in gloom, at Mr Karasselos's hotel, alternately sipping Mr Karasselos's brandy and giving vent to a nervous, retching cough. The Hararis' brief military enthusiasm was over. There were now no volunteers drilling in the streets. Attempts had been made, with small success, to get them to the front. Now the order was that all Abyssinians were to proceed south and leave the Hararis with the task of garrisoning their city.

The ancient antagonism of cross and crescent seemed at last to have been reconciled; red crosses had sprung up everywhere. There was one on the Emperor's Gibbi, another on the Law Courts; another on the Treasury, another on a little tin shed next to the Belgian orderly-room, another, partly obliterated but still clearly visible, on the roof of the wireless station. Two old-established missions – French and Swedish – maintained a medical service, but there was no ambulance corps of any kind in the city. I sent my interpreter out to try and obtain information about what preparations were being made in these other buildings; he returned unsuccessful. He had been refused admission everywhere; by questioning the guards and friends in the town he learned that it was proposed to put wounded there should any arrive. No special steps had been taken for their accommodation. The shed at the barracks was said to house a small fund of money subscribed locally for humane purposes.

There had been a panic in the city on the day of the bombardment of Adowa. Mr Karasselos, among others, had prepared for flight and the journalists quartered in his hotel had taken refuge at the British Consulate. They were still encamped there, although Mr Karasselos had later reopened his door; after two days of sordid discomfort I joined them.

The consul controlled his guests with amiability and tact and, as a result, the acrimonious competition of Addis Ababa hardly existed. The wireless had imposed a limit of fifty words daily on press messages. Every morning the journalists drove into the city and sat with their typewriters in Mr Karasselos's dining-room; here their various informants brought them the news. At noon they returned to the consulate, lunched heavily and dozed away the rest of the day. Even at this dark hour of its history the gentle atmosphere of Harar exercised a benign influence, shaming the toughest go-getters into temporary leisured decency.

My interpreter – 'my name is Mustafa Jimma but gentlemen call me James' – who had been with me now for several weeks, was a 'British-protected person' from the Soudan – an inestimable advantage, for Ethiopian subjects lived in constant fear of police persecution. He spoke English, Amharic, Arabic and Harari. As a Moslem he enjoyed the confidence of the townspeople; he had lived there some years previously, and still had friends in the place.

One day he came to me and said that one of the sheiks of the Mosque wished to talk to me.

The meeting was arranged with the utmost secrecy, in a bedroom at the native inn. I went there first, alone, slipped as unobtrusively as possible from the street into the shady court, and climbed to the gallery. The only inmates were two torpid Arabs, browsing on *khat*. Presently James returned leading a venerable Harari, white-bearded, white-turbaned, white-robed. James had clearly been talking about the importance of his employer. I explained to the old man that I was merely the reporter for a newspaper, but he politely smiled away these subterfuges. He believed that I was an emissary from the British Government and the purpose of his visit was to persuade me, in the name of numerous Moslem elders, to propose the conquest of Harar and its absorption into British Somaliland. Later in the week I had a second interview with him in similar circumstances; on that occasion he brought a friend with him, a cautious old landowner, who had suffered spoliation at Abyssinian hands. We sat in a row on the couch in the little white-washed cell, while James stood before us and interpreted, fluently and, I believe, quite honestly.

In its bare outlines their complaint had a close resemblance to the grumbles of elderly gentlemen in any part of the world – the place was going to the dogs, it was the government's fault, the younger generation were irreligious, disobedient and depraved, over-taxation was ruining them, upstarts of low birth and odious manners were usurping the government offices, the police were corrupt, and so on. But there was this difference, that they were risking their lives to tell me these things and, behind their querulousness, I thought I could distinguish a genuine anxiety for the welfare of their people. Over-taxation was their main complaint; they belonged to a trading community and they saw its life being rapidly stifled by the impositions. They gave the facts in biblical detail – so many yards of cloth for the Governor, so many for the Emperor, so many houses commandeered by Abyssinian officials, so many days' forced labour by the women, so many by the men, such and such a percentage on each corn crop, so much on each basket of produce brought to market. It made a formidable list; a vast, increasing burden borne by everyone in the province, the advantage of which went directly and exclusively to the Abyssinian conquerors. There was no question of social services; the money went straight into the pockets of the officials. These were the arguments they put first as being of obvious practical importance, but later they began to talk in a more general way and I began to understand why they were prepared to risk their lives for the hope of reforms which, if ever possible, could only in the nature of things profit them for a very few years of life. They were concerned about a higher thing, the destruction of a culture. As boys they had known Harar as an independent Emirate; they had grown up in the Koranic law, scholarship and habit of life. They saw their descendants not only reduced to political dependence – that they could have borne; indeed were clearly ready to bear it – but to cultural insignificance, losing both their religion and their racial identity, becoming not only under-dogs but mongrels. Moslem schools were being squeezed out; Moslem law was overruled by Abyssinian; drink was sold openly in the streets; the fasts were broken, ancient customs falling into decay; a Moslem who turned Christian was promoted, a Christian who turned Moslem was flogged; they spoke with horror of the contamination by Christian manners, in almost identical terms as those in which the Bishops' encyclicals denounce 'the New Paganism'.

I asked why, in this case, they wished to be governed by England, and they replied politely that they did not regard England as a really Christian people. We thought all religions of the same value; besides we were rich. The French were licentious and poor, only one degree better than the Abyssinians. They did not know much about the Italians but they understood they were a good people. They frankly hoped they would win the war. 'The Habasha' (Abyssinians) 'order us to pray in the Mosque for victory. Only Allah knows for whose victory we pray.'

What they would most like to see would be a bloodthirsty defeat of the Abyssinians by the Italians, followed by a partition in which the Harar province was added to British Somaliland. It was a statesmanlike aspiration, but I was not able to give them much hope of its fulfilment.

*

No news of any value came from the front. Wehib Pasha's defensive lines seemed to be holding out. There was daily bombing in the Gorahai and Sassa Baneh district. Everyone spoke of a big offensive in the next few days. Desta's and Nasebu's armies were now concentrated against Graziani, who, it seemed, had received no reinforcements. We still believed that the big campaign of the winter would be fought on the southern front. At the beginning of November I returned to Addis with the intention of collecting all my equipment and taking up quarters in the consulate at Harar.

I arrived, however, to find that the long-awaited permission to go to Dessye had at last been granted. Enthusiasm for the trip had simultaneously begun to wane. It was said that the Emperor would not in fact go there; that it was a ruse to get the pressmen under close observation and out of harm's way; that there would be no wireless facilities; that the big southern campaign would begin in our absence. In the end only a small number of those who had been clamouring for permission decided to avail themselves of it. The Radical was among them, and he and I agreed to travel together.

As soon as this was known we became a centre of interest. All the boys at the Deutsches Haus, and the girl of no fixed occupation who pottered about the outbuildings giggling and occasionally appeared in the bedrooms with a broom, applied to accompany us. A saturnine Syrian, named Mr Karam, who had lately formed the habit of waylaying me on Sunday mornings after Mass and asking me to drink coffee with him, offered to sell us a motor lorry. The trouble about this lorry was that it did not in fact belong to Mr Karam. He has secured an option on it from a fellow Syrian and hoped to resell it at a profit. This was not clear until later, when he suffered great embarrassment about the spare parts. We said we would not take the lorry until it was fully equipped; he promised to equip it as soon as the agreement was signed. It was only when we went with him to the store that we discovered that he could not get the spare parts on credit, and could not pay for them until we had paid him an instalment of the price. There was a further embarrassment. We demanded a trial run up Entoto to test the engine. He could not get the petrol for the trip. In the end we filled up the tanks. James, who was not getting the rake-off he expected and had consequently taken up a suspicious attitude to Mr Karam, reported in triumph next morning that Mr Karam had hired out the lorry to a building contractor and was consuming our petrol. Poor Mr Karam was merely trying to raise the money for a new tyre. In the end we hired the machine for a month, at what I suspect was very near its full purchase price. From that moment Mr Karam was obsessed by anxiety that we proposed to make off with his lorry. He hung about the garage, where a gang was at work enhancing its value with a covered top and built-in boxes for petrol cans, pathetically canvassing our signatures to bits of paper on which we guaranteed not to drive beyond Dessye. It happened that the various agreements were made out in my name. When, a month later, the Radical and I separated and I returned to Addis Ababa in another car, poor Mr Karam's suspicions became feverish. He was convinced that there had been a plot against him and that the Radical had deserted with his lorry to the Italians.

With James's help we got together a suitable staff for the journey. He and my own boy, an Abyssinian, had long been at enmity. In the hiring of the servants they frequently came to tears. The most important man was the cook. We secured one who looked, and as it turned out was, all that a cook should be. A fat, flabby Abyssinian with reproachful eyes. His chief claim to interest was that his former master, a German, had been murdered and dismembered in the Issa country. I asked him why he had done nothing to protect him. '*Moi, je ne suis pas soldat, suis cuisinier vous savez.*' That seemed a praiseworthy attitude, so I engaged him. He suffered a great deal from the privations of the journey and cried with cold most evenings, the tears splashing and sizzling among the embers of his fire, but he cooked excellently, with all the native cook's aptitude for producing four or five courses from a single blackened pan over a handful of smoking twigs.

The chauffeur seemed to be suitable until we gave him a fortnight's wages in advance to buy a blanket. Instead he bought cartridges and *tedj*, shot up the bazaar quarter and was put in chains. So we engaged a Harari instead who formed a Moslem alliance with James against the other servants. The Radical and I found ourselves in almost continuous session as a court of arbitration. A cook's boy and chauffeur's boy completed the party. We had brought camping equipment and a fair quantity of stores from England; we supplemented these with flour, potatoes, sugar and rice from the local market; our Press cards were officially endorsed for the journey; our servants had been photographed and provided with special passes; and by November 13, the day announced by the Press Bureau for our departure, everything was ready.

It seemed scarcely possible that any working of the Addis bureaucracy could be so smooth. Eight or nine other parties were being fitted out for the journey, some on a very magnificent scale. One truck was emblazoned with the Lion of Judah and bore the legend '—— *Co. Inc. of New York. EXPEDITION TO THE FRONT WITH H.M. THE EMPEROR OF ETHIOPIA*'. But few of us really believed that we should be allowed to start on the appointed day.

Rumours came back that there were disturbances on the Dessye road. Part of it ran through the fringe of the Danakil country and these unamiable people had been resorting to their traditional sport of murdering runners and stragglers from the Abyssinian forces; there had also been sharp fighting between the Imperial Guard and the irregular troops, causing a number of casualties which reached us in a highly exaggerated form. A Canadian journalist who had arranged to start a week earlier with a caravan of mules had his permission cancelled abruptly and without explanation. David and Lorenzo refused to commit themselves; both were unapproachable for the two days preceding the 13th, but on the night of the 12th no official announcement had been made of postponement, our passes were in order, and the Radical and I decided to see how far we could get. At the best we might arrive before the road had been cleared of traces of the recent troubles; at the worst it would be an interesting experiment with Ethiopian government methods. The correspondent of the *Morning Post* decided to join us.

Most of the loading was done on the day before. That night we kept the lorry in the road outside the Deutsches Haus and put two boys to sleep in it. We meant to start at dawn, but, just as we were ready, James accused the cook of peculation, the Abyssinians refused to be driven by a Harari, and my personal boy burst into tears. I think they had spent the evening saying good-bye to their friends and were suffering from hangovers. The only two who kept their composure were those who had guarded the lorry. It was nearly nine before everyone's honour was satisfied. The streets were then crowded and our lorry, painted with the names of our papers and flying the Union Jack, made a conspicuous object. We drove past the Press Bureau, glancing to see that there was no notice on the door. We let down the side curtains, and the three whites lay low among the cases of stores hoping that we should pass as a government transport.

Our chief fear was that we should find a barrier and military post at the city limits, of the kind which guarded the approach to Harar. For nearly an hour we sprawled under cover in extreme discomfort as the heavily laden lorry jolted and lurched along the rough track. Then James told us that all was clear. We sat up, tied back the curtains, and found we were in open country. Addis was out of sight; a few eucalyptus-trees on the horizon behind us marked the extreme of urban expansion, before us lay a smooth grassy plain and the road, sometimes worn bare, scarred by ruts and hoof marks, sometimes discernible only by the boulders that had been distributed along it at intervals to trace its course. There was brilliant sunshine and a cool breeze. The boys at the back began to unwrap their bundles of luggage and consume large quantities of an aromatic spiced paste. An air of general good humour had succeeded the irritation of early morning.

We drove on for five or six hours without a stop. The way was easy; occasionally we met small streams where loose stones and sometimes a few baulks of timber had been piled to afford a crossing; for the most part we ran over firm, bare earth. This was still Galla country, for Menelik had founded his capital in conquered territory. We passed small farms, many of them stone built, standing beside hedges of euphorbia. Galla girls came out to wave to us, tossing their bundles of plaited hair. The men bowed low, three times; no one had travelled by car on that road for many months except Abyssinian officials or officers, and they had learned to associate motor traffic with authority.

After the first twenty miles we found soldiers everywhere. Some at noon, still encamped; others wandering along in companies of a dozen; some with mules to carry their loads, some with women. These were stragglers from Ras Getatchu's army which had gone through Addis a week before.

The road turned and wandered following the lie of the ground; every now and then we ran across the line of the telephone, a double overhead wire running straight across country. This, we knew, constituted our danger.

The first telephone station was named Koromach. We reached it at three o'clock. A uniformed Abyssinian stood across the road signalling us to stop. James and the Harari were all for running him down; we restrained their enthusiasm and climbed out of our places. The office was a small, lightless *tukal* a hundred yards or so off the road. There were twenty or thirty irregular soldiers there, squatting on their heels with rifles across their knees, and a chief in a new khaki uniform. By means of James the telephone officer explained that he had received an order from Addis to stop two car loads of white men travelling without permits. This constituted the strong point of our argument, for we were clearly only one car load and we had our permits; we showed them to him. He took them away into a corner and studied them at length; yes, he admitted, we had our permits. He showed them to the chief and the two sat for some time in colloquy. 'The chief is a good man,' said James. 'The telephone man very bad man. He is saying we are not to go on. The chief says we have permission and he will not stop us.'

Since the man in charge of the guns was on our side, we took a more arrogant line. What proof had the clerk that he had received a message at all? How did he know who was speaking? How did he know the message, if message there was, referred to us? Here were we being held up in our lawful business by the hearsay statement of the telephone. It was evident that the chief really distrusted the telephone as much as we affected to do. A piece of writing on a printed card had more weight with him than a noise coming out of a hole in the wall. At this stage of the discussion James left us and disappeared into the lorry. He returned a moment later with a bottle

of whisky and a mug. We gave the chief a good half-pint of neat
spirit. He tossed it off, blinked a little, and apologised for the delay
we had been caused; then he conducted us, with his men, to the lorry
and, the telephone man still protesting, waved us a cordial farewell.

We had been held up for half an hour. It got dark soon after six,
so, since we had as yet had no practice in making camp, after an
hour and a half's further drive, we turned off the track and stopped
for the night under the lee of a small hill.

It was deadly cold. None of us slept much that night. I could hear
the boys shivering and chattering round the fire whenever I woke.
An hour before dawn we rose, breakfasted and struck camp under
a blaze of stars. With the first sign of the sun we were on the road.
Our hope was to get through Debra Birhan before the Gibbi officials
at Addis were awake to warn them of our approach. Debra Birhan
was about three hours' drive away. It was the last telephone station
on the road. Once past that the way lay clear to Dessye.

We were out of Galla country now and among true Abyssinians,
but this part was sparsely populated and many of the farms had been
left empty by their owners who were marching to the front. There
were fields of maize here and there, standing high on either side of
the road, many of them showing where they had been trampled
down by passing soldiers; the track was tolerably level and we made
good time. When we were a couple of miles from Debra Birhan,
James warned us that it was time to hide. We drew the curtains, lay
down as before and covered ourselves as well as we could with sacks
and baggage.

It seemed a very long two miles and we had begun to believe that
we were safely past the station when the lorry came to a halt and we
heard a loud altercation going on all round us. We still lay low,
hoping that James would bluff our way through, but after about five
minutes his head appeared through the curtain. It was no good;
rather shamefacedly we crept out of hiding. We found ourselves on
the green of a large village. On one side stood the church of considerable size from which the place took its name. Next to it was the
Governor's compound and courthouse; on all sides irregular clusters
of huts; some sizeable trees; a pretty place. A less agreeable prospect
was the collection of soldiers who surrounded us. They were the

crocks left behind when the young men went to the war. They were ragged and dilapidated, some armed with spears but most of them with antiquated guns. 'I am sorry to disturb you,' said James politely, 'but these people wished to shoot us.'

In the centre stood the mayor – a typical Abyssinian squireen, tall, very fat, one-eyed. It was not clear at first whether he was disposed to be friendly; we tried him with whisky, but he said he was fasting – a bad sign.

He said he had received a message to stop us. We told him we had heard that story before at Koromach; we had cleared the whole matter up there. It was a mistake. We showed him our permits. Yes, he admitted, they were quite in order. He must just make a note of our names and write a letter of commendation for us to the other chiefs on the road; would we come with him to Government House.

It sounded hopeful, but James added to his interpretation 'I think, sir, that this is a liar-man.'

A leper woman had now joined the party; together we all sauntered across the green to the mayor's compound.

The main building was a rectangular, murky hut. We went inside. The telephone operator was not well that day; he lay on his bed in the darkest corner. The chief of police sat by his side: a toothless little old man with an absurd military cap on the side of his head. These three talked at some length about us. 'They do not want to let us go, but they are a little afraid,' said James. 'You must pretend to be angry.' We pretended to be angry. 'They are *very* afraid,' said James. But if this was so they controlled their emotion heroically.

The argument followed much the same course as yesterday's, but the one-eyed mayor was much less impressed by our written permits. First he affected not to be able to read them; then he complained that the signature looked fishy; then he said that although we had indeed permission to go to Dessye we had neglected to get permission to leave Addis Ababa. It was a mere formality, he said; we had better go back and do it.

Then we made a false step. We proposed that he should do this for us by telephone. He jumped at the suggestion. It was exactly what he would do. Only it would take some time. It was unsuitable that people of our eminence should stand about in the sun. Why did we not pitch a tent and rest? His men would help us.

If we had gone on being angry we might still have got through; instead we weakly assented, pitched a tent and sat down to smoke. After an hour I sent James to inquire how things were getting on. He came back to say that no attempt was being made to telephone to Addis. We must come back and be angry again.

We found the chief holding a court, his single, beady eye fixed upon a group of litigants who at a few inches' distance from him were pleading their case with all the frantic energy common in Abyssinian suits. He was not at all pleased at being disturbed. He was a great man, he said. We said we were great men too. He said that the telephone operator was far from well, that the line was engaged, that the Gibbi was empty, that it was a fast day, that it was dinner time, that it was late, that it was early, that he was in the middle of important public business, that James was offensive and untruthful and was not translating what he said and what we said, but instead, was trying to make a quarrel of a simple matter which admitted of only one solution, that we should wait until the afternoon and then come and see him again.

I do not know what James said, but the result was an adjournment of the court and a visit to the telephone hut, where the chief of police demonstrated, by twirling the handle, that the machine was out of order. We wrote out a telegram to Lorenzo protesting in the customary terms of the Foreign Press Association that we were being unjustly held prisoner in defiance of his own explicit permission to proceed. We had little hope of moving Lorenzo; we thought it might impress the mayor. 'They are *very* frightened,' said James. But they proceeded to their luncheon with the utmost composure and our message remained in the hands of the bedridden and now, apparently, moribund telephonist. 'They are too frightened to send it,' said James, trying to put an honourable complexion on the affair.

When we returned to our tent we found that, in our absence, the entire male and female labour of the village had been recruited and a barricade built of stones and tree trunks across the front of the lorry. Walking a little way back along the road we had come, we

found another barricade. Any hopes which we might have entertained of the mayor's goodwill were now dispelled.

The afternoon passed in a series of fruitless negotiations. The
chief would not send our message to Lorenzo, nor subsequent
messages which we wrote to other officials. We tried to get him to
endorse them with a note that they had been presented and refused.
That was no good. We made up our minds to spending the night at
Debra Birhan and pitched the other tents.

Our sudden docility disconcerted the chief and for the first time
he showed some sign of the fears which James had attributed to him.
He clearly feared that we intended to make a sortie by night. To
prevent this he tried to separate us from the lorry; he and the chief of
police came waddling down at the head of their guard – now
reinforced by the village idiot, a stark-naked fellow who loped and
gibbered among them until they drove him away with stones, when
he squatted out of range and spent the rest of the day gesticulating at
them obscenely. They said that we had chosen a very cold and
dangerous camping-ground. We might be attacked by robbers or
lions; the tents might be blown down; would we not prefer to move
to a more sheltered place? We replied that if they had been solicitous
of our comfort earlier, we could no doubt have found a better
camping-ground on the road to Dessye.

Later they tried a stupendous lie. The Emperor was on the
telephone, they said; he had rung up to say that ten lorry loads of
journalists were on the way to join us; would we mind waiting for
them until to-morrow morning, when we could all travel together?

Finally, to make things certain, they set a guard round us; not
a mere posse of sentries but the whole village, leper, idiot, police
chief and the mayor himself. The latter pitched a tent a few paces
from us; a ramshackle square thing which to the loud derision of our
boys, who were enjoying the situation to the full, blew down twice.
The others squatted with spears and rifles in a circle all round us. It
was a bitterly cold night. By dawn they looked frozen. We breakfasted, struck camp, loaded the lorry and waited. At eight the chief
came to say that we must go back. The barrier behind us was
removed. We climbed into the lorry. Even now the chief feared
a sudden dash for Dessye; he drew up his men across the road

with their rifles ready. The chief of police spoiled the gravity of the defence by trotting forward and asking us to take his photograph. Then, in a cheerful mood, we drove back to Addis Ababa, which with some rather ruthless driving we made before nightfall.

Our little trip had caused a mild scandal. As soon as it became known we had gone, officials from the Press Bureau had trotted round all the hotels with typewritten notices, dated the day before, saying that leave for Dessye was indefinitely postponed. A stout barricade and a military post were set up on the road out of Addis. The French journalists had lodged a formal protest that preferential treatment was being given us; Belattingetta Herui announced that we were enjoying a little holiday in camp five miles outside the capital; an American journalist cabled home that we were in chains. Mr Karam hung round us rather tentatively offering a bill for ten pounds; the return trip to Debra Birhan, he claimed, had not been specified in our original contract. We had missed no news of importance and had picked up through James, who had earned the esteem of one of our guards with the present of six matches, some interesting details of the Danakil raids and inter-regimental fighting near Dessye. On the whole it had been an enjoyable excursion.

5

Two days after our return general permission for Dessye was again issued, this time in earnest. Rumours, which proved groundless, of an Italian advance in the Fafan valley, drew a scamper of journalists to Harar, among them the correspondents of *The Times*, the *Morning Post*, and Reuter's. Patrick was still happily cruising round the Red Sea. In the end it was a scratch caravan which set out for Dessye. The Radical, the *Daily Express* correspondent and I were the only regular English journalists; an American preacher, a free-lance communist, and an unemployed German Jew deputised for more august principals. Only the cinema companies travelled impressively.

We started on the 19th and travelled without incident. We went in our own time. There was no possible advantage to be gained by priority, but habitual competition had by now unbalanced many, so that some lorries made a race of it, and neglected the common decencies of travel, passing by without offer of help a rival outfit stuck in a river-bed. An adolescent Canadian far outdistanced the rest of the field and arrived in Dessye a day ahead; I believe that on his return he was accorded a civic reception in his home town for this feat. Others preferred a more leisurely journey; stopped to fish and shoot on the way and compose descriptions of the scenery, which, a few hours after Debra Birhan, became varied and magnificent.

It was intensely cold on the plateau, with a continuous high wind. Sometimes we passed a handful of stragglers from one of the migrating armies; sometimes a slave or a free cultivator working in the fields, but it was mostly desolate country, bounded by a horizon of ever-receding ranges of blue mountain; occasionally the hills to our right fell away and revealed a sensational prospect of the Awash valley and Danakil plain, shimmering in the heat thousands of feet below.

Early in the afternoon of the second day we came suddenly and without warning – for the road was recent and not yet marked on any published map – upon an enormous escarpment, a rocky precipice open before our wheels; far below lay a broad valley, richly cultivated and studded with small hemispherical hills, each crowned with a church or a cluster of huts. Down this awful cliff the track fell in a multitude of hairpin bends; surveyed from above the gradient seemed, in places, almost perpendicular; there was barely clearance for the wheels; on the off-side the edge crumbled away into space; at the corners the road was sharply inclined in the wrong direction. Our Harari driver gave a sigh of despair. Straight down the face of the cliff transecting the road at each turn led a precipitous footpath. Nominally to lighten the truck, actually because we were thoroughly scared, the Radical and I decided to go down on foot. It was a stiff descent; with every step the air became warmer as though we were scrambling across the seasons. When we reached more tolerable ground we waited for the lorry, which presently arrived, the driver speechless but triumphant. All that night, James reported, he was talking in his sleep about braking and reversing.

We found a warm and sheltered camping-place a few miles from the foot of the escarpment, and here, shortly before sundown, we were visited by heralds from the local governor, Dedjasmach Matafara, who was living near by in temporary quarters, to ask us our business. I sent James to explain. He returned rather drunk to say that the Dedjasmach was 'very gentleman'. He was accompanied by slaves bearing a present of *tedj*, native bread and a young sheep; also an invitation to breakfast the next morning.

The Dedjasmach was a very old man, a veteran of the first battle of Adowa, corpulent, ponderous in his movements, with unusually dark skin and a fine white beard. He bore a marked resemblance to the portraits of the Emperor Menelik. His normal residence was some way off at Ankober; he was here on duty patrolling the road.

He occupied a series of huts behind a well-made stockade. There was a circular *tukal* where he slept and where, on our arrival, he was completing his toilet; there was a larger, square building for eating and the transaction of business, a cook-house, women's and soldiers' quarters, and in the centre an open space, part farmyard and part barrack square. Soldiers, slaves and priests thronged the place, disputing it with cattle and poultry.

James stood at our side to interpret. The Dedjasmach greeted us with great politeness and dignity, slipped on a pair of elastic-sided boots and led us across to the dining-room. The preparations were simple. One of the sheets was taken from the Dedjasmach's bed and stretched across the centre of the hut to shield us from public view; behind it, in almost complete darkness, a low wicker table was laid with piles of native bread. The Radical and I, the Dedjasmach and two priests, sat down at little stools. James stood beside us. Two women slaves stood with horsehair whisks, fanning away the flies. Abyssinian bread is made in thin, spongy discs. It is used very conveniently as both plate and spoon. The curry – a fiery but rather delicious dish which forms the staple food of those who can afford it – is ladled out into the centre of the bread; morsels are then wrapped up in pieces torn from the edge and put into the mouth. The Dedjasmach courteously helped us to tit-bits from his own pile. Other slaves brought us horn mugs of *tedj* – a heavy drink at eight in the morning. Conversation was intermittent and rather laborious;

it consisted chiefly of questions addressed to us by our host and the priests. They asked us our ages, whether we were married, how many children. One of the priests recorded this information in a little exercise book. The Dedjasmach said he loved the English because he knew that they too hated the Italians. The Italians were a poor sort of people, he said; one of his friends had killed forty of them, one after the other, with his sword. He asked us if we knew General Harrington; he had been a good man; was he still alive? Then he returned to the question of the Italians. They did not like the smell of blood, he said; when they smelled blood they were afraid; when an Abyssinian smelled blood he became doubly brave; that was why the sword was better than the gun.

Besides, he said, the Italians disliked fighting so much they had to be given food free before they would do it; he knew this for a fact; he had seen it himself forty years ago; they had great carts loaded with food and wine to persuade the men to fight; Abyssinians scorned that; each man brought his own rations and, if he had one, his own mule. He asked us when the Emperor was going to the war; that was where he should be, with his soldiers. The Abyssinians fought better if the Emperor were looking on; each strove to attract his attention with deeds of valour.

Water was brought for us to bathe our hands; then little cups of bitter coffee. Finally we made our adieux. He invited us, when the troubles were over, to come and visit him at Ankober. He asked us to take two soldiers with us to Dessye; we pointed out that our lorry was already overladen, but he insisted, saying that some people had been killed on the road lately. Slightly drunk, we stepped out into the brilliant morning sunshine. One of the soldiers who was accompanying us had to sell his mule before he could start. At last the transaction was complete. He bundled in at the back with the boys; we were saved the embarrassment of the second by the arrival, just as we were starting, of a French journalist. We told him that the Dedjasmach had sent the soldier for him and he accepted the man gratefully.

Then we resumed the journey.

It had been more than a pleasant interlude; it had been a glimpse of the age-old, traditional order that still survived, gracious and sturdy, out of sight beyond the brass bands and bunting, the topees and humane humbug of Tafari's régime; of an order doomed to destruction. Whatever the outcome of the present war: mandate or conquest or internationally promoted native reform – whatever resulted at Geneva or Rome or Addis Ababa, Dedjasmach Matafara and all he stood for was bound to disappear. But we were pleased to have seen it and touched hands across the centuries with the court of Prester John.

On the fourth day we reached Dessye. The second part of the journey was varied and enjoyable. We crossed several streams and one considerable river where we stuck for several hours, unloaded and finally heaved the truck clear on our shoulders, but there were no serious obstacles to compare with the escarpment; we passed a hot spring and an army – Dedjasmach Bayana's, which had left Addis fourteen days before; they had found a sugar plantation, and every man was sucking a cane as he shambled along; Bayana himself maintained the same pomp as when he had paraded before the Emperor; he rode under a black umbrella, surrounded by his domestic slaves and led-mules still adorned with their ceremonial trappings; a team of women followed him carrying jars of *tedj* under crimson cotton veils. We passed through belts of forest, full of birds and game and monkeys and brilliant flowers. Then the road suddenly improved in quality and began to mount. It took an hour to reach the town from the moment when we came into sight. It lay high up in a cup in the mountains, surrounded on all sides by hills; the road from Addis twisted and doubled, led through a narrow pass into the city, and out again to the north, where it led direct to the front for twenty miles and then petered out into the original caravan track.

Dessye is a place of recent creation; an Abyssinian military outpost in the Mohammedan Wollo country. In appearance it was very much like a miniature of Addis Ababa – the same eucalyptus-trees, the same single shopping street, the same tin roofs, a Gibbi built on an eminence dominating the town. There were a few Armenian storekeepers, an American Adventist Mission at the extremity of the town, a French Mission a mile or so distant.

The most solid building was the former Italian consulate, deserted now, and, it was rumoured, under preparation for the Emperor's coming. The inhabitants were Abyssinian squatters; the Wollo Gallas came in for the weekly market but lived in the villages. There was a large Coptic church and a building, ecclesiastical in appearance, which was in reality the private house of the Dedjas-mach. At the time of our arrival this building was flying the Red Cross in honour of the two Irishmen who had lately arrived, and an anti-aircraft gun was mounted on the balcony.

The place was full of soldiers; a detachment of the Imperial Guard was quartered in the grounds of the Italian consulate; the irregulars slept in a ring of encampments along the surrounding hillside. They came into town at dawn and remained until sunset, drinking, quarrelling and sauntering about the streets; more were arriving daily and the congestion was becoming perilous. The chiefs were under orders to leave for the front, but they hung on, saying that they would not move until the Emperor led them in person. It was partly for this purpose that his arrival was expected.

We reported to the mayor, a stocky, bearded figure who had disgraced himself in London and now happily compromised in his costume between the new and old régimes by wearing beard and cloak of a traditional cut and, below them, shorts and red and white ringed football stockings. He passed us on to the chief of police, who, that afternoon, was tipsy. Eventually we found a camping-ground for ourselves in the compound of the local branch of the Ethiopian Bank, an institution of indiscernible value, for it could neither cash cheques, change notes or accept deposits. Here we spent the first night, moving next day to the Adventist Mission, who hospitably threw open their large park to the journalists.

For so many weeks now Dessye had been our goal – a promised land sometimes glimpsed from afar, sometimes impenetrably ob-scured, sometimes seen in a mirage a stone's throw away in crystal detail, always elusive, provocative, desirable – that its pursuit had become an end in itself. Now that, at length, we found ourselves actually there, when the tents were pitched and the stores unpacked and all round us a village of tents had sprung up, we began to wonder what precisely we had gained by the journey. We were two hundred or so miles nearer the Italians, but for any contact we had with the battlefield or information about what was happening, we were worse off than at Addis Ababa. A field wireless had been established on the hillside a mile out of the town. Here we all hurried to enquire about facilities and were told, to our surprise, that messages of any length might be sent. At Addis there had been a limit of two hundred words. All messages from Dessye had to be retransmitted from Addis. It seemed odd, but we were used to unaccountable happenings. That evening all over the camp type-writers were tapping as the journalists spread themselves over five hundred, eight hundred, a thousand words messages describing the perils of the journey. Two days later we were cheerfully informed that none of the messages had been sent, that no more could be accepted until further notice, that when the station reopened there would be a limit of fifty words and a rigid censorship. So there, for the time being, our professional activities ended.

A week passed in complete idleness. The Emperor's arrival was daily predicted and daily postponed. Lij Yasu died, and James, who had been dining with Mohammedan friends in the town, and drinking in Christian fashion, returned in a high state of excitement to say that the Emperor would be murdered if he attempted to show himself among the Wollo Gallas.

An Abyssinian gentleman named Dedjasmach Gugsa Ali enjoyed what must be one of the briefest periods of official favour in recorded history; he was the former governor of a neighbouring district, had been deposed, and had lived for many years in disgrace. He now followed the prevailing fashion and presented himself at the Gibbi and offered his submission. The governing Dedjasmach re-instated him, and in the name of the Emperor embraced him. Bowing low, Gugsa Ali withdrew from his presence, tripped over the doorstep and broke his neck.

The native members of the 'Ethiopian Red Cross' had a beano, stripped to the skin and danced round the tent of their American officer, who had only that evening moved his quarters to avoid contamination from his more worldly Irish colleagues.

The governing Dedjasmach made a strenuous and partly successful attempt to get some of the soldiers to the front. He organised a parade, and himself at their head, drums beating and bugles playing, led them Pied-Piper fashion up the Makale road, returning by himself after dark to the more agreeable accommodation of his own bedroom.

Every item of news became known to us all simultaneously; there was no hope of a scoop; the wireless station remained blandly obstructive. Relieved of the itch to cable the journalists displayed amiable characteristics which they had hitherto concealed. We became house proud; the Radical and I set a popular vogue by erecting the first latrine. Mr Prospero contrived an arc-light. We began to entertain and competed mildly in kitchen and service. Except for a Finnish misanthrope who maintained a front of unbroken hostility – and later on his return to Addis indulged in litigation at the American consular court against a colleague who punched him – the grimmest characters seemed to grow soft in idleness. On November 28 there was a Thanksgiving Dinner, attended by all except the Finn, and after it a drinking competition won – dishonestly we discovered later – by one of the Irishmen.

Next day it was announced officially that the Emperor was on the road, and on the 30th he arrived. The soldiers waited for him all day, squatting along the route, reeling and jostling about the streets. They had been surly and hostile for some days; now, exhilarated at the prospect of the Emperor's arrival, they became menacing, held up the cars of the cinema men, scowled and jeered through the heat of the day; then, towards evening, as it became cold, crowded shivering and morose. The royal mules in brilliant saddle cloths waited to take the Emperor on the last stage of his journey, up the hill to the Crown Prince's Gebbi, but the sun went down, the crowds began to melt away and the photographers were again deprived of a picturesque shot. At length he arrived, unobtrusively, in the darkness. From now on Dessye became his headquarters; in the new year he moved north; he was not to see Addis again until he arrived in the spring, in flight to the coast.

With the Emperor came a small circle of courtiers, including Lorenzo and David, and with them the official news. We had left

Addis in the expectation of a big Italian attack in the Fafan; it was now announced that the attack had completely failed, that Ras Desta had gained a decisive victory and that bands of Ethiopian Somalis were invading Italian territory and carrying out successful raids as far as the coast. In the north the Italian advance had come to an end; the garrison at Makale was almost cut off and a great concentration of troops at Amba Alagi – Imru's, Kassa's and Mou-lugetta's – were preparing to surround it. There was no mistaking the sincerity of the Court's optimism; three weeks before they had professed the same confidence but in a strained and anxious fashion; now, away from the tin and tarmac of Addis, in the keen air of the mountains, reverting to the simpler habits of their upbringing, they were openly jubilant.

Next day the Emperor came to visit the American hospital. The wards were fairly full, but not with war wounded; there were several venereal cases and some of influenza contracted on the journey up (the Imperial Guard seemed to be of lower stamina than the irregular troops); there were a few soldiers who had deserted from Eritrea and got badly cut up by a company of Abyssinian troops deserting in the opposite direction; but there were no heroes upon whom the Emperor could suitably manifest his sympathy. In order to show the equipment of the hospital at its best advantage the doctors staged an operation – the amputation of a gangrened stump of arm. Emperor, Court and journalists crowded into the theatre; the photographers and cinema men took their shots. The Emperor asked, 'And where did this gallant man lose his hand?'

'Here in Dessye. The Dedjasmach had it cut off for stealing two besas' worth of corn.'

Meanwhile in Europe and America the editors and film magnates had begun to lose patience. They had spent large sums of money on the Abyssinian war and were getting very little in return; several journalists had already been recalled; the largest cinema company was beginning to pack up; now a general retreat began. I received my dismissal by cable on the day after the Emperor's arrival. For a few hours I considered staying on independently. That had been my original intention, but now the prospect seemed unendurably dismal. I had long wanted to spend Christmas at Bethlehem. This was the opportunity.

The war seemed likely to drag on without incident until the big rains; peace terms disappointing to both sides and heavy with future dangers would be devised and accepted. There would be an exchange of territory; Italy, after its ceremonious occupation, would clearly keep Adowa, perhaps the whole of the Tigre; Abyssinia would get an outlet to the sea, either at Assab or Zeila. Neither port would be valuable without European or American exploitation. The old wrangle, now acutely embittered, of competing concession hunters, spheres of influence, xenophobic local officials, obstructionist central government – the very situation which had brought about the present war – would begin anew. Disorder in the provinces, immensely aggravated by the recent profuse distribution of arms and munitions, would again challenge intervention. Perhaps there would be an attempt to put into effect the suggestions of the Five Power Conference in September; there might be an administration by international foreign advisers; their work, difficult enough among a people slightly scared at the unknown dangers of mechanised invasion, would be utterly impossible after a successful defence; the natural truculence of the Shoans would be confirmed by an absolute conviction of their superiority and invincibility. Italy would certainly be unrepresented in the foreign régime and her imperialist aspirations unsatisfied. There would be a complete end of any peaceful penetration; there would be a development loan and international bond holders would call for intervention. If it was to be effective, the international régime would find itself transformed into a coercive protectorate; perhaps a mandate would be granted to England and France – or at the worst to both; there might be an expensive war of conquest under League auspices; the sanctionist movement would appear to the whole world – as it already appeared to part of it – as a device of the great imperial powers to cut out a competitor.

There were still plenty of munitions and plenty of men in Abyssinia; there was on all sides an apparent zeal for the Emperor's cause. We knew that there was disaffection and disorganisation, but no one realised how fragile had been the whole structure of order in the country. Neither then in December, nor in the subsequent two months, did anyone in Abyssinia or Rome seriously anticipate the sudden, utter collapse of the Shoa monarchy.

Wherever one's sympathies lay – it was a situation in which an Englishman could have little enthusiasm either way – there seemed grounds for nothing except despond and exasperation. In this mood I left Dessye. There was a car travelling to Addis Ababa on Red Cross business in which I was able, illegally, to purchase a seat. We had to start before dawn in order to avoid notice from the Red Cross authorities. I took one servant, rations for the road, and left everything else with the Radical. James cried. It was an uneventful journey. The German driver – an adventurous young airman who had come to look for good fortune after serving in the Paraguayan war – kept a rifle across the wheel and inflicted slight wounds on the passing farmers at point-blank range.

Addis was dead. With the Emperor's departure the public services had settled into the accustomed coma. The bars were open but empty. A handful of journalists from the south were packing up to return to England. The mystery men had faded away.

After a few days I got down to Djibouti. At Diredawa the French garrison were firmly entrenched; half the town was a French fort. Djibouti was still crowded, still panicky. There were a number of journalists there reporting the war at leisure from their imaginations. One of them waged a pretty little war in his hotel bedroom with flags and a large-scale map; others were still happily photographing scenes of Abyssinian home life in the *quartier toleré*. Soon after I left some bombs had been dropped on Dessye and the chief excitement of Djibouti centred on a race to get the films of them back to Europe. Weeks later in Devon I saw them on the news reel. It was difficult to recapture the excitement, secrecy and competition that had attended their despatch.

News of the Hoare-Laval proposals reached us in the Red Sea; at Port Said we heard of their reception. Next day I was in Jerusalem and visited the Abyssinian monks, perched in their little African village on the roof of the Holy Sepulchre; Christmas morning in Bethlehem; desert and ruined castles in Transjordan; like the rest of the world I began to forget about Abyssinia.

CHAPTER 6

ADDIS ABABA DURING THE FIRST DAYS
OF THE ITALIAN EMPIRE

1

BUT IT WAS not so easy. With the withdrawal of the special correspondents, news from Abyssinia became meagre and inconspicuous;
soon it consisted mainly of the official communiqués issued by the
rival governments. In February, Desta's army was routed on the
Southern front and Graziani pursued him to Negelli. But this was
not the advance we had expected. The Jijiga front was unbroken;
strategists still saw the campaign in terms of the Fafan route and the
railway; it was not yet realised that Badoglio would attempt and
perform the stupendous feat of taking Addis Ababa from the North.
In March, for the first time, English editors began to give preference
to the Italian bulletins. In April it was clear that the Abyssinian
armies were in a bad way, but the Emperor's flight in the beginning
of May surprised the world. Some vivid accounts followed of anarchy and destruction. Then on the arrival of the Italians the last
foreign journalists left the country and the English newspapers
stopped printing Abyssinian news. There were other crises, the
German occupation of the Rhine frontier, the Spanish civil war.

Sanctions were abolished after a few hours' debate. The Liberals,
who in the preceding months had emerged from the shadows, so
swollen with indignation as to become a bogey to their peaceable
fellow citizens, were allowed to deflate, noisily but without much
harm, in the correspondence columns of the Conservative press.
Some memorable phrases were devised; one indignant letter writer
described the areas given over to banditry, where the Italians had
not yet established garrisons, as 'pockets of legitimate government'.

It is by no means the first time in English history that the world
has been almost fatally confused by mistaking the peevish whinny of
the nonconformist conscience for the voice of the nation. It often

happens. Someone is always the loser for it. This time it was the unfortunate Emperor of Abyssinia. The country – except for its perennial distrust of the Mediterranean races – was apathetic.

But for those of us who knew Abyssinia it was not so easy. There were countless loose ends. Why had Abyssinia broken up so suddenly? How was the new régime really working? Where were the Italian garrisons? Had the Government of the West any real existence? Were the submissions of the Rases genuine? What had happened to David and James and M. Idot? I received weekly copies of a paper devoted to Abyssinian propaganda, edited by an English suffragette; it was full of startling stories of the state of the country. The continental papers printed an interview with Ras Seyoum in which he was reported as saying, 'I think your aeroplanes are marvellous.' The missionary who had described in harrowing terms the sufferings of a nation whose women and children were being blinded by gas, now wrote to say that their sight had been restored. What was really happening? Curiosity could only be satisfied by another visit. Accordingly, at the beginning of June, I applied for permission to return. At the end of July it was granted.

I was the first Englishman to get into the country since its occupation and it seemed reasonable to expect that I should be able to sell a few articles to the newspapers. A year before every scrap of information and conjecture had been avidly gobbled up. But now the subject was dead except for the dribble of complaint in the correspondence column. The attitude of Fleet Street was typified when, one morning shortly before my departure, I received a letter from an editor saying, in terms which had then grown familiar, that he regretted that there was no longer any interest in Abyssinian conditions; beside it on the breakfast-tray lay that morning's issue of his paper and prominently displayed on its middle page a letter written from an address in England by an Englishman who, I think, had no possible access to special information, describing the distress prevalent in Abyssinia, and calling upon Italy to redeem her 'tarnished honour' by relieving it.

So, independent of any commissions from Fleet Street, drawn by motives of curiosity which seemed, in the stifling passage of the Red Sea, daily less compelling, I found myself once more in Djibouti, where eight months before I had taken ship with the fervent resolve never, in any circumstances, to set foot there again.

The place was uninhabitable. The hotels were full; rows of Italian officers lying restlessly in camp beds and on tables in the public rooms gave them at night the appearance of improvised hospitals. The shifting population of polyglot refugees was now swollen by recent extraditions from up the line. Sitting in Regas's café one was able to count the familiar figures lounging past, with their familiar, questing faces. I had not been there ten minutes before I was joined by a Greek informer. 'The Italians will not let you go to Addis Ababa. They have even expulsed me.'

I told him that I already had my visa. He shook his head sagely.

'Mr Waugh, do not go there. You have no idea what the conditions are up country. The Italians are starving. The soldiers live on a piece of bread a day. Nothing can be bought in the shops. No one will accept the Italian money. The Abyssinians are encamped all round the town. Dessye has been evacuated. The Italians hold Addis Ababa, the railway-line and the road to Makale – beyond that nothing. Last week they were still attempting to take Ankober. No one can go a hundred yards outside the town. Last month the railway was cut for ten days. Bandits march into the town whenever they like. They are fighting every day in the centre of the town. All the natives have arms hidden. When the Italians made an order for them to be given up they brought in only the old rifles. Every tukal has a new machine gun under the floor. Only last month they captured a train of lorries on the Dessye road and took all the ammunition. At a given signal the people will rise and massacre the Italians. By the twenty-fifth of September Addis will be in the hands of the Abyssinians. This time they will spare no one. Even the Gallas have turned against the Italians. They were given all kinds of promises and nothing has been done. They say in Europe that the war is over. It is only beginning. The people have got rid of Tafari. Now they can fight in their own way.'

It was the old Djibouti story adapted to the new conditions. One had heard it before in another form. It was never credible but it never failed to depress. For half an hour he poured out his warnings.

Then he took his leave. 'I hope to come to England soon. Mr Balfour will be *very* pleased to see me. I will visit you too in your home.'

The Somali hawkers loped in and out among the crowd selling cheroots, shirts and native daggers. Among them were two or three who had seen European service in the preceding year.

'Good evening, sir. I brought you a letter once from Mr Collins when you were staying at the Consulate at Harar.' ... 'Good evening, Mr Waugh, did you find the hat you lost at Direda-wa?' ... 'How is Mr Balfour?' ... 'Do you remember me, sir? I was with Mr Roper. My brother-in-law was shot with the British major.' ... 'How is the American with red hair?' ... 'Good evening, sir, it was I who drove Captain P.'s motor when you had dinner with him at Addis Ababa.'

Their memory and curiosity were amazing. Once they were recognised they forgot about their merchandise and asked searching questions about the subsequent histories of the journalists. Were they married; when were they coming back to Ethiopia. I asked some of them how they liked the new régime. There was plenty of work, they said; some Somalis were making good money. I tried to press the point; did the Somalis like being ruled by the Italians? Some Somalis made plenty of money, they said, others not so much.

'But are you glad the Emperor went away?'

'Those that make money are glad. Some are sorry.'

'Why are they sorry?'

'Because they do not make money.'

The train next day was densely crowded, almost exclusively by Italians – soldiers, government officials, traders, engineers, prospectors. It was impossible at this stage to distinguish them, for they were obliged to travel through French territory in civilian clothes. There was a general in plus-fours. An artillery officer who had been on my ship and who, through the heat of the Red Sea, had paraded the decks in riding-boots and spurs, now appeared in crumpled shorts. It was a curious spectacle to see the rear-guard of a conquering army queueing up, presenting their passports, buying their railway tickets in an unfamiliar foreign currency, struggling with porters over their suitcases, as they made their entry into the new empire. Some, who had not got their mufti unpacked, had to unpick the stars and decorations from their tunics with nail scissors. It was a temporary inconvenience. During my stay in Abyssinia the agreement was made with France about the control of the railway; meanwhile the French officials insisted rigidly on every formality, with, as I found later at Diredawa, a substantial profit to someone over the currency regulations.

There was a perceptible thrill of enthusiasm throughout the train as we crossed into Italian territory. The section of the line between the frontier and Diredawa was fairly secure and the guards were not much larger than they had been under the old régime, but there were patriotic demonstrations at each station, often broken by cordial shouts of recognition as a soldier ran up to the running-board to greet a friend.

Diredawa, like every place I visited in the country, was enormously full. The French garrison – about six hundred strong – was still there. In addition there was a large Italian camp and air-base. Here, too, travellers were sleeping three or four to a room. The streets in the evening were thronged with soldiers, sauntering about in groups, looking like schoolboys on a wet Sunday of term, as soldiers always do look who have few duties and very little pocket-money.

It seemed suitable to begin my tour with a visit to the devastated areas. Accordingly next day I drove over to Harar and spent two nights with my former host at the British Consulate. He is a man who shuns publicity and for that reason alone I have been obliged to omit any detailed description of his achievements during the preceding eighteen months. From the attack on Walwal until the time of his departure, shortly after my visit, he worked alone in circumstances of constant anxiety, aggravated at the end by a grave attack of fever. He dealt with a situation of the utmost delicacy and responsibility, a responsibility out of all proportion to his seniority in his service. It is too little to say – but it is all I dare say without fear of antagonising him and betraying his hospitality – that of the honours distributed among the various Englishmen who distinguished themselves in Abyssinia during this unhappy period, none was more admirably earned than his.

I spent a day walking about the city, calling on people I had known before, visiting the bazaars and public buildings, wandering about in the lanes, peering into the *tedj* houses. A few months before it had been bombarded, burned, and – it was reported in the English press – sacked. Patrick Balfour had written an eloquent lament for it, headed '*This was a City*'. It was practically unchanged. It was a little cleaner. The paving of the main streets was rather smoother. There were a great number of Italians about and fewer Abyssinians. The third best café was now called the Albergo Savoia. Most of the shops displayed pictures of Mussolini and the King of Italy. But in its general aspect it was the same city. The Hararis had come back in crowds; their gay costume filled the streets. The market, which had been almost squeezed out of existence by Abyssinian impositions, was now going merrily. Merrily was the word. There could be no two opinions about whether the Hararis liked the change. They could now bring their produce into the town free of duty; the labour which had before been conscripted was now voluntary and, by local standards, highly paid. The Indians looked sulky. The currency restrictions hit them hard. They were now obliged to spend their money in the country where they earned it and that is not the way of the East African Indian trader. The Abyssinian priests, depleted in number by the religious enthusiasm of the Somali bands, looked less than comfortable. But the Hararis were clearly in the best of humours.

People write and speak as though in the first few hours of the next war all the capital cities of Europe will be turned to dust. The Italian aeroplanes had had the place to themselves without any opposing aircraft or any serious interference from the ground, but the ravages of the bombardment were hard to find. There had always been a large proportion of ruinous houses in Harar. They were still there, many black from the recent fire. The rest had been repaired, almost effortlessly. The town was nearly empty at the time of the attack. When the inhabitants returned they had shovelled out the débris, patched the roofs, and settled down to their normal life. The build-ings which had taken it worst were the Abyssinian church, the drawing-room of the French doctor, and the Catholic church. There government workmen were still engaged in restoration. It was a revelation to me to see how little damage a bomb does. The Catholic church had suffered a direct hit from a standard bomb. The roof was new but there were the same pictures on the walls, the same plaster statues, the same carved woodwork. There were a number of splinter holes, but one had to go round with a guide and have the damage pointed out. Throughout the entire campaign the heaviest casualties from air raids seem always to have been caused not by bombs, but by machine-gunning from the air.

The day was brilliant; the night limpid cool. The consulate garden was full of highly coloured birds. There was no shortage of food; the market was full of fruit, green vegetables and the best possible coffee. The consulate cow was in milk. Even the news that a party of bandits, eight hundred rifles strong, had been sauntering across the Diredawa road a week before, could not destroy the feeling of secure well-being. By contrast Addis was a place of sepulchral gloom.

The approach was miserable. The Somali-Abyssinian borders have always been a paradise for the money changer. At the moment they presented a microcosm of the world monetary chaos. There were seven sorts of currency of fluctuating value. First the lira which had been proclaimed the official money of the country; but notes of 500 or 1,000 lire carried the disadvantage that, though they were current at par within the territory, it was criminal to cross the frontier either way in their possession; they were liable to confiscation at the customs and thus could only be changed for notes of lower denomination at a 20 per cent. discount. There were, as always, the two sorts of franc, Banque de France and Banque d'Indo-Chine, which have long proved a source of petty exaction at Djibouti. These might be exported and imported freely and were thus greatly in demand; one could change them into lire very profitably but illegally. Then there was the Maria Theresa thaler which was still nominally current. This had been fixed at the value of 5 lire, with the result that it had instantly disappeared from circulation. It was still the only coin acceptable to natives outside Addis and Diredawa. Then there were the notes of the Bank of Ethiopia which no one used to want but which had now attained a sudden and temporary vogue, in spite of the liquidation of the Bank, because they were the official currency of the French railway; and finally there were the nickel half- and quarter-thalers which, though they were still legal tender, no one wanted at any price.

The complexity of the situation was impressed on me when I attempted to buy my railway ticket from Diredawa to Addis. I came to the guichet with a wallet full of lire and francs. The clerk informed me I must pay in thalers. Where was I to get them? With a fine imitation of the classic shrug of the French *fonctionnaire* he told me that that was my business. I went to Mohamedaly's. The manager told me that his brother had now been waiting ten days, trying to collect enough thalers for his ticket to Djibouti. I was willing to pay a good price for them, I said. So, remarked the manager, was his brother. Mr Costi, the manager at Bololakos's Hotel, had a good laugh when I tried to change money with him. Everyone in Diredawa wanted thalers, he said. But what must I do? I must stay in Diredawa like everyone else, Mr Costi suggested; he added that it was now a very agreeable town, a military band played there twice a week in the main street.

Eventually a Czecho-Slovak was discovered who had a small cache he was willing to change against sterling; so in great secrecy – we were liable to be gaoled for it – and at an extravagant price, I was able to buy fifty. The transaction took place in a bedroom. It was like buying cocaine.

Rain began soon after we left Diredawa and continued almost without intermission for the two days of the journey. There was a machine-gun section posted at the front of the train; another at the rear. From Awash to Addis the line was heavily guarded. There had been sharp fighting there in the previous month. A train was derailed and sacked, two bridges destroyed and a station besieged for a day and a half. For ten days trains could not get through. The affair was inadequately reported from official sources and enormously exaggerated by rumour. Several lives were lost. When it was all over a Greek woman was discovered under the train, clutching two children, scared almost out of her wits but uninjured except for a black eye. After that Eritrean troops had been sent to 'clean up' the villages in the vicinity. By all accounts they had done the job with relish. Now there were blackshirts and white troops camped in the mud at every station. They called out for newspapers as we passed. At one station we met a group of Italian soldiers talking to each other in English. They were volunteers from the United States who had forgotten their native language. All the white troops, both here and elsewhere, looked very fit and very bored.

The children along the line crowded round the carriages begging in their accustomed manner. But they had learned some new tricks. *Si salute romanamente.* They could all cry *Viva Duce!* Some of them could sing 'Giovanezza'. They were rewarded with handfuls of small change.

The promise of the station-master at Diredawa that another coach would be added at Awash to relieve the acute overcrowding was not fulfilled. Eventually, at sunset on the second day, we came to the end of our journey.

2

I was received two days later by the Viceroy. He lived in temporary quarters at the Emperor's New Gibbi, in the minimum of personal splendour. Indeed it would have been impossible to be splendid in that seedy villa. The structure had suffered little during the days of pillage, but it had been robbed of most of its furniture and looked as woebegone as a bankrupt casino. The floors were stripped of their carpets and the cheap parquet was already buckled and warped; patches of damp discoloured the paint; here and there plaster had cracked and flaked away; curtains had been torn down and windowpanes broken; strands of wire protruded from walls, ceilings and cornices, where the rioters had snatched at sconces and electric fittings. (The mob were fanciful in their depredations. A Swedish doctor, who had given his whole life to the service of the Abyssinians, was shocked to encounter a Galla woman walking out of his surgery with his microscope balanced on her head.)

The Viceroy's own apartments were tolerably furnished with the few gilt chairs and imitation French tables that had been salvaged. Graziani was in his Marshal's field uniform sitting at a desk laden with official papers. The autocratic tradition persisted and he found himself, I was told, responsible for the details of every branch of the administration; every decision, however trivial, was referred to him.

He gave me twenty minutes. I have seldom enjoyed an official audience more. His French was worse than mine, but better than my Italian. Too often when talking to minor fascists one finds a fatal love of oratory. The morning before I had been present when the German Consul-General paid a visit to the fascist headquarters. The officer-in-charge – a blackshirt political boss from Milan – had straddled before us, thrown out his chin, flashed his gold teeth and addressed his audience of half a dozen upon the resurgence of Rome, the iniquity of sanctions and the spirit of civilisation and the Caesars, in a manner carefully modelled upon that of the Duce speaking from the balcony of the Palazzo Venezia. There was no nonsense of that kind about Graziani. He was like the traditional conception of an English admiral, frank, humorous and practical. He asked where I had been, what I had seen, what I wanted to see. Whenever my requests were reasonable he gave his immediate consent. If he had to refuse anything he did so directly and gave his reasons. He did not touch on general politics or the ethics of conquest. He did not ask me to interpret English public opinion. How long had I got for my visit? Did that time include my return journey? He knew exactly how long it would take under existing conditions to reach any particular place, what facilities I should find for transport, what accommodation on arrival. He urged me to go South and see the line of his own advance. I said I preferred, in the limited time at my disposal, to visit the North. He immediately authorised my journey from Asmara as far as Lake Ashangi and, if I wished it, to Dessye; I might use the military air service from Diredawa to Massawa. He made a few caustic and well-deserved criticisms on the war-time press service in Addis Ababa. He declined to commit himself about the ultimate development of the new territory; his immediate concern was the job in hand – pacification. Then, referring to a dossier before him: 'You were here for the Negus' coronation. Would you recognise the crown?'

He called to his clerk, who unlocked a red plush hat-box and produced the crown of Ethiopia, recently recovered from the looters. It was not the old crown of Theodore which we used to keep in London, but the silver-gilt local product used for the coronation, about which reporters at the time had composed such extravagant fables. It had never been very beautiful or very valuable. Now it was a pathetic, commonplace thing, the cross at the top loose and hanging askew; every stone had been prised out of it. But it was still recognisable as the ornament that had been used on that absurd occasion. It recalled the aspect of the assembled dignitaries – the Duke of Gloucester, the Prince of Udine, Marshal d'Esperey, Mr Jacoby from the U.S.A., and all the meaningless good words that had graced the day. He asked about the book I was going to write; said he was sure he would not have time to read it, and dismissed me. I left with the impression of one of the most amiable and sensible men I had met for a long time.

3

It was clear that Asmara, not Addis, would have to be my centre for seeing the battlefields and the working of the new administration in the conquered territories. Meanwhile there was enough to keep me interested, between trains, in renewing acquaintances and observing the changes in the capital.

Addis, as has been already suggested, was never a town of outstanding amenities. At this season of this particular year it seemed preternaturally forbidding. The central square, where the Post Office, the two cinemas and the principal European shops had stood, was still as it had been left by the rioters, a heap of blackened masonry, charred timber and twisted iron. For weeks now the Dessye Road had been impassable; the railway was the sole means of communication with the outside world and this had been working to its utmost capacity to keep the city, whose population was now increased by a garrison of forty thousand troops, in flour and the bare necessaries of life. It had been impossible to import building materials and all work of reconstruction had thus been postponed until after the rains. Every available building had been taken over to provide quarters for the new civil and military population; a ring of temporary forts protected the city, where the men lived under canvas behind timber stockades and waged a ceaseless war on the floodwater which seeped in from all sides and lay everywhere in shallow pools of muck. The commissariat department were faced with a formidable task. They provided an adequate supply of essential food, but no surplus and very few luxuries. Prices, though controlled, were abnormally high; most things were three or four times their usual price, some things ten times; eggs, milk, butter and vegetables were very rare indeed. The private soldier's five lire a day did not go far in supplementing his rations; he had wine once a week and lived mainly on coarse dry bread and spaghetti and meat stew. Petrol was rigidly controlled; an occasional densely crowded bus might be seen, but the taxis, once so numerous, had disappeared from the streets. So had the natives. The crowds of white figures which formerly had filled the streets, teeming in to market, lounging and trotting and brawling from sunrise to dusk, were scattered about the countryside. They were shy of the new regulations. They did not like the new money. They had nothing to sell. Many of the tukals had been destroyed and deserted during the riots. The native population who remained were being humanely treated. Those who had got employment were well paid, but there was an ample supply of white labour for most purposes of the moment. A big school had been established where the children were fed, clothed and taught to sing patriotic songs. They were the happiest people in the city. The Italians, as everyone knows, love children and it was the most common sight to see groups of Italian soldiers playing with small Abyssinians in a manner which shocked the race-conscious of the German colony.

It was difficult to get information about what was going on outside, for beyond the stockades lay a closed country, but people who had lately come to town reported that wherever they went in Shoa and round Addis they found that the fields had not been planted. It seems almost certain that during its first year the new régime will be faced with serious famine throughout the whole district from Addis Ababa to Amba Alagi.

The foreign population were far from easy. They had changed the names of the shops and cafés – Ristorante di Bologna, Vulpa di Roma, etc. – and made the most cordial demonstrations of loyalty, but the authorities were gradually weeding out the undesirables; they had always been a shady lot and few of them can, at heart, have felt much confidence in their own desirable qualities. The Idots had gone. M. Kakophilos remained. M. and Mme Moriatis survived but in sadly reduced circumstances. *Le Select* had been completely sacked in the riots. Moriatis inhabited a temporary shed among the ruins and was struggling through the transition period by selling cups of coffee to lorry drivers. He still spoke hopefully of the chic bar, restaurant and cinema which he would build after the rains. Meanwhile he was being cut out by the most improbable of competitors – Mr and Mrs Heft. The *Deutsches Haus* was now named 'Pensione Germanica'. My bedroom was used for dinner and the former dining-room was metamorphosed. A new, almost modernistic bar ran along one side of it, served by a white barman in a white mess-jacket with scarlet carnation. The faithful Orgi, the only one of Heft's servants to fight for him in the riots, collected hats and sticks at the door. An illuminated aeroplane propeller revolved in the ceiling and Heft in dinner-jacket and stiff shirt presided over a highly decorous and much frequented 'dancing'. There were no geese now in the yard to attack his elegant clientele.

There was a general sense of insecurity – unreasonable but infectious. The raids on the town were futile; the chance of a rising inside it, remote. But all the time there was an illusion of being besieged. The thick groves of eucalyptus which surround Addis on all sides provided perfect cover for attack and retreat; no attempt had been made to cut a defensive boulevard; the bandits could and frequently did advance unobserved to a few yards of the outer defences; more than this, the circumference of the town is so large and its boundaries so ill defined, the ground so broken with water-courses and footpaths, that they could effortlessly penetrate the defences at twenty places. If they left their arms behind them they could walk into the town by the main roads unchallenged. In an attack in July several hundred armed raiders got into the centre of the city before they were discovered and wiped out in one of the gulleys. A few days before my arrival an English acquaintance of mine was visited at his house, on a small matter of business, by a young Abyssinian chief whom he knew to be a bandit. The youth said he had left his machine gun in the charge of his companions a mile or so outside the town and was taking a day's holiday to see how things were going. He was returning that evening to do a little shooting. My friend said: 'You are mad. There are forty thousand fully equipped troops in this town. There are not five thousand Abyssinian soldiers within a week's march. Go back to your farm. Leave your machine gun where it is. Grow food for the coming year and forget about the war.'

'Oh no, you are entirely misinformed. The city will be taken next week or the week after. The English have sent two hundred aeroplanes and they are coming to bomb it.' And he went back confidently to his machine gun in the woods.

We had a raid one evening during the four days of my visit. I had an appointment that afternoon to visit Ras Hailu; drove out to his house beyond the American hospital and was politely informed that his Highness was unable to see me; he had gone out to a battle. From the tukals round Hailu's house his soldiers were scampering about with rifles, buckling on their cartridge belts; others were loading a car with ammunition cases. The official of the Ministero Stampa, who was looking after me, seemed embarrassed. It was the first I had heard of it. Later the news got about. Ras Kassa's son was attacking the aerodrome. Bombers arrived from Diredawa. It was quite a battle. They fought on for some hours and then retreated after robbing a few bodies. At dawn we were disturbed by artillery shelling the woods from the old Gibbi. All that day the European underworld went about with despondent expressions. There was to be another attack that night, in great strength, they said; this time the natives inside would rise and massacre the garrison. Nothing happened; not a shot was fired. But, however extravagant one knew these rumours to be, they made one restless.

I dined that night at our legation and found, when the car came for me, that the Italians had thoughtfully posted a bearded carabinieri, armed with a light machine gun, on the seat beside the chauffeur. On the preceding afternoon the German Consul-General had given me a lift in his car. I was discomfited to find myself sitting on two hand-grenades which he always kept loose in case of emergency on the seat next to him.

Nothing could be easier but, in fact, less candid than to make political copy, as many émigrés have done, of incidents of this kind. It would be easy to write ironically about the Pax Romana and contrast the public utterances in Rome with conditions in the heart of the new Empire. It would be easy to represent the Italian conquest, as the Greek at Djibouti had done, as a bluff which, in the general anxiety of the world, everyone in Europe was eager to accept without investigation. It is for precisely this reason that the Italians have closed the frontier to foreign journalists. I can well imagine what some of the more excitable of my former colleagues could have made of the material.

The truth, I think, is simply this. That the Italians have had a thoroughly dismal wet season. They have never for a moment been in serious danger. Lorries have been ambushed, sentries have been sniped. They do not pretend, at the moment, to effective control of more than the strategic skeleton of the country. There are vast areas which are wholly given over to marauding bands of Abyssinians. These men owe no sort of allegiance to the former Shoan monarchy, or to any leader above their immediate chief. They exist in companies of anything from five thousand to a hundred. They live by pillage. They have a good supply of arms and ammunition, partly the remains of those issued to them by the Emperor, partly what they took from the armouries which he threw open to them when he fled, partly what they have captured from the Italians. At Gore itself and for an infinitesimal radius about it there was something which still claimed to be the legitimate successor to the Emperor's government;[1] the rest of the country is a no-man's-land where the Italians or any European protectors[2] are eagerly awaited by the population who at present are suffering hideous depredations.

This lapse into anarchy is a thing which greatly surprised those who know the country well, and is barely comprehensible to those who do not. When the Abyssinian armies broke the men did

---

1 Imru is now credibly reported to have fled to the Sudan. – E. W., *Oct. 9th*, 1936.
2 See the reports, unobtrusively summarised in *The Times* of September 28th, 1936, of the British Consul at Gore and the Sudan District Commissioner at Gambeila.

not, as might have been expected, make their way home as best they could to their own farms; they formed into small, mutually hostile, bands. It was not merely a question of the subject tribes revolting against the Amharas – nearly everyone had expected that – but of the Amharas savagely at war among themselves. I met in Addis Ababa a European doctor who had had the unique experience of spending the whole of the war with the army of Ayula Berru. He was unconnected with any Red Cross unit. At the beginning of hostilities he had been asked by the Emperor to go North and attend this chief who was ill. He had consented on condition that he was allowed to return immediately. This was promised. He was flown to Berru's camp, where he found 15,000 men, first-class fighting material, well armed. He cured the chief but his application to return was refused. From then onwards he shared the fortunes of the army. They advanced in the highest spirits, won two sharp engagements and by December were in a strong position to harass the Italian lines of communication, then unduly extended and suffering from grave difficulties. This was consistently forbidden by the Emperor, who maintained intermittent relations with them by wireless. The army halted and camped on the Eritrean frontier. From that moment desertions began in ever-increasing numbers. They were bombed regularly but the country was full of caves and casualties were not serious. Gas was used but accounted for only eighteen lives.[1] The men were bored and exasperated with a weapon to which they could make no effective answer. In two months the army had dwindled to 5,000 men. Berru then began his retreat. Once the army was in column it provided an easy target. They were consistently bombed from the air by day. At night they could not make camp because they

---

[1] It is difficult to get reliable figures, but it seems that at no time was gas or ypirite very effective as a lethal weapon. Nor was it primarily used as such. Its value to the invading army was to sterilise the bush along the line of advance, so that the mechanised column could push forward rapidly without fear of ambush. It was not used at Dessye or Harar or, as far as I know, on any town. Great publicity was given at the time to the gas cases which came to the hospitals for treatment. All wounds and all the effects of war are, of course, hideous. Actually those caused by gas and ypirite appear to have been far fewer in number and more temporary in character than those of other weapons. In breaking the Abyssinian morale machine-gunning from the air appears to have proved the most effective arm.

were being followed and attacked at every stage of their journey by their own deserters. They reached Gondar after a frightful march, during which they had been on the move day and night with no provisions other than what they could find in a countryside already pillaged by their former comrades. At Gondar they found the town fortified against them by the inhabitants. They turned North again and for weeks stumbled back along the road they had come, starving, ragged, dwindling daily in number from casualties and desertions, attacked ceaselessly by both races until, some time after the Emperor's flight, Berru surrendered with a handful of men to an Italian military post. That was what was going on all over the country in April and May. In many parts things seem to have been worse. Berru was a fighter and he maintained some sort of authority over some of his men. In districts where the conservative hereditary nobles had been dispossessed and their places taken by the Emperor's nominees – semi-educated, semi-Westernised members of the patriotic party – the men were often left without a semblance of leadership, for the qualities which had enabled the new aristocracy to rise in royal favour were not those which were needed at a time of national disaster.

The collapse of the Shoan system of government and the whole illusion of national unity was so sudden and so complete that no one was prepared for it. The Italians had accomplished in six months a task which they had expected to take two years. They now found themselves faced with opportunities and responsibilities vastly greater than their ambitions at the beginning of the war. It was a triumph in Rome. It was the end of the war as far as Europe was concerned. But it was the beginning of an enormous work in Africa and of work which had to be postponed through tedious months of rain. The conquering army were enjoying few of the fruits of victory. They had still to be maintained at war strength and in war conditions. They were told that peace had been declared but they lived in constant vigilance. There was nothing to do except sit about sheltering from the rain and gaze out from the sentry posts into the dripping eucalyptus; to go into action when it suited the temper of the marauding bands to come and shoot at them. It was a severe test of morale and they stood up to it in a way which should dispel any doubts which still survive of the character of the new Italy. By the time that these words appear in print the period of waiting will be over. The roadmakers and soldiers will have started on the second decisive campaign. Plans are already being drawn up for a new city at Addis. In a few months it will seem incredible that one drove out to dinner with a machine-gunner on the box, that one found hand-grenades in the back seat. The new régime is going to succeed. But I am glad to have seen the town at the moment of the transition.

CHAPTER 7

THE ROAD

1

WE WERE LATE in leaving Diredawa; we stopped to lunch and gossip at Assab; it was four o'clock before we landed at Massawa; an afternoon of burning, breathless heat, far hotter than noon at Assab. We had flown at a great height in the big, three-engined Caproni bomber; there was nothing to see in that country, nor could I have seen it from my place in the gun turret; once or twice I climbed down to the observation pit, but found an unvarying landscape of coast, sand dune and minute, dry watercourses. Currents of icy wind drove through the machine; we sat huddled in leather overcoats. It was an odd feeling to drop suddenly to sea-level and step out on to the blistering sand of the hottest place in the Red Sea; an agreeable feeling for the first few seconds, a tingling all over the skin which made one shiver, succeeded almost immediately by a sense of dead oppression.

I had spent a night in Massawa on the voyage out, and did not wish to repeat the experience. The aerodrome was deserted. We sat for an hour in the shade of a hangar. Then a car arrived and we were able to get a lift to headquarters. There we found a good-natured captain who was on the point of starting for the hills. He offered me a place in his car and a bed in his camp at Gura. We started at dusk.

It was the beginning of the great trunk road that climbs from Massawa to Asmara and then runs through the mountains along the line of Badoglio's advance, through Adigrat, Makale, Kworam and Dessye; within a few weeks of the appearance of these words in print it will have reached Addis Ababa; thence to go through the unconquered territories of the South to the Somali coast and Mogadishu. With its vast tributaries, of which Dessye is to be the point of

705

confluence, it is at once the symbol and the supreme achievement of the Italian spirit. A main road in England is a foul and destructive thing, carrying the ravages of barbarism into a civilised land – noise, smell, abominable architecture and inglorious dangers. Here in Africa it brings order and fertility.

During the succeeding fortnight I travelled the length of it until it petered out into a rough military track South of Lake Ashangi. It is a tremendous work, broad, even, perdurable; a monument of organised labour. It crosses some of the most formidable country in the world; sometimes following the contours, cut in the rock face, borne on great buttresses and ramparts of concrete and faced stone; continually descending into the ravines with which the country is scored, in a multitude of delicately graded hairpin bends; bridging the rivers on Roman arches and climbing again into the mountains beyond; sometimes running dead straight across the plain on high stone embankments.

In all the years of external peace, with European advice and unlimited native labour, the Shoan Government, whose chief need and avowed aim was the improvement of communications, had only succeeded in making the pathetic tracks from Addis Ababa to Dessye, and from Diredawa to Jijiga; there are still English Liberals who maintain that, left to himself, the Emperor would have accomplished all that the Italians hope to do for the development of his country. The Italian road has been built in a few months of exceptional difficulty to last for centuries. The workmen followed literally at the heels of the conquering army. In late summer we sped comfortably at sixty miles an hour over the battlefields of the early spring. At one point we passed the graves of seventy civilian workmen who were surprised, unarmed, by an Abyssinian raiding party, and butchered with every traditional atrocity. (A monk was the leader of that enterprise.) After the fighting came the rains, but the work went on. While the route was still in construction, a continuous stream of transport, taking supplies to the troops, followed as best it could. Much of the country over which it travelled was desert, much depopulated and despoiled. There was constant difficulty in supplying the workmen with food and materials, but they worked on. And when they rested they employed their leisure in embellishing the road they had made with little gardens of saplings and wild flowers, ornamental devices of coloured pebbles, carved eagles and wolves, fasces and heads of Mussolini, inscriptions, in the Roman fashion, recording the dates and details of their passage.

2

Asmara may have been a decent enough little town before the war when it was built to accommodate a white population of 2,000. Now there were 60,000 and it was hell. Dense, aimless, exclusively male, white crowds thronged the streets. Every shop, restaurant and place of entertainment, even the Cathedral, was unendurably over-full. The hotel ran Mr Kakophilos close for the All-Africa booby prize and only failed by a short head through the superiority of the servants; Italians do not seem to know how to wait badly. But it was a revelation to me to find that they can prepare uneatable macaroni. I occupied the same quarters as those described by Mr Mortimer Durand in *Abyssinian Stop Press*. I can assure him that they have in no way improved; have in fact deteriorated by reason of an invasion of fleas. In fact I was so badly bitten that when I showed the marks to Captain Franchi, of the Press Bureau, he could not believe that fleas existed in such numbers anywhere in the world and remarked sceptically 'Perhaps it is your stomach.' It was no fault of Franchi's, to whom were due all the amenities and none of the discomforts of my visit. He proved throughout the most thoughtful and efficient of hosts. This was all the more noble in him since my arrival came as a bitter disappointment.

The Viceroy had telegraphed to him from Addis to expect me. Like many others before him, he was deluded by my Christian name and for two days flitted between airport and railway station, meeting every possible conveyance, in a high state of amorous excitement. His friends declared that he had, with great difficulty, procured a bouquet of crimson roses. The trousered and unshaven figure which finally greeted him must have been a hideous blow, but with true Roman courtesy he betrayed nothing except cordial welcome, and it was only some days later, when we had become more intimate, that he admitted his broken hopes.

For there were only seven unattached white women among the 60,000 men of Asmara and feminine company is a primary need for Italians, the lack of which is for them one of the most severe hardships of the campaign. It is a romantic rather than a physical need; the latter, in a rough and tumble way, has been catered for. Teutons, on the whole, welcome prolonged holidays from their womenfolk and, at home, invent clubs and sports and smoking-rooms where they can escape and get together a male society. But Latins like the presence of women. The simple soldiers missed the domesticity of their cottages – the wives and daughters and grand-mothers and visiting aunts and sisters-in-law; the officers wanted to dance and meet women at dinner and gossip with them. Almost all conversations in Ethiopia reverted very quickly to the subject of women. Everyone had been envying Franchi his privileged oppor-tunities as my guide; there had been the keenest speculation about my age and appearance. I could not have been a keener disappoint-ment; nor could I have been treated with greater consideration if I had in fact been the woman they were all hoping for.

One day Franchi and I drove to Axum. We started before dawn and, as the sun came up over the crest of the mountains and the grey, watery mist that had drifted across the headlights began to clear, we saw the navvies emerging from their camps for work on the roads. We passed them all day, sometimes in gangs, working concrete mixers, sprays of hot asphalt, steam rollers: sometimes holding us up as a charge of dynamite shattered the rock ahead of us, some-times scattered in ones and twos over a mile of road, squatting at the side breaking stones; for the work was being done in sections and there were still places where one diverged from the new route and followed the rough military track made by the sappers. At times all three lines were visible, crossing and recrossing one another – the new highway, the temporary water-bound road of the mechanised army, and the old, precipitous, straggling mule-track along which the caravans still passed.

The men were, for the most part, older than the soldiers; sturdy, middle-aged, apparently indefatigable men (for they were still working when we repassed them at sunset with the same resolute application they had shown early in the day). Some of them were patriarchal, with long grizzled beards. They wore the clothes which they would have worn to work in Italy except for the addition of a sun helmet – in most cases rendered shapeless now by rain and wear.

It was a new thing in East Africa to see white men hard at work on simple manual labour; the portent of a new type of conquest.

To the other imperial races it was slightly shocking. To the Abyssinians it was incomprehensible. To them the fruit of victory is leisure. They fought their wars against the neighbouring tribes, won them as the Italians had done, through superior arms and organisation, and from then onwards settled back to a life of ease. The idea of conquering a country in order to work there, of treating an empire as a place to which things must be brought, to be fertilised and cultivated and embellished instead of as a place from which things could be taken, to be denuded and depopulated; to labour like a slave instead of sprawling idle like a master – was something wholly outside their range of thought. It is the principle of the Italian occupation.

It is something new in Africa; something, indeed, that has not been seen anywhere outside the United States of America for two hundred years. English colonisation has always been the expansion of the ruling class. At the worst it has been the achievement of rich men trying to get richer; at the best it has been the English upper classes practising among the simpler communities of the world the virtues of justice and forbearance and sympathy which they have inherited and for which their own busier civilisation gives less scope. It has always been an aristocratic movement and the emigrant of humble origin in his own home finds himself a man of position in the colonies, with dignity and responsibilities, a host of servants, the opportunities for expensive sport, and the obligation of a strict rule of conduct, simply by reason of his being an Englishman in an English colony. The 'poor white' is a thing to be abhorred, to be pushed out of sight; white men are only permitted to be under-dogs in their own countries. But the Italian occupation of Ethiopia is the expansion of a race. It began with fighting, but it is not a military movement, like the French occupation of Morocco. It began with the annexation of potential sources of wealth, but it is not a capitalistic movement like the British occupation of the South

African gold-fields. It is being attended by the spread of order and decency, education and medicine, in a disgraceful place, but it is not primarily a humane movement, like the British occupation of Uganda. It can be compared best in recent history to the great western drive of the American peoples, the dispossession of the Indian tribes and the establishment in a barren land of new pastures and cities.

Adowa was completely unscarred by war and apparently thoroughly happy. It is a more imposing city than anything in the South. The Tigreans retain a sense of architecture from their ancient civilisation. The houses are often of two stories, built of well-fitted stone with, here and there, an attempt at ornament over a door or window. There are great sycamore-trees and little walled courts round the houses. The people grinned and saluted everywhere; the children in particular were quite fearless and unaffectedly friendly. We went on to Axum, which has been fully described by more adventurous travellers in the past. We saw the antiquities, the great monolithic styles; the dingy old church which is the religious centre of the empire; we lunched at the officers' mess in the grounds of Ras Seyoum's Gibbi. The usual crowd of suitors, litigants and gossips were hanging about, as at an Abyssinian court of the old régime. After luncheon we went out with lanterns and explored the finely built sixth-century mausoleum that lies half buried in the hillside. No doubt it will soon be a tourist resort – marked with one star in Baedeker. We were back in Asmara in time for dinner, having comfortably accomplished in fourteen hours what would, a year before, have been a formidable and painful journey.

Two days later we set out on a three-day trip along the main road (the Axum road branches West at Asmara and will eventually lead to Gondar and Lake Tana) through Adigrat, Makale, Amba Aradam, Amba Alagi, Mai Cio, Lake Ashangi and Kworam – places whose names less than a year ago we had so often read in the bulletins and marked, with so much curiosity, on our maps.

The approach to Makale, at dusk on the first evening, was overpoweringly romantic after the temporary wooden towns, reminiscent of cowboy films, through which we had been travelling all day. It seemed to be a place of castles – Galliano's fort on the hills dominating the city; a lonely, castellated stronghold of the Emperor Theodore in the plain beyond; and, in the centre, the palace of Gugsa, built in baronial Gothic for Theodore by an Italian architect. The officers' mess received us with genial hospitality. There was no talk of politics or of Mr Eden, whose name unjustly but irradicably is now fixed in every Italian mind as the embodiment of personal spite. Instead we spoke of the habits of the Tigreans, the adventures of the campaign, the merits and peculiarities of the native askaris and, inevitably, of women.

Next day from the hill station at Mai Cio an officer who had fought there explained the tactics of the decisive battle in the saucer of land below us; the battle which will go down to history, quite inaccurately, as the Battle of Lake Ashangi. He was still suspicious, in spite of all I could tell him, that British artillery officers had been fighting with the Emperor that morning. The official military history of the campaign is in preparation. I will not attempt an inexpert recapitulation of what he told me. Three facts seemed chiefly to have impressed him – the skill with which the Abyssinians had by then learned to take cover from aircraft, the reckless courage of the advance of the Imperial Guard, and the fatal two days' delay when the Emperor, who was then in personal command, hung back from the attack and allowed Badoglio to get into position and bring up his artillery. After luncheon we followed the valley to Lake Ashangi; it was there that the aeroplanes, which had played only a minor part in the battle, were able to turn the retreat into a rout.

Large herds of oxen were peaceably grazing by the lakeside in charge of a small native. He grinned and gave the fascist salute as we passed him. A few miles further on lay the straggling village of Kworam which had been the Emperor's headquarters; from which he began the retreat which led in a few weeks to Djibouti, Jerusalem and Geneva.

And there, for the moment, the road came to an end. The men were already working between Kworam and Dessye. Soon they would be pushing out from Dessye and Addis Ababa. Now it was a perilous no-man's-land of bog and bandits. They are at work there at this moment, as I write. They will be at work there when these words appear, and in a few months the great metalled highway will run uninterrupted along the way where the Radical and I so painfully travelled a year before, past the hot springs where our servants mistook the bubbles for rising fish, past the camping-ground where Dedjasmach Matafara entertained us to breakfast, up the immense escarpment, past Debra Birhan where the one-eyed chief held us prisoner, to Addis, where a new city will be in growth – a real 'New Flower' – to take the place of the shoddy ruins of Menelik and Tafari. And from Dessye new roads will be radiating to all points of the compass, and along the roads will pass the eagles of ancient Rome, as they came to our savage ancestors in France and Britain and Germany, bringing some rubbish and some mischief; a good deal of vulgar talk and some sharp misfortunes for individual opponents; but above and beyond and entirely predominating, the inestimable gifts of fine workmanship and clear judgement – the two determining qualities of the human spirit, by which alone, under God, man grows and flourishes.

ROBBERY UNDER LAW:

THE MEXICAN OBJECT-LESSON

CONTENTS

FOREWORD

I AM INDEBTED to many friends – old and new, British, American and Mexican – for their abundant kindness to me in London, New York, Washington and Mexico. They provided me with a sequence of delightful introductions, entertained me in their homes, helped plan my journeys, talked to me very freely of their particular problems; but this is an occasion, I believe, where gratitude is best expressed by silence. The appearance of their names here could only be an embarrassment to them. I formed my opinions in their company, but none of them will agree with all I have written, some of them with none of it. It would be idle to pretend that a visit to Mexico, at the present moment, can be wholly agreeable; the pervading atmosphere ranges from vexation to despair, and only the most obtuse traveller could escape infection. That, in spite of the present gloomy spectacle and the still gloomier prospect of the future, there were more good hours than bad for me in Mexico, is entirely due to these friends. If they come to read this I should like them to know that I am sincerely grateful; in particular to two, an Englishman and a Mexican, one of whom, harassed by personal worries, took all mine into his charge; the other who was my constant companion in all my movements. I remember with delight the days at Orizaba and Cuernavaca, a bottle of magnificent claret in Mexico City, the trip down the railway, away from newspapers and wireless, during the European September crisis, the good company in the Ritz bar, the trust with which members of the Catholic laity accepted me. I am sorry that these happy episodes shall have so little reflection in the following pages, but, as my friends know better than I, there is at the moment no opportunity for solid happiness in Mexico.

E. W.

Stinchcombe, 1939.

CHAPTER 1

INTRODUCTION

1

THIS IS A political book; the sketch of a foreign country where I spent a day or so under two months; of a country which has already provoked a huge number of books, many of them by residents of life-long experience. I do not see how it is possible to escape the imputation of presumption. 'The fellow mugs up a few facts in the London Library, comes out here for a week or two with a bare smattering of the language, hangs about bothering us all with a lot of questions, and then proceeds to make money by telling us all our own business.'

It is a charge to which professional writers are commonly exposed and I know no answer except the truth: that this, in fact, is our professional habit. Superficial acquaintance is one of the materials of our trade. Other professions are equally culpable; the barrister spends an evening or two studying his brief, pleads in court as though he had never had any other interest in life than the welfare of the litigants, and, over his luncheon, forgets their names, their faces and everything about them. The medical specialist gives his diagnosis in an hour on a patient he has never seen in health and of whose life history he knows no more than a few routine questions will elicit. Compared with them a journalist is less presumptuous. His trade is to observe, record and interpret. He does not claim that in a month or two of sight-seeing he has made himself an expert on local history and archæology; still less that he has fitted himself for the post of benevolent dictator who can put right troubles which perplex the statesmen. His hope is to notice things which the better experienced accept as commonplace and to convey to a distant

public some idea of the aspect and feel of a place which hitherto has
been merely a geographical or political term, so that subsequent
events reported thence in the newspapers – events which in the
vagaries of contemporary history may quite suddenly have a rude
impact on their own livelihood and lives – may have more interest
and actuality. For this purpose even a few weeks may sometimes be
too long. How many travel books open vividly and end in a mere
catalogue of transport difficulties! The truthful travel book rarely
works to a climax; the climax is sometimes the moment of disembarkation and everything beyond it an attempt to revive artificially,
under the iron lung of rhythmic, day to day observations, the
revelation of first acquaintance.

I went to Mexico in order to write a book about it; in order to
verify and reconsider impressions formed at a distance. To have
travelled a lot, to have spent, as I had done, the first twelve years of
adult life intermittently on the move, is to this extent a disadvantage:
that one's mind falls into the habit of recognising similarities rather
than differences. At the age of thirty-five one needs to go to the
moon, or some such place, to recapture the excitement with which
one first landed at Calais. For many people Mexico has, in the past,
had this lunar character. Lunar it still remains, but in no poetic
sense. It is waste land, part of a dead or, at any rate, a dying planet.
Politics, everywhere destructive, have here dried up the place,
frozen it, cracked it and powdered it to dust. Is civilisation, like a
leper, beginning to rot at its extremities? In the sixteenth century
human life was disordered and talent stultified by the obsession of
theology; today we are plague-stricken by politics. It is a fact;
distressing for us, dull for our descendants, but inescapable. This is
a political book; its aim, roughly, is to examine a single problem; why
it was that last summer a small and almost friendless republic
jubilantly recalled its Minister from London, and, more important,
why people in England thought about this event as they did; why, for
instance, patriotic feeling burst into indignation whenever a freight
ship – British only in name, trading in defiance of official advice –
was sunk in Spanish waters, and remained indifferent when a rich
and essential British industry was openly stolen in time of peace. If
one could understand that problem one would come very near to

understanding all the problems that vex us today, for it has at its origin the universal, deliberately fostered anarchy of public relations and private opinions that is rapidly making the world uninhabitable.

The succeeding pages are notes on anarchy.

2

Travellers from New York to Mexico have a choice of route; they may take either the weekly steamship for Vera Cruz or the faster, more costly, daily train. The inexperienced and economical, of whom I was one, prefer the former; inexperienced, for I was thinking of trains in un-American terms. New York was in the depth of a heat-wave; one stepped right down into it, as into a bath, from the gangway of the liner. Those who have been in New York at such a time – if such a time has ever occurred before, which the daily papers and one's own sense of probability made one doubt – will understand what it means; to those who have not, words are useless. It is enough to say that it seemed inconceivable that anyone could hesitate between a week at sea, with fresh breezes and shady decks, and four days cramped in a sleeper, rattling into the tropics through the burning plains of Texas and St Luis Potosi. Now I know better. There are a number of objections which the jealous European may make to American trains – as that they are slow, that one is knocked off one's feet whenever they stop and start, that one has no assurance of fermented liquor with one's food – but, when all is said, it remains true that they are the most comfortable means of getting across country yet devised by man. I did not know that at the time; nor did I know what to expect on board the steamship.

Half the polite letters of the world take the form of contrasting expectation with realisation. I had formed an image of what the *S.S. Siboney* would be like. I saw her – Heaven knows why, except that the fare was cheap – as a cargo vessel carrying a few heterogeneous passengers in rough and homely comfort; a ship something like the coasters of the Gulf of Corinth, full of traders and prospectors and nondescript adventurers whose table talk would supplement my meagre and purely academic acquaintance with the country to which we were travelling. But the *Siboney* is purely and simply a tourist service, gallantly attempting to reproduce a luxury cruise at cut-price rates; admirable for its purpose, but no manner of use to a writer in search of local colour. The ship was fairly full, of women, mostly, who were on their way to Mexico to have a good time.

Mexico is a long way from England, and you do not meet a great many Englishmen who have been there; it is next door to the U.S.A. and holiday-makers swarm across the border like ants. Tourist traffic was down last year, like every Mexican business, but it is still large and the depreciation of the peso has done a good deal to counteract the – at the moment quite groundless – apprehensions about personal safety. It is doubly important, in Mexico because anything that brings foreign currency into the republic is desperately needed; in the U.S.A. because anything which helps to form American public opinion about its dangerous little neighbour, is, at the moment, of disproportionate interest.

As far as Mexico is concerned the tourists are not popular; I doubt whether they are anywhere in the world except at seaside resorts and in Norway. It is a long abandoned belief that tourism, like competitive athletics, makes for international friendship. The three most hated peoples in the world – Germans, Americans and British – are the keenest sight-seers. There are very few English villagers who have seen an Egyptian; very few Egyptian villagers who have not seen an Englishman; the result is that the English generally are well disposed towards Egypt, while the Egyptians detest us. Sympathy for foreigners varies directly with their remoteness. We were prepared to love the Abyssinians; Italians, for most of us, meant a customs official we had fallen out with, or an avaricious cab-driver. Moreover a race who stay at home and are visited extensively from abroad fall into the error of supposing all foreigners to be very rich and very frivolous. Few Mexicans ever saw a poor Englishman or American; it is not unnatural that they get an impression that they are having the worst of the international deal and are being mulcted. (Twenty years ago, of course, the Monagasques had never seen a poor Mexican, but that is distant history.) Not that the American tourists are big spenders. Mexico is for those who cannot afford the Grand Tour to Europe. They buy round tickets and except for getting a few execrable objects as presents for those at home, they do not want to spend any more; tips and guides are included in their fare. They have a national abhorrence of beggars. The profits are carefully calculated and not much slips into general circulation. It can well be argued, in general terms, that a country is happier without tourists, but Mexico is in no position to be fastidious about its sources of revenue. It values the tourist trade and would feel the loss if the frontier were closed. It has laid out a lot of money in roads and hotels and has even, in late years, modified some of its more conspicuous abuses in deference to tourists' protests; in particular the loot and destruction of Spanish-Colonial art treasures and the persecution of the clergy. Some of the Mexicans in the government party have realised that the tourists do not come simply to exercise their motor cars or, now that Prohibition is more or less over, to drink imported whisky; that seventeenth-century silver-ware is more valuable in its existing shape than melted into a lump; that if you want some proofed canvas to patch a roof it is cheaper in the long run to buy a piece, than to clamber on to the altar of the village church and cut a Cabrera out of the reredos; the enlightenment comes late but it is something gained, and something for which, indirectly, we may thank the jolly young women of the *S.S. Siboney.*

Americans undoubtedly feel a sense of responsibility towards Mexico. Later, on my homeward journey, I fell into conversation with an insurance agent returning across the border from a 'convention' of fellow insurance men who were having a corporate jaunt together twenty strong. He told me in full detail about the prosperity of his business and the terms of affectionate subservience on which he lived with his wife. I asked him after a time if he knew England. No, he said, he had never been abroad.

After two months in Mexico that came as a surprise, for I could conceive of no two countries more foreign to one another than his and the one he had just been visiting. It is true, of course, that he had travelled in an American-built, air-conditioned coach, that he had found ice-water and American cereals on the breakfast table at his hotel, hall porters and barmen who understood his English, and what was in intention and origin, if not in effect, American plumbing, but he could not long have been taken in by these things.

It was not so much kinship as proprietorship that he felt. His was
the attitude of the nineteenth-century Englishman towards Ireland.
He saw Mexico as backward and deficient in many of the advantages of the northern system. In particular he was impressed by
the physical dirt; food being exposed for sale without its decent
wrapping of cellophane shocked his sense of propriety; the place
needed taking in hand; the people should be taught industrious and
hygienic habits. Labour had got a bit out of hand lately; well, they
had had a raw deal before, now they were getting a bit of their own
back; it would all even up soon and better relations be established.
The Church had had too much money and they spent it all on
extravagant building instead of teaching the people; most of
those big buildings *were* schools? He hadn't understood that from
the guide – but, anyhow, what did they teach? Only a lot of Latin
and stuff. The landowners ill-treated the peasants and lived in
Biarritz; pity the peasants were worse off now than they were before,
but that would come right when they'd been taught modern
methods; pity the Government took away Americans' estates, too,
but they had said they would pay for them one day. He knew that
historically and economically the Government was dependent
on his; he thought it a pity that the frontier should have been
drawn where it had been; Mexico was a projection of California
and Texas; it needed no violent imperialism; clean it up a bit and
it would come into the Federation on its own account. Like
the nineteenth-century Englishman in Ireland, he overlooked
the one vital difference – that Mexico was a foreign country. His
attitude, I think, is still in the main that of the State Department
at Washington.

In contrast to this type of transitory visitor there are a large
number of Americans who find, or profess to find in Mexico a
spiritual home. These are the painters and writers who make such
a large and charming section of the English-speaking colony. Here
in the hills they find an antidote for all the ills of their native
civilisation. Although, almost all of them, dependent on invested
capital for their livelihood, they express generous sympathy with
General Cardenas's socialist régime. They see Mexico as they were
first taught to see it by the travel-agencies' folders, as a country of

sunny, indolent peasantry, ancient domes and patios, local feasts that are spontaneous and traditional – a happy change from the more organised junketings of Elks and Shriners in their own home towns; they see a land where ambition, and particularly financial ambition, is not the dominant passion. Though they would vehemently disclaim it, the truth is that they are in love with Europe; they are nostalgic for the Classical-Christian culture from which they remotely spring, which they can find transplanted, transformed in part, but still recognisable in Mexico. They see it, as Dr Munthe saw San Michele, and it is largely due to their sentimental vision, that the legend has spread and earned credence, of the parasitic white tyrant and the patient savage. The new mood in the Mexican governing clique is destructive of all they value but few of them seem to recognise this; quite soon they may have a rude shock but at the moment they are happy with their tropical plants, collections of bric-a-brac, and albums of Diego Rivera. Their books are published in large quantities in the United States; in England seekers of the picturesque have a wider scope and the writer who has given most people their ideas about Mexico is D. H. Lawrence; and he hated it. He was taken in by a great many things, but never by the *San Michele* view of Mexico. He came there hoping for an antidote to the poison of industrialism and he left in disgust; he never forgot it. Every traveller to Mexico must read the *Plumed Serpent*; at any rate the opening chapters. The early, satirical passages about Mexico City – the bull fight, the tea party... 'all jade is bright green'... – are superb. Then his loneliness and lack of humour and his restless, neurotic imagination combine to make one of the silliest stories in recent literature. I defy anyone who has not been hypnotised by Lawrence's reputation to read the account of Kate's marriage – the corpulent, middle-aged Irish woman waddling out into the rain in her homespun shift; the swarthy little bridegroom trotting beside her in his bedraggled white pants; the words of the ceremony, 'This man is my rain from heaven', the rubbing of the roots of her hair and the soles of her feet with salad oil – without being inevitably reminded of 'Beachcomber's' column in the *Daily Express*; and the account of the bogus paganism is sillier, if less funny; when Lawrence describes the secession to it of many of the local clergy – who have been unjustly

accused of many defects but never of lack of tenacity in their faith —
he passes beyond Mexico into a world of stark nonsense.

Nevertheless, for all its folly, the *Plumed Serpent* is a better guide to
Mexico than Mr Philip Terry. His is the standard work; it was on sale
on board the *Siboney* and in every bookshop in Mexico City. In
appearance it has some superficial likenesses to the works of Baedeker . . . I could write at length on my horror of Terry's Guide; enough
to say that it says nothing that could offend any local sentiment, nor
could interest any serious traveller, but is well suited to the requirements of most of the *S.S. Siboney* round-tour passengers, who like
their accommodation the better for seeing it extravagantly praised
in print and have too much on their hands, anyway, to mind missing
the more unobtrusive sights which it is the primary duty of a guide
book to mention.

Besides the holidaymakers and the sentimentalists there is a third
rapidly increasing group of foreign visitors to Mexico. These are the
ideologues; first in Moscow, then in Barcelona, now in Mexico these
credulous pilgrims pursue their quest for the promised land; constantly disappointed, never disillusioned, ever thirsty for the phrases
in which they find refreshment. They have flocked to Mexico in the
last few months for the present rulers have picked up a Marxist
vocabulary so that, from being proverbial for misgovernment, the
republic, now at its nadir of internal happiness and external importance, greatly to the surprise of its citizens, has achieved the oddest of
reputations — that of 'contemporary significance'. But there were
no recognisable ideologues on board the *Siboney* — and they are
usually recognisable.

3

On the eve of our arrival in Mexican waters we were summoned
to the lounge to hear an address from the purser on our behaviour in
a foreign country. Curiosity and the lack of alternative occupation
provided a large attendance. Just outside the door was a tank of iced
drinking-water and a column of cardboard cups. As the passengers
assembled they paused at this national monument and drank; it was
like a congregation coming into church passing the stoop of holy

water. When they were all refreshed and settled the purser entered. He was a personable, rather grim fellow in whom the distaste for passengers, endemic in all good seamen, seemed tempered by compassion. His speech, presumably, was the same every sailing; I wish I had been able to record it verbatim for it was a model of what such speeches should be.

First he explained the arrangements for disembarkation and the requirements of customs and immigration officials; he told them to us succinctly, in detail, more than once, with a tolerant acceptance of our intellectual limitations, like a very patient and experienced schoolmaster. One would have thought he had made himself plain; one would have been wrong as was evident, at the end, when he invited questions ... 'We have to take charge of our own tourist cards?'; 'Yes'; 'You mean when we go ashore we carry them with us?'; 'Yes'; 'Is this what you call a tourist card?'; 'Yes'; 'We can't leave them on the ship?'; 'No'; 'Which of these is my tourist card?'; 'Is *this* my tourist card?'; 'Is this *my* tourist card?'; 'Is this my *tourist card*?' ... When that was over he admonished us about our behaviour ... 'Most of you have never been out of your own country before,' he said. 'Well, you mustn't expect to find things exactly the same as they are back home.' The Mexican, he said, was a charming fellow if you treated him right. He was out to give us a good time; we must do our share too. We wanted a good time; the company wanted us to have a good time; he spoke for the officers, the crew and the staff when he said we ought to have a good time. Well the secret of that was to make up our minds to have a good time. If we didn't complain of the Mexican, he wouldn't get sore with us and then we should not have so much to complain of. The Mexican was very proud. We must remember it was *his* country. If we had any criticisms we had better wait till we were back home and make them there. We might see a lot of things in Mexico that seemed strange to us. We mustn't expect things to be the same as they were back home. 'Don't go taking pictures of the poor.' There were plenty of things to take pictures of if we wanted to take pictures; but not the poor. 'We've got our breadlines back home. We shouldn't like it if anyone took pictures of them ... Don't start any arguments about religion or politics. The Mexicans are doing their best and they like to think they are being appreciated, same as we do . . . '

It was very sound advice, and it provoked reflection. What exactly is the proper mood in which to approach a foreign country in these days? It is an important point, particularly to Americans and English, for we are the great travelling race in whose interest all the tourist bureaux of the world are organised.

It is interesting to read the travel books of fifty years ago and notice their air of tolerant or intolerant superiority. Perhaps at the time there was some justification for it; now there is very little. The words progressive and backward have become confused in their meanings. The old idea was of universal, inevitable progress; the nations were like horses at 'Minaroo', moving at varying speeds towards the same object ; sometimes one nation would have a run of luck, sometimes another. Britain at the moment was leading; other races, like us in ambition, but lacking our courage, integrity and good sense, were just behind; others, such as the hottentots, had barely started; others, such as the Spanish and Chinese, had made fly-away starts but failed to hold the pace. Certain defects, in particular, held people back from success – aristocratic or autocratic forms of government, the Church of Rome, etc. All that they needed was revolution, capitalisation and education. It was the duty of the more prosperous nations to lead and to lend . . . Alas, recent history has made it impossible for a thoughtful European to view the world with the same easy assurance. We have seen devils driven out and replaced by worse. Free Trade and the system of mobile financial credits scarcely exist; representative institutions survive precariously only in the countries of their origin. And as for moral superiority . . . how about ourselves? What were the grounds on which we were used to censure the backward Latin American republics? They neglected to pay their public debts; what European country can afford to be censorious about that today? A political career, in those dissolute communities, more often ended in murder than in a peerage and a pension; Dollfuss? Sotelo? Matteotti? the Romanoffs? Schleicher? the early Bolshevists and the early Nazis? Did a British Prime Minister not win an election with the promise to hang the Kaiser? They neglected their legacy of art and architecture; how about England? Which is worse, the destruction that comes of poverty, or of riches? Bandits were still at large; St Valentine's day in Chicago? The people were credulous and superstitious; what popular English paper can dispense with its astrological column? Education was a monopoly of the Church; which is the sounder, the catechism, or the race-mythology taught in half the schools of Europe today?

No, we must leave our superiority in bond when we cross the frontier; it is no longer for importation to foreign countries.

And there is another form of priggishness, too, with which we can dispense – the humbug of being unbiased. No one can grow to adult age without forming a set of opinions; heredity, environment, education and experience all condition us; the happiest are those who have allowed their opinions and beliefs to grow naturally; the unhappy are those who accept intellectually a system with which they are out of sympathy. When we go abroad we take our opinions with us; it is useless to pretend, as many writers do, that they arrive with minds wholly innocent of other experience; are born anew into each new world. Nor do our readers desire it. There is nothing more repugnant to the English reader than to be obliged to form his own judgement afresh with each book he takes up. Indeed readers, bored with the privilege of a free press, have lately imposed on themselves a voluntary censorship; they have banded themselves into Book Clubs so that they may be perfectly confident that whatever they read will be written with the intention of confirming their existing opinions.

Let me, then, warn the reader that I was a Conservative when I went to Mexico and that everything I saw there strengthened my opinions. I believe that man is, by nature, an exile and will never be self-sufficient or complete on this earth; that his chances of happiness and virtue, here, remain more or less constant through the centuries and, generally speaking, are not much affected by the political and economic conditions in which he lives; that the balance of good and ill tends to revert to a norm; that sudden changes of physical condition are usually ill, and are advocated by the wrong people for the wrong reasons; that the intellectual communists of today have personal, irrelevant grounds for their antagonism to society, which they are trying to exploit. I believe in government;

that men cannot live together without rules but that these should be kept at the bare minimum of safety; that there is no form of government ordained from God as being better than any other; that the anarchic elements in society are so strong that it is a whole-time task to keep the peace. I believe that inequalities of wealth and position are inevitable and that it is therefore meaningless to discuss the advantages of their elimination; that men naturally arrange themselves in a system of classes; that such a system is necessary for any form of cooperative work, more particularly the work of keeping a nation together. I believe in nationality; not in terms of race or of divine commissions for world conquest, but simply this: mankind inevitably organises itself into communities according to its geographical distribution; these communities by sharing a common history develop common characteristics and inspire a local loyalty; the individual family develops most happily and fully when it accepts these natural limits. I do not think that British prosperity must necessarily be inimical to anyone else, but if, on occasions, it is, I want Britain to prosper and not her rivals. I believe that war and conquest are inevitable; that is how history has been made and that is how it will develop. I believe that Art is a natural function of man; it so happens that most of the greatest art has appeared under systems of political tyranny, but I do not think it has a connection with any particular system, least of all with representative government, as nowadays in England, America and France it seems popular to believe; artists have always spent some of their spare time in flattering the governments under whom they live, so it is natural that, at the moment, English, American and French artists should be volubly democratic.

Having read this brief summary of the political opinions I took with me to Mexico, the reader who finds it unsympathetic may send the book back to her library and apply for something more soothing. Heaven knows, she will find plenty there.

CHAPTER 2

TOURIST MEXICO

1

THE COLONIAL FLAVOUR that still lingers everywhere in Mexico for those who care to find it, is nowhere more marked than in the abrupt division between rural and urban life. One is reminded of Africa, where village life, unaltered in centuries, exists within a mile of the new European cities. Mexican culture is not homogeneous; it exists, as it did in the fifteenth century, in a system of towns, which lie scattered like a constellation over the great plateau and beyond it, varying in splendour and importance with their distance from the capital. For the plateau is still the centre of what survives of Mexican culture. Nearly half the whole area of the Republic, it is true, lies North of the most southern point of the United States; South of the plateau are great tracts of tropical forest, and to the East the remote, ill-reputed peninsula of Yucatan, but in common speech and in historical fact, Mexico *is* the tableland – the Mesa Central de Anahuac, a vast, rocky, temperate area tilted towards the Pacific, 1,500 miles long by 500 or 600 miles in width. It is superb country, mountainous, volcanic, cracked and pitted with green cultivable valleys and wooded slopes rising above the snow line, into angular shining peaks; graced, every few miles, by the domes and façades of the conquerors' churches; when the clouds lift, everything is a shade sharper and brighter in the thin, dry air of the highlands than seems natural to Northern eyes. Certainly it is now a spectacle of decay; the little valleys are often rank and deserted, where the peasants have edged in towards the larger centres of population, or have been transported hundreds of miles away to other states to be settled on the unfamiliar, stolen lands of the great proprietors; the wooded slopes have been prodigally stripped for charcoal; the churches and monasteries have been sacked in turn by rebels and government and left to fall in ruin, for the governing Mexicans are ashamed of their Spanish past and, except in the main tourist centres (and pretty shoddily there) do nothing for its preservation, squandering instead the small sums available for the Department of Arts on reconstructing the infinitely tedious pyramids and terraces of their Aztec and Mayan conquerors. But even in its decay the plateau is a spectacle of intoxicating beauty; this is the Mexico of history; of Montezuma, Cortes, Iturbide and Maximilian.

Roughly at the centre of the plateau, lies the capital. Just as the towns have unusual importance in the country, so Mexico City has a unique position among the towns. It shelters nearly a tenth of the whole population of the Republic. It is the centre of government. Mexico, in this respect, is the exact opposite of France, whose government comes from the provinces and revolution from the capital. In Mexico the vice-regal tradition persists; the Federal Constitution has never had very much significance; it was a half-sincere compliment to the powerful neighbour in the North; the political habits of the Republic remain consistently autocratic and centralised. From time to time savages come from the North and South, either in armies or single adventurers to capture the seat of power; from time to time the local governors achieve a temporary independence, but in successive revolutions the people of Mexico City have usually declared for the existing régime, and it is from the city that such order as exists, emanates. It is to Mexico City that the tourist naturally goes, and from there that he plans his journeys.

It is a huge, crowded, cosmopolitan, infernally noisy place where everything contrives to puzzle and stun the stranger, so that in the first days of his visit he lives in a kind of breathless trance – actually breathless, for the altitude plays tricks with even the most robust constitution, so that the even-tempered find themselves liable to sudden, unreasonable explosions of rage, the heartiest eaters lose their appetite, and the most energetic are overcome by lassitude. It is doubtful how much humankind can become properly at ease in this climate; perhaps one may attribute to it a great part of the otherwise unaccountable alternations of listlessness and violence that have made Mexican history.

2

It depends on the circumstances of his arrival whether listlessness or violence is dominant in the stranger's mind during his first hours in the country. If he comes, as most seem to do, in the charge of a tourist agency, or if, as was my own fortunate experience, a friend has heroically risen at dawn to meet him, he passes through the station in an agreeable daze, shielded from too early contact with the inhabitants; if, however, he is travelling on his own, he receives his first rude acquaintance with local conditions from the railway porters.

I remember reading in the *New Statesman* one of those warm-hearted little articles which used to appear in the early days of the Spanish civil war; the author – Mr Cyril Connolly, I think – was describing his emotions when he crossed from capitalist France into the free, proletarian air of Catalonia; the particular mark, he said, of the Workers' State, was the elimination of the outstretched palm. If this is so, the Mexicans, in this matter as in much else, have got their Marxism a little mixed, for the exactions to which the traveller is liable have no parallel elsewhere in the world. Mexico is the only country I know of where one is invited to pay for carrying one's own hand luggage.

But, as I have said, on this first grey and chilly morning, I was relieved from all annoyance and hospitably conducted to my quarters.

The principal hotel stands in the old Spanish town, in the street now named Avenida Madero. There are others larger, more expensive, and more recently built, offering an equal profusion of hot, cold and iced water, but it is to the Ritz that people naturally gravitate who are spending any length of time in the city. It is the only hotel frequented by the Mexicans themselves and it has the somewhat equivocal advantage of standing in the heart of the busiest street.

Busiest street! . . . Mexico is the most shrill and thunderous city in the world. Noise is the first, shattering greeting to the stranger, it is the constant companion of all his days, the abiding memory which he takes home with him to the nordic stillness of London or New York. Noise of every conceivable kind competing for predominance. Noise of traffic; the old-fashioned courtesy for which many Mexicans are justly famous seems to forsake them when they get behind the wheel of a motor car. They move, as all urban drivers must, in a series of rushes, like infantry advancing through machine-gun fire; when they are halted they hoot continuously to be released; when they go, they still hoot to scare off the streets any aged and infirm persons who have got caught, half-way across, by the change of lights; embedded here and there in the turmoil, raised sometimes on little platforms covered in advertisements, stand policemen, whistling.

The sidewalks – they cannot be called pavements, for the greater part of them are not paved but coated with undulating asphalt – are very narrow and full of foot passengers, but, oddly enough, they are the main centre of social life and the noise of human voices is louder, even, than the klaxons; there are few cafés and little café life in Mexico; what there is occurs at night; during the day, at the crowded hours, if a Mexican wants to talk with his friends, he stands in the middle of the sidewalk and yells – politics, politenesses, business negotiations, anything that requires full verbal expression. And above them again – for as the conversationalists seek to out-talk the traffic, so they must interrupt the conversationalists – rise the voices of the street sellers, calling the numbers of lottery tickets and the headlines of the newspapers. In justice to the beggars who throng the side streets, it should be said that they are, when sober, a quiet lot; they rely for their appeal on proximity, pushing their faces very close and muttering confidentially or, in the case of the children, merely swinging on one's coat-tails and reciting the rosary. There are, however, street singers with curiously penetrating tones and I met one old Indian who was well ahead of the traffic, playing an instrument entirely new to me – the nose-organ.

Besides these purely communicative and representational sounds, there is the abstract noise for noise's sake – the bashing together of pieces of wood or iron, preferably in the echoing light-wells of the larger buildings, for no other purpose than the general good; for Mexicans feast on sound, as the more ascetic nordics fast on stillness, and count no man happy until his ear drums are ringing. Thus if one arrives early at the leading restaurant of the place, the head-waiter hospitably puts himself out to set you at ease and relieve the unhomely silence, by grinding the legs of the furniture on the tiled floor till the tables round you fill up and all is Babel again.

At night, in the shabbier parts of the city, and in all quarters of the provincial towns, the stranger is liable to be alarmed by what sounds like rifle fire. Occasionally, no doubt, it is so. In the brave days of Carranza and Calles people were fairly free with firearms; they used to shoot the street lamps after a party and not infrequently their fellow guests. But most of these explosions come from fireworks and from bits of dynamite stolen from the mines. Europeans like fireworks for their visual effect and regard the noise as an inevitable concomitant. The Mexicans like the noise alone and most of their fireworks provide plain, large bangs.

But of all the noises of Mexico City the loudest and most individual was made by the mechanical pile-driver opposite the Opera House. Thud-shriek, thud-shriek; it worked day and night; the hammer fell, the compressed air escaped and the great tree trunks sank foot by foot into the soft sub-soil. While, in the general slump, other major works were at a standstill, this infernal machine pounded on incessantly, dominating a whole quarter of the city. By a peculiar irony it was constructing new vaults for the metallic reserves of the National Bank. The national finances that summer were a joke which was offensive to nobody. Revenue was down, production was down, credit was down, trade was down; the pile-driver seemed to thump home monotonously the simple facts of national bankruptcy. No figures had been published for some time but everyone, whatever his politics, believed that the President was keeping up the peso by buying American dollars at a rate which would completely empty the treasury in a few months; after that lay a prospect of inflation, repudiation, confiscation. Everyone, for various reasons, wanted a crisis (with the possible exception of the American ambassador and it did not occur to him that a crisis was imminent) for when the last of the metal reserves had left the country, the Mexican Government would have to readjust itself, one way or another. And everyone had different ideas of the readjustment that was required. Meanwhile the pile-driver prepared the new vaults.

No description of Mexico City should be complete without some mention of Popocatapetl. The city lies in its shadow and other travellers have felt, or professed to feel, the life of the place dominated by its vast and splendid bulk. Honesty obliges me to confess that I never saw it, as it should be seen, rising above the domes of the city. I saw it only once, late in the evening, returning from the country, before the buildings came into sight. For the remainder of my visit it remained hidden in cloud. Perhaps it is needed to complete the composition; every great city needs some physical features, sea or river or palm belt among surrounding wastes, to give it a shape and purpose; the flatness of Mexico City with its curtain of low cloud gives it, in the rainy season, a ramshackle appearance which is not in its nature, as though for all its solidity and evident age it were a great camping-ground. But it is full of splendid sights.

The area – particularly when you look down on it from the surrounding hills – seems enormous. There is the old colonial town, very large indeed for the age and circumstances in which it was built, beyond which on three sides stretch large, drab, proletarian quarters; on the other side is the new, residential city which grew up in the Diaz-Limantour era of prosperity; broad streets named after the cities of Europe ('Liverpool' is one of the best addresses) flanked by villas in Fitzjohn's Avenue style. Most of them have gardens of a sort – everything grows big and flabby in Mexico – and many English ladies wage a gallant defensive action over patches of grass. These houses no longer suggest opulence, but there is still a certain smugness about them; few are, as yet, actually in decay, though they keep their gates inhospitably padlocked. Beyond, round the palace of Chapultepec a new suburb has grown up; the ring of villas is spreading everywhere on the surrounding plain, for urban house property is one of the few investments that have not yet been attacked by the Government. Railway and utility stock and Government bonds are more or less worthless. The nearest thing to a gilt-edged security is suburban rents and it is in these that the bull-fighters and politicians invest their savings. As a result most people in Mexico City with any money to spare, seem to spend most of it, and of their time, in litigation with tenants, sub-tenants and building contractors.

In style these new houses vary from Hollywood Spanish (wrought iron, tiles, spindly little colonnades, etc.) which – heaven knows why – is thought to be the more aristocratic, to the Nazi-factory manner (concrete and steel) which – heaven knows why – is thought to be the more Marxist. The most painful effort of this latter kind was designed by the painter Diego Rivera and placed, in poignant contrast, next door to the San Angel Convent (now a road-house). As modern suburbs go, they are inoffensive and compare quite favourably with anything in France or England.

The old town is full of entrancing buildings, civil and ecclesi-astical. They stand everywhere in silent reproach of the surrounding chaos, and if contemporary habits of life look shoddier and sillier for their presence, they offer continual compensation and encourage-ment to the distressed stranger.

The city has the advantage of a good, whitish grey building stone and of a material unique to the place – a deep red volcanic clay which rapidly hardens after cutting, somewhat in the manner of West of England cobb. These two are sometimes combined with Puebla tile and majolica work; the sculpture which is used abun-dantly, and, in the best examples, with contrasting alternations of absolutely plain masonry, is the work of Indians copying motifs from imported engravings and pieces of furniture, and adding to them a great deal of their own very peculiar, far from prosaic mentality. For the stone deaf, or for those whose æsthetic enthusiasm is powerful enough to exclude interruption, Mexico City is a delight, for it is not so surveyed and catalogued that one cannot make discoveries for oneself, nor so modernised that there are no discoveries to make.

The Juarez reforms destroyed some fine churches, and spoilt others by driving streets through the monastic gardens and crowding with commercial erections façades which were designed to be seen from a distance, but enough remains to give a very fair idea of the splendour of a century ago. Cultured Mexicans complain a great deal, but they have suffered less than we have. Their countrymen on the whole, have been rather frivolous in their vandalism; they have stolen and neglected and put things to unsuitable uses, but there has been none of the systematic extermination of good architecture the Londoners have enjoyed. When, for instance, the Government took over the charitable foundation of the Vizcainas, they merely bricked up the doors of the famous, rococo chapel; it is still there in the dark; one day someone will find it again with rejoicing. The iconoclasm too is tolerably impartial; the art of the liberators suffers equally with the relics of the oppressors. At the Ministry of Education – the lodging it so happens of the Department of Arts – an acre or so of Diego Rivera fresco is rapidly being reduced to bare plaster by civil servants who beguile their luncheon hour scratching off the paint, and the fine crazy pictures of Orosco at the Preparatory School have already been obliterated as high as a man's hand can reach.

One is reminded again of the Irish who look on the English as the Mexicans do on the Spanish, dislike their art as evidence of their occupation, but let it decay in its own time. 'Thou shalt not kill, yet needs not strive officiously to keep alive' seems to be the principle of both local governments, and we, in England, have no cause to be censorious. I suppose Venice in the last days of the Austrian occupation, when the palaces were turning into tenements and warehouses, must have looked rather like Mexico City. English and American romantics did a great deal for the preservation of Venice. It is not too late to save Mexico. Perhaps one day we shall see it happen. Wealthy Americans may restore and refurnish the old houses. There may be a Mexican season. American heiresses may start marrying Mexicans; a College of Arms may be set up to polish the pedigrees and titles of the colonial families and a new society arise of elegant international Marquesas.

Meanwhile the palaces and all the buildings of the city suffer, however, from one danger that never much troubled Venice; as though in shame of their posterity they are literally sinking into the ground. For Mexico is built on soft mud. Even the new Opera House has gone down a yard or two. This process plays odd tricks in proportion; doors that were designed to rise on steps now stand below street level; plinths have disappeared totally; columns now rise, baseless as Bayswater Doric; windows are at knee height. In the case of the earliest buildings the loss is least felt; it contributes to the general picturesque; but at the end of the eighteenth century a first-class classical architect named Tolsa devised what should have been the finest buildings in the New World. It is impossible now to see anything as he drew it. His School of Mines[1] has not only sunk, but sunk irregularly so that the cornice curves like the lines of a ship, and his severely symmetrical Church of Our Lady of Loreto is full of all the dizzy optical illusions of the Crooked House at Himley.

Of the destruction which comes from the confidence of being able to do better, Mexico has been laudably free since the last days of Spanish rule when there was a craze for tearing out Chirruguer-esque reredoses and replacing them with refined, correct and wholly alien classical structures like Georgian chimney pieces. I only met two examples of attempted improvement, the show house in Puebla which has been Hollywoodised by the Department of Arts, and a project, not yet realised, at Santa Maria del Tule which was can-vassed in the following English inscription.

VISITOR!

The authority of this village, favouring the interesting plan of the Depart-mento Forestal y de Caza y Pesca, *tending to suppress the ugly adobe fence that surrounds this TREE, of worldly reputation, to be substituted by an artistic iron railing that does not obstruct, as at present, the integral view of the admirable GIANT, attentively invites you to help us carry on this noble end, buying the only illustrated and complete monograph that we know of the TREE. It is sold in the Secretary's office of the City Hall that I preside, in Spanish or English, at the low price of one Mexican peso each.*

The tree of worldly reputation was certainly vast, but the wall of the churchyard in which it stood was a sympathetic, rough old thing marked with the traditional Stations of the Cross, so I hope that nothing comes of the plan. Those who know the district say that there is no cause for apprehension.

---

1 Mr T. Philip Terry's popular guide book says of this brilliant design, 'The average traveller will be inclined to think that Tolsa's real genius lay in his ability to spend so much money on so unpretentious a structure.'

Elsewhere in the world revolutionary régimes have usually been manifest in a campaign of public architecture. In Mexico City there are only two post-Diaz buildings of any real prominence. Each of them is significant.

There is the Monument of the Revolution through which most of the innumerable public processions are conducted. It is a formidable structure two hundred feet high, consisting of a single dome supported on four arches. One need not be suspected of political prejudice in condemning its startling ugliness, for it was designed for quite another purpose, to be, in fact, the central lobby of the Houses of Parliament. In 1934 the present president decided to commemorate his election and the topical scepticism of representative institutions in the same ingenious undertaking, of clothing the metal skeleton, which had stood for years, and transforming it into a triumphal arch. It is certainly one of the most tediously hideous buildings in the New World, and Mexicans of all political views regard it with the kind of fascinated horror with which Romans accept the Victor Emmanuel Memorial and which, until a few years ago, used to be devoted in London to the Albert Memorial. It is one of the sights. Another, still more recent 'sight' is the new offices of the Mexican Eagle Company. It is a very different structure, of traditional design and local material. That too was never put to its original purpose, for it was confiscated at the moment of its completion at the same time as the oil fields; the confiscation, indeed, was delayed until the last plasterer had finished work; it is in many ways a worthy member of the long succession of fine buildings which Mexican governments have acquired by theft. After a time, however, it became a great bore. I soon lost count of the number of times this building was pointed out to me. One passed it two or three times a day, for it stands in the main arterial boulevard of the town. Taxi drivers would swing round in their seats and say 'Aguila'; passing strangers would stop one in the street with the same word. It was repeated with every possible inflexion of tone – chagrin, derision, triumph, indignation, awe, venom, regret, apprehension . . . for no one in Mexico City was indifferent to its fate. It seemed to symbolise the precarious condition of all their lives.

Add to this architectural background a number of squares planted with tropical vegetation and ornamented with patriotic statuary, here, as everywhere else in the world, decreasing in merit as it becomes more modern, and you have the physical scene of Mexican life; and yet, reconstructed, say, in a film studio, it would lack a certain essential quality which is hard to describe in other terms than those of shabbiness and untidiness. It is no dirtier than many large cities; you do not return covered in grime after a morning's shopping as you do in most English towns; you do not see more distressing evidence of poverty than in Paris; the smells are no stronger than in Venice. Nevertheless there is a persistent and curiously depressing air of disorder and dirt as of a seaside beach after a Bank Holiday; the side streets tail off into waste land; the sidewalks of the main streets are muddy and littered with cigarette ends and waste paper; broken things never seem to get mended; it is partly the evidence of a race who have ceased to keep up appearances, partly of an invading people who do not quite know what to do with their acquisitions. The people have a kind of listless shabbiness that has nothing to do with poverty; they just do not bother to shave or to wear clean collars; they are always eating; Indian families squat in corners preparing the national dish of pancakes and pepper; men and women wander aimlessly about in groups munching huge dripping fruits; at the government offices pedlars display trays of delicatessen in the colonnades; policemen and sentries have mouths covered in crumbs. The Mexican street crowds are the most inelegant I have ever seen.

By this I do not simply mean that they are not rich. It is not necessary to have big motor cars and fashionably dressed women for a town to have style. There are no motor cars in the old town of Fez and the women except for a few uniformed slaves are invisible, but that town has incomparable grace and dignity. There are, for that matter, quite a number of politicians in Mexico City with substantial American banking accounts; there are numberless cars as expensive as anything one would find in Bath or Cheltenham. The sense of shabbiness comes from something uneconomic, in the way the people move and talk.

It has for some years now ceased to be a gay city. The Jockey Club, which was formerly the centre of expensive life, has been disbanded; the gaming-houses from which former presidents derived part of their incomes have been shut down; gambling of every kind is illegal and there is a strong temperance movement, which is following the laudable programme of substituting the very excellent national beer for the spirits which were formerly the usual drink; on public holidays the bars are shut. There is a large and formidably drab *quartier toleré*, where the licensed prostitutes, each in her separate cabin, stand all day at little guichets soliciting custom; there is a good country club where Mexicans and foreigners mingle on cordial terms; the drug trade which was once extensive and highly profitable is now being efficiently checked. There is one more or less respectable night club and dancing for tourists at some of the large hotels. There is practically no private entertaining on any large scale. There is an occasional concert and an occasional week or two of opera at the great Opera House, but the building is becoming more and more used for purposes of Government propaganda. Those who come to Mexico with picturesque ideas of a voluptuous, Latin American night life, are usually disappointed.

Films, of course, are rapidly driving out other forms of entertainment. There are Cinema Theatres doing brisk business all over the town, showing everything from the latest American products – the dialogue in English, roughly translated in a profusion of Spanish captions – to native works which specialise in costumed orchestras, funny men and a type of beauty refreshingly unlike the established models of Hollywood. Here too one can still find those serial thrillers which seem unhappily to have disappeared in Europe, which leave the hero, at the end of each instalment, in positions of apparently inescapable danger from which he is effortlessly relieved the following week. Prices vary from theatre to theatre but are uniform in each house; a concession to the Mexican's habit of destroying the upholstery when he is dissatisfied with his place and to the bull-ring tradition of climbing the barriers and invading any more expensive seats which are empty or held by people who look pusillanimous. But this is the only democratic feature of the entertainment. There seems little demand for the Russian instructional films which delight

European socialists. Indeed the Mexicans seem to have a disproportionate relish for the spectacle of the stiff shirts and chinchilla that
have disappeared from their own country. While I was there three
films on consecutive weeks were drawing crowded houses; all dealt
with the single theme of a girl who goes to a fashionable hotel with
borrowed clothes and an assumed title and ends by marrying a real
millionaire. But, more curiously still, the film which had the greatest
popularity was *The Drum*, a romantic story of British Imperialism in
the East. How the crowd cheered when the good Highlanders shot
down the bad Afridis!

3

The great majority of tourists in Mexico have either come on
brief, round-ticket visits or they have driven down in their own cars
from the United States; in either case their itinerary is limited to the
motoring-roads which, in the tourist zone, are in good condition and
so decorated with hoardings advertising international products that
they might be part of England or the United States. From Mexico
City one can drive in every comfort to Orizaba, Puebla, Tehuacan,
Cuernavaca, Taxco and with mild discomfort to Acapulco, Guadalajara and up the great north road to Laredo. The stretch of railway
from Tehuacan to Oaxaca is the only piece of line, excepting those
to Vera Cruz and Laredo, which is frequented by tourists. There is
an air service to Yucatan which deposits its passengers to see the
ruins at Chichen-Itza, and whisks them away again as neat and fresh
as they started. Travel in other parts of the country – and that is by
far the larger part – is, with the exception of the oil lands, which at
the time of my visit political events had virtually isolated from all
except Government sympathisers, as tedious and dangerous as in
any inhabited part of the world. The railway system which was one
of the chief achievements of the pre-revolutionary régime, was
practically destroyed during the civil wars; its return to its former
owners was accompanied by labour conditions which made effective
reorganisation impossible. Most of it was confiscated by General
Cardenas in 1937 and handed over to the workmen. The railway
from Mexico to Vera Cruz is still operated by a British company in

increasingly hostile conditions. It has shown no profit since the revolution and has had the utmost difficulty in maintaining its service; the obligation to employ a redundant staff with wages and benefits enormously in excess of those paid by any native concern, make any improvement impossible; it is, however, luxurious compared with the Puebla–Oaxaca line which embodies in their most aggravated form all the jokes people have ever made about railways. Others are said to be incomparably worse. A friend who travelled from Guatemala to Orizaba found it hard to convince people in Mexico City that the feat could be performed at all. His account of it is, I believe, eventually to be published, so I will not filch the gruesome details from him. Nor will I plagiarise from Mr Graham Greene's harrowing description[1] of his recent expedition through Tabasco and Chiapas. My own experiences, I am afraid, were definitely homely. Those who have borrowed this book in anticipation of vicarious endurances, of treacherous guides and blistered toes, pack mules, dysentery, common or amœbic, bandits, official or outlawed, campfires and strange encounters, must, I fear, return it to the library unread. The worst sufferings I can boast were from bed-bugs in two luxury hotels[2] and a film producer at luncheon. I was in Mexico both for a holiday and for work and both kept me in soft conditions.

Soft, let it be said, in contrast with Mr Graham Greene's. There are more thorns than roses everywhere in Mexico. But no one wants to hear about my bed-bugs and my film producer when the country all round one was full of deadly germs and desperadoes. I can only say that the small discomforts and inconveniences that the tourist suffers are prodigally repaid by the beauty and interest of the country.

Various small incidents stand out as typical, if not of the country at least of my trip there:–

The Indian chambermaid at the simple inn at Tenancingo who, as we left, pursued my wife into the street with a 20-peso bill which she had found on the floor of our room.

---

1 *The Lawless Roads.*

2 Neither, I hasten to say, both from fear of libel and in gratitude to a place where I was very comfortable, the Ritz.

The little janitor at the museum in Oaxaca who was learning English; he had transcribed in pencil, in an awkward hand, the verses of the hymn 'All things bright and beautiful' and asked our Mexican companion to explain some of the words to him in Spanish; I see them now against the glass cases full of Mixtec gold construing the poem together.

A very drunk mestizo at the hotel in Oaxaca. The dining-room was the former patio of the house, now roofed with glass, the floor bare tiles; every sound swelled and echoed monstrously; he sat with a friend shouting, spitting and singing uproariously and glaring round the room as if he expected someone to start a fight. He was quite mirthless and curiously lonely in his cups. His sober friend sat opposite him eating impassively. Presently he made the plain and slatternly waitress sit at the table with him. She tried to make him take her to the cinema; instead he took her up to his room where he sang and shouted most of the night. I asked who he was. 'He must be a politician,' they said. 'Otherwise he would not behave like that.' Further enquiry discovered that he was a commercial traveller.

A cloud of dust, a galloping horse, a swarthy figure in a wide sombrero, attended by three or four young men, more modestly mounted. The peasants in the roadsides bowed low as he passed. A brigand? No, the parish priest coming in to say Mass. Another priest, an Englishman who, because he had been born in Mexico, was allowed to remain. He lived in the corner of a deserted cloister. The patio was waste land; once he tried to make a garden there and found in the rubble an old fountain which he re-erected. Then he went to Mexico City for a week. While he was away the soldiers came and stole the fountain; the people of his parish lay down in the street to stop them rolling the stone away; but the soldiers won; now his only ornament is a brilliant and ferocious parrot; he has not been out of Mexico for thirty years.

A ride into the hills above Tenancingo, through pine woods, to a deserted monastery. An Indian family were housed in the porter's lodging; it was Sunday morning and they were washing their heads in the tiled basin of a disused fountain, the lather startlingly white on their dead black hair. We walked round the garden where an elaborate system of irrigation was choked and dry and the monks' fruit-trees sprawled untended, full of dead wood.

A burst tyre on the road to Puebla. While it was being mended we walked round the village; it had once been of some size but most of the houses seemed empty now, and the garden walls were mere heaps of stone; from above – the place sloped sharply up the hillside – one could see that it had once been carefully planned with level terraces and symmetrical, transecting streets. A great fortress-like building stood at the further side of the central square. It had once been an important college, said an old Indian; he had been to school there himself as a child. The fathers had managed a fertile estate there where all the villagers worked. When the fathers had been sent away the village began to disappear. No one looked after the gardens now. He lived by collecting onyx on the hillside and making souvenirs for the shops in Puebla. Tourists never came his way directly and he did not try to sell anything.

Cuernavaca, two hours' drive over the hills from Mexico City, where the foreign business community go for week-ends. All the villas have swimming-pools and frigidaires and verandahs. It is the most uncompetitive and friendliest of communities, both to themselves and to strangers. They have the kind of mutual loyalty that comes of being under siege together. They wander in and out of one another's houses, play cards, drink Coca-Cola and beyond an occasional joke about 'Article 33' (the enactment by which the Mexican Government may expel aliens) seldom talk of their week-day worries. There is a seaside atmosphere in the foreign villas. Outside there always seems to be a wedding in progress. The women in the piazza are smarter than in Mexico City. The recreations are walking round the bandstand and revolver practice. The old shrine in the main street has quite lately been destroyed by communists. Of Borda's famous garden nothing remains except some dry, cement tanks and the great mango-trees. The Cathedral and the group of buildings round it are splendid.

Taxco, the only consciously picturesque place in Mexico. Mr T. Philip Terry becomes lyrical in his descriptions of the hotels. The one where we stayed was certainly admirable. The town is full of silversmiths' shops; every turn of the steep cobbled streets offers a shot for the amateur photographer. The church is one of the few buildings in Mexico whose interior is finer than the exterior. Its pictures and altars have been left intact. It is the only place in Mexico where the children have learned to be impudent. It is no place for the kind of tourists we were. Either you must be very simple indeed and treat the place like Coney Island, or a resident. The residents are said to be the last survivors of the international Bohemianism of the '20s – the army of semi-intellectual good-timers who once overran half Europe; it was, by nature, a mobile force, living on the country; they have moved from Capri, Berlin, Villefranche, Fez, Majorca suffering mass desertions in the slump, and providing material for unnumbered light novels. At the moment they have set up their camp in Taxco – so they say in Mexico City.

Puebla, the only town in Mexico of dignity. It is hard to realise that it has constantly been a centre of revolution and that Toledano is stronger there, probably, than anywhere in the country. Every street is beautiful; there is a good restaurant and antique shops where objects of real antiquity and beauty are for sale – (normally in Mexico 'antique' and 'curiosity' are synonymous terms referring to souvenirs, things as frightful there as I have ever seen anywhere in the world). The San Domingo chapel, which escapes notice in Terry's guide, is the finest of its kind in Mexico.

Chapultepec Palace. It was supposed to be shut for the day, but a soldier let us in. General Cardenas does not live there; he has a villa of his own in a flood-lit pine grove. Chapultepec is full of memories of his predecessors; Maximilian's chosen site, then outside the city, now a suburb; it is his view; his stained-glass windows in the best taste of his time, the worst in the world, his trees billowing below the windows but the windows themselves bear the mark of the Republic – M.R. in frosted, public-house glass; Diaz's billiard-room and brass stair rails; Rubio's swimming-bath. The terrace is curiously like a seaside pier with glass shelters and kiosks where one expects to find cigar sellers; Carranza and his captains used to sprawl about here in the happy vinous interlude between battle-field and firing-squad.

A garden in the outskirts of Mexico City with an eighteenth-century grotto made of Chinese porcelain set in cement; glimpses of crowded patios in the poor quarters; a morning in the prison. Tourists are quite welcome there. There are workshops for about a tenth of the inmates; the others lie in bed or lounge about the yards and beg money from the visitors; some of them have started small retail businesses selling sweets and tobacco. The men are allowed visits from women once a week in cells specially set aside for their meetings; that and other humane privileges are prescribed by law; it depends on your possession of money whether the gaolers allow them; with money you can get most things, from cocaine to an evening's dancing at *el Retiro*. There is an English homicide there, of unsettled mentality, who is said to be often seen treating his gaolers in the fashionable bars. General Cardenas was a gaoler once and stepped into history when he liberated his only prisoner and set out in his company to join the revolutionary army.

The September crisis; all the Mexican papers making the worst of it – *Guerra Inevitabile* on all the posters. As a result no one taking it seriously. We read that children were being sent out of London; that they were digging trenches in Hyde Park. We thought, 'no wonder foreigners think us odd when they are told stories like that about us'. A little later thousands of people in the United States were thrown into panic by the belief that there had been an invasion from Mars; that is how the September crisis looked in Mexico for the first few days. People with wireless sets said they had heard snatches from London; things looked very bad there. In the Ritz bar there was a certain amount of discussion among men of military age as to how they were to get home. Then the papers came out with enormous headlines 'President Cardenas Appeals for Peace'. Shortly after that peace was arranged; many of his supporters believed it was his doing until the American newspapers began to say it was not such a good peace after all. The war in Spain was very much more real to them than any other piece of contemporary history; more real even than Roosevelt's New Deal. They understood the Spanish issue in Spanish terms, without any English and French and American confusions, and felt strongly about it one way or the other. It was like part of their own lives. In the vestibule of the Public Library hung a picture called 'Spain' – a woman in travail among the bombs, painted with Indian ferocity; a really frightful picture. There was a sweet, heady cocktail on sale at the smart bars called a 'Franco'. Even a partisan of Franco like myself, could see something ironical in these two different modes of expressing sympathy. A taxi driver had the Franco flag on the front of his car.

A week of vexations in the attempt to buy a picture. There was a large eighteenth-century, stylised, decorative St Michael on sale at Sanbornes for the very modest price of 100 pesos. They are building a church for my parish at home. It seemed to be just the thing. The lady in charge, who throughout bore my vacillations with heroic patience, warned me that there might be difficulty in getting it out of the country. It had clearly come from a church and as all Church property had been confiscated by the Government its export was forbidden; a sensible law which has done much to preserve what *has* been preserved. We went to the Ministry of Arts for permission to take it away. They were charming and said they would send someone to look at it. Days passed and our departure became imminent. We called and telephoned; if permission was given we should have to have it photographed and obtain a special passport for it. At last we got someone from the Ministry to see it. It was too big, he said, and tried to console us by deploring our taste; an ugly picture, he said, of no value or interest. Then someone told us of a smuggler who could get anything one wanted out of the country. He was blandly reassuring; yes, nothing would be easier; he was sending a cargo of contraband at the moment; if we could bring it at once he would have it crated up and we should find it waiting for us at San Antonio. We told him the day of our train; it would be there in time. We paid for the picture and carried it through the streets to his office; he was quite unembarrassed by the ostentation of its delivery. An old Indian carpenter was summoned to make a crate for it. I was to call next day, when it had been weighed, and pay for transit. I called. The smuggler was not there. His clerk said he might come that day or might not. We called repeatedly and hung about the door. At length we caught him. The picture was crated up. It would be delivered in San Antonio in a week or so. But, we protested, he had promised it for three days' time. We were going straight through to New York. Well, he said, that was impossible. Why had he not told us that before we bought the picture? He had been busy and forgotten the date. It was all one to him whether he handled it or not; he was only trying to be obliging.

Then the deal was off, we said. The lady at Sanbornes patiently received us. Would she take the picture back? Very well. We carried it through the streets and it was re-hung in its place in the gallery.

A lengthy dispute now began with the smuggler. Was it fair to him, he asked, to call the deal off? He had been to great trouble about it. We offered to pay for the crate and the carpenter. That, he said, was of no consequence; the carpenter was his father. But what of the risk?

The risk? Did he mean the risk of the authorities intervening?

No, no, the authorities were his friends. What of the risk he had run in housing the picture all night? Suppose his warehouse had been burned down, he would have been liable for the picture's value. It had been an anxious night for him, housing our picture. Anything might have happened. He was not pressing his claim as a business man but as one gentleman to another. He did not profit by his smuggling; he did it simply to oblige gentlemen. I said, as one gentleman to another, that I thought his anxiety exaggerated.

He began to appeal on grounds of national honour. What about the prestige of England? What would people say if it became known that an Englishman had behaved in this manner? I asked him what price he set on his anxiety. That, he said, was a matter for an English gentleman to decide for himself.

At this stage the Mexican friend who had been my support in every predicament intervened. I was handling this affair from quite the wrong angle. Did the smuggler realise, asked my friend, that England was faced with war? I was returning to fight for my King. How could I, in the circumstances, be expected to concern myself with pictures? The smuggler was moved to sudden affection. Why had I not mentioned this significant fact instead of wrangling about risks of storage? He perfectly understood my predicament. How could I go into action carrying a six-foot canvas of St Michael?

Of course there could be no question between us of payment. To clinch matters I gave a peso to the porter who had done nothing in the matter except wriggle his bare toes among the shavings. This convinced the smuggler of my inherent generosity. We parted friends.

Ironically enough, when we got to the frontier, the Mexican customs officers never came into our carriage. We could have carried off a hundred pictures.

An exhilarating day in search of a *fiesta*. The bulletin issued for tourists in Spanish and English, *This Week in Mexico*, announced a fiesta at a village named Chalma. 'In part,' it said, 'it is a religious fiesta and due to the folk lore, traditions and the hundreds of Indian dancers that come from all over the country it will probably outclass other fiestas during this month.' We decided to go. Our only concern was that we should find it overrun with fellow tourists. We need not have worried.

Chalma was not on any map. Enquiry at the Tourist Bureau elicited the advice to drive in our own car to Toluca, hire another for the bad road to Tenancingo, from where it was two or three hours' ride by horse. We set out the day before. At Toluca we ate delicious little white fish cooked in black butter; the first good food we had met in a restaurant (on our return the fish had doubled in price because, they said, some foreigners had eaten so many – ourselves). The waiter at the restaurant said it was eight hours' ride from Tenancingo to Chalma. We found a car with a negro driver. He knew a man who kept a hat shop who came from Chalma; he would be able to direct us. The hatter said the fiesta was not at Chalma but at another village beyond, a village named Santiago, not through Tenancingo at all. It would be a beautiful fiesta. We could sleep the night at Santiago and go there next day. We drove off over appalling roads, through lovely country to Santiago, a decayed village where no one knew of a fiesta. We went to see the village priest, an old man with a full white beard who was sitting in silence in his sacristy with a younger man in shabby civilian clothes, another visiting priest. There was nowhere to stay in Santiago they said; there *was* a fiesta at Chalma but a very small one, without dancing. The Government did not allow dancing. But at the next village, the one we were going to, there would be a beautiful fiesta next day. How far was it? About two hours.

We stopped in the piazza to ask a soldier the way. How far was it? Ten minutes. It was a question I suppose of the prestige of the motor car. It took us about half an hour. When we reached the village we found a statue of Juarez, a small church, a few houses. The Indians were decorating the church with branches of leaves. We asked about the fiesta. There would be High Mass, they said, in the morning. And afterwards? In the evening some actors were coming from Toluca to sing in a tent. Dances? No, nowadays the soldiers did not allow that outside the church and the priests would not allow it inside. We heard afterwards that they do still dance at these village fiestas, in the yard outside the churches, but the practice has come into vague discredit and they will not talk about it to strangers. We drove on to Tenancingo and arrived there some hours after dark. An enjoyable day.

These were our holidays. There are few countries that still offer so many surprises to the tourist. But there were graver interests which have no part in this chapter.

CHAPTER 3

A COUNTRY WHERE THERE ARE
NO CONSERVATIVES

1

IT MAY BE useful here to give a few notes about Mexican political
history. Various names will occur and recur in the following pages. It
would be tedious for the reader who is already familiar with them, to
find the argument constantly interrupted by explanatory matter. On
the other hand it is perhaps not discourteous to assume that some
readers may be as ignorant as I was myself when the events of last
spring first excited my curiosity about the country. For their sake
I will suggest, with the minimum of comment, the outlines of this
historical structure of which recent incidents are a part; the learned
are invited to skip the next few pages.

The Spanish conquest of Mexico took place between the years
1519 and 1521. The land had been the scene of previous extensive
invasions, the history of which is conjectural and based upon archæological inferences. The Toltec people are believed to have conquered it from the South at the end of the seventh century of our era;
to have lived there for three centuries and to have disappeared again
in circumstances of which nothing is known. In the thirteenth
century savage invaders from the North West overran the country.
About a hundred years later a people of higher culture came, also
from the North, named the Aztecs. They established themselves
mainly in the valley of the Anahuac but extended their rule over
a wider area. It was they whom Cortes found in occupation, with
their king, Montezuma II, on the throne. It has been popular in
recent years to attribute to the Aztecs a higher culture than can be
proved by evidence. They built massively and symmetrically, with
stylised intricate ornament and statuary. Nothing that has survived

is comparable either in beauty or technical skill with the art and craftsmanship of mediæval Europe. (When I read accounts of the splendour of lost civilisations, I always remember the descriptions with which the world's Press was lately full of the Imperial court at Addis Ababa.) They had a system of hieroglyphic record, but no real written language; they were ignorant of the wheel and the plough. Their ascendancy over the surrounding peoples seems to have been precarious. Cortes found ready allies in the neighbouring race of Tlaxcalans.

Cortes landed, after a preliminary brush at Tabasco, at Vera Cruz; his force amounted to 400 men, 15 horses (animals never before seen in Mexico) and 7 pieces of artillery. Before setting out into the unknown continent he sank the fleet that had brought him from Cuba. The stupendous daring of the expedition needs no comment. Its success was helped by the superstitious expectations of the people who had a tradition that an event of the kind would occur. In 1522 Cortes became Governor, Captain General and Chief Justice over the Empire which Spain held for three centuries. In 1524 the chaplains who had accompanied his army were re-inforced by twelve Franciscan friars whose duty was to convert the natives; mass baptisms took place. In 1527 Juan de Zumarraga became first Archbishop of Mexico. In 1531 the work of conversion received what is held to be miraculous sanction in the appearance of the Virgin Mary at Guadalupe.

Notions of independence began to appear among the governing class of the Mexicans towards the end of the eighteenth century. The independence of the English colonies in the North, the spread of Freemasonry in the garrisons, the revolution in France, the weakness of Spain in Europe, all contributed to them. The Napoleonic era in Europe and the Peninsular War confused the issues to such an extent that it was not always clear to a Spanish official overseas where his true loyalty lay. In 1810 a parish priest, Hidalgo, led a peasants' rising which was suppressed; he was executed. In 1813 the army chiefs declared for independence. The leading general, Iturbide, became Emperor in 1822; General Santa Anna at the same time proclaimed a republic. The republicans won and Iturbide was executed.

In 1823 the Monroe doctrine was proclaimed by the United States; by this the continent of America was declared closed to European irredentism. In 1825 the last loyal Spanish garrison evacuated its post. From the death of Iturbide until the French invasion of 1861, Mexico had no settled government and in the confusion lost over half her territory, permanently, to the United States. The bankruptcy of the central government and the peculations of successive soldiers and officials, prompted a series of inroads on Church property which ended in the Reform Laws of 1859, by which Juarez confiscated all that was left. Juarez, still one of the heroes of the governing party, was an Indian from Oaxaca, an advanced radical in opinion and tenacious of character. His candidature had the armed support of the United States against the conservatives.

The French intervention of 1861–1867 had at first been intended to have an international, debt-collecting character. Spain and Great Britain, however, early released themselves from their commitments, and it became a personal adventure of Napoleon III's. Arch-Duke Maximilian of Austria had for some time shown ambitions towards historical prominence that were unsuitable in a younger son. He was induced to accept the crown of Mexico under a false impression of the tranquillity of the country. He found that those who had invited him to come represented only a faction and that the problems created by a generation of anarchy and the Juarez Reforms were not amenable to the mildly liberal, constitutional monarchy he had intended. His power and personal safety were insured only by the French troops which, in 1867, Napoleon III withdrew. Two months after they left General Porfirio Diaz took Puebla. Juarez, who had taken refuge in the United States raised a rebellion in the North. A month later Maximilian surrendered, with his loyal generals Miramon and Mejia, and in spite of protests from all over the world, was shot at Juarez's orders on June 17th. The Arch-Duchess Carlotta had gone to Europe to impress on Napoleon III the gravity of the Mexican situation; he was fully aware of it and would do nothing more. She conceived the notion that he intended to murder her, and in Rome became finally insane, refusing to leave the Vatican for fear of her enemies; she was thus the last woman to spend a night in the papal apartments.

General Diaz took Mexico City for Juarez and after his death became the ruler of the country for thirty-five years. During his reign Mexico became the centre of enormous foreign investment; communications were improved and many of the towns assumed a modern industrial character. By 1906 about £200,000,000 of foreign capital was invested in Mexico; the annual budgets showed an excess of revenue over expenditure; currency was steady and credit high. Limantour was finance minister. A few years later the prospective wealth of the country was enormously increased by the discovery of petroleum in various districts in abundant and convenient form. In 1908 the Mexican Eagle Company was formed by the late Lord Cowdray. Other oil companies, American and Mexican owned, developed valuable properties. In 1910, Porfirio Diaz celebrated his 80th birthday and the zenith of Mexican economic prosperity.

In the same year Francisco Madero, a wealthy landowner of Spanish-Jewish origin, issued a book attacking the principle of re-election which, in effect, made Mexico an autocracy and its representative institutions meaningless. Besides this purely political consideration there was a feeling among many of the more humane Mexicans that the distribution of the new riches of Mexico was outstandingly inequitable; the foreigners had been making huge profits, rich Mexicans had become somewhat richer; poor Mexicans somewhat poorer; there had been connivance at acts of enclosure of public lands committed by the large landowners. Many observers believed that Mexico was now so orderly and prosperous that the time was suitable for social readjustments that would improve the pitiable condition of the poorest class. With Diaz's increasing age the machinery of government had fallen into disrepair; local military governors returned 'padded' army lists; when the revolt – or rather the revolts, for there was little identity of interest or aim on the part of the rebels – against Diaz started, it was found that there was both little will to resist and little means of resistance. Civil riots and military mutinies occurred. Madero's name was that generally used by the rebels. Diaz was old and ill; he resigned on May 25 and on the 31st left the country for Europe, where he died in exile; he left the country rich and himself poor. On June 7th, to the accompaniment of an unusually destructive earthquake, Madero entered Mexico City in triumph.

Madero's rule lasted until February 1913 when he was murdered by the adherents of General Huerta. His period of authority was one of bitter disillusionment for himself and his sympathisers. The elements that had made the revolt successful rendered the country ungovernable. Zapata and Villa led bandit armies which successfully prevented all attempts to restore order. Madero had little administrative talent but failed largely through his own virtues of trustfulness and moderation. After his death authority was divided between rival generals and brigands, among whom President Wilson, vainly attempting to identify a suitable leader, chose Carranza. Atrocities took place all over the country; whole States were captured by criminals; the financial structure built up by Limantour collapsed. Foreign investors found their stocks depreciated or worthless while successive governments were obliged to adopt more and more ruthless and irregular means of raising funds. Most of the prominent figures of this decade were either assassinated or executed. In 1916 General Pershing's expeditionary force from the United States failed to capture Villa. Generals Calles and Obregon emerged as powerful leaders. Carranza was murdered in 1920 while trying to escape from the country. The Calles-Obregon group came into power with the support of the C.R.O.M., a labour union organised on Marxist principles in the industrial cities. The governing party organised itself as the Revolutionary Party of Mexico. Since then it has been the only political party in the country; elections continue to be purely formal; candidates for office and for places in Congress are chosen by the party chiefs; rule is autocratic, though the autocrat continues to be subject to strong extra-constitutional pressure; some members of the Revolutionary Party belong, and some do not, to the international communist party; its avowed aims are substantially communist; it is strongly anti-religious. It was powerful enough to destroy the brigand armies; the various questions at issue with the United States, chiefly relating to damage and confiscation of foreign interests, continued to be acute. The general trend has been a pressure from below by organised labour for a more drastic policy of socialisation and nationalisation, resisted by the office-holders who wish to consolidate their personal careers by coming to terms with the United States. In order to pacify the C.R.O.M. (which later was eclipsed in importance by Lombardo Toledano's union of syndicates, the C.T.M.) Obregon and Calles intensified their anti-religious policy; in 1925 the churches were closed throughout the country; countless outrages against the religious took place during an officially supported persecution, the most famous incident of which was the execution of Father Pro, a Jesuit; there was an armed revolt by the *Cristeros* (followers of El Cristo Rey – Christ the King). Obregon was assassinated, with unsolicited help from his own party, by a religious cartoonist named Tocal, in 1928. Calles continued the persecution of the Church, but under the influence of Dwight Morrow became increasingly amenable to the requirements of foreign finance. Various party nominees held the Presidency but Calles remained the real ruler. In 1934 General Lazaro Cardenas was chosen for the six years term of office under the supposition that he would prove obedient to Calles. He quickly disappointed these expectations. First he made a tour of the country, endearing himself by his simplicity and promising substantial philanthropic innovations; he became a personal figure instead of a party nominee. Finally, with the help of General Cedillo, he expelled Calles from the country. Cedillo retired to his property in San Luis Potosi, where he reigned as more or less benevolent dictator. He became, however, the focus for the aspirations of Cardenas's opponents. Cardenas drove him into rebellion by demanding his removal from his own territory, and succeeded in hunting him down and shooting him in the hills. Cardenas, since his accession, has fallen under the influence of Lombardo Toledano, who has convinced him that the various philanthropic reforms he wishes to introduce, can only be accomplished by a full Marxist policy; Toledano's natural persuasiveness has been reinforced by his power as leader of most of the principal industrial and agrarian organisations. The main features of General Cardenas's policy are the nationalisation of industries, most of which are foreign owned and managed, and the confiscation and division into village holdings of the private landed estates. He has encountered little resistance in the latter; in the former, however, he finds himself at variance with the United States and other foreign governments. In March 1938 he took the grave step of confiscating the whole oil industry. He is, personally, a man of predominantly Indian blood and of simple habits; in early middle age. He was a general at the age of 25. He has never been outside Mexico, has no oratorical powers but a gift of endearing himself with those he meets, particularly the peasants; no one has seriously accused him of venality, though his brother is universally believed to have made a fortune by government contracts for road building. Lombardo Toledano is a lawyer of superior education; he has visited Russia and is in touch with labour leaders all over Europe and the Americas; he is handsome, a vigorous orator, sensitive about his personal prestige and credited by his enemies with a substantial and increasing private fortune deposited abroad. He holds no position in the Government and is distrusted by the majority of the army leaders. He is said to regard himself, with some justice, as the real ruler of Mexico.

2

Questions I often asked myself during my stay in Mexico were: if one were not looking for signs of it, how much would one be aware of the very singular social and political conditions surrounding one? How far would it be possible to lead what in other parts of the world would be considered a normal life? The answer to the last question is that for a Mexican or for anyone doing business of any kind in Mexico, it would be quite impossible. The distressed condition of the country and its uncertain future affect every hour of his day. I think, too, that only a very incurious visitor could be unaware of some of the underlying confusion. Many years ago now, there was a delicious film in which Harold Lloyd, as a convalescent million-aire, arrived in a South American republic in the middle of a revolution and progressed placidly down the main street, bowing left and right, while a battle was raging round him. A few happy visitors no doubt travel through the country engrossed in the antiquities or the natural history of the place, completely oblivious of its condition; but they must be very few. For it is impossible to talk to any inhabitant for five minutes without feeling the obsession of politics. For anyone who troubles to enquire the oddest information is constantly cropping up.

On the first day of my visit traffic leading to the Cathedral square was paralysed at midday. My companion advised leaving our taxi and walking. After passing an enormous block of cars, some drivers hooting furiously, others resigned to an indefinite wait, others causing further confusion by attempting to back out in the side streets, we came upon the cause of the trouble; a huge procession of schoolchildren, of all ages, themselves halted and standing wistfully among their banners. Many of the groups wore distinguishing ribbons and uniforms; the banners seemed merely to state the localities from which they came. I asked, 'Is it some football match?'

'No, it is just a demonstration of the children. They are always having them.'

'What about?'

'I'll ask.' My companion asked one or two spectators who shrugged indifferently, saying it was just a demonstration. Finally he obtained the information. 'It is a children's strike.'

'What about?'

'They do not like one of their teachers. They have come to protest to the President.'

'They seem very well organised.'

'Yes, the children's committees do that. The Ministry of Education teach them to organise like the C.T.M.'

'What will happen?'

'The teacher will be dismissed. They are always changing their teachers in that way.'

Next day the newspapers had a story of a brawl between the schoolboys and some chauffeurs from an omnibus garage.

Strikes are a topic of general discussion, like the weather in England, and like it, the habitual excuse for any failure of plans. The visitor may wonder why the service is so bad even at the leading restaurants; if he enquires he will learn that it is practically impossible for an employer to engage temporary labour; nothing fluctuates more sharply and regularly than the tourist trade, but if a restaurateur engages a waiter for the busy months he must keep him. Under the Labour Law the least that can happen to him for discharging a man is the payment of a bonus of a quarter's wages; it is more likely that a prolonged suit will begin; he will be kept from his business day after day waiting for a hearing at the Labour Courts, paying his own lawyer and one for the man who is suing him, paying the man's wages while the case is pending, and at the end be obliged to re-engage him permanently. So employment drops, the tourist sits hungrily at his table or rings despairingly at his bedroom bell in his hotel, the servants who are employed are worked off their feet and everyone is the worse off. The incurious visitor may merely assume that Mexicans are not very good hotel keepers; and that also is true.

Then there is the Museum. Every tourist visits it; how many bother to enquire how it is managed? Those who are told, find the story incredible. These, as I learned them, are the facts. Until a short time ago the staff was divided into two groups, both directly employed by the State. There were the specialists appointed to the various departments – archæologists, anthropologists and so on, who had mostly been trained in the United States or in Europe and knew a fair amount of their sciences; they were very poorly paid, but it was one of the few appointments open to Mexicans of education who were not active politicians; their work corresponded with that of similar officials in other museums; they were responsible for cataloguing, labelling, arranging, advising about new acquisitions and so forth. Below them were the floor cleaners, janitors and officials in peaked caps who lounged about the rooms guarding the exhibits and ordering foreign tourists to remove their hats. These had no pretensions to education, though in time they picked up a little dubious information from what they heard the guides telling the school-children. These outnumbered the specialists. When the Cardenas régime introduced the classless era, instructions were sent out that all units of workers must organise themselves into a union, which was to be a branch of the national C.T.M. – the 'labour front' over which Sr Lombardo Toledano presides. The Museum workers accordingly formed their union. Next they declared the Museum a closed shop and demanded that the specialists be made to join them. This, too, was decreed. The janitor is the boss; he enjoys meetings, and calls them frequently; he has the power to fine absentees which he uses with relish; the specialists have to come to his meetings, where all points of discipline and conditions of employment are debated and decided. It has just been decided that in future all promotions shall be by seniority alone and that all members of the union are equally eligible for all posts. Thus a floor cleaner may, and probably will, find himself in charge of the Mayan antiquities.

Tales of this kind – many of them no doubt exaggerated – form the staple conversation in Mexico. There is the story, which I believe to be perfectly true, of the woman who was ruined by her door-keeper. The door-keeper is an important man in the Mexican family. In the old days of large households it was keenly competed for. It carried no regular wages, but board, lodging, light work and a position of confidence that could be turned to profit in many ways. In particular he got tips for being awakened after bed time. In a patriarchal Mexican house the younger members were often anxious to conceal from their parents the hours they kept. It was a thoroughly good job. One old Indian had held this post content-edly for twenty-five years when he was caught in some unusual dishonesty and dismissed. He consulted a lawyer about the new Labour Laws and their interpretation in the hope of getting some damages. The lawyer, learning that he had received no regular wages, filed a suit against his employer for accumulated arrears at the new rates, for compensation for their having been withheld, for fines for neglect of the labour legislation, and for overtime for having been expected to get up and open the door at night i.e. for having been on duty, at work, all night, every night of his life. The total, with legal expenses came, I was told, to 40,000 pesos. And he won his case.

It is unlikely that he profited much. It is usual in such cases for lawyers to work on a commission basis which in the case of an illiterate Indian would absorb most of the winnings, or even to purchase the rights in an action for a sum down. Litigation is universal in Mexico. 'I have to see a man about an amparo' (stay of justice) is a normal polite excuse in refusing an invitation. European employers who find themselves constantly involved with the courts, get despondent about it, but I got the impression that Mexicans, on the whole, rather enjoy it. What they do not like is for the game to lose the element of chance which is so dear to them. In the old days you never quite knew what decision you would get; it all depended on the pull your adversary had, on the bribe he had offered, and to whom. Now there is monotony in the judicial decisions. They go on purely ideological grounds. The proletarian is always right; between proletarians the one who is nearest to the C.T.M. boss; between bourgeois the one who is nearest to the governing gang. One of the present President's first reforms was to abolish the independence of the Supreme Court and make its personnel a government committee. Since then no appeal has been of any efficacy where politics are concerned – and politics are concerned in every branch of Mexican life. It is no exaggeration to say that to be an employer in Mexico is to outlaw oneself. It is not surprising that business of every kind is in dissolution. There are indications that Mexicans themselves are getting uneasy about their condition.

At first many of them enjoyed the spectacle of the discomfiture of the foreigners. They disliked them personally; they resented their assumption of superiority; they inherited a belief that their government was under foreign influence, and was being conducted for foreign advantage. There was a certain tradition of misunderstanding between foreign commerce and the Mexican educated class which has had an important influence in Mexican politics. There are of course countless exceptions. There are many English and American business men who are popular on the golf links and even in Mexican homes. There are some Mexicans who have been educated in Europe and return more pro-British than the British themselves. But, generally speaking, there is something of the Chinese mandarin about the Mexican aristocrat in his attitude to the capitalists. In the days of prosperity when the Jockey Club was the centre of an extravagant social life, few English or Americans obtained admission. Now the Mexicans are ruined and they attribute their ruin very largely (and I think unjustly) to the foreigners. They believe that most of the revolutionary confiscations took place with the connivance and encouragement of the United States, who backed Juarez against Maximilian; first made and then drove out Huerta, and even idealised ruffians like Villa and Zapata; who armed Calles when half the country had risen against his religious persecution, who were naturally anti-Catholic and anti-aristocratic, who took huge profits out of the country and lectured the Mexicans on their responsibilities if they went on a holiday at Biarritz; who told successive Presidents that a redivision of land would bring national salvation, who complacently watched the ruin of the Church and of the white land-owning families; and were now getting ruined themselves. They are too polite to put matters so bluntly but this is, I believe, the attitude of most of the Mexican upper class. It is only partly justified by historical facts, but that is their belief, and that the reason why, in the present crisis, the foreign business men found no local party to whom they could appeal.

There is a disposition, in fact, among visiting publicists to ignore them altogether or to treat them as a distressed foreign minority, like White Russians in Paris; to accept the centuries of Spanish rule as a closed incident and to look to pre-conquest elements for the eventual salvation of the country; to speak severely of 'Indo-America' in place of 'Latin-America'. That is the official attitude of the Revolutionary Party which finds expression in the huge and clumsy frescoes of Diego Rivera. It suits the politicians and the archæologists, but it makes nonsense of history. Mr Gruening, for example, who is to many students the standard historian, devotes 18 pages out of 664 to the 'colonial period'. But the Spanish conquest was not a process of mere economic exploitation. Mexico was part of New Spain; for three centuries of undisturbed domination Spaniards lived, married and died in Mexico; they mingled their blood profusely with the various native nations; they taught the people their language, law, religion, crafts and social habits. The whole country was saturated with Spanish influence; then the European source was cut off; the surface became dry and dusty but below it there was still rich, moist soil; for another century Mexico remained essentially Spanish. Four hundred years of history cannot be obliterated. The traditions of Spain are still deep in Mexican character and I believe that it is only by developing them that the country can ever grow happy.

I do not mean, of course, that it is possible or desirable to re-establish the vice-regal government, the *oidores*, and the *encomiendas*, although it was in many ways a better system than Mexico has known since. I believe, in fact, that within a hundred years Mexico will form part of the U.S.A. But I mean that for the understanding of its immediate problems fewer mistakes are made if it is remembered that the Mexicans, though they may sometimes *feel* like Aztecs or Tlaxcalans, *think* like Spaniards; their minds have been formed on the Aristotelean model.

The position of the Spanish-Mexican families has no exact parallel anywhere in the world. At the moment they exhibit many of the defects of an aristocracy that has first been deprived of power and privilege and then of livelihood. For generations, now, there has been little inducement to them to attempt to retain the leadership of their country. Under Porfirio Diaz (1876–1911) they filled the diplomatic posts and local governorships, but the national system was purely autocratic and the army a mere police force. They were precluded by their religion from joining the Freemasons who filled the bureaucracy. Moreover they were rich. Not as rich as English or Americans or French, but comfortably provided. Diaz ensured them their incomes and left them to enjoy themselves. Diaz married into their class. It is significant that when the revolution came it was led by a man far nearer to them than to the peon – Francisco Madero, a rich, white, landed proprietor.

Diaz has been criticised since his fall by all parties – by the patriots on the ground that he parcelled up the national resources and sold them to foreigners, by the socialists on the ground that he introduced modern capitalism and kept the peasants in degraded conditions, by humanitarians because he enslaved the Yaqui Indians, by the religious because he left the problems of the Reforms unsolved.

The general feeling is that he had a unique opportunity to reconstruct the nation and that he did nothing except maintain his own authority and allow troubles to accumulate for his successors. The truth was that he set himself a simpler but no less arduous task. He should be judged as a Mustapha Kemal, not as a Mussolini. He found a country which, after two generations' experiment with independence and democracy was rapidly relapsing into savagery. For two generations the country had not known a government. For the period immediately before Diaz's assumption of power Mexico had been in the occupation of a French Army. While everywhere else in the world the ordinary amenities of civilised life had been making prodigious advances, in Mexico they had actually receded since the Spanish occupation. In particular the United States, which at the beginning of the century was on a lower cultural level than her Spanish neighbour, was now a world power of enormous wealth and potentiality. In Mexico there was no law nor national unity; not only had she not kept abreast of mechanical advance; in matters of communication and personal safety she had fallen behind her colonial standard. For thirty-five years Diaz maintained his personal government. He set an example, unique among Mexican rulers, in the integrity of his private life. He was a faithful husband; he left the country rich, himself poor. He opened up the country with roads and railways, bringing law and wealth to practically unexplored districts. Above all he kept the country's sovereignty intact – at a time when statesmen were openly claiming that the natural boundary of the United States was the isthmus of Panama. He was only able to do this by maintaining the equilibrium of foreign investment; by getting English and French to fight his commercial war with the United States. He saved his country from absorption at the very modest price of the dividends that went to European stock holders. It was a big enough achievement for one man; as time goes on perhaps the Mexicans will come to appreciate it, but as there is not yet a single memorial to Cortes, and his most lovely relic, the old church at Tlaxcala has lately been ruined, perhaps this is too much to hope. (Though, come to think of it, is there anywhere in England a memorial to Julius Cæsar?) At the end of Diaz's reign, when his powers were weakened, he began to concern himself with the problem of a successor and for the moment toyed with the idea (as Kemal did with disastrous results for those who took him seriously) of a constitutional opposition. Mexicans of the time, who had grown up under him, and knew the boredom and inevitable abuses that grow in an autocracy, who had never known the bad days of Juarez, wished to see their country conforming still more closely to the contemporary fashion; they had seen general elections at Stonyhurst and knew them to be lively and bonhomous occasions. So party politics were reintroduced with pleasant expectations of candidates competing with benevolent projects and a party loyalty finding expression in coloured rosettes and rotten eggs. The result has been twenty-five years of graft, bloodshed and bankruptcy. Hardly a single prominent figure in the history of Mexico in the last generation has escaped a violent death; Salas, Reyes, both Maderos, Suarez, Villa, Carranza, Obregon, Orozco, Zapata – the catalogue is almost complete. Now and then a politician gets across the border in time, either to wealthy exile like Calles or to imprisonment and death like Huerta. The constitutional opposition to which the opponents of Diaz aspired, has never come into existence. There is still one political party in Mexico, now the Revolutionary Party; seats and offices are appointed at party head-quarters as in all totalitarian states. The only difference between the Mexican system and the Fascist is that the nation has sacrificed its political liberties without getting internal security or foreign prestige in exchange. Thus it is not surprising that a political career has now few attractions for Mexicans of decent principle. It is difficult to say where the fault lies when the government of a country gets into the hands of its worst elements; there is a natural trend of all political forms in this direction. Those who have wearied of demo-cratic forms forget that history is full of instances of legitimate royalty being ruled by corrupt courtiers; English Whigs in the eighteenth century enriched themselves from the public purse; it is not only in France and the United States that the worst men may get to the top. What is certain, however, is that there is a Gresham's Law active in public life; bad rulers drive out good. In France and the United States it is unusual for respectable citizens to go into politics. In Mexico it is at the moment unknown.

In the United States, however, there is trade as an honourable activity and a source of power; in France there is an army. But in Mexico trade is almost all in foreign hands and the army has a very odd position. There is no recent military tradition among the Span-ish Mexicans. The army forms an independent estate with a relationship to the Government and the people which it is impos-sible for a foreigner to understand.

In the ordinary way it is extremely unobtrusive. One sees far fewer soldiers about the place than in most European countries.

Every town has its barracks – (usually a convent appropriated 'for charitable purposes'; many churches show signs of recent military occupation – bayonet cuts in the pictures, the ashes of campfires made from choir stalls, etc.) – on days of national importance the streets are lined and paraded with glum, fairly smart little figures in uniform; there are guards in field uniform – tin hats and bandoliers – at most government offices; on the main roads one passes little pickets, quartered in peasant huts, employed most of the day in cooking and eating; very, very rarely a high officer appears at a night club where, if sober, he sits shyly in a corner, suffering uncertainty about his knife and fork. But one does not get the impression of a country in which the military are predominant. That, however, according to everyone who ought to know, is the case. It is in the army that revolutions start; it is from the army that rulers rise – General Cardenas, for example. And the army is a very unusual force indeed. It is strongly anti-Catholic, pro-Freemason, anti-aristocratic, anti-foreign. Since the reforms of General Amaro it is highly disciplined – almost ascetic. One hears of local generals who maintain a feudal state, rather like Abyssinian Rases, but for the most part they live rough. The officers are recruited from the half-caste minor bourgeoisie; they go to military schools at an early age and imbibe certain Spartan virtues and vices. The men are pure Indian, recruited in the villages, usually, I am told, by forcible methods. Once enrolled they find themselves detached from the village, the soil, the family, and the parish which have hitherto been the basis of their lives; they seem to accept the new attachment placidly enough. Their loyalty, like that of 'native troops' all the world over, is to their immediate superiors. When the officers declare against the government they march with them. They are inspired by the commander's prestige and popularity which seem to have singularly little dependence on his qualities of justice and humanity, or even on his courage and military skill. If the general is successful they get a kind of vicarious satisfaction; if he loses they either take to the hills with him or wander home to their villages. All the fighting they have seen or heard of or are likely to see or hear of is against fellow Mexicans.

The civil service, which includes the school teachers, is appointed purely on political grounds and reflects the opinions of the governing group in Mexico City. The personnel are subject to close scrutiny in their private lives and are liable to expulsion if, for instance, they are seen to practise their religion. Most of them are mere clerks who find it convenient to profess whatever is the current governing philosophy. Many of them are alarmed at the direction General Cardenas's policy is taking; practically all, if they could keep their posts by so doing, would readily support an opposite policy if an opposition came into power. The whole-hearted doctrinaire communists seem mostly to be employed in the office of education, but even here there are many courageous malcontents who give secret religious instruction to their pupils.

The lawyers are an able and influential class. Apart from the endless litigation which is a feature of Mexican life, they occupy themselves prominently with political controversy in the Press. There are many prominent socialists among them. Lombardo Toledano, the head of the C.T.M., the federation of trades unions which is the chief political force in the country, is a lawyer. The judges, as has been mentioned above, are now political nominees, but the bar is predominantly against the Government, largely no doubt for professional reasons; the presence of the foreign business concerns in Mexico has been a source of splendid revenue to them.

The doctors are said to be highly competent, though the best of them still go abroad for their training. They have for a long time enjoyed a privileged position under the Revolution. Foreigners are forbidden to compete with them. Many of them owe their places to C.T.M. appointment. Medical service is one of the directions in which General Cardenas promises – though up to now he has accomplished very little – unlimited expansion. Hospitals are all in Government hands. They may, therefore, be said to support the present régime as a profession, although individually many are becoming apprehensive.

The shopkeepers and small manufacturers are uniformly allied with the foreign business interests. A large number of them are themselves foreign – German and Jewish principally, but drawn from all races, even Chinese and Syrian. They have suffered most from recent events. They are, however, unorganised and, at the moment, without influence.

The priesthood will be dealt with in a later chapter. They have been driven into the life of the catacombs. They are, of course, opposed to their persecutors but it is generally believed that their political power is completely broken.

These are, roughly, the political groupings of the elements from which a national opposition to General Cardenas might be expected to arise. At present time there is no open opposition of the kind which flourishes in a democratic country, and when one questions those who are most bitter in their complaints of the régime as to how they hope to see it altered, the answer nearly always comes back to the Army.

Judged by recent European standards Mexico seems to be in the condition where a Fascist party is due to rise and conquer. There is a historical cycle which is now becoming familiar and seems almost a part of industrial development; a cycle in which at certain moments malignant non-economic forces are decisive. There is the first phase when labourers, accustomed to a low standard of living and employed in a kind of work which makes only modest profits for their overlords, are employed for the same wages on work which provides enormous profits; this is usually called exploitation. Next comes the phase when the workmen realise their importance and the disproportionate nature of their rewards; they successfully claim a larger and larger share of the profits until the employers are gaining the bare margin which gives an inducement for further capital investment in that particular quarter; with the share in the profits comes an increased opportunity for the workmen to rise to higher economic classes and to become, themselves, employers; the increased purchasing power of the new wages and the taste for a wider range of commodities induced by the new social aspirations, make the marginal profits, in gross, considerable; that is liberal capitalism. Then the devil comes into it. As legitimate trading ceases to offer sensational profits the taste for gambling in fictitious values grows on the part of the rich with consequent sudden fluctuations of prosperity and employment, while at the same time the demands of the workmen cease to be temperate, are political in character instead of economic, and become frivolous and vindictive; that is what is popularly known as the class war. The middle class suffers from both sides and sees itself threatened by extinction while at the same time those whose interests are not exclusively economic and class-conscious, are ashamed at the ignominious aspect their country has in the world at large; there is an ebullition of semi-mystical feeling for race and nation combined with an ascetic disgust for people who compete only for physical comforts. Self-preservation and patriotism combine to produce Fascism. Then the devil comes into that, too; cranks and criminals get into power in the new régime; the patriotic motive becomes neurotic; a people constantly maintained in a condition of high excitement by demagogy has to find some food for its nervous appetite more tasty than draining marshland and maintaining a punctual train service; the nation embarks on a war of expansion, is ruined and reverts to those simple standards of life when, in due course, it will be ready for the cycle to start again with a fresh era of exploitation.

This cycle is, of course, largely conjectural. Mexico has seemed to conform to it in recent years but in her case there are further complications. First, the disparity between the urban proletariat and the peasant is enormous; industrial conditions and communist propaganda have brought the factory workers to a condition more or less analogous with those of pre-Fascist Italy and modern France; the peons on the land have no counterpart in Europe; they belong to another historical era. Secondly, the larger industries are almost exclusively owned and managed by foreigners, so that a purely nationalist movement would not seek its allies, as it has done in Europe, among the industrial magnates. Thirdly, Mexico is used to misgovernment. That is perhaps the most dismal feature of all. A whole generation has grown up since the fall of Porfirio Diaz who has known nothing but pillage, graft and degeneration. It is not shocking to them to hear of scandals in high places; they are not disappointed when promises are repudiated; they have grown accustomed to seeing everything working rather less well year by year. They lack the spur to action which comes from exasperation at seeing something misused which they have seen in proper order. Many of the more thoughtful of them have come to the conclusion

that there is no cure for their ills. It is not unknown in history for the
jungle to recapture its lost provinces; one can see it happening,
today, in the West Indies. It is only by unremitting, concerted
defence and counter-attack that man retains his place on the
earth. Many Mexicans, and those some of the most honourable
and disinterested among them, have despaired of the effort.

CHAPTER 4

OIL

1

THE NATIONAL MUSEUM was full of school-children. Crocodiles threaded their way from Huitzilopochtli to Tlahuizcalpantecuhtli, Chac-Mool and Teotihuacan, pausing and stopping at the command of their guide, gazing about them with that air of sullen bewilderment common to school-children in museums in all parts of the world. An eager, English-speaking guide had attached himself to me in the courtyard.

'There are too many children,' he remarked.

'Yes.'

'It is their holiday.'

Together we struggled to the huge Calendar Stone which is the hall-mark of the more expensive souvenirs. You can get the Calendar Stone in china as an ash-tray, or in gold the size of a threepenny bit on a ring, or in silver the size of a soup-plate as a salver; you can even get it – oddest of all commemorative conceits – engraved on an onyx egg, but no one knows what it means. Ingenious, crossword minds have played with this 24-ton puzzle for 150 years and devised various explanations flattering to its Aztec carvers. It has been the base of a patriotic claim that before the Spanish conquest, the Indians had advanced beyond Europe in the science of chronology. We stood and looked at this stone; the school-children swarmed round us.

'It is better to see this very interesting stone early in the morning,' said the guide. 'There are some beautiful objects in the room across the patio.'

We passed into a very nice jumble of bric-a-brac: costumes, snuff-boxes, Imperial regalia, lace and needlework... 'This,' said my guide, 'is one of the swords of Maximilian's bodyguard.'

773

It was one of those triple daggers, ornamented with cairngorms and silver thistle, that form a part of Highland full-dress. Heaven knows how it had found its way here (or did Maximilian keep a piper? I have not seen him mentioned in any of the biographies, but it is quite conceivable that he imported the idea from Balmoral in his romantic Miramar period.)

'That has come from Scotland,' I said.

'Scotland?'

'A part of Great Britain.'

'Ah.' This gave my guide the chance to satisfy himself on a point that had been puzzling him for some time. 'You are not American?'

'No, English.'

'The English are more elegant.'

'Yes.'

'They have more nobility than the Americans.'

'Very true.'

'I am surprised to see an Englishman here since we took your oil. What do they think in England about that? . . . '

The eternal question, with which all conversations in Mexico began and ended: what was the British Government going to do? What did the British people feel about it? The true answer, I suppose, was that though there was only one large international question for the Mexicans, there were a hundred for the British Government. We had stated our views uncompromisingly and were quite prepared to wait a year or so before discussing them. And as for the feelings of the British public, these are only aroused when they see politics in simple terms of under-dog and oppressor. They have not yet got used to thinking of British Companies as under-dogs. Moreover the confiscations had been accompanied by a number of potent phrases about democracy. If the Japanese, or Nationalist-Spaniards, or Germans or Italians had taken our oil, then there would have been a series of meetings in the Albert Hall; but the Mexicans had a Left Book Club vocabulary. It so happened that the Mexican régime showed features which elsewhere would be damning: the government was autocratic; the autocrat was a general; there was only one political party; educational appointments were political and the teaching purely state-propagandist; history books were being edited on the lines of nationalist self-assertion ... Some of the British public knew these things, some did not; but to the politically minded, vocal minority, one thing was of paramount importance: when the Mexicans saluted their bosses they raised the arm with clenched fist, not with extended fingers. So they were all right; they were democrats, like ourselves and the French.

It is true that the majority of Englishmen do not think in quite such simple terms, but it is the minority who edit the weeklies and hold meetings in Trafalgar Square. It is they who are quoted as expressing 'British opinion'. Sober citizens had more on their minds than Mexico in the summer of 1938. The Oil Question, however, makes a very nice working model of a modern international-economic problem. It has practically all the features of the larger problems that are disturbing our lives and may be examined conveniently in the large, but not overwhelming, volume of conflicting propaganda that has been issued by the opposing sides.

The main facts are not in dispute. On March 18th, 1938, General Cardenas, by Presidential decree, confiscated the properties of a dozen or more oil companies representing British, Dutch, American and other foreign shareholders valued by them at about £80,000,000. Since that date his action has been confirmed by judicial decisions and amplified by the executive officials to include business premises in Mexico City and the Isthmus which had no direct connexion with the production or sale of oil. The decree of expropriation was, in form, the General's answer to the refusal of the companies to accept the award of the Mexican Labour Board in a dispute between them and their employees. The British Foreign Office, unsupported by the State Department at Washington, protested on April 8th, in a note from which the following salient points may be quoted:

> *'His Majesty's Government in the United Kingdom do not question the general right of a Government to expropriate in the public interest and on payment of adequate compensation; but this principle does not serve to justify expropriations essentially arbitrary in character ... The Mexican Eagle Company were, as a result of various proceedings in law, confronted with an award rendered by the Labour Board and confirmed by the Supreme Court, which was not in the view of His Majesty's Government justified on the facts ... Essential evidence had been improperly excluded, inadequately considered and unjustifiably overridden by*

experts and the Labour Board; which evidence was directed to show that the figures of profits and costs of the Company subsequently adopted by experts and the Labour Board were erroneous . . . His Majesty's Government are fully satisfied that the conditions following for non-compliance with the award are not such as have warranted the adoption of such a drastic and far-reaching measure as expropri-ation. The severity of this harsh and arbitrary step was out of all proportion to the exigencies of the situation which it was allegedly designed to meet and went far beyond what was necessary if the real object which the Mexican Government had had before them was merely to secure the execution of the award and what, in their view, would be fair treatment for the wage earners . . . His Majesty's Government have looked in vain for any explicit and adequate statement of such public interest as would be served by nothing less than expropriation; nor do they think it could have been demonstrated that any such public interest existed.

'. . . His Majesty's Government . . . find difficulty in escaping the conclusions that the real motive for the expropriation was a political desire to acquire for Mexico in permanence the advantages of ownership and control of the oil fields; that expropriation was tantamount to confiscation carried out under a veil of legality formed by basing it upon labour issues; and that the consequences have been a denial of justice and a transgression by the Mexican Government of the principles of international law.

'His Majesty's Government see no way in which this situation can be remedied but by the restoration of its properties to the Company itself. This His Majesty's Minister is instructed hereby formally to request.'

The Cardenas Government replied on April 12th.

'. . . The Mexican Government cannot do other than point out that, even on the assumption that numerous British investors are very much interested in the situation in which the Company finds itself, the latter is a Mexican enterprise, and therefore the defence of its interests does not appertain to a foreign State . . . The Mexican Government cannot in any way admit the unjustified limitation which it is sought to place on the right of expropriation . . . The expropriation decree must be appraised separately and must be adjudged legal and valid in itself, although it is recognised that the circumstances preceding it made expropriation indispen-sable . . . The ground of public interest which led directly to it was created in this case by the contempt of court on the part of the companies in the face of a decision rendered by the highest court of the land . . . The firm determination to pay for the properties expropriated has been declared publicly before the whole world and the Republic's capacity to pay is a real and certain fact . . . It cannot be said that there was a denial of justice, so long as the legal resources which the company have for their protection have not yet been exhausted before the Mexican Courts.'

As the result of a further exchange of notes in which certain technicalities were disputed and the fundamental disagreement of the two governments accentuated, diplomatic relations were severed, on the initiative of the Mexicans, on May 13th. Legal proceedings to set aside the expropriations were protracted for months, without hope of redress on the part of the companies. The Mexican Courts enjoy far less independence than those of Nazi Germany, and in recent years have never been known to give a decision, in a matter concerning politics, that was not in accordance with presidential instructions, but the tedious and expensive farce had to be played out, to satisfy the Mexican objection that a denial of justice could not be pleaded so long as there were legal means of appeal open. The proceedings were voluminous and, to the lay mind, futile. No one expected impartial justice to result; no one was surprised by a series of decisions, some of which violated the law, some of them commonsense, and some both. Mexicans are nimble advocates; they settled down to the case luxuriously, like gluttons to a feast. The height of fantasy was reached when the Supreme Court decided that the Companies were guilty, not only of contempt of court, which was technically arguable, but of breach of contract with their employees. The men, no one disputed, had occasioned the quarrel, by striking for a new collective contract when they were already bound by a series of contracts, most of which had some time to run after the date of the stoppage. The Supreme Court, however, held the Companies guilty of breach of contract and liable, not only to the payment of three months' pay but of an undefined but potentially vast compensation. Presumably, in dictating this judgment, the President hoped that, in whatever final reckoning might be made, this sum might, somehow, be introduced into the balance as an asset, and written off as an instalment or as the bulk of the compensation which he had promised to pay. But the lawyers had translated the question to a world of make-believe.

Men, in their attitude to law, may, nowadays, be divided into those who believe that if an act is legal, it is irrelevant whether it is just and expedient, and those who believe that if it is just and expedient, it is irrelevant whether it is legal. Few identify the terms, for respect for Law, as such, is the survival of a much earlier

age and of another conception of Society. Then the Ruler was
conceived of as someone holding a commission to enforce the
Law. Law was the inherited, and in many systems divinely revealed,
wisdom and morality of the people. The good king was the one who
administered it; the bad king let it be broken or broke it himself; he
was himself the subject of the Law, not its creator. Nowadays,
however, Law is merely a formulation of the whims of the party in
power. It is used for social experiment; it is 'tried out' on the people
and lightly abandoned if it proves unpopular. Rulers come into
power largely on their promises to make new laws or repeal old
ones. As a consequence law has become intensely provincial. It has
followed the general break-up of international concepts. In the
drying up of civilisation, cracks appear and widen; the parched
nations shrink away from one another. It becomes, year by year,
more difficult for people of one nationality to make their homes
among those of another. When a man voluntarily submits himself to
the law of the land in which he is living, he cannot predict the
implications of his submission. He is prevented from taking any
part in forming a system which may change dizzily. This is true
among the great and stable powers; it is of graver consequence in
a country like Mexico where any hooligan may get into power,
govern by decree, and assume, by his own dismissals and appointments, a judicature who will give his decrees any interpretation
that an emergency may require. Thus the question of whether
Mexican executive actions can be reconciled with Mexican legislation is purely academic; a source of revenue to the over-
crowded Mexican bar; an opportunity for personal recrimination
in the Mexican weekly papers; but a barren topic as far as practical
politics are concerned.

Thus all serious political discussion, today, must employ extra-
legal terms. It was, I believe, abundantly proved in the Mexican
Courts, that the act of expropriation violated the laws and the
constitution, but these are not the grounds on which the ordinary
English or American observer will find his interest aroused. Some,
indeed, have their minds already closed to discussion. There is the
purely nationalist preconception on either side, which is unshakable;
the English – pretty few of them in these days – who believe that the

world was created to supply the English with physical comforts, and that the armed forces of the Crown exist to ensure the regular payment of dividends – 'if the dagoes don't like it, damme, what's the Fleet for?' There are the Mexicans – thousands of them – who believe that the soil of the country and anything on and below it, was ordained for the exclusive use of the heterogeneous peoples who have been born there; that this possession is inalienable and that any use made of it by a foreigner is an act of theft. Besides these, there are the ideologues, to whom all capitalists are outlaws; they believe that a state of war exists between employer and employed; that any gain for one is a corresponding loss to the other; that all profits are stolen from wages and that there is no solution to the differences that arise, except the extermination of the rival party. With these there is no arguing. But beyond either group remain those who believe that mechanical industry and private property can cause both harm and good, and that each case must be judged on its merits. To these the significant questions are: Did the foreign oil companies establish themselves piratically in Mexico? Did their presence retard the peaceful development of its political and social life? Were the workers in the oil fields neglected and underpaid, and their recent demands based on bona fide social grievances? Was the destruction of the companies the only way of satisfying them? Has the Government any intention of paying compensation?

2

Petroleum is, next to the Cinema, the youngest of the great industries of the world and, unlike it, the most highly organised; for the outsider to attempt to disentangle all the ramifications of allied and subsidiary companies is like tracing the marriages of the royal families of Europe. After a period of intense and very nearly disastrous rivalry during the early years of the century, the numerous private concerns which had begun to deal in oil, decided to combine. Prospecting, mining, refining, and marketing are now co-ordinated by enormously wealthy international groups, whose ramifications are so wide that in many minds they have come to bear a slightly sinister connotation. No doubt this is largely due to the fact that besides being an essential of almost every branch of civil life, oil is also a primary requisite in time of war. By a rare beneficence of providence it so happens that the nations who are at the moment credited with the most war-like disposition, are deficient in oil. But it also happens that the sources of oil are, with the exception of those of Russia and the United States, located in small countries who could not hope to maintain their independence by force unaided, and the strong, peaceful powers control the supply, by arrangements more or less analogous to the one lately repudiated by Mexico. Now these small countries are watching events in Mexico with keen interest. If she is successful in her experiment, they will be tempted to imitate her, and a change in the balance of power may result which will prove the deciding consideration in the unresolved question of whether the war-like powers will settle down to exploit what they have already gained, or push on to further, cataclysmic adventures. This is indeed a sinister aspect and it must be remembered when the industry is being treated as a purely commercial organisation.

But even as a commercial organisation there are certain unique features about the petroleum industry. The potential profits are vast; so are the potential losses. It is a highly speculative business in which it is impossible to predict any relation between capital expenditure and the return. Prodigious sums are spent yearly – and must be spent if production is to be maintained – on the exploration of new fields, which often prove entirely fruitless. It is a business on which only very rich corporations can embark with any reasonable hope of success. The stories of small farmers and Indian villagers who find themselves boundlessly wealthy overnight are romantic material and are copiously used as such by dramatists and scenario-writers; but the real history of the oil industry has been made by arduous, unremitting prospecting, financed by companies who can bear the losses because of their occasional disproportionate gains elsewhere. A small state with a precariously balanced budget could not conscientiously undertake the risks of exploring its own resources out of revenue.

Moreover, petroleum is one of the very few industries who serve the general interest by standardisation. The civilised man today finds the world intolerably monotonous in detail; he travels from country to country, continent to continent, and finds the same firms in almost identical buildings displaying uniform mass-products to uniform, mass-clothed, mass-educated customers. The spectacle is so depressing that he is apt to forget that there are occasions when standardisation is desirable. There is everything to be said for regional cookery, regional architecture, regional craftsmanship, but nothing for regional petrol. The car user wishes to be sure that he can get the identical petrol to which he is accustomed, every ten miles, for thousands of miles and that is what the organisation of the companies assures him. He wants, moreover, to be sure of a constant price. Large and erratic fluctuations in the price of oil would be an annoyance to the private driver; they would be disastrous to the numerous industries who depend on it for their power. If petroleum were improvidently mined and marketed by competing small companies and small states, there might, at the cost of great dislocation and unemployment in the industry itself, be a fall in price for a few years. There are a number of wells which, once they have been found, produce petroleum copiously and easily, with working costs which would enable them to sell at a very low price; at present these profits are being absorbed into the industry to balance less successful districts and finance further exploration. Should the industry disintegrate and fall into the hands of competing small companies or governments these sources would speedily be exhausted; in a year or two there would certainly be a sharp rise in price, possibly a world shortage of oil; a condition which, in the rather precarious economic balance of the world, might well precipitate another vast wave of unemployment. It is not conceivable that a group as improvident and corrupt as the politicians now controlling Mexico would resist the temptation to make immediate profits where it could, or that even supposing that some provision was voted for exploration, the sums granted would ever be properly employed for that purpose. It is to the interest of the world at large that the oil industry should remain an international state, as in effect it is today, and as it certainly would be in the ideal Marxist world. The profits accruing to private individuals are a cheap price to pay in exchange for coherence and stability. But to admit this is not to settle the particular problem that has arisen in Mexico. It often happens with human organisations that though generally beneficent in purpose, they are mishandled in practice. It would not be surprising if by reason of its great power and resource, the international oil industry were ruthless in individual cases. Was this the case in Mexico and has General Cardenas hit upon the happiest solution? We are thus back at the six questions from which we digressed.

3

Did the oil companies, as is commonly asserted, establish themselves piratically in Mexico? The answer, so far as the British interests are concerned, is that they came with every encouragement from the existing government and were at great pains to satisfy every lawful requirement of title. Impersonal corporations are at a disadvantage in dealing with dictators, in that the latter can deny all continuity with their predecessors. General Cardenas, for example, chooses to regard his advent into Mexican politics as the initiation of a new, apocalyptic regime of righteousness and joy. Mussolini, Hitler and Stalin (who would no doubt courteously include Lenin) live under the same rosy illusion. It makes government, in certain respects, vastly more simple if you can repudiate previous history. The fact remains, however, that the oil companies came to Mexico less than forty years ago with the full encouragement of the President, Porfirio Diaz. His successors, transient and often fugitive figures, have been willing from time to time to sign away for ready cash concessions that were not theirs to give. Diaz, at the beginning of the century, was the undisputed ruler of a very prosperous republic. He was the one man since the expulsion of the Viceroys, who could without affectation, claim to speak with authority for the whole Republic. He was, however, antecedent to the Cardenas Six Years Plan and all his acts are now officially anathema.

The man who created the Mexican Eagle Company was very far from being the penurious adventurer who, in popular fiction, seeks his fortune among backward peoples. He was, in fact, the greatest figure in Mexican development, second only to the President in importance and esteem.

Weetman Pearson (later Viscount Cowdray) went to Mexico for the first time at Christmas 1889. He was already one of the most prominent engineers of his time, the head and sole motive force of the firm that had successfully executed great engineering works in many parts of the world, and a man of substantial private fortune. He came to Mexico at the President's invitation to cut the Mexican Grand Canal, the largest public work yet undertaken in the Republic. This contract was the beginning of an association with the country which ended only in his death, during which he left his mark on every aspect of the national organisation. His largest works in Mexico were the reconstruction of the Tehuantepec Railway, and the construction of its terminal ports, Salina Cruz and Coatzacoalos which until the opening of the Panama Canal, provided the main trans-continental route from Atlantic to Pacific, and the creation of a new port at Vera Cruz, where, under his impulse the old city was cleansed, its streets repaved, water and drainage supplied – work so well done as to withstand 25 years of wanton neglect; it is only now beginning to relapse into its original squalor. Wherever his operations moved, improved sanitation followed. He set a new standard of healthy living conditions, draining swamps, clearing bush, tapping sources of pure water. His object was not primarily philanthropic; these things were the requirements of efficient labour and appeared as by-products of his work. The conditions of his labour gangs were not up to the standard of modern European developments, but they were superior to anything yet attempted in Mexico. He worked in close association with the President who found in him and his staff men who could be relied on to keep their word and overcome difficulties rather than plead them as excuses for evading their obligations.

It was not until 1901 that Pearson turned his attention to oil, and he came to the subject without any previous acquaintance with its complexities. More than once there were rumours that he was ruined, which approximated nearly to the truth; only his perseverance, his great financial resources, his ability to learn quickly from experience, and a little luck, brought him to final success. The story of the venture is told in detail by Mr J. A. Spender in the official biography.

He needed oil for the use of his locomotives on the Tehuantepec Railway; his surveyors had lately reported local seepages on the Isthmus near San Cristobal on a tributary of the Coatzacoalos River and at a place on the River Pedregal further East. These reports were no doubt in his mind when, stopping for a day at Laredo in Texas, he found the place in a state of wild excitement over the discovery, two months before, of the famous Lucas Gusher at Spindle Top. This fired his imagination and he promptly cabled his agents to secure options on large areas round his properties where oil had been observed. These instructions were amplified later from New York. He engaged the engineer who had made the lucky drilling at Spindle Top and with the least possible delay had begun the development of the San Cristobal-Capoacan field. He quickly learned, however, that the discovery of oil was only the first stage of the undertaking which needed a continuous series of successes to make profitable; the crude oil had to be controlled, refined, conveyed and sold. For a long time expenses greatly exceeded the returns. In 1902 he was talking of 'cutting his losses and clearing out' when he had spent £1,500,000. Before the end he had spent three times this sum. It was not until 1906 that he felt justified in erecting a refinery and tankage, at the cost of a further £500,000. It was not until 1908 that the refinery began work.

Pearson soon gave up the idea of cutting his losses and clearing out. He had learned the first principle of the industry, that it must be conducted on a huge scale, or not at all. In 1906 he obtained concessions from the Federal Government and the State Governments of Vera Cruz, San Luis Potosi, Tamaulipas, Tabasco and Chiapas for further exploration and exploitation rights. In March 1906 he owned about 600,000 acres of oil land and had 200,000–300,000 acres more on royalty leases. These were not obtained by mere strokes of the Presidential pen, as is popularly believed in Mexico. A staff of lawyers was continuously employed for years verifying titles and scrutinising the transfers. The records of land-ownership were often inextricably confused; every kind of fraudulent imposture was attempted on the Englishman who had gone into the market so extravagantly for land that had hitherto been held as valueless.

And still the business showed no profit. Drilling had been con-tinuous but San Cristobal remained the only workable field as yet discovered. San Cristobal only promised a two years' life and in those two years things grew worse instead of better. Pearson went in for marketing oil in competition with the American firm of Waters Pierce who up till then had enjoyed a profitable monopoly in Mexico; when the produce of his own fields fell short of the market commitment, he was obliged to buy and import; he soon found himself buying more than he produced. In June 1909 he bought 400,000 barrels of oil from Texas, while the input of his refinery was down to 3,000 barrels a day. A further field at Furbero which was allied with Pearson proved a disappointment. In the end, when success did come, it was not in the Isthmus where he had originally started, but 400 miles north of it, where he had not been particularly hopeful. In January 1910 a shallow, highly productive well was struck at Tanhuijo and in February Potrero No I gave promise of a rich field. Now, after he had borne all the costs and anxiety himself, Pearson for the first time felt justified in coming before the public and in May the Mexican Eagle Company made its first public issue of shares.

In December of the same year Potrero No 4 was struck; a mine that has become famous among oilmen. For two months it ran to waste at a rate of 100,000 barrels a day, before the engineers could succeed in getting the immense flow under control. This well ran for eight years before it was exhausted and yielded over 100,000,000 barrels, having narrowly escaped total destruction in 1914 when it was set on fire by lightning and burned for seven months. It was the discovery of Potrero 4 which proved decisive in the competition with Waters Pierce Company, which until then was going none too favourably for Pearson. With the end of this conflict, on Pearson's terms, came the beginning of the great system of commercial alli-ances of which the Mexican Eagle now forms a part. By 1918 Mexico had become the second greatest oil-producing country in the world. It has recently lost its position for reasons which will appear later. Oil is still there when conditions allow its production. The history of its discovery is not the familiar cinematographic tale of the destitute heroine finding a fortune on her mortgaged farmyard and living happily ever afterwards, but it is, in its own way, just as exciting.

4

Did the oil companies exercise a malevolent influence on local life and politics?

Last summer a naïve little pamphlet named *The Good Neighbor*, by Mr Oscar Morineau was being distributed free in Mexico City to tourists, who looked as though they might have bourgeois sympathies. Other, more outspoken literature was kept for fellow socialists. The thesis which Mr Morineau had been turned on to defend was that Mexico was not communist, still welcomed private enterprise and further foreign capital investment, but had been driven to drastic action in the particular case of the oil companies because of their licentious behaviour. '*The origin of the oil industry in Mexico,*' he says, '*is stained with blood, violence, plunder, corruption and intrigue of all kinds. We may forget crimes and mistakes of the past, provided the organisation or industry committing them later justifies its existence from a social point of view. Unfortunately the oil companies did not have the necessary foresight to cooperate in the development of the regions in which they operated . . . they left no traces of culture . . . only saloons and places of prostitution flourished . . . we are firmly determined to prevent private enterprises from becoming positive factors of corruption.*'

General Cardenas in his broadcast message to the nation, of March 18th, 1938 said '. . . *Another inevitable consequence of the presence of the oil companies, strongly characterised by their anti-social tendencies, has been their persistent and improper intervention in national affairs.*

'*The oil companies' support to strong rebel factions against the constituted government in the Huasteca region of Vera Cruz and in the Isthmus of Tehuantepec during the years 1917 to 1920 is no longer a matter for discussion by anyone. Nor is anyone ignorant of the fact that in later periods and even at the present time, the oil companies have almost openly fanned the ambitions of elements discontented with the country's government . . . They have had money, arms and munitions for rebellion . . . but for the progress of the country, for establishing an economic equilibrium with their workers through a just compensation of labour, for maintaining hygienic conditions . . . they have neither money nor the desire to subtract it from the volume of their profits.*'

A few days earlier, Sr Lombardo Toledano, speaking to the C.T.M. General Congress, had said: '*You recall, comrades, how the wealth of the oil companies was acquired in Mexico . . . How many wretched Indians in Vera Cruz, in Tamaulipas, in Tabasco, and in other parts of the country were sacrificed! They employed company police and, during the fateful days of Revolution, even had a whole army at their service. Like the condottieri of Renaissance Italy, these traitors to their country were paid by the companies to protect their properties.*'

Statements of this kind were the fuel for most of the oratory which blazed in Mexico at the time of the expropriation. They were widely accepted in the country and even outside it where so much public opinion is formed by the reading of headlines. Well-intentioned citizens of the U.S.A. and England, who had no special interest in the question, became vaguely aware that 'there was a lot to be said on both sides; the oil companies did not behave at all well'. What is the truth?

The charges are never substantiated by detail against Mexican Eagle and the question is rather philosophic than historic; what ought the behaviour to be, of a large, wealthy corporation in a small and poor State? The oil companies came to Mexico when it was a wealthy and stable country; the revolutionaries brought it to ruin; one by one they obliterated its former sources of wealth except petroleum, which the companies managed to keep going (though from 1921 for ten years with a very heavy decline) until they occupied a position of disproportional importance. It was admittedly an embarrassing position for the republican government to find themselves the sovereigns of a vastly richer subject; as we shall see the solution which commended itself to them was to ruin that industry too and reduce the whole country to uniform squalor. Was it improper for the Companies to resist this solution?

It is manifestly unreasonable for General Cardenas to plead, as he did in his Note to the British Government, that the Mexican Eagle was an exclusively Mexican concern answerable only to local law, and at the same time deny them the right to take any interest in the processes by which the law was made. The General, too, is, like all revolutionary leaders, in a somewhat ambiguous position with regard to revolutions. The crown of Spain might logically claim that all rebellion was of its nature, wrong; no subsequent government of independent Mexico has that right. 'Traitor' has come to mean one who did not support the last successful act of revolution. General Cardenas's personal vanity enables him to take the logical hurdles without a spill. All governments before the splendid day in 1935 when, with clemency unprecedented in Mexican politics, he gave his former boss, General Calles, twelve hours to leave the country alive, have been unjust and their personnel traitors (he would probably make an exception of Juarez and Madero; for the latter, sentiment is still strong; he and General Cardenas would have found few points of agreement). Thus a corporation which has attempted to work harmoniously with his predecessors is damned as an ally of the Enemies of the People.

'Working harmoniously' with any Mexican institution involves a good deal that might be regarded askance in Europe. On occasions no doubt the oil companies, faced with the alternatives of curtailing their work or of paying the customary, irregular levies of the political bosses, conformed to local usage; there are few concerns in Mexico, native or foreign, private or public, which are innocent of this. The majority of the courts and the government officials are venal; that is they expect and are expected to supplement their meagre salaries as best they can. A bought decision is not necessarily an unjust one. The government inspectors whose duty it is to examine machinery and see that the prescribed safety devices are employed, expect large tips not to certify defective factories but to approve efficient ones; if the tip is not paid they refuse their certificate and the company is fined; if the company appeals, they may be left unheard or a higher official may be sent who will expect a correspondingly higher bribe. A wealthy institution like the oil companies naturally becomes the target for a continuous fusillade of malicious and irresponsible litigation. They soon learned to their cost that a clear case did not guarantee a favourable decision. It is cheaper and quicker to conform to the custom of the country however reprehensible it seems.

In the matter of political interference the truth, as far, at any rate, as Mexican Eagle is concerned, seems to be the exact reverse of the popular belief. If the company is censurable with regard to its political behaviour it is that it did too little, not too much. They were in Mexico for the purpose of producing oil and they stuck to their posts resolutely through all the giddy changes of local politics. When the American drillers fled, the British stayed on, continued to drill, store, prospect, though rival armies were manœuvring all round them. They paid their taxes to whomever was in a *de facto* position to demand them. When the whole country was given up to guerilla bands, looting, burning and massacring, they armed their men to defend their own lives and homes and the company's property. When the Federal Government had ceased to function and a revolutionary general was in a position to demand blackmail, they sometimes paid it; that is what General Cardenas means when he talks of their financing rebellion. The Mexican Eagle staff stayed at their work in conditions of imminent danger and concentrated on their work. In the light of recent events it is easy to say that they should have done more; that they owed obligations to the country where they worked and should have defended more than their own possessions; that they were too tolerant of the succession of scoundrels who emerged from anarchy into brief periods of power. When all the decent elements in the country were united against Calles they did nothing and allowed the successful revolt, when it came, to be the work of Cardenas and Toledano. That is, I think, an arguable indictment; but, as many American ambassadors have learned to their cost, it is difficult to meddle profitably in Mexican affairs, very easy to deplore events that take place there, very difficult to foresee them. The companies' moderation may yet be rewarded and the extreme folly of Cardenas and Toledano may turn to their benefit.

Ironically enough, at the early stages of the conflict, one of the charges was that the oil companies were anti-democratic in sentiment and sold their oil to the fascist powers. Nothing has been said about this lately, since the Mexican Government has found little enthusiasm for the confiscated oil in law-loving countries and has been obliged to deal mainly with the fascist states.

The further charge, that the oil companies failed to promote culture among their workmen, is not, I think, seriously made by anyone in Mexico and is intended solely for foreign consumption. What, I wonder, did Mr Morineau expect the companies to do?

They paid high wages and the men spent them in Mexican fashion, on loutish enjoyments. 'Saloons and houses of prostitution flourished'; what does Mr Morineau expect the companies to do about that? When, in time of manifest peril, the companies organised protective guards, Mexican patriots pretended to be outraged; what would they say if the companies had formed vigilance committees and patrolled their workers' homes with squads of women police? That, indeed, would be an intolerable imposition; the workman may well talk of slavery when his employer claims the right to supervise his leisure and direct how his wages are to be spent. The companies did much to secure healthy conditions for their men, and were deliberately prevented from doing more, but this point belongs to the further question of whether the men's claims were *bona fide* grievances. The complaints quoted from Mr Morineau and General Cardenas mean nothing less than that the companies did not usurp the proper functions of local government. They paid high wages and high taxes; the workmen misspent the wages and the politicians misspent the taxes, with the result that the country did not benefit as richly as it might have done had it been differently inhabited. That is hardly the companies' fault; but supposing that they had adopted a different policy and supposing, as would obviously not have happened in fact, the local authorities had allowed them to make their properties in a state within the state, a model settlement standing in perpetual reproach to the ramshackle and savage lands surrounding them. Supposing they had taken their workers in hand from birth to death, had them born in a company's hospital, educated in the company's schools, entertained in the company's playing-fields and theatres, edified in the company's library, pensioned off in the company's alms houses and burned up in the company's crematorium; if they became company's men instead of Cardenas's. There indeed would be an imperialism to enrage a patriotic Mexican; a development that could only end in the political separation of the oil fields from the rest of the country.

One can imagine the charabanc loads of proud tourists driving out to the companies' domains ... 'And here, folks, we turn our backs on the dark ages and come into the light of the twentieth-century progress. You are now leaving Mexico and entering

Petroland. The queue outside the gates are Mexicans applying for Petroland citizenship; since the Toledano-Cardenas war applications for citizenship have greatly exceeded the quota; but temporary working permits are being issued to refugees who satisfy the medical requirements. The block-house on the right is the headquarters of the Petroland gendarmerie. On the left you see the Doheny shrine. This beautiful marble statue was erected at the cost of over a million American dollars by admirers in Tea Pot Dome. On the right is the Ambassador Wilson memorial...note the native woman laying flowers at the feet of Mr Doheny. I am glad to tell you that in Petroland this cult is rapidly replacing the retrograde devotion to saints and crosses which we have noted up country...the Company's post office is here. You may buy Petroland stamps in all denominations. No doubt some of you would like to send a postcard of the late Sir Henri Deterding back home and afterwards, if you step round to the Hail and Farewell Bureau you will each be given an ornamental bottle of crude oil to take away as a souvenir...'

5

But the companies did not create, nor could they without the help of international intervention have created, a Petroland. They remained instead a part of the Mexican Republic, subject to its laws and sharing its diverse fortunes. They left it to the Government to produce its own plans for national salvation, and the plans, when ready, were found to follow the old Mexican precedent that has proved disastrous again and again but remains ineradicable in Mexican statesmanship, of progress through theft.

The simple principle, that a nation becomes rich through the industry, thrift and enterprise of its people and through nothing else, so well accepted elsewhere in the world that it is trite to mention it, remains a paradox to the Mexican politician. For him wealth is, in fact and in theory, the product of theft; when in the early days of the Republic the politicians had reduced the state to bankruptcy, they looked round for something to rob; the Church was physically defenceless so they set themselves to obliterate the single common

bond which united the heterogeneous population; the single institution which transcended provincial limitations and which, however
imperfect in state, provided an acceptable and universally accepted
machinery for infusing international culture; the full implications of
the destruction of the Church in Mexico will be discussed in another
chapter; here the significant fact is that the robbery was a complete
failure in its ostensible object; the sums produced were completely
disproportionate to the damage done, and quickly disappeared into
private pockets, leaving the State in as distressed a condition as it
had been before.

In the present generation when the Government set about the
laudable work of establishing a population of peasant proprietors on
the land, the same predilection was evident. The country is very
sparsely populated and though much of it would require very large
clearance, irrigation, drainage and fertilisation works of the kind so
successfully introduced into Italy, to bring it into cultivation, there
were tracts of country lying empty which required only the plough
and rudimentary attention to make fertile. A land scheme based on
increasing the cultivated area would have had the support of every
reasonable person, there and abroad. That however was not the
Mexican politicians' habit. Instead they adopted the easier course of
revenging themselves on their political opponents by seizing the
estates that were already in profitable occupation. Certain provision
was made in the law for the protection of special crops – sisal, coffee,
sugar, etc. – but they were disregarded in practice. The confiscations
were carried through, and are still being completed, with the usual
accompaniments of graft and jobbery; the white aristocracy Mexican and foreign alike was ruined; that was the only success
achieved; production fell everywhere; the country was increasingly
unable to feed the towns, and in the areas where the Government
had taken a direct share in the enterprise, lending money for seeds
and tools, they were faced with a huge deficit which showed no
promise of improvement. To the Mexican political mind this admitted of only one solution; a new steal. The plunderable assets were
rapidly decreasing; bank accounts were being transferred abroad;
the mining industry was, for the most part, working on a suicidal
policy of getting all they could while there was anything to get;

working only easy seams, cutting down on expansion, failing to renew plant; the railways had mostly been taken over already and were already bankrupt; those which still worked under their former management had ceased for some years to show any profit. One industry alone seemed to offer a substantial temptation – oil.

The steps by which the theft was made, are common knowledge.

Two things were necessary; a change in the law so that the act might be legal, and a campaign of agitation so that it might be popular. General Cardenas personally undertook the first task; the second was entrusted to the very able hands of Lombardo Toledano and the C.T.M. bosses.

One of General Cardenas's first acts when he was put into the presidency was to employ the powers recently conferred on him to rid the Supreme Court of judges likely to be unsympathetic and replace them with his own nominees who, under the new Act, held office only during his own term; to these judges and their subordinates – most especially to the arbitrators who sat in the Court of Conciliation to hear industrial disputes between employers and workers – he dictated as a matter of public policy what had for some time, under fear of the C.R.O.M. and its more violent successor, the C.T.M., been their practice: that judicial favour was the exclusive possession of the manual labourer. 'The modern conception of the functions of the State,' he said, 'requires that doubtful cases be decided in favour of the weaker party. To mete out equal treatment to two parties that are not equal is neither to administer justice nor to act equitably.' Henceforward no complaint of employed against employer was too preposterous for sympathetic hearing and, almost invariably, for success. In a speech at Monterey he suggested the principle that ability to pay was the sole criterion in fixing wages and in a sinister phrase invited the employers who were 'weary of the social struggle' to surrender their businesses. He left it to Toledano and his law courts to provoke the weariness.

Until 1936 the powers of the governing party over private property had not, in theory, been totalitarian. The 'Constitution' of 1917 provided that: 'Private property should not be expropriated except for reasons of public utility and by means of indemnification.' In November 1936 General Cardenas sent to Congress for ratification a new Law which annulled this provision by defining 'public utility' in terms so wide and vague that they could cover any presidential caprice. The Mexican Bar Association protested against the Bill as unconstitutional, but it passed inevitably into Law. From that moment the President's power over every piece of property in the country was absolute.

Meanwhile the C.T.M. had been organising a campaign of agitation among the oil workers. The hold which this organisation had over the workers was complete; the companies had after a struggle accepted the 'closed shop' principle; the local syndicate bosses now held the right of deciding who should be employed and who promoted, and exercised it with all the intimidation and extortion to which the country was accustomed. A man who voted against the wishes of the C.T.M. boss lost his syndicate membership and with it his livelihood. Since the syndicate funds depended on subscriptions, it was the C.T.M. policy to swell its membership by the inclusion of casual labourers who had no interest in the welfare of the industry. These considerations were no doubt effective in some degree in securing local support to Toledano's policy; no doubt there were many workers in the oil fields who found themselves obliged to vote against their convictions, who were content under the companies' rule and distrusted the voluble officials from Mexico City, but to explain the whole movement in these terms, as many of the oil companies' executives are disposed to do, is to disregard a decade of growing animosity and a climax of spontaneous, if brief, exultation. There is an unanswerable case that the indignation was irrational, but it was none the less genuine and its explanation is independent of local considerations. Man is by nature an exile, haunted, even at the height of his prosperity, by nostalgia for Eden; individually and collectively he is always in search of an oppressor who will take responsibility for his ills. The Treaty of Versailles, Sanctions, Jews, Bolshevists, Bankers, the Colour Bar – anything will do so long as he can focus on it his sense of grievance and convince himself that his own inadequacy is due to some exterior cause. It requires neither great oratory nor astute conspiracy to inflame a group with a sense of persecution; a hint is enough; and once a grievance is aroused there is no place for figures and arguments.

The workers in the oil industry were, both in actual wages and benefits, the most highly privileged in the country. The lowest unskilled labourer who, elsewhere, had an average daily wage of 1.13 pesos, was getting from 3 to 3.50 in the oil fields; masons earned from 5.20 to 8.40, elsewhere they averaged 1.89; electricians had 6 to 7.60, against 2.74; carpenters 4 to 8.40 against 2.05, etc. These figures are taken from the *Annual Review* of the Mexican Department of Labour for 1935. At the time of the expropriation the figures for the oil industry were, in most cases, 10 per cent. or 15 per cent. higher. In addition to these wages the men received housing or a housing allowance, schools and dispensaries. The companies had made frequent offers to increase their social services, but a spirit of antagonism had arisen in the men, so that they were met with constant obstruction. The abuses of the medical benefit, for example, made them despair of any sane cooperation. The syndicates claimed and exercised the right to appoint the medical officers, who in most districts became agents for robbery. A man had merely to present himself at the dispensary to claim exemption from work, sick pay, and, most important, prescriptions for expensive patent medicines which he discounted for cash at the drug stores. Large numbers of peons were still living in temporary and wholly unsuitable huts; pictures of these were circulated as propaganda at the time of the expropriation; what was not shown was the great store of building materials which had been lying near them for two years, which the syndicate had forbidden the company to erect, not because they proposed to do so with non-union labour but because they were not employing the particular contractor from whom the syndicate boss had arranged a commission and whose tender had been the most expensive submitted. Vexatious litigation in which the company was invariably the victim, further embittered relations. Now that the oil had been found, and until the present wells were exhausted, conditions were favourable to production. The companies could afford to pay more and still show a reasonable profit provided they were allowed to control their business; at the end of the negotiations they offered concessions which would cost them 25,000,000 pesos a year, conditionally upon the re-establishment of the normal working conditions without which a business of any kind anywhere in the world, must fail. This was refused and even used as a demonstration that the protestation of inability to pay had been made in bad faith. Nowhere in Mexico was there any illusion that the oil workers merited compassion; that was an emotion kept for export so that the foreign governments involved might be embarrassed by sympathisers of their own nationality. No one in the Mexican Government intended that the oil workers should gain anything by expropriation – nor indeed have they. When, however, at the beginning of the strike the companies made the suggestion that any additional charge on the companies should be distributed by way of an excess profits tax, not among the small and already privileged class of oil workers, but among the community as a whole, it was disregarded, for this was precisely what General Cardenas intended to do, while to have admitted it would have been to stultify the whole Toledano campaign of agitation in the oil fields. Throughout the entire controversy there are always these two separate forces: General Cardenas, resolved to avert the disaster which his agricultural policy had provoked, by confiscating the oil properties, and consequently giving complete liberty of action to Toledano to create a state of chaos in the industry. Toledano's policy culminated in the preposterous demands of the strikers in November 1936.

The version of these demands published in English by the Workers' University of Mexico and distributed free to visitors at the Six Year Plan Exhibition, requires considerable correction in matters of fact. The demand was for a new collective contract applicable to the whole industry annulling the various existing contracts by which the workers had willingly bound themselves at various recent dates. As itemised in this pamphlet the principal points of the new contract were:

(1) '*Reduction of the "confidential employees"*,' i.e. administrative, executive and advisory posts not appointed by the syndicate, from 900, a number which had been found barely adequate, '*to 114. All other employees to be appointed and controlled by the Syndicate.*' The Workers' University pamphlet omits to add that 50 per cent. of the legal advisers were to be syndicate nominees.

(2) '*In cases of lay-offs, an indemnity to each worker of 90 days' wages, plus 25 days' wages for each year that he had been in the company's service.*'

(3) '*Workers voluntarily leaving employment after ten years to be paid 25 days' wages for each year. Should his leaving be caused by an abrogation of the labour contract through the employer's fault, an additional indemnity of 90 days' wages.*' With regard to this latter provision it is worth noting that in the existing state of the industrial courts it will be almost certain that a case would go against the employer, i.e. after ten years' work a man could give up his job and receive a bonus of a year's wages plus (see below) a life pension of 60 per cent. of his former earnings.

(4) '*The establishment of the 40-hour week'; with pay for 56 hours.*

(5) '*Medical service on a disease-prevention basis to be furnished at the cost of the employer with the necessary facilities for diagnosis, adequate medical installation, and the elimination of all humiliating red tape.*'

This is the kind of provision which sounds benevolent and unexceptionable but which, to anyone familiar with local conditions, would be intolerable. The doctors were to be syndicate nominees – a fact omitted from the pamphlet – and to serve the workers' dependants as well as themselves. The interpretation which might be put on 'disease-prevention basis' and the 'elimination of all humiliating red tape' might include almost any uncontrolled expenditure. It would in fact commit the companies to the provision of any amenities which the syndicate might think desirable.

(6) '*In cases of death from non-occupational causes, the payment of 60 days' wages, funeral expenses, plus 25 days' wages for each year of service.*'

(7) '*In cases of death from occupational causes, 1,400 days' wages.*'

(8) '*In cases of total and permanent disability from occupational causes, 1,825 days' wages, plus 25 days' wages for every year of service. If the injured worker has been employed for more than ten years, a pension.*' (Unspecified amount.)

(9) '*A pension system varying between full wages after 30 years' service and 60% wages after ten years' employment.*'

(10) '*Eighteen compulsory rest days a year,*' in addition to Sundays, all with full pay.

(11) '*Vacations: for workers of five years' service, 25 days a year; from five to ten years, 40 days; from ten to fifteen years, 50 days; from fifteen years up, 60 days.*' On full pay.

(12) '*The establishment of a Savings Fund, 10% discount from wages, 15% of wages contributed by employer.*'

(13) '*The founding of* 45 *scholarships for workers or their children.*'

(14) '*An opportunity for Mexican workmen to acquire the experience necessary to replace foreign technicians*' and all foreign technicians to be replaced by Mexicans within one year.

(15) '*Sanitary and comfortable housing for all workers or* 2 *pesos a day allowance.*'

(16) '*Wage increases*' totalling 28,149,560 pesos.

The Workers' University omit from this list various provisions tightening the hold of the syndicate on the workers and making it impossible for the company to discharge men for anything except criminal offences and a further privilege of three days' leave of absence on full pay at the worker's demand whenever, and, apparently, as often as he chose.

There was some dispute as to the total cost of these demands. The C.T.M. estimated the increase at 65,474,840 pesos annually; the companies' actuaries at £16½ million. It is impossible to estimate the losses in business efficiency. No one, whatever his political views, can suppose that Toledano intended these demands to be acceptable, or that General Cardenas believed that the nation would benefit by the creation of a class, twenty-five thousand strong in a nation of sixteen millions, enjoying wages out of all proportion to the standard of living in the country, and privileges unknown to any trade or profession in any country in the world. In the controversy that followed the expropriation no serious attempt was made to defend Toledano's demands, nor was any attempt made to put them into effect by the new managers. By then the issue had changed and the appeal was for sacrifice rather than improvement, patriotism rather than privilege. But at the time of the threatened strike, in the winter of 1936 and the spring of 1937, it does seem that the men had been persuaded that the paradisal conditions proposed were in fact realisable, and it was on the basis of these demands that the case was heard by the Court of Conciliation.

The real decision had already been made and the steps taken to legalise it are of purely academic interest. The history of the succeeding months merely demonstrates that the Mexican Government had already dismissed the ideal of a peaceful settlement. The demands were first itemised on November 3rd, 1936, with the intimation that they must be not only discussed but approved by a date finally extended to November 29th at 11 a.m. The draft had taken many months to compile, covered 165 pages of legal script, contained 250 clauses, and 40 pages of figures dealing with the wage-schedule. The companies expressed their willingness to negotiate but pointed out the impossibility of digesting proposals so elaborate and revolutionary within the time limit. Public opinion, neither at home nor abroad, was sympathetic to the syndicate's peremptory tactics and General Cardenas proposed a six months' extension for discussion. The companies pointed out that similar contracts in the past had taken as long as two years to negotiate and never less than eight months. The Labour Delegation insisted on a period of 120 working days and were upheld. The assembly sat almost daily from the beginning of December until the end of May 1937, under the chairmanship of the Head of the Labour Department. The policy of the Labour Delegation was consistently obstructionist; in particular by its contention that the new contract should not be legally binding on the industry as prescribed by the Law of November 27th, but a temporary 'special form of general collective contract' liable to further expansion and providing no guarantee of settled working conditions, by its attempt to coerce the Maritime Workers' Unions into the Petroleum Syndicate, and by an attempt to exclude all lawyers from the Employers' Delegation which they pressed to the point of absenting themselves from the assembly for some days. By the end of March it was clear that the discussion of the clauses seriatim could not possibly end within the prescribed limits. Accordingly there was a recess, at the end of which the Employers produced a counter-proposal, expressly omitting the wage-schedule which in its nature required longer consideration. These proposals were submitted on April 12th. Within twenty-four hours – a time hardly sufficient for their perusal, still less for their study – the proposals were rejected and the strike called for midnight on May 27th. Public opinion, however, was still unprepared for drastic action. The strike was called off in ten days and a year of hopeless, acrimonious discussion followed before General Cardenas felt himself strong enough to decree the expropriation.

The form the campaign now took was an 'economic suit' and the investigations of a commission appointed by the Labour Board into the question of the companies' ability to pay. The Commission, as things turned out, consisted of one man, a local communist professor whose activities form one of the few humorous features of a drab episode. In order to establish the average profits of the industry he confined his enquiry to the years 1934–36, serenely neglecting the previous depression; for these three years he preferred his own purely fanciful assessment of profits averaging £3,100,000 to the figure of £1,200,000 proved in the companies' books, and on the basis of these figures made his recommendations for increases in wages and benefits. So mixed did he get in his arithmetic even then that he calculated the cost of his proposals at £1,400,000 a year, when, in fact, as was abundantly demonstrated, they would have cost £2,300,000, i.e. almost double the actual average profits. He further reaffirmed the administrative demands originally made by the syndicate.

The Labour Board confirmed the professor's findings and the companies appealed to the Supreme Court. Their case, a formidable compilation of 7,000 pages in length, was presented on February 2nd, 1938. Despite the fact that their deliberations were disturbed by popular demonstrations, the judges were able to weigh the evidence with despatch and at the end of the month announced their decision against the appeal. The companies made a final offer to increase wages and benefits by £1,400,000 – the sum which the professor thought his proposals would cost – provided the administration of the business was not interfered with. General Cardenas refused to discuss the offer or to communicate it to the workers. Their part in the affair was over. They had been useful, with their imagined grievances, in bringing about the crisis; from now on they must get back to work and forget their aspirations; forget, too, the tangible benefits which they had won for themselves in the past. It was not to enrich *them* that there had been all the bustle in Mexico City. A few of the bosses, it is true, profited for the time. A Mr Juan Gray, the manager in Mexico City of the petroleum syndicate, increased his salary from 590 pesos a month to 5,300; Mr Viesca Arispe, manager at Tampico, from 600 to 2,800; Mr Rubio, comptroller at Tampico, from 500 to 2,000; the wages of a Mr Azorar rose suddenly from 7.70 a day as chauffeur, to 1,300 a month as manager.

For a dozen or so of the most active politicals, expropriation brought apocalyptic rewards. In the oil fields, however, thousands have been thrown out of work and the sole gain was that some of the houses, bought years before by the companies and boycotted by the syndicate, were hastily fitted together to greet the delegates of the International Labour Congress on their tour of inspection and approval.

6

The expropriations, once decreed, were carried out speedily and effectively; property of all kinds was taken without being inventoried, safes were forced and documents, title deeds and cash carried off. In practice, as in theory, the whole process conformed to the new, Nazi statecraft.

Every feature of the Cardenas régime – except the catch-phrases – is an echo of Central Europe. Government is by a semi-military executive which overrides judicature and legislature; popular consent is achieved by agitation; education is a department of propaganda, religion banned from the schools and its place taken by nationalism and national grievances; the basic assumption of foreign policy is that the democracies will not fight; force may be used to steal what force will not defend. There is the same chain of cause and consequence; the Government tells the people that they are miserable and that the cure of their ills is violent breach of international order; when the beneficial effects do not follow, the breach is held up to admiration as a positive achievement – an end in itself – which must be defended by further sacrifice. That has been the result in Mexico. The expropriations were first proposed as a means of raising social conditions; they are now an excuse for depressing them. Finances are desperate. General Cardenas has found that the law-abiding will not buy his petrol and the outlaws cannot pay for it. The temptation to join the Barter Group would be overwhelming were it not for the question of indemnity. General Cardenas has repeatedly offered to pay compensation for the expropriated properties. Since the fall of Porfirio Diaz, Mexico has been a consistent defaulter on her public debts, which amount to about ten times her total annual revenue; she has paid neither the principal nor the interest on her earlier expropriations of agricultural properties. By taking the oil properties she was adding a sum to her capital liabilities which she could not conceivably pay, but until she has actually defaulted it is difficult for the State Department at Washington to accuse her of a breach of international law. Accordingly, in the face of all facts, she maintains her readiness to pay. Suggestions that she should pay for her theft by returning a percentage of the stolen property are too naïve to be considered seriously anywhere except in the Mexican Press. In March 1938, General Cardenas attempted to cash in on the popular enthusiasm by raising a loan of £5,000,000. These bonds were to bear no interest for ten years but to remain in the subscriber's possession as 'diplomas of patriotism'. Prodigious attempts were made to stimulate generosity. Government agents distributed livestock to the peasants in the vicinity of the capital and what had not been devoured overnight was returned next morning at the Opera House to the accompaniment of military music and news-cameras. About £20,000 was raised. In July the loan was closed and the fund diverted to pay the troops.

The situation at the time of writing is a deadlock, the issue of which must depend on the degree of pressure which the United States can bring. There is a market for bootleg petrol in Japan, Germany and Italy; an exclusive barter agreement on the Central European model might save General Cardenas's finances, but he wants money not material and within his country he has to reckon with the Marxism he has fostered in every department of national life; it would be difficult for Toledano to accept the Nazification of the country; can Cardenas now dispense with him? And, further, would the 'Good Neighbour' policy bear the strain of the transformation?

CHAPTER 5

THE GOOD NEIGHBOUR

1

AS HAS BEEN noted before, the attitude of the ordinary citizen of the United States towards the Mexican has many points of resemblance with that of the nineteenth-century Englishman's towards Ireland. He regards him as disorderly, improvident and superstitious, and behind this condemnation there lurks an undefined feeling of guilt. The history of the two countries consists of a series of misunderstandings and miscalculations, of injudicious interference repeatedly prosecuted up to the point beyond which it might have proved beneficial and then capriciously abandoned, of alternations of arrogance and sentimentality, rapacity and benevolence, domination and neglect, of a kind which forms a close parallel with the English policy in Ireland during the centuries between the Reformation and the Peace Treaty, and the consequent ills have been aggravated rather than mollified by the fact that, throughout, Mexican independence has been sedulously affirmed.

It is difficult for modern Europeans, still more for Americans who tend, by nature, to take a short view of history, to realise that the predominance of the U.S. in the New World is quite a recent development. The inhabitants of Mexico before the conquest lived on an immensely higher plane of civilisation than the aboriginals of the North; in the colonial period the Spanish possessions were preeminent in extent, wealth and culture. It was only after her severance from Spain that the decay of Mexico, threatened before by certain inherent but not ineradicable weaknesses, was consummated by the factional and revolutionary troubles that are still daily debasing her. The splendour of Spanish colonial architecture still stands to remind tourists of this superiority but there are other, less accessible, facts which are sometimes overlooked. By 1575, a century before the first press was set up in British America, books were being printed in Mexico City, not only in Spanish, but in twelve different Indian languages. There were three universities in Spanish America nearly a century before the foundation of Harvard. There was a Medical School at the Royal and Pontifical University of Mexico two hundred years before Harvard's, and anatomy and surgery were taught with dissection eighty-six years before William Hunter opened the first school of dissection in England. Elementary education for Indian children existed wherever there was a mission station; inevitably, in three hundred years, some of the schools languished while others flourished, but the campaign for their extension only ended with the revolution.

At the village schools the peasants were taught not only their religion, but reading, writing, music, handicrafts of all kinds and agriculture. In many centres there were institutions of higher education for the Indians, some of whom even took up teaching posts in Europe. As early as 1541 a disgruntled colonist, Geronimo Lopez, himself no great scholar, was complaining bitterly to the King that there were Indians who spoke Latin 'like another Cicero, and every day the number grows'. Von Humboldt, in 1803, made these observations: 'No city in the new continent, without even excepting those of the United States, can display such great and solid scientific establishments as the capital of Mexico'; 'The capital and several other cities have scientific establishments which will bear a comparison with those of Europe.' 'Instruction is communicated gratis in the Academy of Fine Arts. It is not confined alone to the drawing of landscapes and figures ... the Academy labours successfully to introduce among the artisans a taste for elegance and beautiful forms ... every evening some hundreds of young people draw from reliefs or living models, while others copy drawings of furniture, chandeliers or other ornaments in bronze. In this assemblage rank, colour and race is confounded.' 'No European government has sacrificed greater sums to advance the knowledge of the vegetable kingdom than the Spanish government' (of Mexico). '... All these researches, conducted during twenty years in the most fertile districts of the new continent, have not only enriched science with more than four thousand new species of plants, but have also contributed much to diffuse a taste for natural history among the inhabitants of the country.' 'The best mineralogical work in the Spanish language was printed in Mexico, the *Manual of Oryctognosy* by M. del Rio ... the first Spanish translation of Lavater's *Elements of Chemistry* was also published in Mexico.' While the Puritan settlers in the North were denying all education to their women, nuns had established elementary girls' schools all over Mexico and, in the cities, substantial colleges.

There were, of course, abuses and distortions; Francis Clement Kelly[1] must be read in conjunction with Ernest Gruening;[2] unsuitable men sometimes got themselves appointed to important posts in Church and State; charitable institutions sometimes failed to preserve the energy of their founders; racial and class distinctions often hampered the working of good laws; order was precariously maintained in districts remote from the centres of government; acute poverty existed side by side with splendid wealth; but the records up to the last decade of Spanish rule, give evidence that the normal processes of renewal and expansion were continuously at work and that Mexican civilisation was alive and, in many ways, vigorous.

There was little intercourse with the English colonies, for it was the policy of the Kings of Spain to monopolise all trade and much of the antagonism of the sixteenth century still survived in the New World. The Mexicans despised their neighbours as barbarians and had not yet learned to fear them; thus the Chinese regarded the Japanese in the days of the Manchu Empire. When the English colonists declared their independence the differences between the two races widened; Mexico, now, represented not only the historic dangers of the Armada and the Inquisition, but the more present and obnoxious enemy – European imperialism. From the first the United States were keen proselytisers for republican and puritanical institutions and the natural enemies of the monarchical, feudal,

1 *Blood-drenched Altars* by Francis Clement Kelly: in spite of the intolerable artiness of its illustrations, this book is the best statement of the clerical case.

2 *Mexico and its Heritage* by Ernest Gruening: for most Americans and many English the standard defence of the revolution.

hierarchic, baroque culture of Mexico. Accordingly they sought, encouraged and misinterpreted the elements of revolution.

How far they misinterpreted them may be judged from the interview between President, then Secretary of State, Monroe and Colonel Bernardo Guttierez de Lara. This took place in 1811; Colonel de Lara was a revolutionary refugee who came to Washington to see what help might be forthcoming for his movement. Monroe received him amicably and said: The United States would aid the revolution in the Mexican provinces with all their power and would sustain it to the point, not only of furnishing arms and ammunition but in addition with 27,000 good troops which they would soon have for the purpose. But that Colonel Bernardo and the other revolutionary chiefs should arrange for the establishment of a good Constitution ... He laid stress on that of the United States and gave him to understand that the American Government desired that the same Constitution be adopted in Mexico, and that they then would admit these republics into the Union and that with the addition of the other American provinces it would become the most formidable power in the world.

Colonel de Lara was a fugitive and a suitor. He listened with growing impatience until the Secretary of State raised the question of absorption into the Union, when he left in fury. In the light of subsequent history one may doubt whether his country would not have been the happier for Monroe's suggestion; in 1811, with Mexico still proud and prosperous, it came as an outrageous impertinence.

The Mexican revolution as a popular movement was speedily suppressed; when it came, it was the work of the suppressors; a military movement planned in the Masonic Lodges. Its original aim was to eliminate the cumbrous and dilatory machinery of the Vice-regal government and establish a monarchical and aristocratic régime under which locally born Spaniards might have a full share in the profits of office. The Empire of Iturbide had few features which Monroe could regard with sympathy; it had many weaknesses which it became the policy of Washington to exploit. The first instrument of this policy was Joel Poinsett, who came to Mexico at the establishment of its independence, first as United States agent, later as accredited Minister; the means he chose, perhaps the only efficacious means he could have chosen, was the establishment of a rival secret society – the Yorkist Rite to oppose the dominant Scottish Rite.

By its nature the full history of the secret societies of Mexico can never be known and in the general ignorance vast legends have naturally accumulated. It is certain that most of the disasters of the first generation of independent Mexicans, and it is probable that much of their successors', have been due to the organisations which adopted the vocabulary of European Freemasonry. So far as is known the Grand Lodges of the United States and England have consistently refused recognition to their Mexican brothers. The Scottish Rite, which seems to have no connexion with Scotland, appears to have been introduced into Mexico by the Spanish garrisons of the Napoleonic era who had themselves adopted it from revolutionary France. There is no need to accept sensational stories of a world organisation dedicated to anarchy, to understand how the Lodges became the centres of intrigue; at their meetings men of different positions, whose association elsewhere would attract comment, could meet in circumstances of absolute secrecy and freedom of discussion; since the law of the Church forbade membership, it was natural that their tone should be exclusively agnostic and anti-clerical. The Scottish Rite, however, may have included renegade members of the clergy; so far as it had any policy it seems to have favoured constitutional monarchy, to have been zealous of the privileges of rank and services and tolerant of religious practices for the uninitiated; it concerned itself mainly with personalities and the distribution of public offices to its own members. The Yorkist Rite, introduced by Poinsett, was the natural rallying-point for those who had been disappointed in the share-out of benefits; it was made up of the lawless elements of the revolution – the Villas and Zapatas of the revolution of 1910 – and was republican, proletarian and fiercely irreligious in character. Five lodges were organised with local chiefs. Poinsett's chief office was to coax from the Scottish Rite disgruntled members of more responsible position; the most important of these recruits was Arizpe, the Minister of Justice, a political priest. His presence in the new Rite secured protection for its members before the Courts. The acquittal of a Colonel

Ayestaran on a charge of peculation, advertised this privilege; there was an immediate response from senators, generals, governors. Soon the two Rites were divided not only by political views but by personal vendettas. For fifty years the history of Mexico becomes a series of coups and plots, assassinations and executions; of embezzlement and bribery; the learned and charitable institutions were sacked to provide funds for the rival gangs; the work of three centuries of civilised rule was obliterated in a generation, leaving the nation bankrupt, discredited abroad and divided by irreconcilable hatred at home. By this time doubts began to arise at Washington whether these turbulent neighbours would be a desirable addition to the United States.

The personalities of the various competitors for power during this anarchic period – Santa Anna Alvarez, Comonfort, Farias, Bustamante and the rest – are of purely local interest. Throughout their blood struggles the participation of the United States took two principal forms. There was what may be called the ideological campaign against the Spaniards and the Church, initiated by Poinsett, and there was the purely practical campaign for the acquisition of territory. Both were tolerably successful. The former culminated in the spring of 1860 in armed intervention in favour of Juarez, when he was on the point of defeat, by the confiscation by the United States navy of two of Miramon's ships; this action, and the conviction that it would be repeated if necessary, changed the future of the war and consummated the revolution. Juarez had signed a treaty offering territorial concessions as the price of help, but the United States Senate honourably refused to enforce it.

Less delicacy had been shown in the case of Texas and California. In 1820 the first United States citizen, a Moses Austin, had obtained permission to settle in Texas, then Mexican territory, on the grounds that he was a persecuted Catholic; he died prematurely but his son Stephen carried out his intention, and in 1821 Mexico adopted the practice of granting charters to colonists from the North. As political conditions in Mexico deteriorated the position of these settlers became less enviable, but their numbers increased and they soon formed a vigorous minority somewhat analogous to the *uitlanders* among the Boers. In 1835 they had become self-assertive enough to provoke government notice and Santa Anna abrogated the State Constitution. A revolution, led and supported from the United States, was savagely suppressed. A small force of American soldiers then captured Santa Anna and his whole army; under danger of summary execution he acknowledged the independence of Texas and returned in a dilatory manner by way of the United States. General Houston became first president of Texas, which avowed nominal independence until 1844, when great bitterness was aroused in Mexico by its inevitable annexation. President Herrera issued a call for the defence of the country, and Santa Anna returned from one of his frequent periods of exile to lead a disastrous campaign against the invaders, who had, meanwhile, over-run California. The war was an unrelieved series of defeats for the Mexicans; Mexico City was taken and the Peace of Guadalupe-Hidalgo signed on February 2nd, 1848, on the Americans' terms. By these terms Mexico lost more than half her territory. Compensation, of a kind, was given. The Americans could have taken more and paid nothing; the surviving bitterness was in no way lessened by their moderation; subsequent history would have been very different if, as was proposed at the time, the boundary had been drawn south of Tampico.

2

At the beginning of 1861 Juarez entered Mexico City; he owed his position to support from the United States; he was regarded with detestation by the conservative elements in the country; the government was deeply in debt and without hope of legitimate increase of income. The Church had been despoiled by successive dictators, her plate melted down and her colleges closed; Juarez exiled the Bishops and made a last, desperate attempt to sell off the Church's remaining assets. But few could afford, and still fewer were willing, to purchase property acquired in this way. In Mexico City houses belonging to various religious institutions, assessed at over half a million dollars, realised less than two thousand. In the provinces the sums obtained were further reduced by the peculations of the various officials through whose hands they passed. He succeeded in bringing about the final ruin of the Church without adding appreciably to the national wealth. There was no alternative but to suspend payment on his foreign debt. But for the time his friends in the North were occupied with their own affairs. The civil war in the United States seemed to offer the Mexican conservatives a chance to re-establish themselves without interference, but they were now so demoralised that the only means which seemed suitable was to invite further foreign intervention.

The episode of the Emperor Maximilian is an ideal subject for the cinema and has twice been used as such. In Mexican history it is nothing but an episode. It showed that the country had now deteriorated to a condition in which government could only be maintained by force and that national pride still ferociously preferred anarchy to foreign domination. Juarez still lived and the United States, though preoccupied, still supported him; the Church treasured mediæval traditions of her responsibility, did not recognise a champion in Maximilian, with his sceptical nineteenth-century German culture and his light love affairs, nor accept from him terms she had rejected from Juarez; the patriots in the army resented the French garrisons. Only a man of superlative energy could have enforced his rule. It was agreeable to many, after the brigand-camps from which the country had been governed, to have a Court organised on the most stately European model, to have a Hapsburg in place of the half-breeds, to have an Emperor with a fashionable taste in house decoration and an interest in botany, to see at public functions a gracious figure, head and shoulders above the assembly. But Mexican popular heroes are drawn in another shape – squat, swarthy, passionate, intolerant, vain men who when cornered shoot their way to freedom and take to the mountains, who will steal and promise and give lavishly, sell anything and repudiate the bargain, murder their friends and buy off their enemies, nurse a grudge and forget a kindness, sometimes grossly sacrilegious, sometimes heroically pious, Aztec and Castilian inextricably confounded. It is a significant fact that the Mexican history books and the frescoed caricatures which are the most notable instruments of government propaganda deal gently with the Archduke Maximilian; he was never at all dangerous; he conformed to the Mexican ideal only in his dignified bearing before the firing-squad. Miramon, one of the finest of the Mexican conservatives, was shot with him.

The United States regained their influence; Juarez came back and reigned for five years, until his death, among sporadic but unsuccessful rebellions. His successor, Lerdo de Tejada, attempted to carry on Juarez's system in face of growing odium; in 1876 civil war on a national scale broke out, Tejada fled to the United States, General Porfirio Diaz took Mexico City and retained uninterrupted control, even during the Gonzalez presidency (1880–1884), until 1911. For some time the United States refused recognition of Diaz's government. The American Civil War was over but the South was still in a dangerous state and a war of aggression was seriously suggested as a possible outlet for domestic bitterness. John W. Foster, the U.S. minister, President Hayes and a powerful group in Washington were strongly anti-Mexican. In Foster's *Diplomatic Memoirs*, writing of this time, he says 'Certain gentlemen especially interested in the administration of President Hayes had conceived the idea that in view of the tension in the public mind created by the partisans of Mr Tilden and of the disturbed condition of affairs in the Southern States, it would divert attention from pending issues and tend greatly to consolidate the new administration, if a war could be brought on with Mexico and another slice of its territory added to the Union.'

War, however, would not have been popular in the U.S., and the very cause which rendered it desirable – the weakness of Hayes' popular support – rendered it impossible; General Diaz moreover was a man of vastly superior capacity to the military dictators who preceded and succeeded him. Washington was obliged to recognise him and was soon working with him in tolerable harmony. The chief cause of friction during his reign was a series of police incidents on the frontier; both sides of the line were remote from the law and Mexico became the natural goal of fugitive criminals. Between 1874 and 1882 American posses in pursuit of marauders crossed the frontier twenty-three times, each occasion being, technically, an invasion of national territory. Moreover Mexican citizens, then and later, enjoyed very little protection in American territory; there were lynchings, sometimes in atrocious circumstances, summary executions and fatal brawls for which no effective protests were made in Washington. It is fashionable now, in Mexico, to speak of the régime of Porfirio Diaz as a time when national interests were sacrificed to foreign and the government became a native police force charged with making it easy for foreign capitalists to get rich. In fact Diaz was all the time concerned with keeping, as best he could, the commercial balance of power in the country. It was natural that American interests should predominate but it was an essential part of his policy to set them off, as far as he could, with European and to keep them in their proper place, as commercial undertakings concerned merely in developing natural resources. The conduct of foreign nineteenth-century capitalists and their supporting governments in China made it clear that there was no place in the history of his age, for an exclusive nationalism. He kept the peace and he preserved the integrity of the country; there were no more cessions of territory. For a long time the United States had openly coveted the isthmus of Tehuantepec; it was Diaz himself, with the help of British capital and skill, who developed it and made it, before the opening of the Panama Canal, the main route from the Atlantic to the Pacific. He had a practical, soldier's estimate of the importance of national pride; he did not want to harbour foreign criminals and was quite pleased that their own police should take the trouble of recapturing them; he did not think national honour required Palmerstonian defences of the kind of citizen who got himself into trouble in the Texas saloons. But he went further; one day the Texans roasted alive a Mexican rough named Rodriguez. The newspaper *El Debate* reported the incident indignantly and there was general ill-feeling in Mexico City; instead of protesting, however gently, to Washington, Diaz suppressed *El Debate*. In 1910 the American Ambassador objected to the anti-American tone of two other papers, the *Diario del Hogar* and the *El Pais*: both were suppressed. These actions added nothing to the popularity either of the United States or the President. Moreover, in spite of these efforts to be agreeable, in many sections of America Diaz was not admired; towards the end of his reign he seemed to be sacrificing Mexican interests without gaining a corresponding support in the United States. High-minded Americans began to condemn him on doctrinaire grounds. He had reduced democratic forms to an absurdity; in many districts his police were corrupt and cruel; something barely distinguishable from slavery existed in Yucatan, the American public were tired of eulogies of the dictator and read with zeal the well substantiated denunciations of his tyranny. Thus began the disastrous epoch of American interference in Mexican affairs on humanitarian grounds.

Before Diaz the issue was perfectly simple. The Americans believed in their 'manifest destiny' to rule the entire continent; they were an immensely powerful and sporadically aggressive neighbour to be kept at bay by whatever means seemed possible; from the beginning of this century the issues became infinitely involved; generally speaking they may be summarised in President Wilson's phrase, 'I am going to teach the South American republics to elect good men.' This ambition, equally obnoxious to the Mexicans, is pregnant with ambiguous implications.

'*I am going to teach*'; that is to say: the Mexicans are still in a state of tutelage; it is the duty of the American government to instruct and discipline. '*I*', the party momentarily in power at Washington; what if a different party, with the same coercive powers, shall aspire to teach a different lesson?

'*To elect*'; the basic American assumption, in face of much foreign and democratic evidence to the contrary, that 'election' is more than a convenient method of providing a government; it is divinely ordained. Elections, even in countries of homogeneous race, widespread education, and a tradition of disinterested public service are a capricious guide; in Latin America they have always been farcical. There are, in various parts of the world, various means of securing election; the candidate may buy votes in the old English way of ready money down, in the new English way of promises to pay from the public funds when elected; he may evict opponents from their cottages or shoot them up with machine guns in the streets of Cicero; the Mexicans, for the most part, prefer to leave the voting papers uncounted and draw from the lists made up at the party headquarters. To whom and in what terms was President Wilson proposing to teach this elusive art of election?

'*Good men*'; good for what? To be a strong and independent nation with its own institutions developed from its own traditions and needs, or a political no-man's-land of conflicting foreign influences, with orderly habits, balanced public finances, or a republic on the United States model which one day will earn inclusion in the Union, or a political experimental farm where revolutionary ideas may be tried out with a view to importation into the United States. (Just as the United States earned the gratitude of the world by 'trying out' prohibition, so the Mexicans may be said to be trying out Marxism.) All these aims have variously been attributed to the 'good man' in Mexico and all have received support from Washington at one time or another.

3

I think it is an open point whether, in 1910, a patriotic Mexican – or, for that matter, a disinterested foreigner – should have been a supporter of Porfirio Diaz. It is characteristic of Mexican history that at almost any period one looks at there are abundant reasons for deploring the existing régime; one turns the pages and realises that one was wrong; the cure was always worse than the ill. This consideration alone should make one sceptical of betterment by the overthrow of General Cardenas.

Politically the Diaz régime had the weakness of all autocracies, that are not based on royalty, the difficulty of succession. Socially there was every reason to complain that the peons had not shared at all in the general prosperity and that the Mexicans of the more fortunate classes had not a proportionate place of influence in their country's development. After the long period of peace it seemed reasonable to believe that the people had become accustomed to orderly conditions and would not again lapse into anarchy. The days of bankruptcy seemed over; Mexico was now rich enough to contemplate a more equitable distribution of her property. Wealthier Mexicans had been educated in England, France and the United States – for the Mexican educational system never recovered from the Reforms – and had learned to respect representative institutions; they could be trusted to work a parliamentary system in a public-spirited manner. These were the assumptions of the Maderists; they proved tragically false but they seemed reasonable enough at the time.

It is not the object of this chapter to recount the details of the decline and fall of Mexico, but to trace their connexions with the United States and explain the peculiar relations that in consequence subsist between the two peoples.

Francisco Madero had every reason to believe that his policy would be sympathetic to the greater part of the American people; everything which he represented had long been a boasted feature of their own system. His rebellion was not a proletarian movement; the peasants' revolt in Morelos, which had been growing against Diaz, coincided with his own but developed into a movement against him. The kind of state which Madero hoped to bring into existence was very much like those that existed across the border. He was the type of President Wilson's 'good man'. Yet of the numerous causes to which his failure was due, one of the chief was the open opposition of the American Ambassador, another Wilson, who had a different conception of the country's requirements.

The guilt of Ambassador Wilson has been itemised by Gruening and seems indisputable. He was appointed to Mexico in the last days of the Diaz régime; he had no previous diplomatic career to qualify him for the post; his brother was Senator John M. Wilson, Republican boss of the State of Washington. There is a curiously ambiguous phrase employed in American politics, the 'tie-up'; it may mean a family connexion, a personal friendship, or direct paid employment. Ambassador Wilson was 'tied up' – by means of John M. Wilson and Richard Ballinger, Taft's first secretary of the interior – with the Guggenheims whose American Smelting and Refining Company had great interests in Mexico which were in direct competition with the Maderos. It is impossible for a foreigner to judge how much importance can be attached to these political–commercial 'tie-ups'. What is certain is that from the moment of Wilson's arrival the American Embassy became the headquarters of a group of American business men who had ambitions in the country. It seems possible that at first this group welcomed a change of government in the belief that a weak President might be more amenable to pressure. It soon became clear that Madero had neither the inclination nor the authority to help them. From then on Ambassador Wilson set himself to destroy the administration, embarrassing it directly by peremptory and sometimes unreason-able claims, and undermining its prestige abroad by the information he sent to Washington. It is doubtful whether Madero would have survived long, even if he had been given sympathetic treatment; Ambassador Wilson's opposition made his fall a certainty. In the summer of 1911 he was forecasting Madero's failure. In January 1912 he described the country as 'seething with discontent' and the 'area of actual and open rebellion against the Government' as 'not incon-siderable'. In February of that year his reports persuaded the Gov-ernment at Washington to mobilise the entire regular army of the United States along the border, and to reinforce it with the National Guard and a recruiting campaign. News of this manœuvre, spread-ing throughout Mexico, was interpreted as having only one mean-ing; that public order had broken down and that the American Government believed Madero's régime was about to fall. Immedi-ately, all over the country, politicians who had been suspending judgement declared for rebellion; bands of brigands became armies and a period of seven years, civil war had begun.

On March 1, the Orozco rebellion broke out in Chihuaha; next day, before he had had time to inform himself of the gravity of the situation, and while his colleagues were still waiting on events, Wilson urged American nationals to evacuate large areas of the country. On March 15 he was calling for arms to defend the Ameri-can colony in Mexico City. Three days later he telegraphed for a small armoury – 1,000 rifles and 1,000,000 cartridges – for the use 'for patriotic motives' of two of his American friends. One of these was Mr George Beck, who, among other activities, was a director of a company known as the 'Tampico News Company'; this company, it was found at the beginning of May, was engaged in running guns to Zapata, one of the most ferociously destructive of the rebel leaders. On August 22, he reported conditions in six states to be 'as bad as at any time during the two revolutions, if not worse' and Madero as 'incompetent to meet the situation'. On the same day, two hours later, he was protesting that the President, who, according to his own reports, was no longer in effective control, was evincing a 'growing anti-American spirit' and a 'preference for European markets' and was 'harassing and discriminating against

American interests'. As disorder spread Ambassador Wilson pressed Madero for 'a comprehensive and categorical statement' as to the measures he proposed to protect American interests. At the height of its troubles the administration replied patiently and in detail to all Wilson's complaints, showing such a proportion of them to be unjustified that it is impossible to attribute them to anything but malice. On January 7th, 1913, Wilson opened the new year by describing the whole situation as 'gloomy, if not hopeless'. A week later he called for a warship. On February 9th began the period known as the 'tragic ten days'.

Up to this date, it is difficult to distinguish between cause and effect. Wilson had said the country was lapsing into anarchy; it did lapse into anarchy; it is arguable that he was more foresighted than his colleagues and that he was merely doing his duty in communicating his apprehensions to his Government; that is arguable if not convincing. During the 'tragic ten days' his conduct was grossly irregular.

The course of events is recent and familiar history. The rebellion in Mexico City was the work of a garrison of 800 men, three batteries of artillery and the palace guard. It was enough to suppress normal activity in the city but not enough to dominate it. Wilson wired that public opinion, 'both native and foreign', was 'overwhelmingly' against Madero; he called for 'drastic instructions, perhaps of a menacing character', which were not forthcoming. Instead Wilson persuaded his colleagues to ask for Madero's resignation. The President refused. The American Embassy now became, in the words of the Cuban Minister, Marquez Sterling, 'the centre of a true conspiracy'. The determining event of the ten days was the defection to the rebels of General Victoriano Huerta; the day before this took place Wilson wired 'Huerta notifies me to expect some action that will remove Madero from power.' At noon next day he wired that the coup had taken place; it had been planned for that time but actually took place an hour and a half later. The evidence that Wilson was a party to the plot is overwhelming.

That evening the meeting between the leader of the rebellious garrison, Felix Diaz, and General Huerta, former commander of the defence, took place in the American Embassy. Healths were drunk to the new régime. Someone bothered to ask, 'And what will be the fate of poor Madero?'

'Oh they will put Senor Madero in a madhouse,' said Wilson. 'As for the other' (Pino Suarez) 'if they kill him it will be no great loss . . . We must not meddle in the domestic affairs of Mexico.'

Gustavo Madero and Basso, the *Intendente* of the Palace, had already been murdered. It was clear to everyone in the city that Francisco Madero's life was in danger. Wilson concerned himself only with the recognition of the new government. But suspicions had already been aroused in Washington about the part their ambassador was playing. He was instructed to see that no harm came to Madero. ' . . . This Government earnestly hopes to hear that he has been dealt with in a manner consistent with peace and humanity. You may in your discretion make use of these ideas in your conversation with General Huerta.' Wilson, however, re-assured them that there was 'no prospect of injury' to either the deposed President or Vice-President; he urged the recognition of the new government as constitutional, popular, and, in the unanimous opinion of all observers, the only means to avoid further bloodshed.

It is a gloomy coincidence that in the two blackest crimes of recent Mexican history – the murders of Madero and of Pro – there was in each case an American Ambassador at hand who, alone, could have averted it. In Mexico everyone knew that Madero was in danger. The Cuban Minister, Madero's father and his mother appealed directly to Wilson; at last his wife overcame her resentment and came to him in person; she has left an account of her interview, printed by Gruening, on whom most of the evidence quoted in this section is drawn. She went with her sister-in-law; the two ladies were kept waiting while the Ambassador was summoned from the Palace where he was at that moment in conference with Huerta; when he came his manner was 'brusque'.

Mme Madero said, 'I want you to use your influence to protect the lives of my husband and of the other prisoners.'

'That is a responsibility I do not care to undertake, either for myself or my government.'

'Will you be good enough, then, to send this telegram to President Taft.' She produced the draft of a message which she had attempted unsuccessfully to send through the normal service.

Wilson said, 'It is not necessary to send this,' but on pressure, put it in his pocket saying, 'All right. I will send it.' He then, in her distress, proceeded to lecture Mme Madero on the cause of her husband's downfall.... 'He never wanted to consult with me ... he had peculiar ideas ... the people were not satisfied ... I knew all this was going to happen ... it would not have been good policy to warn him ...'

Mme Madero pressed that, whatever his shortcomings, he should be allowed to leave the country. Wilson would promise no more than that his bodily safety would be seen to.

Two days later the prisoners were murdered in circumstances which left no doubt that the crime was premeditated and condoned. It is charitable to suppose that Wilson was not in Huerta's confidence in this matter, but however shocked he was by the tragedy, he concealed his emotion in the telegrams in which he announced it. 'I am disposed to accept the Government's version of the affair,' he said, 'and consider it a closed incident.'

4

On March 4 the Taft administration retired, Woodrow Wilson became President of the United States, and the policy of the State Department at Washington experienced a radical change. Huerta was now in power – precariously and disgracefully, but with the possibility of redeeming himself and restoring order; his prestige depended very largely on the assumption that he had the support of the United States. The only justification for the means he had taken to get power would be the use he made of it; the only justification of the support which Washington, in the person of their Ambassador, had given him when he was a rebel, would be continued and vigorous support now that he was *de facto* President.

Huerta was the antithesis of Madero; it was possible he might succeed where his predecessor had failed; for generations, now, most Mexican Presidents had reached their position by violence; the sort of problems – Villa and Zapata in particular – which confronted the new government needed ruthless solutions; besides the treacherous guards there were many decent men in Huerta's party – Pedro Lascurain, for example. It was not inconceivable that a tolerable government might emerge. Ambassador Wilson exerted himself in every way to provide Huerta with a fair chance; his dispatches minimised the opposition, misinterpreted the views of his colleagues, suppressed unsympathetic consular reports, and continually urged the State Department to give Huerta their recognition. It was useless. In July he was recalled and retired. President Wilson believed that Huerta had done wrong and should be punished for it, no matter who else suffered with him. The punishment has lasted many years now and no one has suffered more than the innocent.

During the civil wars which followed, American 'recognition' became the label of the *de jure* government; these usually became *de facto* because recognition meant the exclusive right to buy arms. One of President Wilson's first acts was to reply to the message of congratulation from Huerta with a simple acknowledgement addressed to him as 'General'. This was on March 9th. In August, after Ambassador Wilson's recall, the President in his message to Congress said, 'It is now our duty to show what true neutrality will do to enable the people of Mexico to set their affairs in order. We cannot be the partisan of either party . . .'

'Either party' was an unduly simple statement of the situation. There was in fact one party, then in power, Huerta's, which still commanded the adherence of those who preferred stability to revenge or loot and there was ranged against it a multitude of heterogeneous rebels. For a time an attempt was made to give them a semblance of unity by naming them collectively 'Constitutionals' but they had nothing in common except the desire to overthrow the government and were soon at war among themselves. All the leaders of this period – Villa, Zapata, Carranza, Alvarado, Cedillo, Obregon – with the single exception of Calles who lives in affluent exile in the United States, have died violently, all at different times and in different circumstances. Villa, sniped one day during his retirement, Zapata ambushed by his hosts when arriving for a dinner party,

Carranza murdered in his sleep in a lonely hut on the road to exile, Alvarado before a firing-squad, Cedillo hunted to death in the hills; Obregon, most curiously of all, was attacked by a pious young artist at a dinner table surrounded by his own adherents; the boy was tortured before he was executed, but no explanation was ever published of the fact that while five cartridges were fired from his revolver, fourteen bullets were found in Obregon's body. Huerta died of his imprisonment in the U.S.A. It is popularly believed in Mexico that he was poisoned. The various rebels represented different elements of discontent. Cedillo and Carranza were of the type of rebel baron in King Stephen's reign, Zapata led a kind of 'jaquerie'; Villa was an intolerable blackguard, guilty of every conceivable public and private atrocity, who has lately been represented to the cinema-going public as a rough and generous Robin Hood; Alvarado a hooligan of the type of the gangster bosses of Chicago in the '20s; Calles and Obregon appear somewhat more presentable than most of their fellows, with strenuous political ambitions. The armies of these leaders included any kind of follower, fierce Yaqui Indians from the North, simple peons who had been told that by taking arms they would get land and liberty, professional soldiers following their immediate superiors, pure criminals; besides these there was an organisation which was to play an increasingly important part in local affairs – the 'Industrial Workers of the World', later to be renamed less pretentiously the Confederaction Regional de Obreros Mexicanos; this society, popularly known as the CROM, had its headquarters in Vera Cruz with branches in all the industrial centres; it is led by Morones who has made himself very rich by means of it. It was a part of the international communistic organisation which developed in the great cities of the world twenty-five years ago. In recent years its importance has been overshadowed by the rival organization of Lombardo Toledano, the C.T.M., but for ten years it ruled Yucatan, Tabasco and Vera Cruz and exercised predominant influence on many occasions in Mexico City; Obregon was its ally. It differed from other revolutionary organisations in its attitude to the Church; to the Liberals the Church was something to rob; robbery had to be justified by abuse; but the revolutionary leaders often called for priests on the death bed, and encouraged their womenfolk to attend Mass; the CROM was fixedly and militantly atheistic and sought to destroy religion as such. It was also narrower in its aims; the Liberals avowed a zeal for the general welfare, some of them almost exclusively for the majority, who lived on the soil; the CROM aimed purely at the power of the small section who worked in industrial concerns, to destroy the commercial organisation under which they worked and give them control of the wealth, and so of the policy of the nation. It is customary for writers, according to their views, to attach particular obloquy to one or other of these parties. The truth is that the atrocities committed by all were so many and so hideous that it is idle to differentiate. Poor Huerta has gone down to history with the label of 'bloodstained', but his crimes seem mild in comparison with those of his successors.

President Wilson can hardly be blamed for not foreseeing these developments. All he knew was that a bad man was in power in Mexico; he set about looking for a good one. So ill informed was he of local conditions that he flirted with the idea of backing Villa – from every conceivable point of view, patriotic, moral, international, the worst of the lot. Finally he decided on Carranza who had an amiable, almost a venerable appearance. He had been governor of the state of Coahuila under Diaz and ruled with the usual accompaniments of the padded army list, purchasable justice, and commercial graft; he was no worse, perhaps rather better than the usual run of governors. He was prepared to back Madero provided he was left undisturbed; he was prepared to back, had, in fact, already backed Huerta on the same terms. But Madero had squandered the savings of Diaz, Huerta needed money and did not want a disproportionate amount to fall into provincial hands. There was a disagreement about the sum of 50,000 pesos which Carranza had stolen from the banks, so Carranza declared against him and for the 'Constitutionalists'.

Huerta meanwhile carried on government of a kind and it became clear at Washington that more definite steps were needed to upset him. In February 1914 Wilson lifted the embargo on arms, thus ensuring, if not their victory, the ability of the 'Constitutionalists' to remain in the field indefinitely. In April, on the flimsiest provocation, he went very much further; he occupied Vera Cruz, thus stopping a supply of arms that were due to be landed there for Huerta. This decided Huerta's fate, just as, three generations before, Miramon's had been decided at the same place, but the war-like intervention was not particularly welcome to Carranza. A curious situation ensued in which Wilson attempted to assist Carranza, first on certain conditions, then on no conditions at all, and Carranza continued to repudiate his help. Villa was already at war with Carranza; he now cheerfully went to war on his own account with the United States; with the arms the Americans had sent him he began a series of outrages along the border. On January 10th, 1916 he lined up sixteen American engineers at Santa Ysabel and shot them; on March 9th he attacked the town of Columbus and burned it, murdering sixteen citizens. President Wilson ordered an army into Mexican territory to 'get Villa alive or dead'. They failed to get him. Carranza refused all cooperation; General Pershing's expedition marched through empty country and finally withdrew; Villa was pardoned and paid off by Carranza. Still President Wilson continued to 'recognise' him. In March 1917 he was formally inaugurated as President. A party manifesto, known as 'the Constitution of Queretaro' was promulgated. Carranza settled down to a brief but voluptuous period of authority, characterised by orgies, that have become fabulous, in the capital, and an abandonment of the provinces to gangster rule. It was during this period that Yucatan was reduced to permanent ruin by Alvarado. The persecution of the Church will be dealt with in a separate chapter. Here it may be noted that Carranza's attempt to stop it, more than any other cause, brought about his death. President Wilson was reluctant to admit the crimes of his protégés; it was only after the facts had again and again been set before him and Catholic opinion in America was becoming seriously inflamed, that he sent a protest. He asked for three things: freedom for foreigners to pursue their businesses in peace; an amnesty for political opponents; a remission of the persecution of religion. 'Nothing will shock the civilised world more,' he wrote, 'than punitive and vindictive action towards priests or ministers of any Church, whether Catholic or Protestant; and the Government of the United States ventures most respectfully but most earnestly to caution the leaders of the Mexican people on this delicate and vital matter. The treatment already said to have been accorded priests has had a most unfortunate effect on opinion outside of Mexico.'

Carranza accordingly went before the Congress in December 1918 to propose a modification of the 'Constitution of Queretaro' in favour of the Church. But Obregon had now entered into an alliance with the CROM; the price for their support was the continued persecution of the Church. Obregon's supporters in Congress were therefore instructed to reject the amendments. Carranza was driven out and murdered. Once again American intervention had proved disastrous.

For the next few years United States policy took the form of mild hostility. A highly capable and honoured Ambassador, Mr Sheffield, was charged with the disagreeable office of watching the steady deterioration of the country and at the same time of patiently pressing a long series of legal and financial claims against a government who would yield to nothing but force and were perfectly confident that force would not be employed against them. At last a new and very different Ambassador was sent to employ a very different policy.

5

At the time nothing seemed more brilliantly triumphant, in its results nothing has proved more futile than the policy of Dwight Morrow. He came as the bankers' agent to collect the debts which had been accumulating against the Mexican Government and to restore conditions in which American business men would be able to renew their activities. He rightly believed that it was no business of a foreign Ambassador to supervise the morals of the Government to which he was accredited. He arrived just at the time when Calles was not only beginning to weary of the demands of the CROM, but was also becoming scared at the tenacity with which the rural population was resisting CROM rule; he wished to consolidate his private fortune, and put the country into a more workable condition. Morrow showed him a way to make his peace with big business and to keep his face at home. He was unique among not only his countrymen but all human kind, in being able to evince a personal affection for the President; Calles responded and a period of mutual admiration ensued in which many points of disagreement were nominally settled. In fact none of the agreements has proved efficacious. Calles was saved by American assistance from one rebellion when the peasantry rose to defend their churches; he was not saved from the communists. He got away, alive and rich. Morrow's diplomatic achievements collapsed with Calles. What survived was a new tradition of verbal geniality which is known as 'the Good Neighbour Policy'.

It is a policy which has had good results elsewhere and is naturally sympathetic to the warm heart of the race. American business men, as all who have had dealings with them gratefully acknowledge, dispense with both the honeyed flattery of Asia and the ponderous and often chilly courtesies of Europe, practising instead a particular kind of personal, man-to-man cordiality. It is taught I believe in the commercial courses at their Universities. Its aim is to convince the other party in a deal that you are negotiating, not for mutual, still less for exclusive, profit, but out of affection. You like him so much that you would sooner talk prices than not talk to him at all. It is a delightful convention for those who have plenty of time to spare and, in its best exponents, is something more than a convention; it springs from a genuine broad bonhomie and a love of figures. Morrow, it seems, did really like General Calles; and he liked Mexico. If he did not appreciate the highest achievements of Mexican architecture he, at any rate, liked peasant pottery; he gave Sr Diego Rivera an important commission; he went around smiling and shaking hands; the average Mexican was about his height and he was able to face the camera with his arms on people's shoulders, without appearing particularly foolish.

Now the Mexicans were not used to that kind of treatment from Americans. In the course of a hundred years their well-founded pride had changed to an equally well-founded feeling of inferiority. They expected to be treated as 'dagos' and 'greasers', to hear their government denounced as cruel and corrupt, their institutions as antiquated, their beliefs as childish and their domestic habits as disgusting. It was quite a new experience to be praised, and this heady, after-dinner oratory, prolonged next day and the day after in private utterances worked all too well. Those to whom the revolution had simply meant an advancement of personal fortune began to fancy themselves as philanthropists and statesmen; those who had lost by the revolution or had failed to obtain the promised benefits, hearing it praised by their censorious Northern neighbours, suddenly began to wonder whether, after all, there had not been some good in it which they had failed to notice. Every government propagandist could now enliven his speeches with quotations from the U.S.A.

Morrow's present successor, Mr Josephus Daniels, has been at his post during one of the most delicate periods of Mexican history. He has seen the Calles régime with which Morrow had come to terms, overthrown; he has seen the CROM and Morones reduced to secondary importance by the rise of the C.T.M. and Lombardo Toledano, the agriculture of the country failing, the communications dislocated, the currency discredited; he has seen the sensational theft of enormous American and European interests, the development of a will to pure mischief among the industrial workers and of despair among the rest of the population – and throughout has maintained an attitude of imperturbable urbanity. Saved from embarrassment by his ignorance of Spanish, he has sat smiling on platforms where Marxist principles have been preached and applauded; he has let his name be quoted as a supporter of the régime; at the crucial time immediately following the expropriations, when the British Foreign Office was composing the first of its notes which led to the breaking of diplomatic relations; while the State Department at Washington had still given no clear indication of the policy it intended to follow; Mr Daniels received a note from General Cardenas in the following terms: '*My Government considers that the attitude adopted by the Government of the United States in the matter of the expropriation of the petroleum companies reaffirms once more the sovereignty of the peoples of this Continent . . . By this attitude, Mr Ambassador, your President and your people have won the esteem of the people of Mexico. The Mexican nation has lived in these last few days through moments of trial in which it did not know whether it would have to give rein to its patriotic feelings or to applaud an act of justice of the neighbouring country represented by your Excellency. Today my country is happy to celebrate without reservations the proof of friendship which it has received from yours, and which will be carried in the hearts of its people.'*

It was an audacious message. The Mexicans were rejoicing, but for all the fireworks and bonfires there was a feeling of apprehension. Like the infant Edmund Gosse when he said his prayers to a chair and waited to be struck from heaven, the people of Mexico had defied the powers that had dominated them for so long, and were waiting to see what would happen to them; it was thus that they had stood, breathless, while the first Spanish missionaries threw down the old gods from their sanctuaries. A snub at that moment, a reminder that since the promulgation of the Monroe doctrine the United States had peculiar responsibilities for European interests in the continent, a reminder, even, that the State Department at Washington had so far not defined its attitude in any terms which allowed of General Cardenas's interpretation, would have been sobering if not crushing. Mr Daniels replied, 'I am gratified to have thus formally received this important expression of Mexico's deep friendship for my country... this feeling is mutual.' From then onwards, on every government platform, Mr Daniels was quoted as a supporter.

Shortly after this he left for three months' holiday. It was thought in some quarters that he would not return, but at the end of June he was back, with his old infectious charm and benignity. By this time the enthusiasm for the expropriations had cooled. Prices had risen everywhere and Government speakers were finding their audiences less responsive. Mr Cordell Hull had made no decisive statement on the oil question; instead he had pointedly asked for a settlement of the debts incurred by previous revolutionary escapades. Neither the American nor the Mexican Press was either optimistic or cordial. In particular the anti-Nazi *New York Times* had a correspondent in Mexico who was exposing some of General Cardenas's propaganda. It was noticed that Mr Daniels adopted an unusually cautious tone with interviewers. But in the meantime other 'good neighbours' with other motives were appearing. There was an influential little group interested in the marketing of the expropriated oil. The central figure of this group was a Mr Davis, who for many years had been

concerned with oil transactions independently of the main controlling groups. Davis had secured the post of middleman for the
disposal of all the Mexican oil abroad. Negotiations were extremely
difficult. Some oil was indisputably the property of the Mexican
Government – the product of their own wells – and it was impossible
to identify any particular shipment as being stolen property. The
position of buyers and sellers varied at law in different countries;
cargoes had been distrained. Many countries refused to accept the
imports and many buyers were reluctant to expose themselves to
legal proceedings. The countries without scruples were also without
foreign exchanges. It was unlikely that a permanent embargo could
be maintained, but at the moment Davis's most hopeful market
seemed the United States. Politically he was 'tied up' with Senator
Guffey, Mr Walter A. Jones, and, through them, with the labour
leader, John L. Lewis. As has been remarked above, it is difficult
for a foreigner to understand the importance of these political–
commercial alliances. He is disposed either to discount them
altogether or to suppose that a formal conspiracy exists where in
fact there is only an intermittent joviality. A few facts, for what they
are worth, are certain. On August 22nd Davis was taken by Walter
A. Jones to interview Cordell Hull. On September 4th the *Houston
Post* reported the election of Walter A. Jones as President of the
Good Neighbour League. Jones is described as 'Guffey's right
bower'. He had 'a gilded cage at the Mayflower with vintages and
Perfectos galore. Law makers were lured there. He gave a rich
blowout to John L. Lewis, with 50 gilt edged guests . . . Jones knows
all about coal and oil . . . and sees everything including the advantages of the Good Neighbour League as a strictly non-partisan
mechanism for boosting the New Deal.'

On September 11th part of an American delegation arrived in
Mexico City for the International Labour Congress. It consisted of
Mr John L. Lewis, Mr Edwin S. Smith and Miss Mary Van Kleeck.
On the same train with them was Margarita Nelkin, a Spanish
communist. They were received by a guard of honour but with
less popular enthusiasm than greeted Gonzales Peña and Leon
Jouhaux. International socialists were common in Mexico City
that week.

Miss Mary Van Kleeck is a well-known American radical; Mr Edwin S. Smith had been an associate of hers on the Russell Sage Foundation. He was nominally on holiday but his normal work is as a member of the National Labour Relations Board, a body which came into existence under the Wagner Act. This body is in some ways analogous in function to the notorious *Conciliacion* of Mexico. The Cardenas party were quick to seize upon this similarity and represent Smith as the mouthpiece of the New Deal. He was believed to be a close associate of President Roosevelt's and in some circles it was supposed that he had come to keep watch on John L. Lewis with the intention of preventing indiscretions which might embarrass the State Department. Any such expectations were disappointed.

From the first Mr Smith was a very much more interesting figure to the Mexican politicians than Mr Lewis. The Government were already abundantly assured of the goodwill of most of the labour organisations of the world. Cables had come to them in great numbers at the time of the expropriations, from powerful unions and modest study circles. They knew where they stood as far as 'proletarian' sympathies were concerned. What they did not know, and what neither they nor anyone else yet knows, is how powerful 'proletarian' sympathies were in influencing American foreign policy. Mr Lewis travelled with some circumstance and it was noted without enthusiasm that while other delegates lived modestly in rooms that were costing them 10 or 12 pesos a day, Mr Lewis engaged the most expensive suite at the town's principal hotel. Perhaps in this the Mexicans saw a certain likeness to their now discredited Morones. As a public speaker he had a forceful manner and the normal socialist matter. All the delegates at the Congress had much the same message to deliver in their different languages – the solidarity and certain victory of the working classes; the identification of Fascism and capital which in more critical circles is becoming daily less tenable. But there was an element of awkwardness in Mr Lewis's position. One of the chief grievances which the Government agitators had been hammering on, in all their speeches, was the Mexican peon's degraded condition in comparison with the American workman's. Large, transparently intelligible

diagrams had been issued contrasting the rates of wages that per-
tained on opposite sides of the border – the Yankee worker in his cap
and overalls balancing on his palm two great coins representing
16.13 pesos; the peon in jacket and sombrero gazing wistfully at three
little discs representing 4.68. More than this, there had been another, widely circulated diagram showing the relative production of
the two workers; a great pile of 23 and a fraction barrels of oil (each
representing 100 barrels) produced by the Mexican in a year; the
meagre crop of 7 and a bit produced by the Yankee. The various
statistical manipulations required to justify these diagrams need not
be examined here. The significant fact was that over a long period of
time the C.T.M. organisers had been telling their men that the
Yankees were paid enormously more than they for very much less
work. Thus when Mr Lewis sought to inflame a Mexican audience
with tales of the oppression of the fascist-capitalists of his own
country, the indignation he provoked was tepid.

Mr Smith on the other hand was credited with disproportionate
importance. He was a second Josephus Daniels come to judgment.
When on the first day the Peruvian delegate, at a meeting in the
Workers' University advocated the internationalisation of the
Panama Canal, and Mr Smith did not openly dissent, it was construed by many that the United States were agreeable to the proposal. On the second day of the Congress particular attention was
paid, as it well might be, to the example set by the Mexican Labour
Courts. A delegate, Arturo Martinez Adame said that their efficacy
depended on 'correct revolutionary interpretation' of the Labour
Laws. Pressed to explain further, he said, 'Conscience decisions are
based on justice and equity rather than on legal proofs and procedure. Consequently Governors of all states are ordered by the Federal
Government to make sure that labour laws always act in favour to
the workers.' To make the lesson still clearer to Mr Smith another
delegate remarked that the United States would 'begin to get somewhere' when his National Labour Relations Board was 'fully developed'.

Any doubts as to whether Mr Smith found the atmosphere of the
Congress sympathetic, were dispelled by his own speech. He drew
a parallel between the United States and Mexico; in both, he said,

there was a capitalist structure of society and a government, based on proletarian principles, determined to revolutionise it by law. In Mexico the victory was almost won; with the Wagner Act the United States had started on the same triumphal progress; in the United States there was a further problem to be faced – the existence of a provincial bourgeoisie whose sympathies, misled by propaganda from the capitalist, ran counter to those of the proletarian. The official reports of Mr Smith's various speeches were issued in somewhat different form in different languages. The English 'hand out' omitted many of his more violent expressions; the Spanish, which was widely circulated in Mexico City, contained a specific approval of the oil expropriations, coupled with the 'boxed' notice that he was a representative of the United States Government. There seems some uncertainty whether the words were actually uttered in public. A number of questions were put to him which give the impression of having been prearranged; it is likely that in his answers to these he was more explicit than in his actual speeches.

On the following Saturday, General Cardenas formally opened the Congress Against War and Fascism. The fact that his agents were at the moment feverishly negotiating for a trade pact to supply the Nazi bloc with the materials of war, was not mentioned during the proceedings. The meeting was staged with all the heraldry of Marxism. The motto of the Congress was displayed on a huge central banner: '*The alliance of organisations of workers in the service of the State salutes the proletariat of the world at these decisive moments when it is fighting against fascism and for the transformation of the capitalistic régime into a socialistic régime.*' Round it were a circle of banners bearing hammers and sickles, Soviet stars charged with the names of Lenin and Marx, 'Por la Lucha de Clases' (For the Class-war) and similar devices. The *International* was sung and salutes were given with the clenched fist. On the platform with Mr Smith sat other representatives of the United States – Miss Van Kleeck, Mr Abe Isserman, the counsel for the CIO and the Civil Liberties Union, Mr Nathaniel Weil, son-in-law of the New York newspaper proprietor Stein, and the Rev. Mr Swafford representing the American League for Peace and Democracy.

Next morning there was a mass meeting in the Bull Ring which gave greater scope for the display of communist insignia. Mr Smith spoke at the first of the meetings; Mr Lewis at both of them. He said, 'It makes no difference whether these avaricious capitalistic organisations are in the United States or in Mexico or in the countries of Europe, their attitude towards the workers and their tactics are the same. Recently there have appeared on the American continent two great statesmen whose sympathies cause them to extend a generous hand to workers of their respective countries. In the United States that man is President Roosevelt. In Mexico that man is President Cardenas ... In Mexico we have seen under the régime of President Cardenas with profound satisfaction the enormous growth of the labour movement through the C.T.M. .... and have witnessed how the natural resources of this country have been made available to the people of this country. The workers should so organise that what has taken place in the United States and Mexico can be achieved in all countries of Latin America.'

When this speech was delivered the chief concern of thoughtful people in Washington was precisely this; that the successful confiscation of the oil properties in Mexico might lead to a wave of similar actions throughout Latin America and the absorption in the Nazi trade bloc of American interests. From Mr Cordell Hull's point of view few utterances could have been more mischievous than this invitation to emulate Mexico, and the identification of Cardenas with Roosevelt, coming from the representative of 4,000,000 American workers whose livelihood would be the first to be threatened by the loss of South American export trade, in the presence of a representative of the United States administration.

Speaking at another meeting on the terms of Mr Cordell Hull's note, Miss Van Kleeck said: 'In diplomatic relations between Mexico and the United States the way appears now cleared for social and economic approach ... Counter-balancing any suggestion that payment' (for the expropriated properties) 'should be immediate is the thoroughly established policy of the Roosevelt Administration for international cooperation. Cooperation is implied in the good neighbour policy and insistence on immediate payment without regard for the social and economic problems involved is objectionable, not only because it is unneighbourly but because it cannot be carried out ... Mexico having embarked on a path of economic democracy has sovereign right to determine the course of its economic programme.'

What were the delegates to make of all this? They varied in position from simple South American workmen to successful English novelists; the elderly and more astute of them had no doubt heard a great deal of this kind of oratory before; had affirmed proletarian solidarity in other days with Germans and Spanish and Italians; had heard fully accredited representatives of different states hold out hopes of cooperation which, for one reason or another, had come to nothing. But they were all socialists, and socialists live by hope; sometimes in one quarter of the heavens, sometimes another, the messianic dawn seems likely to break; they have learned to look in improbable places, and no one, listening to Mr Smith and Mr Lewis can have doubted that it was now from capitalist America that the lead was coming, and that the patient correspondence of the Washington State Department represented the last faltering tones of a dying régime.

A short time after the Congress, when war seemed imminent in Europe, I was talking to the Trinidadian delegate – who was not at all the ingenuous darky that his position might make one expect. I remarked that a European war would at any rate settle the Mexican question; that the United States, sooner than see a supply of oil going to the central powers, would probably occupy the oil fields in the name of the companies. A kindly smile spread over the Trinidadian delegate's face. 'They might want to,' he said, 'but Lewis would never let them.'

Though nothing in his public statements justified it, Mr Lewis certainly left the impression with many Mexicans that he was able and willing to paralyse any coercive measures against Mexico with a general strike. Americans tell me that such an idea is preposterous and that the American unions would never strike on an international issue. In Mexico, however, strikes are a national habit, extolled in the schools as one of the normal duties of citizenship, and practised for the most capricious reasons. To the Mexicans a boast of that kind, if it were made, would be perfectly credible. And large numbers of influential Mexicans believe it was made.

6

Once more, at a crucial moment in Mexican history, when a choice was imminent between further violent experiment and a return to saner counsels, representatives from the United States have lent their influence to the disorderly side. One can be perfectly certain that of the many confused motives that inspired Mr Smith and Mr Lewis, one that was totally absent was the wish to imperial expansion. And yet it has been defined as America's 'manifest destiny' to extend her rule to the isthmus of Panama. National destiny works out in curious ways; empires seem to grow independently of individual ambitions. Is it conceivable that the historian explaining to future generations the reduction and disappearance of Mexico, may include in the succession of empire builders – Poinsett, Monroe, Houston, Ambassador Wilson and the rest – a chapter on the mid-twentieth-century radicals?

CHAPTER 6

PLAN SEXENAL

1

IN THE FIRST half of September, 1938 the Mexican Government had two separate calls on its hospitality. There was a Cuban delegation who came, complete with a marine band, to take part in the celebrations of Independence Day, and there were the delegates to the Labour Congress. The nature of the entertainment was tactfully varied to suit the interests of the guests, and the impression which General Cardenas wished to make on them. To the Cubans he wished to appear principally as a patriot, the leader of Latin American independence; accordingly the armed forces were paraded with their latest equipment and an official party was given at the Ministry of Foreign Affairs where, for the first time since General Cardenas's accession, evening dress was worn and members of the former aristocracy were coaxed out of their seclusion. It was a very grand party with a gay, costumed band, a splendid display of gold braid and jewellery, bright French dialogue, champagne, caviare, and Press photographers. One might have been in Athens. The President himself did not attend, but all the more presentable members of his Government were there chattering to Japanese admirals and Italian attachés in the most civilised fashion.

For the socialist delegates a different air was assumed. Their entertainment, particularly in the provinces, was profuse but less decorative. For them the President was no narrow patriot, but a lieutenant of the International, chief administrative worker of a Workers' State. An element of edification lay behind all their jaunts; they were shown the swag of the recent confiscations, and, as though this was not enough, their guides enriched it with such imaginary features as a pipe line from the oil fields round Tampico, leading, they explained, to the Pacific coast, whence presumably it could be shipped to help the workers of Japan in their struggle for freedom against fascist China. But the main focus for their interest in Mexico City was the Six Year Plan Exhibition at the *Bellas Artes*.

British and American tourists are now well accustomed to being entertained by governmental exhibitions in which the commonplaces of our own individualist society are presented as the triumphs of one or other of the ideological parties. We even forget that we, too, have hospitals and infant schools and recreation grounds at home, so overwhelming is the gusto with which they are shown us abroad. But the *Plan Sexenal* was remarkable among exhibitions of its kind for its naïveté.

Under what is conveniently but loosely called 'the Mexican Constitution', the President holds office for six years. After that the deluge; sometimes assassination, sometimes execution, sometimes exile; very rarely has a President retired into honourable private life in his own country. General Cardenas's predecessors were mostly content with a six-year plan of collecting as much as they could of the public funds and banking them in their own names abroad. General Cardenas had more disinterested, if more mischievous ambitions. He came into power with the will to do so much damage in his six years to the existing financial structure of his country that it could never be reconstructed on the same lines; primarily this meant doing on a universal scale what many of his predecessors had attempted in individual cases and abandoned in disillusionment; the confiscation and redistribution of the land, the confiscation and socialisation of industry. The word 'plan' is an example of the borrowed and barely understood terminology in which Mexican political utterances abound. It was not a 'plan' in the Soviet or Nazi sense of a vast co-ordination of production, exploitation and administration, the bureaucratic paradise of the Machine State. It merely meant a resolute determination to do as much as he could and damn the consequences. Instead of the ant-hill organisation of Russia and Germany, he had at his service only the old gang of Calles and Obregon reinforced with a few revolutionary orators. It is not surprising that the results have been disastrous, but it is surprising that so much of the failure should be apparent in the Exhibition.

Nevertheless it was well attended; school-children were there, poor mites, led around and harangued by their masters; that is inevitable. There were also numbers of workmen in their overalls – deputations sent up from the provinces by their local C.T.M. but a large proportion of the crowds on the two or three times that I went were, like myself, enquiring foreigners. Some no doubt were misled by the name *Sexenal* and having heard lurid stories of sexual education in the schools, were there in the hope of being shocked. A great number, however, were earnest students of the Left Book Club kind, who, abroad, will stare entranced at a cot or a blackboard if they have been told that they represent proletarian progress.

The Exhibition was divided into sections corresponding with the various departments of government – Health, Education, Agriculture and so on. The *Bellas Artes*, where it was held, is the imposing series of galleries which form part of the Opera House building. English-speaking guides were in attendance in the foyer. There were certain singular exhibits such as a great board on which were stuck the photographs of all the girls employed at the Ministry of Labour, but for the most part they conformed, in intention, to the European model; there were statistics in the form of graphic diagrams, architects' plans for public works, trade exhibits showing the products of various industries, stalls for the distribution of propaganda leaflets and so on. At first sight it all seemed quite normal. Indeed it required some exertion to maintain an attitude of polite interest. On the first landing my guide and I passed a collection of carpentry tools. I am interested in carpentry tools so I paused to admire them. They seemed to be of excellent quality.

'These were made in Mexico?'

'Certainly. Under the present Government Mexican industry is making great progress.'

I looked closer and was surprised to find the trade-mark of a well-known American firm. I pointed it out.

'Many American firms used to work in Mexico in the old days,' the guide explained. 'Now the Government has taken them over.'

'But these are all marked "Made in U.S.A.".'

'Yes,' he said. 'I do not know why that is so. There are many more interesting things further on.'

It is poor sport to bait official guides. Poor drudges, they are more bored than anyone by their work; but I was genuinely puzzled and pressed for further information.

'I will ask one of the officials,' he said, and returned after a time with the man in charge of the department; together they examined the trade-marks and spoke rapidly in Spanish that I was unable to follow. At length the guide turned to me, reassured. 'It is as I told you,' he said. 'They were all made in Mexico.'

And there the matter rested. It had given me, however, a new line of interest. I no longer embarrassed us both by asking questions. I simply looked for trade-marks; there were traffic lights made in U.S.A., hospital equipment from Germany, scientific instruments from Italy. Something like 80 per cent. of the exhibits were made abroad.

Now I do not suppose that in this matter the committee of the Exhibition had a fraudulent intention. I think that each department was asked to show what it had been doing; they merely wanted to show that their cities had traffic lights, that their hospitals had operating-theatres and their carpenters' shops planes and hammers. But there are two wider conclusions to be drawn from the incident; first that the government is completely dependent on foreign imports for every branch of its life and secondly that local patriotism is so simple and ignorant that even quite responsible officials will not admit this primary economic fact.

In the department of Agriculture, however, the conduct of the exhibitors does not allow so charitable an explanation. There is a distinction to be drawn between legitimate propaganda and abso-lute falsehood which is generally observed in matters of commercial advertising and may well be applied to governments. To take an example from the Six Year Plan Exhibition: there was, as might have been expected, a hall devoted to the oil expropriations. The most lively minds in the republic are exercised with this question and this part of the show was more expensively and more cleverly arranged than any other. There was a model of a refinery complete with a toy train which ran ceaselessly round a circular track; this attracted, as working models always do, constant attention, and all round it were placards painted with quotations from speeches, figures and diagrams giving, in admirably concise and intelligible form, the Government's case. There was, for instance, a not wholly fanciful picture of three types of dwelling in existence in the oil fields; the first a moderately roomy, two-storied house, the second a decent bunga-low, and the third a dilapidated hovel. There were beside them diagrams showing what proportion of each kind of house was occu-pied by foreign and by native employees, drawing the apparently inescapable conclusion that the oil companies housed their foreign staff in comparative luxury and left the Mexicans in slums. The diagrams were astutely deceptive and yet, as far as they went, fairly accurate. No one disputed that the most responsible jobs in the old fields were held by foreigners; the reason for this is not flattering to Mexican pride; it was simply that they had learned by experience that they could not always trust the kind of Mexican who took up a commercial career. If a man goes abroad to work he expects to be compensated for his exile by a higher standard of life than he would enjoy in the same post at home; that is a commonplace of commercial societies in all parts of the world. The foreign companies in Mexico do not import expensive employees from any disinterested desire to provide comfortable billets for their fellow countrymen. They do so because they have learned by experience that it is profitable. They can trust them to earn their salaries and to avoid deleterious local entanglements. In any country in the world – individualist, fascist or communist – the more responsible officials live in the more comfort-able houses. That too is a commonplace. Therefore it was quite unexceptionable that the proportion of foreigners living in good houses should be higher than the proportion of Mexicans. But very many more Mexicans were employed than foreigners so that if the figures had been stated in the other way, i.e. the proportion of good houses occupied by Mexicans compared with the proportion occu-pied by foreigners, the result would be to show that Mexicans were greatly in the majority. Thus given a perfectly normal situation, the same figures can be used by either side in the controversy to support its argument, and both are employing legitimate methods of propa-ganda. In this particular matter of housing there are other consider-ations. There was the fact that the companies had been trying for years to build new quarters for their men and had been stopped by the C.T.M. There was also the fact that many Mexican workers preferred the housing allowance which the companies paid to a good house. It is usually an obnoxious, and certainly an outmoded, contention that the poor prefer living in slums. It is true, however, of many Mexican peons. At Orizaba I visited a colony of hovels, constructed, like inverted birds' nests, of bits of palm leaf and sacking and flattened petrol tins, into which well-paid jute operators had moved in preference to the solid and sanitary quarters provided by the mill. It was not the business, however, of the organisers of the Exhibition to weaken their case by calling attention to these points; that was the business of their opponents. They had made a very lively show in the oil section and may be honoured for their work.

The agricultural section, however, was quite another matter. Here, faced with damning and notorious facts, the ministry had resorted to pure invention. The facts were that agriculture was in a disastrous decline; the Exhibition merely stated the reverse, categorically.

In his various public speeches and in his notes to the State Department at Washington, General Cardenas has treated his land policy as a sacred mission to the fulfilment of which all other interests must be subordinate. It is an ambition with which, in general, there seemed grounds for sympathy. It is reasonable to regard the establishment of an independent peasantry as a primary source of national strength. The ills of modern society rise, not from the presence of private property, but from its absence; too few people have tangible possessions; a system in which a very few individuals, or, worse still, corporations, absorb all the sources of wealth, exhibits most of the disadvantages of socialism. In general the wish to see as many people as possible supporting their own families on their own holdings of land, is wholly laudable. Those who enquire no further into General Cardenas's statesmanship than his avowed aims, have seldom any reason for withholding their applause. How far he is personally sincere in his professions no one has yet the right to give an opinion. Doctrinaire philanthropy is responsible for many ills. The outside observer must judge the results, not the motives. The simple fact, which is deducible from the published official figures and universally acknowledged in Mexico – except in the agricultural department of Plan Sexenal Exhibition – is that in the last two years agricultural production of every kind has fallen in volume by about 20 per cent. or 25 per cent. The rural districts are no longer feeding the towns and at a time when other political and economic experiments are straining the national finances unendurably, Mexico is obliged to purchase its food in foreign exchanges. This would seem a surprising result of a land settlement scheme and its cause lies deep in Mexican conditions and history.

In the first place, there is plenty of land in Mexico. It is an enormous country varying in fertility from rich tropical and subtropical soil to bare rock. Experts are no longer as confident as they were twenty-five years ago in their apportionments of cultivable and uncultivable areas. Fascist enterprises in Italy and North Africa in draining marshes, watering deserts, binding loose sand and so on, have shown what land settlement means in efficient hands. Communists are cultivating the Arctic. It may well be that no part of the earth's surface is unredeemably infertile; but in the case of Mexico there was never any need for heroic experiments. The country is sparsely populated; its area is about 500,000,000 acres of which, it is estimated, about 58,000,000 acres can be cultivated by normal methods. Conditions of climate and soil vary so greatly from one part of the country to another that this area can produce crops of every kind – rice, sugar, cotton, coffee, maize, wheat, fruit, vegetables, etc. The population is less than 17,000,000. There is, therefore, no natural reason why there should be any shortage of foodstuffs. The explanation must be sought in social and political causes.

When the Spaniards came to Mexico they found a system of land tenure in the Aztec districts closely analogous to the manorial system of European feudalism; great estates belonged to the crown, the priesthood and the military nobility; the cultivators lived in village communities holding their land in common and paying regular dues in work and kind to their overlords; there was also domestic slavery of the sort that had died out in most parts of Europe.

Under the mediæval Spanish system all property rights emanated from the Crown and reverted to it in default of direct heirs. This system was introduced into New Spain with little disturbance to the existing order. Enormous territories were granted to the heroes of the conquest, with sometimes more than 100,000 dependent natives over whom the recipient exercised almost sovereign powers. The Indians were not only serfs; they were a conquered people, and in the earliest years of the colony there was a danger that they might be enslaved. Against this Pope and King legislated decisively. After mature examination of the specimens submitted the theologians came to the conclusion that they were human beings. Human beings can be treated atrociously and many in their time have envied the lot of well-kept animals. The human nature of the Indians did not in itself ensure them any particular advantage as far as physical conditions were concerned, but certain rights were declared to be inalienable; though they were exempt from the Inquisition (a fact constantly forgotten by the painters of Mexico's modern historical frescoes), they were members of the Church which, as in mediæval Europe, gave them the hope of advancement in the priesthood and in education, and ensured their right to marry and bring up their families; they were never mated like animals as were the negro slaves of the English; they shared in the holidays of the Church which provided frequent and extremely lively intervals in their lives of toil – this privilege was bitterly grudged by many of their overlords and helped to foster an anti-clerical sentiment among the colonists. They were also confirmed in the possession of their village lands. By royal ordinance all communities existing at the time of the conquest were granted land for their support in the immediate neighbourhood, which they worked when they were not fulfilling their duties for their overlords. As long as they remained in their native villages they had a protected position, if a subservient one. New introductions such as the plough, the horse, the wheel and the reduction of silver ore by mercury greatly increased the production of the country. The monasteries, greatly enlarged during the centuries by pious bequests, became in many cases horticultural and agricultural experimental farms as well as centres of learning. The introduction of negro slaves was forbidden, and although it existed in an underhand manner, never made a serious difference to the economy of the country. There was usually a shortage of labour, aggravated by the brutal conditions in many of the mines, and the colonists were constantly in search of devices for evading the laws; against these the Spanish government waged a continual and, when difficulties of communication are considered, surprisingly successful war. The practice of tricking the Indians into slavery by debt was put down and did not re-emerge as a serious problem until after the Independence. The King's courts dealt out impartial justice. Henry Hawks, the first Englishman to visit New Spain, wrote in 1572, '*In Mexico the Indians are favoured by the judges. If any Spaniard does them an injury, despoiling them of anything (as is the common practice) and this happens in a pueblo in which there is a judge, the aggressor is punished just as if it had been done to another Spaniard.*' As the *encomienda* system of feudal holdings was found to be conducive of abuse, it became the royal policy to replace it by direct rule; when from time to time heirs failed and estates escheated, they were not granted to new families, but divided into pueblos ruled by royal officials, the *corregidores*, and the struggle between colonists and crown took the new form, easy in a land of ill-defined boundaries, of attempted usurpations of pueblo lands by neighbouring *hacendados* (large landowners). It was not, however, until the independent nineteenth century that this became a real threat to the Indians' position. There is ample evidence to show that in places remote from the royal justice abominable cruelties were practised from time to time according to the character of the *hacendado*; it has been to the interest of modern historians to emphasise these; similar atrocities were taking place in other parts of the world; in general it seems that until the Independence the case of the Indian villager was little heavier than that of the peasant in many parts of Europe and considerably lighter than that of the negroes on the British, Dutch and American plantations. It was however a condition which allowed of no deterioration without real distress and this deterioration came with Independence; the royal justice was abolished; the wide lands of the monasteries fell into secular hands; political intrigue and civil war brought a grosser type to the top and a process closely analogous to the landlordism of Tudor England squeezed the villagers of their essential rights; in particular debt-slavery became almost universal and the 'enclosures' of common lands proceeded unrestrained. From the middle of the nineteenth century until today the living conditions of the Mexican Indian have been as degraded as can be found in any except notoriously savage countries. At the time when Mexico was prosperous this argued a morbid condition. It is natural that it should inspire compassion, and sympathy for any effort to relieve it. Compassion, however, is not enough. In times of national ruin it is always the lowest class who suffer the most. The duty of a ruler should be to see that the community, as a unit, prospers and then to encourage the equitable distribution of wealth within the community. To ruin the whole nation in order to reduce the disproportionate prosperity of a part of it, is insane. That has been General Cardenas's policy.

Until a year or two ago the country was still organised, as it had been for centuries, on the *hacienda* system. The *haciendas* were great feudal holdings including agricultural, urban and mineral properties. The *hacendados* were mostly of aristocratic Spanish origin, though in the course of the centuries the blood of most families had become mixed with native Indian. The *rancheros* – owners of less than two thousand acres – formed a peculiarly Mexican class, half yeoman half squireen, descended either from Spanish colonists of humbler origin or the illegitimate sons of the great landowners. They were predominantly Indian in blood; in costume, manner and morals they were typical of the picturesque Mexican of the cinematograph. They did not send their sons to Stonyhurst or hold the bank at baccarat on the Riviera.

Those who denounce the old system most vigorously, often weaken their case by emphasising the fewness of the fortunate minority. A handful of families, they point out, owned whole provinces; some had never explored the full area of their possessions; they lived lives of luxury in Paris and Biarritz while their estates were managed by ruthless agents. All this is substantially true in many cases and aroused moral indignation, but it does not provide a solution of the problem of poverty, for, after all, even the most ostentatious individual extravagances are a very small item in the budget of a prosperous nation. Under the Mexican system it needed an estate the size of an English county to keep one family in moderate luxury. No doubt it was very bad for the *hacendados* themselves to lead an idle and *deraciné* existence in Europe but the actual sums misappropriated from the national economy were negligible. Moreover it was only a minority of the minority who led an exclusively cosmopolitan life. The average *hacendado* spent some months every year on his estates. He did not regard them with the sentiment of an English landlord; his principal house was in Mexico City; his country house was his business premises and his holiday camp combined. He entertained there and played the *grand seigneur* among his dependants. Foreign visitors and diplomats have left accounts of these picturesque *barbecues* when the landlord feasted the village. Many *hacendados* took a patriarchal interest in their men and competed with one another in humane improvements. It was against these enlightened landlords, even more than the absentees, that the socialists worked, for they represented an alternative, saner solution to the problem. The agricultural new deal was based on the theory that the land originally belonged to the peasants, had been taken from them unjustly and should be restored. It has constantly been found in history that retrospective acts of justice, even after the lapse of a very few years, involve injustices greater than those they seek to remedy. General Cardenas is attempting to redress grievances of four centuries' standing for which the historical grounds are extremely shadowy. The Spaniards found the Indian villagers in the condition of serfs. In the centuries they have themselves become Mexicans. There is no question of driving out a foreign invader but of dispossessing a class in the nation. The agrarian movement has been a part of the class war and as such has been a victory. Most of the landowners have been successfully stripped of their inherited and purchased property without compensation; and the process is being hurriedly completed.

The process is as follows: A village makes a petition to the Government that they have not enough land for their needs and they are immediately given a grant from the neighbouring estate, which they then work in most cases as small holdings, in a few districts in communal farms. The impetus has come not so much from the peasants themselves as from the Government; official inspectors have been sent all over the country organising the petitions; the Indians are simply told that there is a present of land waiting for them if they ask for it; naturally they sign in enormous numbers; when, however, as is more often the case than might be expected, they are reluctant to do so, either from affection for the *hacendado* or a traditional distrust of official philanthropy, the petition is made up by bogus names and by the importation of families from another district; the original families are then transported to a place where they have no ties with their landlord and where, unless they are given land, they will starve.

A typical case is that of a friend of mine; a middle-aged Mexican of pure Spanish descent, now reduced to extreme penury by the operation of the law. It is true that he was brought up in Europe, but not, in accordance with the popular legend, because his parents were leading a life of idleness in Monte Carlo; they were serving their country as diplomats in various European capitals. He inherited a small estate from an uncle. This estate had not been acquired by graft or grant, but purchased from its previous owner. No Indians were dispossessed; it was uninhabited at the time of the purchase. The uncle invested his capital in making a model plantation where formerly there had been rough pasture. He built a house for himself, a church, a village and a school, and induced landless peons to settle round him. He installed expensive machinery for treating the produce. Here he lived for the greater part of his life, experimenting with various types of plant and methods of culture until he had created a tolerably prosperous concern. When he visited his brother in Europe he came home laden with small presents for his Indians; his return was celebrated with dances and feasts; he personally supervised the education of the children and a simple medical service; he was universally loved and respected. When my friend succeeded he carried on the same tradition. One morning a year or two ago he was visited by a Government 'engineer' from Mexico City who told him that a petition had been made and that his estate was to be divided. He was shown a list of names many of which were strange to him; he challenged the 'engineer' to produce the petitioners; these were not forthcoming for the list was, substantially, a forgery. He appealed to the local governor who promised that he should be undisturbed until a genuine petition was made; nevertheless the confiscation went on uninterrupted. He was left with his house, his mill, a few acres of land, and permission to gather and market the crop then ripening on the property. It was the practice of the planters at the beginning of the season to sell their crop in advance to the buyers; this he had already done. Suddenly, and quite illegally, the 'engineer' announced that the partition would take place immediately, before the harvest; there was a further period of appeal with consequent lawyers' fees; finally the confiscation took place as the engineer had said. In order to repay the money advanced by the buyer, the owner was obliged to sell off, precipitately and at a bad price, the house, machinery and the few acres remaining to him. He was left absolutely destitute.

We went together to visit his former home. The house was empty and the garden in decay; a local politician had built a road-house on part of it. The land immediately round the house, which had been sold as a single unit to reimburse the buyer, was still tolerably well cultivated though the experimental plantation was no longer in use; the remainder of the estate which had been divided into small holdings was already, in places, reverting to waste. Shade trees and cropping bushes, unpruned, were growing together half buried in weeds. In places they had been uprooted to make room for maize; the Indians contented themselves by gathering the little fruit that still grew on the rank bushes; where these had been smothered, the maize clearings would take their place. We found the old gardener who, on the assumption that he was too close to the patron, had not shared in the spoils. We asked him about the conditions of the people. He said they had no wages now and that many of them had left their holdings and drifted into the town. The others did not bother to grow more than a bare subsistence for themselves; if they did the Government claimed it in repayment for the tools and seeds they had been lent; when they were in need of ready cash they set off to the hills and made charcoal.

We drove back in a sombre mood, my friend oppressed not only with his own loss but by the spectacle of wanton neglect; he had lost everything and no one was the better off for it.

Heaven knows, one cannot talk of sympathy being wasted, but sometimes when I find my newspapers day after day full of appeals, handsomely supported and eloquently canvassed, for the victims of totalitarian rule in Central Europe; when I read letters from English socialists, half of whose time is devoted to denying the rights of private property for their fellow countrymen, savagely denouncing Nazi confiscations of Jewish shops and factories; I think of my friends in Mexico who also have been ruined and outlawed, and have received nothing from the democratic peoples except smug suggestions that they and their ancestors have brought things on themselves.

The incident quoted is typical both of the injustice and the futility of the agrarian scheme.

In the case of my friend only a modest ranch was involved; hence the extreme speed with which it was swallowed. The great *haciendas* took longer and the process was perhaps the more painful to their owners. First one area, then another would be taken. The owner was often assured that if he relinquished part of his property without dispute he would be left with the remainder; the policy of the Government officials was to wait until the *hacendado* had concentrated his energy upon developing a particular area and then confiscate it. It was three or four years before he was left quite landless. Even now there are huge territories remaining to be divided. The most reliable figures seem to be as follows: up to August 1938, 54,210,790 acres had been distributed, of which about 23,300,000 acres were cultivated land; that is about 40 per cent. of the total cultivable land of the country. Recent confiscations should account for a further 10 per cent. Agricultural production has fallen by about a quarter; it is therefore to be expected that when the process of confiscation is complete – and there is every indication that it is being hurried forward – production will be at about half its former extent. The estates still remaining in their former hands consist of those owned by generals, local governors and members of parliament and by certain influential German companies in the extreme South. Since my return there have been brief notices in the English papers of the confiscation, against the clearly expressed wishes of the local Indians, of a large and conspicuously benevolent Italian property in the North. No pretence has been made at discrimination against bad landlords; on the contrary those who set the best example have been the first to suffer. Nor has any distinction been made between the various rights of possession. Some properties were undoubtedly illegally augmented in the time of Porfirio Diaz;

some traced undisputed possession to the time of Cortes; some were recently acquired by purchase. All have been treated alike. The Government campaign is against property as such and against landowners as a class politically opposed to themselves.

Of the former landowning class, those still left in possession, or part possession, know that their turn is coming and can only wait gloomily until the 'engineers' have the time to attend to them. I visited a ranch in another State where the owner's son was carrying on a dairy farm on about a third of his former property. He showed me one large piece of land that had been taken from him by the Ministry of Education; a small school had been erected in a corner of it, the rest was lying idle; near the house was another field which, many years before, his father had given at their request to the municipality for the extension of the hospital; some half-finished masonry like an ornamental ruin stood deep in undergrowth. His own house was quarter furnished and his cow houses in bad repair. He was an energetic young man full of plans for their improvement. 'What is the good,' he said. 'If I make it attractive the Government will take it away. My only chance of holding on for a little longer is to escape notice. If it looks worth stealing I shall lose it.'

All round Orizaba we visited partitioned estates. The valley of Orizaba is one of the most beautiful and naturally fertile districts in Mexico. It is particularly well placed for communication. Through it run the main road and the railway between Mexico City and Vera Cruz. Ten years ago there were miles of rich sugar and coffee estates. We drove through a devastated area. The sugar mills and ranch houses were in ruins; acre upon acre of sugar land was lying waste; here and there a few puny animals were grazing; here and there were patches of maize; along the roads came women and donkeys laden with charcoal – most fatally destructive of all industries; soon the hillsides, which might have been terraced into acres of fertile land, would be stripped of their cover and washed bare of soil. Indians who wanted money tramped into town to work in the cotton and jute mills, which the trade union officials were vigorously endeavouring to reduce to bankruptcy. The great industry of Orizaba was the brewery under Government management; the beer is as good as any in the world; work there is being held up because the rice fields, now mostly working under Government auspices, had fallen in production and could not deliver what they had contracted for.

People I talked to in Mexico City had sought to impress me with the decay of agriculture resulting from the partitions. In order to verify this, I had first asked my hosts whether they could show me any of these lands that were going out of cultivation. After a morning's drive round the countryside I had to alter my request; could they show me any of the new holdings which were being properly worked? With some difficulty we found a number. The farming was not of a high order; the conditions of living seemed little, if at all, different from elsewhere in the country; the huts were very like the official caricatures of housing on the oil fields, but there was evidence that the family in their way were taking pride in their property, or at least were content in its possession, and, on inquiry, we found that by selling their surplus produce to the Government clearing-houses, they were making rather more than their former wages, even when they had repaid the Government loans for seed and tools. It was a small proportion but one very well worth legislating for.

It was natural that conversation outside Mexico City should turn continually to the agricultural plan, even to the exclusion of the ever present question of oil. A certain number of Mexicans maintained an uncompromising attitude; the Indians were incapable of looking after themselves; they would not work unless they were made to; they had been happy on the *haciendas*; the *hacendado* had been a father to them; they told anecdotes illustrating the loyalty and love that they had inspired among their former dependants. Government supporters – notably American ladies living on invested capital – quoted Gruening on 'land hunger', accepted the desirability of land distribution as their premise, and judged the Government purely on its record in expediting the work. They admitted that numerous politicians had so far escaped confiscation, deplored the fact as a relic of Calles's day, and looked forward to its speedy redress. Others, indifferent to social conditions, found a melancholy relish in the agricultural figures and plight of the Agricultural Banks, as full evidence of General Cardenas's incapacity. But the vast majority, Mexican and foreign alike, agreed that there was the need for an agricultural policy and that General Cardenas had chosen a particularly unhappy one; chosen, not devised, for the policy was not in fact General Cardenas's invention. In theory it was the work of his predecessors. General Cardenas's guilt merely consists in taking their professions literally, in trying to put them into practice and in persisting in the attempt after its folly had been proved.

There were two aims for a Mexican statesman; first the economic one of maintaining and increasing production. In this General Cardenas's policy has been manifestly disastrous. The reasons for its failure are first that after centuries of peonage only exceptional members of a depressed class will have the initiative, foresight, thrift and resolution to become successful independent farmers; the instinct of the average peon, presented with his land, has been to squat in a corner of it and produce with the least trouble enough to keep himself and his family alive. Secondly, certain crops such as henequen require capital and skill; the peon has little interest in anything that is not immediately edible. Thirdly, after decades of misgovernment and revolution the administration is in the hands of a group who are both incapable and malicious; their aim has been more to destroy the rich than benefit the poor; they have preferred to extinguish sources of wealth rather than leave them in the hands of political opponents; even the peon has an inherited mistrust of the Government, cannot believe that its benefactions are disinterested, and has learned to fear that if he produces any surplus someone will come and steal it. Fourthly, the drastic shiftings of population necessitated by the vindictive nature of the policy have resulted in many agrarians being isolated in small, defenceless colonies in parts of the country where they find the inhabitants foreign and hostile. There have been so many cases of attacks on the new settlers that the Government has in many districts been obliged to arm them and hundreds have drifted to the towns rather than live in such inhospitable surroundings. Thus at a time when General Cardenas's other experiments make it most difficult to purchase supplies abroad he is faced with a grave food shortage. His new Nazi associates can send him cameras and binoculars and aeroplanes, but not grain nor the money with which to buy it.

There was, moreover, the social problem of improving the condition of the peons. The lot of many of them was both to work hard and to live in destitution, thus getting the worst of both worlds; they paid the penalties without enjoying the privilege of idleness. But it is a poor solution simply to encourage them to be idle; it seems certain that some kind of discipline is necessary to keep them at work; the function of government should be to see they are compensated for it; the form of discipline they understood was that of the *hacienda*; those who have the qualities to become yeomen should by all means be enabled to do so; those whose mentality is still formed in the traditional loyalties of parish and *hacienda*, should be ensured a suitable reward for their labour. Above all some sense of security of tenure which at the moment no one in Mexico, peon or *hacendado*, feels, is essential to successful agriculture; no man works to develop land which may be taken from him capriciously by a change of government. When the Cardenas group came into power there was plenty of land to spare in Mexico and there was an existing social structure which was well understood by all. It would not have been impossible to devise a policy which included the aims suggested above. The *hacienda* organisation could have been left substantially intact with the individual patron as the nucleus of social service and discipline; land that was lying idle could have been appropriated and developed, as Italy and North Africa have been, by state-directed enterprises of drainage and irrigation; on these an alternative system of small holdings could have been developed, with whom the *hacendados* would be obliged to compete in amenities in order to maintain their labour supply. The Government could have re-assumed the position of the Spanish Monarchy as a fount of justice to prevent exploitation and the infringement of such laws as were found necessary to protect the Indians' well-being. Special taxation might have been imposed on absentee landlords. It is an open question whether the Indian peon can, in his present position, be treated as a responsible citizen capable of having equal obligations with the *mestizo* and the white, or whether he needs special protection. A policy such as has been suggested above would allow for the emergence of the more self-reliant strains of the population, while ensuring the national food supply, and, properly administered, would have been welcome to most of the *hacendados*. It was not however a policy which could happily be combined with subservience to the C.T.M. and its crusade of class war or with the vendettas of the Lodges.

Meanwhile General Cardenas still represents his land policy as the first aim to which other national interests must be subordinate and advertises the extent to which he has carried it.

2

Another department of the Six Year Plan Exhibition which was of particular significance, was the Educational section. As has been said above, the mid-nineteenth-century confiscations of the educational and charitable endowments of three hundred years created a gap in Mexican development that has never been filled; from being, in its continent, outstandingly cultured, the country became notoriously barbarous. Many *hacendados* maintained small private schools for their dependants; here and there in the time of Diaz the religious orders, though still officially proscribed, returned to their work with the connivance of the governors and began patiently restoring the tradition that had been disturbed. Generally speaking, however, the peons remained illiterate and those Mexicans who could afford it, sent their sons to school abroad. A vigorous educational policy was needed and General Cardenas's zeal is undoubted; a great part of the work he hopes to do is laudable. The truth, however, is that he has been able to do very little, and that little has been largely nullified by weaknesses inherent in the principles on which he is working.

The exhibits included some examples of school furniture, painted with animals from Walt Disney films, examples of children's work and of their textbooks and plans and models of school buildings. With regard to the latter it must be remembered that no very clear distinction was made between what had been done and what was proposed. A cursory inspection was calculated to give the impression that the whole country abounded in new, concrete and glass, functional school houses, a small fraction of which had in fact been erected. Moreover the organisers had been none too

scrupulous in their attribution of the work of others to the Government Plan. For example there is on the road to Guadalupe
a prominent and very imposing girls' school which cannot fail to
attract the notice of passers-by. This great building is the creation of
private charity. A wealthy and pious couple having lost their only
child, decided to devote their fortune to a free boarding school for
poor Mexican girls. They themselves planned every detail of it and
left in their will that its management should be entrusted to
a committee whom they could rely upon to carry out their intention.
It was intended to be more than a single benefaction, but a model
which might be followed by others. It is a magnificent place unlike
anything that had been seen before in Mexico – gardens, swimming-
bath, playing-fields, laundry, kitchens, dormitories, library, class-
rooms, workshops are all equipped on the scale and quality of the
most expensive European and American establishments. The girls,
coming to it, are furnished with clothes, books, even toothbrushes,
entirely free. One feature is absent, a chapel, for religious instruction
or practice of any kind is forbidden in any kind of school; the girls
may not even say grace after their meals. The name, even, had to be
changed by Government order, for the founders had wished to
dedicate it to a saint and that was illegal. For some years this institution has occupied a peculiar and precarious position. It is by law
the property of the state and subject to state inspection; the staff are,
however, still those appointed by the benefactors. At any moment
they may be discharged and replaced by officials from the Ministry
of Education. The Government is watching them for a suitable
excuse; girls have been visited at home and questioned about their
religious beliefs in the hope that they may be trapped into an
admission that their teachers are sympathetic to religion. When,
therefore, some weeks before the Exhibition, the school was unexpectedly visited by a formidable deputation from the office of education, the staff feared the worst. To their relief the invasion proved
to have no more sinister intention than to photograph the place in
order to display it as an example of General Cardenas's initiative.

The Government, with so many expensive projects on its hands,
can scarcely be blamed for not having built more. What it has done,
with abundant energy, is to send out from Mexico City an army of

enthusiastic teachers, many of whom have suffered acutely, losing noses, ears and occasionally their lives at the hands of the ungrateful parents. For the education ordained by the Government is strictly ideological; and its aim primarily to shake surviving religious and moral prejudices and glorify the personnel of the dominant régime.

Alarming stories are told by opponents of General Cardenas about the impropriety of the instruction in his schools. Boys and girls are said to be stripped and exhibited naked to mixed physiology classes. I confess I find it hard to credit. There were numerous examples of the Government's hygienic propaganda on view at the Exhibition and it seemed perfectly inoffensive – lively little drawings commending the use of soap and toothbrush, grim warnings that are certainly needed in Mexico of the dangers of venereal disease, advice about nutritive diets and the extermination of bedbugs – the latter could with advantage be studied by the managers of at least two of the leading tourist hotels. The fact remains, however, that the new school teachers do seem to have aroused storms of spontaneous moral indignation in a people not unaccustomed to libidinous officials. I cannot help thinking that it is in their supercilious attitude of brand-new city-made enlightenment and their avowed wish to make the children critical of their homes that the chief grounds of their unpopularity must be sought.

It is undoubtedly true, however, that the Ministry of Education, which is largely the creation of a fanatical fellow called Portes Gil, does represent the most extreme opinions in the country. This is true nearly everywhere; a great proportion of militant communists are or have been teachers; partly because those who hold their opinions very enthusiastically, rightly regard school teaching as the best chance of propagating them and partly because there is something about the work itself which sensibly inclines the mind to bigotry. The analogy between school and state is facile; the need for reducing all problems to their simplest terms tends to the acceptance of ready-made solutions; the necessity for selecting facts and arranging them memorably; the ambition to provoke enthusiasm of any kind in dull little minds; the unremitting association with the immature; the peculiar social position of the schoolmaster in a remote district – the lonely intellectual closeted of an evening with his books, so like, it is pleasant to believe, the exiled Marx in the British Museum Reading Room; the longing to believe that he is making some mark in the world, preparing a new generation for a new order, not just earning a meagre wage by forcing into unwilling heads facts that will soon be forgotten; the ever present anxiety about keeping order predisposing the mind to a system of absolute decrees, secret police and summary executions – all these considerations, no doubt, contribute to make schoolmasters and -mistresses a subversive race.

At the Six Year Plan Exhibition no attempt was made to disguise the Marxist character of the state education. Even the products of the infant schools showed the hammer and the sickle, and the clenched fist represented in a variety of simple handicrafts. I made a small collection of the publications of the Ministry of Education. They are mostly very well produced. There is a series of alphabets – *Carteles de alfabetizacion* – octavo sheets, printed in red and blue, comprising on one side the characters of the alphabet and on the other certain elementary instruction. One number opens with an exhortation to revere the teacher (and not to cut off his ears). 'The rural master,' it says, 'has been the victim of the tendentious propaganda of Reaction, which attacks the Socialist School. The heroic rural master, nevertheless, has remained at his post, advancing and realising his magnificent, highly patriotic and humane labour. He is the veritable apostle of the Socialist School . . . Countryman, spread in the rural population gratitude for his altruistic and self-denying work which aims only at the well-being of the community.' On the next page is a large drawing of a clenched fist with the legend: 'We protest. The Proletarian protests against physical and moral misery, insufficient salaries, the worst food, etc.' Opposite it is a drawing of a personable young man bearing the banner of the C.T.M. Below it: 'The C.T.M. is a national, syndical front in the class war in the service of the Mexican Proletariat' and a brief, enthusiastic summary of its work against 'the semi-feudal structure of the country', 'the intervention of imperialist powers', 'reaction' and 'fascism'. Another page is decorated with a hammer and sickle and a snake and an exposition of 'the Origin of the Class War'.

Another edition of the alphabet has the picture of a boy under a shower-bath with an appeal against the 'horror which is felt against water and washing' and a list of the benefits of the daily bath which among other things 'stimulates the spirit'. There is also a diagram, in the best fascist spirit, against the evils of slouching, and a page devoted to the dangers of dust. Opposite these salutary lessons are two political pages; one shows a workman carrying the banner of the strike (*Huelga*). 'Comrades, the right to strike is positively a constitutional right'; the other a voter putting his paper into the ballot box of the P.R.M. (*Partido de la Revolution Mexicana*). It is idle to speculate what would be the outcry in a democratic country if the government in power attempted to introduce party politics into the school curriculum in this way.

There is a children's magazine – *Periodico Infantile* named *Palomilla* – issued by the Ministry of Education; it consists largely of contributions by children and articles about hobbies. The centre – like the Tiger Tim supplement in the magazines of English childhood – consists of a double coloured page of picture-story. In the second issue of this magazine the story is as follows: the first eight pictures contrast the lot of the rich and poor; the poor woman works washing clothes while the rich lady, attended by three caddies, foozles her drive at golf; the man dressed as a chef prepares a luxurious dinner while the millionaires dressed in fur coats, white gloves and top hats (an object, never seen in Mexico, whose presence in the cartoon suggests foreign origin) and smoking large cigars are concerned only with 'jokes and holidays'; the daughter of the poor family makes clothes for the rich girl to wear in her motor car; the poor child mends the dolls which the rich one breaks. The last two pictures offer the remedy for this invidious social division. The poor family makes itself into a syndicate; we see their simple room decorated with red flags and hammer and sickle; the father of the family thumps the table commanding the attention of his womenfolk; finally comes the great Mexican panacea – *se declara en huelga*; the black and red flag of the strike is hung across the gates of the rich man's villa and the poor family sits idle outside. It is an interesting variation on the exemplary tales of the Victorian nursery in which by self-denial and industry the poor man raised himself until he, too, was able to treat of 'jokes and holidays' and send his wife out to the links.

It would be tedious to multiply examples to prove a case which no one seriously disputes. Mexican education, like that of all the totalitarian states, is planned with the primary intention of 'conditioning' the children in the interests of the political régime; transpose national expansion for class war and you have a system very similar to that of modern Germany. The school teacher in the small towns is the agent of government propaganda. It is his duty to educate people of all ages, to read them the news from the capital with appropriate comments, to promulgate presidential decrees, to stimulate hostility to foreigners and gentlemen, to nose out and report evidence of religion or political disaffection, to embody, in his own person, the virtues of the Six Year Plan; to his friends he is, in the words quoted above, 'the heroic rural master advancing and realising his magnificent, highly patriotic and humane labour . . . a veritable apostle'; to his enemies he is a professional prig and spy. The reports of travellers from the interior seem to agree that in most places where he has been allowed to remain he is carrying out the work for which he was appointed with greater thoroughness than is shown by most Mexican officials. He has profited by the popularity of the Government in places and at times when it has been popular. He suffers from the general displeasure when things go wrong. As things go progressively more wrong it is probable that he will suffer more and that he will be the victim of the next rising – a martyr to noble principles, – a martyr to General Cardenas's conceit, – just a mischievous ass getting his deserts – according as you like to look at him, – but doomed, I am afraid, to an unhappy end. This is not the place to debate the first principles of politics, and it is by these he must be judged. The practical question does, however, arise; what apparent effect is the educational drive having on the present generation of Mexican children?

The answer, of course, varies in different parts of that vast country. In the rural districts, as has been mentioned above, the reception has been so hostile that the Government has sometimes had to abandon or modify its policy. There is moreover an underground organisation of teachers who refuse to concern themselves with politics and are actively, at great personal risk, continuing religious instruction in spite of the Government ban. As is to be expected, the communist schools are most influential in the large towns where the C.T.M. organisers can keep a watch on them and the C.T.M. parents are sympathetic. Here, the evidence is overwhelming, political theory has so far dominated the ordinary school curriculum that the standard of general culture and information has deteriorated from its previous low standard, while discipline has almost ceased to exist.

The teachers have not made their own lot easier by the principles they support. The right to strike is taught as a civic duty and the children practise it enthusiastically. The formation of school syndicates is far from being a game; every large school has its student organisation analogous to the C.T.M. Meetings are called with great frequency during school hours and the children spend their time lobbying for votes and making speeches to one another. The school becomes a factory in microcosm, reproducing all the disorder of Mexican industrial conditions. A children's committee demands an equal share in the management of the school and to their chagrin the teachers find that in the immature mind, they, more often than not, occupy the position of employers and the children that of the proletariat; the syndicates which they encouraged have become a machinery for enforcing changes of curriculum and personnel. Strikes are called to protest against imagined cases of favouritism, against severity in examinations, against personalities that are generally unsympathetic, and – a still more mischievous source of wasted time – against the doings of foreign governments. While I was in Mexico, Vasconcelos, a journalist and former Mexican minister of education, who had been teaching in the United States, lost his job. Vasconcelos is far from being the model Marxist which General Cardenas's ministry of education is trying to popularise; he was a patriotic rather than a proletarian leader; in his exile he had said some very hard things about General Cardenas. Nevertheless the children of Mexico had a strike and a demonstration against the 'Yankee imperialist fascism' of President Roosevelt in sending him home.

The children do not stop at words. The headmaster of the Preparatory School – the chief secondary school of the country –

was lately physically ejected by his pupils; the girls are said to have taken a ferocious part in maltreating the poor fellow.

It is not surprising that in this atmosphere serious studies languish. The worst results are evident at the University. The Royal and Pontifical University, which held rank with that of Salamanca, and was for centuries the main centre of learning in the New World, had an unhappy history during the nineteenth century. It was closed in 1833 by the radical Gomez Farias, reopened in 1834 by Santa Anna, closed again by Comonfort in 1857, opened again by Zuloaga in 1858, closed by Juarez in 1861, opened and shut again by Maximilian. As on a Sunday in the United States the train bar opens and shuts in accordance with the moral feelings of the State through whose territory one is passing, so the University's existence varied with the prejudices of the governing gang. The existing University is its successor, holding at the moment a somewhat anomalous position of semi-independence; there are 15,000 students few of whom have any ambitions to scholarship; they are qualifying for certificates and diplomas which will enable them to get government posts; they contribute little or nothing towards their education. The institution subsists on some small endowments that have survived its former proud possessions and on capricious grants from the Government. The salaries of the professors and tutors are miserable and, even so, are irregularly paid. The combined salaries of the two important chairs, for example, amount to 130 pesos a month – at the present rate of exchange a little over £6. As works of scholarship have to be bought with foreign currency, there is some considerable difficulty for the professors in keeping abreast of recent research. The total grant for the purchase of books for all subjects, technical and humane, is 400 pesos a year, and there is a recurring annual struggle to secure its payment. Foreign languages have ceased to be an essential part of the curriculum. As almost all the authorities for the courses are in French, English, Latin, German or Italian, lectures are given without bibliographies; the library does not stock the books and the students could not read them if it did. Lectures, in fact, consist purely of dictated notes for the answers to examination questions.

Disorder is grossly rampant. The authority of the University is vested in a Council on which a students' committee has a 50 per cent. voting power. Meetings are held in public, to the accompaniment of munching, singing, whistling, the throwing of ink pellets and fireworks, with the governing body so hemmed that they can barely raise their hands to vote. Last year the entire faculty except two, was expelled by the students, and in the last seven years only one Rector has retired normally with comparative honour.

It is a gloomy atmosphere for those teachers – and there are a few of them left – who have tasted the sweets of a life of real scholarship, but they at least have the compensations of their own finely made minds; what is the prospect for the wretched youths brought up to know nothing better? What equipment have they to inherit the world that General Cardenas is preparing for them?

There is much to be said in a very stable, prosperous, self-satisfied society for the presence of a Bohemian student body. It is a thing we have always lacked in England. One of the good effects of discipline should be to provoke a healthy resistance in the more enterprising and self-reliant spirits. It is impossible to regard the Mexican student disorders in these humane terms. The next generation is growing up without any intellectual or moral standards and they will come to manhood in a country faced with every possible internal and external problem in its most acute form.

3

There are other features of General Cardenas's Six Year Plan whose beginnings could be traced in the Exhibition. The President, in his electional campaign, toured the country, enquired into the particular local needs and promised attention – a road was needed here, a canal there; it should be done. It was in fact begun. Then came the oil confiscations and the cessation of public works all over the country.

The last traveller to publish an account – and a brilliant one – of conditions in the remote provinces of Mexico is Mr Graham Greene. His *Lawless Roads* is an appalling account of the mismanagement and miseries which are kept hidden from less courageous travellers; it is all the more damning for its author's obvious antagonism to capitalist society. This is his description of the public works at Las Casas – the former capital of the State of Chiapas. '*Herr F. led me over the rocks to show me examples of Mexican engineering. First the reservoir half finished standing there to crack into ruin in the winter because there was no more money: all money was diverted to Tampico and the oil-fields . . . Seven years ago there had been a disastrous flood. Herr F. had been in charge of relief operations; he showed me the overgrown, neglected canal he had dug at the cost of only fifty pounds. Then Cardenas visited Las Casas; he was not yet president, he was on his electoral tour, and he had promised, if he were elected, men and money. He kept his promise: money poured into Las Casas: federal engineers began the work all over again: the walls were made of loose rocks stuck into cracking cement: in the next rains the walls themselves would help to block the channel. Then as a contrast he showed me what the Spaniards had built eighty years ago. The fine masonry of General Utrillo stood intact: only the alteration in the level of the land made his works out of date.*'

There's the rub; the hopeless, universal deterioration of things in Mexico; that is what changes General Cardenas's futile little exhibition from farce to tragedy. The purser on board the *Siboney* had cautioned us to be tolerant of Mexican conditions. 'They are doing their best . . .'

If Mexico were a small, new country, just emerging from barbarism, house-proud of its little achievements, pardonably anxious to conceal the evidence where zeal had outrun capacity, then, indeed, it would be ungenerous to wound the national pride and abuse hospitality by uncovering its failures. But it is nothing of the kind. It is a huge country with a long and proud history, taking precedence in its national unity of half the states of Europe; it has been rich and cultured and orderly and has given birth to sons illustrious in every walk of life; now, every year, it is becoming hungrier, wickeder, and more hopeless; the great buildings of the past are falling in ruins; the jungle is closing in and the graves of the pioneers are lost in the undergrowth; the people are shrinking back to the river banks and railheads; they are being starved in the mountains and shot in backyards, dying without God. And General Cardenas and his gang stand on their balcony smirking at the applause of communist delegations; the tourists tramp round the Exhibition of his work marvelling at hammers and sickles in cross-stitch and clenched fists in plaster of Paris and the plans of monstrous public offices that no one is ever going to build.

CHAPTER 7

THE STRAIGHT FIGHT

1

IT IS A common complaint against Catholics that they intrude their religion into every discussion, postulating a 'Church Question' in matters which seem to have no theological connexion. This is, in a way, true; the Catholic's life is bounded and directed by his creed at every turn and reminders of this fact may well prove tedious to his protestant or agnostic neighbours. In the case of Mexico, however, no apology is needed for speaking of the subject. It is not land or oil or race or political organisation but religion which is the single, essential question of the nation, and foreign writers may be judged, as to how far they grasp the character of the place, pretty well by the importance they attach to it. Those who regard the religion of the people as a picturesque, quaint local custom or as a mildly deleterious survival of an earlier age, to be gently discouraged and superseded by a more rational ethical outlook, can have little of interest to say about any Mexican topic. The issue is simple enough. There are, it is true, non-Catholic missions of various sects in Mexico handsomely provided with funds from the United States. It is their good fortune to be able to distribute alms where the native clergy have to ask for them; they collect fair-sized congregations and do considerable work in relieving distress and encouraging hygienic habits; their influence in the life of the people, however, is so slight and the possibility of their ever founding a national, evangelical church which could exist independently of American financial aid, is so inconceivably remote, that the authorities do not take the trouble to suppress them. They provide useful testimony for Government propagandists of the kind that was lately heard from Barcelona, that the Government is not opposed to Christianity as such – only to political priests. There are also pagans; Indians descended from communities where the Spanish missionaries never penetrated, or those who have for generations been cut off from the life of the Church and have lapsed into animism and odd superstitions. But for the purpose of any fruitful discussion the politicians know that the religion of the country is Catholic; and it is in direct conflict with merciless, fanatical atheism – an atheism that at the moment adopts Marxist language, just as in earlier generations it used Liberal language, but which antedates either; the atheism of the impenitent thief at the crucifixion.

This is no place to argue the truth of Christianity. The Catholic believes that in logic and in historical evidence he has grounds for accepting the Church as a society of divine institution, holding a unique commission for her work, privileged on occasions by special revelation, glorified continually by members of supernatural sanctity; he finds in her doctrine a philosophy which explains his own peculiar position in the order of the universe, a way of life which makes the earth habitable during his existence there and, after that, according to his merits, the hope of Heaven or the fear of Hell. He may or may not be deluded in this belief. But this is what the vast majority of Mexicans mean by religion. They either hate it frenetically, or cherish it above life itself.

It is a faith which, within its structure, allows of measureless diversity and this is a fact which those outside it find difficult to realise; the spacious wisdom of St Thomas More, the anxiety about liturgical colours of the convert spinster, the final panic of the gangster calling for the sacraments in the condemned cell, the indignation of the Irish priest contemplating the spread of mixed bathing in his parish, the ingenious proofs of the Parisian æsthete that Rimbaud was at heart a religious poet . . . they are all part of the same thing. The Catholic knows this and others do not, hence the continual, unavailing attempt of the enemies of the Church to represent the religion to which they are opposed as something quite distinct and peculiar to their own part of the world; unavailing as far as Catholics are concerned, but effective enough among the general, indifferent, mildly well-intentioned, ill-informed people of America and England among whom public opinion is formed.

These know their Catholic neighbours to be on the whole reasonable and law-abiding, with certain odd practices on Sundays and an
unaccountable aversion to meat on Fridays, crematoriums, contra-
ceptives and so forth; at elections some Catholics vote Conservative
and some of them vote Labour; there is nothing at all sinister about
them. They know this from their own experience, but when they are
told that this same society in other countries is corrupt and oppressive it does not seem improbable. Foreigners are different. Thus they
are quite ready to accept official explanations for acts of brutality
and injustice which in their own country would inflame them with
angry sympathy.

For three generations now, off and on, the enemies of the Church
in Mexico have had it their own way at home and abroad. The first
question which an intelligent foreigner asks is why, if the Church is
what her adherents claim, she should have enemies at all. The
answers are as diverse as human nature; just as there are infinite
varieties of goodness, there are varieties of wickedness. The Church
makes claims and imposes restrictions which many men find onerous; she reminds rich men that their possessions are temporary and
rulers that there are higher laws than their own. In Mexico, however, in general, anti-clericalism has been based on the single vice of
cupidity. The Church was rich and physically defenceless; robbery
had to be justified; human nature is moved more strongly by guilt
than the will to vengeance; we hate most savagely not those who
have wronged us, but those whom we have ourselves wronged.

When it is said, usually with reproach, that the Church in any
particular place is rich, there are a number of different things which
may be meant and should be distinguished. In Mexico, a hundred
years ago, the Church had great possessions accumulated through
the centuries by good husbandry, pious bequests and state grants.
The figures of her revenue, particularly the diocesan figures, seem
formidable and often the reader of popular history is left with
the impression that these sums were the personal allowance of the
Bishop; they were in fact the income out of which not only the whole
ecclesiastical organisation but what would now be called the
'social services' of the district were maintained. Under the Spanish
system, as in mediæval Europe, education, poor relief, hospitals,

orphanages, lunatic asylums were all managed by the Church; it is always possible, of course, for a bad official to embezzle public funds; no doubt in the long era of colonial rule there were from time to time Bishops who did this, but when accounts are found by contemporary visitors of the magnificence of some episcopal establishments it should be remembered that it was no uncommon thing for a man of private fortune to enter the Church and live in the same style as his lay kinsmen. Urban Englishmen who denounce the system of tithes by which the Mexican Church was in part supported, seem to forget that the same system is still in force in our own country, where the national church represents a very much smaller proportion of the population than it did in Mexico. When I write my cheque for the tithe on my own few fields for the support of a body of which I am not a member I do so reluctantly, but with no personal animosity against our local rector.

In the time of Juarez and Maximilian it may have seemed arguable that the Church might profit by being disembarrassed of some of her duties; that government specialists could better administer the great funds that were then in clerical hands. That, in the light of subsequent history, can no longer be maintained. The clergy may have been slipshod and dilatory in some of their methods, but those who robbed her, squandered the booty on private ends and left nothing in her place. Nor, I think, would anyone seriously maintain that the motive of the robbers was a desire to do better; they simply saw great possessions in the hands of those who could not protect themselves, and they took them; their sole defence has been to blackguard their victim.

Another thing is also meant by the 'riches of the Church'; the splendour of the actual churches. Even in their devastated condition they arouse the tourist's wonder and the official guides are quick to point a moral – 'all this silver and gold round the altars', they say, 'while the people wore rags and slept in hovels', and to those brought up across the border in the austere tradition of the whitewashed meeting-house the contrast is indeed striking. All along the tourist route one heard the same comment, sometimes prompted, more often than not spontaneous. 'Think what it must have cost! Think what good they could have done to the poor with all that money'; it is a cry that echoes back to Judas and Mary of Magdala – 'To what purpose is this waste?' – and when I heard it I thought of another incident in my journey in a church that had nothing about it to attract the tourist.

We stopped at the place by chance on the main road between Puebla and the famous[1] tiled church of San Francisco Cholula. It was a drab little village of Indian houses clustering round a shabby, unremarkable church. The presbytery was empty and desolate, for there had not been a parish priest for ten years; the people were not even sure of a weekly Mass; a priest rode out when he could from Puebla; there were dozens of surrounding villages in his charge; wherever he went there were so many demands on him for christenings and blessings, confessions, marriages, advice, arbitration in disputes – that he could not keep to any time-table. He appeared when he could, a dusty fellow in lay clothes like an impoverished *ranchero* to look at; when he came he rang the bells and the people stopped what they were doing and flocked in to Mass. When we arrived the men at first pretended that they had lost the key of the church; they thought we were 'from the Government' and had come to destroy something or take it off to Mexico City. That was all they knew about the Government; that they were well-dressed people who arrived unexpectedly in motor cars to steal something; (and this was in the most civilised part of the country a few miles out of Puebla). We assured them of our good intentions and at last they gave way; even then half the male population of the place followed us in to keep an eye on us. The dark little building was full of the rough, highly coloured carving in wood and stone in which the country abounds. It would create a stir in a Bond Street gallery, for it has remarkable qualities of design – but after a few weeks in Mexico one gets used to it. Our genuflections to the altar reassured them a little and they began showing us their possessions, explaining, as had been explained to them, the identities of the various saints and telling us the stories of the biblical events portrayed. Then they showed us with great pride what they themselves were doing, for

1 Though not to Dr T. Philip Terry.

districts, remote from effective discipline, a parish priest could sometimes be found living a domestic life as patriarch of a family. Hidalgo declared that chastity was contrary to nature; Morelos, the other priest of the first revolution, had children; it was one of the twenty-three charges made against him in 1815 that he had had the eldest of his three sons brought up a Protestant. A catalogue of known delinquents could undoubtedly be compiled which would be profoundly shocking; a dirty story about a priest is, anywhere, doubly offensive; but considered objectively, what do all these tales amount to? In four hundred years, in an enormous country, where strict surveillance was usually impossible; where the climate in many parts predisposes to indulgence; where the priesthood occupied a position of unique privilege and authority so that many were attracted to it from laziness and the love of power; where the position of priest's mistress was considerably more easy than that of the peasant's wife; where, himself none too well educated, the priest was shut off from educated converse and intellectual interests, it was humanly speaking inevitable that there should be scandals. It is either priggish or malicious to make more of them than this.

But suppose, for the purpose of argument, that in this case the Church's enemies were justified in their denunciations, that the evidence were overwhelming and damning, that it were not possible, as it is, to match every disgrace with a dozen proud achievements, every unworthy priest with a multitude of devoted brothers; suppose that the Mexican clergy had so deteriorated from their high origins that the bad predominated – What was the remedy? In her two thousand years the Church has experienced the changes that are evidence of her life; here seeming to lie fallow, there bursting into sudden flower; a Christian civilisation dies in the Eastern Mediterranean, another rises in the forests of the North; she has her fount of continual renewal. The discipline of Rome is always there to punish her faults; the religious orders to fertilise her virtues. Again and again in history the process of renewal has been accomplished. Had the critics of the Church wished merely to correct abuses and restore her to health, the means were at hand. Nothing, however, could have been further from their ambitions. Their earliest move, before they dared strike at the parochial clergy, was to cut the people off from the life of the Church by suppressing the religious orders with their international organisation, and to forbid papal delegates and foreign clergy of any kind from taking part in a restoration of order. They sought to reduce the clergy to the condition in which they depicted them.

It is the character of the Church that, left undisturbed in her work, she becomes the trustee for great benefactions and also the possessor of splendid works of art. To say that the Church in any place is rich, means primarily that she has been loved and trusted. To her enemies, however, her wealth represents money wrung from a cowed and superstitious people and they are often able to quote examples from personal observation which seem to support this view. It is unedifying but not uncommon in peasant communities to find the parish priest wrangling with his parishioners for the price of his services. Many travellers, particularly in Mexico, Catholics as well as non-Catholics, have been shocked to see, for example, a woman of the poorest class, baby in arms, pleading with an obdurate priest for a remission in the price of its baptism; they have turned from this spectacle to the relics of ecclesiastical grandeur about them and argued plausibly that it was by such hard bargaining as this that the great churches were adorned. In fact, however, the argument depends on a reversal of historical sequence. Where the Church is richly endowed, it is the poorest that profit, not only in the various charitable institutes which it supports, but by the services of the priests who, adequately supported, can afford to be generous. The people come to look upon their priest as the source rather than the recipient of bounty. When the endowments of the Church are confiscated the priest is obliged to rely on direct payment for his services. The peasant likes to give, but he also likes to bargain; the priest, drawn from the same stock, has similar tastes. Hence these heated arguments, both sides pleading poverty with equal justice, which are so strange to visitors who are familiar only with Anglican parish life. Hence, also, on occasions an antagonism between priest and people based not on any dispute of the value of the services offered, but of their price. The woman wants to get her child baptised and she wants to get it done as cheaply as possible; if she knows that a neighbour has been given a special price nothing will induce her to pay more.[1] There have been cases when villagers have driven out an unpopular priest, usually on the charge of avarice, and in general it may be said that the Indian's devotion, which in recent years has found expression in so many unplanned, unled, disastrous risings against the Government's policy, has been centred on the tangible fabric of his parish church, on his God, Our Lady and the saints, and the basic facts of his creed, rather than personal allegiance to his parish priest.

When, however, stories are being related of the unworthiness of the Mexican clergy, there is one, of very recent date, that should always be remembered. A few years ago, when the persecution was at its bloodiest and the resistance to it was becoming increasingly formidable, Calles thought of a solution; it was not a new one; it had worked very well in very similar circumstances in Tudor England; he proposed to found a National Church; buildings should be opened to it, protection and financial support guaranteed; all that the priests had to do was to resign their allegiance to the Pope and transfer it to Calles and, as a guarantee of their good faith, to marry. The alternatives were official favour and advancement and a comfortable domestic life on the one hand; persecution to the death on the other. Hostile propaganda had made the Mexican clergy notorious all over the world; they were said to care only for women and money; in many parts of the world their brothers had found it embarrassing to defend them, had decided to shelve them with the Renaissance Popes, as one of the inexplicable shady parts of history, like the rubbish heaps one sometimes finds, pushed out of sight in odd corners of cathedrals. And yet in that whole maligned society only three old reprobates could be found to accept Calles's offer. One of them is said to be at his job still, at the altar of an empty church somewhere in Mexico City; no one seemed to know exactly where.

---

1 Among negro Christians in the West Indies the satisfactory solution has been found of grading funerals, marriages etc. as first, second and third class, according to the length and gaiety of the service. Thus the essential rites are made accessible to the poorest, while the negro's natural love of display ensures the priest a tolerable income from those who can afford it. The Mexican Indians have little of the competitive spirit on which this system depends for its success.

3

But, say Mr Gruening and his readers, the Indian is not really
Christian. He may be willing to die for his religion but it is not the
religion of Notre Dame and Fordham; it is a hotch-potch of poly-
theism and black magic; with the foreign tongue which the missionary taught him he pays lip service to the Spanish God but in his heart
he still worships the old, bloody gods of the Aztecs. Europeans and
Americans who attempt to stir up sympathy for him are merely
seeking to perpetuate a form of degraded paganism.

It is a disingenuous argument for its ultimate aim is to discredit
not the Indians' religion, but everybody's; it is the familiar thesis of
the professors of 'comparative religion' all over the world; that man's
disposition to worship comes from his awe of natural forces and from
his own dreams; that there has been no special revelation but a cycle
of myths, finding new names in the different stages of man's progress
to rational atheism; just as churches were built on the ruins of
temples, pagan statues christened and given the names of the saints,
and the holidays of the Church synchronised with the pagan calendar, so her sacraments are merely the liturgy of the old mystery-cults.
Most knowledgeable Christians have considered this case at one
time or another and, if they have remained Christians, have rejected
it, but it is an arguable case and this is not the place to attempt its
refutation. What is *not* arguable is Mr Gruening's case; that Christianity is true for the American and the European but untrue for the
Indian. The Christian believes that the particular historical events
from which he takes his chronology – the birth, life and death of
Christ which he calls the Incarnation and the Atonement – meant
the expression in humanly intelligible form of truths beyond his
comprehension; he knows that the society which then arose, which
he calls the Church, owes its form to a variety of human influences –
to Greek speculative philosophy, Jewish poetry and theology,
Roman political organisation and so on – all of which have left
their plain imprint on its history and character. He knows that in
the centuries before the Incarnation, human organisations and
discoveries were converging on this particular point of time.

In just this way, before the coming of the Spanish missionaries, the inhabitants of Mexico were approaching similar ideas. They had, for instance, the conception of sacrifice in a highly developed but monstrous form. For the mass butchery of the Aztec temples the missionaries substituted the conception of a single, unique human sacrifice, daily consummated on the new altars. They found, too, habits of devotion curiously analogous to those they sought to introduce; the old priests employed holy water and incense in their ceremonial, they heard general confessions of sin and dispensed absolution, they taught the existence of a future life divided into heaven, hell and limbo. Some of the simpler missionaries were disconcerted by these resemblances and attributed them to the devil, but they made the new teaching readily acceptable, and the Church followed the policy traditional to her, of accepting all that was assimilable in the existing order; the new churches were built, just as they had been in Europe, on the sites of the old temples. Sometimes the old idols were found among the new statues. Mr Gruening found one still standing in a monastic cloister, still honoured by the presence of a few flowers; there, he says, is the proof that the Indians merely follow their old gods with a new name. But there is another explanation; he is on common ground with many a zealous friar in neglecting it; it is simply another way of regarding the same facts. Before they had heard the story of Jesus and Mary, the Indians worshipped them under other names; in the long memory of the race there is still room for gratitude for the blessings they received in those dark ages and they cherish those earlier, confused intimations of truth as the mother of a family may still cherish the dolls she nursed in her childhood.

The love of statues and holy places plays an enormous part in the Indian's religion, and the great shrine of Guadalupe is, certainly, far more important to him than St Peter's in Rome. It is the Indian Virgin as distinct from the little Spanish Virgin of Los Remedios, and Mr Gruening is able to make great fun, as many have done before him, of the competitive nature of the various popular devotions of the country. It is easy to say that since God is everywhere, there is no reason why any particular place should be more holy than any other; that since all statues and pictures are most inadequate symbols of what they represent, that none should excite special reverence; it is easy, for that matter, to say that there was no reason why God should become man; it is on that central theme that all Christianity depends – word becoming tangible flesh – and those who accept its illimitable implications believe that it is only in material symbols that man is capable of recognising the truth by which he lives, and that, because of his own material nature, he has been allowed occasional glimpses of divinity in material form. One of these is the miraculous picture of Guadalupe.

Its history and its presence in Mexico cannot be treated merely as a pretty piece of folk lore. Mexico abounds in picturesque legends of one kind and another, but the Guadalupe stands entirely apart. It is for all the Indians and for great numbers of whites and mestizos the main focus for their hopes and aspirations.

The story is notable as having no pre-Christian Mexican parallel;[1] the account of its origin is as precise as that of Lourdes. It has been told countless times but never better than in its first, contemporary form. One may well be cautious of saying that any narrative has the 'mark of truth' about it, but the author of the Diego story was either relating what he believed, or else was an extremely accomplished fraud. It is this: On December 9th, 1531, ten years and four months after the conquest, an Indian peasant, fifty-eight years old, was on his way by foot to the mission church of Tlaltelolco, to hear Mass and attend a class in the religion in which he had been christened a few years earlier under the name of Juan Diego. No outstanding sanctity was at the time imputed to him. After the event he became a guardian in the new shrine and died a holy death at the age of 70. He was typical of the thousands of Indians who had accepted the conquerors' religion after a minimum of instruction; accepted it, presumably, in a kind of bemused resignation as part of

---

1 Sahagun, a generation later, states that a temple existed on the site of Guadalupe, dedicated to the Indian maternity goddess. He was a zealous scholar and schoolmaster working in the neighbourhood at Tlaltelolco. No mention, contemporary with Diego, is found of the temple. It is reasonable to suppose that the friars of Tlaltelolco had already destroyed it, before the apparition. It would be a suitable place for the new church to arise among the ruins of the old. '*Whom therefore ye ignorantly worship, him I declare unto you*', has been the text of the missionary Church since the time of Paul.

the many foreign introductions that had suddenly revolutionised his world.

Following the track across the desolate area where the town of Guadalupe now stands, passing, it is likely, the ruins where in youth he had paid homage to the native mother-goddess, he suddenly saw the place transfused with unfamiliar light and colour; there was the sound of music and, on a rock above him, he saw a woman, a fellow Indian in colour and type, who called him to her, addressed him as her son, told him that she was Mary and that she wished a church to be built on the spot where she was standing. He was to tell this to the Bishop.

He was received with the scepticism that such tales usually arouse in the higher clergy, and sent away. He returned to the spot; the Lady was waiting for him; he pointed out that it was no good sending him on a mission of this kind; why did she not send a Spaniard or someone of importance? She told him to go back with the same message. He went. On this second visit Diego aroused the interest if not the sympathy of the Bishop; perhaps this was a case of witchcraft of the kind which the Church was endeavouring to stamp out. He told him to bring some sign with him and sent two men to follow him and see what happened. Next day, the 10th, these men reported that Diego, when he reached the rocks where he claimed to have seen the apparition, mysteriously disappeared from view. Unaware of this himself, he received orders to return next day and receive his sign.

Then in Diego's slow, peasant mind suspicions began to arise. He was getting mixed up in affairs that were beyond his capacity. Besides his uncle was ill. He did not return. On the 12th, however, his uncle was worse and wanted a priest; that meant going to Tlaltelolco again. Diego did not like it and chose a circuitous path. But the Lady was there, too, blocking his way. He told her about his uncle being ill. She knew all about it; he would get well, she said; Diego had another duty to perform. He must take his sign to the Bishop. Above where they stood the rocks rose in a sharp, barren hill; the Lady told him to climb there and pick roses. It was an improbable place but Diego found them, miraculously blooming among the stones; enough to fill his *sarape*. So he trudged off again, back to the suspicious Bishop and spilt the flowers at his feet. He may have thought, on the road, that it was not much of a sign; after all, there was only his word for it that they came from the desert. But he did as he was told and revealed not only the roses but a picture of his lady, Our Lady, imprinted on the *sarape*. That is the picture which now hangs over the high altar at Guadalupe.

The church was begun immediately on the site which Diego showed. In 1532 the picture was solemnly conveyed there. It had already created a sensation; a disagreeable one to the many Spaniards who regarded the Indians as animals. There had already been some distrust of the policy of baptising the Indians, giving them the idea that they, too, had souls equal before God with their conquerors. And now Our Lady had appeared to an Indian, more than this she had appeared *as* an Indian; and here, for all time, was the evidence; a Virgin with an Indian face; a thing no painter would have dared do without incurring the charge of blasphemy. And the Spaniards accepted the miracle. The important feature is not the repugnance it aroused but the fact that the repugnance was overcome. The nobility of the country, from the Viceroy down, solemnly prostrated themselves in the new shrine and from that day until now every Christian ruler of Mexico, even Maximilian, has made his homage there to the fact which it had needed a supernatural revelation to enforce, that the religion of the Spaniard was equally the religion of the Indian.

The shrine has never been closed or pillaged, though the neighbouring convent suffered with the rest of the country. At the height of the Calles persecution the Indians guarded it day and night. A bomb was placed under the altar – the cross may be seen as it was twisted by the explosion – but the picture was undamaged. For the time a reproduction was substituted but now the original is back in its place. While I was there the church was being repaired and redecorated; it is always full of worshippers.

Mr T. Philip Terry, whose *Guide to Mexico* has been mentioned elsewhere in these pages, provides the tourist with the kind of comment which the present Government encourages. '*One cannot but admire,*' he says, '*the positive genius of Zumarraga* (the Bishop) *in planning that the Virgin appear in Mexico not as a carved figure, nor yet in the likeness of a Spanish woman, but rather in the guise of an Indian princess with some resemblance to the revered goddess Tonantzin thus striking the Indian population at the most vulnerable point . . . the picture is perhaps of Spanish origin . . . The fact that the apparition occurred during the incumbency of the Bishop Zumarraga, the bigot . . . is significant . . . It is believed that the Indians regard the image of the Virgin as a divine manifestation of their primitive goddess . . . On the feast day the unhygienic and ignorant Indians overrun the village to such an extent that the problem of preventing pestilence is a serious one to the authorities. The church is usually packed to suffocation: the devotees bring habits and an entomological congress as varied as they are astonishing, all the church decorations within reach are kissed to a high polish and thoroughly fumigated later, and all breathe freer when the frenzied shriners have returned to their different homes. Many of the pilgrims are wretchedly poor and to maintain themselves on the journey – which not a few make on foot – they bring curious home-made knick-knacks . . . A careful scrutiny of the church is difficult on Sundays . . . At these times it presents a very animated and democratic appear- ance. Well dressed Mexicans, foreigners, ragged Indians, crying babies . . . are prominent features. Less visible but just as prominent, in a way, are the agile specimens of the genus pulex which the visitor to this sanctuary usually carries away with him.'*

These smug and facetious passages are an exact expression of the wrong-thinking which the miracle of Guadalupe rebukes. Mr Terry starts with an assumption which stultifies all his subsequent observa- tions, that a miracle is of necessity a fraud . . . 'the positive genius of Zumarraga in planning'. The value of miracles anywhere is not in the direct benefits they confer – a single cripple among millions enabled to walk, one hungry man among millions given a single meal – but in their manifesting the nearness of the supernatural. But most miracles also show an immediate and local purpose. The apparition of Lourdes came at the height of French scepticism; at Guadalupe it came to teach the Spaniards that the Indians were men and women and souls, to teach the Indians that the Spaniards' god was the god of all humankind. Mr Terry by his primary incredu- lity finds himself led into denying these beliefs in order to discredit the revelation that supports them. For what is his argument? The Indians are a dirty lot, they are crawling with fleas, the place has to be fumigated after they have gone, they have no business at Gua- dalupe at all, everyone 'breathes the freer' when they go, they come on foot with 'curious knick-knacks', a pestilential mob with whom no tourist cares to rub shoulders, *animals* . . . And, since they are like this, it is absurd to pretend that they are worshipping the same God as well-fed, expensively educated Americans and Europeans; 'it is believed' they regard the Virgin as 'their primitive goddess'. She has 'some resemblance to the revered Tonantzin'. The innocent reader might imagine that Mr Terry had made an iconographical study, had found an image of Tonantzin and compared it with the Virgin of Guadalupe; what he has really done is to read page 236 of Gruening, and what Gruening has done is to quote what Father Sahagun wrote fifty years after the time of Zumarraga, that the Indians when going to Guadalupe said, and, I believe still say, 'Let us go to the festival of Tonantzin'; and what does this sinister word Tonantzin mean? It is simply the Indian word for 'Our Mother'. What more fitting epithet could be found for the Virgin than this, once unworthily applied to a member of the old pantheon? But the Indian is a subhuman creature; if he once thought a heathen goddess was his mother, he does still; he cannot have learned very much, otherwise he would be rich and clean. This is the basis of the criticism.

The Christian point of view is to admit that miracles are possible but exceedingly rare, and to examine each on its evidence. The Guadalupe stands the test well. Hostile critics have usually weakened their case by preliminary abuse of Archbishop Zumarraga. At the time of the conquest quantities of Aztec painted manuscripts[1] disappeared, which would have been of enormous interest to subsequent historians. Zumarraga is charged with their destruction. The authority for his responsibility is the utterance of an eccentric friar named Mier (who in 1817 disguised himself as a Bishop and landed at Soto la Marina with a small revolutionary force under Francisco Javier Mina which was dispersed after a short guerilla campaign). From him the tale has been copied from book to book, even those published since Francis Clement Kelly's exposure, until it is generally accepted. The Indian historian Ixtlilxochitl of the

1 The Aztecs as has been mentioned before had no alphabet or real written language, but a well-developed system of hieroglyphic record.

seventeenth century mentions the destruction but attributes it, inconsistently, both to missionaries and to the Tlaxcalans who sacked Tezcoco eight years before Zumarraga landed in Mexico. The only certain association of Zumarraga with Aztec manuscripts is that he made a collection of all that had survived and took them to Europe in 1532, where they are now preserved in various libraries. As for the missionaries in general, by giving the Indians the alphabet they made it possible for them to record their oral traditions. Hundreds of volumes of this kind were kept in the monastic libraries until the Liberal revolutions of 1855 and 1861, when they were sold as waste paper.

Zumarraga was outstanding in a generation of devoted missionaries for his zeal in educating, evangelising and humanising the Indians. It was he who petitioned the King against their enslavement, smuggling his message out of the country in a hollow image. 'If it is true,' he wrote, 'that your Majesty has granted permission' for the process of enslavement, 'you should out of reverence to God, do humble penitence for it.' It was he who founded the first school for higher education of Indians, Santa Cruz in Tlaltelolco, who started the education of women there, introduced the first printing-press and laid the foundations of the great educational and charitable system which only came to an end in the revolutions. While others were making their fortunes, the Archbishop died in debt. His ambition was to see a new province of Christendom, in its widest application, rising beyond the Atlantic. He was one to whom the special revelation to the Indians would be intensely welcome. Those who lack strong moral feelings themselves, are ever ready to credit their moral superiors with a disposition to do evil that good may come of it. Earnestly as Zumarraga may have prayed for a sign from Heaven, warmly as we know he accepted it, it is scarcely conceivable that his stern conscience would have bent to a fraud of the kind with which Mr Terry credits him; but even were one to accept this psychological improbability, there are many difficulties to explain.

The ground of the picture is certainly an Indian *sarape* of the normal coarse weave with its central seam clearly visible from the sanctuary rails. This, and the native character of the model make it highly unlikely to have been imported ready made from Europe. It is stretching the imagination too far to conceive of the whole matter being plotted and prepared in Madrid, yet the painters who visited Mexico in the earlier colonial days are well known and none of them did work remotely resembling the Virgin of Guadalupe. Moreover no one has been able to identify the material with which it is painted; it is not oil, water nor tempera colour of any recognisable kind. In 1756 the best-known of Mexican painters, Miguel Cabrera, published the report of a careful technical examination in which he professed himself quite unable to explain the process by which it was made; on two other occasions committees of painters have been allowed to take it out of its glass and have been able to give no explanation. Nothing would suit the present Government better than to be able to expose the thing as a priestly fraud, but they have been obliged to keep silent.

And yet, it must be admitted, the picture is very like a human composition; the folds and pattern of the robe, the rays of glory, the crescent moon at the feet, the cherub below, are all curiously stylised. One cannot imagine a painter sitting down to design the holy shroud of Turin, but one *can* imagine him drawing the Virgin of Guadalupe. Looking at it I wondered whether perhaps some human agency had not intervened to preserve and ornament the true image which Diego and Zumarraga saw. The bodies of saints exposed for veneration are often so overlaid with wax that the surface is nowhere the actual skin of the body; there is no fraud; the body is there but the preservative hides it; I wondered whether this might not be the case with Guadalupe; it was a purely personal doubt and it seemed to leave more unexplained than the frank acceptance of the miracle; it did not explain the actual pigmentation of the material; if one can accept a God who treats with human beings in a way they will understand, one can accept the miraculous appearance of a picture; it is neither more nor less credible for having some of the marks of a human composition.

Anyway, the appearance, or, as the guide books prefer it, the alleged appearance of Our Lady at Guadalupe is one of the important features of Mexican history; to the great majority of Mexicans it is something far more real and personally significant than the coming of Cortes, and anyone who treats of Mexico without considering it, is necessarily superficial. Reproductions of the picture are everywhere; even in the homes of the most sceptical foreign business men. There was an enormous output of replicas, some of them by the greatest painters of the country, and today picture-postcards and medals are sold in millions. But it is to the shrine itself that the people flock. There is an air of gaiety surrounding the village, a perpetual fair day. The path which Diego climbed to pick the roses is lined with photographers' booths and Indians who have tramped for weeks to make the pilgrimage may, by sticking their heads through a canvas screen, take home as a souvenir the picture of themselves sailing over the shrine in an aeroplane. It is, however, not only Indians who come to Guadalupe; it is, as Mr Terry remarks with apparent distaste, very 'democratic'. You see people of all nations there, as you do at any place of pilgrimage. (A great deal of nonsense is talked and repeated about the partisan loyalties of the various shrines. One is told for example that Our Lady of the Remedies is 'the Spanish Virgin'. I went to Los Remedios on the morning of the feast; in the crowd that queued up to kiss the little statue which a soldier of Cortes's had brought with him in his saddle bag, we were the only whites.)

There are votive offerings at Guadalupe, but fewer than in most places of pilgrimage in Mexico or elsewhere. In Mexico they take a form which as far as I know is unique. They are little paintings on tin portraying the danger from which the pilgrim has been preserved – accidents with horses and motor cars and trams, attacks by bandits and soldiers, fires – all graphically represented. Most towns have an artist or two who specialise in this work and will do you a disaster for a peso or so. The Ministry of Fine Arts has collected some from the shrines where they belong and added them as a humorous contribution to the furniture at Churibusco. But there were not many at Guadalupe for it is not principally frequented with a view to particular benefits. Mexicans go there several times in their lives; before journeys abroad and on great occasions as a kind of dedication, but more often I think as an act of pure worship – and for reassurance. As long as the Virgin is there over her altar, however desperate things may seem, there is still hope. If she deserts them, then they are back again, helpless, on the reeking altars of Huitzilopochtli. They believe that it was at Guadalupe that Mexico became a nation and that Our Lady took them in her keeping; she is still there guarding them; and they have to come from time to time to make sure.

For myself, at any rate, the great twilit Cathedral was the most impressive sight in Mexico; it was much the same at all hours of the day and on all days of the week; sometimes it was fuller, but there was always the same atmosphere of hushed veneration; there were workmen high overhead on scaffolding, hammering at the roof, but it made no difference. It was the one place in Mexico that never seemed noisy. People of every conceivable kind were always there, praying. There were family groups of all ages, candles in hand, working their way up the aisle on their knees. There were men who remained apparently interminably on their knees with their arms stretched out on either side of them; they were like that when one came in and still there, in the same position, when one left; rapt, their lips moving, their eyes open fixed on the picture. There were women who, in spite of their shabby civil costume, one knew to be nuns, and swarthy, inconspicuous men dressed like small shop-keepers who, to one's surprise, one found to be priests. There were mothers guiding their children in the sign of the cross. All the limitless variety of the Church seemed to be represented there. No doubt there were also 'members of the *genus pulex*' but it did not seem the least important.

In their way, of course, the Mexicans are superstitious; it is a legacy of the dark origins of the human race that is found in every country; it is only an unfamiliar superstition that seems to us shocking. There, as everywhere, it is the concern of the clergy to distinguish and drive out the harmful superstitions; many of them are innocent enough. The priest of a large parish in Oaxaca was showing me his church; one of the statues had a coin inserted between its painted teeth. The priest sighed resignedly. 'They will do it,' he said. 'I am always trying to stop it.' It was the statue of an early Christian martyr who had had his tongue torn out and who, as a somewhat remote consequence, was credited locally with particular powers against scandal-mongers; when anyone in Oaxaca finds there are rumours going round about him, he puts a coin in the saint's mouth. Sometimes, if no one has noticed it and the gossip seems to have abated, he comes and takes it away again and feels the kind of satisfaction people get after completing a railway journey without a ticket. Customs of this kind are prevalent; Mexicans, like Europeans, resort to special shrines of particular benefits. It is common to hear a certain type of foreigner – Catholic as well as agnostic – say that the saints are more important to the Mexicans than their God; that they still worship a host of deities. The routine of their daily life gives some colour to this misapprehension, just as a stranger might believe that the film-stars and athletes who form so large a part of ordinary English conversation were the real heroes and leaders about whom our national life revolved. The test came a few years ago in the peasants' revolt against Calles, when all over the country people rose in defence of their churches and were massacred by the federal troops. They were fighting for essentials then and they called themselves 'Cristeros'; *Viva Cristo Rey* was the rallying cry of that gallant and disastrous campaign.

Of course by no means all the Cristeros were pious crusaders. There is always present in Mexico a considerable semi-bandit population who will join in any disturbance; there were cases when these usurped the badges and banners of the Cristeros and committed outrages which Gruening has carefully catalogued. Even Gruening, however, is bound to admit that the suppression of religion in Mexico has throughout been the work of a hated minority. It is notable, too, that nearly every amelioration of it has resulted from violent popular protest.

The story of the persecution has often been told but has received curiously little attention in Europe. Aspects of it have been noted from time to time in these pages. It began simply as an act of robbery, with the accompanying campaign of justification by agnostic teaching and the vilification of the clergy. Throughout the nineteenth century the Masonic Lodges remained centres of an antireligious party which ensured for itself influential positions in every department of the state. The old-fashioned Liberal-Mason-Agnostics, however, tolerated the priests as a harmless source of

comfort to their women and their peasants, sent their daughters to
school in convents abroad, and even called for a priest themselves on
their death beds. It was only after the fall of Diaz that the movement
became militantly atheist; it was then a definitely communist,
proletarian revolutionary body under the same international
auspices which caused the Leninist revolution in Russia and the
brief and bloody regime of Bela Khun in Hungary. In a decade of
civil war and anarchy, with rival generals everywhere proclaiming
themselves the government, the communist organisation, soon to be
known as the CROM, represented a single, consistent policy and
achieved an importance quite out of proportion to its numbers. It
became the virtual master of each successive President and the price
of its support, always, was the extinction of the Church.

Its influence may be shown on the change of Carranza's and
Obregon's policy between 1915 and 1917. In the former year they
both declared for religious liberty for all Mexican citizens. In the
latter Carranza assembled his supporters at Queretaro and formulated the decree on which all the subsequent troubles have been
based. The decree is now dignified by the name of the 'Constitution', but the convention which discussed it was nothing more
than Carranza's faction. This 'Constitution' began on a sinister note
by reversing the normal logic of politics; instead of deriving the
powers of the constitution from the will of the people, it derived
the rights of the people from the constitution, defining certain
elementary rights which Carranza's party were disposed to 'grant'.
No attempt has ever been made to ratify this camp pronouncement
by popular vote.

Like the Labour Laws, the Constitution of Queretaro must be
read in the knowledge that subsequent rulings would resolve all
ambiguities in the most drastic terms which they were capable of
bearing, but even in their simplest form the provisions represent
a legal condition for the Church which has no parallel in any
country except Russia. They declare education to be totalitarian
and forbid religious corporations or ministers from establishing or
directing primary schools; any school erected for the purpose of
religious teaching is confiscated; ministers of religion may not maintain institutions for scientific research; religious orders of every kind

are proscribed; '*the Law recognises no juridical personality in the religious institutions known as churches*'; i.e. they are deprived of all legal rights of appeal to Congress or protection by the courts; no one of foreign birth may be a priest in Mexico; any Mexican becoming a priest loses his rights of citizenship, his vote and his right to hold office; '*ministers of religious creeds are incapable legally of inheriting by will from ministers of the same religious creed or from any private individual to whom they are not related by blood within the fourth degree*'; '*no trial by jury shall ever be granted for the infraction of any of the preceding provisions*'; no hospital or poor-house may be under the patronage, administration or supervision of a religious corporation.

There are other provisions of a similar nature, all of which would be intolerable in America or England, but it was some time before matters came to a crisis. At first it was uncertain how long the Calles-Obregon-Carranza alliance would last or who would succeed it; it was also uncertain what force and interpretation would be given to the new constitution. There had been hard laws on the statute book in the time of Diaz, but they had not been enforced and the Church had been able to carry on her work in comparative peace. It was nine years before it became clear that the urban communist party was growing in influence and that the Calles-Obregon government had decided to stave off its economic demands by satisfying its hatred of the Church. The Mexican Bishops then attempted to exert their influence by peaceful and topical means in declaring what amounted to a strike; Calles replied by instituting a régime which made no pretence of any other motive than the total and immediate extermination of Christianity in his country. He was of Syrian extraction, without share in the high traditions of Mexico; today he is an affluent exile in California. There is nothing remarkable about him and he would have gone down to history as a purely local figure, one of a succession of negligible names, the riff-raff of party intrigue and violence that gets to the top in times of disorder, had it not been for this campaign of his. It was not even his; he was merely an instrument, allowed to pile up his private gains so long as he followed the policy ordained for him. When he became reluctant to continue he was sent away. But the few years of his régime will always be known by his name and he will be famous, until the end of the world, as the man who murdered Father Pro.

There were hundreds of others done to death at the same time. Mexico had been infertile of religious heroes for some generations; now she suddenly burst into flower; but popular imagination always seeks to personify its ideals, and it is on Pro, very worthily, that it has fastened as the embodiment of the spirit Calles provoked. Within a few hours of his death he was already canonised in the hearts of the people; with typical ineptitude Calles had photographers on the scene of the execution and issued pictures of it to the Press; within a day or two it was a criminal offence to possess one; they circulated nevertheless from hand to hand and were reproduced in secret all over the country. Today you can buy cards of Pro outside the churches and even Government apologists have stopped trying to justify his death. It was a mistake, they admit; it was indeed; one of those resounding mistakes which make history. While Dwight Morrow and his clown and Calles were off on a trip together in the Presidential train talking of debt settlements, Pro was being shot in a back yard. Dwight Morrow is already forgotten. Pro is the inspiration of thousands through whom the Mexican Church is still alive.

4

The present situation of the Church in Mexico is the result of the truce effected with the mediation of Dwight Morrow. Mexican Catholics profess small gratitude to him for his intervention. The promises then made by the Government have not been kept. The Cristeros were induced to surrender their arms under an amnesty which has been broken by a series of retributive murders. The hierarchy believed that their spiritual work was to be allowed to continue without persecution; they have been bitterly disappointed. For Catholics the unhappy character of the compromise has been emphasised by the grave warning of the late Pope in the encyclical *Firmissiman Constantiam* of Easter 1937. For English radicals the situation was explained in an article in *New Statesman* of February 12th, 1938. 'Although the power of the Church's hierarchy has been broken, freedom of worship continues to exist unhampered in Mexico.'

It is true that for the incurious tourist conditions in the districts he frequents may seem more or less normal. They find a number of churches put to civil uses as garages, libraries, warehouses, fire-stations; 'There were too many of them,' the guides explain, and to one surveying the 365 churches[1] that surround the little village of Cholula, the excuse sounds plausible. The churches that are open are perpetually crowded; priests are at the altars and in the confes-sionals, apparently undisturbed.

Landing at Vera Cruz, with an afternoon to wait before the train left for Mexico City, I set out to look at the town. I had read of Vera Cruz as a state where the Government were particularly anti-religious and expected to find its churches shut. The first I entered had been converted into a public library. It is a curious thing, but churches never seem suitable for any other purpose than the one for which they were built. I have seen secularised churches in many parts of the world being used as museums, mosques, billiard saloons, drawing-rooms – they never looked right. The library at Vera Cruz was damp and stuffy; two or three children of high-school age were doing their lessons there; a few others were lounging over the picture papers. It had a depressing air, but so have most public libraries anywhere in the world. The other church was open and very busy; the decorations were shoddy and shabby; plaster statues had taken the place of the rich colonial sculpture, but at every altar there were people making their devotions, not old women only but quite young men, and in the nave a young catechist was giving instruction to a large class of school-children. They were learning the responses of the Mass, repeating them in unison. It looked as though the com-promise were working quite well. The Church was being allowed to compete with the State on equal terms for support of the new generation. Seeing it the Catholic tourist might be tempted to think that the religious press in his own country was making an unnecessary fuss.

1 This prodigality is exceptional, but is always quoted as the example of clerical superfluity. The churches were built in conformity with missionary custom on the sites of existing shrines.

Vera Cruz, as a matter of fact, is a place where the Church had recently won a considerable victory. A year before every church in the State was shut as they had been in the time of Calles. Dwight Morrow's bonhomie had had no effect there. The Bishop had been forbidden to enter his diocese; a few gallant priests moved in disguise from house to house saying Mass in secret. Then an incident had occurred which suddenly aroused the patient people; it was typical of what had been going on all over the country for more than ten years. Those responsible for it had no reason to expect any trouble. They did no more than murder a little girl, as had often been done before, but for some reason the people who had suffered so much in dumb resentment suddenly asserted themselves.

The child had been to one of the houses in Orizaba where the police rightly believed Mass was being said; she came out alone, in the early morning, straight from her communion; she was not of those for whom the *New Statesman* would have us believe 'freedom of worship continued unhampered'; the police followed her; she took fright and began to run. They shot her down in the street and returned to their quarters for their usual torpid Orizaba Sunday. But it proved different from other Sundays. News of the murder spread in the town, which was full of peasants in for the day. Suddenly they rose, broke open the doors of their church, barricaded themselves there and began ringing the bells. The C.T.M. bosses telegraphed helplessly to Mexico for advice. All over the State news spread of what had happened in Orizaba. Everywhere the churches were reoccupied. General Cardenas was just completing his plans for the confiscation of the oil properties; he dared not risk another Cristero rising. The local governor was made to give way. The Bishop returned; the priests came out of hiding, and the people flocked back to their churches.

It is by means such as these, not by the exchange of cigars in the Presidential train, that the Church is being re-established in Mexico. A European is tempted to write 'Faith' instead of Church. I had, indeed, done so and struck it out, for the Faith has never been lost to the vast majority of the country. But the Faith cannot exist for ever without its tangible expression; it is not a mere system of philosophic propositions and historical facts; though it may sometimes appear as this, in certain intellectual types living in a sympathetic atmosphere. It is a habit of life and a social organisation. The simpler a people, the ruder their living conditions and the more limited their information, so much the more do they need to symbolise their ideas in concrete shapes. They must have buildings in which they consort for worship, statues and pictures to make the ideas of their creed intelligible and memorable; above all they – equally with the most arid theologian – must have the sacraments. The communist may logically maintain that these things are futile and mischievous; tricks invented by his enemies to delude man from his real duty in life, which is to get through the largest possible amount of consumable goods and to produce those goods in the largest possible quantities so that he may consume them. Isolate a people absolutely from tainted contacts; obliterate every monument to the old delusions; exterminate those who remember the old order with regret; educate the children in ignorance of its principles; then, humanly speaking, you will produce a race of atheists, or at any rate of non-Christians. Curious ideas will no doubt take shape in their empty minds, but it is not conceivable that a race, theologically sterilised in this way, will evolve for itself the doctrines of the Trinity and the Incarnation. This was the thesis of the communist gang behind Calles; it is reasonable enough, by purely human standards. What is not reasonable is the attitude of the extreme Nazis and the present Mexican apologists – who have to be double-faced in their apologies, to their too zealous international friends on one side, and the too curious humanitarians on the other – that religion is a purely private business; that if a man is disposed that way he can sit at home and be religious by himself; that he needs no special class to minister to him, no special association with sympathisers, no place to associate and no means of conveying his belief to his descendants. Either his religion will die or it will find concrete expression in these ways.

The Church for her life, has to have a priesthood, an order of men peculiarly educated and consecrated for a specific work; she has to have property where she can preserve her sacred things from outrage; she has to have the opportunity of conveying her teaching to children whose parents desire it. Deny her these elementary claims and you deny her life. Each one of these is still being denied in Mexico.

General Cardenas, himself, seems slightly fuddled on the subject of religion. He is not, of course, a practising Catholic; his party would not leave him in office a day if he were, but there are signs that, in his own classic phrase, he has begun to 'weary of the social struggle'. 'I am tired,' he said, 'of closing churches and finding them full.' He is a man who has spent most of his life in barracks in the masonic-agnostic atmosphere of the revolutionary army; in childhood he worked in a printing-office but entered government service at adolescence; 1913 found him as a gaoler with a single prisoner; he let the man out and together they joined the revolution; since then he has probably never come into contact with anything that can be called Christian life; at the age of 25 he was a general, an ally of Calles and Obregon. He was taught that the Church was invented for their profit by priests and *hacendados*; the priests and *hacendados* have gone, and it seems to come as a genuine surprise to him each time that a popular disturbance brings it to his notice that the people still value their faith. His habit has been – as in the incident at Orizaba quoted above – to give way. He is more interested in pleasing the people than in following any logical policy; but, relying as he does for his position and safety upon the C.T.M., he dare not alter the laws; nor can he, until they are brought forcibly to his notice, take any steps to see that the laws are not exceeded. While I was there two State governments, those of Tabasco and Chiapas, still refused even the meagre freedom that the law prescribed. In Tabasco, the churches were still all shut – those, that is to say, that had not been demolished. The late Governor Garrido had got into trouble for carrying his anti-religious zeal too far; he had sent squads of gunmen far beyond the boundaries of his State to shoot up churchgoers near the tourist zone; that had been too much and he had had to disappear to Costa Rica, but his successors maintained his policy of absolute prohibition of every form of worship. In Chiapas some of the churches were open but all were without priests. There has lately been news of a peasants' rising in Villaher-mosa, the capital of Tabasco, where some peasants were murdered by troops while trying to say their prayers in the ruins of one of the churches Garrido had demolished. General Cardenas has promised redress.

Illegal atrocities may be matched by illegal acts of clemency. In many parts of the country, particularly in the tourist zone, greater indulgence was given than the law allowed. In Oaxaca I met a priest who wore clerical clothes in the streets without molestation. One Sunday, while I was in Mexico City, the Catholic students of the University marched in procession to Guadalupe; the matter was kept out of the newspapers and no action was taken against them. In general, however, the régime in Mexico is still violently anti-religious.

The number of priests permitted in any State is decided by the Governor. This is everywhere grossly inadequate. In the United States and Europe the average is one priest to every seven or eight hundred Catholics; a priest with 1,500 in his charge, particularly if they are scattered in a rural district, would rightly regard himself as overworked. In Mexico the average is said to be one to 10,000; this is a somewhat unsatisfactory figure since some States have no priests at all; in some one is allowed to every 30,000, while Mexico City, Puebla, Oaxaca, Cuernavaca and Taxco are fairly well provided. Many of the priests whom the tourist sees in these places, however, are there in defiance of the law with the temporary connivance of the authorities; they are legally criminals and are liable to arrest at any moment should the temper of the police turn. In the conditions the priesthood have been given exceptional facilities by the hierarchy and say numerous Masses on days of obligation. Seminaries are absolutely forbidden everywhere; this law knows no extenuation and the police are active in searching for and confiscating any house where theological instruction is given. A large seminary has been established in Texas and this has supplied many priests in recent years, but, as well as this, seminaries do exist secretly in most of the dioceses. The lot of the students is miserable, for to the normal austerities and restrictions of their life is added the necessity of keeping completely out of sight during the entire period – two or three years – of their studies. Financial support, moreover, is so meagre and precarious that they live in conditions of genuine privation. In spite of all this there is no shortage of applicants.

Persecution is already having its normal result of producing a priesthood of intense devotion. Only a very small number, however, can be maintained in this way; the law against the immigration of foreign religious is still rigidly enforced and the shortage of priests is acute. Added to this is the fact that in the case of trouble of any kind they have no civil rights.

The religious orders are still forbidden absolutely as they have been since the time of Juarez. One of the show places of Mexico is the hidden convent of Puebla; the place where Mr Graham Greene's acquaintance was disappointed of babies' bones. It is, nevertheless, a thrilling place, and it is singularly obtuse on the part of the Government to make the show of it that they do. Here, in the heart of the town, a community of enclosed nuns lived for over seventy years without the knowledge of the police. It was a seventeenth-century foundation of no particular importance in colonial times; when Juarez drove out the nuns elsewhere this little community escaped notice; they were a poor order, with few possessions to attract the Government agents; they had always led a life of strict retirement; now they disappeared from the knowledge of all but a handful of friends; their little patio was so built that no building overlooked it; they had their chapel and a gallery with eye-holes through which they could see the altar of the neighbouring church and hear Mass on occasions when it was too dangerous for a priest to visit them. The only entrance to the world was through a small private house whose occupants were in the secret. Great ingenuity was used to disguise the two doors, through which provisions were brought to them and needlework taken as payment. Here they were professed, lived the strict rule of their order, and died; their bones were thrown into a common pit which now provides a macabre exhibit for the curious. In the more generous times of Diaz novices were admitted but in the last years of its life this was impossible; about forty elderly women were found there in 1935 when the police broke into the place.

One is shown it, as in a fashionable New York restaurant one is shown the devices of prohibition days which conceal the piping-hot cellars where they ruin their wines. First the living-room of the private house; the guide pulls some shelves from the wall, presses

a button and a door opens leading straight into the cell of the
Mother Superior; there is another concealed door in the house, at
the bottom of the stairs, leading into the patio. The convent is still
kept more or less as it was found; it disappointingly revealed few
treasures and no scandals. The most valuable find was a collection of
very ugly paintings on velvet. There is still enough of the convent
atmosphere left to give an element of outrage to each new intrusion.
The guide himself, recruited with the rest from the local masonic
lodge, had a shamefaced air. It was, to me at any rate, inexpressibly
shocking to see him jingling the little penitential chains which they
had found the nuns wearing; to hear him sneer at the underground
cells where the nuns retired for meditation and at the three-foot door
through which they crept to Mass. It affected others, too, in the same
way; one could hear them arriving jauntily and noisily, with slightly
lubricious expectations; they thoroughly enjoyed the secret doors; it
was all part of a detective story; then, as they tramped round those
secret places, they became ill-at-ease and silent. They knew they had
no business there. A few of them asked questions, 'Why were the
nuns turned out?'

'It is against the law.'

'What harm were they doing?'

'They were breaking the law.'

Some, who had never before had any acquaintance with convent
life, were obviously startled. Their shock found expression in such
phrases as, 'Morbid kind of place'. But I do not think they really
meant this. What they were feeling was a sense of personal guilt.
They were prying into things with which their own lives had no
contact. They came out into the street in subdued little parties.

I do not know what impression the Government seeks to give in
the Hidden Convent; the guile of the religious, the zeal of the
detectives, the uselessness of a devotional life? I suppose all these
things. I am sure nothing could serve their purposes worse. There
are plenty of empty monasteries and convents in the country, now
mere architectural monuments with no keener spiritual associations
than the ruins of Fountains or Glastonbury; but everything is so
recent at Puebla. It is not merely that the sight-seer can picture for
himself the scene of a few years back when the police suddenly burst

into the silence and bundled the old women into the streets which they had not seen for half a lifetime; it is that he feels that in his own trespass the outrage is being daily re-enacted.

There is a repugnance for many people about the idea of monastic life. No one suggests that it is a suitable life for any except a particular and relatively rare religious type; for certain people however it offers the highest happiness and development. To deny these people the right to live in the manner they require is a denial of religious liberty.

The churches, as has already been mentioned, are the property of the state; in some districts they have been demolished; in others locked; in the most favoured localities a proportion of them have been returned on sufferance to the people for the use of their priests; the furniture and decorations, such as have survived, are the property of the state; even in the Cathedral of Mexico City the vestments have been removed to a neighbouring museum. Innocent tourists believe it to be a kind of sacristy. While I was seeing them a lady asked, 'Do the priests often wear those things?'

'No, madam,' the guide replied with a certain grim humour, 'not often.'

'I should think not. They are far too valuable.'

'Yes, far too valuable.'

Pictures and statues are still constantly being removed from churches, ostensibly to be put in museums.

Religious processions or the wearing of clerical dress outside the church walls has long been forbidden. Some thirty years ago the Scottish colony of the city held a banquet on St Andrew's Night. They had a piper; many of them wore the kilt; at the end of the evening they decided to walk home in a body. The police did not like the music or the bare knees. They were run in for causing a disturbance, and innocently pleaded that it was St Andrew's Night. The fine was promptly doubled; they had taken part in a religious procession.

Outside the church walls no association of a religious character is allowed; this is interpreted in the most oppressive way to proscribe any sort of social gathering of Catholics; not only are the bazaars and sewing-parties and recreation clubs that make a part of normal parochial life, illegal; a man's house may be confiscated if he holds family prayers with his own household.

The Government is still active in trying to efface its Christian past by changing the names of streets, cities and natural features, that have Christian associations; pages could be filled with examples of the minor discomforts and humiliations to which practising Catholics are put in every branch of the régime. The most vital question, next to the existence of the priesthood, is education.

As has been mentioned above, the department of education is in openly communist hands and the teaching it prescribes not only omits religious instruction but makes anti-religious instruction a prominent part. No kind of alternative school is allowed and parents are obliged to send their children to be taught doctrines which they abominate. The only place where religious instruction is allowed is in the churches and it is necessary for the catechists to coax the children there during their playtime. It is one of the duties of the Government schoolmaster to watch these classes and whenever he knows that a class is to be held, to arrange other activities; he also holds up to the ridicule of the school those children who attend. They are nevertheless well attended, and it seems to many observers likely that if their success increases new repressive measures will be taken, for the degree of toleration now granted is on the supposition that religious practice was a foible of the elderly that would die out with them. 'I am tired of closing churches and finding them full,' said General Cardenas in a public speech at Oaxaca. 'Now I am going to open the churches and educate the people and in ten years I shall find them empty.'

Will he?

So far I have only given an account of the situation from the outside; the spectacle of an armed minority blockading the Church and starving it to death; the resistance of the people has shown itself only in spasmodic, spontaneous outbursts of indignation, and in a wistful tenacity which, unsupported, must in its nature fail. But out of sight the work of the Church is going on. There are no eucharistic congresses or mass meetings of Catholics in Mexico; but there is, nevertheless, a religious revival in progress that is transforming the Mexican Church; driven into the catacombs, the

Church is recovering their spirit. I was allowed to see something of this work while I was in Mexico; the workers must remain anonymous; they meet in empty houses in shabby streets. They go in constant danger and I must write nothing that can give a clue to their identity. I may, however, say something of the nature of their work. In personnel they are mainly laymen and women of modest means and good education and they are organised under the Bishops to carry out purely spiritual work. There are no *pistoleros* among them; no talk of political disturbance; they seek to train and maintain teachers, within and outside the Government service, to counteract the official atheism; they facilitate the movement and concealment of the priesthood in the proscribed areas; they issue simple doctrinal and devotional pamphlets; they organise study groups where men and girls of undergraduate age can discuss religious questions and examine the official doctrines with which they are stuffed in their classes. They have taken as the basis of their discussions the encyclicals of the late Pope, those relating to the particular problems of Mexico and the '*Quadragesimo Anno*', which owing to local difficulties was never, I believe, fully promulgated in Mexico.[1] It was this pronouncement which defined the Catholic meaning of 'social justice', and offered an alternative solution to the Marxian class-war for the problems of our industrialised world. There is nothing reactionary, in the common use of the word, about the aspirations of this lay organisation in Mexico, nothing that will fit into the idiotic dichotomy of Left and Right. Nor is there anything specifically national. They believe that the remedies they advocate are universal, but that their need is manifestly acute in their own country. For in Mexico nationality, colour and race are so confused, the divisions of class so artificially emphasised and embittered and the whole principle of government so disordered that only some extra-national force can bring relief. Such unity as the country ever enjoyed was the gift of the Church; it was the Church who saved the Indians from slavery and established their fundamental

---

1 Neither conservative nor socialist party was particularly anxious for the people to know how much Catholic doctrine has been borrowed by the socialists. Mr Graham Greene in *Lawless Roads* mentions a Bishop of San Luis Potosi who kept the encyclical *De Rerum Novarum* stacked in his cellar.

equality and identity with their conquerors. It is popular to believe that after the first generation the Church neglected her mission; so far as that was ever true, she has paid for it and is starting her work again on her old, true principles. The problem of rebuilding the Mexican nation is the difficulty of finding any common principle on which to work. Identity of economic interests is a weak enough bond even in a more or less homogeneous country; in Mexico the divisions of the urban, unionised labourer and the peasant are unbridgeable in economic terms. Every class and individual is obsessed by grievances, real or imagined. Only the broadest possible identity provides a common interest; the identity, in fact, which the theologians defined at the time of the conquest; the identity of a common human nature and individual souls. Even in the times when the divisions of caste were most meticulously observed, the Church was a reminder of this equality; tiny, significant incidents recur in her history; to build the shrine of the Pocito ladies of fashion worked with the common labourers; in 1849 Pavil Robertson,[1] a rigid protestant, was particularly struck by the freedom with which classes and races mixed in the Easter festivities; the priesthood was recruited from Spanish and Indian alike; the *hacendado* would confess and take the last sacraments from the son of one of his peons; it was from this fundamental identity that a healthy state might have evolved. That it did not do so is indisputable; so is the fact that those who, in a hundred years, have brought the country to her present pitiable state, were, without exception, enemies of her religion. The lay organisations believe that it is only through the Church that Mexico can recover health and unity. But they do not think this can be done merely by re-establishing the hierarchy and restoring the churches. They do not want a Catholic government of the kind of the Emperor Maximilian, who posed as a Christian prince, while personally breaking the Church's laws and doubting her teaching. They have not, in fact, any particular views on the kind of government they want, believing that a good people will evolve its own political organisation. They are at an earlier stage than that of preparing

[1] *A Visit to Mexico*, 1853.

political programmes; they seek to restore the people to a state of faith without which no political programme has any value.

It is a huge and simple ambition in comparison with the slick new world proclaimed by their enemies, but they are setting about it methodically and devotedly. One could spend all one's time in Mexico among Mexicans and know nothing about it. But it is there and the men and women I met who were engaged upon it were the only genuinely happy and hopeful people I met in Mexico.

CHAPTER 8

INDEPENDENCE

1

SEPTEMBER 16TH IS Independence Day in Mexico. On that day in 1810, Hidalgo, an elderly priest who had for some time attracted the suspicions of the authorities by his neglect of his clerical duties and by his political interests, forestalled arrest by proclaiming to his parishioners at Dolores a 'new dispensation' and summoning the Indians to recover from 'the hated Spaniards' their stolen lands. His proclamation is called the *Grito*, or shout, of Dolores. There is evidence that Hidalgo had few religious convictions, but he used his position as priest to give the revolt the air of a crusade. The Madonna of Guadalupe was used as his standard. He became temporarily master of his district, opened the gaols, and soon found himself at the head of a disorderly army of 80,000, armed with agricultural implements, who overran the countryside looting and murdering. At Guantajuato, in two massacres, they killed about 500. The Indians had brought their women with them to carry the loot, but as they deserted others took their places. They overcame one body of troops and advanced on Guadalajara with 100,000 men and 95 pieces of artillery. At the Bridge of Calderon they met 6,000 trained soldiers and were routed. Hidalgo was caught while attempting to escape towards the United States and executed, leaving behind him a written statement of his repentance. His rebellion lasted less than a year. It is not an incident which many nations would look back to with particular pride; it has nevertheless captivated the Mexican imagination; its anniversary is a public holiday and, on its eve, it has become the practice for the President of the Republic to appear on a balcony of the Palace and repeat Hidalgo's *Grito*.

We were fortunate enough to obtain tickets of admission to the ceremony. Most of the diplomatic corps were there, the leading officials civil and military, and a large assembly representative of all degrees of Mexicans. Our sponsor, a member of the former governing class, suffered a little from social embarrassment which was shared by the acquaintances he met. 'Why, what are *you* doing here?' 'My English friends wished to see it. But what are *you* doing?' Each made some excuse or other.

The whole range of state apartments that give on the Cathedral square were open and crowded. People were shoving one another round the windows trying to get a place as near as possible to the Presidential balcony. The square was full of people, but from the palace one could see very little, for we were blinded by the flood-lights that played full on us. Fireworks went off spasmodically in the darkness, rockets, squibs and now and then a set-piece; a large portrait in coloured fire revolved and was consumed. Mickey Mouse flamed up. There was more or less continual cheering, which grew louder when the President appeared – and drowned his utterance of the *Grito*. Then he came back into the room and it was over. I reflected on the divorce that flood-lighting makes be-tween public men and their audience; we think of them gazing down on a mass of eager faces; all they see is a blaze of electric light and a microphone; they might be speaking to the sea from the promen-ade deck of a liner.

For the first time I saw the President at close quarters; he is certainly a supremely national figure, squat and sturdy and clumsy, with a high narrow head and that peculiar mirthlessness that char-acterises the Mexican Indian. People were crowding round him now shaking hands; he was embracing the men with the awkward, national hug; they were all about his height and weight and build; he seemed to be embracing a succession of relatives at a rather gloomy family gathering.

There had been a presentation of some sort; a relic of one of the revolutionary heroes, the handkerchief, I think, which bound the eyes of Morelos when he was executed. It was in a frame and the photographers were trying to get a picture of him and it together. It is not easy to make a satisfactory picture of a little man with a heavy frame, particularly when he is surrounded with people trying to embrace him; at last they got him isolated for a moment, held the relic like a halo behind his head and flashed their lights at him as he stood, stolid and sombre, but not at all ridiculous because he was not attempting to strike any attitude. He just stood; and then went on with the rough, loveless embraces.

It is obviously impertinent to try to judge a man's character from a glimpse of this kind, but I had been talking about him, off and on, to all kinds of people, for weeks, and the impressions I had formed became concrete that evening. There was nothing of the charlatan or the doctrinaire about General Cardenas. Calles is said to have remarked, as he went into exile, 'I never counted on his vanity', but he does not seem to be a vain man in any ordinary sense of the word. People speak of him, and he speaks of himself, as a socialist, but I do not think he is interested in ideas. He is an excellent tactician; he knows his terrain and he never leaves it; he knows how to become powerful in Mexico. He came into authority in a country that had been reduced to anarchy and acute distress by a generation of revolutions. He knew that the avowed aims of the revolutionaries – the policy of the Party – had never been put into practice. He had been brought up with this policy on every lip as the only one which anyone cared to admit to. Accordingly he set out to consummate it. He has encountered difficulties he never foresaw. It sounded so simple; the capitalists and foreigners are rich; the peons are poor; take the possessions of the capitalists and foreigners and distribute them; then everyone will be happy; if the results are disappointing it is because not enough has been distributed; take some more; then more still until no one is hungry. It is a policy naturally intelligible to a general accustomed to the exigencies of commissariat; let the army live on the country. Much cleverer and more knowledgeable people than himself, men like Lombardo Toledano, have told him that this is the way to repair the ravages of his predecessors.

A question that is often asked with particular reference to oil confiscations but with general application, is how can the President save his face if he finds a reversal of policy necessary? The answer, I think, is that face-saving is not a problem of Mexican politics; the question, there, is to keep in power. Mexicans do not expect much of their leaders; they have been disappointed and betrayed too many times. The leader is not answerable to an informed, critical and effective public opinion; his position depends on maintaining support from a balance of forces – mainly the army and the trades unions. There are no hallowed constitutional uses that he need fear to outrage; there is effective rule and anarchy, and the dual altruistic aim of government in seeing that the people do not starve and that the nation remains independent. The change from the system in force in Mexico to that of Germany is a matter of symbols and of discipline. The people have adopted the clenched fist and the hammer and sickle as Hidalgo's mob adopted the Guadalupe; they have fallen into the habit of regarding the failure of a big industry as a victory in the class war. If these victories, fought under communist symbols, are found to be barren of benefits they can effortlessly proclaim a new allegiance; a few executions perhaps would be needed; then the people would go back to work as Nazi socialists and the nation would adopt new protectors. Democracy, for them, has meant wealthy foreigners getting richer with their help. Atrocity stories do not shock them; they are the commonplaces of their own political history. There is a heresy in the Nazi party that is condemned – but rather leniently punished – under the title of National Bolshevism; a combination of the race-myth with the destruction of private property that seems peculiarly apt for importation into Mexico. And the trade routes for its importation are already established.

2

Independence is perhaps the one national achievement that has not lost its glamour for the Mexicans. It has been accompanied by countless disadvantages, many of which have been noted in earlier chapters of this book – the loss of more than half the national territory, the disappearance of learning, the ascendancy of unworthy rulers, a decay in prosperity which has borne most hardly upon the poorest, the waste of whole provinces. Perhaps it is unjust to attribute these entirely to independence. Mexico has certainly proved quite unamenable to representative government; on the other hand Spain itself, in a less degree, was suffering from similar disasters and experiments; nineteenth- and early-twentieth-century Spain was in no condition to govern a distant empire; the disability was increased by the loss of the empire; it has been a vicious circle in which both peoples have suffered.

It was a natural reflection, on Independence Day, to wonder what precisely Mexico was celebrating. There has not been a period in her century of Independence when her rulers have not been subject to effective foreign pressure; at times, as under Maximilian, she has been occupied by foreign troops. At decisive moments in her history, as when Miramon was forced to raise the siege of Vera Cruz, the United States have intervened in favour of a government they hoped would be sympathetic. In the days of Diaz the country enjoyed the kind of international status which comes from the domination of big business. The last ten years, perhaps, have been the time of greatest freedom and they have been years of almost unrelieved failure. But the Mexicans do mean something by Independence which, I think, works out to mean recognisable identity. A foreigner, wherever he comes from, knows the moment he crosses the frontier that he is a foreigner. The place has its own aspect; the people their own habits; it is easy to say that these things might survive political absorption; the observable fact is that they do not; they vanish inexplicably and have to be kept alive by folk societies and tourist agencies. Mexicans cherish their usages and even those who find the régime antagonistic are reluctant to emigrate. They see what, through annexation, has become of California and obstinately prefer their own comparative disorder and desolation. On the other hand it seems to be the trend of industrial history that small units cannot survive. Fifty years ago it was reasonable to think that a system of universal free exchange in currencies and commodities would result in a civilisation in which political divisions would be mainly sentimental; here a king, there a republic; nationalities would become matters of dialect and costume; a universal banking system would provide a *lingua franca*. Marx accepted this contemporary assumption in one set of terms; the idea of the League of Nations is another. At the same time it was pointed out that man's loyalties did not embrace large systems; Scotsmen were patriotic about

Scotland, not about the British Empire. There was a Scottish national movement and a Welsh national movement, to match the Irish; attempts were even made to revive Cornish as a nationality. The less important political frontiers became, the greater was the attraction of a disintegrating loyalty of each district to the traditions in which it had its origin. Separatism of small nationalities depended on the separation being sentimental. A reasonable man of the last generation might well have welcomed and expected the indefinite multiplication of sovereign states in a single, universal financial structure and a machinery for international litigation and conciliation.

In the last ten years, however, the process has changed. Political frontiers have become more important than at any time in history, rival financial structures have developed and ruthless mergers have consequently extinguished the small political units. Central Europe had broken up; it is now riveted together; Spain began to break, Catalans and Basques have been forced into national unity. More remarkable still, as a symptom of this process a new sentimentality has arisen which infects the younger generations of every race and is unintelligible to most men over thirty – crowd-patriotism. Hitherto the instinctive reaction of a self-respecting man to a crowd has been one of revulsion. In a mob people will applaud oratory and themselves shout words which individually each one of them would regard as ridiculous; worse than that, they will commit atrocities from which they will recoil in horror next morning. Of all forms of intoxication that which comes from participation in mob enthusiasm is the one which should bring the bitterest aftermath of shame. It was one of the great arguments in favour of wider dissemination of general knowledge – that the nineteenth-century liberals called education – that it would produce a race of individual thinkers who would be proof against demagogy and hysteria. By all reasonable expectation the discovery of wireless telegraphy should have contributed to this new individualism; a man could listen to his political leaders at his own fireside, uninfected by the emotions of his neighbours; he had ample time to examine the arguments before acting on them. Ten years ago, or less, this would have seemed a sound assumption. Events, however, have proved the reverse. As traditional sources of intoxication have fallen into increasing disrepute, mass hysteria has grown. People find a masochistic relish in being jostled and stifled in a crowd and in surrendering their individual judgements. Instead of diversity of opinion, they prefer rival orthodoxies. 'How does so-and-so stand, Left or Right?' 'Well, it's hard to say exactly.' 'Ah, sitting on the fence. No contemporary significance.' They love a crisis because a sense of universal danger, real or imagined, draws them closer to the mob. In a world where such influences are dominant, what chance does a country like Mexico have of retaining its independence?

It is not a purely American problem. The outcome of the Spanish war is vital to it. It may affect it directly in more than one way. First, there is the possibility of a large influx of population from the defeated side, who at the time of writing are corralled in France and towards whom cordial if somewhat noncommittal sentiments have been expressed. From the beginning of the Spanish war the Mexican governing party expressed the belief that the Spanish republicans were fighting the battle which they themselves had already won. Their contributions to the republican side were not extensive; they sent some obsolete armaments which were sunk in transit and they received a number of unhappy Basque children – whom one General advised shooting – who are now interned in the State of Morelos in circumstances which are said to be rather similar to those of the legionaries now in France. There were some Mexicans on both sides in the Spanish war, more I believe, on Franco's than the republic's. The responsibility of finding a refuge for the republican army is one which all parties are trying to impose upon one another. When those who fought for local – Catalan or Basque – patriotism, those who were prepared to compromise on their economic doctrines and those who merely found themselves geographically in republican territory and were recruited for that side, have been eliminated, there will remain great numbers of stateless men – Italian and central European communists, intransigent Spanish communists and anarchists and the thousands of criminals who, at the outbreak of the revolution, were liberated from prison and armed – for whom a home must be found. It appears that something like 50,000 men will come into this category. An attempt will certainly be made by the other nations to settle them in Mexico and it is difficult to see on what grounds the present Government can refuse to take them. Their arrival could only mean a vast increase of the anarchical element which might drive the army into revolt. A successful military usurpation would almost certainly be followed by the adherence of Mexico to the German trade group that is being busily built up in Latin America. This is far from being an imaginary danger; it has been little exposed in England except in the socialist press, but it is a development which is causing genuine alarm in Washington. It is to counter this danger, not to preserve European frontiers, that the U.S. armaments programme is directed. There are already large colonies of Germans in various parts of South America, in particular on the Brazil–Argentine border; German and Italian business firms – which under the Nazi system mean the State – control important industries all over the continent; the air lines are predominantly German, with control of the landing-grounds; the steel industry in Chile and the port of Malbrego in Peru are largely German. Italians are training the Bolivian army and the Lima police force; in the South of Peru, in the Chichama valley, Japanese troops protect extensive Japanese sugar properties. British and American interests are still predominant but every German settled constitutes a Nazi unit under the direction of party headquarters; there is a wireless service and a chain of newspapers controlled by Germany and devoted to Nazi propaganda; in certain Brazilian districts the government is virtually in the hands of the German Nazi leader. The competition everywhere is of a totally different order from that of rival British and American firms. At present German penetration in Mexico is mainly confined to the Guatemala border where German planters have imported large quantities of arms and maintain a private defence force. A movement to confiscate these properties might be an international event of the gravest consequences. Nazi negotiations to secure the expropriated oil fields are open and, at the time of writing, still liable to success. It is far from fantastic to believe that in the event of political conditions in Mexico being propitious, Germany is prepared to intervene with vast, ready-made plans for taking control. It must be observed in this connection that the United

States Government will no longer be embarrassed by their radical supporters from taking action.

3

There is another way in which the outcome of the Spanish war may affect Mexico; the re-emergence of Spain as a power with imperial memories. People are now prophesying the disappearance of Spain from international politics; she has, it is thought, internal problems of reorganisation which will keep her employed for a generation, problems for whose solution she will need the help, and consequently the influence, of the individualistic states. She is seen now with her country laid waste and her people divided; her weakness is assured.

But Germany has shown, as revolutionary France showed before, that reconstruction can be accompanied by expansion; that there is no better way of solving the problem of a divided people than in uniting them in a series of dangerous national experiments. In 1920 it would have seemed ridiculous to foretell that in fifteen years Italy was going to defy England and France on an African-Mediterranean issue and do so successfully. War does not always generate war-weariness; it generates, also, a taste for fighting; victory generates victory; there is a centrifugal force which renders further expansion necessary to protect the gains already won. This is not necessarily so, but it is often so in history.

Franco's soldiers have fought under the inspiration of their past; they saw their country disintegrating, as their colonies had done, into a group of republics run by men whose policies were derived from abroad and were antagonistic to national tradition. They fought to prevent Spain becoming like Central America. But to re-establish Spain and make it a single people is, to many Spaniards, only the beginning not the end of a national renaissance.

In 1934 Ramiro de Maeztu published a work called *Defensa de la Hispanidad* – 'the Defence of Spanishness', the Essence of Spain; it was written in the darkest days of the Republic and it expressed defiance of the alien ideas that were permeating the government. It embodies the aspirations of the Phalangist Party. A third edition was issued last year in Valladolid. It has added to it, in this edition, a map of the empire of Philip II. The significance of this, and its obvious affinity with the marble maps of the Roman Empire which Musso-lini has erected in Rome, need no comment. If those maps in Rome have proved an inspiration to the Italian people, relating as they do to a period two thousand years earlier, to the achievements of a people who bore different names, professed a different religion, spoke a rather different tongue and were genealogically of rather uncertain connection with the present occupants of the city, how much more must the dominions of Philip mean to the Spaniard, conquered by the men whose direct descendants are fighting by their side and bearing the titles they won in battles less than four centuries ago; men who are as real and present to them as Shake-speare and Sir Philip Sidney and Elizabeth are to the modern Englishman, who spoke the same language and worshipped the same God in precisely the same forms as they do today.

Hispanidad has been caught up outside Spain in South and Central America, where for a hundred years 'Spanishness' has been subjected to insult and persecution. It is being taken up as the antithesis not only of communist rule but in the words of Cardinal Goma against 'Monroeism, Statism, Protestantism, So-cialism and simple mercantilism'. *Hispanidad* is in the heart of every South American who has been treated as a dago. Italians grew impatient of being treated as picturesque and indolent guitar players, and are now reviled as swash-bucklers. Spanish-Americans have the still less amiable reputation of gigolos. Perhaps they will surprise the world. They are the heirs of those little companies who sank their transports and set out in steel cuirasses through tropical jungle, into lands not even known in legend, to conquer an empire. Much can be said against the Conquistadores for their cruelty and avarice, nothing against their courage and resource. *Hispanidad* represents the view that the Spaniards having driven the Moors out of Europe and having discovered and captured the new world, were betrayed by politicians and driven into temporary obscurity from which it is their birthright and destiny to arise. It will be seen that it has close affinities with the German race-myth. At present, since its opponents have been, in the main, atheists it has been strongly Christian in sentiment, but Christianity and the race-myth cannot long work together.

Until a year or two ago the feeling of *Hispanidad* was dormant in most Spanish-Mexicans because economic security pre-disposed them to acquiesce in their humbled position. Race-myth can only flourish under a sense of persecution; now that they have been dispossessed the emotion has a new face.

This sentiment is there, and growing. I heard it, in one form or another, from many Spanish-Mexicans. When, however, one comes to translate it into real politics the difficulties are enormous. There are only a few thousand native whites in Mexico; perhaps they will shortly be swamped by an immigration of communists from Spain; in any case what can the whites do? Their movement, if it took the form of a caste restoration, could not hope for success. But supposing, which is not inconceivable in the light of the past decade, that Spain emerges once more as a world power and supposing she declares the whites in South America as her special concern, and supposing, as is already to some extent the case, that the Germans seek to overturn the Monroe scheme of American balance ... It is all in the air, and conjectural, but these possibilities should be borne in mind as possibilities.

Another doubt occurs; a mere pencilled query in the margin of current history. Was the *Plumed Serpent* as fantastic as it appeared when we first read it? The Nazis have been able to stimulate a cult of pre-Christian deities; suppose there were a similar revival, of the kind Lawrence predicted, among the mestizos and the Indians. They are a devotional and superstitious people. When people of their kind are deprived for long of their priesthood and their sacraments, all manner of curious beliefs and practices spring up. Mr Graham Greene reports a peculiar oracle in a tea caddy that is widely revered in the Godless State of Chiapas. The Mexicans cannot long get on without an object of worship. Suppose that *Hispanidad* beyond the Atlantic takes on a savage aspect, as European exports often do, there might be an anti-toxin of genuine paganism thrown out in the deceased body.

This again is purely conjectural. The fascination of Mexico lies in the stimulus it gives to the imagination. Anything may happen there;

almost everything has happened there; it has seen every extreme of human nature, good, bad and ridiculous. It has, in a way, the position towards Europe that Africa had to the Romans; a source of novelty... 'always something new out of Africa'... but also a distorting mirror in which objects are reflected in perverse and threatening forms. The Romans sent their great men to Africa; they went to seed and became despots and voluptuaries; they sent their ideas and the Africans turned them into enigmas and paradoxes; the precise statements of Roman law and faith became equivocal in the African mirage; and when the barbarians came, Africa was the first to go; her canals silted up, her buildings fell, the sand swept in from the desert over her fields.

POSTSCRIPT

THE OBJECT AND THE LESSON

1

WE ARE JUSTLY suspicious of people who see the world in terms of the single problem in which they have a personal interest and specialised knowledge. We saw too many of them in the post-Versailles period, people who espoused the cause of neglected minorities or became obsessed by cartographical slips. Their foibles seemed innocent enough, but the result of them has been a series of incongruous alliances which has aggravated every political situation. Thus Catholic anti-semites in France have found themselves defying the Pope and pleading the cause of semitic Arabs against Christian rule, liberal Parliamentarians found themselves identifying the autocratic-imperialist rule of the Amharas with the cause of Democracy, champions of Basque nationalism were allied with international communism. Such are the confusions that arise through a piecemeal view of politics. At the beginning of this book I suggested that the present condition of Mexico had a world wide significance. In subsequent chapters I have tried to sketch the conditions. So what? Why should any ordinary American, still less a European, be interested?

First there is Mexico's geographical position, lying across the continent of North America separating the United States from the Panama Canal and sharing with her an immense, arbitrarily defined frontier which has been the scene, on both sides of it, of a long succession of bloody outrages. Internal disorder in Mexico has always constituted, and will always constitute, a lively physical danger to the United States citizens living near the border. Hundreds of men are still living who followed Villa in his raids into the United States.

913

Secondly there is her financial position. She bears debts of the New and Old World which she will never be able to pay. She is feverishly augmenting them by confiscations. She has great mineral wealth, notably in petroleum, for which the world has a use and which it *will* use one way or another.

Thirdly there is her political condition. For a generation there has been anarchy which has made it clear to herself and to outside observers that she has not the aptitude for the particular kind of individualist representative government which, it was assumed, would afford an eventual solution to her troubles. To President Wilson her only problem was to elect good men; at his time there seemed only two kinds of government, one of which was discredited in 1918; there was democracy, as it was understood in France, England and the United States – government by rich men competing against one another for popular favour – and hereditary monarchy. Since then two forms of proletarian rule have appeared, Nazism and Communism. Mexico is at present enjoying an uneasy compromise between the two. Her adoption of either, or the outbreak of a civil war between them, would be an acute embarrassment to the United States.

Nor does the danger remain local. The Monroe doctrine is being challenged by Germany all over South America. Its peaceful acceptance in the first place by Europe was due to two main considerations. Communications across the Atlantic made a campaign there intolerably expensive and precarious, and, at the end of the last century, Europe was too busy parcelling up Africa to think about South and Central America. Since then an American army has fought in France. South America has become accessible as a battleground while at every point the German–Japanese alliance threatens vital American interests. An anti-Cardenas coup, which his policy increasingly provokes, might well result in Mexico joining the anti-Comintern Pact. She is exactly the kind of country where Nazi methods of government and industrial organisation might be expected to bring substantial results. Germany and Japan know this; so do the United States; so do a few Mexicans.

It is in small countries, not in large ones, that world wars start; particularly in heterogeneous states like Mexico.

But, the reader may object, when there are so many causes for alarm, everywhere, what is the good of multiplying them with purely hypothetical dangers? Because the ordinary news services of paper and wireless bulletins have not the time to keep the public informed of anything beyond day-to-day news. When a crisis is announced we hastily turn to our atlases and look out the new danger spot. We feel that these sudden explosions of international enmity, first in one part of the world, then another, are as wantonly strewn about the map as the bombs of the I.R.A. We have not the time to watch them as historical events in a series of cause and effect. If we have not heard of the problem before, we see it as unimportant; the result of some purely irresponsible and malicious agency. The truth is that, at this moment, when the papers are full of other things, Mexico is as dangerous to us as any part of the world.

2

And secondly, there is the simple cautionary tale of the origin and consequences of Mexico's decadence. Every state has something to learn from that. We were most of us brought up on the historical theory of recurrent waves of civilisation which lasted a few centuries, built massive cities and tombs and were literally buried in the sands; an ebbing and flowing tide, city-desert, city-desert, to which, presumably, our own culture would one day be subject, but at a date so distant that it need no more be considered in practical calculation than the Last Judgment. We were educated in the assumption that things would not only remain satisfactory without our effort but would with the very minimum of exertion on our part become unrecognisably better. The elimination of physical pain and privation was assumed not only by buoyant characters like Mr H. G. Wells but by Mr Aldous Huxley, who limited his apprehensions to pointing out that a life without pain and privation might be compensatingly dreary. Even at the time of writing when tempers are gloomier, the air is one of nervous vexation that progress should be checked by malicious intervention; progress is still regarded as normal, decay as abnormal. The history of Mexico runs clean against these assumptions. We see in it the story of a people whom no great external disaster has overwhelmed. Things have gone wrong with them, as they went right with us, as though by a natural process. There is no distress of theirs to which we might not be equally subject.

Some try to comfort themselves by supposing that the difference of races put Mexico at an initial disadvantage, but, in fact, it is difficult to find any stage at which this was decisive. The white Spaniards interbred freely with the Indians and the prestige and advantages attaching to white blood were little, if at all, more than those attaching to noble and gentle blood in contemporary Europe. As purely heraldic standards of eminence began to decline in Europe, so did those of racial purity in Spanish America. For the last hundred years Mexican leaders of all opinions have been white, Indian and mixed without distinction. Americans and British who see the colour question as vital to Mexico are arguing in terms of their own country and colonies.

Nor has there been any lack of what are generally spoken of as 'enlightened ideas'. Almost every unhappy figure, from Iturbide to Cardenas, who has appeared as a leader of the country, has spoken in the phrases of contemporary advanced thought. The country has known, in form at least, Napoleonic-masonic monarchy, liberal-representative democracy, German-enlightened-constitutional monarchy, international-individualist-capitalism, socialism, dictatorship of the proletariat, and, it seems probable, will shortly develop a species of Hitlerism. There is no question of Mexico decaying, as have other civilisations, by reason of a rigid system that has proved itself inadequate to changing needs. Every marked step in her decline, in fact, has corresponded with an experiment towards 'the Left'.

The reasons for her decline have been primarily moral; the majority of her rulers have not been men of good will and their aims have been purely material; if one starts by assuming that the only real good of which man is capable is the enjoyment of consumable goods – and that has been the assumption of the 'Left' for a hundred years – it is a very easy step – logically an inevitable step – to accumulate the goods exclusively for oneself. Altruism does not flourish long without religion. The rulers of

Mexico have almost all started by denying the primary hypothesis of just government.

Secondly, in the political sphere, there has been no true conservatism in Mexico. There have been rival politicians appealing to the interests of rival groups.

A conservative is not merely an obstructionist who wishes to resist the introduction of novelties; nor is he, as was assumed by most nineteenth-century parliamentarians, a brake to frivolous experiment. He has positive work to do, whose value is particularly emphasised by the plight of Mexico. Civilisation has no force of its own beyond what is given it from within. It is under constant assault and it takes most of the energies of civilised man to keep going at all. There are criminal ideas and a criminal class in every nation and the first action of every revolution, figuratively and literally, is to open the prisons. Barbarism is never finally defeated; given propitious circumstances, men and women who seem quite orderly, will commit every conceivable atrocity. The danger does not come merely from habitual hooligans; we are all potential recruits for anarchy. Unremitting effort is needed to keep men living together at peace; there is only a margin of energy left over for experiment however beneficent. Once the prisons of the mind have been opened, the orgy is on. There is no more agreeable position than that of dissident from a stable society. Theirs are all the solid advantages of other people's creation and preservation, and all the fun of detecting hypocrisies and inconsistencies. There are times when dissidents are not only enviable but valuable. The work of preserving society is sometimes onerous, sometimes almost effortless. The more elaborate the society, the more vulnerable it is to attack, and the more complete its collapse in case of defeat. At a time like the present it is notably precarious. If it falls we shall see not merely the dissolution of a few joint-stock corporations, but of the spiritual and material achievements of our history. There is nothing, except ourselves, to stop our own countries becoming like Mexico. That is the moral, for us, of her decay.

THE HOLY PLACES

POPULE MEUS QUID FECI TIBI?
AUT IN QUO CONTRISTAVI TE?
RESPONDE MIHI

THE
HOLY PLACES

BY

EVELYN WAUGH

WITH WOOD ENGRAVINGS BY

REYNOLDS STONE

★

To Elizabeth and Frank Pakenham

WORK ABANDONED

MY FIRST VISIT to Jerusalem was at Christmas-tide, 1935. I came from embattled Abyssinia. The League of Nations had virtually come to an end that summer. But at Bethlehem and at Calvary were the pilgrims of the world, united in an older and more steadfast friendship. It seemed a place of peace.

Those who lived in Palestine knew otherwise. The Arab Revolt was even then being planned. That Christmas in fact was the last to be celebrated at Bethlehem in complete tranquillity. But the pilgrim was not to know that. The Zionists had not then thrown off their disguise; they showed themselves to the ingenuous as decent, rather cranky young people, innocently occupied in the cultivation of grape-fruit. Jerusalem had all the air of a city of Christendom reclaimed. The prayers which, seventeen years before, had risen in thanks for General Allenby's superbly modest entrance, were still fresh in the memory. The first Christian government since the fall of the Crusaders' kingdom was the purest and the most benevolent which the land had known since the age of Constantine. Fine buildings were being completed everywhere, ancient ones were being restored and embellished. Among the deeper emotions of the pilgrimage was also a deep pride in being English.

I was of an age then – thirty-two – when, after I had struck lucky with three or four light novels, it did not seem entirely absurd, at any rate to myself, to look about for a suitable 'life's work'; (one learns later that life itself is work enough). So elated was I by the beauties about me that I there and then began vaguely planning a series of books – semi-historic, semi-poetic fiction, I did not quite know what – about the long, intricate, intimate relations between England and the Holy Places. The list of great and strange Britons who from time to time embodied the association – Helena, Richard Lionheart, Stratford Canning, Gordon – would without doubt grow with research. Helena above all first began a ferment in my imagination which lasted for fifteen years. I completed a novel about her which failed in most cases to communicate my enthusiasm. I then devised a short explanation for the B.B.C., who were giving a dramatic version of my story. It is this that is here reprinted.

The first, flushed, calf love of my theme has never completely cooled, though I now know that I shall not pursue it further. One element certainly is dead for ever – the pride of country. We surrendered our mandate to rule the Holy Land for low motives: cowardice, sloth and parsimony. The vision of Allenby marching on foot where the Kaiser had arrogantly ridden, is overlaid now by the sorry spectacle of a large, well found force, barely scratched in battle, decamping before a little gang of gunmen. Palestine is no longer a land where an Englishman can walk with pride. But piety, curiosity and my relish for the idiosyncratic splendour of the place, drew me back. The patronage of the editors of *Life* enabled me to make a long visit last year and the second essay in this book is the report on what I saw, originally written for that magazine. It makes clear, I think, why the life's work I planned will never come to fruit.

E.W.

STINCHCOMBE 1952

ST HELENA EMPRESS

WE ARE ADVISED to meditate on the lives of the saints, but the precept originated in the ages when meditation was a more precise and arduous activity than we are tempted to think it today. Heavy apparatus has been at work in the last hundred years to enervate and stultify the imaginative faculties. First, realistic novels and plays, then the cinema have made the urban mentality increasingly subject to suggestion so that it now lapses effortlessly into a trance-like escape from its condition. It is said that great popularity in fiction and film is only attained by works into which readers and audience can transpose themselves and be vicariously endangered, loved and applauded. This kind of reverie is not meditation, even when its objects are worthy of high devotion. It may do little harm, perhaps even some little good, to fall day-dreaming and play the parts of Sir Thomas More, King Lewis IX or Father Damien. There are evident dangers in identifying ourselves with Saint Francis or Saint John of the Cross. We can invoke the help of the saints and study the workings of God in them, but if we delude ourselves that we are walking in their shoes, seeing through their eyes and thinking with their minds, we lose sight of the one certain course of our salvation. There is only one saint that Bridget Hogan can actually become, Saint Bridget Hogan, and that saint she *must* become, here or in the fires of purgatory, if she is to enter heaven. She cannot slip through in fancy-dress, made up as Joan of Arc.

For this reason it is well to pay particular attention to the saints about whom our information is incomplete. There are names in the calendar about which we know nothing at all except those names, and them sometimes in a form that would puzzle their contemporaries. There are others about whom, humanly speaking, we know almost everything, who have left us a conspectus of their minds in their own writings, who were accompanied through life by pious biographers recording every movement and saying, who were conspicuous in the history of their times so that we can see them from all sides as they impressed friends and opponents. And mid-way between these two groups are the saints who are remembered for a single act.

To this class Helena eminently belongs. In extreme old age, as Empress Dowager, she made a journey into one part of her son's immense dominions, to Jerusalem. From that journey spring the relics of the True Cross that are venerated everywhere in Christendom. That is what we know; most else is surmise.

Helena was at a time, literally, the most important woman in the world, yet we know next to nothing about her. Two places claim to be her birthplace: Colchester in England and Drepanum, a seaside resort, now quite vanished, in Turkey. The evidence for neither is so strong that Englishman or Turk need abandon his pretension. She was probably of modest rank, not servile, not illustrious. Constantius married her early in his rise to power and abandoned her later for a royal match. She may have been brought up at one of the post-stables on an Imperial trunk road and have there attracted Constantius's attention on one of his official journeys. Or she may, conceivably, have been what legend makes her, the daughter of a British Chief. She bore one son, Constantine the Great, probably at Nish in Serbia. After her divorce she settled at Trier (Treves) where the Cathedral probably stands on the foundations of her palace. Almost certainly it was there that she became Christian. Lactantius, who was tutor to her grandson Crispus, may have helped instruct her. At the very end of her life she suddenly emerged for her great adventure. She died at Constantinople and her body was thereupon or later moved to Rome. Her tomb never became a great centre of pilgrimage. She, herself, seems never to have attracted great personal devotion; but she was a popular saint. Numberless churches are dedicated to her; numberless girls baptised with her name; she appears everywhere in painting, sculpture and mosaic. She has fitted, in a homely and substantial way, into the family life of Christendom.

There is little of heroism or genius in any of this. We can assume that she was devout, chaste, munificent; a thoroughly good woman in an age when palaces were mostly occupied by the wicked; but she lived grandly and comfortably whereas most of the saints in every age have accepted poverty as the condition of their calling. We know of no suffering of hers, physical, spiritual or mental, beyond the normal bereavements, disappointments and infirmities which we all expect to bear. Yet she lived in an age when Christians had often to choose between flight, apostasy or brutal punishment. Where, one may ask, lies her sanctity? Where the particular lesson for us who live in such very different circumstances?

For the world of Constantine, as we catch glimpses of it, is utterly remote from ours. There are certain superficial similarities. Poetry was dead and prose dying. Architecture had lapsed into the horny hands of engineers. Sculpture had fallen so low that in all his empire Constantine could not find a mason capable of decorating his triumphal arch and preferred instead to rob the two-hundred-year-old arch of Trajan. An enormous bureaucracy was virtually sovereign, controlling taxation on the sources of wealth, for the pleasure of city mobs and for the defence of frontiers more and more dangerously pressed by barbarians from the East. The civilised world was obliged to find a new capital. All this seems familiar; but for the event of supreme importance, the victory of Christianity, we can find no counterpart in contemporary history. We cannot by any effort of the imagination share the emotions of Lactantius or Macarius. Helena, more than anyone, stands in the heart of that mystery.

She might claim, like that other, less prudent queen: 'In my end is my beginning.' But for her final, triumphant journey she would have no fame. We should think of her, if at all, as we think of Constantine: someone who neatly made the best of both worlds. The strong purpose of her pilgrimage shed a new and happier light on the long years of uneventful retirement, showing us that it was by an act of will, grounded in patience and humility, that she accepted her position. Or rather, her positions. We do not know in exactly what state Constantius found her. She certainly did not choose him for his hopes of power. Those hopes, indeed, proved her undoing and dismissed her, divorced, into exile. In a court full of intrigue and murder she formed no party, took no steps against her rival, but quietly accepted her disgrace. Constantine rose to power, proclaimed her empress, struck coins in her honour, opened the whole imperial treasury for her use. And she accepted that, too. Only in her religious practices did she maintain her private station, slipping in to Mass at Rome among the crowd, helping with the housework at the convent on Mount Sion. She accepted the fact that God had His own use for her. Others faced the lions in the circus; others lived in caves in the desert. She was to be St Helena Empress, not St Helena Martyr or St Helena Anchorite. She accepted a state of life full of dangers to the soul in which many foundered, and she remained fixed in her purpose until at last it seemed God had no other need of her except to continue to the end, a kind, old lady. Then came her call to a single peculiar act of service, something unattempted before and unrepeatable – the finding of the True Cross.

We have no absolute certainty that she found it. The old sneer, that there was enough 'wood of the cross' to build a ship, though still repeated, has long been nullified. All the splinters and shavings venerated everywhere have been patiently measured and found to comprise a volume far short of a cross. We know that most of these fragments have a plain pedigree back to the early fourth century. But there is no guarantee which would satisfy an antiquary, of the authenticity of Helena's discovery. If she found the True Cross, it was by direct supernatural aid, not by archæological reasoning. That, from the first, was its patent of title. There are certain elements about the surviving relics which are so odd that they seem to preclude the possibility of imposture. The 'Label', for example – the inscription *Jesus of Nazareth, King of the Jews* – now preserved in Santa Croce seems the most unlikely product of a forger's art. And who would have tried to cheat her? Not St Macarius certainly. But it *is* nevertheless possible that Helena was tricked, or that she and her companions mistook casual baulks of timber, builders' waste long buried, for the wood they sought; that the Label, somehow, got added to her treasure later. Even so her enterprise was something life-bringing.

It is not fantastic to claim that her discovery entitles her to a place in the Doctorate of the Church, for she was not merely adding one more stupendous trophy to the hoard of relics which were everywhere being unearthed and enshrined. She was asserting in sensational form a dogma that was in danger of neglect. Power was shifting. In the academies of the Eastern and South-Eastern Mediterranean sharp, sly minds were everywhere looking for phrases and analogies to reconcile the new, blunt creed for which men had died, with the ancient speculations which had beguiled their minds, and with the occult rites which had for generations spiced their logic.

Another phase of existence which select souls enjoyed when the body was shed; a priesthood; a sacramental system, even in certain details of eating, anointing and washing – all these had already a shadowy place in fashionable thought. Everything about the new religion was capable of interpretation, could be refined and diminished; everything except the unreasonable assertion that God became man and died on the Cross; not a myth or an allegory; true God, truly incarnate, tortured to death at a particular moment in time, at a particular geographical place, as a matter of plain historical fact. This was the stumbling-block in Carthage, Alexandria, Ephesus and Athens, and at this all the talents of the time went to work, to reduce, hide and eliminate.

Constantine was no match for them. Schooled on battlefields and in diplomatic conferences, where retreat was often the highest strategy, where truth was a compromise between irreconcilable opposites; busy with all the affairs of State; unused to the technical terms of philosophy; Constantine, not yet baptised, still fuddled perhaps by dreams of Alexander, not quite sure that he was not himself divine, not himself the incarnation of the Supreme Being of whom Jove and Jehovah were alike imperfect emanations; Constantine was quite out of his depth. The situation of the Church was more perilous, though few saw it, than in the days of persecution. And at that crisis suddenly emerged, God-sent from luxurious retirement in the far north, a lonely, resolute old woman with a single concrete, practical task clear before her; to turn the eyes of the world back to the planks of wood on which their salvation hung.

That was Helena's achievement, and for us who, whatever our difficulties, are no longer troubled by those particular philosophic confusions that clouded the fourth century, it has the refreshing quality that we cannot hope to imitate it. The Cross is very plain for us to-day; plainer perhaps than for many centuries. What we can learn from Helena is something about the workings of God; that He wants a different thing from each of us, laborious or easy, conspicuous or quite private, but something which only we can do and for which we were each created.

THE DEFENCE OF
THE HOLY PLACES

ON ONE SIDE a people possessed by implacable resentment, on the
other by limitless ambition; between them a haphazard frontier
determined by the accidents of battle and still, in spite of the truce,
the scene of recurrent acts of atrocity and revenge; on that line and
cut through by it, the most sacred city in the world.

Publicists and politicians have conspired to forget and to make
forgotten this open wound in international honour. On 11th December, 1948, the General Assembly of the United Nations proclaimed
Jerusalem unique and granted it international status under United
Nations control which neither then nor later was made effective.
Now, by a double act of aggression as flagrant as the invasion of
South Korea, the city has become a battle-ground temporarily
divided between two irreconcilable enemies. One voice only is
heard reproaching the nations with their betrayal – the Pope's; but
he speaks as always in terms of generations and centuries. When he
says that internationalisation is the only proper solution of the
problem he does not mean that it is expedient to evict the usurpers
immediately. The great opportunity has been lost. It will come back
one day on the tide of history. Meanwhile the Holy City stands as
a chilly monument to the moral confusion of our rulers.

It was typical of this confusion that even at the time when it
seemed as though the international politicians were ready to protect
Jerusalem, they spoke of it as being 'sacred to three great world
religions' suggesting that the rights and claims of Christian,
Mohammedan and Jew were similar and equal. In fact there are
decisive theological and historical differences. Christianity and
Mohammedanism may both reasonably be called 'world religions'
in that each offers a cosmic system of the relations of all mankind

934

to God. Judaism is the religion of a particular people, a system of rites and social habits which united and distinguished a nation once dispersed, now partly reassembled in a national state. The Temple of Jerusalem was once the sole focus of Jewish worship. There alone a priestly order sacrificed to the national deity. When the Temple was destroyed by Titus in A.D. 70 the Jewish religion was profoundly changed. Since then there has been no priesthood and no sacrifice. In A.D. 363 the Emperor Julian the Apostate ordered the restoration of the Temple and of its worship, but the work was interrupted by a cataclysm which contemporary witnesses accepted as a divine judgment. Since then no responsible Jew has advocated the rebuilding of the Temple. The meat shortage alone would make the ancient sacrifices impossible. The orthodox Jews, who form some eighteen per cent. of the population of Israel, believe that the work can only be undertaken when there is an unmistakable, apocalyptic summons. The ten per cent. of dogmatic atheists, of course, expect no such event. The majority of Zionists are being encouraged to see the fulfilment of the prophecies in the establishment of the State of Israel. For the first time no Jew has access to the Wailing Wall, but it is not in the temper of the new State to lament past glories but instead to exalt present achievements. There is a strong movement to divert the national disposition for mourning into more topical channels. A shrine has been erected under the walls of the old city where the ashes of Jews murdered by the Germans are unceasingly venerated. It is probable that this will take the place of the Wailing Wall in the minds of the next generation.

The Mohammedans were late-comers. Jerusalem had been the sacred city of Christendom for six hundred years before it fell to Omar. He himself entered with all reverence and chivalrously refrained from entering the Holy Sepulchre, an act commemorated in the neighbouring mosque. It is probable that the Prophet passed through Jerusalem on his way to Damascus. It is certain that he picked up a great respect for the place in the garbled versions of Christianity and Judaism which formed the basis of his meditations. At one time he turned towards Jerusalem to pray. But in the end he left his bones in Medina and appointed Mecca as the prime centre of pilgrimage and devotion. Jerusalem comes third to the

Mohammedan and only one spot there is of supreme importance, the rock over which the great Dome stands, reputed to be the altar on which Abraham prepared to sacrifice Isaac; the foundation of the altar is both the Jewish Holy of Holies and the taking-off place of the Prophet's visionary visit to Paradise. It was a Christian church for three hundred years before Omar and again for a century under the Crusaders, but it is now recognised by all as an inalienable Mohammedan possession. It lies on its great platform on the east of the city with access through the Golden Gate to the Kingdom of Jordan. The barrier of its walls makes a clear frontier between it and the rest of the city and when internationalisation comes, it will be easy to separate it from the zone and make it an integral part of the Arab Kingdom.

The rest of the ancient city comprises a dense constellation of Christian Holy Places. This term can be used loosely to include all properties belonging to various Christian bodies – convents, hostels, churches – many of which sprang up in the Holy Land during the last century of Turkish rule; strictly it should mean only those places which were venerated before the Mohammedan invasion as the sites of Christian history. It is to those that the pilgrims flocked, and it was the chief of these that became the subject of the intricate system of *Status Quo* which was elaborated by the *firmans* of successive Sultans, recognised by international treaty and by the British during their thirty years of rule. Of Holy Places in this strict sense there are some forty in the walled city of Jerusalem and on the Mount of Olives; seven in the adjoining village of Bethany and sixteen in and around Bethlehem, which is five miles distant by the old road, now cut by a Jewish salient. All these lie in the *de facto* authority of the Hasha-mite Kingdom of Jordan. In the State of Israel lie the Church of the Dormition and the Cenacle under the walls of the old city, three Holy Places at Ein Karim, one at Emmaus, nine at Nazareth, five on the Sea of Galilee, three at Cana, one at Carmel. The most import-ant of these is Nazareth, which stands in a peculiar position in Israel. Elsewhere the Jews were able to stampede the inhabitants (who now live in destitution, some half million in the wastes of Jordan alone), and hastily fill their homes with Jewish immigrants. But at Nazareth the Arabs, mostly Christians, remained. They now live under restraint, forbidden to travel outside their area or go to work, as they used, in Haifa. Special police passes are required by foreigners to enter the district. The inhabitants are naturally entirely unsympathetic to the State of Israel and would welcome internationalisation.

To move from one part of the Holy Land to the other is almost impossible for a subject of either part. For the foreign pilgrim it is difficult but possible. He must possess duplicate passports, he must be ferried across the line at a prearranged time, normally by the kind offices of his consul; once across there is no return by that route. He must fly out from Amman or drive up to Syria and Lebanon. It may be added that the fictitious rate of exchange makes travel in Israel more costly than anywhere else in the world. That is the trick by which a modern government exacts the dues which were considered intolerably oppressive in the Middle Ages. Indeed the conditions which provoked the First Crusade were scarcely more offensive to the pilgrim than those existing today.

But we should not protest too much. It is in the nature of a pilgrimage to be uncomfortable. Often they are undertaken as penance and early rules for pilgrims enjoin bare feet and uncombed hair as essential features. St Patrick's Purgatory in Ireland is today the only place in the world which maintains the full discipline of the primitive Church (though even there the brush and comb are permitted), and it is thronged with penitents.

The pilgrim's instinct is deep-set in the human heart. It is indeed an affair of the heart rather than of the head. Reason tells us that Christ is as fully present in one church as in another, but we know by experience that some churches have what we most inadequately call an 'atmosphere' in which we pray easily, while others do not. How much more is this true of the spots marked by great events and by the devotion of the saints. Stern moralists of the Middle Ages were constantly exhorting their flocks to stay at home and warning them that the spiritual dangers of the wanderer might quite undo the benefits. But the tide was not to be stayed. It flowed ceaselessly to Compostella and Canterbury and Rome and Cologne and to countless shrines all over the ancient world. As soon as one place was desecrated by Mohammedan and Reformer other places sprang up. In the last hundred years Lourdes and Fatima have taken rank with the great centres of mediæval devotion. Restlessness and mere curiosity no doubt have a part, but motives for human action are inextricably mixed and far above these is the empty human imagination seeking an object for its attention. In this most natural quest the Holy Land has for the Christian a primacy which Rome itself cannot approach.

Nevertheless it is a fact that many visitors are disconcerted by what they see there. Those who come fresh from the towering splendours of Catholic Europe find architecture which is often ramshackle, often meanly modern. Those who come from the light, spacious, plain conventicles of Protestant worship, find murky caves cluttered with shabby ornament and echoing with exotic liturgies. Those whose imaginations have been filled from childhood by bright biblical illustrations and such hymns as Miss Alexander's '*There is a green hill far away*', find a confusing topography in which the Way of the Cross runs through an oriental bazaar. A little girl remarked at Calvary: 'I never knew Our Lord was crucified indoors'; she was expressing an uneasiness that troubles many minds; that troubled General Gordon so much that he was impelled to seek the tomb elsewhere and to find it in a site – archæologically preposterous – which has comforted many bewildered Nordics. 'The Garden Tomb' is what their Sunday School teachers led them to expect, not the Græco-Russian kiosk of 1809 which now sadly crowns the site unearthed by St Macarius in 326.

This confusion of mind was expounded in the English House of Lords when they debated the antiquities of Jerusalem at the end of the mandate. Their Lordships were then comforted by the suggestion that since there was some doubt in some minds about their authenticity, the Holy Places did not greatly matter. Perhaps most Americans and Englishmen who have not studied the matter, have a vague impression that there has been a good deal of conscious imposture. Certainly no one accepts as *de fide* the authenticity of all.

What I suppose is plain to anyone who accepts the truth of the Gospels, is that Galilee and the district in and around Jerusalem are sacred to the incidents of Our Lord's life, death, resurrection and ascension. It is, moreover, certain that the vast majority of the spots venerated today were those identified by a living tradition in the fourth century and have been continuously recognised ever since. Whether this living tradition erred occasionally and precise spots were over-enthusiastically accepted where a rather vague memory survived, we cannot know. Recent excavations – for example those at the Lithostrotos of Pilate's Judgment Hall – have confirmed tradition. We now know that our forefathers were wrong in suppos- ing that the Ecce Homo Arch was the building from which Christ was exposed to the people. We do know, however, that deep below the present Via Dolorosa there does lie the actual path He trod to Calvary. We cannot know whether the Stations are the exact sites of the various incidents. The Holy Places indeed comprise the whole gamut of credibility from the 'Tomb of Adam' – a fantasy, surely; the fruit of ancient prosaic minds seeking a concrete form for the poetic imagery used of the Atonement – to the rock of Calvary which no one but an ill-informed bigot would attempt to discredit. Between these two extremes the other shrines could be arranged in a rough order of probability, but the question is primarily antiquarian rather than religious. Suppose – though there is no particular reason to do so – that the place of John the Baptist's birth were not where we suppose, but a few yards away, in another street, even, of the same village. The devotion of centuries has made the traditional site a Holy Place in fact.

This last may be taken as typical of the minor shrines and of the surprises that await the pilgrim. He has come to Ein Karim to see the home of the Baptist. He finds a handsome modern church in the Spanish style. He is led down a precipitous staircase into a small cave where he is invited to kiss a marble boss. This, he is told, is the birthplace of St John. His guide is a bearded Franciscan. If they have a language in common, and even perhaps if they have not, the pilgrim will be told at length the stories of St Elizabeth and of Zachary. He may be shown some pottery of Herod's time found on the spot and the mosaic remains of two Byzantine chapels. But the Franciscans of the Custody are seldom archæologists and never æsthetes. Their first characteristic is tenacity. They inherited the flag of the Crusades in 1291. When the knights and barons retreated, the friars remained. They have stayed on for more than six hundred years with absolute singleness of purpose, undisturbed by theological and artistic fashions, holding fast to the Gospel and to the stony places where it was enacted. Their struggle has swayed back and forth. They have often been cheated and brutally dispossessed of their property; they have also from time to time received fine benefactions. They have more than once in all their undertakings seen the full revolution of the cycle, decay, destruction, restoration, and have learned to avoid undue attachment to their own transient structures. Indeed they seem positively to relish the demolition of buildings which anywhere else would be patiently preserved; give them the chance to put up something brand new, strong and convenient, and the Franciscans of the Custody jump to it. They have no sentiment except the highest. No association later than the Apostles interests them. There is only one 'period' for them; the years of Our Lord. It is not for us to look askance. They have had small help from art connoisseurs during their age-long, lonely sentry-duty.

But the cave, too, is not what we might have expected. These sacred grottoes are everywhere; here, at Nazareth, at Bethlehem, on the Mount of Olives, as far away as the old Christian quarter beyond the walls of Cairo. The early painters loved to elaborate them and the poetic imagination may leap delightedly from these places to the catacombs, to St Anthony's cell and St Jerome's, and again to Lourdes; but, by prosaic Franciscan lights, it does seem remarkably odd that St Elizabeth should go down to the cellar for her *accouchement*. The explanation, I think, is that she did nothing of the kind. The houses of this district mostly stand over honeycombs of natural and hewn cisterns and store-rooms. These remain when the houses fall or burn. In identifying a site in the fourth century, villagers would say: 'Here, our fathers have told us, John was born.' Nothing is more natural than that a confusion should occur and the cave usurp the history of the former house. We may explain in the same way such objects of veneration as the block of stone from which Our Lord is said to have mounted the ass for his entry into Jerusalem. It is probable that the stone was first put there simply to mark the spot and that later generations made it a participant in the actual drama. Concessions such as these are all that need be made to the sceptic. We may admit, too, that the sites of the Dormition and Our Lady's

Tomb have strong rivals at Ephesus. But when all these small debts to plausibility have been paid in full, the residual wealth of the Holy Land in authentic gilt-edged association is incomparably large. The supreme treasury is, of course, the great Church of the Holy Sepulchre in Jerusalem.

And here, as one might expect, one finds exemplified and accentuated all the peculiarities of the Holy Land. The first impression, as one enters the courtyard, is that one has come inopportunely. The steps by which one approaches are arched over with a structure of steel girders and wood props; the fine, twelfth-century façade and entrance are entirely obscured by scaffolding. Inside, as one's eyes become accustomed to the gloom, one finds that all the arches of choir and rotunda are reinforced with a dense armature of timber, that everywhere a forest of beams and struts spreads between the ancient columns, and that the walls are bound like a clumsily wrapped parcel with a tangle of steel ties. There has been some recent mishap or some defect has suddenly become apparent, the visitor supposes. Work must be in progress; the men are just on holiday. But such is not the case. The disturbance took place in 1927. Grave danger to the whole fabric was apparent seven years later and these girders and baulks of timber are the hasty improvisations of local British engineers, a first-aid treatment while the ecclesiastical authorities were deciding on a plan. In 1942 further dangers were discerned and further temporary measures taken by the same engineers. Now they have gone away; nothing is being done. The dead hand of the old Ottoman *firmans* and the Treaty of Berlin of 1878 renders the ecclesiastical authorities powerless. They are merely waiting for the inevitable collapse, perhaps in their time, perhaps in the time of their successors, when the Christian world will be obliged to turn its attention to its principal shrine.

Meanwhile one wanders backward through history. One notices first the work of the English sappers, next the reconstruction of the Greek builders of 1803; then, if one has an eye for architecture, one sees that all these encumbrances stand in a great Transitional-Norman Cathedral, still almost intact; then one may find tucked away underground all that is left of the original buildings of Constantine and Helena. That great assembly of buildings was

destroyed by the Persians before the Mohammedan invasions, by
Chosroes in 614, who carried off the True Cross. The Emperor
Heraclius was the first true Crusader. Solemnly dedicating his arms,
he invaded Persia eight years later and brought the relic home in
triumph, while the monk Modestus travelled throughout the Empire
raising funds for the rebuilding. The fortunes of the shrine were
inextricably interlocked with the history of that land of earthquake,
invasion and civil riot. Damage, restoration, damage, succeed one
another through the centuries. Certain events are of determining
importance. This destruction by Chosroes and rebuilding by
Modestus and Heraclius is one of them; next, very soon after, the
surrender of the city to the Caliph Omar in 637. His Mohammedan
successors did not emulate his chivalry. In 1009 the Caliph Hakim,
an Egyptian, tried to extirpate Christianity in his dominions. He was
probably insane. He reversed his policy later but not before the
Church of Modestus had been demolished and the Sepulchre itself,
which until then had preserved its original rock-hewn form, had lost
roof and walls so that nothing now remains except the floor and the
slab upon which Our Lord's body lay. Succeeding *edicules* have been
of masonry. It was not until forty years later that the local Christians,
with the help of the Emperor Monomachus, were able to complete
a rebuilding which lacked most of the splendour of its predecessors
and left half the former shrine in ruins. Hakim's persecution shocked
Christendom. It was thought intolerable that the Holy City should
be at the mercy of the caprices of Mohammedan potentates.

The Emperor of the East had become a reduced and localised
power scarcely able to maintain himself at Constantinople, still less
to reconquer Palestine. The crusade was preached in the West. In
1099 a Christian army recaptured Jerusalem and established a Latin
Kingdom there which survived for barely a century. Under this rule
the church was built which stands to-day, enclosing under a single
roof the sites of the Crucifixion and the Resurrection. But meanwhile the Great Schism had occurred. On 16th July, 1054,
the bickerings of two hundred years took violent form in the ex-
communication by the Papal Legates of the Patriarch of
Constantinople in his own cathedral. The Patriarchs of Alexandria,
Antioch and Jerusalem followed him into schism. This was an event

quite different from any of the previous outbreaks of heresy. From time to time in the preceding centuries individuals, representing every aberration of theology, had broken from the Universal Church, taking with them numbers of adherents. Most of these bodies disappeared in a generation unless kept alive by particular racial loyalties. But the separation of four historic orthodox patriarchates, on personal and political grounds chiefly, was a disaster from which Christendom still terribly suffers to-day. It was recognised as something unnatural and deplorable even when tempers were most exacerbated. There were continual attempts at reconciliation. In 1439 at the Council of Florence peace was made, but by that time the Greek clergy had become crassly sectarian and they repudiated their leaders. Nevertheless when Constantinople fell in 1453 St Sophia was still a Catholic church as it had been in its first days. The last Emperor of the East died a Catholic, gallantly fighting on the walls. Congregations all over the Levant remained loyal to Rome and survive prosperously to-day. But, as the whole of Eastern Christendom fell under the Turk, an iron curtain descended between it and the West behind which the great majority of Orthodox Christians was caught at an unpropitious moment. Their schism became the badge of their loyalty. Untouched by humanism, by the stimulating controversy of the fifteenth century, by the great revitalising power of the Counter-Reformation, cut off from the sap of Christian fellowship, the Eastern Churches dried up and hardened.

Thus were born the disputes over the Holy Places which in their turn produced the *Status Quo*. As the Turkish power matured and softened, the administration relied more and more upon the clever subject peoples for its courtiers and civil servants. Persecution alternated with appeasement in the policy towards Greeks, Armenians and Copts. The cheapest form of appeasement is always to pay with the property of others, and throughout the eighteenth century, as the mind of Europe grew less religious and the sovereigns fought for colonies in the New World and Russia gradually emerged as a great Orthodox Christian power, the Sultans granted more and more licences to the Eastern clergy for encroachment on the rights of the Latins, until by 1757 an immensely complex code was evolved defining precisely how many lamps each cult might hang and on how many feet of ground they might worship at each holy place. France had been the recognised protector of the Catholics in the East. At the Revolution France became atheist. At the height of the Napoleonic régime a fire took place in the Church of the Sepulchre. While the West was indifferent and preoccupied, the Greeks acted, swept away the tombs of the Latin Kings and the Latin choir and reconstructed all they could in their own characteristic style. That is the Church we see today. The Treaties of Paris of 1855, and of Berlin in 1878, reaffirmed the *Status Quo* of 1757 as far as concerned the other Holy Places.

The principle of the *Status Quo* was that property belonged to whoever could prove that he had last exercised the right of repairing it. While certain places were subdivided, others were left as common property of the Catholics, Greeks and Armenians. Nothing can be done to common property, which includes the general fabric of the Church of the Holy Sepulchre, without the consent and participation of all. There is thus a complete *impasse* in which the place is visibly falling to pieces. It may be noted in passing that when a small fire recently occurred in the dome, King Abdullah patched it up without consulting anyone and without anyone minding. He also broke with Turkish precedent in appointing, on 5th January, 1951, an official of his own as Curator of the Holy Places. No one seems to know what this official's duties are. He offers no explanation. What is certain is that King Abdullah had not the means to effect the huge repairs that are urgently needed.

In this situation a totally new plan has been produced under the patronage of the Apostle Delegate in Jerusalem. It is one of total demolition and rebuilding. Two Italian architects – Barluzzi and Marangoni – have produced a pretty album of their designs – *Il Santo Sepolchro di Gerusalemme: Splendori – Miserie – Speranze* – at the Institute of Art at Bergamo; in which is envisaged a scheme of town clearance, demanding a whole quarter of the densely populated city, demolishing two mosques including the historic site of Omar's prayer, and the ancient convents that now cluster round the basilica, and planting in the centre of this space a huge brand-new edifice in the places where Calvary and the Sepulchre stand, as they did under

Constantine, as separate buildings in an open court. Centred in this court would stand the churches of all the rites which have claims in the existing building and also the Anglican Church which does not.

No one, I think, regards this undertaking as practicable; few as desirable. Apart from any æsthetic objection – and there are many – there is the supreme objection that this immense erection would be in effect a monument to the divisions of the Church. These divisions are so much a part of the tradition and daily lives of the Franciscans of the Custody that it is small wonder if they have come to accept them as normal and permanent. But there is all the difference between a quarrelsome family who still share one home and jostle one another on the stairs, and one which has coldly split up into separate, inaccessible households. The extreme animosities of the past have subsided, but it is not impossible that they should break out anew. The clergy of the different rites treat one another with courtesy, but they are constantly vigilant; no quarrels have recently occurred because the *Status Quo* has been rigidly observed. Any infringement of it would provide immediate protest and, perhaps, retaliation. It is, of course, all very unseemly and unedifying. But so also is the division of the Church. Under the proposed reconstruction there will be no fear of friction. It would be a great deal more convenient for everyone concerned. But ease would have been bought by the formal perpetuation of a disgrace.

What is needed, surely, is not the grandiose Franciscan plan, but a patient restoration of the buildings as they stood in 1800? This, indeed, would be no small task, but no greater than the restoration of Rheims Cathedral after the First World War and of far wider significance. If the funds and the direction came from some source quite unconnected with any of the rival religious bodies, their consent would doubtless be obtainable. It is a task for which the United Nations are eminently suited. They owe a heavy debt to the Holy City. This might form a token payment.

But even in its decrepit and defaced condition the great church is an inspiration for the whole history of Christendom and is there to be read by those who trouble to study it. Even the superstitions of early science have their monument there in the stone called 'the centre of the earth'. Every degree of pilgrim and tourist pass and repass all day long, with every degree of piety and insolence, but at night the place really comes to life.

There is only one door now. It shuts at sundown. Just before that hour an Arab soldier clears the darkening aisles of the last penitents and sight-seers. The Arab doorkeeper, whose family have held the office since the time of Suleiman the Magnificent – since Omar some will tell you – climbs a ladder and turns the locks from outside, passes the ladder in through a square trap which a priest locks from his side. The windows fade and disappear, the roof is lost. There is no light except from the oil lamps which glow on Calvary, before the Sepulchre and over the Stone of Unction. Absolute silence falls. The air becomes close and chilly, with the faintest smell of oil and candle wax and incense. The place seems quite empty. But, in fact, there are thirty or more sleeping men tucked away out of sight in various dens and galleries, like bats in a sunless cave. Nothing happens for hours. Some of the oil lamps begin to burn out. You can sit on the doorman's divan and think yourself at the bottom of the sea.

And then, a little before eleven o'clock, lights begin to appear and move in unsuspected apertures and galleries. There is a snuffling and shuffling and from their various lairs – the Greek from a balcony above the rock of Calvary, the Franciscan from a tunnel in the wall beyond the Latin Chapel, the Armenian down an iron fire-escape above the spot of the Stabat Mater – three bearded sacristans appear and begin filling and trimming the lamps. Soon after this there is a sound of door-knocking, knuckles, wooden hammers, a little electric bell somewhere; a yawning, and muttering and coughing and rustling.

At 11.30 something like a jungle war-drum starts up. That is the Greeks. Then a great irregular banging together of planks. That is the Armenians. Then two muted thurifers appear and proceed by opposite routes round the whole building, censing every altar with a chinking of brass and clouds of aromatic smoke. Then here and there raw little electric bulbs flash on. The monks and friars assemble in their choirs and just before midnight the night offices start, the severe monotone of the Latins contrasting with the exuberant gaiety of the Armenians who are out of sight, up their iron staircase in their own bright vault, but whose music sounds like a distant village festival of folk-dancing and peasant ballads.

The Latin Office is the most brief. The friars file out into their tunnels. The Greeks and Armenians sing on. And then something new, unexpected and quite delicious stirs the drowsy senses – the sweet, unmistakable smell of new baked bread. It is the Easterns cooking the Hosts for their Masses. Mass is said daily in the tomb by the three rites. On some days the Copts celebrate at an altar built against the outer wall. On Sunday morning the Syrians, too, have their service. And daily on the roof, in the sad little African hovels to which they were driven by the rich Armenians, the Monophysite Abyssinians perform their own ancient liturgy.

The Greeks' Mass is the first, followed by the Armenian. There is room only for priest and server in the inner chamber of the Sepulchre. Two or three more kneel in the outer room. The remainder of the choir stand outside. While the Armenian Mass is going on the Catholics may be heard not far off in their chapel intoning another office. By 3.30 the *edicule* is clear of the Armenians and the Franciscan sacristan busies himself with a portable altar and the Mass furniture of the West. At four o'clock the door is opened. A servant of the Juded family brings the key, which for convenience he now hangs in the Greek convent on the north of the courtyard, and hands it to the representative of the Musedi family. A monk opens the trap-door and pushes out the ladder. With a squeak and a clang the locks are turned and the door swings open. The monks and the gate-keepers salaam and the gate-keepers shuffle back to bed.

At 4.30 the Catholic Mass is said in the Sepulchre, followed by others through all the early hours of the morning on Calvary, in the Chapel of the Franks, and in the Latin Chapel. And at dawn as one steps out into the courtyard after one's vigil one is met by the cry of the *muezzin* from the minaret of Omar's prayer, proclaiming that there is no God but Allah and Mohammed is his Prophet.

One has been in the core of one's religion. It is all there, with all its human faults and its superhuman triumphs, and one fully realises, perhaps for the first time, that Christianity did not strike its first root at Rome or Canterbury or Geneva or Maynooth, but here in the Levant where everything is inextricably mixed and nothing is

assimilated. In the Levant there works an alchemy the very reverse of the American melting-pot. Different races and creeds jostle one another for centuries and their diversity becomes only the more accentuated. Our Lord was born into a fiercely divided civilisation and so it has remained. But our hope must always be for unity, and as long as the Church of the Sepulchre remains a single building, however subdivided, it forms a memorial to that essential hope.

A TOURIST IN AFRICA

CONTENTS

1. DEPARTURE

Childermas in England – Mrs Stitch in Genoa

28th December 1958. On the third day after Christmas we commemorate the massacre of the Holy Innocents. Few candid fathers, I suppose, can regard that central figure of slate in Breughel's painting in Antwerp without being touched by sympathy. After the holly and sticky sweetmeats, cold steel.

I declare smugly that at 55 I am at the time of life when I have to winter abroad, but in truth I reached that age thirty years ago. Even when I thought I enjoyed fox-hunting my enthusiasm waned by Christmas. I have endured few English Februaries since I became self-supporting. February 1940 found me a probationary temporary second-lieutenant in an asbestos chalet on the English Channel; never again, I resolved. February 1941 was far from luxurious, but it was warm, in a densely crowded troopship steaming through the tropics on the great detour to Egypt; but in 1942 I was in a Nissen hut on a Scottish moor; never again. In those days the politicians had a lot to say about Freedom. They met – few will now recall – and guaranteed everyone Freedom from Fear. Did they also guarantee Freedom from Religion? Something of the sort, I think. All I asked in that horrible camp was freedom to travel. That, I should like to claim, is what I fought for, but I did far too little actual fighting to make that boast effective.

Then when the war was over the politicians did what they could to keep us all wired in; but I escaped regularly. Nowadays, I suppose, if such things were still required, I could get a doctor to certify that I needed to go abroad for my health. I begin to stiffen early in December. Stooping, turning, kneeling, climbing in and out of modern motor cars, which are constructed solely for contortionists, become increasingly painful. By Christmas I look out on the bare trees with something near melancholia.

Childermas is the Sabbat of *cafard*. I have just looked up this popular word in the dictionary and have learned, as no doubt the reader already knows, that its roots come from 'hypocrisy' and 'cant'. It is therefore peculiarly apt for the emotions with which the father of a family performs the jollities of Christmastide. It is at Childermas, as a rule, that I begin to make plans for my escape, for, oddly enough, this regularly recurrent fit of claustrophobia always takes me by surprise as, I am told, the pains of childbirth often surprise mothers. Writing now in high summer (for this is not the diary as I kept it. I am trying to make a book from the notes I took abroad), it seems hardly conceivable that I shall ever want to leave my agreeable house and family. But I *shall*, next Childermas, and no doubt I shall once more find myself with no plans made.

It is not so easy as it was thirty years ago to find a retreat. Tourism and politics have laid waste everywhere. Nor is 55 the best age for travel; too old for the jungle, too young for the beaches, one must seek refreshment in the spectacle of other people at work, leading lives quite different from one's own. There are few more fatiguing experiences than to mingle with the holiday-makers of the Jamaican North Shore, all older, fatter, richer, idler and more ugly than oneself. India is full of splendours that must be seen now or perhaps never, but can a man of 55 long endure a régime where wine is prohibited?

I have worked for eighteen months on the biography of a remarkable but rather low-spirited friend many years older than myself. I have read nothing and met no one except to further my work. Old letters, old dons, old clergymen – charming companions, but a lowering diet when prolonged.

Last year I went to Central Africa, but saw nothing. I flew there and back and spent a month in purely English circumstances cross-examining authorities on the book I was writing. Africa again without preoccupations with eyes reopened to the exotic. That's the ticket.

January 1959. Ticket? Not altogether easy. This is the season when the ships are fullest. The wise man sails before Christmas. A visit to the Union Castle office in London. They are able to offer a cabin in *Rhodesia Castle* at the end of the month. She is a one-class ship sailing on the eastward route through the Suez Canal, stopping at several places I knew in other days and will gladly revisit, and reaching Dar-es-Salaam on 20th February. On 27th March their new flag-ship, *Pendennis Castle*, leaves Cape Town on her fast return voyage to England. That leaves me exactly five weeks in which to wander down by land.

I am told I shall need an inoculation against Yellow Fever and that under the new medical organisation this cannot be given by one's own doctor. Instead one must visit a city. In London a nurse was giving, it seemed, some thirty shots an hour at a guinea a time. I purchased my certificate there. In the course of my journey I crossed many frontiers, but no government official ever asked to see it. The only person to show any concern for my health was the ticket clerk at a tiny airfield in Tanganyika. Medical authorities seem to have grown tamer lately. I remember great annoyance at the hands of the captain of a Belgian lake steamer crossing to the Congo in 1931; who sent me ashore under a blazing sun to find a doctor on a golf links who, as the hooter was sounding for departure, certified my immunity from a variety of contagious diseases. As for the nineteenth century, which is popularly supposed to have been so free, readers of Charles Waterton may remember that in 1841 he was shipwrecked on a voyage from Civita Vecchia to Leghorn and with his fellow passengers obliged to transfer to the ship with which they had collided. When they reached Leghorn they were refused permission to land by the quarantine authorities on the grounds that their original bill of health had gone down with their ship. Only the impassioned intervention of Prince Charles Napoleon saved them from twenty days' incarceration. It is wrong to represent bureaucracy as an evil contrived solely by socialists. It is one of the evidences of original sin. The great alluring false promise of the socialists is that the State will wither away.

When I tell people of my movements, they say either: 'Not a very pleasant time to be going. Everything will be very disturbed after the Accra Conference,' or 'A very interesting time to be going.

Everything will be full of life after the Accra Conference.' No one, when one is going to Paris, warns one of the dangers from Algerian terrorists or envies one the excitements of UNESCO. As a defence I pretend to an interest in archæology. 'I want to have a look at the Persian vestiges in the off-shore islands.' I like showy ruins and am moderately knowledgeable about European architecture, but I can't distinguish periods or races in Mohammedan building. I mean to go to some of these 'off-shore islands' (what is an in-shore island?) if I can. I am grateful to them for turning many conversations from the 'colour problem' and African nationalism.

January 27th. A friend in London gave a dinner party to wish me a good journey and kindly assembled people she thought I should like to see. I was put in mind of Swift's observation: 'When we are old our friends find it difficult to please us, and are less concern'd whether we be pleas'd or no.'

An odious and graceless thought; a wintry thought; high time to be off.

January 28th. It is satisfactory to leave for the tropics in bitter, dingy weather. Sometimes I have left in sun and new snow and felt sorry to be off. I am taking the train to Genoa and boarding my ship there. At Dover no one looked at our luggage or passports, but we were none the less herded into the ritual procession round the customs shed. Why can't the train draw up alongside the ship as at Calais? There are lines laid to the quay. The great majority of the passengers carry their own bags and have a long, unnecessary march.

Ticket troubles at Calais. The train comprises miscellaneous sleeping-cars bound for various destinations; only one for Rome and that full. I have to travel in the Simplon-Orient which leaves Paris later than the Rome Express without a dining-car and shall have to change trains in the early morning at Milan. The conductor and guard assure me that they have information that all sleepers are engaged on the Rome Express.

Paris at the cocktail hour. How gaily I used to jump into a taxi and visit the bars while the train crawled round the *ceinture*. Now-adays, hard of hearing and stiff in the joints, I sit glumly in my compartment. At the Gare de Lyon there is an hour in which to try and change to the Rome Express. Clearly a case of 'où est le Cooks homme?'. The wagon-lit office is shut, but a Dickensian figure in the peaked cap of a travel-agency lurks near it. He falls into a hoarse disquisition about a rebate I can get by avoiding Swiss territory, if I get the *chef de train* – 'chef de train mind – conducteur won't do –' to endorse my ticket and send it to the issuing agency. I persuade the Agent that this is not the primary problem. He pads along with me to the platforms. In the hazy evening the station is an ant heap of sleeping-cars scurrying in all directions. My car has disappeared with my luggage. We find an empty berth on the Rome Express, then that car too wanders abruptly away into the darkness while I am talking to the conductor. 'Oh, so you speak French, eh?' says the Agent resentfully as though I had been imposing on his good nature under false pretences. No porters in view – 'Ah porters, now, you don't see many of them these days.' The Agent, who seems as rheumatic as I, limps off to find one. I stay at the Rome Express platform, where my sleeping-car presently returns and is immediately overrun by Indians, men, women and children all beautifully dressed and talking volubly in English. They fill corridor, steps and platform. Five minutes to go and the Agent appears among them with a porter and my baggage. 'What I haven't got, that's your tickets. Conducteur wouldn't hand them over.' He indicates that our transactions are finished. His tip is bigger than he expected (or deserved) and he leaves me with a faint hint of geniality. Precisely at 8 the conductor from my first train comes swimming through the surge of Indians with my tickets. The train moves and suddenly all the Indians start tumbling out of it, leaving one dapper, waving sweetly-scented couple.

I wonder what Cooks-homme's history is. His French sounded very French to me; his English was the kind of cockney one seldom hears nowadays in London. Most of what I said struck him as densely obscure. An English soldier left over from the first World War perhaps, who had married a French girl and settled down with her? A Frenchman who had worked some years in a British colony and picked up the language of his mates? As happier men watch birds, I watch men. They are less attractive but more various.

Man-watching at dinner. The second service is pleasantly unfrequented. A striking figure sits opposite me, hirsute and swarthy; a Syrian revolutionary? an unfrocked Coptic clergyman? He addresses me in English. I take a shot and he admits to being a Sikh who cut his hair and shaved his beard in Detroit. He is now growing them again, but they will not yet have reached a suitable length when he meets his family. How will they take it? I mention the assembly of Indians at the station and surmise they were diplomats. There are no diplomats in Detroit, the Sikh says; everyone works hard there. Then he gives me a detailed account of his sufferings from the avarice of French taxi-drivers. I tell him he will find things worse in Naples, where he is going. He is stopping on the way at Rome. Is that a good place? He knows nothing whatever about it except that it is the capital of Italy. He has never heard of the Cæsars, of the Popes, of Michelangelo or even of Mussolini. He is an engineer and, I suppose, about thirty years old and quite well off.

January 29*th*. Genoa shortly before 8. I have a friend whom I have more than once attempted to portray in fiction under the name of 'Mrs Stitch'. Mrs Stitch was wintering in Rome and I had told her I was coming to Genoa on the remote chance that she might join me. The main reason for my anxiety to get into the Rome Express was that I should be at the hotel at the time I had told her. Just as I finished shaving after my bath she turned up with four hats, six changes of clothes and a list of complicated chores for her friends, for whom she habitually recovers lost property, books tickets and collects peculiar articles of commerce.

Her first business was at the railway station which, for a reason that was never clear to me, was harbouring a coat of unlovely squalor abandoned somewhere by one of her more irresponsible cronies. Without authority or means of identification Mrs Stitch cajoled a series of beaming officials and possessed herself of the sordid garment. 'How different from the French,' Mrs Stitch said, '*they* would never have let me have it.' I sometimes suspect that one of the reasons she gets on so badly with the French is that she speaks their language well. In Italy she has to rely purely on her looks and always gets her way without argument.

Breakfast in the station. The one perennial dissension between Mrs Stitch and me is that I like to eat in marble halls under lofty chandeliers while Mrs Stitch insists on candlelit garrets and cellars. She thinks my preference hopelessly middle-class and tells me I am like Arnold Bennett. Mrs Stitch's greatest difficulty in Italy is that there are singularly few quiet, murky restaurants; the smaller they are, the noisier and the more brilliantly lighted. The railway station at Genoa provided a happy compromise. For luncheon we found what Mrs Stitch wanted at Olivo's on the old quay. At dinner at Pichin in the new quarter the cooking was admirable but the light blinding. On the second day we drove out to a gay little beach restaurant at Nervi. I was never able to get her into the restaurant of our hotel and wistfully caught only an occasional glimpse of its sumptuous Victor-Emanuel trappings. The cooking of Genoa, like its architecture, is mild-flavoured and wholesome.

From this generalisation I exclude the Campo Santo which for the amateur of cemeteries is one of the Wonders of the modern world. We went there at once and emerged after two hours dazed by its preposterous splendours. When the Genoese lost their independence, the energies that had once taken them on piratical hazards into unknown waters, and the remains of their accumulated wealth, were devoted to the private commemoration of their dead.

We are accustomed to the grandiose tombs of monarchs and national heroes. In Genoa for more than a hundred years professional and mercantile families competed in raising purely domestic temples. They stand round two great quadrangles and extend along the terraced hillside beginning with the strong echo of Canova and ending in a whisper of Mestrovic and Epstein. They are of marble and bronze, massively and intricately contrived. Draped and half-draped figures symbolic of mourning and hope stand in unembarrassed intimacy with portrait-sculptures of uncanny realism. There stand the dead in the changing fashions of a century, the men whiskered, frock-coated, bespectacled, the women in bustles and lace shawls and feathered bonnets, every button and bootlace precisely reproduced, and over all has drifted the fine grey dust of a neighbouring quarry. 'He's taken silk all right', said Mrs Stitch before a gowned barrister, and indeed that is precisely the effect of the dust that has settled in the hollows of the polished white marble. All appear to be lined, flesh and clothing alike, in grey shot-silk.

There are *tableaux* almost *vivants* in which marble angels of consolation emerge from bronze gates to whisper to the kneeling bereaved. In one group there is a double illusion; a marble mother lifts her child to kiss the marble bust of his father. In the 1880s the hand of *art nouveau* softens the sharp chiselling. There is nothing built after 1918 to interest the connoisseur. It is as a museum of mid-nineteenth-century bourgeois art in the full, true sense, that the Campo Santo of Genoa stands supreme. If Père la Chaise and the Albert Memorial were obliterated, the loss would be negligible as long as this great repository survives.

Fortunately it was untouched, or apparently so, in the bombardments of the second World War. It was reported in 1944 that the city was 'flat'. Some fine buildings were irreparably lost, but today, apart from an unexploded British naval shell that is gratefully exhibited in the Cathedral, there is little evidence of damage. I remember when Italy declared war on us in 1940, a politician exultantly proclaiming on the wireless that we should soon add notably to ruins for which that country was so justly famous. (It is worth recalling that before the surrender of Rome the English wished to destroy it and were prevented only by our American allies.) He did not take account of the Italians' genius for restoration. They do not, as do those in authority in England, regard the destruction of a good building as a welcome opportunity to erect something really ugly in its place. They set to work patiently exercising the arts of their ancestors. The palaces and churches of Genoa were, it seems, in ruins in 1945. Now walking the streets with Augustus Hare's guide book of 1875 Mrs Stitch and I could see almost all that he saw, as he saw it.

I did not know Genoa before the war. I went through by owl-light countless times, but the train runs underground and one gets no glimpse of the city's beauties. It is a place much neglected by English and American sight-seers who hurry through on their way to Rome and Florence and Venice. Genoa cannot be compared with these. It has no stupendous works of art and is haunted by few illustrious ghosts. It is stately and rather prosaic and passes almost unnoticed in the incomparable riches of Italy. In another country it would be the focus of æsthetic excitement.

All that is interesting, apart from the Campo Santo, lies in the little triangle between the two railway stations and the water-front. There one may see two streets of palaces and some thirty churches displaying every phase of architecture from early mediæval to late rococo. The palaces are all, I think, in public hands or divided into offices and flats. The shipping agency, where I went to verify my sailing, is housed in a delicate eighteenth-century building whose gates lead into a *cortile* with beyond it, through the further arch, a hanging garden rising into the sunlight on elaborately sculptured terraces. The two important streets, the Via Balbi and the Via Nuova, unpleasantly renamed Via Garibaldi, are narrow and deeply shaded except on the roofs and upper stories, where at dawn and sunset the pediments and cornices reveal their strength. The doorways are immense and through them beyond the quad-rangles and open staircases there is often a bright view, on one side of the sea, on the other of the mountains. Steep populous alleys lead down to the harbour, but they are clean and sweet. The people are as polite as Romans. There are no child-beggars, only the trad-itional, black robed, bead-telling old people on the steps of the churches. The Genoese of the old city go to bed early. After dinner one can promenade the empty streets finding at every corner a lamp-lit shrine and meeting few motor cars.

The chief hotel stands near the railway station. Luggage is carried there through a tunnel under the traffic, which during the day is thick and fast. It is as good an hotel as I have found anywhere. As I have said, I was not allowed to try the cooking; everything I did try was first-class, in particular the two concierges. When one is travelling, one's comfort depends more on concierges than on cooks or managers or head waiters. These functionaries are getting rather rare in England and are quite unknown in America. Outside Europe they tend to be rascals. There is in England a Corps of Commission-aires, who have their own burial ground at Brookwood. They are fine figures, uniformed and bemedalled, who have cost me a lot of sixpences in my time. Concierges, on the other hand, have to be polyglot, omniscient, imperturbable as croupiers, patient as nuns, and endowed with memories as deep and accurate as librarians. Mrs Stitch has some of the requisite qualities, but not all. I should be the worst possible man for the job. The concierges of Genoa romantically assumed that my meeting with Mrs Stitch was clandestine and showed exquisite tact in defending our privacy and concealing our identities from an enquirer whom they took for a private detective. I should like to believe that there is an international corps of concierges, a Sovereign Order like the Knights of Malta, and a splendid cemetery where they can all lie together at the end, but I am told they never resort together and mostly retire quite young and rather rich and blandly fatten ducks in remote, soft valleys.

Mrs Stitch and I took our sight-seeing easy. One night in a wagon-lit did not work in me any miracle of rejuvenation. I was not yet good for more than two miles a day, nor could I eat more than a spoonful or two of the delicious confections of fish that were put before us. I was the same seedy old man who had groaned up to Paddington. But my eyes were opening. For months they had ceased to see; I had moved like a blind man through the lanes and hamlets of Somerset and the familiar little area of London that lies between the London Library and the Hyde Park Hotel. I needed a strong draught to quicken my faculty, and I found it in the Counter-Reformation extravagance of the Gesu. That picked me up and I was ready for the subtler beauties of the Cathedral.

My hope, not I trust wholly presumptuous, in publishing this diary is that the things which amused and interested me on my little tour may amuse and interest some others. I do not attempt to guide them by enumerating all the objects to be seen, nor even all I saw. E. V. Lucas's 'Wanderer' series of descriptions of famous towns, which give so beguiling an air of leisure, of the sensitive eye freely roaming, of mature meditation, of unhurried feet pottering, of the mind richly stored with history and anecdote, were in fact, his daughter has revealed, the fruit of breakneck speed and frantic jottings of the kind most ridiculed in less adroit tourists. During these two days in Genoa I hobbled along beside Mrs Stitch, popped into places that looked interesting, sat down as often as possible and stared hard; and my vision cleared. I was not to see much of architectural beauty during my tour, but I brought to other spectacles eyes sharpened on the stones of Italy.

One little puzzle I met which has often exercised me since. For centuries the most illustrious relic in the very rich treasury of San Lorenzo (it claims also the ashes of St John the Baptist and has furnished them with superb vehicles for exposition and procession) was the Sacro Catino. It is a large dish of green glass, broken and put together with a small piece missing, and handsomely mounted. It is displayed in the treasury still, but the sacristan makes no claims to its authenticity. It has an old history. In 1101 Genoese and Pisan crusaders sacked Cæsarea. The loot was enormous, but the Genoese happily surrendered all their share in exchange for this dish which local pundits assured them was used by Our Lord at the Last Supper for washing the apostles' feet. More than this it was cut from a single prodigious emerald which Solomon had given to the Queen of Sheba.

The Genoese bore it back in triumph, enshrined it and protected it as the greatest possession of the republic. Twelve knights were appointed to the high honour of holding the key of its casket for a month each, year after year. In 1476 a law was passed making it a capital offence to try alchemical experiments with it. So it was guarded and venerated until the Revolution. In 1809 French freethinkers captured the city and bore the Sacro Catino off to Paris with other treasures. In 1815 it was restored, but on the road between Turin and Genoa someone dropped it and broke it and plainly revealed that it was made of glass. By an inexplicable process of the human reason the Genoese at once decided that it was totally spurious. If it was not the Queen of Sheba's emerald, it was not Our Lord's basin. No knights guard it now. It is displayed to profane eyes as an *objet de vertu* among the silver altar fronts and the Byzantine reliquaries, all beautifully arranged and lighted as though in the Victoria and Albert Museum.

After luncheon on the second day I covered my suitcases with the gummy labels of the steamship line and lay down to read. After half an hour I was disturbed by a series of strange noises, cracklings and rustlings. Every one of the labels, whether attached to leather or canvas, was detaching itself and rolling up into a little cylinder. Rum.

Farewell, Mrs Stitch. She returned to Rome with the gruesome coat on her elegant arm.

2. VOYAGE

Embarkation – Port Said – Aden – English at sea
– Americans in Africa

January 31st. The *Rhodesia Castle* is a clean, seaworthy, punctual ship
with a swimming-pool, cinema-screen and all modern amenities,
but no pretensions to *grand luxe*. The food was abundant and seduc-
tively named and seemed to cause general satisfaction. I cannot say
much about it. I was treating this voyage as a cure. A ship is one of
the few places where one can play the ascetic without causing
annoyance to anyone else. Accordingly I subsisted chiefly on fruit
and cold ham. I never entered the bar, where the jollier passengers
forgathered, and eventually landed in Africa lighter and very much
more agile than I had embarked.

The ship was quite full and I was lucky to get a cabin with
a bath-room. Not that I can find much use for a bath at sea. A
ship is as clean as a hospital; except after days on shore, washing is
a formality; for the first days of hot weather the fresh-water shower is
a pleasure; after that the cold water runs hot and one breaks into
sweat anew as one tries to dry. But throughout the voyage
I compared the privacy and spaciousness of this journey with the
squalor of my flight the year before.

At the time of writing (July 1959) there is a correspondence in
The Times about the horrors of third-class air-travel. I had gone
to Rhodesia first class. Perhaps we were objects of envy in our
expensive quarters, but we had little compassion to spare for the
second-class victims forward. We had our own bitter troubles. It was
impossible to sleep and very difficult to get to the lavatory. After dark
it was a strain to read by the little spot lights. All of us, rich and poor
alike, were periodically turned out to wait for refuelling at airports
which ingeniously contrived the utmost gloom with the utmost restlessness. There was nothing to do but drink. It took days to recover.

Looking round the miscellaneous shipping in Genoa harbour, I ponder another contrast. Here are vessels of all ages, many of them shabby and battered, all doing their work safely and surely; unlike aeroplanes which capriciously develop what the engineers prettily dub 'metal fatigue' and incinerate their occupants.

Sunday, February 1st. There are three priests on board, Dutch, Italian and Irish-American, on their way to different mission stations. Also two parties of nuns, Catholic and Anglican. The Anglicans are put out that they are denied Communion, but they hear Mass regularly. The Anglican nuns were unmistakably English spinsters. None of them had developed that round cheerful face whose expression varies from serenity to fatuity which one sees everywhere in Catholic convents. These Anglican sisters are universally respected in Africa for their good works. They did not seem notably joyous. But who am I, of all people, to complain about that?

Most of the passengers came on board at London and have made up their bridge fours and dining-tables and generally got acquainted, so that I am able to study them in solitude. I had expected a predominance of elderly people of the kind one finds on the banana boats in the West Indies, making the round trip for their rheumatism or bronchitis. There are some of these, but very few. The great majority are the young, returning to work; not adventurers seeking a fortune; not, at this late age of Africa, empire builders; but the employees of governments and big commercial firms taking up secure posts as clerks and schoolmasters and conservators of soil; sons of the Welfare State; well qualified, well behaved, enjoying an easy bonhomie with the stewards. Many have young wives, children and infants in arms.

A printed notice proclaims: 'The Captain and his officers will wear Blue Mess Kit White Mess Kit Blue Uniform White Uniform at dinner tonight' with the inapplicable words struck out, but few take advantage of this hint. Mine is one of a dozen dinner-jackets worn in the evening.

The library is reserved for adults. It is also free of wireless. Instead of a single, fatigable orchestra, most ships nowadays have loudspeakers everywhere and the succession of gramophone records is

only interrupted by announcements – test match scores, geographical and meteorological information from the bridge, news of the
ship's recreations. (One exhortation on this voyage was enjoyable:
'At 12.45 today a passenger was observed throwing a basket-chair
overboard from the verandah. If this is an expression of dissatisfaction, the Captain would like the opportunity to put things right.')
The library is a place of refuge. It is also well stocked with some
thousand books of which I possess a dozen only and have read
a further two dozen. The steward tells me that the Line employs
a professional librarian who visits every ship at London and Southampton and distributes books. He must have a peculiarly difficult
task, and he does it admirably. Every taste finds some satisfaction.
For me a voyage is the time to read about the places for which I am
bound and to study the best-sellers of the past year. I got through two
books a day and never found myself without something readable.

February 3rd. The Mediterranean is cool and calm. Clocks go on an
hour. Sir Harold Nicolson has said that he resents this shortening of
his life. I find it exhilarating; the gift of a whole precious hour totally
free of delinquency and boredom. Odd that traditionally the voyage
west, where days and nights get longer and longer, should symbolise
the expedition to the Fortunate Isles.

Found Maurice Baring's '*C*' in the library which I have never
read. It was written in the same room with Ronald Knox; he and
Maurice typed together in the library at Beaufort; one so meticu-
lous, the other so slap-dash. The discrepancies in '*C*' are startling.
Did he never re-read what he wrote? Are his devotees thrown into
a trance by his gentle melancholy and rendered quite unobservant?
The distance of a country house from Oxford varies from page to
page between nine and six miles. Still odder one of the leading
characters, Mrs Evelyn, appears first as an elderly widow, then as
married and middle-aged, then as a siren, the mistress of Leila's
husband and is in her final apotheosis 'the essence of London'.
Maurice's delicious spontaneity, versatility and humility, that
made him one of the most lovable of men, are not the attributes of
an artist, who is more often crabbed and assiduous and touchy and
jealous and generally unclubbable.

February 4th. Port Said at dawn. Over a hundred dauntless passengers left for the gruelling dash to the Sphinx and to Suez. I did not
land. The officials who came on board wore khaki service dress and
Brodrick caps. No tarboushes to be seen. The touts have discarded
their white gowns for shoddy western suits, exemplifying the almost
universal rule that 'Nationalists' obliterate national idiosyncrasies.
Even the 'gully-gully' man wore trousers.

I have often wondered about the history of these performers,
more comedians than conjurers, who, as far as I know, are peculiar
to the Canal. Few tourists in these days go shopping in Port Said or
sit in its cafés. (I remember the days when everyone going out, male
and female, bought a topee at the quayside and those returning to
Europe from the tropics threw them overboard in the basin to be
scavenged by Arab boatmen.) So nowadays the 'gully-gully' men ply
between Port Said and Suez, boarding the ships and giving performances on deck at advertised times. I first saw them in February 1929
when perforce I spent some weeks in the port. Their repertoire is as
immutable as the D'Oyly Carte's. The craft, I have been told, is
hereditary. The man who squatted on the deck of the *Rhodesia Castle*
must be the son of those whose attentions in 1929 became rather
tedious after long repetition; or perhaps he was one of those tiny
children whom I mentioned in a book called *Labels*. 'There was
a little Arab girl,' I noted, 'who had taught herself to imitate them
perfectly, only, with a rare instinct for the elimination of essentials,
she used not to bother about the conjuring at all, but would scramble
from table to table in the cafés, saying "Gully-Gully" and taking
a chicken in and out of a little cloth bag. She was every bit as
amusing as the grown-ups and made just as much money.'

There is a distinctly military tinge about the gully-gully ritual,
which dates perhaps from 1915, much facetious saluting and the
address: 'Oh, you, officer, sir,' when chickens are produced from
waistcoat pockets. There is also the invocation of the name of
Mrs Cornwallis-West derived from a remote and forgotten scandal.
But who began the art, when? Most Oriental and African conjurers
assume converse with the supernatural. No doubt Egyptian conjurers did a hundred years ago. Some unrecorded Charlie Chaplin
or Grock of the water-front must at about the time of *Aida* have first

hit on the idea of introducing farce; perhaps the literal progenitor of all gully-gully men. I wish I knew.

All day in the Canal drifting past the dullest landscape in the world, while the passengers hang fascinated on the taffrails and take spools of snapshots.

I remember once seeing a soldier of the French Foreign Legion desert, jump overboard just before luncheon, and stand rather stupidly in the sand watching the ship sail on without him. Once much later, during the last war, I remember a happy evening on the Canal dining with two sailors whose task was to employ numberless Arab bomb-watchers. When they reported an enemy aeroplane and a splash, traffic was stopped until the missile was found. The clever Italians, I was told, dropped blocks of salt which dissolved, leaving no trace. Divers worked for days in vain searching for them and the Canal was blocked as effectively as by high explosive. But there was nothing of interest during this day's journey. All one could see was a line of behinds as the passengers gazed and photographed nothing.

The Captain tells me he finds the Canal the most interesting part of his voyage.

The weather grows pleasantly warm; not warm enough to justify the outbreak of shorts which both sexes, from now on, inelegantly assume.

February 6*th*. A cool, fresh breeze down the Red Sea. For an Englishman the English make ideal travelling companions. I have been accosted twice only; once by a woman who took me for my brother, Alec, and again by a man who mysteriously claimed to have been at Cambridge with Ronald Knox.

The constant music, I suppose, caused genuine pleasure to five per cent. of the passengers; pain to one per cent.; a vague sense of well-being to fifty per cent.; the rest do not notice it.

February 8*th*. – Anchored off Steamer Point, Aden, after luncheon. The ship stays until midnight. A bazaar is set up on a raft below the gangway. Launches ply to and from the quay.

Since I was last here Aden has grown green; not very green, but there are distinct patches of foliage where there was only dust. We originally occupied Berbera, in Somaliland across the straits, in order to have somewhere to grow cabbages and fruit for the garrison of Aden. Water has at last been struck and piped. The continuous trains of shabby camels no longer pad along the road from Crater Town. There are taps and water-closets now in the settlement. I saw only one camel and that was a sleek riding animal from up country, sitting beside its master at an Arab café feeding on a hamper of green vegetables.

Most of the passengers drove off to see the water-tanks ascribed to King Solomon. In a thousand years' time, will Central African guides show tourists the mighty ruins of the Kariba dam as one of the works of Solomon? I wish I could think so.

I took a taxi to Crater Town and walked its narrow streets for an hour looking for remembered landmarks and finding none. Not that there has been much modernisation, but things have disappeared. I could find no trace of the 'Padre Sahib's Bungalow' where I once spent a week. Nor of Mr Besse's emporium. I was Mr Besse's guest on several occasions in his rooms above his offices and warehouse. I also went with him on an appalling climb to the edge of the crater and across the burning volcanic debris to his shark-infested bathing-beach on the far side of the little peninsula. He was an enchanting man. I described him in a book called *Remote People* as 'Mr Leblanc', and was told later that he greatly relished the portrait. I wish he had shown his gratification by leaving me something. He was a rich man then. His great fortune came later and I was astounded ten years ago to read that he left £2,000,000 to Oxford University, an institution which can never have caused him a moment's pleasure. I do not know what he was by race or religion. They named the college he founded St Anthony's, but, when I enquired here, no one knew or had troubled to conjecture which of the twelve canonised Anthonies they were commemorating.

The smells of Crater Town are unchanged – spices, woodsmoke, coffee, incense, goats, delicious Arab and Indian kitchen smells, garlic and curry, sewage and hair oil. It is always a wonder to me that the English who cheerfully endure the reek of their own country – silage, spaniels, cabbages, diesel fumes, deodorisers, fish and chips, gaspers, ice cream – fight shy of 'native' streets.

Wireless rang out everywhere, I suppose from Cairo. There were portraits of Nasser in many of the Arab shops.

Back to Steamer Point. Here there has settled all the tourist trade which used to flourish in Port Said, but in a sadly standardised form. Simon Arzt's in the 1920s was richly cosmopolitan. You could find most of the luxuries of Europe there. At Aden the shops are all kept by Indians and each has an identical stock of Japanese counterfeits – 'American' fountain-pens, 'Swiss' watches, 'French' scent, 'German' binoculars. I searched for cigars, but found none. There used to be two hotels at the extremes of the crescent. Their verandahs were haunted by touts and money-changers and shirt-tailors, and each possessed a 'mermaid' – a stuffed manatee, I think – which was kept in a chest and exhibited on payment. Now one of these hotels had gone and in its place has arisen a large, modern, air-conditioned building; no place for a mermaid. The other is its old shabby self.

I had a personal interest in the mermaids, because six years ago I suffered briefly from hallucinations in the course of which I imagined myself to be in communication with a girl in Aden. She complained of having nothing to do there. I went into some detail (which I omitted from the account I wrote of the experience) about the rather limited diversions of the settlement. Among them I mentioned the mermaid. 'It's gone, Evelyn, it's gone,' she said later, in tones of reproach as though I had maliciously sought to raise false hopes of pleasure, 'it isn't here any more.'

I was curious to discover whether in this particular as in all others my 'voices' had been deceiving me. But here she spoke the plain truth. The first servant I addressed at the hotel looked blank and shrugged, supposing I was demanding some exotic drink. But a much older man came forward. 'Mermaid finish,' he said.

'How?'

'One man came finish mermaid.'

'When?'

'Not so long.'

The curse of Babel frustrated further enquiries. I should have liked to know how the mermaid was finished – bought, stolen, destroyed by a drunk? – and particularly when it disappeared –

before or after or even during my conversations with my forlorn confidante?

9th February. In the Gulf of Aden we lost the breeze which kept us cool in the Red Sea. Once round Cape Guardafui we are in the steam-bath of a New York heatwave. It is more agreeable and, surely, healthier to come to the tropics gradually than to be deposited there suddenly by an aeroplane in the clothes one wore shivering a few hours before in London.

A great stripping of clothes among the passengers. Cortes marched from Vera Cruz in armour; Stanley crossed Africa in knickerbockers and a braided tunic; I in my humble way have suffered for decency. I have worn starched shirts at Christmas dinners in both Zanzibar and Georgetown, British Guiana; but these young people must be almost naked in order to lie in deck-chairs in the shade. The thighs of middle-aged women quiver horribly at the library-steward's table. How different the three Arabs we have taken on board at Aden, who are travelling to Zanzibar. They wear the light cotton robes of their people and always look cool and elegant and clean. They sit playing dominoes in the smoking-room and three times a day spread little mats on deck, take off their sandals and prostrate themselves in prayer.

I have found a diverting book named *Stars and Stripes in Africa; Being a History of American Achievements in Africa by Explorers, Missionaries, Pirates, Adventurers, Hunters, Miners, Merchants, Scientists, Soldiers, Show-men, Engineers and others with some account of Africans who have played a part in American affairs*, by Eric Rosenthal, 1938.

It begins rather surprisingly with Columbus, who once put into the Gold Coast. Some Americans believe he discovered the United States, but can many, I wonder, suppose he flew the Stars and Stripes? Mr Rosenthal was injudicious only in his choice of title; perhaps his publishers chose it for him; American publishers are more presumptuous than European in these ways; anyway, the sub-title fully explains his achievement. He rejoices to trace every con-nexion, however tenuous, between the two continents and has produced a fascinating collection of uncommon information. In fact, I think, the only time that the Stars and Stripes were taken into Africa was at the head of Stanley's expedition to Livingstone (who appears here among American worthies on the grounds that one of his sons died after the battle of Gettysburg; he had enlisted in the Federal army under an assumed name, was wounded and taken prisoner. It is not quite clear from Mr Rosenthal's account whether he fought in the battle.)

Americans have every excuse for claiming Stanley as a compatriot. He claimed it vehemently himself and was at one brief period a naturalised citizen. But he was born and died a Briton. He was the illegitimate son of Welsh parents, jumped his ship at New Orleans, enlisted in and deserted from both sides in the Civil War. When he became widely advertised and was invited to explain his origins, he hesitated between the embarrassments of admitting his illegitimate birth and his 'illegal entry'. He then formally abjured his country. When he became respectable, rich and married he re-naturalised himself British, sat in Parliament and was knighted.

It is interesting to learn from Mr Rosenthal of the enthusiasm of individual Americans for the establishment of the 'colonialism' in Africa which their grandchildren reprobate. At the time of the Boer War, he tells us – I was about to write in the manner of a book-review, 'he reminds us'; I had no idea of this or of most of the facts he adduces – Theodore Roosevelt wrote to Selous: 'the most melan-choly element in the problem is what you bring out [in the *Spectator*] about Englishmen no longer colonising in the way Boers do'.

In the invasion of Matabeleland in 1893 it was a young American trooper, Burnham, who hoisted the Union Jack over Lobengula's Kraal and three years afterwards his father, Frederick Burnham, later chief Boy Scout of the U.S.A., contributed to the pacification of the area and won loud applause by bringing in the head of what he described as 'the M'Limo'. It was a large claim. The M'Limo is an ancient African deity worshipped and consulted in the Matopo Hills long before the coming of the Matabele and still revered as far south as Bechuanaland; his priests are drawn from the Kalanga tribe; they make rain and pronounce oracles. Burnham, 'at stupendous risk', as Mr Rosenthal remarks, had bagged one of these.

There were eight American members of the Reform Committee in Johannesburg who first invited and then repudiated the Jameson

Raid. One of them, Hammond, was condemned to death but later with his fellows was bought off for £25,000 a head.

A Philadelphian built the first synagogue in Rhodesia.

These and many other facts I have learned from Mr Rosenthal. The most moving narration is of the efforts made in 1900 to solve the problem of the Boers by wholesale evacuation. The Governor of Arkansas offered 5,000,000 acres of his State as a free gift. Colorado followed suit. In Wyoming 300,000 acres were actually irrigated and planted for the Boer immigrants. If these farsighted and generous policies had been realised, much annoyance would have been spared Her Majesty's loyal subjects.

February 10*th*. A fancy-dress ball. The general aim is to be comic rather than seductive. Some jokes are purely verbal – a dress sewn with used matches patiently collected from the ship's ash-trays and labelled: 'No more Strikes'. Many beefy young men assume female clothes with balloon breasts. One of them wears nothing but a towel fastened like a baby's napkin and is pushed round the dance floor by another dressed as a nurse. He carries a large feeding-bottle and the inscription: 'Beer builds bonnie babies'. An elderly woman with whitened face parades in a sheet festooned with empty gin and whisky bottles. She represents 'Departed Spirits'.

For a great many passengers this party celebrates the end of the voyage and the end of leave. We are due at Mombasa on 13th, where they disembark and go to work in Kenya and Uganda.

3. VOYAGE CONTINUED

Mombasa – Kenyan hospitality – Officials and settlers
– Fort Jesus – Gedi – Kibo – Tanga – Zanzibar

February 13*th.* The *Rhodesia Castle* spends five days in Mombasa. Few
passengers stay on board during this hot season. I had made no plans
and knew nobody in the colony. Nearly all my old Kenya friends
have died, some by suicide, or returned to their homelands. (The
generous, genial, unconventional population of the highlands was
by no means exclusively British. There were Americans, Danes,
Swedes, French, many of whom used their Kenya estates as holiday
resorts.) Nairobi, I was told, is now unfriendly, huge and infested by
thieves; the care-free life of the Muthaiga Club is a memory; rather
a scandalous one. A second generation of farmers has grown up with
their own social habits, provincial in experience and opinions, more
industrious than their predecessors in the Happy Valley, but not
such good company. This is the opinion I was given on the *Rhodesia
Castle*. It sounds plausible enough. There was nothing in the Kenya
I knew to suggest that it enjoyed any immunity to change. Why
should not this equatorial Arcadia, so lately and lightly colonised, go
the way of Europe? I did not seek to verify it. I could not hope to see
much in five days. Besides, the Queen Mother was in progress up
country and I surmised that casual trippers might not be particularly
welcome at that time. But in Mombasa, at any rate, I found that
the old tradition of open hospitality flourished as it used to up
country.

A former neighbour of mine in Gloucestershire had served in
the Sappers with a friend now settled in Tanganyika. He wrote to
report my imminent arrival. This second sapper not only, as will
appear, made himself my host and companion in Tanganyika,
he wrote to a third sapper, a highly placed official in Mombasa

977

who came on board the *Rhodesia Castle* with the passport officers, introduced himself and took charge of me with a bounty which is often called 'oriental' but in my experience is particularly African. I was the friend of a friend of a friend and I didn't know anyone in Mombasa, so that was enough for him to lend me his car and his driver, take me to a tailor and to a watchmaker, ask me to luncheon at his home, put me up for his club, advise me about anti-malarial specifics, introduce me to the Provincial Commissioner and the Director of Antiquities and perform all the other kindnesses that I shall shortly record.

In my last visit to Kenya I met few officials. There was a rigid apartheid between them and the settlers, who looked on them almost as enemy agents. Those were the days of the Hartington declaration of policy; that where the interests of the immigrant and native races conflicted, the interests of the natives were 'paramount'. If this had been said by a Socialist Colonial Secretary, it would have passed unnoticed; coming from a Tory (and a future duke), it made the settlers for the first time 'politically-conscious'. They saw the Colonial Office as their declared enemy who sought to rob them of the lands they had cleared and ploughed and watered. The officials, they said, had no stake on the country; they were in transit, thinking only of promotion and pension; they would retire to die in Europe. The settlers were transforming a wilderness where they intended to found families. (Come to think of it, I never heard much hostile criticism of the rich cosmopolitans on these grounds.) There was a popular story at the time of a district officer who seduced a farmer's child and begot twins. He honourably offered marriage. The farmer said: 'I would sooner have two bastards in my family than one official.' I daresay it is a very old story that has been told of Montagus and Capulets, Campbells and Macdonalds for generations. But I first heard it of Kenya during the 'paramountcy' agitation.

All that bitterness seems now to have subsided. There was then a simple division between two groups of Englishmen, one trying to run the country as a Montessori School, the other as a league of feudal estates, each sincerely believing that it understood better the natives, and knew what was best for them. There was then a single, troublesome, alien element comprised of Indians. No one talked of

African 'Nationalism'. Now officials, settlers and Indians have a common uncertainty of their future, and since the Mau-Mau 'emergency' no one pretends to understand the natives. (The suppression of that movement, I was assured by an officer closely concerned with it, was achieved by loyal or mercenary Kikuyus more than by regular forces.)

The city of Mombasa has grown enormously since I last saw it and now covers the whole island. There is a large brand-new 'interracial' hotel. 'Interracial' in practice means mainly Indian, for few Africans can afford it and the Europeans forgather in their houses or at the Club. There is an impressive Muslim Institute, erected by the late Aga Khan and the Sultan of Zanzibar and other pious benefactors for the technical education of East African Mohammedans. (The Government of Kenya provide the staff and the running expenses.) They were unusually fortunate in their architect, Captain G. N. Beaumont, an engineer amateur of Mohammedan art who is splendidly uncorrupted by the influence of Corbusier which pervades the modern east. Dome, minaret, arcade, fretted and crenellated parapets, carved doors, tiled walls and pools stand happily disposed in acres of garden, whispering hints of the Alhambra, of Mena House, of the Anglican Cathedral at Gibraltar, of Brighton, but never the harsh tones of UNO.

These two buildings are the chief architectural additions to the city. There is evidence of what seems to be the universal process of offices becoming larger and private houses smaller. For the first time in Africa I heard complaints of the scarcity and expense of domestic servants. The population of the island is more than ever heterogeneous. There are now poor whites in quite formidable numbers – a thing unknown thirty years ago. There is also in the main street a notorious dancing-bar, part brothel, part thieves' kitchen; everyone spoke of it with awe. When at length after many invitations I found a companion to go there, I found it the genuine thing; not at all the tourists' apache café, but something which awoke nostalgic memories of the Vieux Port of Marseilles. All races and all vices were catered for. I have never been in a tougher or more lively joint anywhere. Gentle readers should keep clear.

Kilindini docks are now enormous and efficient. Everywhere there was every sign of prosperity (I suppose complaints about domestic servants are one of these signs) and of political tranquillity.

I have here run away from my diary and given the impressions of several days. On the day I am ostensibly chronicling I spent a restful afternoon on the club verandah with the intention of reading the news I had missed since leaving England. The club is unchanged since I was last here, a spacious, old-fashioned building designed to catch every breath of air. The monsoon was blowing. It was deliciously cool, but it is not easy to read *The Times* India paper edition in deep shade and a brisk wind. Have the editors, I wonder, considered what a high proportion of their copies are perused under fans?

Opposite the club stands one of the most notable buildings in East Africa, Fort Jesus, built by the Portuguese at the end of the sixteenth century and still bearing the royal escutcheon on its walls. Its base is cut from the rock; its upper stories are faced with hard, coral stucco which changes colour as the sun moves over it, mottled, sometimes dun, sometimes rose-red. It is a massive little castle sited for defence on all fronts, battlemented, pierced by slits, approached by a single narrow flight of steep enfiladed steps. Until lately it was used as a prison and all the visitor could see of it were its noble elevations. He could smell it, when the wind was in the wrong quarter from the club verandah. Now, by means of a grant from the Gulbenkian Foundation, it is being cleaned and restored. By the time that these words appear it will be open to view, furnished with a collection of local antiquities and, more important, inhabited by Mr Kirkman, the official archæologist, who has been in charge of the operation.

At 5 o'clock that evening the fort was at its rosiest under the full blaze of the westering sun when, through the kindness of my new sapper friend, I had an appointment with Mr Kirkman. Few people in Mombasa had had the chance to see the work in progress, and a privileged party of six or seven assembled at the gate and were led up to the ramparts. There is nothing of the dry and solemn official scholar in Mr Kirkman. He is an exuberant enthusiast for the comic as well as for the scientific aspects of his work.

The Public Works Department had built over the old structure a shoddy conglomeration of guard-rooms, cells, latrines, barrack-rooms, wash-houses and exercise yards. All these were being demolished and the original levels were being restored. The Arabs had left a few finely carved inscriptions, but what emerges from the excavation is essentially a Portuguese Government House of the seventeenth century. Mr Kirkman gleefully recounted the history of the settlement which is in microcosm the history of the East African coast from Cape Guardafui to Sofala.

Few of the leading figures led enviable lives. The Arabs were the first comers to the island. In the sixteenth century the Portuguese set up a small trading station under the protection of the Sultan of Mombasa but relying for its defence primarily on an alliance with the Sultan of Malindi. In 1588 a Turkish pirate raided and sacked the coast. The Sultan of Mombasa appealed to Constantinople, the Sultan of Malindi to Goa. The Sultan of Mombasa then decamped. Later the Turk reappeared and occupied the island as a base for attacking Malindi. A fleet was sent against him from Goa. Meanwhile, for several years a ferocious cannibal tribe from south of the Zambesi, called the Zimba, had been making a leisurely progress up the coast, eating their way through the inhabitants. They appeared on the mainland just as the Portuguese fleet anchored off the island. The Turks invited the Zimba to cross over and help against the Portuguese. The Zimba came, ate the Turks and, gorged, shambled away to the north, leaving Mombasa to the Portuguese. They were repulsed at Malindi and disappeared from history.

In 1591 the Portuguese began work on Fort Jesus. It was so attractive that their old ally of Malindi invited himself to stay. His hosts unkindly turned him out and bought his head from the mainland villagers with whom he took refuge. When this deed was reported in Lisbon and Goa, the royal authorities were shocked. It was decided that in reparation the Sultan's son Yussuf, then seven years old, should be educated and Christianised. In 1630 he turned up again at Mombasa in European clothes with a white wife under the name of Don Jeronimo. His reception was not as cordial as he had hoped and he began to regret the simplicities of the faith of his fathers, so at a party given in Fort Jesus he arranged a successful massacre of all Christians. It was his last success. He wandered away first to the Yemen, then to Madagascar and was finally murdered by pirates in the Red Sea. The Portuguese reoccupied Fort Jesus until it fell to the Arabs of Oman. The siege from 1696 to 1698 is one of the memorable feats of human endurance; at the end the garrison was reduced to eleven men and two women. The Governor was so tortured by skin disease that he chose to attack the enemy sword in hand. The relief fleet arrived a day late.

In the next century the Portuguese retook the Fort and held it for a year. It fell to the Muscat Arabs whose representative, the Sultan of Zanzibar, is still the titular ruler. Visitors who see a red flag flying there need not fear un-American activities. It is the Sultan's own standard. The British Protectorate was established after being anticipated by a droll episode in 1824 when a captain of the Royal Navy intervened, at the Sultan of Zanzibar's request, to put down a rising of his subjects on the coast. At that time, while the main body was employed on the mainland, Fort Jesus was commanded by a midshipman. A small civil war broke out under the walls of the fort. The boy sent a stern warning to both sides that unless they desisted, the combatants would be punished 'with all the forces at his command'. They desisted. The forces available at Fort Jesus at the time were five Royal Marines, two of whom were down with fever. The protectorate so light-heartedly proclaimed was repudiated by the home government. General Gordon entertained the whimsical notion of annexing Mombasa to Egypt. It was not until 1887 that British administration was established. There is no record of any African having ever ruled there.

This vivid little history was conveyed to us as we stood on the battlements with infectious but inimitable zest by the Director of Antiquities.

That evening I dined with the Provincial Commissioner. Like everyone I met in Mombasa that day and later he was in a daze of gratification at the Queen Mother's visit. On every occasion she had done more than was asked of her. Unflagging in the steam-heat, she had completely defeated the boycott the politicians had tried to impose. In particular, she had made a conquest of the Arab sailors whose dhows fill the old port at this season. Nasser's wireless had been denouncing her as the symbol of Western imperialism. Dhows came sailing in from Zanzibar and all the little ports of the coast. The Queen Mother went to the water-front and paid them a long, happy call which will be talked of for years in the Hadramaut and in the Persian Gulf.

Politics do not seem to be a major concern in Mombasa. Much of our conversation that evening was about the prospects of developing the Kenya coast as a holiday resort. There are sands, surf, coral reefs, deep-sea fishing for marlin, tunny and shark, an almost unexplored sea-bed for goggle divers, everything in fact that draws tourists to the West Indies. At present Mombasa is used mainly as a port and rail-head; rich sportsmen go straight to Nairobi and set out on safari from there into the game reserves. The Commissioner hopes to see his province become a pleasure coast, not only for visitors from Europe and America but for families from the highlands of Kenya and Rhodesia. Rhodesians at present tend to take their holidays at sea-level which doctors recommend, at Durban, a salubrious but unromantic and expensive city. In the cool months Kenya has far greater natural attractions.

February 14th. Today I was able to see something of these attractions. But first I had to make arrangements to sleep out. Nights in the ship tied up alongside the quay at this season are barely supportable for their heat and the noise of stevedores. But deliverance came in the form of a Frenchwoman of incongruous elegance; she came aboard the moment we docked, dressed in a uniform of her own designing, the representative of her husband's travel-agency, the very antithesis of the Agent at the Gare de Lyon. All yesterday she had been despatching parties of animal-watchers into the interior. She was on duty again this morning, spruce and cool. To her sympathetic ear I disclosed my insomnious problems and she at once, for rather a lot of money, arranged for me to sleep the next two nights at a place named Kibo on the slopes of Kilimanjaro.

But first a jaunt up the coast; at 10 o'clock my sapper friend and his wife called for me at the docks. We picked up Mrs Kirkman at her hotel and drove north over the ferry to the mainland. We crossed with a handful of girls from a neighbouring tribe whose name sounded like Gujama. Amid the slatternly European fashions of Mombasa these pagans still preserve their African grace, bare to the waist, prettily tattooed and decorated with wire and beads. The road north runs through alternations of bush and village plantations of coconut and corn. A few independently minded Europeans live in small holdings cleared from the bush near the ferry. In one of these Mr Kirkman was staying. He joined our party and we drove past Freetown, a settlement of slaves freed in the last century, to the ruined city of Gedi.

Current guide books still speak of this as overgrown and shunned by the natives for fear of the ghosts who abound there. This was true ten years ago, but today much of it has been cleared and some of it excavated. It was Mr Kirkman's first task in Africa. For those who lack the archæologist's constructive imagination and are not easily moved by the contemplation of stratified debris, Gedi is second only to Zimbabwe in charm and mystery. It was abandoned, not destroyed; its dilapidation has been from natural causes, storm and invading vegetation during the centuries in which superstition protected it from men.

It was a large, double-walled Arab city, probably founded in the twelfth century. No one, not even Mr Kirkman, knows why it was built here, so far from the sea. Arab geographers refer to the 'iron mines of Melinde' (Malandi). It may have had some connexion with this industry. It is conceivable that the river Sabaki may once have run to the sea below its walls and that it was a depot for trade with the interior. No one knows why it was suddenly deserted in mid-sixteenth century. Perhaps the Zimba paused and sustained themselves there in the course of their gluttonous migration. Anyway, there is plenty to interest the sight-seer who is not a specialist, arches, streets, six mosques, a palace, three pillar tombs, six mansions complete with bath-rooms and privies, water supplies, drainage, store-rooms and courts, all of the fifteenth century, when it seems to have been completely rebuilt. There is a market and coffee-shop. Porcelain and stone-ware from China, glass-ware and beads from Persia have been unearthed. There is still much to be found, but it is easy enough already to picture the populous, prosperous and pious community which flourished there in its period of greatness. The natives now show no reluctance to take part in the work of exhumation.

Two Swahili families are permanently quartered there as custodians. The women were preparing a meal, a horrible mess of mealies. There has been no improvement in the basic East African diet in the last twenty years. As we are constantly reminded, most Africans are always underfed. Poverty, of course, is the true origin but not always the immediate cause of their wretched food. Most of them, I am told, when they are in funds – on returning, for example, from spells of work in the mines – prefer to spend on showy clothes or strong drink. They enjoy an occasional glut of meat when an animal has been killed, but they have no taste for the balanced and varied diet which the health officers would like to inculcate.

There is no recognisable trace now of the once powerful Sultanate of Malindi, where we drove for luncheon. There is instead a pretty little seaside resort with an excellent beach hotel decorated in the style derived from Rex Whistler.

That evening I went with the captain of the *Rhodesia Castle* to dine with the Union Castle agent. The party was mainly of Mombasa business men and their wives. It was clear that the enthusiasm aroused by the Queen Mother's visit was not confined to officials. All spoke of the notorious Star Bar, but none had been there and I could prevail on none to go with me.

February 15*th.* Set off early on the road to Kibo. A party from the *Rhodesia Castle* were away before me, packed tight in the cars, under the guidance of the English husband of the elegant French travel-agent. I self-indulgently had a big car on my own with a driver from the Chagga tribe who live round Kilimanjaro. As will appear later, the Chagga are a remarkable people, very much more civilised than their neighbours.

The road follows the line of the railway, which is itself the old caravan route to the lakes. Wherever you find old mango-trees in East Africa, you are on the Arab slave-tracks. It is a hot, dull road and I was glad to be alone. At noon we came to Voi – the entrance to the game reserve which had attracted my fellow passengers. Midday is no time for animal watching. At dawn and dusk the bush comes to life. We drove slowly round one of the many routes. Under the glare of the sun the area seemed empty and dead; high, dry, dun grass; low, colourless scrub; here and there small trees uprooted by elephants, ash-white as though struck by lightning. Every few minutes we stopped and my driver dramatically pointed to a colourless swift-moving object in the middle distance – a buck or impala or dik-dik. He had sharp, practised eyes and his regular run was to this Park to show wild life to tourists. I am both ignorant and blasé about tropical fauna. At one time or another I have been at close quarters with most sorts of big game. Baboons seem to me far less interesting than, say, the Gujama women on the ferry yesterday. I disappointed my driver by my languid attention and my insistence on getting to the hotel before the larger and keener party, whom we passed gazing intently at some giraffes. They were spending the night at Voi in order to see the elephants come out to drink at sun-down.

They arrived at the hotel as I was finishing luncheon and went up to their rooms to sleep; I drove on to Kibo.

A breathless, hot road crossing and recrossing the branch railway-line. Nothing of interest on either side. Somewhere on the way we crossed the frontier from Kenya into Tanganyika. There was no police post. No one asked whether I had lately been vaccinated. A few Indian shops round a railway station; then we turned off to the right and began to climb. Within a mile we had reached a different country. The summit of Kilimanjaro was hidden in cloud. All we saw was the green slope of gardens merging into forest. On either side of the lane grew coffee and bananas behind flowering hedges. Sweat dried and the air became cool and thin. At the end of our journey was a small, solid, old-fashioned German hotel, with balconies, a terrace, a lawn, flower garden and a cage of monkeys. The inhabitants of the hotel were youngish European couples, some with children, some it seemed on their honeymoons, but in the evening the terrace became more cosmopolitan. Indians are not allowed to settle in this area, but a motor-party came from Moshi and drank fruit juice. Three parties of local Chagga very well dressed and well behaved came to drink beer.

I slept under a blanket and woke in the exhilaration of the mountain dawn.

February 16*th*. Kilimanjaro was visible in the morning, a snowy camel's hump. Explorers of the last century wrote lyrically of this huge, odd, dead volcano that rises out of the plain. It looks less than its height, perhaps because of the high level of vegetation. From the hotel at Kibo parties set out from time to time to climb it. There are rest-huts for the nights and the tramp is made in three days. Ropes and axes are not needed. It is a heavy walk, not a feat of mountaineering, but many strong men fail in the last lap, overcome by mountain sickness. The successive belts of vegetation are a joy to the botanist.

I spent the day with my driver, who was happy to be at home and proud to act as guide. At every turn we met friends and relations of his. I shall have more to say of the Chagga later, the most prosperous and intelligent of the native peoples of East Africa. The Germans gave them security against their war-like neighbours, Catholic and Lutheran missionaries and a revered commissioner named Charles Douglas taught them the arts of peace, but before the white man appeared they had shown themselves an ingenious people, excavating deep caves for refuge from slave-traders and building a stone-walled canal which follows a valley contour and irrigates a village ten miles distant. Many streams from the snow-line fall in green-fringed cascades to be lost in the torrid plain below. It is a scene of theatrical charm. Save for its sturdy black inhabitants it might be in Polynesia. Then into this arcadia there came strolling two elegant, arrogant old men, each dressed in a single cotton length, very tall, upright and slender. 'Masai', said my driver in the voice he had used to point out the game in the reserve, but with an unmistakable note of fear in it, as though he were warning me of something more dangerous than beautiful, for it is not fifty years since the Masai used to raid here and drive the Chagga literally underground, and the memory survives. These two men had come in from their lands beyond the mountain on a peaceful errand, carrying long wands instead of spears, to visit a doctor; but their shadows cast a brief gloom as they passed.

At lunch time the other tourists from the *Rhodesia Castle* arrived at Kibo. They had been out at the watering-places in the reserve at dusk and dawn, had seen many animals and taken many photographs, and were well content with their experiences.

February 17*th*. Back to Mombasa. That night I found a jolly, bearded doctor who was willing to go with me to the Star Bar. It was his first visit and it was he who decided after a very few minutes that it was no place for us, after a girl from Zanzibar who, he diagnosed, was intoxicated with hashish, had taken an unreasonable and demonstrative dislike to his benign appearance. I must admit I was enjoying it awfully.

February 18*th*. Sailed at dawn and put in at Tanga for the day. I remained on board as I intended to go there later from Dar-es-Salaam, but I may here give advice to those who find themselves, as we did, with a day to spend in this busy provincial capital.

Don't let them take you on a sisal estate unless you have some peculiar interest in this vegetable, which was clearly intended by nature to be a picturesque weed; planted in regular lines of seemingly limitless extent it is deeply depressing.

Don't let them take you to a sulphurous cave they are proud of.

The place to visit from Tanga is Pangani, an Arab town some thirty miles down the coast. There is a good road to it (after Pangani it ceases to be passable at most seasons) and two places of interest on the way, a ruined mosque at Tongoli, rather like all other ruined mosques to the untrained eye, and a Swiss-owned sisal estate quite unlike any other, in that a Swahili workman showed a taste for mural decoration and his employers have kept him, as it were, as their official artist. The village consists of identical rectangular white-washed, concrete habitations, arranged in lines, as practical and as drab as the rows of sisal that surround them. These walls are now almost totally covered with vivid, naïve life-sized scenes of local life – dancers, animals, white men, Indians, natives of various tribes, askaris, police, convicts. They are not painted to survive the centuries, but for the time being they provide a lively spectacle.

The village was full of loungers, many rather drunk, for a good workman can cut his stint of sisal in four hours and if he wishes stop work at ten in the morning, having earned all he needs for the day. If he does a second stint, he can afford great quantities of liquor.

Pangani stands at the mouth of the river of that name which rises on the southern slopes of Kilimanjaro. Opposite it, across a ferry where the road leads uncertainly to Dar-es-Salaam, there is a bright green hill and an old mosque. On the Tanga side there is a fine water-front and promenade, a grand Arab fort, now the District Commissioner's house and office and some tall, impenetrable Arab mansions where the descendants of the slave-traders and dhow-builders live their decadent lives. It is said that a mild form of domestic slavery still survives behind their blind white walls. A small hospital and prison, German built of local materials in the local manner, have a deceptive and agreeable air of antiquity. British occupation is commemorated by a tablet marking the place of a landing during the first World War and by two nasty little buildings erected by the Public Works Department. No European lives there except the Commissioner, and few Indians. There is a 'Lucky Bar' where the younger and more decadent Arabs openly defy the precept of the Prophet. They are said to be weak in intellect and deplorable in morals.

That is all there is to see at Pangani, but it is well worth a visit. Perhaps it will not survive long. It has no function in modern Africa. Should I scruple to disturb its gentle decay by recommending it to tourists? I don't think so. There are no gracious dreams in its present tranquillity. In its heyday the place was cruel and grasping and philistine. There is only physical beauty here and that of a low order – the picturesque. Let it be a target for cameras.

February 19*th*. There has been a change in the character of the passengers. The missionaries and officials and many of the young men going to work got off at Mombasa and were replaced by holiday-makers, many of them from remote Kenyan farms who come down for a few days' cruise to enjoy a change of diet and of company.

We anchored off Zanzibar at dawn. A day of fierce heat. The island is said to enjoy a cool season. I have never struck it. An hour's stroll ashore sufficed to revive old memories; then I retired to the ship for a cold bath and an afternoon under the electric fans.

To elderly Englishmen Zanzibar is most famous for the great Bloomsbury rag, when Virginia Woolf and her friends inspected an English man-of-war at Portsmouth in the guise of the Sultan and his entourage, and for Bishop Weston's occupation of the Anglican see. Weston was the hero of many sermons in Lancing chapel and his Cathedral, built on the site of the old slave-market, the symbol of British beneficence in East Africa. Weston it was who, just before the first World War, threatened a schism in the Church of England by delating his neighbouring bishops for collaboration with nonconformists. Readers of Ronald Knox's *A Spiritual Aeneid* will remember the intense excitement of his coterie about the incident which, he said, the Lambeth committee found 'eminently pleasing to God and on no account to be repeated'. The Cathedral has a rather forlorn appearance today. One clergyman presides where there was a 'mess' of six. The main activities of the mission are now on the mainland and the historic little edifice has, with its brass plates commemorating British officials, the air of a Riviera chaplaincy. No church has made much progress in this last of the Arab sultanates. Eighty years ago it was hoped that a province was being added to Christendom. British rule has merely created an Indian settlement.

It was ironic, too, to find notices in the ship and on the quay requesting European ladies to respect local susceptibilities by dressing modestly. Shades of Mrs Jellaby and of all the sewing parties who used to make 'Mother-Hubbard' gowns to clothe the naked heathen! The French are said to be the most shameless tourists. Unless turned back by the police they parade the bazaar in 'Bikini' bathing-dresses.

There are no beggars or touts in Zanzibar. The narrow lanes are clean and fragrant and shaded. I saw no changes except that the fort has been tidied and made public. It is a pretty town. Few buildings are more than 150 years old, but all are built in the traditional fashion of plastered rubble, painted and repainted, with here and there delicate blue washes relieving the mottled white, with carved doors and hidden gardens, and the streets wander along the paths first traced by pack animals. Besides the usual trash for tourists there are genuine Arab and African antiquities to be found in the shops. The money changers have vanished, who used to produce from their leather bags gold pieces struck all over the world and still current, priced by weight, whenever the Arab dhows put in port. A few trousered figures flick wads of escudos under the noses of passengers bound for Mozambique, where venerable, turbaned obesities once squatted by their scales. There is still no tourists' hotel. Magicians still frequent the north island of Pemba, coming from as far as the lakes for their final schools in the black art. The reigning Sultan succeeded in 1911 and has been on his throne longer than any living ruler. His subjects have no nationality, part Arab, part Indian, part Swahili; British administration is pure, effective and benevolent. No doubt we shall soon read in the papers about 'Zanzibar Nationalism' and colonial tyranny.

What I read in the papers now, at the moment of writing is this:

'One of Zanzibar's tourist attractions – the old stone town with its narrow streets and houses with intricately-carved Arab doors – is to be cleared partially to provide improved living conditions. The inhabitants will be moved to new areas where proper amenities can be provided.

'Part of the cleared area will be used for the development of warehouse space in the port area to encourage the establishment of new industries essential to the island's economy.

'The estimated cost of the scheme, which ensures the balanced progress of housing, communications, commerce, industry, education and all community services is £258,000, but only £58,000 can be allocated because of the lack of funds.'

The last sentence is comforting.

4. TANGANYIKA

Dar-es-Salaam – Bagamoyo – an historic fiasco – Kilwa – the
coronation of Bishop Homer A. Tomlinson

February 20th. Dar-es-Salaam at dawn.

I made a grateful leave-taking with the *Rhodesia Castle*, where
I had recovered from all the malaises of the English winter and
landed in extreme heat in Tanganyika. Dar-es-Salaam, too, has its
cool season during the English summer. Its most loyal citizen could
not claim that the climate in February is pleasant. Nor that the city
has much to divert the sight-seer; less than Mombasa, which it
somewhat resembles; no Fort Jesus, no Star Bar. It is a port, a rail-
head and the seat of government – unlike Mombasa it is the capital
city, a distinction which means more every year as political institutions multiply. Its suburbs extend along pleasant beaches. There is
sailing and fishing and a hospitable British society.

Tanganyika is a pure bureaucracy, the number of officials has
doubled since 1945; they attempt to run a Welfare State on an
exiguous budget. They regard themselves as temporary caretakers
who will quite soon hand over their responsibilities to natives. The
head of the 'Nationalist' movement, Mr Nyerere, is universally well
spoken of (though 'nationality' in a people as heterogeneous as those
arbitrarily assigned to the territory has less meaning there than
almost anywhere in the world). There are very few white settlers of
the sort that abound in Kenya and Southern Rhodesia, a few
farmers, mostly industrious Boers, round Arusha, a few reputedly
eccentric English of the old 'Happy Valley' kind in the Southern
Highlands. There are a few sisal estates owned by Greeks and Swiss.
Over great areas the tsetse fly keeps man away. The great European
settlement was made by the Germans at the turn of the century.
They were evicted in the first World War. In the 1930s the Germans

began to return. They were very uppish, openly making lists of chiefs they would hang when Hitler recovered the land for them. (It was never properly part of the British Empire but a territory held under mandate of the League of Nations.) In 1937 it seemed quite probable he would succeed. The history of Africa and perhaps of Europe would have been very different had he done so. In September 1939 the British authorities neatly arrested the lot, taking them quite by surprise, and interned them for the duration of the war. There are very few of them in the territory now. Whenever one finds a building of any attraction, it usually turns out to be German.

One of these was the Club, where I was kindly lodged. It stands on the sea-front behind a broad terrace. In the time of the German occupation it had a beer-hall, skittle-alley and an adjoining brothel. Now there is instead an excellent library. There are a very few air-conditioned offices in Dar-es-Salaam. The older buildings are designed to catch the breeze. The Dar-es-Salaam Club is solidly built with much fine joinery in dark African timber and heavy brass fittings on doors and windows. In the days I spent there I sat for many hours sitting under the fans, sipping lime-juice (curiously enough limes are almost unprocurable in Tanganyika outside the capital. The hotel managers say, as they do in England, that there is 'no demand' for them) and reading the best-sellers of the last decade. It was very much like being on board ship. At sundown the Club came to life. Tables were set out on the terrace. Women appeared. Sometimes a band played. Shorts gave place to suits.

During the day the officials, who are the main white population, wear white shorts and open shirts, looking like grotesquely overgrown little boys who have not yet qualified for the first eleven at their private schools. Those who wish to add a touch of dandyism to this unimposing uniform sport monocles. I wonder how much the loss of European prestige in hot countries is connected with the craven preference for comfort over dignity.

At Dar-es-Salaam I met the ex-sapper to whom I had originally carried an introduction, and who at 400 miles' range had befriended me in Mombasa. He received me with urbane warmth. I will call him R. To him and to Mr Thompson, the agent of the Union Castle

Line, were due almost all the pleasure and interest of my weeks in the territory.

Saturday, February 21st. A policeman has been murdered in the suburbs because his neighbours thought a witch was enjoying police protection. That, at least, is the current story. I saw a great customs shed full of elephant tusks and rhinoceros horns, all for export to India. In order to discourage poaching, which none the less is prevalent, it is forbidden to work ivory in Tanganyika. The elephant tusks fetch 18s. a pound, the rhino horns 60s. Most of the latter are eventually sent to inflame the passions of the Chinese.

February 22nd. Mass at the Cathedral (another German building), very full, mostly of brilliantly endimanchés Goans, hardly a white face to be seen.

R. drove me out to Bagamoyo, forty-five miles up the coast, to lunch with the government archæologist, a young man not so effervescently happy as his confrère at Mombasa. In R.'s Mercedes-Benz we covered the very bad road in an hour and a half. Word had gone before me of my zest for ruined mosques. There are two – one mediæval, the other of the eighteenth century – some little distance from the present town, which is an agreeable decrepit nineteenth-century place, part German colonial, part Arab-slaver, with the spurious air of greater antiquity typical of the coast. The archæologist has a charming house built in the traditional materials – a sharp contrast to a row of mean concrete villas lately erected for official occupation by the Public Works Department.

Bagamoyo was the starting-point of most of the missionaries and explorers of the last century. The Germans made it their headquarters before they developed Dar-es-Salaam. It will be remembered in history as the scene of a disastrous dinner party given on 4th December 1859 to welcome the return of Stanley and Emin Pasha.

Every feature of Stanley's last expedition was tragic and villainous, tempered only by farce. Stanley himself in *In Darkest Africa* suggests diabolic interference.

Emin, it will be remembered, was a protégé of General Gordon's, who sent him to govern, in the name of the Khedive of Egypt, the equatorial province (to which Egypt had no claim) south of the Sudan. When Gordon fell, Emin remained beleaguered but for a time unmolested. Gordon had picked him up locally and little was known of him in Europe. He was a most likeable man, generous, gentle, deeply versed in natural history, a doting father to his half-caste daughter, but not quite the paladin which the English news-papers made of him. Born a German Jew, he worshipped indiffer-ently in synagogue, church and mosque. He represented himself at times as a Turkish subject, at times as an Egyptian; he seems to have considered becoming both British and Belgian. He had a Turkish wife (deserted in Prussia) and an Abyssinian mistress. Emin was a name he adopted in preference to his patronymic, Schnitzer.

When he found himself cut off, he contrived to send appeals for help addressed to the Egyptian, British and German governments. Private enterprise responded. In 1886 a Relief Fund was opened and generously supported from a medley of motives, humane, patriotic and commercial. The betrayal of Gordon at Khartoum must not be repeated. Gordon's last lieutenant was represented as gallantly holding out against the hordes of the Mahdi with a handful of devoted troops. They must either be brought to safety or reinforced and rearmed to continue their defence. Also, there were a number of North Country business men who were curious about the resources of central Africa, who thought the King of the Belgians had been sharp in snapping up the Congo and were eager to emulate him. An expedition through unexplored country meant a series of treaties and concessions from local potentates that could be turned to profit. Stanley had done it before. He must do it again. He accepted the leadership of the expedition.

As is made clearer in other reports than in Stanley's own, his appearance on the shore of Lake Albert precipitated a mutiny in Emin's army, which was largely commanded by officers who had been sent south to expiate crimes. So far from waging a gallant rearguard action they were very comfortably settled with harems and slaves and grown fat on the spoils of the surrounding country-side. Those who maintained a semblance of loyalty to Emin did so because there were rumours of a relief force. Emin and his staff, smartly dressed, came down the lake in their steamship and found

Stanley ragged and starving at the head of a small advance party
who under any other leadership would have been a rabble. He had
to return to pick up what was left of his wrecked forces. The
Egyptians promptly mutinied and arrested Emin. But the mutiny,
in its turn, and the rumours of Stanley's failure provoked the first
serious attack from the Sudanese. Suddenly the mutineers decided
they would follow Emin anywhere out of range of the fuzzy-wuzzies.
The enchanting story should be read at length (I have done so). It is
amply documented and has been attractively summarised by
Mr Byron Farwell in *The Man who Presumed*. I have given this little
sketch in order to point the disaster of the Bagamoyo dinner party.

Stanley arrived at the coast on 4th December 1889. Of the force
of 708 who had started to relieve Emin 196 returned. No one seems
to have troubled to count the Egyptians he had rescued. They set out
in great numbers with their women and children and household
furniture and they melted away on the road. Not all died. Some
found villages to harbour them. Some 260 eventually reached Cairo.
Controversy about Stanley's treatment of his white officers was long
and bitter. But anyway Emin was safe. There had been sharp
quarrels between them and much matter for mutual recrimination,
but they were ostensibly friends and colleagues. Stanley had reason
to hope that the Pasha would show his gratitude by entering either
the British or the Belgium service.

The Germans in command at Bagamoyo gave them a great
reception. Thirty-four Europeans sat down to dinner. It must,
I think, have been in the present Boma, the government office, but
it was not possible to identify it confidently from the wood-cut in *In
Darkest Africa*. It was certainly in a large building of two stories with
a balcony. Nowhere else in Bagamoyo seems a plausible alternative.

A superb scene for the cinematographer; a great German spread;
fresh meat and fresh fish; lashings of champagne; the multitude of
insects, all dear to Emin, expiring round the lamps; a naval band
below; in the streets the surviving Zanzibari porters celebrating their
return with an orgy; speeches, songs; congratulations in various
tongues made a lingua franca by common conviviality. Emin
moves beaming from place to place with a courteous word for
everyone; sailors, soldiers, consuls, missionaries and the guests of

honour; crimson Teutonic faces and thick necks predominate; a huge contrast to the yellow-bellies on the shores of Lake Albert, now littering the trail inland.

Presently the Pasha is absent. Other men have withdrawn from time to time. The party goes on. Then under the uproar word goes round. The Pasha has taken a header off the balcony. The Zanzibari dancers are stamping round his bloody corpse. It is not quite as bad as that, but it is odder in its sequel. He *has* taken a header and has been picked up for dead, blood oozing from his ears. He is unconscious. The medical men leave the table, but the party goes on.

The Governor of Equatoria is not dead. Perhaps it would suit the cinematographer better if he were. He lies in a coma for many days, and when he comes to his senses it is not Emin, it is not Schnitzer. It is something quite new in his history; he is a junker. He who has acknowledged the ancient thrones of Constantine and Suleiman, of David, of Pharaoh and Cleopatra even, indirectly, of Alfred and Victoria recognises only the brand-new, upstart empire of the Hohenzollerns. A telegram from the Kaiser has done the trick. He renounces all previous loyalties and in due time sets off up country on the quest of treaties on which these transient powers are based. But he was not long happy in his new allegiance. 'Would I had died after my fall on the stones of Bagamoyo,' he wrote in October 1891. His eyesight began to fail. Next year his expedition was as wasted by disease as had been Stanley's. Sitting at his table in camp near the Lilu River, some days' march from Stanley Falls, peering blindly at his specimens of plants and birds, the Arab slavers of the district (who had been chiefly responsible for the collapse of Stanley's rear column) came in and unceremoniously cut his throat.

On the road back we passed a village dance. They would keep it up far into the night, drinking and drumming; a jolly, social party not like the ngomas I used to see, which always had a hint of magic and, it seemed, of menace.

February 23rd. I do not regret my insincere expression of interest in mediæval Arab ruins. It has taken me to some delightful places and introduced me to delightful people. Today I booked to fly to Kilwa.

My resolution to eschew aeroplanes – like Belloc's to eschew trains on the *Path to Rome* – has had to be broken. The road is impassable at this season; a steamship plies from Mombasa but to take that would have extended the expedition by some three weeks and inflicted a visit of unbearable length on my kind hosts – for there is no hotel. Visitors must either bivouac or impose themselves as guests on the District Commissioner. So prejudice, now and later, had to be put aside and at noon I stepped into the suffocating little machine (which of course was late) bearing, what I was told would be acceptable, a leg of mutton frozen, when I put it in the rack, to the consistency of granite but soft as putty when I presented it to my hostess.

My destination is some 200 miles down the coast from Dar. There are three Kilwas – the island of Kilwa Kisiwani, all ruins now and a few huts; the sleepy little nineteenth-century town of Kilwa Kivinje, Arab and German built, eighteen miles to the north on the mainland; and Kilwa Masoko, the new boma, or adminis-trative station, to which I was bound. The aeroplane stopped at Mafia Island, a flat grove of coconut and mangrove which attracts deep-sea fishermen. We passed the Rufigi delta where the wreck of a German warship has lain visible for forty years. The Kilwa airstrip is near the boma. Here I was met by the District Commissioner and his wife and carried off to their house. His isolated position gives him a larger measure of freedom from bureaucratic interference than is enjoyed by any of his colleagues in Tanganyika. With the help of two young district officers he governs 3,000 square miles of territory. Inland it is said, there are more elephants than tax-payers; the few villages are visited on foot in the old colonial style. There are three European bungalows at Kilwa Masoko, an office, a school, two Indian shops and a pier. It is to this pier that the boma owes its existence, for in the heady days of the 'Groundnuts Scheme' it was designed to be the rail-head for the produce of the still virgin bush. The D.C. himself is one of the few benefits of that scheme; the 'groundnutters' have a low reputation, largely I gather deserved, but there was among them an appreciable number of zealous and efficient officers from the army who came out full of the faith that they would be doing something to help feed the victims of the war. These were the first to realise that the scheme was fatuous; some returned to England, others, of whom my host was one, remained in Tanganyika to do valuable work in other services. His wife and he are an exhilarating couple, both devoted to their large, lonely territory, without any regrets for the social amenities of the towns.

February 24th. A narrow channel separates the boma from the island of Kilwa Kisiwani. We crossed early in the morning by motor-launch, embarking at the pier and wading ashore up the sandy beach. Once the Sultan of Kilwa ruled from Mafia in the north to Sofala (near the modern Beira) 900 miles to the south. It was by far the greatest of the East African sultanates. Now, with its neighbour-ing islands of Songo Mnara and Sanji ya Kati, it is inhabited by a few families of fishermen. The Persians probably came here first and set up a dynasty in the tenth century. It was under the Arabs of Oman that the place became great. The Portuguese came there at the beginning of the sixteenth century. In 1589 the Zimba ate all the inhabitants and left a waste that was irregularly reoccupied. Once, in the eighteenth century, it recovered some prosperity, again under the Oman Arabs. It then declined steadily until the last sultan was deported by the Sultan of Zanzibar in the middle of the last century.

Archæologists, notably Sir Mortimer Wheeler and Fr Gervase Matthew, have lately paid professional attention to the district. There is plenty to delight the mere sight-seer.

A very faint, inexpungible tinge of luxury lingers in this desolate island. The goats and the few tiny cows which pasture there have made glades and open spaces of park land between the trees whose flowers scent the steamy air as though in a Rothschild's greenhouse; gaudy little birds flash and call as they used to in the aviary at Hackwood. Phrases from Tennyson's Alcaics come uncertainly and not entirely aptly to mind. 'Me, rather, all that bowery loveli-ness'; there are no 'brooks of Eden mazily murmuring' on Kilwa, nor 'cedar arches'; but 'rich ambrosial ocean isle' and 'the stately palm woods whisper in odorous heights of even' are exact and might have been written here.

The buildings lie along the north shore opposite Kilwa Masoko. The most prominent is the most modern, an eighteenth-century

Arab fort standing on Portuguese foundations, probably on the site of an earlier fort, for it is the obvious place for the defence of the harbour. A seemingly ancient carved wooden doorway is, in fact, dated 1807. Once there was a long wall along the seafront, but this has been washed away; the walls to landward survive in various stages of dilapidation with towers at intervals; in the centre the Sultan's palace, consisting of the long narrow rooms whose dimensions were determined by the available timber beams. There are traces of red paint and ornamental plaster. Outside the walls stand a small, domed mosque, and a much larger one called the 'Friday Mosque'. Domed mediæval buildings are very rare in East Africa. Blue-glazed bowls have been set into the cupolas and the minarets. Beyond these mosques lie a cemetery, another mosque, more fortifications, a huge water-cistern and traces of many unidentified buildings. The only mosque in use is a humble shed which serves the present population of a few fishermen.

The only man of importance is a nonogenarian Dervish, on whom I was taken to call by the D.C. He looked like a black Father Christmas. His chief possession is a large, carved bed which is coveted by the museum at Dar. He was not using it that morning, but was recumbent in a low chair, unable to rise to greet us, but attended by a pretty girl who carried a baby he assured us proudly was his own. I once supposed that Dervishes employed themselves either in spinning like tops or in breaking British squares, but I have since looked them up in the encyclopædia and learned that the term is so wide as to be almost meaningless; they can be orthodox, pantheistic, mystical, political, ascetic, orgiastic, magical, ecstatic; they can live as members of strict communities or as hermits or nomads, mendicants, scholars, revivalists – almost anything it seems.

While the D.C. was exchanging politenesses in Kiswahili I noticed over our host's head a framed picture of King George VI with an inscription signed by a former Governor in the name of His Majesty 'as a record of the valuable services rendered by him to his own Country and People and to the British Government in advancing the Moslem religion'. It seemed an odd tribute from the Defender of the Faith.

On saying good-bye, the genial old man produced from his bosom a hen's egg and presented it to me. That afternoon the D.C.'s wife had a sewing class on her verandah for the few native girls of the station.

February 25th. Drove to Kilwa Kivinje – well laid out, well planted, picturesque, decaying. There are no European inhabitants. An Englishman sometimes visits an office where he transacts business in mangrove bark. He was in fact my fellow passenger from Dar and returned there with me on the next flight. An aged Swahili magistrate sat in the old German court-house. In the ramshackle little German hospital Indian doctors rather ironically displayed their meagre equipment. A few youths squatted on their door-steps playing the endless and unintelligible gambling game of dropping nuts very swiftly and earnestly on a board hollowed out for them as for marbles in solitaire. No crafts survive in the town except, among the women, very simple grass matting; the ancient wood-carvers are represented by a single clumsy joiner. There are a few Indian grocers and a pleasant little market of fish and vegetables. Meat is almost unprocurable; hence my offering of frozen mutton. It was a regrettable and much regretted decision to move the boma to Masoko. Anyone having business at headquarters has a walk of nearly forty miles. There is, I think, no unofficial wheeled vehicle in the district. The D.C. and his wife knew everyone in the place and were plainly welcome at every door. He had lately on his own initiative repaired the sea wall, thus preserving a promenade dear to Arab social tradition.

February 26th. The aeroplane came in the morning to take me back to Dar. There was in it a copy of that day's *East African Standard* containing this paragraph: 'Bishop Homer A. Tomlinson of New York, self-styled "King of the World", flew into Dar-es-Salaam last night from Salisbury. He is to crown himself King of Tanganyika today. He intends to leave the New Africa Hotel at 10 a.m. and walk around the town for two hours crowning himself on a suitable site at noon.'

This seemed a happy confirmation of the theme of Eric Rosenthal's *Stars and Stripes in Africa* which had beguiled my voyage out.

We landed at 11 o'clock. Mr Thompson met me at the aerodrome. He had not heard of Bishop Homer A. Tomlinson's assumption of sovereignty. We drove up and down the main streets of the city looking for him and making enquiries. His progress, if it had occurred, had been unobserved. At noon we came to the New Africa Hotel. This, the leading hotel, is near the Club, separated from the water-front by a little public garden and a war memorial. In the tropic noon the place was quite empty except for half a dozen policemen and two journalists. They were waiting for the Bishop, and we joined them in the scanty shade.

I expected a flamboyant figure from Harlem. Instead there presently emerged from the hotel an elderly white man dressed in a blue kimono. He was unattended and somewhat encumbered by paraphernalia. He gave no indication of expecting any kind of ovation. As purposeful and recollected as a priest going to his altar to say Mass, the Bishop shuffled across under the blazing sun, opened a folding chair and sat down in the garden. The police, the two journalists, Mr Thompson and I collected round him. A representative of the local broadcasting organisation appeared with a tape-recorder. The Bishop ignored him and like a priest or rather, perhaps, like a conjurer, began arranging his properties. He had a bible, a crown which seemed to be light and inexpensive, a flag, not – shade of Rosenthal! – the Stars and Stripes but something simple but unidentifiable of his own design of blue and white stars, and a bladder. The stuff of his little chair was slightly regal, a pattern of red and gold with ornamental tassels. He dropped the flag over his head as though preparing for a nap. Then he blew noisily into the bladder which proved to be an inflatable, plastic terrestrial globe. He blew hard and strong, but there was a puncture somewhere. It took the form of a wizened apple but not of a full sphere. After a few more puffs he despaired and laid it on the ground at his feet. Then he removed the flag from his head and began to address us in calm nasal tones.

He was, he said, the acknowledged leader of the largest religious body in the world about 100,000,000 strong to date. In 1923 he had received the call to be a bishop; in 1953 to be a king. He was the sovereign of fifty-two realms and proposed to complete his vocation by crowning himself in every state in the world, including Russia. Under his simple autarchy peace would be assured to all his subjects. He then prayed for the prosperity of Tanganyika, placed the crown on his head, collected his impedimenta and retired to the New Africa Hotel.

The temperature that day was 90°, humidity 100.

From time to time in the next few weeks I had news of him. The Sultan of Zanzibar did not welcome a rival in his dominions. He was forbidden to crown himself there. He got to Nairobi by air, but the immigration authorities of Kenya suspected him of subversive activities and would not let him leave the aerodrome. They would not even let him crown himself in the waiting-room.

5. TANGANYIKA CONTINUED

Safari – Morogoro – Groundnut Scheme – Dodoma – Kondoa – Arusha – a visit to the Masai – Moshi – the King of the Chagga – Soni – Tanga – the last of the junkers – the Emergency – Iringa

Saturday, February 28th. R. has arranged his business so that I can accompany him on a long 'safari' – a term now used to designate a luxurious motor tour. He has been a racing driver in his time and his affection for his car is tender to the point of infatuation. It is a worthy object of devotion, a large, new, fast and extremely comfortable Mercedes-Benz.

R. has a fixed smile of fascination and an air of self-confidence rarely found in civil servants. He is a large, handsome euphoric man in early middle age, as near a dandy as local custom allows; a late-comer to the colonial service. He has – or rather had, for he has just been promoted – an office requiring great tact, patience and discretion. He is in charge of 'personnel'; that is to say of all postings in the government service; most dissensions, discontents and scandals come to him for treatment and part of his task is to make periodic tours of the 'bomas' and see that everyone is reasonably happy and sane. With us, engaged on some rather similar errand whose precise nature I never learned, is a retired brigadier; a regular soldier of imperturbable geniality. I don't know if they enjoyed my company. I certainly enjoyed theirs.

We set out in the early morning. If brigadiers have an occupational weakness, it is neurotic solicitude about their baggage. Not so our brigadier who was blithe and care-free. Indeed, as will appear later, he was deprived of a portfolio of highly confidential documents during our tour and accepted the loss with admirable equanimity.

We drove due west up the old slave-route, which is now the path of road and railway. A road heavy with wicked association. No one, I suppose, except a zealot of some recondite natural science, can find much pleasure in the coastal plain of East Africa. We sped where, not very long ago, we should have met the caravans of yoked and ivory-laden captives. Plantation soon gave place to bush. It was pleasant to be out of Dar and it was quite joyfully that we reached Morogoro before noon. Here we lunched with the District Commissioner. The conversation was of witchcraft, political agitation, tax-evasion, big game and secret societies – the staple, engrossing topics that greet one anywhere up country in Africa. There is little at Morogoro except the boma, the railway station and a few Indian shops. Yes, I know, I ought to write 'Asian'; Pakistanis don't like to be called 'Indian' nowadays, but I grew up with a simple vocabulary in which 'Asian' did not exist and 'Asiatic' usually meant a sinister Chinaman. I hope this little book will not be banned (like the Oxford Dictionary) in Karachi as the result of my antiquated habits of speech. No offence is intended.

There were no problems at Morogoro for R. or the brigadier. We drove on refreshed, and late in the afternoon came to a huge clearing in the bush, 90,000 acres of grassland. This is all that remains of the Kongwa groundnuts plantation which twelve years ago was a topic of furious debate in London and of bitter recrimination in Africa. The Overseas Food Corporation ceased to exist in March 1955. The Tanganyika Agricultural Corporation is now engaged in saving what it can from the wreck. Some 9,000 head of cattle, in herds of 300, have been put in the care of Gogo families. These tribesmen have reverted to their former scanty dress and rebuilt their houses on the ancestral model, very low rectangles of mud, with flat roofs of turf. Three veterinary and administrative officials are the only white population. The cattle are healthy and may multiply. But the Sodom apple threatens to overrun the pasture if not constantly resisted. If the experts go, the grass will go with them.

At my request R. diverged from the main road to visit the once populous site. It was not easy to find. The roads of Kongwa are breaking up, the railway-lines have been removed, the airstrip is overgrown. Few buildings remain, and those are up for sale. As we drove to the only inhabited bungalow, an Englishman came out to ask if we had come to buy the school hall, for the final failure on this disastrous scene has been that of a secondary boarding-school, the only one in Tanganyika, which that month was reopening in the Southern Highlands after some scandalous goings-on at Kongwa.

On a slight rise stand the empty bungalows which were once called 'Millionaires' Row' and 'Easy Street', where the high officials lived in the intervals of flying to Dar and London; sad sheds with the weed growing high in their gardens. We made our way through the growth and peered through the windows at the empty little rooms. It was hard to conceive that they had ever been the object of derisive envy.

There are two excellent documents, *The Groundnut Affair* by the late Alan Wood, written in 1950, and a brief retrospective paper by Mr A.T.P. Seabrook, the Chief Administrative Officer of the Tanganyika Agricultural Corporation, written in 1957. Wood was a loyal socialist and Public Relations Officer in the early stages of the scheme. When he wrote there still seemed a chance of growing some nuts. When Mr Seabrook wrote, he counted the secondary school, which was now being dismantled under our eyes, as one of the positive gains to the territory.

There was no injustice in treating the fiasco as a matter of party politics. The scheme was conceived in an ideological haze, prematurely advertised as a specifically socialist achievement and unscrupulously defended in London when everyone in Africa knew it was indefensible. No one at the top made a penny out of it. The officials were underpaid and had in some cases given up better jobs to come. I well remember the indignation, some twenty years ago, of a foreign art expert who recounted to me in great detail the transaction by which the National Gallery had acquired a painting of doubtful authenticity. 'And all of them,' he concluded in disgust, 'the Director and his committee are gentlemen of private fortune. Not one of them received even a commission. It could not have happened in any other country.'

Africa has seen many great financial swindles. This was not one of them. The aim was benevolent; the provision of margarine for the undernourished people of Great Britain. The fault was pride; the hubris which leads elected persons to believe that a majority at the polls endues them with inordinate abilities.

Mr Strachey's plan was to clear 5,210,000 acres of virgin bush in 1947 which in 1950 would produce 600,000 tons of groundnuts. The total expenditure, spread over six years, was to be £24,000,000. The estimated profit was £10,000,000 a year. It does not require acute hindsight to discern something improbable in this calculation. In September 1948 the administrative heads of departments in Kongwa submitted a report expressing dismay at the progress of the venture. This was ignored. At the end of that year £18,000,000 had been spent and current expenses were £1,000,000 a month. No considerable quantity of groundnuts was ever produced; nor was there a need for them – they were piling up in mountains in West Africa needing only transport to make them available. Altogether, I believe, some £40,000,000 were squandered by the Overseas Food Corporation. Rival politicians had every reason to make a row about it.

But the imagination is moved by the human elements of the story. The Labour Government conceived it as their duty as trustees of the native races to institute trades unions and sent salaried officials to teach them how to strike for higher pay. In the first year their efforts were rewarded. The Europeans working at Kongwa had to be enrolled as special constables and organised in armed patrols for the protection of themselves and their servants. Bands of African spearmen blocked the roads. The railway stopped running. The tractors lay idle. Police had to be brought in from Dodoma. The union leaders were taken to prison and the strikers' demands remained unsatisfied.

Frantic supply officials saw enormous quantities of derelict army stores accumulate at Dar from the Philippine Islands, brought in unlisted lots, the useful and the useless inextricably confused.

The site at Kongwa had been selected for its emptiness. It was empty because it was waterless.

The encampment at Kongwa housed some 2,000 men and women from Great Britain and some 30,000 natives. Their presence among the simple Wagogo came near to dissolving tribal loyalties.

Their high wages put up the price of food so that natives not employed by the scheme went hungry. Many of the natives who were attracted by the high wages left their own small holdings uncultivated, so that less food was grown in the Territory than ever before. Large quantities were imported to feed those who were supposed to be exporters. It was even proposed to import bees into an area where bees were the principal natural terror, in order to pollinate the sunflowers (which died of drought anyway). A half of all the liquor imported into Tanganyika was consumed at Kongwa. It was a new experience for most natives to see Englishmen demonstratively drunk. It was new, also, to see them convicted of theft. Villages of prostitutes, who charged stupendous fees of five shillings or more, sprang up round the encampment. The hospital orderlies did an illicit trade in injections which they pretended cured syphilis. Thieves infested the stores and workshops. A firm official promise that first priority would be given to the erection of 1,000 African married quarters, resulted by the end of 1948 in 200, and those inferior to what were provided by the Greek sisal planters; respectable Africans refused to move their families into them on the grounds that Kongwa was a bad address. The equalitarian ideas of the home government found no sympathy in Africa. The infinitely graded social distinctions among the workers (there are seven recognised classes of Mauritians alone) came as a surprise to the English socialists. By the end of 1948 there was a turnover in the labour force of twenty per cent. per month.

The pity of it is that many of the original 'groundnutters', like my host at Kilwa, had come out to Africa with high, altruistic motives. These mostly left Kongwa in the first two years. It is ironical now to read what Alan Wood (who himself resigned in protest at the obliquity of public utterances in London) wrote in 1950: 'I believe that in Africa, as in Europe, the only real reply to Communism will be Socialism. The best answer to the Africans who dream of Soviet Russia is to boast that the groundnut scheme can be as remarkable an experiment as anything done under the Five-Year Plans; that it is based on some of the same principles, something new in Colonial development, a huge co-operative venture not run for private profit, which will eventually be run by the people who are working for it;

but which represents an advance on anything in Russia, in that large-scale economic planning is combined with political freedom.'

We turned back to the main road past traditional villages of the Wagogo. The inhabitants waved cheerfully at us. The immigrants have all departed, leaving them much as they were when Living-stone passed through, but the richer for some fine cattle.

That night we slept at Dodoma at the railway hotel. It is a railway town, scattered, unlovely, noisy.

Sunday, March 1st. R. goes out before breakfast to visit his motor car and brood over it fondly. I passed him on my way to Mass at the shabby crowded little church. When I returned he had breakfasted and was giving the windscreen a final caress with chamois leather as attentively as a character from Erle Stanley Gardner wiping finger-prints from a telephone.

From Dodoma we drove north, blank bush on our right, hills on our left, a seedy track, part of what was once hopefully spoken of as the all-British route from the Cape to Cairo. A hundred miles brought us to Kondoa, a pretty oasis with an unfathomable spring, a German fort and granary, Arab houses still largely inhabited by Arabs, and a vertiginous suspension foot-bridge over which daring District Officers have been known to drive their motor-bicycles. The Public Works Department is engaged on replacing the spacious and cool houses which the Germans built for their officials with the cramped, concrete structures which are mysteriously preferred by the authorities in Dar. The District Officer, a young man of an earlier and happier type than his contemporaries, still occupied one of the old houses, but his superior, the District Commissioner, had been moved to an ignoble little villa.

At Kondoa we saw the last of Arab influence until we returned to the coast. From there we had 150 miles to go to Arusha, the road climbing all the way through the Masai steppe, empty, open country; the only incidents on the road were occasional hutted camps of the P.W.D. and at Babati a bar frequented by Field Officers and plump, unbecomingly dressed women from the Seychelles.

Arusha is the provincial capital, a considerable town with two hotels, one of which seeks to attract by the claim to be exactly midway between Cape Town and Cairo. There is a small pocket of white farmers in the district, some of them immigrants from the Union of South Africa. Perhaps because it was Sunday evening they gave an air of festivity to the bar and lounge. The rather large European managerial staff mingled affably with them. I did not see any African or Indian customers. Dogs howled and scuffled under the windows at night. Can I say anything pleasant about this hotel? Yes, it stands in a cool place in a well-kept garden and it stocks some potable South African wines in good condition.

R. and the brigadier have a full day's official business before them. They introduce me to the Acting Provincial Commissioner, who very kindly offers to lend me one of his officers for an excursion among the Masai. It is my rare good fortune, he explains, to arrive at the time when there is a great assembly of this nation for the ceremonial initiation of elders.

The Masai are, I suppose, the most easily recognisable people in Africa. Their physical beauty and the extreme trouble they take to adorn it have popularised their photographs in geographical magazines and tourist advertisements all over the world. Every writer on East Africa has paid his tribute to their pride and courage. A generation back they still carried the long spear, hunted lion with it and defended their grazing rights over a huge region much of which is now the 'white highlands' of Kenya. They gleefully pointed out at the time of the Mau Mau rising that it was the English who introduced the supposedly docile Kikuyu into those lands and they enjoyed their small part in the pacification. For a generation they had been punished for raiding the Kikuyu; now they were paid to do so. The story is told that a patrol was sent out with orders to bring in any Kikuyu 'arms' they could find; next morning the commanding officer's tent was surrounded with a heap of severed limbs. Fighting, hunting and herding cattle, sheep and goats – but primarily cattle – are the only occupations suitable for a man. The Matabele, an equally brave people, when conquered, immediately became the servants of their conquerors. No one has ever made a servant of a Masai; nor were they ever conquered; they have been cheated a little, but they have always negotiated with the white man as equals. They employ a servile tribe as blacksmiths and themselves practise no crafts except those of the beauty parlour. Four Holy Ghost Fathers work among them, but by far the greater part remain pagan and polygamous. Nor have they been influenced by the Mohammedan missionaries who are making more converts than the Christians in some areas round the Lakes. At the time of writing, it is announced that they have elected a Catholic paramount chief. There was no paramount chief before; authority resided in an intricate system of local chiefs and elders; the new office is, I think, that of an ambassador rather than of a ruler. They have found it convenient to appoint an educated spokesman to deal for them, not so much with the British Commissioners who understand them, as with the educated Africans of other tribes who will shortly be assuming power; who would like to despise them because they do not wear shorts but have inherited an ineradicable awe. The Masai are not primitive in the way that pygmies and bushmen are. They are an intelligent people who have deliberately chosen to retain their own way of life. Tobacco, snuff and South African sherry are the only products of white civilisation which they value. Like the French they recognise nationality by social habits rather than by race. Men and women from other tribes who marry among them and conform to local custom are accepted. In one boma near Arusha I saw a head-man who was by origin a Sikh. I had always thought Sikhs a remarkably handsome people until I saw him beside the Masai. Those who have been encouraged to seek higher education outside their pastures usually return and at once eagerly readopt the cos-tume and customs of their people. The few who go to the cities are said to turn criminal. Thirty years ago it was predicted that the Masai would become extinct. In fact they have slightly increased in numbers.

March 2nd. The excursion to the Masai was not quite as exhilarating as I had hoped. Early on the cold grey morning the Acting Provin-cial Commissioner called with the news that the officer who had volunteered to accompany me had gone sick. 'But you'll be all right,' he said, 'your driver knows where to go. You will find the

District Commissioner Peebles in camp there and he will show you everything. The place is called Tinka-Tinka. Better take sandwiches with you.'

He presented a police driver to me and addressed him in Swahili; the words 'Tinka-Tinka' occurred in the introduction. The man, who came from Tanga, repeated 'Tinka-Tinka' in a knowledgeable way. It was arranged that he should return in a Landrover after I had breakfasted.

I secured a packet of food and by 9 I and my monoglot driver were on the road, the main road north to Nairobi. We drove for two hours, passing the police post which marked the Kenya frontier. It struck me as odd that an officer of the Tanganyika service should be presiding in Kenya, but I had no means of communicating my doubts and was dulled by the blank monotony of the countryside. The sun was now out. At length we turned off the road and came to a stop at a clearing where there stood six little tin market stalls. The name of the place was plainly displayed on a painted board 'NGUTATEK'.

'Tinka-Tinka?' I asked.

'Tinka-Tinka.'

I pointed to the sign board but my guide was not only monoglot but illiterate. 'Tinka-Tinka,' he said firmly.

'Bwana Peebles?' I asked.

'Bwana Peebles,' he replied. Then he got out of the car and lay down in the shade of a tree.

Great clouds of flies and bees surrounded the little shops. They were kept by Africans and were stocked with identical, miscellaneous goods. I entered one and asked 'Ngutatek?'

'Ngutatek,' the shopkeeper confirmed.

'No, Tinka-Tinka?'

'Tinka-Tinka.'

'Bwana Peebles?'

An emphatic shake of the head. 'No Bwana Peebles.'

'D.C.?'

'No D.C.'

I went to my supine driver. 'No Bwana Peebles. No D.C.'

He nodded vigorously. 'Bwana Peebles, D.C. Tinka Tinka.'

I despaired and returned to the Landrover. Presently there appeared a small group of unmistakable Masai, young warriors covered in ochre; their hair plaited and coated with red; bracelets and necklaces and ear-rings of copper and beads; spears and knob-kerries in hand; their ruddy togas falling loose and open to reveal their dyed flanks. They stared at me and the car. I attempted my little catechism about Tinka and Bwana Peebles. They spat (a politeness, I was told later) and sauntered away. They swaggered into the shops and bought nothing. They swaggered on to my driver and stared at him. He got up and moved further away to the shade of another tree, plainly scared of them. An hour passed. Then there appeared a Kikuyu boy. I welcomed, as I little expected to do when I set out, the evidence in shorts and shirt of European influence. He had a few words of English.

I began my little catechism. No D.C. here. D.C. not coming here. A big meeting of Masai? Not here. Where? That way; pointing vaguely into the bush. But is this Tinka-Tinka. Tinka that way, just here. He pointed to some huts half a mile distant. Show me. I roused my driver. We bumped along the track and found a well with a mechanical pump. This was Tinka. There was no one about. 'Tell this boy in Swahili where the Masai are meeting.' Some conversation ensued, after which my driver got into the car and drove off very crossly in the opposite direction to the one indicated. We drove another twenty miles into Kenya and came to an Indian shop. Here the driver made some enquiries as the result of which he turned the car round and drove furiously back over the road we had travelled.

'Arusha?' I asked.

'Arusha.'

At a river-crossing near the Tanganyika border we had passed an agreeable-looking little road-house. Here I made him stop. I did not want to accept defeat without one more effort. The hotelier was English and kindly disposed. Yes, he knew about the Masai gathering, but he thought it was to be a week or two later. He knew where the D.C. was in camp. He explained the mystery of Tinka. It is an onomatopoeic word used in those parts for any mechanical device. The pump at the well was a Tinka. There were Tinkas all over the place, one at the site of the D.C.'s camp, which was below the western slopes of Kilimanjaro. The hotelier came out to my driver and explained to him in great detail how to get there. The man repeated the route sullenly but apparently with accuracy. All now seemed set fair. I parted from my rescuer with warm thanks at 1 o'clock. I ate my luncheon which the driver refused to share, whether from religious scruples or sheer bad temper I do not know. We stopped and refilled with petrol at the frontier post. Presently we left the main road and took to dirt tracks. Then it came on to rain.

We were now, it was plain from the quality of the cattle, in an area of European occupation. It seemed an improbable venue for Masai initiation ceremonies. We passed various signs illegible to my driver which indicated farms and government establishments, but he drove on through the mud and rain as fast as he could go with a grim lack of curiosity which suggested confidence. He was following instructions, I assumed. It was three hours before I realised he was completely lost. Then I said 'Arusha', and we were looking for a place to turn in the deep lane when there appeared on foot two uniformed Askaris. These were men from the camp we were seeking. They climbed into the car, directed us and at last, with an hour of daylight left, I met Bwana Peebles, who had expected me at 10 o'clock that morning and now greeted me with good humour.

There was no assembly of the Masai, such as I had been led to expect. That, as the hotelier had said, was in the future. The holy hill where the initiation had to take place was separated from the main tribal grazing-grounds by the European farms and it was to arrange a corridor through which the assembly and its herds could pass that the D.C. and his vet. were now in camp. The holiness of the hill was traditional; the Masai resolutely maintained their rights to its use, despite any inconvenience to the 'immigrant races', but I gathered the initiation ceremony would be convivial rather than devotional. A warrior may not marry, but he enjoys wide privileges among the unmarried girls of the tribe. When he becomes an elder, he marries, his wife's head is shaven to make her unattractive and an operation is performed which is thought to make her impervious to the temptations of love. His diet is reduced, but his influence in conference grows. It was this transition, in early middle age, that was being prepared at this new Tinka. Half a dozen of the prospective candidates for maturity were there, living in a neighbouring boma. I was invited to enter this little enclosure, where each family has its own hut and its own entrance to the thorn stockade, and the cattle are penned at night among the surrounding dwellings. Cow dung was the main constituent of the architecture.

'If only people would realise that the Masai are just men with two legs,' said the D.C. 'Europeans go quite dotty about them one way or another.'

'Doesn't everyone love them?'

'No, indeed.'

As we were talking a neighbouring farmer, of Boer extraction, came into camp. It was plain that he for one did not at all relish the passage of the Masai through his property. Mr Peebles disabused me of many popular fallacies, such as that the Masai bleed their cattle and subsist on their blood as a staple diet. It is only done, he told me, either ceremoniously or to stop them straying in time of drought. Also of the belief that they are totally untouched by the modern world. When he first came to the district, he told me, before he had learned the language, he was confronted in his office by a Masai warrior in full rig, standing on one leg. He turned to his clerk and said in Swahili: 'Can you find someone to interpret?'

'That will not be necessary,' said the Masai in English. 'I have come to ask for a passport to attend a Boy Scouts' Jamboree in London.'

The rain had passed. Under a watery sunset my dull driver, who had refused food from the Askaris also (I suppose he simply lacked appetite), was given instructions for his return journey which he successfully followed.

I found R. and the brigadier weary from a long day spent wrestling with the problems of government employees.

They have no direct connexion with native administration. At the places we visited on this tour their concern is to resolve the reactions which inevitably occur in isolated communities.

The British officials in Tanganyika are of three groups, none wholly sympathetic to one another. Near the top are those who were young men of military age in 1938 and 1939. They considered at that time that they could best serve their country at a great distance from the European war which all foresaw. These are now in many cases being appointed to Provincial Commissionerships, enjoying seniority to men of their own age who came to Africa after serving, often with distinction, in the armed forces. This second group, now District Commissioners, are inclined to resent this precedence. Below them are the young men who have been produced by the Butler Education Act. These fear that before they can rise very high in the Colonial Service their jobs will be taken by natives. Nor are they all entirely happy in their immediate circumstances. The State, it seems, has not inculcated middle-class prudence in the newly created middle class. In the early days of the British Empire young men without private means did not aspire to support white consorts until they had risen above the lowest ranks. Disease made promotion rapid. The young men coming out from England now come from families in which, traditionally, men marry young. They sadly present budgets which prove that they cannot afford wives, children, motor cars and the club bar. It is R.'s task to explain that they have no very bitter grievance.

March 3rd. Our next stage was a short one, less than sixty miles to Moshi, the capital of the Chagga country which I had entered from the other side in my trip from Mombasa. It was downhill into a hot plain. I hoped to persuade R. and the brigadier to spend the night at the German hotel on the other side of Kilimanjaro where I had been so comfortable, but there is a huge, brand-new hotel in Moshi itself, built, owned and managed by a Greek; it is named the Livingstone, though Livingstone never came within 200 miles of it. It is the most up to date in Tanganyika, all concrete and plastic and chromium plate, and has proved very useful to film companies who come to make dramas of African life 'on location'. A film company was in occupation of the greater part of it at that moment and their lure proved irresistible to the brigadier, who hoped to find a galaxy of Hollywood starlets. In this he was disappointed. The heroines had already done their part and packed up, leaving the hero, of international repute, and a large, exclusively male rear column of cameramen and 'executives'. But the Livingstone was well equipped and well served, like a liner unaccountably stranded.

Let me here give a word of advice to fellow tourists in East Africa: keep away from hotels run by the British. We have no calling to this profession. Things are often better further south, but in Tanganyika especially all the defects which distress us at home are accentuated. The forbidding young women who stand behind the 'reception' counters in English provincial hotels have taken the place of post office clerks in the popular imagination for their combination of aloofness with incompetence. Many a weary traveller must have wondered what these wretches do in their hours of leisure. In East Africa he can find out. They sit about with their patrons and make bright conversation. We had suffered from them already and I was to suffer more. Nothing like that happened at the Livingstone. But I felt homesick for the cool verandah of Kibo.

Arusha is a colonial town. Moshi is a model of what liberals hope to see in a self-governing dominion. The Chagga number about 300,000; their land is fertile and healthy. They have in recent years evolved something like a constitutional monarchy. When the Germans came they found a number of local chiefs divided by rivalries which sometimes became violent. They hanged a number of chiefs and appointed one Marealle as paramount. It is his grandson who now reigns as Mshumbree Marealle II, the Mangi Mkuu. He is not infrequently spoken of as 'King Tom'. Under him sits the Chagga Council comprising 3 Divisional Chiefs, 17 Area Chiefs, 17 elected members, 6 nominated and 6 co-opted members. There is an independent judicature. By all accounts it works well and the Chagga have ambitions of absorbing their neighbours, the Pare.

We arrived at Moshi at 9 o'clock in the morning. The brigadier's eyes brightly scanned the hall of the hotel but he was told that the film company had already set out for their day's work. They had hired a number of corner-boys and were dressing them up as Masai and teaching them 'tribal' dances.

I was taken off to the Council Offices and introduced to the paramount chief. The Council Offices are brand-new, spick and span, all paid for from local revenue. Marealle is a very engaging young man, who has qualified himself for his high office by taking courses in Social Administration, Economics, Sociology and Psychology at the London School of Economics, without suffering from any of the radical influences popularly associated with that institution. He has also served in Tanganyika as a Welfare Officer and Programmes Manager of the Tanganyika Broadcasting Station and has translated Kipling's 'If' into Kiswahili. He put me in charge of a subordinate to be shown the beauties of his offices and dismissed me with an invitation to dinner that evening, saying: 'Don't trouble to dress. Come in your tatters and rags.'

I am not much of a connoisseur of social and political progress. Another pen than mine is needed to do justice to the really remarkable achievements of the Chagga government. From the Council building I was taken to the KNCU, the Headquarters of the Coffee Cooperative which is the source of almost all the local prosperity. Missionaries introduced the coffee-bean to the slopes of Kilimanjaro and found that it thrived on their property. Dundas, the first British D.C., persuaded the peasants to grow it. Mr Bennett, an Englishman who has spent most of his life in the district, organised the 'cooperative'. Now it is effectively in Chagga hands. I have 'KNCU' plainly written in my diary. What do these initials stand for? I wish I could remember. Presumably something Chagga or Cooperative Union. Anyway it is a very capacious building in 'contemporary' style. Besides the offices used for the coffee trade it has a shopping arcade, a roof café, a library, bedrooms and a Commercial School, the only one (I think) in Tanganyika. Here I found a mixed class of male and female, Chagga and Indian (male Chaggas predominating), taking a secretarial course. I should have known better than to put my head into that classroom. I have been caught before in this way by nuns. I smirked and attempted to get away when I heard the fateful words '. . . would so much appreciate it if you gave them a little address'.

'I am awfully sorry I haven't anything prepared. There's nothing I could possibly talk about except to say how much I admire everything.'

'Mr Waugh, these boys are all wishing to write good English. Tell them how you learned to write so well.'

Like a P. G. Wodehouse hero I gazed desperately at the rows of dark, curious faces.

'Mr Waugh is a great writer from England. He will tell you how to be great writers.'

'Well,' I said, 'well. I have spent fifty-four years trying to learn English and I still find I have recourse to the dictionary almost every day. English,' I said, warming a little to my subject, 'is incomparably the richest language in the world. There are two or three quite distinct words to express every concept and each has a subtle difference of nuance.'

This was clearly not quite what was required. Consternation was plainly written on all the faces of the aspiring clerks who had greeted me with so broad a welcome.

'What Mr Waugh means,' said the teacher, 'is that English is very simple really. You will not learn all the words. You can make your meaning clear if you know a few of them.'

The students brightened a little. I left it at that.

Dinner that evening was highly enjoyable. R., the brigadier and an English accountant and his newly arrived wife and an elderly Greek doctor and his wife comprised the party. Marealle was in anything but 'tatters and rags'; a dandy with great social grace. His house not fifty miles from the nearest Masai bomas, is of a date with everything in Moshi, entirely European in design and furniture; tiled bath-rooms with towels to match their pastel tints, a radiogram in every room, the latest illustrated papers from England and the U.S.A., a grog tray on the verandah. Only the cooking was African, two delicious curries. I cajoled the accountant's wife into asking our host to turn off the wireless.

Marealle talked with humour of his experiences abroad; of how he had seen people in England eat lobsters, which struck him as peculiarly obscene. 'In Africa,' he said, 'we do not like to eat small things.' He had been sent on a tour of the U.S.A., had addressed meetings of Rotarians and made an enormous collection of neck-ties, which after dinner he displayed, all hanging in a specially constructed cabinet. He is Lutheran by religion, but no bigot; of his brothers, both of whom hold high positions, one is Catholic and the other Mohammedan. 'It simply depends what school you have been to,' he explained. His son, who has spent much of his child-hood in Wales, is now at the school at Tabora which I visited when I first passed through the territory. It was new then and regarded rather quizzically as an attempt, unlikely to succeed, to introduce the English Public School system to Africa. Marealle is as hostile to Makerere (the native university in Uganda) as any die-hard colonial. Outside England I have never heard a good word for Makerere.

After dinner, when we had fully appreciated the ties, we saw the album of souvenirs of his visit to the Queen's Coronation.

We sat on the verandah. Glasses were refilled. The wireless was on. In almost every official utterance homage is paid to the idea of 'the Tanganyikan advance in nationhood'. For someone as unpolit-ical as myself it is difficult to guess what is meant by 'a nation' of peoples as dissimilar as the Chagga, the Masai, the Gogo, the Arabs of Pagani, the fishermen of Kilwa, the Greek and Indian magnates of Dar-es-Salaam, whose frontiers were arbitrarily drawn in Europe by politicians who had never set foot in Africa.

March 4th. Early this morning we caught our only glimpse of the film company. As the brigadier and I stood in the hall settling our bills there swept past us a handsome man surrounded by understrappers. One of the understrappers picked up the brigadier's attaché case and followed the hero. Too quick for pursuit, the party climbed into their cars and drove off to the game reserve beyond the reach of any communication. The brigadier's case contained the confidential reports on the entire secretariat of the district. He accepted the loss in a soldierly fashion as part of the fortunes of war. When I said good-bye to him eight days later in Dar, he had still had no news of his lost property.

We drove south to Same, where R. had business, lunched with the D.C. in the Pare country. Here the talk was once more of witchcraft. We were out of the country of constitutional monarchy and cooperative prosperity.

That evening we celebrated R.'s forty-fifth birthday in an en-chanting rickety little German-kept hotel at Soni, perched above a waterfall on the hill leading to Lushoto, where the Germans had a summer residency, a large garrison and many tea planters. The

British governor has a pleasant house there, but he conscientiously sits out the hot season in Dar and lends the place to invalids.

March 5th. We hoped to drive over the hills to Koragwe, but the road was impassable, so we took the low, main road. At Koragwe we are back in sisal country. The D.C. gave a morning party to his highly cosmopolitan neighbours, a Pole, two Parsees, a man from Natal, a Dutchman, a Swahili mayor and an Irishman late of the Palestine Police. He suffers none of the isolation among officials which saddened the life of Same. We came into the hot belt of Tanga.

March 6th. I have already described the chief pleasure of Tanga – the trip to Pangani. I was also shown a municipal beer hall, the George VI Memorial Library, the German-built government offices. The sisal trade is the paramount concern of the town.

I paid a call on one of the relics of German colonisation, a handsome elderly junker and his wife living in a saw mill they had built for themselves in the bush. Coats-of-arms and hunting-trophies hung round the cabin. His father was an early settler, arriving in the 1880s and being granted huge estates in the Lushoto area and elsewhere. These were confiscated in the first World War in which my host's father fell, serving under von Letow. The family still had estates in Germany but my host returned to Tanganyika, watched the decay of the German system, hoped for the restoration of the territory to Germany, was arrested in 1939 and spent the war in a prison camp. He waits resignedly to see the administration surrendered to the natives. He is not very prosperous now. He does not expect to prosper by the change of government. He makes hard wood blocks for parquet floors, which, he remarks, are of too high quality for the modern market. His grandfather to practise himself in arms had taken a commission in the British army and had fallen at Sebastopol. He spoke with pride of his brother who was one of those Prussians who ensured the integrity of the military tradition by going, after 1918, to train the Russian army. What had become of him? Oh, he had fallen at Sebastopol too in the last war, fighting the soldiers whom he had helped train, who confiscated the estates in Prussia and Saxony. He saw no irony in this fate; merely the fulfilment of his family's warlike vocation. There was no element of self-pity or of self-doubt in this much dispossessed person.

March 7th. A swift uneventful drive back to Dar-es-Salaam, some 350 miles through Koragwe and Morogoro once more, as the coast road is impassable.

March 8th, 9th, 10th, 11th. Peaceful empty days and sociable evenings. I found in the Club library several books I missed when they were first published, among them *Black Lamb and Grey Falcon* by Dame Rebecca West. I notice she repeatedly describes the Croats (in whose affairs I once played a minute and ignoble part) as 'angry young men'. Did she, I wonder, coin the phrase?

The English newspapers, which reached us four days late, reported great excitement about disturbances in Nyasaland. The ladies who worked as cypher-clerks in Government House were sometimes called away in the middle of dinner to deal with incoming despatches. This was the full extent of the 'emergency' as far as I saw it. A socialist Member of Parliament spent some days in the town, in transit. He had been evicted from somewhere, but whether from Nyasaland, Northern Rhodesia or Southern Rhodesia no one seemed to know. I asked what he had said of an inflammatory nature, where, to whom and in what language, but got no answer until eventually *The Times* appeared on the Club table. There was then no noticeable rush of members to inform themselves. A good deal more interest was taken in the outcome of a case then being heard in which the widow of a local Greek magnate was contesting his will. Q.C.s had been flown out from England to argue the matter. Their presence caused more remark than the politician's.

Tourist traffic to Nyasaland was interrupted. I therefore decided to leave across the frontier of Northern Rhodesia.

March 12th. R. drove me on my way as far as Iringa in the southern highlands. We started at dawn and arrived in time for a late luncheon being delayed for half an hour by an elephant who stepped into the road 200 yards ahead of us. We stopped. He stood facing us, twitching his ears – a sign, I am told, of vexation. Elephants have been known to charge cars. He was very large, with fine tusks. R.'s fear for his Mercedes-Benz was controlled but acute. He turned and drove back quarter of a mile. 'I *think* we can go faster than he can over a long distance,' he said. Then we waited until in his own time the elephant ambled away into the bush.

Iringa is a cool, pleasant little town with a railway station but no railway and an excellent Greek restaurant. The natives of the place are called, if I heard aright, 'Hehe', a warlike people who defeated a German column and hold themselves superior to the Masai. When the Masai last invaded, the grandfather of the present chief contemptuously put his sister in command of his forces. She drove them back with great slaughter. Now they mostly go to work in the copper mines and return dressed as cinema cowboys. There were many of them swaggering about the streets with spurs, ornamented leather work, brilliant shirts, huge hats; but most of the inhabitants of the town are Greek and Indian.

There was some jubilation that day in honour of a posse of police who had returned from pacifying Fort Hill across the Nyasa border; one of the few places where the disturbances had seemed formidable.

Here we were joined by Mr Newman, the D.C. from Mbeya, some 150 miles south-west, the place from which I was to take the aeroplane to Rhodesia. Mr Newman is a stalwart ex-airman whose post lies nearest to Nyasa of any in Tanganyika. He was serenely unimpressed by the rumours of danger which had been brought by some Indian refugees from the disturbed area.

There is a current explanation of the reports that European cars are being stoned. The responsible Ministry in Rhodesia is said to have instituted an investigation into traffic. Since the native observers are not handy with paper and pencil, they were instructed to put a stone into a basket for every vehicle that passed them. A journalist finding a man at the side of the road with a basketful of stones asked what they were for and received the answer. 'For cars.'

March 13*th*. I said good-bye to R. and his Mercedes-Benz and drove on with Mr Newman in his Landrover. It is tedious to the reader to be presented with long expressions of gratitude for the kindnesses an author receives in his travels. It must already be abundantly clear that R. had devised nearly all the pleasures of the last weeks. Mr Newman took me from him and for the next two days did all that the oldest friend could have done for the stranger thrust upon him.

The road climbs from Iringa to Mbeya; at the end one is chilly and breathless. We stopped briefly at the Consolata Fathers' mission, a fine group of buildings like a small Italian town. 'They are the most powerful people in the district,' said Mr Newman. With the sinking of heart always accompanying the inspection of school laboratories, I was shown the thriving schools. Then the old priest who was guiding us, an Italian long habituated to Africa, spoke of African 'nationalism'. The mistake, he said, was to introduce 'Africanisation' through politics instead of through service. None of the young men now filling the lower government offices should have been sent from England. Natives should have filled those places and an all-African administration should have been built up from the bottom. Instead we contemplated handing over the highest posts to men who had nothing except the ability to make themselves popular. Like everyone I met he spoke well of Mr Nyerere, but he doubted the ability of his party to govern.

It was not a new point of view, but the speaker gave it authority. British officials say that you cannot leave a native Field Officer in charge of a road-gang. He either cheats them or the government, favours his own tribe or kin, lacks authority and so on. (In fact, in Tanganyika a large number of foremen are half-breeds from the Seychelles, who are found to be more skilful than natives in what used to be called 'man-management'.) It is the debate that occupies all the colonial territories, in which a stranger would be absurd to join. What does seem plain to me is that if the Groundnuts Scheme had been conceived and executed by natives, everyone would point to it as incontrovertible evidence that they were unfit to manage their own affairs.

We came into open downland where the pasture, I was told, is not as good as it looks. Here, in the Sao hills, in a climate rather like that of Kenya, there subsists a little pocket of settlers who live rather as my old friends used to live in the 'Happy Valley'. If I was told the

truth, they are rather more bizarre. One of them has turned Mohammedan; another came to a tea party given for Princess Margaret
with his own teapot full of brandy and ginger ale. There is a field for
research here, I was told, in that sparse grassland, under that kinetic
glare, in that absence of atmosphere, for Kinsey and Wolfenden.
I should have liked to linger, but we drove on. In the next range of
hills Mr Newman had lately been busy arresting and rusticating
a school of witches whose fertility cult required human blood-letting
on a scale which often proved fatal. We reached Mr Newman's
house at tea time.

Mbeya is a little English garden-suburb with no particular reason
for existence. It was built in the 1930s as a Provincial capital at the
time when gold was mined there. Now there is a little aerodrome
and a collection of red roofs among conifers and eucalyptus-trees,
a bank, a post office, a police station. There is also an hotel, named
after the non-existent railway, where at that time, it was reputed,
there lurked some disgruntled English journalists who had been
forbidden entrance to Nyasaland; they were now engaged in causing
annoyance among the reserved and isolated community by interviewing the Indians and American missionaries who had taken
alarm and sought refuge here. Mrs Newman forbade me to go to
this hotel and very kindly put me up for the night in her own cheerful
villa. That evening she collected some of her neighbours for cocktails. All were officials; all on easy, intimate terms with one another.
One of the D.O.s kept guinea-pigs; a doctor had a very numerous
family; the P.C. was Australian. All were most welcoming to a rather
travel-worn stranger.

March 14*th*. Rain. I was taken to the police station to have my
passport stamped, to the bank, to the office of the air line and to
the club, where I again met the policeman, the banker, the official of
the air line; also the guests of the evening before; the disgruntled
journalists were not among those present.

There was a long wait at the aerodrome. The building consisted
of a neat little waiting-room with a good deal of window on which
the rain beat hard. It was pleasant to find a place dedicated to this
form of travel which lacked a loud-speaker, but it was none the less

a drab and depressing spot. Large docks in recent years have become mere tunnels through which one passes from ship to train, but the delights of the water-front of small ports, everywhere in the world, are still unspoiled. Small aerodromes have nothing to offer except shelter and boredom. Presently there was a noise in the sky and the vehicle appeared through the rain. We were off by 3.30 and bumped about above the clouds, seeing nothing.

6. THE RHODESIAS

Statistical obsession in the Federation – Saturday night in
Ndola – Mazoe – Umtali – Zimbabwe

The civilised route to Southern Rhodesia is from Beira in Portuguese East Africa. That is the way Cecil Rhodes came when he visited and scolded the disgruntled body of pioneers who had toiled up from the south. He coveted Beira, which he saw as the natural opening to the new territories, and tried to pick a quarrel with the Portuguese. Lord Salisbury refused to go to war on his behalf. Beira remains Portuguese, and air-conditioned sleepers now carry the wise travellers out of the hot coast to the frontier near Umtali. But, alas, I have never travelled on this route. I have come by train from Elizabethville and by air from London. Now I was committed to a very uncomfortable little vehicle. Had I wished I could have gone straight through to Salisbury, but this would have caused me to arrive at a later hour than was convenient for my hosts, who live some forty miles out. Accordingly I arranged to spend the night at Ndola, in Northern Rhodesia, near the Belgian frontier. As soon as it was impossible to write legibly we were presented with the usual sheaf of official forms to fill. Could they not have been provided during our hour-long vigil in the hut which at least provided chairs and a table?

I say 'the usual official forms', but one was unique in my experience. In order to spend one night in transit at Ndola I was required, among other things, to inform the Federal authorities of the names, ages, sexes, dates and places of birth of children *not* accompanying me (six in my case, whose birthdays I can never remember; they remind me in good time), date and place of marriage. What European languages could I write? The oddest demand was to state 'sex of wife'. No question was asked about 'sex of husband'. A note explained: 'All information asked for is necessary to either comply with the law or for statistical purpose.'

An argumentative man might, I suppose, have refused information which did not comply with the law. I filled it all in obediently in a hand-writing, shaken by the machine, which must I fear be causing over-work to the statisticians at Ndola.

'That fellow who stayed here on 14th March – what do you make the name of the eldest son who didn't accompany him – Might be Audubon?'

'Or Anderson.'

'Pass it to the Department of Epigraphy at Lusaka.'

'Or Salisbury.'

'They will pass it on to Salisbury.'

'At least we've got his birthday.'

'Yes, that's the great thing.'

'But the Immigration Office have no business to let him through leaving an ambiguity of this kind.'

'Not enough men for the job.'

'We ought to increase the establishment.'

'We will.'

Looking at the form again (I kept a copy as a souvenir) I see I was too conscientious. Visitors for periods of less than sixty days need not answer questions 13 to 18. So I need not have affirmed pretensions to write English. Rhodesians have good reason to be suspicious of English journalists, but it is, surely, naïve to suppose that it takes sixty days to compose an article traducing them.

Nor need I have stated that I was free from infectious or communicable diseases. That seems odder still, for it is one of the few sane questions. No country welcomes the plague-stricken. In fifty-nine days an active carrier should be able to broadcast his diseases liberally.

Here fully displayed are the arts of modern government for which, it is popularly believed, the native races are not yet far enough advanced.

For the last hour of the flight there was no cloud and we could see a huge expanse of apparently quite empty country; lake, swamp, bush, no sign of a road or village. The apparent emptiness of Africa seems to belie the popular claims to land-hunger, but no doubt there are good reasons for it which the tourist does not understand.

The sun set and we came in by darkness.

The agent of the statisticians was civil enough. A room had been booked for me in the town. There was a bus to take me there. I was the only transit-passenger.

Ndola is south-east of Mbeya, on the railway which joins the Congo to Cape Town. I passed through it many years ago in a train. We arrived at 7.15 by my watch; 6.15 by local time. The town has grown beyond recognition and is growing fast, spreading itself in the manner of modern Africa, where land is cheap and everybody worth the planners' consideration has a motor car, along broad boulevards in a litter of concrete. The hotel alone, one-storied, stucco-faced, soon no doubt to be demolished and rebuilt, is a relic of pioneer days. The builders had plainly some faint memories of the column and architrave. Everything else in sight was 'contemporary'.

It was a hot, airless evening heavy with the fumes of metallurgy. The real copper-belt where white artisans, it is said, live the life of an American country club and honoured guests are luxuriously feasted, lies at some distance. Ndola, like every part of the continent, is in transition. It is already purely a white man's town. On this Saturday evening there were fewer Africans in the streets than would be seen in London. Most of the white men seemed to be drunk.

I left my bags in a sad little, stuffy bedroom, lit by a single faintly glowing bulb, and I wandered out. Attracted by a neon sign which read: 'TAVERN. OLD ENGLISH ATMOSPHERE', I descended concrete steps to a basement-bar, softly lit and pervaded by 'background music'. The barman was white and wore his hair in the Teddy-boy style. A white lady, whom I took to be a tart, sat before him. She had an odd look of Mrs Stitch. Four or five youngish Rhodesians were drinking with her. The old English atmosphere was provided by chair and tables made to look rather like beer barrels.

The bar of the hotel, to which I adjourned, was more congenial. I had no appetite for dinner and asked for some sandwiches. When they were brought, a frightfully drunk man came and devoured most of them. He was, he told me, a philosopher who had lost his soul.

'He's a nice enough fellow,' said the barman, 'except on Saturday nights.'

While he ate my sandwiches he uttered a great deal of vaguely familiar English verse. I think he was just stringing together as many odd lines of Shakespeare and Macaulay and Wordsworth and Kipling as had remained in his mind from some not very remote period of schooling; he improvising a little in part poetic, part Biblical style on the subject of his own evident unpopularity.

A much less drunk man came to protect me.

'You mustn't mind him. He's a bloody nuisance.'

This new friend was stout and affable. I should have taken him for a military man had he not assured me he had served in the Navy and the Air Force. He later confirmed my first speculation by claiming to having been in the Black Watch. He also said he was Irish.

The philosopher then said: 'Don't believe him, he's not Scotch. He only says he is because he went to Fettes.'

Suddenly, apropos of nothing, the barman said: 'D'you happen to know Ed Stanley of Alderley?'

By what mannerism or turn of phrase had I betrayed this arcane knowledge? Perhaps it was the barman's habitual gambit to all visiting Englishmen.

'Sheffield to me,' I replied.

'I am a great friend of his lordship,' said the barman. He then recited the names of some dozen noblemen of his acquaintance. I could join him in one or two cases. This did not endear him to the philosopher, who had formed a low view of aristocracy without, he was at pains to assure me, indulging any respect for democracy.

My stout champion said wistfully: 'I left all that sort of thing behind when I came out here.'

The barman, however, was so pleased that he fetched the manageress to see me.

'A friend of Lord Stanley of Alderley's.'

'Sheffield's. You know him? He has been here?'

'No, I'm afraid I've never heard of him. I hope you'll be comfortable here. What room have they given you?' I told her. 'Oh, dear, that won't do, will it? I'll have your things moved.'

So when, very early, I escaped from my companions I found myself quartered in a fine suite – sitting-room, bedroom, bright lights, flowing water, where I lay very contented while the sounds of a Ndola Saturday night waxed and raged about me until, before dawn, I slipped out to the aerodrome bus in the now silent street.

15*th March*. The aeroplane from Ndola was rather more comfortable than the machine that brought me from Mbeya and the port-holes afforded glimpses of a less desolate terrain than the swamps of Northern Rhodesia. About half-way through the flight we crossed the border of Southern Rhodesia. As we approached Salisbury we might have been over Surrey. Distance gives a trimness, which I knew from previous experience is largely illusory, to the great commercial suburb which has flooded over Matabeleland and Mashonaland.

The friends I was coming to visit are named John and Daphne. Neither was at the aerodrome to meet me; nor at the office in the city. A telephone call, made through an instrument of novel design, which concealed its dial under its base, disclosed that I was not expected until next week. But with imperturbable goodwill Daphne said she would come for me at once.

I had an hour to wait.

Salisbury is changing dizzily. The air line headquarters where I stood was brand-new since last year. Next to it Meikle's Hotel, which on my last visit had some architectural affinities with the hotel at Ndola, had sprung up into a slightly smaller version of the Rockefeller Center in New York. Behind it a tower, slightly lower than the Empire State Building, crowned by a sphere (luminous and opalescent in the hours of darkness), has arisen to accommodate an insurance company. On this Sunday morning the broad streets were empty. The trees were just shedding their flowers. The air was fresh, the sun brilliant and pleasantly warm. At length Daphne arrived and bore me off to Mazoe, near which she and her huge family have been settled for ten years.

John's fortunes are typical of the new Rhodesia. He returned to England from the army in 1945 eager to work and develop his ancestral estates, found himself frustrated by official regulations, impetuously bought an agricultural property, unseen, forty miles out of Salisbury, and removed there with his wife, children and family portraits and much of his livestock. The estate is very large by English standards, but of moderate, viable size for Africa. There was no Labour Government there to vex him, no elaborate regulations or oppressive taxation, but Africa imposes its own discouragements. The farm does not pay its way. He is now a prosperous business man driving daily to an office in the city as though to London from Sunningdale, preserving a strong link with his former way of life through his racing-stable. He is a director of a bank and several commercial enterprises. His main activity is to manufacture paper bags out of imported materials. His sons go to school in Salisbury and speak in a different accent from their parents, the girls to convents in Umtali and South Africa. They go for seaside holidays to Durban. None of them have any sentimental yearnings for their homeland.

The house is a long bungalow stretching across the hillside, roofed with iron, walled with concrete, making no claim to architectural character. A short distance away is the 'native compound', the village of round huts from which sounds of revelry can often be heard long into the night. All John's labour, house-boys and farm-boys alike, come from Nyasaland. He has built them a school and employs an African teacher and an English chaplain. Many have become Christians.

After the great plantation of fruit and the reservoir which are the chief surviving achievements in this area of the old Charter Company, the road becomes rougher. There is a road-house which was once a stage-post in the days of travel by horse and coach. It has now developed a swimming-pool and café tables. Soon after it we turn into John's drive, a steep earth track. White teeth flash and pink palms flutter in greeting as we pass the groups and couples of Nyasas. Then we stop at the house and emerge into dust or mud according to the season.

Today, Sunday, there are no gardeners at work; usually they can be found deep in weed languidly lopping it with tools like golf-clubs. This morning all are on holiday except a small group who are excavating a swimming-pool. They are in a frenzy of righteous activity for they belong to a peculiar half-Christian sect which holds it to be immoral to rest on Sundays.

The house is always thronged but never, apparently, full. My hostess serenely welcomes all comers, friends from England, neighbours, business associates of her husband, relations; but children predominate. The verandah, here called a 'stoep', is their playground. African nurses are not employed much in Rhodesia. There is no nursery. There is a schoolroom imposingly furnished with desks, blackboard and terrestrial globe, but it never contains its children for more than a few minutes at a time. Tricycle riding round the stoep is the favourite pastime.

It is not a restful house by any ordinary standard, but Daphne's personality mysteriously imposes a kind of overriding peace above the turmoil.

16th March. Though I have taken advantage of every comfort Africa affords, I am travel-worn. I have covered a lot of ground one way and another and am glad of a day's inactivity – it cannot be called repose. The teeming life of the house, as in a back-street of Naples, rages round me from dawn to dusk, but I remain in my chair, subject to interrogation, and the performances of conjuring, dancing and exhibitions of strength, but for one day at least immovable.

17th March. We set out in a party of four – Daphne, her chaplain and a kind young manufacturer of paper bags – to drive to the Eastern Highlands.

First we spent a few minutes at the tobacco sales, which are a great annual event of Salisbury. The tobacco stands baled in long rows in the great warehouses. The buyers follow the auctioneer in swift procession sampling and bidding as they go. The auctioneer saunters from bale to bale with an illusion of nonchalance. He has been imported at great expense from New Orleans and is master of his odd trade. He croons continuously, and to the layman, quite unintelligibly, sometimes in a monotone, sometimes breaking into popular melody. He is running up the prices and knocking down the lots with a precision all the more impressive for being entirely mysterious. This, they tell me, is how tobacco is bought and sold everywhere in the world. It is wildly unlike Mr E. M. Forster's description in *Pharos and Pharillon* of the cotton market in Alexandria. Prices were rather low that morning, I gathered. The tobacco crop is the only prosperous agricultural undertaking in Southern Rhodesia and there were some long faces, but the farmers' ladies sat in hats, gloves and their best clothes, cheerfully drinking coffee.

Some 160 miles of railway and good road lead from Salisbury to Umtali. This, as I have noted, is the route by which the wise traveller enters the country. The Eastern Highlands march with the Portuguese frontier. They comprise some of the finest natural scenery in Africa, wooded mountains, waterfalls, keen air, an area of special fascination to the ornithologist and entomologist; to the archæologist also, for here are the finely built stone terraces and unexplained dens of Inyanga. An undated civilisation once flourished here and today there are for the tourist, to my knowledge, two admirable hotels and, by repute, more.

One, where we lunched – by far the best hotel meal since Malindi – is in the main street of Umtali, the capital and centre of this happy land, a spacious garden-city round which many rich immigrants have built themselves villas and laid out gardens.

The object of our visit was to see Daphne's daughter, Jill, who is at school in a brand-new convent which American nuns, who profess a devotion (unfamiliar to me) to 'the Sacred Heart of Mary', have built in the outskirts of the town – a sumptuous place with a bath-room to every two girls. It was a little depressing to find American pseudo-anatomical charts illustrating the ill effects of wine on the human body; also to find text-books of local history composed for use in the Union of South Africa. A more modern note was struck by the appearance of 'Charm' in the time-table of the curriculum. This, on investigation, proved to be the new name for Deportment. And very engaging the deportment of the girls was as they skidded past us in the corridors with little genuflections.

I tried to buy native artifacts in the shops of Umtali. Some tribes of Portuguese East Africa carve very well, as I had seen in the collection made by one of the district officers at Kilwa. But here, almost on the frontier, there was nothing for sale except the most trashy tourist souvenirs. On advice from one shopkeeper we followed our quest to the native quarter, well built and well kept, but hardly welcoming. As at a military establishment there were notices warning-off unauthorised visitors, summoning new arrivals to medical inspection and registration. And there were no carvings to be found.

We drove on higher into the mountains, past a riding-school and the gates of many handsome properties, through a landscape of stupendous beauty to another excellent hotel named Leopard's Rock.

I have said that the Eastern Highlands are the proper approach to Rhodesia. In fact, the holiday-maker need go no further. A booklet issued by the office of Tourist Development sets out the attractions of the district with a moderation which contrasts pleasantly with the language usually employed in such publications. It is admitted that there is neither snow nor sea, but there is everything else; in Umtali golf, bowls, lawn tennis, riding, a camping-site (with bath-rooms), a theatre, cinemas, a Rotary Club, a Round Table, Lodges of English and Scottish Freemasons, and a Catholic Bishop; at Inyanga, Cecil Rhodes's estate is now a National Park, with a trout-hatchery, a lake for bathing (no bilharzia in the mountain waters) and boating, a camp of log cabins in the Tyrolean style; in the Vumba hills there are pretty Samango monkeys; everywhere there are waterfalls – ferns and great trees – well, there is no need to transcribe the whole official encomium; enough to say that it is true. Charabancs have not yet appeared to despoil the place. It is what the natural beauty spots of Europe must have been sixty years ago.

That evening after dinner we sat before a log fire and went to bed in pretty chintzy rooms surrounded by cool, mountain silence. The bill next morning was not excessive.

I should have liked to linger and go further. I hope to return. Perhaps the development of this district may provide the elderly and well-to-do with a more dignified resort than the beaches where they now exhibit themselves. The craze for sunburn has lasted long enough. On the Riviera the survivors and imitators of the elegant young neurotics of Scott Fitzgerald's *Tender is the Night* have grown into those greasy hulks of flesh which are now being hemmed in and invaded by the proletariat. If fashion is to be true to its metier, it must seek seclusion. Where better than here?

March 18*th*. A long day's drive; back to Umtali first, then seventy-six miles due south through the hills, dropping at midday into the hot valley of the Sabi, turning west over Birchenough bridge for some hundred miles of bush and grass country to Zimbabwe, which we reached just before sunset.

I had been here before from Fort Victoria and had fairly thoroughly surveyed these famous ruins – the most remarkable in Africa south of Egypt. Daphne and the others were on their first visit. There was not time that evening to do more than appreciate the general aspect. The rest of the party returned at dawn next day.

There was once a great stone city here of which two main groups of building survive in impressive form. Their aspect has been too often photographed and described to need a detailed account here. Their origin remains a mystery and the ground of acrimonious dispute. They are unique in their size and state of preservation, but there are other 'Zimbabwes' – a word indifferently translated as a 'court' or 'a stone building'. This is correctly called the Great Zimbabwe.

When the first white man came here in 1868 the elliptical enclosure popularly known as the Temple was deserted and densely overgrown. The hilltop called the Acropolis was used by a neighbouring tribe as a cattle kraal and remained in their use for nearly thirty years longer. In the early days of the Charter Company a concession was given to an 'Ancient Ruins Company' formed with a capital of £25,000 to prospect for gold in all the archæological sites between the Limpopo and the Zambesi. It lasted until 1903. No record survives of its depredations. Doubtless numerous artifacts were unearthed and melted down. The damage done by the excavations is now deeply deplored and recent administrations have been at pains to mitigate it.

At Great Zimbabwe the bush has been cleared. It is admirably kept (part of it, indeed, laid out as a golf links); fallen stones have been replaced, paths and, where necessary, steps laid down. The aspect is of Devon parkland, strewn everywhere with natural boulders, outcrops of rock and lines of masonry.

The Acropolis is a steep little hill some 350 feet high, approached originally only through two narrow clefts in the granite. The custodians have laid out a gentler path, interspersed with seats, for the benefit of elderly visitors. The summit is a mass of fortifications and partitions built among the natural boulders and rock face. It was once, presumably, a place of refuge; also of industry. Gold was smelted here although no gold diggings have been found near it. Many objects of archæological value were probably found here by the white pioneers, most of which were destroyed. Of what remains, some are in the museum at Bulawayo, but much was taken to Cape Town in the days when it seemed likely that that city would be the capital of a great British commonwealth country.

The Temple stands more than a quarter of a mile distant. It is a great oval of massive and highly skilfully laid drystone wall surmounted for 265 feet of its length with an ornamental coping of a double strip of chevron pattern. The entrances have been rebuilt, not as they were. Now they are gaps open to the top with rounded sides suggesting Cotswold buttresses. Originally there were doorways each with a beam, and above the beam continuous wall. The outer wall is sixteen feet thick at the bottom. The guide book does not specify its height; more than twenty feet I should guess. The effect must have been forbidding. As it stands, many who are susceptible – Daphne among them – to such impressions find the place eerie. It is certainly enigmatic. For a large part of the circumference there is an inner wall as high as the outer, leaving between them a narrow sunless lane which leads to a solid conical tower which, of course, has been dubbed 'phallic'. I am sceptical of these modish attributions. Are the objects displayed on some of the new electric railway stations of outer London 'phallic'? Do they attract a cult? The only explicitly phallic symbol of recent construction which I know is Wiegland's obelisk in the suburbs of Oslo. There is no mistaking the inspiration of that erection. But it lacks worshippers.

Inside the walls the ground shows signs of division; what was roofed, what was open, what was a ceremonial court, what a cattle byre, are all conjectural. The appellation 'temple' and the deep shadows have stirred the imagination to thoughts of bloody and obscene ritual, but in fact there is no reason for supposing that this was ever a place of worship. I defy the most ingenious film director to reconstruct it, and people it at all plausibly with priests and priestesses. A visitor from Mars to the Catholic Cathedral in Salisbury, Rhodesia, would recognise that he was in a building made by the same kind of people (living in a debased age) and for the same purpose as in Salisbury, England. But 'the Temple' at Zimbabwe leaves the visitor from Europe without any comparison. It is an example of what so often moved G. K. Chesterton to revulsion. It is the Wrong Shape. Something utterly alien.

Nor do there seem to be any native traditions of sanctity. The latest excavators are inclined to think it was a royal kraal, that the outer wall is later than the inner, that the conical erection was a watch-tower or simply a grandiose monument to personal splendour. They think it was built fairly recently by Bantus.

Recently, that is to say, in comparison to some of the theories current in Rhodesia. King Solomon, of course, has been proposed as its architect; also an aboriginal and mythical white race, Freemasons to a man; also Indians, Arabs, Persians, even Chinese; anyone but natives; for it is an article of the local faith, held even by the most cultivated Rhodesians, that the Bantu throughout all history has been as they found him sixty years ago, a primitive savage, totally ignorant of the arts of peace. The most they will admit is that possibly black men might have built a stone wall if enslaved and directed by Asiatics. They preferred the theory of the lost white tribe. This was shaken by the results of a 'carbon test' applied to a piece of wood taken from a beam over a drain in the outer wall. There is an electrical appliance, it appears, which can determine the age of wood. Two independent examinations gave the age of this specimen as about 700 years. I don't profess to understand the process. There is, experts say, room for great discrepancy according to whether the specimen is taken from the heart of a tree or from near the surface. The thirteenth-century attribution has been cheerfully welcomed because the Bantus had probably not moved into this region at that time. Bushmen could not have built Zimbabwe. Therefore a non-African race of higher culture did so. Thus runs the popular argument. But one need not be a scientist to question the significance of the test. Many modern villas in the home counties incorporate genuine Tudor beams; many ancient houses have been repaired with new timber. Wood has long been scarce in the region of Zimbabwe. Nothing is more likely than that builders of whatever age or race make use of beams from earlier structures. The 'carbon test' has really added nothing to our knowledge of the date of the masonry.

There is a choice of hotels within easy reach of the ruins. We chose badly. I noted in my diary: 'kept by fiend', which meant that we were back in the grip of those affable British manageresses of whom I have already warned the reader. I will not, from respect for the law of libel, identify the place, nor, from respect for my reader's patience, expatiate on our sufferings.

March 19*th*. We escaped early and joined the main road that runs from Beit Bridge through Fort Victoria to Salisbury. Fort Victoria has sentimental associations for Rhodesians as the first settlement, established in 1890 by the Pioneer Column as it marched from Bechuanaland into Mashonaland. A little watch-tower survives of the original defences. Now there are shops, a cinema, an hotel, a new civic hall and a fine little Catholic church designed by the architect whose main work we were on our way to visit. Not many people live in the town. It is a market centre for farmers, and ox-waggons can still be seen in the broad streets.

Serima Mission lies off the main road in the native reserve behind a large European estate named Chatsworth. Here again it was my companions' first visit. I had been there a year ago and was eager to show them what seemed to me one of the most remarkable enterprises in the country; also to see what progress had been made in the year and to meet the architect, Fr Groeber, who had been away when I was last there. Serima does not advertise itself or welcome idle sight-seers. It exists for its own people. None of its products is sent out for sale or for exhibition. As far as I know no photographs have ever been published. There are no sign-posts to direct the traveller along the sandy tracks which run through the flat, sparsely grown country.

It is in the diocese of Gwelo, entrusted to the Swiss Bethlehem Fathers. In 1948 Fr Groeber was sent by his bishop to found and design the Mission. The available funds were, and are, pitifully inadequate. Everything was lacking except space and zeal. The staff at present consists of one other priest, a lay brother skilled in building, and six Mary Ward nuns. They have a school of 170 Mashona boarders and, nearing completion, the large and remarkable church which we had come to see.

It is this that one first notices as one emerges from the bush, and at first sight it affords no pleasure to an eye such as mine which is dull to contemporary taste. Geometrical, economical, constructed of concrete and corrugated iron, it rises from the centre of its bleak site like the hangar of a deserted airfield.

Seen on the drawing-board, Serima is a logical and symmetrical plan. Axial roads converge on the church from the surrounding blocks of dormitories, schoolrooms, workshops, refectory and dispensary. But these roads are scarcely visible tracks and bare feet have traced other straggling paths across the campus. The 'blocks' are represented by low sheds. One day it will be laid out and the intervening areas planted and the architect's conception will be manifested to the layman. At present one needs a keen imagination to appreciate the plan.

Fr Groeber works and sleeps in a single cell opening on the little entrance hall of the main building. His bookshelves are filled with books of ascetic theology and modern art in English, German and French. He is an elderly, serene man. When I said I might be writing something about the place, his welcome became slightly clouded, but he did not forbid me to do so and as he began showing me how he worked, he brightened. In youth he studied architecture in Switzerland and on the day after taking his degree went straight to the seminary, volunteered for the African mission and thought it unlikely he would ever be called to exercise his art. In the last twenty years he has built not only for his own order but for the Jesuits, whose seminary for native priests near Salisbury is from his designs. But Serima is his particular creation. It is here that he has founded the little school of art which is one of the most exhilarating places in Africa.

During the last weeks I have taken every chance of searching bazaars and pedlars' wares for examples of African sculpture. The best, as I have said, were at Kilwa and the work of tribes in Portuguese territory, but they, though skilfully cut, were hopelessly lacking in vision and invention. The same archetypes of animal and human form were repeated again and again. I have seen photographs of figures by natives of the Congo and Uganda which might get exhibited in London and Paris; individual enough, but plainly the work of men who had been shown European sculpture. The savage African art of the eighteenth and early nineteenth centuries which delighted the European and American connoisseurs of the 1920s, seems as dead as the civilised art of Europe.

There is a mission at Cyrene with wall paintings by native artists which I have not visited. From photographs it seems that they were shown conventional European pictures and encouraged to translate them into local idiom, rather as the Mexican Indians of the sixteenth and seventeenth century were set to work on models of the Spanish Renaissance and Baroque – with agreeably picturesque results, certainly, but without planting a living art, capable of free growth. And the Mexican Indians had a long tradition of many ingenious crafts. The Mashona among whom Fr Groeber works have never had an artist, nor any craft except the weaving by the women of grass mats in very simple patterns. Fr Groeber has been at pains to keep all European models away from his pupils. He has none of the illusions of the recent past, that every man is a natural artist, but in the boys passing through his hands he has found a few – as many perhaps as would be found passing through an English Public School – who have the genuine æsthetic impulse. At present he has two master-carvers in their mid-twenties and a dozen apprentices in their teens. The sort of carving they produce is symbolic and didactic, like that of the European Middle Ages; entirely novel and entirely African.

Every boy on arrival from his village is told to draw an account of his journey. Many are capable of nothing; some produce pictures not much different from the nursery scrawlings of European children some years their juniors. Those with discernible talent are then taught to control the pencil, the chalk, the pen, the brush; they make abstract symmetrical patterns, they draw 'matchstick' hiero-glyphics of figures in action. Perhaps all this is a commonplace of 'progressive' education. I don't know. It was quite new to me. Nothing of the kind happened in the drawing-classes of my own youth, which began with copying lithographs of rural scenery and advanced to 'freehand' renderings of still life. Clay modelling is the next stage. The boy's first task is always to make a mask which will 'frighten his little brother'. It is explained to him that it is far easier to make ugly things than beautiful; that, implicitly, the paintings of Mr Francis Bacon are a rudimentary accomplishment which the Mashona boy must outgrow. The highest achievement is to make something lovable, an image of angel or saint, of Our Lady or Our Lord, before which it is easy to pray. Before this stage is approached the use of the chisel is taught and the composition of ornaments that express a moral lesson or a theological tenet. Art is the catechism and prayer in visible form. There is no sugges-tion of self-expression or of æsthetic emotion; nor of acquiring a marketable skill or titillating national pride at doing as well as the white man.

Wood is scarce and not of good quality. Everything is first sketched in clay and the best of the sculptors show themselves sharply critical, modelling many versions before committing one to the chisel.

The first completed work was the main entrance. Here the concrete walls have been painted in simple geometric designs of ochre and umber – earth colours made from the soil of the district. On either side of the door stand crowned effigies of the Pope and the Queen; not attempted portraits, but direct African statements of the African idea of majesty; not remotely comic, very much more august indeed than most modern European official (and non-official) statuary.

The panels of the door display a series carved in high relief illustrating the rewards and dangers of African life. For the industri-ous apprentice there are the skills of husbandry, the dignity of teaching, family love, or, highest aim, the priesthood; for the idle apprentice, gambling, drinking, dancing, witch-doctors and Mohammedanism.

No work was going on in the church, which is nearing completion. In plan it is, as Fr Groeber remarked, like a pair of shorts. Two rectangular naves are laid, one corner of each touching, at an angle of about forty-five degrees. The axes of the naves converge on the high altar, which stands in a very large five-sided sanctuary. This plan was evolved from the cruciform with the purpose of setting the altar in the fullest view of the largest congregation. In a first design the arms of the cross were drawn down so as to make a kind of broad arrow. Then the triangular area between the two naves became the Lady chapel, with an altar at its apex, through which one enters. Two side chapels prolong the back wall of the sanctuary. There will be a central tower standing clear behind and (I think) an appended sacristy.

It is a building designed for use, to be seen from the inside. A ceiling of traditional grass-mats supported on a frame of slender beams painted in chevrons of earth colours hides the pitch and harsh material of the roof, which is borne on open parabolic arches of concrete.

The most important carvings at present are the entrance and the Stations of the Cross. The door is panelled like that of the mission house with figures and scenes from the Old and New Testaments, chosen to illustrate theological doctrines. The choice of subject is always Fr Groeber's. The Stations, new since my last visit, are in the round, standing out from the wall on brackets. They are the most ambitious and successful of the works at Serima.

Like everything else they are designed for use. I thought of the Stations at the much advertised chapel at Vence, which Matisse scrawled over a single wall in a manner that inhibits the devotion they should occasion.

In the workshop a rood screen is in preparation; four tall posts, whole tree trunks, carved from top to bottom with figures, and two equally elaborate cross-beams from which a great crucifix is designed to hang. Sanctuary stools, also, were being carved out of solid drums of timber. Quite soon there will be at Serima one of the most beautiful and original churches of the modern world.

That is the aim of the builder; to make a church, not to found an Art School. The sculptors have been called into existence for the church, not the church for the sculptors.

What will happen when Fr Groeber is no longer there to direct them? They are very much younger than he. Their technical skill will remain ripe for well-intentioned exploitation by collectors and museums. How long can their vision remain uncontaminated by Europe and America? Those eager apprentices I saw today will find that there are larger rewards awaiting them for inferior work. With very little labour they can imitate 'expressionist' or 'abstract' models. Something of the kind, I gather, is happening in parts of the Belgian Congo. In less than a full lifetime one has seen so many promising enterprises come to nothing – for example Walt Disney's cartoon films. It would be absurd presumption to suggest that a tradition has been founded at Serima. But to say that is not to belittle the present achievement. It is the fault of the modern eye to be forever goggling ahead, of the modern mind to concern itself only with 'influences' and 'movements', instead of accepting with gratitude the tangible gifts of the past and present. The artist has no concern with the future. Fr Groeber's achievement has been to make Africans do what none but Africans could have done and what no Africans in this huge region ever did before; to leave a church where they and their descendants can worship, which their descendants will cherish with the pride and awe with which we in Europe survey the edifices of our Middle Ages.

The smiling nuns pressed us to stay for luncheon, but my party had business in Salisbury. Soon we were back on the straight, empty main road. We paused briefly at the restaurant of a little mining town, then on again over the plain, and reached the farm where I was staying, before dark.

7. THE RHODESIAS CONTINUED

Salisbury – the Matopos – Rhodes

March 20th. The changes in the city are greater than a first glance revealed. The streets, as all the inhabitants often remind one, are laid out so that a team of oxen could be turned in them. Last year there was no 'traffic problem'. Now parking-meters have sprung up everywhere and the leading grocer has built a 'park' on his roof, approached by a ramp like the Guggenheim Gallery in New York. Customers go down to the shop by lift, make their purchases and collect them at the door when they drive down. There are 'drive-in cinemas'. Every sign of the early settlers is disappearing. Also the word 'settler', which is now held to be opprobrious and politically tendentious.

I have already remarked on the difficulties that face a modern traveller in the kaleidoscopic charges of euphemism. In the old days 'settlers' were proud of their distinction from officials. Now they wish to be called plain 'Rhodesians' fearing that their original name suggests recent and temporary occupation. The oddest manipulation of vocabulary is the one by which a white American is classified as a European and a black American as an 'alien native'. 'Native', surely the most honourable appellation for white or black, is never used of whites, and some blacks resent it. 'Nigger' (except as a term of affection used among niggers) and 'Kaffir' have long been thought offensive. 'Bantu' is held to be inexact by anthropologists. 'African' is clearly too vague for use. I am told that in the U.S.A. one may say 'negro' but not 'negress'. They like to be called 'coloured'. But 'coloured' in most of Africa means mulatto. In my lifetime I have seen 'Anglo-Indian', which I still use to describe my mother's family, come to mean Eurasian. Goanese for some mysterious reason are huffy if they are not called 'Goans'. There is no end to the flood of gentilisms that are eroding the language. Well, I don't suppose any blackamoors, niggers, Kaffirs, natives, Bantu or Africans will read this diary. Some whites may, so I apologise for calling some of them 'settlers', but I don't know how else without periphrasis to describe those nice, pinkish people who have come to settle here.

Very few indeed of these settlers survive or descend from the original invaders of seventy years ago. Those who do are very proud of it and display certificates of the fact, like armorial bearing, in their houses. Not all the 'pioneers' were riff-raff. Missionary stock provides a number of the present leading citizens. But the immigration which has changed the character of the country occurred since 1945. This change is illustrated in an exhibition now being held.

There is a fine new building in Salisbury named the Rhodes National Gallery, the gift of one of these recent immigrants. There are as yet no permanent exhibits and the managers have to exercise ingenuity in filling it. When I was here last year there was a collection of enlarged photographs on view, sent round the world by some American cultural organisation. The theme appeared to be connected with human progress and the brotherhood of man. The effect was of being enclosed in the pages of a popular magazine. This year there is something more enterprising, a collection of furniture and *objets d'art* lent by private owners in the Federation. The catalogue emphasised its federal character, but everything (I think) comes from Southern Rhodesia and almost everything has been brought here since 1945.

It is organised and introduced by a youngish bachelor who keeps an antique shop, bubbles with the lore of Mr Betjeman and Mr Osbert Lancaster – he has settled at the moment on William IV as the 'nicest' period – and is himself an outstanding example of the change in character of modern Rhodesians from the pioneers. He chose and arranged the exhibits, as far as possible as 'period rooms', the last of which is a sly comment on the taste of his humbler neighbours – a room furnished with pieces of local manufacture more gruesome than anything to be seen even in the shop-windows of England.

There are four collectors in Rhodesia with rich possessions; these have provided the most notable pieces. But there are also single exhibits from many widely dispersed houses. John, for example, had lent the superb embroidered train worn by his great-great-grandmother at the christening of the King of Rome.

Not everything would attract interest or even be accepted for sale at Sotheby's. Indeed, from my own Somerset neighbours in a five-mile radius I could assemble a more varied and valuable exhibition than the whole Federation can afford. But the significance of the Salisbury Exhibition is that anything worth showing should be there at all; that it is now possible to illustrate with reasonably good examples almost every period of European taste. The recent settlers have brought their household gods with them. This, much more than the skyscrapers, impresses the tourist with a sense of the depth of European settlement. Also of its humanity; for the new settlers have not adopted the narrow habits of thought of their predecessors.

The commercial growth of Salisbury, its towering banks and insurance offices, its neatly dressed Rotarians, make one forget that it is also the seat of government – of two Governments, indeed, with two parliaments, two prime ministers, a Governor-General and a Governor. John and Daphne and I were commanded to a large dinner party at Government House for a visiting British Minister. It was a pretty sight when the ladies left the table to see them in their long dresses and long white gloves cluster round the door and curtsey like altar boys to the Governor-General. When they had left I found myself sitting next to a local cultivated bigwig. I attempted something polite about how delightful his country was for a visit. He spoke, as politicians will, of the great progress and potentialities of his country.

I said: 'I think you are a bachelor. I should not care to bring up children here.'

'Why not?' rather sharply scenting politics.

'The accent.'

I think there was a glance of sympathy in his eye. He did not expatiate on the educational advantages, the salubrious climate, the

opportunities for enrichment. Instead he talked of his own upbringing in England.

When the Governor-General thinks a party has lasted long
enough, he sends an A.D.C. to play a record of the Death Song
from 'King Kong'.

March 21st. There was racing this afternoon at Mirandellas. In living
memory lions were shot where the race-course now stands. John had
a horse running. Daphne and I left him and his chaplain there and
drove off into the native reserve in search of a Jesuit missionary I had
known in England. He did not know it then, but it was to be his
brother who was sent out as head of the official enquiry into the riots
in Nyasaland.

One does not see many Africans in Salisbury; fewer it seemed
than in London. There are black porters in the larger shops and the
white shop-girls are abominably rude to them. They are also rather
rude to their white customer, for they are at pains to demonstrate
that under God all white men were created equal. The well-paid
plumber who comes out to work in a private house expects to sit
down in the dining-room with the family. He has a black, ill-paid
assistant who squats outside. Here, as in England, the champions of
the colour bar are the classes whose modest skills many negroes can
master.

Southern Rhodesia differs historically from, say, Uganda and
Nyasaland. Here the whites came as conquerors; there the natives
voluntarily put themselves under the protection of the English
Crown. The conquest was not a feast of arms to be remembered
with pride, but it was an exercise of high chivalry compared with
the occupation of Australia, where the settlers regularly put out
poisoned food for the aborigines. The tribes which were conquered
were, in many cases, themselves recent conquerors. Force of
arms had always been recognised in Africa as giving right of
possession.

The visitor to Rhodesia sees as little of the natives as a visitor in
the United States sees little of the very poor. (But in Rhodesia the
natives are proportionately more numerous than the destitute in
America.) They have no obvious tribal characteristics. They are not

beautiful like the Masai or buoyant like the Wachagga or pictur-
esquely prehistoric like the Wagogo. All wear a drab uniform of shirt
and shorts. They have the hang-dog air of the defeated people,
which indeed they are.

Colonel David Stirling, with whom I served in the war, came
here on a commercial enterprise and was so depressed by the
conditions of the natives that he has devoted the last ten years of
his life to persuading the settlers that a 'multi-racial society' is not
merely a politician's cliché. But his Capricorn Society has made less
impression than he hoped.

As soon as we left the main road Daphne and I found ourselves in
the same dusty, dreary country as surrounds Serima – rough tracks,
low scrub, occasional patches of mealies and clusters of huts – we got
lost; enquiries for a Mission led us to an Anglican school where
boys were playing football; a teacher gave us a guide to the Jesuits.
They were playing football there, too, and some boys were splashing
in an iron water-tank. There were four or five priests, in their
working clothes of shirts and shorts; two at least of them men of
high scholarship. We had lost so much time in getting there that we
could barely greet our friend before setting back. He does not repine
either for Farm Street or for Salisbury. Although they are so near
(when one knows the way) to Mirandellas, he and his companions
see few white people except the Native Commissioner. Their life is
devoted to the Mashona, at the central school and in touring the
villages. I have seen lonelier and more comfortless missions in many
parts of the world – in British Guiana, for instance, where up
country I stayed with a solitary priest whose greeting was: 'You are
most welcome. I have been hoping for someone to come and pull
out two of my teeth' – but the outward aspect of this station has
a penetrating drabness.

What is known of Mashona history is ignominious; they were the
prey of the Matabele before white men appeared in the country.
Like the slum-dwellers of industrial England in the last century, they
get very drunk rather often. They clearly enjoy football and splashing in the water. The missionaries say they have some enthusiasm in
religious exercises. But on the superficial observer – or on me at any
rate – they cast a gloom not easily dispelled. It sat heavy on me as we

bumped back to the race-course, which we reached just as the last race was run, and as we sped back on the high road home.

March 22nd. A last tourist trip, to the Matopos. These famous hills are second only to the Eastern Highlands in natural beauty, and they are much odder. At Leopard's Rock there were comparisons to be made with other scenery in other parts of the world. There is nothing I know at all like the Matopos. They comprise some fifty by thirty miles of bare granite and green valleys. The district caught the particular fancy of Cecil Rhodes, and it is here by his wish that he is buried on a spot which he named 'the View of the World' which he designated as a 'Valhalla' for the heroes of the country. It is therefore a region of particular sanctity to patriotic Rhodesians. Also to the Matabele, who first chose it as a burial place for their king, Mzilikazi, who led them here out of Zululand in 1838. When pioneers rifled this royal cave, Rhodes had it walled up and made formal reparation for the sacrilege with the sacrifice of black oxen. But there are older associations than the Matabele. The rock clefts are covered with bushmen drawings of men, animals and unidentified shapes, categorised by archæologists into periods of varying skill, from, perhaps, before the beginning of the Christian era until shortly before the arrival of the Matabele. There is also an oracle that has spoken for at least 500 years and still speaks. It is in the custody of the noble families of the Kalanga tribe and it is inspired by the mysterious spirit, the Mlimo, which the American, Burnham, claimed to have shot. The Mlimo is much concerned with rain making and diseases of cattle, but he has wider interests. It was he who in 1895 helped foment the rising by assuring the Matabele, who took over his cultus with the country, that the white men's bullets would turn to water before striking them – a delusion which in the last hundred years has afflicted Africans in widely separate and unconnected areas; in the Soudan, for instance, and in the Southern Province of Tanganyika. The priests of the Mlimo are said to have maintained an elaborate intelligence service among the whole Bantu people as far south as the Basutos. Pilgrims came, and still come, to him from there and from Swaziland and Bechuanaland. The precise position of this African Delphi, Njelele Cave, is known to some whites but not publicly proclaimed. The official guide book says: 'Very many Africans look upon Mlimo as a powerful and beneficent deity and upon his worship as an important institution. For that reason we have omitted any details of the location of this cave and visitors are asked to respect its privacy by not searching for it by themselves. To visit Njelele at the invitation of one of the *Abantwana bo Mlimo* is, of course, quite another matter and usually it is not difficult for anyone having the confidence of the local Kalango to receive such an invitation.'

I doubt whether many of the visitors would be particularly interested. They come to picnic, fish, catch butterflies and photograph the game. Most modern Rhodesians seem to me morbidly incurious about native customs and beliefs. Their predecessors fought the natives, stole their cattle, tricked them into making concessions, but they perforce studied them in a rough and ready way and mixed with them. Dr Jameson was sworn as a member of Lobengula's bodyguard and, in violation of his oath, led the attack against him. Selous, the most famous hunter and explorer of Rhodesia, had a black wife; a mulatto daughter of his lives in the outskirts of Salisbury today. The Afrikaan conception of 'apartheid' would have been alien and (I think) outrageous to most of the early adventurers.

I have (or rather had, for his tour of duty ended shortly after my visit) a nephew serving as A.D.C. to the Governor of Southern Rhodesia – a dignitary not to be confused with the Governor-General of the Federation. This dutiful young man arranged my trip to the Matopos with practical efficiency, coming out to fetch me and installing me for the night in great comfort at Government Lodge – the Governor's official residence in Salisbury.

Next day *March 23rd* we left at dawn and took the aeroplane to Bulawayo. A car was waiting there to take us to breakfast at Government House. This is the house built by Rhodes for his own use on the site of Lobengula's kraal. It is a charming, low, shady, building in the Dutch-colonial style. In an outbuilding there is the model of a reconstruction of the kraal as it stood in Lobengula's day, part cantonment, part cattle ranch. In the trim garden stands a surprisingly paltry tree which is pointed out as the one under which he held court. There is nothing else at Government House or anywhere in his kingdom to awake his memory; his grave is unknown, his treasure stolen or lost, his posterity unrecognised. But he haunts it yet, a deeply tragic figure from Shakespearean rather than from classical drama; Lear, Macbeth, Richard II, he has a touch of them all. What a part for Mr Paul Robeson could be written of his doom. He was the victim of history. The Matabele kingdom was a military institution aptly organised to survive and prosper in any age before Lobengula's. He inherited a superb army, and war was the condition of his authority. The young warriors had to blood their spears. If the white men had not entered central Africa his dynasty might have lasted centuries. He was personally brave, majestic, intelligent and honourable. The curious thing is that he genuinely liked white men, protected them when it was in his power to annihilate, kept his word when he might have tricked them. The white men he met were mostly scoundrels. It is generally supposed that it was their avarice alone which overthrew him. Mashonaland proved a disappointment to the prospectors. Driven by the hope of finding another Rand or another Kimberley, they clamoured for Matabeleland. Contemporary accounts of Lobengula's last decade make shameful reading. The white concession hunters camped all round him; they brought him champagne and rifles; Dr Jameson treated him with morphia; a squadron of Life Guards paraded before him in full dress; the Jesuits designed a coat-of-arms for his carriage door. And all the time his regiments watched their huge, naked monarch grow fat and muddled. He wrote personally to Queen Victoria for guidance. He sent ambassadors to Cape Town who were kidnapped or murdered. And the young warriors grew mutinous.

It was not only the fortune hunters who welcomed his fall. Before attacking, Rhodes sought the sanction of the missionaries, and got it. It is hard to realise now that at the time of the Diamond Jubliee many men of goodwill and intelligence thought the Pax Victoriana a reality. The bloody little forays of the Matabele seemed to them a shocking anachronism. Even now you will find people of some goodwill and some intelligence who speak of Europeans as having 'pacified' Africa. Tribal wars and slavery were endemic before they came; no doubt they will break out again when they leave. Meantime, under European rule in the first forty years of this century there have been three long wars in Africa on a far larger scale than anything perpetrated by marauding spearmen, waged by white men against white, and a generation which has seen the Nazi régime in the heart of Europe had best stand silent when civilised and uncivilised nations are contrasted. But the missionaries genuinely believed that the autocrats, their fierce aristocracies and their witches were the only grave impediments to the establishment of the sign of charity. Fr Prestage, S.J., who gave his whole life to natives of Rhodesia, wrote: 'If ever there was a just war, the Matabele War was just.'

Lobengula's flight after defeat, aged and half stupefied; his pathetic attempts to make peace by giving a bag of sovereigns to two troopers (who stole it); his wagon of treasure – carrying what? the rubbishy gifts of his European courtiers? ivory? gold? – driven into some cleft in the rocks, hidden, perhaps pilfered, perhaps still there; his disappearance across the river and death, it is said, by smallpox, in an unknown spot; all this comprises the very stuff of poetic drama.

After breakfast we drove back to Bulawayo. It has a quiet, old-fashioned air which, I am told, the inhabitants do not particularly relish. Not long ago it was the commercial capital of Rhodesia. Now Salisbury has cut it out. There are no skyscrapers here. The shops have a sombre, provincial respectability like those of the Scottish Lowlands. The chemist has a panelled window surmounted by the traditional glass bottles of coloured water and inside the drawers and jars with the Latin labels that used to delight one's childhood. Salisbury chemists are ablaze with advertisements of patent medicines, cosmetics and baby-foods. The tobacconist kept better cigars than I had found in Salisbury. There is a good museum, stocked with fauna below; native weapons and costumes upstairs. Until lately natives were not allowed to look at these relics of their past; now the whole place is open to them and they come in large numbers. (The prohibition had no ideological significance. It was simply that the curator's staff, whose offices were on that floor, did not want to be disturbed by chatter.) We saw the soapstone birds and shards collected at Zimbabwe, visited the mineralogist whose task it is to examine specimens of ore and gems brought in to him – he had something of particular interest that morning; was it an emerald? – visited the archæologist who had spent the previous summer at Zimbabwe and heard from him the tentative opinion that the most impressive parts of the ruins are all of recent, Bantu construction, and then drove up into the Matopos.

Rhodes's original estate, which he left in trust to the colony, consists of 95,700 acres, the agricultural and arable part divided into fifteen farms let to tenants, and the rocky remainder, which is laid out and maintained as a pleasure ground. This is the Matopo Park, entered through gates presented by a member of the Beit family, which encloses Rhodes's grave on his View of the World. Beyond this there are some quarter of a million acres added by proclamation in 1953.

These do not come under the control of the Rhodes Trustees but of the National Parks Department, who have laid out roads, dammed streams, and generally set out to make the place attractive to white tourists. When the project was first investigated in 1946 there were found to be some 17,500 native families in occupation with 13,800 head of stock. The officials decided there was room for only 400 families and 4,000 cattle. The natives had no wish to move. Many of them had quite clear memories of Rhodes's funeral, and of Col. Rhodes's subsequent speech in which, with undisguised emotion, he had said: 'As a proof that I know the white man and the Matabele will be brothers and friends for ever, I leave my brother's grave in your hands. I charge you to hand down this sacred trust to your sons that come after you and from generation to generation and I know if you do this my brother will be pleased.'

Would the Great White Chief be pleased, they asked, to see them turned out in under fifty years to make way for picnic parties from the cities? Eventually the decision was modified; some 700 families with ten head of cattle apiece have been allowed to remain.

There is now a small, demarcated island of 'native reserve' and a large area clear of it to the south, similarly allotted. These areas enjoy the rugged, natural character of the Park from which their inhabitants are excluded. Was this what the Great White Chief and

Col. Rhodes had in mind? Was this, it is perhaps not impertinent to wonder, quite what the great concourse of native mourners were saluting when at the obsequies of 10th April 1902 they broke out into cries of (I quote from the guide book) 'N'Kosi'?

One can now drive to the foot of the hill called 'the View of the World' and an easy climb takes one to the summit. The panorama is indeed stupendous and worthy of all that has been written and said of it. Rhodes in naming it did not claim it was the finest 'view' in the world; he meant rather that from this quite modest eminence one does in that clear light and unbroken horizon get, as the guide book says, 'a strange impression of looking out over the uttermost parts of the earth'. It is a curious fact that aeroplanes have added nothing to our enjoyment of height. The human eye still receives the most intense images when the observer's feet are planted on the ground or on a building. The aeroplane belittles all it discloses.

The most prominent man-made object is the memorial to thirty-four soldiers who were killed at the Shangani River in 1893, the advance party of the force pursuing Lobengula. It was by Rhodes's express wish and in opposition to the sentiment of many of the people round Fort Victoria that the bones were brought here from Zimbabwe, where they were first buried. They were, as the inscription simply states, 'Brave Men'; that is to say, they fought to death in circumstances when neither retreat nor surrender was possible. Their monument is a massive erection of granite over thirty feet in height, bearing their life-sized full-length portraits in bronze high-relief by John Tweed, R.A. It is in striking contrast to the other three graves on the hill which are plain slabs of granite and brass under which lie Rhodes, Jameson and at a little distance and distinguished by the gracious appeal 'R.I.P.', Sir Charles Coghlan, the first Prime Minister of Southern Rhodesia.

At Rhodes's funeral the Bishop of Mashonaland read a poem of four stanzas composed by Kipling for the occasion. The theme was Vision:

> *Dreamer devout by vision led*
> *Beyond our guess and reach,*

The terms of panegyric amount almost to apotheosis:

> *This Power that wrought on us and goes*
> *Back to the Power again.*

And:

> *There till the vision he foresaw*
> *Splendid and whole arise*
> *And unimagined Empires draw*
> *To council neath his skies,*
> *The immense and brooding Spirit still,*
> *Shall quicken and control.*

That was written only fifty-seven years ago and already every prediction has been belied.

In his own lifetime, and largely by his own imprudence and dishonesty, he had seen Afrikaners and British in South Africa hopelessly embittered. Today his great project of the all-British Cape to Cairo route has lost all meaning; the personal, honourable ascendancy of Great White Chiefs has degenerated into 'apartheid'. One is tempted to the trite contrast of the achievements of the politician and of the artist; the one talking about generations yet unborn, the other engrossed in the technical problems of the task at hand; the one fading into a mist of disappointment and controversy, the other leaving a few objects of permanent value that were not there before him and would not have been there but for him. But Rhodes was not a politician; or rather he was a minor one. He was a visionary and almost all he saw was hallucination.

He was not, as Jameson disastrously was, a man of action. He was neither a soldier nor an explorer. Much has been made of the incident of his going out almost alone into the Matopos to make peace with the dissident Matabele. It was a courageous act, admirably performed, but in fact it was precisely what Fr Prestage had done with another group of Matabele chiefs four months earlier. The Matabele were then hopeless and leaderless. The promised immunity to rifle fire had proved to be an illusion. They could have been a considerable nuisance if they had continued to sulk with their spears in the inaccessible hills; but they were a defeated people. The significant feature of the celebrated Indabas was the personal effect Rhodes made. He was known to the Matabele only by repute. There can be no doubt that after those meetings they looked to him with something of the awe they had accorded their kings. African politicians who are now idolised, might with profit remember how capriciously these emotions can be aroused among their people.

Rhodes was a financier. He made a huge fortune very young at a time when other huge fortunes were being made. But the Kimberley millionaires were few and they were not lucky prospectors but assiduous business men. Rhodes's predominant skill was in the market, in negotiating combinations, monopolies and loans, in beguiling shareholders, in keeping up the price of Chartered Company Stock when it never paid a dividend, in using first-hand information to buy and sell, in creating, imposing and preserving a legend of himself that calmed the stockmarket. And money for him was not an end; it was not the means to pleasure or even to personal power; it was the substance of his dreams.

There is a connexion between celibacy and 'vision', both at the lowest – Hitler – and the highest – the contemplative. Rhodes inhabited a half world somewhere between. It is the childless who plan for posterity. Parents are too busy with the concerns of the moment.

There is an attractive side to Rhodes's character; his experimental farms; his taste in the houses he chose to live in; his respect for native pieties. The scholarships he founded at Oxford set a model which has been followed in other countries, whose confidence in their 'way of life' is so strong that they believe they must only be known to be loved. It is noteworthy that his scholarships were for Americans, colonials and Germans. The Latin countries were excluded. For his obsessive imagination was essentially puerile. His first Will, made before he had much to leave, provided for the foundation of a kind of secret society dedicated to the supremacy of the Anglo-Saxon race. He had a schoolboy's silly contempt for 'dagoes'; for the whole Mediterranean-Latin culture. He set out quite deliberately to provoke war with the Portuguese and was only stopped by Lord Salisbury. He saw in his fantastic visions of the future a world state of English, Germans and North Americans. But his most important associates both in South Africa and in

Europe were nearly all Jews. That is the point, so often missed, of Belloc's 'Verses to a Lord'. There was no conceivable reason why Jews as much as Gentiles should not make fortunes in the diamond and gold fields, or why they should not welcome an exercise of force to facilitate their business. What was absurd was Rhodes's promoting their interests with idiotic cries of Anglo-Saxon racialism.

Jameson, who lies near him, is remembered now only for his upsetting of 'the apple cart'. He was a foolish, not very scrupulous, rather engaging adventurer who first made himself popular as a doctor by maintaining the labour supply at the diamond mines by his refusal in his professional capacity to quarantine them at a time of epidemic. Lobengula particularly liked him and his morphia. He was no visionary but a faithful dog and he too was celibate.

There was something noble in his adoration of Rhodes. He took physical risks and endured hardships such as Rhodes never knew. He made no fortune. As far as is known, Rhodes had no communication with him, though he was broken-hearted, from the time of his raid until his release from prison.

We left the View of the World and drove through the hills along the roads which have been admirably devised for the pleasure of sight-seers, pausing to look at clefts in the rocks covered in drawings of men and animals that have now vanished from the hills – giraffe, rhinoceros. The fauna most common there now are baboons. We saw plenty of these but none of the famous sable antelope, nor cobras, puff adders nor pythons. My nephew had provided a fine hamper. We ate our lunch beside a lake; no one else was in sight except a passing Matabele guide in smart uniform.

The afternoon aeroplane took us back to Salisbury in time for tea at Government Lodge. I had been there several times before, but never by daylight. I was able to see and admire the garden that has been the particular contribution of the Governor's wife.

March 25*th*. That evening John and I gave a small dinner party, my own farewell combined with the 'coming-out' of his second daughter. At the table we were predominantly British; there was one Prussian; Rhodes would have approved of that; but there were also French, Hungarians, Greeks, the dagoes he wished to exclude from his mad Anglo-Saxon world; who now form a large and lively part of the population. The restaurant was Portuguese, newly opened at the top of one of the new tall buildings. French cooking has not yet reached Rhodesia (it is, I am told, rapidly disappearing from London), but Salisbury has now reached the degree of sophistication when restaurants go in and out of fashion. The Portuguese cooking and wine were excellent. We were far from the bottled sauces and tinned vegetables that used to encumber so many of the tables of British Africa.

March 26th. The anniversary of Cecil Rhodes's death. Public notices had been inviting the citizens to commemorate the event at his statue in the main square of the town. The Governor was there, some police and some school-children, but it was not an imposing gathering. Rhodes's picture hangs in all public places and in some private ones, but the cultus seems tepid. He is as much revered by the new generation of Salisbury as, perhaps, is Abel Janszoon Tasman in Hobart. The 'immense and brooding Spirit' no longer 'quickens and controls'.

Early that afternoon I took the aeroplane for Cape Town.

8. RETURN

March 26*th* continued.

All airports I know are forbidding; Johannesburg, where we stopped late that afternoon, is surely the worst in the world. We were herded down into a concrete basement; a sort of bomb shelter furnished with half a dozen doors into which, one by one, we were directed. No one was seen to emerge. A lamp over the door gave the signal and a sallow young woman announced through a microphone 'Passenger Waugh will proceed to door number 3'. It was like the play of Dunsany's I once saw, in which a group of criminals were summoned to death by (I think) an oriental idol. When I reached the appointed place I found a civil enough young immigration officer who stamped my passport and released me by a further door into a passage which led to the upper level and a waiting-room of the normal kind.

The aeroplane brought me to Cape Town that night and I drove straight to the *Pendennis Castle* and slept on board in comfort.

March 27*th*. Good Friday. We do not sail until evening, but I do not go ashore. It is pleasanter now to see from the decks the famous view of Table Mountain and the decent old city.

Anyone who travelled by troopship to the Middle East in the days when the Mediterranean was impassable must have grateful – some, I believe, have tender – memories of the hospitality of Cape Town. After weeks at sea with blackened port-holes we found a town all alight, but much more than this we found what seemed to be the whole population extended to welcome us, the whole quay lined with cars to take us into the country. I remember the scene at night with the men returning to the ship, some drunk, some sober, all happy, laden, many of them, with great bunches of grapes like the illustrations in old Bibles of the scouts returning to the Israelites in the desert with evidence of the Land of Promise flowing with milk and honey. It is a memory I prefer to maintain intact. Few peoples anywhere, I suppose, deserve the government they get. Too many English voices are at the moment raised to reproach the South Africans for me to join in the clamour.

There was no religious observance on board. Instead the ship was thrown open to visitors who thronged it all day; ladies dressed as though for Ascot, youths dressed for goodness knows what in shorts, many of them with beards, an emblem apparently of republican sympathies.

The stewards carefully hid the ash-trays and teaspoons from souvenir collectors.

The *Pendennis Castle* is a ship well worth visiting; she is the flagship of the line, now on her second voyage. When the sight-seers went ashore I explored her at leisure; she is spacious, ingeniously planned and brightly decorated, manned by stewards more experienced than most of the young men in *Rhodesia Castle*.

They were hard worked, for the passenger list was completely full; quite different company from my fellow travellers on the east coast, older and more opulent; no missionaries, no officials, no young people going to work. A cinema comedian was the only notable on board. He made himself very popular in leading the mild festivities. I was where I belonged; in the returning migration of those who had fled the English winter.

Comfortable, uneventful days succeed one another; a sense of well-being and repose after not very arduous travel. A half-day's stop at Las Palmas to refuel; a morning pottering round the streets of that charming town. Then on again punctually and smoothly.

April 10*th*. Southampton in the early morning; effortless disembarkation. Nothing to record except appreciation of a happy fortnight. When last I returned from Africa it was by air and I landed, like everyone else, cramped and sleepless and fit only for days of recuperation. Today I came ashore buoyantly; very different from the old fellow who crept into the train south two months ago. That was the object of the trip.

I came abroad, as I noted at the time, with the intention of eschewing 'problems' and of seeking only the diverting and the picturesque. Alas, that is not possible. 'Problems' obtrude. There was in my youth a film which opened superbly with Buster Keaton as an invalid millionaire landing from his yacht in a Central American Republic. He is enjoying a rest-cure. The people of the country are enjoying a revolution. He progresses, if I remember rightly, in a bath-chair, up the main street, totally unaware of the battle raging round him. As the dead and wounded double up before him, he raises his hat in acknowledgement of what he takes to be their bows of welcome. One cannot long travel in that way. From Algeria to Cape Town the whole African continent is afflicted by political activities which it is fatuous to ignore and as fatuous to dub complacently an 'awakening'. Men who have given their lives to the continent can do no more to predict the future than can the superficial tourist. All know that there is no solution in parliamentary democracy. But, ironically enough, the British Empire is being dissolved on the alien principles which we ourselves imported, of nineteenth-century Liberalism.

The foundations of Empire are often occasions of woe; their dismemberment, always.

The Austro-Hungarian Empire fell because the component peoples were urged to attribute their ills to thwarted nationalism. No one, I suppose, in their former dominions had a happier or better life as the result of 'self-determination', though Czechs and Croats and Magyars were enormously more civilised in 1918 than the native nations of Africa today.

I suppose the nearest historical comparison to modern Africa is the reality behind the fiction of Buster Keaton's Latin America. The Spanish monarchy was dispossessed by local revolutionaries who spoke the already antiquated language of the Enlightenment. A century of chaos and tyranny followed and is not yet everywhere abated.

The consciences of the English are unnaturally agitated by Africa. The questions that greet the returned tourist are not: 'Did you have a good time?' but: 'What about apartheid? What about Hola? What about the imprisonment of the politicians?' I can only reply: 'Don't know.'

In Tanganyika I found nothing but good-will towards the Africans darkened with grave doubts of the future. In Rhodesia there is an infection from the south of racial insanity. I heard of a Catholic woman who was offended because an itinerant priest said Mass for her on her stoep with a black server. But the story was told me as something disgusting.

I heard people of 'pioneer stock' say: '*You* can't understand. *We* remember the time when these people threatened to kill us,' while at the same time cordially entertaining Germans. The more recent, more civilised immigrants have none of these unreasoning emotions. They regard the natives as a peasantry and treat them accordingly, but if their sons go to local schools they are in danger of picking up more than an unattractive accent. Every year in Rhodesia the status of the native is being slightly raised. Apartheid is the creation of the Boers. It is the spirit of equalitarianism literally cracked. Stable and fruitful societies have always been elaborately graded. The idea of a classless society is so unnatural to man that his reason, in practice, cannot bear the strain. Those Afrikaner youths claim equality with you, gentle reader. They regard themselves as being a cut above the bushmen. So they accept one huge cleavage in the social order and fantastically choose pigmentation as the determining factor. Cardinal Garcias and the Hottentot are equal on one side; you, gentle reader, and the white oaf equal on the other; and there is no passage across that preposterous frontier.

I was witness, many years ago, to a happy product of this disordered logic, when, having run short of money in Cape Town, I travelled home third class. I embarked with some slight apprehensions, which were quite otiose. Our quarters were clean, our food abundant and palatable; there was only one privation – lack of space. We were four in a cabin and there was simply not enough room for all of us to sit on deck or in the saloon. I forget how many baths and lavatories there were, but I remember there was usually a queue. One black man travelled with us. In deference to South African susceptibilties he had a four-berth cabin to himself. More than this he had a lavatory, a bath-room and an arm-chair all placarded: 'For the use of non-European passengers only'. He was a man of studious disposition and he had a very comfortable voyage. I greatly envied his three weeks' solitude. A similar situation existed on my first visit at the University of Rhodesia, where a single black girl enjoyed quarters designed for many.

In Washington D.C., when I was last there, I visited a segregated Pets' Cemetery. The loved ones were separated not by their own colour but by that of their owners; black and white pets of white women lay indifferently in one quarter; black and white pets of black women in another.

Racialism is dotty and rather modern, but it is widespread. One is certainly not more conscious of it in Africa (except in the Union) than in America.

And acts of violence by the police are also widespread everywhere in the world. It would be interesting to know how often during the last five years the Indian police have (quite properly) opened fire on rioters and charged them with *lathis*. These incidents are not given much prominence in the English papers. It was my impression, when I was in India lately and reading the local press, that there was rioting somewhere in that huge country almost every day. No one in his senses thinks it a good thing that Kenya prison warders should kill their prisoners; but no one in his senses should think it peculiar to Kenya. Cruelty and injustice are endemic everywhere.

It is noble to expiate the sins of mankind vicariously in a hermit's cell. Failing that heroic remedy, let me gratefully accept the good things that the world still offers and do not, I beg you, try and impute guilt for things entirely outside my control.

I have had a happy two months and I won't let the weekly papers spoil them for me.

ABOUT THE INTRODUCER

NICHOLAS SHAKESPEARE is a novelist and the biographer of Bruce Chatwin. He has lived in South America and Africa. In 1987 he wrote and narrated 'The Waugh Trilogy' for BBC Television.

This book is set in BASKERVILLE. John
Baskerville of Birmingham formed his
ideas of letter-design during his
early career as a writing-master
and engraver of inscriptions.
He retired in middle age,
set up a press of his
own and produced
his first book
in 1757.